# PSYCHOLOGY

Almost everyone who sees this image by Lois Greenfield stops, stares, and then whispers the word "Wow." We did too. Why is this image so captivating?

Throughout history, human beings have seen themselves as creatures that exist somewhere between the mundane and the divine. The figure in this image appears to be both descending from the heavens and rising from the earth, briefly suspended between two worlds, engaged in some uniquely human ritual that neither the gods above him nor the beasts below him can fully comprehend. For us, this moment of balance captures the essential tension between the mind and the body, between our higher and lower natures, between the aspirations and the origins of our species.

Lois Greenfield has been photographing dancers and dance movement since 1973. In the last three decades, her work has appeared in such diverse publications as *American Photographer, Dance Magazine, Elle, Esquire, Life, The New York Times, Newsweek, Rolling Stone, Vanity Fair, The Village Voice,* and *Vogue*. She has been featured in one-woman exhibitions in the United States, Europe, China, and most recently Japan. She has published two books, *Breaking Bounds: The Dance Photography of Lois Greenfield* (Chronicle Books, 1992) and *Airborne: The New Dance Photography of Lois Greenfield* (Chronicle Books, 1998). She currently lives in New York City.

# PSYCHOLOGY

DANIEL L. SCHACTER
Harvard University

DANIEL T. GILBERT
Harvard University

DANIEL M. WEGNER
Harvard University

Custom Edition for the
University of Alberta

—WORTH—
Custom Publishing

**Publisher:** Catherine Woods
**Acquisitions Editor:** Charles Linsmeier
**Executive Marketing Manager:** Katherine Nurre
**Senior Development Editor:** Mimi Melek
**Development Editors:** Phyllis Fisher, Barbara Brooks
**Senior Media Editor:** Andrea Musick
**Associate Managing Editor:** Tracey Kuehn
**Project Editor:** Jane O'Neill
**Photo Editor:** Ted Szczepanski
**Photo Researchers:** Elyse Rieder and Lyndall Culbertson
**Art Director and Cover Designer:** Babs Reingold
**Text Designer:** Lissi Sigillo
**Layout Designer:** Lee Mahler
**Illustration Coordinator:** Susan Timmins
**Illustrations:** Matt Holt, Christy Krames, Don Stewart
**Cover Photograph:** Lois Greenfield
**Production Manager:** Sarah Segal
**Composition:** TSI Graphics
**Printing and Binding:** RR Donnelley

ISBN-13: 978-1-4292-5787-9
ISBN-10: 1-4292-5787-3

Printed in the United States of America

Worth Custom Publishing
Worth Publishers
41 Madison Avenue
New York, NY 10010
www.worthpublishers.com/custompub

*To our children and their children*

Hannah Schacter

Emily Schacter

Arlo Gilbert

Shona Gilbert

Daylyn Gilbert

Sari Gilbert

Kelsey Wegner

Haley Wegner

# About the Authors

**DANIEL L. SCHACTER** is a professor of psychology at Harvard University. Schacter received his BA degree from the University of North Carolina at Chapel Hill in 1974. He subsequently developed a keen interest in memory disorders. He continued his research and education at the University of Toronto, where he received his PhD in 1981. He taught on the faculty at Toronto for the next 6 years before joining the psychology department at the University of Arizona in 1987. In 1991, he joined the faculty at Harvard University. His research explores the relation between conscious and unconscious forms of memory and the nature of memory distortions. He has received the Phi Beta Kappa teaching prize and several research awards, including the Troland Award from the National Academy of Sciences. Many of Schacter's studies are summarized in his 1996 book, *Searching for Memory: The Brain, the Mind, and the Past*, and his 2001 book, *The Seven Sins of Memory: How the Mind Forgets and Remembers*, both winners of the APA's William James Book Award.

**DANIEL T. GILBERT** is a professor of psychology at Harvard University. After attending the Community College of Denver and completing his BA at the University of Colorado at Denver in 1981, he earned his PhD from Princeton University in 1985. He taught on the faculty of the University of Texas at Austin for the next 11 years. In 1996, he joined the faculty of Harvard University. Gilbert received the American Psychological Association's Distinguished Scientific Award for an Early Career Contribution to Psychology. He has also won numerous teaching awards, including the Phi Beta Kappa Teaching Prize. His research on "affective forecasting" is an attempt to understand how and how well people predict their emotional reactions to future events. He is the author of the 2006 national best seller *Stumbling on Happiness*, winner of the Royal Society General Book Prize given for the year's best popular science book.

**DANIEL M. WEGNER** is a professor of psychology at Harvard University. He received his BS in 1970 and PhD in 1974, both from Michigan State University. He began his teaching career at Trinity University in San Antonio, Texas, before his appointments at the University of Virginia in 1990 and then Harvard University in 2000. He is Fellow of the American Association for the Advancement of Science and former associate editor of *Psychological Review*. His research focuses on thought suppression and mental control, social memory in relationships and groups, and the experience of conscious will. His seminal work in thought suppression and consciousness served as the basis of two trade titles, *White Bears and Other Unwanted Thoughts* and the *Illusion of Conscious Will*, both of which were named *Choice* Outstanding Academic Books.

# Brief Contents

# Contents

## UNIVERSITY OF ALBERTA
## BEHAVIORAL GENETICS SUPPLEMENTAL CHAPTER

### Genetic and Evolutionary Foundations of Behavior
From PSYCHOLOGY, Fifth Edition, by Peter O. Gray (©2007, WORTH)

The last chapter in this textbook contains coverage of behavioral genetics and evolutionary psychology. This material will be assigned in your course and provides valuable insights into the development of our species and our common behavior. Material found in this chapter contributes to many fields of psychology and is cross-referenced with other chapters (below).

### Chapter Table-of-Contents
### (Cross-Referenced to PSYCHOLOGY by Schacter, Gilbert, Wegner)

# Preface

For most of our adult lives, the three of us have been studying the human mind and teaching our students what we and other psychologists have learned about it. We've each written articles in professional journals to convey our findings and ideas to our colleagues, and we've each published popular nonfiction titles to communicate with the general public. For each of us, though, something important has been missing: a text written specifically for students. Reading a textbook should be just as engaging as reading a popular book, and we've worked hard to make sure that happens in *Psychology*.

## Telling the Story of Psychology from a Fresh Perspective

As we wrote this textbook, we found ourselves confronting a question: Why were we attracted to psychology in the first place? Although we each have different interests in psychology that cover a broad range of the field—from cognitive psychology to social psychology to clinical psychology and neuroscience—we all share a common fascination with the errors, illusions, biases, and other mental mistakes that reveal how the mind works.

We believe psychology is interesting in large part because it offers insights into the errors of human thought and action. Some of these errors are familiar and amusing (why do we forget jokes the moment we've heard them?), and others are exceptional and tragic (what causes a pilot to fail to deploy his landing gear on approach?). But all of them cry out for explanation. Indeed, if our thoughts, feelings, and actions were error free, our lives would be orderly, predictable, and dull—and there would be few mysteries for psychology to illuminate.

But human behavior is endlessly surprising, and its surprises are what motivates us to understand the psychological complexities that produce them. Why is memory so prone to error, and what can be done to improve it? How can people discriminate against others even when they're trying hard not to? How can mobs make normal people behave like monsters? What allows a child with an IQ of 50 to compose a symphony? How can newborn babies know about kinetics and occlusion when they can't even find their own fingers? Psychology offers the possibility of answering such questions from a scientific perspective, and it is this possibility that drew us to the field.

## Troubleshooting the Mindbugs

Every rambunctious child knows that you can learn how a toy works by breaking it. If you want to understand things so that you can eventually fix them and even build new ones, knowing how they break is invaluable. When things break, we learn about the pieces and processes that normally work together. Breakdown and error are not just about destruction and failure—they are paths to knowledge. Psychology has long followed these paths. The "bugs" of the human mind reveal a great deal about its function, structure, and design. For example: Freud and other pioneers studied psychological disorders not only to alleviate human misery, but because the disordered mind provides a window through which to view normal psychological functioning; the social blunders of autistic people teach us how human beings usually manage to have such seamless interactions; depression teaches us how most people deal so effectively with the losses and heartbreaks of everyday life; violence and antisocial behavior teach us how most people manage to live relatively peaceful lives characterized by morality and self-control; visual illusions teach us how the eye and brain normally generate visual experiences that correspond so faithfully to the realities they represent; errors of inference and memory teach us how people ordinarily make successful decisions and how they remember so much, so well, for so long. These and other examples of mindbugs are integrated throughout the chapters:

- Automatic behaviors, such as when an individual says "Thank you" to a machine that has just delivered a stamp, provide important insights into the role of habit in mental life (Chapter 1, page 4)

- The tendency to underestimate the likelihood of coincidences helps us understand why people believe in magical abilities such as ESP (Chapter 2, page 46)

- Phantom limb syndrome, in which amputees can feel their missing limbs moving and even feel pain in their absent limbs, sheds light on plasticity in the brain (Chapter 3, page 100)

- The experience of synesthesia, where certain musical notes can evoke visual sensations of certain colors or certain sounds can produce an experience of specific tastes, provides clues about how perception works (Chapter 4, pages 121–123)

- The "seven sins" of memory are aspects of forgetting and distortion that show how people reconstruct their pasts and also reveal the adaptive functions of memory (Chapter 5, pages 187–203)

- Rewarding an individual can result in a decrease in the rewarded behavior when an external award undermines the intrinsic satisfaction of performing a task, thereby illuminating some of the limits of reinforcement (Chapter 6, page 229)

- Savants, such as an English boy named Christopher who was fluent in 16 languages yet lacked the cognitive capacities to live on his own, provide striking evidence that cognition is composed of distinct abilities (Chapter 7, page 253)

- Trying not to think about something can make you obsessed with it and quickly reveals one of the key problems we have in controlling our minds and actions (Chapter 8, pages 303–304)

- The pattern of people's errors on intelligence tests teaches us about how different abilities—such as language and reasoning—are related (Chapter 9, page 348)

- The mistakes people make when identifying their own emotions helps us understand the role that cognition plays in emotional experience (Chapter 10, page 378)

- The mistakes young children make when trying to answer questions about other people's beliefs and desires tell us how human beings come to understand their own minds and the minds of others (Chapter 11, pages 416–417)

- People often report that their favorite letter of the alphabet is the one that begins their own name, revealing an irrational bias to think of "me" first (Chapter 12, page 483)

- Some personality problems—such as being extremely dramatic, shy, or dishonest—are not recognized by the people who have them, showing how little insight we have into our own disorders (Chapter 13, pages 528–529)

- Placebo treatments such as sugar pills or therapies with no "active ingredients" can still sometimes be effective and so show how susceptible we are to psychological influences on our health (Chapter 14, pages 571–572)

- Students taking a boring class cough more often than those in an exciting class, revealing how disease symptoms can be modified by processes of attention (Chapter 15, pages 604–605)

- Stereotyping teaches us how people use categories to make predictions about objects and events they have never seen before (Chapter 16, pages 652–656)

Our experience as teachers suggests that students are every bit as fascinated by these mental oddities as we are. So we've incorporated these inherently interesting examples of human behavior throughout the text. Derived from the idea of "computer bugs," we refer to these examples as "mindbugs." Mindbugs are useful in illuminating the mechanisms of human psychology: They relate seemingly different topics to one another and highlight the strengths of the human mind as well as its vulnerabilities. We have used these errors, mistakes, and behavioral oddities as a thematic focus in each of the domains traditionally covered by introductory textbooks.

This approach has at least two benefits. First, it provides a conceptual linkage between chapters on normal psychological functions (such as memory, perception, and emotion) and chapters on pathology (such as psychological disorders, therapy, and stress and health). Second, psychologists know that most errors occur when normally adaptive mechanisms temporarily misbehave. For example, the tendency to stereotype others is not merely a bad habit acquired from ignorant parents but rather a misuse of the normally adaptive tendency to categorize objects and then use what one knows about the category to prejudge the object itself. A focus on mindbugs invites students to think of the mind as an adaptive solution to the problems that human beings face in the real world.

## The Brain and the Classic Questions of Psychology

Just as psychologists come to understand the mind by observing the instances in which it fails and by considering the problems that it has adapted to solve, they also understand the mind by examining the brain. Traditionally, psychologists have relied on nature's occasional and inexact experiments to teach them about the function of the brain, and the study of brain-damaged patients continues to be an important source of new information. In the last two decades, emerging neuroimaging technologies (such as functional magnetic resonance imaging and positron emission tomography) have allowed psychologists to peer deep into the healthy, living brain as well. These two methods have led to the birth of a new field called cognitive neuroscience, and the findings from this field are already shedding light on some interesting and familiar problems. Consider these examples:

- When people have hallucinations, do they actually see pink elephants and hear the voice of God? Neuroimaging studies have shown that both visual and auditory hallucinations are accompanied by increased activity in the regions of the brain that are normally activated by real visual and auditory experience. This suggests that people really are seeing and hearing during hallucinatory episodes.

- When people claim to remember satanic rituals and childhood sexual abuse, are they really remembering? Neuroimaging studies have revealed that false memories are accompanied by activity in the regions of the brain that are normally associated with true memories, suggesting that people who claim to remember such events are, in fact, having a memorial experience.

- When people fail to get what they wanted and then claim to like what they got, is this just a case of "sour grapes" or do they really prefer the outcome they received to the one they originally desired? Studies of amnesiac patients have revealed that people like the outcomes they receive even when they cannot remember what those outcomes are, suggesting that unreachable grapes really do taste sour.

Cases such as these provide a natural entry to discussions of fundamental issues in perception, memory, and motivation. The brain is the basis of all psychological phenomena, and imaging technologies reveal how the brain creates the miracle of the mind. Our decision to integrate neuroscience in this way reflects the current direction in which the field of psychology is moving. The brain is no longer just the province of specialists—the widespread use of imaging techniques has allowed a whole generation of researchers who study cognition, development, personality, emotion, and social psychology to become excited about the possibility of learning how the brain and the mind are interrelated. We have attempted to bring this excitement and new knowledge to introductory students through vivid case illustrations, brain images, and nontechnical explanations.

## Choices That Inspire, Teach, and Respect Students' Intelligence

An introduction to psychology should focus on what is most important and what is most compelling. It should not be a rehashing of all things psychological. In fact, no single author—nor any three authors—can be expert in all the various domains of psychology. To ensure that *Psychology* offers the very best of psychological science, we formed our Contributing Consultants board of accomplished researchers and master teachers in areas outside our areas of expertise. They advised us on early drafts and throughout the writing process, explaining what is important, what is true, and how to think about the issues and data in their respective fields. Taking this information, we have addressed topics in each subfield of psychology in the greater context of that field as a whole. Each chapter has a narrative arc that tells the story of that field of psychology and provides a thematic context that will hook students from the start. In writing *Psychology*, we have made informed choices about our topic coverage weighing classic studies and current research to produce a contemporary perspective on the field. We believe that our approach engages students, teaches students, entertains students, and above all inspires them as the three of us are inspired by psychology.

## Effective Pedagogy

Captivating and entertaining our readers are not our only goals in *Psychology*. Helping students learn and remember what they have learned remains paramount. We have devised a pedagogical program that reinforces the book's themes and supports student learning.

**Chapter-Opening Vignette** Each chapter begins with a story of an incident from everyday life or a case study to capture students' attention and preview the topics covered in the chapter. The stories typically describe a mindbug that helps explain the chapter topic.

**Special-Topic Boxes**

- *Hot Science:* Each chapter has one or more boxes that feature exciting, cutting-edge research on one of the chapter's core topics. Often this research points toward some big question that psychologists hope to answer in the next few decades. For example, in the chapter on consciousness (Chapter 8), one of the Hot Science boxes looks at recent research suggesting that decisions made without conscious thought can sometimes be better than those made with intensive conscious deliberation. These boxes are meant to help students see that psychology is a living enterprise with many uncharted territories, an enterprise that has room for "hot" new insights and future contributions—perhaps from the students themselves.

- *The Real World:* Psychology is about things we experience every day. These boxes focus on these experiences and apply the chapter content to some pressing real-world phenomenon. Some of The Real World boxes focus on issues straight from the news (Chapter 3, "Neuroscience and Behavior," includes a box on the legal status of brain death and discusses the Terry Schiavo case), whereas others focus on issues that may be relevant to their personal lives (Chapter 16, "Social Psychology," has a box on secret romantic relationships).

**Where Do You Stand? (End of Chapter)** Each chapter ends with a "critical thinking" feature that discusses a topic related to the chapter content. Students are presented with questions that encourage them to consider more deeply the implications of these topics and require them to report their own experiences or to generate defensible arguments and cogent opinions—rather than to remember factual answers. For example, Chapter 11, "Development," presents students with arguments for and against parental licensing, and Chapter 10, "Emotion and Motivation," asks students whether governments should pay citizens to vote.

**Interim Summaries**  To promote study and learning of the material, each major section concludes with *In Summary* features that recap the major points in the section and provide a transition to the next section.

**Only Human Features**  These funny-but-true accounts of oddities and errors in human behavior provide a bit of comic relief that relates to the issues under discussion.

**Definitions and Glossary**  Each key term—a central concept, experimental procedure, or theory—is set apart from the text in boldface type, with its definition immediately following in italic type. The terms and their definitions are provided in a marginal glossary as well as an alphabetical, end-of-text glossary. The terms themselves appear at the end of the chapter with page numbers for easy reference.

**Chapter Review**  In addition to the interim summaries, a bulleted summary at the end of the chapter summarizes the main concepts in each major section.

**Recommended Readings**  Each chapter concludes with recommended readings, including trade books accessible to students, classic articles from the professional literature, online articles, and occasionally films related to a key concept or phenomenon discussed in the chapter.

## Media and Supplements to Accompany *Psychology*
### Web/CD-ROM

**NEW! Worth Publishers Student Video Tool Kit for *Psychology***
With its superb collection of brief (1 to 13 minutes) clips and emphasis on the biological basis of behavior, the **Student Video Tool Kit** gives students a fresh way to experience both the classic experiments at the heart of psychological science and cutting-edge research conducted by the field's most influential investigators.

The **Student Video Tool Kit** provides 51 video clips with a balance of contemporary news footage and classic experiments (both original and re-created) to help illustrate key concepts of the introductory psychology course. The **Student Video Tool Kit** is correlated to each Worth introductory psychology textbook, providing students with book-specific activities and multiple-choice questions. Students can print their answers to these questions, making the **Student Video Tool Kit** a seamless part of your course.

**NEW! Video Tool Kit for *Psychology*: Online Version**
The online version of the **Video Tool Kit for *Psychology*** includes the 51 video clips found on the student CD and is easily accessible through an access code packaged with *Psychology*. Fully customizable, the **Online Video Tool Kit** offers instructors the option of incorporating videos into assignments as well as annotating each video with notes or instructions, making the tool kit an integral part of the introductory course. Instructors also have the option of assigning the tool kit to students without instructor involvement. Videos are correlated to the textbook, and each video is accompanied by multiple-choice questions so that students can assess their understanding of what

they have seen. Student responses/grades are sent to an online grade book, allowing instructors to easily assign and assess as much of the **Online Video Tool Kit** as desired.

### NEW! PsychInvestigator: Laboratory Learning in Introductory Psychology by Arthur Kohn, PhD, Dark Blue Morning Productions

This exciting new Web-based product is a virtual laboratory environment that enables students to participate in real experiments. Students are introduced—step by step—to the various research techniques that are used in psychology. In **PsychInvestigator**, students participate in classic psychology experiments, generate real data, and are trained to create lab reports that summarize their findings. In each experiment, students participate in compelling video tutorials that are displayed before *and* after the actual experiment. **PsychInvestigator** requires no additional faculty time. Students' quiz scores can be automatically uploaded into an online grade book if instructors wish to monitor students' progress.

### eLibrary to Accompany *Psychology* (worthpublishers.com/elibrary)

The **eLibrary** brings together text and supplementary resources in a single, easy-to-use Web site and includes a sophisticated, straightforward search engine (similar to Google) that allows a quick search for resources related to specific topics (not just by chapter). Through simple browse and search tools, users can quickly access content from the text and ancillary package and either download it or create a Web page to share with students.

### PsychSim 5.0 CD-ROM and Booklet by Thomas Ludwig, Hope College

These 42 interactive simulations involve students in the practice of psychological research by having them play the role of experimenter (conditioning a rat, probing the hypothalamus electrically, working in a sleep lab) or subject (responding to tests of memory or visual illusions, interpreting facial expressions). Other simulations provide dynamic tutorials or demonstrations. In addition, five-question multiple-choice quizzes are available for each activity on the **Book Companion site**.

*Psychology* Book Companion Website at www.worthpublishers.com/schacter
The *Psychology* Book Companion Website offers students a virtual study guide 24 hours a day, 7 days a week. Best of all, these resources are free and do not require any special access codes or passwords. The site includes

- Annotated Web links
- Online quizzing
- Interactive flash cards
- Online version of 20 PsychSim 5.0 modules (by Thomas Ludwig, Hope College), accompanied by five-question, multiple-choice quizzes for each PsychSim activity
- Audio downloads
- A **password-protected Instructor site** offers a full array of teaching resources, including a new suite of PowerPoint slides, electronic lecture guides, an online quiz grade book, and links to additional tools.

**PsychInquiry for *Psychology*: Student Activities in Research and Critical Thinking CD-ROM by Thomas Ludwig, Hope College**
Customized to work specifically with *Psychology,* this CD-ROM contains dozens of interactive activities designed to help students learn about psychological research and to improve their critical-thinking skills.

## Course Management

**NEW! PsychPortal—One click. One place. For all the psychology tools you need!**

- Easy integration of all resources
- Easy-to-assign content
- Easy customization
- Easy to afford

**PsychPortal** is Worth's nationally hosted learning management solution. It combines standard course management features (such as course announcements, a syllabus manager, a calendar, and discussion forums) with state-of-the-art content and interactive-learning features. **PsychPortal** is organized into three main teaching and learning components: the **Interactive eBook and Study Center, Course Materials,** and **Quizzes and Assignments,** all fully customizable by the instructor. In addition, **PsychPortal** includes **PsychInvestigator,** a virtual laboratory environment that enables students to participate in real experiments and introduces them to the various research techniques that are used in psychology.

**PsychPortal Features**

- The **Interactive eBook and Study Center** offers a complete online version of the text, equipped with interactive note taking and highlighting capability and fully integrated with all the media resources available with *Psychology.*
- **Course Materials** organizes all the resources for *Psychology* in one location for both students' and instructors' ease of use. In addition, it allows instructors to post their own materials for use or assignment.
- **Quizzes and Assignments** enable instructors to automatically assign and grade homework and quizzes for their classes. Student assignments are collected in one location and allow students immediate feedback on their progress.

**Enhanced Course Management Solutions: Superior Content All in One Place**
**www.bfwpub.com/lms**
The most powerful course management tools are worthless without solid teaching and learning resources that have been meaningfully integrated. Our enhanced *Psychology*

turnkey course in Blackboard, WebCT (Campus Edition and Vista), and Angel course management systems offers a completely integrated solution that you can easily customize and adapt to meet your teaching goals and course objectives. Student content is organized by book chapters and instructor content by content type (e.g., PowerPoint slides). On demand, we can also provide our enhanced *Psychology* solution to those using Desire2Learn, Sakai, and Moodle.

**Sample Instructor Content**

- Video clip library of more than 40 digitized video clips organized by the text chapters
- Complete test bank
- Complete instructor's resources (in Word and PDF formats)
- Complete suite of PowerPoint slides
- Chapter art PowerPoint slides
- Enhanced lecture PowerPoint slides
- Step-up psychology review game
- Personal response system/clicker questions
- PsychSim 5.0 work sheet answer key
- Link to the instructor's eLibrary

**Sample Student Content**

- PsychSim 5.0 (20 activities, work sheets, and quizzes)
- Interactive flash cards (in both Spanish and English)
- Critical thinking and applications exercises
- Anatomical art self-quizzes (for select chapters)
- Crossword puzzles
- Additional simulations and demonstrations (for select chapters)
- Annotated web links
- Link to American Psychological Association style guide

To learn more about the course management solution to accompany *Psychology,* go to www.bfwpub.com.

**NEW! We Now Offer Customized ePacks and Course Cartridges**
Through the custom program, we can also help you tailor *Psychology* content to meet your course needs as well as provide you with technical support and services such as customizing your tests and quizzes, adding new student premium resources, adding Web links, reorganizing content, and adding a customized course banner. For more details, contact your Worth representative.


## Assessment

**Printed Test Bank by Russell Frohardt and Helen Just, St. Edward's University**
The **Test Bank** provides more than 2,000 multiple-choice, true/false, and essay questions. Each question is keyed to a chapter objective and APA Outcome, referenced to the textbook pages, and rated for level of difficulty. Web quizzes from the Book Companion site and Quick Quizzes from the Study Guide (for instructors who incorporate or require the Study Guide in their courses) are also included.

**Diploma Computerized Test Bank (available in Windows and Macintosh on one CD-ROM)**
The CD-ROM allows you to add an unlimited number of questions, edit questions, format a test, scramble questions, and include pictures, equations, or multimedia links. With the accompanying grade book, you can record students' grades throughout a

course, sort student records and view detailed analyses of test items, curve tests, generate reports, and add weights to grades. This CD-ROM is the access point for **Diploma Online Testing**. Blackboard- and WebCT-formatted versions of the **Test Bank** are also available in the Course Cartridge and ePack.

### Diploma Online Testing at www.brownstone.net

With **Diploma**, you can easily create and administer exams over the Internet with questions that incorporate multimedia and interactivity. Students receive instant feedback and can take the quizzes multiple times. Instructors can sort and view results and can take advantage of various grade-book and result-analysis features as well as restrict tests to specific computers or time blocks.

### Online Quizzing at worthpublishers.com/schacter

Now you can easily and securely quiz students online using prewritten multiple-choice questions for each chapter. Students receive instant feedback and can take the quizzes multiple times. As the instructor, you can view results by quiz, student, or question or you can get weekly results via e-mail.

### iClicker Radio Frequency Classroom Response System
### Offered by Worth Publishers in partnership with iClicker

**i◄clicker**

**iClicker** is Worth's hassle-free new polling system, created by educators for educators. This radio frequency system makes your class time more efficient and interactive. **iClicker** allows you to pause to ask questions and instantly record responses as well as take attendance, direct students through lectures, and gauge students' understanding of the material.

## Presentation

### ActivePsych: Classroom Activities Project and Video Teaching Modules

Recognizing that professors want out-of-the-box tools to make introductory psychology more applied and class presentations more interactive, Worth Publishers is proud to launch **ActivePsych**, a suite of instructor presentation CD-ROMs that include the following:

- Interactive activities designed for in-class presentation and group participation. **ActivePsych** activities require very little instructor preparation (allowing adopters to simply load the CD-ROM and launch the activity) and are designed to foster class discussion. Activities include animations, video clips, illustrations and photographs, and critical thinking questions. A number of activities have been adapted from Martin Bolt's Instructor's Resources and Thomas Ludwig's PsychSim 5.0 (and are now classroom-presentation friendly). **ActivePsych** also includes a significant number of completely original, creative activities all written (and class-tested) by veteran introductory psychology teachers.

- **ActivePsych: Classroom Activities Project** This segment of ActivePsych includes

    *32 flash-based interactive demonstrations* designed to promote classroom discussion and critical thinking.

    *22 PowerPoint-based demonstrations, inventories, and surveys* designed to assess student understanding of various psychological topics. These demonstrations can easily work with the iClicker classroom response systems.

- NEW! **Digital Media Archive, Second Edition** Housed in **ActivePsych** and edited by Joe Morrissey, State University of New York at Binghamton (with the assistance of Ann Merriwether, State University of New York at Binghamton and Meredith Woitach, University of Rochester), the second edition offers 33 sections of completely new short video clips and animations drawn from a variety of sources.

- NEW! *Scientific American* **Frontiers Teaching Modules, Third Edition** Housed in **ActivePsych** and edited by Martin Bolt, Calvin College, the third edition offers 15 edited clips from *Scientific American* Frontiers segments produced between 2003 and 2005.

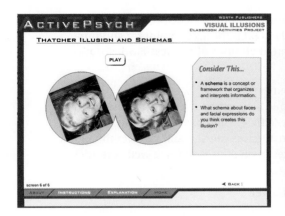

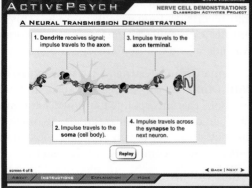

### Instructor's Resource CD-ROM

Customized for *Psychology,* this CD-ROM contains prebuilt PowerPoint presentation slide sets for each chapter, a digital photograph library, an electronic version of the Instructor's Resources, and a complete illustration library. A new intuitive browser interface makes it easy to preview and use all elements in this CD-ROM.

- **Chapter Art PowerPoint Slides** feature all of the text art and illustrations (including tables, charts, and graphs) in a PowerPoint format. We also offer a number of layered PowerPoint slides for key biological processes.

- **Step Up to Psychology: A PowerPoint Review Game** In this PowerPoint-based "game show," teams of students climb the pyramid by answering questions related to chapter material. Questions are ranked for difficulty (four levels) and include both factual/definitional and conceptual/application formats.

- **Lecture PowerPoint Presentation Slides** focus on key concepts and themes from the text and feature tables, graphs, and figures from both the text and outside sources.

- **Digital Photo Library** provides all the photographs from *Psychology* organized by chapter.

### Worth Image and Lecture Gallery at www.worthpublishers.com/ilg

Using the Image and Lecture Gallery, you can browse, search, and download text art, illustrations, outlines, and prebuilt PowerPoint slides for *all* Worth titles. Users can also create personal folders for easy organization of the materials.

## Video/DVD Resources

**NEW! Worth Publishers Video Tool Kit for Introductory Psychology • Available in Dual Platform CD-ROMs, VHS, and DVD**
With its superb collection of brief (1 to 13 minutes) video clips and emphasis on the biological bases of behavior, the **Instructor Video Tool Kit** allows you to introduce central topics, illustrate and reinforce specific core concepts, or stimulate small-group and full-classroom discussions. The **Video Tool Kit** includes a set of 72 digitized video clips combining both research and news footage from the BBC Motion Gallery, CBS News, and other sources. These clips can be easily used with PowerPoint or other presentation resources for classroom lectures and are accompanied by a faculty guide by Martin Bolt (Calvin College).

**Moving Images: Exploring Psychology through Film • Available in VHS and DVD**
Edited by Martin Bolt (Calvin College), this completely new series (drawn from the Films for the Humanities and Sciences) contains 25 1- to 8-minute clips of real people, real experiments, and real patients, combining historical footage with cutting-edge research and news programming. Some highlights include "Brain and Behavior: A Contemporary Phineas Gage," "Firewalking: Mind over Matter," and "Social Rejection: The Need to Belong."

**Worth Digital Media Archive • Available in Dual Platform CD-ROMs, VHS, and DVD**
This rich presentation tool contains 42 digitized video clips of classic experiments and research. Footage includes Bandura's Bobo doll experiment, Takooshian's bystander studies, Piaget's conservation experiment, Harlow's monkey experiments, and Milgram's obedience studies. The **Digital Media Archive** CD-ROM clips are available in MPEG for optimal visual presentation and are compatible with PowerPoint.

*Psychology: The Human Experience* **Teaching Modules • Available in VHS and DVD**
This series includes more than 3 hours of footage from the introductory psychology telecourse *Psychology: The Human Experience,* produced by Coast Learning Systems in collaboration with Worth Publishers. Footage contains noted scholars, the latest research, and striking animations.

*The Many Faces of Psychology* **Video**
**Created and written by Frank J. Vattano, Colorado State University, and Martin Bolt, Calvin College (Produced by the Office of Instructional Services, Colorado State University) • Available in VHS and DVD**
A terrific way to begin your psychology course, *The Many Faces of Psychology* introduces psychology as a science and a profession, illustrating basic and applied methods. This 22-minute video presents some of the major areas in which psychologists work and teach.

*The Brain* **Video Teaching Modules, Second Edition**
**Edited by Frank J. Vattano and Thomas L. Bennet, Colorado State University, and Michelle Butler, United States Air Force Academy • Available in VHS and DVD**
This collection of 32 short clips provides vivid examples for myriad topics in introductory psychology.

*Scientific American* **Frontiers Video Collection, Second Edition • Available in VHS and DVD**
Hosted by Alan Alda, these 8- to-12-minute teaching modules from the highly praised *Scientific American* series feature the work of such notable researchers as Steve Sumi, Renee Baillargeon, Carl Rosengren, Laura Pettito, Steven Pinker, Barbara Rothbaum, Bob Stickgold, Irene Pepperberg, Marc Hauser, Linda Bartoshuk, and Michael Gazzaniga.

*The Mind* **Video Teaching Modules, Second Edition**
**Edited by Frank J. Vattano, Colorado State University, in consultation with Charles Brewer, Furman University, and David Myers, Hope College, in association with WNET • Available in VHS and DVD**
These 35 brief, engaging video clips will dramatically enhance and illustrate your lectures. Examples include segments on language processing, infant cognitive development, genetic factors in alcoholism, and living without memory (featuring a dramatic interview with Clive Wearing).

## Print Supplements

### For Instructors

**Instructor's Resources by Russell Frohardt and Helen Just, St. Edwards University**
Written and compiled by experienced instructors of introductory psychology, the **Instructor's Resources** includes the following:

- An **Outline of Resources** for each chapter, organized by text topic, includes the relevant Instructor's Resources items by type (classroom exercise, lecture/discussion topic, etc.) with a cross-reference to its appropriate Instructor Resource page number.

- **Chapter Outlines** follow the major text section headings (with page references), providing relevant instructional materials for each topic—including dozens of ready-to-use, detailed lecture/discussion ideas, student projects, classroom exercises (many with ready-to-use handouts for in-class or out-of-class use), suggestions of multimedia resources provided by Worth Publishers (see pages xxi–xxvii), and feature films (as they apply to psychological concepts discussed in the text). Other film resources are outlined at the end of each chapter of the Instructor's Resources.

- **Chapter Objectives** from the text highlight main concepts and terms and detail the key points of each text chapter. They can be used as essay questions in classroom examinations. Test Bank and Study Guide questions are keyed to the Chapter Objectives as well.

### Instructor's Media Guide
This handy guide quickly and visually organizes the extensive instructor and student media resources available for *Psychology*, including every video, Web activity (including PsychInvestigator and PsychSim), PowerPoint, and more—all organized by chapter.

## For Students

### Study Guide by Russell Frohardt and Helen Just, St. Edwards University
Following the text's content, the **Study Guide** offers the following for each main chapter:

- **"The Big Picture,"** a brief wrap-up of the chapter's main ideas and concepts
- **Chapter Objectives**, which also appear in the Instructor's Resources and Test Bank
- **Chapter Overview**, a fill-in-the-blank summary that is divided by major section
- Three 10-question **"Quick Quizzes"** and a conceptual/analytical essay question
- **Answers section** with page references, corresponding chapter objectives, and explanations of why a choice is correct or incorrect
- **"Things to Ponder,"** a section that helps students extend and apply knowledge and think about where the material might be going.

### Pursuing Human Strengths: A Positive Psychology Guide by Martin Bolt, Calvin College
By using the scientific method in its efforts to assess, understand, and then build human strengths, positive psychology balances the investigation of weakness and damage with a study of strength and virtue. This brief positive psychology guide gives instructors and students alike the means to learn more about this relevant approach to psychology.

### Critical Thinking Companion, Second Edition
### Jane Halonen, University of West Florida, and Cynthia Gray, Alverno College
Tied to the main topics in psychology, this engaging handbook includes six categories of critical thinking exercises: pattern recognition, practical problem solving, creative problem solving, scientific critical thinking, psychological reasoning, and perspective taking, which connect to the six categories used in the Critical Thinking Exercises available in the student Study Guide.

### *Scientific American* Reader to Accompany *Psychology* by Daniel L. Schacter, Daniel T. Gilbert, and Daniel M. Wegner
Exclusive to Worth Publishers and in partnership with *Scientific American*, this collection of articles features pioneering and cutting-edge research across the fields of psychology. Selected by the authors themselves, this collection provides further insight into the fields of psychology through articles written for a popular audience.

### *Scientific American Mind*
*Scientific American Mind* is a new magazine from the editors of *Scientific American*. The magazine explores riveting breakthroughs in psychology, neuroscience, and related fields. *Scientific American Mind* investigates, analyzes, and reveals new thinking on a variety of contemporary psychological theories and ideas.

### *Improving the Mind and Brain:* A *Scientific American* Special Issue
This single-topic issue from *Scientific American* magazine features findings from the most distinguished researchers in the field.

### *Scientific American Explores the Hidden Mind:* A Collector's Edition
This collector's edition includes feature articles that explore and reveal the mysterious inner workings of our minds and brains.

# Acknowledgments

Despite what you might guess by looking at our photographs, we all found women who were willing to marry us. We thank Susan McGlynn, Marilynn Oliphant, and Toni Wegner for that particular miracle and also for their love and support during the years when we were busy writing this book.

Although ours are the names on the cover, writing a textbook is a team sport, and we were lucky to have an amazing group of professionals in our dugout. Our contributing consultants not only shaped our understanding of key areas of psychology but provided us with original material, expert ideas, and overviews that allowed us to write knowledgeably about topics not our own. We owe them a significant debt of thanks. They are Martin M. Antony, Mark Baldwin, Patricia Csank, Denise D. Cummins, Ian J. Deary, Howard Eichenbaum, Paul Harris, Arthur S. Reber, Alan Swinkels, Richard M. Wenzlaff, and Steven Yantis.

We are grateful for the editorial, clerical, and research assistance we received from Celeste Beck, Amy Cameron, Beth Mela, Betsy Sparrow, Adrian Gilmore, and Alana Wong.

In addition, we would like to thank our core supplements authors from St. Edward's University in Austin, Texas. They provided insight into the role our book can play in the classroom and adeptly developed the materials to support it. Helen Just, Russ Frohardt, and supplements coordinator Alan Swinkels, we appreciate your tireless work in the classroom and the experience you brought to the book's supplements.

Over 1,000 students have class-tested chapters of *Psychology* in various stages of development. Not only are we encouraged by the overwhelmingly positive responses to *Psychology,* but we are also pleased to incorporate these students' insightful and constructive comments. In particular, we would like to thank the introductory psychology students at the following institutions who learned from these chapters in their classrooms and contributed to the development of *Psychology* with a level of engagement we have come to expect from our best students: Baker University; Baldwin Wallace College; Boston University; Bowling Green State University; College of Lake County; College of St. Elizabeth; Curry College; Dominican University; Gainesville College; Hiwassee College; Illinois Wesleyan University; Kennesaw State University; Loyola University, Lakeshore; McKendree College; Morrisville State College, SUNY; Nazareth College of Rochester; Oregon State University; Regis University; Rochester Institute of Technology; Rowan University; Shepherd University; State University of West Georgia; Texas A&M University; University of Arizona; University of Arkansas-Fayetteville; University of Idaho; University of Kansas; University of Minnesota-Duluth; University of Nebraska at Kearney; University of San Diego; University of Texas at Austin; Villanova University; Wake Forest University; Washburn University; Washtenaw Community College.

We also learned a lot from focus group attendees, survey respondents, chapter reviewers, and class testers who read parts of our book, and we thank them for their time and insights, both of which were considerable. They include

George Alder
*Simon Fraser University*

Brad Alford
*University of Scranton*

John Allen
*University of Arizona*

Amber Alliger
*Hunter College*

Erica Altomare
*University of Pittsburgh at Titusville*

Eileen Astor-Stetson
*Bloomsburg University*

Raymond Baird
*University of Texas, San Antonio*

Scott Bates
*Utah State University*

Phillip Batten
*Wake Forest University*

Kyle Baumbauer
*Texas A&M University*

Kimberly Bays-Brown
*Ball State University*

Denise Berg
*UCLA*

Frank Bernieri
*Oregon State University*

Joan Bihun
*University of Colorado, Denver*

Wendi Born
*Baker University*

Deborah Briihl
*Valdosta State University*

Sara Broaders
*Northwestern University*

Cliff Brown
*Wittenberg University*

Krisanne Bursik
*Suffolk University*

Adam Butler
*University of Northern Iowa*

Peter Carole
*Regis University*

Isabelle Cherney
*Creighton University*

Sharon Claffey
*University of Georgia*

Samuel Clay
*BYU-Idaho*

Carl Clements
*University of Alabama*

Lawrence Cohen
*University of Delaware*

David Copeland
*University of Nevada, Las Vegas*

Gregory Corso
*Georgia Institute of Technology*

Renee Countryman
*Illinois Wesleyan University*

Cynthia Craig
*Thomas Jefferson University*

Susan Cross
*Iowa State University*

Mary Ellen Dello Stritto
*Western Oregon University*

Cathy DeSoto
*University of Northern Iowa*

Mary Devitt
*Jamestown College*

Tracy Dunne
*Boston University*

Steven Dworkin
*Jacksonville State University*

Jennifer Dyck
*SUNY Fredonia*

Vanessa Edkins
*University of Kansas*

Tami Eggleston
*McKendree University*

Lisa End-Berg
*Kennesaw State University*

Oney Fitzpatrick
*Lamar University*

Bill Flack
*Bucknell University*

Sandra Frankmann
*Colorado State University–Pueblo*

Phyllis R. Freeman
*SUNY at New Paltz*

Perry Fuchs
*University of Texas, Arlington*

Shira Gabriel
*University at Buffalo, SUNY*

Danielle Gagne
*Alfred University*

Anne Garcia
*Washtenaw Community College*

Luis Garcia
*Rutgers University–Camden*

Wendi Gardner
*Northwestern University*

Afshin Gharib
*Dominican University*

Diane Gillmore
*Loyola University, Lakeshore*

Wendell Goesling
*De Anza College*

Jamie Goldenberg
*University of South Florida*

Nicholas Greco
*College of Lake County*

Erinn Green
*Wilmington College*

Anthony Greene
*University of Wisconsin–Milwaukee*

Sarah Grison
*University of Illinois, Urbana Champaign*

Robert Guttentag
*The University of North Carolina at Greensboro*

Darlene Hannah
*Wheaton College*

Deletha Hardin
*University of Tampa*

David Harrison
*Virginia Tech University*

Mike Havens
*Montana State University, Billings*

Stephen Heinrichs
*Regis College*

Gloria Henderson
*University of San Diego*

Patricia Hinton
*Hiwassee College*

Debra Hollister
*Valencia Community College*

Jeffrey Holmes
*Ithaca College*

Herman Huber
*College of St. Elizabeth*

Allen Huffcutt
*Bradley University*

Linda Jackson
*Michigan State University*

James Jakubow
*Florida Atlantic University*

Norine Jalbert
*Western Connecticut State University*

Alisha Janowsky
*University of Central Florida*

Lance Jones
*Bowling Green State University*

Steve Joordens
*University of Toronto at Scarborough*

Deana Julka
*University of Portland*

Cynthia Kaschub
*University of Florida*

Mary-Louise Kean
*University of California, Irvine*

Craig Kinsley
*University of Richmond*

Michael Knepp
*Virginia Tech University*

Steve Kohn
*Valdosta State University*

Kim Krinsky
*Georgia Perimeter College*

Jose Lafosse
*Regis University*

Pamela Landau
*Eastern Michigan University*

Ann Leonard-Zabel
*Curry College*

Cheyanne Lewis
*Shephard University*

Pam MacDonald
*Washburn University*

Brian Malley
*University of Michigan*

Abe Marrero
*Rogers State University*

Karen Marsh
*University of Minnesota, Duluth*

Rona McCall
*Regis University*

David McDonald
*University of Missouri, Columbia*

Russell McGuff
*Tallahassee Community College*

Dani McKinney
*SUNY Fredonia*

Anca Miron
*University of Wisconsin, Oshkosh*

John Moritsugu
*Pacific Lutheran University*

Jane Noll
*University of South Florida*

Peggy Norwood
*Red Rocks Community College*

Rory O'Brien McElwee
*Rowan University*

Kristy Olin
*Robert E. Lee High School*

John Pierce
*Villanova University*

Joan Porcaro
*Pace University*

Gabriel Radvansky
*University of Notre Dame*

Celia Reaves
*Monroe Community College*

Cynthia Riedi
*Morrisville State College*

Bonnie Rosenblatt
*Kutztown University*

Gail Rothman-Marshall
*Rochester Institute of Technology*

Michael Russell
*Washburn University*

Catherine Sanderson
*Amherst College*

Nelly SantaMaria
*University of Pittsburgh*

Katie Saulsgiver
*University of Florida*

David Schroeder
*University of Arkansas*

Doyce Scott
*Southern University, Shreveport*

Marc Sebrechts
*Catholic University of America*

Janet Seide
*Bridgewater State College*

Ines Segert
*University of Missouri, Columbia*

Don Sharpe
*University of Regina*

David Simpson
*Carroll College*

Alice Skeens
*University of Toledo*

Jeffrey Skowronek
*University of Tampa*

John Skowronski
*Northern Illinois University*

Louisa Slowiaczek
*Bowdoin College*

Christine Smith
*Antioch College*

Claire St. Peter Pipkin
*West Virginia University*

David Steitz
*Nazareth College of Rochester*

Barry Stennett
*Gainesville College*

Deborah Stote
*University of Texas, Austin*

Jim Stringham
*University of Georgia*

George Taylor
*University of Missouri, St. Louis*

Brian Thomas
*Baldwin-Wallace College*

Lisa Thomassen
*Indiana University*

Inger Thompson
*Glendale Community College*

David Topor
*The University of North Carolina at Greensboro*

Michael Trent
*Triton College*

Julie Turchin
*College of San Mateo*

Julie Van Dyke
*Pace University*

Frank Vattano
*Colorado State University*

David Washburn
*Georgia State University*

Shannon Welch
*University of Idaho*

Robin Lea West
*University of Florida*

Julia Whisenhunt
*State University of West Georgia*

Len Williams
*Rowan University*

William Wozniak
*University of Nebraska at Kearney*

John William Wright
*Washington State University*

Jay Wright
*Washington State University*

Karen Yanowitz
*Arkansas State University*

Barbara Young
*Middle Tennessee State University*

Tricia Yurak
*Rowan University*

We are especially grateful to the extraordinary people of Worth Publishers. They include our publisher, Catherine Woods, who provided guidance and encouragement at all stages of the project; our acquisitions editor, Charles Linsmeier, who managed the project with intelligence, grace, and good humor; our senior development editor, Mimi Melek, who beat us mercilessly with her green pen and greatly improved our book in the process, as well as Barbara Brooks, Phyllis Fisher, and Michael Kimball, who also improved the text with their incisive edits; our narrative editor Alan Swinkels, who whipped a lumpy Dan soup into a smooth Dan puree; our associate managing editor Tracey Kuehn, project editor Jane O'Neill, copy editor Karen Taschek, production manager Sarah Segal, and assistant editor Justin Kruger, who through some remarkable alchemy turned a manuscript into a book; our art director Babs Reingold, layout designer Lee Mahler, photo editor Ted Szczepanski, and photo researcher Elyse Rieder, who made that book an aesthetic delight; our senior media editor Andrea Musick, and production manager Stacey Alexander, who guided the development and creation of a superb supplements package; and our executive marketing manager Kate Nurre, and associate director of market development Carlise Stembridge, who served as tireless public advocates for our vision. Thank you one and all. We look forward to working with you again.

Daniel L. Schacter          Daniel T. Gilbert          Daniel M. Wegner

Cambridge, 2007

# PSYCHOLOGY

# 1

# Psychology: The Evolution of a Science

**A LOT WAS HAPPENING IN 1860. ABRAHAM** Lincoln had just been elected president, the Pony Express had just begun to deliver mail between Missouri and California, and a woman named Anne Kellogg had just given birth to a child who would one day grow up to invent the cornflake. But none of this mattered very much to William James, a bright, taciturn, 18-year-old boy who had no idea what to do with his life. He loved to paint and draw but worried that he wasn't talented enough to become a serious artist. He had enjoyed studying biology in school but doubted that a naturalist's salary would ever allow him to get married and have a family of his own. And so like many young people who are faced with difficult decisions about their futures, William abandoned his dreams and chose to do something in which he had little interest but of which his family heartily approved. Alas, within a few months of arriving at Harvard Medical School, his initial disinterest in medicine blossomed into a troubling lack of enthusiasm, and so with a bit of encouragement from the faculty, he put his medical studies on hold to join a biological expedition to the Amazon. The adventure failed to focus his wandering mind (though he learned a great deal about leeches), and when he returned to medical school, both his physical and mental health began to deteriorate. It was clear to everyone that William James was not the sort of person who should be put in charge of a scalpel and a bag of drugs.

Had William become an artist, a biologist, or physician, we would probably remember nothing about him today. Fortunately for us, he was a deeply confused young man who could speak five languages, and when he became so depressed that he was once again forced to leave medical school, he decided to travel around Europe, where at least he knew how to talk to people. And as he talked and listened, he learned about a new science called *psychology* (from a combination of the Greek *psyche*, which means "soul," and *logos*, which means "to study"), which was just beginning to develop. As William read about psychology and talked with those who were developing it, he began to see that this new field was taking a modern, scientific approach to age-old questions about human nature—questions that had become painfully familiar to him during his personal search for meaning, but questions to which only poets and philosophers had ever before offered answers (Bjork, 1983; Simon, 1998). Excited about the new discipline, William returned to America and quickly finished his medical degree. But he never practiced medicine and never intended to do so. Rather, he became a professor at Harvard University and devoted the rest of his life to psychology. His landmark book—*The Principles of Psychology*—is still widely read and remains one of the most influential books ever written on the subject (James, 1890).

William James (1842–1910) was excited by the new field of psychology, which allowed him to apply a scientific approach to age-old questions about the nature of human beings.

A lot has happened since then. Abraham Lincoln has become the face on a penny, the Pony Express has been replaced by a somewhat slower mail system, and the Kellogg Company sells about $9 billion worth of cornflakes every year. If William James (1842–1910) were alive today, he would be amazed by all of these things. But he would probably be even more amazed by the intellectual advances that have taken place in the science that he helped create. Indeed, the sophistication and diversity of modern psychology are nothing short of staggering: Psychologists today are exploring perception, memory, creativity, consciousness, love, anxiety, addictions, and more. They use state-of-the-art technologies to examine what happens in the brain when people feel anger, recall a past experience, undergo hypnosis, or take an intelligence test. They examine the impact of culture on individuals, the origins and uses of language, the ways in which groups form and dissolve, and the similarities and differences between people from different backgrounds. Their research advances the frontiers of basic knowledge and has practical applications as well—from new treatments for depression and anxiety to new systems that allow organizations to function more effectively.

**Psychology** is *the scientific study of **mind and behavior**.* The **mind** refers to our *private inner experience,* the ever-flowing stream of consciousness that is made of perceptions, thoughts, memories, and feelings. **Behavior** refers to *observable actions of human beings and nonhuman animals,* the things that we do in the world, by ourselves or with others. As you will see in the chapters to come, psychology is an attempt to use scientific methods to address fundamental questions about mind and behavior that have puzzled people for millennia. For example, psychologists are curious about the bases of perceptions, thoughts, memories, and feelings, or our subjective sense of self. We'd like to understand how the mind usually functions so effectively in the world, allowing us to accomplish tasks as mundane as tying our shoes, as extraordinary as sending astronauts to the moon, or as sublime as painting the *Mona Lisa.* Importantly, psychologists also want to understand why the mind occasionally functions so *in*effectively in the world, causing us to make errors in reasoning and mistakes in judgment or to experience illusions in perception and gaps in memory. The answers to these questions would have astonished William James. Let's take a look at some examples:

- *What are the bases of perceptions, thoughts, memories, and feelings, or our subjective sense of self?* For thousands of years, philosophers tried to understand how the objective, physical world of the body was related to the subjective, psychological world of the mind, and some philosophers even suggested that the pineal gland in the brain might function as the magic tunnel between these two worlds. Today, psychologists know that there is no magic tunnel, and no need for one, because all of our subjective experiences arise from the electrical and chemical activities of our brains. Our mental lives are nothing more or less than "how it feels to be a brain." (Of course, this is a bit like saying that becoming wealthy involves nothing more or less than making money: It makes something sound simple that isn't.)

As you will see throughout this book, some of the most exciting developments in psychological research focus on how our perceptions, thoughts, memories, and feelings are related to activity in the brain. Psychologists and neuroscientists are using new technologies to explore this relationship in ways that would have seemed like science fiction only 20 years ago. The technique known as *functional magnetic resonance imaging,* or fMRI, allows scientists to "scan" a brain and see which parts are active when a person reads a word, sees a face, learns a new skill, or remembers a personal experience. William James was interested in how people acquire complex skills such as the ability to play the violin, and he wondered how the brain enabled great musicians to produce virtuoso performances. What William James could only ponder, modern psychologists can discover.

As one example, in a recent study, the brains of professional and novice pianists were scanned as they made complex finger movements like those involved in piano playing, and the results showed that professional pianists have *less* activity than novices in those parts of the brain that guide these finger movements (Krings et al.,

**PSYCHOLOGY** The scientific study of mind and behavior.

**MIND** Our private inner experience of perceptions, thoughts, memories, and feelings.

**BEHAVIOR** Observable actions of human beings and nonhuman animals.

2000). This result suggests that extensive practice at the piano changes the brains of professional pianists and that the regions controlling finger movements operate more efficiently than they do in novices. You'll learn more about this in Chapter 6 and see in the coming chapters how studies using fMRI and related techniques are beginning to transform many different areas of psychology.

- *How does the mind usually allow us to function effectively in the world?* Scientists sometimes say that form follows function; that is, if we want to understand *how* something works (e.g., an engine or a thermometer), we need to know what it is working *for* (e.g., powering vehicles or measuring temperature). As William James often noted, "Thinking is for doing," and the function of the mind is to help us do those things that sophisticated animals have to do in order to prosper, such as acquiring food, shelter, and mates. Psychological processes are said to be *adaptive*, which means that they promote the welfare and reproduction of organisms that engage in those processes.

For instance, perception allows us to recognize our families, see predators before they see us, and avoid stumbling into oncoming traffic. Language allows us to organize our thoughts and communicate them to others, which enables us to form social groups and cooperate. Memory allows us to avoid solving the same problems over again every time we encounter them and to keep in mind what we are doing and why. Emotions allow us to react quickly to events that have "life or death" significance, and they enable us to form strong social bonds. The list goes on and on, and as far as anyone can tell, there is no psychological equivalent of the body's appendix; that is, there's no thoroughly useless mental process that we'd all be better off without.

Given the adaptiveness of psychological processes, it is not surprising that those people with deficiencies in those processes often have a pretty tough time. The neurologist Antonio Damasio described the case of Elliot, a middle-aged husband and father with a good job, whose life was forever changed when surgeons discovered a tumor in the middle of his brain (Damasio, 1994). The surgeons were able to remove the tumor and save his life, and for a while Elliot seemed just fine. But then odd things began to happen. At first, Elliot seemed more likely than usual to make bad decisions (when he could make decisions at all), and as time went on, his bad decisions became truly dreadful ones. He couldn't prioritize tasks at work because he couldn't decide what to do first, and when he did, he got it wrong. Eventually he was fired, and so he pursued a series of risky business ventures, all of which failed, and he lost his life's savings. His wife divorced him, he married again, and his second wife divorced him too.

So what ruined Elliot's life? The neurologists who tested Elliot were unable to detect any decrease in his cognitive functioning. His intelligence was intact, and his ability to speak, to think, and to solve logical problems was every bit as sharp as it ever was. But as they probed further, they made a startling discovery: Elliot was no longer able to experience emotions. For example, Elliot didn't experience anxiety when he poured his entire bank account into a foolish business venture, he didn't experience any sorrow when his wives packed up and left him, and he didn't experience any regret or anger when his boss gave him the pink slip and showed him the door. Most of us have wished from time to time that we could be as stoic and unflappable as that; after all, who needs anxiety, sorrow, regret, and anger? The answer is that we all do. Emotions are adaptive because they function as signals that tell us when we are putting ourselves in harm's way. If you felt no anxiety when you thought about an upcoming exam, about borrowing your friend's car without permission, or about cheating on your taxes, you would probably make a string of poor decisions that would leave you without a degree and without a friend, except perhaps for your cellmate. Elliot didn't have those feelings, and he paid a big price for it. The ability of a basic psychological process (i.e., the experience of emotion) to perform its normally adaptive function was missing in poor Elliot's life.

- *Why does the mind occasionally function so ineffectively in the world?* The mind is an amazing machine that can do a great many things quickly. We can drive a car while talking to a passenger while recognizing the street address while remembering the name of the song that just came on the radio. But like all machines, the mind often

 **ONLY HUMAN**

**DÉJÀ VU ALL OVER AGAIN** In Troy, NY, Todd W. Bariteau Sr., 32, pleaded guilty to robbing, for the second time, a store called Déjà vu. In the second robbery, he broke through the same window and stole some of the same kinds of merchandise that he had stolen in the earlier theft.

trades accuracy for speed and versatility. This can produce "bugs" in the system, such as when a doughnut-making machine occasionally spews out gobs of gooey mush rather than dozens of delicious doughnuts. Our mental life is just as susceptible to *mindbugs,* or occasional malfunctions in our otherwise-efficient mental processing. One of the most fascinating aspects of psychology is that we are *all* prone to a variety of errors and illusions. Indeed, if thoughts, feelings, and actions were error free, then human behavior would be orderly, predictable, and dull, which it clearly is not. Rather, it is endlessly surprising, and its surprises often derive from our ability to do precisely the wrong thing at the wrong time.

For example, in two British airline crashes during the 1950s, pilots mistakenly shut down an engine that was operating perfectly normally after they became aware that another engine was failing (Reason & Mycielska, 1982, p. 5). Though the reasons for such catastrophic mental lapses are not well understood, they resemble far more mundane slips that we all make in our day-to-day lives. Consider a few examples from diaries of people who took part in a study concerning mindbugs in everyday life (Reason & Mycielska, 1982, pp. 70–73):

- *I meant to get my car out, but as I passed the back porch on my way to the garage, I stopped to put on my boots and gardening jacket as if to work in the yard.*
- *I put some money into a machine to get a stamp. When the stamp appeared, I took it and said, "Thank you."*
- *On leaving the room to go to the kitchen, I turned the light off, although several people were there.*

If these lapses seem amusing, it is because, in fact, they are. But they are also potentially important as clues to human nature. For example, notice that the person who bought a stamp said, "Thank you," to the machine and not, "How do I find the subway?" In other words, the person did not just do *any* wrong thing; rather, he did something that would have been perfectly right in a real social interaction. As each of these examples suggest, people often operate on "autopilot," or behave automatically, relying on well-learned habits that they execute without really thinking. When we are not actively focused on what we are saying or doing, these habits may be triggered inappropriately. William James thought that the influence of habit could help explain the seemingly bizarre actions of "absentminded" people: "Very absent-minded persons," he wrote in *The Principles of Psychology,* "on going into their bedroom to dress for dinner have been known to take off one garment after another and finally get into bed."

William James understood that the mind's mistakes are as instructive as they are intriguing, and modern psychology has found it quite useful to study such mindbugs. Things that are whole and unbroken hum along nicely and do their jobs while leaving no clue about how they do them. Cars gliding down the expressway might as well be magic carpets as long as they are working properly because we have no idea what kind of magic is moving them along. It is only when automobiles break down that we learn about their engines, water pumps, and other fine pieces and processes that normally work together to produce the ride. Breakdowns and errors are not just about destruction and failure—they are pathways to knowledge. In the same way, understanding lapses, errors, mistakes, and the occasionally buggy nature of human behavior provides a vantage point for understanding the normal operation of mental life and behavior. The story of Elliot, whose behavior broke down after he had brain surgery, is an example that highlights the role that emotions play in guiding normal judgment and behavior.

Psychology is exciting because it addresses fundamental questions about human experience and behavior, and the three questions we've just considered are merely the tip of the iceberg. Think of this book as a guide to exploring the rest of the iceberg. But before we don our parkas and grab our pick axes, we need to understand how the iceberg got here in the first place. To understand psychology in the 21st century, we need to become familiar with the psychology of the past.

# Psychology's Roots:
# The Path to a Science of Mind

When the young William James interrupted his medical studies to travel in Europe during the late 1860s, he wanted to learn about human nature. But he confronted a very different situation than a similarly curious student would confront today, largely because psychology did not yet exist as an independent field of study. As James cheekily wrote, "The first lecture in psychology that I ever heard was the first I ever gave." Of course, that doesn't mean no one had ever thought about human nature before. For 2,000 years, thinkers with scraggly beards and poor dental hygiene had pondered such questions, and in fact, modern psychology acknowledges its deep roots in philosophy. We will begin by examining those roots and then describe some of the early attempts to develop a scientific approach to psychology by relating the mind to the brain. Next we'll see how psychologists divided into different camps or "schools of thought": *structuralists,* who tried to analyze the mind by breaking it down into its basic components, and *functionalists,* who focused on how mental abilities allow people to adapt to their environments.

## Psychology's Ancestors: The Great Philosophers

The desire to understand ourselves is not new. Greek thinkers such as Plato (428 BC–347 BC) and Aristotle (384 BC–322 BC) were among the first to struggle with fundamental questions about how the mind works (Robinson, 1995). Greek philosophers debated many of the questions that psychologists continue to debate today. For example, are cognitive abilities and knowledge inborn, or are they acquired only through experience? Plato argued in favor of **nativism**, which maintains that *certain kinds of knowledge are innate or inborn.* Children in every culture figure out early on that sounds can have meanings that can be arranged into words, which then can be arranged into sentences. Before a child is old enough to poop in the proper place, she has already mastered the fundamentals of language without any formal instruction. Is the propensity to learn language "hardwired"—that is, is it something that children are born with? Or does the ability to learn language depend on the child's experience? Aristotle believed that the child's mind was a *"tabula rasa"* (a blank slate) on which experiences were written, and he argued for **philosophical empiricism**, which holds that *all knowledge is acquired through experience.*

Although few modern psychologists believe that nativism or empiricism is entirely correct, the issue of just how much "nature" and "nurture" explain any given behavior is still a matter of controversy. In some ways, it is quite amazing that ancient philosophers were able to articulate so many of the important questions in psychology and offer many excellent insights into their answers without any access to scientific evidence.

**NATIVISM** The philosophical view that certain kinds of knowledge are innate or inborn.

**PHILOSOPHICAL EMPIRICISM** The philosophical view that all knowledge is acquired through experience.

Many current ideas in psychology can be traced to the theories of two Greek philosophers from the fourth century BC: Plato (left), who believed in nativism, and Aristotle (right), who was Plato's student and believed in empiricism.

Their ideas came from personal observations, intuition, and speculation. Although they were quite good at arguing with one another, they usually found it impossible to settle their disputes because their approach provided no means of testing their theories. As you will see in Chapter 2, the ability to test a theory is the cornerstone of the scientific approach and the basis for reaching conclusions in modern psychology.

## From the Brain to the Mind: The French Connection

We all know that the brain and the body are physical objects that we can see and touch and that the subjective contents of our minds—our perceptions, thoughts, and feelings—are not. Inner experience is perfectly real, but where in the world is it? The French philosopher René Descartes (1596–1650) argued that body and mind are fundamentally different things—that the body is made of a material substance, whereas the mind (or soul) is made of an immaterial or spiritual substance (**FIGURE 1.1**). But if the mind and the body are different things made of different substances, then how do they interact? How does the mind tell the body to put its foot forward, and when the body steps on a rusty nail, why does the mind say, "Ouch"? This is the problem of *dualism,* or how mental activity can be reconciled and coordinated with physical behavior.

Descartes suggested that the mind influences the body through a tiny structure near the bottom of the brain known as the pineal gland. Unfortunately, he was largely alone in this view, as other philosophers at the time either rejected his explanation or offered alternative ideas. For example, the British philosopher Thomas Hobbes (1588–1679) argued that the mind and body aren't different things at all; rather, the mind *is* what the brain *does.* From Hobbes's perspective, looking for a place in the brain where the mind meets the body is like looking for the place in a television where the picture meets the flat panel display.

The French physician Franz Joseph Gall (1758–1828) also thought that brains and minds were linked, but by size rather than by glands. He examined the brains of animals and of people who had died of disease, or as healthy adults, or as children, and observed that mental ability often increases with larger brain size and decreases with damage to the brain. These aspects of Gall's findings were generally accepted (and the part about brain damage still is today). But Gall went far beyond his evidence to develop a psychological theory known as **phrenology**, which held that *specific mental abilities and characteristics, ranging from memory to the capacity for happiness, are localized in specific regions of the brain* (**FIGURE 1.2**). The idea that different parts of the brain are specialized for specific psychological functions turned out to be right; as you'll learn later in the book, a part of the brain called the hippocampus is intimately involved in memory, just as a structure called the amygdala is intimately involved in fear. But phrenology took this idea to an absurd extreme. Gall asserted that the size of bumps or indentations on the skull reflected the size of the brain regions beneath them and that by feeling those bumps, one could tell whether a person was friendly, cautious, assertive, idealistic, and so on.

Gall's phrenological approach was based entirely on anecdotes and casual observations (Fancher, 1979). For example, Gall recalled that someone he knew had a good memory and large protruding eyes, and thus he suggested that the part of the brain behind the eyes must play a special role in memory. Phrenology made for a nice parlor game and gave young people a good excuse for touching each other, but in the end it amounted to a series of strong claims based on weak evidence. Not surprisingly, his critics were galled (so to speak), and they ridiculed many of his proposals. Despite an initially large following, phrenology was quickly discredited (Fancher, 1979).

While Gall was busy playing bumpologist, other French scientists were beginning to link the brain and the mind in a more convincing manner. The biologist Pierre Flourens (1794–1867) was appalled by Gall's far-reaching claims and sloppy methods, and so he conducted experiments in which he surgically removed specific parts of the brain from dogs, birds, and other animals and found (not surprisingly!) that their actions and movements differed from those of animals with intact brains.

LEONARD DE SELVA/CORBIS

**Figure 1.1 René Descartes (1595–1650)** Descartes made contributions to many fields of inquiry, from physiology to philosophy. He is probably best known for his suggestion that the body and soul are fundamentally different.

**Figure 1.2 Phrenology** Francis Gall (1758–1828) developed a theory called phrenology, which suggested that psychological capacities (such as the capacity for friendship) and traits (such as cautiousness and mirth) were located in particular parts of the brain. The more of these capacities and traits a person had, the larger the corresponding bumps on the skull.

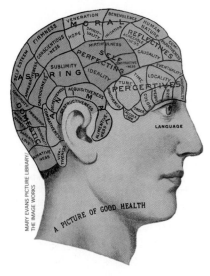

MARY EVANS PICTURE LIBRARY/THE IMAGE WORKS

The surgeon Paul Broca (1825–80) worked with a patient who had suffered damage to a small part of the left side of the brain (now known as Broca's area). The patient, Monsieur Leborgne, was virtually unable to speak and could utter only the single syllable "tan." Yet the patient understood everything that was said to him and was able to communicate using gestures. Broca had the crucial insight that damage to a specific part of the brain impaired a specific mental function, clearly demonstrating that the brain and mind are closely linked. This was important in the 19th century because at that time many people accepted Descartes' idea that the mind is separate from, but interacts with, the brain and the body. Broca and Flourens, then, were the first to demonstrate that the mind is grounded in a material substance; namely, the brain. Their work jump-started the scientific investigation of mental processes.

THE GRANGER COLLECTION

Surgeon Paul Broca (1824–80) worked with a brain-damaged person who could comprehend but not produce spoken language. Broca suggested that the mind is grounded in the material processes of the brain.

## From Physiology to Psychology: A New Science Is Born in Germany

In the middle of the 19th century, psychology benefited from the work of German scientists who were trained in the field of **physiology**, which is *the study of biological processes, especially in the human body.* Physiologists had developed methods that allowed them to measure such things as the speed of nerve impulses, and some of them had begun to use these methods to measure mental abilities. William James was drawn to the work of two such physiologists: Hermann von Helmholtz (1821–94) and Wilhelm Wundt (1832–1920). "It seems to me that perhaps the time has come for psychology to begin to be a science," wrote James in a letter written in 1867 during his visit to Berlin. "Helmholtz and a man called Wundt at Heidelberg are working at it." What attracted James to the work of these two scientists?

### Helmholtz Measures the Speed of Responses

A brilliant experimenter with a background in both physiology and physics, Helmholtz had developed a method for measuring the speed of nerve impulses in a frog's leg, which he then adapted to the study of human beings. Helmholtz trained participants to respond when he applied a **stimulus**—*sensory input from the environment*—to different parts of the leg. He recorded his participants' **reaction time**, or *the amount of time taken to respond to a specific stimulus,* after applying the stimulus. Helmholtz found that people generally took longer to respond when their toe was stimulated than when their thigh was stimulated, and the difference between these reaction times allowed him to estimate how long it took a nerve impulse to travel to the brain. These results were astonishing to 19th-century scientists because at that time just about everyone thought that mental processes occurred instantaneously. When you move your hands in front of your eyes, you don't feel your hands move a fraction of a second before you see them. The real world doesn't appear like one of those late-night movies in which the video and the audio are off by just a fraction of a second. Scientists assumed that the neurological processes underlying mental events *must* be instantaneous for everything to be so nicely synchronized, but Helmholtz showed that this wasn't true. In so doing, he also demonstrated that reaction time could be a useful way to study the mind and the brain.

### Wundt and the Development of Structuralism

Although Helmholtz's contributions were important, historians generally credit the official emergence of psychology to Helmholtz's research assistant, Wilhelm Wundt (Rieber, 1980). Wundt published two books outlining his vision of a scientific

HULTON ARCHIVE/GETTY IMAGES

By measuring a person's reaction times to different stimuli, Hermann von Helmholtz (1821–94) estimated the length of time it takes a nerve impulse to travel to the brain.

**PHRENOLOGY** A now defunct theory that specific mental abilities and characteristics, ranging from memory to the capacity for happiness, are localized in specific regions of the brain.

**PHYSIOLOGY** The study of biological processes, especially in the human body.

**STIMULUS** Sensory input from the environment.

**REACTION TIME** The amount of time taken to respond to a specific stimulus.

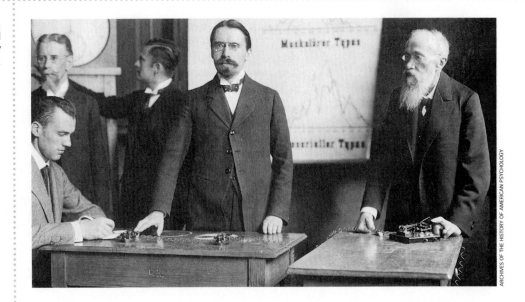

Wilhelm Wundt (1832–1920), far right, founded the first laboratory devoted exclusively to psychology at the University of Leipzig in Germany.

approach to psychology and describing experiments on sensory perception that he had conducted in a makeshift laboratory in his home (Schultz & Schultz, 1987). In 1867, Wundt taught at the University of Heidelberg what was probably the first course in physiological psychology, and this course led to the publication of his book *Principles of Physiological Psychology* in 1874. Wundt called the book "an attempt to mark out [psychology] as a new domain of science" (Fancher, 1979, p. 126). In 1879, at the University of Leipzig, Wundt opened the first laboratory ever to be exclusively devoted to psychological studies, and this event marked the official birth of psychology as an independent field of study. The new lab was full of graduate students carrying out research on topics assigned by Wundt, and it soon attracted young scholars from all over the world who were eager to learn about the new science that Wundt had developed.

Wundt believed that scientific psychology should focus on analyzing **consciousness**, *a person's subjective experience of the world and the mind*. Consciousness encompasses a broad range of subjective experiences. We may be conscious of sights, sounds, tastes, smells, bodily sensations, thoughts, or feelings. As Wundt tried to figure out a way to study consciousness scientifically, he noted that chemists try to understand the structure of matter by breaking down natural substances into basic elements. So he and his students adopted an approach called **structuralism**, or *the analysis of the basic elements that constitute the mind*. This approach involved breaking consciousness down into elemental sensations and feelings, and you can do a bit of structuralism right now without leaving your chair.

Consider the contents of your own consciousness. At this very moment you may be aware of the meaning of these words, the visual appearance of the letters on the page, the key ring pressing uncomfortably against your thigh, your feelings of excitement or boredom (probably excitement), the smell of curried chicken salad, or the nagging question of whether the War of 1812 really deserves its own overture. At any given moment, all sorts of things are swimming in the stream of consciousness, and Wundt tried to analyze them in a systematic way using the method of **introspection**, which involves *the subjective observation of one's own experience*. In a typical experiment, observers (usually students) would be presented with a stimulus (usually a color or a sound) and then be asked to report their introspections. The observers would describe the brightness of a color or the loudness of a tone. They were asked to report on their "raw" sensory experience rather than on their interpretations of that experience. For example, an observer presented with this page would not report seeing words on the page (which counts as an interpretation of the experience), but instead might describe a series of black marks, some straight and others curved, against a bright white background. Wundt also attempted to carefully describe the feelings associated with ele-

**CONSCIOUSNESS** A person's subjective experience of the world and the mind.

**STRUCTURALISM** The analysis of the basic elements that constitute the mind.

**INTROSPECTION** The subjective observation of one's own experience.

ARCHIVES OF THE HISTORY OF AMERICAN PSYCHOLOGY

mentary perceptions. For example, when Wundt listened to the clicks produced by a metronome, some of the patterns of sounds were more pleasant than others. By analyzing the relation between feelings and perceptual sensations, Wundt and his students hoped to uncover the basic structure of conscious experience.

Wundt tried to provide objective measurements of conscious processes by using reaction time techniques similar to those first developed by Helmholtz. Wundt used reaction times to examine a distinction between the perception and interpretation of a stimulus. His research participants were instructed to press a button as soon as a tone sounded. Some participants were told to concentrate on perceiving the tone before pressing the button, whereas others were told to concentrate only on pressing the button. Those people who concentrated on the tone responded about one tenth of a second more slowly than those told to concentrate only on pressing the button. Wundt reasoned that both fast and slow participants had to register the tone in consciousness (perception), but only the slower participants had to also interpret the significance of the tone and press the button. The faster research participants, focusing only on the response they were to make, could respond automatically to the tone because they didn't have to engage in the additional step of interpretation (Fancher, 1979). This type of experimentation broke new ground by showing that psychologists could use scientific techniques to disentangle even subtle conscious processes. In fact, as you'll see in later chapters, reaction time procedures have proven extremely useful in modern research.

## Titchener Brings Structuralism to the United States

The pioneering efforts of Wundt's laboratory launched psychology as an independent science and profoundly influenced the field for the remainder of the 19th century. Many European and American psychologists journeyed to Leipzig to study with Wundt. Among the most eminent was the British-born Edward Titchener (1867–1927), who studied with Wundt for 2 years in the early 1890s. Titchener then came to the United States and set up a psychology laboratory at Cornell University (where, if you'd like to see it, his brain is still on display in the psychology department). Titchener brought some parts of Wundt's approach to America, but he also made some changes (Brock, 1993; Rieber, 1980). For instance, whereas Wundt emphasized the relationship between elements of consciousness, Titchener focused on identifying the basic elements themselves. He trained his students to provide detailed descriptions of their conscious images and sensations—a demanding process that Titchener called "hard introspective labor." In his textbook *An Outline of Psychology* (1896), Titchener put forward a list of more than 44,000 elemental qualities of conscious experience, most of them visual (32,820) or auditory (11,600) (Schultz & Schultz, 1987).

The influence of the structuralist approach gradually faded, due mostly to the introspective method. Science requires replicable observations—we could never determine the structure of DNA or the life span of a dust mite if every scientist who looked through a microscope saw something different. Alas, even trained observers provided conflicting introspections about their conscious experiences ("I see a cloud that looks like a duck"—"No, *I* think that cloud looks like a horse"), thus making it difficult for different psychologists to agree on the basic elements of conscious experience. Indeed, some psychologists had doubts about whether it was even possible to identify such elements through introspection alone. One of the most prominent skeptics was someone you've already met—a young man with a bad attitude and a useless medical degree named William James.

## James and the Functional Approach

After William James pulled out of his downward spiral in the early 1870s, he was still inspired by the idea of approaching psychological issues from a scientific perspective. He received a teaching appointment at Harvard (primarily because the president of the

Edward Titchener (1867–1927) brought structuralism to America, setting up a psychology laboratory at Cornell University. Titchener studied under Wundt in Germany.

**FUNCTIONALISM** The study of the purpose mental processes serve in enabling people to adapt to their environment.

**NATURAL SELECTION** Charles Darwin's theory that the features of an organism that help it survive and reproduce are more likely than other features to be passed on to subsequent generations.

university was a neighbor and family friend) and in 1875 offered a course called "The Relations between Physiology and Psychology." More importantly, his position at Harvard enabled him to purchase laboratory equipment for classroom experiments, making his the first course at an American university to draw on the new experimental psychology developed by Wundt and his German followers (Schultz & Schultz, 1987). These courses and experiments led James to write his masterpiece, *The Principles of Psychology* (James, 1890).

James agreed with Wundt on some points, including the importance of focusing on immediate experience and the usefulness of introspection as a technique (Bjork, 1983), but he disagreed with Wundt's claim that consciousness could be broken down into separate elements. James believed that trying to isolate and analyze a particular moment of consciousness (as the structuralists did) distorted the essential nature of consciousness. Consciousness, he argued, was more like a flowing stream than a bundle of separate elements. So James decided to approach psychology from a different perspective entirely, and he developed an approach known as **functionalism**: *the study of the purpose mental processes serve in enabling people to adapt to their environment.* In contrast to structuralism, which examined the structure of mental processes, functionalism set out to understand the functions those mental processes served. (See The Real World box for some strategies to enhance one of those functions—learning.)

James's thinking was inspired by the ideas in Charles Darwin's recently published book on biological evolution, *The Origin of Species* (1859). Darwin proposed the principle of **natural selection**, which states that *the features of an organism that help it survive and reproduce are more likely than other features to be passed on to subsequent generations.* From this perspective, James reasoned, mental abilities must have evolved because they were adaptive—that is, because they helped people solve problems and increased their chances of survival. Like other animals, people have always needed to avoid predators, locate food, build shelters, and attract mates. Applying Darwin's principle of natural selection, James (1890) reasoned that consciousness must serve an important biological function and the task for psychologists was to understand what those functions are. Wundt and the other structuralists worked in laboratories, and James felt that such work was limited in its ability to tell us how consciousness functioned in the natural environment. Wundt, in turn, felt that James did not focus enough on new findings from the laboratory that he and the structuralists had begun to produce. Commenting on *The Principles of Psychology,* Wundt conceded that James was a topflight writer but disapproved of his approach: "It is literature, it is beautiful, but it is not psychology" (Bjork, 1983, p. 12).

The rest of the world did not agree, and James's functionalist psychology quickly gained followers, especially in North America, where Darwin's ideas were influencing many thinkers. G. Stanley Hall (1844–1924), who studied with both Wundt and James, set up the first psychology research laboratory in North America at Johns Hopkins University in 1881. Hall's work focused on development and education and was strongly influenced by evolutionary thinking (Schultz & Schultz, 1987).

Hall believed that as children develop, they pass through stages that repeat the evolutionary history of the human race. Thus, the mental capacities of a young child resemble those of our ancient ancestors, and children grow over a lifetime in the same way that a species evolves over aeons. Hall founded the *American Journal of Psychology* in 1887 (the first psychology journal in the United States), and he went on to play a key role in founding the American Psychological Association (the first national organization of psychologists in the United States), serving as its first president.

The efforts of James and Hall set the stage for functionalism to develop as a major school of psychological thought in North America. Psychology departments that embraced a functionalist approach started to spring up at many major American universities, and in a struggle for survival that would have made Darwin proud, functionalism became more influential than structuralism had ever been. By the time Wundt and Titchener died in the 1920s, functionalism was the dominant approach to psychology in North America.

G. Stanley Hall (1844–1924) contributed greatly to the growth of psychology in North America. He founded the continent's first psychology laboratory at Johns Hopkins University, the first academic journal devoted to psychology, and the first professional organization (the American Psychological Association).

## { THE REAL WORLD } Improving Study Skills

By reading this book and taking this introductory course, you will learn a great deal about psychology, just as you learn about subjects ranging from religion to literature to history in other courses. Unlike other disciplines, psychology can provide a kind of insight that is applicable to everyday life: Psychology can help you to learn about psychology.

Psychologists have progressed a great deal in understanding how we remember and learn. We'll explore the science of memory and learning in Chapters 5 and 6, but here we focus on the practical implications of psychological research for everyday life: how you can use psychology to improve your study skills. Such knowledge should help you to perform your best in this course and others, but perhaps more importantly, it can help to prepare you for challenges you will face after graduation. With the rapid pace of technological change in our society, learning and memory skills are more important than ever. Experts estimate that the knowledge and skills required for success in a job will change completely every 3 to 7 years during an individual's career (Herrmann, Raybeck, & Gruneberg, 2002). Enhancing your learning and memory skills now should pay off for you later in life in ways we can't even yet predict.

Psychologists have focused on mental strategies that can enhance your ability to *acquire* information, to *retain* it over time, and to *retrieve* what you have acquired and retained. Let's begin with the process of acquiring information—that is, transforming what you see and hear into an enduring memory. Our minds don't work like video cameras, passively recording everything that happens around us. To acquire information effectively, you need to actively manipulate it. One easy type of active manipulation is rehearsal: repeating to-be-learned information to yourself. You've probably tried this strategy already, but psychologists have found that some types of rehearsal are better than others. A particularly effective strategy is called *spaced rehearsal*, where you repeat information to yourself at increasingly long intervals. For example, suppose that you want to learn the name of a person you've just met named Eric. Repeat the name to yourself right away, wait a few seconds and think of it again, wait for a bit longer (maybe 30 seconds) and bring the name to mind once more, then rehearse the name again after a minute and once more after 2 or 3 minutes. Studies show that this type of rehearsal improves long-term learning more than rehearsing the name without any spacing between rehearsals (Landauer & Bjork, 1978). You can apply this technique to names, dates, definitions, and many other kinds of information, including concepts presented in this textbook.

Simple rehearsal can be beneficial, but one of the most important lessons from psychological research is that we acquire information most effectively when we think about its meaning and reflect on its significance. In fact, we don't even have to try to remember something if we think deeply enough about what we want to remember; the act of reflection itself will virtually guarantee good memory. For example, suppose that you want to learn the basic ideas behind Skinner's approach to behaviorism. Ask yourself the following kinds of questions: How did behaviorism differ from previous approaches in psychology? How would a behaviorist like Skinner think about psychological issues that interest you, such as whether a mentally disturbed individual should be held responsible for committing a crime, or what factors would contribute to your choice of a major subject or career path? In attempting to answer such questions, you will need to review what you've learned about behaviorism and then relate it to other things you already know about. It is much easier to remember new information when you can relate it to something you already know.

You'll also learn later in this book about techniques for visualizing information, first developed by the ancient Greeks, that modern psychological research has proven to be effective memory aids (Paivio, 1969). One such technique, known as the *method of loci*, involves "mentally depositing" information you wish to remember into familiar locations and then later searching through those locations to recall the information.

For example, suppose you want to remember the major contributions of Wundt, Freud, and Skinner to the development of psychology. You could use your current or former home as the location and imagine Wundt's reaction time apparatus lying on your bed, Freud's psychoanalysis couch sitting in your living room, and Skinner's rats running around your bathroom. Then when you need this information, you can "pull up" an image of your home and take a mental tour through it in order to see what's there. You can use this basic approach with a variety of familiar locations—a school building you know well, a shopping mall, and so forth—in order to remember many different kinds of information.

You can use each of the mental manipulations discussed here to help you remember and learn the material in this textbook and prepare for your tests:

- Think about and review the information you have acquired in class on a regular basis. Begin soon after class, and then try to schedule regular "booster" sessions.
- Don't wait until the last second to cram your review into one sitting; research shows that spacing out review and repetition leads to longer-lasting recall.
- Don't just look at your class notes or this textbook; test yourself on the material as often as you can. Research also shows that actively retrieving information you've acquired helps you to later remember that information more than just looking at it again.
- Take some of the load off your memory by developing effective note-taking and outlining skills. Students often scribble down vague and fragmentary notes during lectures, figuring that the notes will be good enough to jog memory later. But when the time comes to study, they've forgotten so much that their notes are no longer clear. Realize that you can't write down everything an instructor says, and try to focus on making detailed notes about the main ideas, facts, and people mentioned in the lecture.
- Organize your notes into an outline that clearly highlights the major concepts. The act of organizing an outline will force you to reflect on the information in a way that promotes retention and will also provide you with a helpful study guide to promote self-testing and review.

To follow up on these suggestions and find much more detailed information on learning and study techniques, see the Recommended Reading by Hermann, Raybeck, & Gruneberg (2002).

*"As I get older, I find I rely more and more on these sticky notes to remind me."*

**In summary,** philosophers have pondered and debated ideas about human nature for millennia, but, given the nature of their approach, they did not provide empirical evidence to support their claims. Some of the earliest successful efforts to develop a *science* linking mind and behavior came from the French scientists Pierre Flourens and Paul Broca, who showed that damage to the brain can result in impairments of behavior and mental functions. Hermann von Helmholtz furthered the science of the mind by developing methods for measuring reaction time. Wilhelm Wundt, credited with the founding of psychology as a scientific discipline, created the first psychological laboratory and taught the first course in physiological psychology. His structuralist approach focused on analyzing the basic elements of consciousness. Wundt's student, Edward Titchener, brought structuralism to the United States. William James emphasized the functions of consciousness and applied Darwin's theory of natural selection to the study of the mind, thus helping to establish functionalism and scientific psychology in the United States. Scientific psychology in America got a further boost from G. Stanley Hall, who established the first research laboratory, journal, and professional organization devoted to psychology. ■ ■

## Errors and Illusions Reveal Psychology

At about the same time that some psychologists were developing structuralism and functionalism, other psychologists were beginning to think about how illusions and disorders might illuminate psychological functioning. They began to realize that one can often understand how something works by examining how it breaks. Let's look first at the illusion that launched a new movement known as Gestalt psychology and then consider how observations of mental disorders influenced the development of psychology. In each case, a careful examination of some mindbugs led to a clearer understanding of human mental functioning.

### Illusions of Movement and the Birth of Gestalt Psychology

Magicians and artists could not earn a living unless people were susceptible to **illusions**, that is, *errors of perception, memory, or judgment in which subjective experience differs from objective reality.* For example, if you measure the dark horizontal lines shown in **FIGURE 1.3** with a ruler, you'll see that they are of equal length. And yet, for most of us, the top line appears longer than the bottom one. As you'll learn in Chapter 4, this is because the surrounding vertical lines influence your perception of the horizontal lines. A similar visual illusion fired the imagination of a German psychologist named Max Wertheimer (1880–1943), who was enjoying a train ride during his vacation when he had a sudden insight into the nature of visual perception. Wertheimer was so excited by his idea that he went to a store as soon as he

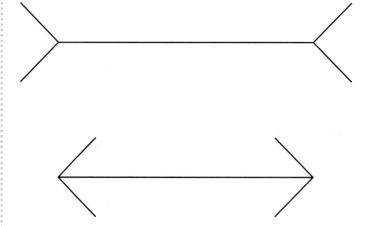

**Figure 1.3 The Mueller-Lyer Line Illusion** Although they do not appear to be, these two horizontal lines are actually the same length. The Gestalt psychologists used illusions like this to show how the perception of a whole object or scene can influence judgments about its individual elements.

http://www.gla.ac.uk/philosophy/CSPE/illusions/Muller-Lyer.GIF

got off the train and purchased equipment for an experiment (Benjamin, 1988). In Wertheimer's experiment, a person was shown two lights that flashed quickly on a screen, one after the other. One light was flashed through a vertical slit, the other through a diagonal slit. When the time between two flashes was relatively long (one fifth of a second or more), an observer would see that it was just two lights flashing in alternation. But when Wertheimer reduced the time between flashes to around one twentieth of a second, observers saw a single flash of light moving back and forth (Fancher, 1979; Sarris, 1989).

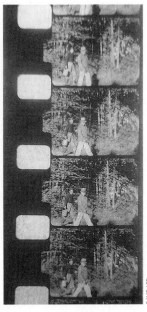

DAVID LEE

Max Wertheimer's (1880–1943) insights about the perception of motion offered a scientific explanation of why we see movement when viewing a series of rapidly flashed still pictures, a method used by moviemakers in the early 1900s.

Creating the illusion of motion was not new. Turn-of-the-century moviemakers already understood that quickly flashing a series of still images, one after the other, could fool people into perceiving motion where none actually existed. But Wertheimer's *interpretation* of this illusion, conceived during his train ride, was the novel element that contributed to the growth of psychology (Benjamin, 1988; Steinman, Pizlo, & Pizlo, 2000). He reasoned that the perceived motion could not be explained in terms of the separate elements that cause the illusion (the two flashing lights) but instead that the moving flash of light is perceived as a *whole* rather than as the sum of its two parts. This unified whole, which in German is called *Gestalt,* makes up the perceptual experience. Wertheimer's interpretation of the illusion led to the development of **Gestalt psychology,** *a psychological approach that emphasizes that we often perceive the whole rather than the sum of the parts.* In other words, the mind imposes organization on what it perceives, so people don't see what the experimenter actually shows them (two separate lights); instead they see the elements as a unified whole (one moving light). This analysis provides an excellent illustration of how illusions can offer clues about the basic principles of the mind.

The Gestaltists' claim was diametrically opposed to the structuralists' claim that experience can be broken down into separate elements. Wertheimer and later Gestalt psychologists such as Kurt Koffka (1886–1941) and Wolfgang Kohler (1887–1967) developed the theory further and came up with additional demonstrations and illusions that strengthened their contention that the mind perceives the whole rather than the sum of its parts. Although Gestalt psychology no longer exists today as a distinct school of thought, its basic claims have influenced the modern study of object perception (as you'll see in Chapter 4) as well as social perception (as you'll see in Chapter 16). Indeed, the notion that the mind imposes structure and organization was a central claim of the philosopher Immanuel Kant (1724–1824), and it remains one of modern psychology's most widely accepted principles. And imagine: All of this came from a lovely little train ride.

## Mental Disorders and Multiple Selves

Just as Gestalt psychologists were discovering that illusions in visual perception can help us understand how the eye and the brain normally work so well, other psychologists were discovering how the bizarre behaviors of patients with psychological disorders could shed light on the workings of the ordinary mind. For example, in 1876 a startling report in a French medical journal described a woman called Felida X (Azam, 1876). Felida was normally shy and quiet, but sometimes she would suddenly become much bolder and more outgoing. Then, without warning, she would just as suddenly return to her usual shy and reserved state. Stranger still, the shy Felida had no memory of what the outgoing Felida had done. Once while riding in a carriage, Felida suddenly switched from outgoing to shy and seemed to completely forget that she had just been to the funeral of a close friend. The barrier between the two states was so strong that the shy Felida forgot that she had become pregnant while in her outgoing state!

**ILLUSIONS** Errors of perception, memory, or judgment in which subjective experience differs from objective reality.

**GESTALT PSYCHOLOGY** A psychological approach that emphasizes that we often perceive the whole rather than the sum of the parts.

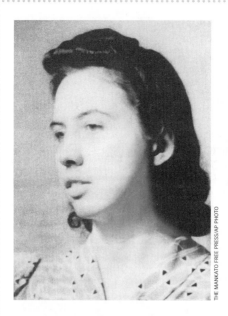

**Figure 1.4 Dissociative Identity Disorder** Shirley Ardell Mason's (left) struggle with dissociative identity disorder was described first in the book *Sybil* (a pseudonym given to protect her privacy), which chronicles her mental illness as revealed through her therapy with Dr. Cornelia Wilbur. Sybil's story was told in the 1973 book (right) and later made into a television movie starring Sally Field, who won an Emmy for her portrayal of Sybil.

Felida X was an early example of an unusual condition now called **dissociative identity disorder** (see Chapter 13), which *involves the occurrence of two or more distinct identities within the same individual* (**FIGURE 1.4**). The French physicians Jean-Marie Charcot (1825–93) and Pierre Janet (1859–1947) reported similar observations when they interviewed patients who had developed a condition known then as **hysteria**, or a *temporary loss of cognitive or motor functions, usually as a result of emotionally upsetting experiences*. Hysterical patients became blind, paralyzed, or lost their memories, even though there was no known physical cause of their problems. However, when the patients were put into a trancelike state through the use of hypnosis (an altered state of consciousness characterized by suggestibility), their symptoms disappeared: Blind patients could see, paralyzed patients could walk, and forgetful patients could remember. After coming out of the hypnotic trance, however, the patients forgot what had happened under hypnosis and again showed their symptoms. Like Felida X, the patients behaved like two different people in the waking versus hypnotic states.

These peculiar disorders were ignored by Wundt, Titchener, and other laboratory scientists, who did not consider them a proper subject for scientific psychology (Bjork, 1983). But William James believed they had important implications for understanding the nature of the mind (Taylor, 2001). He discerned an important mindbug at work, capitalizing on these mental disruptions as a way of understanding the normal operation of the mind. During our ordinary conscious experience we are only aware of a single "me" or "self," but the aberrations described by Charcot, Janet, and others suggested that the brain can create many conscious selves that are not aware of each other's existence (James, 1890, p. 400). These striking observations also fueled the imagination of a young physician from Vienna, Austria, who studied with Charcot in Paris in 1885. His name was Sigmund Freud (1856–1939).

## Freud and Psychoanalytic Theory

After his visit to Charcot's clinic in Paris, Freud returned to Vienna, where he continued his work with hysteric patients. (The word **hysteria**, by the way, comes from the Latin word *hyster*, which means "womb." It was once thought that only women suffered from hysteria, which was thought to be caused by a "wandering womb.") Working with the physician Joseph Breuer (1842–1925), Freud began to make his own observations of hysterics and develop theories to explain their strange behaviors and symptoms. Freud theorized that many of the patients' problems could be traced to the effects of painful childhood experiences that the person could not remember, and he

**DISSOCIATIVE IDENTITY DISORDER** A condition that involves the occurrence of two or more distinct identities within the same individual.

**HYSTERIA** A temporary loss of cognitive or motor functions, usually as a result of emotionally upsetting experiences.

In this photograph, Sigmund Freud (1856–1939) sits by the couch reserved for his psychoanalytic patients.

suggested that the powerful influence of these seemingly lost memories revealed the presence of an unconscious mind. According to Freud, the **unconscious** is *the part of the mind that operates outside of conscious awareness but influences conscious thoughts, feelings, and actions.* This idea led Freud to develop **psychoanalytic theory**, *an approach that emphasizes the importance of unconscious mental processes in shaping feelings, thoughts, and behaviors.* From a psychoanalytic perspective, it is important to uncover a person's early experiences and to illuminate a person's unconscious anxieties, conflicts, and desires. Psychoanalytic theory formed the basis for a therapy that Freud called **psychoanalysis**, which focuses on *bringing unconscious material into conscious awareness.* During psychoanalysis, patients recalled past experiences ("When I was a toddler, I was frightened by a masked man on a black horse") and related their dreams and fantasies ("Sometimes I close my eyes and imagine not having to pay for this session"). Psychoanalysts used Freud's theoretical approach to interpret what their patients said.

In the early 1900s, Freud and a growing number of followers formed a psychoanalytic movement. Carl Gustav Jung (1875–1961) and Alfred Adler (1870–1937) were prominent in the movement, but both were independent thinkers, and Freud apparently had little tolerance for individuals who challenged his ideas. Soon enough, Freud broke off his relationships with both men so that he could shape the psychoanalytic movement himself (Sulloway, 1992). Psychoanalytic theory became quite controversial (especially in America) because it suggested that understanding a person's thoughts, feelings, and behavior required a thorough exploration of the person's early sexual experiences and unconscious sexual desires. In those days these topics were considered far too racy for scientific discussion.

**UNCONSCIOUS** The part of the mind that operates outside of conscious awareness but influences conscious thoughts, feelings, and actions.

**PSYCHOANALYTIC THEORY** Sigmund Freud's approach to understanding human behavior that emphasizes the importance of unconscious mental processes in shaping feelings, thoughts, and behaviors.

**PSYCHOANALYSIS** A therapeutic approach that focuses on bringing unconscious material into conscious awareness to better understand psychological disorders.

This famous psychology conference, held in 1909 at Clark University, was organized by G. Stanley Hall and brought together many notable figures, such as William James and Sigmund Freud. Both men are circled, with James on the left.

Most of Freud's followers, like Freud himself, were trained as physicians and did not conduct psychological experiments in the laboratory (though early in his career, Freud did do some nice laboratory work on the sexual organs of eels). By and large, psychoanalysts did not hold positions in universities and developed their ideas in isolation from the research-based approaches of Wundt, Titchener, James, Hall, and others. One of the few times that Freud met with the leading academic psychologists was at a conference that G. Stanley Hall organized at Clark University in 1909. It was there that William James and Sigmund Freud met for the first time. Although James worked in an academic setting and Freud worked with clinical patients, both men believed that mental aberrations provide important clues into the nature of mind. Each thinker, in his own way, recognized the value of pursuing mindbugs as a clue to human functioning.

## Influence of Psychoanalysis and the Humanistic Response

Most historians consider Freud to be one of the two or three most influential thinkers of the 20th century, and the psychoanalytic movement influenced everything from literature and history to politics and art. Within psychology, psychoanalysis had its greatest impact on clinical practice, but over the past 40 years that influence has been considerably diminished.

This is partly because Freud's vision of human nature was a dark one, emphasizing limitations and problems rather than possibilities and potentials. He saw people as hostages to their forgotten childhood experiences and primitive sexual impulses, and the inherent pessimism of his perspective frustrated those psychologists who had a more optimistic view of human nature. In America, the years after World War II were positive, invigorating, and upbeat: Poverty and disease were being conquered by technology, the standard of living of ordinary Americans was on a sharp rise, and people were landing on the moon. The era was characterized by the accomplishments and not the foibles of the human mind, and Freud's viewpoint was out of step with the spirit of the times.

Freud's ideas were also difficult to test, and a theory that can't be tested is of limited use in psychology or other sciences. Though Freud's emphasis on unconscious processes has had an enduring impact on psychology, psychologists began to have serious misgivings about many aspects of Freud's theory.

It was in these times that psychologists such as Abraham Maslow (1908–70) and Carl Rogers (1902–87) pioneered a new movement called **humanistic psychology**, *an approach to understanding human nature that emphasizes the positive potential of human beings.* Humanistic psychologists focused on the highest aspirations that people had

**HUMANISTIC PSYCHOLOGY** An approach to understanding human nature that emphasizes the positive potential of human beings.

Carl Rogers (1902–87) (left) and Abraham Maslow (1908–70) (right) introduced a positive, humanistic psychology in response to what they viewed as the overly pessimistic view of psychoanalysis.

for themselves. Rather than viewing people as prisoners of events in their remote pasts, humanistic psychologists viewed people as free agents who have an inherent need to develop, grow, and reach their full potential. This movement reached its peak in the 1960s when a generation of "flower children" found it easy to see psychological life as a kind of blossoming of the spirit. Humanistic therapists sought to help people to realize their full potential; in fact, they called them "clients" rather than "patients." In this relationship, the therapist and the client (unlike the psychoanalyst and the patient) were on equal footing. In fact, the development of the humanistic perspective was one more reason why Freud's ideas became less influential.

**In summary,** psychologists have often focused on mindbugs as a way of understanding human behavior. The errors, illusions, and foibles of mental functioning offer a glimpse into the normal operations of the mind. Max Wertheimer founded Gestalt psychology by examining the illusion that causes us to see the whole instead of its parts. Clinicians such as Jean-Marie Charcot and Pierre Janet studied unusual cases in which patients acted like different people while under hypnosis, raising the possibility that each of us has more than one self. Through his work with hysteric patients, Sigmund Freud developed psychoanalysis, which emphasized the importance of unconscious influences and childhood experiences in shaping thoughts, feelings, and behavior. But happily, humanistic psychologists offered a more optimistic view of the human condition, suggesting that people are inherently disposed toward growth and can usually reach their full potential with a little help from their friends. ■ ■

# Psychology in the 20th Century: Behaviorism Takes Center Stage

The schools of psychological thought that had developed by the early 20th century—structuralism, functionalism, psychoanalysis, Gestalt psychology, and humanism—differed substantially from one another. But they shared an important similarity: Each tried to understand the inner workings of the mind by examining conscious perceptions, thoughts, memories, and feelings or by trying to elicit previously unconscious material, all of which were reported by participants in experiments or patients in a clinical setting. In each case it proved difficult to establish with much certainty just what was going on in people's minds, due to the unreliable nature of the methodology. As the 20th century unfolded, a new approach developed as psychologists challenged the idea that psychology should focus on mental life at all. This new approach was called **behaviorism**, which advocated that psychologists should restrict themselves to *the scientific study of objectively observable behavior.* Behaviorism represented a dramatic departure from previous schools of thought.

**BEHAVIORISM** An approach that advocates that psychologists restrict themselves to the scientific study of objectively observable behavior.

In 1894, Margaret Floy Washburn (1871–1939), a student of Edward Titchener at Cornell, became the first woman to receive a PhD degree in psychology. Washburn went on to a highly distinguished career, spent mainly in teaching and research at Vassar College in Poughkeepsie, New York. Washburn wrote an influential book, *The Animal Mind*, developed a theory of consciousness, and contributed to the development of psychology as a profession.

After leaving Johns Hopkins University amid a scandal, John B. Watson (1878–1958) embarked on a successful career with the J. Walter Thompson advertising firm in New York City. He was responsible for developing several memorable ad campaigns, such as this one for toothpaste.

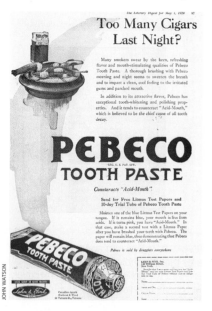

# Watson and the Emergence of Behaviorism

John Broadus Watson (1878–1958) received his PhD in 1904 from the University of Chicago (the first psychology PhD ever awarded there), where he was strongly influenced by James Angell (1869–1949), who had worked within the functionalist tradition. But Watson believed that private experience was too idiosyncratic and vague to be an object of scientific inquiry. Science required replicable, objective measurements of phenomena that were accessible to all observers, and the introspective methods used by structuralists and functionalists were far too subjective for that. So instead of describing conscious experiences, Watson proposed that psychologists focus entirely on the study of behavior—what people *do,* rather than what people *experience*—because behavior can be observed by anyone and it can be measured objectively. Watson thought that a focus on behavior would put a stop to the endless philosophical debates in which psychologists were currently entangled, and it would encourage psychologists to develop practical applications in such areas as business, medicine, law, and education. The goal of scientific psychology, according to Watson, should be to predict and control behavior in ways that benefit society.

Why would someone want to throw the mind out of psychology? This may seem excessive, until you notice that Watson studied the behavior of animals such as rats and birds. In such studies, inferring a mind is a matter of some debate. Shall we say that dogs have minds, for instance, but leave out pigeons? And if we include pigeons, what about worms? Animal behavior specialists staked out claims in this area. In 1908 Margaret Floy Washburn (1871–1939) published *The Animal Mind,* in which she reviewed what was then known about perception, learning, and memory in different animal species. She argued that nonhuman animals, much like human animals, have conscious mental experiences (Scarborough & Furumoto, 1987). Watson reacted to this claim with venom. Because we cannot ask pigeons about their private, inner experiences (well, we can *ask*, but they never tell us), Watson decided that the only way to understand how animals learn and adapt was to focus solely on their behavior, and he suggested that the study of human beings should proceed on the same basis.

Watson was influenced by the work of the Russian physiologist Ivan Pavlov (1849–1936), who carried out pioneering research on the physiology of digestion. In the course of this work, Pavlov noticed something interesting about the dogs he was studying (Fancher, 1979). Not only did the dogs salivate at the sight of food, they also salivated at the sight of the person who fed them. The feeders were not dressed in Alpo suits, so why should the mere sight of them trigger a basic digestive response in the dogs? To answer this question, Pavlov developed a procedure in which he sounded a tone every time he fed the dogs, and after a while he observed that the dogs would salivate when they heard the tone alone. In Pavlov's experiments, the sound of the tone was a stimulus—*sensory input from the environment*—that influenced the salivation of the dogs, which was a **response**—*an action or physiological change elicited by a stimulus*. Watson and other behaviorists made these two notions the building blocks of their theories, which is why behaviorism is sometimes called "stimulus-response" or "S-R" psychology.

Watson applied Pavlov's techniques to human infants. In a famous and controversial study, Watson and his student Rosalie Rayner taught an infant known as "Little Albert" to have a strong fear of a harmless white rat (and other white furry animals and toys) that he had previously not feared. Why would they do such a thing? You'll learn more about this study in Chapter 6, but the short answer is this: Watson believed that human behavior is powerfully influenced by the environment, and the experiments with Little Albert provided a chance to demonstrate such influence at the earliest stage of life. Neither Watson nor later behaviorists believed that the environment was the *only* influence on behavior (Todd & Morris, 1992), but they did think it was the most important one. Consistent with that view, Watson became romantically involved with someone prominent in his environment: Rosalie Rayner. He refused to end the affair when confronted by colleagues, and the resulting scandal forced Watson to leave his position at Johns Hopkins University. He found work in a New York advertising agency, where he applied behaviorist principles to marketing and advertising (which certainly involves manipulating the environment to influence behavior!).

Watson also wrote popular books that exposed a broad general audience to the behaviorist approach (Watson, 1924, 1928). The result of all these developments—Pavlov's work in the laboratory, Watson and Rayner's applications to humans, and Watson's practical applications to daily life—was that by the 1920s, behaviorism had become a dominant force in scientific psychology.

## B. F. Skinner and the Development of Behaviorism

In 1926, Burrhus Frederick Skinner (1904–90) graduated from Hamilton College in upstate New York. Like William James, Skinner was a young man who couldn't decide what to do with his life. He aspired to become a writer, and his interest in literature led him indirectly to psychology. Skinner wondered whether a novelist could portray a character without understanding why the character behaved as he or she did, and when he came across Watson's books, he knew he had the answer. Skinner completed his PhD studies in psychology at Harvard (Wiener, 1996) and began to develop a new kind of behaviorism. In Pavlov's experiments, the dogs had been passive participants that stood around, listened to tones, and drooled. Skinner recognized that in everyday life, animals don't just stand there—they do something! Animals *act* on their environments in order to find shelter, food, or mates, and Skinner wondered if he could develop behaviorist principles that would explain how they *learned* to act in those situations.

Skinner built what he called a "conditioning chamber" but what the rest of the world would forever call a "Skinner box." The box has a lever and a food tray, and a hungry rat could get food delivered to the tray by pressing the lever. Skinner observed that when a rat was put in the box, it would wander around, sniffing and exploring, and would usually press the bar by accident, at which point a food pellet would drop into the tray. After that happened, the rate of bar pressing would increase dramatically and remain high until the rat was no longer hungry. Skinner saw evidence for what he called the principle of **reinforcement**, which states that *the consequences of a behavior determine whether it will be more or less likely to occur again.* The concept of reinforcement became the foundation for Skinner's new approach to behaviorism (see Chapter 6), which he formulated in a landmark book, *The Behavior of Organisms* (Skinner, 1938).

Skinner set out to use his ideas about reinforcement to help improve the quality of everyday life. Skinner often worked with pigeons, and he wanted to see whether he could use reinforcement to teach pigeons to do something that they did not do naturally. Careful scientific observation revealed that pigeons in the wild almost never take up Ping-Pong, so Skinner decided to use the principle of reinforcement to teach some pigeons to play the game. He first broke the task down into small parts and used the principle of reinforcement to teach the pigeons each of the parts—reinforcing them when they made the right move (e.g., turning their paddles toward the ball) but not when they made the wrong one (e.g., yelling at the referee). Soon, the pigeons were able to bat the ball back and forth in a relatively entertaining display of athletic prowess.

Skinner was visiting his daughter's fourth-grade class when he realized that he might be able to improve classroom instruction by

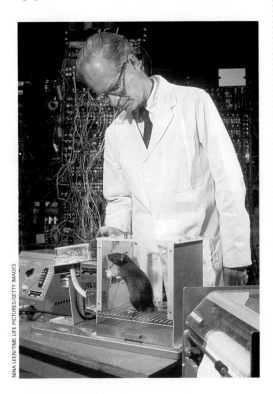

NINA LEEN/TIME LIFE PICTURES/GETTY IMAGES

**RESPONSE** An action or physiological change elicited by a stimulus.

**REINFORCEMENT** The consequences of a behavior that determine whether it will be more likely that the behavior will occur again.

 **ONLY HUMAN**

**"A" TRAIN FROM THE COOP TO HEATHROW** A full page of letters from readers in an issue of *New Scientist* magazine reported sightings by London, England, subway riders of pigeons boarding, and disembarking from, subway cars in "purposeful" ways that suggest they have figured out where they are going.

Inspired by Watson's behaviorism, B. F. Skinner (1904–90) investigated the way an animal learns by interacting with its environment. Here, he demonstrates the "Skinner box," in which rats learn to press a lever to receive food.

breaking a complicated task into small bits and then using the principle of reinforcement to teach children each bit (Bjork, 1993). He developed automatic devices known as "teaching machines" that did exactly that (Skinner, 1958). The teaching machine asked a series of increasingly difficult questions that built on the students' answers to the simpler ones. To learn a complicated math problem, for instance, students would first be asked an easy question about the simplest part of the problem. They would then be told whether the answer was right or wrong, and if a correct response was made, the machine would move on to a more difficult question. Skinner thought that the satisfaction of knowing they were correct would be reinforcing and help students learn.

If fourth graders and pigeons could be successfully trained, then why stop there? In the controversial books *Beyond Freedom and Dignity* and *Walden II,* Skinner laid out his vision of a utopian society in which behavior was controlled by the judicious application of the principle of reinforcement (Skinner, 1971). In those books he put forth the simple but stunning claim that our subjective sense of free will is an illusion and that when we think we are exercising free will, we are actually responding to present and past patterns of reinforcement. We do things in the present that have been rewarding in the past, and our sense of "choosing" to do them is nothing more than an illusion. In this, Skinner echoed the sentiments of the philosopher Benedict Spinoza (1632–1677), who several centuries earlier had noted that "men are deceived in thinking themselves free, a belief that consists only in this, that they are conscious of their actions and ignorant of the causes by which they are determined. As to their saying that human actions depend on the will, these are mere words without any corresponding idea" (1677/1982, p. 86).

Skinner argued that his insights could be used to increase human well-being and solve social problems. Not surprisingly, that claim sparked an outcry from critics who believed that Skinner was giving away one of our most cherished attributes—free will—and calling for a repressive society that manipulated people for its own ends. The criticism even extended to *TV Guide,* which featured an interview with Skinner and called his ideas "the taming of mankind through a system of dog obedience schools for all" (Bjork, 1993, p. 201). Given the nature of Skinner's ideas, the critics' attacks were understandable—he had seriously underestimated how much people cherish the idea of free will—but in the sober light of hindsight, they were clearly overblown. Skinner did not want to turn society into a "dog obedience school" or strip people of their personal freedoms. Rather, he argued that an understanding of the principles by which behavior is generated could be used to increase the social welfare, which is precisely what happens when a government launches advertisements to encourage citizens to drink milk or quit smoking. The result of all the controversy, however, was that Skinner's fame reached a level rarely attained by psychologists. A popular magazine that listed the 100 most important people who ever lived ranked Skinner just 39 points below Jesus Christ (Herrnstein, 1977).

Skinner's well-publicized questioning of such cherished notions as free will led to a rumor that he had raised his own daughter in a Skinner box. This urban legend, while untrue, likely originated from the climate-controlled, glass-encased crib that he invented to protect his daughter from the cold Minnesota winter. Skinner marketed the crib under various names, including the "Air-crib" and the "Heir Conditioner," but it failed to catch on with parents.

**In summary,** behaviorism advocated the study of observable actions and responses and held that inner mental processes were private events that could not be studied scientifically. Ivan Pavlov and John B. Watson studied the association between a stimulus and response and emphasized the importance of the environment in shaping behavior. Influenced by Watson's behaviorism, B. F. Skinner developed the concept of reinforcement using a "Skinner box." He demonstrated that animals and humans repeat behaviors that generate pleasant results and avoid performing those that generate unpleasant results. Skinner extended Watson's contentions about the importance of the environment in shaping behavior by suggesting that free will is an illusion and that the principle of reinforcement can be used to benefit society. ■ ■

# Beyond Behaviorism: Psychology Expands

Watson, Skinner, and the behaviorists dominated psychology from the 1930s to the 1950s. The psychologist Ulric Neisser recalled the atmosphere when he was a student at Swarthmore in the early 1950s:

> Behaviorism was the basic framework for almost all of psychology at the time. It was what you had to learn. That was the age when it was supposed that no psychological phenomenon was real unless you could demonstrate it in a rat (quoted in Baars, 1986, p. 275).

Behaviorism wouldn't dominate the field for much longer, however, and Neisser himself would play an important role in developing an alternative perspective. Why was behaviorism replaced? Although behaviorism allowed psychologists to measure, predict, and control behavior, it did this by ignoring some important things. First, it ignored the mental processes that had fascinated psychologists such as Wundt and James and, in so doing, found itself unable to explain some very important phenomena, such as how children learn language. Second, it ignored the evolutionary history of the organisms it studied and was thus unable to explain why, for example, a rat could learn to associate nausea with food much more quickly than it could learn to associate nausea with a tone or a light. As we shall see, the approaches that ultimately replaced behaviorism met these kinds of problems head-on.

## The Emergence of Cognitive Psychology

For almost two decades, psychologists dismissed the problem of the mind as an intractable fairy tale that could not be studied scientifically. There were some exceptions to this rule (including most clinical and social psychologists, who remained deeply committed to the scientific study of mental processes), but by and large, psychologists happily ignored mental processes until the 1950s, when something important happened: the computer. The advent of computers had enormous practical impact, of course, but it also had an enormous conceptual impact on psychology. Computers are information-processing systems, and the flow of information through their circuits is clearly no fairy tale. If psychologists could think of mental events—such as remembering, attending, thinking, believing, evaluating, feeling, and assessing—as the flow of information through the mind, then they might be able to study the mind scientifically after all. The emergence of the computer led to a reemergence of interest in mental processes all across the discipline of psychology, and it spawned a new approach called **cognitive psychology**, which is *the scientific study of mental processes, including perception, thought, memory, and reasoning.*

### Early Cognitive Pioneers

Even at the height of behaviorist domination, there were a few quiet revolutionaries whose research and writings were focused on mental processes. For example, Sir Frederic Bartlett (1886–1969) was a British psychologist interested in memory. He was dissatisfied with existing research and especially with the research of the German psychologist

**COGNITIVE PSYCHOLOGY** The scientific study of mental processes, including perception, thought, memory, and reasoning.

*"What about that! His brain still uses the old vacuum tubes."*

Hermann Ebbinghaus (1850–1909), who had performed groundbreaking experiments on memory in 1885 that we'll discuss in Chapter 5. Serving as his own research subject, Ebbinghaus had tried to discover how quickly and how well he could memorize and recall meaningless information, such as the three-letter nonsense syllables *dap, kir,* and *sul.* Bartlett believed that it was more important to examine memory for the kinds of information people actually encounter in everyday life, and so he gave people stories to remember and carefully observed the kinds of errors they made when they tried to recall them some time later (Bartlett, 1932). Bartlett discovered many interesting things that Ebbinghaus could never have learned with his nonsense syllables. For example, he found that research participants often remembered what *should* have happened or what they *expected* to happen rather than what actually *did* happen. These and other errors led Bartlett to suggest that memory is not a photographic reproduction of past experience and that our attempts to recall the past are powerfully influenced by our knowledge, beliefs, hopes, aspirations, and desires.

Jean Piaget (1896–1980) was a Swiss psychologist who studied the perceptual and cognitive errors of children in order to gain insight into the nature and development of the human mind. For example, in one of his tasks, Piaget would give a 3-year-old child a large and a small mound of clay and tell the child to make the two mounds equal. Then Piaget would break one of the clay mounds into smaller pieces and ask the child which mound now had more clay. Although the amount of clay remained the same, of course, 3-year-old children usually said that the mound that was broken into smaller pieces was bigger, but by the age of 6 or 7, they no longer made this error. As you'll see in Chapter 9, Piaget theorized that younger children lack a particular cognitive ability that allows older children to appreciate the fact that the mass of an object remains constant even when it is divided. For Piaget, mindbugs such as these provided key insights into the mental world of the child (Piaget & Inhelder, 1969).

The German psychologist Kurt Lewin (1890–1947) was also a pioneer in the study of thought at a time when thought had been banished from psychology. Lewin (1936) argued that one could best predict a person's behavior in the world by understanding the person's subjective experience of the world. A television soap opera is a meaningless series of unrelated physical movements unless one thinks about the characters' experiences—how Karen feels about Bruce, what Van was planning to say to Kathy about Emily, and whether Linda's sister, Nancy, will always hate their mother for meddling in the marriage. Lewin realized that it was not the stimulus, but rather the person's *construal* of the stimulus, that determined the person's subsequent behavior. A pinch on the cheek can be pleasant or unpleasant depending on who administers it, under what circumstances, and to which set of cheeks. Lewin used a special kind of mathematics called *topology* to model the person's subjective experience, and although his topological theories were not particularly influential, his attempts to model mental life and his insistence that psychologists study how people construe their worlds would have a lasting impact on psychology.

BILL ANDERSON/PHOTO RESEARCHERS, INC.

Jean Piaget (1896–1980) studied and theorized about the developing mental lives of children, a marked departure from the observations of external behavior dictated by the methods of the behaviorists.

## Technology and the Development of Cognitive Psychology

Although the contributions of psychologists such as Bartlett, Piaget, and Lewin provided early alternatives to behaviorism, they did not depose it. That job required the army. During World War II, the military had turned to psychologists to help understand how soldiers could best learn to use new technologies, such as radar. Radar operators had to pay close attention to their screens for long periods while trying to decide whether blips were friendly aircraft, enemy aircraft, or flocks of wild geese in need of a good chasing (Aschcraft, 1998; Lachman, Lachman, & Butterfield, 1979). How could radar operators be trained to make quicker and more accurate decisions? The answer to this question clearly required more than the swift delivery of pellets to the radar operator's food tray. It required that those who designed the equipment think about and talk about cognitive processes, such as perception, attention, identification, memory, and decision making. Behaviorism solved the problem by denying it, and thus some psychologists decided to deny behaviorism and forge ahead with a new approach.

This navy radar operator must focus his attention for long stretches of time, while making quick, important decisions. The mental processes involved in such tasks are studied by cognitive psychologists.

The British psychologist Donald Broadbent (1926–93) was among the first to study what happens when people try to pay attention to several things at once. For instance, Broadbent observed that pilots can't attend to many different instruments at once and must actively move the focus of their attention from one to another (Best, 1992). Broadbent (1958) showed that the limited capacity to handle incoming information is a fundamental feature of human cognition and that this limit could explain many of the errors that pilots (and other people) made. At about the same time, the American psychologist George Miller (1956) pointed out a striking consistency in our capacity limitations across a variety of situations—we can pay attention to, and briefly hold in memory, about seven (give or take two) pieces of information. Cognitive psychologists began conducting experiments and devising theories to better understand the mind's limited capacity, a problem that behaviorists had ignored.

As you have already read, the invention of the computer in the 1950s had a profound impact on psychologists' thinking. People and computers differ in many ways, but both seem to register, store, and retrieve information, leading psychologists to wonder whether the computer might be used as a model for the human mind. A computer is made of hardware (e.g., chips and disk drives today, magnetic tapes and vacuum tubes a half century ago) and software (stored on optical disks today and on punch cards a half century ago). If the brain is roughly analogous to the computer's hardware, then perhaps the mind was roughly analogous to a software program. This line of thinking led cognitive psychologists to begin writing computer programs to see what kinds of software could be made to mimic human speech and behavior (Newell, Shaw, & Simon, 1958).

This 1950s computer was among the first generation of digital computers. Although different in many ways, computers and the human brain both process and store information, which led many psychologists at the time to think of the mind as a type of computer. Researchers currently adopt a more sophisticated view of the mind and the brain, but the computer analogy was helpful in the early days of cognitive psychology.

RICK FRIEDMAN/CORBIS

Noam Chomsky's (b. 1928) critique of Skinner's theory of language signaled the end of behaviorism's dominance in psychology and helped spark the development of cognitive psychology.

Ironically, the emergence of cognitive psychology was also energized by the appearance of a book by B. F. Skinner called *Verbal Behavior,* which offered a behaviorist analysis of language (Skinner, 1957). A linguist at the Massachusetts Institute of Technology (MIT), Noam Chomsky (b. 1928), published a devastating critique of the book in which he argued that Skinner's insistence on observable behavior had caused him to miss some of the most important features of language. According to Chomsky, language relies on mental rules that allow people to understand and produce novel words and sentences. The ability of even the youngest child to generate new sentences that he or she had never heard before flew in the face of the behaviorist claim that children learn to use language by reinforcement. Chomsky provided a clever, detailed, and thoroughly cognitive account of language that could explain many of the phenomena that the behaviorist account could not (Chomsky, 1959).

These developments during the 1950s set the stage for an explosion of cognitive studies during the 1960s. Cognitive psychologists did not return to the old introspective procedures used during the 19th century, but instead developed new and ingenious methods that allowed them to study cognitive processes. The excitement of the new approach was summarized in a landmark book, *Cognitive Psychology,* written by someone you met earlier in this chapter: Ulric Neisser (1967). His book provided a foundation for the development of cognitive psychology, which grew and thrived in years that followed.

## The Brain Meets the Mind: The Rise of Cognitive Neuroscience

If cognitive psychologists studied the software of the mind, they had little to say about the hardware of the brain. And yet, as any computer scientist knows, the relationship between software and hardware is crucial: Each element needs the other to get the job done. Our mental activities often seem so natural and effortless—noticing the shape of an object, using words in speech or writing, recognizing a face as familiar—that we fail to appreciate the fact that they depend on intricate operations carried out by the brain. This dependence is revealed by dramatic cases in which damage to a particular part of the brain causes a person to lose a specific cognitive ability. Recall that in the 19th century, the French physician Paul Broca described a patient who, after damage to a limited area in the left side of the brain, could not produce words—even though he could understand them perfectly well. As you'll see later in the book, damage to other parts of the brain can also result in syndromes that are characterized by the loss of specific mental abilities (e.g., prosopagnosia, in which the person cannot recognize human faces) or by the emergence of bizarre behavior or beliefs (e.g., Capgras syndrome, in which the person believes that a close family member has been replaced by an imposter). These striking—sometimes startling—cases remind us that even the simplest cognitive processes depend on the brain. The high level of interest psychologists now have in the link between brain and mind is rooted in the achievements of pioneering researchers working in the middle of the 20th century.

Karl Lashley (1890–1958) conducted experiments that he hoped would reveal a brain area that stores learned information. He removed different parts of animals' brains and observed the effects on the animals' behavior. Though he never found a specific area where learning is stored, his general approach had a major influence on behavioral neuroscience.

YERKES NATIONAL PRIMATE RESEARCH CENTER

Karl Lashley (1890–1958), a psychologist who studied with John B. Watson, took an approach similar to the one that Flourens used a century earlier. By training rats to run mazes, surgically removing parts of their brains, and then measuring how well they could run the maze again, Lashley hoped to find the precise spot in the brain where *learning* occurred. Alas, no one spot seemed to uniquely and reliably eliminate learning (Lashley, 1960). Rather, Lashley simply found that the more of the rat's brain he removed, the more poorly the rat ran the maze. Lashley was frustrated by his inability to identify a specific site of learning, but his efforts inspired other scientists to take up the challenge. They developed a research area called *physiological psychology.* Today, this area has grown into **behavioral neuroscience**, which *links psychological processes to activities in the nervous system and other bodily processes.* To learn about the relationship

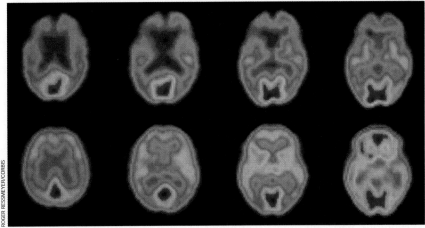

ROGER RESSMEYER/CORBIS

**Figure 1.5** **PET Scans of Healthy and Alzheimer's Brains** PET scans are one of a variety of brain-imaging technologies that psychologists use to observe the living brain. The four brain images on the top each come from a person suffering from Alzheimer's disease; the four on the bottom each come from a healthy person of similar age. The red and green areas reflect higher levels of brain activity compared to the blue areas, which reflect lower levels of activity. In each image, the front of the brain is on the top and the back of the brain is on the bottom. You can see that the patient with Alzheimer's disease, compared with the healthy person, shows more extensive areas of lowered activity toward the front of the brain.

between brain and behavior, behavioral neuroscientists observe animals' responses as they perform specially constructed tasks, such as running through a maze to obtain food rewards. The neuroscientists can record electrical or chemical responses in the brain as the task is being performed or later remove specific parts of the brain to see how performance is affected (**FIGURE 1.5**).

Of course, experimental brain surgery cannot ethically be performed on human beings, and thus psychologists who want to study the human brain often have had to rely on nature's cruel and inexact experiments. Birth defects, accidents, and illnesses often cause damage to particular brain regions, and if this damage disrupts a particular ability, then psychologists deduce that the region is involved in producing the ability. For example, in Chapter 5 you'll learn about a patient whose memory was virtually wiped out by damage to a specific part of the brain, and you'll see how this tragedy provided scientists with remarkable clues about how memories are stored (Scoville & Milner, 1957). (See the Hot Science box on p. 27 for a related example of amnesia.) But in the late 1980s, technological breakthroughs led to the development of noninvasive "brain-scanning" techniques that made it possible for psychologists to watch what happens inside a human brain as a person performs a task such as reading, imagining, listening, and remembering. Brain scanning is an invaluable tool because it allows us to observe the brain in action and to see which parts are involved in which operations (see Chapter 3).

For example, researchers used scanning technology to identify the parts of the brain in the left hemisphere that are involved in specific aspects of language, such as understanding or producing words (Peterson et al., 1989). Later scanning studies showed that people who are deaf from birth but who learn to communicate using American Sign Language (ASL) rely on regions in the right hemisphere (as well as the left) when using ASL. In contrast, people with normal hearing who learned ASL after puberty seemed to rely only on the left hemisphere when using ASL (Newman et al., 2002). These findings suggest that although both spoken and signed language usually rely on the left hemisphere, the right hemisphere also can become involved—but only for a limited period (perhaps until puberty). The findings also provide a nice example of how psychologists can now use scanning techniques to observe people with various kinds of cognitive capacities and use their observations to unravel the mysteries of the mind and the brain (**FIGURE 1.6**). In fact, there's a name for this area of research. **Cognitive neuroscience** is the *field that attempts to understand the links between cognitive processes and brain activity* (Gazzaniga, 2000).

**BEHAVIORAL NEUROSCIENCE** An approach to psychology that links psychological processes to activities in the nervous system and other bodily processes.

**COGNITIVE NEUROSCIENCE** A field that attempts to understand the links between cognitive processes and brain activity.

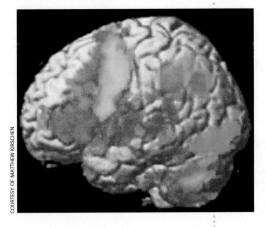

COURTESY OF MATTHEW KIRSCHEN

**Figure 1.6** **More Ways to Scan a Brain** fMRI scanners produce more precise images than PET scans, allowing researchers to more accurately localize brain activity. fMRIs are also quicker at capturing images, allowing researchers to measure brain activity over briefer periods. Here, green areas of the brain were active when research participants remembered information presented visually, and red areas were active when they remembered information presented aurally. Yellow areas were active during both types of presentations.

Today's evolutionary psychologists embrace Charles Darwin's (1809–82) ideas, just as William James did 100 years ago. Darwin's theories of evolution, adaptation, and natural selection have provided insight into why brains and minds work they way they do.

## The Adaptive Mind:
## The Emergence of Evolutionary Psychology

Psychology's renewed interest in mental processes and its growing interest in the brain were two developments that led psychologists away from behaviorism. A third development also pointed them in a different direction. Recall that one of behaviorism's key claims was that organisms are blank slates on which experience writes its lessons, and hence any one lesson should be as easily written as another. But in experiments conducted during the 1960s and 1970s, the psychologist John Garcia and his colleagues showed that rats can learn to associate nausea with the smell of food much more quickly than they can learn to associate nausea with a flashing light (Garcia, 1981). Why should this be? In the real world of forests, sewers, and garbage cans, nausea is usually caused by spoiled food and not by lightning, and although these particular rats had been born in a laboratory and had never left their cages, millions of years of evolution had "prepared" their brains to learn the natural association more quickly than the artificial one. In other words, it was not only the rat's learning history—but the rat's *ancestors'* learning histories—that determined the rat's ability to learn. Although that fact was at odds with the behaviorist doctrine, it was the credo for a new kind of psychology.

**Evolutionary psychology** *explains mind and behavior in terms of the adaptive value of abilities that are preserved over time by natural selection.* Evolutionary psychology has its roots in Charles Darwin's (1809–82) theory of natural selection, which inspired William James's functionalist approach. But it is only since the publication in 1975 of *Sociobiology,* by the biologist E. O. Wilson, that evolutionary thinking has had an identifiable presence in psychology. That presence is steadily increasing (Buss, 1999; Pinker, 1997a; Tooby & Cosmides, 2000). Evolutionary psychologists think of the mind as a collection of specialized "modules" that are designed to solve the human problems our ancestors faced as they attempted to eat, mate, and reproduce over millions of years. According to evolutionary psychology, the brain is not an all-purpose computer that can do or learn one thing just as easily as it can do or learn another; rather, it is a computer that was built to do a few things well and everything else not at all. It is a computer that comes with a small suite of built-in applications that are designed to do the things that previous versions of that computer needed to have done.

Consider, for example, how evolutionary psychology treats the emotion of jealousy. All of us who have been in romantic relationships have been jealous, if only because we noticed our partner noticing someone else. Jealousy can be a powerful, overwhelming emotion that we might wish to avoid, but according to evolutionary psychology, it exists today because it once served an adaptive function. If some of our hominid ancestors experienced jealousy and others did not, then the ones who experienced it might have been more likely to guard their mates and aggress against their rivals and thus may have been more likely to reproduce their "jealous genes" (Buss, 2000).

Critics of the evolutionary approach point out that many current traits of people and other animals probably evolved to serve different functions than those they currently serve. For example, biologists believe that the feathers of birds probably evolved initially to perform such functions as regulating body temperature or capturing prey and only later served the entirely different function of flight. Likewise, people are reasonably adept at learning to drive a car, but nobody would argue that such an ability is the result of natural selection; the learning abilities that allow us to become skilled car drivers must have evolved for purposes other than driving cars.

Complications like these have lead the critics to wonder how evolutionary hypotheses can ever be tested (Coyne, 2000; Sterelny & Griffiths, 1999). We don't have a record of our ancestors' thoughts, feelings, and actions, and fossils won't provide much information about the evolution of mind and behavior. Testing ideas about the evolutionary origins of psychological phenomena is indeed a challenging

**EVOLUTIONARY PSYCHOLOGY** A psychological approach that explains mind and behavior in terms of the adaptive value of abilities that are preserved over time by natural selection.

## { HOT SCIENCE } New Connections

In this chapter we've looked at the development of numerous subfields in psychology, including behaviorism, psychoanalysis, cognitive psychology, cognitive neuroscience, evolutionary psychology, and social psychology. Each takes a different approach to understanding human behavior, and each has its own research journals and scientific jargon. As a result, psychologists in the various subfields usually work separately from one another. No matter how different their approaches, most psychologists have a common goal: understanding the mind and behavior. Instead of tackling this difficult task from just a single viewpoint, combining approaches from different subfields can help generate new insights that might not be obtained otherwise. Research during the past decade bears out this idea: Many of the most exciting new findings in psychology have resulted from making new connections across different subfields.

Two of your textbook authors, Daniel Gilbert and Daniel Schacter, were among the authors of a research study that illustrates the benefits of combining different perspectives: social psychology (Gilbert's area) and cognitive neuroscience (Schacter's area). The study explored the process of *cognitive dissonance*, which is the psychological discomfort that occurs when our behavior conflicts with our beliefs about ourselves (Lieberman, Ochsner, Gilbert, & Schacter, 2001). As you'll learn in Chapter 16, this topic has long interested social psychologists. People will do almost anything to reduce dissonance, such as changing what they believe to fit their behavior or discrediting evidence that threatens their beliefs. An unhappily married woman who believes that her marriage should be successful may distort the past to make the present seem more bearable. A man who purchased an expensive car and then read a bad review

claiming that the car is a lemon might belittle the reviewer as an ignoramus who has no business writing about cars.

Social psychologists have assumed that the experience of cognitive dissonance requires the ability to recall the behavior that produced conflict in the first place. If the man who bought the car doesn't remember making the purchase, presumably the bad magazine review won't bother him, so he won't have any dissonance to reduce. Or will he?

Lieberman and his colleagues examined psychological conflict in a special group of individuals: patients suffering from amnesia as a result of damage to parts of the brain that are needed to form new memories. As you'll see in Chapter 5, these patients have little or no ability to remember their recent experiences. If people with amnesia show cognitive dissonance even though they can't remember the experience that created it, social psychologists would have to modify their ideas about the dissonance process.

To get a sense of the procedure these researchers used, consider the following scenario. You visit an art gallery and fall in love with two prints by the same artist but only have enough money to purchase one. After almost deciding on one and then the other, you finally make your choice. Though you feel conflicted about passing over the remaining print, you rationalize your decision by convincing yourself that you like the print you purchased quite a bit more than the one you passed up. Happily, the dissonance and discomfort created by the difficult decision go away.

Studies have shown that just this sort of dissonance reduction occurs when people are forced to decide between two art prints (Brehm, 1956; Gerard & White, 1983). After making the choice, people

claim to like the chosen print *more* and the bypassed print *less* than they had earlier. We showed art prints to amnesic patients and people without memory problems; they ranked the prints according to how much they liked them. The two groups then made a choice between two prints, indicating which one they would prefer to hang in their homes, and later ranked all the prints again for liking. We found that amnesic patients inflated how much they liked the chosen print relative to the print they had passed over. In other words, people with amnesia reduced the dissonance created by choosing between the two prints in much the same way as non-amnesiacs would. But the patients with amnesia didn't have any conscious memory of making the choice that produced dissonance in the first place! These results suggest that we don't need to *remember* a past conflict in order to be influenced by the rationalizations we used to reduce cognitive dissonance.

By combining a patient population that is usually studied by cognitive neuroscientists with a traditional social psychology procedure, this study encourages us to think in a new way about what happens when people reduce psychological discomfort brought about by cognitive dissonance. When we (or others) rationalize our choices in everyday life, it may seem like we are just "making excuses" for our behavior. Saying that we really like the art print we chose a lot more than the one we bypassed—even though initially we didn't—may seem like a flimsy attempt to make ourselves feel better. The fact that amnesic patients do exactly the same thing, without any memory of the conflict, shows that these rationalizations are much more than just flimsy "excuse making"; they reflect deep and enduring changes in our beliefs.

---

task, but not an impossible one (Buss, Haselton, Shackelford, Bleske, & Wakefield, 1998; Pinker, 1997b). Evolutionary psychologists hold that behaviors or traits that occur universally in all cultures are good candidates for evolutionary adaptations. For example, physical attractiveness is widely valued by both men and women in many cultures, and people from different cultures tend to agree in their judgments of facial attractiveness (Cunningham, Roberts, Barbee, Druen, & Wu, 1995). Several aspects of facial attractiveness, such as symmetrical facial features, have been linked with enhanced physical and mental health, also suggesting the possibility that it is an evolutionary adaptation (Shackelford & Larsen, 1999).

Evolutionary adaptations should also increase reproductive success. So, if a specific trait or feature has been favored by natural selection, it should be possible to find some evidence of this in the numbers of offspring that are produced by the trait's bearers. Consider, for instance, the hypothesis that men tend to be tall because women prefer to mate with tall men. To investigate this hypothesis, researchers conducted a study in which they compared the numbers of offspring from short and tall men. They did their best to equate other factors that might affect the results, such as the level of education attained by short and tall men. Consistent with the evolutionary hypothesis, they found that tall men do indeed bear more offspring than short men (Pawlowski, Dunbar, & Lipowicz, 2000). This kind of study provides evidence that allows evolutionary psychologists to test their ideas. Not every evolutionary hypothesis can be tested, of course, but evolutionary psychologists are becoming increasingly inventive in their attempts.

**In summary,** psychologists such as Frederic Bartlett, Jean Piaget, and Kurt Lewin defied the behaviorist doctrine and studied the inner workings of the mind. Their efforts, as well as those of later pioneers such as Donald Broadbent, paved the way for cognitive psychology to focus on inner mental processes such as perception, attention, memory, and reasoning. Cognitive psychology developed as a field due to the invention of the computer, psychologists' efforts to improve the performance of the military, and Noam Chomsky's theories about language. Cognitive neuroscience attempts to link the brain with the mind through studies of both brain-damaged and healthy people. Evolutionary psychology focuses on the adaptive function that minds and brains serve and seeks to understand the nature and origin of psychological processes in terms of natural selection. ■ ■

# Beyond the Individual: Social and Cultural Perspectives

The picture we have painted so far may vaguely suggest a scene from some 1950s science-fiction film in which the protagonist is a living brain that thinks, feels, hopes, and worries while suspended in a vat of pink jelly in a basement laboratory. Although psychologists often do focus on the brain and the mind of the individual, they have not lost sight of the fact that human beings are fundamentally social animals who are part of a vast network of family, friends, teachers, and coworkers. Trying to understand people in the absence of that fact is a bit like trying to understand an ant or a bee without considering the function and influence of the colony or hive. People are the most important and most complex objects that we ever encounter, and thus it is not surprising that our behavior is strongly influenced by their presence—or their absence. The two areas of psychology that most strongly emphasize these facts are social and cultural psychology.

## The Development of Social Psychology

**Social psychology** is the study of *the causes and consequences of interpersonal behavior.* This broad definition allows social psychologists to address a remarkable variety of topics. Historians trace the birth of social psychology to an experiment conducted in 1895 by the psychologist and bicycle enthusiast, Norman Triplett, who noticed that cyclists seemed to ride faster when they rode with others. Intrigued by this observation, he conducted an experiment that showed that children reeled in a fishing line faster when tested in the presence of other children than when tested alone. Triplett was not trying to improve the fishing abilities of American children, of course, but rather was trying to show that the mere presence of other people can influence performance on even the most mundane kinds of tasks.

Social psychology's development began in earnest in the 1930s and was driven by several historical events. The rise of Nazism led many of Germany's most talented

*"You're certainly a lot less fun since the operation."*

GAHAN WILSON/CARTOONBANK.COM

**SOCIAL PSYCHOLOGY** A subfield of psychology that studies the causes and consequences of interpersonal behavior.

scientists to immigrate to America, and among them were psychologists such as Solomon Asch (1907–96) and Kurt Lewin. These psychologists had been strongly influenced by Gestalt psychology, which you'll recall held that "the whole is greater than the sum of its parts," and though the Gestaltists had been talking about the visual perception of objects, these psychologists felt that the phrase also captured a basic truth about the relationship between social groups and the individuals who constitute them. Philosophers had speculated about the nature of sociality for thousands of years, and political scientists, economists, anthropologists, and sociologists had been studying social life scientifically for some time. But these German refugees were the first to generate theories of social behavior that resembled the theories generated by natural scientists, and more importantly, they were the first to conduct experiments to test their social theories. For example, Lewin (1936) adopted the language of midcentury physics to develop a "field theory" that viewed social behavior as the product of "internal forces" (such as personality, goals, and beliefs) and "external forces" (such as social pressure and culture), while Asch (1946) performed laboratory experiments to examine the "mental chemistry" that allows people to combine small bits of information about another person into a full impression of that person's personality.

Social psychology studies how the thoughts, feelings, and behaviors of individuals can be influenced by the presence of others. Members of Reverend Sun Myung Moon's Unification Church are often married to one another in ceremonies of 10,000 people or more; in some cases couples don't know each other before the wedding begins. Social movements such as this have the power to sway individuals.

Other historical events also shaped social psychology in its early years. For example, the Holocaust brought the problems of conformity and obedience into sharp focus, leading psychologists such as Asch (1956) and others to examine the conditions under which people can influence each other to think and act in inhuman or irrational ways. The civil rights movement and the rising tensions between Black and White Americans led psychologists such as Gordon Allport (1897–1967) to study stereotyping, prejudice, and racism and to shock the world of psychology by suggesting that prejudice was the result of a perceptual error that was every bit as natural and unavoidable as an optical illusion (Allport, 1954). Allport identified a mindbug at work: The same perceptual processes that allow us to efficiently categorize elements of our social and physical world allow us to erroneously categorize entire groups of people. Social psychologists today study a wider variety of topics (from social memory to social relationships) and use a wider variety of techniques (from opinion polls to neuroimaging) than did their forebears, but this field of psychology remains dedicated to understanding the brain as a social organ, the mind as a social adaptation, and the individual as a social creature.

## The Emergence of Cultural Psychology

Americans and Western Europeans are sometimes surprised to realize that most of the people on the planet are members of neither culture. Although we're all more alike than we are different, there is nonetheless considerable diversity within the human species in social practices, customs, and ways of living. Culture refers to the values, traditions, and beliefs that are shared by a particular group of people. Although we usually think of culture in terms of nationality and ethnic groups, cultures can also be defined by age (youth culture), sexual orientation (gay culture), religion (Jewish culture), or occupation (academic culture). **Cultural psychology** is *the study of how cultures reflect and shape the psychological processes of their members* (Shweder & Sullivan, 1993). Cultural psychologists study a wide range of phenomena, ranging from visual perception to social interaction, as they seek to understand which of these phenomena are universal and which vary from place to place and time to time.

**CULTURAL PSYCHOLOGY** The study of how cultures reflect and shape the psychological processes of their members.

Perhaps surprisingly, one of the first psychologists to pay attention to the influence of culture was someone recognized today for pioneering the development of experimental psychology: Wilhelm Wundt. He believed that a complete psychology would have to combine a laboratory approach with a broader cultural perspective. Wundt wrote extensively about cultural and social influences on the mind, producing a 10-volume work on culture and psychology, in which he covered a vast range of topics, such as how people gesture in different cultures or the origins of various myths and religions (Wundt, 1908). But Wundt's ideas failed to spark much interest from other psychologists, who had their hands full trying to make sense of results from laboratory experiments and formulating general laws of human behavior. Outside of psychology, anthropologists such as Margaret Mead (1901–78) and Gregory Bateson (1904–80) attempted to understand the workings of culture by traveling to far-flung regions of the world and carefully observing child-rearing patterns, rituals, religious ceremonies, and the like. Such studies revealed practices—some bizarre from a North American perspective—that served important functions in a culture, such as the painful ritual of violent body mutilation and bloodletting in mountain tribes of New Guinea, which initiates young boys into training to become warriors (Mead, 1935/1968; Read, 1965). Yet at the time, most anthropologists paid as little attention to psychology as psychologists did to anthropology.

Cultural psychology only began to emerge as a strong force in psychology during the 1980s and 1990s, when psychologists and anthropologists began to communicate with each other about their ideas and methods (Stigler, Shweder, & Herdt, 1990). It was then that psychologists rediscovered Wundt as an intellectual ancestor of this area of the field (Jahoda, 1993).

Physicists assume that $e = mc^2$ whether the $m$ is located in Cleveland, Moscow, or the Orion Nebula. Chemists assume that water is made of hydrogen and oxygen and that it was made of hydrogen and oxygen in 1609 as well. The laws of physics and chemistry are assumed to be universal, and for much of psychology's history, the same assumption was made about the principles that govern human behavior (Shweder, 1991). *Absolutism* holds that culture makes little or no difference for most psychological phenomena—that "honesty is honesty and depression is depression, no matter where one observes it" (Segall, Lonner, & Berry, 1998, p. 1103). And yet, as any world traveler knows, cultures differ in exciting, delicious, and frightening ways, and things that are true of people in one culture are not necessarily true of people in another. *Relativism* holds that psychological phenomena are likely to vary considerably across cultures and should be viewed only in the context of a specific culture (Berry, Poortinga, Segall, & Dasen, 1992). Although depression is observed in nearly

The Namgay family from Shingkhey, Bhutan (left), and the Skeen family from Texas, USA (right), display their respective family possessions in these two photos, both taken in 1993. Cultural psychology studies the similarities and differences in psychological processes that arise between people living in different cultures.

every culture, the symptoms associated with it vary dramatically from one place to another. For example, in Western cultures, depressed people tend to devalue themselves, whereas depressed people in Eastern cultures do not (Draguns, 1980).

Today, most cultural psychologists fall somewhere between these two extremes. Most psychological phenomena can be influenced by culture, some are completely determined by it, and others seem to be entirely unaffected. For example, the age of a person's earliest memory differs dramatically across cultures (MacDonald, Uesiliana, & Hayne, 2000), whereas judgments of facial attractiveness do not (Cunningham et al., 1995). As noted when we discussed evolutionary psychology, it seems likely that the most universal phenomena are those that are closely associated with the basic biology that all human beings share. Conversely, the least universal phenomena are those rooted in the varied socialization practices that different cultures evolve. Of course, the only way to determine whether a phenomenon is variable or constant across cultures is to design research to investigate these possibilities, and cultural psychologists do just that (Cole, 1996; Segall et al., 1998).

**In summary,** social psychology recognizes that people exist as part of a network of other people and examines how individuals influence and interact with one another. Social psychology was pioneered by German émigrés, such as Kurt Lewin, who were motivated by a desire to address social issues and problems. Cultural psychology is concerned with the effects of the broader culture on individuals and with similarities and differences among people in different cultures. Within this perspective, absolutists hold that culture has little impact on most psychological phenomena, whereas relativists believe that culture has a powerful effect. Together, social and cultural psychology help expand the discipline's horizons beyond just an examination of individuals. These areas of psychology examine behavior within the broader context of human interaction. ■ ■

# The Profession of Psychology: Past and Present

If ever you find yourself on an airplane with an annoying seatmate who refuses to let you read your magazine, there are two things you can do. First, you can turn to the person and say in a calm and friendly voice, "Did you know that I am covered with strange and angry bacteria?" If that seems a bit extreme, you might instead try saying, "Did you know that I am a psychologist, and I'm forming an evaluation of you as you speak?" as this will usually shut them up without getting you arrested. The truth is that most people don't really know what psychology is or what psychologists do, but they do have some vague sense that it isn't wise to talk to one. Now that you've been briefly acquainted with psychology's past, let's consider its present by looking at psychology as a profession. We'll look first at the origins of psychology's professional organizations, next at the contexts in which psychologists tend to work, and finally at the kinds of training required to become a psychologist.

## Psychologists Band Together: The American Psychological Association

You'll recall that when we last saw William James, he was wandering around the greater Boston area, expounding the virtues of the new science of psychology. In July 1892, James and five other psychologists traveled to Clark University to attend a meeting called by G. Stanley Hall. Each worked at a large university where they taught psychology courses, performed research, and wrote textbooks. Although they were too few to make up a jury or even a decent hockey team, these seven men decided that it was time to form an organization that represented psychology as a profession, and on that day the American Psychological Association (APA) was born. The seven psychologists could scarcely have imagined that today their little club would have more than 150,000 members—approximately the population of a decent-sized city in the United

States. Although all of the original members were employed by universities or colleges, today academic psychologists make up only 20% of the membership, while nearly 70% of the members work in clinical and health-related settings. Because the APA is no longer as focused on academic psychology as it once was, the American Psychological Society (APS) was formed in 1988 by 450 academic psychologists who wanted an organization that focused specifically on the needs of psychologists carrying out scientific research. The APS, renamed the Association for Psychological Science in 2006, grew quickly, attracting 5,000 members within six months; today it comprises nearly 12,000 psychologists.

WELLESLEY COLLEGE ARCHIVES—MARGARET CLAPP LIBRARY

Mary Whiton Calkins (1863–1930), the first woman elected APA president, suffered from the sex discrimination that was common during her lifetime. Despite academic setbacks (such as Harvard University refusing to grant women an official PhD), Calkins went on to a distinguished career in research and teaching at Wellesley College.

### The Growing Role of Women and Minorities

In 1892, APA had 31 members, all of whom were White and all of whom were male. Today, about half of all APA members are women, and the percentage of non-White members continues to grow. Surveys of recent PhD recipients reveal a picture of increasing diversification in the field. The proportion of women receiving PhDs in psychology increased nearly 20% between the mid-1980s and mid-1990s, and the proportion of minorities receiving PhDs in psychology nearly doubled during that same period. Clearly, psychology is increasingly reflecting the diversity of American society.

The current involvement of women and minorities in the APA, and psychology more generally, can be traced to early pioneers who blazed a trail that others followed. In 1905, Mary Calkins (1863–1930) became the first woman to serve as president of the APA. Calkins became interested in psychology while teaching Greek at Wellesley College. She studied with William James at Harvard and later became a professor of psychology at Wellesley College, where she worked until retiring in 1929. In her presidential address to the APA, Calkins described her theory of the role of the "self" in psychological function. Arguing against Wundt's and Titchener's structuralist ideas that the mind can be dissected into components, Calkins claimed that the self is a single unit that cannot be broken down into individual parts. Calkins wrote four books and published over 100 articles during her illustrious career (Calkins, 1930; Scarborough & Furumoto, 1987; Stevens & Gardner, 1982).

ARCHIVES OF THE HISTORY OF AMERICAN PSYCHOLOGY

Francis Cecil Sumner (1895–1954) was the first African American to hold a PhD in psychology, receiving his from Clark University in 1920. Sumner conducted research on race relations, equality, and the psychology of religion.

Today, women play leading roles in all areas of psychology. Some of the men who formed the APA might have been surprised by the prominence of women in the field today, but we suspect that William James, a strong supporter of Mary Calkins, would not be one of them.

Just as there were no women at the first meeting of the APA, there weren't any non-White people either. The first member of a minority group to become president of the APA was Kenneth Clark

A student of Francis Cecil Sumner's, Kenneth B. Clark (1914–2005) studied the developmental effects of prejudice, discrimination, and segregation on children. In one classic study from the 1950s, he found that African American preschoolers preferred white dolls to black ones. Clark's research was cited by the U.S. Supreme Court in its decision for the landmark *Brown v. Board of Education* case that ended school segregation.

WILLIAM E. SAURO/NEW YORK TIMES CO./GETTY IMAGES

(1914–2005), who was elected in 1970. Clark worked extensively on the self-image of African American children and argued that segregation of the races creates great psychological harm. Clark's conclusions had a large influence on public policy, and his research contributed to the Supreme Court's 1954 ruling (*Brown v. Board of Education*) to outlaw segregation in public schools (Guthrie, 2000). Clark's interest in psychology was sparked as an undergraduate at Howard University when he took a course from Francis Cecil Sumner (1895–1954), who was the first African American to receive a PhD in psychology (from Clark University, in 1920). Little known today, Sumner's main interest focused on the education of African American youth (Sawyer, 2000).

## What Psychologists Do: Research Careers

So what should you do if you want to become a psychologist—and what should you fail to do if you desperately want to avoid it? You can become "a psychologist" by a variety of routes, and the people who call themselves psychologists may hold a variety of different degrees. Typically, students finish college and enter graduate school in order to obtain a PhD (or doctor of philosophy) degree in some particular area of psychology (e.g., social, cognitive, developmental). During graduate school, students generally gain exposure to the field by taking classes and learn to conduct research by collaborating with their professors. Although William James was able to master every area of psychology because the areas were so small during his lifetime, today a student can spend the better part of a decade mastering just one.

After receiving a PhD, you can go on for more specialized research training by pursuing a postdoctoral fellowship under the supervision of an established researcher in their area or apply for a faculty position at a college or university or a research position in government or industry. Academic careers usually involve a combination of teaching and research, whereas careers in government or industry are typically dedicated to research alone.

### The Variety of Career Paths

As you saw earlier, research is not the only career option for a psychologist. Most of the people who call themselves psychologists neither teach nor do research, but rather, they assess or treat people with psychological problems. Most of these *clinical psychologists* work in private practice, often in partnerships with other psychologists or with psychiatrists (who have earned an MD, or medical degree, and are allowed to prescribe medication). Other clinical psychologists work in hospitals or medical schools, some have faculty positions at universities or colleges, and some combine private practice

 **ONLY HUMAN**

**A TREASURY OF THERAPEUTIC TECHNIQUES** The *Austin American-Statesman* reported that then Texas treasurer Martha Whitehead had hired a psychologist, for $1,000, to counsel several employees of her office who were despondent about Whitehead's recommendation to abolish her agency.

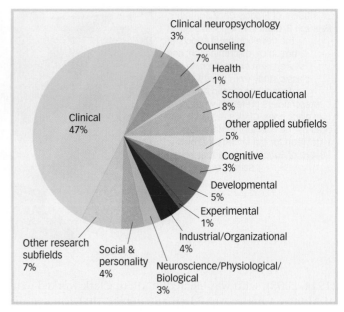

**Figure 1.7 The Major Subfields in Psychology** Psychologists are drawn to many different subfields in psychology. Here are the percentages of people receiving PhDs in various subfields. Clinical psychology makes up almost half of the doctorates awarded in psychology. Source: 2004 Graduate Study in Psychology. Compiled by APA Research Office.

with an academic job. Many clinical psychologists focus on specific problems or disorders, such as depression or anxiety, whereas others focus on specific populations, such as children, ethnic minority groups, or elderly adults (**FIGURE 1.7**).

Just over 10% of APA members are *counseling psychologists,* who assist people in dealing with work or career issues and changes or help people deal with common crises such as divorce, the loss of a job, or the death of a loved one. Counseling psychologists may have a PhD or an MA (master's degree) in counseling psychology or an MSW (master of social work).

Psychologists are also quite active in educational settings. About 5% of APA members are *school psychologists,* who offer guidance to students, parents, and teachers. A similar proportion of APA members, known as *industrial/organizational psychologists,* focus on issues in the workplace. These psychologists typically work in business or industry and may be involved in assessing potential employees, finding ways to improve productivity, or helping staff and management to develop effective planning strategies for coping with change or anticipated future developments.

Even this brief and incomplete survey of the APA membership provides a sense of the wide variety of contexts in which psychologists operate. You can think of psychology as an international community of professionals devoted to advancing scientific knowledge; assisting people with psychological problems and disorders; and trying to enhance the quality of life in work, school, and other everyday settings.

---

**In summary,** the American Psychological Association (APA) has grown dramatically since it was formed in 1892 and now includes over 150,000 members, working in clinical, academic, and applied settings. Psychologists are also represented by professional organizations such as the Association for Psychological Science (APS), which focuses on scientific psychology. Through the efforts of pioneers such as Mary Calkins, women have come to play an increasingly important role in the field and are now as well represented as men. Minority involvement in psychology took longer, but the pioneering efforts of Francis Cecil Sumner, Kenneth B. Clark, and others have led to increased participation of minorities in psychology. Psychologists prepare for research careers through graduate and postdoctoral training and work in a variety of applied settings, including schools, clinics, and industry. ■ ■

## Where Do You Stand?

# The Perils of Procrastination

As you've read in this chapter, the human mind and behavior are fascinating in part because they are not error free. Mindbugs interest us primarily as paths to achieving a better understanding of mental activity and behavior, but they also have practical consequences. Let's consider a mindbug that can have significant consequences in your own life: procrastination.

At one time or another, most of us have avoided carrying out a task or put it off to a later time. The task may be unpleasant, difficult, or just less entertaining than other things we could be doing at the moment. For college students, procrastination can affect a range of academic activities, such as writing a term paper or preparing for a test. Academic procrastination is not uncommon: Over 70% of college students report that they engage in some form of procrastination (Schouwenburg, 1995). Procrastination can be thought of as a mindbug because it prevents the completion of tasks in a timely manner. Although it's fun to hang out with your friends tonight, it's not so much fun to worry for three days about your impending history exam or try to study at 4:00 a.m. the morning before the test. Studying now, or at least a little bit each day, robs the procrastination mindbug of its power over you.

Some procrastinators defend the practice by claiming that they tend to work best under pressure or by noting that as long as a task gets done, it doesn't matter all that much if it is completed just before the deadline. Is there any merit to such claims, or are they just feeble excuses for counterproductive behavior?

A study of 60 undergraduate psychology college students provides some intriguing answers (Tice & Baumeister, 1997). At the beginning of the semester, the instructor announced a due date for the term paper and told students that if they could not meet the date, they would receive an extension to a later date. About a month later, students completed a scale that measures tendencies toward procrastination. At that same time, and then again during the last week of class, students recorded health symptoms they had experienced during the past week, the amount of stress they had experienced during that week, and the number of visits they had made to a health care center during the previous month.

Students who scored high on the procrastination scale tended to turn in their papers late. One month into the semester, these procrastinators reported less stress and fewer symptoms of physical illness than did nonprocrastinators. But at the end of the semester, the procrastinators reported *more* stress and *more* health symptoms than did the nonprocrastinators and also reported more visits to the health center. The procrastinators also received lower grades on their papers and on course exams.

This study shows, then, that procrastination did have some benefits: Procrastinators tended to feel better early on, while they were procrastinating and their deadline was far in the future. But they paid a significant cost for this immediate relief: Procrastinators not only suffered more stress and health problems as they scrambled to complete their work near the deadline, but also reported more stress and health symptoms across the entire semester. There was also no evidence to support the idea that procrastinators do their "best work under pressure," since their academic performance was worse than that of nonprocrastinators. Therefore, in addition to making use of the tips provided in the Real World box on increasing study skills (p. 11), it would seem wise to avoid procrastination in this course and others.

Where do you stand on procrastination? Calculate your procrastination score by rating the statements below on a scale of 1–5, where

1 = not at all; 2 = incidentally;
3 = sometimes; 4 = most of the time;
5 = always

How frequently last week did you engage in the following behaviors or thoughts?

1. Drifted off into daydreams while studying
2. Studied the subject matter that you had planned to do
3. Had no energy to study
4. Prepared to study at some point but did not get any further
5. Gave up when studying was not going well
6. Gave up studying early in order to do more pleasant things
7. Put off the completion of a task
8. Allowed yourself to be distracted from your work
9. Experienced concentration problems when studying
10. Interrupted studying for a while in order to do other things
11. Forgot to prepare things for studying
12. Did so many other things that there was insufficient time left for studying
13. Thought that you had enough time left, so that there was really no need to start studying

# Chapter Review

## Psychology's Roots: The Path to a Science of Mind

- Psychology is the scientific study of mind and behavior. Behavior is usually adaptive because it helps us meet the challenges of daily living; similarly, the brain and mind usually function effectively and efficiently. Disruptions to the mind and behavior, in the form of mindbugs, allow us to better understand the normal functions of the mind and behavior.

- Early efforts to develop a science of mind were pioneered by French scientists Pierre Flourens and Paul Broca, who observed the effects of brain damage on mental abilities of people and animals, and by German scientists such as Hermann von Helmholtz and Wilhelm Wundt, who applied methods from physiology to the study of psychology.

- In Germany, Wilhelm Wundt and Edward Titchener developed a school of thought called structuralism, which focused on analyzing the basic elements of consciousness.

- In America, William James pioneered the school of functionalism, which emphasized the functions of consciousness, and applied Darwin's theory of natural selection to the mind. G. Stanley Hall helped organize psychology with the formation of the first professional laboratory, organization, and journal in the field.

## Errors and Illusions Reveal Psychology

- Max Wertheimer founded Gestalt psychology based on the interpretation of an illusion of apparent motion, in which people perceive flashing lights as a moving whole instead of the sum of its parts.

- Clinicians such as Jean-Marie Charcot and Pierre Janet studied unusual cases in which patients acted like different people while under hypnosis, raising the possibility of more than one conscious self.

- Based on his own observations of clinical patients, Sigmund Freud developed the theory of psychoanalysis, which emphasized the importance of unconscious influences and childhood experiences in shaping thoughts, feelings, and behavior. A more optimistic view of the human condition, espoused by humanistic psychologists such as Abraham Maslow and Carl Rogers, held that people need to grow and reach their full potential.

## Psychology in the 20th Century: Behaviorism Takes Center Stage

- Behaviorism studies observable actions and responses and holds that inner mental processes are private events that cannot be studied scientifically.

- John Watson launched behaviorism in 1913, studied the association between a stimulus and response, and emphasized the importance of the environment over genetics in shaping behavior.

- B. F. Skinner developed the concept of reinforcement, demonstrating that animals and humans will repeat behaviors that generate positive outcomes and avoid those that are associated with unpleasant results.

## Beyond Behaviorism: Psychology Expands

- Cognitive psychology is concerned with inner mental processes such as perception, attention, memory, and reasoning. Cognitive psychology developed as a field due to psychologists' efforts to improve cognitive performance, the invention of the computer, and Noam Chomsky's ideas concerning the development of language.

- Cognitive neuroscience attempts to link the brain with the mind through studies of brain-damaged and healthy patients using neuroimaging techniques that allow glimpses of the brain in action.

- Evolutionary psychology focuses on the adaptive value of the mind and behavior and seeks to understand current psychological processes in terms of abilities and traits preserved by natural selection.

## Beyond the Individual: Social and Cultural Perspectives

- Social psychology recognizes that people exist in a network of other people and examines how individuals influence and interact with one another.

- Cultural psychology is concerned with the effects of the broader culture on individuals and with similarities and differences among people in different cultures.

## The Profession of Psychology: Past and Present

- The American Psychological Association (APA), the largest organization of professional psychologists, has grown dramatically since it was formed in 1892 and now includes over 150,000 members.

- Through the efforts of pioneers such as Mary Calkins, women have come to play an increasingly important role in psychology. Minority involvement in psychology took longer, but the efforts of Francis Cecil Sumner, Kenneth B. Clark, and others have been followed by increased participation by minorities.

- Psychologists prepare for research careers through graduate and postdoctoral training and also work in a variety of applied settings, including schools, clinics, and industry.

## Key Terms

| | | | |
|---|---|---|---|
| psychology (p. 2) | reaction time (p. 7) | dissociative identity disorder (p. 14) | response (p. 18) |
| mind (p. 2) | consciousness (p. 8) | hysteria (p. 14) | reinforcement (p. 19) |
| behavior (p. 2) | structuralism (p. 8) | unconscious (p. 15) | cognitive psychology (p. 21) |
| nativism (p. 5) | introspection (p. 8) | psychoanalytic theory (p. 15) | behavioral neuroscience (p. 24) |
| philosophical empiricism (p. 5) | functionalism (p. 10) | psychoanalysis (p. 15) | cognitive neuroscience (p. 25) |
| phrenology (p. 6) | natural selection (p. 10) | humanistic psychology (p. 16) | evolutionary psychology (p. 26) |
| physiology (p. 7) | illusions (p. 12) | behaviorism (p. 17) | social psychology (p. 28) |
| stimulus (p. 7) | Gestalt psychology (p. 13) | | cultural psychology (p. 29) |

## Recommended Readings

**Fancher, R. E.** (1979). *Pioneers of psychology.* New York: Norton. This engaging book examines the history of psychology by painting portraits of the field's pioneers, including many of the psychologists featured in this chapter. A great way to learn more about the history of psychology is by becoming familiar with the lives of its founders.

**Hermann, D., Raybeck, D., & Gruneberg, M.** (2002). *Improving memory and study skills.* Seattle: Hogrefe and Huber. This excellent book offers a nice introduction to many aspects of cognitive psychology. More importantly, it offers several practical suggestions for improving memory, improving study habits, and mastering material that you are trying to learn.

**James, W.** (1890). *The principles of psychology (1890/1955).* New York: Holt. Considered by many psychologists to be the "bible" of psychology, this masterpiece by William James is still exciting to read over a century after it was published. If you do have a chance to read it, you will understand why thousands of psychologists are so thankful that James bypassed a career in medicine for one in psychology.

**Skinner, B. F.** (1948/1986). *Walden II.* Englewood Cliffs, NJ: Prentice Hall. Skinner's provocative novel describes a modern utopia in which scientific principles from behavioristic psychology are used to shape a model community. This controversial book raises intriguing questions about how knowledge from psychology could or should be used to influence day-to-day living in modern society.

**American Psychological Association Web site:** www.apa.org

**Association for Psychological Science Web site:** www.psychologicalscience.org

These Web sites provide a wealth of information about the APA and the APS and about news and research in all areas of psychology. Both sites have sections specially designed for students and contain many links to other useful and informative sites in psychology. An excellent way to learn about what is going on in the field today.

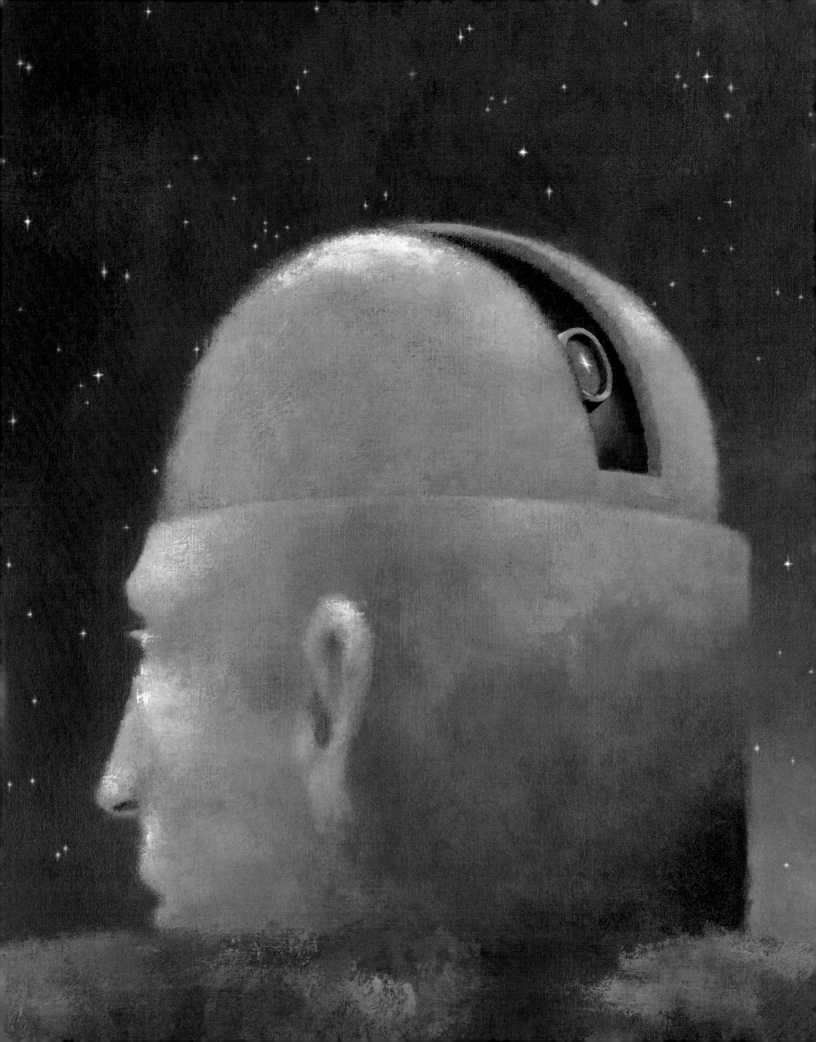

# 2

# The Methods of Psychology

**LORI AND REBA SCHAPPELL ARE HAPPY** to be twins. One is an award-winning country music singer; one is a wisecracking hospital worker who likes strawberry daiquiris. Despite their different interests and different temperaments, they get along quite well and love each other dearly. That's a good thing because Lori and Reba not only share the same parents and the same birthday, but they also share a blood supply, part of a skull, and some brain tissue. Lori and Reba are conjoined twins who have been attached at the forehead since birth. When asked whether they would ever consider being surgically separated, Reba seems perplexed: "Our point of view is no, straight-out no. Why would you want to do that? For all the money in China, why? You'd be ruining two lives in the process" (Angier, 1997). If you find this hard to believe, then welcome to the club. Conjoined twins are routinely separated at birth even when this means crippling both or killing one of them because surgeons and parents—like most of us—can't imagine that a conjoined life is really worth living. And yet, conjoined twins don't seem to share that view. As one medical historian noted, "The desire to remain together is so widespread among communicating conjoined twins as to be practically universal. . . . I have yet to find an instance in which conjoined twins have sought out separation" (Dreger, 1998).

Are conjoined twins really as happy as they claim, or are they simply fooling themselves? Do parents and doctors have the right to impose dangerous surgery on infants who would otherwise grow up to refuse it? Such questions have moral, religious, and philosophical answers, but they can have scientific answers as well. If we could find some way to measure a psychological property such as happiness, then we could use scientific methods to determine who has it and who doesn't and to discover what kinds of lives promote or preclude it. Is a conjoined life a wonderful life, or is it society's responsibility to separate conjoined twins whenever possible? As you are about to see, psychological methods are designed to provide answers to questions like this one.

AP PHOTO//READING EAGLE, JOHN A. SECOGES

Are conjoined twins less happy than singletons? Reba (left) and Lori (right) Schappell are sisters who say that the answer is no.

The 17th-century astronomer Galileo Galilei was excommunicated and sentenced to prison for sticking to his own observations of the solar system rather than accepting the teachings of the church. In 1597 he wrote to his friend and fellow astronomer Johannes Kepler, "What would you say of the learned here, who, replete with the pertinacity of the asp, have steadfastly refused to cast a glance through the telescope? What shall we make of this? Shall we laugh, or shall we cry?" As it turned out, the correct answer was *cry*.

# Empiricism: How to Know Things

When ancient Greeks sprained their ankles, caught the flu, or accidentally set their togas on fire, they had to choose between two kinds of doctors: dogmatists (from *dogmatikos,* meaning "belief"), who thought that the best way to understand illness was to develop theories about the body's functions, and empiricists (from *empeirikos,* meaning "experience"), who thought that the best way to understand illness was to observe sick people. The rivalry between these two schools of medicine didn't last long, however, because the people who chose to see dogmatists tended to die, which wasn't very good for repeat business. It is little wonder that today we use the word *dogmatism* to describe the tendency for people to cling to their assumptions and the word **empiricism** to describe *the belief that accurate knowledge of the world requires observation of it.* The fact that we can answer questions about the world by observation may seem obvious to you, but this obvious fact is actually a relatively new discovery. Throughout most of human history, people have trusted authority to answer important questions about the world, and it is only in the last millennium (and especially in the past three centuries) that people have begun to trust their eyes and ears more than their elders. The shift from dogmatism to empiricism was a long time coming, but when it came, it laid the foundation of modern science.

Of course, some of the sick people who visited empiricists died too because empiricism is by no means infallible. If you glance out the window right now, you will see that the earth is flat and the sun is making a slow circle around it. Neither of these observations is accurate, of course, but until fairly recently most people believed them to be true—not because people were dogmatists, but because they were empiricists who could see the flatness of the earth and the orbit of the sun for themselves. Alas, the naked eye is blind to many things. No matter how long you stare out the window, you will never see a black hole, an atom, a germ, a gene, evolution, gravity, or the true shape of the planet on which you are standing. Empiricism has proved to be a profitable approach to understanding natural phenomena, but using this approach requires a **method**, which is *a set of rules and techniques for observation that allow observers to avoid the illusions, mistakes, and erroneous conclusions that simple observation can produce.*

In many sciences, the word *method* refers primarily to technologies that enhance the powers of the senses. Biologists use microscopes and astronomers use telescopes because the phenomena they seek to explain are invisible to the naked eye. Human behavior, on the other hand, is relatively easy to observe, so you might expect psychology's methods to be relatively simple. In fact, the empirical challenges facing psychologists are among the most daunting in all of modern science, and thus psychological methods are among the most sophisticated. Three things make people especially difficult to study:

- *Complexity:* Psychologists study the single most complex object in the known universe. No galaxy, particle, molecule, or machine is as complicated as the human brain. Scientists can describe the birth of a star or the death of a cell in exquisite detail, but they can barely begin to say how the 500 million interconnected neurons that constitute the brain give rise to the thoughts, feelings, and actions that are psychology's core concerns.
- *Variability:* In almost all the ways that matter, one *E. coli* bacterium is pretty much like another. But people are as varied as their fingerprints. No two individuals ever do, say, think, or feel exactly the same thing under exactly the same circumstances, which means that when you've seen one, you've most definitely not seen them all.

*"Are you just pissing and moaning, or can you verify what you're saying with data?"*

- *Reactivity:* An atom of cesium-133 oscillates 9,192,631,770 times per second regardless of who's watching. But people often think, feel, and act one way when they are being observed and a different way when they are not. When people know they are being studied, they don't always behave as they otherwise would.

In short, human beings are tremendously complex, endlessly variable, and uniquely reactive, and these attributes present a major challenge to the scientific study of their behavior. As you'll see, psychologists have developed a variety of methods that are designed to meet these challenges head-on.

People are variable. Three identical men may stick identical footballs in their ears and still levitate quite differently.

SPENCER RESEARCH LIBRARY, UNIVERSITY OF KANSAS

## The Science of Observation: Saying What

There is no escaping the fact that you have to observe *what* people do before you can try to explain *why* they do it. To *observe* something means to use your senses to learn about its properties. For example, when you observe a round, red apple, your brain is using the pattern of light that is falling on your eyes to draw an inference about the apple's identity, shape, and color. That kind of informal observation is fine for buying fruit but not for doing science. Why? First, casual observations are notoriously unstable. The same apple may appear red in the daylight and crimson at night or spherical to one person and elliptical to another. Second, casual observations can't tell us about many of the properties in which we might be interested. No matter how long and hard you look, you will never be able to discern an apple's crunchiness or pectin content simply by watching it. If you want to know about those properties, you must do more than observe. You must *measure*.

## Measurement

For most of human history, people had no idea how old they were because there was no simple way to keep track of time. Or weight, or volume, or density, or temperature, or anything else for that matter. Today we live in a world of tape measures and rulers, clocks and calendars, odometers, thermometers, and mass spectrometers. Measurement is not just the basis of science, it is the basis of modern life. All of these measurements have two things in common. Whether we want to measure the intensity of an earthquake, the distance between molecules, or the attitude of a registered voter, we must first *define* the property we wish to measure and then find a way to *detect* it.

### Definition and Detection

You probably think you know what *length* is. But if you try to define it without using the word *long,* you get tongue-tied pretty quickly. We use words such as *weight, speed,* or *length* all the time in ordinary conversation without realizing that each of these terms has an **operational definition**, which is *a description of a property in measurable terms.* For example, the operational definition of the property we casually refer to as *length* is "the change in the location of light over time." That's right. When we say that a bookshelf is "a meter long," we are actually saying how long it takes a particle of light to travel from one end of the shelf to the other. (In case you're interested, the answer is 1/299,792,458th of a second. In case you're not interested, that's still the answer.) According to this operational definition, the more time it takes for a photon to travel from one end of a bookshelf to the other, the more "length" that bookshelf has. Operational definitions specify the concrete events that count as instances of an abstract property. The first step in making any measurement is to define the property we want to measure in concrete terms.

**EMPIRICISM** Originally a Greek school of medicine that stressed the importance of observation, and now generally used to describe any attempt to acquire knowledge by observing objects or events.

**METHOD** A set of rules and techniques for observation that allow researchers to avoid the illusions, mistakes, and erroneous conclusions that simple observation can produce.

**OPERATIONAL DEFINITION** A description of an abstract property in terms of a concrete condition that can be measured.

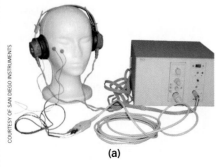

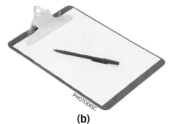

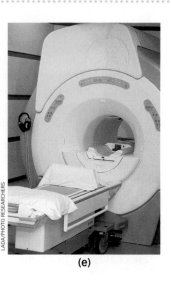

**(a)**

**(b)**

**(c)**

**(d)**

**(e)**

**Figure 2.1 Some Psychological Measures** Psychological measures may take a variety of forms: (a) a modern electromyograph (EMG) measures the electrical activity of muscles in the face; (b) a questionnaire measures preferences, attitudes, and opinions; (c) an 1890 Hipp chronoscope measures reaction times; (d) a 1907 kymograph measures hand movements; and (e) a functional magnetic resonance imaging (fMRI) chamber measures blood flow in the brain; .

*"Are you (a) contented, (b) happy, (c) very happy, (d) wildly happy, (e) deliriously happy?"*

The second step is to find a way to detect the concrete terms that our definition describes. To do this we must use a **measure**, which is *a device that can detect the events to which an operational definition refers*. For example, length is the change in the location of light over time, and we can detect such changes by using a photon detector (which tells us the location of a particle of light) and a clock (which tells us how long it took the particle of light to travel from one location to another). Once we have determined just how far a photon travels in 1/299,792,458th of a second, we can make our next measurement a lot less expensive by marking that distance on a piece of wood and calling it a ruler. Keep in mind that measures (such as clocks and photon detectors) detect the concrete conditions described by our operational definitions (such as "change in the location of light over time"), but *they do not detect the property itself* (such as length). Indeed, properties such as shape, color, length, or duration are best thought of as abstract ideas that can never be measured directly. **FIGURE 2.1** shows a variety of old and new measures used by psychologists.

*Defining* and *detecting* are the two tasks that allow us to measure physical properties, and these same two tasks allow us to measure psychological properties as well. If we wanted to measure Lori Schappell's happiness, for example, our first task would be to develop an operational definition of that property—that is, to specify some concrete, measurable event that will count as an instance of happiness. For example, we might define happiness as the simultaneous contraction of the *zygomatic major* (which is the muscle that makes your mouth turn up when you smile) and the *orbicularis oculi* (which is the muscle that makes your eyes crinkle when you smile). After defining happiness as a specific set of muscular contractions, we would then need to measure those contractions, and the **electromyograph (EMG)**—which is *a device that measures muscle contractions under the surface of a person's skin*—would do splendidly. Once we have defined happiness and found a way to detect the concrete events that our definition supplies, we are in a position to measure it.

But is this the *right* way to measure happiness? That's hard to say. There are many ways to define the same property and many ways to detect the events that this definition supplies. For instance, we could detect the muscular contractions involved in smiling by using EMG, or we could detect them by asking a human observer to watch a participant's face and tell us how often the participant smiled. We could define happiness in terms of muscular contractions, or we could define it as a person's self-assessment of his or her own emotional state, in which case we could measure it by asking people how happy they feel and recording their answers. With so many options for defining and detecting happiness, how are we to choose among them? As you are about to see, there are many ways to define and detect, but some are much better than others.

## Validity

Measurement consists of two tasks: *defining,* which is the process by which properties are linked to operational definitions, and *detecting,* which is the process by which operational definitions are linked to measures. If we do either of these tasks badly, then any measurement we make will lack **validity,** which is *the characteristic of an observation that allows one to draw accurate inferences from it.* Because measurement involves precisely two tasks, there are precisely two ways for a measurement to be invalid (see **FIGURE 2.2**). First, a measurement will be invalid when *the operational definition does not adequately define the property,* and second, a measurement will be invalid when *the measure cannot adequately detect the conditions that the operational definition describes.* Let's consider each of these sources of invalidity more closely.

**Problems of Defining** You can measure a lot of things with a ruler, but happiness isn't one of them because "change in the location of light over time" is not meaningfully related to the emotional experience we call "happiness." We all have some sense of what happiness means, and the distance that a photon travels just isn't it. A good operational definition must have **construct validity,** which is *the tendency for an operational definition and a property to share meaning.* It makes sense to define *wealth* as the amount of money a person has in savings, investments, and real estate because the concrete object we call *money* is meaningfully related to the abstract concept we call *wealth.* It makes no sense to define *wealth* as the number of Junior Mints a person can swallow in one gulp because this ability (as admirable as it may be) has nothing to do with what we mean by the word *wealth.* Some operational definitions are clearly related to their properties, and some are clearly not.

The interesting cases fall between these two extremes. For example, is smiling a valid way to define happiness? Well, this definition certainly has construct validity: We all know from experience that smiling and happiness go together like money and wealth do. But if smiling is a valid definition of happiness, then it should also have **predictive validity,** which is *the tendency for an operational definition to be related to other operational definitions of the same property.* If an operational definition such as smiling is linked to a property such as happiness, then it should also be linked to other operational definitions of the same property. For example, it should be linked to electrical activity in the part of the brain known as the right frontal lobe or to the person's own report of his or her emotional state. If we could demonstrate that people whose right frontal lobes are active and who say, "I sure am happy right now," also tend to smile, then we could be even more certain that smiling is a valid definition of happiness. Predictive validity gets its name from the fact that knowledge of the conditions specified by one operational definition (e.g., knowing whether a person is smiling) should enable us to predict the conditions specified by another operational definition

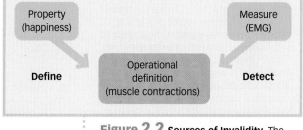

**Figure 2.2 Sources of Invalidity** The process of *defining* links properties to operational definitions, and the process of *detecting* links operational definitions to measures. Invalidity can result from problems in either of these links.

**MEASURE** A device that can detect the measurable events to which an operational definition refers.

**ELECTROMYOGRAPH (EMG)** A device that measures muscle contractions under the surface of a person's skin.

**VALIDITY** The characteristic of an observation that allows one to draw accurate inferences from it.

**CONSTRUCT VALIDITY** The tendency for an operational definition and a property to have a clear conceptual relation.

**PREDICTIVE VALIDITY** The tendency for an operational definition to be related to other operational definitions.

A bathroom scale and a laboratory balance both measure weight, but the balance is more likely to provide exactly the same measurement when it is used to weigh the same object twice (reliability) and more likely to provide different measurements when it is used to weigh two objects that differ by just a fraction of a gram (power). Not surprisingly, the bathroom scale sells for around $30 and the balance for around $3,000. Power and reliability don't come cheap.

**Figure 2.3 Kinds of Validity** Construct validity (pink) refers to the conceptual relationship between a property and a measure. Predictive validity (green) refers to the relationship between different measures. In this example, the property called "happiness" is operationally defined as right frontal lobe (RF) activity (which is measured by functional magnetic resonance imaging, or fMRI) and also as smiling (which is measured by facial electromyography, or EMG).

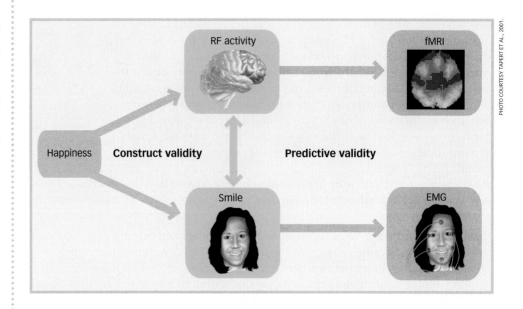

PHOTO COURTESY TAPERT ET AL., 2001.

(e.g., whether the person's right frontal lobe is active or whether the person is claiming to be happy). In short, if we do a good job of defining a property, then our measurement of that property will have validity. **FIGURE 2.3** illustrates the relationship between predictive validity and construct validity.

**Problems of Detection** Yardsticks made of Jell-O have historically been commercial failures. The stiffness of a yardstick is critical because it means that when we repeatedly use the yardstick to measure an object, we repeatedly get the same result. What's more, anyone else who uses the same yardstick to measure the same object will get the same result we did. **Reliability** is *the tendency for a measure to produce the same result whenever it is used to measure the same thing,* and any measure that lacks this tendency is about as useful as a gelatin ruler. For example, if a person's zygomatic muscle did not move for 10 minutes, we would expect the EMG to produce the same reading for 10 minutes. If the EMG produced different readings from one minute to the next, then it would be an unreliable measure that was detecting differences that weren't really there. A good measure must be reliable. The flip side of reliability is **power**, which is *the tendency for a measure to produce different results when it is used to measure different things.* If a person's zygomatic muscle moved continuously for 10 minutes, we would expect the EMG to produce different readings in those 10 minutes. If the EMG instead produced the same reading from one minute to the next, then it would be a weak or powerless measure that was failing to detect differences that were really there. Reliable and powerful measures are those that detect the conditions specified by an operational definition (a) when they happen and (b) *only* when they happen.

Validity, reliability, and power are prerequisites for accurate measurement. But once you've got a good ruler in hand, the next step is to find something to measure with it. Psychologists have developed techniques for doing that too.

## Samples

If a pig flew over the White House, it wouldn't matter whether other pigs could do the same trick. The fact that just one pig flew just one time would challenge our most cherished assumptions about animal physiology, aerodynamics, and national security and would thus be an observation well worth making. Similarly, individuals sometimes do remarkable things that deserve close study, and when psychologists study them closely, they are using the **case method,** which is *a method of gathering scientific knowledge by studying a single individual.* For example, the physician Oliver Sacks described his observations of a brain-damaged patient in a book titled *The Man Who Mistook His Wife for a*

---

**RELIABILITY** The tendency for a measure to produce the same result whenever it is used to measure the same thing.

**POWER** The tendency for a measure to produce different results when it is used to measure different things.

**CASE METHOD** A method of gathering scientific knowledge by studying a single individual.

**POPULATION** The complete collection of participants who might possibly be measured.

**SAMPLE** The partial collection of people who actually were measured in a study.

**LAW OF LARGE NUMBERS** A statistical law stating that as sample size increases, the attributes of a sample will more closely reflect the attributes of the population from which it was drawn.

*Hat,* and those observations were worth making because this is a rather unusual mistake for a man to make. As you saw in Chapter 1, people with unusual abilities, unusual experiences, or unusual deficits often provide important insights about human psychology.

But exceptional cases are the exception, and more often than not, psychologists are in the business of observing *un*exceptional people and trying to explain why they think, feel, and act as they do. When psychologists observe ordinary people, they typically observe *many* of them and then try to explain the *average* of those observations rather than explaining each individual observation itself. This simple technique of averaging many observations is one of psychology's most powerful methodological tools.

*"This fundamentally changes everything we know about elephants!"*

### The Law of Large Numbers

If you sat down and started picking cards from a deck, you would expect to pick as many red cards as black cards over the long run. But *only* over the long run. You would not be surprised if you picked just two cards and they both turned out to be red, but you *would* be surprised if you picked just 20 cards and they all turned out to be red. You would be surprised by 20 red cards and not by two red cards because your intuition tells you that when the number of cards you pick is small, you really can't expect your hand to have the same proportion of red and black cards as does the full deck.

Your intuition is exactly right. A **population** is *the complete collection of objects or events that might be measured,* and a **sample** is *the partial collection of objects or events that is measured*. In this case, the full deck is a population, and the cards in your hand are a sample of that population. Your intuition about the cards is captured by the **law of large numbers**, which states that *as sample size increases, the attributes of the sample more closely reflect the attributes of the population from which the sample was drawn*. The law of large numbers suggests that as the size of a sample (that is, the number cards in your hand) increases, the ratio of black to red cards in the sample will more closely approximate the ratio of black to red cards in the population. In plain English, the more cards you pick, the more likely it is that half the cards in your hand will be red and half will be black.

Precisely the same logic informs the methods of psychology. For example, if we wanted to know how happy people are in Florida, we would begin with an operational definition of happiness. For the sake of simplicity, we might define happiness as a person's belief about his or her own emotional state. Then we'd develop a way to measure that belief, for example, by asking the person to make a checkmark on a 10-point rating scale. If we used this measure to measure the happiness of just one Floridian, our lone observation would tell us little about the happiness of the 15 million people who actually live in that state. On the other hand, if we were to measure the happiness of a hundred Floridians, or a thousand Floridians, or even a million Floridians, the average of our measurements would begin to approximate the average happiness of all Floridians. The law of large numbers suggests that as the size of our sample increases, the average happiness of the people in our sample becomes a better approximation of the average happiness of the people in the population. You can prove this to yourself by considering what would happen if you measured the largest possible sample, namely, every Floridian. In that case, the average happiness of your sample and the average happiness of the population would be identical (see the Real World box on the next page).

Measuring the happiness of just one Floridian could provide a misleading estimate of the happiness of the population.

## { THE REAL WORLD } Taking a Chance

A 2002 CBS NEWS POLL FOUND THAT nearly three out of every five Americans believe in extrasensory perception (ESP). Very few psychologists share this belief, and you might wonder why they tend to be such a skeptical lot. As you have seen, psychology's methods often rely on the laws of probability. Some of these laws, such as the law of large numbers, are intuitively obvious, but others are not, and ignorance of the less obvious laws often leads people to "know what isn't so" (Gilovich, 1991).

Consider the case of the amazing coincidence. One night you dream that a panda is piloting an airplane over the Indian Ocean, and the next day you tell a friend, who says, "Wow, I had exactly the same dream last week!" One morning you are humming an old Green Day tune in the shower, and when you get into your car an hour later, the very same song is on the radio. You and your roommate are wondering what kind of pizza to order when suddenly you both open your mouths and say, "Pepperoni and onions," in perfect unison. Coincidences like these feel truly spooky when they happen. How can we possibly explain them as anything other than instances of precognition (knowing the future before it happens) or telepathy (reading another person's thoughts)?

The same question occurred to Nobel Prize–winning physicist Luis Alverez one day when he was reading the newspaper. A particular story got him thinking about an old college friend whom he hadn't seen in

How easy is it to find a coincidence? One of the authors of this textbook was born on November 5. A few minutes of research revealed that jazz pianist Art Tatum (left) died on November 5 and recorded a song called "Paper Moon," while actress Tatum O'Neal (right) was born on November 5 and starred in a movie called Paper Moon. Should we be amazed?

years. A few minutes later, he turned the page and was shocked to see the very same friend's obituary. Was this a case of precognition (he "saw" 2 minutes into his own future) or telepathy (he read the thoughts of someone who was reading the obituary 2 minutes before he did)? Before jumping to such extraordinary conclusions, Alvarez decided to use probability theory to determine just how amazing this coincidence really was.

First he estimated the number of friends that the average person has, and then he estimated how often the average person thinks about each of those friends. With these estimates in hand, Alvarez did a few simple calculations and determined the

likelihood that someone would think about a friend 5 minutes before learning about that friend's death. The odds, it turned out, were astonishingly high. In a country the size of the United States, for example, this amazing coincidence should happen to 10 people every day (Alvarez, 1965). If this seems surprising to you, then know you are not alone. Research has shown that people routinely underestimate the chance likelihood of coincidences (Diaconis & Mosteller, 1989; Falk & McGregor, 1983; Hintzman, Asher, & Stern, 1978). If you want to profit from this fact, you can bet in any group of 24 or more people that at least 2 of them share the same birthday. The odds are in your favor, and the bigger the group, the better the odds. In fact, in a group of 35, the odds are 85%.

So when *should* we be impressed by an amazing coincidence? When it happens more often than we would expect by chance alone. The problem is that we cannot easily calculate the likelihood that a flying panda, a Green Day tune, or a pepperoni-and-onion pizza will come to mind by chance alone. Science deals with events whose chance occurrence can be estimated, and scientists use this estimate to determine when an event really is or is not surprising. In the real world, we often can't make these estimates with any degree of certainty, which is why we can rarely draw legitimate conclusions about the likelihood of everyday coincidences.

---

 **ONLY HUMAN**

**MAYBE THEY COULD PASS A LAW OF LARGE NUMBERS?** In 1997, David Cook of Caledonian University in Glasgow, Scotland, told the British Psychological Society's annual conference that his 3-year study shows that politicians have significant behavior patterns in common with criminal psychopaths. Cook said that criminals were relatively easy to analyze but that he did not have as much data as he would like on politicians. "They don't like to be studied," he said.

## Averaging

Under the right circumstances, the average of a sample can tell us about the average of a population. But it cannot tell us about the individuals in that population. For example, when psychologists claim that women have better fine motor skills than men (and they do), or that men have better spatial ability than women (and they do), or that children are more suggestible than adults (and they are), or that New Yorkers care more about sex than algebra (well, it seems likely), their claims are not true—and are not *meant* to be true—of every individual in these populations. Rather, when psychologists say that women have better fine motor skills than men, they mean that when the fine motor skills of a large sample of women and men are measured, the average of the women's measurements is reliably higher than the average of the men's.

**FIGURE 2.4** illustrates this point with hypothetical observations that are arranged in a pair of **frequency distributions**, which are *graphic representations of the measurements of a sample that are arranged by the number of times each measurement was observed*. These frequency distributions display every possible score on a fine motor skills test on the horizontal axis and display the number of times (or the *frequency* with which) each score was observed among a sample of men and women on the vertical axis. A frequency distribution can have any shape, but it commonly takes

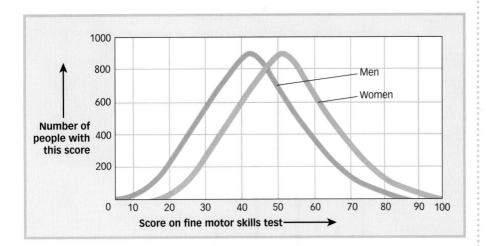

**Figure 2.4** **Frequency Distributions**
This graph shows the hypothetical scores of a sample of men and women who took a test of fine motor skills. The scores are represented along the horizontal axis, and the frequency of each score is represented along the vertical axis. As you can see, the average score of women is a bit higher than the average score of men. Both distributions are examples of normal distributions.

the shape known as a **normal distribution** (sometimes also called a *bell curve*). A normal distribution is *a frequency distribution in which most measurments are concentrated around the mean and fall off toward the tails, and the two sides of the distribution are symmetrical.* As you can see in Figure 2.4, normal distributions are *symmetrical* (i.e., the left half is a mirror image of the right half), have a peak in the middle, and trail off at the ends. Most scores can be found toward the center of a normal distribution, with fewer scores at the extremes. In fact, the point at the very center of a normal distribution is where you'll find the average.

A frequency distribution depicts every measurement in a sample and thus provides a full and complete picture of that sample. But like most full and complete pictures, it is a terribly cumbersome way to communicate information. When we ask a friend how she's been, we don't want her to show us a graph depicting her happiness on each day of the previous six months. Rather, we want a brief summary statement that captures the essential information that such a graph would provide—for example, "I'm doing pretty well," or, "I've been having some ups and downs lately." In psychology, brief summary statements that capture the essential information from a frequency distribution are called *descriptive statistics*. There are two important kinds of descriptive statistics:

■ *Descriptions of central tendency* are summary statements about the value of the measurements that lie near the center or midpoint of a frequency distribution. When a friend says that she has been "doing pretty well," she is describing the central tendency (or approximate location of the midpoint) of the frequency distribution of her happiness measurements. The three most common descriptions of central tendency are the **mode** (*the value of the most frequently observed measurement*), the **mean** (*the average value of the measurements*), and the **median** (*the value that is greater than or equal to the values of half the measurements and less than or equal to half the values of the measurements*). In a normal distribution, the mean, median, and mode are all the same value, but when the distribution departs from normality, these three descriptive statistics can differ. **FIGURE 2.5** on the next page shows how each of these descriptive statistics is calculated.

■ *Descriptions of variability* are statements about the extent to which the measurements in a frequency distribution differ from each other. When a friend says that she has been having some "ups and downs" lately, she is offering a brief summary statement that describes how the measurements in the frequency distribution of her happiness scores over the past six months tend to differ from one another. A mathematically simple description of variability is the **range**, which is *the value of the largest measurement minus the value of the smallest measurement.* There are several other common descriptions of variability that are quite mathematically complicated, such as the *variance* and the *standard deviation,* but all such descriptions give us a sense of how similar or different the scores in a distribution tend to be.

**FREQUENCY DISTRIBUTION** A graphical representation of the measurements of a sample that are arranged by the number of times each measurement was observed.

**NORMAL DISTRIBUTION** A frequency distribution in which most measurements are concentrated around the mean and fall off toward the tails, and the two sides of the distribution are symmetrical.

**MODE** The "most frequent" measurement in a frequency distribution.

**MEAN** The average of the measurements in a frequency distribution.

**MEDIAN** The "middle" measurement in a frequency distribution. Half the measurements in a frequency distribution are greater than or equal to the median and half are less than or equal to the median.

**RANGE** The numerical difference between the smallest and largest measurements in a frequency distribution.

**Figure 2.5 Some Descriptive Statistics**
This frequency distribution shows the scores of 15 individuals on a seven-point test. Descriptive statistics include measures of central tendency (such as the mean, median, and mode) and measures of variability (such as the range).

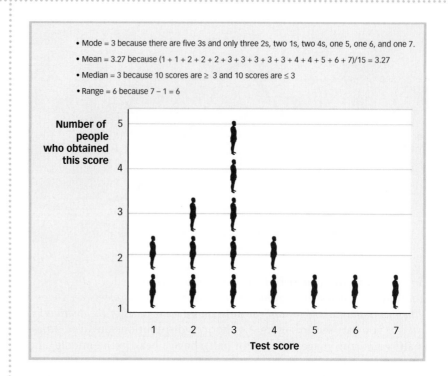

- Mode = 3 because there are five 3s and only three 2s, two 1s, two 4s, one 5, one 6, and one 7.
- Mean = 3.27 because $(1 + 1 + 2 + 2 + 2 + 3 + 3 + 3 + 3 + 3 + 4 + 4 + 5 + 6 + 7)/15 = 3.27$
- Median = 3 because 10 scores are $\geq$ 3 and 10 scores are $\leq$ 3
- Range = 6 because $7 - 1 = 6$

As Figure 2.4, shows, the central tendency and the variability of a frequency distribution jointly determine the kinds of conclusions we can draw from it. The mean of the women's scores is higher than the mean of the men's scores, which suggests that women have better fine motor skills than men *on average*. But both frequency distributions also have considerable variability, which is to say that plenty of men scored higher than plenty of women. Indeed, what is true about people on average is almost never true in every case. As you read about studies in other chapters of this book, you will undoubtedly find yourself thinking of exceptions to the conclusions that the researchers have drawn. *But wait a minute,* you may think, *the book says that women have better fine motor skills than men, but Dad is a surgeon and Mom can't even thread a needle. So how can that be right?* If you have this thought, feel free to come back to page 47 and stare at Figure 2.4, which should remind you that a conclusion can be true on average and still allow for exceptions. One *E. coli* bacterium may be pretty much like the next, but no two people are exactly alike, and because people differ, there is almost nothing interesting that is absolutely true of every one of them at all times. Some New Yorkers probably do like algebra better than sex, but this does not change the fact that *on average* they prefer thinking about lovemaking to the quadratic equation. Psychology's empirical methods allow us to observe the differences between individuals, explain those differences, and, if we wish, look beyond those differences to see underlying patterns of similarity.

Now that you understand *why* psychologists measure samples that are drawn from populations, let's look at *how* they actually do this in everyday life.

On average, men have more upper-body strength than women, but there are still many women with more upper-body strength than many men.

## Bias

People pick their noses, exceed the speed limit, read each other's mail, and skip over major sections of *War and Peace,* and they are especially likely to do these things when they think no one is looking. It is only natural for people to behave a bit differently when they are in the spotlight of each other's attention, but this fact makes people rather difficult to study because while psychologists are trying to discover how people really *do* behave, people are often trying to behave as they think they *should* behave. **Demand characteristics** are *those aspects of a setting that cause people to behave as they think an observer wants or expects them to behave.* They are called demand characteristics because they seem to "demand" or require that people say and do things that they normally might not. If you have ever been asked the question, "Do you think these jeans make me look fat?" then you have experienced a demand characteristic. Demand characteristics hinder our attempts to measure behavior as it normally unfolds, and psychologists have developed a variety of ways to avoid them.

This bar on 10th Avenue in New York City has a "one-way" mirror in its unisex restroom. Customers see their reflections in the restroom's mirror, and people who are walking down the street see the customers. Are the customers influenced by the fact that pedestrians may be watching them? Hard to say, but one observer did notice a suspiciously "high percentage of people who wash their hands" (Wolf, 2003).

### Avoiding Demand Characteristics

People often behave as they think observers want or expect them to behave, and one way to avoid this problem is to observe people without their knowledge. **Naturalistic observation** is *a technique for gathering scientific knowledge by unobtrusively observing people in their natural environments.* For example, naturalistic observation reveals that the biggest groups tend to leave the smallest tips in restaurants (Freeman, Walker, Borden, & Latané, 1975), that hungry shoppers buy the most impulse items at the grocery store (Gilbert, Gill, & Wilson, 2002), that golfers are most likely to cheat when they play several opponents at once (Erffmeyer, 1984), that men do not usually approach the most beautiful woman at a singles' bar (Glenwick, Jason, & Elman, 1978), and that Olympic athletes smile more when they win the bronze rather than the silver medal (Medvec, Madey, & Gilovich, 1995). All of these conclusions are the result of measurements made by psychologists who observed people who didn't know they were being observed. It is unlikely that any of these things would have happened in exactly the same way if the diners, shoppers, golfers, singles, and athletes had known that they were being scrutinized.

Unfortunately, there are two reasons why naturalistic observation cannot by itself solve the problem of demand characteristics. First, some of the things psychologists want to observe simply don't occur naturally. For example, if we wanted to know whether people who have undergone sensory deprivation perform poorly on motor tasks, we would have to hang around the shopping mall for a very long time before a few dozen blindfolded people with earplugs just happened to wander by and start typing. Second, some of the things that psychologists want to observe can only be gathered from direct interaction with a person—for example, by administering a survey, giving tests, conducting an interview, or hooking someone up to an EEG. If we wanted to know how often someone worried about dying, how accurately they could remember their high school graduation, how quickly they could solve a logic puzzle, or how much electrical activity their brain produced when they felt happy, then simply observing them would not do the trick.

When psychologists cannot avoid demand characteristics by hiding in the bushes, they often avoid them by hiding other things instead. For instance, people are less likely to be influenced by demand characteristics when they cannot be identified as the originators of their actions, and psychologists often take advantage of this fact by allowing people to respond privately (e.g., by having them complete questionnaires when they are alone) or anonymously (e.g., by failing to collect personal information, such as the person's name or address). Another technique that psychologists use to avoid demand characteristics is to measure behaviors that are not susceptible to demand. For instance, behaviors can't be influenced by demand characteristics if they

**DEMAND CHARACTERISTICS** Those aspects of an observational setting that cause people to behave as they think an observer wants or expects them to behave.

**NATURALISTIC OBSERVATION** A method of gathering scientific knowledge by unobtrusively observing people in their natural environments.

One way to avoid demand characteristics is to measure behaviors that people are unable or unlikely to control, such as facial expressions, reaction times, eye blink rate, and so on. For example, when people feel anxious they tend to involuntarily compress their lips as President George W. Bush did in this 2006 photo taken as he gave a speech in the Rose Garden.

People's expectations can influence their observations. On September 10, 2002, Mr. Gurdeep Wander boarded an airplane with three other dark-skinned men who had no luggage, switched seats, and got up several times to use the restroom. This was enough to convince the pilot to make an emergency landing in Arkansas and have Mr. Wander arrested as a potential terrorist. Mr. Wander is an American citizen who works at Exxon and was on his way to a convention.

aren't under voluntary control. You may not want a psychologist to know that you are feeling excited, but you can't prevent your pupils from dilating when you feel aroused. Behaviors are also unlikely to be influenced by demand characteristics when people don't know that the demand and the behavior are related. You may want a psychologist to believe that you are concentrating on a task, but you probably don't know that your blink rate slows when you are concentrating and thus you won't fake a slow blink.

All of these tricks of the trade are useful, of course, but the very best way to avoid demand characteristics is to keep the people who are being observed (known as *participants*) from knowing the true purpose of the observation. When participants are kept "blind" to the observer's expectations—that is, when they do not know what the observer expects them to do—then they cannot strive to meet those expectations. If you did not know that a psychologist was studying the effects of baroque music on mood, then you would not feel compelled to smile when the psychologist played Bach's *Air on G String*. This is why psychologists often do not reveal the true purpose of a study to the participants until the study is over.

Of course, people are clever and curious, and when psychologists don't tell them the purpose of their observations, participants generally try to figure it out for themselves ("I wonder why the psychologist is playing the violin and watching me"). That's why psychologists sometimes use *cover stories,* or misleading explanations that are meant to keep participants from discerning the true purpose of an observation. For example, if a psychologist wanted to know how baroque music influenced your mood, he or she might tell you that the purpose of the study was to determine how quickly people can do logic puzzles while music plays in the background. (We will discuss the ethical implications of deceiving people later in this chapter.) In addition, the psychologist might use *filler items,* or pointless measures that are meant to mask the true purpose of the observation. So, for example, he or she might ask you a few questions that are relevant to the study ("How happy are you right now?") and a few that are not ("Do you like cats more or less than dogs?"), which would make it difficult for you to guess the purpose of the study from the nature of the questions you were asked. These are just a few of the techniques that psychologists use to avoid demand characteristics.

### The Blind Observer

Observers are human beings, and like all human beings, they tend to see what they expect to see. This fact was demonstrated in a classic study in which a group of psychology students were asked to measure the speed with which a rat learned to run through a maze (Rosenthal & Fode, 1963). Some students were told that their rat had been specially bred to be "maze dull" (i.e., slow to learn a maze), and others were told that their rat had been specially bred to be "maze bright" (i.e., quick to learn a maze). Although all the rats were actually the same breed, the students who *thought* they were measuring the speed of a dull rat reported that their rats took longer to learn the maze than did the students who *thought* they were measuring the speed of a bright rat. In other words, the rats seemed to do just what the students who observed them expected them to do.

Why did this happen? First, *expectations can influence observations.* It is easy to make errors when measuring the speed of a rat, and expectations often determine the kinds of errors people make. Does putting one paw over the finish line count as "learning the maze"? If the rat falls asleep, should the stopwatch be left running or should the rat be awakened and given a second chance? If a rat runs a maze in 18.5 seconds, should that number be rounded up or rounded down before it is recorded in the log book? The answers to these questions may depend on whether one thinks the rat is bright or dull. The students who timed the rats probably tried to be honest, vigilant, fair, and objective, but their expectations influenced their observations in subtle ways that they could neither detect nor control. Second, *expectations can influence reality.* Students who expected their rats to learn quickly may have unknowingly done things to help that learning along—for example, by muttering, "Oh no!" when the bright rat turned the wrong way in the maze or by petting the bright rat more affectionately than the dull rat and so on. (We shall discuss these phenomena more extensively in Chapter 16.)

# The New York Times

Copyright, 1929, by The New York Times Company.

## STOCK PRICES SLUMP $14,000,000,000 IN NATION-WIDE STAMPEDE TO UNLOAD; BANKERS TO SUPPORT MARKET TODAY

### PREMIER ISSUES HARD HIT

Unexpected Torrent of Liquidation Again Rocks Markets.

DAY'S SALES 9,212,800

Nearly 3,000,000 Shares Are Traded In Final Hour—The Tickers Lag 167 Minutes.

### NEW RALLY SOON BROKEN

Selling by Europeans and "Mob Psychology" Big Factors in Second Big Break.

The second hurricane of liquidation within four days hit the stock market yesterday. It came suddenly, and violently, after holders of stocks had been lulled into a sense of security by the rallies of Friday and Saturday. It was a country-wide collapse of open-market security values in which the declines established and the actual losses taken in dollars and cents were probably the most disastrous and far-reaching in the history of the Stock Exchange.

That the storm has now blown itself out, that there will be organized support to put an end to a reaction which has ripped billions of dollars from market values, appeared certain last night from statements by leading bankers.

Although total estimates of the losses on securities are difficult to make, because of the large number of them not listed on any exchange, it was calculated last night that the total shrinkage in American securities on all exchanges yesterday had aggregated some $14,000,000,000, with a decline of about $10,000,000,000 in New York Stock Exchange securities. The figure is necessarily a rough one, but nevertheless gives an idea of the dollars and cents recessions in one of the most extraordinary declines in the history of American markets.

People's expectations can cause the phenomena they expect. In 1929, investors who expected the stock market to collapse sold their stocks and thereby caused the very crisis they feared. In this photo, panicked citizens stand outside the New York Stock Exchange the day after the crash, which the *New York Times* attributed to "mob psychology."

Observers' expectations, then, can have a powerful influence on both their observations and on the behavior of those whom they observe. Psychologists use many techniques to avoid these influences, and one of the most common is the **double-blind** observation, which is *an observation whose true purpose is hidden from both the observer and the participant.* For example, if the students had not been told which rats were bright and which were dull, then they would not have *had* any expectations about their rats. It is common practice in psychology to keep the observers as blind as the participants. For example, measurements are often made by research assistants who do not know what a particular participant is expected to say or do and who only learn about the nature of the study when it is concluded. Indeed, many modern studies are carried out by the world's blindest experimenter: a computer, which presents information to participants and measures their responses without any expectations whatsoever.

**In summary,** measurement is a scientific means of observation that involves defining an abstract property in terms of some concrete condition, called an operational definition, and then constructing a device, or a measure, that can detect the conditions that the operational definition specifies. A good operational definition shares meaning with the property (construct validity) and is related to other operational definitions (predictive validity). A good measure detects the conditions specified by the operational definition when those conditions occur (power) and not when they don't (reliability).

Psychologists sometimes use the case method to study single, exceptional individuals, but more often they use samples of many people drawn from a population. The law of large numbers suggests that these samples should be relatively large if they are to reflect accurately the properties of the population from which they were drawn. From samples, psychologists draw conclusions about people on average rather than about individuals. Measurements of a sample can be arranged in a frequency distribution, and descriptive statistics can be used to describe some features of that distribution, such as its central tendency (described by the mean, median, and mode) and its variability (described by the range and the standard deviation).

**DOUBLE-BLIND** An observation whose true purpose is hidden from the researcher as well as from the participant.

When people know they are being observed, they may behave as they think they should. Demand characteristics are features of a setting that suggest to people that they should behave in a particular way. Psychologists try to reduce or eliminate demand characteristics by observing participants in their natural habitats or by hiding their expectations from the participant. In double-blind observations, they also hide their expectations from the observer, which ensures that observers are not merely seeing what they expect to see and are not inadvertently causing participants to behave as they expect them to behave. ■ ■

# The Science of Explanation: Saying Why

The techniques discussed so far allow us to construct valid, reliable, powerful, and unbiased measures of properties such as happiness, to use those instruments to measure the happiness of a sample without demand characteristics, and to draw conclusions about the happiness of a population. Although scientific research always begins with the careful measurement of properties, its ultimate goal is typically the discovery of *causal relationships between properties*. We may want to know if happy people are more altruistic than unhappy people, but what we really want to know is whether their happiness is the *cause* of their altruism. We may want to know if children who are spanked are more likely to become depressed than children who aren't, but what we really want to know is whether being spanked *caused* their depression. These are the kinds of questions that even the most careful measurements cannot answer. Measurements can tell us how *much* happiness, altruism, spanking, and depression occur in a particular sample, but they cannot tell us (a) whether these properties are related and (b) whether their relationship is causal. As you will see, scientists have developed some clever ways of using measurement to answer these questions.

## Correlation

If you insult someone, they probably won't give you the time of day. If you have any doubt about this, you can demonstrate it by standing on a street corner, insulting a few people as they walk by ("Hello, you stupid ugly freak . . ."), not insulting others ("Hello . . ."), and then asking everyone for the time of day (". . . could you please tell me what time it is?"). If you did this, the results of your investigation would probably look a lot like those shown in **TABLE 2.1**. Specifically, every person who was not insulted would give you the time of day, and every person who was insulted would refuse. Results such as these would probably convince you that being insulted *causes* people to refuse requests from the people who insulted them. You would conclude that two events—being insulted by someone and refusing to do that person a favor—have a causal relationship. But on what basis did you draw that conclusion? How did you manage to use measurement to tell you not only about *how much* insulting and refusing had occurred, but also about the *relationship* between insulting and refusing?

### Patterns of Variation

Measurements can only tell us about properties of objects and events, but we can learn about the relationships between objects and events by comparing the *patterns of variation in a series of measurements*. Consider what actually happened when you performed your hypothetical study of insults and requests.

| Table 2.1 | Hypothetical Data of the Relationship between Insults and Favors | |
| --- | --- | --- |
| **Participant** | **Treatment** | **Response** |
| 1 | Insulted | Refused |
| 2 | Insulted | Refused |
| 3 | Not insulted | Agreed |
| 4 | Not insulted | Agreed |
| 5 | Insulted | Refused |
| 6 | Insulted | Refused |
| 7 | Not insulted | Agreed |
| 8 | Not insulted | Agreed |
| 9 | Insulted | Refused |
| 10 | Insulted | Refused |
| 11 | Not insulted | Agreed |
| 12 | Not insulted | Agreed |
| 13 | Insulted | Refused |
| 14 | Insulted | Refused |
| 15 | Not insulted | Agreed |
| 16 | Not insulted | Agreed |
| 17 | Insulted | Refused |
| 18 | Insulted | Refused |
| 19 | Not insulted | Agreed |
| 20 | Not insulted | Agreed |

- First, you carefully measured a pair of **variables,** which are *properties whose values can vary across individuals or over time.* (When you took your first algebra course you were probably horrified to learn that everything you'd been taught in grade school about the distinction between letters and numbers was a lie, that mathematical equations could contain *X*s and *Y*s as well as 7s and 4s, and that the letters are called *variables* because they can have different values under different circumstances. Same idea here.) You measured one variable whose value could vary from *not insulted* to *insulted,* and you measured a second variable whose value could vary from *refused* to *agreed.*

- Second, you did this again. And then again. And then again. That is, you made a *series* of measurements rather than making just one.

- Third and finally, you tried to discern a pattern in your series of measurements. If you look at the second column of Table 2.1, you will see that it contains values that vary as your eyes move down the column. That column has a particular *pattern of variation.* If you compare the third column with the second, you will notice that the patterns of variation in the two columns are synchronized. This synchrony is known as a *pattern of covariation* or a **correlation** (as in "co-relation"). Two variables are said to "covary" or to "be correlated" when *variations in the value of one variable are synchronized with variations in the value of the other.* As the table shows, whenever the value in the second column varies from *not insulted* to *insulted,* the value in the third column varies from *agreed* to *refused.*

By looking for synchronized patterns of variation, we can use measurement to discover the relationships between variables. Indeed, this is the only way anyone has *ever* discovered the relationship between variables, which is why most of the facts you know about the world can be thought of as correlations. For example, you know that adults are generally taller than children, but this is just a shorthand way of saying that as the value of *age* varies from *young* to *old,* the value of *height* varies from *short* to *tall.* You know that people who eat a pound of spinach every day generally live longer than people who eat a pound of bacon every day, but this is just a shorthand way of saying that as the value of *daily food intake* varies from *spinach* to *bacon,* the value of *longevity* varies from *high* to *low.* As these statements suggest, correlations are the fundamental building blocks of knowledge.

But correlations do more than just describe the past. They also allow us to predict the future. How long will a person live if she eats a pound of bacon every day? Probably not as long as she would have lived if she'd instead eaten a pound of spinach every day. How tall will Walter be on his next birthday? Probably taller if he is turning 21 than if he is turning 2. Both of these are questions about events that have not yet happened, and their answers are predictions based on correlations. When two variables

**VARIABLE** A property whose value can vary or change.

**CORRELATION** The "co-relationship" or pattern of covariation between two variables, each of which has been measured several times.

When children line up by age, they also tend to line up by height. The pattern of variation in age (from youngest to oldest) is synchronized with the pattern of variation in height (from shortest to tallest).

PETER TURNLEY/CORBIS

are correlated, knowledge of the value of one variable (daily food intake or age) allows us to make predictions about the value of the other variable (longevity or height). Indeed, every time we suspect something ("I think it's going to rain soon"), worry about something ("The psych exam will probably be tough"), or feel excited about something ("Greg's party should be wild"), we are using the value of one variable to predict the value of another variable with which it is correlated.

Every correlation can be described in two equally reasonable ways. A positive correlation describes a relationship between two variables in "more-more" or "less-less" terms. When we say that *more spinach* is associated with *more longevity* or that *less spinach* is associated with *less longevity,* we are describing a positive correlation. A negative correlation describes a relationship between two variables in "more-less" or "less-more" terms. When we say that *more bacon* is associated with *less longevity* or that *less bacon* is associated with *more longevity,* we are describing a negative correlation. How we choose to describe any particular correlation is usually just a matter of simplicity and convenience.

### Measuring Correlation

The hypothetical variables shown in Table 2.1 are perfectly correlated; that is, each and every time *not insulted* changes to *insulted, agreed* also changes to *refused,* and there are no exceptions to this rule. This perfect correlation allows you to make an extremely confident prediction about how pedestrians will respond to a request after being insulted. But perfect correlations are so rare in everyday life that we had to make up a hypothetical study just to show you one. There actually is a correlation between age and height that allows us to predict that a child will be shorter than an adult, and this prediction will be right more often than it is wrong. But it *will* be wrong in some instances because there are *some* tall kids and *some* short adults. So how much confidence should we have in predictions based on correlations?

Statisticians have developed a way to estimate just how accurate a particular prediction is likely to be by measuring the *strength* of the correlation on which it is based. The **correlation coefficient** is *a measure of the direction and strength of a correlation,* and it is symbolized by the letter *r* (as in "relationship"). Like most measures, the correlation coefficient has a limited range. What does that mean? Well, if you were to measure the number of hours of sunshine per day in your hometown, that measure would have a range of 24 because it could only have a value from 0 to 24. Numbers such as –7 and 36.8 would be meaningless. Similarly, the value of *r* can range from –1 to 1, and numbers outside that range are meaningless. What, then, do the numbers *inside* that range mean?

- When $r = 1$, the relationship between the variables is called a *perfect positive correlation,* which means that every time the value of one variable increases by a certain amount, the value of the second variable also increases by a certain amount, and this happens without exception. If every increase in age of $X$ units were associated with an increase in height of $Y$ units, then age and height would be perfectly positively correlated.
- When $r = -1$, the relationship between the variables is called a *perfect negative correlation,* which means that as the value of one variable increases by a certain amount, the value of the second variable *decreases* by a certain amount, and this happens without exception. If every increase in age of $X$ units were associated with a decrease in height of $Y$ units, then age and height would be perfectly negatively correlated.
- When $r = 0$, there is no systematic relationship between the variables, which are said to be *uncorrelated.* This means that the pattern of variation of one variable is not synchronized in any way with the pattern of variation of the other. As the value of one variable increases by a certain amount, the value of the second variable may sometimes increase, sometimes decrease, and sometimes do neither. If increases in age of $X$ units were sometimes associated with changes in height of $Y$ units and sometimes associated with a change in height of $Z$ units, then age and height would be uncorrelated.

**CORRELATION COEFFICIENT** A statistical measure of the direction and strength of a correlation, which is signified by the letter *r*.

The correlations shown in **FIGURE 2.6 a** and **b** are perfect correlations—that is, they show patterns of variation that are perfectly synchronized and without exceptions.

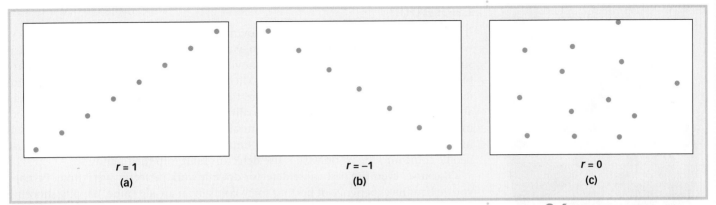

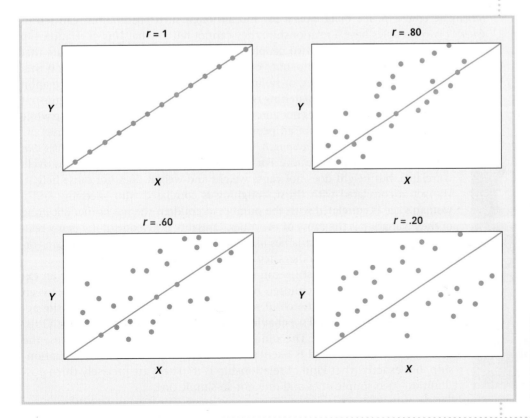

**Figure 2.6** **Three Kinds of Correlations** This figure illustrates pairs of variables that have (a) a perfect positive correlation ($r = +1$), (b) a perfect negative correlation ($r = -1$), and (c) no correlation ($r = 0$).

Such correlations are extremely rare in real life. It may be true that the more bacon you eat, the fewer years you will live, but it's not as though longevity decreases by exactly 1.23 days for every 100 pounds of bacon you put away annually. Bacon eating and longevity are *negatively* correlated (i.e., as one increases, the other decreases), but they are also *imperfectly* correlated, and thus $r$ will lie somewhere between 0 and –1. But where? That depends on how many exceptions there are to the "$X$ more pounds of bacon = $Y$ fewer years of life" rule. If there are just a few exceptions, then $r$ will be much closer to –1 than to 0. But as the number of exceptions increases, then the value of $r$ will begin to move toward 0.

**FIGURE 2.7** shows four cases in which two variables are positively correlated but have different numbers of exceptions, and as you can see, the number of exceptions changes the value of $r$ quite dramatically. Two variables can have a perfect correlation ($r = 1$), a strong correlation (for example, $r = .80$), a moderate correlation (for example, $r = .60$), or a weak correlation (for example, $r = .20$). The correlation coefficient, then, is a measure of both the *direction* and *strength* of the relationship between two variables. The sign of $r$ (plus or minus) tells us the direction of the relationship, and the absolute value of $r$ (between 0 and 1) tells us about the number of exceptions and hence about how confident we can be when using the correlation to make predictions.

**Figure 2.7** **Positive Correlations of Different Strengths** These graphs represent different degrees of positive correlation between two variables. Scores that are on the line adhere strictly to the rule $X = Y$. The more exceptions there are to this rule, the weaker the correlation is.

Although people have smoked tobacco for centuries, only recently has the causal relationship between cigarette smoking and heart and lung disease been detected. By the way, how many physicians said the opposite? And "less irritating" than what?

**NATURAL CORRELATION** A correlation observed between naturally occurring variables.

A woman's age is correlated with the number of children she has borne, but age does not cause women to become pregnant and pregnancy does not cause women to age.

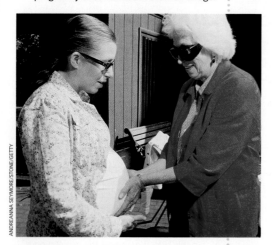

# Causation

If you watched a cartoon in which a moving block collided with a stationary block, which then went careening off the screen, your brain would instantly make a very reasonable assumption, namely, that the moving block was the *cause* of the stationary block's motion (Heider & Simmel, 1944; Michotte, 1963). In fact, studies show that infants make such assumptions long before they have had a chance to learn anything about cartoons, blocks, collisions, or causality (Oakes & Cohen, 1990). For human beings, detecting causes and effects is as natural as sucking, sleeping, pooping, and howling, which is what led the philosopher Immanuel Kant (1781/1965) to suggest that people come into the world with cause detectors built into their brains.

Of course, even the best cause detector doesn't work perfectly every time. Perhaps you've had the experience of putting some coins in an arcade game, happily shooting helicopters or dodging vampires for a minute or so, and then suddenly realizing that you never actually pressed start and that the shooting and dodging you saw on the screen had nothing to do with your nimble handling of the joystick. Mindbugs like this happen all the time (Wegner & Wheatley, 1999). In fact, our brains are so eager to connect causes with effects that they often make connections that aren't really there, which is why astrology continues to be such a popular diversion (Glick, Gottesman, & Jolton, 1989). Conversely, our brains sometimes fail to detect causal relationships that actually do exist. Only in the past century or so have surgeons made it a practice to wash their hands before operating because before that, no one seemed to notice that dirty fingernails were causally related to postsurgical infections. The causal relationships between smoking and lung cancer and between cholesterol and heart disease went undetected for centuries despite the fact that people were smoking tobacco, eating lard, and keeling over with some regularity. The point here is that if we want to discover the causal relationships between variables, then we need more than mere empiricism. What we need is a method for discovering causal relationships. As you're about to see, we've got one.

## The Third-Variable Problem

We observe correlations all the time—between automobiles and pollution, between bacon and heart attacks, between sex and pregnancy. **Natural correlations** are *the correlations we observe in the world around us,* and although such observations can tell us *whether* two variables have a relationship, they cannot tell us what *kind* of relationship these variables have. If you saw two people chatting in a pub, you could be sure that they had some kind of relationship, but you would be hard-pressed to say what it was. They could be spouses, classmates, or siblings, and you would need more information (e.g., matching wedding bands, matching textbooks, or matching parents) to figure out which. Having a relationship does not automatically make them spouses because while all spouses have relationships, not all people who have relationships are spouses. By the same logic, *all variables that are causally related are correlated, but not all variables that are correlated are causally related.* For example, height and weight are positively correlated, but height does not cause weight and weight does not cause height. Hunger is correlated with thirst, coughing is correlated with sneezing, and a woman's age is correlated with the number of children she has borne. But none of these variables is the cause of the other. Causality is just one of the many relationships that correlated variables may have. The fact that two variables are correlated does not tell us whether they are causally related as well.

What kinds of relationships can correlated variables have? Consider an example. Many studies of children have found a positive correlation between the amount of violence the child sees on television (variable *X*) and the aggressiveness of the child's behavior (variable *Y*) (Huesmann, Moise-Titus, Podolski, & Eron, 2003). The more televised violence a child watches, the more aggressive that child is likely to be. These two variables have a relationship, but exactly what kind of relationship is it? There are precisely three possibilities—two simple ones and one not-so-simple one.

- $X \rightarrow Y$. One simple possibility is that watching televised violence ($X$) causes aggressiveness ($Y$). For example, watching televised violence may teach children that aggression is a reasonable way to vent anger and solve problems.

- $Y \rightarrow X$. Another simple possibility is that aggressiveness ($Y$) causes children to watch televised violence ($X$). For example, children who are naturally aggressive may enjoy televised violence more and may seek opportunities to watch it.

- $Z \rightarrow X$ and $Y$. A final and not-so-simple possibility is that a *third variable* ($Z$) causes children both to be aggressive ($Y$) and to watch televised violence ($X$), neither of which is causally related to the other. For example, lack of adult supervision ($Z$) may allow children to get away with bullying others and to get away with watching television shows that adults would normally not allow. If so, then watching televised violence ($X$) and behaving aggressively ($Y$) may not be causally related to each other at all and may instead be the independent effects of a lack of adult supervision ($Z$), just as sneezing and coughing may be independent effects of viral infection, height and weight may be independent effects of nutrition, and so on. In other words, the relation between aggressiveness and watching televised violence may be a case of **third-variable correlation**, which means that *two variables are correlated only because each is causally related to a third variable.*

**FIGURE 2.8** shows the three possible causes of any correlation. How can we determine by simple observation which of these three possibilities best describes the relationship between televised violence and aggressiveness? We can't. When we observe a natural correlation, *the possibility of third-variable correlation can never be dismissed.* Don't take this claim on faith. Let's try to dismiss the possibility of third-variable correlation and you'll see why such efforts are always doomed to fail.

The most straightforward way to dismiss the possibility that a third variable such as lack of adult supervision ($Z$) caused children to watch televised violence ($X$) and behave aggressively ($Y$) would be to eliminate differences in adult supervision among a group of children and see if the correlation between televised violence and aggressiveness remained. For example, we could observe children in **matched samples**, which is *a technique whereby the participants in two samples are identical in terms of a third variable.* For instance, we could observe only children who are supervised by an adult exactly 87% of the time, thus ensuring that every child who watched a lot of televised violence had exactly the same amount of adult supervision as every child who did not watch a lot of televised violence. Alternatively, we could observe children in **matched pairs**, which is *a technique whereby each participant in one sample is identical to one other participant in another sample in terms of a third variable.* For instance, we could observe children who experience different amounts of adult supervision, but we could make sure that for every child we observe who watches a lot of televised violence and is supervised 24% of the time, we also observe a child who doesn't watch a lot of televised violence and is supervised 24% of the time, thus ensuring that the children who do and do not watch a lot of televised violence have the same amount of adult supervision *on average*. Regardless of

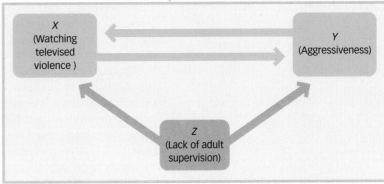

**Figure 2.8** **Causes of Correlation** If $X$ (watching televised violence) and $Y$ (aggressiveness) are correlated, then there are exactly three possible explanations: $X$ causes $Y$, $Y$ causes $X$, or $Z$ (some other factor, such as lack of adult supervision) causes both $Y$ and $X$, neither of which causes the other.

**THIRD-VARIABLE CORRELATION** The fact that two variables may be correlated only because they are both caused by a third variable.

**MATCHED SAMPLES** An observational technique that involves matching the average of the participants in the experimental and control groups in order to eliminate the possibility that a third variable (and not the independent variable) caused changes in the dependent variable.

**MATCHED PAIRS** An observational technique that involves matching each participant in the experimental group with a specific participant in the control group in order to eliminate the possibility that a third variable (and not the independent variable) caused changes in the dependent variable.

How can third-variable correlation explain the fact that the more tattoos a person has, the more likely he or she is to be involved in a motorcycle accident?

which technique we used, we would know that the children who do and don't watch televised violence have equal amounts of adult supervision on average, and thus if those who watch televised violence are more aggressive on average than those who don't, lack of adult supervision cannot be the cause.

Although both of these techniques can be useful, neither allows us to dismiss the possibility of third-variable correlation. Why? Because even if we use matched samples or matched pairs to dismiss a *particular* third variable (such as lack of adult supervision), we would not be able to dismiss *all* third variables. For example, as soon as we finished making these observations, it might suddenly occur to us that emotionally unstable children may gravitate toward violent television programs and may behave aggressively. In other words, "emotional instability" would be a new third variable that we would have to design new observations to dismiss. Clearly, we could dream up new third variables all day long without ever breaking a sweat, and every time we dreamed one up, we would have to rush out and make a whole new set of observations using matched samples or matched pairs to determine whether *this* third variable was the cause of watching televised violence and of behaving aggressively.

The problem, then, is that there are an infinite number of third variables out there and thus an infinite number of reasons why *X* and *Y* might be correlated. Because most of us don't have the time to perform an infinite number of studies with matched samples or matched pairs, we can never be sure that the natural correlation between *X* and *Y* is evidence of a causal relationship between them. This problem is so troubling and pervasive that it has its own name (and one that's easy to remember). The **third-variable problem** refers to the fact that *a causal relationship between two variables cannot be inferred from the natural correlation between them because of the ever-present possibility of third-variable correlation.* In other words, if we care about causality, then natural correlations can never tell us what we really want to know.

### Experimentation

The third-variable problem prevents us from using natural correlations to learn about causal relationships, and so we have to find another method that will. Let's start by considering once again the source of our trouble. We cannot conclude that watching televised violence causes children to behave aggressively because there is some chance that both behaviors are caused by a third variable, such as lack of adult supervision or emotional instability, and there are so many third variables in the world that we could never do enough studies to dismiss them all. Another way of saying this is that children who do watch and don't watch televised violence differ in countless ways, and any one of these countless differences could be the real cause of their different levels of aggressiveness. This suggests that if we could somehow eliminate *all* of these countless differences at once—somehow find a sample of children who are perfect clones, with identical amounts of adult supervision, identical amounts of emotional stability, identical histories, identical physiologies, identical neighborhoods, siblings, toys, schools, teeth, dreams, and so on—then the natural correlation between watching televised violence and aggressiveness *would* be evidence of a causal relationship. If we could somehow accomplish this amazing feat, we would have a sample of children, some of whom watch televised violence and some of whom don't, but all of whom are identical in terms of *every possible* third variable. If we found that the children in this sample who watched televised violence were more aggressive than those who did not, then watching televised violence would *have to be* the cause of their different levels of aggressiveness because, after all, watching televised violence would be the *only* thing that distinguished the most aggressive children from the least aggressive children.

Finding a sample of clones is, of course, not very realistic. But as it turns out, scientists have another way to eliminate all the countless differences between the people in a sample. An **experiment** is *a technique for establishing the causal relationship between variables.* The best way to understand how experiments accomplish this amazing feat is by examining their two key features: manipulation and randomization.

**THIRD-VARIABLE PROBLEM** The fact that the causal relationship between two variables cannot be inferred from the correlation between them because of the ever-present possibility of third-variable correlation.

**EXPERIMENT** A technique for establishing the causal relationship between variables.

## Manipulation

The most important thing to know about experiments is that you already know the most important thing about experiments because you've been doing them all your life. Imagine, for instance, what you would do if you were watching television one day when all of a sudden the picture went fuzzy for 10 minutes, then cleared up, then went fuzzy for a few minutes again, and so on. You might suspect that another electronic device, such as your roommate's new cordless telephone, was interfering with the television reception. Your first step would be to observe and measure carefully, noting the clarity of the television picture when your roommate was and was not using his telephone. But even if you observed a natural correlation between television clarity and telephone use, the third-variable problem would prevent you from drawing a causal conclusion. After all, if your roommate was afraid of storms and tended to rush to the phone and call his mommy whenever a cloud passed over the house, then clouds ($Z$) could be the cause of both the telephone calls ($X$) and the television interference ($Y$).

Because you could not draw a causal conclusion from this natural correlation, you would probably try to create an *artificial* correlation by standing in front of the television with the phone in hand, switching it on and off and observing the clarity of the television picture. If you observed that the artificial pattern of variation you created in the telephone (on for 1 second, off for 3 seconds, on for 8 seconds, off for 2 seconds) was nicely synchronized with the pattern of variation in the television (fuzzy for 1 second, fine for 3 seconds, fuzzy for 8 seconds, fine for 2 seconds), then you would instantly conclude that the telephone was the cause of the interference. Standing in front of the TV and turning the phone on and off may seem to show little common sense, but in doing this, you have discovered and used science's most powerful technique for establishing causal relationships: the experiment. Your actions qualify as an experiment because you used **manipulation**, which is *the creation of an artificial pattern of variation in a variable in order to determine its causal powers.*

Manipulation is one of the critical ingredients of an experiment. Up until now, we have approached science like polite dinner guests, taking what we were offered and making the best of it. Nature offered us children who differed in how much televised violence they watched and who differed in how aggressively they behaved, and we dutifully measured the natural patterns of variation in these two variables and computed their correlations. The problem with this approach is that when all was said and done, we still didn't know what we really wanted to know, namely, whether these variables had a causal relationship. No matter how many matched samples or matched pairs we observed, there was always another third variable that we hadn't yet dismissed. Experiments solve this problem. Rather than *measuring* how much televised violence a child watches, *measuring* the child's aggressiveness, and then computing the correlation between these two naturally occurring variables, experiments require that we *manipulate* how much televised violence a child watches in the same way that you manipulated the telephone. In essence, we need to systematically switch the watching of televised violence on and off in a sample of children and then see if aggressiveness goes on and off too.

We might do this by asking some children to participate in an experiment and exposing half of them to 2 hours of televised violence every day for a month while making sure that the other half saw no televised violence at all (see **FIGURE 2.9** on the next page). At the end of a month, we could measure the aggressiveness of the children and compare the measurements across the two groups. When we compared these measurements, we would be computing the correlation between a variable we measured (aggressiveness) and a variable we manipulated (televised violence). Instead of looking for synchrony in the patterns of variation that nature offered us, we would have caused a pattern of variation in one variable, observed a pattern of variation in another, and looked for synchrony between. In so doing, we would have solved the third-variable problem. After all, if we *manipulated* rather than *measured* a child's exposure to televised violence, then we would never have to ask whether a third variable (such as lack of adult supervision) might have caused it. Why? Because we already *know* what caused the child to watch or not watch televised violence. *We* did!

**MANIPULATION** A characteristic of experimentation in which the researcher artificially creates a pattern of variation in an independent variable in order to determine its causal powers. Manipulation usually results in the creation of an *experimental group* and a *control group*.

**Figure 2.9** **Manipulation** The independent variable is televised violence and the dependent variable is aggressiveness. Manipulation of the independent variable results in an experimental group and a control group. When we compare the behavior of participants in these two groups, we are actually computing the correlation between the independent variable and the dependent variable.

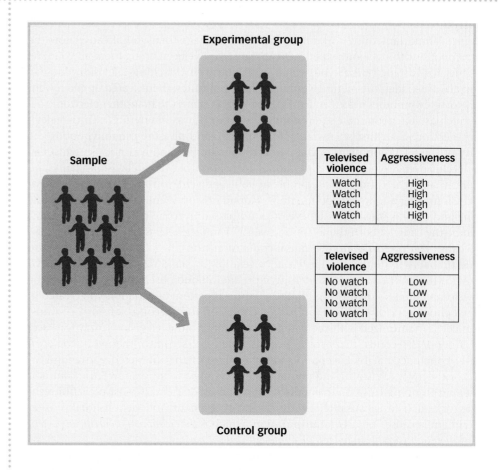

| Televised violence | Aggressiveness |
|---|---|
| Watch | High |
| Watch | High |
| Watch | High |
| Watch | High |

| Televised violence | Aggressiveness |
|---|---|
| No watch | Low |
| No watch | Low |
| No watch | Low |
| No watch | Low |

Doing an experiment, then, involves three critical steps (and several technical terms):

- First, we perform a manipulation. We call *the variable that is manipulated* the **independent variable** because it is under our control, and thus it is "independent" of what the participant says or does. When we manipulate an independent variable (such as watching televised violence), we create at least two groups of participants: an **experimental group**, which is *the group of people who are treated in a particular way,* such as being exposed to televised violence, and a **control group**, which is *the group of people who are not treated in this particular way.*
- Second, having created a pattern of variation in one variable (televised violence), we now measure the pattern of variation in another variable (aggressiveness). We call *the variable that is measured* the **dependent variable** because its value "depends" on what the participant says or does.
- Third and finally, we check to see whether the patterns of variation in the dependent and independent variables are synchronized.

When we have manipulated an independent variable, measured a dependent variable, and looked to see whether their patterns of variation are synchronized, we've done one of the two things that experimentation requires. Now let's talk about the second.

### Randomization

Manipulation is one of the two critical features of experimentation that allow us to overcome the third-variable problem and establish a causal relationship between an independent and a dependent variable. The second feature is a bit less intuitive but equally important. Imagine that we did the televised violence experiment by finding a sample of children and asking each child whether he or she would like to be in the experimental group or the control group. Imagine that, conveniently enough, half of the children volunteered to watch 2 hours of televised violence every day for a

**INDEPENDENT VARIABLE** The variable that is manipulated in an experiment.

**EXPERIMENTAL GROUP** One of the two groups of participants created by the manipulation of an independent variable in an experiment; the experimental group is exposed to the stimulus being studied and the *control group* is not.

**CONTROL GROUP** One of the two groups of participants created by the manipulation of an independent variable in an experiment that is not exposed to the stimulus being studied.

**DEPENDENT VARIABLE** The variable that is measured in a study.

month, and the other half volunteered not to. Imagine that we did as each of the children requested, measured their aggressiveness a month later, and found that the children who watched televised violence were more aggressive than those who did not. Would this experiment allow us to conclude that watching televised violence causes aggressiveness? Definitely not—but *why* not? After all, we switched televised violence on and off and watched to see whether aggressiveness went on and off too. So where did we go wrong?

We went wrong when we let the children decide for themselves how much television they would watch. Many things probably distinguish children who volunteer to watch televised violence from those who don't. For instance, those who volunteer may be older, or stronger, or smarter. Or younger, or weaker, or dumber. Or less often supervised or more emotionally unstable. The list of possible differences goes on and on. The whole point of doing an experiment was to divide children into two groups that differed *in just one way,* namely, in terms of how much televised violence they watched. The moment we allowed the children to select their own groups, the two groups differed in countless ways, and any of those countless differences could have been responsible for differences in their aggressiveness. **Self-selection** is *a problem that occurs when a participant's inclusion in the experimental or control group is determined by the participant.* Just as we cannot allow nature to decide which of the children in our study watches televised violence, we cannot allow the children to decide either. So who decides?

The answer to this question is a bit spooky: *No one decides*. If we want to be sure that there is one and only one difference between the children who do and do not watch televised violence, then their inclusion in these groups must be *randomly determined.* Most of us use the word *random* to mean "without a cause" (as in, "Bill was mad at me today for no reason at all. It was like totally random"). This is precisely how the word should be used, though perhaps without the "like totally" part. If you flipped a coin and a friend asked what had *caused* it to land heads up, you would correctly say that *nothing* had. This is what it means for the outcome of a coin flip to be random. Because the outcome of a coin flip is random, we can put coin flips to work for us to solve the problem that self-selection creates. If we want to be sure that a child's inclusion in the experimental group or the control group was not caused by nature, was not caused by the child, and was not caused by *any* of the infinite number of third variables we could name if we only had the time, then all we have to do is let it be caused by the outcome of a coin flip—which itself has no cause! For example, we could walk up to each child

in our experiment, flip a coin, and, if the coin lands heads up, assign the child to watch 2 hours of televised violence every day for a month. If the coin lands heads down, then we could assign the child to watch no television. **Randomization** is *a procedure that uses random events to ensure that a participant's assignment to the experimental or control group is not determined by any third variable.*

What would happen if we assigned children to groups with a coin flip? As **FIGURE 2.10** on the next page shows, the first thing we would expect is that about half the children would be assigned to watch televised violence and about half would not. That would be convenient. But second—and *much* more importantly—we could expect the experimental group and the control group to have roughly equal numbers of supervised kids and unsupervised kids, roughly equal numbers of

JOIN THE **WAC** NOW!

THOUSANDS OF ARMY JOBS NEED FILLING!    Women's Army Corps United States Army

**SELF-SELECTION** The case in which a participant's inclusion in the experimental or control group is determined by the participant.

**RANDOMIZATION** A procedure to ensure that a participant's inclusion in the experimental or control group is not determined by a third variable.

Self-selection is a problem in experimentation. For example, we could never draw conclusions about the effects of military service by comparing those who joined to those who didn't because those who do and don't join differ in so many ways.

**Figure 2.10 Randomization**
Children with adult supervision are shown in orange and without adult supervision are shown in blue. The independent variable is televised violence and the dependent variable is aggressiveness. Randomization ensures that participants in the experimental and control groups are equal on average in terms of all possible third variables. In essence, it ensures that there is no correlation between a third variable and the dependent variable.

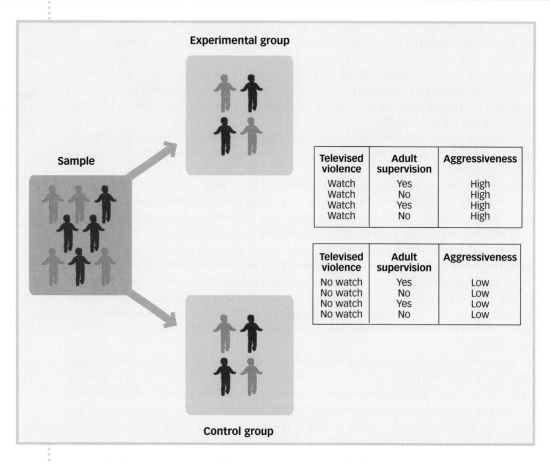

| Televised violence | Adult supervision | Aggressiveness |
|---|---|---|
| Watch | Yes | High |
| Watch | No | High |
| Watch | Yes | High |
| Watch | No | High |

| Televised violence | Adult supervision | Aggressiveness |
|---|---|---|
| No watch | Yes | Low |
| No watch | No | Low |
| No watch | Yes | Low |
| No watch | No | Low |

emotionally stable and unstable kids, roughly equal numbers of big kids and small kids, of active kids, fat kids, tall kids, funny kids, and kids with blue hair named Larry McSweeny. Indeed, we could expect the two groups to have equal numbers of kids who are anything-you-can-ever-name-and-everything-you-can't! Because the kids in the two groups will be the same on average in terms of height, weight, emotional stability, adult supervision, and every other variable in the known universe except the one we manipulated, we can be sure that the variable we manipulated (televised violence) caused changes in the variable we measured (aggressiveness). Watching televised violence was the only difference between the two groups of children when we started the experiment, and thus it *must* be the cause of the differences in aggressiveness we observed a month later (see the Hot Science box).

Randomization ensures that the participants in the experimental and control groups are, on average, identical in every way except one.

## { HOT SCIENCE } Establishing Causality in the Brain

SOMETIMES THE BEST WAY TO LEARN about something is to see what happens when it breaks, and the human brain is no exception. Scientists have studied the effects of brain damage for centuries, and those studies reveal a lot about how the brain normally works so well. As you read in Chapter 1, in the middle of the 19th century, a French surgeon named Paul Broca observed that people who had lost their ability to speak often had damage in a particular spot on the left side of their brains. Broca suggested that this region might control speech production but not other functions such as the ability to understand speech. As it turned out, he was right, which is why this brain region is now known as Broca's area.

Scientists have learned a lot about the brain by studying the behavior of people whose brains are defective or have been damaged by accidents. But the problem with studying brain-damaged patients, of course, is the problem with studying any naturally occurring variable: Brain damage may be related to particular patterns of behavior, but that relationship may or may not be causal. Experimentation is the premiere method for establishing causal relationships between variables, but scientists cannot ethically cause brain damage in human beings, and thus they have not been able to establish causal relationships

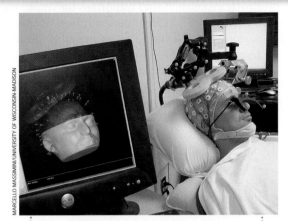

Transcranial magnetic stimulation activates and deactivates regions of the brain with a magnetic pulse, temporarily mimicking brain damage.

between particular kinds of brain damage and particular patterns of behavior.

Until now. Scientists have recently discovered a way to mimic brain damage with a benign technique called *transcranial magnetic stimulation* (or TMS) (Barker, Jalinous, & Freeston, 1985; Hallett, 2000). If you've ever held a magnet under a piece of paper and used it to drag a pin across the paper's surface, you know that magnetic fields can pass through insulating material. The human skull is no exception. TMS delivers a magnetic pulse that passes through the skull and deactivates neurons in the cerebral cortex for a short period. Researchers

can direct TMS pulses to particular brain regions—essentially turning them "off"—and then measure temporary changes in the way a person moves, sees, thinks, remembers, speaks, or feels. By manipulating the state of the brain, scientists can perform experiments that establish causal relationships. For example, scientists have recently discovered that magnetic stimulation of the visual cortex temporarily impairs a person's ability to detect the motion of an object without impairing the person's ability to recognize that object (Beckers & Zeki, 1995). This intriguing discovery suggests that motion perception and object recognition are accomplished by different parts of the brain, but moreover, it establishes that the activity of these brain regions *causes* motion perception and object recognition.

For the first time in human history, the causal relationships between particular brain regions and particular behaviors have been unequivocally established. Rather than relying on observational studies of brain-damaged patients or the snapshots provided by MRI or PET scans, researchers can now manipulate brain activity and measure its effects. Studies suggest that TMS has no harmful side effects (Pascual-Leone et al., 1993), and this new tool promises to revolutionize the study of how our brains create our thoughts, feelings, and actions.

### Significance

Randomization is a powerful tool, but like a lot of tools, it doesn't work every time you use it. When we randomly assigned children to watch or not watch televised violence, we said that we could expect the two groups to have about equal numbers of supervised and unsupervised kids, rich kids and poor kids, thin kids and fat kids, and so on. The key word in that sentence is *about*. If you were to flip a coin 100 times, you would expect it to land heads up *about* 50 times. But every once in a while, 100 coin flips would produce 80 heads, or 90 heads, or even 100 heads, by sheer chance alone. This would not happen often, of course, but it would happen once in a while. Because random assignment is achieved by using a randomizing device such as a coin, every once in a long while the coin will assign all the unsupervised, emotionally disturbed kids to watch televised violence and all the supervised, emotionally undisturbed kids to watch none. When this happens, we say that random assignment has failed—and when random assignment fails, the third-variable problem rises up out of its grave and comes back to haunt us with a vengeance. When random assignment fails, we cannot conclude that there is a causal relationship between the independent and dependent variables.

How can we tell when random assignment has failed? Unfortunately, we can't tell for sure. But we can calculate the *odds* that random assignment has failed in any particular instance. It isn't important for you to know how to do this calculation, but it is important for you to understand how psychologists interpret its results. Psychologists perform this calculation every time they do an experiment, and they do not accept the results of those experiments unless the calculation tells them that there is less than a 5% chance that random assignment failed. In other words, the calculation must allow the psychologist to be 95% certain that random assignment succeeded before the results of the experiment are accepted. When the odds that random assignment failed are less than 5%, an experimental result is said to be *statistically significant*. You've already learned about a few descriptive statistics, such as the mean, the median, and the standard deviation. A second class of statistics—called *inferential statistics*—tells scientists what kinds of conclusions or inferences they can draw from observed differences between the experimental and control groups. For example, $p$ is an inferential statistic that tells psychologists (among other things) the likelihood that random assignment failed in a particular experiment. When psychologists report that $p < .05$, they are saying that according to the inferential statistics they calculated, the odds that random assignment failed are less than 5%, and thus the differences between the experimental and control groups were unlikely to have been caused by a third variable.

## Drawing Conclusions

If we were to apply all the techniques we have discussed so far, we could design an experiment that has **internal validity**, which is *the characteristic of an experiment that allows one to draw accurate inferences about the causal relationship between an independent and dependent variable.* When we say that an experiment is internally valid, we mean that everything *inside* the experiment is working exactly as it must in order for us to draw conclusions about causal relationships. Specifically, an experiment is internally valid when

- An independent variable has been effectively manipulated.
- Participants have been randomly assigned to the groups that this manipulation created.
- A dependent variable has been measured in an unbiased way with a valid, powerful, and reliable measure.
- A correlation has been observed between the pattern of variation created in the independent variable and the pattern of variation measured in the dependent variable.

If we do these things, then we may conclude that manipulated changes in the independent variable caused measured changes in the dependent variable. But we may *not* conclude that one abstract property caused another. For example, even the most well-designed and well-executed study on televised violence and aggressiveness would *not* allow us to conclude that watching televised violence causes aggressiveness. Rather, it would allow us to draw the much more limited conclusion that televised violence *as we defined it* caused aggressiveness *as we defined it* in the people *whom we studied*. The phrases "as we defined it" and "whom we studied" represent important restrictions on the kinds of conclusions that scientists may draw, so let's consider each of them in turn.

### Representative Variables

When we say that we have established a causal relationship between televised violence and aggressiveness *as we have defined them,* we are acknowledging the fact that operational definitions are never perfectly linked to their properties. You will recall that we can never measure an abstract property such as *aggressiveness* but rather can only measure operational definitions of that property, such as *the number of times a child initiates forceful physical contact with other children on the playground during recess.* Because we cannot measure properties, experiments can never be used to make legitimate claims about them. Experiments allow us to draw conclusions about the causal relationship between the particular operational definitions that we manipulated and measured but not about the abstract properties that these particular operational definitions represent.

**INTERNAL VALIDITY** The characteristic of an experiment that allows one to draw accurate inferences about the causal relationship between an independent and dependent variable.

Does piercing make a person more or less attractive? The answer, of course, depends entirely on how you operationally define *piercing*.

Like the interstate speed limit, this is one of those rules to which few people pay serious attention. Consider, for example, the current controversy over the effects of violent video games on children. Some people believe that playing violent video games leads children to behave aggressively, others do not, and both claim that scientific experiments support their arguments (Reichhardt, 2003). So who's right? Nobody is, because experiments do not allow us to draw conclusions about abstractions such as *violent video games* and *aggressive behavior*. Rather, they allow us to draw very particular conclusions about how *playing Pac-Man for 2 minutes* or *playing Blood Sport for 10 hours* influences *the tendency to interrupt when others are speaking* or *the tendency to pummel others with blunt objects*. Not surprisingly, experiments on video games and aggression can produce very different results depending on how the independent and dependent variables are operationally defined. Long exposure to a truly violent game will probably produce more aggressive behavior than will brief exposure to a moderately violent game, and exposure to any kind of violent game will probably influence rudeness more easily than it will influence physical aggression.

What, then, is the right way to operationalize such variables? One obvious answer is that experiments should strive for **external validity**, which is *a property of an experiment in which variables have been operationally defined in a normal, typical, or realistic way*. It seems fairly clear that *interrupting* and *pummeling* are not the kinds of aggressive behaviors with which teachers and parents are normally concerned and that most instances of aggression among children lie somewhere between an insult and a chain saw massacre. If the goal of an experiment is to determine whether the kinds of video games that children typically play cause the kinds of aggression in which children typically engage, then external validity is essential.

Indeed, external validity seems like such a good idea that students are often surprised to learn that most psychology experiments are externally *in*valid—and that most psychologists don't mind. The reason for this is that psychologists are rarely trying to learn about the real world by creating tiny replicas of it in their laboratories. Rather, they are usually trying to learn about the real world by using experiments to test theories and hypotheses (Mook, 1983). A **theory** is *a hypothetical account of how and why a phenomenon occurs*, and a **hypothesis** is *a testable prediction made by a theory*. For example, physicists have a theory stating that heat is the result of the rapid movement of molecules. This theory suggests a hypothesis, namely, that if the molecules that constitute an object are slowed, the object should become cooler. Now imagine that a physicist tested this hypothesis by performing an experiment in which a laser was used to slow the movement of the molecules in a rubber ball, whose temperature was then measured. Would we criticize this experiment by saying, "Sorry, but your experiment teaches us nothing about the real world because in the real world, no one actually uses lasers to slow the movement of the molecules in rubber balls"? Let's hope not. The physicist's theory (molecular motion causes heat) led to a hypothesis about

**EXTERNAL VALIDITY** A characteristic of an experiment in which the independent and dependent variables are operationally defined in a normal, typical, or realistic way.

**THEORY** A hypothetical account of how and why a phenomenon occurs, usually in the form of a statement about the causal relationship between two or more properties. Theories lead to *hypotheses*.

**HYPOTHESIS** A specific and testable prediction that is usually derived from a *theory*.

**RANDOM SAMPLING** A technique for choosing participants that ensures that every member of a population has an equal chance of being included in the sample.

what would happen in the laboratory (slowing the molecules in a rubber ball should cool it), and thus the events that the physicist manipulated and measured in the laboratory served to test the theory.

Similarly, a good theory about the causal relationship between video games and aggression should lead to hypotheses about how people will behave when playing Pac-Man for a few minutes or Blood Sport for many hours. As such, even these unrepresentative forms of video game playing can serve to test the theory. In short, theories allow us to generate hypotheses about what *can* happen, or what *must* happen, or what *will* happen under particular circumstances, and experiments are typically meant to create these circumstances, test the hypotheses, and thereby provide evidence for or against the theories that generated them. Experiments are not meant to be miniature versions of everyday life, and thus external invalidity is not necessarily a problem.

### Representative Samples

You will recall that the law of large numbers advises us to measure many people rather than just one or two so that the average behavior of the people in our sample will closely approximate the average behavior of people in the population. But how do we actually *find* the people in our sample? The best way to do this is to use **random sampling**, which is *a technique for choosing participants that ensures that every member of a population has an equal chance of being included in the sample.* When we randomly sample participants from a population, we earn the right to *generalize* from the behavior of the sample to the behavior of the population, that is, to conclude that what we observed in our experiment would also have been observed if we had measured the entire population. You already have good intuitions about the importance of random sampling. For example, if you stopped at a farm stand to buy a bag of cherries and the farmer offered to let you taste a few that he had specially hand-picked from the bag, you'd be reluctant to generalize from that nonrandom sample to the population of cherries in the bag. But if the farmer invited you to pull a few cherries from the bag without looking, you'd probably be willing to take those cherries as reasonably representative of the cherry population.

Given the importance of random sampling, you may be surprised to learn that psychologists almost never do it. Indeed, virtually every participant in every psychology experiment you will ever read about was a volunteer, and most were college students who were significantly younger, smarter, healthier, wealthier, and whiter than the average earthling. Psychologists sample their participants the "wrong way" (by nonrandom sampling) because it is just about impossible to do it the "right way" (by random sampling). Even if there were an alphabetized list of all the world's human inhabitants from which we could randomly choose our research participants, the likelihood that we could actually perform experiments on those whom we sampled would be depressingly slim. After all, how would we find the 72-year-old Bedouin woman whose family roams the desert so that we could measure the electrical activity in her brain while she watched cartoons? How would we convince the 3-week-old infant in New Delhi to complete a lengthy questionnaire about his political beliefs? Most psychology experiments are conducted by professors and graduate students at colleges and universities in the Western Hemisphere, and as much as they might like to randomly sample the population of the planet, the practical truth is that they are pretty much stuck studying the folks who volunteer for their studies.

Random sampling is always impractical and usually impossible. And yet, if we don't randomly sample, then we can't automatically generalize from our sample to the population from which it was drawn. So how can we learn *anything* from psychology experiments? Isn't the failure to randomly sample a fatal flaw? No, it's not.

*"Hi. You've been randomly selected to participate in a sex survey upstairs in 15 minutes."*

Although we can't automatically generalize from nonrandom samples, there are three reasons why this is not a lethal problem for the science of psychology:

- Sometimes generality does not matter. One flying pig utterly disproves most people's theories of porcine locomotion. Similarly, in psychology it often doesn't matter if *everyone* does something as long as *someone* does it. If playing a violent video game for 1 hour caused a nonrandomly selected group of children to start shoving in the lunch line, then this fact would utterly disprove every theory that claimed that video games cannot cause aggression—and it might even provide important clues about when aggression will and won't occur. An experimental result can be illuminating even when its generality is severely limited.

- Sometimes generality can be determined. When the generality of an experimental result *is* important, psychologists often perform a new experiment that uses the same procedures on a different sample. For example, if we were to measure how some American children behaved after playing Blood Sport for 2 hours, we could then replicate the experiment with Japanese children, or with teenagers, or with adults. In essence, we could treat the attributes of our sample, such as culture and age, as independent variables and do experiments to determine whether these attributes influenced our dependent variable. If the results of our study were replicated in numerous nonrandom samples, we could be more confident (though never completely confident) that the results would generalize to the population at large.

- Sometimes generality can be assumed. Instead of asking, "Is there a compelling reason to generalize from a nonrandom sample?" we might just as easily ask, "Is there a compelling reason not to?" For example, few of us would be willing to take an experimental drug that could potentially make us smarter and happier if a nonrandom sample of seven participants took the drug and died a slow, painful death. Indeed, we would probably refuse the drug even if the seven subjects were mice. Although the study used a nonrandom sample of participants who are different from us in many ways, we are willing to generalize from their experience to ours because we know that even mice share enough of our basic biology to make it a good bet that what harms them can harm us too. By this same reasoning, if a psychology experiment demonstrated that some American children behaved violently after playing Blood Sport for 1 hour, we might ask whether there is a compelling reason to suspect that Ecuadorian college students or middle-aged Australians would behave any differently. If we had a reason to suspect they would, then the experimental method would provide a way for us to investigate that possibility.

**In summary,** to determine whether two variables are causally related, we must first determine whether they are related at all. This can be done by measuring each variable many times and then comparing the patterns of variation within each series of measurements. If the patterns covary, then the variables are correlated. Correlations allow us to predict the value of one variable from knowledge of the value of the other. The direction and strength of a correlation are measured by the correlation coefficient ($r$).

Even when we observe a correlation between two variables, we can't conclude that they are causally related because there are an infinite number of "third variables" that might be causing them both. Experiments solve this third-variable problem by manipulating an independent variable, randomly assigning participants to the experimental and control groups that this manipulation creates, and measuring a dependent variable. These measurements are then compared across groups. If inferential statistics show that there was less than a 5% chance that random assignment failed, then differences in the measurements across groups are assumed to have been caused by the manipulation.

An internally valid experiment establishes a causal relationship between variables as they were operationally defined and among the participants whom they included. When an experiment mimics the real world—that is, when it is externally valid and when its participants are randomly sampled—we may generalize from its results. But most psychology experiments are not attempts to mimic the real world: They are attempts to test hypotheses and theories. ■ ■

**INFORMED CONSENT** A written agreement to participate in a study made by a person who has been informed of all the risks that participation may entail.

**DEBRIEFING** A verbal description of the true nature and purpose of a study that psychologists provide to people after they have participated in the study.

# The Ethics of Science: Saying Please and Thank You

Somewhere along the way, someone probably told you that it isn't nice to treat people like objects. And yet, it may seem that psychologists do just that—creating situations that cause people to feel fearful or sad, to do things that are embarrassing or immoral, and to learn things about themselves that they might not really want to know. Why do psychologists treat people so shabbily? In fact, psychologists go to great lengths to ensure the safety and well-being of their research participants, and they are bound by a code of ethics that is as detailed and demanding as the professional codes that bind physicians, lawyers, and members of the clergy. This code of ethics was formalized by the American Psychological Association in 1958 and offers a number of rules that govern all research conducted with human beings. Here are a few of the most important ones:

- *Informed consent:* Participants may not take part in a psychological study unless they have given **informed consent**, which is *a written agreement to participate in a study made by an adult who has been informed of all the risks that participation may entail*. This doesn't mean that the person must know everything about the study (the hypothesis), but it does mean that the person must know about anything that might potentially be harmful, painful, embarrassing, or unpleasant. If people cannot give informed consent (perhaps because they are minors or are mentally incapable), then informed consent must be obtained from their legal guardians.
- *Freedom from coercion:* Psychologists may not coerce participation. Coercion not only means physical and psychological coercion but monetary coercion as well. It is unethical to offer people large amounts of money to persuade them to do something that they might otherwise decline to do. College students may be invited to participate in studies as part of their training in psychology, but they are ordinarily offered the option of learning the same things by other means.
- *Protection from harm:* Psychologists must take every possible precaution to protect their research participants from physical or psychological harm. If there are two equally effective ways to study something, the psychologist must use the safer method. If no safe method is available, the psychologist may not perform the study.
- *Risk-benefit analysis:* Although participants may be asked to accept small risks, such as a minor shock or a small embarrassment, they may not even be *asked* to accept large risks, such as severe pain or psychological trauma. Indeed, participants may not be asked to take risks that are greater than those they would ordinarily take in their everyday lives. Furthermore, even when participants are asked to take small risks, the psychologist must first demonstrate that these risks are outweighed by the social benefits of the new knowledge that might be gained from the study.
- *Debriefing:* Although psychologists need not divulge everything about a study before a person participates, they must divulge it after the person participates. If a participant is deceived in any way before or during a study, the psychologist must provide a **debriefing**, which is *a verbal description of the true nature and purpose of a study*. If the participant was changed in any way (e.g., made to feel sad), the psychologist must attempt to undo that change (e.g., ask the person to do a task that will make them happy) and restore the participant to the state he or she was in before the study.

These rules require that psychologists show extraordinary concern for their participants' welfare, but how are they enforced? Almost all psychology studies are done by psychologists who work at colleges and universities. These institutions have institutional review boards (IRBs) that are composed of instructors and researchers, university staff, and laypeople from the community (e.g., business leaders or members of the clergy). A psychologist may conduct a study only after the IRB has reviewed and approved it. As you can imagine, the code of ethics and the procedure for approval are so strict that many studies simply cannot be performed anywhere, by anyone, at any

*"I don't usually volunteer for experiments, but I'm kind of a puzzle freak."*

time. For example, psychologists have long wondered how growing up without exposure to language affects a person's subsequent ability to speak and think, but they cannot ethically manipulate such a variable in an experiment. As such, they must be content to study the natural correlations between variables such as language exposure and speaking ability, and they must forever forgo the possibility of firmly establishing causal relationships between these variables. There are many questions that psychologists will never be able to answer definitively because doing so would require unethical experimentation. This is an unavoidable consequence of studying creatures who have fundamental human rights.

Of course, not all research participants have human rights because not all research participants are human. Some are chimpanzees, rats, pigeons, or other nonhuman animals. How does the ethical code of the psychologist apply to nonhuman participants? The question of "animal rights" is one of the most hotly debated issues of our time, and people on opposite sides of the debate rarely have much good to say about each other. And yet, consider three points on which every reasonable person would agree:

- A very small percentage of psychological experiments are performed on nonhuman animals, and a very small percentage of these experiments cause discomfort or death.
- Nonhuman animals deserve good care, should never be subjected to more discomfort than is absolutely necessary, and should be protected by federal and institutional guidelines.
- Some experiments on nonhuman animals have had tremendous benefits for human beings, and many have not.

None of these points is in dispute among thoughtful advocates of different positions, so what exactly is the controversy? The controversy lies in the answer to a single question: Is it morally acceptable to force nonhuman animals to pay certain costs so that human animals can reap uncertain benefits? Most people eat animals, which is to say that most people believe it is morally acceptable to profit at the expense of a nonhuman animal. A small but significant minority of people disagree. Although there are compelling arguments to be made on both sides of this moral dilemma, it is clearly just that—a *moral* dilemma and not a scientific controversy that one can hope to answer with evidence and facts. Anyone who has ever loved a pet can empathize with the plight of the nonhuman animal that is being forced to participate in an experiment, feel pain, or even die when it would clearly prefer not to. Anyone who has ever loved a person with a debilitating illness can understand the desire of researchers to develop drugs and medical procedures by doing to nonhuman animals the same things that farmers and animal trainers do every day. Do animals have rights, and if so, do they ever outweigh the rights of people? This is a difficult question with which individuals and societies are currently wrestling. For now, at least, there is no easy answer.

**ONLY HUMAN**

**THE WELL-BEING OF PARTICIPANTS ALWAYS COMES FIRST!** In 1997 in Mill Valley, California, 10th-grade student Ari Hoffman won first place in the Marin County science fair for doing a study that found that exposure to radiation decreased the offspring of fruit flies. However, he was quickly disqualified for cruelty when it was learned that about 35 of his 200 flies died during the 3-month experiment. Hoffman was disappointed because he had used extraordinary efforts to keep the flies alive, for example, by maintaining a tropical temperature for his flies during the entire experiment.

PAUL MCERLANE/REUTERS/CORBIS

Some people consider it unethical to use animals for clothing or research. Others see an important distinction between these two purposes.

**In summary,** psychologists are acutely aware of the responsibilities that come with conducting research with human and nonhuman animals. Care and consideration are taken to make sure that human research participants give their informed and voluntary consent to participate in studies that pose minimal or no risk. Similar principles guide the humane treatment of nonhuman research subjects. Enforcement of these principles by federal, institutional, and professional governing agencies ensures that the research process is a meaningful one that can lead to significant increases in knowledge. ■ ■

## Where Do You Stand?

## The Morality of Immoral Experiments

Is it wrong to benefit from someone else's wrongdoing? Although this may seem like an abstract question for moral philosophers, it is a very real question that scientists must ask when they consider the results of unethical experiments. During World War II, Nazi doctors conducted barbaric medical studies on prisoners in concentration camps. They placed prisoners in decompression chambers and then dissected their living brains in order to determine how altitude affects pilots. They irradiated and chemically mutilated the reproductive organs of men and women in order to find inexpensive methods for the mass sterilization of "racially inferior" people. They infected prisoners with streptococcus and tetanus in order to devise treatments for soldiers who had been exposed to these bacteria. And in one of the most horrible experiments, prisoners were immersed in tanks of ice water so that the doctors could discover how long pilots would survive if they bailed out over the North Sea. The prisoners were frozen, thawed, and frozen again until they

died. During these experiments, the doctors carefully recorded the prisoners' physiological responses.

These experiments were crimes, hideous beyond all imagining. But the records of these experiments remain, and in some cases they provide valuable information that could never be obtained ethically. For example, because researchers cannot perform controlled studies that would expose volunteers to dangerously cold temperatures, there is still controversy among doctors about the best treatment for hypothermia. In 1988, Dr. Robert Pozos, a physiologist at the University of Minnesota Medical School, who had spent a lifetime studying hypothermia, came across an unpublished report written in 1945 titled "The Treatment of Shock from Prolonged Exposure to Cold, Especially in Water." The report described the results of the horrible freezing experiments performed on prisoners at the Dachau concentration camp, and it suggested that contrary to the conventional medical wisdom, rapid rewarming (rather

than slow rewarming) might be the best way to treat hypothermia.

Should the Nazi medical studies have been published so that modern doctors might more effectively treat hypothermia? Many scientists and ethicists thought they should. "The prevention of a death outweighs the protection of a memory. The victims' dignity was irrevocably lost in vats of freezing liquid forty years ago. Nothing can change that," argued bioethicist Arthur Caplan. Others disagreed. "I don't see how any credence can be given to the work of unethical investigators," wrote Dr. Arnold Relman, editor of the *New England Journal of Medicine*. "It goes to legitimizing the evil done," added Abraham Foxman, national director of the Anti-Defamation League (Siegel, 1988). The debate about this issue rages on (Caplan, 1992). If we use data that were obtained unethically, are we rewarding those who collected it and legitimizing their actions? Or can we condemn such investigations but still learn from them? Where do you stand?

# Chapter Review

### Empiricism: How to Know Things

- Empiricism involves using observation to gain knowledge about the world.

- Because casual observation is prone to error, sciences have methods for observation. These methods are unusually sophisticated in psychology because people are unusually complex, variable, and reactive.

### The Science of Observation: Saying What

- Observation begins with measurement. Researchers generate operational definitions of the properties they wish to measure and develop measures to detect the conditions that those definitions specify.

- Measures must be valid, reliable, and powerful. Validity refers to the relationship between the operational definition and the property (construct validity) and between the operational definition and other operational definitions (predictive validity). Reliability refers to the consistency of a measure, and power refers to the measure's ability to detect differences that do exist and not to detect differences that don't exist.

- Although interesting individuals provide useful information, most measurement is performed on large samples of participants. Larger samples better reflect the characteristics of the population.

- Measurements taken from a sample can be depicted in a frequency distribution, which can be described by various descriptive statistics such as the mean, median, mode, and range.

- Researchers use cover stories and filler items to avoid creating demand characteristics that influence the behavior of participants. They also use double-blind procedures so that the experimenter's expectations do not influence the participant's behavior or the measurement thereof.

## The Science of Explanation: Saying Why

- Psychologists are interested in observing and explaining relationships between variables.

- Correlation refers to a relationship signified by synchronization in the patterns of variation of two variables. The correlation coefficient (*r*) is a statistic that describes both the strength and direction of that relationship.

- Two variables can be correlated for any one of three reasons: $X \rightarrow Y$, $Y \rightarrow X$, or $Z \rightarrow X$ and $Y$.

- Experimentation can determine for which of these three reasons a pair of variables is correlated. It involves the manipulation of an independent variable (which results in an experimental group and a control group) and the measurement of a dependent variable. It requires that participants be randomly assigned to groups.

- Experiments allow one to conclude that changes in an independent variable caused changes in a dependent variable if (a) inferential statistics show that random assignment was unlikely to have failed and (b) the experiment is internally valid.

- Because psychologists rarely sample their participants randomly, most psychology experiments lack external validity. This is rarely a problem because experiments are meant to test theories and not to mimic real-world events.

## The Ethics of Science: Saying Please and Thank You

- Psychologists adhere to a strict code of ethics. People must give their informed consent to participate in any study, they must do so free of coercion, they must be protected from physical and psychological harm, the benefits of the research must outweigh the risks, and participants must be debriefed at the conclusion of the research.

- Institutional review boards must approve all research before it is conducted.

- The treatment of animals is governed by strict rules developed by professional organizations, governmental bodies, and university committees.

## Key Terms

empiricism (p. 40)
method (p. 40)
operational definition (p. 41)
measure (p. 42)
electromyograph (EMG) (p. 42)
validity (p. 43)
construct validity (p. 43)
predictive validity (p. 43)
reliability (p. 44)
power (p. 44)
case method (p. 44)
population (p. 45)

sample (p. 45)
law of large numbers (p. 45)
frequency distribution (p. 46)
normal distribution (p. 47)
mode (p. 47)
mean (p. 47)
median (p. 47)
range (p. 47)
demand characteristics (p. 49)
naturalistic observation (p. 49)
double blind (p. 51)

variable (p. 53)
correlation (p. 53)
correlation coefficient (p. 54)
natural correlation (p. 56)
third-variable correlation (p. 57)
matched samples (p. 57)
matched pairs (p. 57)
third-variable problem (p. 58)
experiment (p. 58)
manipulation (p. 59)
independent variable (p. 60)

experimental group (p. 60)
control group (p. 60)
dependent variable (p. 60)
self-selection (p. 61)
randomization (p. 61)
internal validity (p. 64)
external validity (p. 65)
theory (p. 65)
hypothesis (p. 65)
random sampling (p. 66)
informed consent (p. 68)
debriefing (p. 68)

## Recommended Readings

**Bennett, D. J.** (1998). *Randomness*. Cambridge: Harvard University Press. A mathematician discusses probability theory and games of chance.

**Miller, A. J.** (1986). *The obedience experiments: A case study of controversy in social science*. New York: Praeger. An examination of the most controversial psychology experiment ever conducted: Stanley Milgram's study of obedience.

**Pelham, B. W., & Blanton, H.** (2003). *Conducting research in psychology: Measuring the weight of smoke* (2nd ed.). Pacific Grove, CA: Thomson Wadsworth. A concise, scholarly, and entertaining look at the process of doing psychological research.

**Sobel, D.** (1995). *Longitude: The true story of a lone genius who solved the greatest scientific problem of his time*. New York: Walker. In the 18th century, thousands of people died at sea because no one knew how to measure longitude. This is the story of the man who solved the problem that stumped geniuses from Newton to Galileo.

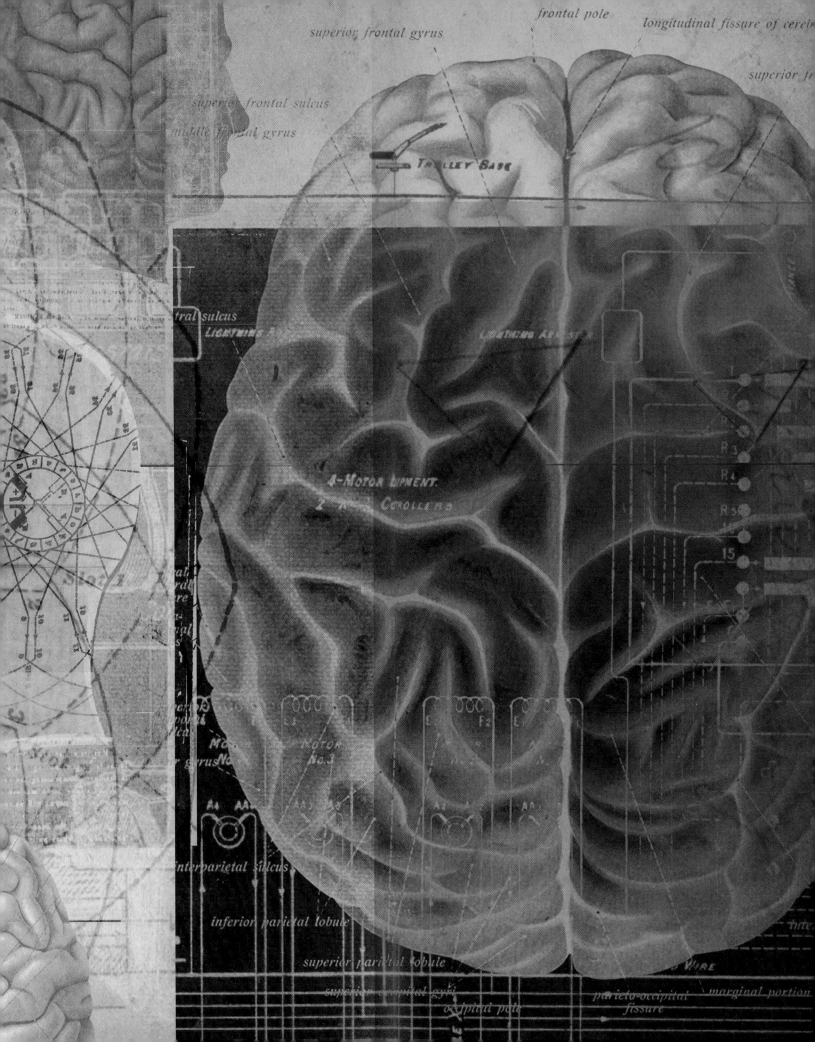

# 3

# Neuroscience and Behavior

TWO PATIENTS WERE ADMITTED TO A hospital emergency room late one evening, complaining of problems with their vision. One patient was a 17-year-old named David, and the other was a 75-year-old named Betty. David saw people who weren't there and Betty didn't recognize her own husband, but these weren't problems with their eyes: They were disorders of their brains.

David was brought in by some fellow members of his gang. They told the doctors that David was usually cool and composed, but he had become frantic, believing he kept seeing members of a rival gang sneaking up on him. At first David's friends listened to his warnings and searched for their rivals. After repeated scares and false alarms, they decided David was seeing shadows and thinking they were enemies. The persistence of these phantom sightings worried David—he thought something was wrong with his vision. His friends thought he had gone crazy.

The doctors didn't find any problems with David's eyes. Instead, they discovered he was suffering from hallucinations—a side effect of abusing methamphetamine (McKetin et al., 2006). David's prolonged crystal meth habit altered the normal functioning of some chemicals in his brain, distorting his perception of reality and "fooling" his brain into perceiving things that were not actually there. After he stopped taking the drug, the hallucinations disappeared and David was back to his normal calm self.

The second patient, Betty, had fainted earlier in the day. After she was revived, Betty no longer recognized her husband, George. Disturbed by this, George called their adult sons, who immediately came over to their house. She didn't recognize her two sons either, but otherwise Betty seemed normal. She insisted it was just a problem with her eyes and had the family bring her to the emergency room for examination.

The doctor who examined Betty's eyes found her vision to be perfectly normal. She could recognize colors and identify common objects, even at a distance. Nonetheless, she was unable to recognize her closest family members or to identify her doctor, whom she had known for 30 years. A brain scan showed that Betty had suffered a stroke that damaged a small area on the right side of her brain. Doctors diagnosed Betty with a rare disorder called *prosopagnosia*, which is an inability to recognize familiar faces (Duchaine et al., 2006; Yin, 1970)—a result of the brain damage caused by her stroke.

David and Betty both complained of problems with their vision, but their symptoms were actually caused by disorders in the brain. David's problem resulted from a malfunction in the brain's system for passing chemical messages between cells. Betty's problem resulted from damage to an area of the brain that integrates and interprets visual information. Our ability to perceive the world around us and recognize familiar people depends not only on information we take in through our senses but, perhaps more importantly, on the interpretation of this information performed by the brain.

**NEURONS** Cells in the nervous system that communicate with one another to perform information-processing tasks.

**CELL BODY** The part of a neuron that coordinates information-processing tasks and keeps the cell alive.

**DENDRITES** The part of a neuron that receives information from other neurons and relays it to the cell body.

**AXON** The part of a neuron that transmits information to other neurons, muscles, or glands.

In this chapter, we'll consider how the brain works, what happens when it doesn't, and how both states of affairs determine behavior. First we'll introduce you to the basic unit of information processing in the brain, the neuron. The electrical and chemical activities of neurons are the starting point of all behavior, thought, and emotion. Next we'll consider the anatomy of the brain, including its overall organization, key structures that perform different functions, and the brain's evolutionary development. Finally, we'll discuss methods that allow us to study the brain and clarify our understanding of how it works. These include methods that examine the damaged brain and methods for scanning the living and healthy brain.

## Neurons: The Origin of Behavior

An estimated 1 billion people watched the final game of the 2006 World Cup. That's a whole lot of people, but to put it in perspective, it's still only 16% of the estimated 6.5 billion people currently living on Earth. A more impressive number might be the 30 billion viewers who tuned in to watch any of the World Cup action over the course of the tournament. But a really, really big number is inside your skull right now, helping you make sense of these big numbers you're reading about. There are approximately *100 billion* cells in your brain that perform a variety of tasks to allow you to function as a human being.

Humans have thoughts, feelings, and behaviors that are often accompanied by visible signals. For example, anticipating seeing a friend waiting up the block for you in the movie ticket line may elicit a range of behaviors. An observer might see a smile on your face or notice how fast you are walking; internally, you might mentally rehearse what you'll say to your friend and feel a surge of happiness as you approach her. But all those visible and experiential signs are produced by an underlying invisible physical component coordinated by the activity of your brain cells. The anticipation you have, the happiness you feel, and the speed of your feet are the result of information processing in your brain. In a way, all of your thoughts, feelings, and behaviors spring from cells in the brain that take in information and produce some kind of output.

The 100 billion cells that perform this function trillions of times a day are called neurons. **Neurons** are *cells in the nervous system that communicate with one another to perform information-processing tasks*. In this section, we'll look at how neurons were discovered, what their components are, and how they are specialized for different types of information processing.

During the 1800s, scientists began to turn their attention from studying the mechanics of limbs, lungs, and livers to studying the harder-to-observe workings of the brain. Philosophers wrote poetically about an "enchanted loom" that mysteriously

wove a tapestry of behavior, and many scientists confirmed the metaphor (Corsi, 1991). To these scientists, the brain looked as though it were composed of a continuously connected lattice of fine threads, leading to the conclusion that it was one big woven web of material. However, in the late 1880s, a Spanish physician named Santiago Ramón y Cajal (1852–1934) tried a new technique for staining neurons in the brain (DeFelipe & Jones, 1988). The stain highlighted the appearance of entire cells, revealing that they came in different shapes and sizes (see **FIGURE 3.1**). Using this

Santiago Ramón y Cajal (1852–1934) discovered the structure of neurons by using a staining technique that allowed a clear view of the cells. He was awarded the Nobel Prize in Physiology in 1906.

SCIENCE SOURCE/PHOTO RESEARCHERS

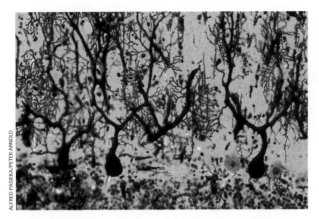

**Figure 3.1** **Golgi-Stained Neurons** Santiago Ramón y Cajal used a Golgi stain to highlight the appearance of neurons. These are Purkinje cells from the cerebellum, known for the elaborate branching of their dendrites.

technique, Cajal was the first to see that each neuron was composed of a body with many threads extending outward toward other neurons. Surprisingly, he also saw that the threads of each neuron did not actually touch other neurons. Cajal believed that neurons are the information-processing units of the brain and that even though he saw gaps between neurons, they had to communicate in some way (Rapport, 2005).

## Components of the Neuron

Cajal discovered that neurons are complex structures composed of three basic parts: the cell body, the dendrites, and the axon (see **FIGURE 3.2**). Like cells in all organs of the body, neurons have a **cell body** (also called the *soma*), the largest component of the neuron that *coordinates the information-processing tasks and keeps the cell alive*. Functions such as protein synthesis, energy production, and metabolism take place here. The cell body contains a *nucleus*; this structure houses chromosomes that contain your DNA, or the genetic blueprint of who you are. The cell body is surrounded by a porous cell membrane that allows molecules to flow into and out of the cell.

Unlike other cells in the body, neurons have two types of specialized extensions of the cell membrane that allow them to communicate: dendrites and axons. **Dendrites** *receive information from other neurons and relay it to the cell body*. The term *dendrite* comes from the Greek word for "tree"; indeed, most neurons have many dendrites that look like tree branches.

The **axon** *transmits information to other neurons, muscles, or glands*. Each neuron has a single axon that sometimes can be very long, even stretching up to a meter from the base of the spinal cord down to the big toe.

**Figure 3.2** **Components of a Neuron** A neuron is made up of three parts: a cell body that houses the chromosomes with the organism's DNA and maintains the health of the cell, dendrites that receive information from other neurons, and an axon that transmits information to other neurons, muscles, and glands.

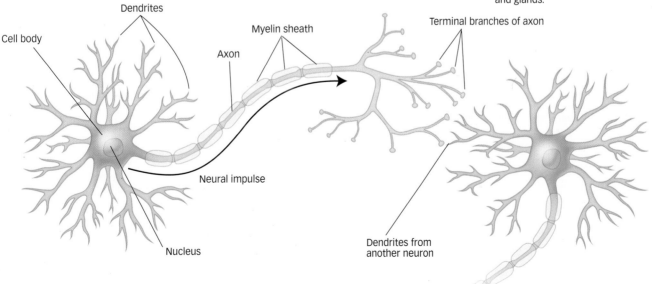

Cell body · Dendrites · Axon · Myelin sheath · Terminal branches of axon · Neural impulse · Nucleus · Dendrites from another neuron

**MYELIN SHEATH** An insulating layer of fatty material.

**GLIAL CELLS** Support cells found in the nervous system.

**SYNAPSE** The junction or region between the axon of one neuron and the dendrites or cell body of another.

In many neurons, the axon is covered by a **myelin sheath**, *an insulating layer of fatty material*. The myelin sheath is composed of **glial cells**, which are *support cells found in the nervous system*. Although there are 100 billion neurons busily processing information in your brain, there are 10 to 50 times that many glial cells serving a variety of functions. Some glial cells digest parts of dead neurons, others provide physical and nutritional support for neurons, and others form myelin to help the axon transmit information more efficiently. Imagine for a minute the pipes coming from the water heater in the basement, leading upstairs to heat a house. When those pipes are wrapped in insulation, they usually perform their task more efficiently: The water inside stays hotter, the heater works more effectively, and so on. Myelin performs this same function for an axon: An axon insulated with myelin can more efficiently transmit signals to other neurons, organs, or muscles.

In fact, in *demyelinating diseases*, such as multiple sclerosis, the myelin sheath deteriorates, causing a slowdown in the transmission of information from one neuron to another (Schwartz & Westbrook, 2000). This leads to a variety of problems, including loss of feeling in the limbs, partial blindness, and difficulties in coordinated movement. In multiple sclerosis there are often cycles of myelin loss and subsequent recovery.

As you'll remember, Cajal observed that the dendrites and axons of neurons do not actually touch each other. There's a small gap between the axon of one neuron and the dendrites or cell body of another. This gap is part of the **synapse**: *the junction or region between the axon of one neuron and the dendrites or cell body of another* (see **FIGURE 3.3**). Many of the 100 billion neurons in your brain have a few thousand synaptic junctions, so it should come as no shock that most adults have between 100 trillion and 500 trillion synapses. As you'll read shortly, the transmission of information across the synapse is fundamental to communication between neurons, a process that allows us to think, feel, and behave.

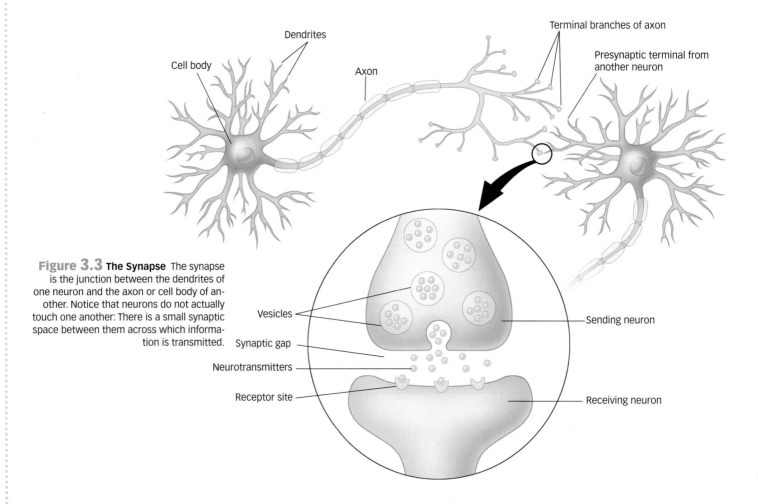

**Figure 3.3 The Synapse** The synapse is the junction between the dendrites of one neuron and the axon or cell body of another. Notice that neurons do not actually touch one another: There is a small synaptic space between them across which information is transmitted.

Cell body
Dendrites
Axon
Terminal branches of axon
Presynaptic terminal from another neuron

Vesicles
Synaptic gap
Neurotransmitters
Receptor site
Sending neuron
Receiving neuron

## Major Types of Neurons

There are three major types of neurons, each performing a distinct function: sensory neurons, motor neurons, and interneurons. **Sensory neurons** *receive information from the external world and convey this information to the brain via the spinal cord.* Sensory neurons have specialized endings on their dendrites that receive signals for light, sound, touch, taste, and smell. For example, in our eyes, sensory neurons' endings are sensitive to light. **Motor neurons** *carry signals from the spinal cord to the muscles to produce movement.* These neurons often have long axons that can stretch to muscles at our extremities. However, most of the nervous system is composed of the third type of neuron, **interneurons**, which *connect sensory neurons, motor neurons, or other interneurons.* Some interneurons carry information from sensory neurons into the nervous system, others carry information from the nervous system to motor neurons, and still others perform a variety of information-processing functions within the nervous system. Interneurons work together in small circuits to perform simple tasks, such as identifying the location of a sensory signal, and much more complicated ones, such as recognizing a familiar face. (See the Hot Science box on the next page for a discussion of a sophisticated type of neuron discovered only recently.)

Besides specialization for sensory, motor, or connective functions, neurons are also somewhat specialized depending on their location (see **FIGURE 3.4**). For example, *Purkinje cells* are a type of interneuron that carries information from the cerebellum to the rest of the brain and spinal cord. These neurons have dense, elaborate dendrites

**SENSORY NEURONS** Neurons that receive information from the external world and convey this information to the brain via the spinal cord.

**MOTOR NEURONS** Neurons that carry signals from the spinal cord to the muscles to produce movement.

**INTERNEURONS** Neurons that connect sensory neurons, motor neurons, or other interneurons.

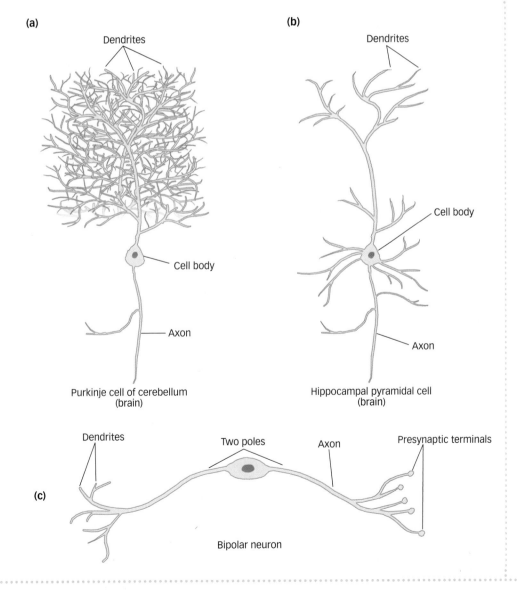

**(a)**

Dendrites

Cell body

Axon

Purkinje cell of cerebellum
(brain)

**(b)**

Dendrites

Cell body

Axon

Hippocampal pyramidal cell
(brain)

**(c)**

Dendrites

Two poles

Axon

Presynaptic terminals

Bipolar neuron

**Figure 3.4 Types of Neurons** Neurons have a cell body, an axon, and at least one dendrite. The size and shape of neurons vary considerably, however. (a) The Purkinje cell has an elaborate treelike assemblage of dendrites. (b) Pyramidal cells have a triangular cell body and a single, long dendrite with many smaller dendrites. (c) Bipolar cells have only one dendrite and a single axon.

## { HOT SCIENCE } Mirror, Mirror, in My Brain

YOU'VE NO DOUBT HEARD THE EXPRESSION, "Monkey see, monkey do." In fact, you may have taunted a sibling or playmate with that line more than once in your life. You probably didn't realize that you were *that close* to making one of the major discoveries in neuroscience when you uttered those prophetic words!

One of the most exciting recent advances in neuroscience is the discovery of the mirror-neuron system. Mirror neurons are found in the frontal lobe (near the motor cortex) and in the parietal lobe (Rizzolatti & Craighero, 2004). They have been identified in birds, monkeys, and humans, and their name reflects the function they serve. Mirror neurons are active when an animal performs a behavior, such as reaching for or manipulating an object. However, mirror neurons are also activated whenever another animal *observes* this animal performing the behavior. In other words, mirror neurons are active both in the animal reaching for the food and in the animal observing this behavior. This kind of mirroring—one monkey sees, one monkey does, but both monkeys' mirror neurons fire—holds intriguing implications for understanding the brain's role in complex social behavior.

A recent study on mirror neurons used fMRI to monitor the brains of humans as they watched each of three presentations (Iacoboni et al., 2005). Sometimes participants saw a hand making grasping motions but without a context; they just saw a hand moving in midair with no "props" or background.

When one animal observes another engaging in a particular behavior, some of the same neurons become active in the observer as well as in the animal exhibiting the behavior. These mirror neurons, documented in monkeys, birds, and humans, seem to play an important role in social behavior.

Sometimes they saw only the context: coffee cups or scrubbing sponges but no hands making motions to go with them. Other times they saw hand motions in two different contexts, either grasping and moving a coffee cup to drink or cleaning dishes with a sponge.

When actions were embedded in a context, such as in the last set of presentations, the participants' mirror neurons responded more strongly than in either of the other two conditions. This suggests that the same set of neurons involved in action recognition are also involved in understanding the intentions of others. Mirror neurons are active when watching someone perform a behavior, such as grasping in midair. But they are more highly activated when that behavior has some purpose or context, such as grasping a cup to take a drink. Recognizing another person's intentions means that the observer has inferred something about that person's goals, wants, or wishes ("Oh, she must be thirsty"). These fMRI results suggest that this kind of recognition occurs effortlessly at a neural level.

Why is this interesting? Admittedly, there is much work to be done to fully understand the function, scope, and purpose of mirror neurons. However, these results suggest a possible inborn neural basis for empathy. Grasping the intentions of another person—indeed, having your brain respond in kind as another person acts—is critical to smooth social interaction. It allows us to understand other people's possible motivations and anticipate their future actions. In fact, these are the kinds of skills that people suffering from autism severely lack. Autism is a developmental disorder characterized by impoverished social interactions and communication skills (Frith, 2001). Psychologists who study autism focus on trying to understand the nature of the disorder and devise ways to help autistic people cope with and function in human society. Research on mirror neurons may offer one avenue for better understanding the origin and prognosis of this disorder (Iacoboni & Dapretto, 2006).

---

that resemble bushes. *Pyramidal cells*, found in the cerebral cortex, have a triangular cell body and a single long dendrite among many smaller dendrites. *Bipolar cells*, a type of sensory neuron found in the retinas of the eye, have a single axon and a single dendrite. The brain processes different types of information, so a substantial amount of specialization at the cellular level has evolved to handle these tasks.

**In summary,** neurons are the building blocks of the nervous system. They process information received from the outside world, they communicate with one another, and they send messages to the body's muscles and organs. Neurons are composed of three major parts: the cell body, dendrites, and the axon. The cell body contains the nucleus, which houses the organism's genetic material. Dendrites receive sensory signals from other neurons and transmit this information to the cell body. Each neuron has only one axon, which carries signals from the cell body to other neurons or to muscles and organs in the body. Neurons don't actually touch: They are separated by a small gap, which is part of the synapse across which signals are transmitted from one neuron to another. Glial cells provide support for neurons, usually in the form of the myelin sheath, which coats the axon to facilitate the transmission of information. In demyelinating diseases, the myelin sheath deteriorates.

Neurons are differentiated according to the functions they perform. The three major types of neurons include sensory neurons, motor neurons, and interneurons. Examples of sensory neurons and interneurons are, respectively, bipolar neurons and Purkinje and pyramidal cells. ■ ■

# Electric Signaling: Communicating Information within a Neuron

Understanding how neurons process information is key to appreciating how the brain works, that is, how these tiny cells make it possible for us to think, feel, and act. The communication of information within and between neurons proceeds in two stages— *conduction* and *transmission*. The first stage is the conduction of an electric signal over relatively long distances within neurons, from the dendrites, to the cell body, then throughout the axon. The second stage is the transmission of electric signals between neurons over the synapse. Together, these stages are what scientists generally refer to as the *electrochemical action* of neurons.

## The Resting Potential: The Origin of the Neuron's Electrical Properties

As you'll recall, the neuron's cell membrane is porous: It allows small electrically charged molecules, called *ions,* to flow in and out of the cell. If you imagine using a strainer while you're preparing spaghetti, you'll get the idea. The mesh of the strainer cradles your yummy dinner, but water can still seep in and out of it. Just as the flow of water out of a strainer enhances the quality of pasta, the flow of molecules across a cell membrane enhances the transmission of information in the nervous system.

Neurons have a natural electric charge called the **resting potential**, which is *the difference in electric charge between the inside and outside of a neuron's cell membrane* (Kandel, 2000). The resting potential is similar to the difference between the "+" and "−" poles of a battery. Biologists discovered the resting potential in the 1930s while studying marine invertebrates—sea creatures that lack a spine, such as clams, squid, and lobsters (Stevens, 1971). They found that squids have giant axons that connect the brain to muscles in the tail. These axons have a very large diameter, about 100 times bigger than the largest axons in humans, making it easier to explore their electrical properties. In the summer of 1939, British biologists Alan Hodgkin and Andrew Huxley inserted a thin wire into the squid axon so that it touched the jellylike fluid inside. Then they placed another wire just outside the axon in the watery fluid that surrounds it. They found a substantial difference between the electric charges inside and outside the axon, which they called the resting potential. They measured the resting potential at about −70 millivolts, or roughly 1/200 of the charge of an AA battery.

The resting potential arises from the difference in concentrations of ions inside and outside the neuron's cell membrane. Ions can carry a positive (+) or a negative (−) charge. In the resting state, there is a high concentration of a positively charged ion, potassium ($K^+$), inside the neuron, compared to the relatively low concentration of $K^+$ outside the neuron. Raising the concentration of $K^+$ in the fluid outside the neuron to match the concentration of $K^+$ inside the neuron causes the resting potential to disappear. This simple test confirms that differences in $K^+$ concentration are the basis of the resting potential (Dowling, 1992).

The concentration of $K^+$ inside and outside an axon is controlled by channels in the axon membrane that allow molecules to flow in and out of the neuron. In the resting state, the channels that allow $K^+$ molecules to flow freely across the cell membrane are open, while channels that allow the flow of other molecules are generally closed. There is a naturally higher concentration of $K^+$ molecules *inside* the neuron, so some $K^+$ molecules move out of the neuron through the open channels, leaving the inside of the neuron with a charge of about −70 millivolts relative to the outside (see **FIGURE 3.5** on the next page).

**RESTING POTENTIAL** The difference in electric charge between the inside and outside of a neuron's cell membrane.

Biologists Alan Hodgkin and Andrew Huxley worked with the squid's axon because it is 100 times larger than the biggest axon in humans and discovered the neuron's resting potential.

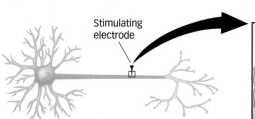

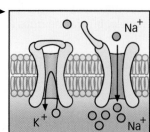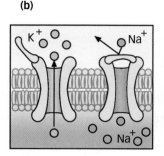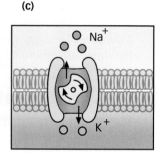

(a) (b) (c)

**Figure 3.5** **The Action Potential**
(a) Electric stimulation of the neuron shuts down the K⁺ channels and opens the Na⁺ channels, allowing Na⁺ to enter the axon. The increase of Na⁺ inside the neuron results in an action potential. (b) In the refractory period after the action potential, the channels return to their original state, allowing K⁺ to flow out of the axon. This leaves an abundance of K⁺ outside and Na⁺ inside the cell. (c) A chemical pump then reverses the ion balance of ions by moving Na⁺ out of the axon and K⁺ into the axon. The neuron can now generate another action potential.

As an example of this process, imagine a field trip to the zoo. Many zoos have turnstiles that allow only one person at a time to enter. The most eager children rush through the turnstiles to see the lions and tigers and bears, while parents hover outside, deciding where to meet later and who's got the sunscreen. With many children on one side of the turnstile, a greater concentration of parents is left on the opposite side. This is like the many small K⁺ ions that move outside the neuron, leaving some large negatively charged molecules inside the neuron, which produces a resting potential across the cell membrane.

## The Action Potential: Sending Signals over Long Distances

The neuron maintains its resting potential most of the time. However, the biologists working with the squid's giant axon noticed that they could produce a signal by stimulating the axon with a brief electric shock, which resulted in the conduction of a large electric impulse down the length of the axon (Hausser, 2000; Hodgkin & Huxley, 1939). This electric impulse is called an **action potential**, which is *an electric signal that is conducted along the length of a neuron's axon to the synapse* (see Figure 3.5). The action potential occurs only when the electric shock reaches a certain level, or *threshold*. When the shock was below this threshold, the researchers recorded only tiny signals, which dissipated rapidly. When the shock reached the threshold, a much larger signal, the action potential, was observed. Interestingly, increases in the electric shock above the threshold did *not* increase the strength of the action potential. The action potential is *all or none*: Electric stimulation below the threshold fails to produce an action potential, whereas electric stimulation at or above the threshold always produces the action potential. The action potential always occurs with exactly the same characteristics and at the same magnitude regardless of whether when the stimulus is at or above the threshold.

The biologists working with the giant squid axon observed another surprising property of the action potential: They measured it at a charge of about +40 millivolts, which is well above zero. This suggests that the mechanism driving the action potential could not simply be the loss of the –70 millivolt resting potential because this would have only brought the charge back to zero. So why does the action potential reach a value above zero?

The action potential occurs when there is a change in the state of the axon's membrane channels. Remember, during the resting potential, only the K⁺ channels are open. However, when an electric charge is raised to the threshold value, the K⁺ channels briefly shut down, and other channels that allow the flow of a *positively* charged ion, sodium (Na⁺), are opened. Na⁺ is typically much more concentrated outside the axon than inside. When the Na⁺ channels open, those positively charged ions flow inside, increasing the positive charge inside the axon relative to that outside. This flow of Na⁺ into the axon pushes the action potential to its maximum value of +40 millivolts.

After the action potential reaches its maximum, the membrane channels return to their original state, and K⁺ flows out until the axon returns to its resting potential. This leaves a lot of extra Na⁺ ions inside the axon and a lot of extra K⁺ ions outside the

**ACTION POTENTIAL** An electric signal that is conducted along an axon to a synapse.

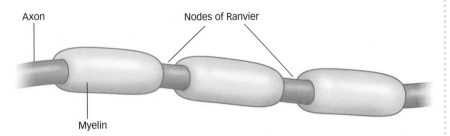

**Figure 3.6 Myelin and Nodes of Ranvier** Myelin is formed by a type of glial cell, and it wraps around a neuron's axon to speed the transmission of the action potential along the length of the axon. Breaks in the myelin sheath are called the nodes of Ranvier. The electric impulse jumps from node to node, thereby speeding the conduction of information down the axon.

axon. During this period where the ions are imbalanced, the neuron cannot initiate another action potential, so it is said to be in a **refractory period**, *the time following an action potential during which a new action potential cannot be initiated*. The imbalance in ions eventually is reversed by an active chemical "pump" in the cell membrane that moves $Na^+$ outside the axon and moves $K^+$ inside the axon.

Earlier, we describe how the action potential occurs at one point in the neuron. But how does this electric charge move down the axon? When an action potential is generated at the beginning of the axon, it spreads a short distance, which generates an action potential at a nearby location on the axon (see Figure 3.5). That action potential also spreads, initiating an action potential at another nearby location, and so on, thus transmitting the charge down the length of the axon. This simple mechanism ensures that the action potential travels the full length of the axon and that it achieves its full intensity at each step, regardless of the distance traveled.

The myelin sheath, which is made up of glial cells that coat and insulate the axon, facilitates the transmission of the action potential. Myelin doesn't cover the entire axon; rather, it clumps around the axon with little break points between clumps, looking kind of like sausage links. These breakpoints are called the *nodes of Ranvier*, after French pathologist Louis-Antoine Ranvier, who discovered them (see **FIGURE 3.6**). When an electric current passes down the length of a myelinated axon, the charge "jumps" from node to node rather than having to traverse the entire axon. This jumping is called *saltatory conduction*, and it helps speed the flow of information down the axon.

---

**In summary,** the neuron's resting potential is due to differences in the $K^+$ concentrations inside and outside the cell membrane. If electric signals reach a threshold, this initiates an action potential, an all-or-none signal that moves down the entire length of the axon. The action potential occurs when sodium channels in the axon membrane open and potassium channels close, allowing the $Na^+$ ions to flow inside the axon. After the action potential has reached its maximum, the sodium channels close and the potassium channels open, allowing $K^+$ to flow out of the axon, returning the neuron to its resting potential. For a brief refractory period, the action potential cannot be re-initiated. Once it is initiated, the action potential spreads down the axon, jumping across the nodes of Ranvier to the synapse. ■ ■

---

# Chemical Signaling:
# Synaptic Transmission between Neurons

When the action potential reaches the end of an axon, you might think that it stops there. After all, the synaptic space between neurons means that the axon of one neuron and the neighboring neuron's dendrites do not actually touch one another. However, the electric charge of the action potential takes a form that can cross the relatively small synaptic gap by relying on a bit of chemistry. We'll look at that process of information transmission between neurons in this section.

Axons usually end in **terminal buttons**, which are *knoblike structures that branch out from an axon*. A terminal button is filled with tiny *vesicles*, or "bags," that contain **neurotransmitters**, *chemicals that transmit information across the synapse to a receiving neuron's dendrites*. The dendrites of the receiving neuron contain **receptors**, *parts of the cell membrane that receive neurotransmitters and initiate a new electric signal*.

**REFRACTORY PERIOD** The time following an action potential during which a new action potential cannot be initiated.

**TERMINAL BUTTONS** Knoblike structures that branch out from an axon.

**NEUROTRANSMITTERS** Chemicals that transmit information across the synapse to a receiving neuron's dendrites.

**RECEPTORS** Parts of the cell membrane that receive the neurotransmitter and initiate a new electric signal.

As K⁺ and Na⁺ flow across a cell membrane, they move the sending neuron, or *presynaptic neuron*, from a resting potential to an action potential. The action potential travels down the length of the axon to the terminal buttons, where it stimulates the release of neurotransmitters from vesicles into the synapse. These neurotransmitters float across the synapse and bind to receptor sites on a nearby dendrite of the receiving neuron, or *postsynaptic neuron*. A new electric potential is initiated in that neuron, and the process continues down that neuron's axon to the next synapse and the next neuron. This electrochemical action, called *synaptic transmission*, allows neurons to communicate with one another and ultimately underlies your thoughts, emotions, and behavior (see **FIGURE 3.7**).

Now that you understand the basic process of how information moves from one neuron to another, let's refine things a bit. You'll recall that a given neuron may make a few thousand synaptic connections with other neurons, so how would the dendrites know which of the neurotransmitters flooding into the synapse to receive and which to ignore? One answer is that neurons tend to form pathways in the brain that are characterized by specific types of neurotransmitters; one neurotransmitter might be prevalent in one part of the brain, whereas a different neurotransmitter might be prevalent in a different part of the brain.

A second answer is that neurotransmitters and receptor sites act like a lock-and-key system. Just as a particular key will only fit in a particular lock, so too will only some neurotransmitters bind to specific receptor sites on a dendrite. The molecular structure of the neurotransmitter must "fit" the molecular structure of the receptor site.

A second reasonable question is what happens to the neurotransmitters left in the synapse after the chemical message is relayed to the postsynaptic neuron. Something must make neurotransmitters stop acting on neurons; otherwise, there'd be no end to the signals that they send. Neurotransmitters leave the synapse through three processes. First, *reuptake* occurs when neurotransmitters are reabsorbed by the terminal buttons of the presynaptic neuron's axon. Second, neurotransmitters can be destroyed by enzymes in the synapse in a process called *enzyme deactivation*; specific enzymes

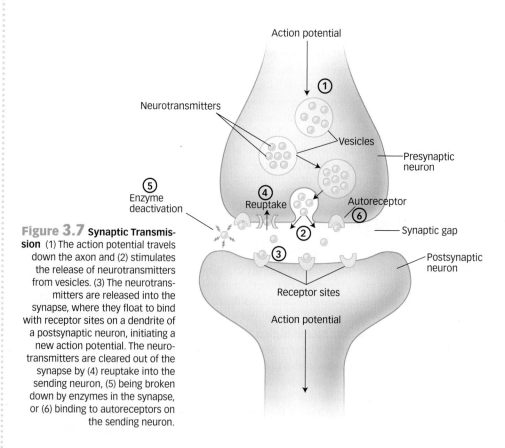

**Figure 3.7 Synaptic Transmission** (1) The action potential travels down the axon and (2) stimulates the release of neurotransmitters from vesicles. (3) The neurotransmitters are released into the synapse, where they float to bind with receptor sites on a dendrite of a postsynaptic neuron, initiating a new action potential. The neurotransmitters are cleared out of the synapse by (4) reuptake into the sending neuron, (5) being broken down by enzymes in the synapse, or (6) binding to autoreceptors on the sending neuron.

break down specific neurotransmitters. Finally, neurotransmitters can bind to the receptor sites called *autoreceptors* on the presynaptic neurons. Autoreceptors detect how much of a neurotransmitter has been released into a synapse and signal the neuron to stop releasing the neurotransmitter when an excess is present.

Finally, you might wonder how many types of neurotransmitters are floating across synapses in your brain right now, helping you to understand all this information about neurotransmitters. For quite some time, scientists thought that only five neurotransmitters contributed to information-processing activities in the brain. Today we know that some 60 chemicals play a role in transmitting information throughout the brain and body and that they differentially affect thought, feeling, and behavior. Let's look more closely at some neurotransmitters and the jobs they do.

## Types of Neurotransmitters

Remember David, the gang member who saw phantom rivals threatening him? The methamphetamine he took altered the function of several neurotransmitters in his brain, which caused his hallucinations. In this case, the actions of chemical messengers at the level of the neurons produced pronounced startling effects in David's behavior. David saw things that weren't there, felt fear that wasn't warranted, and acted oddly without explanation, all of which was eventually traced back to an imbalance in his neurotransmitters. To understand how something like this takes place, let's take a closer look at the major types of neurotransmitters and the tasks they perform (see **TABLE 3.1**).

**Acetylcholine (Ach)**, *a neurotransmitter involved in a number of functions, including voluntary motor control*, was one of the first neurotransmitters discovered. Acetylcholine is found in neurons of the brain and in the synapses where axons connect to muscles and body organs, such as the heart. Acetylcholine activates muscles to initiate motor behavior, but it also contributes to the regulation of attention, learning, sleeping, dreaming, and memory (Gais & Born, 2004; Hasselmo, 2006; Wrenn et al., 2006). These are rather broad effects on a variety of important behaviors, but here are some specific examples. Alzheimer's disease, a medical condition involving severe memory impairments, is associated with the deterioration of Ach-producing neurons. As another example, nicotine excites Ach receptors in the brain, which helps explain why people who wear a nicotine patch often report vivid dreams and why recent ex-smokers often have difficulties thinking or concentrating.

**ACETYLCHOLINE (ACH)** A neurotransmitter involved in a number of functions, including voluntary motor control.

| Table 3.1 | Neurotransmitters and Their Functions | |
|---|---|---|
| **Neurotransmitter** | **Function** | **Examples of Malfunctions** |
| Acetylcholine (Ach) | Enables muscle action; regulates attention, learning, memory, sleeping, and dreaming | With Alzheimer's disease, Ach-producing neurons deteriorate. |
| Dopamine | Influences movement, motivation, emotional pleasure, and arousal | High levels of dopamine are linked to schizophrenia. Lower levels of dopamine produce the tremors and decreased mobility of Parkinson's disease. |
| Glutamate | A major excitatory neurotransmitter involved in learning and memory | Oversupply can overstimulate the brain, producing migraines or seizures. |
| GABA (gamma-aminobutyric acid) | The primary inhibitory neurotransmitter | Undersupply linked to seizures, tremors, and insomnia. |
| Norepinephrine | Helps control mood and arousal | Undersupply can depress mood. |
| Serotonin | Regulates hunger, sleep, arousal, and aggressive behavior | Undersupply linked to depression; Prozac and some other antidepressant drugs raise serotonin levels. |
| Endorphins | Act within the pain pathways and emotion centers of the brain | Lack of endorphins could lower pain threshold or reduce the ability to self-soothe. |

**DOPAMINE** A neurotransmitter that regulates motor behavior, motivation, pleasure, and emotional arousal.

**GLUTAMATE** A major excitatory neurotransmitter involved in information transmission throughout the brain.

**GABA (GAMMA-AMINOBUTYRIC ACID)** The primary inhibitory neurotransmitter in the brain.

**NOREPINEPHRINE** A neurotransmitter that influences mood and arousal.

**SEROTONIN** A neurotransmitter that is involved in the regulation of sleep and wakefulness, eating, and aggressive behavior.

**ENDORPHINS** Chemicals that act within the pain pathways and emotion centers of the brain.

When athletes engage in extreme sports, such as rock climbing, they may experience subjective highs that result from the release of endorphins—chemical messengers acting in emotion and pain centers that elevate mood and dull the experience of pain.

© MARC CHAUVIN

Like acetylcholine, other neurotransmitters in the brain affect a range of behaviors. **Dopamine** is *a neurotransmitter that regulates motor behavior, motivation, pleasure, and emotional arousal*. Because of its role in basic motivated behaviors, such as seeking pleasure or associating actions with rewards, dopamine is involved in regulating some critical human activities. For example, higher levels of dopamine are usually associated with positive emotions. But dopamine can produce different effects in different brain pathways because the effect of any neurotransmitter depends on the type of receptor site it fits. For example, dopamine release in some pathways of the brain plays a role in drug addiction (Baler & Volkow, 2006), whereas in other pathways high levels of dopamine have been linked to schizophrenia (Winterer & Weinberger, 2004); in still other pathways, dopamine contributes to decision making, attention, or movement (Tamminga, 2006). As you can see, the level of the neurotransmitter is not as crucial as the location of the receptor sites it unlocks and the associated processes it triggers.

Neurotransmitters can excite or inhibit synaptic transmission, thereby profoundly changing behavior. **Glutamate** is *a major excitatory neurotransmitter involved in information transmission throughout the brain*. This means that glutamate enhances the transmission of information. Glutamate is used by interneurons; hence, it plays an important role in all kinds of information processing. However, glutamate is especially crucial to learning and the formation of memories (Schmitt et al., 2004). **GABA (gamma-aminobutyric acid)**, in contrast, is *the primary inhibitory neurotransmitter in the brain*. Inhibitory neurotransmitters stop the firing of neurons, an activity that also contributes to the function of the organism. GABA works throughout the brain, and without it, the excitation of synapses could proceed unchecked, sending messages through the brain in a crescendoing circuit (Trevelyan et al., 2006). Thus, it makes sense that drugs that enhance GABA are used as anticonvulsants to combat seizures and are also being explored as treatments for conditions such as anxiety (Post, 2004).

**Norepinephrine**, *a neurotransmitter that influences mood and arousal*, is particularly involved in states of vigilance, or a heightened awareness of dangers in the environment (Ressler & Nemeroff, 1999). Similarly, **serotonin** is *involved in the regulation of sleep and wakefulness, eating, and aggressive behavior* (Kroeze & Roth, 1998). For example, because both neurotransmitters affect mood and arousal, low levels of each have been implicated in mood disorders (Tamminga et al., 2002). Remember, though, that as with dopamine, the actions of these neurotransmitters depend on the receptor sites they unlock and the pathways where they are used, as shown in Figure 3.7.

Another class of chemical messengers is the **endorphins**, *chemicals that act within the pain pathways and emotion centers of the brain* (Keefe, Lumley, Anderson, Lynch, & Carson, 2001). The term *endorphin* is a contraction of *endogenous morphine*, and that's a pretty apt description. Morphine is a synthetic drug that has a calming and pleasurable effect; an endorphin is an internally produced substance that has similar properties, such as dulling the experience of pain and elevating moods. The "runner's high" experienced by many athletes as they push their bodies to painful limits of endurance can be explained by the release of endorphins in the brain.

Each of these neurotransmitters affects thought, feeling, and behavior in different ways, so normal functioning involves a delicate balance of each. Even a slight imbalance—too much of one neurotransmitter or not enough of another—can dramatically affect behavior. These imbalances sometimes occur naturally: The brain doesn't produce enough serotonin, for example, which contributes to depressed or anxious moods. Other times a person may actively seek to cause imbalances. People who smoke, drink alcohol, or take drugs, legal or not, are altering the balance of neurotransmitters in their brains. The drug LSD, for example, is structurally very similar to serotonin, so it binds very easily with serotonin receptors in the brain, producing similar effects on thoughts, feelings, or behavior. In the next section, we'll look at how some drugs are able to "trick" receptor sites in just this way.

## How Drugs Mimic Neurotransmitters

Many drugs that affect the nervous system operate by increasing, interfering with, or mimicking the manufacture or function of neurotransmitters (Cooper, Bloom, & Roth, 2003; Sarter, 2006). **Agonists** are *drugs that increase the action of a neurotransmitter*. **Antagonists** are *drugs that block the function of a neurotransmitter*. Some drugs alter a step in the production or release of the neurotransmitter, whereas others have a chemical structure so similar to a neurotransmitter that the drug is able to bind to that neuron's receptor. If, by binding to a receptor, a drug activates the neurotransmitter, it is an agonist; if it blocks the action of the neurotransmitter, it is an antagonist (see **FIGURE 3.8**).

Many drugs have been developed to mimic or block the actions of certain neurotransmitters (Barchas, Berger, Ciranello, & Elliot, 1980). For example, a drug called L-dopa has been developed to treat Parkinson's disease, a movement disorder involving the loss of neurons that use the neurotransmitter dopamine. Dopamine is created in neurons by a modification of a common molecule called L-dopa. Ingesting L-dopa will elevate the amount of L-dopa in the brain and spur the surviving neurons to produce more dopamine. In other words, L-dopa acts as an agonist for dopamine. The use of L-dopa has become a major success in the alleviation of Parkinson's disease symptoms (Muenter & Tyce, 1971).

Some unexpected evidence also highlights the central role of dopamine in regulating movement and motor performance. In 1982, six people ranging in age from 25 to 45 from the San Francisco Bay area were admitted to emergency rooms with a bizarre set of symptoms: paralysis, drooling, and an inability to speak (Langston, 1995). A diagnosis of advanced Parkinson's disease was made, as these symptoms are consistent with

**AGONISTS** Drugs that increase the action of a neurotransmitter.

**ANTAGONISTS** Drugs that block the function of a neurotransmitter.

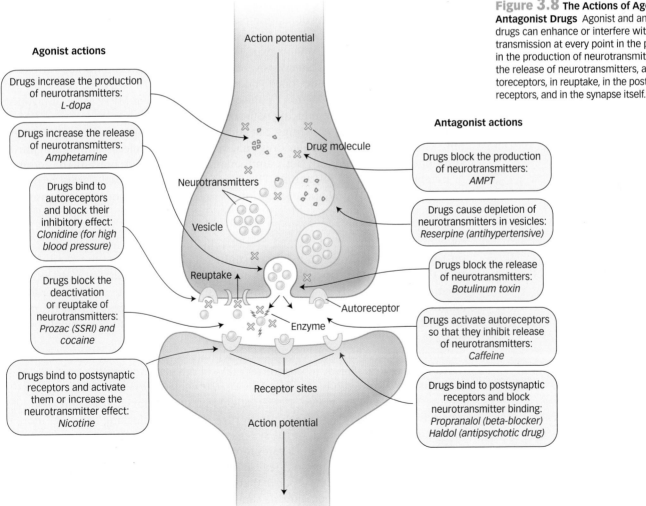

**Figure 3.8 The Actions of Agonist and Antagonist Drugs** Agonist and antagonist drugs can enhance or interfere with synaptic transmission at every point in the process: in the production of neurotransmitters, in the release of neurotransmitters, at the autoreceptors, in reuptake, in the postsynaptic receptors, and in the synapse itself.

**Agonist actions**

Drugs increase the production of neurotransmitters: *L-dopa*

Drugs increase the release of neurotransmitters: *Amphetamine*

Drugs bind to autoreceptors and block their inhibitory effect: *Clonidine (for high blood pressure)*

Drugs block the deactivation or reuptake of neurotransmitters: *Prozac (SSRI) and cocaine*

Drugs bind to postsynaptic receptors and activate them or increase the neurotransmitter effect: *Nicotine*

Action potential

Drug molecule

Neurotransmitters

Vesicle

Reuptake

Autoreceptor

Enzyme

Receptor sites

Action potential

**Antagonist actions**

Drugs block the production of neurotransmitters: *AMPT*

Drugs cause depletion of neurotransmitters in vesicles: *Reserpine (antihypertensive)*

Drugs block the release of neurotransmitters: *Botulinum toxin*

Drugs activate autoreceptors so that they inhibit release of neurotransmitters: *Caffeine*

Drugs bind to postsynaptic receptors and block neurotransmitter binding: *Propranalol (beta-blocker) Haldol (antipsychotic drug)*

Many people suffer from Parkinson's disease, including these well-known personalities: former world heavyweight boxing champion Muhammad Ali; actor Michael J. Fox; the late Pope John Paul II; and, at least according to a diagnosis offered by the CIA, Cuban leader Fidel Castro. The greater visibility of these famous figures has brought with it a greater awareness of the disease and, perhaps, greater efforts directed toward finding a cure.

the later stages of this degenerative disease. It was unusual for six fairly young people to come down with advanced Parkinson's at the same time in the same geographical area. Indeed, none of the patients had Parkinson's, but they were all heroin addicts.

These patients thought they were ingesting a synthetic form of heroin (called MPPP), but instead they ingested a close derivative called MPTP, which unfortunately had the effects of destroying dopamine-producing neurons in an area of the brain crucial for motor performance. Hence, these "frozen addicts" exhibited paralysis and masklike expressions. The patients experienced a remarkable recovery after they were given L-dopa. In fact, it was later discovered that chemists who had worked with MPTP early in their careers later developed Parkinson's disease. Just as L-dopa acts as an agonist by enhancing the production of dopamine, drugs such as MPTP act as antagonists by destroying dopamine-producing neurons.

Like MPTP, other street drugs can alter neurotransmitter function. Amphetamine, for example, is a popular drug that stimulates the release of norepinephrine and dopamine. In addition, both amphetamine and cocaine prevent the reuptake of norepinephrine and dopamine. The combination of increased release of norepinephrine and dopamine and prevention of their reuptake floods the synapse with those neurotransmitters, resulting in increased activation of their receptors. Both of these drugs therefore are strong agonists, although the psychological effects of the two drugs differ somewhat because of subtle distinctions in where and how they act on the brain. Norepinephrine and dopamine play a critical role in mood control, such that increases in either neurotransmitter result in euphoria, wakefulness, and a burst of energy. However, norepinephrine also increases heart rate. An overdose of amphetamine or cocaine can cause the heart to contract so rapidly that heartbeats do not last long enough to pump blood effectively, leading to fainting and sometimes to death.

Prozac, a drug commonly used to treat depression, is another example of a neurotransmitter agonist. Prozac blocks the reuptake of the neurotransmitter *serotonin*, making it part of a category of drugs called *selective serotonin reuptake inhibitors*, or *SSRIs* (Wong, Bymaster, & Engelman, 1995). Patients suffering from clinical depression typically have reduced levels of serotonin in their brains. By blocking reuptake, more of the neurotransmitter remains in the synapse longer and produces greater activation of serotonin receptors. Serotonin elevates mood, which can help relieve depression.

An antagonist with important medical implications is a drug called *propranalol*, one of a class of drugs called *beta-blockers* that obstruct a receptor site for norepinephrine in the heart. Because norepinephrine cannot bind to these receptors, heart rate slows down, which is helpful for disorders in which the heart beats too fast or irregularly.

Beta-blockers are also prescribed to reduce the agitation, racing heart, and nervousness associated with stage fright (Mills & Dimsdale, 1991).

As you've read, many drugs alter the actions of neurotransmitters. Think back to David: His paranoid hallucinations were induced by his crystal meth habit. The actions of methamphetamine involve a complex interaction at the neuron's synapses—it affects pathways for dopamine, serotonin, and norepinephrine—making it difficult to interpret exactly how it works. But the combination of its agonist and antagonist effects alters the functions of neurotransmitters that help us perceive and interpret visual images. In David's case, it led to hallucinations that called his eyesight, and his sanity, into question.

**In summary,** the action potential triggers synaptic transmission through the release of neurotransmitters from the terminal buttons of the sending neuron's axon. The neurotransmitter travels across the synapse to bind with receptors in the receiving neuron's dendrite, completing the transmission of the message. Neurotransmitters bind to dendrites based on existing pathways in the brain and specific receptor sites for neurotransmitters. Neurotransmitters leave the synapse through reuptake, through enzyme deactivation, and by binding to autoreceptors. Some of the major neurotransmitters are acetylcholine (Ach), dopamine, glutamate, GABA, norepinephrine, serotonin, and endorphins. Drugs can affect behavior by acting as agonists, that is, facilitating or increasing the actions of neurotransmitters, or as antagonists by blocking the action of neurotransmitters. ■ ■

# The Organization of the Nervous System

Our glimpse into the microscopic world of neurons reveals a lot about their structure and how they communicate with one another. It's quite impressive that billions of tiny engines cause our thoughts, feelings, and behaviors. Nonetheless, billions of anything working in isolation suggests a lot of potential but not much direction. Neurons work by forming circuits and pathways in the brain, which in turn influence circuits and pathways in other areas of the body. Without this kind of organization and delegation, neurons would be churning away with little purpose. Neurons are the building blocks that form *nerves*, or bundles of axons and the glial cells that support them. The **nervous system** *is an interacting network of neurons that conveys electrochemical information throughout the body*. In this section, we'll look at the major divisions of the nervous system, focusing particularly on structures in the brain and their specific functions.

## Divisions of the Nervous System

There are two major divisions of the nervous system: the central nervous system and the peripheral nervous system (see **FIGURE 3.9** on the next page). The **central nervous system (CNS)** *is composed of the brain and spinal cord*. The central nervous system receives sensory information from the external world, processes and coordinates this information, and sends commands to the skeletal and muscular systems for action. At the top of the CNS rests the brain, which contains structures that support the most complex perceptual, motor, emotional, and cognitive functions of the nervous system. The spinal cord branches down from the brain; nerves that process sensory information and relay commands to the body connect to the spinal cord.

The **peripheral nervous system (PNS)** *connects the central nervous system to the body's organs and muscles*. The peripheral nervous system is itself composed of two major subdivisions, the somatic nervous system and the autonomic nervous system. The **somatic nervous system** *is a set of nerves that conveys information into and out of the central nervous system*. Humans have conscious control over this system and use it to perceive, think, and coordinate their behaviors. For example, directing your hand to reach out and pick up a coffee cup involves the elegantly orchestrated activities of the somatic nervous system: Information from the receptors in your eyes travels to your brain, registering that a cup is on the table; signals from your brain travel to the

**NERVOUS SYSTEM** An interacting network of neurons that conveys electrochemical information throughout the body.

**CENTRAL NERVOUS SYSTEM (CNS)** The part of the nervous system that is composed of the brain and spinal cord.

**PERIPHERAL NERVOUS SYSTEM (PNS)** The part of the nervous system that connects the central nervous system to the body's organs and muscles.

**SOMATIC NERVOUS SYSTEM** A set of nerves that conveys information into and out of the central nervous system.

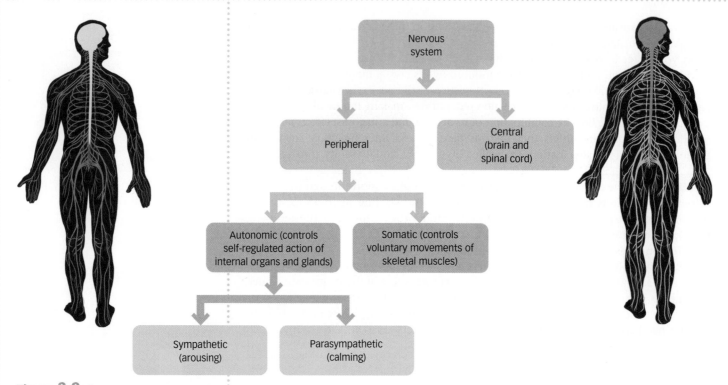

**Figure 3.9 The Human Nervous System**
The nervous system is organized into the peripheral and central nervous systems. The peripheral nervous system is further divided into the automatic and somatic nervous systems.

**AUTONOMIC NERVOUS SYSTEM (ANS)** A set of nerves that carries involuntary and automatic commands that control blood vessels, body organs, and glands.

**SYMPATHETIC NERVOUS SYSTEM** A set of nerves that prepares the body for action in threatening situations.

**PARASYMPATHETIC NERVOUS SYSTEM** A set of nerves that helps the body return to a normal resting state.

muscles in your arm and hand; feedback from those muscles tells your brain that the cup has been grasped; and so on. The somatic nervous system is kind of an "information superhighway," linking the external world of experience with the internal world of the central nervous system.

In contrast, the **autonomic nervous system (ANS)** is *a set of nerves that carries involuntary and automatic commands that control blood vessels, body organs, and glands.* As suggested by its name, this system works on its own to regulate bodily systems, largely outside of conscious control. The ANS has two major subdivisions, the sympathetic nervous system and the parasympathetic nervous system. Each exerts a different type of control on the body. The **sympathetic nervous system** is *a set of nerves that prepares the body for action in threatening situations* (see **FIGURE 3.10**). The nerves in the sympathetic nervous system emanate from the top and bottom of the spinal cord and connect to a variety of organs, such as the eyes, salivary glands, heart and lungs, digestive organs, and sex organs. The sympathetic nervous system coordinates the control of these organs so that the body can take action by fleeing the threatening situation or preparing to face it and fight.

For example, imagine that you hear footsteps behind you in a dark alley. You feel frightened and turn to see someone approaching you from behind. Your sympathetic nervous system kicks into action at this point: It dilates your pupils to let in more light, increases your heart rate and respiration to pump more oxygen to muscles, diverts blood flow to your brain and muscles, and activates sweat glands to cool your body. To conserve energy, the sympathetic nervous system inhibits salivation and bowel movements, suppresses the body's immune responses, and suppresses responses to pain and injury. The sum total of these fast, automatic responses is that they increase the likelihood that you can escape.

The **parasympathetic nervous system** *helps the body return to a normal resting state.* When you're five blocks away from your would-be attacker, your body doesn't need to remain on red alert. Now the parasympathetic nervous system kicks in to reverse the effects of the sympathetic nervous system and return your body to its normal state. The parasympathetic nervous system generally mirrors the connections of the sympathetic nervous system. For example, the parasympathetic nervous system

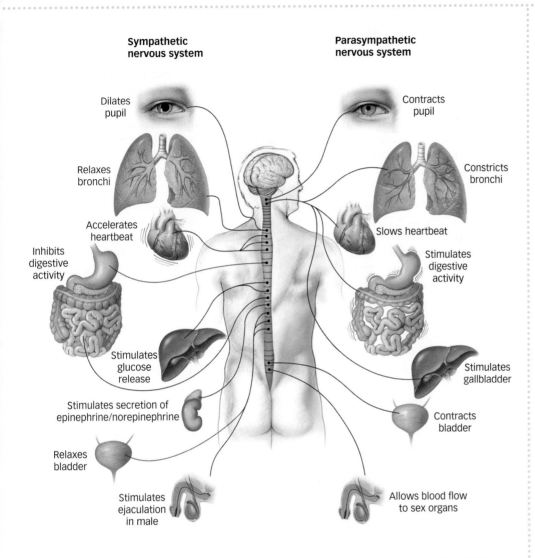

**Sympathetic nervous system**

Dilates pupil

Relaxes bronchi

Accelerates heartbeat

Inhibits digestive activity

Stimulates glucose release

Stimulates secretion of epinephrine/norepinephrine

Relaxes bladder

Stimulates ejaculation in male

**Parasympathetic nervous system**

Contracts pupil

Constricts bronchi

Slows heartbeat

Stimulates digestive activity

Stimulates gallbladder

Contracts bladder

Allows blood flow to sex organs

**Figure 3.10 Sympathetic and Parasympathetic Systems** The autonomic nervous system is composed of two subsystems that complement each other. Activation of the sympathetic system serves several aspects of arousal, whereas the parasympathetic nervous system returns the body to its normal resting state.

constricts your pupils, slows your heart rate and respiration, diverts blood flow to your digestive system, and decreases activity in your sweat glands.

As you might imagine, the sympathetic and parasympathetic nervous systems coordinate to control many bodily functions. One example is sexual behavior. In men, the parasympathetic nervous system engorges the blood vessels of the penis to produce an erection, but the sympathetic nervous system is responsible for ejaculation. In women, the parasympathetic nervous system produces vaginal lubrication, but the sympathetic nervous system underlies orgasm. In both men and women, a successful sexual experience depends on a delicate balance of these two systems; in fact, anxiety about sexual performance can disrupt this balance. For example, sympathetic nervous system activation caused by anxiety can lead to premature ejaculation in males and lack of lubrication in females.

Let's return briefly to an earlier point. Without some kind of coordinated effort, billions and billions of neurons would simply produce trillions and trillions of independent processes. The nervous system has evolved so that the sympathetic and parasympathetic nervous systems work in concert, which in turn allows the autonomic nervous system to function rather effortlessly and, in coordination with the somatic nervous system, allows information to be gathered from the external world. This information travels through the peripheral nervous system and is eventually sent to the brain via the spinal cord, where it can be sorted, interpreted, processed, and acted on. Like the organizational chart of a complex corporation, the organization of the human nervous system is a triumph of delegation of responsibilities.

**SPINAL REFLEXES** Simple pathways in the nervous system that rapidly generate muscle contractions.

## Components of the Central Nervous System

Compared to the many divisions of the peripheral nervous system, the central nervous system may seem simple. After all, it has only two elements: The brain and the spinal cord. But those two elements are ultimately responsible for most of what we do as humans.

The spinal cord often seems like the brain's poor relation: The brain gets all the glory and the spinal cord just hangs around, doing relatively simple tasks. Those tasks, however, are pretty important: keeping you breathing, responding to pain, moving your muscles, allowing you to walk. What's more, without the spinal cord, the brain would not be able to put any of its higher processing into action.

For some very basic behaviors, the spinal cord doesn't need input from the brain at all. Connections between the sensory inputs and motor neurons in the spinal cord mediate **spinal reflexes**, *simple pathways in the nervous system that rapidly generate muscle contractions*. For example, if you touch a hot stove, the sensory neurons that register pain send inputs directly into the spinal cord (see **FIGURE 3.11**). Through just a few synaptic connections within the spinal cord, interneurons relay these sensory inputs to motor neurons that connect to your arm muscles and direct you to quickly retract your hand. In other words, you don't need a whole lot of brainpower to rapidly pull your hand off a hot stove!

More elaborate tasks require the collaboration of the spinal cord and the brain. The peripheral nervous system communicates with the central nervous system through nerves that conduct sensory information into the brain, carry commands out of the brain, or both. The brain sends commands for voluntary movement through the spinal cord to motor neurons, whose axons project out to skeletal muscles and send the message to contract. (See the Hot Science box on page 92 for a description of a novel type of movement control.) Damage to the spinal cord severs the connection from the brain to the sensory and motor neurons that are essential to sensory perception and movement. The location of the spinal injury often determines the extent of the abilities that are lost. As you can see in **FIGURE 3.12,** different regions of the spinal cord control different systems of the body. Patients with damage at a particular level of the spinal cord lose sensation of touch and pain in body parts below the level of the injury as well as a loss of motor control of the muscles in the same areas. A spinal injury higher up the cord usually predicts a much poorer prognosis, such as quadriplegia (the loss of sensation and motor control over all limbs), breathing through a respirator, and lifelong immobility.

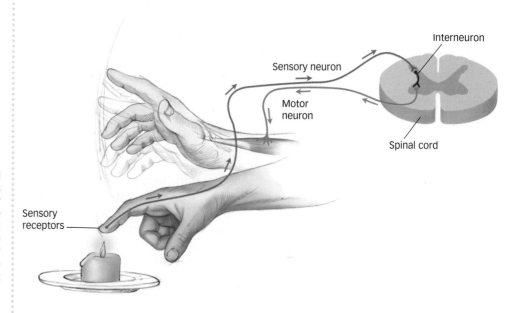

**Figure 3.11 The Pain Withdrawal Reflex** Many actions of the central nervous system don't require the brain's input. For example, withdrawing from pain is a reflexive activity controlled by the spinal cord. Painful sensations (such as a pin jabbing your finger) travel directly to the spinal cord via sensory neurons, which then issue an immediate command to motor neurons to retract the hand.

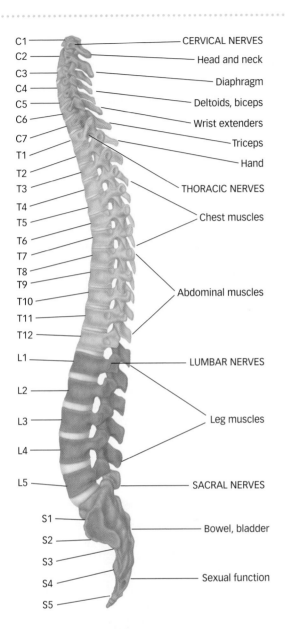

C1 — CERVICAL NERVES
C2 — Head and neck
C3
C4 — Diaphragm
C5 — Deltoids, biceps
C6 — Wrist extenders
C7 — Triceps
T1 — Hand
T2
T3 — THORACIC NERVES
T4
T5 — Chest muscles
T6
T7
T8
T9
T10 — Abdominal muscles
T11
T12
L1 — LUMBAR NERVES
L2
L3 — Leg muscles
L4
L5 — SACRAL NERVES
S1
S2 — Bowel, bladder
S3
S4 — Sexual function
S5

**Figure 3.12 Regions of the Spinal Cord** The spinal cord is divided into four main sections, each of which controls different parts of the body. Damage higher on the spinal cord usually portends greater impairment.

The late actor Christopher Reeve, who starred as Superman in four Superman movies, damaged his spinal cord in a horseback riding accident in 1995, resulting in loss of sensation and motor control in all of his body parts below the neck. Despite great efforts over several years, Reeve made only modest gains in his motor control and sensation, highlighting the extent to which we depend on communication from the brain through the spinal cord to the body and showing how difficult it is to compensate for the loss of these connections (Edgerton et al., 2004). Sadly, Christopher Reeve died at age 52 in 2004 from complications due to his paralysis.

## Exploring the Brain

The human brain is really not much to look at. It's about 3 pounds of slightly slimy, pinkish grayish stuff that sits there like a lump. You already know,

The late actor Christopher Reeve, shown on the left as Superman in 1984 and on the right in 2004, severely damaged his spinal cord in a horseback riding accident in 1995. Reeve worked tirelessly to advocate for greater funding of stem cell research, which could potentially provide enormous breakthroughs for the treatment of spinal cord injuries.

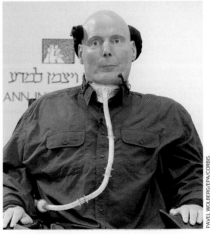

CANNON/THE KOBAL COLLECTION

PAVEL WOLBERG/EPA/CORBIS

## { HOT SCIENCE } Thought Control

IN THE STEVEN SPIELBERG REMAKE OF THE movie *War of the Worlds,* small, squishy aliens control gigantic robots to wreak havoc on humankind. You've probably seen more than one science-fiction movie with that kind of theme: An intruder from another planet steers a monstrous machine through downtown San Francisco or an evil scientist uses brain waves to direct a malevolent robot's actions. You've probably also watched with a fair amount of disbelief. After all, how can a slimy alien or scrawny inventor control that much machinery to do that much damage?

Recently, some *good* scientists have been bringing that science-fiction fantasy closer to reality. Experiments with monkeys provide evidence that mechanical devices can be controlled by thoughts alone. Researchers at Duke University implanted multiple wires into the monkeys' motor cortices (Carmena et al., 2003; Nicolelis, 2001). They then trained the monkeys to move a joystick that controlled a cursor on a computer screen. On each trial, a small target would appear on the screen, and whenever the monkey moved the cursor

from an arbitrary starting position to that target, it was rewarded with fruit juice. After the monkeys had learned the task well, the researchers recorded the action potentials from the motor cortex neurons. Using the activity patterns of many neurons, they created a computer model of the neural activity that corresponded to different directions of joystick movements. Then they disconnected the joystick from the computer and instead connected the signals that their model extracted from the monkey's motor cortex activity directly to the computer.

Now when the monkeys attempted to perform the task, physically manipulating the joystick had no effect. However, their motor cortex cells still produced the neural firings that corresponded to the movement of the joystick, and now these activity patterns directly moved the cursor. At first the motor cortex activity was somewhat crude,

and the monkeys were successful in moving the cursor appropriately only some of the time. With just a few days of practice, however, the monkeys learned to adjust their motor cortex activity patterns to successfully hit the targets. It is as if the monkeys were controlling the cursor with their thoughts.

This finding suggests an exciting direction in brain research. The use of multiple cortical recordings and state-of-the-art computer programs could, in principle, be developed for people with spinal injuries. Great advances have already been made in this area: Wheelchairs can be controlled by puffs of air blown from a paralyzed person's mouth, and speech synthesizers exist that allow a paralyzed person to "talk" to others. However, this research suggests a way to eliminate those intermediary devices. A person's thoughts alone might one day be able to effectively control the movements of a wheelchair, compose e-mail messages to loved ones, or steer a vehicle down to the corner store. Let's just hope no one decides to use thoughts to control a murderous robot instead.

**Monkey Using a Joystick to Control a Cursor** (a) The monkey with electrodes implanted in its motor cortex first learns to move a cursor on a computer screen with a joystick. The electrodes are connected to a device that records activity in the motor cortex cells produced when the monkey moves the cursor. After the monkey learns to control the cursor with the joystick, it is disconnected and the activity patterns in the monkey's motor cortex move the cursor to the target. (b) One of the tasks in which the monkey moves the cursor to the green target that appears at random on the screen.

Data acquisition box

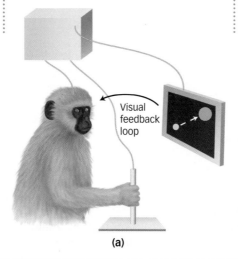

Visual feedback loop

(a)

(b)

The human brain weighs only 3 pounds and isn't much to look at, but its accomplishments are staggering.

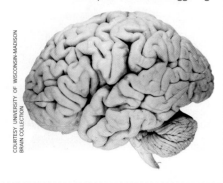

of course, that the neurons and glial cells that make up that lump are busy humming away, giving you consciousness, feelings, and potentially brilliant ideas. But to find out which neurons in which parts of the brain control which functions, scientists first had to divide and conquer: that is, find a way of describing the brain that allows researchers to communicate with one another.

There are several ways that neuroscientists divide up the brain. It can be helpful to talk about areas of the brain from "bottom to top," noting how the different regions are specialized for different kinds of tasks. In general, simpler functions are performed at the "lower levels" of the brain, whereas more complex functions are performed at successively "higher" levels (see **FIGURE 3.13**). As you'll see shortly, the brain can also be approached in a "side-by-side" fashion: although each side of the brain is roughly analogous, one half of the brain specializes in some tasks that the other half doesn't.

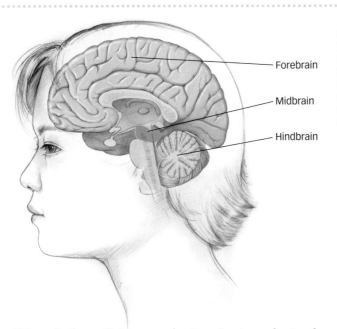

**Figure 3.13 The Major Divisions of the Brain** The brain can be organized into three parts, moving from the bottom to the top, from simpler functions to the more complex: the hindbrain, the midbrain, and the forebrain.

Forebrain

Midbrain

Hindbrain

**HINDBRAIN** An area of the brain that coordinates information coming into and out of the spinal cord.

**MEDULLA** An extension of the spinal cord into the skull that coordinates heart rate, circulation, and respiration.

**RETICULAR FORMATION** A brain structure that regulates sleep, wakefulness, and levels of arousal.

**CEREBELLUM** A large structure of the hindbrain that controls fine motor skills.

Although these divisions make it easier to understand areas of the brain and their functions, keep in mind that none of these structures or areas in the brain can act alone: They are all part of one big, interacting, interdependent whole.

Let's look first at the divisions of the brain and the responsibilities of each part, moving from the bottom to the top. Using this view, we can divide the brain into three parts: the hindbrain, the midbrain, and the forebrain (see Figure 3.13).

### The Hindbrain

If you follow the spinal cord from your tailbone to where it enters your skull, you'll find it difficult to determine where your spinal cord ends and your brain begins. That's because the spinal cord is continuous with the **hindbrain,** *an area of the brain that coordinates information coming into and out of the spinal cord.* The hindbrain is sometimes called the *brain stem*; indeed, it looks like a stalk on which the rest of the brain sits. The hindbrain controls the most basic functions of life: respiration, alertness, and motor skills. There are three anatomical structures that make up the hindbrain: the medulla, the cerebellum, and the pons (see **FIGURE 3.14**).

The **medulla** is *an extension of the spinal cord into the skull that coordinates heart rate, circulation, and respiration.* Inside the medulla is a small cluster of neurons called the **reticular formation,** which *regulates sleep, wakefulness, and levels of arousal.* Damage to this tiny area of the brain can produce dramatically large consequences for behavior. For example, in one early experiment, researchers stimulated the reticular formation of a sleeping cat. This caused the animal to awaken almost instantaneously and remain alert. Conversely, severing the connections between the reticular formation and the rest of the brain caused the animal to lapse into an irreversible coma (Moruzzi & Magoun, 1949). The reticular formation maintains the same delicate balance between alertness and unconsciousness in humans. In fact, many general anesthetics work by reducing activity in the reticular formation, rendering the patient unconscious.

Behind the medulla is the **cerebellum,** *a large structure of the hindbrain that controls fine motor skills. Cerebellum* is Latin for "little brain," and the structure does look like a small replica of the brain. The cerebellum orchestrates the proper sequence of movements when we ride a bike, play the piano, or maintain balance while walking and running. The cerebellum contains a layer of *Purkinje cells*, the elaborate, treelike neurons you read about earlier in the chapter. Purkinje cells are some of the largest neurons in the brain, and they are the sole output for motor coordination originating in the cerebellum and spreading to the rest of the brain.

Damage to the cerebellum produces impairments in coordination and balance, although not the paralysis or immobility you might think would be associated with a

**Figure 3.14 The Hindbrain** The hindbrain coordinates information coming into and out of the spinal cord and controls the basic functions of life. It includes the medulla, the reticular formation, the cerebellum, and the pons.

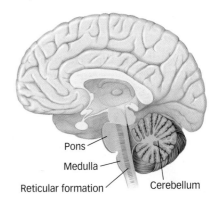

Pons

Medulla

Reticular formation

Cerebellum

**PONS** A brain structure that relays information from the cerebellum to the rest of the brain.

**TECTUM** A part of the midbrain that orients an organism in the environment.

**TEGMENTUM** A part of the midbrain that is involved in movement and arousal.

Olympic medalist Apolo Anton Ohno relies on his cerebellum to execute graceful, coordinated motions on the ice. The cerebellum, part of the hindbrain, helps direct the smooth action of a variety of motor behaviors.

motor control center. This highlights an important role for the cerebellum: It contributes to the "fine tuning" of behavior, smoothing our actions to allow their graceful execution rather than initiating the actions (Smetacek, 2002). The initiation of behavior involves other areas of the brain; as you'll recall, different brain systems interact and are interdependent with one another.

The last major area of the hindbrain is the **pons**, *a structure that relays information from the cerebellum to the rest of the brain*. *Pons* means "bridge" in Latin. Although the detailed functions of the pons remain poorly understood, it essentially acts as a "relay station" or bridge between the cerebellum and other structures in the brain.

### The Midbrain

Sitting on top of the hindbrain is the *midbrain*, which is relatively small in humans. As you can see in **FIGURE 3.15,** the midbrain contains two main structures: the tectum and the tegmentum. The **tectum** *orients an organism in the environment*. The tectum receives stimulus input from the eyes, ears, and skin and moves the organism in a coordinated way toward the stimulus. For example, when you're studying in a quiet room and you hear a *click* behind and to the right of you, your body will swivel and orient to the direction of the sound; this is your tectum in action.

The **tegmentum** is *involved in movement and arousal*; it also helps to orient an organism toward sensory stimuli. However, parts of the tegmentum are involved in pleasure seeking and motivation. It makes sense, then, that an abundance of dopamine-producing neurons is found in this midbrain structure. You'll recall that dopamine contributes to motor behavior, motivation, and pleasure; all are tasks that the tegmentum coordinates. What's more, another structure of the brain loaded with

**Figure 3.15 The Midbrain** The midbrain is important for orientation and movement. It includes structures such as the tectum and tegmentum.

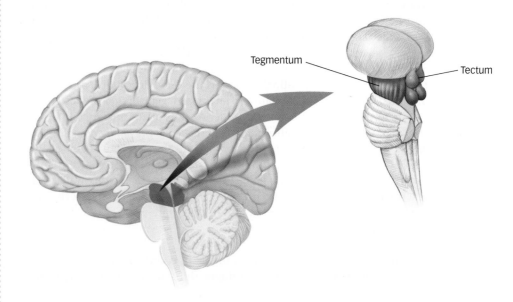

dopamine neurons, the *substantia nigra*, is found in this area. Serotonin, a neurotransmitter that contributes to mood and arousal, is also plentiful in the midbrain. The midbrain may be relatively small, but it is a central location of neurotransmitters involved in arousal, mood, and motivation and the brain structures that rely on them (White, 1996).

You could survive if you had only a hindbrain and a midbrain. The structures in the hindbrain would take care of all the bodily functions necessary to sustain life, and the structures in the midbrain would orient you toward or away from pleasurable or threatening stimuli in the environment. But this wouldn't be much of a life. To understand where the abilities that make us fully human come from, we need to consider the last division of the brain.

## The Forebrain

When you appreciate the beauty of a poem, detect the sarcasm in a friend's remark, plan to go skiing next winter, or notice the faint glimmer of sadness on a loved one's face, you are enlisting the forebrain. The *forebrain* is the highest level of the brain—literally and figuratively—and controls complex cognitive, emotional, sensory, and motor functions (see **FIGURE 3.16**). The forebrain itself is divided into two main sections: the cerebral cortex and the subcortical structures. The **cerebral cortex** is *the outermost layer of the brain, visible to the naked eye, and divided into two hemispheres*. We'll have much more to say about these cerebral hemispheres and the functions they serve in a little bit. First we'll examine the **subcortical structures**, *areas of the forebrain housed under the cerebral cortex near the very center of the brain*.

The subcortical structures are nestled deep inside the brain, where they are quite protected. If you imagine sticking an index finger in each of your ears and pushing inward until they touch, that's about where you'd find the thalamus, hypothalamus, pituitary gland, limbic system, and basal ganglia (see **FIGURE 3.17** on the next page). Each of these subcortical structures plays an important role in relaying information throughout the brain, as well as performing specific tasks that allow us to think, feel, and behave as humans.

The **thalamus** *relays and filters information from the senses and transmits the information to the cerebral cortex*. The thalamus receives inputs from all the major senses except smell, which has direct connections to the cerebral cortex. The thalamus acts as a kind of computer server in a networked system, taking in multiple inputs and relaying them to a variety of locations (Guillery & Sherman, 2002). However, unlike the mechanical operations of a computer—"send input A to location B"—the thalamus actively filters sensory information, giving more weight to some inputs and less weight to others. The thalamus also closes the pathways of incoming sensations during sleep, providing a valuable function in *not* allowing information to pass to the rest of the brain.

The **hypothalamus**, located below the thalamus (*hypo-* is Greek for "under"), *regulates body temperature, hunger, thirst, and sexual behavior*. Although the hypothalamus is a tiny area of the brain, clusters of neurons in the hypothalamus oversee a wide range of basic behaviors. For example, the hypothalamus makes sure that body temperature, blood sugar levels, and metabolism are kept within an optimal range for normal human functioning. Lesions to some areas of the hypothalamus result in overeating, whereas lesions to other areas leave an animal with no desire for food at all. Also, when you think about sex, messages from your cerebral cortex are sent to the hypothalamus to trigger the release of hormones. Finally, electric stimulation of the hypothalamus in cats can produce hissing and biting, whereas stimulation of other areas in the hypothalamus can produce what appears to be intense pleasure for an animal (Siegel, Roeling, Gregg, & Kruk, 1999). Researchers James Olds and Peter Milner found that a small electric current delivered to a certain region of a rat's hypothalamus was extremely rewarding for the animal (Olds & Milner, 1954). In fact, when allowed

**CEREBRAL CORTEX** The outermost layer of the brain, visible to the naked eye and divided into two hemispheres.

**SUBCORTICAL STRUCTURES** Areas of the forebrain housed under the cerebral cortex near the very center of the brain.

**THALAMUS** A subcortical structure that relays and filters information from the senses and transmits the information to the cerebral cortex.

**HYPOTHALAMUS** A subcortical structure that regulates body temperature, hunger, thirst, and sexual behavior.

**Figure 3.16 The Forebrain** The forebrain is the highest level of the brain and is critical for complex cognitive, emotional, sensory, and motor functions. The forebrain is divided into two parts: the cerebral cortex and the underlying subcortical structures. These include the thalamus, hypothalamus, pituitary gland, amygdala, and hippocampus. The corpus callosum connects the two hemispheres of the brain.

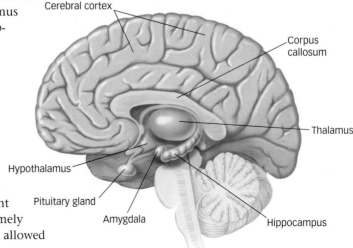

Cerebral cortex

Corpus callosum

Thalamus

Hypothalamus

Hippocampus

Pituitary gland

Amygdala

**PITUITARY GLAND** The "master gland" of the body's hormone-producing system, which releases hormones that direct the functions of many other glands in the body.

**LIMBIC SYSTEM** A group of forebrain structures including the hypothalamus, the amygdala, and the hippocampus, which are involved in motivation, emotion, learning, and memory.

**HIPPOCAMPUS** A structure critical for creating new memories and integrating them into a network of knowledge so that they can be stored indefinitely in other parts of the cerebral cortex.

**AMYGDALA** A part of the limbic system that plays a central role in many emotional processes, particularly the formation of emotional memories.

**BASAL GANGLIA** A set of subcortical structures that directs intentional movements.

Figure **3.17** **The Limbic System** The limbic system includes the hippocampus and the amygdala, as well as the hypothalamus. These structures are involved in motivation, emotion, learning, and memory.

Hypothalamus

Pituitary gland

Amygdala

Hippocampus

to press a bar attached to the electrode to initiate their own stimulation, rats would do so several thousand times an hour, often to the point of exhaustion! It's been suggested, then, that the hypothalamus is in charge of the "four Fs" of behavior: (1) fighting, (2) fleeing, (3) feeding, and (4) mating.

Located below the hypothalamus is the **pituitary gland**, *the "master gland" of the body's hormone-producing system, which releases hormones that direct the functions of many other glands in the body*. The hypothalamus sends hormonal signals to the pituitary gland, which in turn sends hormonal signals to other glands to control stress, digestive activities, and reproductive processes. For example, when a baby suckles its mother's breast, sensory neurons in her breast send signals to her hypothalamus, which then signals her pituitary gland to release a hormone called *oxytocin* into the bloodstream (McNeilly, Robinson, Houston, & Howie, 1983). Oxytocin, in turn, stimulates the release of milk from reservoirs in the breast. The pituitary gland is also involved in the response to stress. When we sense a threat, sensory neurons send signals to the hypothalamus, which stimulates the release of adrenocorticotropic hormone (ACTH) from the pituitary gland. ACTH, in turn, stimulates the adrenal glands (above the kidneys) to release hormones that activate the sympathetic nervous system (Selye & Fortier, 1950). As you read earlier in this chapter, the sympathetic nervous system prepares the body to either meet the threat head-on or flee from the situation.

The thalamus, hypothalamus, and pituitary gland, located in the center of the brain, make possible close interaction with several other brain structures: They receive information, process it, and send it back out again. The hypothalamus is part of the **limbic system**, *a group of forebrain structures including the hypothalamus, the amygdala, and the hippocampus, which are involved in motivation, emotion, learning, and memory* (Maclean, 1970; Papez, 1937). The limbic system is found in a bagel-shaped area around the hypothalamus, where the subcortical structures meet the cerebral cortex (see Figure 3.17). The two remaining structures of the limbic system are the hippocampus (from the Latin for "sea horse," due to its shape) and the amygdala (from the Latin for "almond," also due to its shape).

The **hippocampus** is *critical for creating new memories and integrating them into a network of knowledge so that they can be stored indefinitely in other parts of the cerebral cortex*. Patients with damage to the hippocampus can acquire new information and keep it in awareness for a few seconds, but as soon as they are distracted, they forget the information and the experience that produced it (Scoville & Milner, 1957). This kind of disruption is limited to everyday memory for facts and events that we can bring to consciousness; memory of learned habitual routines or emotional reactions remains intact (Squire, Knowlton, & Musen, 1993). As an example, people with damage to the hippocampus can remember how to drive and talk, but they cannot recall where they have recently driven or a conversation they have just had. You will read more about the hippocampus and its role in creating, storing, and combining memories in Chapter 5.

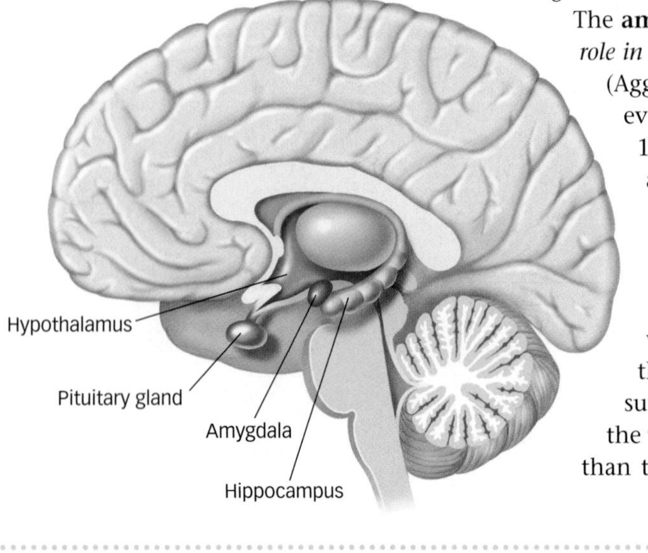

The **amygdala**, *located at the tip of each horn of the hippocampus, plays a central role in many emotional processes, particularly the formation of emotional memories* (Aggleton, 1992). The amygdala attaches significance to previously neutral events that are associated with fear, punishment, or reward (LeDoux, 1992). As an example, think of the last time something scary or unpleasant happened to you: A car came barreling toward you as you started walking into an intersection or a ferocious dog leapt out of an alley as you passed by. Those stimuli—a car or a dog—are fairly neutral; you don't have a panic attack every time you walk by a used car lot. The emotional significance attached to events involving those stimuli is the work of the amygdala. When we are in emotionally arousing situations, the amygdala stimulates the hippocampus to remember many details surrounding the situation (Kensinger & Schacter, 2005). For example, after the terrorist attacks of September 11, 2001, most people recalled much more than the fact that planes crashed into the World Trade Center in New York

City; the Pentagon in Washington, D.C.; and a field in western Pennsylvania. People who lived through the attacks remember vivid details about where they were, what they were doing, and how they felt when they heard the news, even years later. In particular, the amygdala seems to be especially involved in encoding events as *fearful* (Adolphs et al., 1995). We'll have more to say about the amygdala's role in emotion and motivated behavior in Chapter 10. For now, keep in mind that a group of neurons the size of a lima bean buried deep in your brain help you to laugh, weep, or shriek in fright when the circumstances call for it.

There are several other structures in the subcortical area, but we'll consider just one more. The **basal ganglia** are *a set of subcortical structures that directs intentional movements*. The basal ganglia are located near the thalamus and hypothalamus; they receive input from the cerebral cortex and send outputs to the motor centers in the brain stem (see **FIGURE 3.18**). One part of the basal ganglia, the *striatum*, is involved in the control of posture and movement. Patients who suffer from Parkinson's disease typically show symptoms of uncontrollable shaking and sudden jerks of the limbs and are unable to initiate a sequence of movements to achieve a specific goal. This happens because the dopamine-producing neurons in the substantia nigra (found in the tegmentum of the midbrain) have become damaged (Dauer & Przedborski, 2003). The undersupply of dopamine then affects the striatum in the basal ganglia, which in turn leads to the visible behavioral symptoms of Parkinson's.

So, what's the problem in Parkinson's—the jerky movements, the ineffectiveness of the striatum in directing behavior, the botched interplay of the substantia nigra and the striatum, or the underproduction of dopamine at the neuronal level? The answer is "all of the above." This unfortunate disease provides a nice illustration of two themes regarding the brain and behavior. First, invisible actions at the level of neurons in the brain can produce substantial effects at the level of behavior. Second, the interaction of hindbrain, midbrain, and forebrain structures shows how the various regions are interdependent.

## The Cerebral Cortex

Our tour of the brain has taken us from the very small (neurons) to the somewhat bigger (major divisions of the brain) to the very large: the cerebral cortex. The cortex is the highest level of the brain, and it is responsible for the most complex aspects of perception, emotion, movement, and thought (Fuster, 2003). It sits over the rest of the brain, like a mushroom cap shielding the underside and stem, and it is the wrinkled surface you see when looking at the brain with the naked eye.

The smooth surfaces of the cortex—the raised part—are called *gyri* (*gyrus* if you're talking about just one), and the indentations or fissures are called *sulci* (*sulcus* when singular). Sulci and gyri represent a triumph of evolution. The cerebral cortex occupies about 2,500 cubic centimeters of space, or roughly the area of a newspaper page. Fitting that much cortex into a human skull is a tough task. But if you crumple a sheet of newspaper, you'll see that the same surface area now fits compactly into a much smaller space. The cortex, with its wrinkles and folds, holds a lot of brainpower in a relatively small package that fits comfortably inside the human skull (see **FIGURE 3.19**).

The functions of the cerebral cortex can be understood at three levels: the separation of the cortex into two hemispheres, the functions of each hemisphere, and the role of specific cortical areas. The first level of organization divides the cortex into the left and right hemispheres. The two hemispheres are more or less symmetrical in their appearance and, to some extent, in their functions. However, each hemisphere controls the functions of the opposite side of the body. This is called *contralateral control*, meaning that your right cerebral hemisphere perceives stimuli from and controls movements on the left side of your body, whereas your left cerebral hemisphere perceives stimuli from and controls movement on the right side of your body (see **FIGURE 3.20** on the next page).

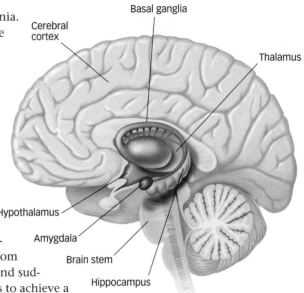

**Figure 3.18** **The Basal Ganglia** The basal ganglia are a group of subcortical brain structures that direct intentional movement. They receive input from the cerebral cortex and send output to the motor centers in the brain stem.

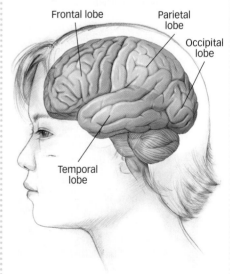

**Figure 3.19** **Cerebral Cortex and Lobes** The four major lobes of the cerebral cortex are the occipital lobe, the parietal lobe, the temporal lobe, and the frontal lobe.

**CORPUS CALLOSUM** A thick band of nerve fibers that connects large areas of the cerebral cortex on each side of the brain and supports communication of information across the hemispheres.

**OCCIPITAL LOBE** A region of the cerebral cortex that processes visual information.

**PARIETAL LOBE** A region of the cerebral cortex whose functions include processing information about touch.

**Figure 3.20** **Cerebral Hemispheres** Top view of the brain with part of the right cerebral hemisphere pulled away to expose the corpus callosum.

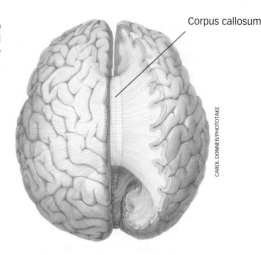

Corpus callosum

CAROL DONNER/PHOTOTAKE

The cerebral hemispheres are connected to each other by *commissures*, bundles of axons that make possible communication between parallel areas of the cortex in each half. The largest of these commissures is the **corpus callosum**, which *connects large areas of the cerebral cortex on each side of the brain and supports communication of information across the hemispheres*. This means that information received in the right hemisphere, for example, can pass across the corpus callosum and be registered, virtually instantaneously, in the left hemisphere.

The second level of organization in the cerebral cortex distinguishes the functions of the different regions within each hemisphere of the brain. Each hemisphere of the cerebral cortex is divided into four areas or *lobes*: From back to front, these are the occipital lobe, the parietal lobe, the temporal lobe, and the frontal lobe, as shown in Figure 3.19. We'll examine the functions of these lobes in more detail later, noting how scientists have used a variety of techniques to understand the operations of the brain. For now, here's a brief overview of the main functions of each lobe.

The **occipital lobe,** located at the back of the cerebral cortex, *processes visual information.* Sensory receptors in the eyes send information to the thalamus, which in turn sends information to the primary areas of the occipital lobe, where simple features of the stimulus are extracted. These features are then processed into a more complex "map" of the stimulus onto the occipital cortex, leading to comprehension of what's being seen. As you might imagine, damage to the primary visual areas of the occipital lobe can leave a person with partial or complete blindness. Information still enters the eyes, which work just fine. But without the ability to process and make sense of the information at the level of the cerebral cortex, the information is as good as lost (Zeki, 2001).

The **parietal lobe,** located in front of the occipital lobe, carries out functions that include *processing information about touch.* The parietal lobe contains the *somatosensory cortex,* a strip of brain tissue running from the top of the brain down to the sides (see **FIGURE 3.21**). Within each hemisphere, the somatosensory cortex represents the skin areas on the contralateral surface of the body. Each part of the somatosensory cortex maps onto a particular part of the body. If a body area is more sensitive, a larger part of the somatosensory cortex is devoted to it. For example, the part of the somatosensory cortex that corresponds to the lips and tongue is larger than the area corresponding to the feet. The somatosensory cortex can be illustrated as a distorted figure, called a *homunculus* ("little man"), in which the body parts are rendered according to how much of the somatosensory cortex is devoted to them (Penfield & Rasmussen, 1950).

Directly in front of the somatosensory cortex, in the frontal lobe, is a parallel strip of brain tissue called the *motor cortex.* Like the somatosensory cortex, different parts of the motor cortex correspond to different body parts. The motor cortex initiates voluntary movements and sends messages to the basal ganglia, cerebellum, and spinal cord. The motor and somatosensory cortices, then, are like sending and receiving areas of the cerebral cortex, taking in information and sending out commands as the case might be.

The homunculus is a rendering of the body in which each part is shown in proportion to how much of the somatosensory cortex is devoted to it.

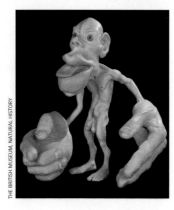

THE BRITISH MUSEUM, NATURAL HISTORY

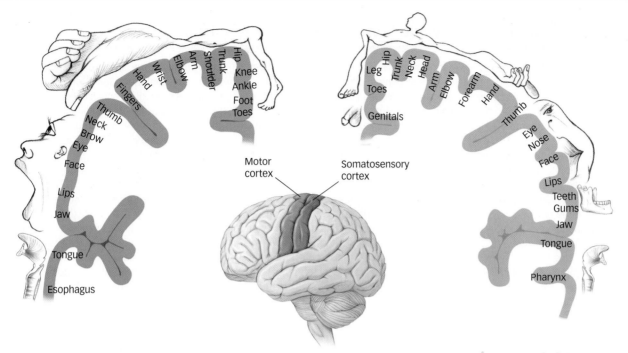

Motor cortex

Somatosensory cortex

The **temporal lobe**, located on the lower side of each hemisphere, is *responsible for hearing and language*. The *primary auditory cortex* in the temporal lobe is analogous to the somatosensory cortex in the parietal lobe and the primary visual areas of the occipital lobe—it receives sensory information from the ears based on the frequencies of sounds. Secondary areas of the temporal lobe then process the information into meaningful units, such as speech and words. The temporal lobe also houses the visual association areas that interpret the meaning of visual stimuli and help us recognize common objects in the environment (Martin, 2007).

The **frontal lobe**, which sits behind the forehead, has *specialized areas for movement, abstract thinking, planning, memory, and judgment*. As you just read, it contains the motor cortex, which coordinates movements of muscle groups throughout the body. Other areas in the frontal lobe coordinate thought processes that help us manipulate information and retrieve memories, which we can use to plan our behaviors and interact socially with others. In short, the frontal cortex allows us to do the kind of thinking, imagining, planning, and anticipating that sets humans apart from most other species (Stuss & Benson, 1986).

The third level of organization in the cerebral cortex involves the representation of information within specific lobes in the cortex. There is a hierarchy of processing stages from primary areas that handle fine details of information all the way up to **association areas**, which are *composed of neurons that help provide sense and meaning to information registered in the cortex*. For example, neurons in the primary visual cortex are highly specialized—some detect features of the environment that are in a horizontal orientation, others detect movement, and still others process information about human versus nonhuman forms. The association areas of the occipital lobe interpret the information extracted by these primary areas—shape, motion, and so on—to make sense of what's being perceived; in this case, perhaps a large cat leaping toward your face. Similarly, neurons in the primary auditory cortex register sound frequencies, but it's the association areas of the temporal lobe that allow you to turn those noises into the meaning of your friend screaming, "Look out for the cat!!" Association areas, then, help stitch together the threads of information in the various parts of the cortex to produce a meaningful understanding of what's being registered in the brain. Neurons in the association areas are usually less specialized and more flexible than neurons in the primary areas. As such, they can be shaped by learning and experience to do their job more effectively. This kind of shaping of neurons by environmental forces allows the brain flexibility, or "plasticity," our next topic.

**Figure 3.21** **Somatosensory and Motor Cortices** The motor cortex, a strip of brain tissue in the frontal lobe, represents and controls different skin and body areas on the contralateral side of the body. Directly behind the motor cortex, in the parietal lobe, lies the somatosensory cortex. Like the motor cortex, the somatosensory cortex represents skin areas of particular parts on the contralateral side of the body.

**TEMPORAL LOBE** A region of the cerebral cortex responsible for hearing and language.

**FRONTAL LOBE** A region of the cerebral cortex that has specialized areas for movement, abstract thinking, planning, memory, and judgment.

**ASSOCIATION AREAS** Areas of the cerebral cortex that are composed of neurons that help provide sense and meaning to information registered in the cortex.

## { THE REAL WORLD } Brain Plasticity and Sensations in Phantom Limbs

LONG AFTER A LIMB IS AMPUTATED, MANY patients continue to experience sensations where the missing limb would be, a phenomenon called *phantom limb syndrome*. Patients can feel their missing limbs moving, even in coordinated gestures such as shaking hands. Some even report feeling pain in their phantom limbs. Why does this happen? Some evidence suggests that phantom limb syndrome may arise in part because of plasticity in the brain.

Researchers stimulated the skin surface in various regions around the face, torso, and arms while monitoring brain activity in amputees and non-amputated volunteers (Ramachandran & Blakeslee, 1998; Ramachandran, Rodgers-Ramachandran, & Stewart, 1992). Brain-imaging techniques displayed the somatosensory cortical areas activated when the skin was stimulated. This allowed the researchers to map how touch is represented in the somatosensory cortex for different areas of the body. For example, when the face was touched, the researchers could determine which areas in the somatosensory cortex were most active; when the torso was stimulated, they could see which areas responded; and so on.

Brain scans of the amputees revealed that stimulating areas of the face and upper arm activated an area in the somatosensory cortex that previously would have been activated by a now-missing hand. The face and arm were represented in the somatosensory

cortex in an area adjacent to where the person's hand—now amputated—would have been represented. Stimulating the face or arm produced phantom limb sensations in the amputees; they reported "feeling" a sensation in their missing limbs.

Brain plasticity can explain these results (Pascual-Leone et al., 2005). The cortical representations for the face and the upper arm normally lie on either side of the representation for the hand. The somatosensory areas for the face and upper arm were larger in amputees and had taken over the part of the cortex normally representing the hand. Indeed, the new face and arm representations were now contiguous with each

other, filling in the space occupied by the hand representation. Some of these new mappings were quite concise. For example, in some amputees, when specific areas of the facial skin were activated, the patient reported sensations in just *one finger* of the phantom hand!

This and related research suggest one explanation for a previously poorly understood phenomenon. How can a person "feel" something that isn't there? Brain plasticity, an adaptive process through which the brain reorganizes itself, offers an answer (Flor, Nikolajsen, & Jensen, 2006). The brain established new mappings that led to novel sensations.

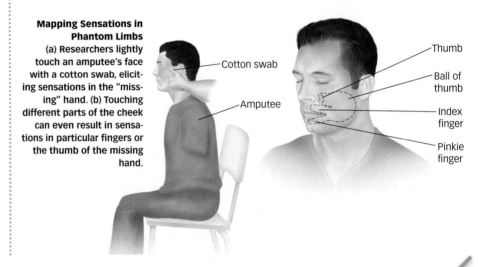

**Mapping Sensations in Phantom Limbs**
**(a)** Researchers lightly touch an amputee's face with a cotton swab, eliciting sensations in the "missing" hand. **(b)** Touching different parts of the cheek can even result in sensations in particular fingers or the thumb of the missing hand.

Cotton swab

Amputee

Thumb

Ball of thumb

Index finger

Pinkie finger

### Brain Plasticity

The cerebral cortex may seem like a fixed structure, one big sheet of neurons designed to help us make sense of our external world. Remarkably, though, sensory cortices are not fixed. They can adapt to changes in sensory inputs, a quality researchers call *plasticity* (i.e., "the ability to be molded"). As an example, if you lose your middle finger in an accident, the part of the somatosensory area that represents that finger is initially unresponsive (Kaas, 1991). After all, there's no longer any sensory input going from that location to that part of the brain. You might expect the "left middle finger neurons" of the somatosensory cortex to wither away. However, over time, that area in the somatosensory cortex becomes responsive to stimulation of the fingers *adjacent* to the missing finger. The brain is plastic: Functions that were assigned to certain areas of the brain may be capable of being reassigned to other areas of the brain to accommodate changing input from the environment. This suggests that sensory inputs "compete" for representation in each cortical area. (See the Real World box for a striking illustration of "phantom limbs.")

Plasticity doesn't only occur to compensate for missing digits or limbs, however. An extraordinary amount of stimulation of one finger can result in that finger "taking over" the representation of the part of the cortex that usually represents other, adjacent fingers (Merzenich, Recanzone, Jenkins, & Grajski, 1990). For example, concert pianists have highly developed cortical areas for finger control: The continued input from the fingers commands a larger area of representation in the somatosensory cortices in the brain. Similar findings have been obtained with quilters (who may have highly developed areas for the thumb and forefinger, which are critical to their profession) and taxi drivers (who have overdeveloped brain areas in the hippocampus that are used during spatial navigation; Maguire, Woollett, & Spiers, 2006).

---

**In summary,** neurons make up nerves, which in turn form the human nervous system. The nervous system is divided into the peripheral and the central nervous system. The peripheral nervous system connects the central nervous system with the rest of the body, and it is itself divided into the somatic nervous system and the autonomic nervous system. The somatic nervous system, which conveys information into and out of the central nervous system, controls voluntary muscles, whereas the autonomic nervous system automatically controls the body's organs. The autonomic nervous system is further divided into the sympathetic and parasympathetic nervous systems, which complement each other in their effects on the body. The sympathetic nervous system prepares the body for action in threatening situations, and the parasympathetic nervous system returns it to its normal state.

The central nervous system is composed of the spinal cord and the brain. The spinal cord can mediate some basic behaviors such as spinal reflexes without input from the brain. The brain can be divided into the hindbrain, midbrain, and forebrain. The hindbrain generally coordinates information coming into and out of the spinal cord with structures such as the medulla, the reticular formation, the cerebellum, and the pons. These structures respectively coordinate breathing and heart rate, regulate sleep and arousal levels, coordinate fine motor skills, and communicate this information to the cortex. The midbrain, with the help of structures such as the tectum and tegmentum, generally coordinates functions such as orientation to the environment and movement and arousal toward sensory stimuli. The forebrain generally coordinates higher-level functions, such as perceiving, feeling, and thinking. The forebrain houses subcortical structures, such as the thalamus, hypothalamus, limbic system (including the hippocampus and amygdala), and basal ganglia; all these structures perform a variety of functions related to motivation and emotion. The cerebral cortex, composed of two hemispheres with four lobes each (occipital, parietal, temporal, and frontal) performs tasks that help make us fully human: thinking, planning, judging, perceiving, and behaving purposefully and voluntarily. Finally, neurons in the brain can be shaped by experience and the environment, making the human brain amazingly plastic. ■ ■

## The Development and Evolution of Nervous Systems

Other ways to understand the organization of the nervous system are to consider its development in the uterus and its evolution over time. The first approach reveals how the nervous system develops and changes within each member of a species, whereas the second approach reveals how the nervous system in humans evolved and adapted from other species. Both approaches help us understand how the human brain came to be the way it is, which is surprisingly imperfect. Far from being a single, elegant machine—the enchanted loom the philosophers wrote so poetically about—the human brain is instead a system composed of many distinct components that have been added at different times during the course of evolution. The human species has retained what worked best in earlier versions of the brain, then added bits and pieces to get us to our present state through evolution. We'll look at that process after we first consider how an individual nervous system develops.

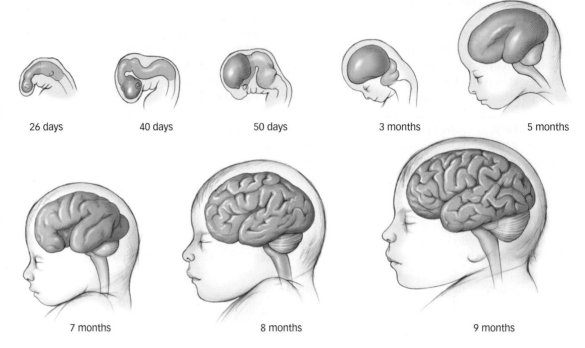

**Figure 3.22 Prenatal Brain Development** The more primitive parts of the brain, the hindbrain and midbrain, develop first, followed by successively higher levels. The cerebral cortex with its characteristic fissures doesn't develop until the middle of the pregnancy. The cerebral hemispheres undergo most of their development in the final trimester.

26 days   40 days   50 days   3 months   5 months

7 months   8 months   9 months

## Prenatal Development of the Central Nervous System

The nervous system is the first major bodily system to take form in an embryo (Moore, 1977). It begins to develop within the third week after fertilization, when the embryo is still in the shape of a sphere. Initially, a ridge forms on one side of the sphere and then builds up at its edges to become a deep groove. The ridges fold together and fuse to enclose the groove, forming a structure called the *neural tube*. The tail end of the neural tube will remain a tube, and as the embryo grows larger, it forms the basis of the spinal cord. The tube expands at the opposite end, so that by the fourth week the three basic levels of the brain are visible; during the fifth week, the forebrain and hindbrain further differentiate into subdivisions. During the seventh week and later, the forebrain expands considerably to form the cerebral hemispheres.

As the embryonic brain continues to grow, each subdivision folds onto the next one and begins to form the structures easily visible in the adult brain (see **FIGURE 3.22**): The hindbrain forms the cerebellum and medulla, the midbrain forms the tectum and the tegmentum, and the forebrain subdivides further, separating the thalamus and hypothalamus from the cerebral hemispheres. Over time, the cerebral hemispheres undergo the greatest development, ultimately covering almost all the other subdivisions of the brain.

The *ontogeny* of the brain—how it develops within a given individual—is pretty remarkable. In about half the time it takes you to complete a 15-week semester, the basic structures of the brain are in place and rapidly developing, eventually allowing a newborn to enter the world with a fairly sophisticated set of abilities. In comparison, the *phylogeny* of the brain—how it developed within a particular species—is a much slower process. However, it too has allowed humans to make the most of the available brain structures, enabling us to perform an incredible array of tasks.

## Evolutionary Development of the Central Nervous System

The central nervous system evolved from the very simple one found in simple animals to the elaborate nervous system in humans today. Even the simplest animals have sensory neurons and motor neurons for responding to the environment (Shepherd,

1988). For example, single-celled protozoa have molecules in their cell membrane that are sensitive to food in the water. These molecules trigger the movement of tiny threads called *cilia*, which help propel the protozoa toward the food source. The first neurons appeared in simple invertebrates, such as jellyfish; the sensory neurons in the jellyfish's tentacles can feel the touch of a potentially dangerous predator, which prompts the jellyfish to swim to safety. If you're a jellyfish, this simple neural system is sufficient to keep you alive.

The first central nervous system worthy of the name, though, appeared in flatworms. The flatworm has a collection of neurons in the head—a simple kind of brain—that includes sensory neurons for vision and taste and motor neurons that control feeding behavior. Emerging from the brain are a pair of tracts that form a spinal cord. They are connected by *commissures*, neural fibers that cross between the left and right side of the nervous system to allow communication between neurons at symmetrical positions on either side of the body. The tracts are also connected by smaller collections of neurons called *ganglia*, which integrate information and coordinate motor behavior in the body region near each ganglion.

During the course of evolution, a major split in the organization of the nervous system occurred between invertebrate animals (those without a spinal column) and vertebrate animals (those with a spinal column). The central nervous system of invertebrates continued along the "flatworm plan," but the nervous system in vertebrates changed dramatically.

In all vertebrates, the central nervous system is a single tubular structure, and the brain is a series of expansions of the tube that forms in the embryo. Also, the central nervous system in vertebrates separates sensory and motor processing. Sensory processing occurs mainly in the back of the brain and spinal cord, whereas motor coordination is controlled by the front of the brain and spinal cord, although as you have already seen, there is considerable communication between the sensory and motor areas. Furthermore, the central nervous system is organized into a hierarchy: The lower levels of the brain and spinal cord execute simpler functions, while the higher levels of the nervous system perform more complex functions. As you saw earlier, in humans, reflexes are accomplished in the spinal cord. At the next level, the midbrain executes the more complex task of orienting toward an important stimulus in the environment. Finally, a more complex task, such as imagining what your life will be like 20 years from now, is performed in the forebrain (Addis, Wong, & Schacter, 2007; Szpunar, Watson, & McDermott, 2007).

The forebrain undergoes further evolutionary advances in vertebrates. In lower vertebrate species such as amphibians (frogs and newts), the forebrain consists only of small clusters of neurons at the end of the neural tube. In higher vertebrates, including reptiles, birds, and mammals, the forebrain is much larger, and it evolves in two different patterns. In reptiles and birds, large groups of neurons develop along the inside edge of the neural tube and form the striatum, which controls their most complex behaviors. The neurons on the outside edge of the neural tube develop into paperlike layers that form the cerebral cortex, which is quite small and thin compared to the striatum. Birds, in particular, have almost no cerebral cortex, but their striatum is developed enough to control complex behavioral patterns, including learning, song production, social behavior, and reproductive behavior (Farries, 2004). The striatum is also fairly well developed in mammals, but even more impressive is the cerebral cortex, which develops multiple areas that serve a broad range of higher mental functions. This forebrain development has reached its peak—so far—in humans.

The human brain, then, is not so much one remarkable thing; rather, it is a succession of extensions from a quite serviceable foundation. Like other species, humans have a hindbrain, and like those species, it performs important tasks to keep us alive. For some species, that's sufficient. All flatworms need to do to ensure their species survival is eat, reproduce, and stay alive a reasonable length of time. But as the human brain

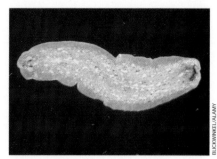

Flatworms don't have much of a brain, but then again, they don't need much of a brain. The rudimentary brain areas found in simple invertebrates eventually evolved into the complex brain structures found in humans.

*"You're making more at this firm than anyone else whose brain is the size of a walnut."*

**GENE** The unit of hereditary transmission.

**CHROMOSOMES** Strands of DNA wound around each other in a double-helix configuration.

evolved, structures in the midbrain and forebrain developed to handle the increasingly complex demands of the environment. The forebrain of a bullfrog is about as differentiated as it needs to be to survive in a frog's world. The human forebrain, however, shows substantial refinement, which allows for some remarkable, uniquely human abilities: self-awareness, sophisticated language use, social interaction, abstract reasoning, imagining, and empathy, among others.

There is intriguing evidence that the human brain evolved more quickly than the brains of other species (Dorus et al., 2004). Researchers compared the sequences of 200 brain-related genes in mice, rats, monkeys, and humans and discovered a collection of genes that evolved more rapidly among primates. What's more, they found that this evolutionary process was more rapid along the lineage that led to humans. That is, primate brains evolved quickly compared to those of other species, but the brains of the primates who eventually became humans evolved even more rapidly. These results suggest that in addition to the normal adaptations that occur over the process of evolution, the genes for human brains took particular advantage of a variety of mutations (changes in a gene's DNA) along the evolutionary pathway. These results also suggest that the human brain is still evolving—becoming bigger and more adapted to the demands of the environment (Evans et al., 2005; Mekel-Bobrov et al., 2005).

Genes may direct the development of the brain on a large, evolutionary scale, but they also guide the development of an individual and, generally, the development of a species. Let's take a brief look at how genes and the environment contribute to the biological bases of behavior.

## Genes and the Environment

You may have heard the phrase "nature vs. nurture," as though these twin influences grapple with each other for supremacy in directing a person's behavior. This suggests that either genetics ("nature") or the environment ("nurture") played a major role in producing particular behaviors, personality traits, psychological disorders, or pretty much any other thing that a human does. The emerging picture from current research is that both nature *and* nurture play a role in directing behavior, and the focus has shifted to examining the relative contributions of each influence rather than the absolute contributions of either influence alone. In short, it's the interaction of genes and environmental influences that determines what humans do (Gottesman & Hanson, 2005; Rutter & Silberg, 2002).

A **gene** is *the unit of hereditary transmission*. Genes are built from strands of DNA (deoxyribonucleic acid) and are organized into large threads called **chromosomes**, which are *strands of DNA wound around each other in a double-helix configuration* (see **FIGURE 3.23**). Chromosomes come in pairs, and humans have 23 pairs each. These pairs of chromosomes are similar but not identical: You inherit one of each pair from your father and one from your mother. There's a twist, however: The selection of *which* of each pair is given to you is random.

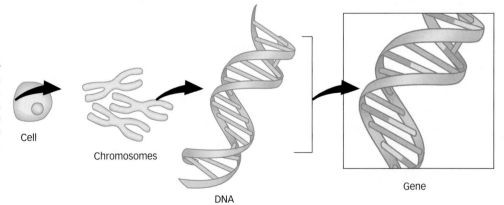

**Figure 3.23 Genes, Chromosomes, and Their Recombination** The cell nucleus houses chromosomes, which are made up of double-helix strands of DNA. Every cell in our bodies has 23 pairs of chromosomes. Genes are segments on a strand of DNA with codes that make us who we are.

Cell

Chromosomes

DNA

Gene

Perhaps the most striking example of this random distribution is the determination of sex. The chromosomes that determine sex are the X and Y chromosomes; females have two X chromosomes, whereas males have one X and one Y chromosome. You inherited an X chromosome from your mother since she has only X chromosomes to give. Your biological sex, therefore, was determined by whether you received an additional X chromosome or a Y chromosome from your father.

There is considerable variability in the genes that individual offspring receive. Nonetheless, children share a higher proportion of their genes with their parents than with more distant relatives or with nonrelatives. Children share half their genes with each parent, a quarter of their genes with their grandparents, an eighth of their genes with cousins, and so on. The probability of sharing genes is called *degree of relatedness*. The most genetically related people are *monozygotic twins* (also called *identical twins*), who develop from the splitting of a single fertilized egg and therefore share 100% of their genes. *Dizygotic twins* (*fraternal twins*) develop from two separate fertilized eggs and share 50% of their genes, the same as any two siblings born separately.

Many researchers have tried to determine the relative influence of genetics on behavior. One way to do this is to compare a trait shown by monozygotic twins with that same trait among dizygotic twins. This type of research usually enlists twins who were raised in the same household, so that the impact of their environment—their socioeconomic status, access to education, parental child-rearing practices, environmental stressors—remains relatively constant. Finding that monozygotic twins have a higher prevalence of a specific trait suggests a genetic influence (Boomsma, Busjahn, & Peltonen, 2002).

As an example, the likelihood that the dizygotic twin of a person who has schizophrenia (a mental disorder we'll discuss in greater detail in Chapter 13) will *also* develop schizophrenia is 27%. However, this statistic rises to 50% for monozygotic twins. This observation suggests a substantial genetic influence on the likelihood of developing schizophrenia. Monozygotic twins share 100% of their genes, and if one assumes environmental influences are relatively consistent for both members of the twin pair, the 50% likelihood can be traced to genetic factors. That sounds scarily high . . . until you realize that the remaining 50% probability must be due to environmental influences. In short, genetics can contribute to the development, likelihood, or onset of a variety of traits. But a more complete picture of genetic influences on behavior must always take the environmental context into consideration. Genes express themselves within an environment, not in isolation.

Genes set the range of possibilities that can be observed in a population, but the characteristics of any individual within that range are determined by environmental factors and experience. Genetically, it's possible for humans to live comfortably 12,000 feet above sea level. The residents of La Paz, Bolivia, have done so for centuries. But chances are *you* wouldn't enjoy gasping for breath on a daily basis. Your environmental

Monozygotic twins (left) share 100% of their genes in common, while dizygotic twins (right) share 50% of their genes, the same as other siblings. Studies of monozygotic and dizygotic twins help researchers estimate the relative contributions of genes and environmental influences on behavior.

*"The title of my science project is 'My Little Brother: Nature or Nurture.'"*

experiences have made it unlikely for you to live that way, just as the experience and environment of the citizens of La Paz have made living at high altitude quite acceptable. Genetically, you and the Bolivians come from the same species, but the range of genetic capabilities you share is not expressed in the same way. What's more, neither you nor a Bolivian can breathe underwater in Lake Titicaca, which is also 12,000 feet above sea level. The genetic capabilities that another species might enjoy, such as breathing underwater, are outside the range of *your* possibilities, no matter how much you might desire them.

With these parameters in mind, behavioral geneticists use calculations based on relatedness to compute the heritability of behaviors (Plomin et al., 2001). **Heritability** is *a measure of the variability of behavioral traits among individuals that can be accounted for by genetic factors.* Heritability is calculated as a proportion, and its numerical value (index) ranges from 0 to 1.00. A heritability of 0 means that genes do not contribute to individual differences in the behavioral trait; a heritability of 1.00 means that genes are the *only* reason for the individual differences. As you might guess, scores of 0 or 1.00 occur so infrequently that they serve more as theoretical limits than realistic values; almost nothing in human behavior is completely due to the environment or owed *completely* to genetic inheritance. Scores between 0 and 1.00, then, indicate that individual differences are caused by varying degrees of genetic and environmental contributions—a little stronger influence of genetics here, a little stronger influence of the environment there, but each always within the context of the other.

For human behavior, almost all estimates of heritability are in the moderate range, between .30 and .60. For example, a heritability index of .50 for intelligence indicates that half of the variability in intelligence test scores is attributable to genetic influences and the remaining half is due to environmental influences. Smart parents often (but not always) produce smart children; genetics certainly plays a role. But smart and not-so-smart children attend good or not-so-good schools, practice their piano lessons with more or less regularity, study or not study as hard as they might, have good and not-so-good teachers and role models, and so on. Genetics is only half the story in intelligence. Environmental influences also play a significant role in predicting the basis of intelligence (see Chapter 9).

Heritability has proven to be a theoretically useful and statistically sound concept in helping scientists understand the relative genetic and environmental influences on behavior. However, there are four important points about heritability to bear in mind.

First, remember that *heritability is an abstract concept*: It tells us nothing about the *specific* genes that contribute to a trait. A heritability index of .40 gives us a reasonable approximation of the extent to which genes influence a behavior, but it says nothing about *which* genes are responsible. Flipping that around also illustrates the point. Heritability of .40 means that there's also an "environmentality" of .60 in predicting the behavior in question. Most people would find it extremely difficult, however, to pinpoint what *one exact factor* in the environment contributed to that estimate. With further decoding of the human genome and a greater understanding of each gene's specific roles, scientists someday may be able to isolate the exact genes that contribute to a specific behavior, but they have not yet attained that degree of precision.

Second, *heritability is a population concept*: It tells us nothing about an individual. For example, a .50 heritability of intelligence means that, on average, about 50% of the differences in intellectual performance are attributable to genetic differences among individuals in the population. It does *not* mean that 50% of any given person's intelligence is due to her or his genetic makeup. Heritability provides guidance for understanding differences across individuals in a population rather than abilities within an individual.

Third, *heritability is dependent on the environment*. Just as behavior occurs within certain contexts, so do genetic influences. For example, intelligence isn't an unchanging quality: People are intelligent within a particular learning context, a social setting, a

**HERITABILITY** A measure of the variability of behavioral traits among individuals that can be accounted for by genetic factors.

family environment, a socioeconomic class, and so on. Heritability, therefore, is meaningful only for the environmental conditions in which it was computed, and heritability estimates may change dramatically under other environmental conditions. At present, heritability estimates for intelligence, to stick with our example, are computed across a range of environments and have a fair amount of stability. But if all the earth's population suddenly had access to better nutrition, higher-quality schooling, and good health care, that change in the environmental context would necessitate a recalculation of heritability within those contexts.

Finally, *heritability is not fate*. It tells us nothing about the degree to which interventions can change a behavioral trait. Heritability is useful for identifying behavioral traits that are influenced by genes, but it is not useful for determining how individuals will respond to particular environmental conditions or treatments.

---

**In summary,** examining the development of the nervous system over the life span of an individual—its ontogeny—and across the time within which a species evolves—its phylogeny—presents further opportunities for understanding the human brain. The nervous system is the first system that forms in an embryo, starting as a neural tube, which forms the basis of the spinal cord. The neural tube expands on one end to form the hindbrain, midbrain, and forebrain, each of which folds onto the next structure. Within each of these areas, specific brain structures begin to differentiate. The forebrain shows the greatest differentiation, and in particular, the cerebral cortex is the most developed in humans.

Nervous systems evolved from simple collections of sensory and motor neurons in simple animals, such as flatworms, to elaborate centralized nervous systems found in mammals. The evolution of the human nervous system can be thought of as a process of refining, elaborating, and expanding structures present in other species. In reptiles and birds, the highest processing area is the striatum; in mammals, the highest processing area is the cerebral cortex. The human brain appears to have evolved more quickly compared to other species to become adapted to a more complex environment.

The gene, or the unit of hereditary transmission, is built from strands of DNA in a double-helix formation that is organized into chromosomes. Humans have 23 pairs of chromosomes—half come from each parent. A child shares 50% of his or her genes with each parent. Monozygotic twins share 100% of their genes, while dizygotic twins share 50%, the same as any other siblings. Because of their genetic relatedness, twins are often participants in genetic research.

The study of genetics indicates that both genes and the environment work together to influence behavior. Genes set the range of variation in populations within a given environment, but they do not predict individual characteristics; experience and other environmental factors play a crucial role as well. ■ ■

---

# Investigating the Brain

So far, you've read a great deal about the nervous system: how it's organized, how it works, what its components are, and what those components do. But one question remains largely unanswered—*how* do we know all of this? Anatomists can dissect a human brain and identify its structures, but they cannot determine which structures play a role in producing which behaviors by dissecting a nonliving brain. In this section, we'll look at some of the methods psychologists and neuroscientists have developed for linking brain structures with the thoughts, feelings, and behaviors they direct.

Scientists use a variety of methods to understand how the brain affects behavior. Let's consider three of the main ones: testing people with brain damage and observing their deficits, studying electrical activity in the brain during behavior, and conducting brain scans while people perform various tasks. Studying people with

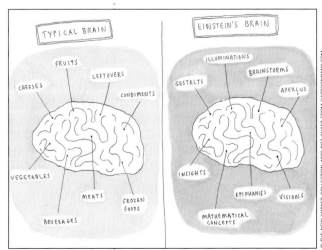

brain damage highlights one of the central themes of this book: To better understand the normal operation of a process, it is instructive to understand what happens when that process fails. Observing the behavioral mindbugs that result from damage to certain areas of the brain enables researchers to identify the functions of those areas. The second approach, studying the brain's electrical activity, has a long history and has produced a wealth of information about which neurons fire when behavior is enacted. The modern extensions of that technique are the various ways that the brain can be scanned, mapped, and coded using a variety of sophisticated instruments, which is the third approach we'll consider. Let's examine each of these ways of investigating the brain.

## Learning about Brain Organization by Studying the Damaged Brain

Remember Betty, the 75-year-old grandmother admitted to the emergency room because she couldn't recognize her own husband? She had suffered a stroke from a blood clot that deprived her brain of oxygen and caused the death of neurons in the afflicted area. Betty's stroke affected part of the association area in her temporal lobe, where complex visual objects are identified. Betty's occipital lobe, the main area where visual processing takes place, was unaffected, so Betty could see her husband and two sons, but because of the damage to her temporal lobe, she could not recognize them.

In Betty's case, the damage was small, and no other visual capacities were affected; the brain areas that process simple visual forms, color, motion, and other features were still intact. So, her vision was not affected, but she had lost her ability to identify familiar faces, even her husband's. Betty thought she was having problems with her vision, but her neuropsychologist recognized the symptoms of *agnosia*, a term that means "without knowledge." Betty's case involved a specific version of this affliction called *prosopagnosia*, which means "without knowledge of faces" (Kleinschmidt & Cohen, 2006).

Much research in neuroscience correlates the loss of specific perceptual, motor, emotional, or cognitive functions with specific areas of brain damage (Andrewes, 2001; Kolb & Whishaw, 2003). By studying these mindbugs, neuroscientists can theorize about the functions those brain areas normally perform. The modern history of neuroscience can be dated to the work of Paul Broca (see Chapter 1). In 1861, Broca described a patient who had lost the capacity to produce spoken language (but not the ability to understand language) due to damage in a small area in the left frontal lobe. In 1874, Carl Wernicke (1848–1905) described a patient with an impairment in language comprehension (but not the ability to produce speech) associated with damage to an area in the upper-left temporal lobe. These areas were named, respectively, *Broca's area* and *Wernicke's area,* and they provided the earliest evidence that the brain locations for speech production and speech comprehension are separate and that for most people, the left hemisphere is critical to producing and understanding language (Young, 1990).

### The Emotional Functions of the Frontal Lobes

As you've already seen, the human frontal lobes are a remarkable evolutionary achievement. However, psychology's first glimpse at some functions of the frontal lobes came from a rather unremarkable fellow; so unremarkable, in fact, that a single event in his life defined his place in the annals of psychology's history (Macmillan, 2000).

Phineas Gage was a muscular 25-year-old boss of the Rutland and Burlington Railroad excavating crew. On September 13, 1848, in Cavendish, Vermont, he was packing an explosive charge into a crevice in a rock when disaster struck. Here is an account of the event in the words of John M. Harlow, the physician who examined him:

> The powder and fuse had been adjusted in the hole, and he was in the act of "tamping it in," as it is called. . . . While doing this, his attention was attracted by his men in the pit behind him. Averting his head and looking over his right shoulder, at the same instant dropping the iron upon the charge, it struck fire upon the rock, and the

explosion followed, which projected the iron obliquely upwards . . . passing completely through his head, and high into the air, falling to the ground several [meters] behind him, where it was afterwards picked up by his men, smeared with blood and brain (Harlow, 1848).

In short, Phineas Gage had a 3-foot, 13-pound iron rod propelled through his head at high speed. As **FIGURE 3.24** shows, the rod entered through his lower left jaw and exited through the middle top of his head. Gruesome but unremarkable; industrial accidents unfortunately happen quite often.

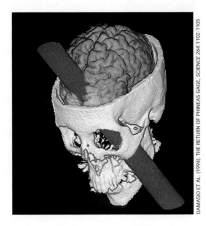

The remarkable part of this story is that Gage lived to tell the tale. After the accident, Gage sat up, climbed in the back of a wagon, and journeyed to town to seek medical treatment. He lived for another 12 years, residing in various parts of the United States and abroad and even joining P. T. Barnum's museum of oddities for a brief stint. He died in 1860 after a series of seizures, whereupon his skull and the iron rod were donated to the Warren Anatomical Museum of the Harvard University Medical School, where they are still displayed today.

Before the accident, Gage had been mild mannered, quiet, conscientious, and a hard worker. After the accident, however, Gage's personality underwent a significant change. He became irritable, irresponsible, indecisive, and given to profanity. The sad decline of Gage's personality and emotional life nonetheless provided an unexpected benefit to psychology. His case study was the first to allow researchers to investigate the hypothesis that the frontal lobe is involved in emotion regulation, planning, and decision making. Furthermore, because the connections between the frontal lobe and the subcortical structures of the limbic system were affected, scientists were able to better understand how the amygdala, hippocampus, and related brain structures interacted with the cerebral cortex (Damasio, 2005).

## The Distinct Roles of the Left and Right Hemispheres

You'll recall that the cerebral cortex is divided into two hemispheres, although typically the two hemispheres act as one integrated unit. Sometimes, though, disorders can threaten the ability of the brain to function, and the only way to stop them is with radical methods. This is sometimes the case with patients who suffer from severe, intractable epilepsy. Seizures that begin in one hemisphere cross the corpus callosum (the thick band of nerve fibers that allows the two hemispheres to communicate) to the opposite hemisphere and start a feedback loop that results in a kind of firestorm in the brain.

To alleviate the severity of the seizures, surgeons can sever the corpus callosum in a procedure called a *split-brain procedure*. This meant that a seizure that starts in one hemisphere is isolated in that hemisphere since there is no longer a connection to the other side. This procedure helps the patients with epilepsy but also produces some unusual, if not unpredictable, behaviors.

Nobel laureate Roger Sperry (1913–94) and his colleagues designed several experiments that investigated the behaviors of split-brain patients and in the process revealed a great deal about the independent functions of the left and right hemispheres (Sperry, 1964). Normally, any information that initially enters the left hemisphere is also registered in the right hemisphere and vice versa: The information comes in and travels across the corpus callosum, and both hemispheres understand what's going on. But in a split-brain patient, information entering one hemisphere stays there. Without an intact corpus callosum,

**Figure 3.24 Phineas Gage** Phineas Gage's traumatic accident allowed researchers to investigate the functions of the frontal lobe and its connections with emotion centers in the subcortical structures. The likely path of the metal rod through Gage's skull is reconstructed here.

 **ONLY HUMAN**

**DO-IT-YOURSELF ANATOMY LESSON**
1995—Troy Harding, 19, was released from a Portland, Oregon, hospital 3 weeks after he turned around abruptly when talking to friends and walked into the radio antenna of his car. The antenna went up his nose almost four inches, pierced his sinus, and entered his brain, coming to rest in his pituitary gland.

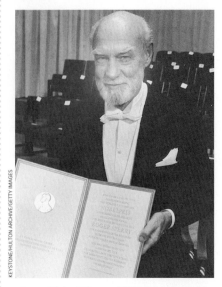

Roger Wolcott Sperry (1913–94) received the Nobel Prize in Physiology in 1981 for his pioneering work investigating the independent functions of the cerebral hemispheres.

there's no way for that information to reach the other hemisphere. Sperry and his colleagues used this understanding of lateralized perception in a series of experiments. For example, they had patients look at a spot in the center of a screen and then projected a stimulus on one side of the screen, isolating the stimulus to one hemisphere.

The hemispheres themselves are specialized for different kinds of tasks. You just learned about Broca and Wernicke's areas, which revealed that language processing is a left-hemisphere activity. So imagine that some information came into the left hemisphere of a split-brain patient, and she was asked to verbally describe what it was. No problem: The left hemisphere has the information, it's the "speaking" hemisphere, so the patient should have no difficulty verbally describing what she saw. But suppose the patient was asked to reach behind a screen with her left hand and pick up the object she just saw. Remember that the hemispheres exert contralateral control over the body, meaning that the left hand is controlled by the right hemisphere. But this patient's right hemisphere has no clue what the object was because that information was received in the left hemisphere and was unable to travel to the right hemisphere! So, even though the split-brain patient saw the object and could verbally describe it, she would be unable to use the right hemisphere to perform other tasks regarding that object, such as correctly selecting it from a group with her left hand (see **FIGURE 3.25**).

Of course, information presented to the right hemisphere would produce complementary deficits. In this case, a patient might be presented with a familiar object in her left hand (such as a key), be able to demonstrate that she knew what it was (by twisting and turning the key in midair), yet be unable to verbally describe what she was holding. In this case, the information in the right hemisphere is unable to travel to the left hemisphere, which controls the production of speech.

Furthermore, suppose a split-brain person was shown the unusual face in **FIGURE 3.26**. This is called a *chimeric face*, and it is assembled from half-face components of the full faces also shown in the figure. When asked to indicate which face was presented, a split-brain person would indicate that she saw *both* faces because information about the face on the left is recorded in the right hemisphere and information about the face on the right is recorded in the left hemisphere (Levy, Trevarthen, & Sperry, 1972).

These split-brain studies reveal that the two hemispheres perform different functions and can work together seamlessly as long as the corpus callosum is intact. Without a way to transmit information from one hemisphere to the other, information gets "stuck" in the hemisphere it initially entered and we become acutely aware of

Figure **3.25** **Split-Brain Experiment** When a split-brain patient is presented with the picture of a ring on the right and that of a key on the left side of a screen, she can verbalize *ring*, but not *key* because the left hemisphere "sees" the ring and language is usually located in the left hemisphere. This patient would be able to choose a key with her left hand from a set of objects behind a screen. She would not, however, be able to pick out a ring with her right hand since what the left hemisphere "sees" is not communicated to the right side of her body.

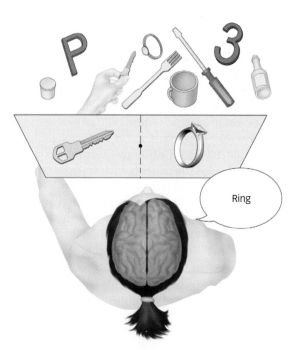

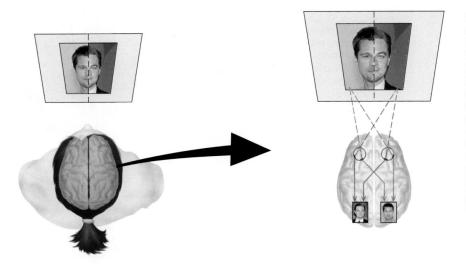

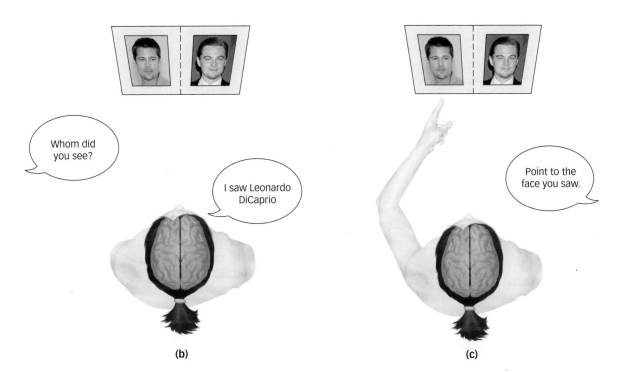

**Figure 3.26** **Chimeric Faces and the Split Brain** (a) When a split-brain patient views a chimeric face of Brad Pitt and Leonardo DiCaprio, her left hemisphere is aware only of Leonardo DiCaprio and her right hemisphere sees only Brad Pitt. (b) When asked who she sees, the patient answers, "Leonardo DiCaprio," because speech is controlled by the left hemisphere. (c) When asked to point to the face she saw with her left hand, she points to Brad Pitt because her right hemisphere is only aware of the left half of the picture.
PHOTO OF BRAD PITT: AP PHOTO/ALEX BRANDON; PHOTO OF LEONARDO DICAPRIO: AP PHOTO/TAMMIE ARROYO

the different functions of each hemisphere. Of course, a split-brain patient can adapt to this by simply moving her eyes a little so that the same information independently enters both hemispheres. Split-brain studies have continued over the past few decades and continue to play an important role in shaping our understanding of how the brain works (Gazzaniga, 2006).

## Listening to the Brain: Single Neurons and the EEG

A second approach to studying the link between brain structures and behavior involves recording the pattern of electrical activity of neurons. An **electroencephalogram (EEG)** is *a device used to record electrical activity in the brain*. Typically electrodes are placed on the outside of the head, and even though the source of electrical activity in synapses and action potentials is far removed from these wires, the electric signals can be amplified several thousand times by the EEG. This provides a visual record of the

**ELECTROENCEPHALOGRAM (EEG)**
A device used to record electrical activity in the brain.

**Figure 3.27 EEG** The electroencephalogram (EEG) records electrical activity in the brain. Many states of consciousness, such as wakefulness and stages of sleep, are characterized by particular types of brainwaves.

underlying electrical activity, as shown in **FIGURE 3.27**. Using this technique, researchers can determine the amount of brain activity during different states of consciousness. For example, as you'll read in Chapter 8, the brain shows distinctive patterns of electrical activity when awake versus asleep; in fact, there are even different brain-wave patterns associated with different stages of sleep. EEG recordings allow researchers to make these fundamental discoveries about the nature of sleep and wakefulness (Dement, 1974). The EEG can also be used to examine the brain's electrical activity when awake individuals engage in a variety of psychological functions, such as perceiving, learning, and remembering.

A different approach to recording electrical activity resulted in a more refined understanding of the brain's division of responsibilities, even at a cellular level. Nobel laureates David Hubel and Torsten Wiesel used a technique that inserted electrodes into the occipital lobes of anesthetized cats and observed the patterns of action potentials of individual neurons (Hubel, 1988). Hubel and Wiesel amplified the action potential signals through a loudspeaker so that the signals could be heard as clicks as well as seen on an oscilloscope. While flashing lights in front of the animal's eye, Hubel and Wiesel recorded the resulting activity of neurons in the occipital cortex. What they discovered was not much of anything: Most of the neurons did not respond to this kind of general stimulation.

Nearing the end of what seemed like a failed set of experiments, they projected a glass slide that contained a shadow (caused by the edge of the slide) to show an image in front of the cat's eyes, reasoning that the flaw wouldn't make much difference to the already unimpressive experimental outcomes. Instead, they heard a brisk flurry of clicks as the neurons in the cat's occipital lobe fired away! They discovered that neurons in the primary visual cortex are activated whenever a contrast between light and dark occurs in part of the visual field, seen particularly well when the visual stimulus was a thick line of light against a dark background. In this case, the shadow caused

David Hubel (left, b. 1926) and Torsten Wiesel (right, b. 1924) received the Nobel Prize in Physiology in 1981 for their work on mapping the visual cortex.

by the edge of the slide provided the kind of contrast that prompted particular neurons to respond. They then found that each neuron responded vigorously only when presented with a contrasting edge at a particular orientation. Since then, many studies have shown that neurons in the primary visual cortex represent particular features of visual stimuli, such as contrast, shape, and color (Zeki, 1993).

These neurons in the visual cortex are known as *feature detectors* because they selectively respond to certain aspects of a visual image. For example, some neurons fire only when detecting a vertical line in the middle of the visual field, other neurons fire when a line at a 45-degree angle is perceived, and still others in response to wider lines, horizontal lines, lines in the periphery of the visual field, and so on (Livingstone & Hubel, 1988). The discovery of this specialized function for neurons was a huge leap forward in our understanding of how the visual cortex works. Feature detectors identify basic dimensions of a stimulus ("slanted line . . . other slanted line . . . horizontal line"); those dimensions are then combined during a later stage of visual processing to allow recognition and perception of a stimulus ("oh, it's a letter *A*").

Other studies have identified a variety of features that are detected by sensory neurons. For example, some visual processing neurons in the temporal lobe are activated only when detecting faces (Kanwisher, 2000; Perrett, Rolls, & Caan, 1982). These neurons lie in the same area of the temporal cortex that was damaged in Betty's stroke. Neurons in this area are specialized for processing faces; damage to this area results in an inability to perceive faces. These complementary observations—showing that the type of function that is lost or altered when a brain area is damaged corresponds to the kind of information processed by neurons in that cortical area—provide the most compelling evidence linking the brain to behavior.

## Brain Imaging: Watching the Brain in Action

The third major way that neuroscientists can peer into the workings of the human brain has only become possible within the past several decades. EEG readouts give an overall picture of a person's level of consciousness, and single-cell recordings shed light on the actions of particular clumps of neurons. The ideal of neuroscience, however, has been the ability to see the brain in operation while behavior is being enacted. This goal has been steadily achieved thanks to a wide range of *neuroimaging techniques* that use advanced technology to create images of the living, healthy brain (Posner & Raichle, 1994; Raichle & Mintun, 2006).

One of the first neuroimaging techniques developed was the *computerized axial tomography (CT) scan*. In a CT scan, a scanner rotates a device around a person's head and takes a series of x-ray photographs from different angles. Computer programs then combine these images to provide views from any angle. CT scans show different densities of tissue in the brain. For example, the higher-density skull looks white on a CT scan, the cortex shows up as gray, and the least dense fissures and ventricles in the brain look dark (see **FIGURE 3.28** on the next page). CT scans are used to locate lesions or tumors, which typically appear darker since they are less dense than the cortex.

*Magnetic resonance imaging (MRI)* involves applying brief but powerful magnetic pulses to the head and recording how these pulses are absorbed throughout the brain. For very short periods, these magnetic pulses cause molecules in the brain tissue to twist slightly and then relax, which releases a small

**off the mark** .com    by Mark Parisi

offthemark.com

**ONLY HUMAN**

**JUST LET US KNOW IF YOU EXPERIENCE ANY DISCOMFORT . . .** 1996—Employees of the Advanced Medical Imaging clinic in Newburgh, New York, forgot that Brenda Revella, 42, was in the claustrophobia-inducing MRI machine when they locked up for the night. (The patient lies in a tube 27 inches wide with the top of the tube only 4 inches from his or her face.) Revella managed to wiggle out 3 hours later.

**Figure 3.28** Structural Imaging Techniques (CT and MRI) CT (left) and MRI (right) scans are used to provide information about the structure of the brain and can help to spot tumors and other kinds of damage. Each scan shown here provides a snapshot of a single slice in the brain. Note that the MRI scan provides a clearer, higher resolution image than the CT scan (see the text for further discussion of how these images are constructed and what they depict).

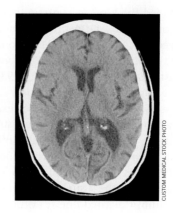
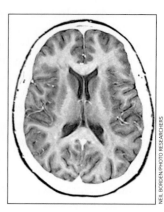

amount of energy. Differently charged molecules respond differently to the magnetic pulses, so the energy signals reveal brain structures with different molecular compositions. Magnetic resonance imaging produces pictures of soft tissue at a better resolution than a CT scan, as you can see in Figure 3.28. These techniques give psychologists a clearer picture of the structure of the brain and can help localize brain damage (as when someone suffers a stroke), but they reveal nothing about the functions of the brain.

Two newer techniques show researchers much more than just the structure of the brain. *Functional-brain-imaging* techniques allow us to actually watch the brain in action. These techniques rely on the fact that activated brain areas demand more energy for their neurons to work. This energy is supplied through increased blood flow to the activated areas. Functional-imaging techniques can detect such changes in blood flow. In *positron emission tomography* (PET), a harmless radioactive substance is injected into a person's bloodstream. Then the brain is scanned by radiation detectors as the person performs perceptual or cognitive tasks, such as reading or speaking. Areas of the brain that are activated during these tasks demand more energy and greater blood flow, resulting in a higher amount of the radioactivity in that region. The radiation detectors record the level of radioactivity in each region, producing a computerized image of the activated areas (see **FIGURE 3.29**). Note that PET scans differ from CT scans and MRIs in that the image produced shows activity in the brain while the person performs certain tasks. So, for example, a PET scan of a person speaking would show activation in Broca's area in the left frontal lobe.

For psychologists, the most widely used functional-brain-imaging technique nowadays is *functional magnetic resonance imaging (fMRI)*, which detects the twisting of hemoglobin molecules in the blood when they are exposed to magnetic pulses. Hemoglobin is the molecule in the blood that carries oxygen to our tissues, including the brain. When active neurons demand more energy and blood flow, oxygenated hemoglobin concentrates in the active areas. fMRI detects the oxygenated hemoglobin and provides a picture of the level of activation in each brain area (see Figure 3.29). Just as MRI was a major advance over CT scans, *functional* MRI represents a similar leap in our ability to record the brain's activity during behavior. Both fMRI and PET allow researchers to localize changes in the brain very accurately. However, fMRI has a couple of advantages over PET. First, fMRI does not require any exposure to a radioactive substance. Second, fMRI can localize changes in brain activity across briefer periods than PET, which makes it more useful for analyzing psychological processes that occur extremely quickly, such as reading a word or recognizing a face. With PET, researchers often have to use experimental designs different from those they would use in the psychological laboratory in order to adapt to the limitations of PET technology. With fMRI, researchers can design experiments that more closely resemble the ones they carry out in the psychological laboratory.

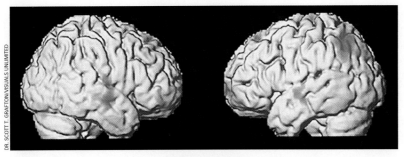

Gesture preparation

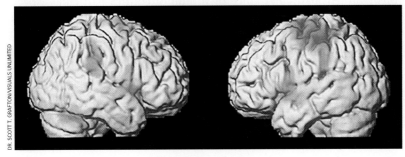

Gesture production

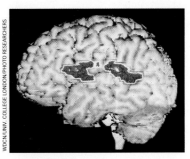

**Figure 3.29** **Functional-Imaging Techniques (PET fMRI)** PET and fMRI scans provide information about the functions of the brain by revealing which brain areas become more or less active in different conditions. The PET scan (directly above) shows areas in the left hemisphere (Broca's area, left; lower parietal-upper temporal area, right) that become active when people hold in mind a string of letters for a few seconds. The fMRI scans (all views to the left) show several different regions in both hemispheres that become active when someone is thinking about a gesture (top) and when performing a gesture (bottom).

PET and fMRI provide remarkable insights into the types of information processing that take place in specific areas of the brain. For example, when a person performs a simple perceptual task, such as looking at a circular checkerboard, the primary visual areas are activated. As you have read, when the checkerboard is presented to the left visual field, the right visual cortex shows activation, and when the checkerboard is presented to the right visual field, the left visual cortex shows activation (Fox et al., 1986). Similarly, when people look at faces, fMRI reveals strong activity in a region in the visual association cortex called the *fusiform gyrus* (Kanwisher, McDermott, & Chun, 1997). When this structure is damaged, people experience problems with recognizing faces, as Betty did in the opening vignette. Finally, when people perform a task that engages emotional processing, for example, looking at sad pictures, researchers observe significant activation in the amygdala, which you learned earlier is linked with emotional arousal (Phelps, 2006). There is also increased activation in parts of the frontal lobe that are involved in emotional regulation, in fact, in the same areas that were most likely damaged in the case of Phineas Gage (Wang et al., 2005).

As you may have noticed, then, the most modern brain-imaging techniques confirm what studies of brain damage from over 100 years ago suspected. When Broca and Wernicke reached their conclusions about language production and language comprehension, they had little more to go on than some isolated cases and good hunches. PET scans have since confirmed that different areas of the brain are activated when a person is listening to spoken language, reading words on a screen, saying words out loud, or thinking of related words. This suggests that different parts of the brain are activated during these related but distinct functions. Similarly, it was pretty clear to the physician who examined Phineas Gage that the location of Gage's injuries played a major role in his drastic change in personality and emotionality. fMRI scans have since confirmed that the frontal lobe plays a central role in regulating emotion. It's always nice when independent methods—in these instances, very old case studies and very recent technology—arrive at the same conclusions. As you'll also see at various points in the text, brain-imaging techniques such as fMRI are also revealing new and surprising findings, such as the insights described in the Where Do You Stand? box. Although the human brain still holds many mysteries, researchers are developing increasingly sophisticated ways of unraveling them.

**In summary,** there are three major approaches to studying the link between the brain and behavior. Neuroscientists observe how perceptual, motor, intellectual, and emotional capacities are affected following brain damage. By carefully relating specific psychological and behavioral disruptions to damage in particular areas of the brain, researchers can better understand how the brain area normally plays a role in producing those behaviors. A second approach looks at global electrical activity in the brain and the activity patterns of single neurons. The patterns of electrical activity in large brain areas can be examined from outside the skull using the electroencephalograph (EEG). Single-cell recordings taken from specific neurons can be linked to specific perceptual or behavioral events, suggesting that those neurons represent particular kinds of stimuli or control particular aspects of behavior. With brain imaging, the third major approach, researchers can scan the brain as people perform different perceptual or intellectual tasks. Correlating energy consumption in particular brain areas with specific cognitive and behavioral events suggests that those brain areas are involved in specific types of perceptual, motor, cognitive, or emotional processing. ▪ ▪

## Where Do You Stand?

# Brain Death

A story shrouded in mystery follows the memory of Andreas Vesalius (1514–64), a Belgian physician regarded as one of the founders of modern anatomy. According to the story, Vesalius conducted an autopsy in 1564 in front of a large crowd in Madrid, Spain. When the cadaver's chest was opened, the audience saw that the man's heart was still beating! The possibility that the patient was still alive created a scandal that forced Vesalius to leave Spain, where he was serving as the imperial physician at the time. He died during his exodus in a shipwreck, on a pilgrimage to Jerusalem under the pressures of the Spanish Inquisition.

We may never know whether this story is accurate. However, it raises a question related to the brain and behavior that is still fiercely debated today. In Vesalius's time, if a patient didn't appear to be breathing, was generally unresponsive, or gave no strong evidence of a heartbeat, the person could safely be considered dead (despite the occasional misdiagnosis). Modern resuscitative techniques can keep the heart, lungs, and other organs functioning for days, months, or even years, so physicians have identified measures of brain function that allow them to decide more definitively when someone is dead.

In 1981, the President's Commission for the Study of Ethical Problems in Medicine and Biomedical and Behavioral Research defined brain death as the *irreversible loss of all functions of the brain*. Contrary to what you may think, brain death is not the same as being in a coma or being unresponsive to stimulation. Indeed, even a flat-line EEG does not indicate that all brain functions have stopped; the reticular formation in the hindbrain, which generates spontaneous respiration and heartbeat, may still be active.

Brain death came to the forefront of national attention during March 2005 in the case of Terri Schiavo, a woman who had been kept alive on a respirator for nearly 15 years in a Florida nursing home. She died on March 31, 2005, after the feeding tube that sustained her was removed. A person like Schiavo is commonly referred to as brain dead, but such an individual is more accurately described as being in a *persistent vegetative state*. In fact, people in a persistent vegetative state are still considered to be alive by some. Respiration is controlled by structures in the hindbrain, such as the medulla, and will continue as long as this area is intact. A heartbeat does not require input from any area of the brain, so the heart will continue to beat as long it continues to receive oxygen, either by intact respiration or if the patient is artificially ventilated. Also, a patient who is brain dead may continue to have muscle spasms, twitches, or even sit up. This so-called *Lazarus reflex* is coordinated solely by the spinal cord.

Terri Schiavo's parents thought she had a substantial level of voluntary consciousness; they felt that she appeared to smile, cry, and turn toward the source of a voice. Terri's parents hired physicians who claimed that she had a primitive type of consciousness. However, neurologists who specialize in these cases emphasized that these responses could be automatic reflexes supported by circuits in the thalamus and midbrain. These neurologists considered Schiavo to be in a persistent vegetative state; they failed to see conclusive evidence of consciousness or voluntary behavior.

Terri's husband, Michael, agreed with the neurologists and asked the courts to remove the feeding tube that kept her alive, a decision a Florida court accepted. Nonetheless, Florida governor Jeb Bush decreed in 2003 that doctors retain Terri's feeding tube and continue to provide medical care. Eventually, the court again ordered her feeding tube removed, and this time it was not replaced, resulting in her death.

Where do you stand on this issue? Should Terri Schiavo have been kept alive indefinitely? The definition of brain death includes the term "irreversible," suggesting that as long as *any* component of the brain can still function—with or without the aid of a machine—the person should be considered alive. But does a persistent vegetative state qualify as "life"? Is a simple consensus of qualified professionals—doctors, nurses, social workers, specialists—sufficient to decide whether someone is "still living" or at least "still living enough" to maintain whatever treatments may be in place? How should the wishes of family members be considered? For that matter, should the wishes of lawmakers and politicians play a role at all? What is your position on these questions of the brain and the ultimate behavior: staying alive?

After you've considered your answers to these questions, consider this: A recent study found evidence that a person diagnosed as being in a vegetative state showed intentional mental activity (Owen et al., 2006). Researchers used fMRI to observe the patterns of brain activity in a 25-year-old woman with severe brain injuries as the result of a traffic accident. When the researchers spoke ambiguous sentences ("The creak came from a beam in the ceiling") and unambiguous sentences ("There was milk and sugar in his coffee"), fMRI revealed that the activated areas in the woman's brain were comparable to those areas activated in the brains of normal volunteers. What's more, when the woman was instructed to imagine playing a game of tennis and then imagine walking through the rooms of her house, the areas of her brain that showed activity were again indistinguishable from those brain areas in normal, healthy volunteers.

The researchers suggest that these findings are evidence for, at least, conscious understanding of spoken commands and, at best, a degree of intentionality in an otherwise vegetative person. The patient's brain activity while "playing tennis" and "walking through her house" revealed that she could both understand the researchers' instructions and willfully complete them. Unfortunately, it's too early to tell how these and other research findings may impact decisions regarding the brain and when life ends (Laureys, Giacino, Schiff, Schabus, Power, 2006).

# Chapter Review

## Neurons: The Origin of Behavior

- Neurons are the information processing elements of the nervous system. They are composed of three main elements: the cell body, dendrites, and the axon. The cell body contains the nucleus and the machinery necessary for cell metabolism. Multiple dendrites receive signals from other neurons, whereas axons conduct a signal to the synapse.

- The synapse is a junction between neurons. Electrochemical "messages" cross the synapse to allow neurons to communicate with one another.

- Glial cells serve a support function in the nervous system. As one example, glial cells form a myelin sheath, which is insulating material that speeds the transmission of information down an axon.

- There are three main types of neurons. Sensory neurons receive information from the external world and convey this information to the brain via the spinal cord. Motor neurons carry signals from the spinal cord to the muscles to produce movement. Interneurons connect sensory neurons, motor neurons, or other interneurons.

## Electric Signaling: Communicating Information within a Neuron

- Neurons have a resting potential that is created by the balance of electrical forces on charged molecules that can pass through the cell membrane. In particular, there is a high concentration of potassium ions inside the neuron, relative to outside the neuron.

- At the start of an axon, electric potentials build to produce a depolarization that is above threshold, which is called an action potential. Action potentials fire in a consistent "all-or-none" fashion and are conducted down the entire length of the axon.

In myelinated axons, the electric signal "jumps" from breakpoint to breakpoint in the myelin sheath.

## Chemical Signaling: Synaptic Transmission between Neurons

- When an action potential arrives at the end of an axon, it stimulates the release of neurotransmitters, which are stored in terminal buttons in the axon. The neurotransmitter enters the synapse and then attaches to the dendrite of the receiving cell.

- Neurotransmitters and receptor sites operate in a lock-and-key fashion; only certain neurotransmitters can be taken up by certain receptors.

- An overflow of neurotransmitters in the synapse can be dealt with in one of three ways: reuptake, enzyme deactivation, or the action of autoreceptors.

- Some of the major neurotransmitters are acetylcholine, norepinephrine, serotonin, dopamine, glutamate, and GABA.

- Many drugs work by facilitating or interfering with a step in the cycle of a neurotransmitter. Drugs that enhance or mimic neurotransmitters are called agonists, whereas those that block neurotransmitters are called antagonists.

## The Organization of the Nervous System

- The nervous system is divided into the central nervous system, which is composed of the brain and spinal cord, and the peripheral nervous system, which is composed of the somatic nervous system and the autonomic nervous system. The somatic nervous system receives sensory information and controls the contractions of voluntary muscles. The autonomic nervous system controls the body's organs.

- The autonomic nervous system is divided further into the sympathetic nervous system that prepares the body for action in threatening circumstances and the parasympathetic nervous system that helps return the body to its normal resting state.

- The spinal cord controls basic reflexes and helps transmit information to and from the brain. Injuries to the spinal cord often result in varying degrees of paralysis or other incapacities.

- The brain can be conceptually divided into three main sections: the hindbrain, the midbrain, and the forebrain.

- The hindbrain is responsible for life-sustaining functions, such as respiration and consciousness, and contains the medulla, pons, and cerebellum. The midbrain contains the tectum and the tegmentum, which help to orient an organism in the environment.

- The forebrain is divided into the cerebral cortex and subcortical structures. The subcortical structures include the thalamus, hypothalamus, pituitary gland, hippocampus, amygdala, and basal ganglia. The motivational and emotional functions of some of the subcortical structures are interrelated, suggesting they could be grouped into an overall organization called the limbic system.

- The cerebral cortex is divided into two hemispheres that exert contralateral control over the body. The cortex can also be divided into lobes: occipital, temporal, parietal, and frontal. Each lobe coordinates different kinds of behaviors.

- Association areas are parts of the cortex that perform higher-level operations. There is also evidence of brain plasticity, or the ability of the brain to reassign functions to other brain areas.

## The Development and Evolution of Nervous Systems

- The nervous system initially develops as a neural tube in the embryo. Over time, the tube enlarges at one end to form the hindbrain, midbrain, and forebrain.

- From an evolutionary perspective, the human brain represents successive developments from previous models. In reptiles and birds, the highest processing area of the brain is the striatum. In mammals, the highest processing area is the cerebral cortex. The structures and functions of the hindbrain and midbrain seen in other species are retained in humans. There is also some evidence that the human forebrain evolved at a comparatively faster rate, compared to other mammals.

- Both genes and environmental factors exert influence on people's behaviors. Genes set the range of possible behaviors within a given environment, but they do not predict individual characteristics.

- Heritability is a measure of the variability in behavioral traits that can be accounted for by genetic variation. Despite its utility, there are several cautions to interpreting heritability.

## Investigating the Brain

- The field of neuroscience investigates the links between the brain and behavior. Three main approaches to this topic are studies of brain damage, electrical recording of brain activity, and imaging techniques of the brain in action.

- Careful case studies of people with brain damage allow researchers to piece together the normal functioning of the brain. When an area is damaged and a specific deficit results, investigators can work backward to discover the likely responsibilities of that brain area. Functions such as speech, language use, emotionality, decision making, and the independent nature of the cerebral hemispheres benefited from this approach.

  An electroencephalograph (EEG) lets researchers measure the overall electrical activity of the brain. However, more recent techniques such as CT scans, MRI, PET, and fMRI provide an increasingly sophisticated way of observing how the brain responds when a variety of tasks are performed.

## Key Terms

neurons (p. 74)
cell body (p. 75)
dendrites (p. 75)
axon (p. 75)
myelin sheath (p. 76)
glial cell (p. 76)
synapse (p. 76)
sensory neurons (p. 77)
motor neurons (p. 77)
interneurons (p. 77)
resting potential (p. 79)
action potential (p. 80)
refractory period (p. 81)
terminal buttons (p. 81)
neurotransmitters (p. 81)
receptors (p. 81)
acetylcholine (Ach) (p. 83)

dopamine (p. 84)
glutamate (p. 84)
GABA (gamma-aminobutyric acid) (p. 84)
norepinephrine (p. 84)
serotonin (p. 84)
endorphins (p. 84)
agonists (p. 85)
antagonists (p. 85)
nervous system (p. 87)
central nervous system (CNS) (p. 87)
peripheral nervous system (PNS) (p. 87)
somatic nervous system (p. 87)
autonomic nervous system (ANS) (p. 88)

sympathetic nervous system (p. 88)
parasympathetic nervous system (p. 88)
spinal reflexes (p. 90)
hindbrain (p. 93)
medulla (p. 93)
reticular formation (p. 93)
cerebellum (p. 93)
pons (p. 94)
tectum (p. 94)
tegmentum (p. 94)
cerebral cortex (p. 95)
subcortical structures (p. 95)
thalamus (p. 95)
hypothalamus (p. 95)
pituitary gland (p. 96)

limbic system (p. 96)
hippocampus (p. 96)
amygdala (p. 96)
basal ganglia (p. 97)
corpus callosum (p. 98)
occipital lobe (p. 98)
parietal lobe (p. 98)
temporal lobe (p. 99)
frontal lobe (p. 99)
association areas (p. 99)
gene (p. 104)
chromosomes (p. 104)
heritability (p. 106)
electroencephalograph (EEG) (p. 111)

## Recommended Readings

**Damasio, A.** (2005). *Descartes' error: Emotion, reason, and the human brain*. New York: Penguin. Emotion and reason seem like competing forces in directing our behavior: One force wants to feel good, while the other wants to think things through. Antonio Damasio, a distinguished neuroscientist, considers how emotion and reason relate to each other and how both cooperate to allow the brain to function efficiently.

**Diamond, M., & Schiebel, A. B.** (1986). *The human brain coloring book*. New York: Collins. Marian Diamond is a professor of anatomy; who better to assemble a book on the structure of the brain? This is a fun way to quiz yourself on the various parts of the brain and a good reason to break out your crayons.

**Johnson, S.** (2004). *Mind wide open: Your brain and the neuroscience of everyday life*. New York: Scribner. Steven Johnson is a science writer who synthesizes scholarly research for a popular audience. In this book, he explores a range of findings related to neuroscience, including techniques for studying the brain (such as MRI), the purposes and functions of brain structures (such as the amygdala), and the meaning behind what the brain does and why it does it.

**LeDoux, J.** (2002). *The synaptic self: How our brains become who we are*. New York: Viking. Joseph LeDoux is a neuroscientist who studies how cortical and subcortical structures direct behavior. In this book, he takes us on a journey from a basic understanding of what neurons are to a proposal that our synaptic connections make us who we are: Personality, self, and related concepts stem from the interwoven connections that make up our brains.

**Ramachandran, V. S., & Blakeslee, S.** (1998). *Phantoms in the brain: Probing the mysteries of the human mind*. New York: Morrow. Vilayanur Ramachandran is a leading theorist in understanding how the brain produces the mind. Susan Blakeslee is a *New York Times* science writer. Together they explore the sometimes bizarre world of the usual and not-so-usual workings of the brain. This book is a good survey of several topics discussed in the current chapter and a nice introduction to some related ideas.

# 4

# Sensation and Perception

*N is sort of . . . rubbery . . . smooth, L is sort of the consistency of watery paint . . . Letters also have vague personalities, but not as strongly as numerals do.*

—Julieta

*The letter A is blue, B is red, C is kind of a light gray, D is orange. . . .*

—Karen

*I hear a note by one of the fellows in the band and it's one color. I hear the same note played by someone else and it's a different color. When I hear sustained musical tones, I see just about the same colors that you do, but I see them in textures.*

—Jazz musician Duke Ellington (George, 1981, p. 226)

*Basically, I taste words.*

—Amelia

THESE COMMENTS ARE NOT FROM A recent meeting of the Slightly Odd Society. They're the remarks of otherwise perfectly normal people describing what seem to be perfectly bizarre experiences except to them—they think these experiences are quite commonplace and genuine. After all, if you can't trust Duke Ellington, an internationally acclaimed jazz composer and band-leader, who can you trust? Perhaps Stevie Wonder? Eddie Van Halen? Vladimir Nabokov, the author of *Lolita*? Franz Liszt, the classical composer? Richard Feynman, the Nobel Prize–winning physicist? Take your pick because these and many other notable people have at least one thing in common: Their perceptual worlds seem to be quite different from most of ours.

What do these people have in common? Duke Ellington, Stevie Wonder, Eddie Van Halen, and Franz Liszt are all musicians, but Richard Feynman was a physicist. All of these people are men, but that has little to do with it. Some are living; some are dead. In fact, all of these people have fairly well-documented experiences of synesthesia, the experience of one sense that is evoked by a different sense.

Duke Ellington

Stevie Wonder

Eddie Van Halen

Franz Liszt

Richard Feynman

**SYNESTHESIA** The perceptual experience of one sense that is evoked by another sense.

These unusual perceptual events are varieties of **synesthesia**, *the perceptual experience of one sense that is evoked by another sense* (Hubbard & Ramachandran, 2003). For some synesthetes, musical notes evoke the visual sensation of color. Other people with synesthesia see printed letters (**FIGURE 4.1**) or numbers in specific, consistent colors (always seeing the digit 2 as pink and 3 as green, for example). Still others experience specific tastes when certain sounds are heard.

For those of us who don't experience synesthesia, the prospect of tasting sounds or hearing colors may seem unbelievable or the product of some hallucinogenic experience. Indeed, for many years scientists dismissed synesthesia either as a rare curiosity or a case of outright faking. But recent research indicates that synesthesia is far more common than previously believed. Synesthesia was once thought to occur in as few as one in every 25,000 people, but it is now clear that some forms of synesthesia are not as rare as others and may be found in as many as one in every 100 people (Hubbard & Ramachandran, 2005). The experience of seeing colors evoked by sounds or of seeing letters in specific colors is much more common among synesthetes than, say, a smell evoked by touching a certain shape.

Recent research has documented the psychological and neurobiological reality of synesthesia. For example, a synesthete who sees the digits 2 and 4 as pink and 3 as green will find it easier to pick out a 2 among a bunch of 3s than among a bunch of 4s, whereas a nonsynesthete will perform these two tasks equally well (Palmieri, Ingersoll, & Stone, 2002). Brain-imaging studies also show that in some synesthetes, areas of the brain involved in processing colors are more active when they hear words that evoke color than when they hear tones that don't evoke color; no such differences are seen among people in a control group (Nunn, Gregory, & Brammer, 2002).

So, synesthesia is neither an isolated curiosity nor the result of faking. In fact, it may indicate that in some people, the brain is "wired" differently than in most, so that brain regions for different sensory modalities cross-activate one another (Ramachandran & Hubbard, 2003). Whatever the ultimate explanations for these fascinating phenomena, this recent wave of research shows that synesthesia is a mindbug that can shed new light on how the brain is organized and how we sense and perceive the world.

In this chapter we'll explore key insights into the nature of sensation and perception. These experiences are basic to survival and reproduction; we wouldn't last long without the ability to accurately make sense of the world around us. Indeed, research on sensation and perception is the basis for much of psychology, a pathway toward understanding more complex cognition and behavior such as memory, emotion, motivation, or decision making. Yet sensation and perception also sometimes reveal mindbugs, ranging from the complexities of synesthesia to various kinds of perceptual illusions that you might see at a science fair or in a novelty shop. These mindbugs are reminders that the act of perceiving the world is not as simple or straightforward as it might seem.

We'll look at how physical energy in the world around us is encoded by our senses, sent to the brain, and enters conscious awareness. Vision is predominant among our

**Figure 4.1 Synesthesia** Most of us see letters printed in black as they appear in (a). Some people with synesthesia link their perceptions of letters with certain colors and perceive letters as printed in different colors, as shown in (b). In synesthesia, brain regions for different sensory modalities cross-activate one another.

**(a) Usual appearance**

**(b) Appearance to a person with synesthesia**

senses; correspondingly, we'll devote a fair amount of space to understanding how the visual system works. Then we'll discuss how we perceive sound waves as words or music or noise, followed by the body senses, emphasizing touch, pain, and balance. We'll end with the chemical senses of smell and taste, which together allow you to savor the foods you eat. But before doing any of that, we will provide a foundation for examining all of the sensory systems by reviewing how psychologists measure sensation and perception in the first place.

## The Doorway to Psychology

From the vantage point of our own consciousness, sensation and perception appear to be one seamless event. Information comes in from the outside world, gets registered and interpreted, and triggers some kind of action: no breaks, no balks, just one continuous process. Psychologists know, however, that sensation and perception are two separate activities.

**Sensation** is *simple awareness due to the stimulation of a sense organ*. It is the basic registration of light, sound, pressure, odor, or taste as parts of your body interact with the physical world. After a sensation registers in your central nervous system, **perception** takes place at the level of your brain: It is *the organization, identification, and interpretation of a sensation in order to form a mental representation*. As an example, your eyes are coursing across these sentences right now. The sensory receptors in your eyeballs are registering different patterns of light reflecting off the page. Your brain, however, is integrating and processing that light information into the meaningful perception of words, such as "meaningful," "perception," and "words." Your eyes—the sensory organ—aren't really seeing words; they're simply encoding different shapes and patterns of ink on a page. Your brain—the perceptual organ—is transforming those shapes into a coherent mental representation of words and concepts.

If all of this sounds a little peculiar, it's because from the vantage point of your conscious experience, it *seems* as if you're reading words directly; again, sensation and perception feel like one single event. If you think of the discussion of brain damage in Chapter 3, however, you'll recall that sometimes a person's eyes can work just fine, yet the individual is still "blind" to faces she has seen for many years. Damage to the visual-processing centers in the brain can interfere with the interpretation of information coming from the eyes: The senses are intact, but perceptual ability is compromised. Sensation and perception are related—but separate—events.

We all know that sensory events involve vision, hearing, touch, taste, and smell. Arguably, we possess several more senses besides these five. Touch, for example, encompasses distinct body senses, including sensitivity to pain and temperature, joint position and balance, and even the state of the gut—perhaps to sense nausea via the autonomic nervous system. Despite the variety of our senses, they all depend on the process of **transduction**, which occurs *when many sensors in the body convert physical signals from the environment into neural signals sent to the central nervous system*.

In vision, light reflected from surfaces provides the eyes with information about the shape, color, and position of objects. In audition, vibrations (from vocal cords or a guitar string, perhaps) cause changes in air pressure that propagate through space to a listener's ears. In touch, the pressure of a surface against the skin signals its shape, texture, and temperature. In taste and smell, molecules dispersed in the air or dissolved in saliva reveal the identity of substances that we may or may not want to eat. In each case physical energy from the world is converted to neural energy inside the central nervous system. We've already seen that synesthetes experience a mixing of these perceptions; however, even during synesthesia the processes of transduction that begin those perceptions are the same. Despite "hearing colors," your eyes simply can't transduce sound waves, no matter how long you stare at your stereo speakers!

**SENSATION** Simple awareness due to the stimulation of a sense organ.

**PERCEPTION** The organization, identification, and interpretation of a sensation in order to form a mental representation.

**TRANSDUCTION** What takes place when many sensors in the body convert physical signals from the environment into neural signals sent to the central nervous system.

# Psychophysics

It's intriguing to consider the possibility that our basic perceptions of sights or sounds might differ fundamentally from those of other people. One reason we find synesthetes fascinating is because their perceptual experiences are so different from most of ours. But we won't get very far in understanding such differences by simply relying on casual self-reports. As you learned in Chapter 2, to understand a behavior researchers must first *operationalize* it, and that involves finding a reliable way to measure it.

Any type of scientific investigation requires objective measurements. Measuring the physical energy of a stimulus, such as the color and brightness of a light, is easy enough: You can probably buy the necessary instruments online to do that yourself. But how do you quantify a person's private, subjective *perception* of that light? It's one thing to know that a flashlight produces "100 candlepower" or gives off "8,000 lumens," but it's another matter entirely to measure a person's psychological experience of that light energy.

The structuralists, led by Wilhelm Wundt and Edward Titchener, tried using introspection to measure perceptual experiences (see Chapter 1). They failed miserably at this task. After all, you can describe your experience to another person in words, but that person cannot know directly what you perceive when you look at a sunset. You both may call the sunset "orange" and "beautiful," but neither of you can directly perceive the other's experience of the same event. Evoked memories and emotions intertwine with what you are hearing, seeing, and smelling, making your perception of an event—and therefore your experience of that event—unique.

Given that perception is different for each of us, how could we ever hope to measure it? This question was answered in the mid-1800s by the German scientist and philosopher Gustav Fechner (1801–87). Fechner was originally trained as a physicist but developed strong interests in philosophy and psychology, especially the study of perception. He began conducting informal studies of visual perception on himself during the 1830s. However, he got a bit carried away with his research and temporarily blinded himself while staring at the sun for a prolonged time. Fechner's eyes became so sensitive to light that he had to bandage them before leaving the house, and they bothered him the rest of his life. Limited in his abilities, Fechner took on extra work to help support his family, such as translating works from French to German and even writing much of an encyclopedia of household knowledge (Watson, 1978). His workload and eye problems resulted in a psychological breakdown and severe depression, leading him to resign his professorship at the University of Leipzig and go into seclusion.

Although this was a difficult period in his life, it was of great importance to psychology. In his isolation, Fechner was free to think deeply about the issues that interested him the most, especially how it might be possible to link psychology and physics. His efforts led him to develop an approach to measuring sensation and perception called **psychophysics:** *methods that measure the strength of a stimulus and the observer's sensitivity to that stimulus* (Fechner, 1860). In a typical psychophysics experiment, researchers ask people to make a simple judgment—whether or not they saw a flash of light, for example. The psychophysicist then relates the measured stimulus, such as the brightness of the light flash, to each observer's yes-or-no response.

# Measuring Thresholds

Psychophysicists begin the measurement process with a single sensory signal to determine precisely how much physical energy is required to evoke a sensation in an observer.

## Absolute Threshold

The simplest quantitative measurement in psychophysics is the **absolute threshold,** *the minimal intensity needed to just barely detect a stimulus.* A *threshold* is a boundary. The doorway that separates the inside from the outside of a house is a threshold, as is the

**PSYCHOPHYSICS** Methods that measure the strength of a stimulus and the observer's sensitivity to that stimulus.

**ABSOLUTE THRESHOLD** The minimal intensity needed to just barely detect a stimulus.

| Table 4.1 | Approximate Sensory Thresholds |
|---|---|
| **Sense** | **Absolute Threshold** |
| Vision | A candle flame 30 miles away on a clear, dark night |
| Hearing | A clock's tick 20 feet away when all is quiet |
| Touch | A fly's wing touching the cheek from 1 centimeter away |
| Smell | A single drop of perfume diffused through an area equivalent to the volume of six rooms |
| Taste | A teaspoon of sugar dissolved in two gallons of water |

*Source:* Adapted from Galanter (1962).

boundary between two psychological states ("awareness" and "unawareness," for example). In finding the absolute threshold for sensation, the two states in question are *sensing* and *not sensing* some stimulus. **TABLE 4.1** lists the approximate sensory thresholds for each of the five senses.

To measure the absolute threshold for detecting a sound, for example, an observer sits in a soundproof room wearing headphones linked to a computer. The experimenter presents a pure tone (the sort of sound made by striking a tuning fork) using the computer to vary the loudness or the length of time each tone lasts and recording how often the observer reports hearing that tone under each condition. The outcome of such an experiment is graphed in **FIGURE 4.2**. Notice from the shape of the curve that the transition from *not hearing* to *hearing* is gradual rather than abrupt. Investigators typically define the absolute threshold as the loudness required for the listener to say she or he has heard the tone on 50% of the trials.

If we repeat this experiment for many different tones, we can observe and record the thresholds for tones ranging from very low pitch to very high. It turns out that people tend to be most sensitive to the range of tones corresponding to human conversation. If the tone is low enough, such as the lowest note on a pipe organ, most humans cannot hear it at all; we can only feel it. If the tone is high enough, we likewise cannot hear it, but dogs and many other animals can.

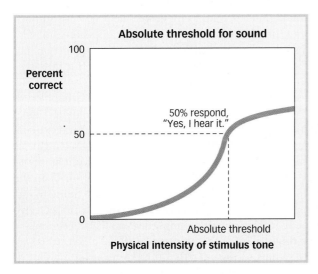

**Figure 4.2 Absolute Threshold** Some of us are more sensitive than others, and we may even detect sensory stimulation below our own absolute threshold. Absolute threshold is graphed here as the point where the increasing intensity of the stimulus enables an observer to detect it on 50% of the trials. As its intensity gradually increases, we detect the stimulation more frequently.

**JUST NOTICEABLE DIFFERENCE (JND)** The minimal change in a stimulus that can just barely be detected.

**WEBER'S LAW** The just noticeable difference of a stimulus is a constant proportion despite variations in intensity.

## Difference Thresholds

The absolute threshold is useful for assessing how sensitive we are to faint stimuli, but most everyday perception involves detecting differences among stimuli that are well above the absolute threshold. Most people are pretty adept at noticing that a couch is red, but they're likely to want to know if the couch is redder than the drapes they're considering. Similarly, parents can usually detect their own infant's cry from the cries of other babies, but it's probably more useful to be able to differentiate the "I'm hungry" cry from the "I'm cranky" cry from the "something is biting my toes" cry. In short, the human perceptual system excels at detecting *changes* in stimulation rather than the simple onset or offset of stimulation.

As a way of measuring this difference threshold, Fechner proposed the **just noticeable difference**, or **JND**, *the minimal change in a stimulus that can just barely be detected*. The JND is not a fixed quantity; rather, it depends on how intense the stimuli being measured are and on the particular sense being measured. Consider measuring the JND for a bright light. An observer in a dark room is shown a light of fixed intensity, called the *standard* (S), next to a comparison light that is slightly brighter or dimmer than the standard. When S is very dim, observers can see even a very small difference in brightness between the two lights: The JND is small. But if S is bright, a much larger increment is needed to detect the difference: The JND is larger.

In fact, the just noticeable difference can be calculated for each sense. It is roughly proportional to the magnitude of the standard stimulus. This relationship was first noticed in 1834 by a German physiologist named Ernst Weber, who taught at the University of Leipzig around the time that Fechner was a student there and likely influenced Fechner's thinking (Watson, 1978). Fechner applied Weber's insight directly to psychophysics, resulting in a formal relationship called **Weber's law**, which states that *the just noticeable difference of a stimulus is a constant proportion despite variations in intensity*. As an example, the JND for weight is about 2%. If you picked up a one-ounce envelope, then a two-ounce envelope, you'd probably notice the difference between them. But if you picked up a five-pound package, then a five-pound, one-ounce package, you'd probably detect no difference at all between them. In fact, you'd probably need about a five-and-a-half-pound package to detect a JND. When calculating a difference threshold, it is the proportion between stimuli that is important; the measured size of the difference, whether in brightness, loudness, or weight, is irrelevant.

## Signal Detection

Measuring absolute and difference thresholds requires a critical assumption: that a threshold exists! But much of what scientists know about biology suggests that such a discrete, all-or-none change in the brain is unlikely. Humans don't suddenly and rapidly switch between perceiving and not perceiving; in fact, recall that the transition from *not sensing* to *sensing* is gradual (see Figure 4.2). The very same physical stimulus, such as a dim light or a quiet tone, presented on several different occasions, may be perceived by the same person on some occasions but not on others. Remember, an absolute threshold is operationalized as perceiving the stimulus 50% of the time . . . which means the other 50% of the time it might go undetected.

Our accurate perception of a sensory stimulus, then, can be somewhat haphazard. Whether in the psychophysics lab or out in the world, sensory signals face a lot of competition, or *noise*, which refers to all the other stimuli coming from the internal and external environment. Memories, moods, and motives intertwine with what you are seeing, hearing, and smelling at any given time. This internal "noise" competes with your ability to detect a stimulus with perfect, focused attention. Other sights, sounds, and smells in the world at large also compete for attention; you rarely have the luxury of attending to just one stimulus apart from everything else. As a consequence of noise, you may not perceive everything that you sense, and you may even perceive things that you haven't sensed.

To see how these mismatches might happen, imagine measuring the electrical activity of a single neuron sending signals from the eye to the brain. As a dim spot of light is flashed onto an observer's eye, the number of subsequent action potentials fluctuates from one presentation to the next even when the light is exactly the same brightness each time. Occasionally, the neuron might fire even if no light is presented—a *spontaneous action potential* has occurred. Sensory systems are noisy; when the signals are very small, dim, or quiet, the senses provide only a "fuzzy" indicator of the state of the world.

This variability among neural responses helps explain why Figure 4.2 shows a gradual rise in the likelihood of hearing a tone. For a fixed tone intensity, the evoked neural response varies a little from one presentation to the next. On some presentations, the auditory neurons' responses will be a bit greater than average, and the listener will be more likely to detect the tone. On other presentations, the neural response will, by chance, be a bit less than average, and the listener will be less likely to detect the tone. On still other occasions, the neurons might produce spontaneous action potentials, leading the observer to claim that a tone was heard when none was presented.

Given the variability in neural responses, observers are faced with a decision. If they say, "Yes, I heard a tone," anytime there is any activity in the auditory system, they will often respond "yes" when no tone is presented. So observers might adopt a more conservative response criterion, deciding to say, "Yes, I heard a tone," only when the sensory experience is quite obvious. The problem now is that an observer will often miss fainter tones that were actually presented. Think of the last time you had a hearing test. You no doubt missed some of the quiet beeps that were presented, but you also probably said you heard beeps that weren't really there.

An approach to psychophysics called **signal detection theory** holds that *the response to a stimulus depends both on a person's sensitivity to the stimulus in the presence of noise and on a person's response criterion.* That is, observers consider the sensory evidence evoked by the stimulus and compare it to an internal decision criterion (Green & Swets, 1966; Macmillan & Creelman, 2005). If the sensory evidence exceeds the criterion, the observer responds by saying, "Yes, I detected the stimulus," and if it falls short of the criterion, the observer responds by saying, "No, I did not detect the stimulus."

Signal detection theory allows researchers to quantify an observer's response in the presence of noise. In a signal detection experiment, a stimulus, such as a dim light, is randomly presented or not. If you've ever taken an eye exam that checks your peripheral vision, you have an idea about this kind of setup: Lights of varying intensity are flashed at various places in the visual field, and your task is to respond anytime you see one. Observers in a signal detection experiment must decide whether they saw the light or not, leading to the four possible outcomes shown in **FIGURE 4.3a**. If the light is presented and the observer correctly responds, "Yes," the outcome is a *hit*. If the light is presented and the observer says, "No," the result is a *miss*. However, if the light is *not* presented and the observer nonetheless says it was, a *false alarm* has occurred. Finally, if the light is *not* presented and the observer responds, "No," a *correct rejection* has occurred: The observer accurately detected the absence of the stimulus.

Observers can adopt a very liberal response criterion, saying, "Yes," at the slightest hint of evidence for the stimulus (see **FIGURE 4.3b**). Notice that this strategy will produce a lot of hits but also a lot of false alarms. Conversely, adopting a very conservative criterion—saying, "Yes," only when the stimulus is clear, strong, and unambiguous—should minimize the rate of false alarms but increase the proportion of misses (see **FIGURE 4.3c**).

**Figure 4.3** **Signal Detection Criteria** Sensation depends not only on our sensitivity to stimulation but also on how we make decisions. Of the four possible outcomes on the grid in (a), we may correctly report the presence (a hit) or absence (correct rejection) of a stimulus, fail to detect it (a miss), or say we detect it when it's not there (false alarm). People may be equally sensitive to stimulation but adopt very different decision criteria. Those who tend to say they detect a signal produce many false alarms as well as many hits (b). Those who tend to say they detect no signal minimize false alarms but often miss the stimulus (c). Decision criteria have wide application in areas as diverse as drug trials and dating.

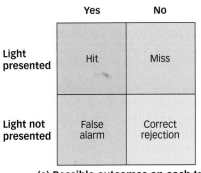

|  | Yes | No |
|---|---|---|
| **Light presented** | Hit | Miss |
| **Light not presented** | False alarm | Correct rejection |

**(a) Possible outcomes on each trial**

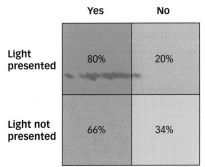

|  | Yes | No |
|---|---|---|
| **Light presented** | 80% | 20% |
| **Light not presented** | 66% | 34% |

**(b) Purely liberal criterion response**

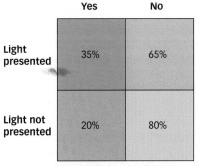

|  | Yes | No |
|---|---|---|
| **Light presented** | 35% | 65% |
| **Light not presented** | 20% | 80% |

**(c) Purely conservative criterion response**

Signal detection theory is a more sophisticated approach than was used in the early days of establishing absolute thresholds. Back then, it might have been assumed that everyone (or at least a majority of observers) heard a tone or saw a flickering candle flame with equal facility. Signal detection theory, in contrast, explicitly takes into account observers' response tendencies, such as liberally saying, "Yes," or reserving identifications only for obvious instances of the stimulus. It's interesting, then, to learn that the ideas behind signal detection theory were developed first by none other than Fechner (1860). It's not clear why such important ideas were not grasped by later psychologists who appreciated other aspects of Fechner's work, but it's possible that most of those researchers lacked the mathematical training required to appreciate Fechner's insights (Link, 1994). In short, Fechner anticipated long ago that both the characteristics of the stimulus *and* the characteristics of the observer need to be taken into account, producing a better understanding of the perceptual process.

Signal detection theory proposes a way to measure *perceptual sensitivity*—how effectively the perceptual system represents sensory events—separately from the observer's decision-making strategy. Two observers with opposite decision criteria and correspondingly distinct hit rates and false alarm rates may exhibit similar levels of sensitivity. That is, even though one person says, "Yes," much more often than another, both may be equally accurate in distinguishing between the presence or absence of a stimulus. Even though the purely conservative and liberal strategies represent two poles on a long continuum of possible decision criteria, signal detection theory has practical applications at home, school, work, and even while driving.

For example, a radiologist may have to decide whether a mammogram shows that a patient has breast cancer. The radiologist knows that certain features, such as a mass of a particular size and shape, are associated with the presence of cancer. But noncancerous features can have a very similar appearance to cancerous ones. The radiologist may decide on a strictly liberal criterion and check every possible case of cancer with a biopsy. As shown in Figure 4.3b, this decision strategy minimizes the possibility of missing a true cancer but leads to many false alarms. A strictly conservative criterion will cut down on false alarms but will miss some treatable cancers (see Figure 4.3c).

As another example, imagine that police are on the lookout for a suspected felon who they have reason to believe will be at a crowded soccer match. Although the law enforcement agency provided a fairly good description—6'0", sandy brown hair, beard, glasses—there are still thousands of people to scan. Rounding up all men between 5'5" and 6'5" would probably produce a hit (the felon is caught) but at the expense of an extraordinary number of false alarms (many innocent people are detained and questioned).

These different types of errors have to be weighed against one another in setting the decision criterion. Signal detection theory offers a practical way to choose among criteria that permit decision makers to take into account the consequences of hits, misses, false alarms, and correct rejections (McFall & Treat, 1999; Swets, Dawes, & Monahan, 2000). (For an example of a common everyday task that can interfere with signal detection, see The Real World box on the next page.)

## Sensory Adaptation

When you walk into a bakery, the aroma of freshly baked bread overwhelms you, but after a few minutes the smell fades. If you dive into cold water, the temperature is shocking at first, but after a few minutes you get used to it. When you wake up in the middle of the night for a drink of water, the bathroom light blinds you, but after a few minutes you no longer squint.

These are all examples of **sensory adaptation**, the observation that *sensitivity to prolonged stimulation tends to decline over time as an organism adapts to current conditions*. Imagine that while you are studying in a quiet room, your neighbor in the apartment next door turns on the stereo. That gets your attention, but after a few minutes the sounds fade from your awareness as you continue your studies. But remember that our perceptual systems emphasize *change* in responding to sensory events: When the music stops, you notice.

**SENSORY ADAPTATION** Sensitivity to prolonged stimulation tends to decline over time as an organism adapts to current conditions.

## { THE REAL WORLD } **Multitasking**

BY ONE ESTIMATE, USING A CELL PHONE while driving makes having an accident four times more likely (McEvoy et al., 2005). In response to highway safety experts and statistics such as this, state legislatures are passing laws that restrict, and sometimes ban, using mobile phones while driving. You might think that's a fine idea . . . for everyone else on the road. But surely *you* can manage to punch in a number on a phone, carry on a conversation, or maybe even text-message while simultaneously driving in a safe and courteous manner. Right?

In a word, *wrong*. The issue here is *selective attention,* or perceiving only what's currently relevant to you. Try this. Without moving a muscle, think about the pressure of your skin against your chair right now. Effortlessly you shifted your attention to allow a sensory signal to enter your awareness. This simple shift shows that your perception of the world depends both on what sensory signals are present and on your choice of which signals to attend to and which to ignore. Perception is an active, moment-to-moment exploration for relevant or interesting information, not a passive receptacle for whatever happens to come along.

Talking on a cell phone while driving demands that you juggle two independent sources of sensory input—vision and audition—at the same time. Normally this kind of *multitasking* works rather well. It's only when you need to react suddenly that your driving performance may suffer. Researchers

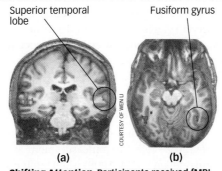

Superior temporal lobe

Fusiform gyrus

COURTESY OF WEN LI

(a)     (b)

**Shifting Attention** Participants received fMRI scans as they performed tasks that required them to shift their attention between visual and auditory information. (a) When focusing on auditory information, a region in the superior (upper) temporal lobe involved in auditory processing showed increased activity (yellow/orange). (b) In striking contrast, a visual region, the fusiform gyrus, showed decreased activity when participants focused on auditory information (blue).

have tested experienced drivers in a highly realistic driving simulator, measuring their response times to brake lights and stop signs while they listened to the radio or carried on phone conversations about a political issue, among other tasks (Strayer, Drews, & Johnston, 2003).

These experienced drivers reacted significantly slower during phone conversations than during the other tasks. This is because a phone conversation requires memory retrieval, deliberation, and planning what to say and often carries an emotional stake in the conversation topic. Tasks such as

listening to the radio require far less attention or none at all.

The tested drivers became so engaged in their conversations that their minds no longer seemed to be in the car. Their slower braking response translated into an increased stopping distance that, depending on the driver's speed, would have resulted in a rear-end collision. Whether the phone was handheld or hands free made little difference. This suggests that laws requiring drivers to use hands-free phones may have little effect on reducing accidents.

Other researchers have measured brain activity using fMRI while people were shifting attention between visual and auditory information. The strength of visual and auditory brain activity was affected: When attention was directed to audition, activity in visual areas decreased compared to when attention was directed to vision (Shomstein & Yantis, 2004). It was as if the participants could adjust a mental "volume knob" to regulate the flow of incoming information according to which task they were attending to at the moment.

So how well do we multitask in several thousand pounds of metal hurtling down the highway? Experienced drivers can handle divided attention to a degree, yet most of us have to acknowledge that we have had close calls due to driving while distracted. Unless you have two heads with one brain each—one to talk and one to concentrate on driving—you might do well to keep your eyes on the road and not on the phone.

---

Sensory adaptation is a useful process for most organisms. Imagine what your sensory and perceptual world would be like without it. When you put on your jeans in the morning, the feeling of rough cloth against your bare skin would be as noticeable hours later as it was in the first few minutes. The stink of garbage in your apartment when you first walk in would never dissipate. If you had to constantly be aware of how your tongue feels while it is resting in your mouth, you'd be driven to distraction. Our perceptual systems respond more strongly to changes in stimulation rather than to constant stimulation. A stimulus that doesn't change usually doesn't require any action; your car probably emits a certain hum all the time that you've gotten used to. But a change in stimulation often signals a need for action. If your car starts making different kinds of noises, you're not only more likely to notice them, but you're also more likely to do something about it.

---

**In summary,** sensation and perception are critical to survival. Sensation is the simple awareness that results from stimulation of a sense organ, whereas perception organizes, identifies, and interprets sensation at the level of the brain. All sensory modalities depend on the process of transduction, which converts physical signals from the environment into neural signals carried by sensory neurons into the central nervous system. In the 19th century, researchers developed psychophysics, an approach to studying perception that measures the strength of a stimulus and an observer's sensitivity to that

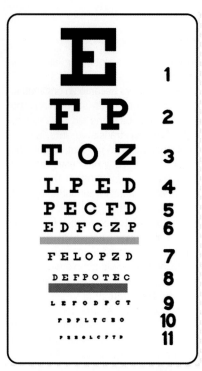

The Snellen chart is commonly used to measure visual acuity. Chances are good you've seen one yourself on more than one occasion.

stimulus. Psychophysicists have developed procedures for measuring an observer's absolute threshold, or the smallest intensity needed to just barely detect a stimulus, and the just noticeable difference (JND), or the smallest change in a stimulus that can just barely be detected. Signal detection theory allows researchers to distinguish between an observer's perceptual sensitivity to a stimulus and criteria for making decisions about the stimulus. Sensory adaptation occurs because sensitivity to lengthy stimulation tends to decline over time. ■ ■ ■

## Vision: More Than Meets the Eye

You might be proud of your 20/20 vision, even if it is corrected by glasses or contact lenses. *20/20* refers to a measurement associated with a Snellen chart, named after Hermann Snellen (1834–1908), the Dutch ophthalmologist who developed it as a means of assessing **visual acuity**, *the ability to see fine detail;* it is the smallest line of letters that a typical person can read from a distance of 20 feet. But if you dropped into the Birds of Prey Ophthalmologic Office, your visual pride would wither. Hawks, eagles, owls, and other raptors have much greater visual acuity than humans; in many cases, about eight times greater, or the equivalent of 20/2 vision. That's handy if you want to spot a mouse from a mile away, but if you simply need to see where your roommate left the big bag of Fritos, you can probably live with the fact that no one ever calls you "Ol' Eagle Eye."

Although you won't win any I Spy contests against a hawk, your sophisticated visual system has evolved to transduce visual energy in the world into neural signals in the brain. Humans have sensory receptors in their eyes that respond to wavelengths of light energy. When we look at people, places, and things, patterns of light and color give us information about where one surface stops and another begins. The array of light reflected from those surfaces preserves their shapes and enables us to form a mental representation of a scene (Rodieck, 1998). Understanding vision, then, starts with understanding light.

### Sensing Light

Visible light is simply the portion of the electromagnetic spectrum that we can see, and it is an extremely small slice. You can think about light as waves of energy. Like ocean waves, light waves vary in height and in the distance between their peaks, or *wavelengths,* as **TABLE 4.2** shows.

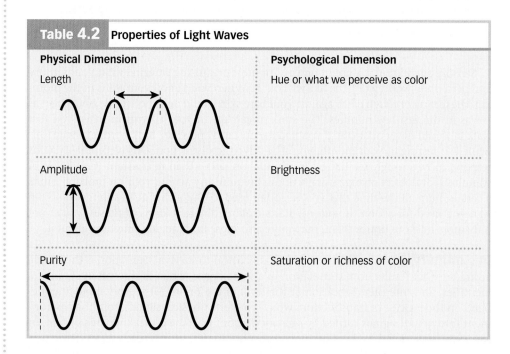

| Table 4.2 | Properties of Light Waves |
|---|---|
| **Physical Dimension** | **Psychological Dimension** |
| Length | Hue or what we perceive as color |
| Amplitude | Brightness |
| Purity | Saturation or richness of color |

**VISUAL ACUITY** The ability to see fine detail.

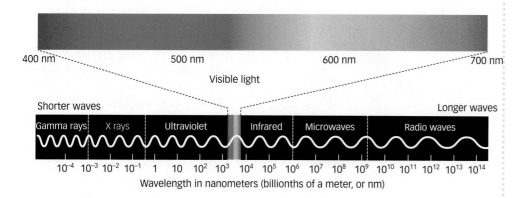

Figure **4.4** **Electromagnetic Spectrum**
The sliver of light waves visible to humans as a rainbow of colors from violet-blue to red is bounded on the short end by ultraviolet rays, which honeybees can see, and on the long end by infrared waves, upon which night-vision equipment operates. Someone wearing night-vision goggles, for example, can detect another person's body heat in complete darkness. Light waves are minute, but the scale along the bottom of this chart offers a glimpse of their varying lengths, measured in nanometers (nm; 1 nm = 1 billionth of a meter).

There are three properties of light waves, each of which has a physical dimension that produces a corresponding psychological dimension. The *length* of a light wave determines its hue, or what humans perceive as color. The intensity or *amplitude* of a light wave—how high the peaks are—determines what we perceive as the brightness of light. The third property is *purity,* or the number of wavelengths that make up the light. Purity corresponds to what humans perceive as saturation, or the richness of colors (see **FIGURE 4.4**). In other words, light doesn't need a human to have the properties it does: Length, amplitude, and purity are properties of the light waves themselves. What humans perceive from those properties are color, brightness, and saturation.

To understand how the properties of waves affect how we sense light, it's helpful to understand how our eyes detect light in the first place.

## The Human Eye

**FIGURE 4.5** shows the human eye in cross-section. Light that reaches the eyes passes first through a clear, smooth outer tissue called the *cornea,* which bends the light wave and sends it through the *pupil,* a hole in the colored part of the eye. This colored part is the *iris,* which is a translucent, doughnut-shaped muscle that controls the size of the pupil and hence the amount of light that can enter the eye.

When you move from the dim illumination of a movie theater into the bright sunshine outside, your irises contract, reducing the size of the pupils and the amount of light passing through them. You may still have to shade your eyes until their light-sensitive cells adapt to the brighter light level. This process is a type of sensory adaptation called *light adaptation.*

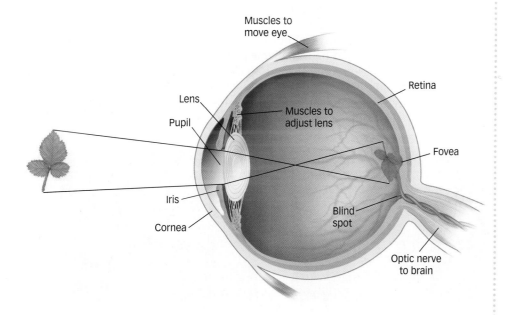

Figure **4.5** **Anatomy of the Human Eye**
Light reflected from a surface enters the eye via the transparent cornea, bending to pass through the pupil at the center of the colored iris. Behind the iris, the thickness and shape of the lens adjust to focus the light on the retina, where the image appears upside down and backward. Basically, this is how a camera lens works. Light-sensitive receptor cells in the retinal surface, excited or inhibited by spots of light, influence the specialized neurons that convey nerve impulses to the brain's visual centers through their axons, which make up the optic nerve.

**(a)**
Normal vision

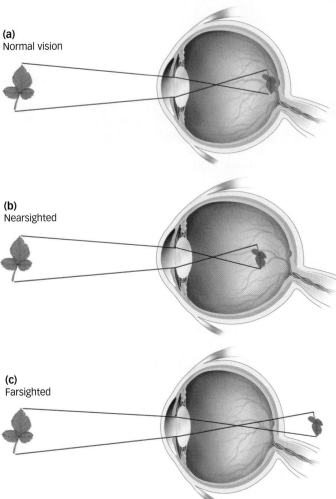

**(b)**
Nearsighted

**(c)**
Farsighted

**Figure 4.6 Accommodation** Inside the eye, the lens changes shape to focus nearby or faraway objects on the retina. (a) People with normal vision focus the image on the retina at the back of the eye, both for near and far objects. (b) Nearsighted people see clearly what's nearby, but distant objects are blurry because light from them is focused in front of the retina, a condition called myopia. (c) Farsighted people have the opposite problem: Distant objects are clear, but those nearby are blurry because their point of focus falls beyond the surface of the retina, a condition called hyperopia.

Immediately behind the iris, muscles inside the eye control the shape of the *lens* to bend the light again and focus it onto the **retina**, *light-sensitive tissue lining the back of the eyeball*. The muscles change the shape of the lens to focus objects at different distances, making the lens flatter for objects that are far away or rounder for nearby objects. This is called **accommodation**, *the process by which the eye maintains a clear image on the retina*. **FIGURE 4.6a** shows how accommodation works.

If your eyeballs are a little too long or a little too short, the lens will not focus images properly on the retina. If the eyeball is too long, images are focused in front of the retina, leading to nearsightedness (*myopia*), which is shown in **FIGURE 4.6b.** If the eyeball is too short, images are focused behind the retina, and the result is farsightedness (*hyperopia*), as shown in **FIGURE 4.6c.** Eyeglasses, contact lenses, and surgical procedures can correct either condition. For example, eyeglasses and contacts both provide an additional lens to help focus light more appropriately, and procedures such as LASIK physically reshape the eye's existing lens.

**RETINA** Light-sensitive tissue lining the back of the eyeball.

**ACCOMMODATION** The process by which the eye maintains a clear image on the retina.

**CONES** Photoreceptors that detect color, operate under normal daylight conditions, and allow us to focus on fine detail.

**RODS** Photoreceptors that become active only under low-light conditions for night vision.

## Phototransduction in the Retina

The retina is the interface between the world of light outside the body and the world of vision inside the central nervous system. Two types of *photoreceptor cells* in the retina contain light-sensitive pigments that transduce light into neural impulses. **Cones** *detect color, operate under normal daylight conditions, and allow us to focus on fine detail.* **Rods** *become active only under low-light conditions for night vision* (see **FIGURE 4.7**).

Rods are much more sensitive photoreceptors than cones, but this sensitivity comes at a cost. Because all rods contain the same photopigment, they provide no information about color and sense only shades of gray. Think about this the next time you wake up in the middle of the night and make your way to the bathroom for a drink of water. Using only the moonlight from the window to light your way, do you see the room in color or in shades of gray?

The full-color image on the left is what you'd see when your rods and cones were fully at work. The grayscale image on the right is what you'd see if only your rods were functioning.

**Figure 4.7** **Close-up of the Retina** The surface of the retina is composed of photoreceptor cells, the rods and cones, beneath a layer of transparent neurons, the bipolar and retinal ganglion cells, connected in sequence. Viewed close up in this cross-sectional diagram is the area of greatest visual acuity, the fovea, where most color-sensitive cones are concentrated, allowing us to see fine detail as well as color. Rods, the predominant photoreceptors activated in low-light conditions, are distributed everywhere else on the retina.

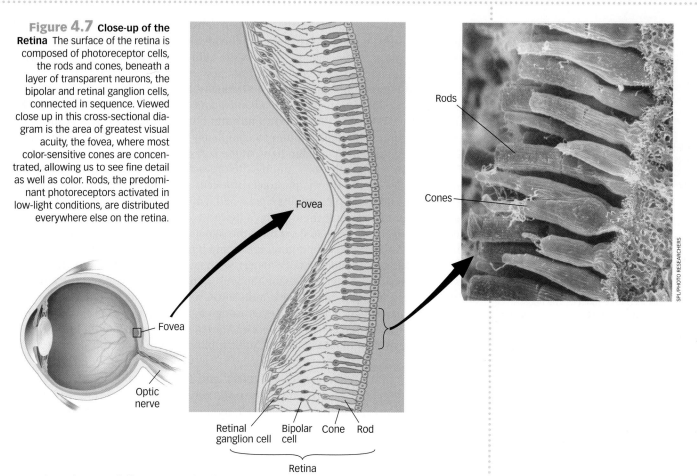

Rods and cones differ in several other ways as well, most notably in their numbers. About 120 million rods are distributed more or less evenly around each retina except in the very center, the **fovea,** *an area of the retina where vision is the clearest and there are no rods at all.* The absence of rods in the fovea decreases the sharpness of vision in reduced light, but it can be overcome. For example, when amateur astronomers view dim stars through their telescopes at night, they know to look a little off to the side of the target so that the image will fall not on the rod-free fovea but on some other part of the retina that contains many highly sensitive rods.

In contrast to rods, each retina contains only about 6 million cones, which are densely packed in the fovea and much more sparsely distributed over the rest of the retina, as you can see in Figure 4.7. The high concentration of cones in the fovea directly affects visual acuity and explains why objects off to the side, in your *peripheral vision,* aren't so clear. The light reflecting from those peripheral objects has a difficult time landing in the fovea, making the resulting image less clear. The more fine detail encoded and represented in the visual system, the clearer the perceived image. The process is analogous to the quality of photographs taken with a six-megapixel digital camera versus a two-megapixel camera.

**FOVEA** An area of the retina where vision is the clearest and there are no rods at all.

The image on the left was taken at a higher resolution than the image on the right. The difference in quality is analogous to light falling on the fovea versus not.

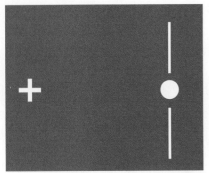

**Figure 4.8 Blind Spot Demonstration**
To find your blind spot, close your left eye and stare at the cross with your right eye. Hold the book six to 12 inches (15 to 30 centimeters) away from your eyes and move it slowly toward and away from you until the dot disappears. The dot is now in your blind spot and so is not visible. At this point the vertical lines may appear as one continuous line because the visual system fills in the area occupied by the missing dot. To test your left-eye blind spot, turn the book upside down and repeat with your right eye closed.

Rods and cones also differ in the way their sensitivity changes when the overall light level changes. Remember that the pupil constricts when you move from dim to bright illumination. Now consider the reverse: When you enter a dark theater after being outside on a sunny day, your pupil enlarges to let in more light, but at first you will be almost blind to the seating layout. Gradually, however, your vision adapts. This form of sensory adaptation is called *dark adaptation* (Hecht & Mandelbaum, 1938). Cones adapt to the dark within about 8 minutes but aren't too sensitive at low light levels. Rods require about 30 minutes to completely adapt to the dark, but they provide much better sensitivity in dim light, at the cost of color vision.

The retina is thick with cells. Among the different neuron types that occupy the retina's three distinct layers, the photoreceptor cells (rods and cones) form the innermost layer. The middle layer contains *bipolar cells,* which collect neural signals from the rods and cones and transmit them to the outermost layer of the retina, where neurons called *retinal ganglion cells* (RGCs) organize the signals and send them to the brain.

The axons and dendrites of photoreceptors and bipolar cells are relatively short (just a few microns long, or millionths of a meter), whereas the axons of the retinal ganglion cells span several centimeters. RGCs are the sensory neurons that connect the retina to various centers within the brain. The bundled RGC axons—about 1.5 million per eye—form the *optic nerve,* which leaves the eye through a hole in the retina called the **blind spot**, which *contains neither rods nor cones and therefore has no mechanism to sense light*. Try the demonstration in **FIGURE 4.8** to find the blind spot in each of your own eyes.

### Receptive Fields and Lateral Inhibition

Each axon in the optic nerve originates in an individual retinal ganglion cell, as shown at the bottom of **FIGURE 4.9.** Most RGCs respond to input not from a single retinal cone or rod but from an entire patch of adjacent photoreceptors lying side by side, or laterally, in the retina. A particular RGC will respond to light falling anywhere within that small patch, which is called its **receptive field**, *the region of the sensory surface that, when stimulated, causes a change in the firing rate of that neuron.* Although we'll focus on vision here, the general concept of receptive fields applies to all sensory systems. For example, the cells that connect to the touch centers of the brain have receptive fields, which are the part of the skin that, when stimulated, causes that cell's response to change in some way.

Within a receptive field, neighboring photoreceptors respond to stimulation differently: Some cells are excited, whereas some are inhibited. These opposing responses interact, which means that the signals they send through the bipolar cells to the RGC are based on differing levels of receptor activation, a process called *lateral inhibition.* Moving from top to bottom in Figure 4.9, a spot of light that covers any or all of the cones will activate one or more bipolar cells, which in turn causes the ganglion cell to change the rate at which it sends action potentials.

A given RGC responds to a spot of light projected anywhere within a small, roughly circular patch of retina (Kuffler, 1953). Most receptive fields contain either a central excitatory zone surrounded by a doughnut-shaped inhibitory zone, which is called an *on-center cell,* or a central inhibitory zone surrounded by an excitatory zone, which is called an *off-center cell* (see **FIGURE 4.10**). The doughnut-shaped regions represent patches of retina, as if the top of the diagram in Figure 4.9 were tilted forward so we could look at the cones end-on.

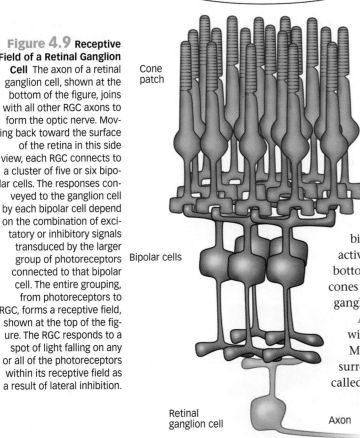

Receptive field

Cone patch

To retina

Bipolar cells

Retinal ganglion cell

Axon

To optic nerve

**Figure 4.9 Receptive Field of a Retinal Ganglion Cell** The axon of a retinal ganglion cell, shown at the bottom of the figure, joins with all other RGC axons to form the optic nerve. Moving back toward the surface of the retina in this side view, each RGC connects to a cluster of five or six bipolar cells. The responses conveyed to the ganglion cell by each bipolar cell depend on the combination of excitatory or inhibitory signals transduced by the larger group of photoreceptors connected to that bipolar cell. The entire grouping, from photoreceptors to RGC, forms a receptive field, shown at the top of the figure. The RGC responds to a spot of light falling on any or all of the photoreceptors within its receptive field as a result of lateral inhibition.

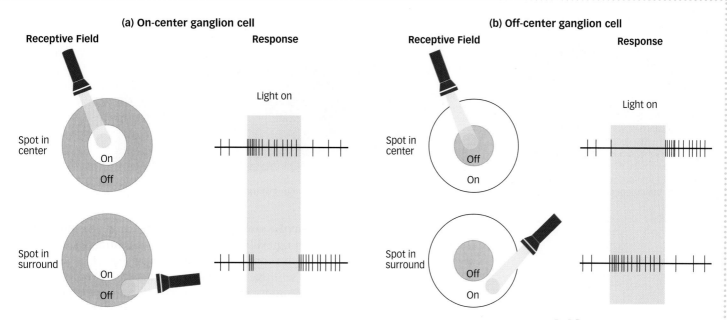

**(a) On-center ganglion cell**

Receptive Field

Response

Spot in center

Light on

Spot in surround

**(b) Off-center ganglion cell**

Receptive Field

Response

Spot in center

Light on

Spot in surround

Think about the response of an on-center retinal ganglion cell when its receptive field is stimulated with spots of light of different sizes (**FIGURE 4.10a**). A small spot shining on the central excitatory zone increases the RGC's firing rate. When the spot exactly fills the excitatory zone, it elicits the strongest response, whereas light falling on the surrounding inhibitory zone elicits the weakest response or none at all. The response of an off-center cell, shown in **FIGURE 4.10b**, is just the opposite. A small spot shining on the central inhibitory zone elicits a weak response, and a spot shining on the surrounding excitatory zone elicits a strong response in the RGC.

If a spot of light "spills over" into the inhibitory zone of either receptive-field type, the cell's response decreases somewhat, and if the entire receptive field is stimulated, excitatory and inhibitory activations cancel out due to lateral inhibition and the RGC's response will look similar to its response in the dark. Why would the RGC respond the same way to a uniformly bright field as to a uniformly dark field? The answer is related to the idea of difference thresholds: The visual system encodes *differences* in brightness or color. In other words, the RGC is a kind of "spot detector," recording the relative changes in excitation and inhibition of receptive fields.

Lateral inhibition reveals how the visual system begins to encode the spatial structure of a scene and not merely the point-by-point light intensity sensed at each location in the retina. The retina is organized in this way to detect edges—abrupt transitions from light to dark or vice versa. Edges are of supreme importance in vision. They define the shapes of objects, and anything that highlights such boundaries improves our ability to see an object's shape, particularly in low-light situations.

**Figure 4.10** RGC Receptive Fields Viewed End-on Imagine that you're looking down on the receptive field represented at the top of Figure 4.9. (a) An on-center ganglion cell increases its firing rate when the receptive field is stimulated by light in the central area but decreases its firing rate when the light strikes the surrounding area. Both neural response levels are shown in the right column. (b) The off-center ganglion cell decreases its firing rate when its receptive field is stimulated by light in the central area but increases its firing rate when the light strikes the surrounding area. Both responses are shown at the right.

## Perceiving Color

We thrill to the burst of colors during a fireworks display, "ooh" and "aah" at nature's palette during sunset, and marvel at the vibrant hues of a peacock's tail feathers. Color indeed adds zest to the visual world, but it also offers fundamental clues to an object's identity. A black banana or blue lips are color-coded calls to action—to avoid or sound the alarm, as the case might be.

### Seeing Color

Sir Isaac Newton pointed out around 1670 that color is not something "in" light. In fact, color is nothing but our perception of light's wavelength (see **FIGURE 4.11** on page 136). We perceive the shortest visible wavelengths as deep purple. As wavelengths increase, the color perceived changes gradually and continuously to blue, then green, yellow, orange, and, with the longest visible wavelengths, red. This rainbow of hues and accompanying wavelengths is called the *visible spectrum,* illustrated in Figure 4.11.

**BLIND SPOT** An area of the retina that contains neither rods nor cones and therefore has no mechanism to sense light.

**RECEPTIVE FIELD** The region of the sensory surface that, when stimulated, causes a change in the firing rate of that neuron.

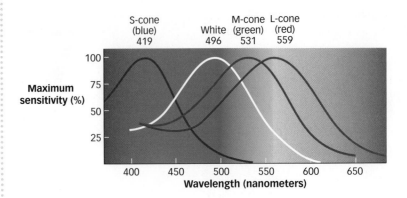

**Figure 4.11** **Seeing in Color** We perceive a spectrum of color because objects selectively absorb some wavelengths of light and reflect others. Color perception corresponds to the summed activity of the three types of cones. Each type is most sensitive to a narrow range of wavelengths in the visible spectrum—short (bluish light), medium (greenish light), or long (reddish light). Rods, represented by the white curve, are most sensitive to the medium wavelengths of visible light but do not contribute to color perception.

You'll recall that all rods contain the same photopigment, which makes them ideal for low-light vision but bad at distinguishing colors. Cones, by contrast, contain any one of three types of pigment. Each cone absorbs light over a range of wavelengths, but its pigment type is especially sensitive to visible wavelengths that correspond to red (long-wavelength), green (medium-wavelength), or blue (short-wavelength) light. Red, green, and blue are the primary colors of light, and the idea that color perception relies on three components in the retina dates to the 19th century, when it was first proposed by the English scientist Thomas Young (1773–1829). Young produced staggering accomplishments—he was a practicing physician and a distinguished physicist, and in his spare time he contributed to solving the mystery of the Rosetta stone (a tablet that allowed archeologists to translate Egyptian hieroglyphics to Greek, a language they actually understood!). He knew so much about so many topics that a recent biographer called him "the last man who knew everything" (Robinson, 2006). Happily for psychology, Young had some pretty good ideas abut how color vision works. But it was the great German scientist Hermann von Helmholtz (1821–94) who more fully developed Young's idea that color perception results from different combinations of the three basic elements in the retina that respond to the wavelengths corresponding to the three primary colors of light. This insight has several implications and applications.

For example, lighting designers add primary colors of light together, such as shining red and green spotlights on a surface to create a yellow light, as shown in **FIGURE 4.12a**. Notice that in the center of the figure, where the red, green, and blue lights overlap, the surface looks white. This demonstrates that a white surface really is reflecting all visible wavelengths of light. Increasing light to create color in this way is called *additive color mixing*.

Centuries before Newton first experimented with light, Renaissance painters in Italy had learned that they could re-create any color found in nature simply by mixing only three colors: red, blue, and yellow. You may have discovered this process for

**Figure 4.12** **Color Mixing** The millions of shades of color that humans can perceive are products not only of a light's wavelength but also of the mixture of wavelengths a stimulus absorbs or reflects. We see a ripe banana as yellow because the banana skin reflects the light waves that we perceive as yellow but absorbs the wavelengths that we perceive as shades of blue to green and those that make us see red. (a) Additive color mixing works by increasing the reflected wavelengths—by adding light to stimulate the red, blue, or green photopigments in the cones. When all visible wavelengths are present, we see white. (b) Subtractive color mixing removes wavelengths, thus absorbing light waves we see as red, blue, or yellow. When all visible wavelengths are absorbed, we see black.

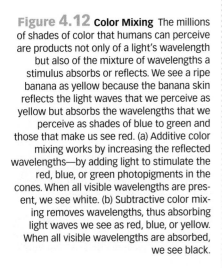

Fritz Goro, Life Magazine, 1971, Time Warner, Inc.

**(a) Additive color mixing**
**(red, blue, green)**

**(b) Subtractive color mixing**
**(red, blue, yellow)**

yourself by mixing paints. This *subtractive color mixing* works by removing light from the mix, such as when you combine yellow and red to make orange or blue and yellow to make green, shown in Figure 4.12b. The darker the color, the less light it contains, which is why black surfaces reflect no light.

When you perceive color, then, the cone receptors in your retina encode the wavelengths of light reflected from a surface. But color processing in the human visual system occurs in two stages. The first stage—encoding—occurs in the retina, whereas the second stage—processing—requires the brain (Gegenfurtner & Kiper, 2003).

## Trichromatic Color Representation in the Cones

Light striking the retina causes a specific pattern of response in the three cone types (Schnapf, Kraft, & Baylor, 1987). One type responds best to short-wavelength (bluish) light, the second type to medium-wavelength (greenish) light, and the third type to long-wavelength (reddish) light. Researchers refer to them as S-cones, M-cones, and L-cones, respectively (see Figure 4.11).

This **trichromatic color representation** means that *the pattern of responding across the three types of cones provides a unique code for each color.* Researchers can "read out" the wavelength of the light entering the eye by working backward from the relative firing rates of the three types of cones. A genetic disorder in which one of the cone types is missing—and, in some very rare cases, two or all three—causes a *color deficiency*. This trait is sex-linked, affecting men much more often than women.

Color deficiency is often referred to as *color blindness,* but in fact, people missing only one type of cone can still distinguish many colors, just not as many as someone who has the full complement of three cone types. Like synesthetes, people whose vision is color deficient often do not realize that they experience color differently from others.

Trichromatic color representation is well established as the first step of encoding color in the visual system (Abromov & Gordon, 1994). Sensory adaptation helps to explain the second step.

## Color-Opponent Representation into the Brain

Recall that sensory adaptation occurs because our sensitivity to prolonged stimulation tends to decline over time. Just like the rest of your body, cones need an occasional break too. Staring too long at one color fatigues the cones that respond to that color, producing a form of sensory adaptation called *color afterimage*. To demonstrate this effect for yourself, follow these instructions for **FIGURE 4.13**:

- Stare at the small cross between the two color patches for about 1 minute. Try to keep your eyes as still as possible.
- After a minute, look at the lower cross. You should see a vivid color aftereffect that lasts for a minute or more. Pay particular attention to the colors in the afterimage.

Were you puzzled that the red patch produces a green afterimage and the green patch produces a red afterimage? This result may seem like nothing more than a curious mindbug, but in fact it reveals something important about color perception. The explanation stems from the second stage of color representation, the **color-opponent system**, where *pairs of visual neurons work in opposition;* red-sensitive cells against green-sensitive (as in Figure 4.13) and blue-sensitive cells against yellow-sensitive (Hurvich & Jameson, 1957). How do opponent pairs of *four* colors make sense if we have just *three* cone types?

It may be that opponent pairs evolved to enhance color perception by taking advantage of excitatory and inhibitory stimulation. Red-green cells are excited (they increase their firing rates) in response to wavelengths corresponding to red and inhibited (they decrease their firing rates) in response to wavelengths corresponding to green. Blue-yellow cells increase their firing rate in response to blue wavelengths (excitatory) and decrease their firing rate in response to yellow wavelengths (inhibitory). The color pairs are linked to each other as opposites.

**TRICHROMATIC COLOR REPRESENTATION** The pattern of responding across the three types of cones that provides a unique code for each color.

**COLOR-OPPONENT SYSTEM** Pairs of visual neurons that work in opposition.

**Figure 4.13** **Color Afterimage Demonstration** Follow the accompanying instructions in the text, and sensory adaptation will do the rest. When the afterimage fades, you can get back to reading the chapter.

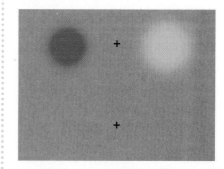

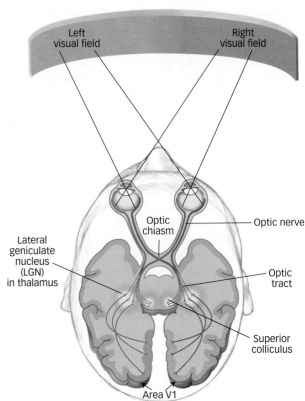

**Figure 4.14** **Visual Pathway from Eye through Brain** Objects in the right visual field stimulate the left half of each retina, and objects in the left visual field stimulate the right half of each retina. The optic nerves, one exiting each eye, are formed by the axons of retinal ganglion cells emerging from the retina. Just before they enter the brain at the optic chiasm, about half the nerve fibers from each eye cross. The left half of each optic nerve, representing the *right* visual field, runs through the brain's left hemisphere via the thalamus, and the right halves, representing the *left* visual field, travel this route through the right hemisphere. So information from the right visual field ends up in the left hemisphere and information from the left visual field ends up in the right hemisphere.

The color-opponent system explains color aftereffects. When you view a color, let's say, green, the cones that respond most strongly to green become fatigued over time. Fatigue leads to an imbalance in the inputs to the red-green color-opponent neurons, beginning with the retinal ganglion cells: The weakened signal from the green-responsive cones leads to an overall response that emphasizes red. A similar explanation can be made for other color aftereffects; find a bright blue circle of color and get ready to make your roommate see yellow spots!

Working together, the trichromatic and color-opponent systems begin the process of color perception. S-, M-, and L-cones connect to color-opponent RGCs with excitatory and/or inhibitory connections that produce the color-opponent response. Color-opponent, excitatory-inhibitory processes then continue down the visual pathways to the brain, first to neurons in the thalamus and then to the occipital cortex, as mapped in **FIGURE 4.14** (De Valois, Abramov, & Jacobs, 1966).

## The Visual Brain

A great deal of visual processing takes place within the retina itself, including the encoding of simple features such as spots of light, edges, and color. More complex aspects of vision, however, require more powerful processing, and that enlists the brain.

Streams of action potentials containing information encoded by the retina travel to the brain along the optic nerve. Half of the axons in the optic nerve that leave each eye come from retinal ganglion cells that code information in the right visual field, whereas the other half code information in the left visual field. These two nerve bundles link to the left and right hemispheres of the brain, respectively (see Figure 4.14). The optic nerve travels from each eye to the *lateral geniculate nucleus* (*LGN*), located in the thalamus. As you will recall from Chapter 3, the thalamus receives inputs from all of the senses except smell. From there the visual signal travels to the back of the brain, to a location called **area V1**, the *part of the occipital lobe that contains the primary visual cortex.* Here the information is systematically mapped into a representation of the visual scene. There are about 30 to 50 brain areas specialized for vision, located mainly in the occipital lobe at the back of the brain and in the temporal lobes on the sides of the brain (Orban, Van Essen, & Vanduffel, 2004; Van Essen, Anderson, & Felleman, 1992).

**AREA V1** The part of the occipital lobe that contains the primary visual cortex.

## Neural Systems for Perceiving Shape

One of the most important functions of vision involves perceiving the shapes of objects; our day-to-day lives would be a mess if we couldn't distinguish individual shapes from one another. Imagine not being able to reliably differentiate between a warm doughnut with glazed icing and a straight stalk of celery and you'll get the idea; breakfast could become a traumatic experience if you couldn't distinguish shapes. Perceiving shape depends on the location and orientation of an object's edges. It is not surprising, then, that area V1 is specialized for encoding edge orientation.

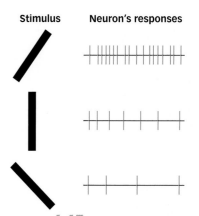

As you read in Chapter 3, neurons in the visual cortex selectively respond to bars and edges in specific orientations in space (Hubel & Weisel, 1962, 1998). In effect, area V1 contains populations of neurons, each "tuned" to respond to edges oriented at each position in the visual field. This means that some neurons fire when an object in a vertical orientation is perceived, other neurons fire when an object in a horizontal orientation is perceived, still other neurons fire when objects in a diagonal orientation of 45 degrees are perceived, and so on (see **FIGURE 4.15**). The outcome of the coordinated response of all these feature detectors contributes to a sophisticated visual system that can detect where a doughnut ends and celery begins.

**Figure 4.15** **Single Neuron Feature Detectors** Area V1 contains neurons that respond to specific orientations of edges. Here a single neuron's responses are recorded (at right) as the monkey views bars at different orientations (left). This neuron fires continuously when the bar is pointing to the right at 45 degrees, less often when it is vertical, and not at all when it is pointing to the left at 45 degrees.

## Pathways for What, Where, and How

In Chapter 2 you learned how brain researchers have used transcranial magnetic stimulation (TMS) to demonstrate that a person who can recognize what an object is may not be able to perceive that the object is moving. This observation implies that one brain system identifies people and things and another tracks their movements, or guides our movements in relation to them. Two functionally distinct pathways, or *visual streams,* project from the occipital cortex to visual areas in other parts of the brain (see **FIGURE 4.16**):

- The *ventral* ("below") *stream* travels across the occipital lobe into the lower levels of the temporal lobes and includes brain areas that represent an object's shape and identity—in other words, what it is. The damage caused by Betty's stroke that you read about in Chapter 3 interrupted this "what pathway" (Tanaka, 1996). As a result, Betty could not recognize familiar faces even though she could still see them.
- The *dorsal* ("above") *stream* travels up from the occipital lobe to the parietal lobes (including some of the middle and upper levels of the temporal lobes), connecting with brain areas that identify the location and motion of an object—in other words, where it is. Because the dorsal stream allows us to perceive spatial relations, researchers originally dubbed it the "where pathway" (Ungerleider & Mishkin, 1982).

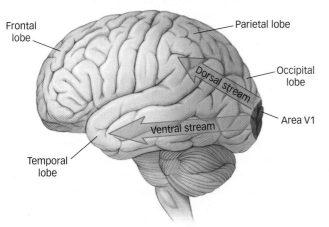

**Figure 4.16** **Visual Streaming** One interconnected visual system forms a pathway that courses from the occipital visual regions into the lower temporal lobe. This ventral pathway enables us to identify what we see. Another interconnected pathway travels from the occipital lobe through the upper regions of the temporal lobe into the parietal regions. This dorsal pathway allows us to locate objects, to track their movements, and to move in relation to them.

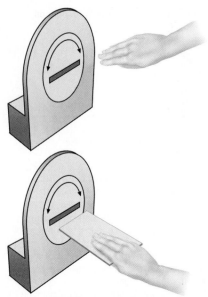

**Figure 4.17 Testing Visual Form Agnosia** When researchers asked patient D. F. to orient her hand to match the angle of the slot in the testing apparatus, as shown at the top, she was unable to comply. Asked to insert a card into the slot at various angles, as shown at the bottom, however, D. F. accomplished the task virtually to perfection.

More recently, neuroscientists have argued that because the dorsal stream is crucial for guiding movements, such as aiming, reaching, or tracking with the eyes, the "where pathway" should more appropriately be called the "how pathway" (Milner & Goodale, 1995).

Some of the most dramatic evidence for two distinct visual streams comes from studying the mindbugs that result from brain injury. A patient known as D. F. suffered permanent brain damage following exposure to toxic levels of carbon monoxide (Goodale, Milner, Jakobson, & Carey, 1991). A large region of the lateral occipital cortex was destroyed, an area in the ventral stream that is very active when people recognize objects. D. F.'s ability to recognize objects by sight was greatly impaired, although her ability to recognize objects by touch was normal. This suggests that the *visual representation* of objects, and not D. F.'s *memory* for objects, was damaged. Like Betty's inability to recognize familiar faces, D. F.'s brain damage belongs to a category called **visual-form agnosia**, *the inability to recognize objects by sight* (Goodale & Milner, 1992, 2004).

Oddly, although D. F. could not recognize objects visually, she could accurately *guide* her actions by sight. D. F. was shown a display board with a slot in it, as in **FIGURE 4.17**. The researchers could adjust the orientation of the slot. In one version of the task, shown at the top in the figure, they asked D. F. to report the orientation of the slot by holding her hand up at the same angle as the slot. D. F. performed very poorly at this task, almost randomly, suggesting that she did not have a reliable representation of visual orientation.

In another version of the task, shown at the bottom in Figure 4.17, D. F. was asked to insert a flat block into the slot, as if she were posting a letter into a mail slot. Now she performed the task almost perfectly! The paradox is that D. F.'s explicit or conscious understanding of what she was seeing was greatly impaired, but her ability to use this very same information nonconsciously to guide her movements remained intact. When D. F. was scanned with fMRI, researchers found that she showed normal activation of regions within the dorsal stream during guided movement (James et al., 2003).

Other patients with brain damage to the parietal section of the dorsal stream have difficulty using vision to guide their reaching and grasping movements, a condition termed *optic ataxia* (Perenin & Vighetto, 1988). However, these patients' ventral streams are intact, meaning they recognize what objects are. We can conclude from these two patterns of impairment that the ventral and dorsal visual streams are functionally distinct; it is possible to damage one while leaving the other intact.

---

**In summary,** light initially passes through several layers in the eye, with the retina linking the world of light outside and the world of visual perception inside the central nervous system. Two types of photoreceptor cells in the retina transduce light into neural impulses: cones, which operate under normal daylight conditions and sense color, and rods, which are active only under low-light conditions for night vision.

The retina contains several layers, and the outermost consists of retinal ganglion cells (RGCs) that collect and send signals to the brain. A particular RGC will respond to light falling anywhere within a small patch that constitutes its receptive field. Light striking the retina causes a specific pattern of response in each of three cone types that are critical to color perception: short-wavelength (bluish) light, medium-wavelength (greenish) light, and long-wavelength (reddish) light. The overall pattern of response across the three cone types results in a unique code for each color, known as its trichromatic color representation. Information encoded by the retina travels to the brain along the optic nerve, which connects to the lateral geniculate nucleus in the thalamus and then to the primary visual cortex, area V1, in the occipital lobe.

Two functionally distinct pathways project from the occipital lobe to visual areas in other parts of the brain. The ventral stream travels into the lower levels of the temporal lobes and includes brain areas that represent an object's shape and identity. The dorsal stream goes from the occipital lobes to the parietal lobes, connecting with brain areas that identify the location and motion of an object. ■ ■ ■

**VISUAL-FORM AGNOSIA** The inability to recognize objects by sight.

## Recognizing Objects by Sight

Take a quick look at the letters in the accompanying illustration. Even though they're quite different from one another, you probably effortlessly recognized them as all being examples of the letter *G*. Now consider the same kind of demonstration using your best friend's face. Your friend might have long hair, but one day she decides to get it cut dramatically short. Even though your friend now looks strikingly different, you still recognize that person with ease. Add glasses. A dye job, producing reddish hair. Maybe your friend grows a beard or mustache. Or he uses colored contact lenses. Perhaps she gets piercings to accommodate a nose ring. Any or all of these elements have the effect of producing a distinctly different-looking face, yet just like the variability in *G*s you somehow are able to extract the underlying features of the face that allow you to accurately identify your friend.

This thought exercise may seem trivial, but it's no small perceptual feat. If the visual system were somehow stumped each time a minor variation occurred in an object being perceived, the inefficiency of it all would be overwhelming. We'd have to effortfully process information just to perceive our friend as the same person from one meeting to another, not to mention laboring through the process of knowing when a *G* is really a *G*. In general, though, object recognition proceeds fairly smoothly, in large part due to the operation of the feature detectors we discussed earlier.

How do feature detectors help the visual system get from a spatial array of light hitting the eye to the accurate perception of an object, such as your friend's face? Some researchers argue for a *modular view:* that specialized brain areas, or modules, detect and represent faces or houses or even body parts. Using fMRI to examine visual processing in healthy young adults, researchers found a subregion in the temporal lobe that responds selectively to faces compared to just about any other object category, while a nearby area responds selectively to buildings and landscapes (Kanwisher, McDermott, & Chun, 1997). This view suggests we not only have feature detectors to aid in visual perception but also "face detectors," "building detectors," and possibly other types of neurons specialized for particular types of object perception (Kanwisher & Yovel, 2006).

Psychologists and researchers who argue for a more *distributed representation* of object categories challenge the modular view. Researchers have shown that although a subregion in the temporal lobes does respond more to faces than to any other category, parts of the brain outside this area may also be involved in face recognition. In this view, it is the pattern of activity across multiple brain regions that identifies any viewed object, including faces (Haxby et al., 2001). Each of these views explains some data better than the other one, and researchers are continuing to debate their relative merits.

### Representing Objects and Faces in the Brain

Investigations of how the brain responds to complex objects and to faces began in the 1980s with experiments using primates as research subjects. Researchers recorded from single cells in the temporal lobes of macaque monkeys and found that different neurons respond selectively to different object shapes (Tanaka, 1996). Other investigators found neurons that respond best to other monkey faces or to human faces.

In the mid-1990s, neuroscientists began using fMRI to investigate whether specialized neurons like these operate in the human brain. They showed healthy participants photographs of faces, houses, and other object categories—shoes, tools, or dogs, for example. During the past decade, fMRI studies have revealed that some brain regions in the occipital and temporal lobes do respond selectively to specific object categories (Downing, Chan, Peelen, Dodds, & Kanwisher, 2006).

Another perspective on this issue is provided by experiments designed to measure precisely where seizures originate; these experiments have provided insights on how single neurons in the human brain respond to objects and faces (Quiroga, Reddy, Kreiman, Koch, & Fried, 2005). Electrodes were placed in the temporal lobes of people who suffer from epilepsy. Then the volunteers were shown photographs of faces and objects as the researchers recorded their neural responses. The researchers found that neurons in the temporal lobe respond to specific objects viewed from multiple angles and to people wearing different clothing and facial expressions and photographed

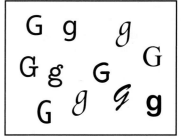

A quick glance and you recognize all these letters as *G*, but their varying sizes, shapes, angles, and orientations ought to make this recognition task difficult. What is it about the process of object recognition that allows us to perform this task effortlessly?

**PERCEPTUAL CONSTANCY** A perceptual principle stating that even as aspects of sensory signals change, perception remains consistent.

from various angles. In some cases, the neurons also respond to the words for the objects they prefer. For example, a neuron that responded to photographs of the Sydney Opera House also responded when the words *Sydney Opera* were displayed but not when the words *Eiffel Tower* were displayed (Quiroga et al., 2005).

Taken together, these experiments demonstrate the principle of **perceptual constancy:** *Even as aspects of sensory signals change, perception remains consistent.* Think back once again to our discussion of difference thresholds early in this chapter. Our perceptual systems are sensitive to relative differences in changing stimulation and make allowances for varying sensory input. This general principle helps explain why you still recognize your friend despite changes in hair color or style or the addition of facial jewelry. It's not as though your visual perceptual system responds to a change with, "Here's a new and unfamiliar face to perceive." Rather, it's as though it responds with, "Interesting . . . here's a deviation from the way this face usually looks." Perception is sensitive to changes in stimuli, but perceptual constancies allow us to notice the differences in the first place.

## Principles of Perceptual Organization

Before object recognition can even kick in, the visual system must perform another important task: to group the image regions that belong together into a representation of an object. The idea that we tend to perceive a unified, whole object rather than a collection of separate parts is the foundation of Gestalt psychology, which you read about in Chapter 1. Gestalt principles characterize many aspects of human perception. Among the foremost are the Gestalt *perceptual grouping rules,* which govern how the features and regions of things fit together (Koffka, 1935). Here's a sampling:

- *Simplicity:* A basic rule in science is that the simplest explanation is usually the best. This is the idea behind the Gestalt grouping rule of *Pragnanz,* which translates as "good form." When confronted with two or more possible interpretations of an object's shape, the visual system tends to select the simplest or most likely interpretation (see **FIGURE 4.18a**).
- *Closure:* We tend to fill in missing elements of a visual scene, allowing us to perceive edges that are separated by gaps as belonging to complete objects (see **FIGURE 4.18b**).
- *Continuity:* Edges or contours that have the same orientation have what the Gestaltists called "good continuation," and we tend to group them together perceptually (see **FIGURE 4.18c**).
- *Similarity:* Regions that are similar in color, lightness, shape, or texture are perceived a belonging to the same object (see **FIGURE 4.18d**).
- *Proximity:* Objects that are close together tend to be grouped together (see **FIGURE 4.18e**).
- *Common fate:* Elements of a visual image that move together are perceived as parts of a single moving object (see **FIGURE 4.18f**).

**Figure 4.18** **Perceptual Grouping Rules** Principles first identified by Gestalt psychologists and now supported by experimental evidence demonstrate that the brain is predisposed to impose order on incoming sensations. One neural strategy for perception involves responding to patterns among stimuli and grouping like patterns together.

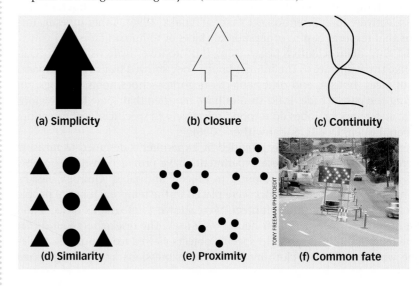

(a) Simplicity   (b) Closure   (c) Continuity

(d) Similarity   (e) Proximity   (f) Common fate

## Separating Figure from Ground

Perceptual grouping is a powerful aid to our ability to recognize objects by sight. Grouping involves visually separating an object from its surroundings. In Gestalt terms, this means identifying a *figure* apart from the (back)*ground* in which it resides. For example, the words on this page are perceived as figural: They stand out from the ground of the sheet of paper on which they're printed. Similarly, your instructor is perceived as the figure against the backdrop of all the other elements in your classroom. You certainly can perceive these elements differently, of course: The words *and* the paper are all part of a thing called "a page," and your instructor *and* the classroom can all be perceived as "your learning environment." Typically, though, our perceptual systems focus attention on some objects as distinct from their environments.

Size provides one clue to what's figure and what's ground: Smaller regions are likely to be figures, such as tiny letters on a big paper. Movement also helps: Your instructor is (we hope) a dynamic lecturer, moving around in a static environment. Another critical step toward object recognition is *edge assignment*. Given an edge, or boundary, between figure and ground, which region does that edge belong to? If the edge belongs to the figure, it helps define the object's shape, and the background continues behind the edge. Sometimes, though, it's not easy to tell which is which.

Edgar Rubin (1886–1951), a Danish psychologist, capitalized on this ambiguity in developing a famous illusion called the *Rubin vase* or, more generally, a *reversible figure-ground relationship*. You can view this "face-vase" illusion in **FIGURE 4.19** in two ways, either as a vase on a black background or as a pair of silhouettes facing each other. Your visual system settles on one or the other interpretation and fluctuates between them every few seconds. This happens because the edge that would normally separate figure from ground is really part of neither: It equally defines the contours of the vase as it does the contours of the faces. Evidence from fMRIs shows, quite nicely, that when people are seeing the Rubin image as a face, there is greater activity in the face-selective region of the temporal lobe we discussed earlier than when they are seeing it as a vase (Hasson, Hendler, Bashat, & Malach, 2001).

## Theories of Object Recognition

Researchers have proposed two broad explanations of object recognition, one based on the object as a whole and the other on its parts. Each set of theories has strengths and weaknesses, making object recognition an active area of study in psychology.

According to *image-based object recognition* theories, an object you have seen before is stored in memory as a **template**, *a mental representation that can be directly compared to a viewed shape in the retinal image* (Tarr & Vuong, 2002). Shape templates are stored along with name, category, and other associations to that object. Your memory compares its templates to the current retinal image and selects the template that most closely matches the current image. For example, supermarket scanners use a form of template matching to identify the bar codes on grocery labels.

Image-based theories are widely accepted, yet they do not explain everything about object recognition. For one thing, the time it takes to recognize a familiar object does not depend on its current orientation relative to the object's standard orientation: You can quickly recognize that a cup is a cup even when it is tilted on its side. Correctly matching images to templates suggests that you'd have to have one template for cups in a normal orientation, another template for cups on their side, another for cups upside down, and so on. This makes for an unwieldy and inefficient system and therefore one that is unlikely to be effective, yet seeing a cup on its side rarely perplexes anyone for long. Another limitation is that image-based theories cannot account for objects you have never seen before. How can you correctly identify an object by matching it to a template if you don't have a template because you've never seen the object before? This roundabout reasoning suggests that people would be mystified when encountering unfamiliar objects, yet actually we make sense of even unfamiliar objects quite readily.

*Parts-based object recognition* theories propose instead that the brain deconstructs viewed objects into a collection of parts (Marr & Nishihara, 1978). One important

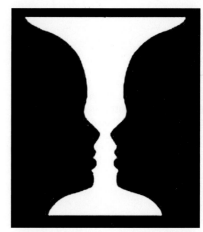

**Figure 4.19 Ambiguous Edges** Here's how Rubin's classic reversible figure-ground illusion works: Fixate your eyes on the center of the image, and your perception will alternate between a vase and facing silhouettes, even as the sensory stimulation remains constant.

**TEMPLATE** A mental representation that can be directly compared to a viewed shape in the retinal image.

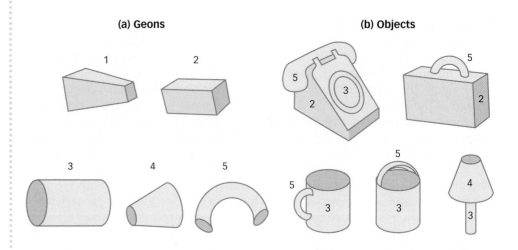

**(a) Geons**    **(b) Objects**

**Figure 4.20** **An Alphabet of Geometric Elements** Parts-based theory holds that objects such as those shown in (b) are made up of simpler three-dimensional components called geons, shown in (a), much as letters combine to form different words.

parts-based theory contends that objects are stored in memory as structural descriptions: mental inventories of object parts along with the spatial relations among those parts (Biederman, 1987). The parts inventories act as a sort of "alphabet" of geometric elements called *geons* that can be combined to make objects, just as letters are combined to form words (see **FIGURE 4.20**). For example, elements such as *curved, cylindrical,* or *pointy* might be indexed in an inventory, along with their relations to each other. In parts-based theories, object recognition constructs an image into its visible parts, notes the spatial relations among these parts, and then compares this structural description to inventories stored in memory (see Figure 4.20).

Like image-based theories, parts-based object recognition has major limitations. Most importantly, it allows for object recognition only at the level of categories and not at the level of the individual object. Parts-based theories offer an explanation for recognizing an object such as a face, for example, but are less effective at explaining how you distinguish between your best friend's face and a stranger's face.

As you can see, there are strengths and weaknesses of both image-based and parts-based explanations of object recognition. Researchers are developing hybrid theories that attempt to exploit the strengths of each approach (Peissig & Tarr, 2007).

## Perceiving Depth and Size

You've probably never appreciated the mundane benefits of knowing where you are at any given time. If you've ever been in an unfamiliar environment, though, the benefits of knowing what's around you become readily apparent. Think of being in a house of mirrors: Is the exit to your left or to your right, or are you completely turned around? Imagine being in a new shopping mall: Was Abercrombie and Fitch on the top floor of the west wing, or was that American Eagle? Are those your friends over there at the food court or just some people who look like them? Knowing what's around you is important. Knowing where each object is located is important too. Whether one object is above, below, or to the left or right of another is first encoded in the retinal image.

Objects in the world are arranged in three dimensions—length, width, and depth—but the retinal image contains only two dimensions, length and width. How does the brain process a flat, two-dimensional retinal image so that we perceive the depth of an object and how far away it is? The answer lies in a collection of *depth cues* that change as you move through space. Monocular, binocular, and motion-based depth cues all help visual perception (Howard, 2002).

### Monocular Depth Cues

If you had to wear an eye patch for a few hours each day, perhaps in your role as Salty the Pirate at the local fast-food joint, you might predict you'd have a difficult time perceiving things. After all, there must be a good reason for having two eyes! However,

THE PHOTO WORKS

©THE PHOTO WORKS

**Figure 4.21** **Familiar Size and Relative Size** When you view images of people, such as the men in the left-hand photo, or of things you know well, the object you perceive as smaller appears farther away. With a little image manipulation, you can see in the right-hand photo that the relative size difference projected on your retinas is far greater than you perceive. The image of the man in the blue vest is exactly the same size in both photos.

some aspects of visual perception involve **monocular depth cues,** *aspects of a scene that yield information about depth when viewed with only one eye.* These cues rely on the relationship between distance and size. Even with one eye closed, the retinal image of an object you're focused on grows smaller as that object moves farther away and larger as it moves closer. Our brains routinely use these differences in retinal image size, or *relative size,* to perceive distance.

This works particularly well in a monocular depth cue called *familiar size.* Most adults, for example, fall within a familiar range of heights (perhaps five to seven feet tall), so retinal image size alone is usually a reliable cue to how far away they are. Our visual system automatically corrects for size differences and attributes them to differences in distance. **FIGURE 4.21** demonstrates how strong this mental correction for familiar size is.

Monocular cues are often called *pictorial depth cues* because they are present even in two-dimensional paintings, photographs, and videos where the third dimension of depth is not really there. In addition to relative size and familiar size, there are several more monocular depth cues, such as

- *Linear perspective,* which describes the phenomenon that parallel lines seem to converge as they recede into the distance (see **FIGURE 4.22a** on the next page).
- *Texture gradient,* which arises when you view a more or less uniformly patterned surface because the size of the pattern elements, as well as the distance between them, grows smaller as the surface recedes from the observer (see **FIGURE 4.22b**).
- *Interposition,* which occurs when one object partly blocks another (see **FIGURE 4.22c**). You can infer that the block*ing* object is closer than the block*ed* object. However, interposition by itself cannot provide information about how far apart the two objects are.
- *Relative height in the image* depends on your field of vision (see **FIGURE 4.22d**). Objects that are closer to you are lower in your visual field, while faraway objects are higher.

**MONOCULAR DEPTH CUES** Aspects of a scene that yield information about depth when viewed with only one eye.

**BINOCULAR DISPARITY** The difference in the retinal images of the two eyes that provides information about depth.

**MOTION PARALLAX** A depth cue based on the movement of the head over time.

**(a)**

**(b)**

**(c)**

**Figure 4.22** **Pictorial Depth Cues** Visual artists rely on a variety of monocular cues to make their work come to life. You can rely on cues such as (a) linear perspective, (b) texture gradient, (c) interposition, and (d) relative height in an image to infer distance, depth, and position, even if you're wearing an eye patch.

**(d)**

## Binocular Depth Cues

Portraying pirates is not a hot occupation, mainly because two eyes are better than one, especially when it comes to depth perception. *Binocular depth cues* exist because we have stereoscopic vision: Having space between our eyes means that each eye registers a slightly different view of the world.

Hold your right index finger up about two feet in front of your face, close one eye, and look at your finger. Now alternate, opening and closing each eye rapidly. Your finger appears to jump back and forth as you do this.

The difference in these two views provides direct and compelling information about depth. The closer the object you're looking at, the greater the **binocular disparity**, *the difference in the retinal images of the two eyes that provides information about depth.* Your brain computes the disparity between the two retinal images to perceive how far away objects are, as shown in **FIGURE 4.23.** Viewed from above in the figure, the images of the more distant square and the closer circle each fall at different points on each retina.

Binocular disparity as a cue to depth perception was first discussed by Sir Charles Wheatstone in 1838. Wheatstone went on to invent the stereoscope, essentially a holder for a pair of photographs or drawings taken from two horizontally displaced locations (Wheatstone did not lack for

**Figure 4.23** **Binocular Disparity** We see the world in three dimensions because our eyes are a distance apart and the image of an object falls on the retinas of each eye at a slightly different place. In this two-object scene, the images of the square and the circle fall on different points of the retina in each eye. The disparity in the positions of the circle's retinal images provides a compelling cue to depth.

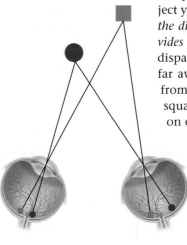

The View-Master has been a popular toy for decades. It is based on the principle of binocular disparity: Two images taken from slightly different angles produce a stereoscopic effect.

original ideas—he also invented the accordion and an early telegraph and coined the term *microphone*). When viewed, one by each eye, the pairs of images evoked a vivid sense of depth. The View-Master toy is the modern successor to Wheatstone's invention, and 3-D movies are based on this same idea.

### Motion-Based Depth Cues

When you're riding in a car, bus, or train, the scene changes systematically and continuously. Nearby objects appear to zip by quickly, but faraway objects appear to move slowly or not at all. This phenomenon is called **motion parallax**, *a depth cue based on the movement of the head over time*. The speed and direction of the images on your retina depend on where you are looking and on how far away the objects you see are.

The depth perception you experience from motion parallax is essentially the same as that provided by binocular disparity. Both involve mentally comparing retinal image information from multiple viewpoints. In the case of binocular disparity, two slightly different viewpoints are sampled simultaneously by the two eyes. In motion parallax, the two viewpoints are sampled in succession, over time.

As you move forward through a scene, the motion cues to depth behave a little differently: As objects get closer, their image sizes on the retina increase, and their contours move outward on the retina, toward the side. *Optic flow*, the pattern of motion that accompanies an observer's forward movement through a scene, is a form of motion parallax. At any given point, the scene ahead moves outward from the point toward which the observer is moving. This kind of motion parallax is therefore useful for navigation while walking, driving, or landing an airplane.

If you have ever watched an old episode of Star Trek, you will recognize as optic flow the visual effect on the view screen when the spaceship jumps to warp speed. Trails of starlight out ahead expand outward from a central point. Back on Earth, you can see this effect when you look out the windshield as you drive through a snowstorm at night. As your headlights illuminate the onrushing snowflakes, the flakes at the center are farthest away (near the horizon) and the flakes on the periphery are closest to you.

### Illusions of Depth and Size

We all are vulnerable to *illusions,* which, as you'll remember from Chapter 1, are errors of perception, memory, or judgment in which subjective experience differs from objective reality (Wade, 2005). These mindbugs inspired the Gestalt psychologists, whose contributions continue to influence research on object perception. Recall the Mueller-Lyer illusion from Chapter 1 (see Figure 1.3). Even though the horizontal lines in that figure are exactly the same length, the top horizontal line looks longer than the bottom one. That's because you don't perceive the horizontal lines in isolation: Your perception of them is related to and influenced by the surrounding vertical lines.

 **ONLY HUMAN**

**I KNOW IT'S AROUND HERE SOMEPLACE. . .** A 44-year-old man was arrested for DUI in Australia's Northern Territory after he asked a police officer how to get to the hard-to-miss Uluru (Ayers Rock, the huge, 1,000-foot-high rock formation that appears red in sunlight), which was about 300 feet in front of him, illuminated in his headlights.

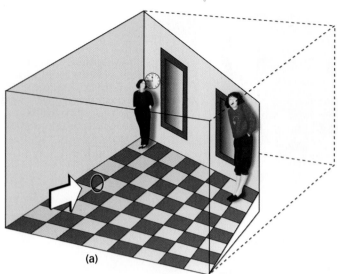

(a)

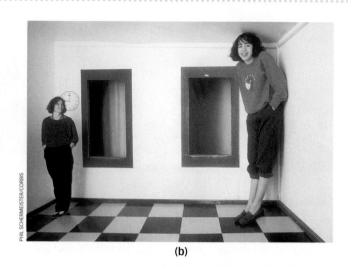

(b)

PHIL SCHERMEISTER/CORBIS

**Figure 4.24 The Amazing Ames Room** (a) A diagram showing the actual proportions of the Ames room reveals its secrets. The sides of the room form a trapezoid with parallel sides but a back wall that's way off square. The uneven floor makes the room's height in the far back corner shorter than the other. Add misleading cues such as specially designed windows and flooring and position the room's occupants in each far corner and you're ready to lure an unsuspecting observer. (b) Looking into the Ames room through the viewing port with only one eye, the observer infers a normal size-distance relationship—that both girls are the same distance away. But the different image sizes they project on the retina leads the viewer to conclude, based on the monocular cue of familiar size, that one girl is very small and the other very large.

The moon at the horizon appears to be much larger than when it is high in the sky. This illusion happens because of visual cues at the horizon such as buildings and trees.

DAVID NUNUK/PHOTO RESEARCHERS

The relation between size and distance has been used to create elaborate illusions that depend on fooling the visual system about how far away objects are. All these illusions depend on the same principle: When you view two objects that project the same retinal image size, the object you perceive as farther away will be perceived as larger.

One of the most famous illusions is the *Ames room,* constructed by the American ophthalmologist Adelbert Ames in 1946. The room is trapezoidal in shape rather than square: Only two sides are parallel (see **FIGURE 4.24a**). A person standing in one corner of an Ames room is physically twice as far away from the viewer as a person standing in the other corner. But when viewed with one eye through the small peephole placed in one wall, the Ames room looks square because the shapes of the windows and the flooring tiles are carefully crafted to *look* square from the viewing port (Ittelson, 1952).

The visual system perceives the far wall as perpendicular to the line of sight so that people standing at different positions along that wall appear to be at the same distance, and the viewer's judgments of their sizes are based directly on retinal image size. As a result, a person standing in the right corner appears to be much larger than a person standing in the left corner (see **FIGURE 4.24b**).

The *moon illusion* is another case where incorrectly perceived distance affects the perception of size (Hershenson, 1989). The full moon often appears much larger when it is near the horizon than when it is directly overhead. In fact, the moon projects identical retinal image sizes in both positions. What accounts for this compelling mindbug? When the moon is near the horizon, it appears farther away because many features—hills, trees, buildings—intervene between the viewer and the moon. Nothing intervenes when the moon is directly overhead, so it appears smaller.

## Perceiving Motion

You should now have a good sense of how we see what and where objects are, a process made substantially easier when the objects stay in one place. But real life, of course, is full of moving targets; objects change position over time. To sense motion, the visual system must encode information about both space and time. The simplest case to consider is an observer who does not move trying to perceive an object that does.

As an object moves across an observer's stationary visual field, it first stimulates one location on the retina, and then a little later it stimulates another location on the retina. Neural circuits in the brain can detect this change in position over time and respond to specific speeds and directions of motion (Emerson, Bergen, & Adelson, 1992). A region in the middle of the temporal lobe referred to as *MT* ( (part of the dorsal stream we discussed earlier) is specialized for the visual perception of motion (Born & Bradley, 2005; Newsome & Paré, 1988), and brain damage in this area leads to a deficit in normal motion perception (Zihl, von Cramon, & Mai, 1983).

Of course, in the real world, rarely are you a stationary observer. As you move around, your head and eyes move all the time, and motion perception is not as simple. The motion-perception system must take into account the position and movement of your eyes, and ultimately of your head and body, in order to perceive the motions of objects correctly and allow you to approach or avoid them. The brain accomplishes this by monitoring your eye and head movements and "subtracting" them from the motion in the retinal image.

Motion perception, like color perception, operates in part on opponent processes and is subject to sensory adaptation. A motion aftereffect called the *waterfall illusion* is analogous to color aftereffects. If you stare at the downward rush of a waterfall for several seconds, you'll experience an upward motion aftereffect when you then look at stationary objects near the waterfall such as trees or rocks. What's going on here?

The process is similar to seeing green after staring at a patch of red. Motion-sensitive neurons are connected to motion detector cells in the brain that encode motion in opposite directions. A sense of motion comes from the difference in the strength of these two opposing sensors. If one set of motion detector cells is fatigued through adaptation to motion in one direction, then the opposing sensor will take over. The net result is that motion is perceived in the opposite direction. Evidence from fMRIs indicates that when people experience the waterfall illusion while viewing a stationary stimulus, there is increased activity in region MT, which plays a key role in motion perception (Tootell et al., 1995).

The movement of objects in the world is not the only event that can evoke the perception of motion. The successively flashing lights of a Las Vegas casino sign can evoke a strong sense of motion, exactly the sort of illusion that inspired Max Wertheimer to investigate the *phi phenomenon,* discussed in Chapter 1. Recall, too, the Gestalt grouping rule of *common fate:* People perceive a series of flashing lights as a whole, moving object (see Figure 4.18f). This *perception of movement as a result of alternating signals appearing in rapid succession in different locations* is called **apparent motion.**

Video technology and animation depend on apparent motion. A sequence of still images sample the continuous motion in the original scene. In the case of motion pictures, the sampling rate is 24 frames per second (fps). A slower sampling rate would produce a much choppier sense of motion; a faster sampling rate would be a waste of resources because we would not perceive the motion as any smoother than it appears at 24 fps.

---

**In summary,** some regions in the occipital and temporal lobes respond selectively to specific object categories, supporting the modular view that specialized brain areas represent particular classes of objects. The principle of perceptual constancy holds that even as sensory signals change, perception remains consistent. Gestalt principles of perceptual grouping, such as simplicity, closure, and continuity, govern how the features and regions of things fit together. Depth perception depends on monocular cues, such as familiar size and linear perspective; binocular cues, such as retinal disparity; and motion-based cues, such as motion parallax, which is based on the movement of the head over time. We experience a sense of motion through the differences in the strengths of output from motion-sensitive neurons. These processes can give rise to illusions such as apparent motion. ■ ■

**APPARENT MOTION** The perception of movement as a result of alternating signals appearing in rapid succession in different locations.

# Audition: More Than Meets the Ear

Vision is based on the spatial pattern of light waves on the retina. The sense of hearing, by contrast, is all about *sound waves*—changes in air pressure unfolding over time. Plenty of things produce sound waves: the collision of a tree hitting the forest floor, the impact of two hands clapping, the vibration of vocal cords during a stirring speech, the resonance of a bass guitar string during a thrash metal concert. Except for synesthetes who "hear colors," understanding most people's auditory experience requires understanding how we transform changes in air pressure into perceived sounds.

Motorhead is the loudest band in the world. Oddly, front man Lemmy Kilmister reports little hearing loss despite more than 30 years of standing in front of a huge stack of amplifiers. Most of the rest of us would suffer severe damage to our hearing under such circumstances.

## Sensing Sound

Plucking a guitar string or striking a tuning fork produces a *pure tone,* a simple sound wave that first increases air pressure and then creates a relative vacuum. This cycle repeats hundreds or thousands of times per second as sound waves propagate outward in all directions from the source.

Just as there are three dimensions of light waves corresponding to three dimensions of visual perception, so too there are three physical dimensions of a sound wave. Frequency, amplitude, and complexity determine what we hear as the pitch, loudness, and quality of a sound (see **TABLE 4.3**).

The *frequency* of the sound wave, or its wavelength, depends on how often the peak in air pressure passes the ear or a microphone, measured in cycles per second, or hertz (abbreviated Hz). Changes in the physical frequency of a sound wave are perceived by humans as changes in **pitch**, *how high or low a sound is.*

The *amplitude* of a sound wave refers to its height, relative to the threshold for human hearing (which is set at zero decibels, or dBs). Amplitude corresponds to **loudness**, or *a sound's intensity*. To give you an idea of amplitude and intensity, the rustling of leaves in a soft breeze is about 20 dB, normal conversation is measured at about 40 dB, shouting

**PITCH** How high or low a sound is.

**LOUDNESS** A sound's intensity.

**TIMBRE** A listener's experience of sound quality or resonance.

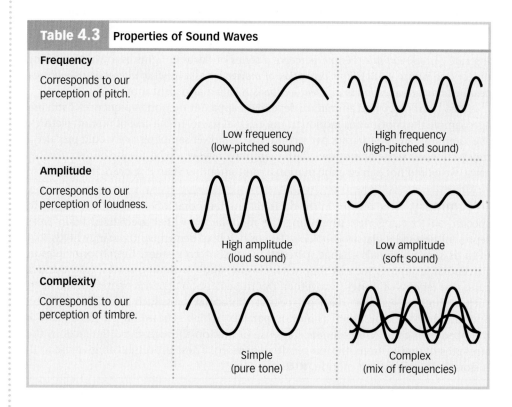

| Table 4.3 | Properties of Sound Waves | |
|---|---|---|
| **Frequency**<br>Corresponds to our perception of pitch. | Low frequency<br>(low-pitched sound) | High frequency<br>(high-pitched sound) |
| **Amplitude**<br>Corresponds to our perception of loudness. | High amplitude<br>(loud sound) | Low amplitude<br>(soft sound) |
| **Complexity**<br>Corresponds to our perception of timbre. | Simple<br>(pure tone) | Complex<br>(mix of frequencies) |

produces 70 dB, a Slayer concert is about 130 decibels, and the sound of the space shuttle taking off one mile away registers at 160 dB or more. That's loud enough to cause permanent damage to the auditory system and is well above the pain threshold; in fact, any sounds above 85 decibels can be enough to cause hearing damage, depending on the length and type of exposure.

Differences in the *complexity* of sound waves, or their mix of frequencies, correspond to **timbre,** *a listener's experience of sound quality or resonance.* Timbre (pronounced "TAM-ber") offers us information about the nature of sound. The same note played at the same loudness produces a perceptually different experience depending on whether it was played on a flute versus a trumpet, a phenomenon due entirely to timbre. Many "natural" sounds also illustrate the complexity of wavelengths, such as the sound of bees buzzing, the tonalities of speech, or the babbling of a brook. Unlike the purity of a tuning fork's hum, the drone of cicadas is a clamor of overlapping sound frequencies.

Of the three dimensions of sound waves, frequency provides most of the information we need to identify sounds. Amplitude and complexity contribute texture to our auditory perceptions, but it is frequency that carries their meaning. Sound-wave frequencies blend together to create countless sounds, just as different wavelengths of light blend to create the richly colored world we see.

Moreover, sound-wave frequency is as important for audition as spatial perception is for vision. Changes in frequency over time allow us to identify the location of sounds, an ability that can be crucial to survival and also allow us to understand speech and appreciate music, skills that are valuable to our cultural survival. The focus in our discussion of hearing, then, is on how the auditory system encodes and represents sound-wave frequency (Kubovy, 1981).

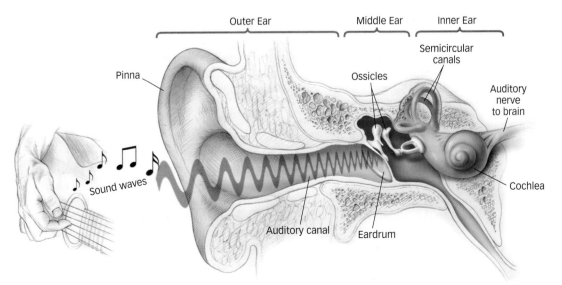

*"The ringing in your ears—I think I can help."*

## The Human Ear

How does the auditory system convert sound waves into neural signals? The process is very different from the visual system, which is not surprising, given that light is a form of electromagnetic radiation whereas sound is a physical change in air pressure over time: Different forms of energy suggest different processes of transduction. The human ear is divided into three distinct parts, as shown in **FIGURE 4.25.** The *outer ear* collects sound waves and funnels them toward the *middle ear,* which transmits the vibrations to the *inner ear,* embedded in the skull, where they are transduced into neural impulses.

Outer Ear   Middle Ear   Inner Ear

Semicircular canals

Ossicles

Pinna

Auditory nerve to brain

Sound waves

Cochlea

Auditory canal   Eardrum

**Figure 4.25** **Anatomy of the Human Ear** The pinna funnels sound waves into the auditory canal to vibrate the eardrum at a rate that corresponds to the sound's frequency. In the middle ear, the ossicles pick up the eardrum vibrations, amplify them, and pass them along by vibrating a membrane at the surface of the fluid-filled cochlea in the inner ear. Here fluid carries the wave energy to the auditory receptors that transduce it into electro-chemical activity, exciting the neurons that form the auditory nerve, leading to the brain.

**Figure 4.26** **Auditory Transduction** Inside the cochlea, shown here as though it were uncoiling, the basilar membrane undulates in response to wave energy in the cochlear fluid. Waves of differing frequencies ripple varying locations along the membrane, from low frequencies at its tip to high frequencies at the base, and bend the embedded hair cell receptors at those locations. The hair-cell motion generates impulses in the auditory neurons, whose axons form the auditory nerve that emerges from the cochlea.

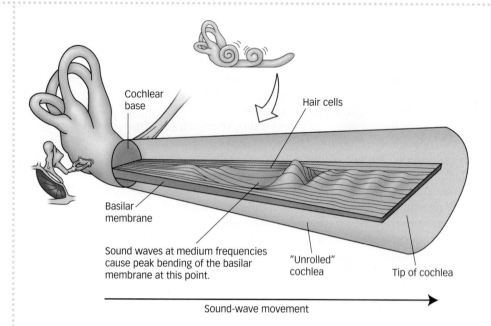

Cochlear base

Hair cells

Basilar membrane

Sound waves at medium frequencies cause peak bending of the basilar membrane at this point.

"Unrolled" cochlea

Tip of cochlea

Sound-wave movement

The outer ear consists of the visible part on the outside of the head (called the *pinna*); the auditory canal; and the eardrum, an airtight flap of skin that vibrates in response to sound waves gathered by the pinna and channeled into the canal. The middle ear, a tiny, air-filled chamber behind the eardrum, contains the three smallest bones in the body, called *ossicles*. Named for their appearance as hammer, anvil, and stirrup, the ossicles fit together into a lever that mechanically transmits and intensifies vibrations from the eardrum to the inner ear.

The inner ear contains the spiral-shaped **cochlea** (Latin for "snail"), *a fluid-filled tube that is the organ of auditory transduction*. The cochlea is divided along its length by the **basilar membrane**, *a structure in the inner ear that undulates when vibrations from the ossicles reach the cochlear fluid* (see **FIGURE 4.26**). Its wavelike movement stimulates thousands of tiny **hair cells**, *specialized auditory receptor neurons embedded in the basilar membrane*. The hair cells then release neurotransmitter molecules, initiating a neural signal in the auditory nerve that travels to the brain. You might not want to think that the whispered "I love you" that sends chills up your spine got a kick start from lots of little hair cells wiggling around, but the mechanics of hearing are what they are!

## Perceiving Pitch

From the inner ear, action potentials in the auditory nerve travel to the thalamus and ultimately to the contralateral ("opposite side"; see Chapter 3) hemisphere of the cerebral cortex. This is called **area A1**, *a portion of the temporal lobe that contains the primary auditory cortex* (see **FIGURE 4.27**). For most of us, the auditory areas in the left hemisphere analyze sounds related to language and those in the right hemisphere specialize in rhythmic sounds and music.

Neurons in area A1 respond well to simple tones, and successive auditory areas in the brain process sounds of increasing complexity (Schreiner, Read, & Sutter, 2000). Like area V1 in the visual cortex, area A1 has a topographic organization: Similar frequencies activate neurons in adjacent locations (see Figure 4.27, inset). A young adult with normal hearing ideally can detect sounds between about 20 and 20,000 Hz, although the ability to hear at the upper range decreases with age; an upper limit of about 16,000 Hz may be more realistic. The human ear is most sensitive to frequencies around 1,000 to 3,500 Hz. But how is the frequency of a sound wave encoded in a neural signal?

**COCHLEA** A fluid-filled tube that is the organ of auditory transduction.

**BASILAR MEMBRANE** A structure in the inner ear that undulates when vibrations from the ossicles reach the cochlear fluid.

**HAIR CELLS** Specialized auditory receptor neurons embedded in the basilar membrane.

**AREA A1** A portion of the temporal lobe that contains the primary auditory cortex.

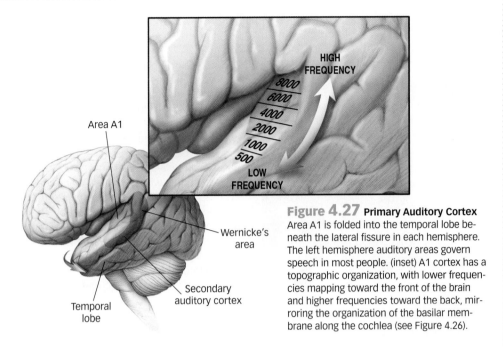

Area A1

HIGH
FREQUENCY

8000
6000
4000
2000
1000
500

LOW
FREQUENCY

Wernicke's
area

Secondary
auditory cortex

Temporal
lobe

**Figure 4.27 Primary Auditory Cortex**
Area A1 is folded into the temporal lobe beneath the lateral fissure in each hemisphere.
The left hemisphere auditory areas govern
speech in most people. (inset) A1 cortex has a
topographic organization, with lower frequencies mapping toward the front of the brain
and higher frequencies toward the back, mirroring the organization of the basilar membrane along the cochlea (see Figure 4.26).

Our ears have evolved two mechanisms to encode sound-wave frequency, one for high frequencies and one for low frequencies. The **place code**, used mainly for high frequencies, is active when *the cochlea encodes different frequencies at different locations along the basilar membrane.* In a series of experiments carried out from the 1930s to the 1950s, Nobel laureate Georg von Békésy (1899–1972) used a microscope to observe the basilar membrane in the inner ear of cadavers that had been donated for medical re-search (Békésy, 1960). Békésy found that the movement of the basilar membrane re-sembles a traveling wave (see Figure 4.26). The wave's shape depends on the frequency of the stimulating pitch. When the frequency is low, the wide, floppy tip (*apex*) of the basilar membrane moves the most; when the frequency is high, the narrow, stiff end (*base*) of the membrane moves the most.

The movement of the basilar membrane causes hair cells to bend, initiating a neural signal in the auditory nerve. Axons fire the strongest in the hair cells along the area of the basilar membrane that moves the most; in other words, the place of activation on the basilar membrane contributes to the perception of sound. The place code works best for relatively high frequencies that resonate at the basilar membrane's base and less well for low frequencies that resonate at the tip because low frequencies produce a broad traveling wave and therefore an imprecise fre-quency code.

A complementary process handles lower frequencies. A **temporal code** *registers low frequencies via the firing rate of action potentials entering the auditory nerve.* Action poten-tials from the hair cells are synchronized in time with the peaks of the incoming sound waves (Johnson, 1980). If you imagine the rhythmic *boom-boom-boom* of a bass drum, you can probably also imagine the *fire-fire-fire* of action potentials correspon-ding to the beats. This process provides the brain with very precise information about pitch that supplements the information provided by the place code.

However, individual neurons can produce action potentials at a maximum rate of only about 1,000 spikes per second, so the temporal code does not work as well as the place code for high frequencies. (Imagine if the action potential has to fire in time with the *rat-a-tat-a-tat-a-tat* of a snare drum roll!) Like trichromatic representation and opponent processes in color processing, the place code and the temporal code work together to cover the entire range of pitches that people can hear. (For research on how to combat hearing loss, see the Hot Science box on the next page.)

**PLACE CODE** The cochlea encodes different frequencies at different locations along the basilar membrane.

**TEMPORAL CODE** The cochlea registers low frequencies via the firing rate of action potentials entering the auditory nerve.

## { HOT SCIENCE } Cochlear Implants

TEN DAYS AFTER NATALIE WAS BORN, SHE developed a persistent, high fever. Her pediatrician's diagnosis was meningitis, an inflammation of the lining around the brain and spinal cord. Natalie spent several weeks in the hospital, at times close to death. Finally, the fever broke and Natalie seemed to recover fully.

During the next several months, Natalie's parents grew increasingly concerned because she was not responding to sound. They took her to a pediatric audiologist for assessment and learned that the meningitis had damaged the hair cells in Natalie's cochleas. The damage was irreversible.

Broadly speaking, hearing loss has two main causes. *Conductive hearing loss* arises because the eardrum or ossicles are damaged to the point that they cannot conduct sound waves effectively to the cochlea. The cochlea itself, however, is normal, making this a kind of "mechanical problem" with the moving parts of the ear: the hammer, anvil, stirrup, or eardrum. In many cases, medication or surgery can correct the problem. Sound amplification from a hearing aid also can improve hearing through conduction via the bones around the ear directly to the cochlea.

*Sensorineural hearing loss* is caused by damage to the cochlea, the hair cells, or the auditory nerve. This was Natalie's affliction, rare in an infant but commonly experienced

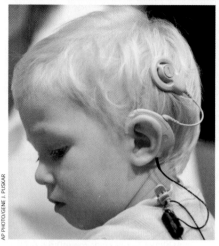

A microphone picks up sounds and sends them to a small speech-processing computer worn on the user's belt or behind the ear. The electric signals from the speech processor are transmitted to an implanted receiver, which sends the signals via electrodes to the cochlea, where the signals directly stimulate the auditory nerve.

by people as they grow older. Sensorineural hearing loss can be heightened in people regularly exposed to high noise levels (such as rock musicians or jet mechanics). Simply amplifying the sound does not help because the hair cells can no longer transduce sound waves. In these cases a *cochlear implant* may offer some relief.

A cochlear implant is an electronic device that replaces the function of the hair cells (Waltzman, 2006). The external parts of the device include a microphone, a small speech processor the size of an iPod (worn on a belt), and an external transmitter worn behind the ear. The implanted parts include a receiver just inside the skull and a thin wire containing electrodes inserted into the cochlea to stimulate the auditory nerve. Sound picked up by the microphone is transformed into electric signals by the speech processor, which is essentially a small computer. The signal is transmitted to the implanted receiver, which activates the electrodes in the cochlea.

Cochlear implants are now in routine use and can improve hearing to the point where speech can be understood. As of 2006, some 60,000 people worldwide have received cochlear implants. Young infants like Natalie, who have not yet learned to speak, are especially vulnerable because they may miss the critical period for language learning (see Chapter 7). Without auditory feedback during this time, normal speech is nearly impossible to achieve. Efforts are under way to introduce cochlear implants to children as early as 12 months or younger to maximize their chances of normal language development (DesJardin, Eisenberg, & Hodapp, 2006).

## Localizing Sound Sources

Just as the differing positions of our eyes give us stereoscopic vision, the placement of our ears on opposite sides of the head give us stereophonic hearing. The sound arriving at the ear closer to the sound source is louder than the sound in the farther ear, mainly because the listener's head partially blocks sound energy. This loudness difference decreases as the sound source moves from a position directly to one side (maximal difference) to straight ahead (no difference).

Another cue to a sound's location arises from timing: Sound waves arrive a little sooner at the near ear than at the far ear. The timing difference can be as brief as a few microseconds, but together with the intensity difference, it is sufficient to allow us to perceive the location of a sound. When the sound source is ambiguous, you may find yourself turning your head from side to side to localize it. By doing this, you are changing the relative intensity and timing of sound waves arriving in your ears and collecting better information about the likely source of the sound.

**In summary,** perceiving sound depends on three physical dimensions of a sound wave: The frequency of the sound wave determines the pitch; the amplitude determines the loudness; and differences in the complexity, or mix, of frequencies determines the sound quality or timbre. Auditory perception begins in the ear, which consists of an outer ear that funnels sound waves toward the middle ear, which in turn sends the vibrations to the inner ear, which contains the cochlea. Action potentials from the inner ear travel along an auditory pathway through the thalamus to the contralateral primary auditory cortex, area A1, in the temporal lobe. Auditory perception depends on both a place code and a temporal code, which together cover the full range of pitches that people can hear. Our ability to localize sound sources depends critically on the placement of our ears on opposite sides of the head. ■■ ■

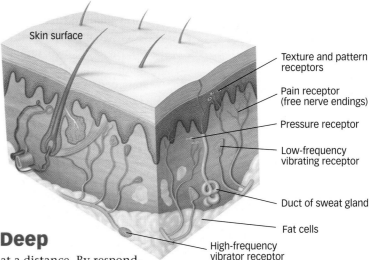

Skin surface

Texture and pattern receptors

Pain receptor (free nerve endings)

Pressure receptor

Low-frequency vibrating receptor

Duct of sweat gland

Fat cells

High-frequency vibrator receptor

# The Body Senses: More Than Skin Deep

Vision and audition provide information about the world at a distance. By responding to light and sound energy in the environment, these "distance" senses allow us to identify and locate the objects and people around us. In comparison, the body senses, also called *somatosenses* (*soma* from the Greek for "body"), are up close and personal. **Haptic perception** results from our *active exploration of the environment by touching and grasping objects with our hands*. We use sensory receptors in our muscles, tendons, and joints as well as a variety of receptors in our skin to get a feel for the world around us (see **FIGURE 4.28**).

**Figure 4.28 Touch Receptors** Specialized sensory neurons form distinct groups of haptic receptors that detect pressure, temperature, and vibrations against the skin. Touch receptors respond to stimulation within their receptive fields, and their long axons enter the brain via the spinal or cranial nerves. Pain receptors populate all body tissues that feel pain: They are distributed around bones and within muscles and internal organs as well as under the skin surface. Both types of pain receptors—the fibers that transmit immediate, sharp pain sensations quickly and those that signal slow, dull pain that lasts and lasts—are free nerve endings.

This rather unimposing geodesic dome sits on the floor of the Exploratorium, a world-renowned science museum in San Francisco. Called the Tactile Dome, it was created in 1971 by August Coppola (brother of director Francis Ford Coppola and father of actor Nicholas Cage) and Carl Day, who wanted to create an environment in which only haptic perception could be used. The inside of the dome is pitch black; visitors must crawl, wiggle, slide, and otherwise navigate the unfamiliar terrain using only their sense of touch. How would you feel being in that environment for an hour or so?

©EXPLORATORIUM

## Touch

Four types of receptors located under the skin's surface enable us to sense pressure, texture, pattern, or vibration against the skin (see Figure 4.28). The receptive fields of these specialized cells work together to provide a rich tactile (from Latin, "to touch") experience when you explore an object by feeling it or attempt to grasp it. In addition, *thermoreceptors,* nerve fibers that sense cold and warmth, respond when your skin temperature changes. All these sensations blend seamlessly together in perception, of course, but detailed physiological studies have successfully isolated the parts of the touch system (Johnson, 2002).

Touch begins with the transduction of skin sensations into neural signals. Like cells in the retina of each eye, touch receptors have receptive fields with central excitatory zones surrounded by doughnut-shaped inhibitory zones that, when stimulated, cause that cell's response to change. The representation of touch in the brain follows a topographic scheme, much as vision and hearing do. Think back to the homunculus you

**HAPTIC PERCEPTION** The active exploration of the environment by touching and grasping objects with our hands.

read about in Chapter 3; you'll recall that different locations on the body project sensory signals to different locations in the somatosensory cortex in the parietal lobe.

There are two important principles regarding the neural representation of the body's surface. First, there is contralateral organization: The left half of the body is represented in the right half of the brain and vice versa. Second, just as more of the visual brain is devoted to foveal vision where acuity is greatest, more of the tactile brain is devoted to parts of the skin surface that have greater spatial resolution. Regions such as the fingertips and lips are very good at discriminating fine spatial detail, whereas areas such as the lower back are quite poor at that task. These perceptual abilities are a natural consequence of the fact that the fingertips and lips have a relatively dense arrangement of touch receptors and a large topographical representation in the somatosensory cortex; comparatively, the lower back, hips, and calves have a relatively small representation (Penfield & Rasmussen, 1950).

## Pain

Although pain is arguably the least pleasant of sensations, this aspect of touch is among the most important for survival: Pain indicates damage or potential damage to the body. The possibility of a life free from pain might seem appealing, but without the ability to feel pain, we might ignore infections, broken bones, or serious burns. Congenital insensitivity to pain, a rare inherited disorder that specifically impairs pain perception, is more of a curse than a blessing: Children who experience this disorder often mutilate themselves (biting into their tongues, for example, or gouging their skin while scratching) and are at increased risk of dying during childhood (Nagasako, Oaklander, & Dworkin, 2003).

Tissue damage is transduced by pain receptors, the free nerve endings shown in Figure 4.28. Researchers have distinguished between fast-acting *A-delta fibers,* which transmit the initial sharp pain one might feel right away from a sudden injury, and slower *C fibers,* which transmit the longer-lasting, duller pain that persists after the initial injury. If you were running barefoot outside and stubbed your toe against a rock, you would first feel a sudden stinging pain transmitted by A-delta fibers that would die down quickly, only to be replaced by the throbbing but longer-lasting pain carried by C fibers. Both the A-delta and C fibers are impaired in cases of congenital insensitivity to pain, which is one reason why the disorder can be life threatening.

As you'll remember from Chapter 3, the pain withdrawal reflex is coordinated by the spinal cord. No brainpower is required when you touch a hot stove; you retract your hand almost instantaneously. But neural signals for pain—such as wrenching your elbow as you brace yourself from falling—travel to two distinct areas in the brain and evoke two distinct psychological experiences (Treede, Kenshalo, Gracely, & Jones, 1999). One pain pathway sends signals to the somatosensory cortex, identifying where the pain is occurring and what sort of pain it is (sharp, burning, dull). The second pain pathway sends signals to the motivational and emotional centers of the brain, such as the hypothalamus and amygdala, and to the frontal lobe. This is the aspect of pain that is unpleasant and motivates us to escape from or relieve the pain.

Pain typically feels as if it comes from the site of the tissue damage that caused it. If you burn your finger, you will perceive the pain as originating there. But we have pain receptors in many areas besides the skin—around bones and within muscles and internal organs as well. When pain originates internally, in a body organ, for example, we actually feel it on the surface of the body. This kind of **referred pain** occurs when *sensory information from internal and external areas converge on the same nerve cells in the spinal cord.* One common example is a heart attack: Victims often feel pain radiating from the left arm rather than from inside the chest.

Pain intensity cannot always be predicted solely from the extent of the injury that causes the pain (Keefe, Abernathy, & Campbell, 2005). For example, *turf toe* sounds like the mildest of ailments; it is pain at the base of the big toe as a result of bending or pushing off repeatedly, as a runner or football player might do during a sporting

**REFERRED PAIN** Feeling of pain when sensory information from internal and external areas converge on the same nerve cells in the spinal cord.

**GATE-CONTROL THEORY** A theory of pain perception based on the idea that signals arriving from pain receptors in the body can be stopped, or *gated*, by interneurons in the spinal cord via feedback from two directions.

event. This small-sounding injury in a small area of the body can nonetheless sideline an athlete for a month with considerable pain. On the other hand, you've probably heard a story or two about someone treading bone-chilling water for hours on end, or dragging their shattered legs a mile down a country road to seek help after a tractor accident, or performing some other incredible feat despite searing pain and extensive tissue damage. Pain type and pain intensity show a less-than-perfect correlation, a fact that has researchers intrigued.

Some recent evidence indicates subjective pain intensity may differ among ethnic groups. A study that examined responses to various kinds of experimentally induced pain, including heat pain and cold pain, found that compared to White young adults, Black young adults had a lower tolerance for several kinds of pain and rated the same pain stimuli as more intense and unpleasant (Campbell, Edward, & Fillingim, 2005).

How do psychologists account for this puzzling variability in pain perception? According to **gate-control theory**, *signals arriving from pain receptors in the body can be stopped, or gated, by interneurons in the spinal cord via feedback from two directions* (Melzack & Wall, 1965). Pain can be gated by the skin receptors, for example by rubbing the affected area. Rubbing your stubbed toe activates neurons that "close the gate" to stop pain signals from traveling to the brain. Pain can also be gated from the brain by modulating the activity of pain-transmission neurons. This neural feedback is elicited not by the pain itself, but rather by activity deep within the thalamus.

The neural feedback comes from a region in the midbrain called the *periaqueductal gray* (PAG). Under extreme conditions, such as high stress, naturally occurring endorphins can activate the PAG to send inhibitory signals to neurons in the spinal cord that then suppress pain signals to the brain, thereby modulating the experience of pain. The PAG is also activated through the action of opiate drugs, such as morphine.

A different kind of feedback signal can *increase* the sensation of pain. This system is activated by events such as infection and learned danger signals. When we are quite ill, what might otherwise be experienced as mild discomfort can feel quite painful. This pain facilitation signal presumably evolved to motivate people who are ill to rest and avoid strenuous activity, allowing their energy to be devoted to healing.

Gate-control theory offers strong evidence that perception is a two-way street. The senses feed information, such as pain sensations, to the brain, a pattern termed *bottom-up control* by perceptual psychologists. The brain processes this sensory data into perceptual information at successive levels to support movement, object recognition, and eventually more complex cognitive tasks, such as memory and planning. But there is ample evidence that the brain exerts plenty of control over what we sense as well. Visual illusions and the Gestalt principles of filling in, shaping up, and rounding out what isn't really there provide some examples. This kind of *top-down control* also explains the descending pain pathway initiated in the midbrain.

In 2003, Aron Ralston was hiking in a remote canyon in Utah when tragedy struck. A 1,000-pound boulder pinned him in a three-foot-wide space for 5 days, eventually leaving him no choice but to amputate his own arm with a pocketknife. He then applied a tourniquet, rappelled down the canyon, and hiked out to safety. These and similar stories illustrate that the extent of an injury is not perfectly correlated with the amount of pain felt. Although self-amputation is undoubtedly excruciating, luckily in this case it was not debilitating.

## Body Position, Movement, and Balance

It may sound odd, but one aspect of sensation and perception is knowing where parts of your body are at any given moment. It's not as though your arm sneaks out of the bedroom window at night to meet some friends. Your body needs some way to sense its position in physical space other than moving your eyes to constantly visually check the location of your limbs. Sensations related to position, movement, and balance depend on stimulation produced within our bodies. Receptors in the muscles, tendons, and joints signal the position of the body in space, whereas information about balance and head movement originates in the inner ear.

Sensory receptors provide the information we need to perceive the position and movement of our limbs, head, and body. These receptors also provide feedback about whether we are performing a desired movement correctly and how resistance from held objects may be influencing the movement. For example, when you swing a baseball bat, the weight of the bat affects how your muscles move your arm as well as the change in sensation when the bat hits the ball. Muscle, joint, and tendon

Hitting a ball with a bat or racket provides feedback as to where your arms and body are in space as well as how the resistance of these objects affects your movement and balance. Successful athletes, such as Serena Williams, have particularly well-developed body senses.

**VESTIBULAR SYSTEM** The three fluid-filled semicircular canals and adjacent organs located next to the cochlea in each inner ear.

**OLFACTORY RECEPTOR NEURONS (ORNS)** Receptor cells that initiate the sense of smell.

feedback about how your arms actually moved can be used to improve performance through learning.

Maintaining balance depends primarily on the **vestibular system,** *the three fluid-filled semicircular canals and adjacent organs located next to the cochlea in each inner ear* (see Figure 4.25). The semicircular canals are arranged in three perpendicular orientations and studded with hair cells that detect movement of the fluid when the head moves or accelerates. This detected motion enables us to maintain our balance, or the position of our bodies relative to gravity. The movements of the hair cells encode these somatic sensations (Lackner & DiZio, 2005).

Vision also helps us keep our balance. If you see that you are swaying relative to a vertical orientation, such as the contours of a room, you move your legs and feet to keep from falling over. Psychologists have experimented with this visual aspect of balance by placing people in rooms that can be tilted forward and backward (Bertenthal, Rose, & Bai, 1997; Lee & Aronson, 1974). If the room tilts enough—particularly when small children are tested—people will topple over as they try to compensate for what their visual system is telling them. When a mismatch between the information provided by visual cues and vestibular feedback occurs, motion sickness can result. Remember this discrepancy the next time you try reading in the backseat of a moving car!

---

**In summary,** touch is represented in the brain according to a topographic scheme in which locations on the body project sensory signals to locations in the somatosensory cortex, a part of the parietal lobe. The experience of pain depends on signals that travel along two distinct pathways. One sends signals to the somatosensory cortex to indicate the location and type of pain, and another sends signals to the emotional centers of the brain that result in unpleasant feelings that we wish to escape. The experience of pain varies across individuals, which is explained by bottom-up and top-down aspects of gate-control theory. Balance and acceleration depend primarily on the vestibular system but are also influenced by vision. ▨ ▨

---

## The Chemical Senses: Adding Flavor

Somatosensation is all about physical changes in or on the body: Vision and audition sense energetic states of the world—light and sound waves—and touch is activated by physical changes in or on the body surface. The last set of senses we'll consider shares a chemical basis to combine aspects of distance and proximity. The chemical senses of *olfaction* (smell) and *gustation* (taste) respond to the molecular structure of substances floating into the nasal cavity as you inhale or dissolving in saliva. Smell and taste combine to produce the perceptual experience we call *flavor.*

### Smell

Olfaction is the least understood sense and the only one directly connected to the forebrain, with pathways into the frontal lobe, amygdala, and other forebrain structures (recall from Chapter 3 that the other senses connect first to the thalamus). This mapping indicates that smell has a close relationship with areas involved in emotional and social behavior. Smell seems to have evolved in animals as a signaling sense for the familiar—a friendly creature, an edible food, or a sexually receptive mate.

Countless substances release odors into the air, and some of their *odorant molecules* make their way into our noses, drifting in on the air we breathe. Situated along the top of the nasal cavity shown in **FIGURE 4.29** is a mucous membrane called the *olfactory epithelium,* which contains about 10 million **olfactory receptor neurons (ORNs),** *receptor cells that initiate the sense of smell.* Odorant molecules bind to sites on these specialized receptors, and if enough bindings occur, the ORNs send action potentials into the olfactory nerve (Dalton, 2003).

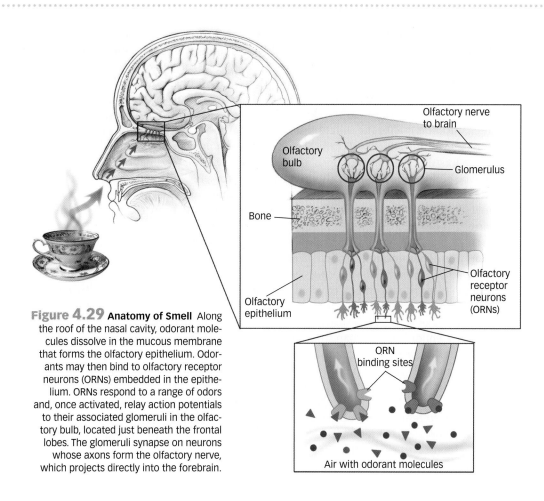

**Figure 4.29** **Anatomy of Smell** Along the roof of the nasal cavity, odorant molecules dissolve in the mucous membrane that forms the olfactory epithelium. Odorants may then bind to olfactory receptor neurons (ORNs) embedded in the epithelium. ORNs respond to a range of odors and, once activated, relay action potentials to their associated glomeruli in the olfactory bulb, located just beneath the frontal lobes. The glomeruli synapse on neurons whose axons form the olfactory nerve, which projects directly into the forebrain.

Each olfactory neuron has receptors that bind to some odorants but not to others, as if the receptor is a lock and the odorant is the key (see Figure 4.29). Groups of ORNs send their axons from the olfactory epithelium into the **olfactory bulb,** *a brain structure located above the nasal cavity beneath the frontal lobes.* Humans possess about 350 different ORN types that permit us to discriminate among some 10,000 different odorants through the unique patterns of neural activity each odorant evokes. This setup is similar to our ability to see a vast range of colors based on only a small number of retinal cell types or to feel a range of skin sensations based on only a handful of touch receptor cell types.

The axons of all ORNs of a particular type converge at a site called a *glomerulus* within the olfactory bulb; thus, humans have about 350 glomeruli. Different odorant molecules produce varied patterns of activity (Rubin & Katz, 1999). A given odorant may strongly activate some glomeruli, moderately activate others, and have little effect on still others. The genetic basis for this olfactory coding was worked out in large part by Linda Buck and Richard Axel (1991), who were awarded the Nobel Prize in 2004 for their efforts.

Some dogs have as many as 100 times more ORNs than humans do, producing a correspondingly sharpened ability to detect and discriminate among millions of odors. Nevertheless, humans are sensitive to the smells of some substances in extremely small concentrations. For example, a chemical compound that is added to natural gas to help detect gas leaks can be sensed at a concentration of just 0.0003 parts per million. By contrast, acetone (nail polish remover), something most people regard as pungent, can be detected only if its concentration is 15 parts per million or greater.

**OLFACTORY BULB** A brain structure located above the nasal cavity beneath the frontal lobes.

**PHEROMONES** Biochemical odorants emitted by other members of their species that can affect an animal's behavior or physiology.

The olfactory bulb sends outputs to various centers in the brain, including the parts that are responsible for controlling basic drives, emotions, and memories. This explains why smells can have immediate, strongly positive or negative effects on us. If the slightest whiff of an apple pie baking brings back fond memories of childhood or the unexpected sniff of vomit mentally returns you to a particularly bad party you once attended, you've got the idea. Thankfully, sensory adaptation is at work when it comes to smell, just as it is with the other senses. Whether the associations are good or bad, after just a few minutes the smell fades. Smell adaptation makes sense: It allows us to detect new odors that may require us to act, but after that initial evaluation has occurred, it may be best to reduce our sensitivity to allow us to detect other smells. Evidence from fMRIs indicates that experience with a smell can modify odor perception by changing how specific parts of the brain involved in olfaction respond to that smell (Li, Lexenberg, Parrish, & Gottfried, 2006).

Smell may also play a role in social behavior. Humans and other animals can detect odors from **pheromones**, *biochemical odorants emitted by other members of their species that can affect the animal's behavior or physiology.* Parents can distinguish the smell of their own children from other people's children. An infant can identify the smell of its mother's breast from the smell of other mothers. Even though the recognition of these smells occurs outside of conscious awareness, it nonetheless influences behavior: Parents pick up their own children rather than strangers' children, and breast feeding becomes a personal connection between mother and child. Pheromones also play a role in reproductive behavior in insects and in several mammalian species, including mice, dogs, and primates (Brennan & Zufall, 2006). Can the same thing be said of human reproductive behavior?

Studies of people's preference for the odors of individuals of the opposite sex have produced mixed results, with no consistent tendency for people to prefer them over other pleasant odors. Recent research, however, has provided a link between sexual orientation and responses to odors that may constitute human pheromones. Researchers used positron emission tomography (PET) scans to study the brain's response to two odors, one related to testosterone, which is produced in men's sweat, and the other related to estrogen, which is found in women's urine. The testosterone-based odor activated the hypothalamus (a part of the brain that controls sexual behavior; see Chapter 3) in heterosexual women but not heterosexual men, whereas the estrogen-based odor activated the hypothalamus in heterosexual men but not women. Strikingly, homosexual men responded to the two chemicals in the same way as women did: The hypothalamus was activated by the testosterone- but not estrogen-based odor (Savic, Berglund, & Lindstrom, 2005; see **FIGURE 4.30**). Other common odors unrelated to sexual arousal were processed similarly by all three groups. A follow-up study with lesbian women showed that their responses to the testosterone- and estrogen-based odors were largely similar to those of heterosexual men (Berglund, Lindstrom, & Savic, 2006). Taken together, the two studies suggest that some human pheromones are related to sexual orientation.

Other evidence also indicates that pheromones can affect human physiology. Women who live in close proximity for extended periods—living together in a college dormitory, for example—tend to synchronize menstrual periods. To test the hypothesis that this synchrony might be mediated by pheromones, a group of women wore cotton pads in their armpits to collect sweat (McClintock, 1971). The secretions were

Figure **4.30** **Smell and Social Behavior**
In a PET study, heterosexual women, homosexual men, and heterosexual men were scanned as they were presented with each of several odors. During the presentation of a testosterone-based odor (referred to in the figure as AND), there was significant activation in the hypothalamus for heterosexual women (left) and homosexual men (center) but not for heterosexual men (right) (Savic et al., 2005).

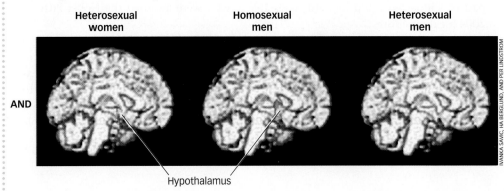

Heterosexual women  Homosexual men  Heterosexual men

AND

Hypothalamus

transferred to the upper lip (under the nose) of women with whom they had no other contact. This procedure did indeed cause the menstrual cycles of the pairs to synchronize over time, although the mechanism remains a mystery. It does not appear to involve any conscious awareness of the smell: The recipient women in these studies reported that they could not discriminate between the smell of the pads worn by the donor women from pads that had not been treated. Nonetheless, the introduction of these pheromones contributed to the regulation of the women's bodily states.

## Taste

One of the primary responsibilities of the chemical sense of taste is identifying things that are bad for you—as in "poisonous and lethal." Many poisons are bitter, and we avoid eating things that nauseate us for good reason, so taste aversions have a clear adaptive significance. Some aspects of taste perception are genetic, such as an aversion to extreme bitterness, and some are learned, such as an aversion to a particular food that once caused nausea. In either case, the direct contact between a tongue and possible foods allows us to anticipate whether something will be harmful or palatable.

The tongue is covered with thousands of small bumps, called *papillae,* which are easily visible to the naked eye. Within each papilla are hundreds of **taste buds,** *the organ of taste transduction* (see **FIGURE 4.31**). Most of our mouths contain between 5,000 and 10,000 taste buds fairly evenly distributed over the tongue, roof of the mouth, and upper throat (Bartoshuk & Beauchamp, 1994; Halpern, 2002). Each taste bud contains 50 to 100 taste receptor cells. Taste perception fades with age: On average, people lose half their taste receptors by the time they turn 20. This may help to explain why young children seem to be "fussy eaters," since their greater number of taste buds brings with it a greater range of taste sensations. (For a striking example of extreme taste sensitivity, see The Real World box on the next page.)

The human eye contains millions of rods and cones, the human nose contains some 350 different types of olfactory receptors, but the taste system contains just five main types of taste receptors, corresponding to five primary taste sensations: salt, sour, bitter, sweet, and umami (savory). The first four are quite familiar, but *umami* may not be. In fact, perception researchers are still debating its existence. The umami receptor was discovered by Japanese scientists who attributed it to the tastes evoked by foods containing a high concentration of protein, such as meats and cheeses (Yamaguchi, 1998). If you're a meat eater and you savor the feel of a steak topped with butter or a cheeseburger as it sits in your mouth, you've got an idea of the umami sensation.

Each taste bud contains several types of taste receptor cells whose tips, called *microvilli,* react with *tastant molecules* in food. Salt taste receptors are most strongly activated by sodium chloride—table salt. Sour receptor cells respond to acids, such as vinegar or lime juice. Bitter and sweet taste receptors are more complex. Some 50 to 80 distinct binding sites in bitter receptors are activated by an equal number of different

**TASTE BUDS** The organ of taste transduction.

**Figure 4.31** **A Taste Bud** (a) Taste buds stud the bumps (papillae) on your tongue, shown here, as well as the back, sides, and roof of the mouth. (b) Each taste bud contains a range of receptor cells that respond to varying chemical components of foods called tastants. Tastant molecules dissolve in saliva and stimulate the microvilli that form the tips of the taste receptor cells. (c) Each taste bud contacts the branch of a cranial nerve at its base.

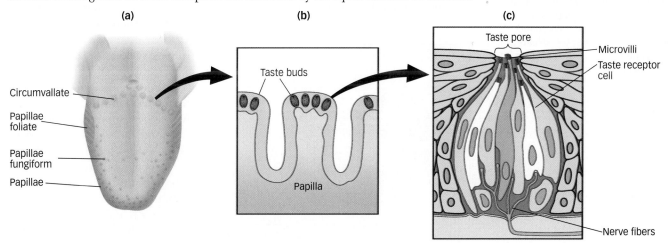

(a)

Circumvallate
Papillae foliate
Papillae fungiform
Papillae

(b)

Taste buds
Papilla

(c)

Taste pore
Microvilli
Taste receptor cell
Nerve fibers

## { THE REAL WORLD } Supertasters

WE ALL KNOW FUSSY EATERS. CHILDREN who don't like to eat their vegetables quickly come to mind. Even some adults shun dark green vegetables such as Brussels sprouts, kale, and broccoli throughout their lifetimes. If you enjoy these vegetables, such taste preferences may seem a little irrational.

But what if different people actually experience the taste of broccoli differently; not like the lie your parents told you—"It tastes like ice cream!"—but in a qualitatively different way from other folks? About 50% of people report a mildly bitter taste in caffeine, saccharine, certain green vegetables, and other substances, while roughly 25% report no bitter taste. Members of the first group are called *tasters* and members of the second group are called *nontasters*. The remaining 25% of people are *supertasters*, who report that such substances, especially dark green vegetables, are extremely bitter, to the point of being inedible.

There's an evolutionary rationale for this. Aversion to bitter tastes is present at birth; not too surprising, since bitter-tasting substances often are poisons. However, many foods that taste bitter—those dark green veggies included—are beneficial in promoting health and protecting us from disease. Ironically, the very evolutionary mechanism that may keep you from poisoning yourself

**Fussy eater or just too many taste buds? Our taste perception declines with age: We lose about half of our taste receptors by the time we're 20 years old. That can make childhood either a time of savory delight or a sensory overload of taste.**

may also keep you from ingesting some of the most healthy food available.

There are substantial individual differences in taste preference as well. For example, not everyone has taste receptors for bitter sensations, based on their genetics (Bartoshuk, Duffy, & Miller, 1994). As another example, people from Asia, Africa, and South America are more likely to be supertasters than are others. Women's sensitivity

to bitter tastes tends to intensify during pregnancy but to diminish after menopause. Children start out as tasters or supertasters, which could help explain their early tendency toward fussiness in food preference. However, some children grow up to become nontasters.

Supertasters also experience other flavors differently from nontasters. Supertasters get more "burn" from chili peppers and more creaminess from fats and thickeners in food than others do. They also experience oral pain more intensely than nontasters (Bartoshuk, 2000). Because supertasters tend to avoid fruits and vegetables that contain tastes they experience as extremely bitter, they may be at increased health risk for diseases such as colon cancer. On the other hand, because they also tend to avoid fatty, creamy foods, they tend to be thinner and may have decreased risk of cardiovascular disease (Bartoshuk, 2000).

The difference between the experiences of nontasters and supertasters can be compared to the difference in experiences among people with normal color vision and those with genetic color deficiencies, where at least one of the three cone types is missing. In each case, personal perceptual experiences differ in ways that may be impossible for others to grasp. A color-deficient supertaster, in fact, has probably learned to avoid the gray broccoli.

**ONLY HUMAN**

**I LOVE THE TASTE OF ASPHALT IN THE MORNING** In April 2006, Jim Werych of the Wednesday Night Classics car club in Brookfield, Wisconsin, ritually dragged his tongue, in a deep lick, across Lisbon Road (with traffic stopped in both directions) to verify, and proclaim, that the streets are free of winter salt and thus safe for the club's delicate classics.

bitter-tasting chemicals. Sweet receptor cells likewise can be activated by a wide range of substances in addition to sugars.

Although umami receptor cells are the least well understood, researchers are honing in on their key features (Chandrashekar, Hoon, Ryba, & Zuker, 2006). They respond most strongly to glutamate, an amino acid in many protein-containing foods. Recall from Chapter 3, glutamate acts as a neurotransmitter; in fact, it's a major excitatory neurotransmitter. The food additive *monosodium glutamate* (MSG), which is often used to flavor Asian foods, particularly activates umami receptors. Some people develop headaches or allergic reactions after eating MSG.

Of course, the variety of taste experiences greatly exceeds the five basic receptors discussed here. Any food molecules dissolved in saliva evoke specific, combined patterns of activity in the five taste receptor types. Although we often think of taste as the primary source for flavor, in fact, taste and smell collaborate to produce this complex perception.

*"We would like to be genetically modified to taste like Brussels sprouts."*

As any wine connoisseur will attest, the full experience of a wine's flavor cannot be appreciated without a finely trained sense of smell. Odorants from substances outside your mouth enter the nasal cavity via the nostrils, and odorants in the mouth enter through the back of the throat. This is why wine aficionados are taught to pull air in over wine held in the mouth: It allows the wine's odorant molecules to enter the nasal cavity through this "back door."

You can easily demonstrate the contribution of smell to flavor by tasting a few different foods while holding your nose, preventing the olfactory system from detecting their odors. If you have a head cold, you probably already know how this turns out. Your favorite spicy burrito or zesty pasta probably tastes as bland as can be.

**In summary,** our experience of smell, or olfaction, is associated with odorant molecules binding to sites on specialized olfactory receptors, which converge at the glomerulus within the olfactory bulb. The olfactory bulb in turn sends signals to parts of the brain that control drives, emotions, and memories, which helps to explain why smells can have immediate and powerful effects on us. Smell is also involved in social behavior, as illustrated by pheromones, which are related to reproductive behavior and sexual responses in several species. Sensations of taste depend on taste buds, which are distributed across the tongue, roof of the mouth, and upper throat and on taste receptors that correspond to the five primary taste sensations of salt, sour, bitter, sweet, and umami.

Together, taste and smell produce what we perceive as flavor. This is why smelling the "bouquet" of a wine is an essential part of the wine-tasting ritual. Without smell, it would be difficult to taste subtle differences between wines.

## Where Do You Stand?

# Perception and Persuasion

In the 1950s, movie theater owners experimented with a new and controversial marketing technique: subliminal advertising. They screened films into which studios had spliced single frames containing photographs of popcorn and soda or word images such as *I'm thirsty*. At normal projection speed, these images were too brief for moviegoers to perceive consciously, but theater owners hoped that projecting the messages would register with viewers and thus increase concession sales during intermissions. However, scientific evidence for this kind of subliminal persuasion has been mixed at best.

These days, marketers advocate a more subtle form of advertising known as *sensory branding* (Lindstrom, 2005). The idea is to exploit all the senses to promote a product or a brand. We're used to seeing advertisements that feature exciting, provocative, or sexual images to sell products. In television commercials these images are accompanied by popular music that advertisers hope will evoke an overall mood favorable to the product. The notion is that the sight and sound of exciting things will become associated with what might be an otherwise drab product.

But sensory branding goes beyond sight and sound by enlisting smell, taste, and touch as well as vision and hearing. You probably recognize the distinctive aroma of a newly opened can of Play-Doh or a fresh box of Crayola crayons. Their scents are unmistakable, but they're also somewhat inadvertent: Play-Doh was first sold in 1956 and Crayola crayons appeared in 1903, both long before there was any thought given to marketing as a total sensory experience.

Sensory branding is a much more intentional approach to marketing. That new-car smell you anticipate while you take a test drive? Actually, it's a manufactured fragrance sprayed into the car, carefully tested to evoke positive feelings among potential buyers. Bang and Olufsen, a Danish high-end stereo manufacturer, carefully designed its remote control units to have a certain distinctive "feel" in a user's hand. Singapore Airlines, which has consistently been rated "the world's best airline," has actually patented the smell of their airplane cabins (it's called Stefan Floridian Waters).

Another form of advertising that has grown dramatically in recent years is product placement: Companies pay to have their products appear prominently in motion pictures and television productions. Do you notice when the star of a film drinks a can of a well-known beverage or drives a particular model of automobile in a car chase? Although viewers may not notice or even be aware of the product, advertisers believe that product placement benefits their bottom lines.

Video technology has advanced even to the point where products can be placed in motion pictures after the fact. Princeton Video, using its L-VIS (live-video insertion) system, placed a Snackwell's cookie box on the kitchen counter of a Bewitched rerun from the 1960s, long before the Snackwell's brand existed (Wenner, 2004)! Currently, there's a wave of interest in developing product placement advertising for multiplayer online games, even to the extent that ads can be tailored to specific users based on their preferences and previous buying habits.

Is there any harm in marketing that bombards the senses or even sneaks through to perception undetected? Advertising is a business, and like any business it is fueled by innovation in search of a profit. Perhaps these recent trends are simply the next clever step to get potential buyers to pay attention to a product message. On the other hand, is there a point when "enough is enough"? Do you want to live in a world where every sensory event is trademarked, patented, or test-marketed before reaching your perceptual system? Does the phrase, "Today's sunset was brought to you by the makers of . . ." cause you alarm? Where do you stand?

# Chapter Review

## The Doorway to Psychology

- Sensation and perception are separate events that, from the vantage point of the perceiver, feel like one single process. Sensation is simple awareness due to the stimulation of a sense organ, whereas perception is a brain activity that organizes, identifies, and interprets a sensation in order to form a mental representation.

- Transduction is the process that converts physical energy in the world into neural signals in the central nervous system. All senses rely on transduction, although the types of energy being sensed differ (e.g., light waves for vision, sound waves for audition).

- Psychophysics was a field of study during the mid- to late-1800s that sought to understand the link between properties of a physical stimulus and people's psychological reactions to them.

- Psychophysics researchers developed the idea of an absolute threshold, the minimal intensity needed to just barely detect a stimulus, and the difference threshold, the minimal change in a stimulus that can just barely be detected. The difference threshold is also referred to as the just noticeable difference (JND). Signal detection theory represents a refinement of these basic approaches and takes into account a perceived hit, miss, false alarm, and correct rejection rates.

- Sensory adaptation occurs when sensitivity to prolonged stimulation tends to decline over time as an organism adapts to current conditions. This adaptive process illustrates that the perceptual system is more sensitive to changes in stimulation than to constant levels of stimulation.

## Vision: More Than Meets the Eye

- Vision takes place when light waves are transduced by cells in the eye. Light waves have the properties of length, amplitude, and purity. These physical properties are perceived as color, brightness, and saturation, respectively.

- Light enters the eye through the cornea and pupil, landing on the retina, tissue that lines the back of each eyeball. The retina is composed of three layers of cells: photoreceptors, bipolar cells, and retinal ganglion cells (RGCs). Photoreceptors take the form of rods and cones; rods are specialized for low-light vision, whereas cones are specialized for color vision.

- The optic nerve is composed of bundled axons from the retinal ganglion cells; it leaves the eye via the blind spot at the back of each eyeball. Retinal ganglion cells have a receptive field that responds to light falling anywhere in it; some responses are excitatory, whereas others are inhibitory.

- Cones specialized to sense red, green, or blue wavelengths begin the process of color vision. Combinations of these cones firing produces the spectrum of colors we can see. Cones also operate in red-green and blue-yellow opponent combinations to contribute to color vision. Both additive and subtractive color mixing determine how shades of color can be produced.

- The optic nerve makes its way through various parts of the brain to terminate in area V1, the primary visual cortex, located in the occipital lobe. There specialized neurons respond to the sensation of bars and edges in different orientations. The ventral stream leaves the occipital cortex to provide a "what" visual pathway to other parts of the brain. The dorsal stream provides a "where" and "how" pathway.

- Both the modular view and the distributed representation view offer explanations of how we perceive and recognize objects in the world. At a minimum, humans show a great deal of perceptual constancy: Even as aspects of sensory signals change, perception remains consistent. We are rarely misled to think that distant objects are actually tiny, that the moon increases in physical size as it rises, or that a friend who grew a mustache is a totally different person.

- Gestalt psychologists delineated basic perceptual principles long ago, such as simplicity, closure, continuity, and proximity. Gestalt psychologists also observed that we tend to perceive figures set against some kind of background. Many visual illusions capitalize on perceptual ambiguities related to these principles.

- Both template-matching and parts-based explanations of object recognition have strengths and weaknesses. Neither account fully captures how humans correctly and efficiently perceive objects in their environment.

- Monocular, binocular, and motion-based cues all enable us to perceive size and depth, although we sometimes fall prey to visual illusions. Humans are also quite adept at perceiving motion through a variety of mechanisms.

## Audition: More Than Meets the Ear

- Hearing takes place when sound waves are transduced by receptors in the ear. Sound waves have the properties of frequency, amplitude, and complexity. These physical properties are perceived as pitch, loudness, and timbre.

- There are three parts of the human ear: the outer ear, the middle ear, and the inner ear. The outer ear channels sound waves toward the middle ear, where tiny bones (called ossicles) mechanically transmit and intensify vibrations from the eardrum to the inner ear.

- The inner ear contains the cochlea, which is divided along its length by the basilar membrane. The undulation of the basilar membrane stimulates thousands of tiny hair cells, specialized auditory receptor neurons embedded in the basilar membrane. The hair cells then release neurotransmitter molecules, initiating a neural signal in the auditory nerve.

- Both a place code and a temporal code are involved in transducing sound frequencies. A place code is used for high-frequency sounds, whereas a temporal code is used for low-frequency sounds. Auditory signals travel to area A1, the primary auditory cortex in the temporal lobe.

- The placement of the ears on the head enables us to localize sounds in the environment.

## The Body Senses: More Than Skin Deep

- Haptic perception involves the active exploration of the environment through touching and grasping. Four types of specialized receptor cells are located under the surface of the skin to trans-duce pressure, texture, pattern, or vibration. There are also receptor cells for sensing temperature and pain.

- The somatosensory strip is organized like a homunculus; areas of the body that are more sensitive occupy a greater area in the somatosensory strip. For example, fingertips have a greater representation than do the calves of the legs.

- Pain is a useful body sense; without it, we might quickly succumb to the effects of unnoticed wounds. A-delta fibers and C fibers are two types of pathways by which pain signals reach the brain.

- Gate-control theory proposes both a bottom-up and a top-down way of controlling pain signals in the body. This helps to account for individual differences in the experience of pain.

- Body position and movement are regulated by receptors located in the muscles, joints, and tendons. Balance is regulated by the semicircular canals in the inner ear and to some extent by visual cues.

## The Chemical Senses: Adding Flavor

- Smell and taste are both chemical senses; smell occurs when molecules enter the nose, and taste occurs when molecules are dissolved in saliva. Smell and taste combine to produce the experience of flavor.

- The olfactory epithelium, located at the top of the nasal cavity, contains about 10 million olfactory receptor neurons (ORNs). Each olfactory neuron has receptors that operate like a lock and key with odorant molecules. Groups of ORNs send their axons to a glomerulus within the olfactory bulb.

- Pheromones are biochemical odorants that affect behavior and physiology. There is mixed evidence that pheromones affect some aspects of human sexual behavior.

- The tongue is covered with papillae, which contain taste buds, the organs of taste transduction. Each taste bud contains taste receptor cells that respond to either salty, sweet, bitter, sour, or umami taste sensations. Umami refers to the savoriness of foods.

- Both taste and smell contribute to the perception of flavor. Odorants from food enter the nasal cavity both through the nose and through the back of the mouth. Plugging your nose while you eat can make palatable foods taste bland or make unpalatable foods taste acceptable.

## Key Terms

synesthesia (p. 122)
sensation (p. 123)
perception (p. 123)
transduction (p. 123)
psychophysics (p. 124)
absolute threshold (p. 124)
just noticeable difference (JND) (p. 126)
Weber's law (p. 126)
signal detection theory (p. 127)
sensory adaptation (p. 128)
visual acuity (p. 130)

retina (p. 132)
accommodation (p. 132)
cones (p. 132)
rods (p. 132)
fovea (p. 133)
blind spot (p. 134)
receptive field (p. 134)
trichromatic color representation (p. 137)
color-opponent system (p. 137)
area V1 (p. 138)
visual-form agnosia (p. 140)

perceptual constancy (p. 142)
template (p. 143)
monocular depth cues (p. 145)
binocular disparity (p. 146)
motion parallax (p. 147)
apparent motion (p. 149)
pitch (p. 150)
loudness (p. 150)
timbre (p. 151)
cochlea (p. 152)
basilar membrane (p. 152)
hair cells (p. 152)

area A1 (p. 152)
place code (p. 153)
temporal code (p. 153)
haptic perception (p. 155)
referred pain (p. 156)
gate-control theory (p. 157)
vestibular system (p. 158)
olfactory receptor neurons (ORNs) (p. 158)
olfactory bulb (p. 159)
pheromones (p. 160)
taste buds (p. 161)

## Recommended Readings

**Cytowic, R.** (2003). *The man who tasted shapes.* Cambridge: MIT Press. Richard Cytowic is a neurologist and author who offers insights on synesthesia. Interspersed with first-person accounts of synesthetic experiences are Cytowic's views on how and why the brain developed as it did and the implications of that evolutionary process for the mind, behavior, and social interaction.

**Enns, J. T.** (2004). *The thinking eye, the seeing brain.* New York: Norton. James Enns offers a tour through the visual system, focusing both on sensations in the eye and perception in the brain. This is a fine summary of the key points mentioned in the current chapter and a nice starting point for branching out to other topics in the science of vision.

**Goodale, M., & Milner, D.** (2004). *Sight unseen.* Oxford: Oxford University Press. Melvyn Goodale and David Milner explore conscious and unconscious vision in this intriguing book. Their arguments from studies of brain damage and neuroscience lead to the proposal of dual systems in visual perception.

**Illusions**

http://www.philomel.com/phantom_words/description.html

http://www.faculty.ucr.edu/~rosenblu/VSMcGurk.html

http://www.psychologie.tu-dresden.de/i1/kaw/diverses%20 Material/www.illusionworks.com/html/hall_of_illusions.html

Visual illusions trick the eye and the brain, and they're admittedly fun to demonstrate and intriguing in their operation. However, there are other types of sensory and perceptual illusions that you may find interesting. Visit some of these websites for demonstrations and more information.

# 5

# Memory

**A POPULAR PHRASE HAS IT, "IF YOU CAN** remember the '60s, then you weren't there." Let's meet a man who *can* remember the '60s even though he *was* there. But that's not what makes his story interesting.

In the late 1960s, many young people decided to turn on, tune in, and drop out. Greg was one of those people. He quit school; let his hair grow to his shoulders; tried a variety of soft and not-so-soft drugs; and moved to New York City's Greenwich Village, where his primary occupation seemed to be attending Grateful Dead concerts. But getting high and listening to music didn't prove to be quite as fulfilling as Greg had hoped, and in

1971 he joined the International Society for Krishna Consciousness and moved to their temple in New Orleans. At about that same time, Greg began having trouble with his vision. The trouble worsened, and by the time he sought medical attention, he was completely blind. His doctors discovered a tumor the size of a small orange in Greg's brain, and although they were able to remove it, the damage had already been done. Greg lost his sight, but because the tumor had also destroyed a part of the temporal lobe that is crucial for forming and retaining memories of everyday experience, Greg lost much of his memory as well.

**MEMORY** The ability to store and retrieve information over time.

In 1977, Greg was admitted to a hospital for patients requiring long-term care. When the neurologist Oliver Sacks interviewed him, Greg had no idea why he was in the hospital but suspected that it might be due to his past drug abuse. Dr. Sacks noticed piles of rock albums in Greg's room and asked him about his interest in music, whereupon Greg launched into a version of his favorite Grateful Dead song, "Tobacco Road," and then shared a vivid memory of a time when he had heard the group perform in New York's Central Park. "When did you hear them in Central Park?" asked Dr. Sacks. "It's been a while, over a year maybe," Greg replied. In fact, the concert had taken place 8 years earlier (Sacks, 1995, p. 48). Dr. Sacks conducted more tests, asking Greg to recall lists of words and simple stories. He noticed that Greg could hold on to the information for a few seconds but that within just a few minutes, he would forget nearly everything he had been told. Greg could sometimes learn songs and jingles if they were repeated over and over, but even when he learned them, he had no recollection of how or when he had done so.

Greg was upset when he was told that his father had died, but then he seemed quickly to forget about it. However, his demeanor changed after he learned of his father's death. He became increasingly sad and no longer wanted to go home for special occasions such as Thanksgiving, although he couldn't say why.

It is sometimes said of middle-aged men with bald spots and ponytails that they are "stuck in the '60s," but for Greg this was literally true. He was unaware that his favorite member of the Grateful Dead, the keyboard player Pigpen, had died in 1973. He knew nothing of President Nixon's visit to China, the death of Janis Joplin, the Arab-Israeli War, or Elvis Presley's divorce. When asked to name the president of the United States (who at that time was Jimmy Carter), he guessed that it was either Lyndon Johnson or John F. Kennedy. When Dr. Sacks gave Greg a hint—"The president's first name is Jimmy"—Greg perked up. "Jimi Hendrix?" he asked hopefully.

After 14 years in the hospital, Dr. Sacks took Greg to a Grateful Dead concert at Madison Square Garden. When the band performed their well-known songs from the 1960s, Greg sang along enthusiastically, but he was puzzled when the band played more recent songs, which he thought sounded "futuristic" and strange. "That was fantastic," Greg told Dr. Sacks as they left the concert. "I will always remember it. I had the time of my life." When Dr. Sacks saw Greg the next morning, he asked him about the Grateful Dead concert. "I love them. I heard them in Central Park and at the Fillmore East," replied Greg, recalling concerts he had seen more than 2 decades ago. "Didn't you just hear them at Madison Square Garden?" asked Dr. Sacks. "No," replied Greg, "I've never been to the Garden" (Sacks, 1995, pp. 76–77).

**Memory** is *the ability to store and retrieve information over time,* and as Greg's story suggests, it is more than just a handy device that allows us to find our car keys and schedule our dental appointments. In a very real way, our memories define us. Each of us has a unique identity that is intricately tied to the things we have thought, felt, done, and experienced. Memories are the residue of those events, the enduring

Greg's brain damage interfered with his ability to form new memories, so he was able to remember the Grateful Dead only as they sounded and performed in the early 1970s, not as they appeared more recently.

changes that experience makes in our brains and leaves behind when it passes. If an experience passes without leaving a trace, it might just as well not have happened. For Greg, the last 20 years of his life have come and gone without a trace, leaving him forever frozen in 1969. He can revisit old memories, but he cannot make new ones, and so he himself can never change. What he says and does, what he feels and imagines, is there and then gone, like smoke in the wind. As he admitted to Dr. Sacks one day, "It's not much of a life" (Sacks, 1995, p. 68).

Those of us who *can* remember what we did yesterday often fail to appreciate just how complex that act of remembering really is because it occurs so easily. But just consider the role that memory plays in the simplest act, such as arranging to meet a friend at the movies. You must recall your friend's name and telephone number and how to make a call. You must remember what her voice sounds like so that you'll recognize who answers the phone, and you need to remember how to talk to her and how to make sense of the things she says. You need to remember which movies are currently playing, as well as the types of movies that you and your friend enjoy. To find a convenient day and time, you need to remember everything else that is happening in your life as well. Eventually, you will need to remember how to get to the theater, how to drive your car, and what your friend looks like so you can recognize her among the people standing in front of the theater. And finally, you'll have to remember which movie you just saw so that you don't accidentally do this all this over again tomorrow. These are ordinary tasks, tasks so simple that you never give them a second thought. But the fact is that the most sophisticated computer could not even begin to accomplish them as efficiently as any average human.

Because memory is so remarkably complex, it is also remarkably fragile (Schacter, 1996). Every one of us has had the experience of forgetting something we desperately wanted to remember or of remembering something that never really happened. Why does memory serve us so well in some situations and play such cruel tricks on us in other cases? When can we trust our memories and when should we view them skeptically? Is there just one kind of memory, or are there many? These are among the questions that psychologists have asked and answered.

As you've seen in other chapters, the mind's errors and misfires provide key insights into its fundamental nature, and there is no better illustration of these mindbugs than in the realm of memory. Though often fascinating and sometimes frustrating, the mindbugs of memory teach us much about how we remember our pasts and hence about who we are. In this chapter we shall consider the three key functions of memory: **encoding,** *the process by which we transform what we perceive, think, or feel into an enduring memory;* **storage,** *the process of maintaining information in memory over time;* and **retrieval,** *the process of bringing to mind information that has been previously encoded and stored.* We shall then examine several different kinds of memory and focus on the ways in which errors, distortions, and imperfections can reveal the nature of memory itself.

## Encoding: Transforming Perceptions into Memories

For at least 2,000 years, people have thought of memory as a recording device, like some sort of video camera that makes exact copies of information that comes in through our senses and then stores those copies for later use. This idea is simple and intuitive. In fact, the only thing wrong with this idea it is that it is thoroughly and completely incorrect. Consider the case of Bubbles P., a professional gambler with no formal education, who spent most of his time shooting craps at local clubs or playing high-stakes poker. If you take the digit memory test shown in **FIGURE 5.1,** you will probably find that you can recall about seven numbers after one look back at the digits. But Bubbles had no difficulty rattling off 20 numbers, in either forward or backward order, after just a single glance (Ceci, DeSimone, & Johnson, 1992). You might conclude that Bubbles must have had a "photographic memory" that allowed him to make an instant copy of the information that he could "look at" later. In fact, that isn't at all how Bubbles accomplished his astounding feats of memory.

**ENCODING** The process by which we transform what we perceive, think, or feel into an enduring memory.

**STORAGE** The process of maintaining information in memory over time.

**RETRIEVAL** The process of bringing to mind information that has been previously encoded and stored.

**Figure 5.1 Digit Memory Test** How many digits can you remember? Start on the first row and cover the rows below it with a piece of paper. Study the numbers in the row for 1 second and then cover that row back up again. After a couple of seconds, try to repeat the numbers. Then uncover the row to see if you were correct. If so, continue down to the next row, using the same instructions, until you can't recall all the numbers in a row. The number of digits in the last row you can remember correctly is your digit span. Bubbles P. could remember 20 random numbers, or about 5 rows deep. How did you do?

2 8
6 9 1
0 4 7 3
8 7 4 5 4
9 0 2 4 8 1
5 7 4 2 2 9 6
6 4 7 1 9 3 0 4
3 5 6 7 1 8 4 8 5
1 0 2 8 8 3 4 7 2 9
4 7 2 0 8 2 7 4 2 6 4
7 3 1 0 9 3 4 3 5 1 3 8

**ELABORATIVE ENCODING** The process of actively relating new information to knowledge that is already in memory.

**VISUAL IMAGERY ENCODING** The process of storing new information by converting it into mental pictures.

To understand how Bubbles did this, we must abandon the notion that memories are copies of sensory experience. On the contrary, memories are made by combining information we *already* have in our brains with new information that comes in through our senses. In this way memory is much less like photography and much more like cooking. Like starting from a recipe but improvising along the way, we add old information to new information, mix, shake, bake, and out pops a memory. Memories are *constructed*, not recorded, and encoding is the process by which we transform what we perceive, think, or feel into an enduring memory. Let's look at three types of encoding processes: elaborative encoding, visual imagery encoding, and organizational encoding.

## Elaborative Encoding

Memories are a combination of old and new information, so the nature of any particular memory depends as much on the old information already in our memories as it does on the new information coming in through our senses. In other words, how we remember something depends on how we think about it at the time. In one study, researchers presented participants with a series of words and asked them to make one of three types of judgments (Craik & Tulving, 1975). *Semantic judgments* required the participants to think about the meaning of the words ("Is *hat* a type of clothing?"), *rhyme judgments* required the participants to think about the sound of the words ("Does *hat* rhyme with *cat*?"), and *visual judgments* required the participants to think about the appearance of the words ("Is *HAT* written uppercase or lowercase?"). The type of judgment task influenced how participants thought about each word—what old information they combined with the new—and thus had a powerful impact on their memories (**FIGURE 5.2**). Those participants who made semantic judgments (i.e., had thought about the meaning of the words) had much better memory for the words than did participants who had thought about how the word looked or sounded. The results of these and many other studies have shown that long-term retention is greatly enhanced by **elaborative encoding**, which involves *actively relating new information to knowledge that is already in memory* (Brown & Craik, 2000).

These findings would not have surprised Bubbles P. As a professional gambler, Bubbles found numbers unusually meaningful, and so when he saw a string of digits, he tended to think about their meanings. For example, he might have thought about how they related to his latest bet at the racetrack or to his winnings after a long night at the poker table. Whereas you might try to memorize the string 22061823 by saying it over and over, Bubbles would think about betting $220 at 6 to 1 odds on horse number 8 to place 2nd in the 3rd race. Indeed, when Bubbles was tested with materials other than numbers—faces, words, objects, or locations—his memory performance was no better than average.

You may consciously use Bubbles's strategy when you study for exams ("Well, if Napoleon was born in 1769, that would have made him 7 years old when America declared independence"), but you also use it automatically every day. Have you ever wondered why you can remember 20 experiences (your last summer vacation, your 16th birthday party, your first day at college) but not 20 digits? The reason is that most of the time we think of the meaning behind our experiences, and so we elaboratively encode them without even trying to (Craik & Tulving, 1975). Your 16th birthday party, for example, was probably not just an occasion for cake but rather signaled a transition to being able to drive a car, maybe having a meaningful dating relationship, or buying that electric guitar you never really played after a few months because it was hard to learn. The significance and deeper meaning

**Figure 5.2 Levels of Processing** Elaborative encoding enhances subsequent retention. Thinking about a word's meaning (making a *semantic judgment*) results in deeper processing—and better memory for the word later—than merely attending to its sound (*rhyme judgment*) or shape (*visual judgment*). (From Craik & Tulving, 1975)

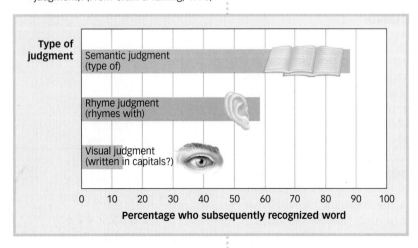

Type of judgment

Semantic judgment (type of)

Rhyme judgment (rhymes with)

Visual judgment (written in capitals?)

0    10    20    30    40    50    60    70    80    90    100

**Percentage who subsequently recognized word**

attached to the experience of your 16th birthday allowed you to encode that event more readily and thereby commit it to memory. The point is that Bubbles's amazing memory for numbers and your amazing memory for experiences are both due to elaborative encoding and not to some mysterious kind of "photographic memory."

So where does this elaborative encoding take place? What's going on in the brain when this type of information processing occurs? Studies reveal that elaborative encoding is uniquely associated with increased activity in the inner part of the left temporal lobe and the lower left part of the frontal lobe (**FIGURE 5.3a, b**) (Demb et al., 1995; Kapur et al., 1994; Wagner et al., 1998). In fact, the amount of activity in each of these two regions during encoding is directly related to whether people later remember an item. The more activity there is in these areas, the more likely the person will remember the information.

## Visual Imagery Encoding

At a banquet in Athens in 477 BC, the Greek poet Simonides regaled his audience with some stand-up poetry. Moments after the emcee announced, "Simonides has left the building!" the banquet hall collapsed and killed all the people inside. Talk about bringing down the house! Simonides was able to name every one of the dead simply by visualizing each chair around the banquet table and recalling the person who had been sitting there. Simonides wasn't the first, but he was among the most proficient, to use **visual imagery encoding**, which involves *storing new information by converting it into mental pictures* (**FIGURE 5.4**).

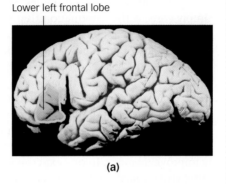
Lower left frontal lobe

**(a)**

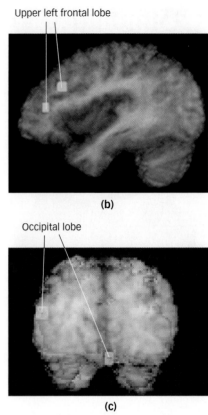
Upper left frontal lobe

**(b)**

Occipital lobe

**(c)**

**Figure 5.3** **Brain Activity during Different Types of Judgments** fMRI studies reveal that different parts of the brain are active during different types of judgments: (a) During semantic judgments, the lower left frontal lobe is active; (b) during organizational judgments, the upper left frontal lobe is active; and (c) during visual judgments, the occipital lobe is active.

(a) Courtesy of Anthony Wagner; (b) Savage et al., 2001, *Brain, 124*(1), pp. 219–231, Fig. 1c, p. 226. Courtesy of C. R. Savage; (c) Kosslyn et al., *Science, 284,* pp. 167–170, Fig. 2, p. 168. Courtesy of Stephen M. Kosslyn.

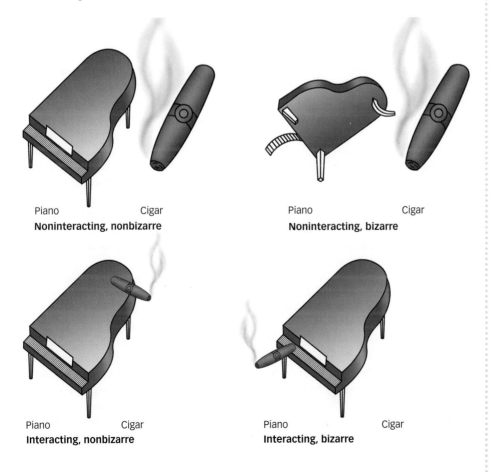

Piano　　　　Cigar
**Noninteracting, nonbizarre**

Piano　　　　Cigar
**Noninteracting, bizarre**

Piano　　　　Cigar
**Interacting, nonbizarre**

Piano　　　　Cigar
**Interacting, bizarre**

**Figure 5.4** **Visual Imagery** One way to better remember something is by relating it to something else using visual imagery. Here it is easier to remember a piano and a cigar when they are interacting than as individual items. This strategy works well, whether the images are bizarre or not (Wollen, Weber, & Lowry, 1972).

No one remembers how the Greek poet Simonides actually looked, but his memory improvement method, which uses visual images to encode new information, has never been forgotten.

If you wanted to use Simonides' method to create an enduring memory, you could simply convert the information that you wanted to remember into a visual image and then "store it" in a familiar location. For instance, if you were going to the grocery store and wanted to remember to buy Coke, popcorn, and cheese dip, you could use the rooms in your house as locations and imagine your living room flooded in Coke, your bedroom pillows stuffed with popcorn, and your bathtub as a greasy pond of cheese dip. When you arrived at the store, you could then take a "mental walk" around your house and "look" into each room to remember the items you needed to purchase. While you're at the store, you might also want to buy a mop to clean up the mess at home.

Numerous experiments have shown that visual imagery encoding can substantially improve memory. In one experiment, participants who studied lists of words by creating visual images of them later recalled twice as many items as participants who just mentally repeated the words (Schnorr & Atkinson, 1969). Another experiment found similar results for people who studied lists composed of concrete words that are easily visualized, such as *tree, battleship,* or *sun,* compared to abstract words, such as *idea, democracy,* or *will* (Paivio, 1969). Why does visual imagery encoding work so well? First, visual imagery encoding does some of the same things that elaborative encoding does: When you create a visual image, you relate incoming information to knowledge already in memory. For example, a visual image of a parked car might help you create a link to your memory of your first kiss.

Second, when you use visual imagery to encode words and other verbal information, you end up with two different mental "placeholders" for the items—a visual one and a verbal one—which gives you more ways to remember them than just a verbal placeholder alone (Paivio, 1971, 1986). How do we know these multiple placeholders are created? As you just read, elaborative encoding seems to activate the frontal and temporal lobes of the brain, but visual imagery encoding activates regions in the occipital lobe (Kosslyn et al., 1993), which as you'll recall from Chapter 3, is the center of visual processing. This finding suggests that people indeed enlist the visual system when forming memories based on mental images (see **FIGURE 5.3c**).

## Organizational Encoding

Have you ever ordered dinner with a group of friends and watched in amazement as your server took the order without writing anything down? To find out how this is done, one researcher spent 3 months working in a restaurant where waitresses routinely wrote down orders but then left the check at the customer's table before proceeding to the kitchen and *telling* the cooks what to make (Stevens, 1988). The researcher wired each waitress with a microphone and asked her to think aloud, that is, to say what she was thinking as she walked around all day doing her job. The researcher found that as soon as the waitress left a customer's table, she immediately began *grouping* or *categorizing* the orders into hot drinks, cold drinks, hot foods, and cold foods. The waitresses grouped the items into a sequence that matched the layout of the kitchen, first placing drink orders, then hot food orders, and finally cold food orders. The waitresses remembered their orders by relying on **organizational encoding**, which involves *noticing the relationships among a series of items.*

For example, how easily do you think you could memorize the words *peach, cow, chair, apple, table, cherry, lion, couch, horse, desk*? If you are like most people, this doesn't seem like a particularly easy list to remember. But if you organized the items into three categories—*peach, apple, cherry* and *cow, lion, horse* and *chair, couch, desk*—you would likely have no problems. Studies have shown that instructing people to sort items into categories like this is an effective way to enhance their subsequent recall of those items (Mandler, 1967). Even more complex organizational schemes have been used, such as the hierarchy in **FIGURE 5.5** (Bower et al., 1969). As you can see, people improved their recall of individual items by organizing them into multiple-level categories, all the way from a general category such as *animals,* through intermediate categories such as *birds* and *songbirds,* down to specific examples such as *wren* and *sparrow.*

**ORGANIZATIONAL ENCODING** The act of categorizing information by noticing the relationships among a series of items.

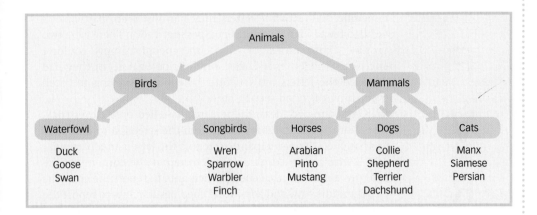

**Figure 5.5** **Organizing Words into a Heirarchy** Organizing words into conceptual groups and relating them to one another—such as in this example of a hierarchy—makes it easier to reconstruct the items from memory later (Bower et al., 1969). Keeping track of the 17 items in this example can be facilitated by remembering the hierarchical groupings they fall under.

Organizing by categories encourages you to focus on the similarities among items. But organizational encoding can also take advantage of the differences between items (Hunt & McDaniel, 1993). Look at the following items for a couple of seconds each, and then try to recall them: VRZ, BGR, HPL, WQM, 247, SWY, RNB, PLB. In this list, "247" is the oddball item, and because it stands out from the others, you will probably tend to remember it best—better, in fact, than if it appeared in a list with other numbers (von Restorff, 1933). The relationships between things—how they fit together and how they differ—can help us remember them.

Just as elaborative and visual imagery encoding activate distinct regions of the brain, so too does organizational encoding. As you can see in Figure 5.3b, organizational encoding activates the upper surface of the left frontal lobe (Fletcher, Shallice, & Dolan, 1998; Savage et al., 2001). Different types of encoding strategies appear to rely on different areas of brain activation.

---

**In summary,** encoding is the process by which we transform what our senses take in, and what we experience, into a lasting memory. Most instances of spectacular memory performance reflect the skillful use of encoding strategies rather than so-called photographic memory. Memory is influenced by the type of encoding we perform regardless of whether we consciously intend to remember an event or a fact. Elaborative encoding, visual imagery encoding, and organizational encoding all increase memory, but they use different parts of the brain to accomplish that. ■ ■

---

## Storage: Maintaining Memories over Time

Encoding is the process of turning perceptions into memories. But one of the hallmarks of a memory is that you can bring it to mind on Tuesday, not on Wednesday, and then bring it to mind again on Thursday. So where are our memories when we aren't using them? Clearly, those memories are *stored* somewhere in your brain. **Memory storage** is *the process of maintaining information in memory over time*. We can think of a memory store as a place in which memories are kept when we are not consciously experiencing them. The memory store has three major divisions—sensory, short-term, and long-term. As these names suggest, the three divisions are distinguished primarily by the amount of time in which a memory can be kept inside them.

### Sensory Storage

The **sensory memory store** is *the place in which sensory information is kept for a few seconds or less*. In a series of classic experiments, research participants were asked to remember rows of letters (Sperling, 1960). In one version of the procedure, participants viewed three rows of four letters each, as shown in **FIGURE 5.6** on the next page. The researcher flashed the letters on a screen for just 1/20th of a second. When asked to

**MEMORY STORAGE** The process of maintaining information in memory over time.

**SENSORY MEMORY STORE** The place in which sensory information is kept for a few seconds or less.

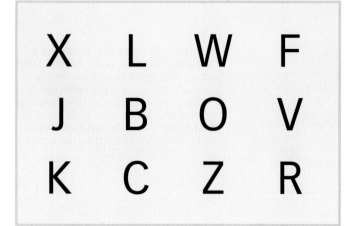

**Figure 5.6 Iconic Memory Test** When a grid of letters is flashed on-screen for only 1/20th of a second, it is difficult to recall individual letters. But if prompted to remember a particular row immediately after the grid is shown, research participants will do so with high accuracy. Sperling used this procedure to demonstrate that although iconic memory stores the whole grid, the information fades away too quickly for a person to recall everything (Sperling, 1960).

remember all 12 of the letters they had just seen, participants recalled fewer than half of them (Sperling, 1960). There were two possible explanations for this: Either people simply couldn't encode all the letters in such a brief period of time, or they had encoded the letters but forgotten them while trying to recall everything they had seen.

To test the two ideas, the researchers relied on a clever trick. Just after the letters disappeared from the screen, a tone sounded that cued the participants to report the letters in a particular row. A *high tone* cued participants to report the contents of the top row, a *medium* tone cued participants to report the contents of the middle row, and a *low* tone cued participants to report the contents of the bottom row. When asked to report only a single row, people recalled almost all of the letters in that row! Because the tone sounded *after* the letters disappeared from the screen, the researchers concluded that people could have recalled the same number of letters from *any* of the rows had they been asked to. Participants had no way of knowing which of the three rows would be cued, so the researchers inferred that virtually all the letters had been encoded. In fact, if the tone was substantially delayed, participants couldn't perform the task; the information had slipped away from their sensory memories. Like the afterimage of a flashlight, the 12 letters flashed on a screen are visual icons, a lingering trace stored in memory for a very short period.

Because we have more than one sense, we have more than one kind of sensory memory. **Iconic memory** is *a fast-decaying store of visual information.* A similar storage area serves as a temporary warehouse for sounds. **Echoic memory** is *a fast-decaying store of auditory information.* When you have difficulty understanding what someone has just said, you probably find yourself replaying the last few words—listening to them echo in your "mind's ear," so to speak. When you do that, you are accessing information that is being held in your echoic memory store. The hallmark of both the iconic and echoic memory stores is that they hold information for a very short time. Iconic memories usually decay in about a second or less, and echoic memories usually decay in about five seconds (Darwin, Turvey, & Crowder, 1972). These two sensory memory stores are a bit like doughnut shops: The products come in, they sit briefly on the shelf, and then they are discarded. If you want one, you have to grab it fast.

## Short-Term Storage and Working Memory

A second kind of memory store is the **short-term memory store**, which is *a place where nonsensory information is kept for more than a few seconds but less than a minute.* For example, if someone tells you a telephone number, you can usually wait a few seconds and repeat it back with ease. But if you wait too long, you can't. How long is too long? In a study that examined how long people can hold information in short-term memory, research participants were given consonant strings to remember, such as DBX and HLM. After seeing each string, participants were asked to count backward from 100 by 3s for varying amounts of time and were then asked to recall the strings (Peterson & Peterson, 1959). As shown in **FIGURE 5.7,** memory for the consonant strings declined rapidly, from approximately 80% after a 3-second delay to less than 20% after a 20-second delay.

These results suggest that information can be held in the short-term memory store for about 15 to 20 seconds, but for most of us, that's not nearly long enough. So we use a trick that allows us to get around the natural limitations of our short-term memories. If someone gives us a telephone number and we don't have a pencil, we say it over and over to ourselves until we find one. **Rehearsal** is *the process of keeping information in short-term memory by mentally repeating it.* Why does rehearsal work so well? Because each time you repeat the number, you are putting it back or "reentering" it into short-term memory, thus giving it another 15 to 20 seconds of shelf life.

**ICONIC MEMORY** A fast-decaying store of visual information.

**ECHOIC MEMORY** A fast-decaying store of auditory information.

**SHORT-TERM MEMORY STORE** A place where nonsensory information is kept for more than a few seconds but less than a minute.

**REHEARSAL** The process of keeping information in short-term memory by mentally repeating it.

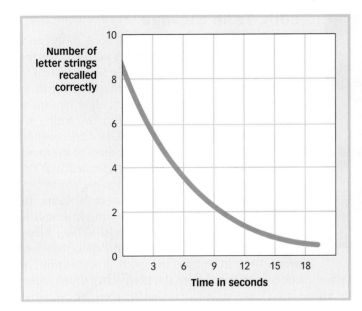

**Figure 5.7** **The Decline of Short-Term Memory** A 1959 experiment showed how quickly short-term memory fades without rehearsal. On a test for memory of three-letter strings, research participants were highly accurate when tested a few seconds after exposure to each string, but if the test was delayed another 15 seconds, people barely recalled the strings at all (Peterson & Peterson, 1959).

Short-term memory is naturally limited in how *long* it can hold information, but it is also naturally limited in how *much* information it can hold. Experiments suggest that most people can keep approximately seven numbers in short-term memory, and if they put more new numbers in, then old numbers begin to fall out (Miller, 1956). It is no accident that telephone numbers were (until recently) limited to seven digits. But there is something puzzling here. If we can keep only seven numbers in short-term memory, then how is it that we can also keep seven words? After all, seven words could easily involve more than 50 letters. The answer is that short-term term memory can hold about seven *meaningful items,* and therefore one way to circumvent its natural limitations is to group several letters into a single meaningful item. **Chunking** involves *combining small pieces of information into larger clusters or chunks*. Short-term memory can hold about seven chunks of information, and although a word may contain more than 10 letters, it is still considered a single chunk (Miller, 1956). Recall the waitresses who organized the customers' orders into groups. These waitresses were essentially chunking the information, thus giving themselves less to remember.

Just as sensory memory can be subdivided into iconic and echoic components, short-term memory can also be conceptualized as having different elements. Short-term memory was originally conceived of as a kind of "place" where information is kept for a limited amount of time. Indeed, the language that researchers use to talk about memory (e.g., *store, storage area*) illustrates that approach. A more dynamic model of a limited-capacity memory system has been developed and refined over the past few decades. **Working memory** refers to *active maintenance of information in short-term storage* (Baddeley & Hitch, 1974). It differs from the traditional view that short-term memory is simply a place to hold information and instead includes the operations and processes we use to work with information in short-term memory.

Working memory includes subsystems that store and manipulate visual images or verbal information. If you wanted to keep the arrangement of pieces on a chessboard in mind as you contemplated your next move, you'd be relying on working memory. Working memory includes the visual representation of the positions of the pieces, your mental manipulation of the possible moves, and your awareness of the flow of information into and out of memory ("Is my time almost up?" "Wait; there's a better move!" "The pawn might work over there."), all stored for a limited amount of time. In short, the working memory model acknowledges both the limited nature of this kind of memory storage and the activities that are commonly associated with it.

**CHUNKING** Combining small pieces of information into larger clusters or chunks that are more easily held in short-term memory.

**WORKING MEMORY** Active maintenance of information in short-term storage.

Even years after leaving home in Pontito, Italy, painter Franco Magnani was able to create a near-perfect reproduction of what he'd seen there. Magnani's painting (left), based on a memory of a place he hadn't seen for years, is remarkably similar to the photograph Susan Schwartzenberg took of the actual scene (right).

 **ONLY HUMAN**

**HELP! I'VE EATEN AND I CAN'T GET HOME!** In Oslo, Norway, Jermund Slogstad, 50, was moving into his new apartment when he took a break to get something to eat. He went to a nearby café but forgot to take his wallet, which contained his new address. He was unable to find his way home. "This is embarrassing," he told a newspaper a month later, hoping word of his plight would reach his new landlady, whom he had paid a month's rent in advance.

## Long-Term Storage

The artist Franco Magnani was born in Pontito, Italy, in 1934. In 1958, he left his village to see the rest of the world, and he settled in San Francisco in the 1960s. Soon after arriving, Magnani began to suffer from a strange illness. Every night he experienced feverish dreams of Pontito, in which he recalled the village in vivid detail. The dreams soon penetrated his waking life in the form of overpowering recollections, and Magnani decided that the only way to rid himself of these images was to capture them on canvas. For the next 20 years, he devoted much of his time to painting in exquisite detail his memories of his beloved village. Many years later, photographer Susan Schwartzenberg went to Pontito, armed with a collection of Magnani's paintings, and photographed each scene from the perspective of the paintings. As you can see in the images above, the correspondence between the paintings and the photographs was striking (Sacks, 1995; Schacter, 1996).

Many years intervened between Magnani's visual perception and artistic reconstruction of the village, suggesting that very detailed information can sometimes be stored for a very long time. The **long-term memory store** is *a place in which information can be kept for hours, days, weeks, or years.* In contrast to both the sensory and short-term memory stores, the long-term store has no known capacity limits (see **FIGURE 5.8**). For example, most people can recall 10,000 to 15,000 words in their native language, tens of thousands of facts ("Columbus discovered America in 1492" and "$3 \times 3 = 9$"), and an untold number of personal experiences. Just think of all the song lyrics you can recite by heart, and you'll understand that you've got a lot of information tucked away in long-term memory!

Amazingly, people can recall items from the long-term memory store even if they haven't recalled them for years. For example, do you think you would you be able to recognize your classmates if their high school photographs showed up, say, on *America's Most Wanted* 10 years from now? Researchers have found that even 50 years after graduation, people can accurately recognize about 90% of their high school classmates from yearbook photographs (Bahrick, 2000). Although Franco Magnani's memories are impressive, we are all capable of quite remarkable feats of long-term storage.

Not everybody has the ability to put information into the long-term memory store. In 1953, a 27-year-old man, known by the initials HM, suffered from intractable epilepsy (Scoville & Milner, 1957). To prevent further spread of epileptic tissue, HM had parts of his temporal lobes removed, including the hippocampus and some surrounding regions (**FIGURE 5.9**). After the operation, HM could converse easily, use and understand language, and perform well on intelligence tests. Indeed, the only thing

You probably have a pretty good memory for the names and faces of the people who went to your high school. That information got stored in long-term memory, and you will likely still remember most of the people in your high school in 50 years' time.

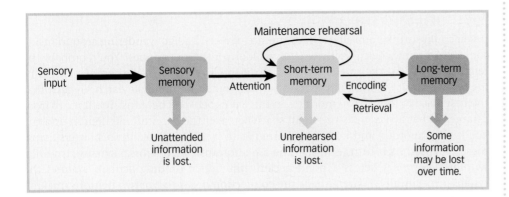

**Figure 5.8 The Flow of Information through the Memory System** Information moves through several stages of memory as it gets encoded, stored, and made available for later retrieval.

HM could *not* do was remember things that happened to him *after* the operation. For example, he would often forget that he had just eaten a meal or fail to recognize the hospital staff who helped him on a daily basis. Like Greg, who was stuck in the 1960s, HM lacked the ability to hang on to the new memories he created. HM could repeat a telephone number with no difficulty, suggesting that his short-term memory store was just fine (Corkin, 1984, 2002; Hilts, 1995). But after information left the short-term store, it was gone forever. For HM, everything that had ever happened had either happened in the last few moments or prior to 1953.

Studies of HM and others have shown that the hippocampal region of the brain is critical for putting new information into the long-term store. When this region is damaged, patients suffer from a condition known as **anterograde amnesia**, which is *the inability to transfer new information from the short-term store into the long-term store*. Some amnesic patients also suffer from **retrograde amnesia**, which is *the inability to retrieve information that was acquired before a particular date, usually the date of an injury or operation*. Although HM could not store new memories, he was generally able to recall knowledge acquired during adolescence and childhood and could also recall some of his youthful experiences, although his early personal memories lacked detail (Corkin, 2002). The fact that HM had much worse anterograde than retrograde amnesia suggests that the hippocampal region is not the site of long-term memory; indeed, research has shown that different aspects of a single memory are stored in different places in the cortex (Damasio, 1989; Schacter, 1996; Squire & Kandel, 1999). Consider, for example, your memory of the first concert you ever attended. Memories of the band's appearance are probably stored in your visual cortex, perhaps in the occipital lobe or inferior temporal lobe (see Chapters 3 and 4). Memories of the tunes they played are probably stored in your auditory cortex.

If different parts of a memory are stored in different parts of the brain, then why does hippocampal damage cause any kind of amnesia at all? Think about it: If bits and pieces of experience are scattered throughout the cortex, then *something* has to gather them together in order for us to have a single, integrated memory. Psychologists now believe that the hippocampal region serves this function, acting as a kind of "index" that links together all of these otherwise separate bits and pieces so that we remember them as one (Schacter, 1996; Squire, 1992; Teyler & DiScenna, 1986). If you were making a pie, the recipe would serve as an index—it would tell you to retrieve eggs and butter from the refrigerator, flour from the pantry, and rhubarb from the garden and then to mix them all together to produce the pie. But if the hippocampus is a memory index, then why was HM able to recall scenes from his childhood? Good question! It appears that when people recall experiences over and over again, the bits and pieces start to become integrated, and they no longer need the hippocampal index to tie them together. If you made rhubarb pies every day, you wouldn't need a recipe after only a week or so. When the butter came out, so would the eggs. Scientists are still debating the extent to which the hippocampal regions helps us to remember details of our old memories (Bayley et al., 2005; Moscovitch et al., 2006), but the notion of the hippocampus as an index explains why people like HM *cannot* make new memories and why they *can* remember old ones.

**LONG-TERM MEMORY STORE** A place in which information can be kept for hours, days, weeks, or years.

**ANTEROGRADE AMNESIA** The inability to transfer new information from the short-term store into the long-term store.

**RETROGRADE AMNESIA** The inability to retrieve information that was acquired before a particular date, usually the date of an injury or operation.

**Figure 5.9 The Hippocampus Patient** HM had his hippocampus and adjacent structures of the medial temporal lobe (indicated by the shaded area) surgically removed to stop his epileptic seizures. As a result, he could not remember things that happened after the surgery.

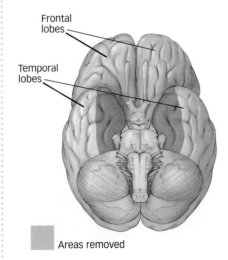

Frontal lobes

Temporal lobes

Areas removed

**LONG-TERM POTENTIATION (LTP)**
Enhanced neural processing that results from the strengthening of synaptic connections.

**NMDA RECEPTOR** A hippocampal receptor site that influences the flow of information from one neuron to another across the synapse by controlling the initiation of long-term potentiation.

# Memories in the Brain

If you could shrink yourself down to the size of a cell and go wandering around inside someone's brain, where exactly would you look for their memories? You'd probably be tempted to look at their neurons; after all, at the level of the cell, there's really nothing *but* neurons to look at. But that isn't where you'd find them. Research suggests that the best place to look for memories is in the *spaces* between neurons. You'll recall from Chapter 3 that a *synapse* is the small space between the axon of one neuron and the dendrite of another, and neurons communicate by sending neurotransmitters across these synapses. As it turns out, sending a neurotransmitter across a synapse isn't like sending a toy boat across a pond because the act of sending actually *changes* the synapse. Specifically, it strengthens the connection between the two neurons, making it easier for them to transmit to each other the next time. This is why researchers sometimes say, "Cells that fire together wire together" (Hebb, 1949).

The idea that the connections between neurons are strengthened by their communication, thus making communication easier the next time, provides the neurological basis for long-term memory, and much of what we know about this comes from the tiny sea slug *Aplysia*. Having an extremely simple nervous system consisting of only 20,000 neurons (compared to roughly 100 billion in the human brain), *Aplysia* has been attractive to researchers because it is relatively uncomplicated. When an experimenter stimulates *Aplysia*'s tail with a mild electric shock, the slug immediately withdraws its gill, and if the experimenter does it again a moment later, *Aplysia* withdraws its gill even more quickly. If the experimenter comes back an hour later and shocks *Aplysia,* the withdrawal of the gill happens as slowly as it did the first time, as if *Aplysia* can't "remember" what happened an hour earlier (Abel et al., 1995). But if the experimenter shocks *Aplysia* over and over, it does develop an enduring "memory" that can last for days or even weeks. Research suggests that this long-term storage involves the growth of new synaptic connections between neurons (Abel et al., 1995; Squire & Kandel, 1999). So, learning in *Aplysia* is based on changes involving the synapses for both short-term storage (enhanced neurotransmitter release) and long-term storage (growth of new synapses). Any experience that results in memory produces physical changes in the nervous system—even if you're a slug.

If you're something more complex than a slug—say, a mammal or your roommate—a similar process of synaptic strengthening happens in the hippocampus, which we've seen is an area crucial for storing new long-term memories. In the early 1970s, researchers applied a brief electrical stimulus to a neural pathway in a rat's hippocampus (Bliss & Lømo, 1973). They found that the electrical current produced a stronger connection between synapses that lay along the pathway and that the strengthening lasted for hours or even weeks. They called this **long-term potentiation**, more commonly known as **LTP**, which is *enhanced neural processing that results from the strengthening of synaptic connections.* Long-term potentiation has a number of properties that indicate to researchers that it plays an important role in long-term memory storage: It occurs in several pathways within the hippocampus; it can be induced rapidly; and it can last for a long time. In fact, drugs that block LTP can turn rats into rodent versions of patient HM: The animals have great difficulty remembering where they've been recently and become easily lost in a maze (Bliss, 1999; Morris, Anderson, Lynch, & Baudry, 1986).

So how does LTP take place? What's going on in the neurons in the hippocampus to produce these stronger synaptic connections? The primary agent is a neural receptor site called NMDA, known more formally as *N*-methyl-D-aspartate. The **NMDA receptor** *influences the flow of information from one neuron to another across the synapse by controlling the initiation of LTP in most hippocampal pathways* (Bliss, 1999). Here's how it works. The hippocampus contains an abundance of NMDA receptors, more so than in other areas of the brain. This is not surprising because the hippocampus is intimately involved in the formation of long-term memories. But for these NMDA receptors to become activated, two things must happen at roughly the same time. First, the presynaptic, or "sending," neuron releases a neurotransmitter called *glutamate* (a major

The sea slug *Aplysia californica* is useful to researchers because it has an extremely simple nervous system that can be used to investigate the mechanisms of short- and long-term memory.

GERALD & BUFF CORSI/VISUALS UNLIMITED

excitatory neurotransmitter in the brain), which attaches to the NMDA receptor site on the postsynaptic, or "receiving," neuron. Second, excitation takes place in the postsynaptic neuron. Together, these two events initiate LTP, which in turn increases synaptic connections by allowing neurons that fire together to wire together (**FIGURE 5.10**).

Don't get lost wandering around all these neurons . . . in fact, un-shrink yourself from the size of a cell and look at the big picture for a minute. It's easy to say that humans and other animals can form long-term memories. We can tell from a person's behavior that information has been stored and is able to be called up again and acted on. But it's another matter to understand *how* and *why* long-term memories are formed. The neural research on LTP and NMDA receptors helps us link an observable mental phenomenon ("Look! The squirrel remembered where the nuts were! She went right back to the correct tree!") with the biological underpinnings that produce it. More work remains to be done in this area to conclusively show how LTP leads to the formation of long-term memories, but the implications of this line of research are considerable. You can read about some of those implications in the Hot Science box.

**Figure 5.10 Long-Term Potentiation in the Hippocampus** The presynaptic neuron (top of figure) releases the neurotransmitter glutamate into the synapse. Glutamate then binds to the NMDA receptor sites on the postsynaptic neuron (bottom). At about the same time, excitation in the postsynaptic neuron takes place. The combined effect of these two processes initiate long-term potentiation and the formation of long-term memories.

Presynaptic neuron

Vesicles containing glutamate

Glutamate

NMDA receptors

Postsynaptic neuron

## { HOT SCIENCE } A Memory Drug?

IT'S DIFFICULT TO IMAGINE MANY THINGS that people would welcome more than a memory-enhancing drug. A memory enhancer could help eliminate forgetting associated with aging and disease. Furthermore, such a drug could help people remember past experiences more clearly and help us acquire new information more easily for school and at work. As scientists learn more about memory, we are closing in on this tantalizing goal.

Some of the most exciting evidence comes from research that has built on earlier findings linking LTP and memory to identify a gene that improves memory in mice (Tang et al., 1999). The gene makes a protein that assists the NMDA receptor, which plays an important role in long-term memory by helping to initiate LTP. Mice bred to have extra copies of this gene showed more activity in their NMDA receptors, more LTP, and improved performance on several different memory tasks—learning a spatial layout, recognizing familiar objects, and recalling a fear-inducing shock (Tang et al., 1999).

If these basic insights about genes, LTP, and the synaptic basis of memory can be translated to people—and that remains to be seen—they could pave the way for memory-enhancing treatments. Like steroids for bulking up the muscles, these drugs would bulk up memory. As exciting as this may sound, it also raises troubling issues. Consider the potential educational implications of memory-enhancing drugs. If memory enhancers were available, children who used them might be able to acquire and retain extraordinary amounts of information, allowing them to progress far more rapidly in school than they could otherwise. How well could the brain handle such an onslaught of information? What happens to children who don't have access to the latest memory enhancers? Are they left behind in school—and as a result handicapped later in life?

What are the potential implications of memory-enhancing drugs for the workplace? Imagine that you are applying for a job that requires a good memory, such as a manager at a technology company or a sales position that requires remembering customers' names as well as the attributes of different products and services. Would you take a memory-enhancing drug to increase your chances of landing the position? Would people who felt uncomfortable taking such a drug find themselves cut out of lucrative career opportunities?

Memory drugs might also help take the sting out of disturbing memories that we wish we could forget but can't. The 2004 hit movie *Eternal Sunshine of the Spotless Mind* told the story of a young man seeking just such freedom from the painful memories of a romantic breakup. As you will see in the section on persistence later in the chapter, emotionally arousing events often create intrusive memories, and researchers have already muted emotional memories with drugs that block the action of key hormones. Should emergency workers who must confront horrifying accident scenes that can burden them with persisting memories be provided with such drugs? Should such drugs be given to rape victims who can't forget the trauma? Memory drugs might provide some relief to such individuals. But could they also interfere with an individual's ability to assimilate and come to terms with a difficult experience? We may find ourselves struggling with these kinds of questions in the not-too-distant future.

**The film *Eternal Sunshine of the Spotless Mind* builds on the premise that erasing some memories might be a good idea.**

LEE DAVID/FOCUS FEATURES/THE KOBAL COLLECTION

**RETRIEVAL CUE** External information that is associated with stored information and helps bring it to mind.

**ENCODING SPECIFICITY PRINCIPLE** The idea that a retrieval cue can serve as an effective reminder when it helps re-create the specific way in which information was initially encoded.

**STATE-DEPENDENT RETRIEVAL** The tendency for information to be better recalled when the person is in the same state during encoding and retrieval.

**TRANSFER-APPROPRIATE PROCESSING** The idea that memory is likely to transfer from one situation to another when we process information in a way that is appropriate to the retrieval cues that will be available later.

 **ONLY HUMAN**

**PERHAPS BAKERS GET UP A BIT TOO EARLY** Burglars broke into the safe in the Wonder-Hostess Thrift Shop bakery in Davenport, Iowa. Police said the burglars had an easy time because the bakery employees could not remember the safe's combination: They had written it out and posted it on the nearby bulletin board.

A particular light, odor, or melody can make a memory reappear vividly, with all its force and its precision, as if a window opened on the past.

**In summary,** there are several different types of memory storage: Sensory memory holds information for a second or two; short-term or working memory retains information for about 15 to 20 seconds; and long-term memory stores information for anywhere from minutes to years or decades. The hippocampus and nearby structures play an important role in long-term memory storage, as shown by the severe amnesia of patients such as HM. Memory storage depends on changes in synapses, and long-term potentiation (LTP) increases synaptic connections. ■ ■

# Retrieval: Bringing Memories to Mind

There is something fiendishly frustrating about piggy banks. You can put money in them, you can shake them around to assure yourself that the money is there, but you can't easily get the money out, which is why no one carries a piggy bank instead of a wallet. If memory were like a piggy bank, it would be similarly useless. We could make memories, we could store them, and we could even shake our heads around and listen for the telltale jingle. But if we couldn't bring our memories out of storage and use them, then what would be the point of saving them in the first place? Retrieval is the process of bringing to mind information that has been previously encoded and stored, and it is perhaps the most important of all memorial processes (Roediger, 2000; Schacter, 2001a).

## Retrieval Cues: Reinstating the Past

When someone asks you to juggle three apples, you know exactly what to do. You keep one apple in the air at all times, you keep your mind focused, you get a good rhythm going, and you hope you can juggle long enough to impress any potential dating partners who might be watching. But what do you do when you try to *remember* how to juggle? The answer is that you probably seek help. One of the best ways to retrieve information from *inside* your head is to encounter information *outside* your head that is somehow connected to it. The information outside your head is called a **retrieval cue**, which is *external information that is associated with stored information and helps bring it to mind*. Retrieval cues can be incredibly effective.

In one experiment, undergraduates studied lists of words, such as *table, peach, bed, apple, chair, grape,* and *desk* (Tulving & Pearlstone, 1966). Later, the students took a test in which they were simply asked to write down all the words from the list that they could remember. The students remembered and wrote and remembered some more, and when they were absolutely sure that they had emptied their memory stores of every last word that was in them, they took another test. This time the experimenter asked them to remember the words on the list, but he provided them with retrieval cues, such as "furniture" or "fruit." The students who were sure that they had done all the remembering they possibly could were suddenly able to remember more words (Tulving & Pearlstone, 1966). These results suggest that information is sometimes *available* in memory even when it is momentarily *inaccessible* and that retrieval cues help us bring inaccessible information to mind. Of course, this is something you already knew. How many times have you said something like, "I *know* who starred in *Charlie and the Chocolate Factory,* but I just can't remember it"? only to have a friend give you a hint ("Wasn't he in *Pirates of the Caribbean*?"), which instantly brings the answer to mind ("Johnny Depp!").

Although hints are a form of retrieval cue, not all retrieval cues come in the form of hints. The **encoding specificity principle** states that *a retrieval cue can serve as an effective reminder when it helps re-create the specific way in which information was initially encoded* (Tulving & Thomson, 1973). In other words, the thoughts or feelings we had at the time we encoded information are associated with the information we encoded, and so those thoughts and feelings can also help us retrieve it. For example, you'd probably expect a fellow student who studied for an exam while drunk to perform poorly, and you would probably be right—but only if he made the mistake of taking the exam while sober! Studies suggest that if the student studied while drunk, he would probably perform poorly the next day, but he'd perform better if he'd had a six-pack instead of Cheerios for breakfast. Why should that be? Because a person's physiological or psychological state at the time of encoding is associated with the information being encoded. If the person's state at the time of retrieval matches the person's state at the time of encoding, the state itself serves as a retrieval cue—a bridge that connects the moment at which we experience something to the moment at which we remember it.

**State-dependent retrieval** is *the tendency for information to be better recalled when the person is in the same state during encoding and retrieval.* State-dependent retrieval has been documented with both alcohol and marijuana (Eich, 1980; Weissenborn, 2000). Similar effects occur with natural (as opposed to drug-induced) states. For example, retrieving information when you are in a sad or happy mood increases the likelihood that you will retrieve sad or happy episodes (Eich, 1995), which is part of the reason it is so hard to "look on the bright side" when you're feeling low. And by the way, you'd probably do *much* better on an exam if you were alert and sober when you studied and alert and sober when you took the test!

Almost any similarity between the context in which an item is encoded and the context in which it is retrieved can serve as a retrieval cue. For example, in one study divers learned some words on land and some other words underwater; they recalled the words best when they were tested in the same dry or wet environment in which they had initially learned them because the environment itself served as a retrieval cue (Godden & Baddely, 1975). Recovering alcoholics often experience a renewed urge to drink when visiting places in which they once drank because these places serve as retrieval cues. There may even be some wisdom to finding a seat in a classroom, sitting in it every day, and then sitting in it again when you take the test because the feel of the chair and the sights you see may help you remember the information you learned while you sat there. Retrieval cues need not be inner states and they need not be external environments—they can even be thoughts themselves, as when one thought calls to mind another, related thought (Anderson et al., 1976).

Consider just one more unusual consequence of the encoding specificity principle. You learned earlier that making semantic judgments about a word (e.g., "What does *orange* mean?") usually produces more durable memory for the word than does making rhyme judgments (e.g., "What rhymes with *orange*?"). So if you were asked to think of a word that rhymes with *brain* and your friend was asked to think about what *brain* means, we would expect your friend to remember the word better the next day if we simply asked you both, "Hey, what was that word you saw yesterday?" However, if instead of asking that question, we asked you both, "What was that word that rhymed with *train*?" we would expect you to remember it better than your friend did (Fisher & Craik, 1977). This is a fairly astounding finding. Semantic judgments almost always yield better memory than rhyme judgments. But in this case, the typical finding is turned upside down because the retrieval cue matched your encoding context better than it matched your friend's. The principle of **transfer-appropriate processing** states that *memory is likely to transfer from one situation to another when we process information in a way that is appropriate to the retrieval cues that will be available later* (Morris, Bransford, & Franks, 1977; Roediger, Weldon, & Challis, 1989) (**FIGURE 5.11**).

**Callahan**

*"I wonder if you'd mind giving me directions. I've never been sober in this part of town before."*

**High recall minus baseline**   **Low recall minus baseline**

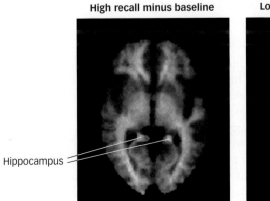
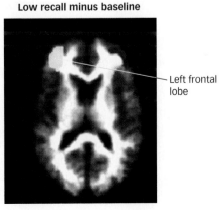

Hippocampus

Left frontal lobe

**Figure 5.11** **PET Scans of Successful and Unsuccessful Recall** When people successfully remembered words they saw earlier in an experiment, achieving high levels of recall on a test, the hippocampus showed increased activity. When people tried but failed to recall words they had seen earlier, achieving low levels of recall on a test, the left frontal lobe showed increased activity (Schacter et al., 1996a).

## Separating the Components of Retrieval

Finally, let's look at how the process of retrieval works. There is reason to believe that *trying* to recall an incident and *actually* recalling one are fundamentally different processes that occur in different parts of the brain (Moscovitch, 1994; Schacter, 1996). For example, regions within the right frontal lobe show heightened activity when people retrieve information that was presented to them earlier (Shallice et al., 1994; Squire et al., 1992; Tulving et al., 1994), and many psychologists believe that this activity reflects the mental effort that people put forth when they struggle to dredge up the past event (Lepage et al., 2000). However, successfully remembering a past experience tends to be accompanied by activity in the hippocampal region and also in parts of the brain that play a role in processing the sensory features of an experience (Eldridge et al., 2000; Nyberg et al., 1996; Schacter et al., 1996a). For instance, recall of previously heard sounds is accompanied by activity in the auditory cortex (the upper part of the temporal lobe), whereas recall of previously seen pictures is accompanied by activity in the visual cortex (in the occipital lobe) (Wheeler, Petersen, & Buckner, 2000). Although retrieval may seem like a single process, brain studies suggest that separately identifiable processes are at work.

---

**In summary,** whether we remember a past experience depends on whether retrieval cues are available to trigger recall. Retrieval cues are effective when they help reinstate how we encoded an experience. Moods and inner states can serve as retrieval cues. Retrieval can be separated into the effort we make while trying to remember what happened in the past and the successful recovery of stored information. Neuroimaging studies suggest that trying to remember activates the right frontal lobe, whereas successful recovery of stored information activates the hippocampus and regions in the brain related to sensory aspects of an experience. ■ ■

---

# Multiple Forms of Memory: How the Past Returns

If someone offered to give you a quick lesson in farming, you'd be suspicious. After all, how could farming be taught in a single lesson when it includes everything from raising sheep to raising barns? True, all these things *are* components of farming, but farming itself is much more than any one of them. The same is true of memory. We say that we cannot remember what happened to us last May 13, we will always remember what happened to Abraham Lincoln in Ford's Theatre on April 14, 1865, we ought to remember that China is bigger than Thailand, we hope to remember that you can't divide anything by zero, and we must remember to take out the trash. Sometimes we even *behave* as though we are remembering things while claiming to remember nothing at all. Although each of these is an example of memory, the diversity of the examples suggests that there must be many different kinds of memory (Eichenbaum & Cohen, 2001; Schacter & Tulving, 1994; Schacter, Wagner, & Buckner, 2000; Squire & Kandel, 1999). Indeed, there are; let's consider some of them.

## Implicit and Explicit Memory

Although Greg was forever stranded in the Summer of Love and unable to make new memories, some of the new things that happened to him seemed to leave a mark. For example, Greg did not recall learning that his father had died, but he did seem sad and withdrawn for years after hearing the news. Similarly, HM could not make new memories after his surgery, but if he played a game in which he had to track a moving target, his performance gradually improved with each round (Milner, 1962). Greg could not consciously remember hearing about his father's death, and HM could not consciously remember playing the tracking game, but both showed clear signs of having been permanently changed by experiences that they so rapidly forgot. Research suggests that this

**EXPLICIT MEMORY** The act of consciously or intentionally retrieving past experiences.

**IMPLICIT MEMORY** The influence of past experiences on later behavior and performance, even though people are not trying to recollect them and are not aware that they are remembering them.

**PROCEDURAL MEMORY** The gradual acquisition of skills as a result of practice, or "knowing how," to do things.

nebulous sauerkraut vagueness

is not unusual. For example, when patients with amnesia practice a task, they generally show improvements similar to those of healthy volunteers, despite the fact that they cannot remember ever having performed the task. For instance, to figure out the identities of the mirror-inverted words above, you have to mentally manipulate the spatial positions of the letters until you "see" the word. With practice, most people can read the inverted words faster and faster. But so can people who have amnesia—despite the fact that such patients generally cannot remember having ever seen the words (Cohen & Squire, 1980). Amnesic patients have even proved capable of learning how to program computers despite having no conscious recollection of their training (Glisky, Schacter, & Tulving, 1986)!

The fact that people can be changed by past experiences without having any awareness of those experiences suggests that there must be at least two different kinds of memory. **Explicit memory** occurs *when people consciously or intentionally retrieve past experiences*. Recalling last summer's vacation, incidents from a novel you just read, or facts you studied for a test all involve explicit memory. Indeed, anytime you start a sentence with, "I remember . . ." you are talking about an explicit memory. **Implicit memory** occurs when *past experiences influence later behavior and performance, even though people are not trying to recollect them and are not aware that they are remembering them* (Graf & Schacter, 1985; Schacter, 1987). Implicit memories are not consciously recalled, but their presence is "implied" by our actions. Greg's persistent sadness after his father's death, even though he had no conscious knowledge of the event, is an example of implicit memory. So is HM's improved performance on a tracking task that he didn't consciously remember doing (**FIGURE 5.12**).

All of this makes implicit memory sound mysterious, but really we all have implicit memories. For example, how do you balance on a two-wheeled bicycle? You might be tempted to say, "Gee, I don't know," but if you don't know, why can you do it so easily? Your knowledge of how to balance on a bicycle is a particular kind of implicit memory called **procedural memory**, which refers to *the gradual acquisition of skills as a result of practice, or "knowing how," to do things*. One of the hallmarks of procedural memory is that the things you remember (e.g., how to shift gears in a car, how to play a G chord on the guitar) are automatically translated into actions. All you have to do is will the action and it happens, but it happens because you have implicit memories of how to make it happen. Sometimes you can explain how it is done ("Put one finger on the third fret of the E string, one finger . . .") and sometimes you can't ("Get on the bike and . . . well, uh . . . just balance"). The fact that people who have amnesia can acquire new procedural memories suggests that the hippocampal structures

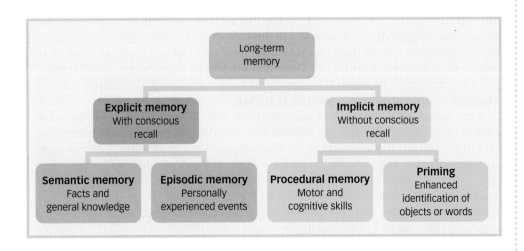

**Figure 5.12 Multiple Forms of Memory** Explicit and implicit memories are distinct from each other. Thus, a person with amnesia may lose explicit memory yet display implicit memory for material that she or he cannot consciously recall learning.

**PRIMING** An enhanced ability to think of a stimulus, such as a word or object, as a result of a recent exposure to the stimulus.

**SEMANTIC MEMORY** A network of associated facts and concepts that make up our general knowledge of the world.

**EPISODIC MEMORY** The collection of past personal experiences that occurred at a particular time and place.

that are usually damaged in these patients may be necessary for explicit memory, but they aren't needed for implicit procedural memory. In fact, it appears that brain regions outside the hippocampal area (including areas in the motor cortex) are involved in procedural memory. Chapter 6, on learning, discusses this evidence further, where you will also see that procedural memory is crucial for learning various kinds of motor, perceptual, and cognitive skills.

Not all implicit memories are "how to" memories. For example, in one study, participants were asked to memorize a list of words, and for some people, that list included the word *moon* (Nisbett & Wilson, 1977). Later, they were asked to name their favorite brands of several grocery items, including laundry detergent. The results showed that those participants who had earlier memorized the word *moon* were more likely to say that their favorite detergent was Tide, but none of them was aware that the memorization task had influenced their answer. This is an example of **priming**, which refers to *an enhanced ability to think of a stimulus, such as a word or object, as a result of a recent exposure to the stimulus* (Tulving & Schacter, 1990). Just as priming a pump makes water flow more easily, priming the memory system makes some information more accessible.

In one experiment, college students were asked to study a long list of words, including items such as *avocado, mystery, climate, octopus,* and *assassin* (Tulving, Schacter, & Stark, 1982). Later, explicit memory was tested by showing participants some of these words along with new ones they hadn't seen and asking them which words were on the list. To test for priming, participants received word fragments and were asked them to come up with a word that fit the fragment.

Try the test yourself: ch–––nk      o–t–p––      –og–y–––      –l–m–te.

You probably had difficulty coming up with the answers for the first and third fragments (*chipmunk, bogeyman*) but had little problem coming up with answers for the second and fourth (*octopus, climate*). Seeing *octopus* and *climate* on the original list primed your ability to generate them on the fragment completion test. In the experiment, people showed priming for studied words even when they failed to consciously remember that they had seen them earlier.

In a sense, the healthy participants in this study behaved like patients with amnesia. Many experiments have shown that amnesic patients can show substantial priming effects—often as large as healthy, nonamnesic people—even though they have no explicit memory for the items they studied. In one study, researchers showed patients with amnesia and healthy volunteers in the control group a list of words, including *table* and *motel,* and then gave them two different types of tests (Graf, Squire, & Mandler, 1984). One of these tested their explicit memory by providing them with the first three letters of a word (e.g., *tab___*) and asking them to remember a word from the list that began with those letters. On this test, amnesic patients remembered fewer words than the healthy volunteers.

The second test was identical to the first, except that people were given the first three letters of a word and simply asked to write down any word that came to mind. On this test, the people who had amnesia produced words from the study list just as often as the healthy volunteers did. As you can see, the two tests were the same, but in one case the participants were asked to produce words from the list (which requires explicit memory) and in the other case they were asked to produce any word at all (which requires implicit memory). These and other similar results suggest that priming, like procedural memory, does not require the hippocampal structures that are damaged in cases of amnesia (Schacter & Curran, 2000).

If the hippocampal region isn't required for procedural memory and priming, what parts of the brain are involved? Experiments have revealed that priming is associated with *reduced* activity in various regions of the cortex that are activated when people perform an unprimed task. For instance, when research participants are shown the word stem *mot___* or *tab___* and are asked to provide the first word that comes to mind, parts of the occipital lobe involved in visual processing and parts of the frontal lobe involved in word retrieval become active. But if people perform the same task after being primed by seeing *motel* and *table,* there's less activity in these same regions (Buckner et al., 1995; Schacter, Dobbins, & Schnyer, 2004; Wiggs & Martin, 1998). Something similar happens when

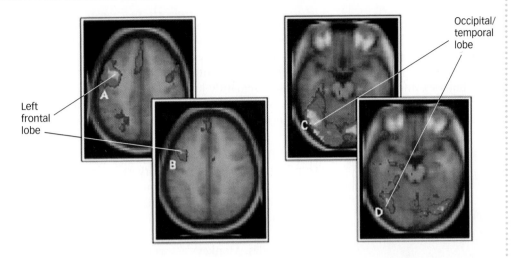

Left frontal lobe

Occipital/temporal lobe

**Figure 5.13 Primed and Unprimed Processing of Stimuli** Priming is associated with reduced levels of activation in the cortex on a number of different tasks. In each pair of fMRIs, the images on the upper left (A, C) show brain regions in the frontal lobe (A) and occipital/temporal lobe (C) that are active during an unprimed task (in this case, providing a word response to a visual word cue). The images on the lower right within each pair (B, D) show reduced activity in the same regions during the primed version of the same task.

D. L. Schacter & R. L. Buckner, 1998, Priming and the Brain, *Neuron, 20*, pp. 185–195.

people see pictures of everyday objects on two different occasions. On the second exposure to a picture, there's less activity in parts of the visual cortex that were activated by seeing the picture initially. Priming seems to make it easier for parts of the cortex that are involved in perceiving a word or object to identify the item after a recent exposure to it. This suggests that the brain "saves" a bit of processing time after priming (**FIGURE 5.13**).

## Semantic and Episodic Memory

Consider these two questions: (1) Why do we celebrate on July 4? and (2) what is the most spectacular celebration you've ever seen? Every American knows the answer to the first question (we celebrate the signing of the Declaration of Independence on July 4, 1776), but we all have our own answers to the second. For instance, *you* might remember the time your neighbor bought two shopping bags' worth of illegal fireworks from out of state and shot them off in his backyard, at which point his wife yelled at him for scaring the dog, the police came, and there was a seriously scorched spot on the lawn for the rest of that summer. However, it is unlikely that anyone else (other than the neighbor, the wife, the police, and the dog) has precisely that same memory. Although both of these questions required you to search your long-term memory and explicitly retrieve information that was stored there, one required you to revisit a particular time and place—or episode—from your personal past, and one required you to dredge up a fact that everyone knows and that is not part of your personal autobiography. These memories are called *episodic* and *semantic* memories, respectively (Tulving, 1972, 1983, 1998). **Semantic memory** is *a network of associated facts and concepts that make up our general knowledge of the world,* whereas **episodic memory** is *the collection of past personal experiences that occurred at a particular time and place.*

This contestant on the game show *Who Wants to Be a Millionaire?* is consulting her semantic memory in order to answer the question. The answer is B: Bulgaria.

### Episodic Memory in Humans

Episodic memory is special because it is the only form of memory that allows us to engage in "mental time travel," projecting ourselves into the past and revisiting events that have happened to us. This ability allows us to connect our pasts and our presents and construct a cohesive story of our lives. People who have amnesia can usually travel back in time and revisit episodes that occurred before they became amnesiac, but they are unable to revisit episodes that happened later. For example, Greg couldn't travel back to any time after 1969 because that's when he stopped being able to create new episodic memories. But can people with amnesia create new semantic memories?

Researchers have studied three young adults who suffered damage to the hippocampus during birth as a result of difficult deliveries that interrupted the oxygen supply to their brains (the hippocampus is especially sensitive to the lack of oxygen) (Vargha-Khadem et al., 1997). Their parents noticed that the children could not recall what happened during a typical day, had to be constantly reminded of appointments, and often became lost and disoriented. Beth (14 years old), Jon (19 years old), and Kate (22 years old) all showed clear evidence of episodic memory problems on laboratory tests. In view of their hippocampal damage, you might also expect that each of the three would perform poorly in school and might even be classified as learning disabled. Remarkably, however, all three learned to read, write, and spell; developed normal vocabularies; and acquired other kinds of semantic knowledge that allowed them to perform well at school. Based on this evidence, researchers have concluded that the hippocampus is not necessary for acquiring new *semantic* memories.

Clark's nutcracker shows a remarkable ability to remember thousands of seed hiding spots months after storing the seeds. Researchers are debating whether this type of memory indicates an ability for humanlike episodic memory.

### Do Animals Have Episodic Memory?

Thinking about episodic memory as mental time travel raises an intriguing question: Can monkeys, rats, birds, or other nonhuman animals revisit their pasts as people do? We know that animals *behave* as though they can retrieve information acquired during specific past episodes. Monkeys act as though they are recalling objects they've seen only once during experimental tests (Zola & Squire, 2000). Rats seem to remember places they've visited recently in a maze (Olton & Samuelson, 1976). And birds that store food (such as Clark's nutcracker) can store as many as 30,000 seeds in 5,000 locations during the fall and then retrieve them all the next spring (Kamil & Jones, 1997; Shettleworth, 1995). But do these smart pet tricks involve the same kind of mental time travel that we all do when we relive the July 4 picnic when Uncle Harry spilled barbecue sauce all over Aunt Norma? Or are the episodic memories of animals more similar to the kinds of memory available to people who have amnesia; for example, are they simply implicit procedural memories?

It's difficult to say. Explicit memory always has a subjective component: When information "comes to mind," it *feels* like something. Animals cannot tell us whether they are having this subjective experience, and we can never tell by watching them whether they are actually having that experience or just behaving as though they are. Some researchers believe that even birds possess abilities closely related to episodic memory. Food-storing scrub jays act as though they can recall what type of food they've stored (a worm or a peanut), where they stored it (on one side of a storage tray or another), and when they stored it (hours or days prior to a test) (Clayton & Dickinson, 1998). Other researchers remain skeptical that demonstrations of highly detailed memories in birds or other animals truly signal the presence of mental time travel (Tulving, 1998). Human episodic memory involves a conscious experience of the self at different points in time. Does a scrub jay project itself backward in time when the bird recalls where and when it stored a worm or a peanut? No one knows for sure. The only reason we are so confident that other *people* engage in mental time travel is that they tell us they do. Because animals can't talk, it seems likely that we will never have a definitive answer to this intriguing question.

**In summary,** long-term memory consists of several different forms. Explicit memory is the collection of our conscious retrieval of past experiences, whereas implicit memory refers to the unconscious influences of past experiences on later behavior and performance, such as procedural memory and priming. Procedural memory involves the acquisition of skills as a result of practice, and priming is a change in the ability to recognize or identify an object or a word as the result of past exposure to it. People who have amnesia are able to retain implicit memory, including procedural memory and priming, but they lack explicit memory. Episodic memory is the collection of personal experiences from a particular time and place, whereas semantic memory is a networked, general, impersonal knowledge of facts, associations, and concepts. Animals possess extensive memory abilities, but it is still a matter of debate as to whether they can engage in the "mental time travel" characteristic of human episodic memory. ■ ■

# Memory Failures: The Seven Sins of Memory

You probably haven't given much thought to breathing today, and the reason is that from the moment you woke up, you've been doing it effortlessly and well. But the moment breathing fails, you are reminded of just how important it is. Memory is like that. Every time we see, think, notice, imagine, or wonder, we are drawing on our ability to use information stored in our brains, but it isn't until this ability fails that we become acutely aware of just how much we should treasure it. Like a lot of human behavior, we can better understand how a process works correctly by examining what happens when it works incorrectly. We've seen in other contexts how an understanding of mindbugs—those foibles and errors of human thought and action—reveals the normal operation of various behaviors. It's useful to think of memory mindbugs as the "seven sins" of memory (Schacter, 1999, 2001b). These "sins" include *transience* (forgetting over time), *absentmindedness* (lapses in attention that result in forgetting), *blocking* (temporary inability to retrieve information), *memory misattribution* (confusing the source of a memory), *suggestibility* (incorporating misleading information into a memory), *bias* (the influence of present knowledge, beliefs, and feelings on recollections of the past), and *persistence* (recalling unwanted memories we would prefer to forget).

## Transience

The investigation and eventual impeachment of former president Bill Clinton held the nation spellbound in the late 1990s. Aside from political jockeying and tabloid revelations about Clinton's relationship with White House intern Monica Lewinsky, the investigation also produced a lot of discussion about Clinton's claims to have forgotten a variety of things. Based on his own intuitions about what a person might reasonably be expected to forget, the special prosecutor, Kenneth Starr, decided that Clinton's apparent memory lapses were self-serving conveniences designed to avoid embarrassing admissions.

Starr was especially interested in what Clinton said in January 1998, when he testified in a sexual harassment lawsuit brought against him by Paula Jones (Schacter, 2001b). In that deposition, Clinton discussed a meeting he held 3 weeks earlier with his good friend Vernon Jordan, who had on the same evening met with Lewinsky. She told Jordan that she had received a subpoena from the independent counsel's office to testify in their investigation. Jordan testified that he discussed these matters with Clinton, but the president claimed he did not recall exactly what had happened. But when he testified in the Jones case, about three weeks after that meeting, the president said, "I didn't remember all the details of all this. I didn't remember what—when Vernon talked to me about Monica Lewinsky, whether she talked to him on the telephone or had a meeting, I didn't remember all those details."

Was Clinton's claim to have forgotten a credible one, or was it just the feeble excuse of someone caught in a transparent lie? The culprit in this incident is **transience:** *forgetting what occurs with the passage of time*. Transience occurs during the storage phase of memory, after an experience has been encoded and before it is retrieved. You've already seen the workings of transience—rapid forgetting—in sensory storage and short-term storage. Transience also occurs in long-term storage, as illustrated dramatically by amnesic patients such as Greg and HM. But transience affects all our memories to some extent. To understand transience, we need to address some key questions: How quickly do our memories fade over time? What kinds of information are we most likely to forget as time passes?

The psychological study of transience dates to the late 1870s, when a young German philosopher named Hermann Ebbinghaus measured his own memory for lists of nonsense syllables at different delays after studying them (Ebbinghaus, 1885/1964). The first researcher to study memory, Ebbinghaus charted his recall of nonsense syllables over time, creating the forgetting curve shown in **FIGURE 5.14**. on the next page. Ebbinghaus noted a rapid drop-off in retention during the first few tests, followed by a slower rate of forgetting on later tests—a general pattern confirmed by many subsequent memory

**TRANSIENCE** Forgetting what occurs with the passage of time.

President Clinton hugs Monica Lewinsky as he greets the crowd at a public appearance. Clinton's claims to have forgotten several incidents related to their affair may be an example of transience.

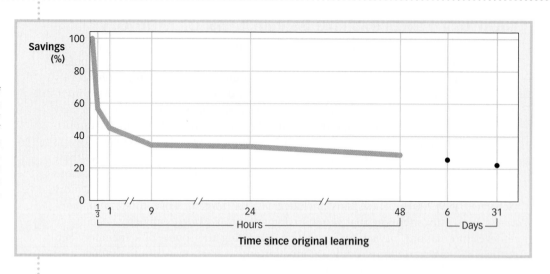

**Figure 5.14 The Curve of Forgetting** Hermann Ebbinghaus measured his retention at various delay intervals after he studied lists of nonsense syllables. Retention was measured in percent savings, that is, the percentage of time needed to relearn the list compared to the time needed to learn it initially.

Hermann Ebbinghaus (1850–1909), a German philosopher and psychologist, conducted some of the first scientific studies of memory. Ebbinghaus trained himself to memorize lists of nonsense syllables, then kept track of how long he could retain the information. Ebbinghaus's research revealed a great deal about the nature of remembering and forgetting.

researchers (Wixted & Ebbesen, 1991). This consistent finding shows that memories don't fade at a constant rate as time passes; most forgetting happens soon after an event occurs, with increasingly less forgetting as more time passes.

Memory doesn't just erode with the passage of time: The quality of our memories also changes. At early time points on the forgetting curve—minutes, hours, and days—memory preserves a relatively detailed record, allowing us to reproduce the past with reasonable if not perfect accuracy. But with the passing of time, we increasingly rely on our general memories for what usually happens and attempt to reconstruct the details by inference and even sheer guesswork. Transience involves a gradual switch from specific to more general memories (Brewer, 1996; Eldridge, Barnard, & Bekerian, 1994; Thompson et al., 1996). These findings illuminate President Clinton's memory lapse. The government attorney might have been appropriately skeptical had Clinton claimed to have entirely forgotten an important meeting with Vernon Jordan three weeks after it happened. But Clinton's confusion about the details of that meeting—whether Lewinsky spoke to Jordan on the telephone or face-to-face—is exactly the sort of confusion that we would expect based on both naturalistic and laboratory studies.

There's an important research basis for these conclusions as well. After Ebbinghaus developed his nonsense syllable task, many researchers thought that was a dandy way of studying memory. By stripping the to-be-remembered information of all meaning, the *process* of remembering and forgetting could be examined, uncontaminated by any meaning associated with the information itself. One researcher who disagreed with that approach did some pioneering work that addresses transience. Sir Frederick Bartlett (1932) asked British research participants to read a brief Native American folktale that had odd imagery and unfamiliar plots in it and then recount it as best they could after 15 minutes and sometimes after longer periods. The readers made interesting but understandable errors, often eliminating details that didn't make sense to them or adding elements to make the story more coherent. As the specifics of the story slipped away, the general meaning of the events stayed in memory but usually with elaborations and embellishments that were consistent with the readers' worldview. Because the story was unfamiliar to the readers, they raided their stores of general information and patched together a reasonable recollection of what *probably* happened.

Why does transience happen? Do details of experience simply disappear or decay as time passes? The simple answer is yes. In a study of memory for Spanish vocabulary acquired by English speakers during high school or college courses, participants were tested for retention of Spanish at different times (ranging from 1 year to 50 years) after the students stopped taking Spanish courses (Bahrick, 1984, 2000). There was a rapid drop-off in memory for the Spanish vocabulary during the first three years after the students' last class, followed by tiny losses in later years. But research suggests that the decay caused by the mere passage of time is not nearly as important as *what* happens as time passes (**FIGURE 5.15**). As time goes by, new experiences occur and new memories are created, and these new memories can interfere with our retrieval of old ones.

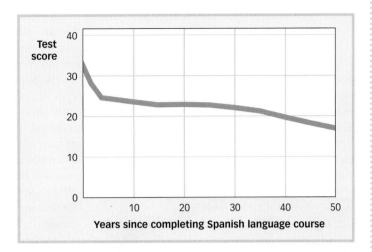

**Figure 5.15** **The Decline of Spanish Language Skills** Language skills (measured here as scores on a language exam) decay rapidly for the first few years after instruction ends, followed by a much slower decline over the next few decades. Like many other memories, the knowledge of Spanish is transient unless it is rehearsed or remains actively used (Bahrick, 1984, 2000).

**Retroactive interference** occurs when *later learning impairs memory for information acquired earlier* (Postman & Underwood, 1973). If you carry out the same activities at work each day, by the time Friday rolls around, it may be difficult to remember what you did on Monday because later activities blend in with earlier ones. **Proactive interference**, in contrast, refers to situations in which *earlier learning impairs memory for information acquired later.* If you use the same parking lot each day at work or school, you've probably gone out to find your car and then stood there confused by the memories of having parked it on previous days.

**RETROACTIVE INTERFERENCE** Situations in which later learning impairs memory for information acquired earlier.

**PROACTIVE INTERFERENCE** Situations in which earlier learning impairs memory for information acquired later.

**ABSENTMINDEDNESS** A lapse in attention that results in memory failure.

## Absentmindedness

The great cellist Yo-Yo Ma put his treasured $2.5 million instrument in the trunk of a taxicab in Manhattan and then rode to his destination. After a 10-minute trip, he paid the driver and left the cab, forgetting his cello. Minutes later, Ma realized what he had done and called the police. Fortunately, they tracked down the taxi and recovered the instrument within hours (Finkelstein, 1999). But how had the celebrated cellist forgotten about something so important that had occurred only 10 minutes earlier? Transience is not a likely culprit. If someone had reminded Mr. Ma about his instrument, he surely would have recalled where he had put it. This information had not disappeared from his memory (which is why he was able to tell the police where the cello was). Instead, Yo-Yo Ma was a victim of **absentmindedness**, which is *a lapse in attention that results in memory failure.*

What makes people absentminded? Attention plays a vital role in encoding information into long-term memory. In studies of "divided attention," research participants are given materials to remember, such as a list of words, a story, or a series of pictures. At the same time, they are required to perform an additional task that draws their attention away from the material. For example, in one study, participants listened to lists of 15 words for a later memory test (Craik et al., 1996). They were allowed to pay full attention to some of the lists, but while they heard other lists, they simultaneously viewed a visual display containing four boxes and pressed different keys to indicate where an asterisk was appearing and disappearing. On a later test, participants recalled far fewer words from the list they had heard while their attention was divided.

ROBERT E. KLEIN/AP PHOTO

Yo-Yo Ma with his $2.5 million cello. The famous cellist lost it when he absentmindedly forgot that he'd placed the instrument in a taxi's trunk minutes earlier.

Many everyday instances of absentmindedness probably result from a kind of "divided attention" that occurs frequently in our daily lives. Mentally consumed with planning for a psychology test the next day, you might place your keys in an unusual spot as you are reading over your notes. Because your attention was focused on the test and not your keys, you do not encode where you put the keys. So, you later have no memory of the incident and must frantically search before finding the keys. Attentional lapses that lead to absentminded forgetting are particularly common during routine activities, such as driving or typing, that do not require elaborative encoding. When you first learn to drive a car, you pay careful attention to every step of the activity. As your skill increases with practice, you rely more and more on procedural memory, and less and less attention is required to perform the same tasks (Anderson & Fincham, 1994; Logan,

1988). Most experienced drivers, for example, are familiar with the unsettling experience of cruising along at 65 miles per hour on a six-lane interstate and suddenly realizing that they have no recollection of the road for the past 5 miles. Experienced drivers rely on the well-learned skills that allow them to drive safely even when on "automatic." Absorbed with other concerns, they remember nothing of it, until they face a prosecutor.

Talking on a cell phone while driving is a common occurrence of divided attention in everyday life. This can be dangerous, and an increasing number of states have banned the practice.

What happens in the brain when attention is divided? In one study, volunteers tried to learn a list of word pairs while researchers scanned their brains with positron emission tomography (PET) (Shallice et al., 1994). Some people simultaneously performed a task that took little attention (they moved a bar the same way over and over), whereas other people simultaneously performed a task that took a great deal of attention (they moved a bar over and over but in a novel, unpredictable way each time). The researchers observed less activity in the participants' lower left frontal lobe when their attention was divided. As you saw earlier, greater activity in the lower left frontal region during encoding is associated with better memory. Dividing attention, then, prevents the lower left frontal lobe from playing its normal role in elaborative encoding, and the result is absentminded forgetting.

Neuroimaging evidence also links the lower left frontal lobe with automatic behavior. Researchers performed PET scans while they showed volunteers a series of common nouns and asked them to generate related verbs (Raichle et al., 1994). For example, when shown the noun *dog*, participants might generate the verb *bark* or *walk*. When the volunteers first performed this task, it was associated with extensive activity in the lower left frontal lobe (and many other parts of the brain). This activity probably reflected a kind of elaborative encoding related to thinking about properties of dogs and the kinds of actions they perform. Remembering dog facts requires a bit of mental work. But as the volunteers practiced the task repeatedly with the same nouns and generated the verbs more quickly and automatically, activity in the lower left frontal lobe gradually decreased. This suggests that automatic behaviors, which are the cause of many absentminded errors, are associated with low levels of left prefrontal activity.

Many errors of absentmindedness involve forgetting to carry out actions that we planned to do in the future. You may think of memory as a link to the past, but in everyday life, you rely on memory to deal with the future as much as the past. On any given day, you need to remember the times and places that your classes meet, you need to remember with whom and where you are having lunch, you need to remember which grocery items to pick up for dinner, and you need

*"It says, 'Please disregard this reminder if your check is in the mail.'"*

to remember which page of this book you were on when you fell asleep. Forgetting these things would leave you uneducated, friendless, hungry, and with an unsettling desire to start reading this book from the beginning. In other words, you have to remember to remember, and this is called **prospective memory**, or *remembering to do things in the future* (Einstein & McDaniel, 1990).

Failures of prospective memory are a major source of absentmindedness. Avoiding these mindbugs often requires having a cue available at the moment you need to remember to carry out an action. For example, air traffic controllers must sometimes postpone an action but remember to carry it out later, such as when they cannot immediately grant a pilot's request to change altitude. In a simulated air traffic control experiment, researchers provided controllers with electronic signals to remind them to carry out a deferred request 1 minute later. The reminders were made available either during the 1-minute waiting period, at the time the controller needed to act on the deferred request, or both. Compared with a condition in which no reminder was provided, controllers' memory for the deferred action improved only when the reminder was available at the time needed for retrieval. Providing the reminder during the waiting period did not help (Vortac, Edwards, and Manning, 1995). An early reminder, then, is no reminder at all.

## Blocking

Look at the definitions in **TABLE 5.1** and try to think of the correct word for each one. Chances are that you will recall some of the words and not others. Some of the unrecalled words will cause you to draw a complete blank, but others will feel as though they are "on the tip of your tongue." For example, you may remember the first letter or two

Many people rely on memory aids such as calendars—and, more recently, personal digital assistants (PDAs)—to help them remember to perform a particular activity in the future.

ILENE MACDONALD/ALAMY

### ONLY HUMAN

**MONEY TO BURN** Chef Albert Grabham of the New House Hotel in Wales hid the restaurant's New Year's Eve earnings in the oven. He failed to remember that when he lit the same oven to prepare New Year's Day lunch.

| Table 5.1 | Inducing a Tip-of-the-Tongue Experience |
|---|---|

**Instructions**

Below are the dictionary definitions of 10 uncommon words. Please look at each definition and try to think of the word it defines. If you can't think of the word but it seems like it's on the "tip of your tongue," try this: Try to guess the first letter of the word, or try to think of one or two words that sound similar to the one you're trying to find. The answers are given below. No peeking!

**Definitions**

1. A blood feud in which members of the family of a murdered person try to kill the murderer or members of his family.

2. A protecting charm to ward off spirits.

3. A dark, hard, glassy volcanic rock.

4. A person who makes maps.

5. A building used for public worship by Moslems.

6. An Egyptian ornament in the shape of a beetle.

7. The staff of Hermes, symbol of a physician or of the medical corps.

8. A sword with a short curved blade, used by the Turks and Arabs.

9. House of rest for travelers or for the terminally ill, often kept by a religious order.

10. Something out of keeping with the times in which it exists.

**Answers:** 1. Vendetta, 2. Amulet, 3. Obsidian, 4. Cartographer, 5. Mosque, 6. Scarab, 7. Caduceus, 8. Scimitar, 9. Hospice, 10. Anachronism

**PROSPECTIVE MEMORY**
Remembering to do things in the future.

of the word and feel certain that it is rolling around in your head *somewhere* but that you just can't retrieve it at the moment. This problem is called **blocking**, which is *a failure to retrieve information that is available in memory even though you are trying to produce it.* The sought-after information has been encoded and stored, and a cue is available that would ordinarily trigger recall of it. The information has not faded from memory, and you aren't forgetting to retrieve it. Rather, you are experiencing a full-blown retrieval failure, which makes this memory mindbug especially frustrating. It seems absolutely clear that you should be able to produce the information you seek, but the fact of the matter is that you can't. How can you know you know something but not know what it is?

The most common type of blocking is known as the **tip-of-the-tongue experience**, which is *the temporary inability to retrieve information that is stored in memory, accompanied by the feeling that you are on the verge of recovering the information.* The tip-of-the-tongue state has been described as "a mild torment, something like [being] on the brink of a sneeze" (Brown & McNeil, 1966, p. 326). Researchers have found that when people are in tip-of-the-tongue states, they often know something about the item they can't recall, such as the meaning of a word. For example, knowing the number of syllables in a blocked word is very common. People frequently know the first letter of the blocked word, less frequently know the final letter, and even less often know the middle letters. During tip-of-the-tongue states, people also frequently come up with words that are related in sound or meaning to the sought-after item. If you blocked on any of the items in Table 5.1, you might have thought of a word that was similar to the one you were seeking even though you were sure that it was not the blocked word itself.

When experimenters induced tip-of-the-tongue states by playing participants theme songs from 1950s and 1960s television shows and asking for the names of the shows, people who were blocked on *The Munsters* often came up with the similarly themed *The Addams Family*. Likewise, some of those who blocked on *Leave It to Beaver* thought of *Dennis the Menace* (Riefer, Kevari, & Kramer, 1995) (**FIGURE 5.16**). If these titles mean anything at all to you, then you are either middle-aged or watching too much *Nick-at-Nite*.

Blocking and tip-of-the-tongue states occur especially often for the names of people and places (Cohen, 1990; Valentine, Brennen, & Brédart, 1996). Why? Because their links to related concepts and knowledge are weaker than for common names. That somebody's last name is Baker doesn't tell us much about the person, but saying that he *is* a baker does. To illustrate this point, researchers showed people pictures of cartoon and comic strip characters, some with descriptive names that highlight key features of the character (e.g., Grumpy, Snow White, Scrooge) and others with arbitrary names (e.g., Aladdin, Mary Poppins, Pinocchio) (Brédart and Valentine, 1998). Even though the two types of names were equally familiar to participants in the experiment, they blocked less often on the descriptive names than on the arbitrary names.

**Figure 5.16 Blocking** Suppose you were asked to name a classic television comedy from hearing the show's theme music. The tip-of-the-tongue experience might cause you to block the Munsters, pictured on the left, for their close counterparts the Addams Family, on the right.

CBS/PHOTOFEST

ABC-TV/THE KOBAL COLLECTION

Although it's frustrating when it occurs, blocking is a relatively infrequent event for most of us. However, it occurs more often as we grow older, and it is a very common complaint among people in their sixties and seventies (Burke et al., 1991). Even more striking, some brain-damaged patients live in a nearly perpetual tip-of-the-tongue state. One patient could recall the names of only 2 of 40 famous people when she saw their photographs, compared to 25 out of 40 for healthy volunteers in the control group (Semenza & Zettin, 1989). Yet she could still recall correctly the occupations of 32 of these people—the same number as healthy people could recall. This case and similar ones have given researchers important clues about what parts of the brain are involved in retrieving proper names. Name blocking usually results from damage to parts of the left temporal lobe on the surface of the cortex, most often as a result of a stroke. In fact, studies that show strong activation of regions within the temporal lobe when people recall proper names support this idea (Damasio et al., 1996; Tempini et al., 1998).

## Memory Misattribution

Shortly after the devastating 1995 bombing of the federal building in Oklahoma City, police set about searching for two suspects they called John Doe 1 and John Doe 2. John Doe 1 turned out to be Timothy McVeigh, who was quickly apprehended and later convicted of the crime and sentenced to death. The FBI believed that John Doe 2 had accompanied McVeigh when he rented a van from Elliott's Body Shop in Junction City, Kansas, 2 days before the bombing, but the FBI never found John Doe 2. They later learned that John Doe 2 was a product of the memory of Tom Kessinger, a mechanic at Elliott's Body Shop who was present when McVeigh rented the van. He recalled seeing two men that day and described them in great detail. Kessinger's description of John Doe 2, however, is a near perfect fit to a man he encountered at Elliott's Body Shop a day later, when Army Sergeant Michael Hertig and his friend Private Todd Bunting also rented a van in Kessinger's presence. Hertig, like McVeigh, was tall and fair. Bunting was shorter and stockier, was dark haired, wore a blue-and-white cap, and had a tattoo beneath his left sleeve—a match to the description of John Doe 2. Tom Kessinger had confused his recollections of men he had seen on separate days in the same place. He was a victim of **memory misattribution:** *assigning a recollection or an idea to the wrong source* (**FIGURE 5.17**).

Memory misattribution errors are some of the primary causes of eyewitness misidentifications. The memory researcher Donald Thomson was accused of rape based on the victim's detailed recollection of his face, but he was eventually cleared when it turned out he had an airtight alibi. At the time of the rape, Thompson was giving a live television interview on the subject of distorted memories! The victim had been watching the show just before she was assaulted and misattributed her memory of Thomson's face to the rapist (Schacter, 1996; Thomson, 1988).

**BLOCKING** A failure to retrieve information that is available in memory even though you are trying to produce it.

**TIP-OF-THE-TONGUE EXPERIENCE** The temporary inability to retrieve information that is stored in memory, accompanied by the feeling that you are on the verge of recovering the information.

**MEMORY MISATTRIBUTION** Assigning a recollection or an idea to the wrong source.

DAVID GLASS/AP PHOTO

FBI/THE OKLAHOMAN/AP PHOTO

**Figure 5.17 Memory Misattribution** In 1995, the Murrah Federal Building in Oklahoma City was bombed in an act of terrorism. The police sketch shows "John Doe 2," who was originally thought to have been culprit Timothy McVeigh's partner in the bombing. It was later determined that the witness had confused his memories of different men whom he had encountered at Elliott's Body Shop on different days.

**Doonesbury**

**SOURCE MEMORY** Recall of when, where, and how information was acquired.

**FALSE RECOGNITION** A feeling of familiarity about something that hasn't been encountered before.

Part of memory is knowing where our memories came from. This is known as **source memory:** *recall of when, where, and how information was acquired* (Johnson, Hashtroudi, & Lindsay, 1993; Schacter, Harbluk, & McLachlan, 1984). People sometimes correctly recall a fact they learned earlier or accurately recognize a person or object they have seen before but misattribute the source of this knowledge. Experiments have shown, for instance, that people can remember perfectly well that they saw a previously presented face yet misremember the time or place that they saw it, as happened to Tom Kessinger and the rape victim in the Donald Thomson incident (Davies, 1988). Such misattribution could be the cause of déjà vu experiences, where you suddenly feel that you have been in a situation before even though you can't recall any details. A present situation that is similar to a past experience may trigger a general sense of familiarity that is mistakenly attributed to having been in the exact situation previously (Reed, 1988).

Patients with damage to the frontal lobes are especially prone to memory misattribution errors (Schacter et al., 1984; Shimamura & Squire, 1987). This is probably because the frontal lobes play a significant role in effortful retrieval processes, which are required to dredge up the correct source of a memory. These patients sometimes produce bizarre misattributions. In 1991, a British photographer in his mid-40s known

Patient MR probably would have felt that the unfamiliar man on the left is as famous as professional basketball player Shaquille O'Neal (Ward et al., 1999).

as MR was overcome with feelings of familiarity about people he didn't know. He kept asking his wife whether each new passing stranger was "somebody"—a screen actor, television newsperson, or local celebrity. MR's feelings were so intense that he often could not resist approaching strangers and asking whether they were indeed famous celebrities. When given formal tests, MR recognized the faces of actual celebrities as accurately as did healthy volunteers in the control group. But MR also "recognized" more than 75% of unfamiliar faces, whereas healthy controls hardly ever did. Neurological exams revealed that MR suffered from multiple sclerosis, which had caused damage to his frontal lobes (Ward et al., 1999).

Psychologists call the type of memory misattribution made by MR **false recognition**, which is *a feeling of familiarity about something that hasn't been encountered before.* We are all vulnerable to false recognition.

Take the following test and there is a good chance that you will experience false recognition for yourself. First study the two lists of words presented in **TABLE 5.2** by reading each word for about 1 second. When you are done, return to the paragraph you were reading for more instructions, but don't look back at the table!

Now take a recognition test by indicating which of these words—*taste, bread, needle, king, sweet, thread*—appeared on the lists you just studied. If you think that *taste* and *thread* were on the lists you studied, you're right. And if you think that *bread* and *king* weren't on those lists, you're also right. But if you think that *needle* or *sweet* appeared on the lists, you're dead wrong.

Most people make exactly the same mistake, claiming with confidence that they saw *needle* and *sweet* on the list. Experiments have shown that undergraduates claim to recognize *needle* and *sweet* about as often (84%) as they claim to recognize words that really were on the list (86%). (Undergraduates claimed to recognize unrelated words such as *bread* or *king* only 20% of the time.) This type of false recognition occurs because all the words in the lists are associated with *needle* or *sweet*. Seeing each word in the study list activates related words. Because *needle* and *sweet* are related to all of the associates, they become more activated than other words—so highly activated that only minutes later, people swear that they actually studied the words. But they are misattributing a powerful feeling of familiarity to having seen (or heard) the word (Deese, 1959; Roediger & McDermott, 1995, 2000).

Brain scanning studies using PET and fMRI have shown one reason why people are so easily fooled into "remembering" words such as *needle* and *sweet:* Many of the same brain regions are active during false recognition and true recognition, including the hippocampus (Cabeza et al., 2001; Schacter et al., 1996b; Slotnick & Schacter, 2004). However, there are some differences in brain activity. For example, a PET scanning experiment revealed that a part of the auditory cortex (on the surface of the temporal lobe) showed greater activity for words that had actually been heard earlier in the experiment than for associated words such as *needle* or *sweet,* which had not been heard previously (Schacter et al., 1996b). A later fMRI study showed that true recognition of previously studied visual shapes produced more activity in parts of the visual cortex than false recognition of new shapes that looked similar to those previously studied (Slotnick & Schacter, 2004) (**FIGURE 5.18**).

It is possible, however, to reduce or avoid false recognition by presenting distinctive information, such as a picture of *thread,* and encouraging participants to require specific recollections of seeing the picture before they say "yes" on a recognition test (Schacter, Israel, & Racine, 1999). Unfortunately, we do not always demand specific recollections before we say that we encountered a word in an

| Table 5.2 | False Recognition |
|-----------|-------------------|
| Sour | Thread |
| Candy | Pin |
| Sugar | Eye |
| Bitter | Sewing |
| Good | Sharp |
| Taste | Point |
| Tooth | Prick |
| Nice | Thimble |
| Honey | Haystack |
| Soda | Pain |
| Chocolate | Hurt |
| Heart | Injection |
| Cake | Syringe |
| Tart | Cloth |
| Pie | Knitting |

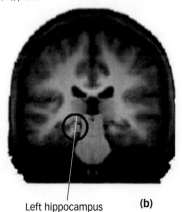

**Figure 5.18 Hippocampal Activity during True and False Recognition** Many brain regions show similar activation during true and false recognition, including the hippocampus. The figure shows results from an fMRI study of true and false recognition of visual shapes (Slotnick & Schacter, 2004). (a) A plot showing the activity level in the strength of the fMRI signal from the hippocampus over time. This shows that after a few seconds, there is comparable activation for true recognition of previously studied shapes (red line) and false recognition of similar shapes that were not presented (yellow line). Both true and false recognition show increased hippocampal activity compared with correctly classifying unrelated shapes as new (purple line). (b) A region of the left hippocampus.

(b) Slotnick & Schacter, *Nature Neuroscience*, 2004, 7(61), p. 669.

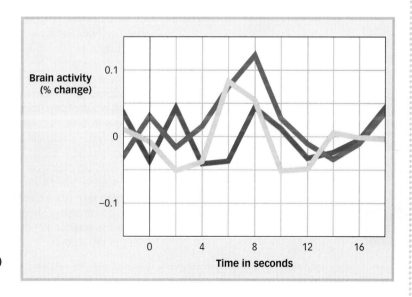

(a)

Left hippocampus  (b)

**SUGGESTIBILITY** The tendency to incorporate misleading information from external sources into personal recollections.

experiment or—more importantly—make a positive identification of a suspect. When people experience a strong sense of familiarity about a person, object, or event but lack specific recollections, a potentially dangerous recipe for memory misattribution is in place. Understanding this point may be a key to reducing the dangerous consequences of misattribution in eyewitness testimony (see the Real World box).

---

## { THE REAL WORLD } Deadly Misattributions

ON JULY 25, 1984, A 9-YEAR-OLD GIRL WAS found dead in the woods near Baltimore after being brutally beaten and sexually assaulted. A witness identified 23-year-old Kirk Bloodsworth as the killer, based on a sketch police generated from five other witness accounts. Although Bloodsworth passionately maintained his innocence, a jury convicted him of first-degree murder and the judge sentenced him to death. After Bloodsworth spent 2 years on death row, the sentence was reduced to life in prison on an appeal. In 1993, DNA testing revealed that Bloodsworth was not the source of incriminating semen stains in the victim's underwear. He was released from prison after serving 9 years, later received a full pardon, and returned to his quiet life as a crab fisherman (Chebium, 2000; Connors, Lundregan, Miller, & McEwen, 1997; Wells et al., 1998). In addition to losing nearly a decade of his young adulthood, Bloodsworth's mother did not live to see him freed: She died of a heart attack several months before his release.

Bloodsworth is not alone. The first 40 cases in which DNA evidence led to the release of wrongfully imprisoned individuals revealed that 36 of the convictions—

90%—were based partly or entirely on mistaken eyewitness identification (Wells et al., 1998). Fifty separate eyewitnesses were involved in these cases; they were all confident in their memories but seriously mistaken. These statistics are especially troubling because eyewitness testimony is frequently relied on in the courtroom: Each year more than 75,000 criminal trials are decided on the basis of eyewitness testimony (Ross et al., 1994, p. 918). Why do memory misattribution errors occur, and what can be done to avoid them?

Common lineup identification practices may often promote misattribution because people are encouraged to rely on general familiarity (Wells et al., 1998, 2000). In standard lineup procedures, witnesses are shown several suspects; after seeing all of them, they attempt to identify the culprit. Under these conditions, witnesses tend to rely on "relative judgments": They choose the person who, relative to the others in the lineup, looks most like the suspect. The problem is that even when the suspect is *not in* the lineup, witnesses still tend to choose the person who looks most like the suspect. Witnesses rely on general similarities between a face in a lineup and the

actual culprit, even when they lack specific recollections of the culprit. There are ways to minimize reliance on relative judgments: Ask witnesses to make a "thumbs-up or thumbs-down" decision about each suspect immediately after seeing each face instead of waiting until all suspects' faces have been displayed (Wells et al., 1998, 2000). This procedure encourages people to examine their memories more carefully and evaluate whether the pictured suspect matches the details of their recollections.

One encouraging development is that law enforcement officials are listening to what psychologists have to say about the construction of lineups and other identification procedures that could promote inaccurate identification. In early 1998, then attorney general Janet Reno formed a working group of psychologists, police, and attorneys to develop guidelines for collecting eyewitness evidence. This group eventually published a set of guidelines based on rigorous psychological studies that provide law enforcement officials with specific steps to take when questioning witnesses or constructing lineups in order to reduce the likelihood of eyewitness errors (Wells et al., 2000).

**Kirk Bloodsworth spent 9 years behind bars for a crime he didn't commit. He was released after DNA evidence led to the reversal of his conviction based on mistaken eyewitness testimony. Here he holds up the book that tells his story, by author and attorney Tim Junkin.**

## Suggestibility

On October 4, 1992, an El Al cargo plane crashed into an apartment building in a southern suburb of Amsterdam, killing 39 residents and all four members of the airline crew. The disaster dominated news in the Netherlands for days as people viewed footage of the crash scene and read about the catastrophe. Ten months later, Dutch psychologists asked a simple question of university students: "Did you see the television film of the moment the plane hit the apartment building?" Fifty-five percent answered "yes." In a follow-up study, 66% responded affirmatively (Crombag et al., 1996). The students also recalled details concerning the speed and angle of the plane when it hit the building and what happened to the body of the plane right after the collision. All of this might seem perfectly normal except for one key fact: There was no television film of the moment when the plane actually crashed. The researchers had asked a suggestive question that implied that television film of the crash had been shown. Respondents may have viewed television film of the post-crash scene, and they may have read, imagined, or talked about what might have happened when the plane hit the building, but they most definitely did not see it. The suggestive question led participants to misattribute information from these or other sources to a film that did not exist. **Suggestibility** is the *tendency to incorporate misleading information from external sources into personal recollections.* Suggestibility is closely related to memory misattribution in the sense that converting suggestions into inaccurate memories must involve misattribution. Unlike suggestibility, however, memory misattribution often occurs in the absence of specific suggestions.

Research evidence of suggestibility abounds. For example, in one study, Elizabeth Loftus and her colleagues showed participants a videotape of an automobile accident involving a white sports car (Loftus, 1975; Loftus et al., 1978). Some participants were then asked how fast the car was going when it passed the barn. Nearly 20% of these individuals later recalled seeing a barn in the videotape—even though there was no barn (participants who weren't asked about a barn almost never recalled seeing one). In later experiments, Loftus showed that people who received a misleading suggestion that they had earlier seen a car stop at a yield sign (they had actually seen the car at a stop sign) often claimed later to remember seeing a yield sign. Misleading suggestions do not eliminate the original memory (Berkerian & Bowers, 1983; McCloskey & Zaragoza, 1985). Instead, they cause participants to make source memory errors: They have difficulty recollecting whether they actually saw a yield sign or only learned about it later.

If misleading details can be implanted in people's memories, is it also possible to suggest entire episodes that never occurred? Could you be convinced, for example, that you had once been lost in a shopping mall as a child or spilled a bowl of punch at a wedding—even though these events never actually happened? The answer seems to be "yes" (Loftus, 1993, 2003). In one study, the research participant, a teenager named Chris, was asked by his older brother, Jim, to try to remember the time Chris had been lost in a shopping mall at age 5. He initially recalled nothing, but after several days, Chris produced a detailed recollection of the event. He recalled that he "felt so scared I would never see my family again" and remembered that a kindly old man wearing a flannel shirt found him crying (Loftus, 1993, p. 532). But according to Jim and other family members, Chris was never lost in a shopping mall. Of 24 participants in a larger study on implanted memories, approximately 25% falsely remembered being lost as a child in a shopping mall or in a similar public place (Loftus & Pickrell, 1995).

In 1992, an El Al cargo plane crashed into an apartment building in a suburb of Amsterdam. When Dutch psychologists asked students if they'd seen the television film of the plane crashing, most said they had. In fact, no such footage exists (Crombag, Wagenaar, & Koppen, 1996).

In a classic experiment by Elizabeth Loftus, people were shown a videotape of a car at a stop sign. Those who later received a misleading suggestion that the car had stopped at a yield sign often claimed they had seen the car at a yield sign (Loftus, Miller, & Burns, 1978).

Other researchers have also successfully implanted false memories of childhood experiences in a significant minority of participants (Hyman & Billings, 1998; Hyman & Pentland, 1996). In one study, college students were asked about several childhood events that, according to their parents, actually happened. But they were also asked about an event that never happened. For instance, the students were asked if they remembered a wedding reception they attended when they were 5, running around with some other kids and bumping into a table and spilling the punch bowl on the parents of the bride. Students remembered nearly all of the true events and initially reported no memory for the false events. However, with repeated probing, approximately 20% to 40% of the participants in different experimental conditions eventually came to describe some memory of the false event.

People develop false memories in response to suggestions for some of the same reasons memory misattribution occurs. We do not store all the details of our experiences in memory, making us vulnerable to accepting suggestions about what might have happened or should have happened. In addition, visual imagery plays an important role in constructing false memories (Goff & Roediger, 1998). Asking people to imagine an event like spilling punch all over the bride's parents at a wedding increases the likelihood that they will develop a false memory of it (Hyman & Pentland, 1996).

Imagery also had a dramatic effect on false memories in a study that examined people's earliest recollections. What is the first thing you can recall from childhood? For most of us, first memories date from 3 to 5 years of age. People generally cannot remember incidents that occurred before they were 2 years old, probably because the brain regions necessary for episodic memory are not yet fully mature (Nadel & Zola-Morgan, 1984; Schacter & Moscovitch, 1984). But when researchers introduced a suggestive procedure by asking participants to visualize themselves as toddlers, they got reports of earliest memories as dating to approximately 18 months, well before the presumed end of childhood amnesia (Malinoski & Lynn, 1999; for more on childhood amnesia, see the Where Do You Stand? box on pp. 204–205). In fact, one-third of those exposed to the suggestive procedure reported an earliest recollection from prior to 12 months, whereas nobody did so without visualization suggestions.

So is this what happens when adults suddenly develop memories of childhood events that involve disturbing behavior or even crimes that have gone unpunished? This question was at the center of a controversy that arose during the 1980s and 1990s concerning the accuracy of childhood memories that people recall during psychotherapy. Suggestibility played an important role in the controversy. Diana Halbrooks was a happily married woman from Texas who started psychotherapy in the late 1980s. As her treatment progressed, she began recalling disturbing incidents from her childhood—for example, that her mother had tried to kill her and that her father had abused her sexually. Although her parents denied that these events had ever occurred, her therapist encouraged her to believe in the reality of her memories. Had Halbrooks retrieved terrible memories of events that had actually occurred, or were the memories inaccurate, perhaps the result of suggestive probing during psychotherapy?

In the early 1990s, more and more American families found themselves coping with similar stories. Educated middle-class women (and some men) entered psychotherapy for depression or related problems, only to emerge with recovered memories of previously forgotten childhood sexual abuse, typically perpetrated by fathers and sometimes by mothers. Families and psychologists were split by these controversies. Patients believed their memories were real, and many therapists supported those beliefs, but accused parents contended that the alleged abuses had never happened and that they were instead the products of false memories. A number of prominent memory researchers, as well as some therapists, raised doubts about the accuracy of recovered memories, noting that memory is susceptible to suggestion and distortion (Lindsay & Read, 1994; Loftus, 1993). But others questioned whether people would ever falsely recall such a traumatic event as childhood sexual abuse (Freyd, 1996; Herman, 1992).

Who was right? A few recovered memories of childhood abuse have been corroborated and appear to be accurate (Gleaves, Smith, Butler, & Spiegel, 2004; Pendergrast, 1995). In these cases, individuals who experienced an episode (or episodes) of abuse did not think about the incident until they were reminded of it years later. For example, a Massachusetts man named Frank Fitzpatrick suddenly recalled one day that he had been abused by a priest as a child and later recorded the priest confessing to what he had done (Pendergrast, 1995).

Several kinds of evidence suggest that many recovered memories are inaccurate. First, some people have recovered highly implausible memories of being abused repeatedly during bizarre practices in satanic cults, and yet there is no proof of these practices or even that the cults exist (Pendergrast, 1995; Wright, 1994). Second, a number of the techniques used by psychotherapists to try to pull up forgotten childhood memories are clearly suggestive. A survey of 145 therapists in the United States revealed that approximately 1 in 3 tried to help patients remember childhood sexual abuse by using hypnosis or by encouraging them to imagine incidents that might or might not have actually happened (Poole et al., 1995). Yet imagining past events and hypnosis can help create false memories (Garry, Lindsay, Memor, & Boll, 1996; Hyman & Pentland, 1996; McConkey, Barnier, & Sheehan, 1998).

Finally, a growing number of patients eventually retracted their recovered memories after leaving therapy or returned to their families (McHugh, Lief, Freyd, & Fetkewicz, 2004). This is just what happened to Diana Halbrooks: She stopped therapy and eventually came to realize that the "memories" she had recovered were inaccurate. By the end of the 1990s, the number of new cases of disputed recovered memories of childhood sexual abuse had slowed to a trickle (McHugh et al., 2004). This probably occurred, at least in part, because some of the therapists who had been using suggestive procedures stopped doing so (McNally, 2003).

## Bias

In 2000, the outcome of a very close presidential race between George W. Bush and Al Gore was decided by the Supreme Court 5 weeks after the election had taken place. At issue were dangling chads and recounts in Florida, all of which led to a high degree of uncertainty for the candidates and voters alike. Eventually, Al Gore conceded the election on December 15, 2000, sending George Bush to the first of his two terms in office.

The day after the election (when the result was still in doubt), supporters of Bush and Gore were asked to predict how happy they would be after the outcome of the election was determined (Wilson, Meyers, & Gilbert, 2003). These same respondents reported how happy they felt with the outcome on the day after Al Gore conceded. And 4 months later, the participants recalled how happy they had been right after the election was decided. In short, both Bush and Gore supporters predicted their future happiness, reported their current happiness, and recalled their previous happiness with the election outcomes.

Bush supporters, who eventually enjoyed a positive result (their candidate took office), were understandably happy on the day after the Supreme Court's decision. However, their retrospective accounts *over*estimated how happy they were at the time. Conversely, Gore supporters were not pleased with the outcome. But

How happy do you think you'd be if the candidate you supported won an election? Do you think you'd accurately remember your level of happiness if you recalled it several months later? Chances are good that bias in the memory process would alter your recollection of your previous happiness. Indeed, 4 months after they heard the outcome of the 2000 presidential election, Bush supporters *over*estimated how happy they were, while Gore supporters *under*estimated how happy they were.

**BIAS** The distorting influences of present knowledge, beliefs, and feelings on recollection of previous experiences.

when polled 4 months after the election was decided, Gore supporters *under*estimated how happy they actually were at the time of the result. In both groups, recollections of happiness were at odds with existing reports of their actual happiness at the time (Wilson et al., 2003).

These results illustrate the problem of **bias,** which is *the distorting influences of present knowledge, beliefs, and feelings on recollection of previous experiences.* Sometimes what people remember from their pasts says less about what actually happened than about what they think, feel, or believe now. Both Bush and Gore supporters re-scripted their memories of December 2000 to fit how they felt months afterward. Other researchers have also found that our current moods can bias our recall of past experiences (Bower, 1981; Eich, 1995). So, in addition to helping you recall actual sad memories (as you saw earlier in this chapter), a sad mood can also bias your recollections of experiences that may not have been so sad. Bias can influence memory in three ways: by altering the past to fit the present (*consistency bias*), by exaggerating differences between past and present (*change bias*), and by distorting the past to make us look better (*egocentric bias*).

### Consistency Bias

In addition to moods, current knowledge and beliefs can produce biasing effects. Several researchers have described a *consistency bias,* in which people reconstruct the past to fit what they presently know or believe. One researcher asked people in 1973 to rate their attitudes toward a variety of controversial social issues, including legalization of marijuana, women's rights, and aid to minorities (Marcus, 1986). They were asked to make the same rating again in 1982 and also to indicate what their attitudes had been in 1973. Researchers found that participants' recollections of their 1973 attitudes in 1982 were more closely related to what they believed in 1982 than to what they had actually said in 1973.

The consistency bias is often quite striking in romantically involved couples. In a study of dating couples, participants were asked to evaluate themselves, their dating partner, and their relationship twice—first in an initial session and then again 2 months later (McFarland & Ross, 1987). During the second session, participants were also asked to recall their earlier evaluations. Researchers found that participants whose relationships had soured over time recalled their initial evaluations as more negative than they really were. However, when participants reported a positive or deeper relationship in the present, they also recalled having felt more liking or loving in the past.

The way each member of this happy couple recalls earlier feelings toward the other depends on how each currently views their relationship.

### Change Bias

Just as we sometimes exaggerate the similarity of the past and the present, we sometimes exaggerate the *difference* between what we feel or believe now and what we felt or believed in the past. In other words, *change biases* also occur. For example, most of us would like to believe that our romantic attachments grow stronger over time. In one study, dating couples were asked, once a year for 4 years, to assess the present quality of their relationships and to recall how they felt in past years (Sprecher, 1999). Couples who stayed together for the 4 years recalled that the strength of their love had increased since they last reported on it. Yet their actual ratings at the time did not show any increases in love and attachment. Objectively, the couples did not love each other more today than yesterday. But they did from the subjective perspective of memory.

### Egocentric Bias

Sometimes we exaggerate the change between present and past in order make ourselves look good in retrospect, thus revealing a *self-enhancing* or *egocentric bias.* For example, students sometimes remember feeling more anxious before taking an exam than they actually reported at the time (Keuler & Safer, 1998), and blood donors sometimes recall being more nervous about giving blood than they actually were (Breckler, 1994). In both cases, change biases color memory and make people feel that they behaved more bravely or courageously than they actually did. Our memories for grades that we achieved in school also reflect an egocentric bias. Can you recall your grades from high school courses? Do you remember how many As and Ds appeared on your report card? Chances are that you will recall more of the good grades than the bad ones. When college students tried to remember high school grades and their memories were checked against actual transcripts, they were highly accurate for grades of A (89% correct) and extremely inaccurate for grades of D (29% correct) (Bahrick, Hall, & Berger, 1996). The students were remembering the past as they wanted it to be rather than the way it was.

## Persistence

The artist Melinda Stickney-Gibson awoke in her Chicago apartment to the smell of smoke. She jumped out of bed and saw black plumes rising through cracks in the floor. Melinda tried to call the fire department, but the phone lines had already burned out. Raging flames had engulfed the entire building, and there was no chance to escape except by jumping from her third-floor window. Shortly after she crashed to the ground, the building exploded into a brilliant fireball. She lost all her possessions and her beloved dog, but she saved her own life. Alas, that life was never the same. Melinda became overwhelmed by memories of the fire and frequently could think of little else. Her paintings, which were previously bright, colorful abstractions, became dark meditations that included only black, orange, and ochre—the colors of the fire. When Melinda sat down in front of a blank canvas to start a new painting, her memories of that awful night intruded. She remembered the incident vividly for years, even after she had recovered physically from the injuries suffered in her fall (Schacter, 1996).

Melinda Stickney-Gibson's experiences illustrate memory's seventh and most deadly sin: **persistence,** or *the intrusive recollection of events that we wish we could forget.* Melinda's experience is far from unique: Persistence frequently occurs after disturbing or traumatic incidents, such as the fire that destroyed her home. Although being able to quickly call up memories is usually considered a good thing, in the case of persistence, that ability mutates into a bedeviling mindbug.

Controlled laboratory studies have revealed that emotional experiences tend to be better remembered than nonemotional ones. For instance, memory for unpleasant pictures, such as mutilated bodies, or pleasant ones, such as attractive men and women, is more accurate than for emotionally neutral pictures, such as household objects (Ochsner, 2000). Emotional arousal seems to focus our attention on the central features of an event. In one experiment, people who viewed an emotionally arousing sequence of slides involving a bloody car accident remembered more of the central themes and fewer peripheral details than people who viewed a nonemotional sequence (Christianson & Loftus, 1987).

Intrusive memories are undesirable consequences of the fact that emotional experiences generally lead to more vivid and enduring recollections than nonemotional experiences do. One line of evidence comes from the study of **flashbulb memories,** which are *detailed recollections of when and where we heard about shocking events.* In one study, all but 1 of 40 people who were questioned about the assassination of President John F. Kennedy in November 1963 reported specific, vivid recollections of when and where they heard the news (Brown & Kulik, 1977). It was as if a mental flashbulb had gone off and recorded the event. Many of us can remember where we were and how we heard about the September 11, 2001, terrorist attack on the World Trade Center and the Pentagon.

Several studies have shown that flashbulb memories are not always entirely accurate, but they are generally better remembered than mundane news events from the same time (Neisser & Harsch, 1992; Larsen, 1992). Enhanced retention of flashbulb memories is partly attributable to the emotional arousal elicited by events such as the

**PERSISTENCE** The intrusive recollection of events that we wish we could forget.

**FLASHBULB MEMORIES** Detailed recollections of when and where we heard about shocking events.

Some events are so emotionally charged, such as the Kennedy assassination and the terrorist attack on the World Trade Center, that we form unusually detailed memories of when and where we heard about them. These flashbulb memories generally persist much longer than memories for more ordinary events.

September 11 terrorist attacks and partly attributable to the fact that we tend to talk and think a lot about these experiences. Recall that elaborative encoding enhances memory: When we talk about flashbulb experiences, we elaborate on them and thus further increase their memorability (and decrease their accuracy).

Why do our brains succumb to persistence? A key player in the brain's response to emotional events is a small almond-shaped structure called the amygdala, shown in **FIGURE 5.19.** Buried deep in the inner regions of the temporal lobe, the amygdala is located next to the hippocampus but performs different functions. Damage to the amygdala does not result in a general memory deficit. Patients with amygdala damage, however, do not remember emotional events any better than nonemotional events (Cahill & McGaugh, 1998).

For example, consider what happened when people viewed a series of photographic slides that began with a mother walking her child to school and later included an emotionally arousing event: the child being hit by a car. When tested later, the research participants remembered the arousing event better than the mundane ones. But patients with amygdala damage remembered the mundane and emotionally arousing events equally well (Cahill & McGaugh, 1998). PET and fMRI scans show that when healthy people view a slide sequence that includes an emotionally arousing event, the level of activity in their amygdalas at the time they see it is a good predictor of their subsequent memory for the slide. When there is heightened activity in the amygdala as people watch emotional events, there's a better chance that they will recall those events on a later test (Cahill et al., 1996; Kensinger & Schacter, 2005).

The amygdala influences hormonal systems that kick into high gear when we experience an arousing event. The release of stress-related hormones, such as adrenaline and cortisol, mobilizes the brain and the body in the face of threat or other sources of stress. These hormones also enhance memory for the experience. For instance, administering stress-related hormones heightens a rat's memory for an electrical shock or for places in a maze that it has visited recently (LeDoux, 1996). When the

Hippocampus

Amygdala

**Figure 5.19 The Amygdala's Influence on Memory** The amygdala, located next to the hippocampus, responds strongly to emotional events. Patients with amygdala damage are unable to remember emotional events any better than nonemotional ones (Cahill & McGaugh, 1998).

amygdala is damaged, it no longer releases the stress-related hormones that enhance memory. When people are given a drug that interferes with the release of stress-related hormones, their memory for the emotional sections of a slide sequence is no better than their memory for the mundane sections. It seems, then, that the amygdala influences memory storage by turning on the hormones that allow us to respond to and vividly remember emotionally arousing events.

## Are the Seven Sins Vices or Virtues?

You may have concluded that evolution burdened us with an extremely inefficient memory system that is so prone to error that it often jeopardizes our well-being. Not so. The seven sins are the price we pay for the many benefits that memory provides (Schacter, 2001b). These mindbugs are the occasional result of the normally efficient operation of the human memory system.

Consider the seemingly buggy nature of transience, for example. Wouldn't it be great to remember all the details of every incident in your life, no matter how much time had passed? Not necessarily. It is helpful and sometimes important to forget information that isn't current, like an old phone number. If we didn't gradually forget information over time, our minds would be cluttered with details that we no longer need (Bjork & Bjork, 1988). Information that is used infrequently is less likely to be needed in the future than information that is used more frequently over the same period (Anderson & Schooler, 1991, 2000). Memory, in essence, makes a bet that when we haven't used information recently, we probably won't need it in the future. We win this bet more often than we lose it, making transience an adaptive property of memory. But we are acutely aware of the losses—the frustrations of forgetting—and are never aware of the wins. This is why people are often quick to complain about their memories: The drawbacks of forgetting are painfully evident, but the benefits of forgetting are hidden.

Absentmindedness can also be irritating, but we would be even more irritated without it. Absentminded errors happen in part because events that receive little attention and elaboration when they occur are difficult to recall later. But if all events were registered in elaborate detail, our minds would be cluttered with useless information. This is just what happened in the unusual case of a journalist named Solomon Shereshevskii (Luria, 1968). He formed and retained highly detailed memories of almost everything that happened to him, important or not. Because Shereshevskii's mind was always populated with trivia, he was unable to generalize or function at an abstract level. The struggle to forget plagued him throughout his life, and he used elaborate rituals to try to rid himself of the mass of information competing for space in his mind. The details of past experiences that left Shereshevskii overwhelmed by information are best denied entry to memory in the first place.

Similarly, although blocking is such a frustrating mindbug that we are often tempted to bite the tips of our tongues clean off, it has adaptive features (Bjork & Bjork, 1988). People generally block information that has not been used recently because the odds are that such information will not be needed in the future. In general, blocking helps the memory system to run smoothly and efficiently but occasionally causes embarrassing incidents of retrieval failure.

Memory misattribution and suggestibility both occur because we often fail to recall the details of exactly when and where we saw a face or learned a fact. This is because memory is adapted to retain information that is most likely to be needed in the environment in which it operates. We seldom need to remember all the precise contextual details of every experience. Our memories carefully record such details only when we think they may be needed later, and most of the time we are better off for it. We pay the price, however, when we are required to recollect specific information about an experience that did not elicit any special effort to encode details about its source.

Bias is also a problem, skewing our memories so that we depict ourselves in an overly favorable light. This mindbug may seem self-serving and unduly optimistic, but it can produce the benefit of contributing to our overall sense of contentment. Holding positive illusions about ourselves can lead to greater psychological well-being (Taylor, 1989).

Finally, persistence has both a dark and light side. Although it can cause us to be haunted by traumas that we'd be better off forgetting, overall, it is probably adaptive to remember threatening or traumatic events that could pose a threat to survival. If you could conveniently forget being burned on a hot stove, you might fail to avoid stoves in the future.

---

**In summary,** memory's mindbugs can be classified into seven "sins." *Transience* is reflected by a rapid decline in memory followed by more gradual forgetting. With the passing of time, memory switches from detailed to general. Both decay and interference contribute to transience. *Absentmindedness* results from failures of attention, shallow encoding, and the influence of automatic behaviors and is often associated with forgetting to do things in the future. *Blocking* occurs when stored information is temporarily inaccessible, as when information is on the tip of the tongue. *Memory misattribution* happens when we experience a sense of familiarity but don't recall, or mistakenly recall, the specifics of when and where an experience occurred. Misattribution can result in eyewitness misidentification or false recognition. Patients suffering from frontal lobe damage are especially susceptible to false recognition. *Suggestibility* gives rise to implanted memories of small details or entire episodes. Suggestive techniques such as hypnosis or visualization can promote vivid recall of suggested events, and therapists' use of suggestive techniques may be responsible for some patients' false memories of childhood traumas. *Bias* reflects the influence of current knowledge, beliefs, and feelings on memory or past experiences. Bias can lead us to make the past consistent with the present, exaggerate changes between past and present, or remember the past in a way that makes us look good. *Persistence* reflects the fact that emotional arousal generally leads to enhanced memory, whether we want to remember an experience or not. Persistence is partly attributable to the operation of hormonal systems influenced by the amygdala. Although each of the seven sins can cause trouble in our lives, they have an adaptive side as well. You can think of the seven sins as costs we pay for benefits that allow memory to work as well as it does most of the time. ■ ■

---

## Where Do You Stand?

## The Mystery of Childhood Amnesia

As you have seen, transience is a pervasive characteristic of memory. Nonetheless, you can easily recall many experiences from different times in your life, such as last summer's job or vacation, the sights and sounds of a favorite concert, or the most exciting sporting event you've ever attended. But there is one period of time from which you likely have few or no memories: the first few years of your life. This lack of memory for our early years is called *childhood amnesia* or *infantile amnesia*.

Psychoanalyst Sigmund Freud was one of the first psychologists to comment on childhood amnesia (see Chapter 1). In 1905, he

described a "peculiar amnesia which, in the case of most people, though by no means all, hides the earliest beginnings of their childhood up to their sixth or eighth year" (Freud, 1905/1953, p. 174). Freud's assessments of childhood amnesia were based on observations of individual patients from his psychoanalytic practice.

In the 1930s and 1940s, psychologists carried out systematic studies in which they asked large samples of individuals to report their earliest memories with the dates when they occurred. Contrary to Freud's suggestion that most people cannot remember childhood experiences prior to their sixth or eighth

year, these studies revealed that, on average, an individual's earliest memory dates to about 3½ years of age (Dudycha & Dudycha, 1933; Waldfogel, 1948). Later studies suggested that women report slightly earlier first memories (3.07 years of age) than men (3.4 years) (Howes, Siegel, & Brown, 1993).

Try to recall your own earliest memory. As you mentally search for it, you may encounter a problem that has troubled researchers: How do you know the exact time when your recollection took place? Memory for dates is notoriously poor, so it is often difficult to determine precisely when your earliest memory occurred (Friedman,

1993). To address this problem, researchers asked people about memories for events that have clearly definable dates, such as the birth of a younger sibling, the death of a loved one, or a family move (Sheingold & Tenney, 1982; Usher & Neisser, 1993). In one study researchers asked individuals between 4 and 20 years old to recall as much as they could about the birth of a younger sibling (Sheingold & Tenney, 1982). Participants who were at least 3 years old at the time of the birth remembered it in considerable detail, whereas participants who were younger than 3 years old at the time of the birth remembered little or nothing. A more recent study found that individuals can recall events surrounding the birth of a sibling that occurred when they were about 2.4 years old; some people even showed evidence of recall from ages 2.0 to 2.4 years, although these memories were very sketchy (Eacott & Crawley, 1998).

It is difficult to draw firm conclusions from these kinds of studies. On the one hand, they suggest that people can come up with memories from earlier in life than was previously thought. On the other hand, memories of early events may be based on family conversations that took place long after the events occurred. An adult or a child who remembers having ice cream in the hospital as a 3-year-old when his baby sister was born may be recalling what his parents told him after the event. Consistent with this idea, cross-cultural studies have turned up an interesting finding. Individuals from cultures that emphasize talking about the past, such as North American culture, tend to report earlier first memories than individuals from cultures that place less emphasis on talking about the past, such as Korean and other Asian cultures (MacDonald, Uesilana, & Hayne, 2000; Mullen, 1994).

Recent research has examined whether the events that people say they remember from early childhood really are *personal recollections,* which involve conscious re-experiencing of some aspect of the event, or whether people *just know* about these events (perhaps from family photos and discussions), even though they don't truly possess personal recollections (Multhaup, Johnson, & Tetirick, 2005). Several experiments revealed that personal recollections tend to emerge later than memories based on "just knowing," with the transition from mostly "know" memories to mostly "recollect" memories occurring at 4.7 years.

Some events in your personal history are personal recollections. In other words, you actually remember the occurrence of the event. Personal recollections are ones in which you can become consciously aware again of some aspects of the event, of what happened, or of what you experienced at the time. Perhaps you have an image of the event or can re-experience some specific details.

Other events from your past are ones that you know happened but are not personal recollections. In other words, you know the event occurred, but you cannot consciously recollect any aspect of what happened or of what you experienced at the time. Instead, your knowledge of the event is based on an external source of information, perhaps your parents and/or other family members, friends, pictures, photo albums, diaries, or family stories. To find out about your own "recollected" versus "known" memories, complete the items listed below from the 2005 study by Multhaup et al.

| Instructions | Event | Recollect | Know | Age | Don't Know |
|---|---|:---:|:---:|:---:|:---:|
| Please label each of the events listed as a personal "recollection" or as an event that you "know" happened but that is not a personal memory. If you neither "recollect" nor "know" the event (perhaps because you never experienced it), please label it as "don't know." For each event you "recollect" or "know," indicate your age at the time the event occurred, as best you can determine, with the year followed by month (e.g., 4.0 is 4 years old exactly, 4.6 is 4½ years old, 4.9 is 4¾, and so forth). | You read your first book with chapters. | ❏ | ❏ | ❏ | ❏ |
| | You went to your first sleepover. | ❏ | ❏ | ❏ | ❏ |
| | You saw your first movie in a movie theater. | ❏ | ❏ | ❏ | ❏ |
| | You took your first swimming lesson. | ❏ | ❏ | ❏ | ❏ |
| | You joined your first organized sports team. | ❏ | ❏ | ❏ | ❏ |
| | You learned to write in cursive. | ❏ | ❏ | ❏ | ❏ |
| | You stopped taking naps. | ❏ | ❏ | ❏ | ❏ |
| | You learned to spell your name. | ❏ | ❏ | ❏ | ❏ |
| | You went to an amusement park for the first time. | ❏ | ❏ | ❏ | ❏ |
| | You were toilet trained. | ❏ | ❏ | ❏ | ❏ |
| | Your first permanent tooth came in. | ❏ | ❏ | ❏ | ❏ |
| | You learned to ride a bicycle (2 wheels, no training wheels). | ❏ | ❏ | ❏ | ❏ |
| | You slept in a bed instead of a crib. | ❏ | ❏ | ❏ | ❏ |

(Items are sampled from experiments 1 and 2 of Multhaup et al., 2005, p. 172.)

# Chapter Review

## Encoding: Transforming Perceptions into Memories

- Memories are not passive recordings of the world but instead result from combining incoming information with previous experiences. Encoding is the process of linking new and old information.

- Elaborative encoding (actively linking incoming information to existing associations and knowledge), visual imagery encoding (converting incoming information into mental pictures), and organizational encoding (noticing relationships among items you want to encode) all benefit memory.

- Different regions within the frontal lobe play important roles in elaborative encoding and organizational encoding, whereas the visual cortex (occipital lobe) appears to be important for visual imagery encoding.

## Storage: Maintaining Memories over Time

- Three major forms of memory storage hold information for different amounts of time: sensory memory (a second or two), short-term or working memory (less than a minute), and long-term memory (minutes, hours, weeks, and years).

- The hippocampus puts information into long-term storage so that it can later be consciously remembered. Amnesic patients with damage to the hippocampal region have little ability to remember their recent experiences.

- Memories are most likely stored in the synapses that connect neurons to one another.

## Retrieval: Bringing Memories to Mind

- Recall of past experiences depends critically on retrieval cues, which trigger recall by reinstating what we thought or how we felt during the encoding of an experience.

- Information or experiences we can't recall on our own are sometimes only temporarily inaccessible and can be brought to mind with appropriate retrieval cues.

- Different parts of the brain seem to be activated when we put forth the mental effort to try to call up a past experience and when we actually remember the experience.

## Multiple Forms of Memory: How the Past Returns

- Memory can be broadly divided into explicit memory, involving conscious, intentional retrieval of previous experiences, and implicit memory, which is a nonconscious, unintentional form of memory.

- Priming (an enhanced ability to think of a stimulus as a result of recent exposure to the stimulus) and procedural memory (learning skills from practice) both draw on implicit memory.

- Episodic memory (recollection of specific personal experiences) and semantic memory (general knowledge of the world) involve explicit recall information.

## Memory Failures: The Seven Sins of Memory

- There are seven major ways in which memory can cause us trouble: transience, absentmindedness, blocking, memory misattribution, suggestibility, bias, and persistence. The first three sins all involve different types of forgetting, the next three involve different types of distortion, and the final sin involves remembering what we wish we could forget.

- Each of the seven sins has adaptive features. The sins are prices we pay for benefits in memory that generally serve us well. Understanding these memory mindbugs helps researchers better understand the normal operations of memory.

## Key Terms

Memory (p. 168)
Encoding (p. 169)
Storage (p. 169)
Retrieval (p. 169)
Elaborative encoding (p. 170)
Visual imagery encoding (p. 171)
Organizational encoding (p. 172)
Memory storage (p. 173)
Sensory memory store (p. 173)
Iconic memory (p. 174)
Echoic memory (p. 174)
Short-term memory store (p. 174)

Rehearsal (p. 174)
Chunking (p. 175)
Working memory (p. 175)
Long-term memory store (p. 176)
Anterograde amnesia (p. 177)
Retrograde amnesia (p. 177)
Long-term potentiation (LTP) (p. 178)
NMDA receptor (p. 178)
Retrieval cue (p. 180)
Encoding specificity principle (p. 180)
State-dependent retrieval (p. 181)

Transfer-appropriate processing (p. 181)
Explicit memory (p. 183)
Implicit memory (p. 183)
Procedural memory (p. 183)
Priming (p. 184)
Semantic memory (p. 185)
Episodic memory (p. 185)
Transience (p. 187)
Retroactive interference (p. 189)
Proactive interference (p. 189)
Absentmindedness (p. 189)

Prospective memory (p. 191)
Blocking (p. 192)
Tip-of-the-tongue experience (p. 192)
Memory misattribution (p. 193)
Source memory (p. 194)
False recognition (p. 194)
Suggestibility (p. 197)
Bias (p. 200)
Persistence (p. 201)
Flashbulb memories (p. 201)

## Recommended Readings

**Brainerd**, C. J., & **Reyna**, V. F. (2005). *The science of false memory*. New York: Oxford University Press. Written by two of the leading researchers into the nature of false memories, this volume provides a readable summary of what we know about false memories and how they differ from true memories.

**McNally**, R. J. (2003). *Remembering trauma*. Cambridge, MA: Harvard University Press. This is the single most comprehensive source concerning traumatic memories. McNally explains the characteristics and origins of traumatic memories and also provides a useful discussion of the controversy concerning the accuracy of repressed and recovered traumatic memories.

**Neisser**, U., & **Hyman**, I. E. (Eds.). (2000). *Memory observed: Remembering in natural contexts*. New York: Worth. A fascinating collection of articles and essays concerned with how people remember and forget in the real world.

**Schacter**, D. L. (2001). *The seven sins of memory*. New York and Boston: Houghton Mifflin. This book provides a more in-depth treatment of memory's seven sins than that provided in this chapter, including many more examples of how the seven sins affect us in everyday life.

**Wearing**, D. (2006). *Forever today*. London: Corgi Books. Clive Wearing is a gifted musician who also has the dubious distinction of having one of the most severe cases of amnesia ever documented. His memory lasts for about 7 seconds, making every experience seem new to him. His wife, Deborah, wrote a book about their relationship and the challenges associated with coping with this kind of brain damage.

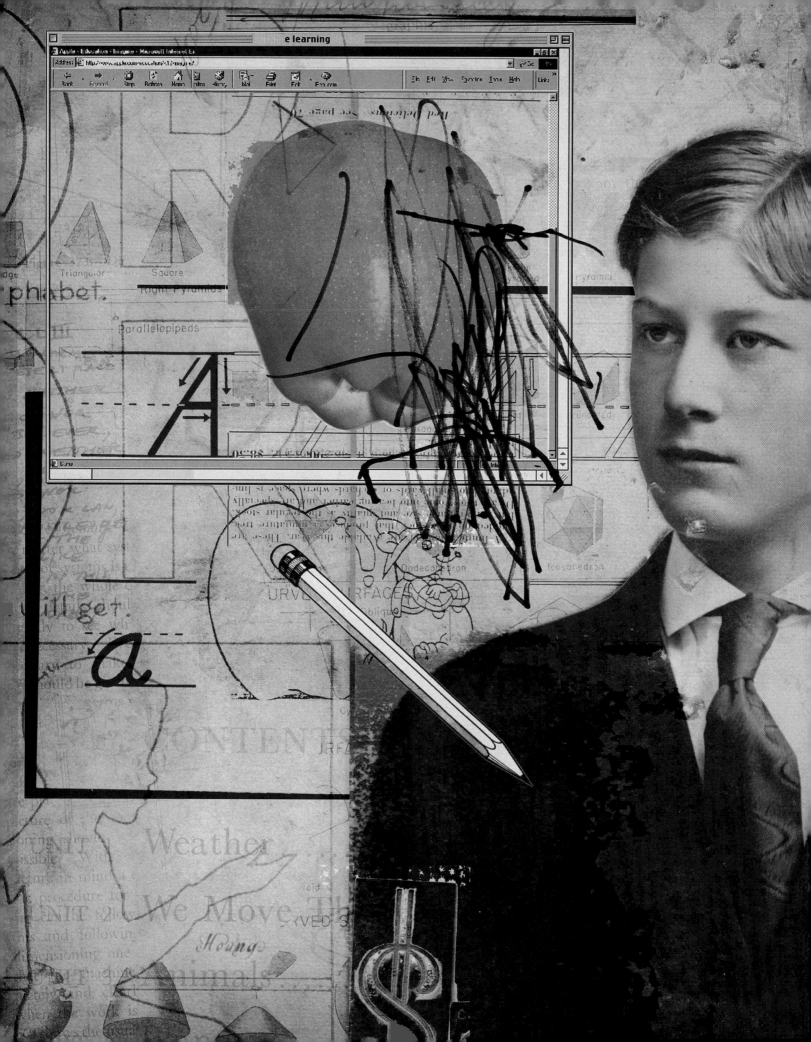

# 6

# Learning

**ADAM AND TERI'S DAUGHTER, CARLY, WAS** born at 2:00 p.m. on September 11, 2000. This fact is unremarkable in itself, except that it means Carly celebrated her first birthday on September 11, 2001. The family happened to be living in Boston at the time, and they awoke that morning (on a 1-year-old's early-rising schedule) full of anticipation for a fun-filled day of birthday celebration.

What they got instead was a phone call from a friend in Texas, urging them to turn on the local news. Like many Americans, Adam and Teri watched with sadness and horror as terrorist attacks in New York, Pennsylvania, and the nation's capital took place before their eyes. American Airlines Flight 11, which crashed into the North Tower of the World Trade Center, had originated from Boston that morning, heightening the sense of uncertainty and anxiety that already had begun to define the day. Adam and Teri watched in shock as United Airlines Flight 175 crashed into the South Tower on live television. As the news reports filtered in throughout the day, each more disturbing than the last, the couple could scarcely avert their eyes from the television, and they ended up having CNN on all day long.

Yet through it all, young Carly played with her presents, blissfully unaware of the events unfolding on the TV screen. One gift, a small yellow soccer goal, turned out to be a favorite. When the ball hit the back of the net, it triggered a voice that yelled, "Goooooaaaallll!" and then played one of several songs at random. Carly loved to hear the music, and she would repeatedly whack the toy to make it play a song. In a surreal scene, fire, turmoil, and carnage were set to the strains of "John Jacob Jingleheimer Schmidt."

And that's what makes this a story about learning.

As baby Carly played with her new soccer goal, television images showed the horrifying events of September 11, 2001. Carly's parents, Adam and Teri, learned an association between the baby's toy and the 9/11 events that lasted for years.

uite a curious thing happened. As the weeks turned to months and 2001 turned to 2002, the immediate emotional impact of 9/11 faded for Adam. Carly grew and developed, and she continued to love playing with her soccer goal. Each time it played a song, though, Adam felt a chill run through his body and saw images of burning buildings in his mind's eye. It was as though John Jacob Jingleheimer Schmidt was a madman bent on bedeviling his life. Carly is much older now, and her baby toys have been put up on a shelf. But just the sight of that little yellow goal can still bring back a flood of sad memories and call up a welter of unpleasant emotions for her parents.

What's at work here is a type of learning based on association. Adam and Teri came to associate a unique historical tragedy and a child's toy, and as a result, either of the two stimuli produced certain mental and emotional reactions. The fear and sadness that were triggered by watching the events of 9/11 came to be triggered by an innocuous plaything, and it was an effect that lasted for years. In this chapter, we'll consider this type of learning as well as other ways that knowledge is acquired and stored.

## Defining Learning: Experience That Causes a Permanent Change

Learning is shorthand for a collection of different techniques, procedures, and outcomes that produce changes in an organism's behavior. Learning psychologists have identified and studied as many as 40 different kinds of learning. However, there is a basic principle at the core of all of them. **Learning** involves *some experience that results in a relatively permanent change in the state of the learner.* This definition emphasizes several key ideas: Learning is based on experience; learning produces changes in the organism; and these changes are relatively permanent. Think back to Adam and Teri's experiences on September 11, 2001—seeing the horrors of 9/11 unfold on their TV screen and hearing Carly's toy changed their response to what had been a harmless child's toy. Furthermore, the association they learned lasted for years.

Learning can be conscious and deliberate or unconscious. For example, memorizing the names of all the U.S. presidents is a conscious and deliberate activity, with an explicit awareness of the learning process as it is taking place. In comparison, the kind of learning that associated Carly's toy with images of horror is much more implicit. Adam and Teri certainly weren't aware of or consciously focused on learning as it was taking place. Some other forms of learning start out explicitly but become more implicit over time. When you first learned to drive a car, for example, you probably devoted a lot of attention to the many movements and sequences that needed to be carried out simultaneously ("step lightly on the accelerator while you push the turn indicator and look in the rearview mirror while you turn the steering wheel"). That complex interplay of motions is now probably quite effortless and automatic for you. Explicit learning has become implicit over time.

These distinctions in learning might remind you of similar distinctions in memory and for good reason. In Chapter 5, you read about the differences between *implicit* and *explicit* memories as well as *procedural, semantic,* and *episodic* memories. Do different forms of learning mirror different types of memory? It's not that simple, but it is true that learning and memory are inextricably linked. Learning produces memories, and conversely, the existence of memories implies that knowledge was acquired, that experience was registered and recorded in the brain, or that learning has taken place.

## The Case of Habituation

Adam and Teri's learning is certainly not simple, but let's consider some of the simplest forms of learning. If you've ever lived under the flight path of your local airport, near railroad tracks, or by a busy highway, you probably noticed the deafening roar as a Boeing 737 made its way toward the landing strip, the clatter of a train speeding down the track, or the sound of traffic when you first moved in. You probably also noticed that after a while, the roar wasn't quite so deafening anymore and that eventually you ignored the sounds of the planes, trains, or automobiles in your vicinity.

**Habituation** is *a general process in which repeated or prolonged exposure to a stimulus results in a gradual reduction in responding.* For example, a car that backfires unexpectedly as you walk by will produce a startle response: You'll jump back; your eyes will widen; your muscles will tense; and your body will experience an increase in sweating, blood pressure, and alertness. If another car were to backfire a block later, you may show another startle response, but it will be less dramatic and subside more quickly. If a third backfire should occur, you will likely not respond at all. You will have become *habituated* to the sound of a car backfiring.

Habituation is a simple form of learning. An experience results in a change in the state of the learner: In the preceding example, you begin by reacting one way to a stimulus and, with experience, your reactions change. However, this kind of change usually isn't permanent. In most cases of habituation, a person will exhibit the original reaction if enough time has gone by. To continue our example, if another car backfires a week later, you will almost certainly have a full-blown startle response. Similarly, when you return home from a 2-week vacation, the roar of the jets will probably be just as loud as ever.

A simple experiment explored the question of just how robust habituation to a loud sound could be (Leaton, 1976). One group of rats was exposed to several hundred loud tones within a 5-minute span. Another group was exposed to one loud tone each day over an 11-day period. The researchers found that the two groups reacted quite differently. The rats in the first group showed the expected startle response at first, but it quickly gave way to a rather indifferent attitude toward the tones. However, this reaction didn't last. When the tone was presented 24 hours later, the rats showed a full-blown startle response. The rats in the other group, however, showed a slow, continuous decline in the startle response over the entire 11 days of the experiment. The second outcome reflects the basic principle underlying most types of learning—that change in behavior has some permanence to it.

MICHAEL KLINEC/ALAMY

Living near a busy highway can be unpleasant. Most people who live near major highways become habituated to the sound of traffic.

## Learning and Behaviorism

As you'll recall from Chapter 1, a sizable chunk of psychology's history was devoted to a single dominant viewpoint. Behaviorism, with its insistence on measuring only observable, quantifiable behavior and its dismissal of mental activity as irrelevant and unknowable, was the major outlook of most psychologists working from the 1930s through the 1950s. This was also the period during which most of the fundamental work on learning theory took place.

You might find the intersection of behaviorism and learning theory a bit surprising. After all, at one level learning seems abstract: Something intangible happens to you, and you think or behave differently thereafter. It seems that you'd need to explain that transformation in terms of a change in mental outlook, the development of a new way of thinking, or any of several other phrases that evoke mental processes that behaviorists do not consider in their learning theories. In fact, most behaviorists argued that the "permanent change in experience" that resulted from learning could be demonstrated equally well in almost any organism: rats, dogs, pigeons, mice, pigs, or humans. From this perspective, behaviorists viewed learning as a purely behavioral, eminently observable activity that did not necessitate any mental activity.

As you'll see shortly, in many ways the behaviorists were right. Much of what we know about how organisms learn comes directly from the behaviorists' observations of behaviors. However, the behaviorists also overstated their case. There are some important cognitive considerations—that is, elements of mental activity—that need to be addressed in order to understand the learning process.

**LEARNING** Some experience that results in a relatively permanent change in the state of the learner.

**HABITUATION** A general process in which repeated or prolonged exposure to a stimulus results in a gradual reduction in responding.

**CLASSICAL CONDITIONING** When a neutral stimulus evokes a response after being paired with a stimulus that naturally evokes a response.

**UNCONDITIONED STIMULUS (US)** Something that reliably produces a naturally occurring reaction in an organism.

**UNCONDITIONED RESPONSE (UR)** A reflexive reaction that is reliably elicited by an unconditioned stimulus.

**CONDITIONED STIMULUS (CS)** A stimulus that is initially neutral and produces no reliable response in an organism.

**CONDITIONED RESPONSE (CR)** A reaction that resembles an unconditioned response but is produced by a conditioned stimulus.

*"Perhaps, Dr. Pavlov, he could be taught to seal envelopes."*

**Figure 6.1 Pavlov's Apparatus for Studying Classical Conditioning** Pavlov presented auditory stimuli to the animals using a bell or a tuning fork. Visual stimuli could be presented on the screen. The inset shows a close-up of the tube inserted in the dog's salivary gland for collecting saliva.

# Classical Conditioning: One Thing Leads to Another

You'll recall from Chapter 1 that American psychologist John B. Watson kick-started the behaviorist movement, arguing that psychologists should "never use the terms *consciousness, mental states, mind, content, introspectively verifiable, imagery,* and the like" (Watson, 1913, p. 166). Watson's firebrand stance was fueled in large part by the work of a Russian physiologist, Ivan Pavlov (1849–1936).

Pavlov was awarded the Nobel Prize in Physiology in 1904 for his work on the salivation of dogs. Pavlov studied the digestive processes of laboratory animals by surgically implanting test tubes into the cheeks of dogs to measure their salivary responses to different kinds of foods. Serendipitously, however, his explorations into spit and drool revealed the mechanics of one form of learning, which came to be called classical conditioning. **Classical conditioning** occurs *when a neutral stimulus evokes a response after being paired with a stimulus that naturally evokes a response.* In his classic experiments, Pavlov showed that dogs learned to salivate to neutral stimuli such as a bell or a tone after that stimulus had been associated with another stimulus that naturally evokes salivation, such as food.

## Pavlov's Experiments on Classical Conditioning

Pavlov's basic experimental setup involved cradling dogs in a harness to administer the foods and to measure the salivary response, as shown in **FIGURE 6.1.** He noticed that dogs that previously had been in the experiment began to produce a kind of "anticipatory" salivary response as soon as they were put in the harness, before any food was presented. Pavlov and his colleagues regarded these responses as annoyances at first because they interfered with collecting naturally occurring salivary secretions. In reality, the dogs were behaving in line with the four basic elements of classical conditioning.

When the dogs were initially presented with a plate of food, they began to salivate. No surprise here—placing food in front of most animals will launch the salivary process. Pavlov called the presentation of food an **unconditioned stimulus (US),** or *something that reliably produces a naturally occurring reaction in an organism.* He called the dogs' salivation an **unconditioned response (UR),** or *a reflexive reaction that is reliably elicited by an unconditioned stimulus.* As a shorthand, these elements are often abbreviated US and UR, and the whole thing is quite natural and sensible: Food makes animals salivate.

Pavlov soon discovered that he could make the dogs salivate to stimuli that don't usually make animals salivate, such as the sound of a buzzer. In various experiments, Pavlov paired the presentation of food with the sound of a buzzer, the ticking of a metronome, the humming of a tuning fork, or the flash of a light (Pavlov, 1927). Sure enough, he found that the dogs salivated to the sound of a buzzer, the ticking of a

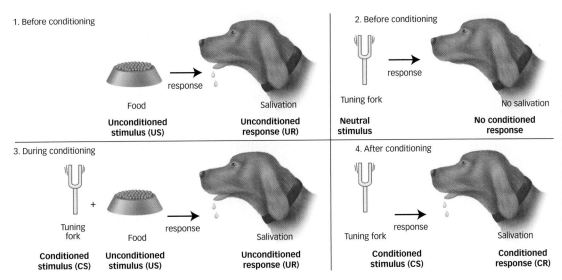

1. Before conditioning

Food
**Unconditioned stimulus (US)**

response

Salivation
**Unconditioned response (UR)**

2. Before conditioning

Tuning fork
**Neutral stimulus**

response

No salivation
**No conditioned response**

3. During conditioning

Tuning fork + Food
**Conditioned stimulus (CS)**   **Unconditioned stimulus (US)**

response

Salivation
**Unconditioned response (UR)**

4. After conditioning

Tuning fork
**Conditioned stimulus (CS)**

response

Salivation
**Conditioned response (CR)**

**Figure 6.2 The Elements of Classical Conditioning** In classical conditioning, a previously neutral stimulus (such as the sound of a tuning fork) is paired with an unconditioned stimulus (such as the presentation of food). After several trials associating the two, the conditioned stimulus (the sound) alone can produce a conditioned response.

metronome, the humming of a tuning fork, or the flash of a light, each of which had become a **conditioned stimulus (CS)**, or *a stimulus that is initially neutral and produces no reliable response in an organism* (see **FIGURE 6.2**). When dogs hear the sound of a buzzer in the wild, they're not known to salivate: There's nothing natural or predictable about the sound of a buzzer producing a particular kind of behavior in a dog. However, when the conditioned stimulus (CS), in this case the sound of a buzzer, is paired over time with the unconditioned stimulus (US), or the food, the animal will learn to associate food with the sound and eventually the CS is sufficient to produce a response, or salivation. This response resembles the UR, but Pavlov called it the **conditioned response (CR)**, or *a reaction that resembles an unconditioned response but is produced by a conditioned stimulus*. In this example, the dogs' salivation (CR) was eventually prompted by the sound of the buzzer (CS) alone because the sound of the buzzer and the food (US) had been associated so often in the past. Technically, though, the salivation is not a UR (the naturally occurring, reflexive reaction to the presentation of food) because it is produced instead by the CS (the sound of the buzzer). As you can imagine, a range of stimuli might be used as a CS, and as we noted earlier, several different stimuli became the CS in Pavlov's experiment.

Let's apply these four basic elements of the classical-conditioning process—the US, UR, CS, and CR—to a couple of examples. First, consider your own dog (or cat). You probably think you have the only dog that can tell time because she always knows when dinner's coming and gets prepared, stopping short of pulling up a chair and tucking a napkin into her collar. It's as though she has one eye on the clock every day, waiting for the dinner hour. Sorry to burst your bubble, but your dog is no clock-watching wonder hound. Instead, the presentation of food (the US) has become associated with a complex CS—your getting up, moving into the kitchen, opening the cabinet, working the can opener—such that the CS alone signals to your dog that food is on the way and therefore initiates the CR of her getting ready to eat.

Another example comes from the popular film *Super Size Me* (2004), director Morgan Spurlock's documentary about fast-food consumption and obesity in America. In one scene, Spurlock is lamenting to an interviewee about the perils of childhood obesity and how restaurants seem to lure children with playscapes, Fun Meals, and birthday celebrations. Reflecting the seeming impossibility of steering young children clear of such fast-food attractions, Spurlock jokingly comments that if he had a child, he would punch him each time they passed a McDonald's. This shocking but facetious image is classical conditioning in action. The painful US (a punch) should become associated with a CS (the sight of McDonald's) so that eventually the CS alone produces the CR (feelings of fear and avoidance whenever the restaurant is in view). Even though it might be an effective method to keep kids away from fast food, it's not one that any parent should ever consider.

**DENNIS THE MENACE**

*"I think Mom's using the can opener."*

**ACQUISITION** The phase of classical conditioning when the CS and the US are presented together.

Finally, think back to Adam, Teri, and Carly's experiences on September 11, 2001. As Adam and Teri watched the World Trade Center collapsing on television, they felt sadness, fear, and anxiety. The images of devastation and horror were the US and the negative feelings were the UR: Seeing horrible things usually makes people feel horrible. However, Carly's soccer goal acted as the CS. The toy—and especially, the songs it played—was an initially neutral stimulus that was associated with the US that day. As the horrific images flashed across the screen, "Skip to My Lou," "Twinkle, Twinkle, Little Star," and "She's a Grand Old Flag" provided an endless sound track. As Adam experienced, eventually the CS all by itself—the music played by the toy—was sufficient to produce the CR—feelings of sadness, fear, and anxiety.

## The Basic Principles of Classical Conditioning

When Pavlov's findings first appeared in the scientific and popular literature (Pavlov, 1923a, b), they produced a flurry of excitement because psychologists now had demonstrable evidence of how conditioning produced learned behaviors. This was the kind of behaviorist psychology John B. Watson was proposing: An organism experiences events or stimuli that are observable and measurable, and changes in that organism can be directly observed and measured. Dogs learned to salivate to the sound of a buzzer, and there was no need to resort to explanations about why it had happened, what the dog wanted, or how the animal thought about the situation. In other words, there was no need to consider the mind in this classical-conditioning paradigm, which appealed to Watson and the behaviorists. Pavlov also appreciated the significance of his discovery and embarked on a systematic investigation of the mechanisms of classical conditioning. Let's take a closer look at some of these principles. (As the Real World box on the facing page shows, these principles help explain how drug overdoses occur.)

### Acquisition

Remember when you first got your dog? Chances are she didn't seem too smart, especially the way she stared at you vacantly as you went into the kitchen, not anticipating that food was on the way. That's because learning through classical conditioning requires some period of association between the CS and US. This period is called **acquisition**, or *the phase of classical conditioning when the CS and the US are presented together*. During the initial phase of classical conditioning, typically there is a gradual increase in learning: It starts low, rises rapidly, and then slowly tapers off, as shown on the left side of **FIGURE 6.3**. Pavlov's dogs gradually increased their amount of salivation over several trials of pairing a tone with the presentation of food, and similarly, your dog eventually learned to associate your kitchen preparations with the subsequent appearance of food. After learning has been established, the CS by itself will reliably elicit the CR.

**Figure 6.3** **Acquisition, Extinction, and Spontaneous Recovery** In classical conditioning, the CS is originally neutral and produces no specific response. After several trials pairing the CS with the US, the CS alone comes to elicit the salivary response (the CR). Learning tends to take place fairly rapidly and then levels off as stable responding develops. In extinction, the CR diminishes quickly until it no longer occurs. A rest period, however, is typically followed by spontaneous recovery of the CR. In fact, a well-learned CR may show spontaneous recovery after more than one rest period even though there have been no additional learning trials.

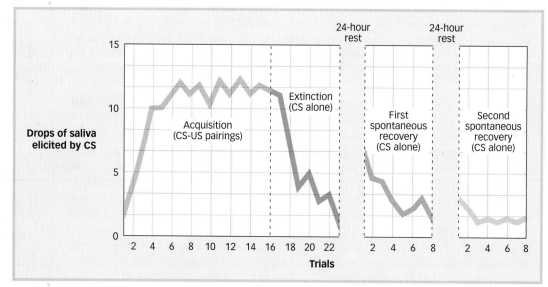

## { THE REAL WORLD } Understanding Drug Overdoses

ALL TOO OFTEN, POLICE ARE CONFRONTED with a perplexing problem: the sudden death of addicts from a drug overdose. These deaths are puzzling for at least three reasons: The victims are often experienced drug users, the dose taken is usually not larger than what they usually take, and the deaths tend to occur in unusual settings. Experienced drug users are just that: experienced! You'd think that if a heroin addict or crack cocaine user were ingesting a typical amount of a substance they'd used many times before, the chances of an overdose would be *lower* than usual.

Classical conditioning provides some insight into how these deaths occur. First, when classical conditioning takes place, the CS is more than a simple bell or tone: It also includes the overall *context* within which the conditioning takes place. Indeed, Pavlov's dogs often began to salivate even as they approached the experimental apparatus. Second, many CRs are compensatory reactions to the US. In some of Pavlov's early experiments, he used a very mild acid solution as the US because it produces large amounts of saliva that dilute the acid in the dog's mouth. When that salivary response is eventually conditioned to the sound of a tone, in a way it represents the remnants of the body's natural reaction to the presentation of the US.

These two finer points of classical conditioning help explain what happens when someone takes a drug such as heroin (Siegel, 1984). When the drug is injected, the entire setting (the drug paraphernalia, the room, the lighting, the addict's usual companions) functions as the CS, and the addict's brain reacts to the heroin by secreting

AP PHOTO/CHRIS GARDNER

**Although opium dens and crack houses may be considered blight, it is often safer for addicts to use drugs there. The environment becomes part of the addict's CS, so ironically, busting crack houses may contribute to more deaths from drug overdose when addicts are pushed to use drugs in new situations.**

neurotransmitters that counteract its effects. Over time, this protective physiological response becomes part of the CR, and like all CRs, it occurs in the presence of the CS but prior to the actual administration of the drug. These compensatory physiological reactions are also what make drug abusers take increasingly larger doses to achieve the same effect; ultimately, these reactions produce *drug tolerance,* discussed in Chapter 8.

Based on these principles of classical conditioning, taking drugs in a new environment can be fatal for a longtime drug user. If an addict injects the usual dose in a setting that is sufficiently novel or where heroin has never been taken before, the CS is now altered. What's more, the physiological compensatory CR either does not occur or is substantially decreased. As a result, the addict's usual dose becomes an overdose and death often results. This effect has also been shown experimentally: Rats that have had extensive experience with morphine in one setting were much more likely to survive dose increases in that same setting than in a novel one (Siegel, 1976).

The basic principles of classical conditioning help explain this real-world tragedy of drug overdose. Intuitively, addicts may stick with the crack houses, opium dens, or "shooting galleries" with which they're familiar for just this reason.

## Second-Order Conditioning

After conditioning has been established, a phenomenon called **second-order conditioning** can be demonstrated: *conditioning where the US is a stimulus that acquired its ability to produce learning from an earlier procedure in which it was used as a CS.* For example, in an early study Pavlov repeatedly paired a new CS, a black square, with the now-reliable tone. After a number of training trials, his dogs produced a salivary response to the black square even though the square itself had never been directly associated with the food. You could do the same thing with your own dog. After she has learned the association between your kitchen noises and the presentation of food, you might try humming a particular tune each time you walk into the kitchen for any reason. After a while you should find that humming the tune by itself causes your dog to salivate.

Psychologists quickly appreciated the applications of second-order conditioning to daily life. For example, it can help explain why some people desire money to the point that they hoard it and value it even more than the objects that it can be used to purchase. Money is initially used to purchase objects that produce gratifying outcomes, such as expensive cars or big-screen televisions. Although money is not directly associated with the thrill of a high-speed drive in a new sports car or the amazing clarity of a high-definition TV, through second-order conditioning money can become linked with these desirable qualities.

**SECOND-ORDER CONDITIONING**
Conditioning where the US is a stimulus that acquired its ability to produce learning from an earlier procedure in which it was used as a CS.

Some people desire money to the extent that they hoard it and value it more than the things it can buy. Multibillionaire technology executives Lawrence Ellison (left) and Paul Allen (right) donated considerably less than 1% of their personal fortunes in 2006, instead hoarding the money for themselves. Such people may be showing the effects of second-order conditioning.

### Extinction

After Pavlov and his colleagues had explored the process of acquisition extensively, they turned to the next logical question: What would happen if they continued to present the CS (tone) but stopped presenting the US (food)? Repeatedly presenting the CS without the US produces exactly the result you might imagine. As shown on the right side of the first panel in Figure 6.3, behavior declines abruptly and continues to drop until eventually the dog ceases to salivate to the sound of the tone. This process is called **extinction**, *the gradual elimination of a learned response that occurs when the US is no longer presented.* The term was introduced because the conditioned response is "extinguished" and no longer observed. If you make noises in the kitchen without subsequently presenting a meaty plate of Alpo, eventually your dog will stop salivating or even getting aroused every time you walk into the kitchen.

### Spontaneous Recovery

Having established that he could produce learning through conditioning and then extinguish it, Pavlov wondered if this elimination of conditioned behavior was permanent. Is a single session of extinction sufficient to knock out the CR completely, or is there some residual change in the dog's behavior so that the CR might reappear?

To explore this question, Pavlov extinguished the classically conditioned salivation response and then allowed the dogs to have a short rest period. When they were brought back to the lab and presented with the CS again, they displayed **spontaneous recovery**, *the tendency of a learned behavior to recover from extinction after a rest period.* This phenomenon is shown in the middle panel in Figure 6.3. Notice that this recovery takes place even though there have not been any additional associations between the CS and US. Some spontaneous recovery of the conditioned response even takes place in what is essentially a second extinction session after another period of rest (see the right-hand panel in Figure 6.3 on p. 214). Clearly, extinction had not completely wiped out the learning that had been acquired. The ability of the CS to elicit the CR was weakened, but it was not eliminated.

Pavlov proposed that spontaneous recovery came about because the extinction process has two distinct effects. First, it weakened the associations formed during acquisition, and second, it inhibited the conditioned response. If this explanation was correct, how often could spontaneous recovery occur? Is it possible to ever completely extinguish a conditioned response after it was learned? As you see from Figure 6.3, some spontaneous recovery can be seen after a second rest period and, occasionally, a third. Eventually, however, the conditioned response will cease to occur.

But consider this. Even if a sufficient number of extinction trials are conducted so that there is no longer any evidence of spontaneous recovery, can we still conclude that any residual associations have been completely eliminated? The answer is no. If

**EXTINCTION** The gradual elimination of a learned response that occurs when the US is no longer presented.

**SPONTANEOUS RECOVERY** The tendency of a learned behavior to recover from extinction after a rest period.

**GENERALIZATION** A process in which the CR is observed even though the CS is slightly different from the original one used during acquisition.

**DISCRIMINATION** The capacity to distinguish between similar but distinct stimuli.

the CS-US pairings are introduced again, the animal will show rapid conditioning, much more rapid than during the initial acquisition phase. This effect is known as savings, since it suggests that some underlying neural changes that occurred during the initial learning are "saved" no matter how many extinction trials are conducted.

## Generalization

Suppose you decide to break down and buy a new can opener, replacing the crummy one that you've had for years. Let's say the new one makes a slightly different sound. Did you consider your dog at any point in this decision making? After all, Fido had associated the sound of the old can opener with the onset of food, and now you've gone and changed things. Do you think your dog will be stumped, unable to anticipate the presentation of her food? Will a whole new round of conditioning need to be established with this modified CS?

Probably not. It wouldn't be very adaptive for an organism if each little change in the CS-US pairing required an extensive regimen of new learning. Rather, the phenomenon of **generalization** tends to take place, in which *the CR is observed even though the CS is slightly different from the original one used during acquisition*. This means that the conditioning "generalizes" to stimuli that are similar to the CS used during the original training. As you might expect, the more the new stimulus changes, the less conditioned responding is observed. If you replaced the can opener with an electric can opener, your dog would probably show a much weaker conditioned response (Pearce, 1987; Rescorla, 2006).

Some generalization studies used a 1,000-hertz (Hz) tone as the CS during the acquisition phase. The test stimuli used were tones of higher or lower pitches. As you might expect, an animal gives the maximum response to the original stimulus of 1,000 Hz, with a systematic drop-off as the pitch of the replacement stimulus is farther away from the original tone of 1,000 Hz regardless of whether the tone was higher or lower. Interestingly, when the stimulus is one of the octaves of the original stimulus (octaves in music are tones that are direct multiples of each other), either 500 Hz or 2,000 Hz, there is a slight increase in responding. In these cases, the rate of responding is lower than that of the original CS but higher than it is in other cases of dissimilar tones. The animals clearly show that they detect octaves just like we do, and in this case, responding has generalized to those octaves (see **FIGURE 6.4**).

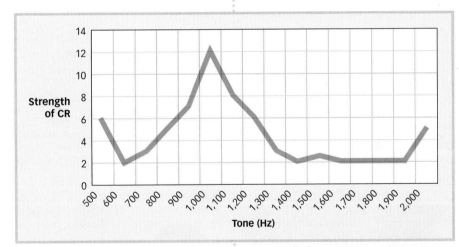

**Figure 6.4 Stimulus Generalization** In this experiment, an animal was conditioned using a 1,000-Hz tone (the CS) and tested with a variety of tones of higher and lower pitches. As the pitches move farther away from the original CS, the strength of the CR drops off systematically. However, when the tone is an octave of the original (i.e., either 500 or 2,000 Hz), there is an increase in the CR.

## Discrimination

When an organism generalizes to a new stimulus, two things are happening. First, by responding to the new stimulus used during generalization testing, the organism demonstrates that it recognizes the similarity between the original CS and the new stimulus. Second, by displaying *diminished* responding to that new stimulus, it also tells us that it notices a difference between the two stimuli. In the second case, the organism shows **discrimination**, or *the capacity to distinguish between similar but distinct stimuli*.

Here's a true story about a talented golden retriever named Splash. Splash was very well trained to perform a number of behaviors when his name was called, as in, "Go, Splash," to fetch a ball. The sound of his name was the CS, and running after a target was the US. Repeated attempts to trick him, by yelling, "Go, Splat!" or, "Go, Crash!" or even, "Go, Spla!" resulted in predictable outcomes. Splash would start to move, but then hesitate, showing that he discriminated between the appropriate stimulus ("Splash!") and the substituted ones ("Splat!").

Conceptually, generalization and discrimination are two sides of the same coin. The more organisms show one, the less they show the other, and training can modify the balance between the two.

## Conditioned Emotional Responses: The Case of Little Albert

Before you conclude that classical conditioning is merely a sophisticated way to train your dog, let's revisit the larger principles of Pavlov's work. Classical conditioning demonstrates that durable, substantial changes in behavior can be achieved simply by setting up the proper conditions. By skillfully associating a naturally occurring US with an appropriate CS, an organism can learn to perform a variety of behaviors, often after relatively few acquisition trials. There is no reference to an organism's *wanting* to learn the behavior, *willingness* to do it, *thinking* about the situation, or *reasoning* through the available options. We don't need to consider internal and cognitive explanations to demonstrate the effects of classical conditioning: The stimuli, the eliciting circumstances, and the resulting behavior are there to be observed by one and all.

It was this kind of simplicity that appealed to behaviorists such as John B. Watson. His rallying cry for a behaviorist psychology was based, in large part, on his dissatisfaction with what he saw as mysterious, philosophical, and unverifiable internal explanations for behavior that were being offered by Wundt, Freud, and others during the early days of psychology (see Chapter 1). In fact, Watson and his followers thought that it was possible to develop general explanations of pretty much *any* behavior of *any* organism based on classical-conditioning principles.

As a step in that direction, Watson embarked on a controversial study with his research assistant Rosalie Rayner (Watson & Rayner, 1920). To support his contention that even complex behaviors were the result of conditioning, Watson enlisted the assistance of 9-month-old "Little Albert." Albert was a healthy, well-developed child, and, by Watson's assessment, "stolid and unemotional" (Watson & Rayner, 1920, p. 1). Watson wanted to see if such a child could be classically conditioned to experience a strong emotional reaction—namely, fear.

Watson presented Little Albert with a variety of stimuli: a white rat, a dog, a rabbit, various masks, and a burning newspaper. Albert's reactions in most cases were curiosity or indifference, and he showed no fear of any of the items. Watson also established that something *could* make him afraid. While Albert was watching Rayner, Watson unexpectedly struck a large steel bar with a hammer, producing a loud noise. Predictably, this caused Albert to cry, tremble, and be generally displeased.

Watson and Rayner then led Little Albert through the acquisition phase of classical conditioning. Albert was presented with a white rat. As soon as he reached out to touch it, the steel bar was struck. This pairing occurred again and again over several trials. Eventually, the sight of the rat alone caused Albert to recoil in terror, crying and clamoring to get away from it. In this situation, a US (the loud sound) was paired with a CS (the presence of the rat) such that the CS all by itself was sufficient to produce the CR (a fearful reaction). Little Albert also showed stimulus generalization. The sight of a white rabbit, a seal-fur coat, and a Santa Claus mask produced the same kinds of fear reactions in the infant.

What was Watson's goal in all this? First, he wanted to show that a relatively complex reaction could be conditioned using Pavlovian techniques. Unlike a dog returning a ball or salivating at the

John Watson and Rosalie Rayner show Little Albert an unusual bunny mask. Why doesn't the mere presence of these experimenters serve as a conditioned stimulus in itself?

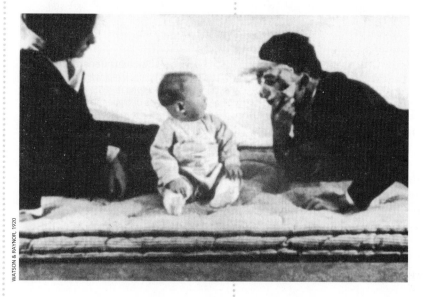

WATSON & RAYNOR, 1920

sight of food, an organism showing a fearful, anxious, and avoidant response is a bit more sophisticated. Second, he wanted to show that emotional responses such as fear and anxiety could be produced by classical conditioning and therefore need not be the product of deeper unconscious processes or early life experiences as Freud and his followers had argued (see Chapter 1). Instead, Watson proposed that fears could be learned, just like any other behavior. Third, Watson wanted to confirm that conditioning could be applied to humans as well as to other animals. Work with dogs, rats, birds, and other species had shown the utility of classical conditioning as a form of learning, but an application to humans demonstrated the universality of the principles. This bolstered Watson's view that psychology was the study of behavior and that it didn't matter if that behavior was enacted by a dog, a rat, or a little boy.

This study was controversial in its cavalier treatment of a young child, especially given that Watson and Rayner did not follow up with Albert or his mother during the ensuing years (Harris, 1979). Modern ethical guidelines that govern the treatment of research participants make sure that this kind of study could not be conducted today. At the time, however, it was consistent with a behaviorist view of psychology. As Watson (1930) summarized his position several years later:

> Give me a dozen healthy infants, well-formed, and my own specified world to bring them up in and I'll guarantee to take any one at random and train him to become any type of specialist I might select— doctor, lawyer, artist, merchant-chief and, yes, even beggar-man and thief, regardless of his talents, penchants, tendencies, abilities, vocations, and race of his ancestors. (p. 104)

In the very next sentence, Watson added: "I am going beyond my facts and I admit it, but so have the advocates of the contrary and they have been doing it for many thousands of years" (Watson, 1930, p. 104). In short, Watson was promoting a staunch view that learning and the environment were responsible for determining behavior, more so than genetics or personality, as "advocates to the contrary" might have believed at the time. Watson intended his statements to be extreme in order to shake up the young discipline of psychology and highlight the importance of acquired experiences in shaping behavior.

## A Deeper Understanding of Classical Conditioning

As a form of learning, classical conditioning could be reliably produced, it had a simple set of principles, and it had applications to real-life situations. In short, classical conditioning offered a good deal of utility for psychologists who sought to understand the mechanisms underlying learning, and it continues to do so today.

Like a lot of strong starters, though, classical conditioning has been subjected to deeper scrutiny in order to understand exactly how, when, and why it works. Let's examine three areas that give us a closer look at the mechanisms of classical conditioning.

### The Neural Elements of Classical Conditioning

Pavlov saw his research as providing insights into how the brain works. After all, he was trained in medicine, not psychology, and was a bit surprised when psychologists became excited by his findings. Recent research has clarified some of what Pavlov hoped to understand about conditioning and the brain.

The case of Little Albert and the earlier discussion of Adam, Teri, and Carly share a common theme: They are both examples of fear conditioning. In Chapter 3, you saw that the amygdala plays an important role in the experience of emotion, including fear and anxiety. So, it should come as no surprise that the amygdala, particularly an area known as the *central nucleus,* is also critical for emotional conditioning.

Consider a rat who is conditioned to a series of CS-US pairings where the CS is a tone and the US is a mild electric shock. When rats experience sudden painful stimuli in nature, they show a defensive reaction, known as *freezing,* where they crouch down and sit motionless. In addition, their autonomic nervous systems go to work: Heart rate and blood pressure increase, and various hormones associated with stress are released. When fear conditioning takes place, these two components—one behavioral and one physiological—occur, except that now they are elicited by the CS.

The central nucleus of the amygdala plays a role in producing both of these outcomes through two distinct connections with other parts of the brain. If connections linking the amygdala to a particular part of the midbrain are disrupted, the rat does not exhibit the behavioral freezing response. If the connections between the amygdala and the lateral part of the hypothalamus are severed, the autonomic responses associated with fear cease (LeDoux et al., 1988). Hence, the action of the amygdala is an essential element in fear conditioning, and its links with other areas of the brain are responsible for producing specific features of conditioning. The amygdala is involved in fear conditioning in people as well as rats and other animals (Phelps & LeDoux, 2005).

## The Cognitive Elements of Classical Conditioning

Pavlov's work was a behaviorist's dream come true. In this view, conditioning is something that *happens to* a dog, a rat, or a person, apart from what the organism thinks about the conditioning situation. However, eventually someone was bound to ask an important question: *Why didn't Pavlov's dogs salivate to Pavlov?* After all, he was instrumental in the arrival of the CS. If Pavlov delivered the food to the dogs, why didn't they form an association with him? Indeed, if Watson was present whenever the unpleasant US was sounded, why didn't Little Albert come to fear *him*?

Maybe classical conditioning isn't such an unthinking, mechanical process as behaviorists originally had assumed (Rescorla, 1966, 1988). Somehow, Pavlov's dogs were sensitive to the fact that Pavlov was not a *reliable* indicator of the arrival of food. Pavlov was linked with the arrival of food, but he was also linked with other activities that had nothing to do with food, including checking on the apparatus, bringing the dog from the kennel to the laboratory, and standing around and talking with his assistants. These observations suggest that perhaps cognitive components are involved in classical conditioning after all.

Robert Rescorla and Allan Wagner (1972) were the first to theorize that classical conditioning only occurs when an animal has learned to set up an *expectation*. The sound of a tone, because of its systematic pairing with food, served to set up this cognitive state for the laboratory dogs; Pavlov, because of the lack of any reliable link with food, did not. In fact, in situations such as this, many responses are actually being conditioned. When the tone sounds, the dogs also wag their tails, make begging sounds, and look toward the food source (Jenkins et al., 1978). In short, what is really happening is something like the situation shown in **FIGURE 6.5**. (See also the Hot Science box on the facing page, which explains one dog's remarkable learning abilities.)

The *Rescorla-Wagner model* introduced a cognitive component that accounted for a variety of classical-conditioning phenomena that were difficult to understand from a simple behaviorist point of view. For example, the model predicted that conditioning would be easier when the CS was an *unfamiliar* event than when it was familiar. The reason is that familiar events, being familiar, already have expectations associated

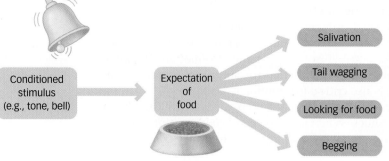

**Figure 6.5**
**Expectation in Classical Conditioning** In the Rescorla-Wagner model of classical conditioning, a CS serves to set up an expectation. The expectation in turn leads to an array of behaviors associated with the presence of the CS.

Conditioned stimulus (e.g., tone, bell) → Expectation of food → Salivation, Tail wagging, Looking for food, Begging

DON MASON/CORBIS

## { HOT SCIENCE } Can Animals Learn Language?

THE SOUND TRACK FOR THE CHILDREN'S film *Dr. Doolittle* featured a rousing little ditty called "Talk to the Animals," which crescendoed in the line, "And they could squeak and squawk and speak and talk to us!" Toe-tapping fun for many a 6-year-old, to be sure, but for the rest of us, the idea that an animal can learn a language seems a little dubious.

Nonetheless, a recent study has produced the fascinating finding that Rico, a border collie living in Leipzig, Germany, may have a remarkable word-learning ability (Kaminski, Call, & Fischer, 2004). Rico appears capable of learning new words using a process called *fast mapping,* which refers to the burst of learning that toddlers go though as they acquire the meanings of the tens of thousands of words that will make up their mature vocabulary (see Chapter 7). One way that fast mapping works is by simple association. A child is presented with a new object and told that it's called a "mouse." The child links the sound with the object and the word is learned. A different technique is based on the ability to make inferences. For example, suppose a child already knows the meaning of the words *dog* and *cat*. While on a walk, Dad points to a group of three animals containing a dog and cat and an unknown creature and says, "Oh, look at the duck." The child immediately infers that this new word is the name of the unfamiliar creature.

Psychologists have long known that some animals are capable of the first kind of learning, although their vocabularies tend to be rather limited. Rico, however, has shown that he knows the names of over 200 objects and can fetch any of them on command, a number that is far beyond anything seen before in dogs and matched only by a few rather talented chimps, dolphins, and parrots. Rico, by the way, only understands German, so if you want him to fetch a flower, you must ask him for a *Blume*. However, it is not clear whether Rico really has a cognitive sense that *Blume means* "flower" or whether he simply has learned a simple associative link between the sound and the object and embedded them in a game of go fetch.

One way to answer this question is to see if he can learn by inference, as children do. To test this, a novel item was placed in a room along with nine familiar objects. Rico was then told to fetch using the name of

**Rico—one smart collie.**

REUTERS/MANUELA HARTLING/NEWSCOM

the unknown object. Rico returned with the unfamiliar object on 7 out of 10 trials. Moreover, when he was tested for these newly learned objects 4 weeks later, he was able to pick them out of a display containing 4 well-known objects and 4 objects he had never seen before on 3 of 6 trials. That's a performance level comparable to that of an average 3-year-old child.

Before you trade in your 3-year-old nephew for a border collie, realize that Rico is far from developing into a native German *speaker.* Your nephew at least stands a good chance of developing real language skills someday. Nonetheless, Rico's impressive performance has three implications. First, it indicates that fast mapping may not be a strictly human ability. We're all pretty amazed when toddlers add word after word to their vocabularies in short order and rightly so. But save some of your amazement: Other species may have the same capacity. Second, the results imply that the ability to attach meaning to an arbitrary sound evolved earlier than and independently of the ability to speak. Rico's not going to speak anytime soon, except for maybe a "voof" in response to the familiar, "Speak, boy!" He does, however, have the ability to match meanings with sounds.

Finally, the results suggest that the basic perceptual and cognitive processes that underlie the learning of a language are a good deal older than believed, evolutionarily speaking. Understanding concepts is a building block of learning language, and it's a foundation that Rico sits proudly on.

---

with them, making new conditioning difficult. For example, Adam didn't recoil in horror every time he saw his daughter Carly, even though she was present during the acquisition phase of 9/11/2001. The familiarity of Carly in multiple contexts made her, thankfully, a poor CS for Adam's fear conditioning. In short, classical conditioning might appear to be a primitive and unthinking process, but it is actually quite sophisticated and incorporates a significant cognitive element.

### The Evolutionary Elements of Classical Conditioning

In addition to this cognitive component, evolutionary mechanisms also play an important role in classical conditioning. As you learned in Chapter 1, evolution and natural selection go hand in hand with adaptiveness: Behaviors that are adaptive allow an organism to survive and thrive in its environment. In the case of classical conditioning, psychologists began to appreciate how this type of learning could have adaptive value. Research exploring this adaptiveness has focused on three main areas: conditioned food aversions, conditioned food preferences, and biological preparedness.

Under certain conditions, people may develop food aversions. This serving of hummus looks inviting and probably tastes delicious, but at least one psychologist avoids it like the plague.

Rats can be difficult to poison because of learned taste aversions, which are an evolutionarily adaptive element of classical conditioning. Here a worker tries his best in the sewers of France.

Food aversions can occur for quite sensible reasons, as when Aunt Dolly offers you her famous eel-and-kidney pie and you politely decline. Food aversions can also be classically conditioned. A psychology professor was once on a job interview in Southern California, and his hosts took him to lunch at a Middle Eastern restaurant. Suffering from a case of bad hummus, he was up all night long. Needless to say, he was in pretty rough shape the following day, and he didn't get the job offer.

This colleague developed a lifelong aversion to hummus. Why would one bad incident taint food preferences in such a lasting way? On the face of it, this looks like a case of classical conditioning. The hummus was the CS, its apparent toxicity was the US, and the resulting gastric distress was the UR. The UR (the nausea) became linked to the once-neutral CS (the hummus) and became a CR (an aversion to hummus). However, there are several unusual aspects in this case.

For starters, all of the psychologist's hosts also ate the hummus, yet none of them reported feeling ill. It's not clear, then, what the US was; it couldn't have been anything that was actually in the food. What's more, the time between the hummus and the distress was several hours; usually a response follows a stimulus fairly quickly. Most baffling, this aversion was cemented with a single acquisition trial. Usually it takes several pairings of a CS and US to establish learning.

These peculiarities are not so peculiar from an evolutionary perspective. What seems like a mindbug is actually the manifestation of an adaptive process. Any species that forages or consumes a variety of foods needs to develop a mechanism by which it can learn to avoid any food that once made it ill. To have adaptive value, this mechanism should have several properties.

First, there should be rapid learning that occurs in perhaps one or two trials. If learning takes more trials than this, the animal could die from eating a toxic substance. Second, conditioning should be able to take place over very long intervals, perhaps up to several hours. Toxic substances often don't cause illness immediately, so the organism would need to form an association between food and the illness over a longer term. Third, the organism should develop the aversion to the smell or taste of the food rather than its ingestion. It's more adaptive to reject a potentially toxic substance based on smell alone than it is to ingest it. Finally, learned aversions should occur more often with novel foods than familiar ones. It is not adaptive for an animal to develop an aversion to everything it has eaten on the particular day it got sick. Our psychologist friend didn't develop an aversion to the Coke he drank with lunch or the scrambled eggs he had for breakfast that day; however, the sight and smell of hummus do make him uneasy.

John Garcia and his colleagues illustrated the adaptiveness of classical conditioning in a series of studies with rats (Garcia & Koelling, 1966). They used a variety of CSs (visual, auditory, tactile, taste, and smell) and several different USs (injection of a toxic substance, radiation) that caused nausea and vomiting hours later. The researchers found weak or no conditioning when the CS was a visual, auditory, or tactile stimulus, but a strong food aversion developed with stimuli that have a distinct taste and smell. In one experiment, they presented water accompanied by bright lights and tinkling sounds as the CS, and little or no conditioned aversion was observed. However, if the CS was water laced with a harmless but distinctly flavored novel substance (such as strawberry), the researchers found a strong aversion to the smell and taste of strawberries. Moreover, if the CS was a familiar food that the animal had eaten before, the aversion was much less likely to develop. Other researchers have shown that these food aversions can be acquired even when the organism is unconscious. Rats that were administered a toxic substance while under total anesthesia developed a taste aversion to foods they had eaten earlier when awake (Rabin & Rabin, 1984).

This research had an interesting application. It led to the development of a technique for dealing with an unanticipated side effect of radiation and chemotherapy: Cancer patients who experience nausea from their treatments often develop aversions to foods they ate before the therapy. Broberg and Bernstein (1987) reasoned that, if the findings with rats generalized to humans, a simple technique should minimize the negative consequences of this effect. They gave their patients an unusual food (coconut or root-beer-flavored candy) at the end of the last meal before undergoing treatment. Sure enough, the conditioned food aversions that the patients developed were overwhelmingly for one of the unusual flavors and not for any of the other foods in the meal. Other than any root beer or coconut fanatics among the sample, patients were spared developing aversions to more common foods that they are more likely to eat. Understanding the basis of mindbugs can have practical as well as theoretical value.

Other research has revealed a parallel mechanism, one that allows organisms to learn to *prefer* particular substances over others (Sclafani, 1995). In one study, rats were given flavored water (e.g., cherry). As they drank, a nutritive substance (such as sucrose) was delivered directly into their stomachs. On other occasions, another flavor (e.g., orange) was used, but it was paired with the delivery of water to their stomachs. After only a few trials, the rats developed a strong preference for the flavor paired with sucrose over that paired with water. The effect also occurs with substances other than sucrose: Recent work shows that conditioned food preferences can be produced by sources of fat, such as corn oil and safflower oil (Ackroff, Lucas, & Sclafani, 2005).

Studies such as these suggest that evolution has provided each species with a kind of **biological preparedness**, *a propensity for learning particular kinds of associations over others*, so that some behaviors are relatively easy to condition in some species but not others. For example, the taste and smell stimuli that produce food aversions in rats do not work with most species of birds. Birds depend primarily on visual cues for finding food and are relatively insensitive to taste and smell. However, as you might guess, it is relatively easy to produce a food aversion in birds using an unfamiliar visual stimulus as the CS, such as a brightly colored food (Wilcoxon, Dragoin, & Kral, 1971). Indeed, most researchers agree that conditioning works best with stimuli that are biologically relevant to the organism (Domjan, 2005).

Humans also have biological predispositions for conditioning, as in the case of phobias. As you'll see in Chapter 13, phobias are strong, irrational, emotional reactions to some stimulus or situation. Early behaviorists, such as Watson, viewed them as the result of simple classical conditioning: A CS is paired with a threatening US and that's that. However, research on learned aversions and preferences suggests that his perspective may have been a bit naive. Humans do indeed suffer from a variety of phobias, but not all phobias occur with the same frequency: Some phobias are common, whereas others are quite rare, and some are relatively mild, whereas others can be debilitating. Virtually everyone has cut himself or herself with a kitchen knife, yet phobias associated with knives are so rare that they are almost nonexistent. But fear of the dark and fear of heights are common and often show up in individuals who have never had any particularly unpleasant experiences associated with the dark or with heights.

Humans have a biological preparedness to develop phobias of situations that, in our evolutionary past, were potentially dangerous to survival (Ohman & Mineka, 2001). A species that is relatively physically vulnerable and has poor night vision needs to be wary of predators that lurk in the night. A species that spends a good bit of time in trees will live longer if it develops a healthy appreciation of the dangers of falling. Hence, we are biologically prepared for easy classical conditioning to fear circumstances such as darkness or heights that, ironically, are no longer as life threatening as they were for our ancestors.

**In summary,** classical conditioning can be thought of as an exercise in pairing a neutral stimulus with a meaningful event or stimulus. Ivan Pavlov's initial work paired a neutral tone (a conditioned stimulus) with a meaningful act: the presentation of food to a hungry animal (an unconditioned stimulus). As he and others demonstrated, the pairing of a CS and US during the acquisition phase of classical conditioning eventually allows the CS all by itself to elicit a response called a conditioned response (CR).

Classical conditioning was embraced by behaviorists such as John B. Watson, who viewed it as providing a foundation for a model of human behavior. As a behaviorist, Watson believed that no higher-level functions, such as thinking or awareness, needed

**BIOLOGICAL PREPAREDNESS** A propensity for learning particular kinds of associations over others.

Some phobias in humans might be the result of biological predispositions. Fear of the dark is one example. In fact, part of the synopsis for this horror movie states *"Fear of the Dark is a tightly woven tale that taps into our universal fear of what lies hidden in the dark. It's what scares you the most."*

to be invoked to understand behavior. As later researchers showed, however, the underlying mechanism of classical conditioning turned out to be more complex (and more interesting) than the simple association between a CS and a US. As Pavlov assumed, the brain is involved in many types of conditioning, as in the case of fear conditioning and the action of the amygdala. Researchers discovered that even simple species set up expectations and are sensitive to the degree to which the CS functions as a genuine predictor of the US, indicating that classical conditioning involves some degree of cognition. The evolutionary aspects of classical conditioning show that each species is biologically predisposed to acquire particular CS-US associations based on its evolutionary history. In short, classical conditioning is not an arbitrary mechanism that merely forms associations. Rather, it is a sophisticated mechanism that evolved precisely because it has adaptive value. ■ ■

# Operant Conditioning: Reinforcements from the Environment

The learned behaviors you've seen so far share a common feature: They all occurred beyond the voluntary control of the organism. Most animals don't voluntarily salivate or feel spasms of anxiety; rather, these animals exhibit these responses involuntarily during the conditioning process. In fact, these reflexlike behaviors make up only a small portion of our behavioral repertoires. The remainder are behaviors that we voluntarily perform, behaviors that modify and change the environment around us. The study of classical conditioning is the study of behaviors that are *reactive*. We turn now to a different form of learning: **operant conditioning**, *a type of learning in which the consequences of an organism's behavior determine whether it will be repeated in the future.* The study of operant conditioning is the exploration of behaviors that are *active*.

## The Early Days: The Law of Effect

The study of how active behavior affects the environment began at about the same time as classical conditioning. In fact, Edward L. Thorndike (1874–1949) first examined active behaviors back in the 1890s, before Pavlov published his findings. Thorndike's research focused on *instrumental behaviors,* that is, behavior that required an organism to *do* something, solve a problem, or otherwise manipulate elements of its environment (Thorndike, 1898). For example, Thorndike completed several experiments using a puzzle box, which was a wooden crate with a door that would open when a concealed lever was moved in the right way (see **FIGURE 6.6**). A hungry cat

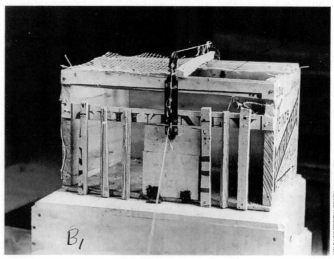

**Figure 6.6 Thorndike's Puzzle Box** In Thorndike's original experiments, food was placed just outside the door of the puzzle box, where the cat could see it. If the cat triggered the appropriate lever, it would open the door and let the cat out.

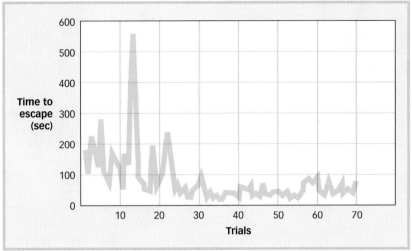

**Figure 6.7** **The Law of Effect**
Thorndike's cats displayed trial-and-error behavior when trying to escape from the puzzle box. They made lots of irrelevant movements and actions until, over time, they discovered the solution. Once they figured out what behavior was instrumental in opening the latch, they stopped all other ineffective behaviors and escaped from the box faster and faster.

placed in a puzzle box would try various behaviors to get out—scratching at the door, meowing loudly, sniffing the inside of the box, putting its paw through the openings—but only one behavior opened the door and led to food: tripping the lever in just the right way. After this happened, Thorndike placed the cat back in the box for another round. Don't get the wrong idea. Thorndike probably *really liked* cats. Far from teasing them, he was after an important behavioral principle.

Fairly quickly, the cats became quite skilled at triggering the lever for their release. Notice what's going on. At first, the cat enacts any number of likely (but ultimately ineffective) behaviors, but only one behavior leads to freedom and food. That behavior is *instrumental* for the cat in achieving the desired outcome: escape from the box and access to food. Over time, the ineffective behaviors become less and less frequent, and the one instrumental behavior (going right for the latch) becomes more frequent (see **FIGURE 6.7**). From these observations, Thorndike developed the **law of effect**, which states that *behaviors that are followed by a "satisfying state of affairs" tend to be repeated and those that produce an "unpleasant state of affairs" are less likely to be repeated.*

The circumstances that Thorndike used to study learning were very different from those in studies of classical conditioning. Remember that in classical-conditioning experiments, the US occurred on every training trial no matter what the animal did. Pavlov delivered food to the dog whether it salivated or not. But in Thorndike's work, the behavior of the animal determined what happened next. If the behavior was "correct" (i.e., the latch was triggered), the animal was rewarded with food. Incorrect behaviors produced no results and the animal was stuck in the box until it performed the correct behavior. Although different from classical conditioning, Thorndike's work resonated with most behaviorists at the time: It was still observable, quantifiable, and free from explanations involving the mind (Galef, 1998).

Oddly, John B. Watson, the founder of behaviorism, originally rejected Thorndike's ideas about the potential of rewards to influence behavior. Watson thought this was some kind of magic, possibly akin to some cognitive explanation of "wanting" or "willing" to perform a behavior. It took a different kind of behaviorist promoting a different kind of behaviorism to develop Thorndike's ideas into a unified explanation of learning.

## Reinforcement, Punishment, and the Development of Operant Conditioning

Several decades after Thorndike's work, B. F. Skinner (1904–90) coined the term **operant behavior** to refer to *behavior that an organism produces that has some impact on the environment.* In Skinner's system, all of these emitted behaviors "operated" on the environment in some manner, and the environment responded by providing events that

**OPERANT CONDITIONING** A type of learning in which the consequences of an organism's behavior determine whether it will be repeated in the future.

**LAW OF EFFECT** The principle that behaviors that are followed by a "satisfying state of affairs" tend to be repeated and those that produce an "unpleasant state of affairs" are less likely to be repeated.

**OPERANT BEHAVIOR** Behavior that an organism produces that has some impact on the environment.

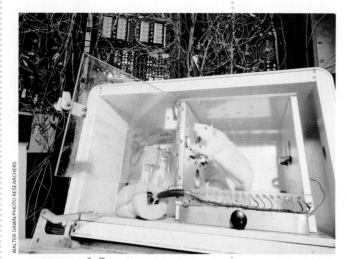

**Figure 6.8 Skinner Box** In a typical Skinner box, or *operant conditioning chamber,* a rat, pigeon, or other suitably sized animal is placed in this environment and observed during learning trials that use operant conditioning principles.

either strengthened those behaviors (i.e., they *reinforced* them) or made them less likely to occur (i.e., they *punished* them). Skinner's elegantly simple observation was that most organisms do *not* behave like a dog in a harness, passively waiting to receive food no matter what the circumstances. Rather, most organisms are like cats in a box, actively engaging the environment in which they find themselves to reap rewards (Skinner, 1938, 1953).

In order to study operant behavior scientifically, Skinner developed a variation on Thorndike's puzzle box. The *operant chamber,* or *Skinner box,* as it is commonly called, shown in **FIGURE 6.8**, allows a researcher to study the behavior of small organisms in a controlled environment. In his early experiments, Skinner preferred using rats, but he quickly shifted to using pigeons. Pigeons turned out to be easily trained; they display remarkable persistence, they need relatively little sleep, and they will work for the most meager of rewards. And, being a staunch behaviorist, Skinner assumed that studying one organism was as good as studying another. With a focus on behavior and no recourse for mental processes to get in the way, Skinner could easily conduct research with participants that were readily available and easy to manage.

Skinner's approach to the study of learning focused on *reinforcement* and *punishment.* These terms, which have commonsense connotations, turned out to be rather difficult to define. For example, some people love roller coasters, whereas others find them horrifying; the chance to go on one will be reinforcing for one group but punishing for another. Dogs can be trained with praise and a good belly rub—procedures that are nearly useless for most cats. Skinner settled on a "neutral" definition that would characterize each term by its effect on behavior. Therefore, a **reinforcer** is *any stimulus or event that functions to increase the likelihood of the behavior that led to it,* whereas a **punisher** is *any stimulus or event that functions to decrease the likelihood of the behavior that led to it.*

Whether a particular stimulus acts as a reinforcer or punisher depends in part on whether it increases or decreases the likelihood of a behavior. Presenting food is usually reinforcing, producing an increase in the behavior that led to it; removing food is often punishing, leading to a decrease in the behavior. Turning on an electric shock is typically punishing (the behavior that led to it); turning it off is rewarding (and increases the behavior that led to it).

To keep these possibilities distinct, Skinner used the term *positive* for situations in which a stimulus was presented and *negative* for situations in which it was removed. Consequently, there is *positive reinforcement* (where something desirable is presented) and *negative reinforcement* (where something undesirable is removed), as well as *positive punishment* (where something unpleasant is administered) and *negative punishment* (where something desirable is removed). Here the words *positive* and *negative* mean, respectively,

**REINFORCER** Any stimulus or event that functions to increase the likelihood of the behavior that led to it.

**PUNISHER** Any stimulus or event that functions to decrease the likelihood of the behavior that led to it.

B. F. Skinner with some of his many research participants.

| Table 6.1 | Reinforcement and Punishment | |
|---|---|---|
| | **Increases the Likelihood of Behavior** | **Decreases the Likelihood of Behavior** |
| **Stimulus is presented** | Positive reinforcement | Positive punishment |
| **Stimulus is removed** | Negative reinforcement | Negative punishment |

something that is *added* or something that is *taken away.* As you can see from **TABLE 6.1**, positive and negative reinforcement increase the likelihood of the behavior and positive and negative punishment decrease the likelihood of the behavior.

These distinctions can be confusing at first; after all, "negative reinforcement" and "punishment" both sound like they should be "bad" and produce the same type of behavior. There are a couple of ways to keep track of these distinctions. First, remember that *positive* and *negative* simply mean *presentation* or *removal,* and the terms don't necessarily mean "good" or "bad" as they do in everyday speech. Negative reinforcement, for example, involves something pleasant; it's the *removal* of something unpleasant, like a shock, and the absence of a shock is indeed pleasant.

Second, bear in mind that reinforcement is generally more effective than punishment in promoting learning. There are many reasons (Gershoff, 2002), but one reason is this: Punishment signals that an unacceptable behavior has occurred, but it doesn't specify what should be done instead. Spanking a young child for starting to run into a busy street certainly stops the behavior—which, in this case, is probably a good idea. But it doesn't promote any kind of learning about the *desired* behavior. Should the child never venture into a street, wait for an adult, hold someone's hand, walk slowly into the busy street, or what? A more effective strategy would be to skillfully administer reinforcement for desired behaviors. Each time the child waits for an adult and holds that person's hand, for example, reinforcement would be given, perhaps in the form of verbal praise ("That's the right thing to do!"), a warm smile, a big hug, or the presentation of some other stimulus that the child finds desirable. Remember the law of effect: The intended behavior of waiting for an adult should become more frequent, and unwanted behaviors such as running into the street should decrease.

Negative reinforcement involves the removal of something undesirable from the environment. When Daddy stops the car, he gets a reward: His little monster stops screaming. However, from the perspective of the child, this is positive reinforcement. The child's tantrum results in something positive added to the environment—stopping for a snack.

## Primary and Secondary Reinforcement and Punishment

Reinforcers and punishers often gain their functions from basic biological mechanisms. A pigeon who pecks at a target in a Skinner box is usually reinforced with food pellets, just as an animal who learns to escape a mild electric shock has avoided the punishment of tingly paws. Food, comfort, shelter, or warmth are examples of *primary reinforcers* because they help satisfy biological needs. However, the vast majority of reinforcers or punishers in our daily lives have little to do with biology: Handshakes, verbal approval, an encouraging grin, a bronze trophy, or money all serve powerful reinforcing functions, yet none of them taste very good or help keep you warm at night. The point is, we learn to perform a lot of behaviors based on reinforcements that have little or nothing to do with biological satisfaction.

These *secondary reinforcers* derive their effectiveness from their associations with primary reinforcers through classical conditioning. For

*"Oh, not bad. The light comes on, I press the bar, they write me a check. How about you?"*

Secondary reinforcers often aren't valuable in themselves. After all, money is just pieces of paper—as illustrated by this virtually worthless currency that was used during the German hyperinflation in 1923. The reinforcing quality of secondary reinforcers derives from their association with primary reinforcers.

example, money starts out as a neutral CS that, through its association with primary USs like acquiring food or shelter, takes on a conditioned emotional element. Flashing lights, originally a neutral CS, acquire powerful negative elements through association with a speeding ticket and a fine. Under normal circumstances, as long as the CS-US link is maintained, the secondary reinforcers and punishers can be used to modify and control behavior. If the links are broken (that is, an extinction procedure is introduced), they typically lose these functions. Money that is no longer backed by a solvent government quickly loses its reinforcing capacity and becomes worth no more than the paper it is printed on.

## The Neutrality of Reinforcers

Some reinforcers are more effective than others, but this is not always easy to discern. However, as David Premack (1962) pointed out, there is a simple and practical way to check. The *Premack principle* states that discerning which of two activities someone would rather engage in means that the preferred activity can be used to reinforce a nonpreferred one. For example, many children prefer to spend more time watching TV than doing their homework. As many parents have discovered, the preferred activity can be a useful reinforcer for the performance of the nonpreferred activity: No TV until the homework's done! Of course, this reinforcement will not work for all children. There are some who prefer doing their homework to watching TV; for these children, the effectiveness of the reinforcers will be reversed. In short, it's important to establish a hierarchy of behaviors for an individual in order to determine which kinds of events might be maximally reinforcing.

The Premack principle makes it clear why Skinner's neutral definitions of reinforcement and punishment make sense. A stimulus or event will be *relatively* reinforcing based on a host of factors, many of which are specific to the individual. What's more, the effectiveness of particular stimuli can be manipulated. For example, it seems pretty obvious that water can be used to reinforce a thirsty rat for running in an exercise wheel. However, the relationship between these two activities can be reversed. Depriving a rat of exercise for several days but allowing it free access to water creates a situation in which the rat will now drink in order to be given the opportunity to spend time running in the wheel.

## Some Limiting Conditions of Reinforcement

Any card-carrying behaviorist during the 1930s through 1960s would tell you that providing rewards for performing a behavior should make that behavior more likely to occur again in the future. Unfortunately, this isn't always the case, and sometimes the presentation of rewards can cause the exact opposite effect: a decrease in performing the behavior. This mindbug occurs because extrinsic reinforcement—rewards that come from external sources—doesn't always capture the reasons why people engage in behavior in the first place. Many times people engage in activities for intrinsic rewards, such as the pure pleasure of simply doing the behavior.

The **overjustification effect,** *when external rewards can undermine the intrinsic satisfaction of performing a behavior,* captures this mind-bug for examination. In one study nursery school children were given colored pens and paper and were asked to draw whatever they wanted (Lepper & Greene, 1978). For a young child, this is a pretty satisfying event: The pleasures of drawing and creative expression are rewarding all by themselves. Some children, though, received a "Good Player Award" for their efforts at artwork, whereas other children did not. As you may have guessed, the Good Players spent more time at the task than the other children. As you may not have guessed, when the experimenters stopped handing out the Good Player certificates to the first group, the amount of time the children spent drawing dropped significantly below that of the group that never received any external reinforcements.

This was a case of *over*justification, or too much reinforcement. The children who received the extrinsic reinforcement of the certificate came to view their task as one that gets rewards. The children who didn't receive the extrinsic reinforcement continued to perform the task for its own sake. When the extrinsic rewards were later removed, children in the first group found little reason to continue engaging in the task. Other researchers have found that when people are paid for tasks such as writing poetry, drawing, or finding solutions to economic and business problems, they tend to produce *less* creative solutions when monetary rewards are offered (Amabile, 1996). You can weigh in on these issues in the Where Do You Stand? box at the end of this chapter.

Drawing pictures is fun. Drawing pictures for external rewards might, oddly enough, make drawing pictures seem like much less fun.

## The Basic Principles of Operant Conditioning

After establishing how reinforcement and punishment produced learned behavior, Skinner and other scientists began to expand the parameters of operant conditioning. This took the form of investigating some phenomena that were well known in classical conditioning (such as discrimination, generalization, and extinction) as well as some practical applications, such as how best to administer reinforcement or how to produce complex learned behaviors in an organism. Let's look at some of these basic principles of operant conditioning.

### Discrimination, Generalization, and the Importance of Context

Here are some things you probably haven't given much thought to: We all take off our clothes at least once a day, but usually not in public. We scream at rock concerts but not in libraries. We say, "Please pass the gravy," at the dinner table but not in a classroom. Although these observations may seem like nothing more than common sense, Thorndike was the first to recognize the underlying message: Learning takes place *in contexts,* not in the free range of any plausible situation. As Skinner rephrased it later, most behavior is under *stimulus control,* which develops when a particular response only occurs when the appropriate stimulus is present.

It's easy to demonstrate this simple truth. If a pigeon is reinforced for pecking a key whenever a particular tone is sounded but never reinforced if the tone is absent, that tone will quickly become a *discriminative stimulus,* or a stimulus that is associated with reinforcement for key pecking in that situation. Pigeons, reinforced under these conditions, will quickly learn to engage in vigorous key pressing whenever the tone sounds but cease if it is turned off. The tone sets the occasion for the pigeon to emit the operant response, much like being at a rock concert sets the occasion for your loud, raucous behavior.

Stimulus control, perhaps not surprisingly, shows both discrimination and generalization effects similar to those we saw with classical conditioning. To demonstrate this, researchers used either a painting by the French Impressionist Claude Monet or one of Pablo Picasso's paintings from his Cubist period for the discriminative stimulus

**OVERJUSTIFICATION EFFECT**
Circumstances when external rewards can undermine the intrinsic satisfaction of performing a behavior.

In research on stimulus control, participants trained with Picasso paintings, such as the one on the left, responded to other paintings by Picasso or even to paintings by other Cubists. Participants trained with Monet paintings, such as the one on the right, responded to other paintings by Monet or by other French Impressionists. Interestingly, the participants in this study were pigeons.

TATE GALLERY, LONDON/ART RESOURCE, NY

TATE GALLERY, LONDON/ART RESOURCE, NY

(Watanabe, Sakamoto, & Wakita, 1995). Participants in the experiment were only reinforced if they responded when the appropriate painting was present. After training, the participants discriminated appropriately; those trained with the Monet painting responded when other paintings by Monet were presented and those trained with a Picasso painting reacted when other Cubist paintings by Picasso were shown. And as you might expect, Monet-trained participants did not react to Picassos and Picasso-trained participants did not respond to Monets. What's more, the research participants showed that they could generalize *across* painters as long as they were from the same artistic tradition. Those trained with Monet responded appropriately when shown paintings by Auguste Renoir (another French Impressionist), and the Picasso-trained participants responded to artwork by Cubist painter Henri Matisse, despite never having seen these paintings before. If these results don't seem particularly startling to you, it might help to know that the research participants were pigeons who were trained to key-peck to these various works of art. Stimulus control, and its ability to foster stimulus discrimination and stimulus generalization, is effective even if the stimulus has no meaning to the respondent.

### Extinction

As in classical conditioning, operant behavior undergoes extinction when the reinforcements stop. Pigeons cease pecking at a key if food is no longer presented following the behavior. You wouldn't put more money into a vending machine if it failed to give you its promised candy bar or soda. Warm smiles that are greeted with scowls and frowns will quickly disappear. On the surface, extinction of operant behavior looks like that of classical conditioning: The response rate drops off fairly rapidly and, if a rest period is provided, spontaneous recovery is typically seen.

However, there is an important difference. In classical conditioning, the US occurs on every trial no matter what the organism does. In operant conditioning, the reinforcements only occur when the proper response has been made, and they don't always occur even then. Not every trip into the forest produces nuts for a squirrel, auto salespeople don't sell to everyone who takes a test drive, and researchers run many experiments that do not work out and never get published. Yet these behaviors don't weaken and gradually extinguish. In fact, they typically become stronger and more resilient. Curiously, then, extinction is a bit more complicated in operant conditioning than in classical conditioning because it depends in part on how often reinforcement is received. In fact, this principle is an important cornerstone of operant conditioning that we'll examine next.

**FIXED INTERVAL SCHEDULE (FI)**
An operant conditioning principle in which reinforcements are presented at fixed time periods, provided that the appropriate response is made.

**VARIABLE INTERVAL SCHEDULE (VI)** An operant conditioning principle in which behavior is reinforced based on an average time that has expired since the last reinforcement.

## Schedules of Reinforcement

Skinner was intrigued by the apparent paradox surrounding extinction, and in his autobiography, he described how he began studying it (Skinner, 1979). He was laboriously rolling ground rat meal and water to make food pellets to reinforce the rats in his early experiments. It occurred to him that perhaps he could save time and effort by not giving his rats a pellet for every bar press but instead delivering food on some intermittent schedule. The results of this hunch were dramatic. Not only did the rats continue bar pressing but they also shifted the rate and pattern of bar pressing depending on the timing and frequency of the presentation of the reinforcers. Unlike classical conditioning, where the sheer *number* of learning trials was important, in operant conditioning the *pattern* with which reinforcements appeared was crucial.

Skinner explored dozens of what came to be known as *schedules of reinforcement* (Ferster & Skinner, 1957) (see **FIGURE 6.9**). The two most important are *interval schedules,* based on the time intervals between reinforcements, and *ratio schedules,* based on the ratio of responses to reinforcements.

Under a **fixed interval schedule (FI)**, *reinforcements are presented at fixed time periods, provided that the appropriate response is made.* For example, on a 2-minute fixed interval schedule, a response will be reinforced, but only after 2 minutes have expired since the last reinforcement. Rats and pigeons in Skinner boxes produce predictable patterns of behavior under these schedules. They show little responding right after the presentation of reinforcement, but as the next time interval draws to a close, they show a burst of responding. If this pattern seems odd to you, consider that virtually every undergraduate has behaved exactly like this. They do relatively little work until just before the upcoming exam, then engage in a burst of reading and studying.

Under a **variable interval schedule (VI)**, a *behavior is reinforced based on an average time that has expired since the last reinforcement.* For example, on a 2-minute variable interval schedule, responses will be reinforced every 2 minutes *on average* but not after each 2-minute period. Variable interval schedules typically produce steady, consistent responding because the time until the next reinforcement is less predictable. Variable interval schedules are not encountered that often in real life, although one example might be radio promotional giveaways. A radio station might advertise that they give

Students cramming for an exam often show the same kind of behavior as pigeons being reinforced under a fixed interval schedule.

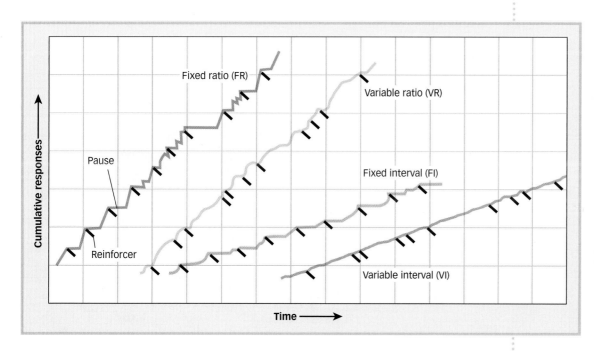

**Figure 6.9** **Reinforcement Schedules** Different schedules of reinforcement produce different rates of responding. These lines represent the amount of responding that occurs under each type of reinforcement. The black slash marks indicate when reinforcement was administered. Notice that ratio schedules tend to produce higher rates of responding than do interval schedules, as shown by the steeper lines for fixed ratio and variable ratio reinforcement.

Radio station promotions and giveaways often follow a variable interval schedule of reinforcement.

away concert tickets every hour, which is true, but the DJs are likely to say, "Sometime this hour, I'll be giving away a pair of tickets to see the Arctic Monkeys in concert!" which is also true. The reinforcement—getting the tickets—might average out to once an hour across the span of the broadcasting day, but the presentation of the reinforcement is variable: It might come early in the 10:00 o'clock hour, later in the 11:00 o'clock hour, immediately into the 12:00 o'clock hour, and so on.

Both fixed interval schedules and variable interval schedules tend to produce slow, methodical responding because the reinforcements follow a time scale that is independent of how many responses occur. It doesn't matter if a rat on a fixed interval schedule presses a bar 1 time during a 2-minute period or 100 times: The reinforcing food pellet won't drop out of the shoot until 2 minutes have elapsed, regardless of the number of responses.

Under a **fixed ratio schedule (FR)**, *reinforcement is delivered after a specific number of responses have been made.* One schedule might present reinforcement after every fourth response, a different schedule might present reinforcement after every 20 responses; the special case of presenting reinforcement after *each* response is called *continuous reinforcement,* and it's what drove Skinner to investigate these schedules in the first place. Notice that in each example, the ratio of reinforcements to responses, once set, remains fixed.

There are many situations in which people, sometimes unknowingly, find themselves being reinforced on a fixed ratio schedule: Book clubs often give you a "freebie" after a set number of regular purchases, pieceworkers get paid after making a fixed number of products, and some credit card companies return to their customers a percent of the amount charged. When a fixed ratio schedule is operating, it is possible, in principle, to know exactly when the next reinforcer is due. A laundry pieceworker on a 10-response fixed ratio schedule who has just washed and ironed the ninth shirt knows that payment is coming after the next shirt is done.

Under a **variable ratio schedule (VR)**, *the delivery of reinforcement is based on a particular average number of responses.* For example, if a laundry worker was following a 10-response variable ratio schedule instead of a fixed ratio schedule, she or he would still be paid, on average, for every 10 shirts washed and ironed but not for *each* 10th shirt. Most people who work in sales find themselves operating under variable ratio schedules. Real estate brokers won't sell every house they show but will establish an average ratio of houses shown to houses sold. Slot machines in a modern casino pay off on variable ratio schedules that are determined by the random number generator that controls the play of the machines. A casino might advertise that they pay off on "every 100 pulls on average," which could be true. However, one player might hit a jackpot after 3 pulls on a slot machine, whereas another player might not hit until after 80 pulls. The ratio of responses to reinforcements is variable, which probably helps casinos stay in business.

These pieceworkers in a textile factory get paid following a fixed ratio schedule: They receive payment after some set number of shirts have been sewn.

All ratio schedules encourage high and consistent rates of responding because the number of rewards received is directly related to the number of responses made. Unlike a rat following a fixed interval schedule, where food is delivered at a specified time regardless of the number of responses, rats following a ratio schedule should respond quickly and often. Not surprisingly, variable ratio schedules produce slightly higher rates of responding than fixed ratio schedules primarily because the organism never knows when the next reinforcement is going to appear. What's more, the higher the ratio, the higher the response rate tends to be; a 20-response variable ratio schedule will produce considerably more responding than a 2-response variable ratio schedule. All of these schedules of reinforcement provide **intermittent reinforcement**, *when only some of the responses made are followed by reinforcement.* They all produce behavior that is much more resistant to extinction than a continuous reinforcement schedule. One way to think about this effect is to recognize that the more irregular and intermittent a schedule is, the more difficult it becomes for an organism to detect when it has actually been placed on extinction.

COURTESY OF HTTP://PHILIP.GREENSPUN.COM

Slot machines in casinos pay out following a variable ratio schedule. This helps explain why some gamblers feel incredibly lucky, whereas others (like this chap) can't believe they can play a machine for so long without winning a thing.

For example, if you've just put a dollar into a soda machine that, unbeknownst to you, is broken, no soda comes out. Because you're used to getting your sodas on a continuous reinforcement schedule—one dollar produces one soda—this abrupt change in the environment is easily noticed and you are unlikely to put additional money into the machine: You'd quickly show extinction. However, if you've put your dollar into a slot machine that, unbeknownst to you, is broken, do you stop after one or two plays? Almost certainly not. If you're a regular slot player, you're used to going for many plays in a row without winning anything, so it's difficult to tell that anything is out of the ordinary. Under conditions of intermittent reinforcement, all organisms will show considerable resistance to extinction and continue for many trials before they stop responding. The effect has even been observed in infants (Weir et al., 2005).

This relationship between intermittent reinforcement schedules and the robustness of the behavior they produce is called the **intermittent-reinforcement effect**, *the fact that operant behaviors that are maintained under intermittent reinforcement schedules resist extinction better than those maintained under continuous reinforcement.* In one extreme case, Skinner gradually extended a variable ratio schedule until he managed to get a pigeon to make an astonishing 10,000 pecks at an illuminated key for one food reinforcer! Behavior maintained under a schedule like this is virtually immune to extinction.

## Shaping through Successive Approximations

Have you ever been to AquaLand and wondered how the dolphins learn to jump up in the air, twist around, splash back down, do a somersault, and then jump through a hoop, all in one smooth motion? Well, they don't. Wait—of course they do; you've seen them. It's just that they don't learn to do all those complex aquabatics in *one* smooth motion. Rather, elements of their behavior get shaped over time until the final product looks like one smooth motion.

Skinner noted that the trial-by-trial experiments of Pavlov and Thorndike were rather artificial. Behavior rarely occurs in fixed frameworks where a stimulus is presented and then an organism has to engage in some activity or another. We are continuously acting and behaving, and the world around us reacts in response to our actions. Most of our behaviors, then, are the result of **shaping**, or *learning that results from the*

**FIXED RATIO SCHEDULE (FR)** An operant conditioning principle in which reinforcement is delivered after a specific number of responses have been made.

**VARIABLE RATIO SCHEDULE (VR)** An operant conditioning principle in which the delivery of reinforcement is based on a particular average number of responses.

**INTERMITTENT REINFORCEMENT** An operant conditioning principle in which only some of the responses made are followed by reinforcement.

**INTERMITTENT-REINFORCEMENT EFFECT** The fact that operant behaviors that are maintained under intermittent reinforcement schedules resist extinction better than those maintained under continuous reinforcement.

**SHAPING** Learning that results from the reinforcement of successive approximations to a final desired behavior.

Training animals by shaping their behavior through successive approximations can result in some extraordinary feats, such as this tiger's daring jump through fire during the Hangzhou Sapphire Circus in China.

*reinforcement of successive approximations to a final desired behavior.* The outcomes of one set of behaviors shape the next set of behaviors, whose outcomes shape the next set of behaviors, and so on.

To illustrate the effects of shaping, Skinner noted that if you put a rat in a Skinner box and wait for it to press the bar, you could end up waiting a very long time: Bar pressing just isn't very high in a rat's natural hierarchy of responses. However, it is relatively easy to "shape" bar pressing. Watch the rat closely: If it turns in the direction of the bar, deliver a food reward. This will reinforce turning toward the bar, making such a movement more likely. Now wait for the rat to take a step toward the bar before delivering

B. F. Skinner shaping a dog named Agnes. In the span of 20 minutes, Skinner was able to use reinforcement of successive approximations to shape Agnes's behavior. The result was a pretty neat trick: to wander in, stand on hind legs, and jump.

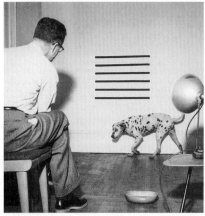

**1 Minute**

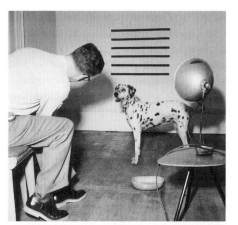

**4 Minutes**

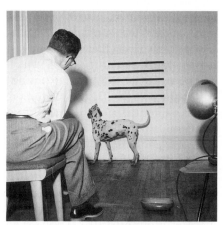

**8 Minutes**

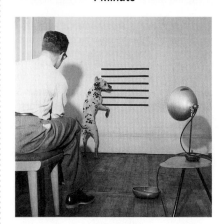

**12 Minutes**

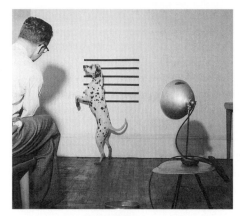

**16 Minutes**

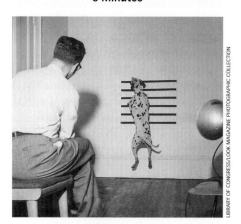

**20 Minutes**

food; this will reinforce moving toward the bar. After the rat walks closer to the bar, wait until it touches the bar before presenting the food. Notice that none of these behaviors is the final desired behavior—reliably pressing the bar. Rather, each behavior is a *successive approximation* to the final product, or a behavior that gets incrementally closer to the overall desired behavior. In the dolphin example—and indeed, in many instances of animal training in which relatively simple animals seem to perform astoundingly complex behaviors—you can think through how each smaller behavior is reinforced until the overall sequence of behavior gets performed reliably.

## Superstitious Behavior

Everything we've discussed so far suggests that one of the keys to establishing reliable operant behavior is the correlation between an organism's response and the occurrence of reinforcement. In the case of continuous reinforcement, when every response is followed by the presentation of a reinforcer, there is a one-to-one, or perfect, correlation. In the case of intermittent reinforcement, the correlation is weaker (i.e., not every response is met with the delivery of reinforcement), but it's not zero. As you read in Chapter 2, however, just because two things are correlated (that is, they tend to occur together in time and space) doesn't imply that there is causality (that is, the presence of one reliably causes the other to occur).

Skinner (1947) designed an experiment that illustrates this distinction. He put several pigeons in Skinner boxes, set the food dispenser to deliver food every 15 seconds, and left the birds to their own devices. Later he returned and found the birds engaging in odd, idiosyncratic behaviors, such as pecking aimlessly in a corner or turning in circles. He referred to these behaviors as "superstitious" and offered a behaviorist analysis of their occurrence. The pigeons, he argued, were simply repeating behaviors that had been accidentally reinforced. A pigeon that just happened to have pecked randomly in the corner when the food showed up had connected the delivery of food to that behavior. Because this pecking behavior was "reinforced" by the delivery of food, the pigeon was likely to repeat it. Now pecking in the corner was more likely to occur, and it was more likely to be reinforced 15 seconds later when the food appeared again.

For each pigeon, the behavior reinforced would most likely be whatever the pigeon happened to be doing when the food was first delivered. Skinner's pigeons acted as though there was a causal relationship between their behaviors and the appearance of food when it was merely an accidental correlation. Superstitious behavior is not limited to pigeons, of course. Baseball players who enjoy several home runs on a day when they happened to have not showered are likely to continue that tradition, laboring under the belief that the accidental correlation between poor personal hygiene and a good day at bat is somehow causal. This "stench causes home runs" hypothesis is just one of many examples of human superstitions (Gilbert, Brown, Pihel, & Wilson, 2000; Radford & Radford, 1949).

 **ONLY HUMAN**

**SHAPING YES, WRITING NO** 1991—Last summer, a class of 25 psychology students at Kalamazoo College in Michigan trained 14 rats as part of a class project in lieu of writing term papers. Among the tricks the rats mastered were the broad jump, tightrope walking, and playing soccer.

People believe in many different superstitions and engage in all kinds of superstitious behaviors. Many major league baseball players, for example, maintain a superstition of not stepping on the baselines when they enter or leave the field, as illustrated by Baltimore Orioles pitcher Daniel Cabrera. Skinner thought superstitions resulted from the unintended reinforcement of inconsequential behavior.

AP PHOTO/CHRIS GARDNER

# A Deeper Understanding of Operant Conditioning

Like classical conditioning, operant conditioning also quickly proved powerful. It's difficult to argue this fact when a rat learns to perform relatively complex behaviors after only 20 minutes of practice, prompted by little more than the skillful presentation of rat chow. The results are evident: "Learning" in its most fundamental sense is a change in behavior brought about by experience. In this case, the rat didn't perform the task at first, and then, after a little training, it learned to perform the task very well indeed. Case closed.

Well, case closed to the satisfaction of behaviorists. Like the behaviorism of John Watson, the behaviorism of B. F. Skinner didn't include the mind in its analysis of an organism's actions. Skinner was satisfied to observe an organism perform the behavior; he didn't look for a deeper explanation of mental processes (Skinner, 1950). In this view, an organism behaved in a certain way as a response to stimuli in the environment, not because there was any wanting, wishing, or willing by the animal in question. However, some research on operant conditioning digs deeper into the underlying mechanisms that produce the familiar outcomes of reinforcement. Let's examine three elements that expand our view of operant conditioning beyond strict behaviorism: the neural, cognitive, and evolutionary elements of operant conditioning.

## The Neural Elements of Operant Conditioning

Soon after psychologists came to appreciate the range and variety of things that could function as reinforcers, they began looking for underlying brain mechanisms that might account for these effects. The first hint of how specific brain structures might contribute to the process of reinforcement came from the discovery of what came to be called *pleasure centers*. James Olds and his associates inserted tiny electrodes into different parts of a rat's brain and allowed the animal to control electric stimulation of its own brain by pressing a bar. They discovered that some brain areas, particularly those in the limbic system (see Chapter 3), produced what appeared to be intensely positive experiences: The rats would press the bar repeatedly to stimulate these structures. The researchers observed that these rats would ignore food, water, and other life-sustaining necessities for hours on end simply to receive stimulation directly in the brain. They then called these parts of the brain "pleasure centers" (Olds, 1956) (see **FIGURE 6.10**).

Based on this research, researchers implanted stimulating electrodes into the brains of patients who suffered from disorders such as intractable epilepsy in the hope that they could be used to develop new therapeutic techniques. In a number of cases, these patients did indeed experience a distinct sense of pleasure, most often when the electrodes were placed in limbic areas. Some patients reported feelings that were sexual in nature, but most merely responded that they "felt good" in some vague sense. These studies have been abandoned for various reasons ranging from questions about their ethics to failures to find any particularly useful therapeutic applications (Valenstein, 1973, 1986).

In the years since these early studies, researchers have identified a number of structures and pathways in the brain that deliver rewards through stimulation (Wise, 1989, 2005). The neurons in the *medial forebrain bundle,* a pathway that meanders its way from the midbrain through the *hypothalamus* into the *nucleus accumbens,* are the most susceptible to stimulation that produces pleasure. This is not surprising as psychologists have identified this bundle of cells as crucial to behaviors that clearly involve pleasure, such as eating, drinking, and engaging in sexual activity. Second, the neurons all along this pathway and especially those in the nucleus accumbens itself are all *dopaminergic;* that is, they secrete the neurotransmitter *dopamine.* Remember from Chapter 3 that higher levels of dopamine in the brain are usually associated with positive emotions.

**Figure 6.10 Pleasure Centers in the Brain** The nucleus accumbens, medial forebrain bundle, and hypothalamus are all major pleasure centers in the brain.

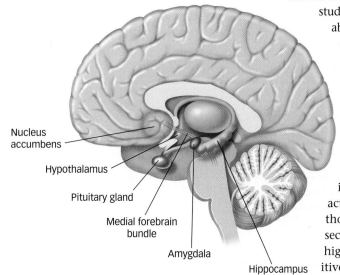

Nucleus accumbens

Hypothalamus

Pituitary gland

Medial forebrain bundle

Amygdala

Hippocampus

Researchers have found good support for this "reward center." First, as you've just seen, rats will work to stimulate this pathway at the expense of other basic needs (Olds & Fobes, 1981). However, if drugs that block the action of dopamine are administered to the rats, they cease stimulating the pleasure centers (Stellar, Kelley, & Corbett, 1983). Second, drugs such as cocaine, amphetamine, and opiates activate these pathways and centers (Moghaddam & Bunney, 1989), but dopamine-blocking drugs dramatically diminish their reinforcing effects (White & Milner, 1992). Third, fMRI studies (see Chapter 3) show increased activity in the nucleus accumbens in heterosexual men looking at pictures of attractive women (Aharon et al., 2001) and in individuals who believe they are about to receive money (Knutson, Adams, Fong, & Hommer, 2001). Finally, rats given primary reinforcers such as food or water or who are allowed to engage in sexual activity show increased dopamine secretion in the nucleus accumbens—but only if the rats are hungry, thirsty, or sexually aroused (Damsma, Pfaus, Wenkstern, Phillips, & Fibiger, 1992). This last finding is exactly what we might expect given our earlier discussion of the complexities of reinforcement. After all, food tastes a lot better when we are hungry and sexual activity is more pleasurable when we are aroused. These biological structures underlying rewards and reinforcements probably evolved to ensure that species engaged in activities that helped survival and reproduction.

## The Cognitive Elements of Operant Conditioning

In Skinner's day, most operant-conditioning researchers argued for a strict behaviorist interpretation of learning. All they required was a complete description of the stimuli, the subsequent response, and the associations between them. As you've already seen, in the case of classical conditioning, this strict behaviorist model was enhanced by considering the role of cognitive activities in learning. Several lines of research suggest that considering the role of cognition can better explain operant conditioning.

Edward Chace Tolman (1886–1959) was the strongest early advocate of a cognitive approach to operant learning. Tolman was dissatisfied with the simple stimulus-response (S-R) approach to understanding learning, arguing that there was more to learning than just knowing the circumstances in the environment (the properties of the stimulus) and being able to observe a particular outcome (the reinforced response). Instead, Tolman proposed that an animal established a means-ends relationship. That is, the conditioning experience produced knowledge or a belief that, in this particular situation, a specific reward (the end state) will appear if a specific response (the means to that end) is made.

Tolman's means-ends relationship may remind you of another paradigm you've read about in this chapter—the Rescorla-Wagner model of classical conditioning. Rescorla argued that the CS functions by setting up an expectation about the arrival of a US—and "expectations" are most certainly mental states. In both Rescorla and Tolman's theories, the stimulus does not directly evoke a response; rather, it establishes an internal cognitive state, which then produces the behavior. These cognitive theories of learning focus less on the S-R connection and more on what happens in the organism's mind when faced with the stimulus. In contrast to staunch S-R behaviorists, cognitively oriented psychologists such as Tolman are more concerned with what goes on between the S and the R.

Edward Chace Tolman advocated a cognitive approach to operant learning and provided evidence that in maze learning experiments, rats develop a mental picture of the maze, which he called a cognitive map.

Early studies with rats and mazes supported the influence of cognition on operant conditioning. Rats that had learned to run through a maze for a small reward ran much faster when they were switched to a larger reward; in fact, they ran faster than a comparable group that had always had the large reward (Crespi, 1942). Similarly, rats that were switched from the large reward to the small one ran slower than those who always had the smaller rewards. In both cases, the rats acted as though they had a pretty good idea

**LATENT LEARNING** A condition in which something is learned but it is not manifested as a behavioral change until sometime in the future.

**COGNITIVE MAP** A mental representation of the physical features of the environment.

about what to expect at the end of the maze. Their behavior revealed a cognitive element: The rats appeared to be either excited or annoyed about changes in the reward and seemed to make corresponding changes in their behavior.

During the 1930s and 1940s, Tolman and his students conducted studies that focused on *latent learning* and *cognitive maps,* two phenomena that strongly suggest that simple stimulus-response interpretations of operant learning behavior are inadequate.

In **latent learning,** *something is learned but it is not manifested as a behavioral change until sometime in the future.* Latent learning can easily be established in rats and occurs without any obvious reinforcement, a finding that posed a direct challenge to the then-dominant behaviorist position that all learning required some form of reinforcement (Tolman & Honzik, 1930a).

Tolman gave three groups of rats access to a complex maze every day for over 2 weeks. The control group never received any reinforcement for navigating the maze. They were simply allowed to run around until they reached the goal box at the end of the maze. In **FIGURE 6.11** you can see that over the 2 weeks of the study, this group (in green) got a little better at finding their way through the maze but not by much. A second group of rats received regular reinforcements; when they reached the goal box, they found a small food reward there. Not surprisingly, these rats showed clear learning, as can be seen in blue in Figure 6.11. A third group was treated exactly like the control group for the first 10 days and then rewarded for the last 7 days. This group's behavior (in orange) was quite striking. For the first 10 days, they behaved like the rats in the control group. However, during the final 7 days, they behaved a lot like the rats in the second group that had been reinforced every day. Clearly, the rats in this third group had learned a lot about the maze and the location of the goal box during those first 10 days even though they had not received any reinforcements for their behavior. In other words, they showed evidence of latent learning.

These results suggested to Tolman that beyond simply learning "start here, end here," his rats had developed a sophisticated mental picture of the maze. Tolman called this a **cognitive map,** or *a mental representation of the physical features of the environment.* Beyond simply learning "start here, end here," Tolman thought that the rats had developed a mental picture of the maze, more along the lines of "make two lefts, then a right, then a quick left at the corner." He devised several experiments to test this idea (Tolman & Honzik, 1930b; Tolman, Ritchie, & Kalish, 1946).

One simple experiment provided support for Tolman's theories and wreaked havoc with the noncognitive explanations offered by staunch behaviorists. Tolman trained a group of rats in the maze shown in **FIGURE 6.12a.** As you can see, rats run down a straightaway, take a left, a right, a long right, and then end up in the goal box at the end of the maze. Because we're looking at it from above, we can see that the rat's position at the end of the maze, relative to the starting point, is "diagonal to the upper

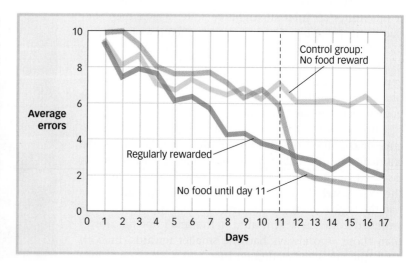

**Figure 6.11 Latent Learning** Rats in a control group that never received any reinforcement (in green) improved at finding their way through the maze over 17 days but not by much. Rats that received regular reinforcements (in blue) showed fairly clear learning; their error rate decreased steadily over time. Rats in the latent learning group (in orange) were treated exactly like the control group rats for the first 10 days and then like the regularly rewarded group for the last 7 days. Their dramatic improvement on day 12 shows that these rats had learned a lot about the maze and the location of the goal box even though they had never received reinforcements. Notice also that on the last 7 days, these latent learners actually seem to make *fewer* errors than their regularly rewarded counterparts.

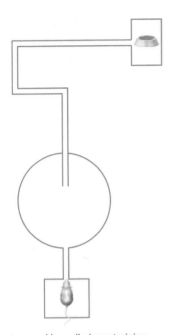

(a) Apparatus used in preliminary training

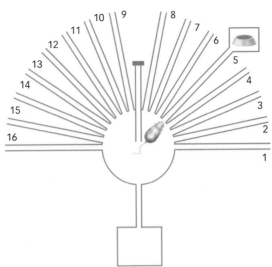

(b) Apparatus used in test trial

**Figure 6.12** **Cognitive Maps**
(a) Rats trained to run from a start box to a goal box in the maze on the left mastered the task quite readily. When these rats were then placed in the maze on the right (b), in which the main straightaway had been blocked, they did something unusual. Rather than simply backtrack and try the next closest runway (i.e., those labeled 8 or 9 in the figure), which would be predicted by stimulus generalization, the rats typically chose runway 5, which led most directly to where the goal box had been during their training. The rats had formed a cognitive map of their environment and so knew where they needed to end up, spatially, compared to where they began.

right." Of course, all the rat in the maze sees are the next set of walls and turns until it eventually reaches the goal box. Nonetheless, rats learned to navigate this maze without error or hesitation after about four nights. Clever rats. But they were more clever than you think.

After they had mastered the maze, Tolman changed things around a bit and put them in the maze shown in Figure 6.12b. The goal box was still in the same place relative to the start box. However, many alternative paths now spoked off the main platform, and the main straightaway that the rats had learned to use was blocked. Most behaviorists would predict that the rats in this situation—running down a familiar path only to find it blocked—would show stimulus generalization and pick the next closest path, such as one immediately adjacent to the straightaway. This was not what Tolman observed. When faced with the blocked path, the rats instead ran all the way down the path that led directly to the goal box. The rats had formed a sophisticated cognitive map of their environment and behaved in a way that suggested they were successfully following that map after the conditions had changed. Latent learning and cognitive maps suggest that operant conditioning involves much more than an animal responding to a stimulus. Tolman's experiments strongly suggest that there is a cognitive component, even in rats, to operant learning.

## The Evolutionary Elements of Operant Conditioning

As you'll recall, classical conditioning has an adaptive value that has been fine-tuned by evolution. Not surprisingly, we can also view operant conditioning from an evolutionary perspective. This viewpoint grew out of a set of curious observations from the early days of conditioning experiments. Several behaviorists who were using simple T mazes like the one shown in **FIGURE 6.13** to study learning in rats discovered that if a rat found food in one arm of the maze on the first trial of the day, it typically ran down the *other* arm on the very next trial. A staunch behaviorist wouldn't expect the rats to behave this way. After all, the rats in these experiments were hungry and they had just been reinforced for turning in a particular direction. According to operant conditioning, this should *increase* the likelihood of turning in that same direction, not reduce it. With additional trials the rats eventually learned to go to the arm with the food, but they had to learn to overcome this initial tendency to go "the wrong way." How can we explain this mindbug?

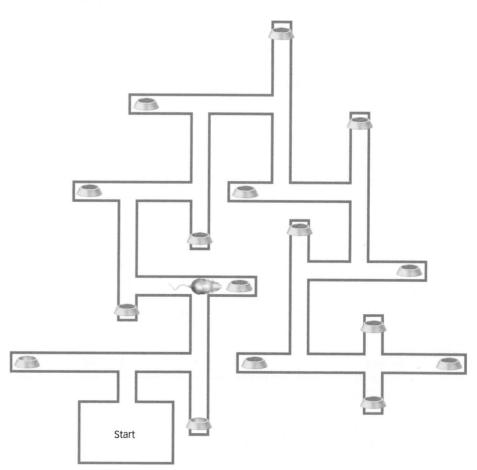

**Figure 6.13** **A Simple T Maze** When rats find food in the right arm of a typical T maze, on the next trial, they will often run to the *left* arm of the maze. This contradicts basic principles of operant conditioning: If the behavior of running to the right arm is reinforced, it should be more likely to occur again in the future. However, this behavior is perfectly consistent with a rat's evolutionary preparedness. Like most foraging animals, rats explore their environments in search of food and seldom return to where food has already been found. Quite sensibly, if food has already been found in the right arm of the T maze, the rat will search the left arm next to see if *more* food is there.

Start

What was puzzling from a behaviorist perspective makes sense when viewed from an evolutionary perspective. Rats are foragers, and like all foraging species, they have evolved a highly adaptive strategy for survival. They move around in their environment looking for food. If they find it somewhere, they eat it (or store it) and then go look somewhere else for more. If they do not find food, they forage in another part of the environment. So, if the rat just found food in the *right* arm of a T maze, the obvious place to look next time is the *left* arm. The rat knows that there isn't any more food in the right arm because it just ate the food it found there! Indeed, foraging animals such as rats have well-developed spatial representations that allow them to search their environment efficiently. If given the opportunity to explore a complex environment like the multi-arm maze shown in **FIGURE 6.14**, rats will systematically go from arm to arm collecting food, rarely returning to an arm they have previously visited (Olton & Samuelson, 1976). So, in this case it's not the rat who is the victim of a mindbug; it's the behaviorist theorist!

Two of Skinner's former students, Keller Breland and Marian Breland, were among the first researchers to discover that it wasn't just rats in T mazes that presented a problem for behaviorists (Breland & Breland, 1961). The Brelands pointed out that psychologists and the organisms they study often seemed to "disagree" on what the organisms should be doing. Their argument was simple: When this kind of dispute develops, the animals are always right, and the psychologists had better rethink their theories.

**Figure 6.14** **A Complex T Maze** Like many other foraging species, rats placed in a complex T maze such as this one show evidence of their evolutionary preparedness. These rats will systematically travel from arm to arm in search of food, never returning to arms they have already visited.

Start

The Brelands, who made a career out of training animals for commercials and movies, often used pigs because pigs are surprisingly good at learning all sorts of tricks. However, they discovered that it was extremely difficult to teach a pig the simple task of dropping coins in a box. Instead of depositing the coins, the pigs persisted in rooting with them as if they were digging them up in soil, tossing them in the air with their snouts and pushing them around. The Brelands tried to train raccoons at the same task, with different but equally dismal results. The raccoons spent their time rubbing the coins between their paws instead of dropping them in the box.

Having learned the association between the coins and food, the animals began to treat the coins as stand-ins for food. Pigs are biologically predisposed to root out their food, and raccoons have evolved to clean their food by rubbing it with their paws. That is exactly what each species of animal did with the coins.

The Brelands' work shows that each species, including humans, is biologically predisposed to learn some things more readily than others and to respond to stimuli in ways that are consistent with its evolutionary history (Gallistel, 2000). Such adaptive behaviors, however, evolved over extraordinarily long periods and in particular environmental contexts. If those circumstances change, some of the behavioral mechanisms that support learning can lead an organism astray. Raccoons that associated coins with food failed to follow the simple route to obtaining food by dropping the coins in the box; "nature" took over and they wasted time rubbing the coins together. The point is that although much of every organism's behavior results from predispositions sharpened by evolutionary mechanisms, these mechanisms sometimes can have ironic consequences.

A clever series of studies showed how evolved predispositions to learn can backfire on an animal (Thomas, 1981). Rats were placed in a Skinner box and the timer was set to deliver food every 20 seconds, no matter what the rats did. (You'll recall that this is a fixed interval schedule of reinforcement.) In fact, if they just lay around doing absolutely nothing, they were guaranteed to get three food pellets every minute. However, the feeding mechanism was rigged so that if a rat actually *did* press the bar before the full 20 seconds was up, a food pellet would be delivered immediately. Aside from not having to wait for their first pellet, the rats gained nothing else from these preemptive bar presses; they still had to wait for the 20-second period to elapse before they could get the next pellet. Because the feedings were controlled in this manner, in

The misbehavior of organisms: Pigs are biologically predisposed to root out their food, just as raccoons are predisposed to wash their food. Trying to train either species to behave differently can prove to be an exercise in futility.

any 1-hour session exactly 180 food pellets were delivered, and nothing the rats did could increase that amount. In short, bar pressing was absolutely useless in the long run. Nevertheless, over several hours of training, the rats increased bar pressing from an average of 0 presses per minute to nearly 30. The rats learned that there was an association between bar pressing and food, even though this association was worthless in terms of the number of reinforcements delivered.

A second experiment showed just how counterproductive this tendency to find associations can be. In this experiment, everything was kept the same except for one important modification. Now those preemptive bar presses that made food immediately available had a severe negative consequence. If a rat pressed the bar, it got food right away, but it was docked food in the next 20-second interval, whether it pressed the bar during this period or not. In other words, a rat that pressed the bar regularly would lose out on every other reinforcement. It could only get a food pellet half the time, and its overall rations would be cut in half, reduced from 3 pellets every minute to an average of only 1.5 pellets. Yet the association between the bar press and the immediate delivery of food was sufficiently strong that the rats still showed systematic increases in bar pressing, some of them averaging over 25 bar presses a minute.

These rats showed the perils of impatience. By opting for immediate rewards, they ended up losing out in the long run. What seems to be a perverse mindbug is a consequence of the usually adaptive tendency to discover the associations between events in the environment. In this case, acting too readily on the association between bar pressing and food delivery backfired as a long-term adaptive strategy.

---

**In summary,** operant conditioning, as developed by B. F. Skinner, is a process by which behaviors are reinforced and therefore become more likely to occur, where complex behaviors are shaped through reinforcement, and where the contingencies between actions and outcomes are critical in determining how an organism's behaviors will be displayed. Like Watson, Skinner tried to explain behavior without considering cognitive or evolutionary mechanisms. However, as with classical conditioning, this approach turned out to have serious shortcomings. Operant conditioning has clear cognitive components: Organisms behave as though they have expectations about the outcomes of their actions and adjust their actions accordingly. Moreover, the associative mechanisms that underlie operant conditioning have their roots in evolutionary biology. Some things are relatively easily learned and others are difficult; the history of the species is usually the best clue as to which will be which. ■ ■

---

## Observational Learning: Look at Me

The guiding principle of operant conditioning is that reinforcement determines future behavior. That tenet fit well with behaviorism's insistence on observable action as the appropriate level of explanation and the behaviorists' reluctance to consider what was going on in the mind. As we've already seen, however, cognition helps explain why operant conditioning doesn't always happen as behaviorists would expect. The next section looks at learning by keeping one's eyes and ears open to the surrounding environment and further chips away at strict behaviorist doctrine.

### Learning without Direct Experience

Consider this story about 4-year-old Rodney and his 2-year-old sister, Margie. Their parents had always told them to keep away from the stove, and that's good advice for any child and many an adult. Being a mischievous imp, however, Rodney decided one day to heat up a burner, place his hand over it, and slowly press down . . . until the singeing of his flesh led him to recoil, shrieking in pain. Rodney was just fine—more scared than hurt, really—and no one hearing this story doubts that he learned something important that day. But no one doubts that little Margie, who stood by watching each of these events unfold, *also* learned the same lesson. Rodney's story is a behaviorist's textbook example: The administration of punishment led to a learned change in his behavior. But how can we explain Margie's learning? She received neither punishment nor reinforcement—indeed, she didn't even have direct experience with the wicked appliance—yet it's arguable that she's just as likely to keep her hands away from stoves in the future as Rodney is.

Margie's is a case of **observational learning**, in which *learning takes place by watching the actions of others*. Observational learning challenges behaviorism's reinforcement-based explanations of classical and operant conditioning, but there is no doubt that this type of learning produces changes in behavior. In all societies, appropriate social behavior is passed on from generation to generation largely through observation (Bandura, 1965). The rituals and behaviors that are a part of our culture are acquired by each new generation, not only through deliberate training of the young but also through young people observing the patterns of behaviors of their elders. Tasks such as using chopsticks or learning to operate a TV's remote control are more easily acquired if we watch these activities being carried out before we try ourselves. Even complex motor tasks, such as performing surgery, are learned in part through extensive observation and imitation of models. And anyone who is about to undergo surgery is grateful for observational learning. Just the thought of a generation of surgeons acquiring their surgical techniques using the trial-and-error techniques studied by Thorndike or the shaping of successive approximations that captivated Skinner would make any of us very nervous.

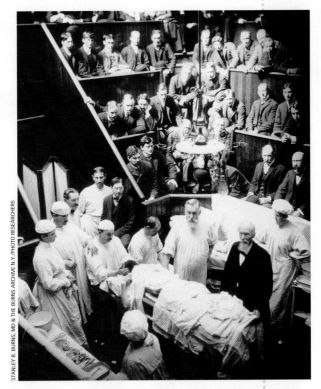

STANLEY B. BURNS, MD & THE BURNS ARCHIVE N.Y./PHOTO RESEARCHERS

Observational learning plays an important role in surgical training, as illustrated by the medical students observing famed German surgeon Vincenz Czerny (beard and white gown) perform stomach surgery in 1901 at a San Francisco hospital.

## Observational Learning in Humans

In a series of studies that have become landmarks in psychology, Albert Bandura and his colleagues investigated the parameters of observational learning (Bandura, Ross, & Ross, 1961). The researchers escorted individual preschoolers into a play area, where they found a number of desirable toys that they could play with: stickers, ink stamps, crayons, all things that 4-year-olds typically like. An adult *model,* someone whose behavior might serve as a guide for others, was then led into the room and seated in the opposite corner, where there were several adult toys. There were Tinkertoys, a small mallet, and a Bobo doll, which is a large inflatable plastic toy with a weighted bottom that allows it to bounce back upright when knocked down. The adult played quietly for a bit but then started aggressing toward the Bobo doll, knocking it down, jumping on it, hitting it with the mallet, kicking it around the room, and yelling "Pow!" and "Kick him!" When the children who observed these actions were later allowed to play with a variety of toys, including a child-size Bobo doll, they were more than twice as likely to interact with it in an aggressive manner as a group of children who hadn't observed the aggressive model.

**OBSERVATIONAL LEARNING** A condition in which learning takes place by watching the actions of others.

© ALBERT BANDURA, DEPT. OF PSYCHOLOGY, STAMFORD UNIVERSITY

**Figure 6.15** **Beating Up Bobo** Children who were exposed to an adult model who behaved aggressively toward a Bobo doll were likely to behave aggressively themselves. This behavior occurred in the absence of any direct reinforcement. Observational learning was responsible for producing the children's behaviors.

So what? Kids like to break stuff, and after all, Bobo dolls are made to be punched. Although that's true, as **FIGURE 6.15** shows, the degree of imitation that the children showed was startling. In fact, the adult model purposely used novel behaviors such as hitting the doll with a mallet or throwing it up in the air so that the researchers could distinguish aggressive acts that were clearly the result of observational learning. The children in these studies also showed that they were sensitive to the consequences of the actions they observed. When they saw the adult models being punished for behaving aggressively, the children showed considerably less aggression. When the children observed a model being rewarded and praised for aggressive behavior, they displayed an increase in aggression (Bandura, Ross, & Ross, 1963).

The observational learning seen in Bandura's studies has implications for social learning, cultural transmission of norms and values, and psychotherapy, as well as moral and ethical issues (Bandura, 1977, 1994). For example, a recent review of the literature on the effects of viewing violence on subsequent behavior concluded that viewing media violence has both immediate and long-term effects in increasing the likelihood of aggressive and violent behavior among youth (Anderson et al., 2003). This conclusion speaks volumes about the impact of violence and aggression as presented on TV, in movies, and in video games on our society, but it is hardly surprising in light of Bandura's pioneering research more than 40 years earlier.

Video games have become a must-have device in many households. Research on observational learning suggests that seeing violent images—in video games, on television, or in movies—can increase the likelihood of enacting violent behavior.

ALEX SEGRE/ALAMY

## Observational Learning in Animals

Humans aren't the only creatures capable of learning through observing. A wide variety of species learns by observing. In one study, for example, pigeons watched other pigeons get reinforced for either pecking at the feeder or stepping on a bar. When placed in the box later, the pigeons tended to use whatever technique they had observed other pigeons using earlier (Zentall, Sutton, & Sherburne, 1996).

In an interesting series of studies, researchers showed that laboratory-raised rhesus monkeys that had never seen a snake would develop a fear of snakes simply by observing the fear reactions of other monkeys (Cook & Mineka, 1990; Mineka & Cook, 1988). In fact, the fear reactions of these lab-raised monkeys were so authentic and pronounced that they could function as models for still *other* lab-raised monkeys, creating a kind of observational learning "chain." These results also support our earlier discussion of how each species has evolved particular biological predispositions for specific behaviors. Virtually every rhesus monkey raised in the wild has a fear of snakes, which strongly suggests that such a fear is one of this species' predispositions. This research also helps to explain why some phobias that humans suffer from, such as a fear of heights (acrophobia) or enclosed spaces (claustrophobia), are so common, even in people who have never had unpleasant experiences in these contexts (Mineka & Ohman, 2002). The fears may emerge not from specific conditioning experiences but from observing and learning from the reactions of others.

Observational learning may involve a neural component as well. As you read in Chapter 3, *mirror neurons* are a type of cell found in the brains of primates (including humans). Mirror neurons fire when an animal performs an action, such as when a monkey reaches for a food item. More importantly, however, mirror neurons also fire when an animal watches someone *else* perform the same specific task (Rizzolatti & Craighero, 2004). Although this "someone else" is usually a fellow member of the same species, some research suggests that mirror neurons in monkeys also fire when they observe humans performing an action (Fogassi et al., 2005). For example, monkeys' mirror neurons fired when they observed humans grasping for a piece of food, either to eat it or to place it in a container.

Mirror neurons, then, may play a critical role in the imitation of behavior as well as the prediction of future behavior (Rizzolatti, 2004). If the neurons fire when another organism is seen performing an action, it could indicate an awareness of intentionality, or that the animal is anticipating a likely course of future actions. Both of these elements—rote imitation of well-understood behaviors and an awareness of how behavior is likely to unfold—contribute to observational learning.

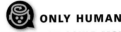 **ONLY HUMAN**

**IF ONLY WE COULD MODEL THIS BEHAVIOR AT HOME** A female chimpanzee, Judy, escaped at the Little Rock, Arkansas, zoo in January and as she moved about was observed entering a bathroom, grabbing a brush, and cleaning a toilet. She also wrung out a sponge and cleaned off a refrigerator, according to an Associated Press report.

---

**In summary,** classical and operant conditioning are forms of learning that are best understood as having cognitive and functional components that are the result of evolutionary processes. The same is true for observational learning. The cognitive component is fairly clear; the very process itself is based on cognitive mechanisms such as attention, perception, memory, or reasoning. But observational learning also has roots in evolutionary biology and for the most basic of reasons: It has survival value. Observational learning is an important process by which species gather information about the world around them. Shaping by successive approximations can be slow and tedious, and trial-and-error learning often results in many errors before learning is complete. However, when one organism patterns its actions on another organism's successful behaviors, learning is speeded up and potentially dangerous errors are prevented. What's more, such observational learning can save an organism from situations that might prove harmful. Learning by observing another individual successfully negotiate a dangerous environment, deciding not to eat a food that has made others ill, or avoiding conflicts with those who have been seen to vanquish all their opponents are all behavioral advantages that can save an organism considerable pain . . . or even its life. ▪ ▪

# Implicit Learning: Under the Wires

So far, we have covered a lot of what is known about learning with only the briefest consideration of *awareness* in the learning process. You may remember we distinguished between explicit learning and implicit learning at the beginning of the chapter. People often know that they are learning, are aware of what they're learning, and can describe what they know about a topic. If you have learned something concrete, such as doing arithmetic or typing on a computer keyboard, you know that you know it and you know *what* it is you know.

But did Pavlov's dogs *know* that they had been conditioned to salivate to a bell? Did Adam and Teri in our opening vignette understand that they had learned to associate their child's toy with an emotional event? Were Bandura's young research participants aware that the adult model was affecting their behavior? Would their behavior have been any different if they were? It certainly makes sense to ask whether these basic learning processes in humans require an awareness on the part of the learner. Perhaps some permanent changes in experience can be acquired without the benefit of awareness.

Researchers began to investigate how children learned such complex behaviors as language and social conduct (Reber, 1967). Most children, by the time they are 6 or 7 years old, are linguistically and socially fairly sophisticated. Yet most children reach this state with very little explicit awareness that they have learned something and with equally little awareness of what it was they have actually learned.

This simple observation poses theoretical challenges to traditional learning theories. As you'll recall from Chapter 1, linguist Noam Chomsky challenged behaviorist explanations of complex processes such as language acquisition and socialization (Chomsky, 1959). Learning to speak and understand English, for example, involves more than acquiring a series of stimulus-response associations or reinforcing successive approximations to grammatical sentences. Using a language is a creative process. Virtually every sentence we speak, hear, write, or read is new. You understand this sentence that you are now reading, although this is almost certainly the first time you have encountered these words in this particular order. In fact, virtually every sentence in this textbook is new to you, yet you understand them with little difficulty. Behaviorism cannot account for this kind of abstract process, so how can we tackle this problem?

For starters, it's safe to assume that people are sensitive to the patterns of events that occur in the world around them. Most people don't stumble through life thoroughly unaware of what's going on. Okay, maybe your roommate does. But people usually are attuned to linguistic, social, emotional, or sensorimotor events in the world around them so much so that they gradually build up internal representations of those patterns that were acquired without explicit awareness. This process is often called **implicit learning**, or *learning that takes place largely independent of awareness of both the process and the products of information acquisition.* As an example, although children are often given explicit rules of social conduct ("Don't chew with your mouth open"), they learn how to behave in a civilized way through experience. They're probably not aware of when or how they learned a particular course of action and may not even be able to state the general principle underlying their behavior. Yet most kids have learned not to eat with their feet, to listen when they are spoken to, and not to kick the dog. Implicit learning is knowledge that sneaks in "under the wires."

## Ways to Study Implicit Learning

Early studies of implicit learning showed research participants 15 or 20 letter strings and asked them to memorize them. The letter strings, which at first glance look like nonsense syllables, were actually formed using a complex set of rules called an *artificial grammar* (see **FIGURE 6.16**). Participants were not told anything about the rules, but with experience, they gradually developed a vague, intuitive sense of the "correctness" of particular letter groupings. These letter groups became familiar to the participants, and they processed these letter groupings more rapidly and efficiently than the "incorrect" letter groupings (Reber, 1967, 1996).

**IMPLICIT LEARNING** Learning that takes place largely independent of awareness of both the process and the products of information acquisition.

Take a look at the letter strings shown in Figure 6.16. The ones on the left are "correct" and follow the rules of the artificial grammar; the ones on the right all violated the rules. The differences are pretty subtle, and if you haven't been through the learning phase of the experiment, both sets look a lot alike. In fact, each nongrammatical string only has a single letter violation. Research participants are asked to classify new letter strings based on whether they follow the rules of the grammar. People turn out to be quite good at this task (usually they get between 60 and 70 percent correct), but they are unable to provide much in the way of explicit awareness of the rules and regularities that they are using. The experience is like when you come across a sentence with a grammatical error—you are immediately aware that something is wrong and you can certainly make the sentence grammatical. But unless you are a trained linguist, you'll probably find it difficult to articulate which rules of English grammar were violated or which rules you used to repair the sentence.

Other studies of implicit learning have used a *serial reaction time* task (Nissen & Bullemer, 1987). Here research participants are presented with five small boxes on a computer screen. Each box lights up briefly, and when it does, the person is asked to press the button that is just underneath that box as quickly as possible. Immediately after the button is pressed, a different box lights up, the person has to press the corresponding button, and so on. As with the artificial grammar task, the sequence of lights appears to be random, but in fact it follows a pattern. Research participants eventually get faster with practice as they learn to anticipate which box is most likely to light up next. If the sequence is changed or the patterns are modified, people's reaction times slow down, indicating that they were actually learning the sequence and not simply learning to press buttons quickly.

In these experiments, people are not looking for rules or patterns; they are "blind" to the goals of the experiments. The participants' learning takes place outside of their awareness. These studies establish implicit learning as a distinct form of learning (Stadler & Frensch, 1998).

Implicit learning has some characteristics that distinguish it from explicit learning. For example, when asked to carry out implicit tasks, people differ relatively little from one another, but on explicit tasks, such as conscious problem solving, they show large individual-to-individual differences (Reber, Walkenfeld, & Hernstadt, 1991). Implicit learning also seems to be unrelated to IQ: People with high scores on standard intelligence tests are no better at implicit-learning tasks, on average, than those whose scores are more modest (Reber & Allen, 2000). Implicit learning changes little across the life span. Researchers discovered well-developed implicit learning of complex, rule-governed auditory patterns in 8-month-old infants (Saffran, Aslin, & Newport, 1996). Infants heard streams of speech that contained experimenter-defined nonsense words. For example, the infants might hear a sequence such as "bidakupadotigolabu-bidaku," which contains the nonsense word *bida*. The infants weren't given any explicit clues as to which sounds were "words" and which were not, but after several repetitions, the infants showed signs that they had learned the novel words. Infants tend to prefer novel information, and they spent more time listening to novel nonsense words that had not been presented earlier than to the nonsense words such as *bida* that had been presented. Remarkably, the infants in this study were as good at learning these sequences as college students. At the other end of the life span, researchers have found that implicit-learning abilities extend well into old age and that they decline more slowly than explicit-learning abilities (Howard & Howard, 1997).

Implicit learning is remarkably resistant to various disorders that are known to affect explicit learning. A group of patients suffering from various psychoses were so severely impaired that they could not solve simple problems that college students had little difficulty with. Yet these patients were able to solve an artificial grammar learning task about as well as college students (Abrams & Reber, 1988). Other studies have found that profoundly amnesic patients not only show normal implicit memories but also display virtually normal implicit learning of artificial grammar (Knowlton,

| Grammatical Strings | Nongrammatical Strings |
|---|---|
| VXJJ | VXTJJ |
| XXVT | XVTVVJ |
| VJTVXJ | VJTTVTV |
| VJTVTV | VJTXXVJ |
| XXXXVX | XXXVTJJ |

**Figure 6.16** **Artificial Grammar and Implicit Learning** These are examples of letter strings formed by an artificial grammar. Research participants are exposed to the rules of the grammar and are later tested on new letter strings. Participants show reliable accuracy at distinguishing the valid, grammatical strings from the invalid, nongrammatical strings even though they usually can't explicitly state the rule they are following when making such judgments. Using an artificial grammar is one way of studying implicit learning (Reber, 1996).

## { THE REAL WORLD } Can You Sleep on It?

FOR A LOT OF PEOPLE, SLEEP SEEMS LIKE A waste of time. After all, you don't *do* anything important—like reading comic books, watching TV, or maybe finishing homework—for 5 to 10 hours every night. It's true that your television watching is cut drastically by needing to sleep (a good reason to get yourself a DVR), but it's not true that sleep is a waste of time. In fact, some scientists have proposed that sleep plays a role in learning.

There are two theories for sleep learning. The first theory is that a person can learn something while asleep. Imagine that you settle down for the night with a CD player next to your pillow playing the basic principles of chemistry. When you wake in the morning, you now know more than you ever wanted to about covalent and ionic bonds simply by having it processed by your sleeping brain. The second theory is that while a person is asleep, information that person has experienced during the day is processed and coded by the brain, thereby strengthening learning. Both of these are fascinating scientific hypotheses; if either is true, they would tell us a great deal about how the brain goes about acquiring knowledge.

Unfortunately, the first proposal doesn't hold up since it has proven difficult to document actual learning while people are asleep. When people report some success in using sleep-learning programs (and they occasionally do), it is because they recall items that were playing during the short periods of wakefulness that occur during sleep. You'd be well advised to resist buying any of the various sleep-learning programs touted in magazines and on the Internet. You should also start going to your chemistry class more often.

Researchers have been able to find support for the second hypothesis. As you learned in Chapter 5, experiences that become part of our permanent memories are those that undergo a variety of neurological modifications, and there are good reasons for believing that many of these changes take place during sleep. For example, researchers asked participants to complete a task that involved learning a series of digits presented as stimulus-response sequences but didn't tell them that the series of digits followed a complex rule. Participants exhibited implicit learning—they got faster as they practiced the task—but only about 25% of

them showed awareness of the rule. However, after a night's sleep, nearly 60% of the participants discovered the rule! It wasn't just the passage of time that caused this dramatic increase in learning and insight. Participants in the control group, who stayed awake for the same 8 hours after learning, showed a rate of insight comparable to that shown by the original data; that is, only about 25% of them discovered the rule. It also didn't matter what time of day these events took place. Eight hours awake during the day produced the same outcomes as 8 hours awake during the night (Wagner, Gais, Haider, Verleiger, & Born, 2004). These striking results suggest that sleep can promote the restructuring of knowledge, providing the backdrop for what later appear as sudden and spontaneous insights.

Overall, the latest research shows that sleep plays an important role in promoting learning. From a practical perspective, it is probably a good idea to make sure that you get a full night's sleep after you've engaged in practice or studied novel information. From a theoretical perspective, psychologists now need to develop better theories of exactly how sleep enhances learning.

Ramus, & Squire, 1992). In fact, these patients made accurate judgments about novel letter strings even though they had essentially no explicit memory of having been in the learning phase of the experiment! (The Real World box above discusses research indicating that implicit learning can occur even during sleep.)

## Implicit and Explicit Learning Use Distinct Neural Pathways

The fact that patients suffering from psychoses or amnesia show implicit learning strongly suggests that the brain structures that underlie implicit leaning are distinct from those that underlie explicit learning. What's more, it appears that distinct regions of the brain may be activated depending on how people approach a task.

Researchers found that distinct parts of the brain are activated when people approach a learning task in either an implicit or an explicit manner (Reber, Gitelman, Parrish, & Mesulam, 2003). Participants completed a simple pattern perception procedure. During the initial phase of the study, everyone saw a series of dot patterns, each of which looked like an array of stars in the night sky. Actually, all the stimuli were constructed to conform to an underlying prototypical dot pattern. The dots, however, varied so much that it was virtually impossible for a viewer to guess that they all had this common structure. Before the experiment began, half of the participants were told about the existence of the prototype; in other words, they were given instructions that encouraged explicit processing. The others were given standard implicit-learning instructions: They were told nothing other than to attend to the dot patterns.

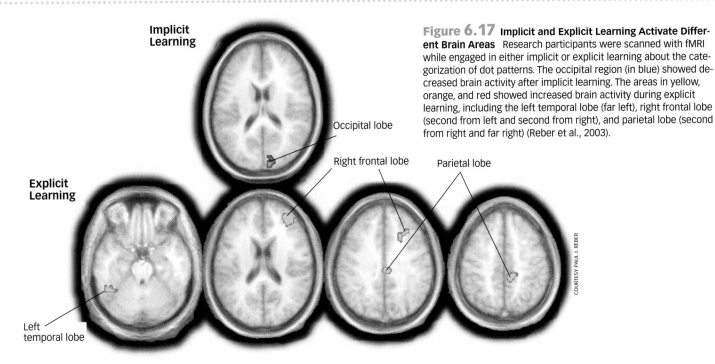

Implicit
Learning

Figure **6.17** **Implicit and Explicit Learning Activate Different Brain Areas** Research participants were scanned with fMRI while engaged in either implicit or explicit learning about the categorization of dot patterns. The occipital region (in blue) showed decreased brain activity after implicit learning. The areas in yellow, orange, and red showed increased brain activity during explicit learning, including the left temporal lobe (far left), right frontal lobe (second from left and second from right), and parietal lobe (second from right and far right) (Reber et al., 2003).

Occipital lobe

Right frontal lobe        Parietal lobe

Explicit
Learning

Left
temporal lobe

The participants were then scanned as they made decisions about new dot patterns, attempting to categorize them into those that conformed to the prototype and those that did not. Interestingly, both groups performed equally well on this task, correctly classifying about 65% of the new dot patterns. However, the brain scans revealed that the two groups were making these decisions using very different parts of their brains (see **FIGURE 6.17**). Participants who were given the explicit instructions showed *increased* brain activity in the prefrontal cortex, parietal cortex, hippocampus, and a variety of other areas known to be associated with the processing of explicit memories. Those given the implicit instructions showed *decreased* brain activation primarily in the occipital region, which is involved in visual processing. This finding suggests that participants recruited distinct brain structures in different ways depending on whether they were approaching the task using explicit or implicit learning.

**In summary,** implicit learning is a process that detects, learns, and stores patterns without the application of explicit awareness on the part of the learner. Complex behaviors, such as language use or socialization, can be learned through this implicit process. Tasks that have been used to document implicit learning include artificial grammar and serial reaction time tasks. Implicit and explicit learning differ from each other in a number ways: There are fewer individual differences in implicit than explicit learning, psychotic and amnesic patients with explicit-learning problems can exhibit intact implicit learning, and neuroimaging studies indicate that implicit and explicit learning recruit distinct brain structures, sometimes in different ways. ■ ■

## Where Do You Stand?

# Learning for Rewards or for Its Own Sake?

The principles of operant conditioning and the merits of reinforcement have more than found their way into mainstream culture. The least psychology-savvy parent intuitively understands that rewarding a child's good behavior should make that behavior more likely to occur in the future; the "law of effect" may mean nothing to this parent, but the principle and the outcome are readily appreciated nonetheless. And what parent wouldn't want the best for her or his child? If reward shapes good behavior, then more reward must be the pathway to exemplary behavior, often in the form of good grades, high test scores, and overall clean living. So, bring on the rewards!

Maybe, maybe not. As you learned earlier in this chapter, the *overjustification effect* predicts that sometimes too much external reinforcement for performing an intrinsically rewarding task can undermine future performance. Rewarding a child for getting good grades or high test scores might backfire: The child may come to see the behavior as directed toward the attainment of rewards rather than for its own satisfying outcomes. In short, learning should be fun for its own sake,

not because new toys, new clothes, or cash are riding on a set of straight A's.

Many parents seem to think differently. You probably have friends whose parents shower them with gifts whenever a report card shows improvement; in fact, you may have experienced this yourself. Nobody objects to a little recognition now and then, and it's nice to know that others appreciate your hard work. In fact, if you'd like to know the many, many others who'll appreciate your hard work, pay a visit to www.rewardsforgrades.com. It's a website that lists organizations that will give students external reinforcements for good grades, high test scores, perfect school attendance, and other behaviors that students are usually expected to produce just because they're students. Krispy Kreme offers a free doughnut for each A, Blockbuster gives free kids' movie rentals, Chick-fil-A rewards honor roll membership and perfect attendance with free kids' meals, and Limited Too offers a $5 discount on merchandise if you present a report card "with passing grades" (which, in many school districts, might mean all D's).

Before you get too excited by visions of a "grades for junk food" scam, you should know that there are often age limits on these offers. However, if you're a precocious fourth grader reading this textbook, feel free to cash in on the goods. Or if you happen to be enrolled at Wichita State University, you already might be familiar with the Cash for Grades initiative (www.cashforgrades.com). The proposal is that an 8%-per-credit-hour increase to student fees would be used to then reward good student performance: $624 to a student with a 3.5 GPA at the end of a semester, $804 for straight A's.

Where do you stand on this issue? Is this much ado about nothing or too much of a good thing? Some proponents of rewarding good academic performance argue that it mirrors the real world that, presumably, academic performance is preparing students to enter. After all, in most jobs, better performance is reinforced with better salaries, so why not model that in the school system? On the other hand, shouldn't the search for knowledge be reward enough? Is the subtle shift away from wanting to learn for its own sake to wanting to learn for a doughnut harmful in the long run?

# Chapter Review

### Defining Learning: Experience That Causes a Permanent Change

- Learning refers to any of several processes that produce relatively permanent changes in an organism's behavior.
- Habituation is a process by which an organism changes the way it reacts to external stimuli. Short-term habituation is distinguished from learning because the changes are not long lasting; long-term habituation is generally regarded as learning.

### Classical Conditioning: One Thing Leads to Another

- Classical conditioning is a kind of learning in which a reflexlike reaction (conditioned response) becomes associated with a previously neutral stimulus (conditioned stimulus).
- Stimulus generalization occurs if a CS that is similar to the one used in the original training is introduced. Stimulus discrimination is the flip side of generalization.
- Extinction of a learned response will occur if the CS is presented repeatedly without being followed by the US. Spontaneous recovery occurs if an organism is allowed a rest period following extinction.

- Classical conditioning originally was viewed as an automatic and mechanical process. However, it was soon discovered that neural, cognitive, and evolutionary elements were involved in the process.

### Operant Conditioning: Reinforcements from the Environment

- Operant conditioning is a kind of learning in which behaviors are shaped by reinforcement.
- Whereas classical conditioning involves reflexlike behaviors elicited from an organism, operant conditioning deals with overt, controlled, and emitted behaviors.
- Reinforcement is any operation that functions to increase the likelihood of the behavior that led to it. Punishment functions to decrease the likelihood of the behavior.
- Like classical conditioning, operant conditioning shows acquisition, generalization, discrimination, and extinction. The schedule with which reinforcements are delivered has a dramatic

effect on how well an operant behavior is learned and how resistant it is to extinction.

- Like classical conditioning, operant conditioning is better understood by taking into account underlying neural, cognitive, and evolutionary components.

- Latent learning and the development of cognitive maps in animals clearly implicate cognitive factors underlying operant learning. The evolutionary histories of individual species promote different patterns of operant learning.

### Observational Learning: Look at Me

- Learning can take place through the observation of others and does not necessarily require that the acquired behaviors be performed and reinforced. Observational learning does not simply result in imitation; it can also show creative elements. A child who sees an adult behave in a gentle manner with a toy will often show a variety of gentle reactions, including ones that were not exhibited by the adult model.

- Observational learning occurs in various animal species, including pigeons and monkeys. At a neural level, mirror cells are implicated in the imitation and expectation of behavior.

### Implicit Learning: Under the Wires

- Implicit learning takes place largely in the absence of awareness of either the actual learning or the knowledge of what was learned. Infants show intact implicit learning long before they develop conscious awareness. Various patient populations, such as psychotics and those with severe neurological disorders, show virtually normal implicit learning.

- Implicit learning is mediated by areas in the brain that are distinct from those activated during explicit learning. The brain structures that regulate the implicit-learning system evolved much earlier than those that regulate explicit processing.

## Key Terms

learning (p. 210)
habituation (p. 211)
classical conditioning (p. 212)
unconditioned stimulus (US) (p. 212)
unconditioned response (UR) (p. 212)
conditioned stimulus (CS) (p. 213)
conditioned response (CR) (p. 213)
acquisition (p. 214)

second-order conditioning (p. 215)
extinction (p. 216)
spontaneous recovery (p. 216)
generalization (p. 217)
discrimination (p. 217)
biological preparedness (p. 223)
operant conditioning (p. 224)
law of effect (p. 225)
operant behavior (p. 225)
reinforcer (p. 226)

punisher (p. 226)
overjustification effect (p. 229)
fixed interval schedule (FI) (p. 231)
variable interval schedule (VI) (p. 231)
fixed ratio schedule (FR) (p. 232)
variable ratio schedule (VR) (p. 232)

intermittent reinforcement (p. 233)
intermittent-reinforcement effect (p. 233)
shaping (p. 233)
latent learning (p. 238)
cognitive map (p. 238)
observational learning (p. 243)
implicit learning (p. 246)

## Recommended Readings

**Animal Training at SeaWorld.** http://www.seaworld.org/animal-info/info-books/training/how-animals-learn.htm. This website offers a glimpse at the operant conditioning techniques used to train Shamu, porpoises, and the occasional squid or two. There are solid, research-based discussions of the principles of reinforcement, observational learning, and other concepts in this chapter.

**Bandura, A.** (1986). *Social foundations of thought and action: A social cognitive theory.* Englewood Cliffs, NJ: Prentice Hall. This book is a classic statement of Albert Bandura's ideas on the origins of human functioning. Drawing from the beginnings of observational learning, Bandura sketches an elegant and comprehensive theory of how behavior develops and the determinants that shape it.

**Buckley, K. W.** (1989). *Mechanical man: John Broadus Watson and the beginnings of behaviorism.* New York: Guilford Press. There are many biographies of Watson available; Kerry Buckley's one of the best. Buckley is a historian specializing in the history of psychology, and he has published numerous scholarly works on Watson's life and ideas.

**Hartley, M., & Commire, A.** (1990). *Breaking the silence.* New York: Putnam Group. Mariette Hartley is a well-known television actress and the granddaughter of John B. Watson. Her autobiography focuses on . . . well, *her* life, mainly. But there are some references to Watson and what it's like growing up as a relative of a controversial figure.

**Skinner, B. F.** (1971). *Beyond freedom and dignity.* New York: Bantam Books. This book, reprinted by Hackett Publishing in 2002, is largely considered Skinner's definitive statement on humankind and its behavior. Skinner argues that most of society's problems can be better addressed by reshaping the environment following the principles of operant conditioning. Outmoded concepts such as "freedom" and "human dignity" should be abandoned in favor of developing more effective cultural practices. A controversial book when it first appeared, it remains so today.

**Todes, D. P.** (2000). *Pavlov: Exploring the animal machine.* New York: Oxford University Press. This overview of Pavlov's life and work is part of the Oxford Portraits in Science series, a set of titles that provide easy access to information about key scientists in all disciplines. This title should provide a bit more background about Pavlov's discoveries and the events in his life that helped shape his work.

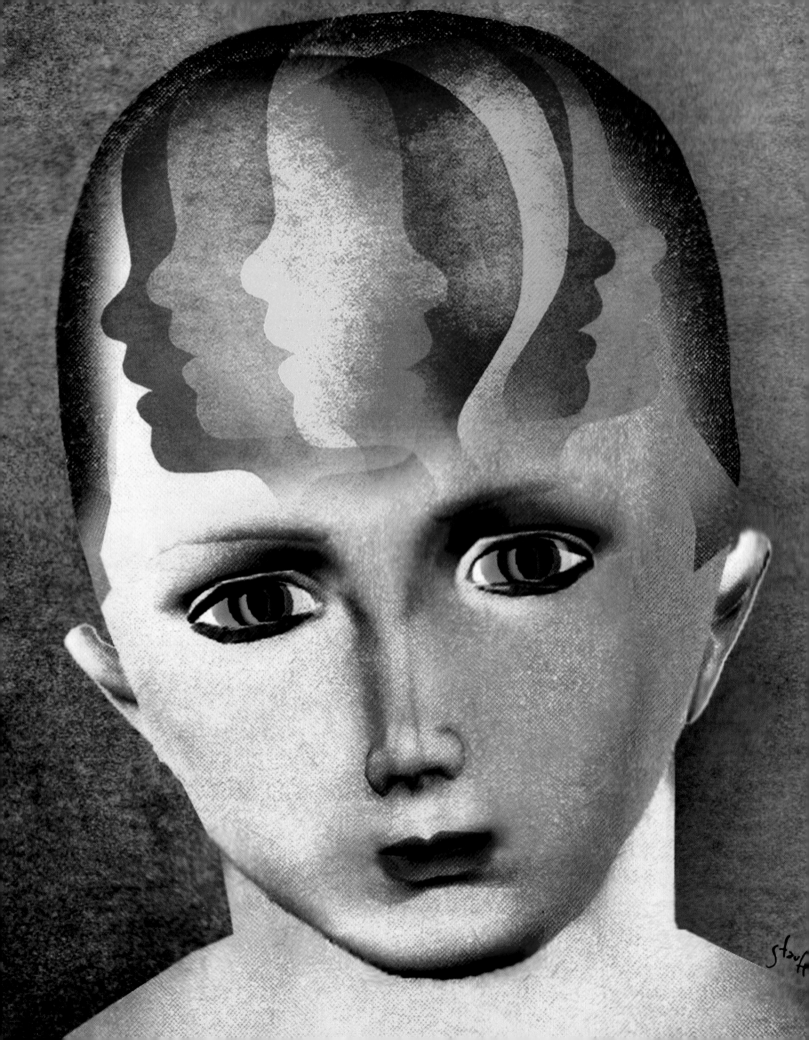

# 8

# Consciousness

**UNCONSCIOUSNESS IS SOMETHING YOU** don't really appreciate until you need it. Belle Riskin needed it one day on an operating table, when she awoke just as doctors were pushing a breathing tube down her throat. She felt she was choking, but she couldn't see, breathe, scream, or move. Unable even to blink an eye, she couldn't signal to the surgeons that she was conscious. "I was terrified. Why is this happening to me? Why can't I feel my arms? I could feel my heart pounding in my head. It was like being buried alive, but with somebody shoving something down your throat," she explained later. "I knew I was conscious, that something was going on during the surgery. I had just enough awareness to know I was being intubated" (Groves, 2004).

How could this happen? Anesthesia for surgery is supposed to leave the patient unconscious, "feeling no pain," and yet in this case—and in about one in a thousand other operations (Sandin et al., 2000)—the patient regains consciousness at some point and even remembers the experience. Some patients remember pain; others remember the clink of surgical instruments in a pan or the conversations of doctors and nurses. There may be lingering memories of being pushed, pulled, cut, or stitched. This is *not* how modern surgery is supposed to go, but the problem arises because muscle-relaxing drugs are used to keep the patient from moving involuntarily and making unhelpful contributions

to the operation. Then, when the drugs that are given to induce unconsciousness fail to do the job, the patient with extremely relaxed muscles is unable to show or tell doctors that there is a problem.

Waking up in surgery sounds pretty rough all by itself, but this could cause additional complications. The conscious patient could become alarmed and emotional during the operation, spiking blood pressure and heart rate to dangerous levels. Awareness also might lead to later emotional problems. Fortunately, new methods of monitoring wakefulness by measuring the electrical activity of the brain are being developed. One system uses sensors attached to the person's head and gives readings on a scale from 0 (no electrical activity signaling consciousness in the brain) to 100 (fully alert), providing a kind of "consciousness meter." Anesthesiologists

When it's time for surgery, it's great to be unconscious.

TIM PANNELL/CORBIS

293

**CONSCIOUSNESS** The person's subjective experience of the world and the mind.

**CARTESIAN THEATER** (after philosopher René Descartes) A mental screen or stage on which things appear to be presented for viewing by the mind's eye.

using this index deliver anesthetics to keep the patient in the recommended range of 40 to 65 for general anesthesia during surgery; they have found that this system reduces postsurgical reports of consciousness and memory for the surgical experience (Sigl & Chamoun, 1994). One of these devices in the operating room might have helped Belle Riskin settle into the unconsciousness she so dearly needed.

Most of the time, of course, consciousness is something we cherish. How else could we experience a favorite work of art; the mellow strains of an oldie on the radio; the taste of a sweet, juicy peach; or the touch of a loved one's hand? **Consciousness** is *a person's subjective experience of the world and the mind*. Although you might think of consciousness as simply "being awake," the defining feature of consciousness is *experience*, which you have when you're not awake but experiencing a vivid dream. Conscious experience is essential to what it means to be human. The anesthesiologist's dilemma in trying to monitor Belle Riskin's consciousness is a stark reminder, though, that it is impossible for one person to experience another's consciousness. Your consciousness is utterly private, a

world of personal experience that only you can know.

How can this private world be studied? One way to explore consciousness is to examine it directly, trying to understand what it is like, how it seems to be created, how it works, and how it compares with the mind's *un*conscious processes. We'll begin with this direct approach, looking at the mysteries of consciousness and its known properties. Another way to explore consciousness is to examine its altered states, in other words, the cases in which the experience of being human departs from normal, everyday waking. We will probe these changes, beginning with the major alterations that happen during sleep, when waking consciousness steals away only to be replaced by the surreal form of consciousness experienced in dreams. Then we'll look into how we alter our consciousness through intoxication with alcohol and other drugs, and other changes in consciousness that occur during hypnosis and meditation. Like the traveler who learns the meaning of *home* by roaming far away, we can learn the meaning of consciousness by exploring its exotic variations.

## Conscious and Unconscious: The Mind's Eye, Open and Closed

What does it feel like to be you right now? It probably feels as though you are somewhere inside your head, looking out at the world through your eyes. You can feel your hands on this book, perhaps, and notice the position of your body or the sounds in the room when you orient yourself toward them. If you shut your eyes, you may be able to imagine things in your mind, even though all the while thoughts and feelings come and go, passing through your imagination. The philosopher Daniel Dennett called this "place in your head" where "you" are the **Cartesian Theater** (after philosopher René Descartes), *a mental screen or stage on which things appear to be presented for viewing by your mind's eye* (Dennett, 1991). But where are "you," really? And how is it that this theater of consciousness gives you a view of some things in your world and your mind but not others? The Cartesian Theater unfortunately isn't available on DVD, making it difficult to share exactly what's on our mental screen with our friends, a researcher, or even ourselves in precisely the same way a second time. As you'll recall from Chapter 1, Wilhelm Wundt encountered similar problems when studying consciousness in the earliest days of psychology. We'll look at the difficulty of studying consciousness directly but also move along to examine the nature of consciousness (what it is that can be seen in this mental theater) and then explore the unconscious mind (what is *not* visible to the mind's eye).

*"We keep this section closed off."*

# The Mysteries of Consciousness

Other sciences, such as physics, chemistry, and biology, have the great luxury of studying *objects,* things that we all can see. Psychology studies objects too, looking at people and their brains and behaviors, but it has the unique challenge of also trying to make sense of *subjects.* A physicist is not concerned with what it is like to be a neutron, but psychologists hope to understand what it is like to be a human, that is, grasping the subjective perspectives of the people that they study. Psychologists hope to include an understanding of **phenomenology,** *how things seem to the conscious person,* in their understanding of mind and behavior. After all, consciousness is an extraordinary human property that could well be unique to us. But including phenomenology in psychology brings up mysteries pondered by great thinkers almost since the beginning of thinking. Let's look at two of the more vexing mysteries of consciousness: the problem of other minds and the mind/body problem.

## The Problem of Other Minds

One great mystery is called the **problem of other minds,** *the fundamental difficulty we have in perceiving the consciousness of others.* How do you know that anyone else is conscious? They tell you that they are conscious, of course, and are often willing to describe in depth how they feel, how they think, what they are experiencing, and how good or how bad it all is. But perhaps they are just *saying* these things. There is no clear way to distinguish a conscious person from someone who might do and say all the same things as a conscious person but who is *not* conscious. Philosophers have called this hypothetical nonconscious person a "zombie," in reference to the living-yet-dead creatures of horror films (Chalmers, 1996). A philosopher's zombie could talk about experiences ("The lights are so bright!") and even seem to react to them (wincing and turning away) but might not be having any inner experience at all. No one knows whether there could be such a zombie, but then again, because of the problem of other minds, none of us will ever know for sure that another person is *not* a zombie.

Even the "consciousness meter" used by anesthesiologists falls short. It certainly doesn't give the anesthesiologist any special insight into what it is like to be the patient on the operating table; it only predicts whether patients will *say* they were conscious. We simply lack the ability to directly perceive the consciousness of others. In short, you are the only thing in the universe you will ever truly know what it is like to be.

The problem of other minds also means there is no way you can tell if another person's experience of anything is at all like yours. Although you know what the color red looks like to you, for instance, you cannot know whether it looks the same to other people. Maybe they're seeing what you see as blue and just *calling* it red in a consistent way. If their inner experience "looks" blue, but they say it looks hot and is the color of a tomato, you'll never be able to tell that their experience differs from yours. Of course, most people have come to trust each other in describing their inner lives, reaching the general assumption that other human minds are pretty much like their own. But they don't know this for a fact, and they can't know it directly.

The problem of other minds is not just a matter of how we perceive people. In an essay asking, What is it like to be a bat?, philosopher Thomas Nagel (1974) wondered

**PHENOMENOLOGY** How things seem to the conscious person.

**PROBLEM OF OTHER MINDS** The fundamental difficulty we have in perceiving the consciousness of others.

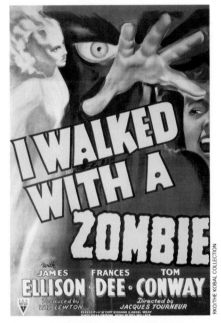

How would you know if you walked with a zombie? Could you perceive its lack of consciousness?

Does a computer have a mind? Champion chess player Gary Kasparov may have thought so as he played against the computer X3D Fritz during a virtual reality match in New York, Tuesday, November 18, 2003. After the third game in a four-game match, Kasparov and computer were tied one-and-a-half games each.

*Noreldo, the mental marvel, reads the mind of his cat, Ned.*

what it's like flying around in a dark cave, sensing the walls through the echoes made by your ultrasonic screeches. Would your experience of the cave include visual images, or sounds, or something else entirely? It's difficult to imagine; we're not bats. And if bat consciousness is hard to imagine, what about all the other animals? When a puppy looks up at you with those warm brown eyes, seemingly saying, "I love you and everything you stand for," you can't really know what it's like in there—so your appreciation of the puppy's mind reflects what's going on in *your* head more than in the puppy's. The perception of other minds is in fact something that happens in the mind of the perceiver.

How do people perceive other minds? Researchers conducting a large online survey asked people to compare the minds of 13 different targets, such as a baby, chimp, robot, man, and woman, on 18 different mental capacities, such as feeling pain, pleasure, hunger, and consciousness (see **FIGURE 8.1**) (Gray, Gray, & Wegner, 2007). Respondents who were judging the mental capacity to feel pain, for example, compared pairs of targets: Is a frog or a dog more able to feel pain? Is a baby or a robot more able to feel pain? Is a 7-week-old fetus or a man in a persistent vegetative state more able to feel pain? When the researchers examined all the comparisons on the different mental capacities with the computational technique of factor analysis (see Chapter 9), they found two dimensions of mind perception. People judge minds according to the capacity for *experience* (such as the ability to feel pain, pleasure, hunger, consciousness, anger, or fear) and the capacity for *agency* (such as the ability for self-control, planning, memory, or thought). As shown in Figure 8.1, respondents rated some targets as having little experience or agency (the dead person), others as having experiences but little agency (the baby), and yet others as having both experience and agency (adult humans). Still others were perceived to have agency without experiences (the robot, God). The perception of minds, then, involves more than just whether something has a mind. People appreciate that minds both have experiences and act as agents that perform actions.

Ultimately, the problem of other minds is a problem for psychological science. As you'll remember from Chapter 2, the scientific method requires that any observation made by one scientist should, in principle, be available for observation by any other scientist. But if other minds aren't observable, how can consciousness be a topic of scientific study? One radical solution is to eliminate consciousness from psychology entirely and follow the other sciences into total objectivity by renouncing the study of *anything* mental. This was the solution offered by behaviorism, and it turned out to have its own shortcomings, as you saw in Chapter 1. Despite the problem of other minds, modern psychology has embraced the study of consciousness. The astonishing richness of mental life simply cannot be ignored.

**Figure 8.1 Dimensions of Mind Perception** When participants judged the mental capacities of 13 targets, two dimensions of mind perception were discovered (Gray et al., 2007). Participants perceived minds as varying in the capacity for experience (such as abilities to feel pain or pleasure) and in the capacity for agency (such as abilities to plan or exert self-control). They perceived normal adult humans (male, female, or "you," the respondent) to have minds on both dimensions, whereas other targets were perceived to have reduced experience or agency. The man in a persistent vegetative state ("PVS man"), for example, was judged to have only some experience and very little agency.

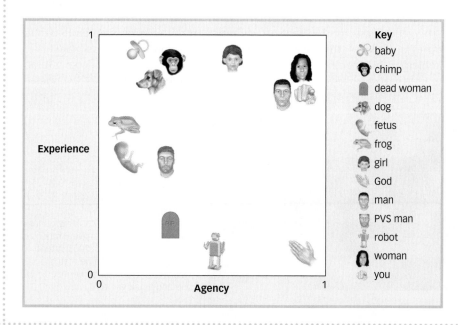

**Key**
- baby
- chimp
- dead woman
- dog
- fetus
- frog
- girl
- God
- man
- PVS man
- robot
- woman
- you

## The Mind/Body Problem

Another mystery of consciousness is the **mind/body problem**, *the issue of how the mind is related to the brain and body.* French philosopher and mathematician René Descartes (1596–1650) is famous, among other things, for proposing that mind and body are made of different substances. As you read in Chapter 1, Descartes believed that the human body is a machine made of physical matter but that the human mind or soul is a separate entity made of a "thinking substance." He proposed that the mind has its effects on the brain and body through the pineal gland, a small structure located near the center of the brain. It has the appealing property of being unitary, whereas the rest of the brain is split into right and left halves (see **FIGURE 8.2**). In fact, the pineal gland is not even a nerve structure but rather is an endocrine gland quite poorly equipped to serve as a center of human consciousness.

But Descartes was right in pointing out the difficulty of reconciling the physical body with the mind. Most psychologists assume that mental events are intimately tied to brain events, such that every thought, perception, or feeling is associated with a particular pattern of activation of neurons in the brain (see Chapter 3). Thinking about a particular duck, for instance, occurs with a unique array of neural connections and activations. If the neurons repeat that pattern, then you must be thinking of the duck; conversely, if you think of the duck, the brain activity occurs in that pattern. Far from the tiny connection between mind and brain in the pineal gland that was proposed by Descartes, instead the mind and brain are connected everywhere to each other! In other words, "the mind is what the brain does" (Minsky, 1986, p. 287). Studies of the brain structures associated with conscious thinking in particular (as opposed to all the other mental efforts that go on in the background of the mind) suggest that conscious thought is supported widely in the brain by many different structures (Koch, 2004).

One telling set of studies, however, suggests that the brain's activities *precede* the activities of the conscious mind. The electrical activity in the brains of volunteers was measured using sensors placed on their scalps as they repeatedly decided when to move a hand (Libet, 1985). Participants were also asked to indicate exactly when they consciously chose to move by reporting the position of a dot moving rapidly around the face of a clock just at the point of the decision (**FIGURE 8.3a**). As a rule, the brain begins to show electrical activity around half a second before a voluntary action (535 milliseconds, to be exact). This makes sense since brain activity certainly seems to be necessary to get an action started.

What this experiment revealed, though, was that the brain also started to show electrical activity before the person's conscious decision to move. As shown in **FIGURE 8.3b**, these studies found that the brain becomes active more than 300 milliseconds before participants report that they are consciously trying to move. The feeling that you are consciously willing your actions, it seems, may be a result rather than a cause of your brain activity. Although your personal intuition is that you *think* of an action and *then* do it, these experiments suggest that your brain is getting started before *either* the thinking or the doing, preparing the way for both thought and action. Quite simply, it may appear to us that our minds are leading our brains and bodies, but the order of events may be the other way around (Wegner, 2002).

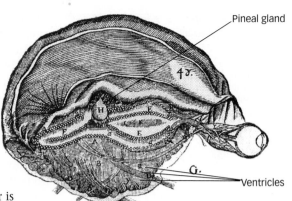

Pineal gland

Ventricles

**Figure 8.2 Seat of the Soul** Descartes imagined that the seat of the soul—and consciousness—might reside in the pineal gland located in the ventricles of the brain. This original drawing from Descartes (1662) shows the pineal gland (H) nicely situated for a soul, right in the middle of the brain.

**MIND/BODY PROBLEM** The issue of how the mind is related to the brain and body.

**Figure 8.3 The Timing of Conscious Will** (a) In Benjamin Libet's experiments, the participant was asked to move fingers at will while simultaneously watching a dot move around the face of a clock to mark the moment at which the action was consciously willed. Meanwhile, EEG sensors timed the onset of brain activation and EMG sensors timed the muscle movement. (b) The experiment showed that brain activity (EEG) precedes the willed movement of the finger (EMG) but that the reported time of consciously willing the finger to move follows the brain activity.

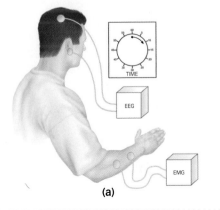

(a)

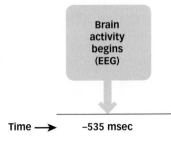

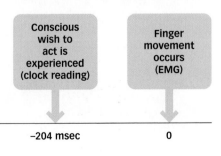

| Brain activity begins (EEG) | Conscious wish to act is experienced (clock reading) | Finger movement occurs (EMG) |
|---|---|---|

Time → −535 msec −204 msec 0

(b)

**DICHOTIC LISTENING** A task in which people wearing headphones hear different messages presented to each ear.

**COCKTAIL PARTY PHENOMENON** A phenomenon in which people tune in one message even while they filter out others nearby.

Consciousness has its mysteries, but psychologists like a challenge. Although researchers may not be able to see the consciousness of others or know exactly how consciousness arises from the brain, this does not prevent them from collecting people's reports of conscious experiences and learning how these reports reveal the nature of consciousness. We'll consider that topic next.

## The Nature of Consciousness

How would you describe your own consciousness? Researchers examining people's descriptions suggest that consciousness has four basic properties—intentionality, unity, selectivity, and transience of consciousness—that it occurs on different levels, and that it includes a range of different contents. Let's examine each of these points in turn.

### Four Basic Properties

Consciousness is always *about* something. Philosophers call this first property the *intentionality of consciousness,* the quality of being directed toward an object. Psychologists, in turn, have tried to measure the relationship between consciousness and its objects, examining the size and duration of the relationship. How long can consciousness be directed toward an object, and how many objects can it take on at one time? Researchers have found that conscious attention is limited. Despite all the lush detail you see in your mind's eye, the kaleidoscope of sights and sounds and feelings and thoughts, the object of your consciousness at any one moment is just a small part of all of this (see **FIGURE 8.4**). To describe how this limitation works, psychologists refer to three other properties of consciousness: unity, selectivity, and transience.

The *unity of consciousness* is its resistance to division. This property becomes clear when you try to attend to more than one thing at a time. You may wishfully think that you can study and watch TV simultaneously, for example, but research suggests not. One study had research participants divide their attention by reacting to two games superimposed on a television screen (see **FIGURE 8.5**). They had to push one button when one person slapped another's hands in the first game and push another button when a ball was passed in the second game. The participants were easily able to follow one game at a time, but their performance took a nosedive when they tried to follow both simultaneously. Their error rate when attending to the two tasks was eight times greater than when attending to either task alone (Neisser & Becklen, 1975). Your attempts to study, in other words, could seriously interfere with a full appreciation of your TV show.

The *selectivity of consciousness* is its capacity to include some objects and not others. This property is shown through studies of **dichotic listening,** *in which people wearing headphones are presented with different messages in each ear.* Research participants were instructed to repeat aloud the words they heard in one ear while a different message

**Figure 8.4 Bellotto's Dresden and Close-up** The people on the bridge in the distance look very finely detailed in *View of Dresden with the Frauenkirche at Left,* by Bernardo Bellotto (1720–80) (left). However, when you examine the detail closely (right), you find that the people are made of brushstrokes merely *suggesting* people—an arm here, a torso there. Consciousness produces a similar impression of "filling in," as it seems to consist of extreme detail even in areas that are peripheral (Dennett, 1991).

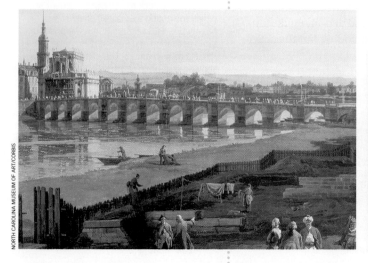

NORTH CAROLINA MUSEUM OF ART/CORBIS

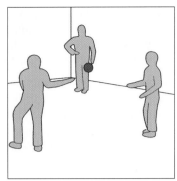

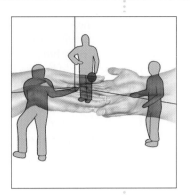

**A**　　　　　　　　　　**B**　　　　　　　　　　**C**

**Figure 8.5** **Divided Attention** Research participants presented with two different games (A and B) could easily follow each game separately. When participants tried to follow the action in the two different games simultaneously (C), they performed remarkably poorly (Neisser & Becklen, 1975).

was presented to the other ear (Cherry, 1953). As a result of focusing on the words they were supposed to repeat, participants noticed little of the second message, often not even realizing that at some point it changed from English to German! So, consciousness *filters out* some information. At the same time, participants did notice when the voice in the unattended ear changed from a male's to a female's, suggesting that the selectivity of consciousness can also work to *tune in* other information.

How does consciousness decide what to filter in and what to tune out? The conscious system is most inclined to select information of special interest to the person. For example, in what has come to be known as the **cocktail party phenomenon,** *people tune in one message even while they filter out others nearby.* In the dichotic listening situation, for example, research participants are especially likely to notice if their own name is spoken into the unattended ear (Moray, 1959). Perhaps you too have noticed how abruptly your attention is diverted from whatever conversation you are having when someone else within earshot at the party mentions your name. Selectivity is not only a property of waking consciousness, however; the mind works this way in other states. People are more sensitive to their own name than others' names, for example, even during sleep (Oswald, Taylor, & Triesman, 1960). This is why when you are trying to wake someone up, it is best to use the person's name (particularly if you want to sleep with that person again).

A final basic property is the *transience of consciousness,* or its tendency to change. Consciousness wiggles and fidgets like that toddler in the seat behind you on the airplane. The mind wanders not just sometimes, but incessantly, from one "right now" to the next "right now" and then on to the next (Wegner, 1997). William James, whom you met way back in Chapter 1, famously described consciousness as a stream: "Consciousness . . . does not appear to itself chopped up in bits. Such words as 'chain' or 'train' do not describe it. . . . It is nothing jointed; it flows. A 'river' or a 'stream' are the metaphors by which it is most naturally described" (James, 1890, Vol. 1, p. 239). Books written in the "stream of consciousness" style, such as James Joyce's *Ulysses,* illustrate the whirling, chaotic, and constantly changing flow of consciousness. Here's an excerpt:

> I wished I could have picked every morsel of that chicken out of my fingers it was so tasty and browned and as tender as anything only for I didn't want to eat everything on my plate those forks and fishslicers were hallmarked silver too I wish I had some I could easily have slipped a couple into my muff when I was playing with them then always hanging out of them for money in a restaurant for the bit you put down your throat we have to be thankful for our mangy cup of tea itself as a great compliment to be noticed the way the world is divided in any case if its going to go on I want at least two other good chemises for one thing and but I dont know what kind of drawers he likes none at all I think didn't he say yes and half the girls in Gibraltar never wore them either naked as God made them that Andalusian singing her Manola she didn't make much secret of what she hadnt yes and the second pair of silkette stockings is laddered after one days wear I could have brought them back to Lewers this morning and kicked up a row and made that one change them only not to upset myself and run the risk of walking into him and ruining the whole thing and one of those kidfitting corsets Id want advertised

Participants in a dichotic listening experiment hear different messages played to the right and left ear and may be asked to "shadow" one of the messages by repeating it aloud.

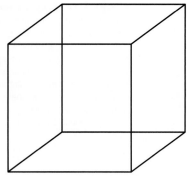

**Figure 8.6 The Necker Cube** This cube has the property of reversible perspective in that you can bring one or the other of its two square faces to the front in your mind's eye. Although it may take awhile to reverse the figure at first, once people have learned to do it, they can reverse it regularly, about once every 3 seconds (Gomez et al., 1995). The stream of consciousness flows even when the target is a constant object.

cheap in the Gentlewoman with elastic gores on the hips he saved the one I have but thats no good what did they say they give a delightful figure line 11/6 obviating that unsightly broad appearance across the lower back to reduce flesh my belly is a bit too big Ill have to knock off the stout at dinner or am I getting too fond of it (1994, p. 741)

The stream of consciousness may flow in this way partly because of the limited capacity of working memory. Remember from Chapter 5 that you can hold only so much information in your mind, so when more information is selected, some of what is currently there must disappear. As a result, your focus of attention keeps changing. The Necker cube (see **FIGURE 8.6**) is the visual counterpart to stream of consciousness writing. Although the cube is a constant object, the stream of consciousness flows, reversing the figure.

The basic properties of consciousness are reminiscent of the "bouncing ball" that moves from word to word when the lyrics of a sing-along tune are shown on a karaoke machine. The ball always bounces on something (intentionality), there is only one ball (unity), the ball selects one target and not others (selectivity), and the ball keeps bouncing all the time (transience).

## Levels of Consciousness

Consciousness can also be understood as having levels, ranging from minimal consciousness to full consciousness to self-consciousness. These levels of consciousness would probably all register as "conscious" on that wakefulness meter for surgery patients you read about at the beginning of the chapter. The levels of consciousness that psychologists distinguish are not a matter of degree of overall brain activity but instead involve different qualities of awareness of the world and of the self.

In its minimal form, consciousness is just a connection between the person and the world. When you sense the sun coming in through the window, for example, you might turn toward the light. Such **minimal consciousness** is *consciousness that occurs when the mind inputs sensations and may output behavior* (Armstrong, 1980). This level of consciousness is a kind of sensory awareness and responsiveness, something that could even happen when someone pokes you during sleep and you turn over. Something seems to register in your mind, at least in the sense that you experience it, but you may not think at all about having had the experience. It could be that animals or, for that matter, even plants can have this minimal level of consciousness. But because of the problem of other minds and the notorious reluctance of animals and plants to talk to us, we can't know for sure that they *experience* the things that make them respond. At least in the case of humans, we can safely assume that there is something it "feels like" to be them and that when they're awake, they are at least minimally conscious.

Human consciousness is often more than this, of course, but what exactly gets added? Consider the glorious feeling of waking up on a spring morning as rays of sun stream across your pillow. It's not just that you are having this experience; being fully conscious means that you are also *aware* that you are having this experience. The critical ingredient that accompanies **full consciousness** is that you *know and are able to report your mental state*. That's a subtle distinction; being fully conscious means that you are aware of having a mental state while you are experiencing the mental state itself.

**MINIMAL CONSCIOUSNESS** A low-level kind of sensory awareness and responsiveness that occurs when the mind inputs sensations and may output behavior.

**FULL CONSCIOUSNESS** Consciousness in which you know and are able to report your mental state.

**SELF-CONSCIOUSNESS** A distinct level of consciousness in which the person's attention is drawn to the self as an object.

It's easy to zone out while reading: Your eyes continue to follow the print, but you're not processing the content and your mind has drifted elsewhere. Hello? Are you still paying attention while you're reading this?

STOCKBYTE/GETTY

When you have a hurt leg and mindlessly rub it, for instance, your pain may be minimally conscious. After all, you seem to be experiencing pain because you are indeed rubbing your leg. It is only when you realize that it hurts, though, that the pain becomes fully conscious. Full consciousness involves not only thinking about things but also thinking about the fact that you are thinking about things (Jaynes, 1976).

Full consciousness fluctuates over time, coming and going throughout the day. You've no doubt had experiences of reading and suddenly realizing that you have "zoned out" and are not processing what you read. When people are asked to report each time they zone out during reading, they report doing this every few minutes. Even then, when an experimenter asks these people at other random points in their reading whether they are zoned out at that moment, they are sometimes caught in the state of having "zoned out" even before they've noticed it (Schooler, Reichle, & Halpern, 2001). It's at just this point—when you are zoned out but don't know it—that you seem to be unaware of your own mental state. You are minimally conscious of wherever your mind has wandered, and you return with a jolt into the full consciousness that your mind had drifted away. Thinking about thinking allows you to realize that you weren't thinking about what you wanted to be thinking.

Full consciousness involves a certain consciousness of oneself; the person notices the self in a particular mental state ("Here I am, reading this sentence"). However, this is not quite the same thing as *self*-consciousness. Sometimes consciousness is entirely flooded with the self ("Gosh, I'm such a good reader!"), focusing on the self to the exclusion of almost everything else. William James (1890) and other theorists have suggested that **self-consciousness** is yet another distinct level of consciousness in which *the person's attention is drawn to the self as an object*. Most people report experiencing such self-consciousness when they are embarrassed; when they find themselves the focus of attention in a group; when someone focuses a camera on them; or when they are deeply introspective about their thoughts, feelings, or personal qualities.

Self-consciousness brings with it a tendency to evaluate yourself and notice your shortcomings. Looking in a mirror, for example, is all it takes to make people evaluate themselves—thinking not just about their looks but also about whether they are good or bad in other ways. People go out of their way to avoid mirrors when they've done something they are ashamed of (Duval & Wicklund, 1972). Self-consciousness can certainly spoil a good mood, so much so that a tendency to be chronically self-conscious is associated with depression (Pyszczynski, Holt, & Greenberg, 1987). However, because it makes people self-critical, the self-consciousness that results when people see their own mirror images can make them briefly more helpful, more cooperative, and less aggressive (Gibbons, 1990). Perhaps everyone would be a bit more civilized if mirrors were held up for them to see themselves as objects of their own scrutiny.

Most animals can't follow this path to civilization. The typical dog, cat, or bird seems mystified by a mirror, ignoring it or acting as though there is some other critter back there. However, chimpanzees that have spent time with mirrors sometimes behave in ways that suggest they recognize themselves in a mirror. To examine this, researchers painted an odorless red dye over the eyebrow of an anesthetized chimp and then watched when the awakened chimp was presented with a mirror (Gallup, 1977). If the chimp interpreted the mirror image as a representation of some other chimp with an unusual approach to cosmetics, we would expect it just to look at the mirror or perhaps to reach toward it. But the chimp reached toward its *own eye* as it looked into the mirror—not the mirror image—suggesting that it recognized the image as a reflection of itself.

Versions of this experiment have now been repeated with many different animals (Gallup, 1997), and it turns out that like humans, animals such as chimpanzees and orangutans, possibly dolphins (Reiss & Marino, 2001), and maybe even elephants (Plotnik, de Waal, & Reiss, 2006) recognize their own mirror images. Dogs, cats, birds, monkeys, and gorillas have been tested and don't seem to know they are looking at themselves. Even humans don't have self-recognition right away. Infants don't recognize themselves in mirrors until they've reached about 18 months of age (Lewis & Brooks-Gunn, 1979). The experience of self-consciousness, as measured by self-recognition in mirrors, is limited to a few animals and to humans only after a certain stage of development.

Self-consciousness is a curse and a blessing. Looking in a mirror can make people evaluate themselves on deeper attributes such as honesty as well as superficial ones such as looks.

A chimpanzee tried to wipe off the red dye on its eyebrow in the Gallup experiment. This suggests that some animals recognize themselves in the mirror.

**Dilbert**

## Conscious Contents

What's on your mind? For that matter, what's on everybody's mind? The contents of consciousness are, of course, as rich and varied as human experience itself. But there are some common themes in the topics that occupy consciousness and in the form that consciousness seems to take as different contents come to mind.

One way to learn what is on people's minds is to ask them, and much research has called on people simply to *think aloud.* A more systematic approach is the *experience sampling technique,* in which people are asked to report their conscious experiences at particular times. Equipped with electronic beepers, for example, participants are asked to record their current thoughts when beeped at random times throughout the day (Csikszentmihalyi & Larson, 1987). Experience sampling studies show that consciousness is dominated by the immediate environment, what is seen, felt, heard, tasted, and smelled—all are at the forefront of the mind. Much of consciousness beyond this orientation to the environment turns to the person's *current concerns,* or what the person is thinking about repeatedl*y* (Klinger, 1975). **TABLE 8.1** shows the results of a Minnesota study where 175 college students were asked to report their current concerns (Goetzman, Hughes, & Klinger, 1994). The researchers sorted the concerns into the categories shown in the table. Keep in mind that these concerns are ones the students didn't mind reporting to psychologists; their private preoccupations may have been different and probably far more interesting.

Think for a moment about your own current concerns. What topics have been on your mind the most in the past day or two? Your mental "to do" list may include things you want to get, keep, avoid, work on, remember, and so on (Little, 1993). Items on the list often pop into mind, sometimes even with an emotional punch

| Table **8.1** | What's on Your Mind? College Students' Current Concerns | |
|---|---|---|
| **Current Concern Category** | **Example** | **Frequency of Students Who Mentioned the Concern** |
| Family | Gain better relations with immediate family | 40% |
| Roommate | Change attitude or behavior of roommate | 29% |
| Household | Clean room | 52% |
| Friends | Make new friends | 42% |
| Dating | Desire to date a certain person | 24% |
| Sexual intimacy | Abstaining from sex | 16% |
| Health | Diet and exercise | 85% |
| Employment | Get a summer job | 33% |
| Education | Go to graduate school | 43% |
| Social activities | Gain acceptance into a campus organization | 34% |
| Religious | Attend church more | 51% |
| Financial | Pay rent or bills | 8% |
| Government | Change government policy | 14% |

("The test in this class is tomorrow!"). People in one study had their skin conductance level (SCL) measured to assess their emotional responses (Nikula, Klinger, & Larson-Gutman, 1993). SCL sensors attached to their fingers indicated when their skin became moist—a good indication that they were thinking about something distressing. Once in a while, SCL would rise spontaneously, and at these times the researchers quizzed the participants about their conscious thoughts. These emotional moments, compared to those when SCL was normal, often corresponded with a current concern popping into mind. Thoughts that are not emotional all by themselves can still come to mind with an emotional bang when they are topics of our current concern.

Current concerns do not seem all that concerning, however, during *daydreaming*, a state of consciousness in which a seemingly purposeless flow of thoughts comes to mind. When thoughts drift along this way, it may seem as if you are just wasting time. However, psychologists have long suspected that daydreams reflect the mind's attempts to deal with difficult projects and problems. A computer program designed to simulate daydreams, for example, works on the basis of this assumption to produce passages that resemble human daydreams (Mueller, 1990). The program draws on the idea that people learn from past experiences by "replaying" them in daydreams, that they discover creative approaches to the future by imaging fanciful scenarios, and that all this helps them to control and channel their emotions.

In one case, the Daydreamer program was given the information that it had been turned down for a date by a famous Hollywood actress and then was allowed to "daydream" in response. In a daydream, it imagined that going out with the actress would have been a hassle because of the reporters; this daydream helped rationalize the failure and make it less disappointing. Another daydream by the program envisioned a new way of asking her out, one that would have secured her phone number so she could have been approached again later on; this response created new information that would be helpful in similar situations in the future. Human daydreams and fantasies, like these computer-simulated versions, may be more useful than they appear at first glance.

The current concerns that populate consciousness can sometimes get the upper hand, transforming daydreams or everyday thoughts into rumination and worry. Thoughts that return again and again, or problem-solving attempts that never seem to succeed, can come to dominate consciousness. When this happens, people may exert **mental control**, *the attempt to change conscious states of mind.* For example, someone troubled by a recurring worry about the future ("What if I can't get a decent job when I graduate?") might choose to try not to think about this because it causes too much anxiety and uncertainty. Whenever this thought comes to mind, the person engages in **thought suppression**, the *conscious avoidance of a thought.* This may seem like a perfectly sensible strategy because it eliminates the worry and allows the person to move on to think about something else.

Or does it? The great Russian novelist Fyodor Dostoevsky (1863–1955) remarked on the difficulty of thought suppression: "Try to pose for yourself this task: not to think of a polar bear, and you will see that the cursed thing will come to mind every minute." Inspired by this observation, Daniel Wegner and his colleagues gave people this exact task in the laboratory (1987). Participants were asked to try not to think about a white bear for 5 minutes while they recorded all their thoughts aloud into a tape recorder. In addition, they were asked to ring a bell if the thought of a white bear came to mind. On average, they mentioned the white bear or rang the bell (indicating the thought) more than once per minute. Thought suppression simply didn't work and instead produced a flurry of returns of the unwanted thought. What's more, when some research participants later were specifically asked to change tasks and deliberately *think* about a white bear, they became oddly preoccupied with it. A graph of their bell rings in **FIGURE 8.7** on the next page shows that these participants had the white bear come to mind far more often than did people who had only been asked to think about the bear from the outset, with no prior suppression. This **rebound effect of thought suppression**, *the tendency of a thought to return to consciousness with greater frequency following suppression,* suggests that attempts at mental control may be difficult indeed. The act of trying to suppress a thought may itself cause that thought to return to consciousness in a robust way.

**MENTAL CONTROL** The attempt to change conscious states of mind.

**THOUGHT SUPPRESSION** The conscious avoidance of a thought.

**REBOUND EFFECT OF THOUGHT SUPPRESSION** The tendency of a thought to return to consciousness with greater frequency following suppression.

*"Are you not thinking what I'm not thinking?"*

**Figure 8.7 Rebound Effect** Research participants were first asked to try not to think about a white bear, and then they were asked to think about it and to ring a bell whenever it came to mind. Compared to those who were simply asked to think about a bear without prior suppression, those people who *first* suppressed the thought showed a rebound of increased thinking (Wegner et al., 1987).

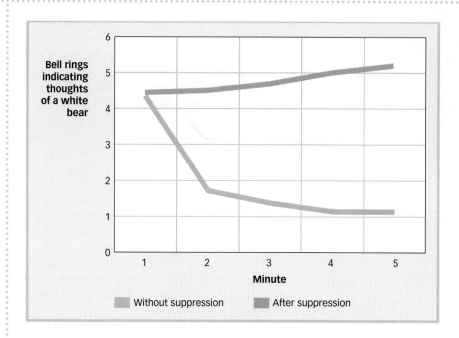

As with thought suppression, other attempts to "steer" consciousness in any direction can result in mental states that are precisely the opposite of those desired. How ironic: Trying to consciously achieve one task may produce precisely the opposite outcome! These ironic effects seem most likely to occur when the person is distracted or under stress. People who are distracted while they are trying to get into a good mood, for example, tend to become sad (Wegner, Erber, & Zanakos, 1993), and those who are distracted while trying to relax actually become more anxious than those who are not trying to relax (Wegner, Broome, & Blumberg, 1997). Likewise, an attempt not to overshoot a golf putt, undertaken during distraction, often yields the unwanted overshot (Wegner, Ansfield, & Pilloff, 1998). The theory of **ironic processes of mental control** proposes that such *ironic errors occur because the mental process that monitors errors can itself produce them* (Wegner, 1994). In the attempt not to think of a white bear, for instance, a small part of the mind is ironically *searching* for the white bear.

This ironic-monitoring process is not present in consciousness. After all, trying *not* to think of something would be useless if monitoring the progress of suppression required keeping that target in consciousness. For example, if trying not to think of a white bear meant that you consciously kept repeating to yourself, "No white bear! No white bear!" then you've failed before you've begun: That thought is present in consciousness even as you strive to eliminate it. Rather, the ironic monitor is a process of the mind that works *outside* of consciousness, making us sensitive to all the things we do not want to think, feel, or do so that we can notice and consciously take steps to regain control if these things come back to mind. The person trying not to think about a white bear, for

**IRONIC PROCESSES OF MENTAL CONTROL** Mental processes that can produce ironic errors because monitoring for errors can itself produce them.

**DYNAMIC UNCONSCIOUS** An active system encompassing a lifetime of hidden memories, the person's deepest instincts and desires, and the person's inner struggle to control these forces.

**REPRESSION** A mental process that removes unacceptable thoughts and memories from consciousness.

Go ahead, look away from the book for a minute and try not to think about a white bear.

example, would unconsciously monitor any signs of the thought and so be prompted to try consciously to think of something else if it returns. As this unconscious monitoring whirs along in the background, it unfortunately increases the person's sensitivity to the very thought that is unwanted. Ironic processes are mental functions that are needed for effective mental control—they help in the process of banishing a thought from consciousness—but they can sometimes yield the very failure they seem designed to overcome. Ironic processes of mental control are among the mindbugs that the study of psychology holds up for examination. And because ironic processes occur outside of consciousness, they remind us, too, that much of the mind's machinery may be hidden from our view, lying outside the fringes of our experience.

## The Unconscious Mind

Many mental processes are unconscious, in the sense that they occur without our experience of them. When we speak, for instance, "We are not really conscious either of the search for words, or of putting the words together into phrases, or of putting the phrases into sentences. . . . [The] actual process of thinking . . . is not conscious at all . . . only its preparation, its materials, and its end result are consciously perceived" (Jaynes, 1976). Just to put the role of consciousness in perspective, think for a moment about the mental processes involved in simple addition. What happens in consciousness between hearing a problem ("What's 4 plus 5?") and thinking of the answer ("9")? Probably nothing—the answer just appears in the mind. But this is a piece of calculation that must take at least a bit of thinking. After all, at a very young age you may have had to solve such problems by counting on your fingers. Now that you don't have to do that anymore (. . . right?), the answer seems to pop into your head automatically, by virtue of a process that doesn't require you to be aware of any underlying steps, and, for that matter, doesn't even *allow* you to be aware of the steps. The answer just suddenly appears.

In the early part of the 20th century, when structuralist psychologists, such as Wilhelm Wundt, believed that introspection was the best method of research (see Chapter 1), research volunteers trained in describing their thoughts tried to discern what happens in such cases—when a simple problem brings to mind a simple answer (e.g., Watt, 1905). They drew the same blank you probably did. Nothing conscious seems to bridge this gap, but the answer comes from somewhere, and this emptiness points to the unconscious mind. To explore these hidden recesses, we can look at the classical theory of the unconscious introduced by Sigmund Freud and then at the modern cognitive psychology of unconscious mental processes.

### Freudian Unconscious

The true champion of the unconscious mind was Sigmund Freud. As you read in Chapter 1, Freud's psychoanalytic theory viewed conscious thought as the surface of a much deeper mind made up of unconscious processes. Far more than just a collection of hidden processes, Freud described a **dynamic unconscious**—*an active system encompassing a lifetime of hidden memories, the person's deepest instincts and desires, and the person's inner struggle to control these forces.* The dynamic unconscious might contain hidden sexual thoughts about one's parents, for example, or destructive urges aimed at a helpless infant—the kinds of thoughts people keep secret from others and may not even acknowledge to themselves. According to Freud's theory, the unconscious is a force to be held in check by **repression**, *a mental process that removes unacceptable thoughts and memories from consciousness and keeps them in the unconscious.* Without repression, a person might think, do, or say every unconscious impulse or animal urge, no matter how selfish or immoral. With repression, these desires are held in the recesses of the dynamic unconscious.

Freud looked for evidence of the unconscious mind in speech errors and lapses of consciousness, or what are commonly called "Freudian slips." Forgetting the name of someone you dislike, for example, is a mindbug that seems to have special meaning. Freud believed that errors are not random and instead have some surplus meaning that may appear to have been created by an intelligent unconscious mind, even though the person consciously disavows them. For example, when Condoleezza Rice, serving as the National Security Advisor for President George W. Bush, was addressing an audience at a Washington, DC, dinner party, she reportedly said, "As I was telling my husba—" before breaking off and correcting herself: "As I was telling President Bush . . . ." Although no one seriously believes the single Rice and married Bush are an "item," you can almost hear her dynamic unconscious trumpeting the psychological intimacy they enjoy.

One experiment revealed that slips of speech can indeed be prompted by a person's pressing concerns (Motley & Baars, 1979). Research participants in one group were told they might receive minor electric shocks, whereas those in another group heard no mention of this. Each person was then asked to read quickly through a series of word pairs, including *shad bock*. Those in the group warned about shock more often slipped in pronouncing this pair, blurting out *bad shock*.

Unlike errors created in experiments such as this one, many of the meaningful errors Freud attributed to the dynamic unconscious were not predicted in advance and so seem to depend on clever after-the-fact interpretations. That's not so good. Suggesting a pattern to a series of random events is quite clever, but it's not the same as scientifically predicting and explaining when and why an event should happen. Anyone can offer a reasonable, compelling explanation for an event after it has already happened, but the true work of science is to offer testable hypotheses that are evaluated based on reliable evidence. Freud's book *The Psychopathology of Everyday Life* (Freud, 1901/1938) suggests not so much that the dynamic unconscious produces errors but that Freud himself was a master at finding meaning in errors that might otherwise have seemed random. Condi Rice's curious slip about being married to President Bush may have been a random error, only meaningful in the minds of news commentators who found it amusing and worthy of explanation.

### Cognitive Unconscious

Modern psychologists share Freud's interest in the impact of unconscious mental processes on consciousness and on behavior. However, rather than Freud's vision of the unconscious as a teeming menagerie of animal urges and repressed thoughts, the current study of the unconscious mind views it as the factory that builds the products of conscious thought and behavior (Kihlstrom, 1987; Wilson, 2002). The **cognitive unconscious** includes *all the mental processes that are not experienced by the person but that give rise to the person's thoughts, choices, emotions, and behavior* (see the Hot Science box on the facing page).

One indication of the cognitive unconscious at work is when the person's thought or behavior is changed by exposure to information outside of consciousness. This happens in **subliminal perception**, when *thought or behavior are influenced by stimuli that a person cannot consciously report perceiving*. Worries about the potential of subliminal influence were first provoked in 1957, when a marketer, James Vicary, claimed he had increased concession sales at a New Jersey theater by flashing the words "Eat Popcorn" and "Drink Coke" briefly on-screen during movies. It turns out his story was a hoax, and many attempts to increase sales using similar methods have failed. But the very idea of influencing behavior outside of consciousness created a wave of alarm about insidious "subliminal persuasion" that still concerns people (Epley, Savitsky, & Kachelski, 1999; Pratkanis, 1992).

Subliminal perception does occur, but the degree of influence it has on behavior is not very large (Dijksterhuis, Aarts, & Smith, 2005). One set of studies examined whether beverage choices could be influenced by brief visual exposures to thirst-related words (Strahan, Spencer, & Zanna, 2002). Research volunteers were asked to perform a computer task that involved deciding whether each of 26 letter strings was a word or not. This ensured that they would be looking intently at the screen when, just before each letter string appeared, a target was shown that could not be consciously perceived: A word was flashed for 16 milliseconds just off the center of the screen, followed by a row of *x*'s in that spot to mask any visual memory of the word. For half the participants, this subliminal word was thirst related (such as *thirst* and *dry*) and for the other half it was unrelated (such as *pirate* and *won*). When the volunteers afterward were

**COGNITIVE UNCONSCIOUS** The mental processes that give rise to the person's thoughts, choices, emotions, and behavior even though they are not experienced by the person.

**SUBLIMINAL PERCEPTION** A thought or behavior that is influenced by stimuli that a person cannot consciously report perceiving.

# How Smart Is the Unconscious Mind?

A BASKETBALL PLAYER ON A HOT STREAK IS sometimes described as "unconscious," in the sense that the play is so good that the player doesn't even seem to be thinking about it. Although a truly unconscious player might be a serious liability for the team, lying there on the floor and all, a player whose *moves* appear to be unconscious is usually an asset. No doubt you trust the talents of your unconscious mind as well. When you type, for example, your unconscious mind takes care of remembering what finger movements stand for what letters on your keyboard so you only have to worry consciously about what to write. Your unconscious mind knows, too, that when you extend your arm out in front of you, your body must lean backward just slightly to balance the movement, or you would fall over forward. The unconscious mind can be a kind of "mental butler," taking over background tasks that are too tedious, subtle, or bothersome for consciousness to trifle with (Bargh & Chartrand, 1999; Bower, 1999).

Psychologists have long debated just how smart this mental butler might be. Freud attributed great intelligence to the unconscious, believing that it harbors complex motives and inner conflicts and that it expresses these in an astonishing array of thoughts and emotions, as well as psychological disorders (see Chapter 12). Contemporary cognitive psychologists wonder whether the unconscious is so smart, however, and point out that some unconscious processes even seem downright stupid (Loftus & Klinger, 1992). For example, the unconscious processes that underlie the perception of subliminal visual stimuli do not seem able to understand the combined meaning of word pairs, although they can understand single words. To the *conscious* mind, for example, a word pair such as *enemy loses* is somewhat positive—it is good to have your enemy lose. However, subliminal presentations of this word pair make people think of negative things, as though the unconscious mind is simply adding together the unpleasantness of the single words *enemy* and *loses* (Greenwald, 1992). Perhaps the mental butler is not all that bright.

New research suggests, however, that at least in some cases the unconscious mind makes better decisions than the conscious mind. Participants in an experiment were asked to choose which of three hypothetical people they would prefer to have as a roommate (Dijksterhuis, 2004). Each candidate was described with 12 attributes, so the participants saw lots of information—36 items such as "Roommate A has fun friends," "Roommate B is messy," "Roommate C has a

**Choosing a roommate can be like playing the lottery: Sometimes you win, many times you lose.**

good CD collection," and so on, each item presented for just 2 seconds on a computer screen. The research participants weren't told that the information was rigged to make one roommate a good choice (eight positive qualities, four negative), another one a fair choice (six positive qualities, six negative), and the third a poor choice (four positive qualities, eight negative). You may have guessed that people would pick up on this, and you're right—many did—preferring the good choice to the fair choice and the fair choice to the poor choice.

The participants were divided into three groups, and each group was instructed to arrive at the best decision using a different method. One group of people was prompted to make a *conscious decision;* after seeing the information they were given 4 minutes to think about what their answer should be. A second group was given no time at all to make a wise decision; this *immediate decision* group was asked for their answer as soon as the information display was over. Finally, the third group was encouraged to reach an *unconscious decision.* This group was allowed the same 4 minutes of time

after the display ended to give their answer (as the conscious group had been given), but during this interval their conscious minds were occupied with solving a set of anagrams (for example, what word can be made from the letters *icpeb?*). They were distracted from thinking consciously about what to do. And by the way, the anagram spells *bicep.*

As you can see in the figure below, the unconscious decision group showed a stronger preference for the good roommate than did the immediate decision or conscious decision groups. Unconscious minds seemed *better able* than conscious minds to sort out the information and arrive at the best choice. Dijksterhuis found in other studies that people making unconscious decisions remember the information about their choice alternatives in a more organized way than do those making conscious or hurried decisions, which may be why the unconscious decision is a better one. In some cases, consciousness can even hurt by drawing attention to idiosyncratic ideas and taking attention away from your "gut feeling" (Wilson & Schooler, 1991). This may be why you sometimes end up more satisfied with decisions you make after just "letting it happen" than with the decisions you consciously agonize over.

Should all decisions be made unconsciously? It is important to remember that even gut feelings can be wrong. After all, an unconscious mind that can't appreciate when an "enemy loses" may not always be a wise leader. On balance, this new research on the apparent intelligence of unconscious decisions suggests simply that devoting more time and thought to a decision is no guarantee that the smartest choice will be made.

**People making roommate decisions who had some time for unconscious deliberation chose better roommates than those who thought about the choice consciously or those who made snap decisions (Dijksterhuis, 2004).**

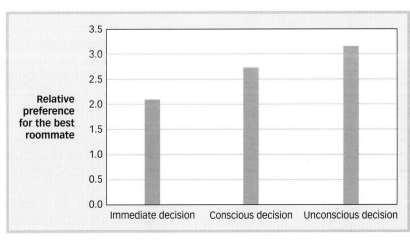

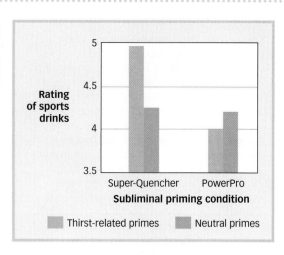

**Figure 8.8** Subliminal Influence
Preference for a thirst-quenching beverage, "Super-Quencher," increased relative to another sports drink, "PowerPro," among people subliminally primed with thirst words (Strahan et al., 2002).

President George W. Bush denied that Republican Party commercials used subliminal messages (which he called "subliminable") after Democrats complained that the word *RATS* subtly flashed on-screen in a TV spot criticizing his opponent Al Gore in the 2000 election. "One frame out of 900 hardly makes a conspiracy," he said in the ad's defense—although the ad was pulled off the air.

given a choice of free coupons toward the purchase of possible new sports beverages *Super-Quencher* ("the best thirst-quenching beverage ever developed") and *PowerPro* ("the best electrolyte-restoring beverage ever developed"), those who had been subliminally exposed to thirst words more often chose Super-Quencher (see **FIGURE 8.8**).

There are two important footnotes to this research. First, the influence of the subliminal persuasion was primarily found for people who reported already being thirsty when the experiment started. The subliminal exposure to thirst words had little effect on people who didn't feel thirsty, suggesting that Vicary's "Drink Coke" campaign, even if it had actually happened, would not have drawn people out to the lobby unless they were already inclined to go. Second, the researchers also conducted a study in which other participants were shown the target words at a slower speed (300 milliseconds) so the words could be seen and consciously recognized. Their conscious perception of the thirst words had effects just like subliminal perception. Subliminal influences might be worrisome because they can change behavior without our conscious awareness but not because they are more powerful in comparison to conscious influences.

Unconscious influences on behavior are not limited to cases of subliminal persuasion—they can happen when you are merely reminded of an idea in passing. For example, the thought of getting old can make a person walk more slowly. John Bargh and his colleagues discovered this by having college students complete a survey that called for them to make sentences with various words (1996). The students were not informed that most of the words were commonly associated with aging (Florida, gray, wrinkled), and even afterward they didn't report being aware of this trend. In this case, the "aging" idea wasn't presented subliminally, just not very noticeably. As these research participants left the experiment, they were clocked as they walked down the hall. Compared with those not exposed to the aging-related words, these people walked more slowly! Just as with subliminal perception, a passing exposure to ideas can influence actions without conscious awareness.

**In summary,** consciousness is a mystery of psychology because other people's minds cannot be perceived directly and because the relationship between mind and body is perplexing. Nonetheless, people's reports of their consciousness can be studied, and these reveal basic properties such as intentionality, unity, selectivity, and transience. Consciousness also can be understood in terms of levels—minimal consciousness, full consciousness, and self-consciousness—and can be investigated for contents such as current concerns, daydreams, and unwanted thoughts. There are mental processes that are not conscious as well, and there are two main views of these. Unconscious processes are sometimes understood as expressions of the Freudian dynamic unconscious but are more commonly viewed as processes of the cognitive unconscious that create and influence our conscious thoughts and behaviors. The cognitive unconscious is at work when subliminal perception influences a person's thought or behavior without the person's awareness. ■ ■

# Sleep and Dreaming: Good Night, Mind

What's it like to be asleep? Sometimes it's like nothing at all. Sleep can produce a state of unconsciousness in which the mind and brain apparently turn off the functions that create experience: The Cartesian Theater is closed. But this is an oversimplification because the theater actually seems to reopen during the night for special shows of bizarre cult films—in other words, dreams. Dream consciousness involves a transformation of experience that is so radical it is commonly considered an **altered state of consciousness**—*a form of experience that departs significantly from the normal subjective experience of the world and the mind*. Such altered states can be accompanied by changes in thinking, disturbances in the sense of time, feelings of the loss of control, changes in emotional expression, alterations in body image and sense of self, perceptual distortions, and changes in meaning or significance (Ludwig, 1966). The world of sleep and dreams, then, provides two unique perspectives on consciousness: a view of the mind without consciousness and a view of consciousness in an altered state.

## Sleep

Consider a typical night. As you begin to fall asleep, the busy, task-oriented thoughts of the waking mind are replaced by wandering thoughts and images, odd juxtapositions, some of them almost dreamlike. This presleep consciousness is called the *hypnagogic state*. On some rare nights you might experience a *hypnic jerk,* a sudden quiver or sensation of dropping, as though missing a step on a staircase. (No one is quite sure why these happen, but there is no truth to the theory that you are actually levitating and then fall.) Eventually, your presence of mind goes away entirely. Time and experience stop, you are unconscious, and in fact there seems to be no "you" there to have experiences. But then come dreams, whole vistas of a vivid and surrealistic consciousness you just don't get during the day, a set of experiences that occur with the odd prerequisite that there is nothing "out there" you are actually experiencing. More patches of unconsciousness may occur, with more dreams here and there. And finally, the glimmerings of waking consciousness return again in a foggy and imprecise form as you enter postsleep consciousness (the *hypnopompic state*) and then awake, often with bad hair.

### Sleep Cycle

The sequence of events that occurs during a night of sleep is part of one of the major rhythms of human life, the cycle of sleep and waking. This **circadian rhythm** is *a naturally occurring 24-hour cycle*—from the Latin *circa,* "about," and *dies,* "day." Even people who are sequestered in underground buildings without clocks ("time-free environments") and are allowed to sleep when they want to tend to have a rest-activity cycle of about 25.1 hours (Aschoff, 1965). This slight deviation from 24 hours is not easily explained (Lavie, 2001), but it seems to underlie the tendency many people have to want to stay up a little later each night and wake up a little later each day. We're 25.1-hour people living in a 24-hour world.

**ALTERED STATES OF CONSCIOUSNESS** Forms of experience that depart from the normal subjective experience of the world and the mind.

**CIRCADIAN RHYTHM** A naturally occurring 24-hour cycle.

MOORE: ALBERT JOSEPH/BIRMINGHAM MUSEUMS AND ART GALLERY/ THE BRIDGEMAN ART LIBRARY

*Dreamers,* by Albert Joseph Moore (1879/1882). Without measuring REM sleep, it's hard to know whether Moore's "Dreamers" are actually dreaming.

**REM SLEEP** A stage of sleep characterized by rapid eye movements and a high level of brain activity.

**ELECTROOCULOGRAPH (EOG)** An instrument that measures eye movements.

The sleep cycle is far more than a simple on/off routine, however, as many bodily and psychological processes ebb and flow in this rhythm. In 1929 researchers made EEG (electroencephalograph) recordings of the human brain for the first time (Berger, 1929; see Chapter 3). Before this, many people had offered descriptions of their nighttime experiences, and researchers knew that there are deeper and lighter periods of sleep, as well as dream periods. But no one had been able to measure much of anything about sleep without waking up the sleeper and ruining it. The EEG recordings revealed a regular pattern of changes in electrical activity in the brain accompanying the circadian cycle. During waking, these changes involve alternation between high-frequency activity (called *beta waves*) during alertness and lower-frequency activity (*alpha waves*) during relaxation.

The largest changes in EEG occur during sleep. These changes show a regular pattern over the course of the night that allowed sleep researchers to identify five sleep stages (see **FIGURE 8.9**). In the first stage of sleep, the EEG moves to frequency patterns even lower than alpha waves (*theta waves*). In the second stage of sleep, these patterns are interrupted by short bursts of activity called *sleep spindles* and *K complexes,* and the sleeper becomes somewhat more difficult to awaken. The deepest stages of sleep are 3 and 4, known as slow-wave sleep, in which the EEG patterns show activity called *delta waves*.

During the fifth sleep stage, **REM sleep,** *a stage of sleep characterized by rapid eye movements and a high level of brain activity,* EEG patterns become high-frequency saw-tooth waves, similar to beta waves, suggesting that the mind at this time is as active

**Figure 8.9 EEG Patterns during the Stages of Sleep** The waking brain shows high-frequency beta wave activity, which changes during drowsiness and relaxation to lower-frequency alpha waves. Stage 1 sleep shows lower-frequency theta waves, which are accompanied in Stage 2 by irregular patterns called sleep spindles and K complexes. Stages 3 and 4 are marked by the lowest frequencies, delta waves. During REM sleep, EEG patterns return to higher-frequency sawtooth waves that resemble the beta waves of waking.

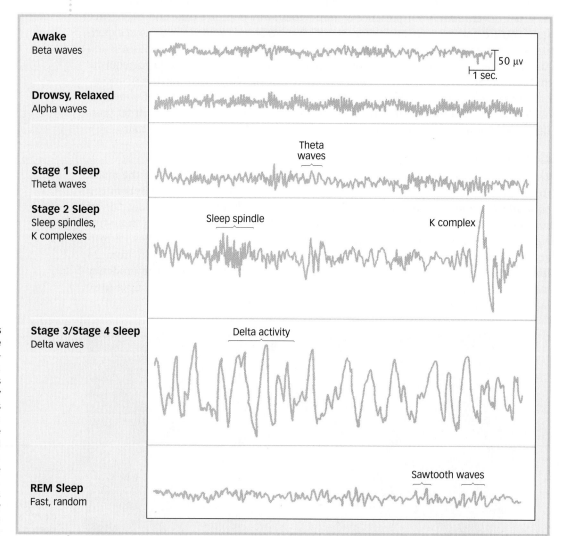

as it is during waking (see Figure 8.9). Using an **electrooculograph (EOG)**, *a device to measure eye movements,* during sleep, researchers found that sleepers wakened during REM periods reported having dreams much more often than those wakened during non-REM periods (Aserinsky & Kleitman, 1953). During REM sleep, the pulse quickens, blood pressure rises, and there are telltale signs of sexual arousal. At the same time, measurements of muscle movements indicate that the sleeper is very still, except for a rapid side-to-side movement of the eyes. (Watch someone sleeping and you may be able to see the REMs through their closed eyelids. Be careful doing this with strangers down at the bus depot.)

Although many people believe that they don't dream much (if at all), some 80% of people awakened during REM sleep report dreams. If you've ever wondered whether dreams actually take place in an instant or whether they take as long to happen as the events they portray might take, the analysis of REM sleep offers an answer. Sleep researchers William Dement and Nathaniel Kleitman (1957) woke volunteers either 5 minutes or 15 minutes after the onset of REM sleep and asked them to judge, on the basis of the events in the remembered dream, how long they had been dreaming. Sleepers in 92 of 111 cases were correct, suggesting that dreaming occurs in "real time." The discovery of REM sleep has offered many insights into dreaming, but not all dreams occur in REM periods. Some dreams are also reported in other sleep stages (non-REM sleep, also called *NREM sleep*) but not as many—and the dreams that occur at these times are described as less wild than REM dreams and more like normal thinking.

Putting EEG and REM data together produces a picture of how a typical night's sleep progresses through cycles of sleep stages (see **FIGURE 8.10**). In the first hour of the night, you fall all the way from waking to the fourth and deepest stage of sleep, the stage marked by delta waves. These slow waves indicate a general synchronization of neural firing, as though the brain is doing one thing at this time rather than many—the neuronal equivalent of "the wave" moving through the crowd at a stadium, as lots of individuals move together in synchrony. You then return to lighter sleep stages, eventually reaching REM and dreamland. Note that although REM sleep is lighter than that of lower stages, it is deep enough that you may be difficult to awaken. You then continue to cycle between REM and slow-wave sleep stages every 90 minutes or so throughout the night. Periods of REM last longer as the night goes on, and lighter sleep stages predominate between these periods, with the deeper slow-wave stages 3 and 4 disappearing halfway through the night. Although you're either unconscious or dream-conscious at the time, your brain and mind cycle through a remarkable array of different states each time you have a night's sleep.

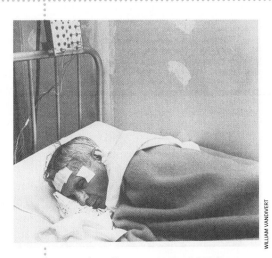

REM sleep discoverer Nathaniel Kleitman as a participant in his own sleep experiment with REM and EEG measurement electrodes in place.

WILLIAM VANDIVERT

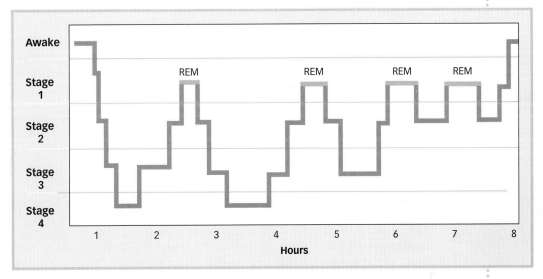

**Figure 8.10 Stages of Sleep during the Night** Over the course of the typical night, sleep cycles into deeper stages early on and then more shallow stages later. REM periods become longer in later cycles, and the deeper slow-wave sleep of stages 3 and 4 disappears halfway through the night.

## Sleep Needs and Deprivation

How much do people sleep? The answer depends on the age of the sleeper (Dement, 1999). Newborns will sleep 6 to 8 times in 24 hours, often totaling more than 16 hours. Their napping cycle gets consolidated into "sleeping through the night," usually sometime between 9 and 18 months, but sometimes even later. The typical 6-year-old child might need 11 or 12 hours of sleep, and the progression to less sleep then continues into adulthood, when the average is about 7 to 7½ hours per night. With aging, people can get along with even a bit less sleep than that. Over a whole lifetime, we get about 1 hour of sleep for every 2 hours we are awake.

This is a lot of sleeping, and you might wonder whether less than this might be tolerable. Rather than sleeping our lives away, perhaps we can stay awake and enjoy life. The world record for staying awake belongs to Randy Gardner, who at age 17 stayed up for 264 hours and 12 minutes in 1965 for a science project. Randy was followed around for much of the 11 days and nights by sleep researchers, who noted that he seemed remarkably chipper and easy to keep awake during the day—but that he struggled mightily at night, when fighting drowsiness required heroic measures. Along with the researchers, he spent the last night in a penny arcade playing hundreds of games on a baseball machine. He won easily, suggesting that even extreme sleep deprivation is not entirely debilitating or that sleep researchers are lousy at arcade games. The main symptom of his deprivation was sleepiness, along with a couple of minor hallucinatory experiences. When Randy finally did go to sleep, he slept only 14 hours and 40 minutes and awakened essentially recovered (Dement, 1978).

Feats like this one suggest that sleep might be expendable. This is the theory behind the classic "all-nighter" that you may have tried on the way to a rough exam. But it turns out that this theory is mistaken. Robert Stickgold and his colleagues (2000b) found that when people learning a difficult perceptual task are kept up all night after they finished practicing the task, their learning of the task is wiped out. Even after two nights of catch-up sleep, they show little indication of their initial training on the task. Sleep following learning appears to be essential for memory consolidation (see Chapter 5). It is as though memories normally deteriorate unless sleep occurs to help keep them in place. Studying all night may help you cram for the exam, but it won't make the material stick—which pretty much defeats the whole point.

Sleep turns out to be a necessity rather than a luxury in other ways as well. At the extreme, sleep loss can be fatal. When rats are forced to break Randy Gardner's human waking record and stay awake even longer, they have trouble regulating their body temperature and lose weight although they eat much more than normal. Their bodily systems break down and they die, on average, in 21 days (Rechsthaffen et al., 1983). Shakespeare called sleep "nature's soft nurse," and it is clear that even for healthy young humans, a few hours of sleep deprivation each night can have a cumulative detrimental effect: reducing mental acuity and reaction time, increasing irritability and depression, and increasing the risk of accidents and injury (Coren, 1997).

Some studies have deprived people of different sleep stages selectively by waking them whenever certain stages are detected. Studies of REM sleep deprivation indicate that this part of sleep is important psychologically, as memory problems and excessive aggression are observed in both humans and rats after only a few days of being wakened whenever REM activity starts (Ellman et al., 1991). The brain must value something about REM sleep because REM deprivation causes a rebound of more REM sleep the next night (Brunner et al., 1990). Deprivation from slow-wave sleep (in stages 3 and 4), in turn, has more physical effects, with just a few nights of deprivation leaving people feeling tired, fatigued, and hypersensitive to muscle and bone pain (Lentz et al., 1999).

It's clearly dangerous to neglect the need for sleep. But why would we have such a need in the first place? Insects don't seem to sleep, but most "higher" animals do, including fish and birds. Giraffes sleep less than 2 hours daily, whereas brown bats snooze for almost 20 hours. These variations in sleep needs, and the very existence of a need, are hard to explain. Is the restoration

Sleep deprivation can often be diagnosed without the help of any psychologists or brain-scanning equipment.

SONDA DAWES/THE IMAGE WORKS

that happens during the unconsciousness of sleep something that simply can't be achieved during consciousness? Sleep is, after all, potentially costly in the course of evolution. The sleeping animal is easy prey, so the habit of sleep would not seem to have developed so widely across species unless it had significant benefits that made up for this vulnerability. Theories of sleep have not yet determined why the brain and body have evolved to need these recurring episodes of unconsciousness.

## Sleep Disorders

In answer to the question, "Did you sleep well?" comedian Stephen Wright said, "No, I made a couple of mistakes." Sleeping well is something everyone would love to do, but for many people, sleep disorders are mindbugs that can get in the way. Disorders that plague sleep include insomnia, sleep apnea, somnambulism, narcolepsy, sleep paralysis, nightmares, and night terrors. Perhaps the most common sleep disorder is **insomnia**, *difficulty in falling asleep or staying asleep.* About 15% of adults complain of severe or frequent insomnia, and another 15% report having mild or occasional insomnia (Bootzin, Manber, Perlis, Salvio, & Wyatt, 1993). Although people often overestimate their insomnia, the distress caused even by the perception of insomnia can be significant. There are many causes of insomnia, including anxiety associated with stressful life events, so insomnia may sometimes be a sign of other emotional difficulties.

Insomnia can be exacerbated by worry about insomnia (Borkevec, 1982). No doubt you've experienced some nights on which sleeping was a high priority, such as before a class presentation or an important interview, and you've found that you were unable to fall asleep and may have even stayed up later than usual. In this situation, sleeping seems to be an emergency, and every wish to sleep takes you further from that goal. The desire to sleep initiates an ironic process of mental control—a heightened sensitivity to signs of sleeplessness—and this sensitivity interferes with sleep. In fact, participants in an experiment who were instructed to go to sleep quickly became hypersensitive and had more difficulty sleeping than those who were not instructed to hurry (Ansfield, Wegner, & Bowser, 1996). The paradoxical solution for insomnia in some cases, then, may be to give up the pursuit of sleep and instead find something else to do.

Giving up on trying so hard to sleep is probably better than another common remedy—the use of sleeping pills. Although sedatives can be useful for brief sleep problems associated with emotional events, their long-term use is not effective. To begin with, most sleeping pills are addictive. People become dependent on the pills to sleep and may need to increase the dose over time to achieve the same effect. Even in short-term use, sedatives can interfere with the normal sleep cycle. Although they promote sleep, they reduce the proportion of time spent in REM and slow-wave sleep (Nishino, Mignot, & Dement, 1995), robbing people of dreams and their deepest sleep stages. As a result, the quality of sleep achieved with pills may not be as high as without, and there may be side effects such as grogginess and irritability during the day. Finally, stopping the treatment suddenly can produce insomnia that is worse than before.

**Sleep apnea** is *a disorder in which the person stops breathing for brief periods while asleep.* A person with apnea usually snores, as apnea involves an involuntary obstruction of the breathing passage. When episodes of apnea occur for over 10 seconds at a time and recur many times during the night, they may cause many awakenings and sleep loss or insomnia. Apnea occurs most often in middle-age overweight men (Partinen, 1994) and may go undiagnosed because it is not easy for the sleeper to notice. Bed partners may be the ones who finally get tired of the snoring and noisy gasping for air when the sleeper's breathing restarts, or the sleeper may eventually seek treatment because of excessive sleepiness during the day. Therapies involving weight loss, drugs, or surgery may solve the problem.

Another sleep disorder is **somnambulism**, commonly called sleepwalking, which occurs when *a person arises and walks around while asleep.* Sleepwalking is more common in children, peaking around the age of 11 or 12, with as many as 25% of children experiencing at least one episode (Empson, 1984). Sleepwalking tends to happen early

**INSOMNIA** Difficulty in falling asleep or staying asleep.

**SLEEP APNEA** A disorder in which the person stops breathing for brief periods while asleep.

**SOMNAMBULISM** (sleepwalking) Occurs when the person arises and walks around while asleep.

**ONLY HUMAN**

**DUBIOUS TEENAGER EXCUSE #53**
Authorities are investigating how a sleepwalking teenage London girl ended up asleep atop a 130-foot crane in the middle of the night. A passerby spotted the girl around 1:30 a.m. on June 25 and called the police, thinking she was going to jump. A firefighter climbed up and inched along the beam to where the girl was sleeping. He was very cautious about startling her as he secured the unidentified teen in a safety harness. A special rescue truck was called, which deployed a hydraulic ladder to get the girl down after 2½ hours. The girl's parents were called to the scene and told police their daughter is a frequent sleepwalker (Sleepwalker found dozing high atop crane, 2005).

**NARCOLEPSY** A disorder in which sudden sleep attacks occur in the middle of waking activities.

**SLEEP PARALYSIS** The experience of waking up unable to move.

**NIGHT TERRORS** (or sleep terrors) Abrupt awakenings with panic and intense emotional arousal.

in the night, usually in slow-wave sleep, and sleepwalkers may awaken during their walk or return to bed without waking, in which case they will probably not remember the episode in the morning. The sleepwalker's eyes are usually open in a glassy stare, although walking with hands outstretched is uncommon except in cartoons. Sleepwalking is not usually linked to any additional problems and is only problematic in that sleepwalkers can hurt themselves. People who walk while they are sleeping do not tend to be very coordinated and can trip over furniture or fall down stairs. Contrary to popular belief, it is safe to wake sleepwalkers or lead them back to bed.

There are other sleep disorders that are less common. **Narcolepsy** is *a disorder in which sudden sleep attacks occur in the middle of waking activities.* Narcolepsy involves the intrusion of a dreaming state of sleep (with REM) into waking and is often accompanied by unrelenting excessive sleepiness and uncontrollable sleep attacks lasting from 30 seconds to 30 minutes. This disorder appears to have a genetic basis, as it runs in families, and can be treated effectively with medication. **Sleep paralysis** is *the experience of waking up unable to move* and is sometimes associated with narcolepsy. This eerie experience usually lasts only a few moments, happens in hypnagogic or hypnopompic sleep, and may occur with an experience of pressure on the chest (Hishakawa, 1976). **Night terrors** (or sleep terrors) are *abrupt awakenings with panic and intense emotional arousal.* These terrors, which occur mainly in boys ages 3 to 7, happen most often in NREM sleep early in the sleep cycle and do not usually have dream content the sleeper can report.

To sum up, there is a lot going on when we close our eyes for the night. Humans follow a pretty regular sleep cycle, going through five stages of NREM and REM sleep during the night. Disruptions to that cycle, either from sleep deprivation or sleep disorders, can produce consequences for waking consciousness. But something else happens during a night's sleep that affects our consciousness, both while asleep and when we wake up. It's dreaming, and we'll look at what psychologists know about dreams next.

## Dreams

Pioneering sleep researcher William C. Dement (1959) said, "Dreaming permits each and every one of us to be quietly and safely insane every night of our lives." Indeed, dreams do seem to have a touch of insanity about them. We experience crazy things in dreams, but even more bizarre is the fact that we are the writers, producers, and directors of the crazy things we experience. Just what are these experiences, and how can the experiences be explained?

### Dream Consciousness

Dreams depart dramatically from reality. You may dream of being naked in public, of falling from a great height, of sleeping through an important appointment, of your teeth being loose and falling out, of being chased, or even of flying (Holloway, 2001). These things don't happen much in reality unless you have a very bad life.

The quality of consciousness in dreaming is also altered significantly from waking consciousness. There are five major characteristics of dream consciousness that distinguish it from the waking state (Hobson, 1988). For one, we intensely feel *emotion,* whether it is bliss or terror or love or awe. Second, dream *thought* is illogical: The continuities of time, place, and person don't apply. You may find you are in one place and then another, for example, without any travel in between—or people may change identity from one dream scene to the next. Third, *sensation* is fully formed and meaningful; visual sensation is predominant, and you may also deeply experience sound, touch, and movement (although pain is very uncommon). A fourth aspect of dreaming is *uncritical acceptance,* as though the images and events were perfectly normal rather than bizarre. A final feature of dreaming is the *difficulty of remembering* the dream after it is over. People often remember dreams only if they are awakened during the dream and even then may lose recall for the dream within just a few minutes of waking. If waking memory were this bad, you'd be standing around half naked in the street much of the time, having forgotten your destination, clothes, and probably your lunch money.

**Maxine**

Some of the most memorable dreams are nightmares, as these frightening dreams often wake up the dreamer. One set of daily dream logs from college undergraduates suggested that the average student has about 24 nightmares per year (Wood & Bootzin, 1990), although some people may have them as often as every night. Children have more nightmares than adults, and people who have experienced traumatic events are inclined to have nightmares that relive those events. Following the 1989 earthquake in the San Francisco Bay Area, for example, college students who had experienced the quake reported more nightmares than those who had not and often reported that the dreams were about the quake (Wood et al., 1992). This effect of trauma may not only produce dreams of the traumatic event: When police officers experience "critical incidents" of conflict and danger, they tend to have more nightmares in general (Neylan et al., 2002).

Not all of our dreams are fantastic and surreal, however. We also dream about mundane topics that reflect prior waking experiences or "day residue." Current conscious concerns pop up (Nikles et al., 1998), along with images from the recent past. A dream may even incorporate sensations experienced during sleep, as when sleepers in one study were led to dream of water when drops were sprayed on their faces during REM sleep (Dement & Wolpert, 1958). The day residue does not usually include episodic memories, that is, complete daytime events replayed in the mind. Rather, dreams that reflect the day's experience tend to single out sensory experiences or objects from waking life. After watching a badminton tournament one evening, for example, you might dream about shuttlecocks darting through the air. One study had research participants play the computer game Tetris and found that participants often reported dreaming about the Tetris geometrical figures falling down—even though they seldom reported dreams about being in the experiment or playing the game (Stickgold et al., 2001). Even severely amnesic patients who couldn't recall playing the game at all reported Tetris-like images appearing in their dreams (Stickgold et al., 2000b). The content of dreams takes snapshots from the day rather than retelling the stories of what you have done or seen. This means that dreams often come without clear plots or storylines, and so they may not make a lot of sense.

### Dream Theories

Dreams are puzzles that cry out to be solved. How could you *not* want to make sense out of these experiences—although dreams are fantastic and confusing, they are emotionally riveting, filled with vivid images from your own life, and they seem very real. The search for dream meaning goes all the way back to biblical figures, who interpreted dreams and looked for prophecies in them. In the Old Testament, the prophet Daniel (a favorite of the authors of this book) curried favor with King Nebuchadnezzar of Babylon by interpreting the king's dream. The question of what dreams mean has been burning since antiquity, mainly because the meaning of dreams is usually far from obvious.

*The Nightmare,* by Henry Fuseli (1790). Fuseli depicts not only a mare in this painting but also an incubus—an imp perched on the dreamer's chest that is traditionally associated with especially horrifying nightmares.

## { HOT SCIENCE } Dreaming and the Brain

WHAT HAPPENS IN THE BRAIN WHEN WE dream? Several studies have made fMRI scans of people's brains during sleep, focusing on the areas of the brain that show changes in activation during REM periods. These studies show that the brain changes that occur during REM sleep correspond clearly with certain alterations of consciousness that occur in dreaming. The figure to the right shows some of the patterns of activation and deactivation found in the dreaming brain (Schwartz & Maquet, 2002).

One notable feature that distinguishes dreams from waking consciousness, for instance, is their scariness. Nightmares by definition are terrifying, but even your common, run-of-the-mill dream is often populated with anxiety-producing images (Neilson, Deslauriers, & Baylor, 1991). There are heights to look down from, dangerous people lurking, the occasional monster, lots of minor worries, and at least once in a while that major exam you've forgotten about until you walk into class. These thoughts suggest that the brain areas responsible for fear or emotion somehow work overtime in dreams, and it turns out that this is clearly visible in fMRI scans. The amygdala is involved in responses to threatening or stressful events, and indeed the amygdala is quite active during REM sleep.

The typical dream is also a visual wonderland, with visual events present in almost all dreams. However, there are fewer auditory sensations, even fewer tactile sensations, and almost no smells or tastes. This dream "picture show" doesn't involve actual perception, of course, just the imagination of visual events. It turns out that the areas of the brain responsible for visual perception are *not* activated during dreaming, whereas the visual association areas in the occipital lobe that are responsible for visual imagery *do* show activation (Braun et al., 1998), as shown in the figure. Your brain is smart enough to realize that it's not really seeing bizarre images but acts instead as though it's imagining bizarre images.

During REM, the prefrontal cortex shows relatively less arousal than it usually does during waking consciousness. What does this mean for the dreamer? As a rule, the prefrontal areas are associated with planning

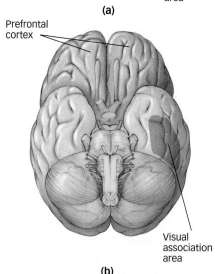

(a)

(b)

**Brain activation and deactivation during REM sleep. Brain areas shaded red are activated during REM sleep; those shaded blue are deactivated. (a) The medial view shows the activation of the amygdala, the visual association areas, the motor cortex, and the brain stem and the deactivation of the prefrontal cortex. (b) The ventral view shows the activation of other visual association areas and the deactivation of the prefrontal cortex (Schwartz & Maquet, 2002).**

and executing actions, and often dreams seem to be unplanned and rambling. Perhaps this is why dreams often don't have very sensible storylines—they've been scripted by an author whose ability to plan is inactive.

Another odd fact of dreaming is that while the eyes are moving rapidly, the body

is otherwise very still. During REM sleep, the motor cortex is activated, but spinal neurons running through the brain stem inhibit the expression of this motor activation (Lai & Siegal, 1999). This turns out to be a useful property of brain activation in dreaming; otherwise, you might get up and act out every dream! In fact, when this inhibitory area is lesioned in cats, they become highly active during REM sleep (Jouvet & Mounier, 1961). People who are thrashing around during sleep are probably not dreaming. If they were dreaming, they'd be very still. The brain specifically inhibits movement during dreams, perhaps to keep us from hurting ourselves.

Brain scans may also someday help solve the intriguing question of whether people can be aware that they are dreaming. Some people claim that they only become aware they have been dreaming when they wake up and realize "it was all a dream." The dream state in this case seems to be like the waking state of minimal consciousness, in that the person is not aware of being in the mental state. Other individuals report, however, that they sometimes know they are dreaming while the dream is ongoing—they experience the dream equivalent of full consciousness. Such *lucid dreaming*, the awareness of dreaming during the dream, has been described often (LaBerge & Rheingold, 1990) but is still a matter of controversy because evidence of such dreams comes only from these descriptions reported by the dreamers. One goal of brain imaging research is to examine how the brain may be involved in the creation of such elusive states of mind. Researchers have not yet established whether there are differences in brain activation between minimal consciousness and full consciousness during waking, but perhaps if they do, brain research can corroborate the reports of lucid dreamers.

At present, studies of the activities of the dreaming brain yield a picture of dreaming as a unique state of mind. The brain's activities in dreaming underlie extensive visual activity, reductions of other sensations, increased sensitivity to emotions such as fear, lessened capacities for planning, and the prevention of movement.

In the first psychological theory of dreams, Freud (1900/1965) proposed that dreams are confusing and obscure because the dynamic unconscious creates them precisely *to be* confusing and obscure. According to Freud's theory, dreams represent wishes, and some of these wishes are so unacceptable, taboo, and anxiety producing that the mind can only express them in disguised form. Freud believed that many of the most unacceptable wishes are sexual, so he interpreted a dream of a train going into a tunnel as symbolic of sexual intercourse. According to Freud, the **manifest content** of a dream, *a dream's apparent topic or superficial meaning,* is a smoke screen for its **latent content**, *a dream's true underlying meaning.* For example, a dream about a tree burning down in the park across the street from where a friend once lived (the manifest content) might represent a camouflaged wish for the death of the friend (the latent content). In this case, wishing for the death of a friend is unacceptable, so it is disguised as a tree on fire. The problem with this approach is that there are an infinite number of potential interpretations of any dream and finding the correct one is a matter of guesswork—and of convincing the dreamer that one interpretation is superior to the others.

Although dreams may not represent elaborately hidden wishes, there is evidence that they do feature the return of suppressed thoughts. Researchers asked volunteers to think of a personal acquaintance and then to spend 5 minutes before going to bed writing down whatever came to mind (Wegner, Wenzlaff, & Kozak, 2004). Some participants were asked to suppress thoughts of this person as they wrote, others were asked to focus on thoughts of the person, and yet others were asked just to write freely about anything. The next morning, participants wrote dream reports. Overall, all participants mentioned dreaming more about the person they had named than about other people. But they most often dreamed of the person they named if they were in the group that had been assigned to suppress thoughts of the person the night before. This finding suggests that Freud was right to suspect that dreams harbor unwanted thoughts. Perhaps this is why actors dream of forgetting their lines, travelers dream of getting lost, and football players dream of fumbling the ball.

Another key theory of dreaming is the **activation-synthesis model** (Hobson & McCarley, 1977). This theory proposes that *dreams are produced when the mind attempts to make sense of random neural activity that occurs in the brain during sleep.* During waking consciousness, the mind is devoted to interpreting lots of information that arrives through the senses. You figure out that the odd noise you're hearing during class is your cell phone vibrating, for example, or you realize that the strange smell in the hall outside your room must be from burned popcorn. In the dream state, the mind doesn't have access to external sensations, but it keeps on doing what it usually does: interpreting information. Because that information now comes from neural activations that occur without the continuity provided by the perception of reality, the brain's interpretive mechanisms can run free (see the Hot Science box on the facing page). This might be why, for example, a person in a dream can sometimes change into someone else. There is no actual person being perceived to help the mind keep a stable view. In the mind's effort to perceive and give meaning to brain activation, the person you view in a dream about a grocery store might seem to be a clerk but then change to be your favorite teacher when the dream scene moves to your school. The great interest people have in interpreting their dreams the next morning may be an extension of the interpretive activity they've been doing all night.

The Freudian theory and the activation-synthesis theory differ in the significance they place on the meaning of dreams. In Freud's theory, dreams begin with meaning, whereas in the activation-synthesis theory, dreams begin randomly—but meaning can be added as the mind lends interpretations in the process of dreaming. Dream research has not yet sorted out whether one of these theories or yet another might be the best account of the meaning of dreams.

---

**In summary,** sleep and dreaming present a view of the mind with an altered state of consciousness. EEG and EOG measures have revealed that during a night's sleep, the brain passes through a five-stage sleep cycle, moving in and out of lighter sleep stages, from slow-wave sleep stages to the REM sleep stage, in which most dreaming occurs.

**MANIFEST CONTENT** A dream's apparent topic or superficial meaning.

**LATENT CONTENT** A dream's true underlying meaning.

**ACTIVATION-SYNTHESIS MODEL** The theory that dreams are produced when the brain attempts to make sense of activations that occur randomly during sleep.

BRENT MADISON

The seat of consciousness.

Sleep needs decrease over the life span, but deprivation from sleep and dreams has psychological and physical costs. Sleep can be disrupted through disorders that include insomnia, sleep apnea, somnambulism, narcolepsy, sleep paralysis, and night terrors. Dreaming is an altered state of consciousness in which the dreamer uncritically accepts changes in emotion, thought, and sensation but poorly remembers the dream on awakening. Dream consciousness is paralleled by changes in brain activation, and theories of dreaming include Freud's psychoanalytic theory and more current views such as the activation-synthesis model. ■ ■

# Drugs and Consciousness: Artificial Inspiration

The author of the anti-utopian novel *Brave New World,* Aldous Huxley, once wrote of his experiences with the drug mescaline. His essay "The Doors of Perception" described the intense experience that accompanied his departure from normal consciousness. He described "a world where everything shone with the Inner Light, and was infinite in its significance. The legs, for example, of [a] chair—how miraculous their tubularity, how supernatural their polished smoothness! I spent several minutes—or was it several centuries?—not merely gazing at those bamboo legs, but actually *being* them" (Huxley, 1954).

Being the legs of a chair? This is better than being a seat cushion, but it still sounds like an odd experience. Still, many people seek out such experiences, often through using drugs. **Psychoactive drugs** are *chemicals that influence consciousness or behavior by altering the brain's chemical message system.* As you read in Chapter 3, information is communicated in the brain through neurotransmitters that convey neural impulses to neighboring neurons. Some of the most common neurotransmitters are serotonin, dopamine, gamma aminobutyric acid (GABA), and acetylcholine. Drugs alter these neural connections by preventing the bonding of neurotransmitters to sites in the postsynaptic neuron or by inhibiting the reuptake of or enhancing the bonding and transmission of neurotransmitters. Different drugs can intensify or dull transmission patterns, creating changes in brain electrical activity that mimic natural operations of the brain. For example, a drug such as Valium (benzodiazepine) induces sleep but prevents dreaming and so creates a state similar to slow-wave sleep, that is, what the brain naturally develops several times each night. Other drugs prompt patterns of brain activity that do not occur naturally, however, and their influence on consciousness can be dramatic. Like Huxley experiencing himself becoming the legs of a chair, people using drugs can have experiences unlike any they might find in normal waking consciousness or even in dreams. To understand these altered states, let's explore how people use and abuse drugs and examine the major categories of psychoactive drugs.

## Drug Use and Abuse

Why do children sometimes spin around until they get dizzy and fall to the ground? There is something strangely attractive about states of consciousness that depart from the norm, and people throughout history have sought out these altered states by dancing, fasting, chanting, meditating, and ingesting a bizarre assortment of chemicals to intoxicate themselves (Tart, 1969). People pursue altered consciousness even when there are costs, from the nausea that accompanies dizziness to the life-wrecking obsession with a drug that can come with addiction. In this regard, the pursuit of altered consciousness can be a malicious mindbug.

Often, drug-induced changes in consciousness begin as pleasant and spark an initial attraction. Researchers have measured the attractiveness of psychoactive drugs by seeing how much laboratory animals will work to get them. In one study researchers allowed rats to intravenously administer cocaine to themselves by pressing a lever (Bozarth & Wise, 1985). Rats given free access to cocaine increased their use over the course of the 30-day study. They not only continued to self-administer at a high rate but also occasionally binged to the point of giving themselves convulsions. They stopped grooming themselves and eating until they lost on average almost a third of their body weight. About 90% of the rats died by the end of the study.

Rats are not tiny little humans, of course, so such research is not a firm basis for understanding human responses to cocaine. But these results do make it clear that cocaine is addictive and that the results of such addiction can be dire. Studies of self-administration of drugs in laboratory animals show that animals will work to obtain not only cocaine but also alcohol, amphetamines, barbiturates, caffeine, opiates (such as morphine and heroin), nicotine, phenylcycladine (PCP), MDMA (ecstasy), and THC (tetrahydrocannabinol, the active ingredient in marijuana). There are some psychoactive drugs that animals won't work for (such as mescaline or the antipsychotic drug phenothiazine), suggesting that these drugs have less potential for causing addiction (Bozarth, 1987).

People usually do not become addicted to a psychoactive drug the first time they use it. They may experiment a few times, then try again, and eventually find that their tendency to use the drug increases over time due to several factors, such as drug tolerance, physical dependence, and psychological dependence. **Drug tolerance** is *the tendency for larger drug doses to be required over time to achieve the same effect.* Physicians who prescribe morphine to control pain in their patients are faced with tolerance problems because steadily greater amounts of the drug may be needed to dampen the same pain. With increased tolerance comes the danger of drug overdose; recreational users find they need to use more and more of a drug to produce the same high. But then, if a new batch of heroin or cocaine is more concentrated than usual, the "normal" amount the user takes to achieve the same high can be fatal.

Self-administration of addictive drugs can also be prompted by withdrawal symptoms, which result when the drug is abruptly discontinued. Some withdrawal symptoms signal *physical dependence,* when pain, convulsions, hallucinations, or other unpleasant symptoms accompany withdrawal. People who suffer from physical dependence seek to continue drug use to avoid getting physically ill. A common example is the "caffeine headache" some people complain of when they haven't had their daily jolt of java. Other withdrawal symptoms result from *psychological dependence,* a strong desire to return to the drug even when physical withdrawal symptoms are gone. Drugs can create an emotional need over time that continues to prey on the mind, particularly in circumstances that are reminders of the drug. Some ex-smokers report longing wistfully for an after-dinner smoke, for example, even years after they've successfully quit the habit.

Drug addiction reveals a human mindbug: our inability to look past the immediate consequences of our behavior. Although we would like to think that our behavior is guided by a rational analysis of future consequences, more typically occasions when we "play first, pay later" lead directly to "let's just play a lot right now." There is something intensely inviting about the prospect of a soon-to-be-had pleasure and something pale, hazy, and distant about the costs this act might bring at some future time. For example, given the choice of receiving $1 today or $2 a week later, most people will take the $1 today. However, if the same choice is to be made for some date a year in the future (when the immediate pleasure of today's windfall is not so strong), people choose to wait and get the $2 (Ainslie, 2001). The immediate satisfaction associated with taking most drugs may outweigh a rational analysis of the later consequences that can result from taking those drugs, such as drug addiction.

The psychological and social problems stemming from addiction are major. For many people, drug addiction becomes a way of life, and for some, it is a cause of death. Like the cocaine-addicted rats in the study noted earlier (Bozarth & Wise, 1985), some people become so attached to a drug that their lives are ruled by it. However, this is not always the end of the story. This ending is most well known because the addict becomes a recurrent, visible social problem, "publicized" through repeated crime and repeated appearances in prisons and treatment programs. But a life of addiction is not the only possible endpoint of drug use. Stanley Schachter (1982) suggested that the visibility of addiction is misleading and that in fact many people overcome addictions. He found that 64% of a sample of people who had a history of cigarette smoking had quit successfully, although many had to try again and again to achieve their success. One study of soldiers who became addicted to heroin in Vietnam found that 3 years after

**PSYCHOACTIVE DRUG** A chemical that influences consciousness or behavior by altering the brain's chemical message system.

**DRUG TOLERANCE** The tendency for larger doses of a drug to be required over time to achieve the same effect.

The antique espresso machine, a sight that warms the hearts of caffeine lovers around the world.

JOHN LANDER/ALAMY

**DEPRESSANTS** Substances that reduce the activity of the central nervous system.

People will often endure significant inconveniences to maintain their addictions.

their return, only 12% remained addicted (Robins et al., 1980). The return to the attractions and obligations of normal life, as well as the absence of the familiar places and faces associated with their old drug habit, made it possible for returning soldiers to successfully quit. Although addiction is dangerous, it may not be incurable.

It may not be accurate to view all recreational drug use under the umbrella of "addiction." Many people at this point in the history of Western society, for example, would not call the repeated use of caffeine an addiction, and some do not label the use of alcohol, tobacco, or marijuana in this way. In other times and places, however, each of these has been considered a terrifying addiction worthy of prohibition and public censure. In the early 17th century, for example, tobacco use was punishable by death in Germany, by castration in Russia, and by decapitation in China (Corti, 1931). Not a good time to be traveling around waving a cigar. By contrast, cocaine, heroin, marijuana, and amphetamines have each been popular and even recommended as medicines at several points throughout history, each without any stigma of addiction attached (Inciardi, 2001).

Although addiction has a certain meaning here and now, this meaning is open to interpretation (Cherry, Dillon, & Rugh, 2002). Indeed, the concept of addiction has been extended to many human pursuits, giving rise to such terms as "sex addict," "gambling addict," "workaholic," and, of course, "chocoholic." Societies react differently at different times, with some uses of drugs ignored, other uses encouraged, others simply taxed, and yet others subjected to intense prohibition (see the Real World box on pp. 324–325). Rather than viewing *all* drug use as a problem, it is important to consider the costs and benefits of such use and to establish ways to help people choose behaviors that are informed by this knowledge (Parrott, Morinan, Moss, & Scholey, 2004).

*"Hi, my name is Barry, and I check my E-mail two to three hundred times a day."*

## Types of Psychoactive Drugs

Four in five North Americans use caffeine in some form every day, but not all psychoactive drugs are this familiar. To learn how both the well-known and lesser-known drugs influence the mind, let's consider several broad categories of drugs: depressants, stimulants, narcotics, hallucinogens, and marijuana. **TABLE 8.2** summarizes what is known about the potential dangers of these different types of drugs.

| Table 8.2 | Dangers of Drugs | | |
|---|---|---|---|
| | **Dangers** | | |
| | **Overdose** | **Physical Dependence** | **Psychological Dependence** |
| **Drug** | (Can taking too much cause death or injury?) | (Will stopping use make you sick?) | (Will you crave it when you stop using it?) |
| **Depressants** | | | |
| Alcohol | X | X | X |
| Barbiturates/benzodiazepines | X | X | X |
| Toxic inhalants | X | X | X |
| **Stimulants** | | | |
| Amphetamines | X | X | X |
| MDMA (Ecstasy) | X | | ? |
| Cocaine | X | X | X |
| Narcotics (opium, heroin, morphine, methadone, codeine) | X | X | X |
| Hallucinogens (LSD, mescaline, psilocybin, PCP, ketamine) | X | | ? |
| Marijuana | | | ? |

## Depressants

**Depressants** are *substances that reduce the activity of the central nervous system.* The most commonly used depressant is alcohol, and others include barbiturates, benzodiazepines, and toxic inhalants (such as glue or gasoline). Depressants have a sedative or calming effect, tend to induce sleep in high doses, and can arrest breathing in extremely high doses. Depressants can produce both physical and psychological dependence.

## Alcohol

Alcohol is "king of the depressants," with its worldwide use beginning in prehistory, its easy availability in most cultures, and its widespread acceptance as a socially approved substance. Fifty-two percent of Americans over 12 years of age report having had a drink in the past month, and 15% have binged on alcohol (over five drinks in succession) in that time. Young adults (ages 18 to 25) have even higher rates, with 60% reporting a drink last month and 31% reporting a binge (*Health, United States,* 2001; National Center for Health Statistics, 2001).

Alcohol's initial effects, euphoria and reduced anxiety, feel pretty positive. As it is consumed in greater quantities, drunkenness results, bringing slowed reactions, slurred speech, poor judgment, and other reductions in the effectiveness of thought and action. The exact way in which alcohol influences neural mechanisms is still not understood, but like other depressants, alcohol increases activity of the neurotransmitter GABA (De Witte, 1996). As you read in Chapter 3, GABA normally inhibits the transmission of neural impulses, so one effect of alcohol is as a disinhibitor—a chemical that lets transmissions occur that otherwise would be held in check. But there are many contradictions. Some people using alcohol become loud and aggressive, others become emotional and weepy, others become sullen, and still others turn giddy—and the same person can experience each of these effects in different circumstances. How can one drug do this? Two theories have been offered to account for these variable effects: *expectancy theory* and *alcohol myopia.*

**Expectancy theory** suggests that *alcohol effects are produced by people's expectations of how alcohol will influence them in particular situations* (Marlatt & Rohsenow, 1980). So,

**EXPECTANCY THEORY** The idea that alcohol effects can be produced by people's expectations of how alcohol will influence them in particular situations.

*"Hey, what is this stuff? It makes everything
I think seem profound."*

for instance, if you've watched friends or family drink at weddings and notice that this often produces hilarity and gregariousness, you could well experience these effects yourself should you drink alcohol on a similarly festive occasion. Seeing people getting drunk and fighting in bars, in turn, might lead to aggression after drinking.

The expectancy theory has been tested in studies that examine the effects of actual alcohol ingestion independent of the *perception* of alcohol ingestion. In experiments using a **balanced placebo design**, *behavior is observed following the presence or absence of an actual stimulus and also following the presence or absence of a placebo stimulus.* In such a study, participants are given drinks containing alcohol or a substitute liquid, and some people in each group are led to believe they had alcohol and others are led to believe they did not. People told they are drinking alcohol when they are not, for instance, might get a touch of vodka on the plastic lid of a cup to give it the right odor when the drink inside is merely tonic water. These experiments often show that the belief that one has had alcohol can influence behavior as strongly as the ingestion of alcohol itself (Goldman, Brown, & Christiansen, 1987). You may have seen people at parties getting rowdy after only one beer—perhaps because they expected this effect rather than because the beer actually had this influence.

Another approach to the varied effects of alcohol is the theory of **alcohol myopia**, which proposes that *alcohol hampers attention, leading people to respond in simple ways to complex situations* (Steele & Josephs, 1990). This theory recognizes that life is filled with complicated pushes and pulls, and our behavior is often a balancing act. Imagine that you are really attracted to someone who is dating your friend. Do you make your feelings known or focus on your friendship? The myopia theory holds that when you drink alcohol, your fine judgment is impaired. It becomes hard to appreciate the subtlety of these different options, and the inappropriate response is to veer full tilt one way or the other. So, alcohol might lead you to make a wild pass at your friend's date or perhaps just cry in your beer over your timidity—depending on which way you happened to tilt in your myopic state.

In one study on the alcohol myopia theory, men, half of whom were drinking alcohol, watched a video showing an unfriendly woman and then were asked how acceptable it would be for a man to act sexually aggressive toward a woman (Johnson, Noel, & Sutter-Hernandez, 2000). The unfriendly woman seemed to remind them that sex was out of the question, and indeed, men who were drinking alcohol and had seen this video were no more likely to think sexual advances were acceptable than men who were sober. However, when the same question was asked of a group of men who had seen a video of a *friendly* woman, those who were drinking were more inclined to recommend sexual overtures than those who were not, even when these overtures might be unwanted. Apparently, alcohol makes the complicated decisions involved in relationships seem simple ("Gee, she was so friendly")—and potentially open to serious misjudgments.

Both the expectancy and myopia theories suggest that people using alcohol will often go to extremes. In fact, it seems that drinking is a major contributing factor to social problems that result from extreme behavior. Drinking while driving is a main cause of auto accidents, for example, contributing to 39% of crash fatalities in 1997 (National Center for Injury Prevention and Control, 2001–2002). A survey of undergraduates revealed that alcohol contributes to as many as 90% of rapes and 95% of violent crimes on campus (Wechsler et al., 1994). Of the binge drinkers in the student sample, 41% reported that they had had unplanned sex due to drinking, and 22% said their drinking led to unprotected sex.

### Barbiturates, Benzodiazepines, and Toxic Inhalants

Compared to alcohol, the other depressants are much less popular but still are widely used and abused. Barbiturates such as Seconal or Nembutal are prescribed as sleep aids and as anesthetics before surgery. Benzodiazepines such as Valium and Xanax are also called minor tranquilizers and are prescribed as antianxiety drugs. These drugs are prescribed by physicians to treat anxiety or sleep problems, but they are dangerous when

**BALANCED PLACEBO DESIGN** A study design in which behavior is observed following the presence or absence of an actual stimulus and also following the presence or absence of a placebo stimulus.

**ALCOHOL MYOPIA** A condition that results when alcohol hampers attention, leading people to respond in simple ways to complex situations.

used in combination with alcohol. Physical dependence is possible since withdrawal from long-term use can produce severe symptoms (including convulsions), and psychological dependence is common as well. Finally, toxic inhalants are perhaps the most alarming substances in this category. These drugs are easily accessible even to children in the vapors of glue, gasoline, or propane. Sniffing or "huffing" these vapors can promote temporary effects that resemble drunkenness, but overdoses are sometimes lethal, and continued use holds the potential for permanent brain damage (Fornazzari, Wilkinson, Kapur, & Carler, 1983).

## Stimulants

The **stimulants** are *substances that excite the central nervous system, heightening arousal and activity levels.* They include caffeine, amphetamines, nicotine, cocaine, and ecstasy (MDMA) and sometimes have a legitimate pharmaceutical purpose. Amphetamines (also called "speed"), for example, were originally prepared for medicinal uses and as diet drugs; however, amphetamines such as Methedrine and Dexedrine are widely abused, causing insomnia, aggression, and paranoia with long-term use. Stimulants increase the levels of dopamine and norepinephrine in the brain, thereby inducing higher levels of activity in the brain circuits that depend on these neurotransmitters. As a result, they increase alertness and energy in the user, often producing a euphoric sense of confidence and a kind of agitated motivation to get things done. All stimulants produce physical and psychological dependence, and their withdrawal symptoms involve depressive effects such as fatigue and negative emotions.

Ecstasy is an amphetamine derivative also known as MDMA, "X," or "e." It is a stimulant, but it has added effects somewhat like those of hallucinogens (we'll talk about those shortly). Ecstasy is particularly known for making users feel empathic and close to those around them. It is used often as a party drug to enhance the group feeling at dances or raves, but it has unpleasant side effects such as causing jaw clenching and interfering with the regulation of body temperature. The rave culture has popularized pacifiers and juices as remedies for these problems, but users remain highly susceptible to heatstroke and exhaustion. Although ecstasy is not as likely as some other drugs to cause physical or psychological dependence, it nonetheless can lead to some dependence. What's more, the impurities sometimes found in "street" pills are also dangerous (Parrott, 2001). Ecstasy's potentially toxic effect on serotonin-activated neurons in the human brain is under intense debate, and a good deal of research attention is being devoted to studying the effects of this drug on humans.

Cocaine is derived from leaves of the coca plant, which has been cultivated by indigenous peoples of the Andes for millennia and chewed as a medication. Yes, the urban legend is true: *Coca-Cola* contained cocaine until 1903 and still may use coca leaves (with cocaine removed) as a flavoring—although the company's not telling (*Pepsi-Cola* never contained cocaine and is probably made from something brown).

Coca-Cola has been a popular product for more than 100 years. In the early days, one of the fatigue-relieving ingredients was a small amount of cocaine.

## { THE REAL WORLD }  Drugs and the Regulation of Consciousness

WHY DOES EVERYONE HAVE AN OPINION about drug use? Given that it's not possible to perceive what happens in anyone else's mind (that pesky "other minds" mystery of consciousness), why does it matter so much to us what people do to their own consciousness? Is consciousness something that governments should be able to legislate—or should people be free to choose their own conscious states (McWilliams, 1993)? After all, how can a "free society" justify regulating what people do inside their own heads?

Individuals and governments alike answer these questions by pointing to the costs of drug addiction, both to the addict and to the society that must "carry" unproductive people, pay for their welfare, and often even take care of their children. Drug users appear to be troublemakers and criminals, the culprits behind all those "drug-related" shootings, knifings, robberies, and petty thefts you see in the news day after day. It makes sense that their behavior appears to be caused by drug use, and you might even be able to understand the frustration that led Darryl Gates, then chief of the Los Angeles Police Department, to remark to the U.S. Senate Judiciary Committee in 1990 that "casual drug users should be taken out and shot." Although most government officials are more compassionate than this, widespread anger about the drug problem has surfaced in the form of the "War on Drugs," a federal

**Prohibition was an attempt to legislate self-control that eventually produced so many problems that people campaigned in the streets to repeal the law.**

government program that has focused on drug use as a criminal offense and has attempted to stop drug use through the imprisonment of users.

Social commentators such as economist Milton Friedman and psychiatrist Thomas Szasz believe that the War on Drugs is much like the era of Prohibition, the federal government's 1920–33 ban on alcohol (Trebach & Zeese, 1992). This famous experiment failed because the harm produced by the policy outweighed the damage produced by legal alcohol consumption. Illegal alcohol became wildly expensive, and the promise of large profits led to the rapid growth of organized criminal suppliers, an entire criminal subculture complete with gang killings and turf wars over distribution rights. With the huge jump in organized crime came a parallel wave of crime by "users"—illegal alcohol was so expensive that people who were dependent on it begged, stole, or sold anything to get money to buy it.

The current War on Drugs has led to the same buildup of criminal supply systems, along with an increase in crimes committed by users to get drug money—and an unprecedented increase in the incarceration of drug offenders. From 1990 to 1999, for example, the number of drug offenders in state and federal prisons increased from 179,070 to 319,560—a jump of 78% (Bureau of Justice Statistics, 2001)—not because of a measurable increase in drug use, but because of the rapidly increasing use of

Sigmund Freud tried cocaine and wrote effusively about it for a while. Cocaine (usually snorted) and crack cocaine (smoked) produce exhilaration and euphoria and are seriously addictive, both for humans and the rats you read about earlier in this chapter. Withdrawal takes the form of an unpleasant "crash," cravings are common, and antisocial effects like those generated by amphetamines—aggressiveness and paranoia—are frequent with long-term use. Although cocaine has enjoyed popularity as a "party drug," its extraordinary potential to create dependence should be taken very seriously.

### Narcotics

Opium, which comes from poppy seeds, and its derivatives heroin, morphine, methadone, and codeine (as well as prescription drugs such as Demerol and Oxycontin) are known as **narcotics** or **opiates**, *drugs derived from opium that are capable of relieving pain.* Narcotics induce a feeling of well-being and relaxation that is enjoyable but can also induce stupor and lethargy. The addictive properties of narcotics are powerful, and long-term use produces both tolerance and dependence. Because these

**NARCOTICS** or **OPIATES** Highly addictive drugs derived from opium that relieve pain.

imprisonment for drug offenses. Many people who are being prevented from ruining their lives with drugs are instead having their lives ruined by prison. These observations bring up the question of whether it is the drug use that causes social problems or the *prohibition* of drug use that causes these problems.

What should be done? One possibility is the **harm reduction approach,** *a response to high-risk behaviors that focuses on reducing the harm such behaviors have on people's lives* (Marlatt, 1998). This approach (which originated in the Netherlands and England) focuses on reducing drug harm rather than reducing drug use. Harm reduction involves tactics such as providing intravenous drug users with sterile syringes to help them avoid contracting HIV and other infections from shared needles. Harm reduction may even involve providing drugs for addicts to reduce the risks of poisoning and overdose they face when they get impure drugs of unknown dosage from criminal suppliers. A harm reduction idea for alcoholics, in turn, is to allow moderate drinking; the demand to be cold sober may keep many alcoholics on the street and away from any treatment at all (Marlatt et al., 1993). Harm reduction strategies may not always find public support because they challenge the popular idea that the solution to drug and alcohol problems must always be prohibition: stopping use entirely.

The mistaken belief in prohibition is fueled, in part, by the worry that drug use turns people into criminals and causes psy-

In the Netherlands, marijuana use is not prosecuted. The drug is sold in "coffee shops" to those over 18.

chological disorders. A key study that followed 101 children as they grew from the age of 3 to 18 did not confirm this theory (Shedler & Block, 1990). Personality assessments given to participants showed that those who were frequent drug users at 18 indeed were the most irresponsible, inconsiderate, irritable, rebellious, low in self-esteem, and so on. However, the adjustment problems of the frequent users were *already present* in early childhood, long before they started using drugs. Some other factor (a poor family environment as a child, perhaps) caused both their adjustment problems *and* their frequent drug use. As you read in Chapter 2, in this case, a third variable was at work in producing a correlation. It may be that allowing some limited forms of drug use—and instead focusing greater attention on reducing harm—would not create the problems we fear.

Harm reduction seems to be working in the Netherlands. The Netherlands Ministry of Justice (1999) reported that the decriminalization of marijuana there in 1979 has not led to increased use and that the use of other drugs remains at a level far below that of other European countries and the United States. Conversely, in the United States, the War on Drugs seems to have had little real impact. A comparison of drug users in Amsterdam and San Francisco revealed that the city in which marijuana is criminalized—San Francisco—had higher rates of drug use for both marijuana and other drugs (Reinarman, Cohen, & Kaal, 2004). Separating the markets in which people buy marijuana and alcohol from those in which they get "hard" drugs such as heroin, cocaine, or methamphetamine may create a social barrier that reduces interest in the hard drugs. There may be solutions that involve reasonable responses to drugs, a middle ground between prohibition and deregulation, as a way of reducing harm. Perhaps we can eliminate some casualties in the War on Drugs by fighting drug harm rather than heaping further harm on drug users. Regulating consciousness may be less important for society than reducing the harm that is caused when individuals try to regulate their own consciousness through drug use.

**HARM REDUCTION APPROACH** A response to high-risk behaviors that focuses on reducing the harm such behaviors have on people's lives.

drugs are often administered with hypodermic syringes, they also introduce the danger of diseases such as HIV when users share syringes. Unfortunately, these drugs are especially alluring because they are external mimics of the brain's own internal relaxation and well-being system.

The brain produces **endorphins** or **endogenous opiates,** which are *neurotransmitters that are closely related to opiates.* Endorphins play a role in how the brain copes internally with pain and stress. These substances reduce the experience of pain naturally. When you exercise for a while and start to feel your muscles burning, for example, you may also find that there comes a time when the pain eases—sometimes even *during* the exercise. Endorphins are secreted in the pituitary gland and other brain sites as a response to injury or exertion, creating a kind of natural remedy (like the so-called runner's high) that subsequently reduces pain and increases feelings of well-being. When people use narcotics, the brain's endorphin receptors are artificially flooded, however, reducing receptor effectiveness and possibly also depressing the production of endorphins. When external administration of narcotics stops, withdrawal symptoms are likely to occur.

**ENDORPHINS** or **ENDOGENOUS OPIATES** Neurotransmitters that have a similar structure to opiates and that appear to play a role in how the brain copes internally with pain and stress.

Psychedelic art and music of the 1960s were inspired by some visual and auditory effects of drugs such as LSD.

**HALLUCINOGENS** Drugs that alter sensation and perception and often cause visual and auditory hallucinations.

**MARIJUANA** The leaves and buds of the hemp plant.

**HYPNOSIS** An altered state of consciousness characterized by suggestibility and the feeling that one's actions are occurring involuntarily.

 **ONLY HUMAN**

**JUSTICE FOR ALL? In** Salt Lake City, Federal Judge Paul G. Cassell, remarking that mandatory minimum-sentencing laws gave him no choice, sent a 25-year-old, small-quantity marijuana dealer to prison for 55 years (because he had a gun during two of the transactions). Two hours before that, in a crime Cassell described as far more serious but not subject to the same mandatory sentencing minimums, he sentenced a man to 22 years in prison for beating an elderly woman to death with a log (Berman, 2005).

## Hallucinogens

The drugs that produce the most extreme alterations of consciousness are the **hallucinogens**, *drugs that alter sensation and perception, often causing hallucinations.* These include LSD (lysergic acid diethylamide), or acid; mescaline; psilocybin; PCP (phencycladine); and ketamine (an animal anesthetic). Some of these drugs are derived from plants (mescaline from peyote cactus, psilocybin or "shrooms" from mushrooms) and have been used by people since ancient times. For example, the ingestion of peyote plays a prominent role in some Native American religious practices. The other hallucinogens are largely synthetic. LSD was first made by chemist Albert Hofman in 1938, leading to a rash of experimentation that influenced popular culture in the 1960s. Timothy Leary, at the time a Harvard psychology professor, championed the use of LSD to "turn on, tune in, and drop out"; the Beatles sang of *Lucy in the sky with diamonds* (denying, of course, that this might be a reference to LSD); and the wave of interest led many people to experiment with hallucinogens.

The experiment was not a great success. These drugs produce profound changes in perception. Sensations may seem unusually intense, objects may seem to move or change, patterns or colors may appear, and these perceptions may be accompanied by exaggerated emotions ranging from blissful transcendence to abject terror. These are the "I've-become-the-legs-of-a-chair!" drugs. But the effects of hallucinogens are dramatic and unpredictable, creating a psychological roller-coaster ride that some people find intriguing but others find deeply disturbing. Hallucinogens are the main class of drugs that animals *won't* work to self-administer, so it is not surprising that in humans these drugs are unlikely to be addictive. Hallucinogens do not induce significant tolerance or dependence, and overdose deaths are rare. Although hallucinogens still enjoy a marginal popularity with people interested in experimenting with their perceptions, they have been more a cultural trend than a dangerous attraction.

## Marijuana

The *leaves and buds of the hemp plant* contain THC, the active ingredient in **marijuana**. When smoked or eaten, either as is or in concentrated form as *hashish,* this drug produces an intoxication that is mildly hallucinogenic. Users describe the experience as euphoric, with heightened senses of sight and sound and the perception of a rush of ideas. Marijuana affects judgment and short-term memory and impairs motor skills and coordination— making driving a car or operating heavy equipment a poor choice during its use ("Where did I leave the darn bulldozer?"). Researchers have found that receptors in the brain that respond to THC (Stephens, 1999) are normally activated by a neurotransmitter called *anandamide* that is naturally produced in the brain (Wiley, 1999). Anandamide is involved in the regulation of mood, memory, appetite, and pain perception and has been found temporarily to stimulate overeating in laboratory animals, much as marijuana does in humans (Williams & Kirkham, 1999). Some chemicals found in dark chocolate also mimic anandamide, although very weakly, perhaps accounting for the well-being some people claim they enjoy after a "dose" of chocolate.

The addiction potential of marijuana is not strong, as tolerance does not seem to develop, and physical withdrawal symptoms are minimal. Psychological dependence is possible, however, and some people do become chronic users. Marijuana use has been widespread throughout the world for recorded history, both as a medicine for pain and/or nausea and as a recreational drug, but its use remains controversial. States such as California and Oregon have passed legislation favoring medical uses, as has British Columbia in Canada, but the U.S. federal government classifies marijuana as a "Schedule I Controlled Substance," recognizing no medical use and maintaining that marijuana has the same high potential for abuse as heroin. All told, it seems that the greatest danger of marijuana is that its use is illegal.

**In summary,** psychoactive drugs influence consciousness by altering the brain's chemical messaging system and intensifying or dulling the effects of neurotransmitters. The altered consciousness brought about by drug use is attractive to many people, but in many cases drugs cause serious harm. Drug tolerance can result in overdose, and physical and psychological dependence can lead to addiction. Although people can sometimes overcome addiction, it is a serious human weakness that reveals the difficulty people have in acting with their best long-term interests in mind. The most commonly used and abused psychoactive drugs include depressants, stimulants, narcotics, hallucinogens, and marijuana. The varying effects of alcohol, a depressant, are explained by theories of alcohol expectancy and alcohol myopia. Each of the major classes of psychoactive drugs was developed for medical, social, or religious reasons, but each has different effects and presents a different array of dangers. ■ ■

# Hypnosis: Open to Suggestion

You may have never been hypnotized, but you have probably heard or read about it. Its wonders are often described with an air of amazement, and demonstrations of stage hypnosis make it seem very powerful and mysterious. When you think of hypnosis, you may envision people down on all fours acting like farm animals or perhaps "regressing" to early childhood and talking in childlike voices. Some of what you might think is true, but many of the common beliefs about hypnosis are false. **Hypnosis** is *an altered state of consciousness characterized by suggestibility and the feeling that one's actions are occurring involuntarily.* In other words, it is mainly a state of mind in which people follow instructions readily and feel that their actions are things that are happening to them rather than things they are doing (Lynn, Rhue, & Weekes, 1990).

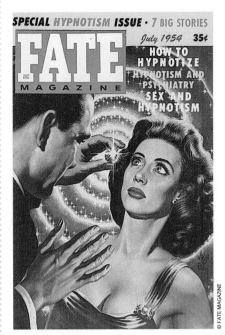

As you gaze at this magazine cover, you are getting sleepy . . . very sleepy. . . .

## Induction and Susceptibility

How do people get hypnotized? An early form of hypnotic induction is credited to Franz Anton Mesmer (1734–1815), a physician working in Paris. He attempted to cure people of illness through contact with what he called "animal magnetism." He introduced patients to his theory that a force could be generated from water and iron to rejuvenate their health and then proceeded to get them involved in several curious rituals. Patients held on to iron rods immersed in a large water tub, sometimes with their waists loosely tied to the tub with rope, and were asked to sit quietly while Mesmer passed his hands lightly over their bodies (Gauld, 1992). These theatrical gestures led many patients to believe that their ailments were cured. Some patients reported miraculous cures of chronic stomach problems, headaches, paralysis, and even blindness, and those whose cures were less dramatic still often agreed that they too felt better for all this. *Mesmerism* became a major sensation. Although Mesmer's theory was eventually discredited and he was dismissed as a charlatan (it turned out that none of the water tubs or paraphernalia were even needed for the effect), his technique of influencing people developed into what is now called hypnosis.

The essence of Mesmer's technique was persuading people that his actions would influence them. In a modern hypnotic induction, many people already know enough about hypnosis to suspect that something the hypnotist does might indeed have an effect on them. To induce hypnosis, then, a hypnotist may ask the person to be hypnotized to sit quietly and focus on some item (such as a spot on the wall) and then suggest to the person what effects hypnosis will have (for example, "Your eyelids are slowly closing" or "Your arms are getting heavy"). Modern hypnosis shares a common theme with mesmerism: In both cases, the hypnotist and participant engage in a social interaction in which the participants are led to expect that certain things will happen to them that are outside of their conscious will (Wegner, 2002).

The induction of hypnosis usually involves a number of different "suggestions," ideas the hypnotist mentions to the volunteer about what the volunteer will do. Some of

Stage hypnotists often perform an induction on a whole audience and then bring some of the more susceptible members onstage for further demonstrations. This hypnotist seems to think it is entertaining to see people slump over.

these ideas seem to cause the actions—just thinking about their eyelids slowly closing, for instance, may make many people shut their eyes briefly or at least blink. Just as you may find yawning contagious when you think about someone else yawning, many different behaviors can be made more common just by concentrating on them. In hypnosis, a series of behavior suggestions can induce in some people a state of mind that makes them susceptible to even very unusual suggestions, such as getting down on all fours and sniffing in the corner.

Not everyone is equally hypnotizable. Susceptibility varies greatly, such that some hypnotic "virtuosos" are strongly influenced, most people are only moderately influenced, and some people are entirely unaffected. Susceptibility is not easily predicted by a person's personality traits, so tests of hypnotic susceptibility are made up of a series of suggestions in a standard hypnotic induction. One of the best indicators of a person's susceptibility is the person's own judgment. So, if you think you might be hypnotizable, you may well be (Hilgard, 1965). People with active, vivid imaginations, or who are easily absorbed in activities such as watching a movie, are also somewhat more prone to be good candidates for hypnosis (Sheehan, 1979; Tellegen & Atkinson, 1974).

## Hypnotic Effects

From watching stage hypnotism, you might think that the major effect of hypnosis is making people do peculiar things. In fact, there are some impressive demonstrations. At the 1849 festivities for Prince Albert of England's birthday, for example, a hypnotized guest was asked to ignore any loud noises and then didn't even flinch when a pistol was fired near his face. The real effects of hypnosis are often clouded, however, by extravagant claims—that hypnotized people can perform extraordinary physical stunts, for example, or that they can remember things they have forgotten in normal consciousness.

Hypnotists often claim that their volunteers can perform great feats not possible when the volunteers are fully conscious. One of the claims for superhuman strength involves asking a hypnotized person to become "stiff as a board" and lie unsupported with shoulders on one chair and feet on another. However, many people can do this without hypnosis. Similarly, the claim that people will perform extreme actions when hypnotized fails to take into account that people will also perform these actions when they are simply under a lot of social pressure. Some early studies reported, for instance,

An 1849 demonstration of hypnosis at the festivities for Prince Albert's birthday. A pistol is discharged near the face of a young man in a trance, and he does not even flinch.

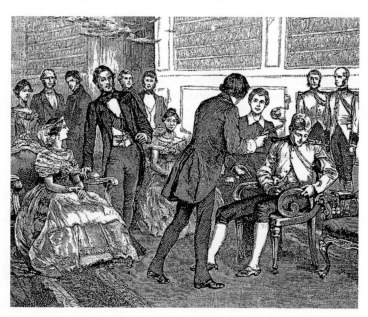

A hypnotist stands on a subject who has been rendered "stiff as a board" by hypnosis.

HULTON-DEUTSCH COLLECTION/CORBIS

that hypnotized people could be led to throw what they thought was a flask of acid in an experimenter's face (Rowland, 1939; Young, 1948). In further examinations of this phenomenon, participants who were not hypnotized were asked to *simulate* being hypnotized (Orne & Evans, 1965). They were instructed to be so convincing in faking their hypnosis that they would fool the experimenter. These people, just like the hypnotized participants, threw what they thought was acid in the experimenter's face! Clearly, hypnotic induction was not a necessary requirement to produce this behavior in the research participants.

Other strong claims for hypnosis have arisen because of the extraordinary agreeableness of many hypnotized people. When a susceptible person under hypnosis is asked to go back in time to childhood, for example, the person may become remarkably childlike, even to the point of babbling like an infant or breaking down in tears. One young man whose first language was Japanese but who was raised speaking English from the age of 8 reverted to Japanese spontaneously when under hypnosis; it was suggested that he was only 3 years old (Hilgard, 1986). Such cases have made psychologists wonder whether there is true "hypnotic age regression" or whether such cases are matters of playacting. (After all, does the hypnotized person who barks like a dog actually *become* a dog?) It turns out that the mental abilities of adults who have been age-regressed in hypnosis do not truly revert to early developmental stages or show childlike ways of thinking (Nash, 1987).

Hypnosis also has been touted as a cure for lost memory. The claim that hypnosis helps people to unearth memories that they are not able to retrieve in normal consciousness, however, seems to have surfaced because hypnotized people often make up memories to satisfy the hypnotist's suggestions. For example, Paul Ingram, a sheriff's deputy accused of sexual abuse by his daughters in the 1980s, was asked by interrogators in session after session to relax and imagine having committed the crimes. He emerged from these sessions having confessed to dozens of horrendous acts of "satanic ritual abuse." These confessions were called into question, however, when independent investigator Richard Ofshe used the same technique to ask Ingram about a crime that Ofshe had simply made up out of thin air, something of which Ingram had never been accused. Ingram produced a three-page handwritten confession, complete with dialogue (Ofshe, 1992). Still, prosecutors in the case accepted Ingram's guilty plea, and he was only released in 2003 after a public outcry and years of work on his defense. After a person claims to remember something, even under hypnosis, it is difficult to convince others that the memory was false (Loftus & Ketcham, 1994).

**POSTHYPNOTIC AMNESIA** The failure to retrieve memories following hypnotic suggestions to forget.

**HYPNOTIC ANALGESIA** The reduction of pain through hypnosis in people who are susceptible to hypnosis.

Hypnosis can also undermine memory. People susceptible to hypnosis can be led to experience **posthypnotic amnesia**, *the failure to retrieve memories following hypnotic suggestions to forget.* Ernest Hilgard (1986) taught a hypnotized person the populations of some remote cities, for example, and then suggested that he forget the study session. The person was quite surprised after the session at being able to give the census figures correctly. (Asked how he knew the answers, the individual decided he might have learned them from a TV program.) Such amnesia can then be reversed in subsequent hypnosis.

However, research does *not* find that people can retrieve through hypnosis memories that were not originally lost through hypnosis. Instead, hypnotized people try to report memories in line with the hypnotist's questioning. In one study, 27 hypnotizable research volunteers were given suggestions during hypnosis that they had been awakened by loud noises in the night a week before. After hypnosis, 13 of them—roughly 50%—reported that they had been awakened by loud noises (Laurence & Perry, 1983). Hypnosis does not enhance the accuracy of memory and instead only increases the person's *confidence* in false memory reports (Kihlstrom, 1985).

Although all the preceding claims for hypnosis are somewhat debatable, one well-established effect is **hypnotic analgesia**, *the reduction of pain through hypnosis in people who are hypnotically susceptible.* For example, one study (see **FIGURE 8.11**) found that for pain induced in volunteers in the laboratory, hypnosis was more effective than morphine, diazepam (Valium), aspirin, acupuncture, or placebos (Stern et al., 1977). For people who are hypnotically susceptible, hypnosis can be used to control pain in surgeries and dental procedures, in some cases more effectively than any form of anesthesia (Druckman & Bjork, 1994; Kihlstrom, 1985). Evidence for pain control supports the idea that hypnosis is a different state of consciousness and not entirely a matter of skillful role-playing on the part of highly motivated people.

The conscious state of hypnosis is accompanied by unique patterns of brain activation. In one study, researchers prescreened highly hypnotizable people for their ability to hallucinate during hypnosis (Szechtman et al., 1998). After a standard hypnotic induction, these participants were tested in a PET (positron emission tomography) scanner while performing each of three tasks: perception, imagination, and hypnotic hallucination. For the perception task, participants heard a recording of the sentence "The man did not speak often, but when he did, it was worth hearing what he had to say." For the imagination task, they were asked to imagine hearing this line again. For the hypnotic hallucination task, they listened as the hypnotist suggested that the tape was playing once more (although it was not). The researchers expected this last suggestion to prompt an auditory hallucination of the line, and participants indeed reported thinking they heard it.

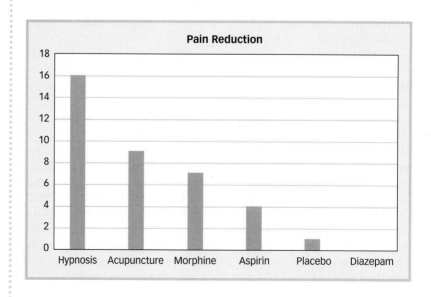

**Figure 8.11 Hypnotic Analgesia** The degree of pain reduction reported by people using different techniques for the treatment of laboratory-induced pain. Hypnosis wins.
From Stern et al., 1977.

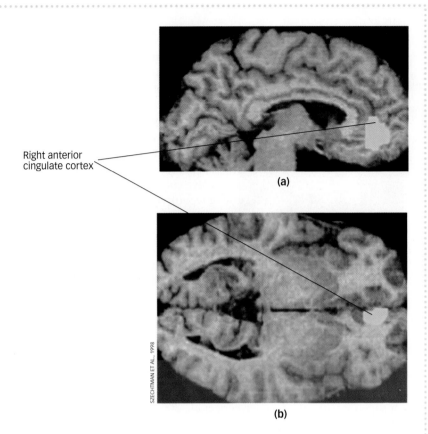

Right anterior
cingulate cortex

(a)

SZECHTMAN ET AL., 1998

(b)

**Figure 8.12** **Brain Activity during Hypnosis** Researchers found right anterior cingulate cortex activation in hypnotized research participants both when they were hearing a target sentence and when they were following the suggestion to hallucinate the sentence. The right anterior cingulate cortex is involved in the regulation of attention. The brain is viewed here in two cross-sectional scans: (a) upright and (b) horizontal.

The PET scan revealed that the right anterior cingulate cortex, an area involved in the regulation of attention, was just as active while the participants were hallucinating as when they were actually hearing the line. However, there was less activation in this brain area when participants were merely imagining the sentence. **FIGURE 8.12** shows where the right anterior cingulate area was activated in the hypnotizable participants both during hearing and hallucinating. This pattern of activation was not found in people who were not highly hypnotizable. The researchers concluded that hypnosis stimulated the brain to register the hallucinated voice as real rather than as imagined.

---

**In summary,** although there are many claims for hypnosis that overstate its effects, this altered state of consciousness characterized by suggestibility does have a range of real effects on individuals who are susceptible. Inductions of hypnosis can create the experience that one's actions are occurring involuntarily, influence memory reports, lead people to experience posthypnotic amnesia, create analgesia, and even change brain activations in ways that suggest that hypnotic experiences are more than imagination. ■ ■

---

# Meditation and Religious Experiences: Higher Consciousness

Some altered states of consciousness occur without hypnosis, without drugs, and without other external aids. In fact, the altered states of consciousness that occur naturally or through special practices such as meditation can provide some of the best moments in life. Abraham Maslow (1962) described these "peak experiences" as special states of mind in which you feel fully alive and glad to be human. Sometimes these come from simple pleasures—a breathtaking sunset or a magical moment of personal creativity— and other times they can arise through meditative or religious experiences.

Meditation can confer physical and psychological benefits on its practitioners—but research has not yet determined how it might work.

## Meditation

**Meditation** is *the practice of intentional contemplation*. Techniques of meditation are associated with a variety of religious traditions and are also practiced outside religious contexts. The techniques vary widely. Some forms of meditation call for attempts to clear the mind of thought, others involve focusing on a single thought (for example, thinking about a candle flame), and still others involve concentration on breathing or on a mantra, a repetitive sound such as *om*. At a minimum, the techniques have in common a period of quiet.

Why would someone meditate? The time spent meditating can be restful and revitalizing, and according to meditation enthusiasts, the repeated practice of meditation can enhance psychological well-being. The evidence for such long-term positive effects of meditation is controversial (Druckman & Bjork, 1994), but meditation does produce temporarily altered patterns of brain activation. Meditation influences EEG recordings of brain waves, usually producing patterns known as *alpha waves* that are associated with relaxation (Dillbeck & Orme-Johnson, 1987). A brain-scanning study of Buddhist practitioners during meditation found especially low levels of activation in the posterior superior parietal lobe (Newberg et al., 2001). This area is normally associated with judging physical space and orienting oneself in space—knowing angles, distances, and the physical landscape and distinguishing between the self and other objects in space. When this area is deactivated during meditation, its normal function of locating the self in space may subside to yield an experience of immersion and a loss of self.

## Ecstatic Religious Experiences

In some religious traditions, people describe personal experiences of altered consciousness—feelings of ecstasy, rapture, conversion, or mystical union. Members of a religious group may "speak in tongues," or the celebrants may go into trances, report seeing visions, or feel as though they are possessed by spirits. These altered states may happen during prayer or worship or without any special religious activity. Over 40% of one sample of Americans reported having a profound experience of this kind at least once in their lives (Greeley, 1975), and altered states of consciousness of one sort or another are associated with religious practices around the world (Bourguignon, 1968).

Whirling dervishes of the Mevlevi order of Sufism perform the Sema, a spiritual ceremony that aids in their quest for divine illumination.

**MEDITATION** The practice of intentional contemplation.

Like meditation, certain brain activation patterns are associated with ecstatic religious experiences. Some people who experience religious fervor show the same type of brain activation that occurs in some cases of epilepsy. Several prophets, saints, and founders of religions have been documented as having epilepsy—Joan of Arc, for example, had symptoms of epilepsy accompanying the religious visions that inspired her and her followers (Saver & Rabin, 1997). People asked to describe what it is like to have a seizure, in turn, sometimes report feeling what they call a religious "aura." One patient described his seizures as consisting of feelings of incredible contentment, detachment, and fulfillment, accompanied by the visualization of a bright light and soft music; sometimes he also saw a bearded man he assumed was Jesus Christ (Morgan, 1990). Surgery to remove a tumor in the patient's right anterior temporal lobe eliminated the seizures but also stopped his religious ecstasies. Cases such as this suggest the right anterior temporal lobe might be involved when people without epilepsy experience profound religious feelings. The special moments of connection that people feel with God or the universe may depend on the way in which brain activation promotes a religious state of consciousness.

The states of religious ecstasy and meditation are just two of the intriguing varieties of experience that consciousness makes available to us. Our consciousness ranges from the normal everyday awareness of walking, thinking, or gazing at a picture to an array of states that are far from normal or every day—sleep, dreams, drug intoxication, hypnosis, and beyond. These states of mind stand as a reminder that the human mind is not just something that students of psychology can look at and study. The mind is something each of us looks *through* at the world and at ourselves.

---

**In summary,** meditation and religious ecstasy can be understood as altered states of consciousness. Meditation involves contemplation that may focus on a specific thought, sound, or action (such as breathing) or may be an attempt to avoid any focus. The practice of meditation promotes relaxation in the short term, but the long-term benefits claimed by enthusiasts have not been established. Ecstatic religious experiences may have a basis in the same brain region—the right anterior temporal lobe—associated with some forms of epilepsy. ■ ■

---

# Where Do You Stand?

## Between NORML and MADD: What Is Acceptable Drug Use?

Where is the line between drug use and abuse, between acceptable chemical alteration of consciousness and over-the-top drug-crazed insanity? Some people think that the line is drawn too strictly—organizations such as NORML (National Organization for the Reform of Marijuana Laws) lobby for the legalization of marijuana. Others think the line is too loose—MADD (Mothers Against Drunk Driving) asks bars and restaurants to end "happy hours" that promote alcohol consumption. At the extremes, some people advocate the legalization of cocaine and heroin (for instance, Jenny Tonge, member of the British Parliament), and others propose to fight caffeine addiction (for example, Rosemarie Ives, mayor of Redmond, Washington). Where do you stand?

It may not be entirely clear where you stand after all because you may not have thought this through. Drug use is a controversial topic, and whenever it comes up, you may find yourself face-to-face with people who have very strong opinions. Talking with some people about drugs and alcohol may feel like talking with interrogators under a bright light down at the police station, and you may find yourself taking sides that do not reflect how you really feel. On the other hand, people you know who drink or use drugs may make you feel like a stick-in-the-mud if you don't always approve of what they're doing. Where do you stand? Should people be legally allowed to use psychoactive drugs and if yes, which ones? What about alcohol? Should there be restrictions on when or where these substances are used? For a legal drug, how old should a person be to use it?

# Chapter Review

## Conscious and Unconscious: The Mind's Eye, Open and Closed

- Consciousness is a mystery of psychology because other people's minds cannot be perceived directly and also because the relationship between mind and body is perplexing.

- Consciousness is intentional, unified, and selective but transient and can be viewed as having levels of minimal consciousness, full consciousness, and self-consciousness. The contents of the stream of consciousness include current concerns, daydreams, and unwanted thoughts.

- Unconscious processes are sometimes understood as expressions of the Freudian dynamic unconscious but are more commonly seen as processes of the cognitive unconscious that create and influence conscious thoughts and behaviors.

## Sleep and Dreaming: Good Night, Mind

- The sleep cycle involves a regular pattern of sleep and dreaming that creates altered states of consciousness. Humans progress through stages of NREM and REM sleep throughout the night.

- There are several sleep disorders that influence the quality of both sleep and dreams, including insomnia, sleep apnea, somnambulism, narcolepsy, sleep paralysis, nightmares, and night terrors.

- Sleep deprivation and dream deprivation are both detrimental to psychological effectiveness and physical health.

- The contents of dreams are related to waking life and can be understood by examining the areas of the brain that are activated when people dream. Different theories about why dreams occur and their potential meanings have been proposed. Older views focus on symbolism and the unconscious, whereas more recent accounts approach dreaming as an aspect of normal brain activity.

## Drugs and Consciousness: Artificial Inspiration

- Psychoactive drugs influence consciousness and sometimes produce addiction. Addiction to drugs involves drug tolerance and drug withdrawal, which may include both physical and psychological dependence.

- Specific effects on consciousness and behavior occur with different classes of psychoactive drugs. These classes include depressants, stimulants, narcotics, hallucinogens, and marijuana.

- Depressants are substances that reduce the activity of the central nervous system, producing a sedative or calming effect. Examples of depressants are alcohol, barbiturates, benzodiazepines, and toxic inhalants. Stimulants are substances that excite the nervous system and include caffeine, amphetamines, nicotine, cocaine, and ecstasy (MDMA).

- Narcotics are highly addictive drugs derived from opium, such as heroin, morphine, methadone, and codeine. Hallucinogens produce altered sensations and perceptions. Examples include LSD, psilocybin, mescaline, PCP, and ketamine.

- Marijuana, the leaves and buds of the hemp plant, produces heightened sensations but impairs memory and motor skills.

## Hypnosis: Open to Suggestion

- Inductions of hypnosis can alter consciousness in people who are susceptible, making them feel that their actions are occurring involuntarily and leading them to follow the hypnotist's suggestions.

- Hypnosis can cause amnesia and lead people to make up memories but is useful as an analgesic for pain.

## Meditation and Religious Experiences: Higher Consciousness

- Changes in consciousness away from the normal state may be attained through meditation, yielding short-term relaxation but no clearly measured long-term effects.

- Religious experiences are sometimes associated with brain regions that are also affected by epilepsy.

## Key Terms

consciousness (p. 294)

Cartesian Theater (p. 294)

phenomenology (p. 295)

problem of other minds (p. 295)

mind/body problem (p. 297)

dichotic listening (p. 298)

cocktail party phenomenon (p. 299)

minimal consciousness (p. 300)

full consciousness (p. 300)

self-consciousness (p. 301)

mental control (p. 303)

thought suppression (p. 303)

rebound effect of thought suppression (p. 303)

ironic processes of mental control (p. 304)

dynamic unconscious (p. 305)

repression (p. 305)

cognitive unconscious (p. 306)

subliminal perception (p. 306)

altered state of consciousness (p. 309)

circadian rhythm (p. 309)

REM sleep (p. 310)

electrooculograph (EOG) (p. 311)

insomnia (p. 313)

sleep apnea (p. 313)

somnambulism (p. 313)

narcolepsy (p. 314)

sleep paralysis (p. 314)

night terrors (p. 314)

manifest content (p. 317)

latent content (p. 317)

activation-synthesis model (p. 317)

psychoactive drugs (p. 318)

drug tolerance (p. 319)

depressants (p. 321)

expectancy theory (p. 321)

balanced placebo design (p. 322)

alcohol myopia (p. 322)

stimulants (p. 323)

narcotics or opiates (p. 324)

harm reduction approach (p. 325)

endorphins or endogenous opiates (p. 325)

hallucinogens (p. 326)

marijuana (p. 326)

hypnosis (p. 327)

posthypnotic amnesia (p. 330)

hypnotic analgesia (p. 330)

meditation (p. 332)

## Recommended Readings

**Blackmore, S.** (2004). *Consciousness: An introduction*. New York: Oxford University Press. Susan Blackmore is the sort of writer whom you might expect would show up every few weeks with her hair freshly dyed in a new pattern of rainbow colors, and in fact this is exactly what she does. Her book blends philosophy, psychology, and neuroscience in a clear, enjoyable, and colorfully written introduction to the field of consciousness.

**Hobson, A.** (1988). *The dreaming brain*. New York: Basic Books. This book's subtitle is "How the Brain Creates Both the Sense and the Nonsense of Dreams." Hobson examines the history of dream theories, including psychoanalytic theory, and then provides his own "activation synthesis" hypothesis—that dreaming is the brain's way of making sense of its own nighttime activations.

**Wegner, D. M.** (1994). *White bears and other unwanted thoughts: Suppression, obsession, and the psychology of mental control.*

New York: Guilford Press. Why it is that we have so much trouble controlling our own minds? This book describes the initial experiments in which people were asked to try to stop thinking about a white bear—and found they could not.

**Wegner, D. M.** (2002). *The illusion of conscious will*. Cambridge: MIT Press. This book describes how it is that we come to believe that we consciously will our own actions and examines along the way such anomalies as phantom limbs, Ouija board spelling, spirit possession, and hypnosis.

**Zeman, A.** (2002). *Consciousness: A user's guide*. New Haven, CT: Yale University Press. The author is a neurologist, and his wide-ranging interests in everything from Shakespeare to the architecture of the brain make for exhilaratingly broad reading—and a high-level introduction to the science of consciousness.

# 10

# Emotion and Motivation

"WHY? WHY? WHY? WHY? THAT'S THE question I think everyone is asking."

At 6:02 p.m. on October 2, 2002, James Martin was walking across the Shoppers Food Warehouse parking lot in Wheaton, Maryland, with a bag of groceries in his arms. He'd left his office at the usual time that evening and stopped at the grocery store to pick up a few things for the youth group at his church. His wife, Billie, and their 11-year-old son, Ben, were waiting for him at home, but their wait would be in vain. As Martin approached his truck, there was a sudden, loud pop, and a bullet from a Bushmaster XM15 semiautomatic rifle severed his spinal cord and perforated his aorta. He crumpled to the pavement and bled to death.

James Martin was the first, but he would not be the last. The next day, in a period of less than 90 minutes, James Buchanan was shot while mowing the lawn, Premkumar Walekar was shot while pumping gas, Sarah Ramos was shot while sitting at a bus stop, Lori Ann Lewis-Rivera was shot while vacuuming her car, and Pascal Charlot was shot while taking a walk. In the days that followed, there were more shootings and more deaths. The serial killer whom the media called the "Beltway Sniper" seemed to select his victims at random and shoot them from afar, leaving authorities to guess at his motive. "The thrill of the kill," speculated one FBI agent. "Playing God. Having the power over these individuals. Life and death. That's a real heady rush" (Horwitz & Ruane, 2003). The sniper's motive seemed to become clear when authorities received a note demanding that they pay him $10 million to stop killing people. The note provided clues that led police to 42-year-old John Allen Muhammad and 17-year-old Lee Boyd Malvo, who were arrested in a blue Chevrolet Caprice whose trunk had been modified to serve as a sniper's perch.

What motivated John Allen Muhammad (left) and Lee Boyd Malvo (right), to spend 22 days killing people at random?

STEVE HELBER/AP/GETTY IMAGES

AP PHOTO/SUSAN WALSH, FILE

367

Why did two men ride around in a car for 22 days, slaughtering innocent people at random? Authorities discovered that the plot to extort money had been hatched only *after* the men had killed most of their victims. Prosecutors claimed that, in fact, Muhammad had come to Maryland to kill his ex-wife and that when he was unable to locate her, he went mad and "began shooting people around her" (Ahlers, 2003). Muhammad's attorney argued that his client was a troubled veteran for whom "something went terribly wrong. He came back from Desert Storm a different man" (Sipe, 2006). A psychologist described Muhammad as a "very, very angry individual," but added, "Of course there are a lot of angry people who don't explode. So there must have been something in his social interaction—in his marriage or his military career—that pulled the trigger" (Leonard, 2002).

The teenage Malvo claimed that he had not wanted to kill anyone and that he participated in the slaughter in order to please Muhammad, whom he called "Father." Not everyone believed that the two men were motivated by greed, by rage, or by filial loyalty. "Muhammad might have seen himself as a foot soldier in the jihad against the United States and he took up arms to terrorize Americans," wrote one commentator (Pipes, 2002). "In a society that celebrates celebrity above all, they were seeking to enter the Hall of Fame in the only category where they stood a chance, as criminals and serial killers," wrote another (Buchanan, 2002).

"**W**hy? Why? Why? Why? That's the question I think everyone is asking," said Malvo's brother (Pipes, 2002). And indeed it was. Serial killers fascinate us—not because of a morbid curiosity, but because we are fascinated by people whose motives we can't fathom and whose emotions we can't comprehend. What led Muhammad to select another human being at random and put a bullet through his heart? What compelled Malvo to take aim at a pregnant woman simply because his surrogate father asked him to? How could these men have pulled the triggers of their rifles; watched helpless men, women, and children fall to the ground; and then driven away calmly? How could they not have felt sadness, remorse, or disgust? The behaviors in question are mercifully rare, but the questions themselves are not. When we ask why people feel and act as they do, we are asking questions about their emotions and motivations. As you will see, emotions and motivations are intimately connected, and understanding their connection allows us to answer the "Why?" question that everyone is asking.

## Emotional Experience: The Feeling Machine

Trying to describe love to someone who had never experienced it would be a bit like trying to describe green to someone who was born blind. You could tell them about its

For most people, these pictures evoke emotional experiences. Having these experiences is easy, but describing them is difficult.

sources ("It's that feeling you get when you see your sweetheart across the room") and you could describe its physiological correlates ("It makes your pupils dilate"), but in the end, your descriptions would largely miss the point because the essential feature of love—like the essential feature of all emotions—is the *experience*. It *feels* like something to love, and what it feels like is love's defining attribute.

## What Is Emotion?

What can we do when we want to study something whose defining attribute resists description? Psychologists have developed a clever technique that capitalizes on the fact that while people can't always say what an emotional experience feels like ("Love is . . . um . . . uh . . ."), they can usually say how similar it is to another ("Love is more like happiness than like anger"). By asking people to rate the similarity of dozens of emotional experiences, psychologists have been able to map those experiences using a sophisticated technique known as *multidimensional scaling*. The mathematics behind this technique is complex, but the logic is simple. If you listed the distances between a dozen U.S. cities and then handed the list to a friend and challenged him to draw a map on which every city was the listed distance from every other, your friend would be forced to draw a map of the United States because there is no other map that allows every city to appear at precisely the right distance from every other. Sure, there are lots of ways to draw a map so that San Francisco is 344 miles from Los Angeles, but there is only one way to draw a map so that San Francisco is 344 miles from Los Angeles *and* 1,863 miles from Chicago *and* 2,582 miles from New York, and so on. The point is that a map of the physical landscape can be generated from nothing but a list of distances between cities.

The same logic can be used to generate a map of the emotional landscape. If you listed the similarity of a dozen emotional experiences (giving smaller numbers to those that were conceptually "close" to each other and larger numbers to those that are conceptually "far away" from each other) and then challenged a friend to draw a map on which every experience was the listed "distance" from every other, your friend would draw a map like the one shown in **FIGURE 10.1**. This is the unique map that allows every emotional experience to be precisely the right "distance" from every other.

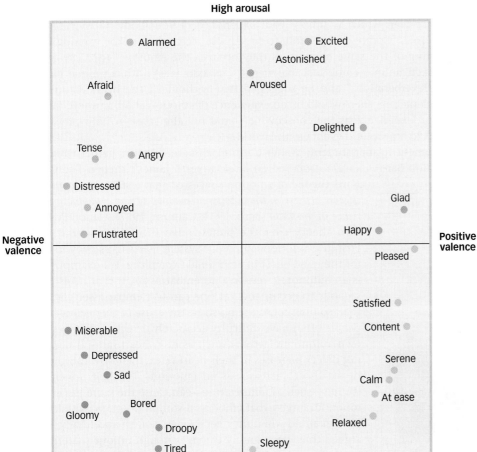

**Figure 10.1 Two Dimensions of Emotion** Just as cities can be mapped by their longitude and latitude, emotions can be mapped by their arousal and valence.

**EMOTION** A positive or negative experience that is associated with a particular pattern of physiological activity.

**JAMES-LANGE THEORY** A theory about the relationship between emotional experience and physiological activity suggesting that stimuli trigger activity in the autonomic nervous system, which in turn produces an emotional experience in the brain.

**CANNON-BARD THEORY** A theory about the relationship between emotional experience and physiological activity suggesting that a stimulus simultaneously triggers activity in the autonomic nervous system and emotional experience in the brain.

**TWO-FACTOR THEORY** A theory about the relationship between emotional experience and physiological activity suggesting that emotions are inferences about the causes of undifferentiated physiological arousal.

What good is this map? As it turns out, maps don't just show how close things are to each other: They also reveal the *dimensions* on which those things vary. For example, a U.S. map reveals that cities differ on two dimensions called longitude and latitude, and thus every city can be described by its unique coordinates in this two-dimensional space. Similarly, an emotion map reveals that emotional experiences differ on two dimensions that are called *valence* (how positive or negative the experience is) and *arousal* (how active or passive the experience is), and every emotional experience can be described by its unique coordinates in this two-dimensional space (Russell, 1980; Watson & Tellegen, 1985).

This map of emotional experience suggests that any definition of emotion must include two things: first, the fact that emotional experiences are always good or bad, and second, the fact that these experiences are associated with characteristic levels of bodily arousal. As such, **emotion** can be defined as *a positive or negative experience that is associated with a particular pattern of physiological activity*. As you are about to see, the first step in understanding emotion involves understanding how experience and physiological activity are related.

## The Emotional Body

You probably think that if you walked into your kitchen right now and saw a bear nosing through the cupboards, you would feel fear, your heart would start to pound, and the muscles in your legs would prepare you for running. Presumably away. But William James and Carl Lange suggested that the events that produce an emotion might actually happen in the opposite order (Lange & James, 1922). The **James-Lange theory** of emotion asserts that *stimuli trigger activity in the autonomic nervous system, which in turn produces an emotional experience in the brain*. In other words, first you see the bear, then your heart starts pounding and your leg muscles contract, and *then* you experience fear, which is simply your experience of your body's activity. As James (1884) wrote, "Bodily changes follow directly the perception of the exciting fact. . . . And feeling of the same changes as they occur *is* the emotion" (pp. 189–190). For James, each unique emotional experience was associated with a unique pattern of "bodily reverberation," and he suggested that without all the heart pounding and muscle clenching, there would be no experience of emotion at all. In short, James saw emotional experience as the consequence—and not the cause—of our physiological reactions to objects and events in the world.

But James's former student, Walter Cannon, disagreed, and together with *his* student, Philip Bard, Cannon proposed an alternative to James's theory. The **Cannon-Bard theory** of emotion suggested that *a stimulus simultaneously triggers activity in the autonomic nervous system and emotional experience in the brain* (Bard, 1934; Cannon, 1927). Canon favored his own theory over the James-Lange theory for several reasons. First, the autonomic nervous system reacts too slowly to account for the rapid onset of emotional experience. For example, a blush is an autonomic response to embarrassment that takes 15 to 30 seconds to occur, and yet one can feel embarrassed long before that, so how could the blush be the cause of the feeling? Second, people often have difficulty accurately detecting changes in their own autonomic activity, such as their heart rates. If people cannot detect increases in their heart rates, then how can they experience those increases as an emotion? Third, if nonemotional stimuli—such as temperature—can cause the same pattern of autonomic activity that emotional stimuli do, then why don't people feel afraid when they get a fever? Fourth and finally, Cannon argued that there simply weren't enough unique patterns of autonomic activity to account for all the unique emotional experiences people have. If many different emotional experiences are

*"I never realized they had feelings."*

associated with the same pattern of autonomic activity, then how could that pattern of activity be the sole determinant of the emotional experience?

These are all good questions, and about 30 years after Cannon asked them, psychologists Stanley Schachter and Jerome Singer supplied some answers (Schachter & Singer, 1962). James and Lange were right, they claimed, to equate emotion with the perception of one's bodily reactions. Cannon and Bard were also right, they claimed, to note that there are not nearly enough distinct bodily reactions to account for the wide variety of emotions that human beings can experience. Whereas James and Lange had suggested that different emotions are *different experiences* of *different patterns* of bodily activity, Schachter and Singer claimed that different emotions are merely *different interpretations* of *a single pattern* of bodily activity, which they called "undifferentiated physiological arousal" (see **FIGURE 10.2**).

Schachter and Singer's **two-factor theory** of emotion claimed that *emotions are inferences about the causes of undifferentiated physiological arousal*. When you see a bear in your kitchen, your heart begins to pound. Your brain quickly scans the environment, looking for a reasonable explanation for all that pounding, and it finds, of all things, a bear. Having noticed both a bear and a pounding heart, your brain then does what brains do so well: It puts two and two together, makes a logical inference, and interprets your arousal as fear. In other words, when people are physiologically aroused in the presence of something that they think should scare them, they label their arousal as *fear*. But if they have precisely the same bodily response in the presence of something that they think should delight them, they may label that arousal as *excitement*. According to Schachter and Singer, people have the same physiological reaction to all emotional stimuli, but they interpret that reaction differently on different occasions.

To demonstrate their claim, Schachter and Singer gave participants in an experiment an injection of epinephrine, a neurotransmitter that mimics the action of the sympathetic nervous system, causing increases in blood pressure, heart rate, blood flow to the brain, blood sugar levels, and respiration. Some participants were correctly informed that side effects of the injection would include trembling hands, a flushed face, and an increased heart rate. Other participants were incorrectly informed that the side effects of the injection would include numb feet, an itching sensation all over the body, and a slight headache. Next, participants were given the opportunity to interact with one of two people who, unbeknownst to them, were confederates of the experimenter. In one condition of the experiment, the confederate acted giddy, doodling on some paper, crumbling it into a makeshift basketball, constructing paper airplanes, and swinging some hula hoops he found. In the other condition, the confederate acted surly, spending his time grousing and harrumphing his way through a

England's Prince William blushes with embarrassment as he arrives at his hotel and finds a throng of adoring female fans. Because the experience of embarrassment precedes blushing by up to 30 seconds, it is unlikely that blushing is the cause of the experience.

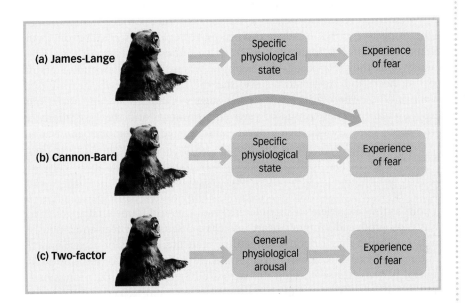

(a) **James-Lange** → Specific physiological state → Experience of fear

(b) **Cannon-Bard** → Specific physiological state → Experience of fear

(c) **Two-factor** → General physiological arousal → Experience of fear

**Figure 10.2 Classic Theories of Emotion** Classic theories make different claims about the origins of emotion. (a) The James-Lange theory suggests that stimuli trigger specific physiological states, which are then experienced as emotions. (b) The Cannon-Bard theory suggests that stimuli trigger both specific physiological states and emotional experiences independently. (c) The two-factor theory suggests that stimuli trigger general physiological arousal whose cause the brain interprets, and this interpretation leads to emotional experience.

Some of the pioneers of emotion theory are William James, Carl Lange, and Walter Cannon (top row, left to right), and Phillip Bard, Stanley Schachter, and Jerome Singer (bottom row, left to right).

questionnaire before finally ripping up the paper and storming out of the room. Schachter and Singer predicted that participants who were correctly informed about the side effects would correctly interpret their arousal ("I'm feeling a little revved up because of the shot") but that participants who were not correctly informed about the side effects would seek an explanation for their arousal—and that the confederate's behavior would supply it. Specifically, they predicted that when the confederate acted goofy, the misinformed participants would conclude that they were feeling *happy* but that when the confederate acted nasty, they would conclude that they were feeling *angry*. And that's just what happened.

How has the two-factor model fared in the last half century? In one sense, it has fared quite well. Research has shown that when people are aroused, say, by having them ride an exercise bike in the laboratory, they subsequently find attractive people more attractive, annoying people more annoying, and funny cartoons funnier—as if they were interpreting their exercise-induced arousal as attraction, annoyance, and delight, respectively (Byrne, Allgeier, Winslow, & Buckman, 1975; Dutton & Aron, 1974; Zillmann, Katcher, & Milausky, 1972). Indeed, these effects occur even when people merely *think* they're aroused—for example, when they hear an audiotape of a rapidly beating heart and are led to believe that the heartbeat they're hearing is their own (Valins, 1966). These and other studies suggest that people can indeed misattribute their arousal to other stimuli in their environments and that the inferences people draw about the causes of their arousal can influence their emotional experience.

On the other hand, one of the model's central claims is that all emotional experiences derive from the same pattern of bodily activity, namely, undifferentiated physiological arousal. Research has not been so kind to this part of the theory. Paul Ekman, Robert Levenson, and Wallace Friesen (1983) measured participants' physiological reactions as they experienced six different emotions and found that anger, fear, and sadness each produced a higher heart rate than disgust; that fear and disgust produced higher galvanic skin response (sweating) than did sadness or anger; and that anger produced a larger increase in finger temperature than did fear (see **FIGURE 10.3**). This general pattern has been replicated across different age groups, professions, genders, and cultures (Levenson et al., 1991; Levenson, Ekman, & Friesen, 1990; Levenson et

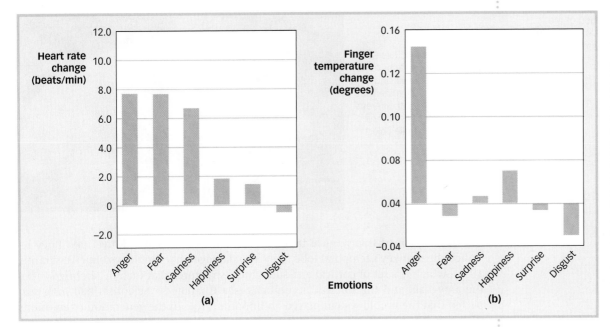

**Figure 10.3**
**Different Physiological Patterns of Emotion** Contrary to the claims of the two-factor theory, different emotions do seem to have different underlying patterns of physiological arousal. (a) Anger, fear, and sadness all produce higher heart rates compared to happiness, surprise, and disgust. (b) Anger produces a much larger increase in finger temperature than any other emotion.

al., 1992). In fact, some physiological responses seem unique to specific emotions. For example, a blush is the result of increased blood volume in the subcutaneous capillaries in the face, neck, and chest, and research suggests that people blush when they feel embarrassment but not when they feel any other emotion (Leary et al., 1992). Similarly, certain patterns of activity in the parasympathetic branch of the autonomic nervous system (which is responsible for slowing and calming rather than speeding and exciting) seem uniquely related to prosocial emotions such as compassion (Oately, Keltner, & Jenkins, 2006).

It now appears that James and Lange were right when they suggested that patterns of physiological response are not the same for all emotions. But it appears that Cannon and Bard were right when they suggested that people are not perfectly sensitive to these patterns of response, which is why people must sometimes make inferences about what they are feeling. Our bodily activity and our mental activity are both the causes and the consequences of our emotional experience. The precise nature of their interplay is not yet fully understood, but as you are about to see, much progress has been made over last few decades by following the trail of emotion from the beating heart to the living brain.

## The Emotional Brain

Psychologist Heinrich Klüver was curious: Why do monkeys smack their lips after being given hallucinogenic drugs? So on the afternoon of December 7, 1936, he and the physician Paul Bucy removed the temporal lobe of a particularly aggressive rhesus monkey named Aurora and ultimately learned nothing whatsoever about lip smacking. They did, however, produce what Klüver would later call "the most striking behavior changes ever produced by a brain operation in animals" (Klüver, 1951, p. 151). Their surgical experiments revealed that monkeys whose temporal lobes had been removed would eat just about anything and have sex with just about anyone or anything—as though they could no longer distinguish between good and bad food or good and bad mates. But the most striking thing about these monkeys was their extraordinary lack of fear. They were eerily calm when being handled by experimenters or being confronted by snakes, both of which rhesus monkeys typically find alarming (Klüver & Bucy, 1937, 1939). This constellation of behaviors became known as "temporal lobe syndrome" or "Klüver-Bucy syndrome" (though it was later pointed out that the syndrome had been described in 1888 by Brown and Schafer).

**APPRAISAL** An evaluation of the emotion-relevant aspects of a stimulus that is performed by the amygdala.

Animals with Klüver-Bucy syndrome become hypersexual and will attempt to mate with members of different species and even inanimate objects.

What explained this surgical taming? As it turned out, when Klüver and Bucy lesioned the monkey's temporal lobe, they also damaged her limbic system (Weiskrantz, 1956), which is a set of cortical and subcortical structures that include, among others, the amygdala and the nucleus accumbens (see Chapter 3). Scientists had long suspected that the limbic system played an important role in the generation of emotions (Papez, 1937), and these experiments confirmed that speculation in the case of fear. A few decades later, psychologists James Olds and Peter Milner implanted electrodes in the brains of rats to see how the rats would respond to direct electrical stimulation of their brains (Olds & Milner, 1954). When Olds and Milner stimulated the rat's limbic system, they found that it quickly returned to whatever part of the cage it had just been in—as though the rat were trying to re-create the circumstances that had led to the electric stimulation. When they allowed the rat to stimulate its own brain by pressing a lever, the rat did so for hours on end, often choosing electric stimulation over food. These studies suggested that the limbic system was also implicated in the experience of emotions such as pleasure.

More recent research has demonstrated that a particular limbic structure—the amygdala—plays a key role in the production of emotion. William James (1884) claimed that "bodily changes follow directly the perception of the exciting fact" (p. 189), which means that some part of the brain decides which facts are exciting. Between the moment that information about an approaching bear enters our eye and the moment our heart starts pounding, our brain has to decide that a bear is something to be afraid of. That decision is called an **appraisal**, which is *an evaluation of the emotion-relevant aspects of a stimulus* (Arnold, 1960; Lazarus, 1984; Roseman, 1984; Roseman & Smith, 2001; Scherer, 1999, 2001), and research suggests that making appraisals is the amygdala's primary job (see **FIGURE 10.4**). For example, in one study,

**Figure 10.4 Emotion Recognition and the Amygdala** Facial expressions of emotion were morphed into a continuum that ran from happiness to surprise to fear to sadness to disgust to anger and back to happiness. This sequence was shown to a patient with bilateral amygdala damage and to a group of 10 people without brain damage. Although the patient's recognition of happiness, sadness, and surprise was generally in line with that of the undamaged group, her recognition of anger, disgust, and fear was impaired. (Calder et al., 1996)

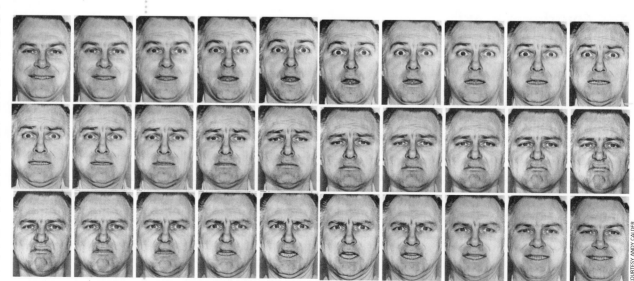

researchers performed an operation on monkeys so that information entering the monkey's left eye could be transmitted to the amygdala but information entering the monkey's right eye could not (Downer, 1961). When these monkeys were allowed to see a threatening stimulus with only their left eye, they responded with fear and alarm, but when they were allowed to see the threatening stimulus with only their right eye, they were calm and unruffled. These results suggest that if visual information doesn't reach the amygdala, then its emotional significance cannot be assessed. Klüver and Bucy's monkeys were calm in the presence of a snake because their amygdalae had been damaged, so the sight of a snake was no longer coded as threatening. Research on human beings has reached a similar conclusion. For example, normal people have superior memory for emotionally evocative words such as *death* or *crap,* but people whose amygdalae are damaged (LaBar & Phelps, 1998) or who take drugs that temporarily impair neurotransmission in the amygdala (van Stegeren et al., 1998) do not.

The amygdala's job is to make a very rapid appraisal of a stimulus, and thus it does not require much information (Zajonc, 1980, 1984). When people are shown fearful faces at speeds so fast that they are unaware of having seen them, their amygdalae show increased activity (Whalen et al., 1998). Psychologist Joseph LeDoux (2000) mapped the route that information about a stimulus takes through the brain and found that it is transmitted simultaneously along two distinct routes: the "fast pathway," which goes from the thalamus directly to the amygdala, and the "slow pathway," which goes from the thalamus to the cortex and *then* to the amygdala (see **FIGURE 10.5**). This means that while the cortex is slowly using the information to conduct a full-scale investigation of the stimulus's identity and importance ("This seems to be an animal . . . probably a mammal . . . perhaps a member of the genus *Ursus . . .*"), the amygdala has already received the information directly from the thalamus and is making one very fast and very simple decision: "Is this bad for me?" If the amygdala's answer to that question is "yes," it initiates the neural processes that ultimately produce the bodily reactions and conscious experience that we call fear.

When the cortex finally finishes processing the information, it sends a signal to the amygdala telling it to maintain fear ("We've now analyzed all the data up here, and sure enough, that thing is a bear—and bears bite!") or decrease it ("Relax, it's just some guy in a bear costume"). When people are asked to *experience* emotions such as happiness, sadness, fear, and anger, they show increased activity in the limbic system and decreased activity in the cortex (Damasio et al., 2000), but when people are asked to *inhibit* these emotions, they show increased cortical activity and decreased limbic

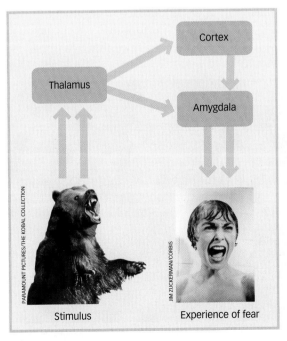

**Figure 10.5** **The Fast and Slow Pathways of Fear** According to Joseph LeDoux, information about a stimulus takes two routes simultaneously: the "fast pathway" (shown in pink), which goes from the thalamus directly to the amygdala, and the "slow pathway" (shown in green), which goes from the thalamus to the cortex and then to the amygdala. Because the amygdala receives information from the thalamus before it receives information from the cortex, people can be afraid of something before they know what it is.

**EMOTION REGULATION** The use of cognitive and behavioral strategies to influence one's emotional experience.

**REAPPRAISAL** A strategy that involves changing one's emotional experience by changing the meaning of the emotion-eliciting stimulus.

activity (Ochsner Burge, Gross, & Gabrieli, 2002). In a sense, the amygdala presses the emotional gas pedal and the cortex then hits the brakes. That's why adults with cortical damage and children (whose cortices are not well developed) have difficulty inhibiting their emotions (Stuss & Benson, 1986).

Studies of the brain confirm what psychologists have long suspected: Emotion is a primitive system that prepares us to react rapidly and on the basis of little information to things that are relevant to our survival and well-being. While our newly acquired cortex identifies a stimulus, considers what it knows about it, and carefully plans a response, our ancient limbic system does what it has done so well for all those millennia before the cortex evolved: It makes a split-second decision about the significance of the objects and events in our environment and, when necessary, prepares our hearts and our legs to get our butts out of the woods.

## The Regulation of Emotion

No one is agnostic about their own emotional experience. We may not care whether we have cereal or eggs for breakfast, whether we play cricket or cards this afternoon, or whether we spend a few minutes thinking about hedgehogs, earwax, or the War of 1812. But we always care whether we are feeling happy or fearful, angry or relaxed, joyful or disgusted. Because we care so much about our emotional experiences, we take an active role in determining which ones we will have. **Emotion regulation** refers to *the cognitive and behavioral strategies people use to influence their own emotional experience.* Although emotion regulation is typically an attempt to turn negative emotions into positive ones, there are times when people feel a bit too chipper for their own good and seek ways to "cheer down" (Erber, Wegner, & Therriault, 1996; Parrott, 1993). A patient who is feeling depressed may whistle a silly song while waiting for his doctor, and a doctor who is feeling silly may think a few depressing thoughts before entering the room to give the patient bad news. Both are regulating their emotional experience.

Nine out of 10 people report that they attempt to regulate their emotional experience at least once a day (Gross, 1998), and they describe more than a thousand different strategies for doing so (Parkinson & Totterdell, 1999). Some of these are behavioral strategies (e.g., avoiding situations that trigger unwanted emotions, doing distracting activities, or taking drugs) and some are cognitive strategies (e.g., trying not to think about the cause of the unwanted emotion or recruiting memories that trigger the desired emotion). Research suggests that one of the most effective strategies for emotion regulation is **reappraisal**, which involves *changing one's emotional experience by changing the meaning of the emotion-eliciting stimulus.* How people think about an event can determine how they feel about it. For example, participants who watched a circumcision that was described as a joyous religious ritual had slower heart rates, had lower skin

Taking heroin and singing in church would seem to have little in common, but both can be forms of emotion regulation.

conductance levels, and reported less distress than did participants who watched the circumcision but did not hear the same description (Lazarus & Alfert, 1964). Everyone knows that the phrase "Don't forget your umbrella" elicits annoyance when it is construed as nagging and gratitude when it is construed as caring, and we can regulate our emotional experience by construing it in one of these ways rather than the other.

More than two millennia ago, Roman emperor Marcus Aurelius wrote: "If you are distressed by anything external, the pain is not due to the thing itself, but to your estimate of it; and this you have the power to revoke at any moment." But is that true? Do we have the power to change how we think about events in order to change our emotional experiences? Research suggests that to some extent we do. In one study, participants' brains were scanned as they saw photos that induced negative emotions, such as a photo of a woman crying during a funeral. Some participants were then asked to reappraise the picture, for example, by imagining that the woman in the photo was at a wedding rather than a funeral. The results showed that when participants initially saw the photo, their amygdalae became active. But as they reappraised the picture, several key areas of the cortex became active, and moments later, their amygdalae were deactivated (Ochsner et al., 2002). In other words, participants consciously and willfully turned down the activity of their own amygdalae simply by thinking about the photo in a different way.

Studies such as these demonstrate at the neural level what psychologists have observed for centuries at the behavioral level: Because emotions are reactions to the appraisals of an event and not to the event itself, changes in appraisal bring about changes in emotional experience. As you will learn in Chapter 14, therapists often attempt to alleviate depression and distress by helping people find new ways to think about the events that happen to them. Indeed, reappraisal appears to be important for both mental and physical health (Davidson, Putnam, & Larson, 2000), and the inability to reappraise events lies at the heart of psychiatric disorders, such as depression (Gross & Munoz, 1995).

 **ONLY HUMAN**

**WHO ENFORCES THE EMOTION REGULATION?** In 1991, the mayor of Sund, Norway, proposed a resolution to the town council that banned crankiness and required people to be happy and think positively. The resolution contained an exemption for those who had a good reason to be unhappy.

---

**In summary,** emotional experiences are difficult to describe, but psychologists have identified their two underlying dimensions: arousal and valence. Psychologists have spent more than a century trying to understand how emotional experience and physiological activity are related. The James-Lange theory suggests that a stimulus causes a physiological reaction, which leads to an emotional experience; the Cannon-Bard theory suggests that a stimulus causes both an emotional experience and a physiological reaction simultaneously; and Schachter and Singer's two-factor theory suggests that a stimulus causes undifferentiated physiological arousal about which people draw inferences. None of these theories is entirely right, but each has elements that are supported by research.

Emotions are produced by the complex interaction of limbic and cortical structures. Information about a stimulus is sent simultaneously to the amygdala (which makes a quick appraisal of the stimulus's goodness or badness) and the cortex (which does a slower and more comprehensive analysis of the stimulus). In some instances, the amygdala will trigger an emotional experience that the cortex later inhibits. People care about their emotional experiences and use many strategies to regulate them. Reappraisal involves changing the way one thinks about an object or event, and it is one of the most effective strategies for emotion regulation (see the Hot Science box on the next page). ■ ■

---

# Emotional Communication: Msgs w/o Wrds

Emotions may be private events, but the "bodily reactions" they produce are not. An **emotional expression** is *an observable sign of an emotional state,* and human beings exhibit many such signs. For example, people's emotional states influence the way they talk—from intonation and inflection to loudness and duration—and research shows

**EMOTIONAL EXPRESSION** Any observable sign of an emotional state.

## { HOT SCIENCE } The Pleasures of Uncertainty

WOULD YOU RATHER WIN THE LOTTERY OR become permanently disabled? You probably think that's the easiest question you've ever been asked. After all, isn't it *obvious* that one of these events would make you deliriously happy for years to come and the other would make you hopelessly depressed? Obvious, yes—but not necessarily true. Research shows that just a year after the event, lottery winners and paraplegics are about equally happy (Brickman, Coates, & Janoff-Bulman, 1978). If you find that hard to believe, then you're not alone. Timothy Wilson and Daniel Gilbert have studied **affective forecasting**, which is *the process by which people predict their emotional reactions to future events,* and they've found that people are not particularly good at predicting how they will feel after experiencing positive or negative events (Gilbert, Driver-Linn, & Wilson, 2002; Wilson & Gilbert, 2003). People routinely overestimate the joy of falling in love and the pain of falling out of it, the thrill of winning a football game and the agony of losing one, the delight of getting promoted and the distress of getting fired—and many other good and bad events (Gilbert, Pirel, Wilson, Blumberg, & Wheatley, 1998; Wilson Wheatley, Meyers, Gilbert, & Axsom, 2000). The fact is that you could know exactly what your future will hold and still not know how much you're going to like it when you get there.

Why are we so poor at forecasting our emotional reactions to future events? One reason is that most of us have a poor understanding of how our own emotions work. For example, imagine that you are studying in the library when a fellow student walks up to you, hands you a card that has a dollar coin attached to it, and then walks away. If you received the card shown on the left, how happy do you think you'd be 20 minutes later? Okay, how about if you received the card on the right?

Most people believe that getting a dollar from a stranger would make them feel happy, but they don't think it matters whether the card is the one on the left or the right. But most people are wrong. When researchers actually did this experiment, they found that people were happier if they had received the card on the left than if they had received the card on the right (Wilson, Centerbar, Kerner, & Gilbert, 2005).

Why? Although both cards contain declarative statements such as, "We like to promote random acts of kindness," the card on the right also contains questions to which those declarative statements are the answers. The card on the right provides no extra information, but because it uses a question-and-answer format, it makes people *feel* as though they understand why the experimenter gave them the card ("Aha, now I see—that guy is from the Smile Society, and the reason he does this is to promote acts of kindness"). One of the basic laws of emotion is that people have stronger emotional reactions to events whose causes they don't understand ("Yikes! What was that thumping noise?") than to events whose causes they do understand ("The washing machine is making that thumping noise again"). Because the card on the right makes us feel that we understand *why* the stranger walked up to us and gave us a dollar, our emotional reaction to that event subsides more quickly. But most people don't know about this law of emotion, and thus they can't accurately predict their own reactions to explained and unexplained events.

Indeed, people typically *prefer* to have an explanation than to remain in mystery, and thus they may choose things that undermine their own happiness. In one study, participants were college students who were linked to an Internet chat room where they had conversations with several other students (Wilson et al., 2005). After a little while, the experimenter asked everyone in the chat room to send a private e-mail message to the person whom they liked best explaining why they liked that person so much. What participants didn't know was that all the "other students" with whom

they were chatting were actually confederates of the experimenter. As soon as the participants sent off their e-mail messages, they received e-mail messages from *every one* of the "other students" explaining why the other student had chosen the participant as the person they liked most. In one condition of the study, every e-mail message was clearly identified so that the participant could tell which of the other students had sent it. In another condition of the experiment, the e-mail messages were anonymous so that the participant couldn't tell which student had sent which message. The results revealed two things. First, participants were happier when they could *not* identify the sender of the messages than when they could. Because unexplained events produce more intense and enduring emotions, the students who were "in the dark" about this happy event were happier for longer. Second, when a new group of participants were asked whether they would prefer to be able to identify the sender of each e-mail or to be kept in the dark, every one of them said they would prefer to know the sender's identity.

Studies such as these suggest that most people don't know enough about the nature of their own emotions to predict how happy they will be in different situations or to choose the situations that will make them happiest. Our emotional blind spots, it seems, can make us strangers to ourselves (Gilbert, 2006; Wilson, 2002).

**AFFECTIVE FORECASTING** The process by which people predict their emotional reactions to future events.

that listeners can infer a speaker's emotional state from vocal cues alone with better-than-chance accuracy (though vocal signs of anger, happiness, and sadness are somewhat easier to recognize than are vocal signs of fear and disgust; Banse & Scherer, 1996; Frick, 1985). The voice is not the only clue to a person's emotional state. In fact, observers can often estimate a person's emotional state from the direction of the person's gaze, gait, posture, and even from a person's touch (Dittrich, Troscianko, Lea, & Morgan, 1996; Keltner & Shiota, 2003; Wallbott, 1998). In some sense, we are walking, talking advertisements for what's going on inside us.

No part of the body is more exquisitely designed for communicating emotion than the face. Underneath every face lie 43 muscles that are capable of creating more than 10,000 unique configurations, which enables a face to convey information about its owner's emotional state with an astonishing degree of subtlety and specificity (Ekman, 1965). Psychologists Paul Ekman and Wallace Friesen (1978) spent years cataloguing the muscle movements of which the human face is capable. They isolated 46 unique movements, which they called *action units,* and they gave each one a number and a memorable name, such as "cheek puffer" and "dimpler" and "nasolabial deepener" (all of which, oddly enough, are also the names of heavy metal bands). Research has shown that combinations of these action units are reliably related to specific emotional states (Davidson, Ekman, Savon, Senulis, & Friesen, 1990). For example, when someone feels happy, the movements of the *zygomatic major* (a muscle that pulls the lip corners up) and the *obicularis oculi* (a muscle that crinkles the outside edges of the eyes) produce a unique facial expression that psychologists describe as "action units 6 and 12" and that the rest of us simply call smiling (Ekman & Friesen, 1982; Frank, Ekman, & Friesen, 1993; Steiner, 1986).

## Communicative Expression

Why are our emotions written all over our faces? In 1872, Charles Darwin published a book titled *The Expression of the Emotions in Man and Animals,* in which he speculated about the evolutionary significance of emotional expression (Darwin, 1998). Darwin noticed that people and animals seem to share certain facial and postural expressions, and he suggested that these expressions are a means by which organisms communicate information about their internal states to each other. If a dominant animal can bare its teeth and communicate the message "I am angry at you" and if a subordinate animal can lower its head and communicate the message "I am afraid of you," then the two may be able to establish a pecking order without actually spilling blood. Emotional expressions are a convenient way for one animal to let another animal know how it is feeling and hence how it is prepared to act. In this sense, emotional expressions are a bit like the words or phrases of a nonverbal language.

### The Universality of Expression

Of course, a language only works if everybody speaks the same one, and that fact led Darwin to develop the **universality hypothesis,** which suggests that *emotional expressions have the same meaning for everyone.* In other words, everyone expresses happiness

**UNIVERSALITY HYPOTHESIS** The hypothesis that emotional expressions have the same meaning for everyone.

Some animals looking soothed, angry, and sulky, according to Charles Darwin.

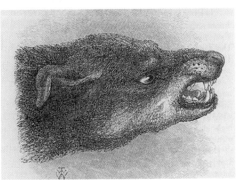
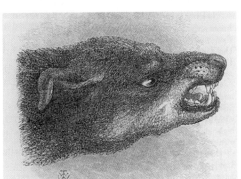

FROM DARWIN, C. (1872). THE EXPRESSION OF THE EMOTIONS IN MAN AND ANIMALS, LONDON: MURRAY. COURTESY OF UNIVERSITY OF CAMBRIDGE, DARWIN-ONLINE.ORG.UK

An Israeli woman cries at the funeral of a relative who was killed in a suicide attack in 2005. The universality hypothesis suggests that any human being who looks at this picture will know what she is feeling.

with a smile and everyone understands that a smile signifies happiness. Two lines of evidence suggest that Darwin was largely correct. First, people are quite accurate at judging the emotional expressions of members of other cultures (Boucher & Carlson, 1980; Ekman & Friesen, 1971; Ekman et al., 1987; Elfenbein & Ambady, 2002; Frank & Stennet, 2001; Haidt & Keltner, 1999; Izard, 1971; McAndrew, 1986; Shimoda, Argyle, & Ricci-Bitt, 1978). Not only do Chileans, Americans, and Japanese all recognize a smile as a sign of happiness and a frown as a sign of sadness, but so do members of preliterate cultures. In the 1950s, researchers showed photographs of people expressing anger, disgust, fear, happiness, sadness, and surprise to members of the South Fore, a people who lived a Stone Age existence in the highlands of Papua New Guinea and who had had little contact with the outside world. The researchers discovered that the Fore could recognize the emotional expressions of Americans about as accurately as Americans could and vice versa. The one striking exception to this rule was that the Fore had trouble distinguishing expressions of surprise from expressions of fear, perhaps because for people who live in the wild, surprises are rarely pleasant.

The second line of evidence in favor of the universality hypothesis is that people who have never seen a human face make the same facial expressions as those who have. For instance, congenitally blind people make all the facial expressions associated with the basic emotions, and though their expressions are not quite as recognizable as those made by sighted individuals, the underlying action of the facial muscles is quite similar (Galati, Scherer, & Ricci-Bitt, 1997). Two-day-old infants (who have had virtually no exposure to human faces) react to sweet tastes with a smile and to bitter tastes with an expression of disgust (Steiner, 1973, 1979). In short, a good deal of evidence suggests that the facial displays of at least six emotions—anger, disgust, fear, happiness, sadness, and surprise—are universal. Recent evidence suggests that some other emotions, such as embarrassment, amusement, guilt, or shame, may have a universal pattern of facial expression as well (Keltner, 1995; Keltner & Buswell, 1996; Keltner & Haidt, 1999; Keltner & Harker, 1998).

## The Cause and Effect of Expression

Why do so many people seem to express so many emotions in the same ways? After all, people in different cultures don't speak the same languages, so why do they smile the same smiles and frown the same frowns? The answer is that words are *symbols* and facial expressions are *signs*. Symbols are arbitrary designations that have no causal relationship with the things they symbolize. We English speakers use the word *cat* to indicate a particular animal, but there is nothing about felines that actually causes this particular sound to pop out of our mouths, and we aren't

Why is Stevie Wonder smiling? Perhaps it's the 22 Grammy awards he's won since 1974. Research shows that people who are born blind express emotion on their faces in the same ways that sighted people do.

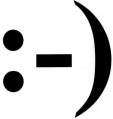

On September 19, 1982, Scott Fahlman posted a message to an Internet user's group that read, "I propose the following character sequence for joke markers: :-) Read it sideways." And so the emoticon was born. Fahlman's smile (above left) is a sign of happiness, whereas his emoticon is a symbol.

surprised when other human beings make different sounds—such as *popoki* or *gatto*—to indicate the same thing. Facial expressions, on the other hand, are not arbitrary symbols of emotion. They are signs of emotion, and signs are *caused* by the things they signify. The feeling of happiness *causes* the contraction of the zygomatic major and thus its contraction is a sign of that feeling in the same way a footprint in the snow is a sign that someone walked there.

Although emotional experiences cause emotional expressions, there are instances in which the causal path runs in the other direction. The **facial feedback hypothesis** (Adelmann & Zajonc, 1989; Izard, 1971; Tomkins, 1981) suggests that *emotional expressions can cause the emotional experiences they signify.* For instance, people feel happier when they are asked to make the sound of a long *e* or to hold a pencil in their teeth (both of which cause contraction of the zygomatic major) than when they are asked to make the sound of a long *u* or to hold a pencil in their lips (Strack, Martin, & Stepper, 1988; Zajonc, 1989) (see **FIGURE 10.6**). Some researchers believe that this happens because the muscle contractions of a smile change the temperature of the brain, which in turn brings about a pleasant affective state (Zajonc, 1989). Others believe that the smile and the feeling of happiness become so strongly associated through experience that one always brings about the other. Although no one is sure why it happens, smiling does seem to be a cheap cure for the blues.

The fact that emotional expressions can cause the emotional experiences they signify may help explain why people are generally so good at recognizing the emotional expressions of others. Some studies suggest that observers unconsciously mimic the body postures and facial expressions of the people they are watching (Chartrand & Bargh, 1999; Dimberg, 1982). When we see someone lean forward and smile, we lean very slightly and slightly contract our zygomatic major. What purpose does this subtle mimicry serve? If making a facial expression brings about the feeling it signifies, then one can tell what others are feeling simply by imitating

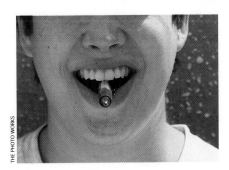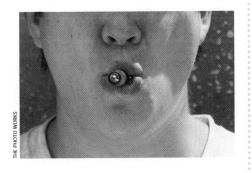

**Figure 10.6 The Facial Feedback Hypothesis** Research shows that people who hold a pen in their teeth feel happier than those who hold a pen in their lips. Holding a pen in the teeth contracts the zygomatic major muscles of the face in the same way a smile does.

their expressions and thereby experiencing their feelings oneself (Lipps, 1907). If this is actually what happens, then we would expect people who have trouble experiencing emotions to have trouble recognizing the emotional expressions of others. In fact, people with amygdala damage are typically quite poor at recognizing facial expressions of fear and anger (Adolphs, Russell, & Tranel, 1999), and this is especially true if their brain damage was sustained early in life (Adolphs, Cahill, Schol, & Babinsky, 1997). Similarly, people who are low in empathy find it difficult to know what others are feeling, and research shows that they are less likely to mimic the facial expressions of those with whom they interact (Sonnby-Borgstrom, Jonsson, & Svensson, 2003). All of this suggests that our emotional expressions play an important role in both sending and receiving information (see the Real World box).

## { THE REAL WORLD } That's Gross!

IF YOU WANT TO FEEL ONE OF THE MOST powerful, most irrational, and most poorly understood of all emotions, just spit in a glass of water. Then drink it. Despite the fact that the spit is yours and despite the fact that it was in your mouth just a moment ago, you will probably experience disgust.

Psychologist Paul Rozin has spent a lifetime disgusting people in order to understand the nature of this emotion, which is produced by the prospect of incorporating an offensive substance into one's body (Rozin & Fallon, 1987). The disgust reaction is characterized by feelings of nausea, a facial expression marked by distinct actions of the nose and mouth, and an etymology meaning "bad taste" (Rozin, Haidt, & Mc-Cauley, 1999). In this sense, disgust is a kind of defensive response that ensures that improper substances do not enter our bodies through our mouths, noses, or other orifices. For Americans, these improper substances include certain animals (such as rats and roaches), certain body products (such as vomit, feces, or blood), and certain foods (such as dog meat). The thought of eating a sumptuous meal of stewed monkey brains or of biting into an apple teeming with maggots makes most Americans feel nauseated, despite the fact that people in many other countries find both dishes quite palatable. Things that remind us of our animal nature, such as poor hygiene (body odor), inappropriate sex (i.e., with animals or family members), body boundary violations (open sores, amputated limbs), or contact with death (touching a corpse, watching an autopsy) also elicit disgust (Rozin & Fallon, 1987; Rozin et al., 1999). We like to distance ourselves from the rest of the animal kingdom, so reminders of our own animal origins, from belching to blood to barbarity, get tagged as disgusting.

COURTESY ALAN SWINKELS

San Francisco's Exploratorium features an exhibit on disgust that invites visitors to drink clean water from a toilet. Casual observation suggests that 5-year-olds are generally willing and 55-year-olds are not.

Disgust plays an important role, but it can be quite irrational, and its irrationality seems to follow two rules. The first is the rule of *contagion*, which suggests that any two things that were once in contact will continue to share their properties. So, for example, would you be willing to lick raisins off a flyswatter? Of course not. The flyswatter may have invisible traces of roach legs and fly guts on it, and those things can make you sick. Okay, then, what if the flyswatter were washed in alcohol, heated to within a degree of melting, and cooled to within a degree of breaking, making it the most sterile and hygienic thing in your entire house? Would you lick raisins off it then? Most people still say no (Rozin, Millman, & Nemeroff, 1986b). And the reason is that the swatter once touched a bug and thus it will forever have a disgusting "bugness" that cannot be cleansed away. The second irrational rule is the rule of *similarity*, which suggests that things that share appearances also share properties. If someone whipped up a batch of fudge that was shaped to look convincingly like dog poop, chances are you'd turn down the opportunity to sample it. Fudge is fudge, of course, and its shape shouldn't matter, but most people still balk at this proposition (Rozin et al., 1986b)—most people, that is, except children. Children under 2 years of age will readily put any number of disgusting things in their mouths, which suggests that disgust (unlike many emotions) develops late in life (Rozin et al., 1986a). A 4-year-old will avoid eating human hair because it doesn't taste very good, but a 10-year-old child will avoid eating it because . . . well, it's haaaaaaaaair—and that's gross!

If you want to observe the irrationality of disgust for yourself, just offer your friends some guacamole in a disposable diaper or some lemonade in a bedpan. And make sure to stir it with a comb.

# Deceptive Expression

Given how important emotional expressions are, it's no wonder that people have learned to use them to their advantage. Because you can control most of the muscles in your face, you don't have to display the emotion you are actually feeling or actually feel the emotion you are displaying. When your roommate makes a sarcastic remark about your haircut, you may make the facial expression for contempt (accompanied, perhaps, by a reinforcing hand gesture), but when your boss makes the same remark, you probably swallow hard and display a pained smile. Your expressions are moderated by your knowledge that it is permissible to show contempt for your peers but not for your superiors. **Display rules** are *norms for the control of emotional expression* (Ekman, 1972; Ekman & Friesen, 1968), and following them requires using several techniques:

Can you tell what this woman is feeling? She hopes not. Helen Duann is a champion poker player who knows how to keep a "poker face," which is a neutral expression that provides little information about her emotional state.

**DISPLAY RULES** Norms for the control of emotional expression.

- *Intensification* involves exaggerating the expression of one's emotion, as when a person pretends to be more surprised by a gift than she really is.
- *Deintensification* involves muting the expression of one's emotion, as when the loser of a contest tries to look less distressed than he really is.
- *Masking* involves expressing one emotion while feeling another, as when a poker player tries to look distressed rather than delighted as she examines a hand with four aces.
- *Neutralizing* involves feeling an emotion but displaying no expression, as when judges try not to betray their leanings while lawyers make their arguments.

Although people in different cultures all use the same techniques, they use them in the service of different display rules. For example, in one study, Japanese and American college students watched an unpleasant film of car accidents and amputations (Ekman, 1972; Friesen, 1972). When the students didn't know that the experimenters were observing them, Japanese and American students made similar expressions of disgust, but when they realized that they were being observed, the Japanese students (but not the American students) masked their disgust with pleasant expressions. In many Asian societies, there is a strong cultural norm against displaying negative emotions in the presence of a respected person, and people in these societies may mask or neutralize their expressions. The fact that different cultures have different display rules may also help explain the fact that people are better at recognizing the facial expressions of people from their own cultures (Elfenbein & Ambady, 2002).

Our attempts to obey our culture's display rules don't always work out so well. Darwin (1898/1998) noted that "those muscles of the face which are least obedient to the will, will sometimes alone betray a slight and passing emotion" (p. 79). Despite our best attempts to smile bravely when we receive a poor grade on an exam or appear concerned when a friend receives the same, our voices, bodies, and faces are "leaky" instruments that may betray our emotional states even when we don't want them to. Four sets of features can allow a careful observer to tell whether our emotional expression is sincere (Ekman, 2003a):

**Figure 10.7 Genuine and Fake Smiles**
Both spontaneous smiles (left) and voluntary smiles (right) raise the corners of the mouth, but only a spontaneous smile crinkles the corners of the eye.

- *Morphology:* Certain facial muscles tend to resist conscious control, and for a trained observer, these so-called *reliable muscles* are quite revealing. For example, the zygomatic major raises the corners of the mouth, and this happens when people smile spontaneously or when they force themselves to smile. But only a genuine, spontaneous smile engages the obicularis oculi, which crinkles the corners of the eyes (see **FIGURE 10.7**.

- *Symmetry:* Sincere expressions are a bit more symmetrical than insincere expressions. A slightly lopsided smile is less likely to be genuine than is a perfectly even one.

- *Duration:* Sincere expressions tend to last between a half second and 5 seconds, and expressions that last for shorter or longer periods are more likely to be insincere.

- *Temporal patterning:* Sincere expressions appear and disappear smoothly over a few seconds, whereas insincere expressions tend to have more abrupt onsets and offsets.

Our emotions don't just leak on our faces: They leak all over the place. Research has shown that many aspects of our verbal and nonverbal behavior are altered when we tell a lie (DePaulo et al., 2003). For example, liars speak more slowly, take longer to respond to questions, and respond in less detail than do those who are telling the truth. Liars are also less fluent, less engaging, more uncertain, more tense, and less pleasant than truth tellers. Oddly enough, one of the telltale signs of a liar is that his or her performances tend to be just a bit too good: Liars' speech lacks the imperfections of truthful speech, such as superfluous details ("I noticed that the robber was wearing the same shoes that I saw on sale last week at Bloomingdale's and I found myself wondering what he paid for them"), spontaneous corrections ("He was six feet tall . . . well, no, actually more like six-two"), and expressions of self-doubt ("I think he had blue eyes, but I'm really not sure").

Given the reliable differences between sincere and insincere expressions, you might think that people would be quite good at telling one from the other. In fact, studies show that human lie detection ability is fairly awful. In studies in which a score of 100% represents perfect accuracy and a score of 50% represents pure chance, some trained professionals can attain scores of 80% (Ekman & O'Sullivan, 1991; Ekman, O'Sullivan, & Frank, 1999) (see **FIGURE 10.8**). But under most conditions, most people score barely better than chance (DePaulo, Stone, & Lassiter, 1985; Ekman, 1992; Zuckerman, DePaulo, & Rosenthal, 1981; Zuckerman & Driver, 1985). One reason for this is

**Figure 10.8 Jobs and Lie Detection** Most people are poor lie detectors, but some professionals aren't so bad. In tasks in which merely guessing would produce an accuracy rate of 50%, federal officers are 73% accurate. No one knows if the training for such jobs improves people's lie detection ability or if people who happen to be good lie detectors tend to get such jobs. (Ekman & O'Sullivan, 1991; Ekman, O'Sullivan & Frank, 1999).

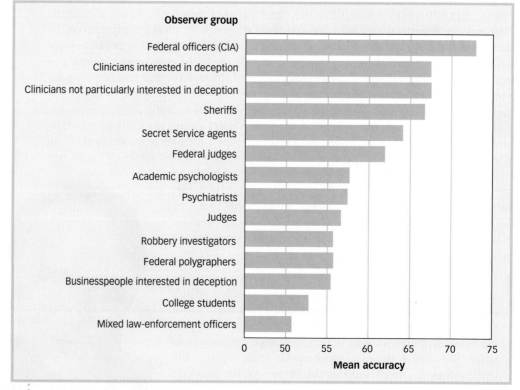

that people have a strong bias toward believing that others are sincere. In everyday life, most people are sincere most of the time, so it makes sense that we are predisposed to believe what we see and hear. This may explain why people tend to mistake liars for truth tellers but not the other way around (Gilbert, 1991). A second reason why people are such poor lie detectors is that they don't seem to know which pieces of information to attend to and which to ignore. People seem to think that certain things—such as whether a person speaks quickly or averts her gaze—are associated with lying when, in fact, they are not, and people seem to think that certain other things—such as talking too little or repeating words—are not associated with lying when, in fact, they are. These instances of myth and ignorance may explain why the correlation between a person's ability to detect lies and the person's confidence in that ability is essentially zero (DePaulo, Charlton, Cooper, Lindsay, & Muhlenbruck, 1997).

When people can't do something well (e.g., adding numbers or picking up 10-ton rocks), they typically turn the job over to machines (see **FIGURE 10.9**). Can machines detect lies better than we can? The answer is yes, but that's not saying much. The most widely used lie detection machine is the *polygraph,* which measures a variety of physiological responses that are associated with stress, which people often feel when they are afraid of being caught in a lie. In fact, the machine is so widely used by governments and businesses that the National Research Council recently met to consider all the scientific evidence on its validity. After much study, they concluded that the polygraph can indeed detect lies at a rate that is significantly better than chance (National Research Council, 2003). However, they also concluded that "almost a century of research in scientific psychology and physiology provides little basis for the expectation that a polygraph test could have extremely high accuracy" (p. 212).

The council went on to note the dangers of using a test that has the polygraph's error rate. Imagine, for example, that in a group of 10,000 people, 10 are terrorists and that when hooked up to a polygraph, all 10,000 people proclaim their innocence.

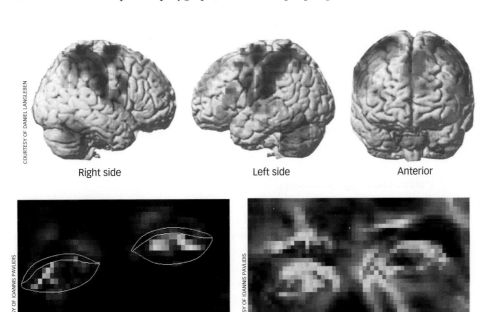

Right side    Left side    Anterior

COURTESY OF DANIEL LANGLEBEN

COURTESY OF IOANNIS PAVLIDIS

COURTESY OF IOANNIS PAVLIDIS

**Figure 10.9** **Lie Detection Machines** Some researchers hope to replace the polygraph with more accurate machines, such as those that measure changes in blood flow in the brain and the face. As the top panel shows, some areas of the brain are more active when people tell lies than when they tell the truth (shown in red), and some are more active when people tell the truth than when they tell lies (shown in blue) (Langleben et al., 2005). The bottom panel shows images taken by a thermal camera that detects the heat caused by blood flow to different parts of the face. The images show a person's face before (left) and after (right) telling a lie (Pavlidus, Eberhardt, & Levine, 2002). Although neither of these new techniques is extremely accurate, that could soon change.

Given the machine's error rate, a polygraph operator who caught 8 of the 10 terrorists would also "catch" 1,598 innocent people. If the operator were willing to use more stringent criteria for guilt, he could reduce the number of innocent people he caught to 39—but then he'd only catch 2 of the 10 terrorists! Furthermore, these numbers assume that the terrorists don't know how to fool the polygraph, which is something that people can, in fact, be trained to do. The council warned: "Given its level of accuracy, achieving a high probability of identifying individuals who pose major security risks in a population with a very low proportion of such individuals would require setting the test to be so sensitive that hundreds, or even thousands, of innocent individuals would be implicated for every major security violator correctly identified" (p. 6). In short, neither people nor machines are particularly good at lie detection, which is why lying continues to be a staple of human social interaction.

---

**In summary,** the voice, the body, and the face all communicate information about a person's emotional state. Darwin suggested that these emotional expressions are the same for all people and are universally understood, and research suggests that this is generally true. Emotional expressions are caused by the emotions they signify, but they can also cause those emotions. Emotional mimicry allows people to experience and hence identify the emotions of others.

Not all emotional expressions are sincere because people use display rules to help them decide which emotions to express. Cultures have different display rules, but people obey them by using the same set of techniques. There are reliable differences between sincere and insincere emotional expressions, just as there are reliable differences between truthful and untruthful utterances, but people are generally poor at determining when an expression or an utterance is sincere. Although machines such as the polygraph can make this determination with better-than-chance accuracy, their error rates are dangerously high. ■ ■

---

# Motivation: Getting Moved

You now know something about how emotions are produced, experienced, and communicated. But what in the world are they *for*? Emotions have several functions, and one of the most important is that they motivate behavior. **Motivation** refers to *the purpose for or cause of an action,* and it is no coincidence that the words *emotion* and *motivation* share a common linguistic root that means "to move." We act because our emotions move us to do so, and they move us in two different ways: First, emotions provide us with *information* about the world, and second, emotions are the *objectives* toward which we strive. Let's examine each of these in turn.

## The Function of Emotion

In the film *Invasion of the Body Snatchers,* a young couple suspects that most of the people they know have been kidnapped by aliens and replaced with replicas. This bizarre belief is the trope of many sci-fi movies, but it is also the primary symptom of Capgras syndrome (see **FIGURE 10.10**). People who suffer from this syndrome typically believe that one or more of their family members are imposters. As one Capgras sufferer told her doctor, "He looks exactly like my father, but he really isn't. He's a nice guy, but he isn't my father. . . . Maybe my father employed him to take care of me, paid him some money so he could pay my bills" (Hirstein & Ramachandran, 1997, p. 438). The patient's father had not been body-snatched, of course, nor had he hired his own stand-in. Rather, the patient had sustained damage to the neural

**MOTIVATION** The purpose for or cause of an action.

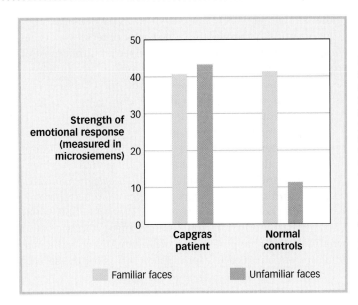

Figure **10.10** **Capgras Syndrome** This graph shows the emotional responses (as measured by skin conductance) of a patient with Capgras syndrome and a group of control participants to a set of familiar and unfamiliar faces. Although the controls have stronger emotional responses to the familiar than to the unfamiliar faces, the Capgras patient has similar emotional responses to both. (Hirstein & Ramachandran, 1997)

connections between her temporal lobe (where people's faces are identified) and her limbic system (where emotions are generated). As a result, when she saw her father's face, she could easily recognize it, but because this information was not transmitted to her limbic system, she didn't feel the warm emotions that her father's face once produced. Her father "looked right" but didn't "feel right," and so she concluded that the man before her was an imposter.

The patient's conclusions were wrong, of course, but her logic was sound. The patient used her emotional experience as information about the world, and studies show that most of us do the same thing. For example, people report being more satisfied with their lives in general when they are asked the question on a sunny day rather than a rainy day. Why? Because people feel happier on sunny days, and they use their happiness as information about the quality of their lives (Schwarz & Clore, 1983). People who are in good moods believe that they have a higher probability of winning a lottery than do people who are in bad moods. Why? Because people use their moods as information about the likelihood of succeeding at a task (Isen & Patrick, 1983). We all know that satisfying lives and bright futures make us feel good—so when we feel good, we naturally conclude that our lives must be satisfying and our futures must be bright. Because the world influences our emotions, our emotions provide information about the world (Schwarz, Mannheim, & Clore, 1988).

Indeed, without this information, we wouldn't know what to do next. When neurologist Antonio Damasio was asked to examine a patient with an unusual form of brain damage, he asked the patient to choose between two dates for an appointment. As Damasio (1994) later noted:

> For the better part of a half-hour, the patient enumerated reasons for and against each of the two dates: Previous engagements, proximity to other engagements, possible meteorological conditions, virtually anything that one could reasonably think about concerning a simple date. . . . He was walking us through a tiresome cost-benefit analysis, an endless outlining and fruitless comparison of options and possible consequences. (p. 193)

The patient's inability to make a simple decision was not due to any impairment of his ability to think or reason. On the contrary, he could think and reason all too well. What he couldn't do was feel. The patient's injury had left him unable to experience emotion, and thus when he entertained one option ("If I come next Tuesday, I'll have to cancel my lunch with Fred"), he didn't feel any better or any worse than when he entertained another ("If I come next Wednesday, I'll have to get up early to catch the bus"). And because he *felt* nothing when he thought about an option, he couldn't

**HEDONIC PRINCIPLE** The notion that all people are motivated to experience pleasure and avoid pain.

decide which was better. Studies show that when patients with this particular kind of brain damage are given the opportunity to gamble, they make a lot of reckless bets because they don't feel the twinge of anxiety that most of us would feel and that most of us would take to mean we're about to do something stupid. (It's only fair to note that under certain circumstances, these patients are superior investors, precisely because they are willing to take risks that others will not; Shiv et al., 2005.)

Emotions motivate us by providing information about the world, but they also motivate us more directly. People strongly prefer to experience positive rather than negative emotions, and the emotional experiences that we call happiness, satisfaction, pleasure, and joy are often the goals, the ends, the objectives that our behavior is meant to accomplish. The **hedonic principle** is *the notion that all people are motivated to experience pleasure and avoid pain,* and some very smart people have argued that this single principle can explain all human behavior. For example, Aristotle (350 BC/1998) observed that if one traces any human motivation to its source, one will always find the desire for pleasure, or what he called "happiness." According to Aristotle, the pursuit of pleasure and the avoidance of pain "is a first principle, for it is for the sake of this that we all do all that we do."

This may sound a bit extreme, but it isn't hard to convince yourself that Aristotle was on to something. If a friend asked you why you went to the mall, you might explain that you wanted to buy a new pair of mittens. If your friend then asked why you wanted to buy a new pair of mittens, you might explain that you wanted to keep your hands warm. If your friend then asked why you wanted to keep your hands warm, you might explain that warm hands are a pleasure and cold hands are a pain. Each of these motivations rests on another, and thus each of your answers would make sense.

But if your friend then asked you why you wanted to experience pleasure instead of pain, you'd find yourself tongue-tied. There is no answer to this question because there is no other motivation on which the desire for pleasure rests. The desire for pleasure is at the bottom of the pile—it holds everything else up and nothing lies beneath it. We want many other things, of course, from peace and prosperity to health and security, but the reason we want these things is that they (like new mittens) help us experience pleasure and avoid pain. As Aristotle's teacher, Plato (380 BC/1956), asked about all the many things that human beings call *good:* "Are these things good for any other reason except that they end in pleasure, and get rid of and avert pain? Are you looking to any other standard but pleasure and pain when you call them good?" Plato was suggesting that pleasure doesn't just matter to us—it is what *mattering* means.

According to the hedonic principle, then, our emotional experience can be thought of as a gauge that ranges from bad to good, and our primary motivation—perhaps even our *sole* motivation—is to keep the needle on the gauge as close to *g* as possible. Even when we voluntarily do things that tilt the needle in the opposite direction, such as letting the dentist drill our teeth or waking up early for a boring class, we are doing these things because we believe that they will nudge the needle toward *g* in the future and keep it there longer.

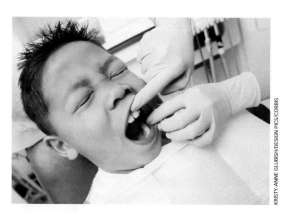

Many people voluntarily do things that cause them pain. According to the hedonic principle, people would not visit the dentist unless the pain of having dental work was ultimately outweighed by the pleasure of having had it done.

KRISTY-ANNE GLUBISH/DESIGN PICS/CORBIS

# The Conceptualization of Motivation

The hedonic principle sets the stage for an understanding of motivation but leaves many questions unanswered. For example, if our primary motivation is to keep the needle on *g*, so to speak, then which things push the needle in that direction and which things push it away? And where do these things get the power to push our needle around, and exactly how do they do the pushing? The answers to such questions lie in two concepts that have played an unusually important role in the history of psychology: *instincts* and *drives*.

## Instincts

When a newborn baby is given a drop of sugar water, it smiles, but when it is given a check for $10,000, it acts like it couldn't care less. By the time the baby gets into college, these responses pretty much reverse. It seems clear that nature endows us with certain motivations and that experience endows us with others. Almost a century ago, William McDougall (1908) argued that "observation of animals of any one species shows that all members of the species seek and strive toward a limited number of goals of certain types . . . and all members of the species seek these goals independently of example and of prior experience of attainment of them. . . . We are justified, then, in inferring that each member of the species inherits the tendencies of the species to seek goals of these several types" (p. 458). William James (1890) called the inherited tendency to seek a particular goal an *instinct,* which he defined as "the faculty of acting in such a way as to produce certain ends, without foresight of the ends, and without previous education in the performance" (p. 383). According to both McDougall and James, nature hardwired penguins, parrots, puppies, and people to want certain things without training and to execute the behaviors that produce these things without thinking. They and other psychologists of their time tried to make a list of what those things were.

Unfortunately, they were quite successful, and in just a few decades the list of instincts they generated had grown preposterously long, coming to include some rather exotic entries such as "the instinct to be secretive" and "the instinct to grind one's teeth" (both of which were contributed by James himself). In his 1924 survey of the burgeoning literature on instinct, sociologist Luther Bernard counted 5,759 instincts and concluded that after three decades of list making, the term seemed to be suffering from "a great variety of usage and the almost universal lack of critical standards" (Bernard, 1924, p. 21). Furthermore, to explain the fact that people befriend each other by claiming that people have an "affiliation instinct" didn't seem like much of an explanation at all. When Aristotle explained the downhill movement of water and the upward movement of fire by claiming that the former had "gravity" and the latter had "levity," it didn't take long for his fellow philosophers to catch on to the fact that Aristotle had merely named these tendencies and not really explained them. Psychologists worried that instincts were explanatory tautologies of Aristotelian proportion (Ayres, 1921; Dunlap, 1919; Field, 1921).

By 1930, the concept of instinct had taken "a sharp turn toward obscurity" (Herrnstein, 1972, p. 23). Yes, the concept was somewhat vague and vacuous, but that wasn't its real problem. Its real problem was that it flew in the face of American psychology's newest and most unstoppable force: behaviorism. Behaviorists rejected the concept of instinct on two grounds. First, they believed that behavior should be explained by the external stimuli that evoke it and not by reference to the hypothetical internal states on which it depends. John Watson (1913) had written that "the time seems to have come when psychology must discard all reference to consciousness" (p. 163), and behaviorists saw instincts as just the sort of unnecessary "internal talk" that Watson forbade. Second, behaviorists wanted nothing to do with the notion of inherited behavior because for them all complex behavior was learned. Because instincts were inherited tendencies that resided inside the organism, behaviorists considered them doubly repugnant.

All animals are born with both the motivation and the ability to perform certain complex behaviors. Spiders don't teach their offspring how to build elaborate webs, but their offspring build them nonetheless.

JOHN MCNALLY/PHOTOLIBRARY

All mammals experience sex drives and hunger drives. This one seems to experience Sunday drives as well.

### Drives

But within a few decades, some of Watson's younger followers began to realize that the strict prohibition against the mention of internal states made certain phenomena difficult to explain. For example, if all behavior is a response to an external stimulus, then why does a rat that is sitting still in its cage at 9:00 a.m. start wandering around and looking for food by noon? Nothing in the cage has changed, so why has the rat's behavior changed? What visible, measurable external stimulus is the wandering rat responding to? The obvious answer (obvious, at least, to any ordinary person) is that the rat is responding to something inside itself, which meant that one should look inside the rat if one wanted to explain its wandering. Because the right answer obviously had something to do with internal states and because Watson had forbidden behaviorists to talk about internal states, his young followers—the "new behaviorists"—had to use code words. The code word chosen by their leader, B. F. Skinner (1932a, 1932b), was *drive.*

The new behaviorists began by noting that bodies are like thermostats. When thermostats detect that the room is too cold, they send signals that initiate corrective actions such as turning on a furnace. Similarly, when bodies detect that they are underfed, they send signals that initiate corrective actions such as eating. **Homeostasis** is *the tendency for a system to take action to keep itself in a particular state,* and two of the new behaviorists, Clark Hull and Kenneth Spence, suggested that rats, people, and thermostats are all homeostatic mechanisms. To survive, an organism needs to maintain precise levels of nutrition, warmth, and so on, and when these levels depart from an optimal point, the organism receives a signal to take corrective action. That signal is called a **drive**, which is *an internal state generated by departures from physiological optimality.* According to Hull and Spence, it isn't food per se that organisms find rewarding; it is the reduction of the drive for food. Hunger is a drive, a drive is an internal state, and when organisms eat, they are attempting to change their internal state. It is important to understand that behaviorists had to use a great many words in order to avoid using the forbidden ones. So if "an internal state whose amelioration is rewarding" sounds suspiciously like a "bad feeling" to you, then join the club.

## Eating and Mating

The words *instinct* and *drive* are no longer widely used in psychology, but the concepts remain part of the modern conception of motivation. The concept of instinct reminds us that nature endows organisms with a tendency to seek certain things, and the concept of drive reminds us that this seeking is initiated by an internal state. Psychologist William McDougall (1930) called the study of motivation "hormic psychology," which is a term derived from the Greek word for "urge," and people clearly have urges—some of which they acquire through experience and some of which they do not—that motivate them to take action. What kinds of urges do we have, and what kinds of actions do we take to satisfy them?

Abraham Maslow (1954) attempted to organize the list of human urges—or, as he called them, *needs*—in a meaningful way (see **FIGURE 10.11**). He noted that some needs (such as the need to eat) must be satisfied before others (such as the need to mate), and he built a hierarchy of needs that had the strongest and most immediate needs at the bottom and the weakest and most deferrable needs at the top. Maslow suggested that as a rule, people will not experience a need until all the needs below it are met. So when people are hungry or thirsty or exhausted, they will not seek intellectual fulfillment or moral clarity, which is to say that philosophy is a luxury of the well fed. Although many aspects of Maslow's theory failed to win empirical support (e.g., a person on a hunger strike may value her principles more than her physical needs; see

**HOMEOSTASIS** The tendency for a system to take action to keep itself in a particular state.

**DRIVE** An internal state generated by departures from physiological optimality.

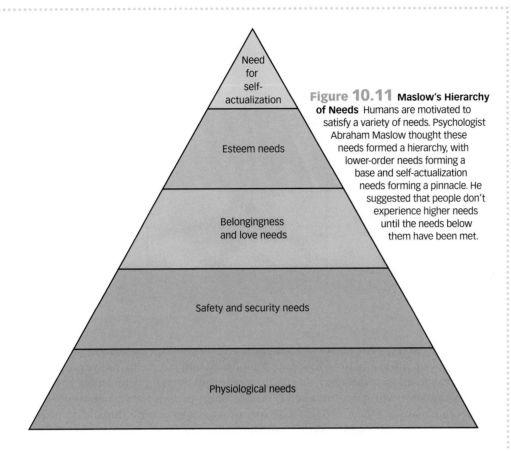

**Figure 10.11 Maslow's Hierarchy of Needs** Humans are motivated to satisfy a variety of needs. Psychologist Abraham Maslow thought these needs formed a hierarchy, with lower-order needs forming a base and self-actualization needs forming a pinnacle. He suggested that people don't experience higher needs until the needs below them have been met.

Wahba & Bridwell, 1976), the idea that some needs take precedence over others is clearly right. And although there are exceptions, those that typically take precedence are those that we share with other mammals and that are related to our common biology. Two of these needs—the need to eat and the need to mate—are among the most powerful and well studied, so let's see how they work.

### The Hunger Signal

Hunger tells an organism to eat. But how does hunger arise? At every moment, your body is sending signals to your brain about its current energy state. If your body needs energy, it sends an *orexigenic* signal to tell your brain to switch hunger on, and if your body has sufficient energy, it sends an *anorexigenic* signal to tell your brain to switch hunger off (Gropp et al., 2005). No one knows precisely what these signals are or how they are sent and received, but research has identified a variety of candidates. For example, *leptin* is a chemical secreted by fat cells, and it appears to be an anorexigenic signal that tells the brain to switch hunger off. *Ghrelin* is a chemical that is produced in the stomach, and it appears to be an orexigenic signal that tells the brain to switch hunger on (Inui, 2001; Nakazato et al., 2001). Blood concentrations of ghrelin increase just before eating and decrease as eating proceeds (Cummings et al., 2001), and when people are injected with ghrelin, they become intensely hungry and eat about 30% more than usual (Wren et al., 2001). These are just two of the chemical messengers that tell the brain when to switch hunger on or off. Some researchers believe that there is no general state called hunger but rather that there are many different hungers, each of which is a response to a unique nutritional deficit and each of which is switched on by a unique chemical messenger (Rozin & Kalat, 1971). For example, rats that are deprived of protein will turn down fats and carbohydrates and specifically seek proteins, suggesting that they are experiencing a specific "protein hunger" and not a general hunger (Rozin, 1968).

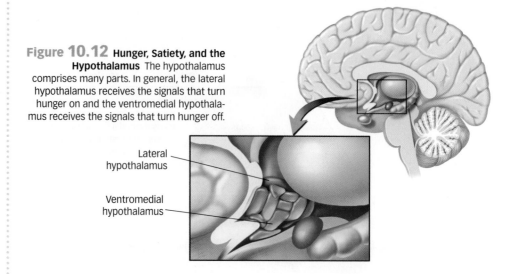

**Figure 10.12 Hunger, Satiety, and the Hypothalamus** The hypothalamus comprises many parts. In general, the lateral hypothalamus receives the signals that turn hunger on and the ventromedial hypothalamus receives the signals that turn hunger off.

Lateral hypothalamus

Ventromedial hypothalamus

Whether hunger is one signal or many, the primary receiver of these signals is the hypothalamus. Different parts of the hypothalamus receive different signals (see **FIGURE 10.12**). The *lateral hypothalamus* receives orexigenic signals, and when it is destroyed, animals sitting in a cage full of food will starve themselves to death. The *ventromedial hypothalamus* receives anorexigenic signals, and when it is destroyed, animals will gorge themselves to the point of illness and obesity (Miller, 1960; Steinbaum & Miller, 1965). These two structures were once thought to be the "hunger center" and "satiety center" of the brain, but recent research has shown that this view is far too simple. For example, some studies suggest that damage to the ventromedial hypothalamus causes animals to eat because it increases insulin production, which causes a larger percentage of the animal's meal to be turned into fat. This means that a smaller percentage of the animal's meal is available to meet its immediate energy needs, and thus the animal must eat more to compensate (Woods et al., 1998). It is tempting to think of different brain areas as hunger and satiety centers, but as psychologist Douglas Mook (1996) noted, "A map of the brain will not look like a map of Europe: Spain for satiety, France for feeding, Denmark for drinking. It will look more like a map of the Los Angeles freeway system, with routes diverging, converging, and crossing over, and many different destinations even for those all traveling the same route at the moment" (p. 98). Hypothalamic structures play an important role in turning hunger on and off, but the way they execute these functions is complex and poorly understood (Stellar & Stellar, 1985).

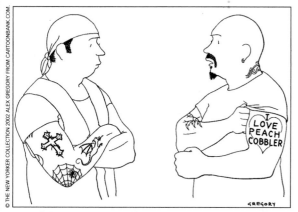

*"Never get a tattoo when you're drunk and hungry."*

### Eating Problems

Feelings of hunger tell us when to eat and when to stop. But for the 10 to 30 million Americans who have eating disorders, eating is a much more complicated affair (Hoek & van Hoeken, 2003). For instance, **bulimia nervosa** is *a disorder characterized by binge eating followed by purging.* Bulimics typically ingest large quantities of food in a relatively short period and then take laxatives or induce vomiting to purge the food from their bodies. Bulimics are caught in a cycle: They eat to ameliorate negative emotions such as sadness and anxiety, but then concern about weight gain leads them to experience negative emotions such as guilt and self-loathing, and these emotions then lead them to purge.

**Anorexia nervosa** is *a disorder characterized by an intense fear of being fat and severe restriction of food intake.* Anorexics tend to have a distorted body image that leads them to believe they are fat when they are actually emaciated, and they tend to be high-achieving perfectionists who see their severe control of eating as a triumph of will over

**BULIMIA NERVOSA** An eating disorder characterized by binge eating followed by purging.

**ANOREXIA NERVOSA** An eating disorder characterized by an intense fear of being fat and severe restriction of food intake.

impulse. Contrary to what you might expect, anorexics have extremely *high* levels of ghrelin in their blood, which suggests that their bodies are trying desperately to switch hunger on, but that hunger's call is being suppressed, ignored, or overridden (Ariyasu et al., 2001). Like most eating disorders, anorexia strikes more women than men, and 40% of newly identified cases of anorexia are among females who are 15 to 19 years old. Anorexics believe that thinness equals beauty, and it isn't hard to understand why. The average American woman is 5′4″ tall and weighs 140 pounds, but the average American fashion model is 5′11″ tall and weighs 117 pounds. Indeed, most college-age women want to be thinner than they are (Rozin, Trachtenberg, & Cohen, 2001), and nearly one in five reports being *embarrassed* to buy a chocolate bar (Rozin, Bauer, & Catanese, 2003).

Bulimia and anorexia are problems for many people. But America's most pernicious and pervasive eating-related problem is obesity, which is defined as having a body mass index of 30 or greater. **TABLE 10.1** allows you to compute your body mass index, and the odds are that you won't like what you learn. Approximately 3 million Americans die each year from obesity-related illnesses (Allison, Fontaine, Manson, Stevens, & VanItallie, 1999), and that number is growing fast. Obese people are viewed negatively by others, have lower self-esteem, and have a lower quality of life (Hebl & Heatherton, 1997; Kolotkin, Meter, & Williams, 2001). Indeed, the stigma of obesity is so powerful that average-weight people are viewed negatively if they even have a relationship with someone who is obese (Hebl & Mannix, 2003).

Obesity can result from biochemical abnormalities, and it seems to have a strong genetic component, but overeating is often a part of its cause. If the brain has a complex system of on and off switches that regulate hunger, why does anyone overeat? Hunger is just one of the reasons why people eat—and not always the most important one. For example, whether a person eats depends on their knowledge of when they last ate, which is why amnesiacs will happily eat a second lunch shortly after finishing an unremembered first one (Rozin, Dow, Moscovitch, & Rajaram, 1998). People often eat to reduce negative emotions such as sadness or anxiety, and they often eat out of habit ("It's noon") or obligation ("Everyone else is ordering lunch"), all of which can cause people to eat more than they should.

CHRISTOPHER LAMARCA/REDUX

Although people who suffer from anorexia are dangerously thin, they typically see themselves as fat. Sixteen-year-old Hannah Hartney has been suffering from anorexia since she was 9 years old.

**Table 10.1** | **Body Mass Index Table**

| | Normal | | | | | | Overweight | | | | | Obese | | | | | | | | | | Extreme Obesity | | | | | | | | | | | | | | | |
|---|---|---|---|---|---|---|---|---|---|---|---|---|---|---|---|---|---|---|---|---|---|---|---|---|---|---|---|---|---|---|---|---|---|---|---|---|
| BMI | 19 | 20 | 21 | 22 | 23 | 24 | 25 | 26 | 27 | 28 | 29 | 30 | 31 | 32 | 33 | 34 | 35 | 36 | 37 | 38 | 39 | 40 | 41 | 42 | 43 | 44 | 45 | 46 | 47 | 48 | 49 | 50 | 51 | 52 | 53 | 54 |
| Height (Inches) | Body Weight (pounds) | | | | | | | | | | | | | | | | | | | | | | | | | | | | | | | | | | | |
| 58 | 91 | 96 | 100 | 105 | 110 | 115 | 119 | 124 | 129 | 134 | 138 | 143 | 148 | 153 | 158 | 162 | 167 | 172 | 177 | 181 | 186 | 191 | 196 | 201 | 205 | 210 | 215 | 220 | 224 | 229 | 234 | 239 | 244 | 248 | 253 | 258 |
| 59 | 94 | 99 | 104 | 109 | 114 | 119 | 124 | 128 | 133 | 138 | 143 | 148 | 153 | 158 | 163 | 169 | 173 | 178 | 183 | 188 | 193 | 198 | 203 | 308 | 212 | 217 | 222 | 227 | 232 | 237 | 242 | 247 | 252 | 257 | 262 | 267 |
| 60 | 97 | 102 | 107 | 112 | 116 | 123 | 128 | 133 | 138 | 143 | 148 | 153 | 156 | 163 | 168 | 174 | 179 | 184 | 189 | 194 | 199 | 204 | 209 | 215 | 220 | 225 | 230 | 235 | 240 | 245 | 250 | 256 | 261 | 266 | 271 | 278 |
| 61 | 100 | 108 | 111 | 116 | 122 | 127 | 132 | 137 | 143 | 148 | 153 | 156 | 164 | 169 | 174 | 180 | 186 | 190 | 195 | 201 | 206 | 211 | 217 | 222 | 227 | 232 | 238 | 243 | 248 | 254 | 259 | 264 | 269 | 275 | 280 | 285 |
| 62 | 104 | 109 | 115 | 120 | 126 | 131 | 138 | 142 | 147 | 153 | 158 | 164 | 169 | 175 | 180 | 186 | 191 | 196 | 202 | 207 | 213 | 218 | 224 | 229 | 235 | 240 | 248 | 251 | 258 | 262 | 267 | 273 | 278 | 264 | 289 | 295 |
| 63 | 107 | 113 | 118 | 124 | 130 | 135 | 141 | 148 | 152 | 158 | 163 | 169 | 175 | 180 | 188 | 191 | 197 | 203 | 208 | 214 | 220 | 225 | 231 | 237 | 242 | 248 | 254 | 260 | 265 | 270 | 278 | 282 | 287 | 293 | 299 | 304 |
| 64 | 110 | 118 | 122 | 128 | 134 | 140 | 145 | 151 | 157 | 163 | 169 | 174 | 180 | 188 | 192 | 197 | 204 | 209 | 215 | 221 | 227 | 232 | 238 | 244 | 250 | 258 | 262 | 267 | 273 | 279 | 285 | 291 | 298 | 302 | 308 | 314 |
| 65 | 114 | 120 | 128 | 132 | 138 | 144 | 150 | 156 | 162 | 168 | 174 | 180 | 186 | 192 | 193 | 204 | 210 | 218 | 222 | 228 | 234 | 240 | 246 | 252 | 258 | 264 | 270 | 278 | 282 | 288 | 294 | 300 | 308 | 312 | 318 | 324 |
| 66 | 118 | 124 | 130 | 138 | 142 | 148 | 155 | 161 | 167 | 173 | 179 | 186 | 192 | 198 | 204 | 210 | 216 | 223 | 229 | 235 | 241 | 247 | 253 | 260 | 266 | 272 | 278 | 284 | 291 | 297 | 303 | 309 | 315 | 322 | 328 | 334 |
| 67 | 121 | 127 | 134 | 140 | 146 | 153 | 159 | 166 | 172 | 178 | 185 | 191 | 198 | 204 | 211 | 217 | 223 | 230 | 238 | 242 | 249 | 256 | 261 | 268 | 274 | 280 | 287 | 293 | 299 | 308 | 312 | 319 | 325 | 331 | 338 | 344 |
| 68 | 125 | 131 | 138 | 144 | 151 | 158 | 164 | 171 | 177 | 184 | 190 | 197 | 203 | 210 | 216 | 223 | 230 | 236 | 243 | 249 | 256 | 262 | 269 | 278 | 282 | 289 | 295 | 302 | 303 | 315 | 322 | 328 | 335 | 341 | 348 | 354 |
| 69 | 128 | 135 | 142 | 149 | 155 | 162 | 169 | 176 | 182 | 189 | 195 | 203 | 209 | 218 | 223 | 230 | 236 | 243 | 250 | 257 | 263 | 270 | 277 | 284 | 291 | 297 | 304 | 311 | 318 | 324 | 331 | 338 | 345 | 351 | 358 | 365 |
| 70 | 132 | 139 | 146 | 153 | 160 | 167 | 174 | 181 | 188 | 195 | 202 | 209 | 216 | 222 | 229 | 236 | 243 | 250 | 257 | 264 | 271 | 278 | 285 | 292 | 299 | 308 | 313 | 320 | 327 | 334 | 341 | 348 | 355 | 362 | 369 | 378 |
| 71 | 138 | 143 | 150 | 157 | 166 | 172 | 179 | 186 | 193 | 200 | 208 | 215 | 222 | 229 | 235 | 243 | 250 | 257 | 265 | 272 | 279 | 288 | 293 | 301 | 308 | 315 | 322 | 329 | 338 | 343 | 351 | 358 | 365 | 372 | 379 | 388 |
| 72 | 140 | 147 | 154 | 162 | 169 | 177 | 184 | 191 | 199 | 208 | 213 | 221 | 228 | 235 | 242 | 250 | 258 | 265 | 272 | 279 | 287 | 294 | 302 | 309 | 316 | 324 | 331 | 338 | 346 | 353 | 361 | 368 | 375 | 383 | 390 | 397 |
| 73 | 144 | 151 | 159 | 166 | 174 | 182 | 189 | 197 | 204 | 212 | 219 | 227 | 236 | 242 | 250 | 257 | 266 | 272 | 280 | 288 | 295 | 302 | 310 | 318 | 326 | 333 | 340 | 348 | 355 | 363 | 371 | 378 | 388 | 393 | 401 | 408 |
| 74 | 148 | 155 | 163 | 171 | 179 | 188 | 194 | 202 | 210 | 218 | 225 | 233 | 241 | 249 | 258 | 264 | 272 | 280 | 287 | 295 | 303 | 311 | 319 | 328 | 335 | 343 | 351 | 359 | 367 | 375 | 383 | 391 | 399 | 407 | 415 | 423 | 431 |
| 75 | 152 | 160 | 166 | 178 | 184 | 192 | 200 | 208 | 216 | 224 | 232 | 240 | 248 | 256 | 264 | 272 | 279 | 287 | 295 | 303 | 311 | 319 | 327 | 335 | 343 | 351 | 359 | 367 | 375 | 383 | 391 | 399 | 407 | 415 | 423 | 431 |
| 76 | 158 | 164 | 172 | 180 | 189 | 197 | 205 | 213 | 221 | 230 | 238 | 246 | 254 | 263 | 271 | 279 | 287 | 295 | 304 | 312 | 320 | 328 | 338 | 344 | 353 | 361 | 369 | 377 | 385 | 394 | 402 | 410 | 418 | 428 | 436 | 443 |

*Source:* Adapted from National Institutes of Health, 1998, *Clinical Guidelines on the Identification, Evaluation, and Treatment of Overweight and Obesity in Adults: The Evidence Report.* This and other information about overweight and obesity can be found at www.nhlbi.nih.gov/guidelines/obesity/ob_home.htm.

KAREN KASMAUSKI/CORBIS

Prejudice against obese people is powerful and widespread. In this photo, members of the self-proclaimed "Bod Squad" protest against weight loss surgery in front of a San Francisco hospital.

Moreover, nature seems to have designed us for overeating. For most of our evolutionary history, the kinds and amounts of food available to people made it rather unlikely that anyone would eat too much, and the main food-related problem facing our ancestors was starvation. Their brains and bodies evolved two strategies to avoid it. First, they developed a strong attraction to foods that provide large amounts of energy per bite—in other words, foods that are calorically rich—which is why most of us prefer hamburgers and milk shakes to celery and water. Second, they developed an ability to store excess food energy in the form of fat, which enabled them to eat more than they needed when food was plentiful and then live off their reserves when food was scarce. We are beautifully engineered for a world in which food is generally low cal and scarce, and the problem is that we don't live in that world anymore. Rather, most of us live in a world in which the calorie-laden miracles of modern technology—from chocolate cupcakes to sausage pizzas—are inexpensive and readily available.

It is all too easy to overeat and become overweight or obese, and it is all too difficult to reverse course. The human body resists weight loss in two ways. First, when we gain weight, we experience an increase in both the size and the number of fat cells in our bodies (usually in our abdomens if we are male and in our thighs and buttocks if we are female). But when we lose weight, we experience a decrease in the size of our fat cells but no decrease in their number. Once our bodies have added a fat cell, that cell is pretty much there to stay. It may become thinner when we diet, but it is unlikely to die. Second, our bodies respond to dieting by decreasing our **metabolism**, which is *the rate at which energy is used.* When our bodies sense that we are living through a famine (which is what they conclude when we refuse to feed them), they find more efficient ways to turn food into fat—a great trick for our ancestors but a real nuisance for us. Indeed, when rats are overfed, then put on diets, then overfed again and put on diets again, they gain weight faster and lose it more slowly the second time around, which suggests that with each round of dieting, their bodies become increasingly efficient at converting food to fat (Brownell, Greenwood, Stellar, & Shrager, 1986). The bottom line is that avoiding obesity is much easier than overcoming it.

## Sexual Interest

Essayist Florence King (1990) once remarked, "I've had sex and I've had food, and I'd rather eat." Indeed, food motivates us more strongly than sex because food is essential to our survival. But sex is essential to our DNA's survival, and thus evolution has ensured that a healthy desire for sex is wired deep into the brain of every mammal. In

**METABOLISM** The rate at which energy is used by the body.

some ways, that wiring scheme is simple: Glands secrete hormones, which travel through the blood to the brain and stimulate sexual desire. But which hormones, which parts of the brain, and what triggers the launch in the first place?

A hormone called dihydroepiandosterone (DHEA) seems to be involved in the initial onset of sexual desire. Both males and females begin producing this slow-acting hormone at about the age of 6, which may explain why boys and girls both experience their initial sexual interest at about the age of 10 despite the fact that boys reach puberty much later than girls. Two other hormones have more gender-specific effects. Both males and females produce testosterone and estrogen, but males produce more of the former and females produce more of the latter. As you will learn in Chapter 11, these two hormones are largely responsible for the physical and psychological changes that characterize puberty. But are they also responsible for the waxing

*"Come back, young man. He needs a booster shot."*

and waning of sexual desire in adults? The answer appears to be yes—as long as those adults are rats. Testosterone increases the sexual desire of male rats by acting on a particular area of the hypothalamus, and estrogen increases the sexual desire of female rats by acting on a different area of the hypothalamus. Lesions to these areas reduce sexual motivation in the respective genders, and when testosterone or estrogen is applied to these areas, sexual motivation increases. In short, testosterone regulates sexual desire in male rats and estrogen regulates both sexual desire and fertility in female rats.

The story for human beings is far more interesting. The females of most mammalian species—for example, dogs, cats, and rats—have little or no interest in sex except when their estrogen levels are high, which happens when they are ovulating (i.e., when they are "in estrus" or "in heat"). In other words, estrogen regulates both ovulation and sexual interest in these mammals. But female human beings—like female monkeys and apes—can be interested in sex at any point in their monthly cycles. Although the level of estrogen in a woman's body changes dramatically over the course of her monthly menstrual cycle, studies suggest that sexual desire changes little if at all. Somewhere in the course of our evolution, it seems, women's sexual interest became independent of their ovulation. Some theorists have speculated that the advantage of this independence was that it made it more difficult for males to know whether a female was in the fertile phase of her monthly cycle. Male mammals often guard their mates jealously when their mates are ovulating but go off in search of other females when their mates are not. If a male cannot use his mate's sexual receptivity to tell when she is ovulating, then he has no choice but to stay around and guard her all the time. For females who are trying to keep their mates at home so that they will contribute to the rearing of children, sexual interest that is continuous and independent of fertility may be an excellent strategy.

If estrogen is not the hormonal basis of women's sex drives, then what is? Two pieces of evidence suggests that the answer is testosterone—the same hormone that drives male sexuality. First, when women are given testosterone, their sex drives increase. Second, men naturally have more testosterone than women do, and they clearly have a stronger sex drive. Men are more likely than women to think about sex, have sexual fantasies, seek sex and sexual variety (whether positions or partners), masturbate, want sex at an early point in a relationship, sacrifice other things for sex, have permissive attitudes toward sex, and complain about low sex drive in their partners. Indeed, a group of researchers summarized decades of research on sex drive by concluding that "by all measures, men have a stronger sex drive than women . . . [and] there were no measures that showed women having stronger sex drives than men" (Baumeister, Cantanese, & Vohs, 2001, pp. 263–264). All of this suggests that testosterone may be the hormonal basis of sex drive in both men and women.

The red coloration on the female gelada's chest indicates she is in estrus and thus amenable to sex. The sexual interest of female human beings is not limited to a particular time in their monthly cycle, and they do not clearly advertise their fertility.

## Sexual Activity

Men and women may have different levels of sexual drive, but their physiological responses during sex are fairly similar. Prior to the 1960s, data on human sexual behavior consisted primarily of people's answers to questions about their sex lives—and you may have noticed that this is a topic about which people don't always tell the truth. William Masters and Virginia Johnson changed all that by conducting groundbreaking studies in which they actually measured the physical responses of many hundreds of volunteers as they masturbated or had sex in the laboratory (Masters & Johnson, 1966). Their work led to many discoveries, including a better understanding of the **human sexual response cycle**, which refers to *the stages of physiological arousal during sexual activity* (see **FIGURE 10.13**). Human sexual response has four phases:

- During the *excitement phase,* muscle tension and blood flow increase in and around the sexual organs, heart and respiration rates increase, and blood pressure rises. Both men and women may experience erect nipples and a "sex flush" on the skin of the upper body and face. A man's penis typically becomes erect or partially erect and his testicles draw upward, while a woman's vagina typically becomes lubricated and her clitoris becomes swollen.

- During the *plateau phase,* heart rate and muscle tension increase further. A man's urinary bladder closes to prevent urine from mixing with semen, and muscles at the base of his penis begin a steady rhythmic contraction. A man's Cowper gland may secrete a small amount of lubricating fluid (which often contains enough sperm to cause pregnancy). A woman's clitoris may withdraw slightly, and her vagina may become more lubricated. Her outer vagina may swell, and her muscles may tighten and reduce the diameter of the opening of the vagina.

- During the *orgasm* phase, breathing becomes extremely rapid and the pelvic muscles begin a series of rhythmic contractions. Both men and women experience quick cycles of muscle contraction of the anus and lower pelvic muscles, and women often experience uterine and vaginal contractions as well. During this phase, men ejaculate about 2 to 5 milliliters of semen (depending on how long it has been since their last orgasm and how long they were aroused prior to ejaculation). Ninety-five percent of heterosexual men and 69% of heterosexual women reported having an orgasm during their last sexual encounter (Richters, de Visser, Rissel, & Smith, 2006), though it is worth noting that roughly 15% of women never experience orgasm, less than half experience orgasm from intercourse alone, and roughly half report having "faked" an orgasm at least once (Wiederman, 1997). The frequency with which women have orgasms seems to have a relatively large genetic component (Dawood et al., 2005). When men and women do have orgasms, they typically experience them as intensely pleasurable, and although many of us assume that these pleasurable experiences are different for men and for women, studies suggest that they are similar (Mah & Binik, 2002). Indeed, when gynecologists, psychologists, and medical students read people's descriptions of their orgasmic experiences, they cannot reliably tell whether those descriptions were written by men or by women (Vance & Wagner, 1976).

- During the *resolution phase,* muscles relax, blood pressure drops, and the body returns to its resting state. Most men and women experience a *refractory period,* during which further stimulation does not produce excitement. This period may last from minutes to days and is typically longer for men than for women.

   Men and women are similar in their responses during sexual activity, and they are also similar in their reasons for engaging in sexual activity in the first place. Sex is necessary for reproduction, of course, but the vast majority of sexual acts are performed for other reasons, which include experiencing pleasure, coping with negative emotions, increasing emotional intimacy between partners, pleasing one's partner, impressing one's friends, and reassuring oneself of one's own attractiveness (Cooper, Shapiro, & Powers, 1998). Both women and men report that their primary motivation for having sex is to create intimacy with their partners. Women are less likely than

**HUMAN SEXUAL RESPONSE CYCLE** The stages of physiological arousal during sexual activity.

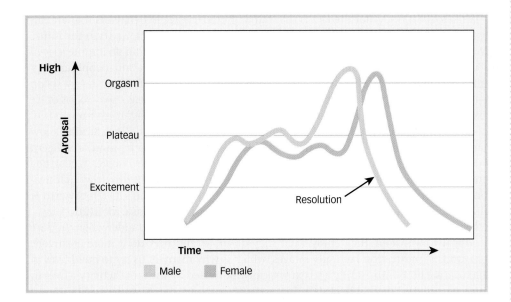

men to have sex to impress their friends, and men become less likely to have sex for this reason as they get older. Interestingly, as they age, both men and women are more likely to have sex for pleasure but no less likely to have sex to reassure themselves of their attractiveness. It is worth noting that not all sex is motivated by one of these reasons: About half of college-age women and a quarter of college-age men report having unwanted sexual activity in a dating relationship (O'Sullivan & Allegeier, 1998). We will have much more to say about sexual attraction and relationships in Chapter 16.

## Kinds of Motivation

Without Carolus Linnaeus, there would be no *Homo sapiens*. Linnaeus was the eighteenth-century Swedish naturalist who developed the classification system, or "taxonomy," by which all living things are described. For example, he decided that your genus would be called *Homo* and your species would be called *sapiens,* and his organizational scheme made modern biology possible. Eating and mating are two things that human beings are strongly motivated to do—but what are the others, and how do they relate to each other? Alas, there is no widely accepted taxonomy of human motivations, which has made it difficult for psychologists to develop theories about where motivations come from and how they operate. Nonetheless, psychologists have made initial progress by identifying several of the dimensions on which motivations differ.

### Intrinsic vs. Extrinsic

Taking a psychology exam is not like eating a french fry. One makes you tired and the other makes you fat, one requires that you move your lips and one requires that you don't, and so on. But the key difference between these activities is that one is a means to an end and one is an end in itself. An **extrinsic motivation** is *a motivation to take actions that lead to reward.* When we floss our teeth so we can avoid gum disease (and get dates), when we work hard for money so we can pay our rent (and get dates), and when we take an exam so we can get a college degree (and get money to get dates), we are extrinsically motivated. None of these things directly brings pleasure, but all may lead to pleasure in the long run. An **intrinsic motivation** is *a motivation to take actions that are themselves rewarding.* When we eat a french fry because it tastes good, exercise because it feels good, or listen to music because it sounds good, we are intrinsically motivated. These activities don't have to *have* a payoff because they *are* a payoff.

Extrinsic motivation gets a bad rap. Americans tend to believe that people should "follow their hearts" and "do what they love," and we feel sorry for or disdainful of students who choose courses just to please their parents and parents who choose jobs just

**EXTRINSIC MOTIVATION** A motivation to take actions that are not themselves rewarding but that lead to reward.

**INTRINSIC MOTIVATION** A motivation to take actions that are themselves rewarding.

**CONSCIOUS MOTIVATION** A motivation of which one is aware.

**UNCONSCIOUS MOTIVATION** A motivation of which one is not aware.

**NEED FOR ACHIEVEMENT** The motivation to solve worthwhile problems.

to earn a lot of money. But the fact is that our ability to engage in behaviors that are un-rewarding in the present because we believe they will bring greater rewards in the future is one of our species' most significant talents, and no other species can do it quite as well as we can (Gilbert, 2006). In research on the ability to delay gratification, people are typically faced with a choice between getting something they want right now (e.g., a scoop of ice cream) or waiting and getting more of what they want later (e.g., two scoops of ice cream). Waiting for ice cream is a lot like taking an exam or flossing: It isn't much fun, but you do it because you know you will reap greater rewards in the end. Studies show that 4-year-old children who can delay gratification are judged to be more intelligent and socially competent 10 years later and that they have higher SAT scores when they enter college (Mischel, Shoda, & Rodriguez, 1989). In fact, the ability to delay gratification is a better predictor of a child's grades in school than is the child's IQ (Duckworth & Seligman, 2005). Apparently there is something to be said for extrinsic motivation.

There is a lot to be said for intrinsic motivation too. People work harder when they are intrinsically motivated, they enjoy what they do more, and they do it more creatively. Both kinds of motivation have advantages, which is why many of us try to build lives in which we are both intrinsically and extrinsically motivated by the same activity—lives in which we are paid the big bucks for doing exactly what we like to do best. Who hasn't fantasized about becoming a professional artist, a professional athlete, or a professional chocolatier? Alas, research suggests that it is difficult to eat your chocolate and have it too because extrinsic rewards can undermine intrinsic rewards (Deci, Koestner, & Ryan, 1999; Henderlong & Lepper, 2002). For example, in one study, college students who were intrinsically interested in a puzzle were either paid to complete it or completed it for free, and those who were paid were less likely to play with the puzzle later on (Deci, 1971). In a similar study, children who enjoyed drawing with Magic Markers were either promised or not promised an award for using them, and those who were promised the award were less likely to use the markers later (Lepper, Greene, & Nisbett, 1973). It appears that under some circumstances, people take rewards to indicate that an activity isn't inherently pleasurable ("If they had to pay me to do that puzzle, it couldn't have been a very fun one") and thus rewards can cause people to lose their intrinsic motivation.

Just as rewards can undermine intrinsic motivation, punishments can create it. In one study, children who had no intrinsic interest in playing with a toy suddenly gained an interest when the experimenter threatened to punish them if they touched it (Aronson, 1963). College students who had no intrinsic motivation to cheat on a test were more likely to do so if the experimenter explicitly warned against it (Wilson & Lassiter, 1982). Threats can suggest that a forbidden activity is desirable, and they can also have the paradoxical consequence of promoting the very behaviors they are meant to discourage. For example, when a group of day-care centers got fed up with parents who arrived late to pick up their children, some of them instituted a financial penalty for tardiness. As **FIGURE 10.14** shows, the financial penalty caused an *increase*

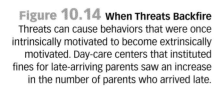

**Figure 10.14 When Threats Backfire** Threats can cause behaviors that were once intrinsically motivated to become extrinsically motivated. Day-care centers that instituted fines for late-arriving parents saw an increase in the number of parents who arrived late.

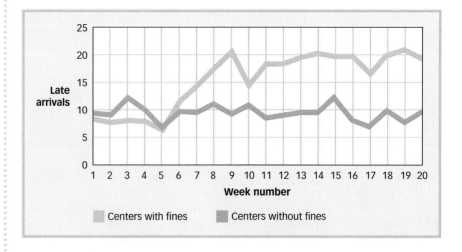

in late arrivals (Gneezy & Rustichini, 2000). Why? Because parents are intrinsically motivated to fetch their kids and they generally do their best to be on time. But when the day-care centers imposed a fine for late arrival, the parents became extrinsically motivated to fetch their children—and because the fine wasn't particularly large, they decided to pay a small financial penalty in order to leave their children in day care for an extra hour. When threats and rewards change intrinsic motivation into extrinsic motivation, unexpected consequences can follow.

Will this child enjoy swimming when he grows up? Studies suggest that extrinsic motivators, such as money, can undermine a person's intrinsic interest in performing activities such as swimming.

## Conscious vs. Unconscious

When prizewinning artists or scientists are asked to explain their achievements, they typically say things like "I wanted to liberate color from form" or "I wanted to cure diabetes." They almost never say, "I wanted to exceed my father's accomplishments, thereby proving to my mother that I was worthy of her love." A **conscious motivation** is *a motivation of which one is aware,* and an **unconscious motivation** is *a motivation of which one is not aware.* Freud believed that people have unconscious motivations, but do they? In one sense, this is a trivial question. As you learned in Chapter 8, people often can't identify the reasons for or causes of their own behavior, and in this sense, people clearly have motivations of which they are unaware. We may avoid movies that star a particular actor without also knowing that the reason why we can't stand his face is that he resembles our eighth-grade algebra teacher.

But some psychologists have suggested that people have unconscious motivations that are anything but trivial. For example, David McClelland and John Atkinson argued that people vary in their **need for achievement**—which is *the motivation to solve worthwhile problems* (McClelland et al., 1953). They argued that this basic motivation is unconscious and thus must be measured with special techniques such as the *Thematic Apperception Test,* which presents people with a series of drawings and asks them to tell stories about them. The amount of "achievement-related imagery" in the person's story ostensibly reveals the person's unconscious need for achievement. (You'll learn more about these sorts of tests in Chapter 14.) Although there has been much controversy about the validity and reliability of measures such as these (Lilienfeld, Wood, & Garb, 2000; Tuerlinckx, De Boeck, & Lens, 2002), research shows that a person's responses on this test reliably predict the person's behavior in certain circumstances. For example, they can predict a child's grades in school (Khalid, 1991). Research also suggests that this motivation can be "primed" in much the same way that thoughts and feelings can be primed. For example, when words such as *achievement* are presented on a computer screen so rapidly that people cannot consciously perceive them, those people will work especially hard to solve a puzzle (Bargh, Gollwitzer, Lee-Chai, Barndollar, & Trötschel, 2001) and will feel especially unhappy if they fail (Chartrand & Kay, in press).

Some of our motivations are conscious and some are not. So which are which? A person who is shopping for mittens may be simultaneously motivated to increase her happiness, to keep her hands warm, and to find the mitten aisle in the store. Which of these motives will she be aware of? You'll notice that some of these motivations are quite general (increasing happiness) and some are quite specific (looking for mittens). Robin Vallacher and Daniel Wegner have suggested that people tend to be aware of their general motivations unless the complexities of executing an action force them to become aware of their specific motivations (Vallacher & Wegner, 1985, 1987). For example, if a person is changing a lightbulb and is asked about her motivation, she may say something like, "I'm helping my dad out." But the moment the lightbulb gets stuck, her answer will change to, "I'm trying to get these threads aligned." The person

 **ONLY HUMAN**

**ACHIEVEMENT MOTIVATION GONE WILD** Vitaly Klimakhin dropped out of high school in 1991 to become a writer, and over a period of 107 days, he turned out a book that consisted entirely of the word *Ford* written 400,000 times. Klimakhin explained, "For a time, I would get up every morning and think, 'I've got to stop doing this before I lose my mind.' But ultimately my determination to finish won out."

**APPROACH MOTIVATION** A motivation to experience positive outcomes.

**AVOIDANCE MOTIVATION** A motivation not to experience negative outcomes.

has both motivations, of course, but she is conscious of her more general motivation when her action is easy and of her more specific motivation when her action is difficult. In one experiment, participants drank coffee either from a normal mug or from a mug that had a heavy weight attached to the bottom, which made the mug difficult to manipulate. When asked what they were doing, those who were drinking from the normal mug explained that they were "satisfying my needs," whereas those who were drinking from the weighted mug explained that they were "swallowing" (Wegner Vallacher, Macomber, Wood, & Arps, 1984).

### Approach vs. Avoidance

The poet James Thurber (1956) wrote: "All men should strive to learn before they die / what they are running from, and to, and why." The hedonic principle describes two conceptually distinct motivations: a motivation to "run to" pleasure and a motivation to "run from" pain. These correspond to what psychologists call an **approach motivation**, which is *a motivation to experience a positive outcome,* and an **avoidance motivation**, which is *a motivation not to experience a negative outcome.* Although pleasure and pain seem like two sides of the same coin, they are independent phenomena that occur in different parts of the brain (Davidson et al., 1990), so it's not surprising that the motivation to experience positive emotions and the motivation not to experience negative emotions behave a bit differently.

For example, research suggests that, all else being equal, avoidance motivations tend to be more powerful than approach motivations. As you learned in Chapter 4, most people will turn down a chance to bet on a coin flip that would pay them $10 if it came up heads but would require them to pay $8 if it came up tails because they believe that the pain of losing $8 will be more intense than the pleasure of winning $10 (Kahneman & Tversky, 1979). Because people expect losses to have more powerful emotional consequences than equal-size gains, they will take more risks to avoid a loss than to achieve a gain. When participants are told that a disease is expected to kill 600 people and that one vaccine will definitely save 400 people, whereas another has a one-third chance of saving 600 people and a two-thirds chance of saving no one, they typically say that the government should play it safe and use the first vaccine. But when people are told that one vaccine will definitely allow 200 people to die, whereas the other has a one-third chance of letting no one die and a two-thirds chance of letting 600 people die, they say that the government should gamble and use the second vaccine (Tversky & Kahneman, 1981). If you whip out your calculator, you will quickly see that these are just two ways of describing the same thing—and yet when the vaccines are described in terms of the number of lives lost instead of the number of lives gained, most people are ready to take a big risk in order to avoid the horrible loss of 600 human lives.

Although avoidance motivation tends to be stronger than approach motivation overall, there are people for whom this is more or less true. For instance, people with a high need for achievement tend to be somewhat more motivated by their hope for success, whereas people with a low need for achievement tend to be somewhat more motivated by their fear of failure. This causes the "highs" to set reasonable goals that maximize their chances of achieving a worthwhile, meaningful success, and it causes "lows" to set goals that are either too easy (which ensures their success) or too difficult (which provides an excuse for their failure). When participants in one study were invited to play a game in which they had to toss a ring onto a pole and were allowed to stand as close to the pole as they wished, participants who had a high need for achievement tended to stand an intermediate distance from the pole—close enough to make success a good possibility, but far enough to make success worthwhile. Participants who were low in the need for achievement, on the other hand, were more likely to stand very close to the pole or very far from it (Atkinson & Litwin, 1960).

In another study, participants were given an anagram task. Some were told that they would be paid $4 for the experiment, but they could earn an extra dollar by finding 90% or more of all the possible words. Others were told that they that they would

People are motivated to avoid losses and achieve gains, but whether an outcome is seen as a loss or a gain often depends on how it is described. Smart retailers refer to price discrepancies such as this one as a "cash discount" rather than a "credit card surcharge."

MICHAEL BROWN/GETTY IMAGES

be paid $5 for the experiment, but they could avoid losing a dollar by not missing more than 10% of all the possible words. People who had a "promotion focus"—which is a tendency to think in terms of achieving gains—performed better in the first case than in the second. But people who had a "prevention focus"—which is a tendency to think in terms of avoiding losses—performed better in the second case than in the first (Shah, Higgins, & Friedman, 1998).

---

**In summary,** emotions motivate us indirectly by providing information about the world, but they also motivate us directly. The hedonic principle suggests that people approach pleasure and avoid pain and that this basic motivation underlies all others. All organisms are born with some motivations and acquire others through experience.

When the body experiences a deficit, we experience a drive to remedy it. Biological drives such as eating and mating generally take precedence over others. Hunger is the result of a complex system of physiological processes, and problems with this system can lead to eating disorders and obesity, both of which are very difficult to overcome. With regard to sexual drives, men and women tend to be more similar than different. Both genders experience the same sequence of physiological arousal, engage in sex for most of the same reasons, and have sex drives that are regulated by testosterone.

People have many motivations that can be classified in many ways. Intrinsic motivations can be undermined by extrinsic rewards and punishments. People tend to be aware of their more general motivations unless difficulty with the production of action forces them to be aware of their more specific motivations. Avoidance motivations are generally more powerful than approach motivations, but this is more true for some people than for others. ■ ■

---

## Where Do You Stand?

# Here Comes the Bribe

Americans prize their right to vote. They talk about it, they sing about it, and they die for it. They just don't use it very much.

The U.S. Census Bureau estimates that about 60% of American citizens who are eligible to vote in a presidential election actually do so, and the numbers are significantly lower for "off-year" elections. Everyone seems to agree that this is a problem, including the people who don't vote, so what can be done? Government officials and social scientists have investigated numerous ways to increase voter turnout, and some of their efforts have had modest effects, but none has come close to solving the problem. And yet not all countries have this problem. Belgium, for instance, has a voter turnout rate close to 100% because for the better part of a century, failing to vote in Belgium has been illegal. (If you failed to vote in Belgium, don't worry; this only applies to Belgians.) Belgians who fail to vote may be fined, and if they fail to vote several times in a

row, they may be "legally disenfranchised," which makes it difficult for them to get a job. Although some people have suggested that America should join the long list of countries that have compulsory voting, Americans generally don't like the threat of punishment.

But they sure do love the possibility of reward—and that's what led Arizona ophthalmologist Mark Osterloh to propose the Arizona Voter Reward Act, which would have awarded $1 million to a randomly selected voter in every election. As soon as Osterloh announced his idea, principled people lined up against it. "People should not go vote because they might win a lottery," said Curtis Gans, the director of the Center for the Study of the American Electorate in Washington. "We need to rekindle the religion of civic duty, and that is a hard job, but we should not make voting crassly commercial" (Archibold, 2006). An editorial in the *Yuma Sun* stated: "A jackpot is not the right motivator for voting. . . . People should vote because they

want to and because they think it is important. . . . Bribing people to vote is a superficial approach that will have no beneficial outcome to the process, except to make some people feel good that the turnout numbers are higher" (Editorial, 2006). Nonetheless, 185,902 of Osterloh's fellow Arizonans thought his idea had merit, and they signed their names to get his measure on the ballot.

In November 2006, Arizonans defeated the measure by a sound margin, but Osterloh wasn't dejected. "I believe somebody is eventually going to bring this back and get this approved somewhere around the world, and it's going to spread," he said days after the election. "If anybody has a better idea of how to get people to vote, let me know and I will support it" (Rotstein, 2006).

Should our government motivate people to vote with extrinsic rewards or punishments? We know where Arizonans stand on this issue. How about you?

# Chapter Review

## Emotional Experience: The Feeling Machine

- Emotional experiences are difficult to describe, but psychologists have identified their two underlying dimensions: arousal and valence.

- Psychologists have spent more than a century trying to understand how emotional experience and physiological activity are related. The James-Lange theory suggests that a stimulus causes a physiological reaction, which leads to an emotional experience; the Cannon-Bard theory suggests that a stimulus causes both an emotional experience and a physiological reaction simultaneously; and Schachter and Singer's two-factor theory suggests that a stimulus causes undifferentiated physiological arousal about which people draw inferences.

- Emotions are produced by the complex interaction of limbic and cortical structures. Information about a stimulus is sent simultaneously to the amygdala (which makes a quick appraisal of the stimulus's goodness or badness) and the cortex (which does a slower and more comprehensive analysis of the stimulus). In some instances, the amygdala will trigger an emotional experience that the cortex later inhibits.

- People care about their emotional experiences and use many strategies to regulate them. Reappraisal involves changing the way one thinks about an object or event, and it is one of the most effective strategies for emotion regulation.

## Emotional Communication: Msgs w/o Wrds

- Darwin suggested that emotional expressions are the same for all people and are universally understood, and research suggests that this is generally true.

- Emotional expressions are caused by the emotions they signify, but they can also cause those emotions.

- Emotional mimicry allows people to experience and hence identify the emotions of others.

- Not all emotional expressions are sincere because people use display rules to help them decide which emotions to express. Cultures have different display rules, but people obey them by using the same set of techniques.

- There are reliable differences between sincere and insincere emotional expressions, just as there are reliable differences between truthful and untruthful utterances, but people are generally poor at determining when an expression or an utterance is sincere. Although machines such as the polygraph can make this determination with better-than-chance accuracy, their error rates are dangerously high.

## Motivation: Getting Moved

- Emotions motivate us indirectly by providing information about the world, but they also motivate us directly. The hedonic principle suggests that people approach pleasure and avoid pain and that this basic motivation underlies all others.

- All organisms are born with some motivations and acquire others through experience.

- When the body experiences a deficit, we experience a drive to remedy it. Biological drives such as eating and mating generally take precedence over others.

- Hunger is the result of a complex system of physiological processes, and problems with this system can lead to eating disorders and obesity, both of which are very difficult to overcome.

- With regard to sexual drives, men and women tend to be more similar than different. Both genders experience the same sequence of physiological arousal, engage in sex for most of the same reasons, and have sex drives that are regulated by testosterone.

- Intrinsic motivations can be undermined by extrinsic rewards and punishments.

- People tend to be aware of their more general motivations unless difficulty with the production of action forces them to be aware of their more specific motivations.

- Avoidance motivations are generally more powerful than approach motivations, but this is more true for some people than for others.

## Key Terms

emotion (p. 370)
James-Lange theory (p. 370)
Cannon-Bard theory (p. 370)
two-factor theory (p. 371)
appraisal (p. 374)
emotion regulation (p. 376)
reappraisal (p. 376)
emotional expression (p. 377)

affective forecasting (p, 378)
universality hypothesis (p. 379)
facial feedback hypothesis (p. 381)
display rules (p. 383)
motivation (p. 386)
hedonic principle (p. 388)
homeostasis (p. 390)

drive (p. 390)
bulimia nervosa (p. 392)
anorexia nervosa (p. 392)
metabolism (p. 394)
human sexual response cycle (p. 396)
extrinsic motivation (p. 397)
intrinsic motivation (p. 397)

conscious motivation (p. 399)
unconscious motivation (p. 399)
need for achievement (p. 399)
approach motivation (p. 400)
avoidance motivation (p. 400)

# Recommended Readings

**Ekman, P.** (2003b). *Emotions revealed: Recognizing faces and feelings to improve communication and emotional life.* New York: Times Books. Psychologist Paul Ekman explains the roots of our emotions and their expressions and answers such questions as: How does our body signal to others whether we are slightly sad or anguished, peeved or enraged? Can we learn to distinguish between a polite smile and the genuine thing? Can we ever truly control our emotions? A fascinating and fun book, packed with unique exercises and photographs.

**Gilbert, D. T.** (2006). *Stumbling on happiness.* New York: Knopf. In this award-winning international best seller, psychologist Daniel Gilbert examines our uniquely human ability to imagine the future and predict how much we will like it when we get there. *New Scientist* described it as "a witty,

insightful and superbly entertaining trek through the foibles of human imagination."

**LeDoux, J.** (1996). *The emotional brain: The mysterious underpinnings of emotional life.* New York: Simon & Schuster. Neuroscientist Joseph LeDoux explains how the human brain processes information and generates emotions. The amygdala, he argues, processes information more quickly than other parts of the brain, thus allowing a rapid "fear response" that can save our lives before other parts of the brain have had a chance to react. Amazon.com called it "a compelling read about the mysteries of emotions and the workings of the brain."

# THE ADAPTIVENESS OF BEHAVIOR

We are the products of our genes and our environments. Our genes have been shaped by millions of years of evolution, adapting us to the general conditions of human life on earth. Through this process, we have acquired, among other things, an immense capacity to learn. In this unit, Chapter 3 examines the role of genes and evolution in the production of the underlying mechanisms of behavior, and Chapter 4 deals with basic processes of learning, through which an individual's behavior is constantly modified to meet the unique conditions of that person's life.

part 2

# Genetic and Evolutionary Foundations of Behavior

chapter 3

Have you ever stood before a chimpanzee enclosure at a zoo and watched for a while? If you haven't, I urge you to seize the next opportunity to do so. It is impossible, I think, to look for long without sensing strongly the animal's kinship to us. Its facial expressions, its curiosity, even its sense of humor, are so like ours that we intuitively see it as a hairy, long-armed cousin. Indeed, the chimpanzee is our cousin. It—along with the bonobo, a chimp-like ape discussed later in this chapter—is one of our two closest animal relatives. Geneticists have lined up the DNA of chimpanzees against that of humans and found that they match at 98.8 percent of the nearly three billion individual base units that make up the DNA molecules for each species (Cryanoski, 2002). In genetic material, you and I are just 1.2 percent different from a chimpanzee. Language and culture, and the knowledge these have given us, have in some ways separated us markedly from our cousins. But in our genes—and in our basic drives, emotions, perceptual processes, and ways of learning, which are partly products of those genes—we are kin not just to chimpanzees, but in varying degrees to all of the mammals, and in lesser degrees to other animals as well.

Nearly 150 years ago, in *On the Origin of Species,* Charles Darwin (1859/1963) presented a theory of evolution that explains both the similarities and the differences among the animal species. According to Darwin, all species are to varying degrees similar to one another because of common ancestry, and all species are to some degree unique because natural selection has adapted each species to the unique aspects of the environment in which it lives and reproduces. Darwin presented massive amounts of evidence for his theory, and essentially everything that scientists have learned since, about our own and other species, is consistent with it.

This chapter is primarily about the application of evolutionary theory to the behavior of humans and other animals. It is also the first of a two-chapter sequence on the *adaptiveness of behavior*. Adaptation refers to modification to meet changed life circumstances. Evolution is the long-term adaptive process, spanning generations, that equips each species for life in its ever-changing natural habitat. The next chapter is on learning, a set of shorter-term adaptive processes that occur within the life span of each individual. The mechanisms that permit learning to occur are themselves products of evolution.

Darwin developed his theory of evolution without any knowledge of genes, but the theory is best understood today in the light of such knowledge. Therefore, the chapter begins with a discussion of basic genetic mechanisms and their implications for the inheritance of behavioral characteristics. With that as background, the rest of the chapter is concerned with the evolution of behavior and with ways in which we can learn about our own behavior by comparing it to that of our animal relatives.

# Review of Basic Genetic Mechanisms

You have almost certainly studied the mechanisms of gene action and reproduction in a biology course at one time or another, so I will not go into detail on these processes here. But a brief review of them, focused on their implications for psychology, may be useful.

## How Genes Affect Behavior

**1**

How can genes affect behavioral traits through their role in protein synthesis?

<<< Sometimes, as a sort of shorthand (which I will use occasionally in this book), researchers speak of genes "for" particular behavioral traits. For example, they might speak of genes *for* singing ability, *for* aggression, or *for* cooperation. But genes never produce or control behavior directly. All the effects that genes have on behavior occur through their role in building and modifying the physical structures of the body. Those structures, interacting with the environment, produce behavior. Thus, a gene might influence musical ability by promoting the development of a brain system that analyzes sounds or by promoting certain physical aspects of the vocal cords. Similarly, a gene might affect aggressiveness by fostering the growth of brain systems that organize aggressive behavior in response to irritating stimuli. In a sense, all genes that contribute to the body's development are "for" behavior, since all parts of the body are involved in behavior. Especially relevant for behavior, however, are genes that contribute to the development of sensory systems, motor systems (muscles and other organs involved in movement), and, most especially, the nervous system (which includes the brain).

## Genes Provide the Codes for Proteins

Genes affect the body's development through, and only through, their influence on the production of *protein molecules*. We are what we are, biologically speaking, because of our proteins. A class of proteins called *structural proteins* forms the structure of every cell of the body. Another, much larger class called *enzymes* controls the rate of every chemical reaction in every cell.

How do genes organize the production of proteins? Physically, genes are components of extremely long molecules of a substance called DNA (deoxyribonucleic acid). These molecules exist in the egg and sperm cells that join to form a new individual, and they replicate themselves during each cell division in the course of the body's growth and development. A replica of your whole unique set of DNA molecules exists in the nucleus of each of your body's cells, where it serves as a template (that is, a mold or pattern) for producing another molecular substance called RNA (ribonucleic acid), which in turn serves as a template for producing protein molecules. Each protein molecule consists of a long chain of smaller molecules called amino acids. The 20 distinct amino acids can be arranged in countless sequences to form different protein molecules. The job of each gene is to provide the code that dictates the particular sequence of amino acids for a single type of protein. From a molecular vantage point, a *gene* can be defined as the segment of a DNA molecule that contains the code for manufacturing a particular type of protein molecule. With this definition, geneticists have determined that humans, chimpanzees, and mice all have nearly the same number of genes—about 30,000 of them (Tecott, 2003).

## Genes Work Only Through Interaction with the Environment

At every level, from biochemical to behavioral, the effects of genes are entwined with the effects of the environment. *Environment,* as used in this context, refers to every aspect of an individual and his or her surroundings except the genes themselves. It includes the nourishing womb and maternal bloodstream before birth; the internal chemical environment of the developing individual; and all the events, objects, and other individuals encountered after birth. Foods—a part of the environment—supply genes with amino acids, which are needed to manufacture proteins. Environmental effects also turn genes "on" and "off," resulting in bodily changes that alter the individual's behavioral capacity. Such changes can occur in adulthood as well as earlier in development. For example, physical exercise modifies the chemical environment of muscle cells in a way that activates genes that promote further growth of the muscle. One's body and behavioral capacities result from a continuous, complex interplay between genes and environment (see Figure 3.1). In no sense is one more basic than the other.

Researchers have begun recently to learn about specific mechanisms through which experiences can activate genes and thereby alter the individual's brain and behavior. A well-studied example has to do with parental behavior in mice and rats. Adult mice and rats that have not given birth will normally avoid newborns of their species that are placed in their cage. However, if exposed to newborns continuously for several hours or more, they gradually begin to care for them. This change in behavior involves the environmental induction of gene activity (Brown & others, 1996; Stack & Numan, 2000). The sight, sound, or smell of newborns activates a particular gene. The activated gene produces a protein molecule that stimulates activity in a specific cluster of brain cells that are known to be crucial for the motivation and organization of such behaviors as retrieving young to a nest and hovering over them. The result is that a mouse or rat that previously did not take care of young is transformed into a mouse or rat that does.

There is good reason to believe that all sorts of prolonged behavioral effects that derive from experience, including those that we call "learning," involve the activation of genes (Johnston & Edwards, 2002). The experience activates genes, which produce proteins, which in turn alter the function of some of the neural circuits in the brain and thereby change the manner in which the individual behaves. More about this is discussed in Chapter 5.

## Distinction Between Genotype and Phenotype

Geneticists use the term **genotype** to refer to the set of genes that the individual inherits and the term **phenotype** to refer to the observable properties of the body and behavioral traits. The same genes can have different effects, depending on the environment and the mix of other genes. Two individuals with the same genotype can be quite different in phenotype as a result of differences in their environments. Genetically identical rats will differ phenotypically in their behavior toward infant rats if one has been previously exposed to infant rats and the other has not. Genetically identical human twins will differ in size if they have been exposed differently to growth-promoting factors in their environments (see Figure 3.2 on the next page) and will differ in behavior if they have been subjected to different learning experiences.

>>> ——————————————— 2

What does it mean to say that genes can influence behavioral traits only through interaction with the environment? How, in general, are genes involved in long-term behavioral changes that derive from experience?

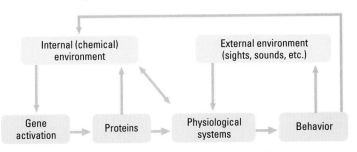

**| FIGURE 3.1 | Route through which genes affect behavior** Genes build proteins, which form or alter the body's physiological systems (including brain systems), which, in turn, produce behavior. Each step in this process involves interaction with the environment. Aspects of the internal environment control gene activation, and aspects of both the internal and the external environments act on physiological systems to control behavior. Behavior, in turn, can affect gene activation through direct and indirect effects on the internal environment.

>>> ——————————————— 3

How can the same genotype produce various phenotypes?

Van Bucher / Photo Researchers

**| FIGURE 3.2 |** Identical twins
These 13-year-old girls have the same genotype, but they obviously differ in at least one aspect of their phenotype. It is uncertain what caused this difference. It may have derived from their occupying different positions in the womb such that one received more early nutrition than the other, which activated genes promoting more growth.

**4** ————————————————
How does meiosis produce egg or sperm cells that are all genetically different from one another?

## How Genes Are Passed Along in Sexual Reproduction

Genes not only provide the codes for building proteins; they also serve as the biological units of heredity. They are replicated and passed along from parents to offspring, and they are the cause of offsprings' resemblance to parents.

To understand how genes are passed along in sexual reproduction, it is useful to know something about their arrangement within cells. The genetic material (strands of DNA) exists in each cell in structures called **chromosomes,** which are usually dispersed throughout the cell nucleus and are not visible. Just prior to cell division, however, the chromosomes condense into compact forms that can be stained, viewed through a microscope, and photographed. The normal human cell has 23 pairs of chromosomes. Twenty-two of these are true pairs in both the male and the female, in the sense that each chromosome looks like its mate. The remaining pair is made up of the sex chromosomes. In the normal human male cell, that pair consists of a large chromosome labeled X and a small chromosome labeled Y (see Figure 3.3). Genetically, the only difference between the sexes is that females have two X chromosomes (XX) rather than the XY of the male.

## The Production of Genetically Diverse Egg and Sperm Cells

When cells divide to produce new cells *other than* egg or sperm cells, they do so by a process called **mitosis.** In mitosis, each chromosome precisely replicates itself and then the cell divides, with one copy of each chromosome moving into each of the two cell nuclei thus formed. Because of the faithful copying of genetic material in mitosis, all your body's cells, except your egg or sperm cells, are genetically identical to one another. The differences among different cells in your body—such as muscle cells and skin cells—arise from the differential activation of their genes, not from different gene content.

When cells divide to produce egg or sperm cells, they do so by a different process, called **meiosis,** which results in cells that are not genetically alike. During meiosis, each chromosome replicates itself once, but then the cell divides twice. Before the first cell division, the chromosomes of each pair line up next to one another and exchange genetic material in a random manner. Although the chromosomes in each pair look the same, they do not contain precisely the same genes.

The result of this random exchange of genetic material and of the subsequent cell divisions is that each egg or sperm cell produced is genetically different from any other egg or sperm cell and contains only half of the full number of chromosomes (one member of each of the 23 pairs).

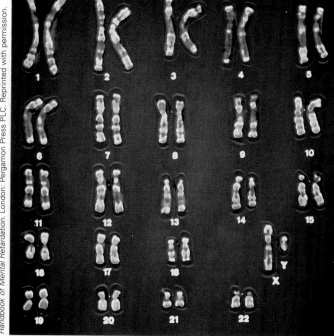

Pueschel, S. M., & Goldstein, A. (1983). Genetic counseling. In J. L. Maton & J. A. Mulick (Eds.), *Handbook of Mental Retardation.* London: Pergamon Press PLC. Reprinted with permission.

## The Genetic Diversity of Offspring

It may seem ironic that the very cells you use for "reproduction" are the only cells in your body that cannot, in theory, reproduce you. They are the only cells in your body that do not have all your genes. In sexual reproduction you are, of course, not really reproducing yourself. Rather, you are creating a genetically unique individual who has half of your genes and half of your partner's. When a sperm and an egg unite, the result is a single new cell, the **zygote,**

**| FIGURE 3.3 |** Chromosomes of a normal human male cell  The 22 numbered pairs of chromosomes are the same in a normal female cell as they are in a normal male cell. The remaining two, labeled X and Y, are the sex chromosomes. The normal human female cell (not shown) has a second X chromosome instead of a Y.

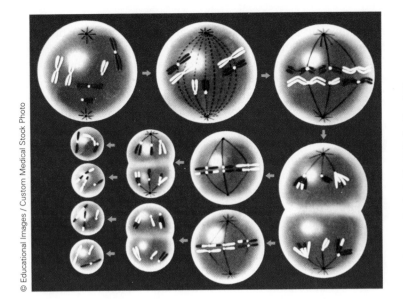

**Schematic illustration of meiosis in sperm production**
This illustration is for a creature that has only three pairs of chromosomes rather than the 23 pairs that humans have. At the beginning of this sequence (top left), each chromosome has already replicated itself and remains attached to its replica. The pairs of replicated chromosomes (one blue and one white in the diagram) then line up next to one another and exchange genetic material. The cell then divides twice, resulting in four sperm cells, each with just one member of each pair of chromosomes. Notice that each sperm cell is genetically different from the others, having a different mix of the original (blue and white) material from the parental pairs of chromosomes. Meiosis in egg production is similar to that in sperm production, but only one of the two cells produced at each division survives.

which contains the full complement of 23 paired chromosomes. One member of each of these pairs comes from each parent. The zygote then grows, through mitosis, eventually to become a new person. Because each sperm or egg is different from any other sperm or egg (even from the same parent), each zygote is different from any other.

The value of sex, as opposed to simple cloning (the asexual production of genetically identical offspring), apparently lies in the production of genetically diverse offspring. In a world where the environment keeps changing, genes have a better chance of surviving if they are rearranged at each generation in many different ways, to produce different kinds of bodies, than if they are all put into the same kind of body. This is an almost literal example of the old saying, "Don't put all your eggs in the same basket." By producing diverse offspring, parents are reducing the chance that all of their offspring will die as a result of some unforeseen change in the environment. In Chapter 15 you will see how this idea—that there is value in genetic diversity—may apply in the realm of human personality.

The only people who are genetically identical to each other are **identical twins.** They are formed when two bundles of cells separate from each other during the early mitotic divisions following the formation of a zygote. Because they originate from one zygote, identical twins are also known as *monozygotic twins.* **Fraternal twins,** or *dizygotic twins,* originate from two zygotes, formed from two different egg and sperm cells. Fraternal twins are no more or less similar to each other genetically than are any two non-twin siblings. In later chapters (especially Chapter 10), you will see how psychologists make use of twins in research aimed at understanding how much of the variability among people, in certain psychological traits, results from differences in their genes and how much results from differences in their environments.

>>> ————————————— 5

What is the advantage of producing genetically diverse offspring?

## Consequences of the Fact That Genes Come in Pairs

You have seen that genes exist on long DNA strands in chromosomes, rather like beads on a string, and that chromosomes come in pairs. The two genes that occupy the same **locus** (location) on a pair of chromosomes are sometimes identical to each other and sometimes not. When they are identical, the individual is said to be **homozygous** [**home**-oh-**zai**-gus] at that locus, and when they are not identical, the individual is said to be **heterozygous** [**het**-er-oh-**zai**-gus] at that locus (see Figure 3.4). Different genes that can occupy the same locus, and thus can potentially pair with each other, are referred to as **alleles.**

**6**

What is the difference between a dominant and a recessive gene (or allele)?

**|FIGURE 3.4 |** Schematic illustration of gene loci on a pair of chromosomes Successive genes are depicted here as beads on a string. This pair of chromosomes is homozygous at loci 1, 3, and 5 (the paired genes there are identical to each other) and heterozygous at loci 2 and 4 (the paired genes there are not identical to each other). Nonidentical genes that can occupy the same locus on a pair of chromosomes are referred to as alleles of each other. Thus the two genes at locus 2 are alleles, as are the two at locus 4.

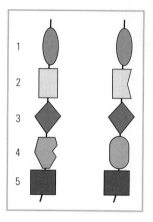

<<< For example, a gene for brown eyes and a gene for blue eyes in humans are alleles because they can occupy the same locus. If you are homozygous for brown eyes, you have two copies of a gene that manufactures an enzyme that makes your eyes brown. What if you were heterozygous for eye color, with one copy of the allele for brown eyes and one copy for blue eyes? In this case, you would have brown eyes, no different from the eye color you would have if you were homozygous for brown eyes. This effect is described by saying that the allele for brown eyes is *dominant* and the one for blue eyes is *recessive*. A **dominant** gene (or allele) is one that will produce its observable effects in either the homozygous or the heterozygous condition, and a **recessive** gene (or allele) is one that will produce its effects in the homozygous condition only. But not all pairs of alleles manifest dominance or recessiveness. Some pairs blend their effects. For example, if you cross red four-o'clocks (a kind of flower) with white four-o'clocks, the offspring will be pink, because neither the red nor the white allele is dominant over the other.

## Mendelian Pattern of Heredity

The idea that the units of heredity come in pairs and that one member of a pair can be dominant over the other was developed in the mid-nineteenth century by an Austrian monk named Gregor Mendel. In a typical experiment, Mendel would start with two purebred strains of peas that differed in one or more easily observed traits. He could cross-pollinate them to observe the traits of the offspring, called the $F_1$ (first filial) generation. Then he would pollinate the $F_1$ peas with pollen from other $F_1$ peas to produce the $F_2$ (second filial) generation. In one experiment, for example, Mendel cross-pollinated a strain of peas that regularly produced round seeds with a strain that regularly produced wrinkled seeds. His famous findings were that (a) all of the $F_1$ generation had round seeds and (b) three-fourths of the $F_2$ generation had round seeds and one-fourth had wrinkled seeds.

**7**

Why do three-fourths of the offspring of two heterozygous parents show the dominant trait and one-fourth show the recessive trait?

<<< Mendel's findings make perfect sense if we assume that seed texture is controlled by a single pair of genes, with the allele for round dominant over that for wrinkled. To illustrate this, let us use the capital letter $R$ to stand for the dominant, round-producing allele and the small letter $r$ for the recessive, wrinkle-producing allele. The purebred round strain is homozygous for the "round" allele ($RR$), and the purebred wrinkled strain is homozygous for the "wrinkled" allele ($rr$). (Purebred strains are homozygous for all traits.) Because one allele must come from each parent, the only possible result for the $F_1$ generation, produced by crossing the two purebred strains, is the heterozygous condition ($Rr$). This explains why all the $F_1$ peas in Mendel's experiment were round. At the next step, when $Rr$ peas receive pollen from other $Rr$ peas to produce the $F_2$ generation, four equally likely combinations can occur: (1) an $R$ from each parent ($RR$), (2) an $R$ from the female parent and an $r$ from the male ($Rr$), (3) an $r$ from the female parent and an $R$ from the male ($rR$), and (4) an $r$ from each parent ($rr$). (See Figure 3.5.) Since only one of these possible outcomes ($rr$) is wrinkled, the expectation is that one-fourth of the $F_2$ generation will be wrinkled and the other three-fourths, round. This is just what Mendel found.

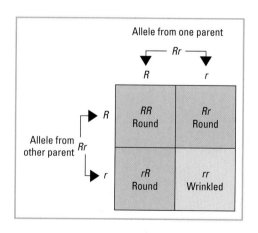

**|FIGURE 3.5 |** Explanation of Mendel's 3:1 ratio When a pea plant that is heterozygous for round versus wrinkled seeds is pollinated by another pea plant that is similarly heterozygous, four possible gene combinations occur in the offspring. Here $R$ stands for the dominant, round-producing allele, and $r$ for the recessive, wrinkle-producing allele. The phenotype of three of the offspring will be round and that of one, wrinkled. This 3:1 ratio was Mendel's famous finding.

Whenever a trait is inherited in a pattern like that observed by Mendel, we can assume that the trait results from variation at a single gene locus.

## SECTION REVIEW

| Genes affect behavior by affecting the bodily structures involved in behavior. | | |
| --- | --- | --- |
| **Nature of Genetic Influence** | **Meiosis and Sexual Reproduction** | **Gene Pairing** |
| • Genes affect bodily structures, and thereby affect behavior, by influencing protein synthesis.<br><br>• Genes act in concert with the environment, not in isolation. For example, environmental cues can activate genes that make rats or mice nurturant to newborns. | • Meiosis results in egg and sperm cells that contain just one member of each pair of genes.<br><br>• Meiosis involves random assortment of paired genes.<br><br>• Genetic diversity produced by sexual reproduction promotes the genes' survival. | • Paired genes, which occupy the same locus (location) on a pair of chromosomes, may be identical (homozygous) or different (heterozygous). Gene variations that can occupy the same locus are called alleles.<br><br>• Mendel's discovery of consistent ratios of traits in offspring of cross-pollinated strains of peas led to the gene concept and to the concepts of dominance and recessiveness. |

# Inheritance of Behavioral Traits

Variation in genes contributes to the variation in behavior that one sees in any animal species. Some behavioral characteristics are inherited in accordance with the same pattern that Mendel observed, indicative of control by a single pair of genes. Most behavioral characteristics, however, depend on many genes. In this section we shall look first at two examples of single-gene traits and then at traits that are affected by many genes.

## Examples of Single-Gene (Mendelian) Behavioral Traits

### Mendelian Inheritance of Fearfulness in Dogs

One of the first demonstrations of single-gene control of a behavioral trait in dogs occurred more than 40 years ago. In pioneering research on the role of genes in behavior, John Paul Scott and John Fuller (1965) studied the behavior of basenji [buh-**sen**-jee] hounds, cocker spaniels, and their mixed-breed offspring. Basenjis are timid dogs, showing fear of people until they have received much gentle handling. Cockers, in contrast, show little fear under normal rearing conditions. In a standard test with 5-week-old puppies, Scott and Fuller found that all the basenji puppies yelped and/or ran away when approached by a strange person, whereas only a few of the cocker puppies showed these reactions. When cockers and basenjis were crossbred (see Figure 3.6 on the next page), the offspring ($F_1$ hybrids) were like basenjis in this test: All showed signs of fear when approached. Since this was as true of hybrids raised by cocker mothers as of those raised by basenji mothers, Scott and Fuller concluded that the effect stemmed from the hybrid dogs' genes and not from the way their mothers treated them.

The fact that the $F_1$ hybrids were as fearful as the purebred basenjis suggested to Scott and Fuller that the difference in fearfulness between the two purebred strains might be controlled by a single gene locus, with the allele promoting fear dominant over that promoting confidence. If this were so, then mating $F_1$ hybrids with each other should produce a group of offspring ($F_2$ generation) in which three-fourths would show basenji-like fear and one-fourth would show cocker-like confidence—

>>>────────────── **8**

How did Scott and Fuller show that the difference in fearfulness between cocker spaniels and basenji hounds is controlled by a single gene locus, with the "fear" allele dominant over the "non-fear" allele?

Scott, J. P. & Fuller, J. L. (1965). *Genetic and social behavior of the dog.* Chicago: University of Chicago Press.

**│ FIGURE 3.6 │ Dogs used in Scott and Fuller's research** At left are a male basenji and a female cocker spaniel; at right are two $F_1$ (first-generation) hybrids resulting from a basenji-cocker cross.

the same ratios that Mendel had found with seed texture in peas. Scott and Fuller did this experiment and, indeed, found ratios very close to those predicted. As additional evidence, they also mated $F_1$ hybrids with purebred cockers. About half the offspring of those *backcrosses* were basenji-like in fear, and the other half were cocker-like in confidence—just as can be expected if the "fear" allele is dominant over the "non-fear" allele (see Figure 3.7).

**9**

Why would it be a mistake to conclude, from Scott and Fuller's work, that fear in dogs is caused just by one gene or that it is caused just by genes and not by the environment?

<<< Be careful not to misinterpret this finding. It concerns a difference between two breeds of dogs in certain behavioral tests. It would not be reasonable to conclude that fear in all its various forms is controlled by a single gene. Many different genes must contribute to building the complex neural structure needed to experience fear and express it in behavior. Scott and Fuller's work demonstrates only that the difference between cocker spaniels and basenji hounds in a particular test of fear is controlled by a single gene. Recognize also that their studies do not diminish the role of environmental influences. Scott and Fuller could detect the effect of a specific gene pair because they raised all the dogs in similar environments. In other research, Scott (1963) showed that any puppy isolated from people for the first 4 months of life will be fearful of humans. Had Scott and Fuller isolated the cockers from all human contact and given the basenjis lots of kind handling before the behavioral test, they might well have found the cockers to be more fearful than the basenjis, despite the genetic predispositions toward the opposite behavior.

**Allele from cocker-basenji hybrid**

┌─── *Ff* ───┐

|  | *F* | *f* |
|---|---|---|
| **Allele from purebred *ff* cocker** → *f* | *fF* Fearful | *ff* Not fearful |
| → *f* | *fF* Fearful | *ff* Not fearful |

**│ FIGURE 3.7 │ Explanation of Scott and Fuller's results of mating basenji-cocker hybrids with purebred cockers** The finding that half the offspring were fearful and half were not makes sense if fearfulness results from a dominant allele (*F*) and lack of fearfulness results from a recessive allele (*f*). Because half the offspring receive *F* from their hybrid parent and all receive *f* from the purebred parent, half the offspring will be *Ff* (phenotypically fearful) and the other half, *ff* (not fearful).

## Mendelian Inheritance of a Specific Language Disorder

Most of the behaviorally relevant traits in humans that derive from alteration at a single gene locus are brain disorders, caused by relatively rare, mutant, malfunctioning genes that are passed from generation to generation.

A particularly interesting example is a specific language impairment that has been studied extensively in three generations of one family, known as the KE family. The disorder, which is very rare outside of the KE family, is characterized primarily by difficulty in articulating words, distinguishing speech sounds from other sounds, and learning grammatical rules (Gopnik, 1999; Marcus & Fisher, 2003). With much effort, people with this disorder learn to speak and understand language well enough to get along, but language never becomes natural to them. For example, they never develop the intuitive understanding of grammatical categories and rules that even normal 3-year-olds manifest. Brain scans of people with this disorder have revealed underdevelopment in several areas of the brain that are known to be critical for producing and understanding language (Liégeois & others, 2003).

The pattern of heredity of this disorder in the KE family is depicted in Figure 3.8. As you can see by examining the results for the third generation, when neither parent had the specific language impairment (SLI), no child had it, and when one parent had it, about half of the offspring had it—just what you would expect if the impairment results from a single dominant gene. The logic behind this expectation is identical to that shown in Figure 3.7 for fearfulness in dogs. If one parent has one copy of the abnormal gene and the other parent lacks the abnormal gene, each offspring has a 50 percent chance of inheriting a copy of that gene. Because the abnormal gene is dominant, each person inheriting it is linguistically impaired.

Recently, researchers have isolated the gene that causes this language impairment (Fisher, 2003; Lai & others, 2001). It is located on Chromosome 7, and in its normal (unimpaired) form it codes for a type of protein known as a *transcription factor*. Transcription factors are proteins that interact with the regulatory regions of other genes and in that way control the rate at which those genes produce their protein molecules. Apparently, the normal version of this gene is responsible for activating a set of other genes that are involved in the development of various areas

>>> ————————————————— **10**

How did the pattern of inheritance of a disorder in language ability, in a particular family, show that the disorder is caused by a single dominant gene? Also, what other general ideas about genetic influences are illustrated by this example?

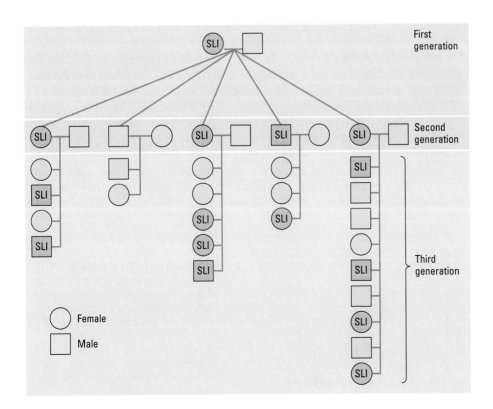

| FIGURE 3.8 | Inheritance of a specific language impairment This diagram shows the members of three generations of a family in which a specific language impairment (SLI) recurred. Circles depict females; squares, males; horizontal lines, marriage bonds; and slanted or vertical lines, lines of descent. "SLI" indicates presence of the disorder. Notice that approximately half (10 of 21) of the third-generation children who had one parent with the disorder also had the disorder. This pattern is consistent with the theory that the disorder is inherited through a single dominant gene. (Based on Gopnik & Crago, 1991.)

of the brain that are crucial for human language. The mutated (SLI) version of the gene fails to activate the other genes. Two copies of the normal gene are required to activate the other genes sufficiently for normal development of the language areas of the brain. Thus the disorder appears in people who have one normal gene and one SLI gene.

The normal human version of this gene appears to be unique to humans. The chimpanzee version of the same gene is slightly different from that of the human version and produces a slightly different protein molecule (Marcus & Fisher, 2003). Apparently, modification of this particular gene was one of the evolutionary steps that enabled language to occur in humans and helped to distinguish us from chimpanzees and other apes.

I chose this particular example of a single-gene trait not just because it illustrates Mendelian inheritance in human behavior but also because it illustrates four other general ideas about genes:

- Genes can influence behavior by influencing the development of particular areas of the brain.

- A single gene can have multiple effects (in this case the gene affects various aspects of linguistic ability by altering the brain in various locations).

- Some genes exert their effects by activating sets of other genes, thereby controlling the production of several or many different protein molecules.

- The evolution of human beings (and of other species) involves alterations in anatomy and behavior that derive from alterations in genes.

## Polygenic Characteristics and Selective Breeding

11
How does the distribution of scores for a polygenic trait differ from that usually obtained for a single-gene trait?

<<< Characteristics that derive from variation at a single gene locus are typically *categorical* in nature. That is, they are characteristics that sharply differentiate one group (category) from another. Peas are either round or wrinkled; mixed-breed basenji-cockers differ so sharply from one another in fearfulness that they can be categorized into two distinct groups; members of the KE family either have or do not have the specific language disorder (none of them "sort of have it").

But most measurable anatomical and behavioral differences among individuals of any species are in degree, not type. They are *continuous* rather than categorical. That is, the measures taken from individuals do not fall into two or more distinct groups but can lie anywhere within the observed range of scores. Most often, the set of scores obtained on such measures approximate a **normal distribution,** meaning that most scores fall near the middle of the range and the frequency tapers off toward the two extremes (see Figure 3.9). Measures of aggressiveness in mice, of maze learning in rats, and of conscientiousness in people are just a few of the behavioral measures that are consistently found to fit a normal distribution.

Characteristics that vary in a continuous way are generally affected by many genes and are therefore called **polygenic characteristics** (the prefix *poly-* means "many"). Of course, these traits are also influenced by variation in the environment, so the variability observed in a graph such as Figure 3.9 results from a combination

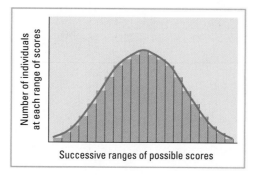

**| FIGURE 3.9 |** Normal distribution When many individuals are tested for a polygenic characteristic, the majority usually fall in the middle of the range of scores and the frequency tapers off toward zero at the extremes. Mathematically, this defines a normal curve. (For a more complete description, see the Statistical Appendix at the end of the book.)

of genetic differences at many gene loci and environmental differences. In animals it is possible to study the role of genes in polygenic traits through the procedure of selective breeding.

## Selective Breeding for Behavioral Characteristics in Animals

To the degree that individuals within a species differ in any measurable character-istic because of differences in their genes, that characteristic can be modified over successive generations through *selective breeding.* This procedure involves the mating of individuals that lie toward the desired extreme on the measure in ques-tion. For single-gene characteristics the effects of selective breeding are immediate, but for polygenic characteristics the effects are gradual and cumulative over generations.

The basic procedure of selective breeding is by no means new. For thousands of years before a formal science of genetics existed, plant and animal breeders used selective breeding to produce new and better strains of every sort of domesticated species. Grains were bred for plumper seeds; cows, for docility and greater milk production; horses, along separate lines for working and racing; canaries, for their song; and dogs, along dozens of different lines for such varied purposes as following a trail, herding sheep (running around them instead of at them), and being gentle playmates for children. The procedure in every case was essentially the same: The members of each generation that best approximated the desired type were mated to produce the next generation, resulting in a continuous genetic molding toward the varieties we see today.

Under controlled laboratory conditions, researchers have used selective breeding to produce many behaviorally specialized strains of animals. Fruit flies have been bred to move instinctively either toward or away from a source of light, mice to be either more or less inclined to fight, and rats to either prefer or not prefer alcohol over water (Crabbe & others, 1999a; Wimer & Wimer, 1985). That selective breeding can influence es-sentially any behavioral trait should come as no surprise. It follows logically from the fact that all behaviors depend on particular sensory, motor, and neural struc-tures, all of which are built from proteins whose production depends on genes.

## Selective Breeding for Maze Learning: Tryon's Classic Research

The first long-term, systematic study of selective breeding in psychology was begun in the 1920s by Robert Tryon (1942), partly in reaction to the belief then held by some psychologists that individual differences in behavior are due entirely to environmental, not at all to genetic, differences. Tryon wanted to demonstrate that a type of behavior frequently studied by psychologists could be strongly influ-enced by variation in genes.

Tryon began by testing a genetically diverse group of rats for their ability to learn a particular maze. Then he mated the males and females that had made the fewest errors in the maze to begin what he called the "maze bright" strain and those that had made the most errors to begin the "maze dull" strain. When the offspring of succeeding generations reached adulthood, he tested them in the same maze and mated the best-performing members of the bright strain, and the worst-performing members of the dull strain, to continue the two lines.

Some of his results are shown in Figure 3.10 on the next page. As you can see, with each generation the two strains became increasingly distinct, until by the sev-enth there was almost no overlap between them. Almost all seventh-generation bright rats made fewer errors in the maze than even the best dull rats. To control for the possibility that the offspring were somehow learning to be bright or dull from their mothers, Tryon cross-fostered the rats so that some of the offspring from each strain were raised by mothers in the other strain. He found that rats in the bright strain were equally good in the maze, and those in the dull strain equally poor, regardless of which mothers raised them.

>>> ———————————— **12**

How are the characteristics of animals shaped through selective breeding?

**A fox bred for tameness** Since 1959, researchers in Russia have been selec-tively breeding silver foxes for tame-ness. At each generation, only those foxes that show the least fear and aggression and the most affection to humans have been bred. The result, after 30 to 35 generations, is a breed of foxes that are as friendly to humans as are dogs (Trut, 1999).

>>> ———————————— **13**

How did Tryon produce "maze bright" and "maze dull" strains of rats? How did he show that the difference was the result of genes, not rearing?

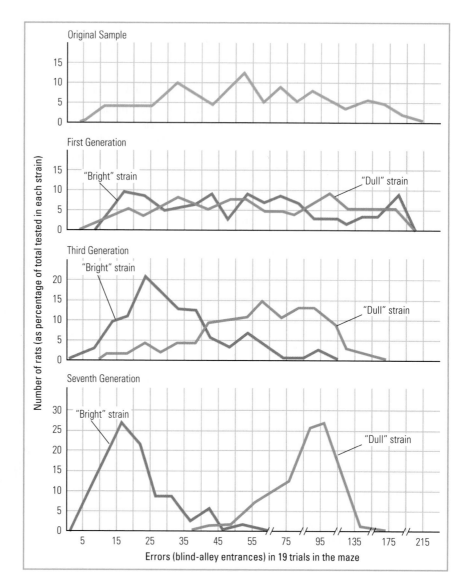

| FIGURE 3.10 | Selective breeding for "maze brightness" and "maze dullness" in rats The top graph shows, for the original parent stock, the distribution of rats according to the number of errors they made in the maze. Subsequent graphs show this distribution for the "bright" and "dull" rats. With successive generations, an increasing percentage in the "bright" strain made few errors and an increasing percentage in the "dull" strain made many errors. (From Tryon, 1942.)

**14**

Why is the strain difference produced by Tryon not properly characterized in terms of "brightness" or "dullness"?

<<< Once a strain has been bred to show some behavioral characteristic, the question arises as to what other behavioral or physiological changes accompany it. Tryon referred to his two strains of rats as "bright" and "dull," but all he had measured was their performance in a particular type of maze. Performance in the maze no doubt depended on many sensory, motor, motivational, and learning processes, and specific changes in any of them could in theory have mediated the effects that Tryon observed. In theory, Tryon's "dull" rats could simply have been those that had less acute vision, or were less interested in the variety of food used as a reward, or were more interested in exploring the maze's blind alleys.

In later studies, another researcher found that Tryon's "dull" rats were as good as the "bright" ones, and sometimes even better, at other learning tasks (Searle, 1949). We do not know what underlying abilities or dispositions changed in Tryon's two strains of rats to produce their difference in maze performance, but the change was apparently not one of general learning ability. This problem still occurs in modern behavioral genetics research, in which new strains of animals (usually mice) are created by adding, deleting, or modifying known genes using sophisticated genetic-engineering methods. The behavioral differences between two strains found in one laboratory often fail to occur in another laboratory, apparently because of subtle differences in the way the animals are housed or tested (Cabib & others, 2000; Crabbe & others, 1999b).

## Polygenic Behavioral Characteristics in Humans

Most of the measures of human traits that interest psychologists—such as scores on personality tests—are continuous and normally distributed, and are affected by many genes as well as by environmental variables. Some psychologists are interested in the degree to which the differences in such scores, for a particular group of people, are the result of differences in their genes or differences in their environmental experiences. Of course, psychologists can't perform selective breeding studies with humans, but they have developed other methods to estimate that degree. Those methods involve comparing the average difference in test scores for people who are closely related to one another with that for people who are less closely related, using people who are chosen in such a way that the environments of the closely related people are no more similar to one another than are those of the less closely related people. Comparisons of identical twins with fraternal twins, and of biologically related siblings with adoptive siblings, have proven particularly useful. In Chapters 10, 15, and 16 you will read about such methods as they apply, respectively, to intelligence tests, personality tests, and predisposition to various mental disorders.

### SECTION REVIEW

---

**Hereditary effects on behavioral traits can involve just one gene, but usually involve many.**

| Single-Gene Traits | Polygenic Traits |
|---|---|
| • Single-gene traits (controlled by one pair of genes) are categorical (all or none) in nature. | • Polygenic traits (influenced by many gene pairs) are continuous (present in varying degrees) and often fit a normal distribution. |
| • Mendelian patterns of inheritance indicate single-gene control. | • Through selective breeding, a trait can be strengthened or weakened gradually over generations. |
| • Examples are breed differences in fearfulness in dogs and a language disorder in the KE family. General lessons concerning inheritance are illustrated with each example. | • An example is Tryon's breeding of rats for maze ability, which illustrates certain general lessons. |

---

# Evolution by Natural Selection

## Darwin's Insight: Selective Breeding Occurs in Nature

The idea that plants and animals can be modified by selective breeding was understood long before Darwin was born. In the first chapter of *On the Origin of Species*, Darwin (1859/1963) referred to such human-controlled selective breeding as ***artificial selection,*** and he reminded readers of the enormously diverse varieties of plants and animals that had been produced through that procedure. He then pointed out—and this was his true, original insight—that breeding in nature is also selective and can also produce changes in living things over generations.

>>> ———————————— 15

What insight led Darwin to his theory of evolution? How is natural selection similar to and different from artificial selection?

Selective breeding in nature, which Darwin labeled ***natural selection,*** is dictated not by the needs and whims of humans but by the obstacles to reproduction that are imposed by the natural environment. Those obstacles include predators, limited food supplies, extremes of temperature, difficulty in finding and attracting mates for sexual reproduction—anything that can cut life short or otherwise prevent an organism from producing offspring. Animals and plants that have characteristics that help them overcome such obstacles are, by definition, more likely to have offspring than those that don't have these characteristics.

Darwin's essential point was this: Individuals of a species vary in the number of offspring they produce. Some produce none, because they die early or fail to mate,

**NON SEQUITUR** by Wiley

HOW NATURAL SELECTION REALLY WORKS...

WELL, I'M NOT MOVING UNTIL SOMEONE CAN EXPLAIN WHY *WE* SHOULD RUN WHEN WE HAVE HIM OUT-NUMBERED..

Non Sequitur by Wiley
© 1997 Washington Post Writers Group

and others produce many. Any inherited trait that increases the number of off-spring that an individual produces is automatically "selected for," as the trait is passed on to those offspring. Conversely, any inherited trait that decreases the number of one's offspring is automatically "selected against," appearing in fewer members of the next generation. Thus, as long as inheritable differences exist among individuals in an interbreeding population, and as long as some of those differences affect survival and reproduction, evolution will occur.

## Genetic Diversity Provides the Fodder for Natural Selection

<<< Darwin knew nothing of genes. He realized that something, passed along through eggs and sperm, must provide the hereditary foundation for evolution, but he did not know what. Mendel's work, which was the first step toward our modern knowledge of genes, was unknown to most scientists until about 1900. Today we know that genes are the units of heredity and that evolution entails changes, from generation to generation, in the frequencies of particular genes in an interbreeding population. Genes that improve an individual's ability to survive and reproduce in the existing environment increase from generation to generation, and genes that impede this ability decrease from generation to generation.

The genetic variability on which natural selection acts has two main sources: (1) the reshuffling of genes that occurs in sexual reproduction (already discussed) and (2) mutations.

*Mutations* are errors that occasionally and unpredictably occur during DNA replication, causing the "replica" to be not quite identical to the original. In the long run of evolution, mutation is the ultimate source of all genetic variation. As would be expected of any random change in a complex, organized structure, new mutations are more often harmful than helpful, and natural selection usually weeds them out. But occasionally a mutation is useful, producing a protein that affects the organism's development in a way that increases its ability to reproduce. Because of its effect on reproduction, the gene arising from such a mutation increases in frequency from generation to generation. At the level of the gene, that is evolution.

Prior to the modern understanding of genes, many people believed that changes in an individual that stem from practice or experience could be inherited and therefore provide a basis for evolution. For example, some argued that early giraffes, by frequently stretching their necks to reach leaves in trees, slightly elongated their necks in the course of their lives and that this change was passed on to their offspring, resulting, over many generations, in the long-necked giraffes we see today. That idea, referred to as the *inheritance of acquired characteristics,* is most often attributed to Jean-Baptiste de Lamarck (1744–1829), although many other evolutionists, both before and after Lamarck, held the same view (Futuyma, 1997). Even Darwin did not reject that idea but added to it the concepts of random variation and natural selection.

Now, however, we know that evolution is based entirely on genetic changes and that no amount of practice or experience can change one's genes in a way that affects the next generation. Random change in genes followed by natural selection, not directed change stemming from individual experience, provides the basis for evolution.

**16**

How are genes involved in evolution? What are the sources of genetic diversity on which natural selection acts?

## Environmental Change Provides the Force for Natural Selection

Evolution is spurred by changes in the environment. If the environment were completely stable, organisms would adapt as fully as possible and change little or not at all thereafter. But the environment keeps changing. Climates change, sources of food change, predators change, and so on. When the conditions of life change, what was previously a useful characteristic may become harmful, and vice versa.

Darwin believed that evolution was a slow and steady process. But today we know that it can occur rapidly, slowly, or almost not at all, depending on the rate and nature of environmental change and on the degree to which genetic variability already exists in a population (Gould & Eldredge, 1993). Environmental change spurs evolution *not* by causing the appropriate mutations to occur but by promoting natural selection. Some mutations that previously would not have been advantageous, and would have been weeded out by natural selection, are advantageous in the new environment, so they are passed along in increasing numbers from generation to generation. Evolution sometimes occurs so quickly that people can see it happen. In fact, scientists since Darwin's time have reported more than a hundred cases of observed evolution (Endler, 1986; Weiner, 1994).

One of the most well-documented examples of observed evolution comes from the work of Peter and Rosemary Grant, who for 30 years studied a species of finch that inhabits one of the Galápagos Islands, about 600 miles off the coast of Ecuador (Grant, 1991; Weiner, 1994). The Grants found that the members of this species differ somewhat in body size, that the variation is inheritable, and that environmental changes sometimes result in selection for large size and other times for small size. During years of drought, when most of the finches died because the plants that produce the seeds they eat failed to grow, the birds that survived and produced offspring tended to be the larger ones, apparently because their beaks were thick and powerful enough to crack open the large, hard-shelled seeds that were last to be consumed (see Figure 3.11). During rainy years, when an abundance of seeds caused a population explosion among the finches, the smaller birds did better. Apparently, in those conditions, their young could grow to full size and reproduce more quickly than the young of the larger finches.

The evolution of simple or small changes, such as in skin pigmentation or in body size, can occur in a few generations when selection conditions are strong, but more complex changes require much more time. The difference between, say, a chimpanzee brain and a human brain could not have come about in a few generations, as it must have involved many mutations, each of which would have promoted a slight selective advantage to the chimpanzee (in its environment) or to the human (in our environment). When evolutionists talk about "rapid" evolution of complex changes, they are usually talking about periods measured in hundreds of thousands of years (Gould & Eldredge, 1993).

>>> ———————————— **17**

How does change in the environment affect the direction and speed of evolution? How did a study of finches illustrate the role of environmental change in evolution?

*Natural History Magazine*

**❘ FIGURE 3.11 ❘** Rapid evolution
During years of drought, natural selection quickly produces the larger body size and the thicker beak, shown at right, in the finches studied by Peter and Rosemary Grant.

## Evolution Has No Foresight

People sometimes mistakenly think of evolution as a mystical force working toward a predetermined end. One manifestation of this belief is the idea that evolution could produce changes for some future purpose, even though they are useless or harmful at the time that the change occurs. But evolution has no foresight. The finches studied by the Grants could not have evolved thicker beaks in anticipation of drought. Only genetic changes that increase survival and reproduction in the immediate environment can proliferate through natural selection.

Another manifestation of the belief in foresight is the idea that present-day organisms can be ranked according to the distance they have moved along a set evolutionary route, toward some planned end (Gee, 2002). For example, some may think of humans as the "most evolved" creatures, with chimpanzees next and amoebas way down on the list. But evolution has no set route or planned end. Humans, chimps, and amoebas have taken their different forms and behavioral

>>> ———————————— **18**

What are three mistaken beliefs about evolution, all related to the misconception that foresight is involved?

characteristics because of chance events that led them to occupy different niches in the environment, where the selection criteria differed. The present-day amoeba is not an early step toward humans but a creature that is at least as well adapted to its environment as we are to ours. The amoeba has no more chance of evolving to become like us than we have of evolving to become like it.

A third manifestation of the belief in foresight is the idea that natural selection is a moral force, that its operation and its products are in some sense right or good. In everyday talk, people sometimes imply that whatever is natural (including natural selection) is good and that evil stems from society or human contrivances that go beyond nature. But nature is neither good nor bad, moral nor immoral. To say that natural selection led to such and such a characteristic does not lend any moral virtue to that characteristic. As you will see, fighting is as much a product of evolution as is cooperation, but that is no reason to consider them morally equivalent.

## SECTION REVIEW

### Natural selection is the mechanism that produces evolutionary change.

| How Natural Selection Works | Role of Environmental Change | Evolution Lacks Foresight |
|---|---|---|
| • To the degree that a trait enhances survival and reproduction, genes producing that trait are passed on to offspring. The result is that such genes become more frequent over generations. | • The rate and nature of environmental change affect the rate and course of evolution. An example is the effect of drought on the evolution of beak thickness in finches. | • Natural selection can only lead to changes that are immediately adaptive; it cannot anticipate future needs. |
| • Mutations and reshuffling of genes in sexual reproduction provide genetic diversity on which natural selection operates. | • Complex changes, requiring many mutations, require a long time to evolve. | • There is no preset pathway for evolution.<br><br>• Natural selection is not a moral force. |

# Natural Selection as a Foundation for Functionalism

19
How does an understanding of evolution provide a basis for functionalism in psychology?

<<< The mechanisms underlying behavior are products of natural selection, and, like all products of natural selection, they came about because they promoted survival and reproduction. Just as Tryon, through artificial selection, bred rats to be better at learning a particular maze, natural selection automatically breeds animals to be better at doing what they must to survive and reproduce in their natural environments. This idea provides a foundation for the psychological approach known as *functionalism*—the attempt to explain behavior in terms of what it accomplishes for the behaving individual.

When applied to understanding the behavioral traits of a species, the functionalist approach in psychology is essentially the same as the functionalist approach in anatomy: Why do giraffes have long necks? Why do humans lack fur? Why do male songbirds sing in the spring? Why do humans have such an irrepressible ability to learn language? The anatomist trying to answer the first two questions, and the behavioral researcher or psychologist trying to answer the latter two, would look for ways by which each trait helped ancestral members of the species to survive and reproduce.

## Ultimate and Proximate Explanations of Behavior

Biologists and psychologists who think in evolutionary terms find it useful to distinguish between two kinds of explanations of behavior—ultimate and proximate:

- *Ultimate explanations* are functional explanations at the evolutionary level. In
other words, they are statements of the role that the behavior plays in the animal's survival and reproduction. Viewed from the vantage point of the gene, they are statements of how the behavior helps the individual's genes make it into the next generation.

- *Proximate explanations* are explanations that deal not with function but with mechanism; they are statements of the immediate conditions, both inside and outside the animal, that bring on the behavior.

**20**

How are ultimate explanations of behavior different from, but complementary to, proximate explanations?

## Illustration of the Complementarity of Ultimate and Proximate Explanations

As an illustration of these two modes of explanation, consider how they might be applied to the question of why male songbirds (of many species) sing in the spring. An *ultimate explanation* goes something like this (Koodsma & Byers, 1991): Over the course of evolution, songbirds have adapted to a mating system that takes place in the spring. The male's song serves to attract a female with which to mate and to warn other males to stay away from the singer's territory in order to avoid a fight. In the evolution of these birds, males whose genes promoted such singing produced more offspring (more copies of their genes) than did males whose genes failed to promote such singing.

A *proximate explanation,* in contrast, might go as follows (Ball & Hulse, 1998): The increased period of daylight in the spring triggers, through the birds' visual system, a physiological mechanism that leads to the increased production of the sex hormone testosterone, which in turn acts on certain areas of the brain (which we might call the "song areas"), promoting the drive to sing. Notice the complementary nature of these explanations. The ultimate explanation states the survival or reproductive value of the behavior, and the proximate explanation states the stimuli and physiological mechanisms through which the behavior occurs.

**A yellow-throated western blackbird at home** This male's singing warns other males of the species to stay away.

## The Search for Ultimate Explanations in Human Psychology

All of the complex biological mechanisms underlying human behavior and experience—including the basic mechanisms of perception, learning, memory, thought, motivation, and emotion—are products of evolution by natural selection. They all came about because each small step in their evolution tended to promote the survival and reproduction of our ancestors. Thus for any basic psychological characteristic that is part of human nature—for any basic drive or emotion, for example—it is legitimate to ask: How did this characteristic improve the survival and reproductive chances of our ancestors? How did it help our ancestors get their genes into the next generation?

The ultimate explanations of some human traits (especially those that we share with all other mammals) are relatively obvious. We have strong drives to breathe air, drink fluids, and consume foods because our bodies need these things to remain alive. We have strong drives to copulate, under certain conditions, because that is the means by which our genes get from one generation to the next. Individuals who lacked such drives are ancestors to nobody today; their genes died out. The ultimate explanations of some other human traits, however, are not so obvious. It is not obvious, for example, why humans everywhere tend to sleep about eight hours each night (discussed in Chapter 6), or why humans everywhere under certain conditions experience the painful emotion of guilt (discussed in Chapter 14). In various places in this book, including in the last sections of this chapter, you will encounter examples of ultimate explanations that are not intuitively obvious but are supported by research evidence. As you will see, evidence for or against any particular ultimate explanation can come from detailed analysis of the behavior or trait in question, from cross-species comparisons, and sometimes from studies showing what happens when the behavior or trait is missing.

## Limitations on Functionalist Thinking

**21**

What are four reasons for the existence of traits or behaviors that do not serve survival and reproductive functions?

<<< Before we go deeper into discussions of ultimate functions, it is useful to know something about the limitations of functionalist thinking. It is not the case that every detail of every trait serves a useful function, and some traits that were once functional may not be so today. Here are four reasons why a particular trait or behavior may not be functional.

### Some Traits Are Vestigial

Some traits that evolved to serve the needs of our ancestors are no longer functional today, yet they remain. These remnants of our past are called **vestigial characteristics.** As an example, consider the *grasp reflex* by which newborn infants close their fingers tightly around objects in their hands. This reflex may well be useful today in the development of the infant's ability to hold and manipulate objects, but that does not explain why prematurely born infants grasp so strongly that they can support their own weight, why they grasp with their toes as well as their hands (see Figure 3.12), and why the best stimulus for eliciting the response is a clump of hair (Eibl-Eibesfeldt, 1975). These aspects of the reflex make more sense when we observe them in other primates. To survive, infant monkeys and apes cling tightly with hands and feet to their mother's fur while she swings in trees or goes about her other daily business. In the course of our evolution from ape-like ancestors, we lost our fur, so our infants can no linger cling to us in this way, but the reflex remains.

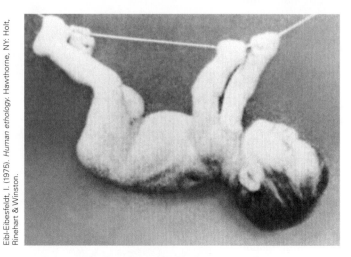

Eibl-Eibesfeldt, I. (1975). *Human ethology.* Hawthorne, NY: Holt, Rinehart & Winston.

**I FIGURE 3.12 I** Premature infant clinging with hands and toes This ability may be a vestigial carryover from an earlier evolutionary time, when the infants of our ancestors clung to their parents' fur.

The concept of vestigial traits becomes especially relevant to psychologists when applied to our inherited drives, or motives. Because of culture, our habitats and lifestyles have changed dramatically in just a few centuries, a speck on the evolutionary time scale. Essentially all of our evolution as a species occurred in conditions that were quite different from those present today, and some of our inherited tendencies may be harmful, rather than helpful, in the habitat that we occupy today. An example is our great appetite for sugar. In the world of our ancestors, sugar was a rare and valuable commodity. It existed primarily in fruits and provided energy needed for life in the wild, as we can see by looking at the diets of present-day monkeys and apes. But today sugar is readily available in most areas of the world, and life (for many of us) is less physically strenuous. Yet our preference for sugar persists as strong as ever, despite such negative consequences as tooth decay and obesity.

### Some Traits Are Side Effects of Natural Selection for Other Traits

Useless changes can come about in evolution as by-products of natural selection for other, useful changes. A simple example, in humans, is the belly button (suggested by Buss & others, 1998). To the best of anybody's knowledge, the belly button serves no function related to survival or reproduction. It is simply a remnant left from the umbilical cord. The umbilical cord, of course, does serve a survival and reproductive function, that of conveying nutrients from the mother to the developing fetus. An anatomist from Mars who observed belly buttons on adult earthlings, but who never observed a fetus or the birth process, would be at a loss to explain why such a structure would have evolved.

It seems quite possible that some human psychological capacities, even some that are so general that we would consider them to be part of human nature, came about as side effects of the evolution of other capacities. It is reasonable to ask, for example, whether the universal human proclivities for art and music are direct effects of natural selection or side effects. Perhaps these proclivities served to attract mates during much of our evolutionary history (as they seem to today), and were therefore selected for directly, much as song was selected for in birds. It is also possible, however, that they emerged simply as by-products of selection for other proclivities, such as those for planning, constructing tools, and communicating through language. A third possibility, combining the first two, is that proclivities for art and music may have initially emerged as by-products and then been selected for because of their usefulness for attracting mates or other helpers. At present, we do not have evidence to support strongly any of these theories over the others.

## Some Traits Result Simply from Chance

Some inheritable characteristics that result from just one or two mutations are inconsequential for survival and reproduction. Different races of people have somewhat differently shaped noses. *Maybe* that variation is caused by natural selection. Perhaps one shape worked best in one climate and another worked best in another climate, so natural selection molded the noses differently. But we can't automatically assume that. The different shapes might be a result of mutations that didn't matter and therefore were never weeded out by natural selection. Maybe the small group of people who migrated to a specific part of the world, and who were the ancestors of a particular racial group, just happened to carry along genes for a nose shape that was different from the average for the group they left. Such variation, due to chance alone without selection, is referred to as *genetic drift*.

Many years ago, researchers discovered that the incidence of schizophrenia (a serious mental disorder, discussed in Chapter 16) is three times greater among people living in northern Sweden, above the Arctic Circle, than among people in most other parts of the world (Huxley & others, 1964). There are at least three possible explanations of this observation: (a) Environmental conditions, such as the harsh climate or the isolation it produces, might tend to bring on schizophrenia in people who are prone to it. (b) Natural selection might have increased the frequency of schizophrenia-promoting genes among these people, perhaps because such genes help protect people from harmful effects of physical stressors such as cold climate. (This was the hypothesis suggested by Huxley and his colleagues.) (c) The Arctic population may have been founded by a small group of Swedish migrants who, just by chance, had a higher proportion of schizophrenia-promoting genes than the population at large. This last possibility (also mentioned by Huxley and his colleagues) would be an example of genetic drift. To this day, scientists do not know which of these theories is correct.

## Evolved Mechanisms Cannot Deal Effectively with Every Situation

Our basic drives, emotions, and other behavioral tendencies came about in evolution because, on balance, they promoted survival and reproduction more often than they interfered with survival and reproduction. That does not mean, however, that every instance of activation of such a drive, emotion, or tendency serves survival or reproductive ends. In Chapter 14 I will present evidence that the emotion of guilt serves the ultimate function of helping us to preserve our relationships with people whose help we need for survival and reproduction. When we hurt someone on whom we depend, we feel guilty, which motivates us to make amends and patch up the relationship. That does not mean, however, that every manifestation of guilt in every person serves that function. Sometimes guilt can be crippling; sometimes our capacity for guilt is exploited by others for their ends at the expense of ours. The best that natural selection could do was to develop a guilt mechanism that is triggered by certain general conditions. It could not build a mechanism capable of distinguishing every possible condition from every other and triggering guilt only when it is useful, never when it is harmful. The same is true for all of our other evolved emotions and drives (and that is why we have psychotherapists).

## SECTION REVIEW

**The concept of natural selection provides a secure footing for functionalism.**

| The Functionalist Approach | Limitations of Functionalism |
|---|---|
| • Functionalism is an approach to psychology that focuses on the usefulness of a particular behavior to the individual engaging in it. | • Some traits are vestigial; they once served a function but no longer do. |
| • Ultimate explanations are functional explanations, stating the role that specific behaviors play in survival and reproduction. | • Some traits are side effects of other traits that arose through natural selection. |
| • Proximate explanations are complementary to ultimate explanations; they are concerned with mechanisms that bring about behavior. | • Some traits that require few mutations are products just of chance, not natural selection. |
| | • Even evolved mechanisms, such as that for guilt, are not useful in every situation in which they are active. |

# Natural Selection as a Foundation for Understanding Species-Typical Behaviors

Suppose you saw an animal that looked exactly like a dog, but it went "meow," climbed trees, and ignored the mail carrier. Would you call it a dog or a cat? Clearly, we identify animals as much by their behavior as by their anatomy. Every species of animal has certain characteristic ways of behaving. These are commonly called *instincts,* but a more technical term for them is ***species-typical behaviors.*** Meowing, tree climbing, and acting aloof are species-typical behaviors of cats. Dam building is species-typical of beavers. Smiling, talking, and two-legged walking are species-typical of humans.

## Species-Typical Behaviors in Humans

Species-typical behaviors are products of evolution, but that does not mean that they are necessarily rigid in form or uninfluenced by learning. To understand more fully the concept of species-typical behaviors, let us examine some examples in humans.

### Human Emotional Expressions as Examples of Species-Typical Behaviors

**22**

What evidence supports the idea that many human emotional expressions are examples of species-typical behaviors?

<<< Darwin noted that humans, like other animals, automatically communicate moods and behavioral intentions to one another through body postures, movements, and facial expressions. In his book *The Expression of the Emotions in Man and Animals,* Darwin (1872/1965) argued that specific facial expressions accompany specific emotional states in humans and that these expressions are universal, occurring in people throughout the world and even in people who were born blind and thus could not have learned them through observation.

In an extension of Darwin's pioneering work, Paul Ekman and Wallace Friesen (1975, 1982) developed an atlas that describes and depicts the exact facial-muscle movements that make up each of six basic emotional expressions in people: surprise, fear, disgust, anger, happiness, and sadness (see Figure 3.13). They then showed photographs of each expression to individuals in many different cultures—including members of a preliterate tribe in the highlands of New Guinea who had little previous contact with other cultures—and found that people in every culture described each depicted emotion in a way that was consistent with descriptions in the United States (Ekman, 1973; Ekman & others, 1987). In a reversal of this proce-

Elkman, P. & Friesen, W. (1975). *Unmasking the face.* Englewood Cliffs, NJ: Prentice Hall.

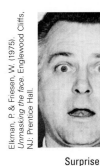
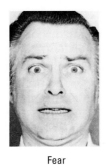

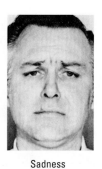

| Surprise | Fear | Disgust | Anger | Happiness | Sadness |

**I FIGURE 3.13 I** Six basic human emotional expressions
These expressions, taken from Ekman and Friesen's atlas of emotional expressions, were produced by a model who was asked to move specific facial muscles in specific ways. As you study each figure, try to describe the positions of the facial features for each expression. For example, surprise can be described as follows: The brows are pulled upward, producing horizontal wrinkles across the forehead; the eyes are opened wide, revealing white above the iris; and the lower jaw is dropped, with no tension around the mouth.

dure, they also photographed members of the New Guinea tribe who had been asked to act out various emotions and showed the photographs to college students in the United States. The college students were quite accurate in labeling the emotions portrayed by the New Guineans.

In a further extension of Darwin's work, Irenäus Eibl-Eibesfeldt documented the cross-cultural universality of many nonverbal signals, including one that he labeled the *eyebrow flash,* a momentary raising of the eyebrows lasting about one-sixth of a second, usually accompanied by a smile and an upward nod of the head (see Figure 3.14). He observed this expression in every culture he studied—including those in New Guinea, Samoa, and various parts of Africa, Asia, South America, and Europe—and concluded that it is a universal sign of greeting among friends (Eibl-Eibesfeldt, 1989). Raised eyebrows are also a component of the emotional expression of surprise (look at Figure 3.13 again), so the eyebrow flash with its accompanying smile might be interpreted as a nonverbal way of saying, "What a happy surprise to see you."

Eibl-Eibesfeldt (1975) also filmed children who were born blind, or both blind and deaf, and found that they manifest emotions in the same basic ways as sighted children do (see Figure 3.15 on the next page). Such observations provide the most direct evidence that at least some human expressions do not have to be learned through observing them in others or hearing descriptions of them.

Taking all the evidence together, there can be little doubt that we are biologically predisposed to express certain emotions in certain species-typical ways. It is also clear, however, that we can control and modify our emotional expressions and

>>> ——————— 23
How do human emotional expressions illustrate the point that species-typical behaviors can be modified by learning?

(a)    (b)

Eibl-Eibesfeldt, I. (1989). *Human ethology.* Hawthorne, NY: Walter de Gruyter, Inc.

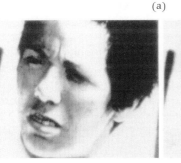

**I FIGURE 3.14 I** The eyebrow flash This universal signal of greeting is shown in adjacent frames from films of (a) a French woman and (b) a Yanomami man (of the Brazil-Venezuela border).

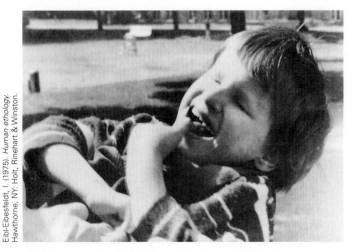

Eibl-Eibesfeldt, I. (1975). *Human ethology.* Hawthorne, NY: Holt, Rinehart & Winston.

| FIGURE 3.15 | Some emotional expressions need not be learned through observation This young girl, manifesting joy, has been blind and deaf since birth.

learn new ones. Even researchers who focus on universal expressions are quick to point out cross-cultural differences. For example, Eibl-Eibesfeldt (1975) found that despite its cross-cultural similarity in form and general meaning, large cultural differences exist in the use of the eyebrow flash. The Japanese, who are reserved in social expressions among adults, use it mainly when greeting young children, whereas Samoans, at the other extreme, greet nearly everyone in this way. More recently, Hillary Elfenbein and Nalini Ambady (2002, 2003) have shown that cultural dialects occur in the emotional expressions that Ekman and Friesen included in their atlas. In general, people can identify each emotion more easily and accurately when it is expressed by other members of their own culture than when it is expressed by members of a very different culture.

## The Role of Learning in the Development of Species-Typical Behaviors

To say that a behavior is instinctive, or species-typical, is not to say that it is unaffected by learning. As I just pointed out, our basic emotional expressions are species-typical, but cultural differences among them are learned. The role of learning is even more obvious in two of our most characteristic species-specific behaviors—our manner of walking and our use of language.

**24**

How is the point that species-typical behaviors may depend on learning illustrated by the examples of two-legged walking and language in humans, and singing in white-crowned sparrows?

<<< A scientist from Mars would almost certainly point to two-legged walking and use of a grammar-based language as being among the defining behavioral characteristics of the human species. These characterize humans everywhere and clearly depend on inherited predispositions, yet their development also clearly depends on learning. During the peak months of learning to walk (generally during the second year of life), infants spend an average of about six hours per day practicing balancing and walking and, on a typical day, take about 9,000 walking steps and travel the length of 29 football fields (Adolph & others, 2003). By the time they are proficient walkers, they have spent thousands of hours practicing, on their own initiative. During those same months, infants also, on their own initiative, intensely practice talking. With language, infants do not just learn the motor coordination needed to produce the sounds, but they also, and more amazingly, learn the basic vocabulary and grammar of the language that they hear around them (to be discussed in Chapter 11). Two-legged walking and talking are species-typical behaviors in humans, but a human raised in an environment where either of these capacities was impossible to practice would not develop that capacity. Such an inhuman environment would not produce a normal human being.

Learning plays crucial roles in the development of species-specific behaviors in other animals as well. For example, white-crowned sparrows develop the ability to sing their species-typical song only if they are permitted to hear it during the first summer after hatching (Marler, 1970). Indeed, populations of the species living in different areas have somewhat different dialects, and a white-crowned sparrow learns to sing the dialect of the adult that it hears (usually its father). Yet the range of possible songs that the birds can learn is limited by their biology. No matter what environmental experiences it has, a white-crowned sparrow cannot learn to sing like a canary or like any species other than a white-crowned sparrow. In Chapter 4 you will encounter other examples of species-typical behaviors that require specific learning experiences to develop normally.

## Biological Preparedness as the Basis for Species-Typical Behaviors

**25**

How is the concept of biological preparedness related to that of species-typical behavior? How is biological preparedness illustrated with the examples of human walking and talking?

The difference between behaviors that we call instinctive, or species typical, and those that we do not so label has to do with the degree of *biological preparedness*. <<< Evolution has equipped each species with anatomical structures, in the brain and

**Biological preparedness** Infants are born with a "stepping reflex," which shows that they have, inborn, the neural mechanisms for two-legged walking. Perfecting that behavior, however, requires extensive practice, during the toddling stage, when the legs have become strong enough to support the child's weight.

elsewhere, that operate to ensure that normal individuals of the species, raised in a normal environment for that species, will be physically able to perform the species-typical behaviors and will be motivated to learn what they must for adequate performance.

Human beings clearly come into the world biologically prepared to learn to walk on two legs. Evolution has provided us with anatomical features—such as strong hindlimbs with feet, weaker forelimbs without feet, an upwardly tilted pelvis, and a short, stiff neck—that combine to make it more convenient for us to walk upright than on all fours. Moreover, we are born with neural systems in the brain and spinal cord that enable us to move our legs correctly for coordinated two-legged walking and with neural structures that motivate us to practice this behavior at the appropriate stage in our development. Consider the difference between two-legged walking in humans and in dogs. Dogs are capable of learning to walk on two legs, and much is made of that fact by circus trainers, but they are never very good at it. They do not have the appropriate muscular and skeletal systems to co-ordinate the behavior properly, and they have no natural impulse to walk in this manner. A dog, unlike a human child, will practice two-legged walking only if it re-ceives immediate rewards, such as food, for doing so. Thus two-legged walking is not a species-typical behavior in dogs.

The same is true for talking. Humans are born with anatomical structures, in-cluding a tongue and larynx, that can produce a wide range of sounds and with a brain that has special neural centers for understanding and producing language (discussed in Chapter 5). Infants begin talking at a certain stage even if they re-ceive little encouragement from those around them. Chimpanzees can be taught to simulate some aspects of human language, just as dogs can be taught to walk on their hind legs, but they require lots of encouragement and are never very good at it (discussed in Chapter 11).

## The Relative Nature of the Concept of Species-Typical Behavior

Having characterized the concept of species-typical behavior in terms of biological preparedness, I must now add that the concept is relative rather than absolute. No behavior stems just from biological preparation; some sort of experience with the environment is always involved. Conversely, any behavior that an animal can produce—no matter how artificial it may seem or how much training is required—must make use of the animal's inherited biological capacities. The concept of

>>> ————————— **26**

Why is the concept of species-typical behavior relative rather than absolute?

species-typical behavior is useful as long as we accept it as relative and do not argue about whether one or another behavior really should or should not be called species-typical. *Big* and *little* are useful words in our vocabulary, but there is no point in arguing about whether a breadbox is properly called one or the other. Two-legged walking is more species-typical for humans than for dogs, as a breadbox is bigger than a matchbox.

The question to ask when we study a particular behavior is not, Is this a species-typical behavior? Rather, the meaningful questions are these:

● What are the environmental conditions needed for the full development of this behavior?

● What internal mechanisms are involved in producing this behavior?

● What consequences does this behavior have in the individual's daily life?

● In the course of evolution, why would the genes that make this behavior possible have been favored by natural selection?

These questions can be asked of any behavior, regardless of whether or not it is thought of as species-typical.

## The Value of Cross-Species Comparisons of Species-Typical Behaviors

In psychology as well as biology, scientists have learned a lot about human beings by comparing humans to other animals. The basic rationales for learning about any one species by comparing it with other species are found in the principle of evolution by natural selection.

### Two Forms of Cross-Species Comparison: Homologies and Analogies

27
What is the difference between a homology and an analogy, and how can researchers tell whether a similarity between two species in some trait is one or the other?

<<< An understanding of evolution makes it clear that two conceptually different classes of similarities exist across species: homologies and analogies.

A **homology** is any similarity that exists because of the different species' common ancestry. All animals originated from a common ancestor, so it is not surprising that some homologies—such as those in the basic structure of DNA molecules and of certain enzymes—can be found between any two species. But the more closely related two species are, the more homologies they will show.

An **analogy,** in contrast, is any similarity that stems not from common ancestry but from *convergent evolution*. Convergent evolution occurs when different species, because of some similarity in their habitats or lifestyles, independently evolve a common characteristic.

As an illustration, consider some comparisons among species that can fly. Flying has arisen separately in three taxonomic groups: birds, some insects (such as butterflies), and some mammals (bats). Similarities across these three groups in

| **FIGURE 3.16** | Analogous wings
Similarities in the wings and flying behavior of birds, bats, and butterflies are considered to be analogies, not homologies, because they arose independently in evolution.

Joe McDonald / Earth Scenes / Animals, Animals

M. Tuttle / Photo Researchers

James Carmich / Bruce Coleman

their flying motions, and in the anatomical structures that permit flight, are examples of analogies because they do not result from common ancestry (see Figure 3.16). However, similarities in flight and wings among species within any of these groups, such as between crows and sparrows, are likely to be homologies. The last common ancestor between a crow and a sparrow was itself a bird with wings, but the last common ancestor between a crow and a butterfly, or between a crow and a bat, did not have wings.

Aside from evidence based on knowledge about the degree of relatedness of the compared species, analogies and homologies can often be distinguished by the nature of the observed similarity (Lorenz, 1974). Analogies entail similarity in function and gross form, but not in detail and underlying mechanism. Thus the wings of birds, bats, and butterflies are similar at the functional and gross anatomical level in that they provide broad, flappable surfaces that enable flight; but they are very different from one another in the details of their construction and in the neural and muscular mechanisms that control them. The difference in detail is great because they evolved independently, through different sets of genetic mutations. In contrast, because homologies arise from shared genes, they entail similarities in their underlying construction and physiological mechanisms, even when, because of divergent evolution, large differences have emerged in gross form or function (for example, see Figure 3.17).

## The Value for Psychology of Studying Homologies

Homologies are useful for research on the physiological mechanisms of behavior (that is, research on how the brain and other biological structures operate to produce the behavior being studied). Because convergent evolution can produce similar behaviors that operate through different mechanisms, researchers who seek to understand the physiological mechanism of some behavior in humans through experiments on other species must study species in which the relevant behavior is homologous, not analogous, to that in humans. You will find many examples of such research in Chapters 4 to 8 of this book. Many basic mechanisms of learning, motivation (such as hunger), and sensation (such as vision) are homologous across all or at least most species of mammals, and we have learned much about these by studying them in mice, rats, cats, and other laboratory mammals.

Homologies are also useful for inferring the pathways along which species-typical behaviors evolved. By comparing the different forms of a particular species-typical behavior in closely related species, it is often possible to reconstruct how the more complex of these forms evolved through a series of steps from the simpler form. Darwin (1859/1963) himself used this method to figure out the evolutionary steps through which honeybees acquired their marvelous ability to construct complex hives consisting of wax combs of closely fitting hexagonal cells in which to store honey and larvae (see Figure 3.18 on the next page).

## Homologies as Clues to the Evolutionary Origins of Two Human Smiles

In research that is more directly relevant to psychology, Darwin also used homologies to understand the origins of species-typical emotional expressions in humans. At the London Zoo, he watched monkeys and apes and noted that a number of their expressions seemed to be homologous to human expressions, including the smile (Darwin, 1872/1965). Research following up on Darwin's work has suggested that people may produce two kinds of smiles, which may have separate evolutionary origins.

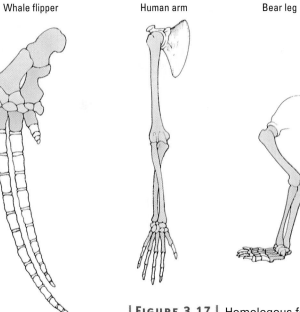

Whale flipper    Human arm    Bear leg

**| FIGURE 3.17 |** Homologous forelimbs Similarities in the forelimbs of different species of mammals are considered to be homologies because they arose from common ancestry. Although the limbs of the whale, human, and bear differ in function and gross structure, they are similar in certain structural details, as is characteristic of homologies. Behaviors, too, can be homologous, and a key to their homology is similarity in mechanism and detail, even when function differs. (Adapted from Lorenz, 1974.)

⟫⟫⟫ ——————————— **28**

How are homologies used for learning about (a) the physiological mechanisms and (b) the evolutionary pathways of species-typical traits?

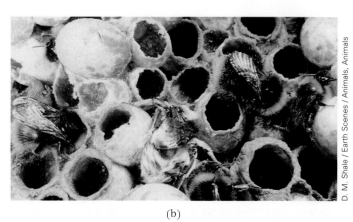

(a)

(b)

**I FIGURE 3.18 I Cells built by honeybees and bumblebees**
Honeybees build hives with hexagonally shaped cells (a), which are the optimal shape for storing large amounts of honey and larvae using the least amount of precious wax. In order to understand how such behavior might have come about through small steps in natural selection, Darwin studied the homologous but simpler storage structures built by related bee species. The simplest, produced by bumblebees (b), consists simply of a cluster of spherical cells, which the bees easily build by sweeping their abdomens compass-like to carve out the spheres. Other species, more closely related to honeybees, build intermediate structures, with spherical cells that intersect and are patched up with flat wax walls at the places of intersection. From such observations, Darwin suggested that ancestors of modern honeybees built their hives in a way similar to that of modern bumblebees but, through evolution, began placing their cells ever closer together and more regularly spaced and patching up the intersections, resulting eventually in the hexagonal cells that honeybees build today.

People smile in two quite different contexts: (1) when genuinely happy and (2) when wishing to show another person that they are favorably disposed toward that person. The latter situation need not entail happiness at all; in fact, people are especially likely to smile at others in potentially tense circumstances, apparently as a means of reducing the tension (Goldenthal & others, 1981). Darwin (1872/1965) pointed out that these two smiles are anatomically distinct. The *happy smile* involves not just the turning up of the corners of the lips but also the pulling in of the skin near the outside corners of the eyes. This creates the creases called crow's feet, which radiate from the eyes and seem to make them sparkle. The other smile, in contrast, typically involves the lips alone, without the eyes. This distinction has been confirmed in many studies with both adults and young children (Ekman, 1992; Sarra & Otta, 2001). In one study, for example, 10-month-old infants smiled with eyes and mouth when approached by their mother (presumably a happy situation) but smiled with mouth alone when approached by a stranger (a possibly tense situation) (Fox & Davidson, 1988).

Ekman (1992) considers the mouth-alone smile to be a derivative of the happy smile. He emphasizes its use in masking one's true feelings and calls it a "false smile." An alternative possibility, supported by research with monkeys and apes, is that the mouth-alone smile is a unique expression—let's call it the *greeting smile*—that arrived through a different evolutionary route from the happy smile (Redican, 1982; van Hooff, 1976).

**29**

How do studies of homologies between humans and other primates support the view that the human greeting smile and the human happy smile have separate evolutionary origins?

<<< **Possible Origin of the Greeting Smile** Nonhuman primates manifest two distinct smile-like displays. The one that seems most clearly to be homologous to the human greeting smile is the *silent bared-teeth display* (see Figure 3.19a). If you have ever watched a cage of macaque monkeys at a zoo, you have almost certainly observed this display, a grimace usually shown by the more submissive of two monkeys as it glances nervously toward the more dominant. A direct stare in macaques (and other primates) is an aggressive signal, which precedes attack and can precipitate an attack by the other, and the silent bared-teeth display seems to have evolved as a means for a more submissive monkey to look at a more dominant one without provoking a fight. If it could be translated into words, it might be rendered

| FIGURE 3.19 | Possible homologues to two types of **human smiles** The silent bared-teeth display (a) is believed to be homologous to the human greeting smile, and the relaxed open-mouth display (b) is believed to be homologous to the human laugh and happy smile. The animals in both photos are chimpanzees.

(a)

as, "I'm looking at you but I'm not going to attack, so please don't attack me." In some monkey species, it is also used to promote affiliation after an aggressive encounter (Preuschoft & van Hooff, 1997).

J. A. van Hooff (1972, 1976) found that among chimpanzees this display takes on a new function, more similar to that of the human smile of greeting. *Both* the more submissive and the more dominant of two chimpanzees show the display upon meeting, and it usually precedes friendly interaction between them. From such observations, van Hooff proposed that the silent bared-teeth display originated in monkeys as a submissive gesture, but in the evolutionary line leading to chimpanzees and humans it evolved further into a general form of greeting. As used by the more submissive individual, it may retain its original meaning, "Please don't attack me," but as used by the more dominant, it may mean, "Rest assured, I won't attack," and as used by both it may mean, "Let's be friends."

**Possible Origin of Laughter and the Happy Smile**  The other primate smile-like expression is the *relaxed open-mouth display,* or *play face* (see Figure 3.19b), which occurs mostly in young primates during playful fighting and chasing and may be homologous to both laughter and the happy smile in humans. In chimpanzees, it is often accompanied by a vocalized *ahh ahh ahh,* which sounds like a throaty human laugh. Van Hooff believes that this display originated as a means for young primates to signal to each other that their aggressive-like behavior is not to be taken seriously; nobody will really get hurt. Interestingly, in human children, laughter occurs during playful fighting and chasing more reliably than during any other form of play (Blurton-Jones, 1967), and even among us "sophisticated" adults, pie throwing, chase scenes, mock insults, and other forms of fake aggression are among the most reliable ways to elicit laughter. Thus our laughter not only is similar in form to the relaxed open-mouth display of other primates but, at least in some cases, seems to serve a similar function as well.

(b)

The smile of laughter is similar in form to the non-laughing happy smile, so the latter, too, may have its roots in the relaxed open-mouth display (Redican, 1982). There is, it seems to me, some poetry in the thought that the smile of happiness may have originated from a signal indicating that, although the world can be frightening and full of conflict, the aggression going on now is just in fun and we are safe.

## The Value, for Psychology, of Studying Analogies

You have just seen examples of how homologies can be used to make inferences about the evolutionary origins of species-typical behaviors. Analogies, in contrast, are not useful for tracing evolutionary origins, but are useful for making inferences about the ultimate functions of species-typical behaviors. If different species have independently evolved a particular behavioral trait, then comparing the species may reveal commonalities of habitat and lifestyle that are clues to the ultimate function of that trait. You will see examples of this use of analogies in the remaining sections of this chapter, as applied to patterns of mating, patterns of aggression, and patterns of helping.

>>> ——————————— **30**

How can analogies be used to make inferences about the ultimate functions of species-typical traits?

**Species-typical behaviors have come to exist through natural selection.**

| Species-Typical Behaviors | Homologies and Analogies |
|---|---|
| • Commonly called instincts, species-typical behaviors are ways of behaving that characterize a species—such as cats meowing and humans walking upright. | • Homologies are similarities due to common ancestry. They are useful for studying underlying mechanisms and for tracing the evolutionary course of species-typical behaviors, exemplified by research on the greeting smile and happy smile in humans. |
| • They may be influenced by learning or even require learning, as exemplified by cultural differences in the eyebrow flash, human language learning, and white-crowned sparrows' song development. | • Analogies are similarities due to convergent evolution (independent evolution of similar traits). They are useful for inferring ultimate functions. |
| • They depend upon biological preparedness—i.e., upon having anatomical structures that permit and motivate the behavior. | |

# Evolutionary Analyses of Mating Patterns

From an evolutionary perspective, no class of behavior is more important than mating. Mating is the means by which all sexually reproducing animals get their genes into the next generation. Mating is also interesting because it is the most basic form of social behavior. Sex is the foundation of society. Were it not necessary for female and male to come together to reproduce, members of a species could, in theory, go through life completely oblivious to one another.

Countless varieties of male–female arrangements for sexual reproduction have evolved in different species of animals. One way to classify them is according to the number of partners a male or female typically mates with over a given period of time, such as a breeding season. Four broad classes are generally recognized: *polygyny* [pah-**lij**-inee], in which one male mates with more than one female; *polyandry* [pah-lee-**an**-dree], in which one female mates with more than one male; *monogamy,* in which one male mates with one female; and *polygynandry* [pah-lee-**jin**-an-dree], in which members of a group consisting of more than one male and more than one female mate with one another (Rees & Harvey, 1991). (These terms are easy to remember if you know that *poly-* means "many"; *mono-*, "one"; *-gyn,* "female"; and *-andr,* "male." Thus, for example, *polygynandry* literally means "many females and males.") As illustrated in Figure 3.20, a feature of both polygyny and polyandry is that some individuals are necessarily deprived of a mating opportunity—a state of affairs associated with considerable conflict.

## A Theory Relating Mating Patterns to Parental Investment

**31**

What is Trivers's theory of parental investment?

<<< In a now-classic article, Robert Trivers (1972) outlined a theory relating courtship and mating patterns to sex differences in amount of **parental investment.** Parental investment can be defined roughly as the time, energy, and risk to survival that are involved in producing, feeding, and otherwise caring for each offspring. More precisely, Trivers defined it as the loss, to the adult, of future reproductive capacity that results from the production and nurturance of any given offspring. Every offspring in a sexually reproducing species has two parents, one of each sex, but the amount of parental investment from the two is usually not equal. The essence of Trivers's theory is this: *In general, for species in which parental investment is unequal, the more parentally invested sex will (a) be more vigorously competed for than the other and (b) be more discriminating than the other when choosing mates.*

To illustrate and elaborate on this theory—and to see how it is supported by cross-species comparisons focusing on analogies—let us apply it to each of the four general classes of mating patterns.

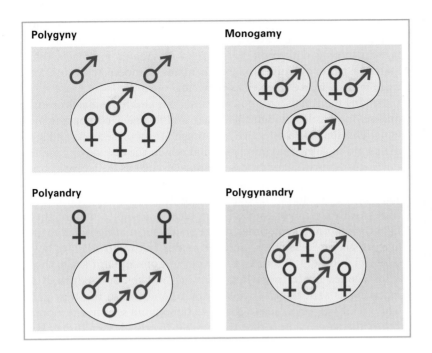

**| FIGURE 3.20 |** Four mating systems  In a polygynous system (common in mammals), the unmated males are a threat to the mated male, and in a polyandrous system (present in some birds and fishes), the unmated females are a threat to the mated female. Threat is reduced by monogamy and polygynandry, because with those systems, most individuals find mates.

## Polygyny Is Related to High Female and Low Male Parental Investment

Most species of mammals are polygynous, and Trivers's theory helps explain why. Mammalian reproductive physiology is such that the female necessarily invests a great deal in the offspring she bears. The young must first develop within her body and then must obtain nourishment from her in the form of milk. Because of the female's high investment, the number of offspring she can produce in a breeding season or a lifetime is limited. A female whose gestation and lactation periods are such that she can bear at most four young a year can produce no more than that regardless of the number of different males with which she mates.

Things are different for the male. His involvement with offspring is, at minimum, simply the production of sperm cells and the act of copulation. These require little time and energy, so his maximum reproductive potential is limited not by parental investment but by the number of fertile females with which he mates.

>>> ———————————— 32

Based on Trivers's theory of parental investment, why does high investment by the female lead to (a) polygyny, (b) large size of males, and (c) high selectivity in the female's choice of mate?

Ben Osborne / Earth Scenes / Animals, Animals

**Who's bigger and stronger?** These male elephant seals are sizing each other up for possible battle over mating rights to the many females in the background. Because the larger combatant usually wins, male elephant seals have through natural selection become huge compared with females.

*Natural History, August 1995, p. 57. Photo by Tom Vezo.*

**An aggressive female** The spotted sandpiper is a polyandrous species. The female mates with several males and defends her territory from invading females. This female is stretching her wings in a threat display.

A male that mates with 20 females, each of which can bear four young, can in theory produce 80 offspring a year. When the evolutionary advantage in mating with multiple partners is greater for males than for females, a pattern evolves in which males compete with one another to mate with as many females as they can.

Among mammals, competition among males for females often involves one-on-one battles, which the larger and stronger combatant most often wins. This leads to a selective advantage for increased size and strength in males, up to some maximum beyond which the size advantage in obtaining mates is outweighed by disadvantages, such as difficulty in finding sufficient food to support the large size. In general, the more polygynous a species, the greater is the average size difference between males and females. An extreme example is the elephant seal. Males of this species fight one another, sometimes to the death, for mating rights to groups averaging about 50 females, and the males outweigh females several-fold (Hoelzel & others, 1999). In the evolution of elephant seals, those males whose genes made them large, strong, and ferocious enough to defeat other males sent many copies of their genes on to the next generation, while their weaker or less aggressive opponents sent few or none.

For the same reason that the female mammal usually has less evolutionary incentive than the male to mate with many individuals, she has more incentive to be discriminating in her choice of mate (Trivers, 1972). Because she invests so much, risking her life and decreasing her future reproductive potential whenever she becomes pregnant, her genetic interests lie in producing offspring that will have the highest possible chance themselves to survive and reproduce. To the degree that the male affects the young, either through his genes or through other resources he provides, females would be expected to select males whose contribution will be most beneficial. In elephant seals, it is presumably to the female's evolutionary advantage to mate with the winner of battles. The male victor's genes increase the chance that the female's sons will win battles in the future and produce many young themselves.

## Polyandry Is Related to High Male and Low Female Parental Investment

**33**

What conditions promote the evolution of polyandry? How do sex differences within polyandrous species support Trivers's theory?

<<< Polyandry is not the primary mating pattern for any species of mammal, but it is for some species of fishes and birds (Clutton-Brock & Vincent, 1991; Erckmann, 1983). Polyandry is more likely to evolve in egg-laying species than in mammals, because a smaller proportion of an egg layer's reproductive cycle is tied to the female's body. Once the eggs are laid, they can be cared for by either parent, and, depending on other conditions, evolution can lead to greater male than female parental investment.

Consistent with Trivers's theory, females of polyandrous species are the more active and aggressive courters, and they have evolved to be larger, stronger, and in some cases more brightly colored than the males (Berglund & Rosenqvist, 2001). An example is the spotted sandpiper, a common freshwater shorebird. A female spotted sandpiper can lay up to three clutches of eggs in rapid succession, each cared for by a different male that has mated with her (Oring, 1995). At the beginning of the breeding season, the females—which outweigh the males by about 20 percent and have somewhat more conspicuous spots—stake out territories where they actively court males and drive out other females.

## Monogamy Is Related to Equivalent Male and Female Parental Investment

**34**

What conditions promote the evolution of monogamy? Why are sex differences in size and strength generally lacking in monogamous species?

<<< According to Trivers's theory, when the two sexes make approximately equal investments in their young, their degree of competition for mates will also be approximately equal, and monogamy will prevail. Equal parental investment is most likely to come about when conditions make it impossible for a single adult to raise

the young but quite possible for two to raise them. Under these circumstances, if either parent leaves, the young fail to survive, so natural selection favors genes that lead parents to stay together and care for the young together. Because neither sex is much more likely than the other to fight over mates, there is little or no natural selection for sex differences in size and strength, and, in general, males and females of monogamous species are nearly identical in these characteristics.

Consistent with the view that monogamy arises from the need for more than one adult to care for offspring, over 90 percent of bird species are predominantly monogamous (Cézilly & Zayan, 2000; Lack, 1968). Among most species of birds, unlike most mammals, a single parent would usually not be able to raise the young. Birds must incubate and protect their eggs until they hatch and then must guard the hatchlings and fetch food for them until they can fly. One parent alone cannot simultaneously guard the nest and leave it to get food, but two together can. Among mammals, monogamy has arisen in some species that are like birds in the sense that their young must be given food other than milk, of a type that the male can provide. The best-known examples are certain carnivores, including foxes and coyotes (Malcolm, 1985). Young carnivores must be fed meat until they have acquired the necessary strength, agility, and skills to hunt on their own, and two parents are much better than one at accomplishing this task. Monogamy also occurs in several species of rodents, where the male may play a crucial role in protecting the young from predators while the mother forages (Sommer, 2000).

With modern DNA techniques to determine paternity, researchers have learned that social monogamy (the faithful pairing of female and male for raising young) does not necessarily imply sexual monogamy (fidelity in copulation between that female and male). Researchers commonly find that between 5 and 35 percent of offspring in socially monogamous birds are sired by a neighboring male rather than by the male at the nest (Birkhead & Moller, 1992); for one species, the superb fairy wren, that average is 75 percent (Mulder, 1994). Why does such extra-mate copulation occur? From the female's evolutionary perspective, copulation with a male that is genetically superior to her own mate (as manifested in song and feathers) results in genetically superior young, and copulation with any additional male increases the chance that all her eggs will be fertilized by viable sperm (Zeh & Zeh, 2001). For the male, evolutionary advantage rests in driving neighboring males away from his own mate whenever possible and in copulating with neighboring females whenever possible. Genes that build brain mechanisms that promote such behaviors are passed along to more offspring than are genes that do not.

*Natural History, November 1994, p. 60. Photo by C. Allan Morgan.*

**A not-so-faithful couple** The superb fairy wren is socially but not sexually monogamous. The male (at the left) and the female stay together at the nest and raise the young together, but DNA testing has shown that about 75 percent of the offspring, on average, are sired by neighboring males.

>>> ──────────────── **35**

For what evolutionary reasons might monogamously mated females and males sometimes copulate with partners other than their mates?

## Polygynandry Is Related to Investment in the Group

Among the clearest examples of polygynandrous species are chimpanzees and bonobos, which happen to be our two closest animal relatives (see Figure 3.21 on the next page). Bonobos are similar in appearance to chimpanzees but are rarer and have only recently been studied in the wild. The basic social structure of both species is the colony, which consists usually of two to three dozen adults of both sexes and their offspring. When the female is ovulating, she develops on her rump a prominent pink swelling, which she actively displays to advertise her condition. During the time of this swelling, which lasts about a week in chimps and 3 weeks in bonobos, she is likely to mate with most of the adult males of the colony, though she may actively choose to mate with some more often than with others (Goodall, 1986; Kano, 1992; Stumpf & Boesch, 2005).

Polygynandry has apparently evolved in these ape species because it permits a group of adult males and females to live together in relative harmony, without too much fighting over who mates with whom. A related advantage, from the female's perspective, is paternity confusion (Hrdy, 1981, 2000). Among many species of

>>> ──────────────── **36**

What appear to be the evolutionary advantages of polygynandry for chimpanzees and bonobos, and in what ways is polygynandry more fully developed for the latter than the former?

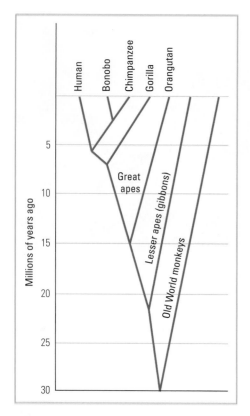

**| FIGURE 3.21 |** Relationship of humans to apes and Old World monkeys The ancestral line leading to humans split off from that leading to Old World monkeys 30 million years ago, and it split off from that leading to bonobos and chimpanzees 5.6 million years ago. (Data from Corballis, 1999.)

**Bonobo sex** Bonobos seem to live by the motto, "Make love, not war." Research suggests that they are the most sexually active and the most peaceful of all primates. Here a male has mounted a female in a face-to-face position—a position long thought to be unique to humans. But bonobo sex occurs in all possible partner combinations (homosexual as well as heterosexual) and essentially all imaginable positions.

primates, males kill young that are not their own, and such behavior has been observed in chimpanzees when a female migrates into a colony bringing with her an infant that was sired elsewhere (Wrangham, 1993). Because almost any chimp or bonobo male in the colony could be the father of any infant born within the colony, each male's evolutionary interest lies not in attacking the young but in helping to protect and care for the group as a whole.

Polygynandry seems to be more fully developed in bonobos than in chimps. Male chimps do fight with one another over females that are at peak fertility, and sometimes a single male manages to monopolize the sexual activity of a female throughout her ovulatory cycle (Goodall, 1986; Wrangham, 1993). In contrast, bonobo males rarely compete physically to copulate. In fact, for bonobos sex appears to be more a reducer of aggression than a cause of it (Parish & de Waal, 2000; Wrangham, 1993). Unlike any other apes, female bonobos copulate at all times of their reproductive cycle, not just near the time of ovulation. In addition to their frequent heterosexual activity, bonobos of the same sex often rub their genitals together, and genital stimulation of all types occurs most often following conflict and in situations that could potentially elicit conflict, such as when a favorite food is discovered (Hohmann & Fruth, 2000; Parish, 1996). Field studies suggest that bonobos are the most peaceful of primates and that their frequent polygynandrous sexual activity helps keep them that way (Kano, 1992).

## What About Human Mating Patterns?

**37**

What evidence suggests that humans evolved as a partly monogamous, partly polygynous species? How is this consistent with Trivers's parental investment theory?

<<< When we apply the same criteria that are used to classify the mating systems of other species, we find that humans fall on the boundary between monogamy and polygyny (Dewsbury, 1988). In no culture are human beings as sexually promiscuous as are our closest ape relatives, the chimpanzees and bonobos. In every culture people form long-term mating bonds, which are usually legitimized through some sort of culturally recognized marriage contract. Anthropologists have found that the great majority of non-Western cultures, where Western influence has not made

polygyny illegal, practice a mixture of monogamy and polygyny (Marlowe, 2000; Murdock, 1981). In such cultures, a few men, who have sufficient wealth or status, have two or more wives, while the great majority of men have one wife and a few have none. Thus, even in cultures that permit and idealize polygyny, most marriages are monogamous.

Human children, more so than the young of any other primates, require an extended period of care before they can play full adult roles in activities such as food gathering. Cross-cultural research shows that in every culture mothers provide most of the direct physical care of children, but fathers contribute in various ways. In many cultures—especially in hunter-gatherer cultures—fathers share to some degree in the physical care of their offspring (Marlowe, 2000), and in nearly all cultures fathers provide indirect care in the form of food and other material provisions. In fact, in 77 percent of the cultures for which data are available, fathers provide more of the provisions for young than do mothers (Marlowe, 2000). Taking both direct and indirect care into account, we are a species in which fathers typically lag somewhat behind mothers, but not greatly behind them, in degree of parental investment. This, in line with Trivers's parental investment theory, is consistent with our being a primarily monogamous but moderately polygynous species. The moderate size difference between men and women is also consistent with this conclusion (Dewsbury, 1988). The average size difference between males and females in humans is nowhere near that observed in highly polygynous species, such as elephant seals and gorillas, but is greater than that observed in monogamous species.

©1994 Ruben Bolling. Distributed by Quaternary Features.

Our biological equipment that predisposes us for mating bonds includes brain mechanisms that promote the twin emotions of romantic love and sexual jealousy. These emotions are found in people of every culture that has been studied (Buss, 2000; Fisher, 1992). People everywhere develop strong emotional ties to those toward whom they are sexually drawn. This is experienced as a need to be constantly near the other person. People also, everywhere, feel intensely jealous when "their" mates appear to be sexually drawn to others. While love tends to create mating bonds, jealousy tends to preserve such bonds by motivating each member of a mated pair to act in ways designed to prevent the other from having an affair with someone else.

Other animals that form long-term mating bonds show evidence of emotions that are functionally similar to human love and jealousy. In this sense, we are more like monogamous birds than we are like our closest ape relatives. The similarities between humans and birds in sexual love and jealousy are clearly analogies, not homologies (Lorenz, 1974). These evolved separately in humans and birds as means to create and preserve mating bonds long enough to promote biparental care of offspring. Chimpanzees and bonobos (especially the latter) can engage in open, promiscuous sex with little emotional consequence, because they have not evolved strong emotions of sexual love and jealousy, but humans and monogamous birds cannot. The difference ultimately has to do with species differences in the need for care from both parents.

At the same time that love and jealousy tend to promote bonding, lust (another product of evolution) tends to motivate both men and women to engage surreptitiously in sex outside of such bonds. In this sense we are like those socially monogamous birds that are sexually unfaithful. A man who can inseminate women beyond his wife may send more copies of his genes into the next generation than a completely faithful man. A woman who has sex with men other than her husband may benefit, evolutionarily, by (a) increasing her chances of conception (hedging

>>> ──────────── 38

From an evolutionary perspective, what are the functions of romantic love and sexual jealousy, and how is this supported by cross-species comparisons? How is sexual unfaithfulness explained?

against the possibility that her husband's sperm are not viable or are genetically incompatible with her eggs); (b) increasing the evolutionary fitness of her offspring (by mating with a man who has evolutionarily superior genes compared to those of her husband); and/or (c) gaining provisions from more than one man (Hrdy, 2000). And so the human soap opera continues, much like that of the superb fairy wren, though not to such an extreme. Studies involving DNA testing, in cultures ranging from hunter-gatherer groups to modern Western societies, suggest that somewhere between 2 and 10 percent of children in socially monogamous families are sired by someone other than the mother's husband (Marlowe, 2000).

## SECTION REVIEW

### An evolutionary perspective offers functionalist explanations of mating patterns.

| Mating Patterns Related to Parental Investment | Human Mating Patterns |
|---|---|
| • Trivers theorized that sex differences in parental investment (time, energy, risk involved in bearing and raising young) explain mating patterns and sex differences in size, aggressiveness, competition for mates, and selectivity in choosing mates. | • Parental investment is somewhat lower for fathers than for mothers, consistent with the human mix of monogamy and polygyny. |
| • Consistent with Trivers's theory, polygyny is associated with high female and low male parental investment; polyandry is associated with the opposite; and monogamy is associated with approximately equal investment by the two sexes. | • Romantic love and jealousy help promote and preserve bonding of mates, permitting two-parent care of offspring. |
| • Polygynandry, common to chimps and bonobos, seems to be associated with high investment in the group. | • Sex outside of mating bonds may yield evolutionary benefits. |

# Evolutionary Analyses of Hurting and Helping

Human beings, like other animals, are motivated both to hurt and to help one another in the struggle to survive and reproduce. From an evolutionary perspective, other members of one's species are competitors for food, mates, safe places to live, and other limited resources. Ultimately, such competition is the foundation of aggression. Yet, at the same time, others of one's kind are potential helpmates. Many life-promoting tasks can be accomplished better by two or more individuals working together than by one struggling alone. The human drama, like that of other social species, involves the balancing of competitiveness with the need for others' help. Let us look first at the grim topic of aggression and then end, more pleasantly, with cooperation.

## Sex Differences in Aggression

*Aggression,* as the term is used here, refers to fighting and threats of fighting among members of the same species. Brain mechanisms that motivate and organize such behavior have evolved because they help animals acquire and retain resources needed to survive and reproduce. As you saw in the previous section, much animal aggression centers on mating. Polygynous males and polyandrous females fight for mates; monogamous males fight to prevent other males from copulating with their mates; and monogamous females fight to keep other females from leading their mates away (Slagsvold & others, 1999; Tobias & Seddon, 2000). Aggression can also serve to protect a feeding ground for oneself and one's offspring, to drive away individuals that may be a threat to one's young, and to elevate one's status within a social group. Much could be said from an evolutionary perspective about all aspects of aggression, but here I will focus just on sex differences in how aggression is manifested.

## Why Male Primates Are Generally More Violent Than Female Primates

Among most species of mammals, and especially among primates, males are much more violently aggressive than are females. Female primates are not unaggressive, but their aggression is typically aimed directly toward obtaining resources and defending their young. When they have achieved their ends, they stop fighting. Male primates, in contrast, seem at times to go out of their way to pick fights, and they are far more likely to maim or kill their opponents than are females.

Most of the violence perpetrated by male primates has to do directly or indirectly with sex. Male monkeys and apes of many species have been observed to kill infants fathered by others, apparently as a means to get the females to stop lactating so they will ovulate again and become sexually active. Males also fight with one another, sometimes brutally, to raise their ranks in the dominance hierarchy of the colony. High rank generally increases both their attractiveness to females and their ability to intimidate sexual rivals (Cowlishaw & Dunbar, 1991). Males are also often violent toward females; they use violence to force copulation or to prevent the female from copulating with other males. All of these behaviors have been observed in chimpanzees and many other primate species (Goodall, 1986; Smuts, 1992; Wittig & Boesch, 2003).

Evolution, remember, is not a moral force. It promotes those behaviors that tend to get one's genes passed on to the next generation. Female primates, because of their higher parental investment, don't need to fight to get the opposite sex interested in them. Moreover, aggression may have a higher cost for females than for males. The female at battle risks not just her life but also that of any fetus she is gestating or young she is nursing—the repositories of her genes. The male at battle risks just himself, and, in the cold calculus of evolution, his life isn't worth anything unless he can get a female to mate with him. Genes that promote mating, by whatever means, proliferate, and genes that fail to promote it vanish.

Humans are no exception to the usual primate rule. Cross-cultural studies show that everywhere men are more violent, more likely to maim or kill, than are women. In fact, in a survey of cross-cultural data on this issue, Martin Daly and Margo Wilson (1988) were unable to find any society in which the number of women who killed other women was even one-tenth as great as the number of men who killed other men. On average, in the data they examined, male–male killings outnumbered female–female killings by more than 30 to 1. One might construe a scenario through which such a difference in violence would be purely a product of learning in every culture, but the hypothesis that the difference resides at least partly in inherited sex differences seems more plausible.

According to Daly's and Wilson's analyses, the apparent motives underlying male violence and homicide are very much in accord with predictions from evolutionary theory. Among the leading motives for murder among men in every culture is sexual jealousy. In some cultures, men are *expected* to kill other men who have sex with their wives (Symons, 1979), and in others, such murders are common even though they are illegal (Daly & Wilson, 1988). Men also fight over issues of status (Daly & Wilson, 1990). One man insults another and then the two fight it out—with fists, knives, or guns. And men, like many male monkeys and apes, often use violence to control females. In the United States and Canada between 25 and 30 percent of women are battered by their current or former mate at some time in their lives

>>> ————————————— **39**

How is male violence toward infants, toward other males, and toward females explained from an evolutionary perspective?

**Tough young males** Male mammals of many species compete with one another for dominance. Much of their competition, however, involves threat and bluff rather than bloodshed, as illustrated by these two young mountain gorillas.

(Randall & Haskell, 1995; Williams & Hawkins, 1989). Analyses of domestic violence cases indicate that much of it has to do with the man's belief (often unfounded) that his partner has been or might become sexually unfaithful (Peters & others, 2002; Wilson & Daly, 1993).

## How Female Bonobos Dominate Males

**40**

How have bonobo females countered the mammalian tendency for males to control females through violence?

<<< Bonobos are an exception to the primate rule that males are the more violent sex. Bonobos, as you recall, are as closely related to us as are chimpanzees, and bonobos and chimpanzees are more closely related to each other than either species is to us (look back at Figure 3.21). Yet, in terms of their patterns of aggression, bonobos are very different from chimpanzees. They are much less aggressive than chimpanzees overall, and, to the degree that they are aggressive, females dominate males. It took researchers a long time to come to this conclusion, because it was so unexpected, but by now the researchers who are most familiar with bonobo behavior agree that female bonobos are aggressively dominant over males, despite the fact that the males are physically larger and stronger than the females (Kano, 1998; Parish & de Waal, 2000).

The females dominate because they form strong alliances with one another and help one another whenever one of them has a dispute with a male (Parish & de Waal, 2000). A single female bonobo generally cannot defeat a male in a fight, but a group of two or three can easily do so. When a valued but limited source of food is found by a colony of bonobos, the females eat first. A male who attempts to violate that rule is beaten off by the females as a group. If a male attempts to mount a female who does not want to be mounted, she screams and other females come to her rescue. A male who offends a female in any way—even one who offends by refusing a female's invitation to mount her—risks serious attack and possible injury at the hands and teeth of the female's friends (Parish & de Waal, 2000). Even the most dominant male is subject to such attacks.

In bonobos, a strong tendency for females to form close alliances to control males seems to derive largely from the genetic makeup of the species. It is seen among all bonobo groups that have been studied, both in the wild and in captivity. You might wonder why the males don't form alliances for counterattack; nobody knows the answer. Human females, by contrast, don't universally form alliances to control males, yet such alliances are within human capacity. In a cross-cultural analysis, Barbara Smuts (1992) showed that men's violence toward women is lowest in those cultures and communities in which women have strong alliances with one another and men have relatively weak alliances with one another. In those communities, women hear about and come to the aid of a woman who is being abused by a man, and, through humiliation or other means (usually not physical violence), teach the offending man a lesson. Other cross-cultural analyses reveal that women have relatively more control over economic resources in societies where alliances among women are strong than in societies where such alliances are weak (Yanca & Low, 2004).

## Patterns of Helping

From an evolutionary perspective, *helping* can be defined as any behavior that increases the survival chance or reproductive capacity of another individual. Given this definition, it is useful to distinguish between two categories of helping: cooperation and altruism.

*Cooperation* occurs when an individual helps another while helping itself. This sort of helping happens all the time in the animal world and is easy to understand from an evolutionary perspective. It occurs when a mated pair of foxes work together to raise their young, a pack of wolves work together to kill an antelope, or a group of chimpanzees work together to chase off a predator or a rival group of chimpanzees. Most of the advantages of social living lie in cooperation. By working with others for common ends, each individual has a better chance of survival and reproduction than it would have alone. Whatever costs accrue are more than re-paid by the benefits. Human beings everywhere live in social groups and derive the benefits of cooperation. Those who live as our ancestors did cooperate in hunting and gathering food, caring for children, building dwellings, defending against predators and human invaders, and, most human of all, in exchanging, through language, information that bears on all aspects of the struggle for survival.

*Altruism,* in contrast, occurs when an individual helps another while *decreasing* its own survival chance or reproductive capacity. This is less common than cooperation, but many animals do behave in ways that at least appear to be altruistic. For example, some animals, including female ground squirrels, emit a loud, distinctive call when they spot an approaching predator. The cry warns others of the predator's approach and, at the same time, tends to attract the predator's attention to the caller (Sherman, 1977). (See Figure 3.22.) The selfish response would be to remain quiet and hidden, or to move away quietly, rather than risk being detected by warning others. How can such behavior be explained from an evolutionary perspective? As Trivers (1971) pointed out long ago, any evolutionary account of apparent altruism must operate by showing that from a broader perspective, focusing on the propagation of one's genes, the behavior is not truly altruistic. Evolutionists have developed two broad theories to account for ostensible altruism in animals: the kin selection theory and the reciprocity theory.

## The Kin Selection Theory of Altruism

The **kin selection theory** holds that behavior that seems to be altruistic came about through natural selection because it preferentially helps close relatives, who are genetically most similar to the helper (Hamilton, 1964). What actually survives over evolutionary time, of course, is not the individual but the individual's genes. Any gene that promotes the production and preservation of copies of itself can be a fit gene, from the vantage point of natural selection, even if it reduces the survival chances of a particular carrier of the gene.

Imagine a ground squirrel with a rare gene that promotes the behavior of calling out when a predator is near. The mathematics of inheritance are such that, on average, one-half of the offspring or siblings of the individual with this gene would be expected to have the same gene, as would one-fourth of the nieces or nephews and one-eighth of the cousins. Thus if the altruist incurred a small risk ($\Delta$) to its own life while increasing an offspring's or a sibling's chances of survival by more than $2\Delta$, a niece's or nephew's by more than $4\Delta$, or a cousin's by more than $8\Delta$, the gene would increase in the population from one generation to the next.

Many research studies have shown that animals do help kin more than non-kin. For example, ground squirrels living with kin are more likely to emit alarm calls than are those living with non-kin (Sherman, 1977). Chimpanzees and other primates are more likely to help kin than non-kin in all sorts of ways, including sharing food, providing assistance in fights, and helping take care of young (Goodall, 1986; Nishida, 1990; Silk, 2002). Consistent with the mathematics of genetic relatedness, macaque monkeys have been observed to help their brothers and sisters more readily than their cousins and their cousins more readily than more distant relatives (Silk, 2002). For these and many other examples, helpers can apparently distinguish kin from non-kin, and this ability allows them to direct help selectively to kin (Pfennig & Sherman, 1995; Silk, 2002). In theory, however, altruistic behavior can evolve through kin selection even without such discrimination. A tendency to help any member of one's species, indiscriminately, can evolve if the animal's usual living arrangements are such that, by chance alone, a sufficiently high percentage of help is directed toward kin.

Among humans, the selective aiding of kin is called *nepotism,* and cross-cultural research shows that such behavior is common everywhere (Essock-Vitale & McGuire, 1980). If a mother dies or for other reasons is unable to care for a child, the child's grandmother, aunt, or other close relative is by far the most likely adopter (Kurland, 1979). Close kin are also most likely to share dwellings or land,

>>> ———————————— 41

How do the kin selection and reciprocity theories take the altruism out of "altruism"? What observations show that both theories apply to humans as well as to other animals?

L. D. Klein / Photo Researchers

**| FIGURE 3.22 |** An alarm-calling ground squirrel When they spot a predator, female ground squirrels often emit an alarm call, especially if they are living in a group of close kin. Males are less likely to live near close kin and do not show this response.

hunt together, or form other collaborative arrangements. On the other side of the same coin, studies in Western culture indicate that genetic kin living in the same household are less often violent toward one another than are non-kin living in the same household (Daly & Wilson, 1988), and studies in other cultures have shown that villages in which most people are closely related have less internal friction than those in which people are less closely related (Chagnon, 1979). People report feeling emotionally closer to their kin than to their non-kin friends, even if they live farther away from the former than from the latter and see them less often (Neyer & Lang, 2003).

When leaders call for patriotic sacrifice or universal cooperation, they commonly employ kinship terms (Johnson, 1987). At times of war, political leaders ask citizens to fight for the "motherland" or "fatherland"; at other times, religious leaders and humanists strive to promote world peace by speaking of our "brothers and sisters" everywhere. The terms appeal to our instincts to be kind to relatives. Our imagination and intelligence allow us, at least sometimes, to extend our concept of kinship to all humanity.

## The Reciprocity Theory of Apparent Altruism

The *reciprocity theory* provides an account of how acts of apparent altruism can arise even among non-kin. According to this theory, behaviors that seem to be altruistic are actually forms of long-term cooperation (Trivers, 1971). Computer simulations of evolution have shown that a genetically induced tendency to help non-kin can evolve if it is tempered by (a) an ability to remember which individuals have reciprocated such help in the past and (b) a tendency to refrain from helping again those who failed to reciprocate previous help (discussed in Chapter 14). Under these conditions, helping another is selfish because it increases the chance of receiving help from that other in the future. Behavior fitting this pattern is found in various niches of the animal world. As one example, vampire bats frequently share food with unrelated members of their species that have shared food with them in the past (Wilkinson, 1988). As another example, bonobo females that establish friendship coalitions and are so very effective in helping one another are often unrelated to one another, having immigrated from different natal colonies (Kano, 1992; Parish & de Waal, 2000). The help each gives the others, in such acts as chasing off offending males, is reciprocated at another time.

Gunter Ziesler / Peter Arnold, Inc.

**Helpful little demons** Vampire bats are gregarious mammals that demonstrate reciprocal altruism. After gorging itself on a blood meal, a bat will share some of what it has ingested with another bat, usually one that has fed it in the past.

The greatest reciprocal helpers of all, by far, are human beings. People in every culture feel a strong drive to return help that is given to them (Gouldner, 1960; Hill, 2002). Humans, more than any other species, can keep track of help given, remember it over a long period of time, and think of a wide variety of ways of reciprocating. Moreover, to ensure reciprocity, people everywhere have a highly developed sense of fairness and behave in ways that punish those who fail to fulfill their parts in reciprocal relationships (Fehr & Fischbacher, 2003). Certain human emotions seem to be well designed, by natural selection, to promote reciprocity. We feel gratitude (a sense of wanting to give) toward those who help us, pride when we return such help, guilt when we fail to return help, and anger when someone fails repeatedly to return help that we have given (as discussed more fully in Chapter 14). Humans also help others, including others who may never be able to reciprocate, in order to develop a good reputation in the community at large, and those with a good reputation are valued and helped by the community (Fehr & Fischbacher, 2003).

# Final Words of Caution: Two Fallacies to Avoid

Before closing this chapter it would be worthwhile to reiterate and expand on two points that I have already made: (1) Natural selection is not a moral force, and (2) our genes do not control our behavior in ways that are independent of the environment. These statements contradict two fallacious ideas that often creep into the evolutionary thinking of people who don't fully understand natural selection and the nature of genetic influences.

## The Naturalistic Fallacy

The **naturalistic fallacy** is the equation of "natural" with "moral" or "right." If male mammals in nature dominate females through force, then aggressive dominance of women by men is right. If natural selection promotes self-interested struggle among individuals, then selfishness is right. Such equations are logically indefensible, because nature itself is neither moral nor immoral except as judged so by us. Morality is a product of the human mind. We have acquired, in our evolution, the capacity to think in moral terms, and we can use that ability to develop moral philosophies that go in many possible directions, including those that favor real altruism and constrain individual self-interest for the good of the larger community.

>>> ———————————— 42
Why is the equation of "natural" with "right" considered a fallacy? How did that fallacy figure into the philosophy of Herbert Spencer?

The term *naturalistic fallacy* was coined by the British philosopher G. E. Moore (1903) as part of an argument against the views of another British philosopher, Herbert Spencer (1879). A contemporary of Darwin, Spencer considered himself a strong believer in Darwin's theory, and his goal was to apply it to the spheres of social philosophy and ethics. Unlike Darwin, Spencer seemed to imply in his writings that natural selection is guided by a moral force. He distinguished between "more evolved" and "less evolved" behaviors in nature and suggested that "more evolved" meant more moral. Although Spencer discussed cooperation as highly evolved and virtuous, his philosophy leaned more toward the virtues of individualism and competition. Spencer's writings were especially popular in the United States, where they were championed by such industrialists as John D. Rockefeller and Andrew Carnegie (Rachels, 1990). It was Spencer, not Darwin, who popularized the phrase "survival of the fittest," and some of the so-called *social Darwinists,* who were inspired by Spencer, used that phrase to justify even the most ruthless extremes of capitalism. In their view, the fittest were those who rose to the top in unchecked capitalism, and the unfit were those who fell into poverty or starvation.

Darwin himself was not seduced by the naturalistic fallacy. He was repulsed by much of what he saw in nature and marveled at the human ability to rise, sometimes, above it. He conscientiously avoided phrases such as "more evolved" that would imply that evolution is a moral force, and he felt frustrated by his inability to stop others from assuming that it is. In a letter to a friend, shortly after publication of *On the Origin of Species,* he wrote wryly, "I have noted in a Manchester newspaper a rather good squib, showing that I have proved 'might is right' and therefore Napoleon is right and every cheating tradesman is also right" (Rachels, 1990).

## The Deterministic Fallacy

The second general error, called the **deterministic fallacy,** is the assumption that genetic influences on our behavior take the form of genetic control of our behavior, which we can do nothing about (short of modifying our genes). The mistake here is assuming or implying that genes influence behavior directly, rather than through the indirect means of working with the environment to build or modify biological structures that then, in interplay with the environment, produce behavior. Some popular books on human evolution have exhibited the deterministic fallacy by implying that one or another form of behavior—such as fighting for territories—is unavoidable because it is controlled by our genes. That implication is unreasonable even when applied to nonhuman animals. Territorial birds, for example, defend territories only when the environmental conditions are ripe for them to do so. We humans can control our environment and thereby control ourselves. We can

>>> ———————————— 43
Why is it a mistake to believe that characteristics that are influenced by genes cannot be changed except by modifying genes?

either enhance or reduce the environmental ingredients needed for a particular behavioral tendency to develop and manifest itself.

We also can and regularly do, through conscious self-control and well-learned social habits, behave in ways that are contrary to biases built into our biology. One might even argue that our capacity for self-control is the essence of our humanity. In our evolution, we acquired that ability in a greater dose than seems apparent in any other species, perhaps because of its role in permitting us to live in complex social groups. Our ability for self-control, itself, is part of our biological heritage, and it liberates us to some degree—but by no means completely—from that heritage.

Our great capacity for knowledge, including knowledge of our own biological nature, can also be a liberating force. Most evolutionary psychologists contend that an understanding of human nature, far from implying fatalism, can be a step toward human betterment. For example, in her evolutionary analysis of men's violence against women, Smuts (1992) wrote:

> Although an evolutionary analysis assumes that male aggression against women reflects selection pressures operating during our species' evolutionary history, it in no way implies that male domination of women is genetically determined, or that frequent male aggression toward women is an immutable feature of human nature. In some societies male aggressive coercion of women is very rare, and even in societies with frequent male aggression toward women, some men do not show these behaviors. Thus, the challenge is to identify the situational factors that predispose members of a particular society toward or away from the use of sexual aggression. I argue that an evolutionary framework can be very useful in this regard.

As you review all of the human species-typical behaviors and tendencies discussed in this chapter, you might consider how each depends on environmental conditions and is modifiable by changes in those conditions.

## SECTION REVIEW

### An evolutionary perspective offers functionalist explanations of aggression and helping.

| Male Violence | Helping | Common Fallacies |
|---|---|---|
| • Male primates, including men, are generally more violent than are females of their species. | • Helping (promoting another's survival or reproduction) takes two forms—cooperation and altruism. | • The naturalistic fallacy is the equation of what is natural with what is right. It was indulged in by social Darwinists. |
| • Most aggression and violence in male primates relate directly or indirectly to sex. Genes that promote violence are passed to offspring to the degree that they increase mating. | • Cooperation (helping others while also helping oneself, as in the case of wolves hunting together) is easy to understand evolutionarily. | • The deterministic fallacy is the belief that genes control behavior in ways that cannot be altered by environmental experiences or conscious decisions. |
| • Among bonobos, female alliances counter male violence. | • Apparent acts of altruism (helping others at a net cost to oneself) make evolutionary sense if explained by the kin selection or reciprocity theories. | |

# Concluding Thoughts

**1. The indirect nature of genetic influences on behavior** Genes are simply DNA molecules that provide the code for building the body's proteins. Variation in genes across species provides the basis for species-typical behaviors, and variation in genes among members of a species is one source of individual differences in behavior within a species. But genes never produce behaviors directly. Genes always work in conjunction with the environment, and so their effects depend on environmental conditions. Neither genes nor environment "deter-

mines" our behavior. Our behavior results from an interplay between the environment in which we live and our bodies' biological mechanisms, which themselves were built through an interplay between genes and environment.

**2. The unconscious nature of ultimate functions** Sigmund Freud (discussed in Chapters 15 and 17) is famous for his claim that we are often unconscious of the real reasons for our actions. On that point, at least, modern evolutionary psychologists and Freud agree. Our species-typical drives and behavioral tendencies evolved to promote functions related to survival and reproduction, but we rarely think of those functions, and we are often completely ignorant of them. Toddlers toddle and play with words because it is "fun" to do so, without any thought about the value of such play in learning to walk and talk. We all smile, instinctively or because it seems like the right thing to do, when we are happy or when we meet someone, without thinking about the functions that smiling might serve. When we fall in love, we are far more likely to attribute that feeling to the sweet, charming, and irresistible nature of the beloved person than to anything having to do with the value of bonding for producing and raising children. When we feel jealous because of attention another is paying to our beloved, we think angry thoughts about betrayal and unfaithfulness, not about the role of jealousy in preserving monogamy. The reasons we give ourselves for what we do are an aspect of the proximate causation of our behavior. We are often no more aware of the ultimate functions of our actions than the cabbage fly is of why it is irresistibly drawn to the cabbage plant as the only proper place to lay its eggs.

**3. Evolution as an integrative theme in psychology** The evolutionary perspective provides the broadest view that we can take in psychology. It is concerned with the origins and ultimate functions of all aspects of human nature (and the nature of other animals). It is a perspective that can be applied to the whole vast range of topics with which psychology is concerned. All of the complex biological mechanisms that underlie our psychological nature came about because they helped our ancestors to survive and reproduce. We can expect, therefore, that all of our basic motivational and emotional mechanisms are biased toward generating behaviors that promote survival and reproduction; and we can expect that our sensory, perceptual, memory, and reasoning mechanisms are biased toward picking up and using information essential to those purposes. We are not general learning or thinking machines that indiscriminately analyze all information available; we are biological survival machines designed to use information selectively to achieve our ends. As you go through the rest of this book, crossing the whole range of psychology, you will see this idea applied in every chapter.

## Further Reading

**CHARLES DARWIN** (1859; reprinted 1963). *The origin of species.* New York: Washington Square Press.

Darwin was an engaging writer as well as a brilliant thinker. Why not read at least part of this book, which revolutionized the intellectual world? The most relevant chapter for psychologists is Chapter 8, entitled "Instinct," which includes Darwin's research on hive building in bees and many other insights about the behavior of wild and domesticated animals.

**MATT RIDLEY** (2003). *Nature via nurture.* New York: HarperCollins.

The recent explosion of research on human genetics—including the full sequencing of the human genome—is greatly increasing our knowledge of the genetic differences and similarities between humans and other animals and of the pathways by which genes influence behavior. Ridley summarizes, in highly readable and well-documented form, some of the most dramatic recent discoveries. As the title implies, the more we know about genes the more we realize that nature (genetic influence) and nurture (environmental influence) are inextricably entwined.

**BOBBI S. LOW** (2000). *Why sex matters: A Darwinian look at human behavior.* Princeton, NJ: Princeton University Press.

Low is an anthropologist who has conducted wide-ranging research into sex differences in animals and people, the latter across cultures and historical time. This scholarly but highly readable book is about sex, the differences between the sexes, and all that relates to these—beauty, bonding, reproduction, parenting, division of labor, cooperation, competition, wealth, power, and politics. It's an excellent introduction to evolutionary psychology from an anthropological perspective.

**JANE GOODALL** (1988). *In the shadow of man* (rev. ed.). Boston: Houghton Mifflin.

Goodall's study of wild chimpanzees, which began in 1960, ranks as one of the most courageous and scientifically valuable studies of animal behavior ever undertaken. This book, first published in 1971, is an exciting account of her early struggle to locate and study the animals and of her early findings about their behavior. For a more complete and scientific account of her research, I recommend Goodall's 1986 book, *The Chimpanzees of Gombe.*

**FRANS DE WAAL, WITH PHOTOGRAPHS BY FRANS LANTING** (1997). *Bonobo: The forgotten ape.* Berkeley: University of California Press.

Bonobos—the apes that are tied with chimpanzees as our closest animal relatives—were rediscovered in the 1980s, after decades of scientific neglect. Among the scientists who have studied them intensively is Frans de Waal, and here he describes their ecology and habits in a narrative that is accompanied by dozens of full-color, full-page photographs of these endangered apes, famous for their make-love-not-war style of life. Chapter 4 is X-rated.

# Glossary

**absentmindedness** A lapse in attention that results in memory failure. (p. 189)

**absolute threshold** The minimal intensity needed to just barely detect a stimulus. (p. 124)

**accommodation** The process by which infants revise their schemas in light of new information. (p. 413)

**accommodation** The process by which the eye maintains a clear image on the retina. (p. 132)

**acetylcholine (ach)** A neurotransmitter involved in a number of functions, including voluntary motor control. (p. 83)

**acquisition** The phase of classical conditioning when the CS and the US are presented together. (p. 214)

**action potential** An electric signal that is conducted along an axon to a synapse. (p. 80)

**activation-synthesis model** The theory that dreams are produced when the brain attempts to make sense of activations that occur randomly during sleep. (p. 317)

**actor-observer effect** The tendency to make situational inferences for our own behaviors while making dispositional inferences for the identical behavior of others. (p. 659)

**adolescence** The period of development that begins with the onset of sexual maturity (about 11 to 14 years of age) and lasts until the beginning of adulthood (about 18 to 21 years of age). (p. 430)

**adulthood** The period of development that begins around 18 to 21 years and ends at death. (p. 438)

**affective forecasting** The process by which people predict their emotional reactions to future events. (p. 378)

**aggression** Behavior whose purpose is to harm another. (p. 623)

**agonists** Drugs that increase the action of a neurotransmitter. (p. 85)

**agoraphobia** An extreme fear of venturing out into public places. (p. 505)

**alcohol myopia** A condition that results when alcohol hampers attention, leading people to respond in simple ways to complex situations. (p. 322)

**algorithm** A well-defined sequence of procedures or rules that guarantees a solution to a problem. (p. 275)

**altered states of consciousness** Forms of experience that depart from the normal subjective experience of the world and the mind. (p. 309)

**altruism** Behavior that benefits another without benefiting oneself. (p. 627)

**amygdala** A part of the limbic system that plays a central role in many emotional processes, particularly the formation of emotional memories. (p. 96)

**anal stage** The second psychosexual stage, which is dominated by the pleasures and frustrations associated with the anus, retention and expulsion of feces and urine, and toilet training. (p. 468)

**analogical problem solving** Solving a problem by finding a similar problem with a known solution and applying that solution to the current problem. (p. 281)

**anorexia nervosa** An eating disorder characterized by an intense fear of being fat and severe restriction of food intake. (p. 392)

**antagonists** Drugs that block the function of a neurotransmitter. (p. 85)

**anterograde amnesia** The inability to transfer new information from the short-term store into the long-term store. (p. 177)

**antianxiety medications** Drugs that help reduce a person's experience of fear or anxiety. (p. 562)

**antidepressants** A class of drugs that help lift people's mood. (p. 563)

**antipsychotic drugs** Medications that are used to treat schizophrenia and related psychotic disorders. (p. 560)

**antisocial personality disorder (APD)** A pervasive pattern of disregard for and violation of the rights of others that begins in childhood or early adolescence and continues into adulthood. (p. 529)

**anxiety disorder** The class of mental disorder in which anxiety is the predominant feature. (p. 501)

**aphasia** Difficulty in producing or comprehending language. (p. 262)

**apparent motion** The perception of movement as a result of alternating signals appearing in rapid succession in different locations. (p. 149)

**appraisal** An evaluation of the emotion-relevant aspects of a stimulus that is performed by the amygdala. (p. 374)

**approach motivation** A motivation to experience positive outcomes. (p. 400)

**area A1** A portion of the temporal lobe that contains the primary auditory cortex. (p. 152)

**area V1** The part of the occipital lobe that contains the primary visual cortex. (p. 138)

**assimilation** The process by which infants apply their schemas in novel situations. (p. 413)

**association areas** Areas of the cerebral cortex that are composed of neurons that help provide sense and meaning to information registered in the cortex. (p. 99)

**attachment** The emotional bond that forms between newborns and their primary caregivers. (p. 422)

**attitude** An enduring positive or negative evaluation of an object or event. (p. 645)

**attribution** An inference about the cause of a person's behavior. (p. 657)

**autonomic nervous system (ANS)** A set of nerves that carries involuntary and automatic commands that control blood vessels, body organs, and glands. (p. 88)

**availability bias** Items that are more readily available in memory are judged as having occurred more frequently. (p. 275)

**aversion therapy** A form of behavior therapy that uses positive punishment to reduce the frequency of an undesirable behavior. (p. 548)

**avoidance motivation** A motivation not to experience negative outcomes. (p. 400)

**axon** The part of a neuron that transmits information to other neurons, muscles, or glands. (p. 75)

**balanced placebo design** A study design in which behavior is observed following the presence or absence of an actual stimulus and also following the presence or absence of a placebo stimulus. (p. 322)

**basal ganglia** A set of subcortical structures that directs intentional movements. (p. 97)

**basilar membrane** A structure in the inner ear that undulates when vibrations from the ossicles reach the cochlear fluid. (p. 152)

**behavior** Observable actions of human beings and nonhuman animals. (p. 2)

**behavior therapy** A type of therapy that assumes that disordered behavior is learned, and symptom relief is achieved through changing overt maladaptive behaviors to more constructive behaviors. (p. 548)

**behavioral neuroscience** An approach to psychology that links psychological processes to activities in the nervous system and other bodily processes. (p. 24)

**behaviorism** An approach that advocates that psychologists restrict themselves to the scientific study of objectively observable behavior. (p. 17)

**belief** An enduring piece of knowledge about an object or event. (p. 645)

**belief bias** People's judgments about whether to accept conclusions depend more on how believable the conclusions are than on whether the arguments are logically valid. (p. 287)

**bias** The distorting influences of present knowledge, beliefs, and feelings on recollection of previous experiences. (p. 200)

**Big Five** The traits of the five-factor model: conscientiousness, agreeableness, neuroticism, openness to experience, and extraversion. (p. 457)

**binocular disparity** The difference in the retinal images of the two eyes that provides information about depth. (p. 146)

**biofeedback** The use of an external monitoring device to obtain information about a bodily function and possibly gain control over that function. (p. 598)

**biological preparedness** A propensity for learning particular kinds of associations over others. (p. 223)

**bipolar disorder** An unstable emotional condition characterized by cycles of abnormal, persistent high mood (mania) and low mood (depression). (p. 515)

**blind spot** An area of the retina that contains neither rods nor cones and therefore has no mechanism to sense light. (p. 134)

**blocking** A failure to retrieve information that is available in memory even though you are trying to produce it. (p. 192)

**bulimia nervosa** An eating disorder characterized by binge eating followed by purging. (p. 392)

**burnout** A state of physical, emotional, and mental exhaustion created by long-term involvement in an emotionally demanding situation and accompanied by lowered performance and motivation. (p. 594)

**bystander intervention** The act of helping strangers in an emergency situation. (p. 629)

**Cannon-Bard theory** A theory about the relationship between emotional experience and physiological activity suggesting that a stimulus simultaneously triggers activity in the autonomic nervous system and emotional experience in the brain. (p. 370)

**Cartesian Theater** (after philosopher René Descartes) A mental screen or stage on which things appear to be presented for viewing by the mind's eye. (p. 294)

**case method** A method of gathering scientific knowledge by studying a single individual. (p. 44)

**catatonic behavior** A marked decrease in all movement or an increase in muscular rigidity and overactivity. (p. 521)

**categorization** The process by which people identify a stimulus as a member of a class of related stimuli. (p. 652)

**category-specific deficit** A neurological syndrome that is characterized by an inability to recognize objects that belong to a particular category while leaving the ability to recognize objects outside the category undisturbed. (p. 268)

**cell body** The part of a neuron that coordinates information-processing tasks and keeps the cell alive. (p. 75)

**central nervous system (CNS)** The part of the nervous system that is composed of the brain and spinal cord. (p. 87)

**cephalocaudal rule** The "top-to-bottom" rule that describes the tendency for motor skills to emerge in sequence from the head to the feet. (p. 411)

**cerebellum** A large structure of the hindbrain that controls fine motor skills. (p. 93)

**cerebral cortex** The outermost layer of the brain, visible to the naked eye and divided into two hemispheres. (p. 95)

**childhood** The stage of development that begins at about 18 to 24 months and lasts until adolescence. (p. 415)

**chromosomes** Strands of DNA wound around each other in a double-helix configuration. (p. 104)

**chronic stressor** A source of stress that occurs continuously or repeatedly. (p. 584)

**chunking** Combining small pieces of information into larger clusters or chunks that are more easily held in short-term memory. (p. 175)

**circadian rhythm** A naturally occurring 24-hour cycle. (p. 309)

**classical conditioning** When a neutral stimulus evokes a response after being paired with a stimulus that naturally evokes a response. (p. 212)

**cochlea** A fluid-filled tube that is the organ of auditory transduction. (p. 152)

**cocktail party phenomenon** A phenomenon in which people tune in one message even while they filter out others nearby. (p. 299)

**cognitive behavioral therapy (CBT)** A blend of cognitive and behavioral therapeutic strategies. (p. 552)

**cognitive development** The emergence of the ability to understand the world. (p. 412)

**cognitive dissonance** An unpleasant state that arises when a person recognizes the inconsistency of his or her actions, attitudes, or beliefs. (p. 650)

**cognitive map** A mental representation of the physical features of the environment. (p. 238)

**cognitive neuroscience** A field that attempts to understand the links between cognitive processes and brain activity. (p. 25)

**cognitive psychology** The scientific study of mental processes, including perception, thought, memory, and reasoning. (p. 21)

**cognitive restructuring** A therapeutic approach that teaches clients to question the automatic beliefs, assumptions, and predictions that often lead to negative emotions and to replace negative thinking with more realistic beliefs. (p. 551)

**cognitive therapy** A form of psychotherapy that involves helping a client identify and correct any distorted thinking about self, others, or the world. (p. 550)

**cognitive unconscious** The mental processes that give rise to the person's thoughts, choices, emotions, and behavior even though they are not experienced by the person. (p. 306)

**color-opponent system** Pairs of visual neurons that work in opposition. (p. 137)

**comorbidity** The co-occurrence of two or more disorders in a single individual. (p. 496)

**companionate love** An experience involving affection, trust, and concern for a partner's well-being. (p. 638)

**comparison level** The cost-benefit ratio that people believe they deserve or could attain in another relationship. (p. 638)

**concept** A mental representation that groups or categorizes shared features of related objects, events, or other stimuli. (p. 267)

**concrete operational stage** The stage of development that begins at about 6 years and ends at about 11 years, in which children acquire a basic understanding of the physical world and a preliminary understanding of their own and others' minds. (p. 415)

**conditioned response (CR)** A reaction that resembles an unconditioned response but is produced by a conditioned stimulus. (p. 213)

**conditioned stimulus (CS)** A stimulus that is initially neutral and produces no reliable response in an organism. (p. 213)

**cones** Photoreceptors that detect color, operate under normal daylight conditions, and allow us to focus on fine detail. (p. 132)

**conformity** The tendency to do what others do simply because others are doing it. (p. 643)

**conjunction fallacy** When people think that two events are more likely to occur together than either individual event. (p. 276)

**conscious motivation** A motivation of which one is aware. (p. 399)

**consciousness** A person's subjective experience of the world and the mind. (pp. 8, 294)

**conservation** The notion that the properties of an object are invariant despite changes in the object's appearance. (p. 415)

**construct validity** The tendency for an operational definition and a property to have a clear conceptual relation. (p. 43)

**control group** One of the two groups of participants created by the manipulation of an independent variable in an experiment that is not exposed to the stimulus being studied. (p. 60)

**conventional stage** A stage of moral development in which the morality of an action is primarily determined by the extent to which it conforms to social rules. (p. 427)

**conversion disorder** A disorder characterized by apparently debilitating physical symptoms that appear to be voluntary—but that the person experiences as involuntary. (p. 607)

**cooperation** Behavior by two or more individuals that leads to mutual benefit. (p. 625)

**corpus callosum** A thick band of nerve fibers that connects large areas of the cerebral cortex on each side of the brain and supports communication of information across the hemispheres. (p. 98)

**correlation** The "co-relationship" or pattern of covariation between two variables, each of which has been measured several times. (p. 53)

**correlation coefficient** A statistical measure of the direction and strength of a correlation, which is signified by the letter *r*. (p. 54)

**correspondence bias** The tendency to make a dispositional attribution even when a person's behavior was caused by the situation. Also known as the fundamental attribution error. (p. 658)

**crystallized intelligence** The accuracy and amount of information available for processing (see *fluid intelligence*). (p. 348)

**cultural psychology** The study of how cultures reflect and shape the psychological processes of their members. (p. 29)

**debriefing** A verbal description of the true nature and purpose of a study that psychologists provide to people after they have participated in the study. (p. 68)

**deep structure** The meaning of a sentence. (p. 256)

**defense mechanisms** Unconscious coping mechanisms that reduce anxiety generated by threats from unacceptable impulses. (p. 466)

**deindividuation** A phenomenon that occurs when immersion in a group causes people to become less aware of their individual values. (p. 629)

**delusion** A patently false belief system, often bizarre and grandiose, that is maintained in spite of its irrationality. (p. 520)

**demand characteristics** Those aspects of an observational setting that cause people to behave as they think an observer wants or expects them to behave. (p. 49)

**dendrites** The part of a neuron that receives information from other neurons and relays it to the cell body. (p. 75)

**dependent variable** The variable that is measured in a study. (p. 60)

**depressants** Substances that reduce the activity of the central nervous system. (p. 321)

**developmental psychology** The study of continuity and change across the life span. (p. 406)

**deviation IQ** A statistic obtained by dividing a person's test score by the average test score of people in the same age group and then multiplying the quotient by 100 (see *ratio IQ*). (p. 340)

**diathesis-stress model** Suggests that a person may be predisposed for a mental disorder that remains unexpressed until triggered by stress. (p. 498)

**dichotic listening** A task in which people wearing headphones hear different messages presented to each ear. (p. 298)

**diffusion of responsibility** The tendency for individuals to feel diminished responsibility for their actions when they are surrounded by others who are acting the same way. (p. 629)

**discrimination** Positive or negative behavior toward another person based on their group membership. (p. 628)

**discrimination** The capacity to distinguish between similar but distinct stimuli. (p. 217)

**disorganized speech** Severe disruption of verbal communication in which ideas shift rapidly and incoherently from one to another unrelated topic. (p. 521)

**displacement** A defense mechanism that involves shifting unacceptable wishes or drives to a neutral or less-threatening alternative. (p. 467)

**display rules** Norms for the control of emotional expression. (p. 383)

**dissociative amnesia** The sudden loss of memory for significant personal information. (p. 510)

**dissociative disorder** A disorder in which normal cognitive processes are severely disjointed and fragmented, creating significant disruptions in memory, awareness, or personality that can vary in length from a matter of minutes to many years. (p. 508)

**dissociative fugue** The sudden loss of memory for one's personal history, accompanied by an abrupt departure from home and the assumption of a new identity. (p. 510)

**dissociative identity disorder (DID)** The presence within an individual of two or more distinct identities that at different times take control of the individual's behavior. (p. 508)

**dissociative identity disorder** A condition that involves the occurrence of two or more distinct identities within the same individual. (p. 14)

*DMS-IV-TR* Diagnostic and Statistical Manual of Mental Disorders (Fourth Edition, Text Revision). (p. 491)

**door-in-the-face technique** A strategy that uses reciprocating concessions to influence behavior. (p. 642)

**dopamine** A neurotransmitter that regulates motor behavior, motivation, pleasure, and emotional arousal. (p. 84)

**dopamine hypothesis** The idea that schizophrenia involves an excess of dopamine activity. (p. 524)

**double depression** A moderately depressed mood that persists for at least 2 years and is punctuated by periods of major depression. (p. 512)

**double-blind** An observation whose true purpose is hidden from the researcher as well as from the participant. (p. 51)

**drive** An internal state generated by departures from physiological optimality. (p. 390)

**drug tolerance** The tendency for larger doses of a drug to be required over time to achieve the same effect. (p. 319)

**dynamic unconscious** An active system encompassing a lifetime of hidden memories, the person's deepest instincts and desires, and the person's inner struggle to control these forces. (pp. 305, 463)

**dysthymia** A disorder that involves the same symptoms as in depression only less severe, but the symptoms last longer, persisting for at least 2 years. (p. 512)

**echoic memory** A fast-decaying store of auditory information. (p. 174)

**eclectic psychotherapy** Treatment that draws on techniques from different forms of therapy, depending on the client and the problem. (p. 543)

**ego** The component of personality, developed through contact with the external world, that enables us to deal with life's practical demands. (p. 464)

**egocentrism** The failure to understand that the world appears differently to different observers. (p. 416)

**elaborative encoding** The process of actively relating new information to knowledge that is already in memory. (p. 170)

**electroconvulsive therapy (ECT)** A treatment that involves inducing a mild seizure by delivering an electric shock to the brain. (p. 567)

**electroencephalogram (EEG)** A device used to record electrical activity in the brain. (p. 110)

**electromyograph (EMG)** A device that measures muscle contractions under the surface of a person's skin. (p. 42)

**electrooculograph (EOG)** An instrument that measures eye movements. (p. 311)

**embryonic stage** The period of prenatal development that lasts from the second week until about the eighth week. (p. 407)

**emotion** A positive or negative experience that is associated with a particular pattern of physiological activity. (p. 307)

**emotion regulation** The use of cognitive and behavioral strategies to influence one's emotional experience. (p. 376)

**emotional expression** Any observable sign of an emotional state. (p. 377)

**empiricism** Originally a Greek school of medicine that stressed the importance of observation, and now generally used to describe any attempt to acquire knowledge by observing objects or events. (p. 40)

**encoding** The process by which we transform what we perceive, think, or feel into an enduring memory. (p. 169)

**encoding specificity principle** The idea that a retrieval cue can serve as an effective reminder when it helps re-create the specific way in which information was initially encoded. (p. 180)

**endorphins** or **endogenous opiates** Neurotransmitters that have a similar structure to opiates and that appear to play a role in how the brain copes internally with pain and emotion. (pp. 84, 325)

**episodic memory** The collection of past personal experiences that occurred at a particular time and place. (p. 185)

**equity** A state of affairs in which the cost-benefit ratios of two partners are roughly equal. (p. 638)

**evolutionary psychology** A psychological approach that explains mind and behavior in terms of the adaptive value of abilities that are preserved over time by natural selection. (p. 26)

**exemplar theory** A theory of categorization that argues that we make category judgments by comparing a new instance with stored memories for other instances of the category. (p. 272)

**existential approach** A school of thought that regards personality as governed by an individual's ongoing choices and decisions in the context of the realities of life and death. (p. 472)

**expectancy theory** The idea that alcohol effects can be produced by people's expectations of how alcohol will influence them in particular situations. (p. 321)

**experiment** A technique for establishing the causal relationship between variables. (p. 58)

**experimental group** One of the two groups of participants created by the manipulation of an independent variable in an experiment; the experimental group is exposed to the stimulus being studied and the *control group* is not. (p. 60)

**explicit memory** The act of consciously or intentionally retrieving past experiences. (p. 183)

**exposure therapy** An approach to treatment that involves confronting an emotion-arousing stimulus directly and repeatedly, ultimately leading to a decrease in the emotional response. (p. 549)

**expressed emotion** Emotional overinvolvement (intrusiveness) and excessive criticism directed toward the former patient by his or her family. (p. 525)

**external validity** A characteristic of an experiment in which the independent and dependent variables are operationally defined in a normal, typical, or realistic way. (p. 65)

**extinction** The gradual elimination of a learned response that occurs when the US is no longer presented. (p. 216)

**extrinsic motivation** A motivation to take actions that are not themselves rewarding but that lead to reward. (p. 397)

**facial feedback hypothesis** The hypothesis that emotional expressions can cause the emotional experiences they signify. (p. 381)

**factor analysis** A statistical technique that explains a large number of correlations in terms of a small number of underlying factors. (p. 345)

**false recognition** A feeling of familiarity about something that hasn't been encountered before. (p. 194)

**family resemblance theory** Members of a category have features that appear to be characteristic of category members but may not be possessed by every member. (p. 269)

**fast mapping** The fact that children can map a word onto an underlying concept after only a single exposure. (p. 258)

**fetal alcohol syndrome** A developmental disorder that stems from heavy alcohol use by the mother during pregnancy. (p. 408)

**fetal stage** The period of prenatal development that lasts from the ninth week until birth. (p. 408)

**fight-or-flight response** An emotional and physiological reaction to an emergency that increases readiness for action. (p. 586)

**fixation** A phenomenon in which a person's pleasure-seeking drives become psychologically stuck, or arrested, at a particular psychosexual stage. (p. 468)

**fixed interval schedule (FI)** An operant conditioning principle in which reinforcements are presented at fixed time periods, provided that the appropriate response is made. (p. 231)

**fixed ratio schedule (FR)** An operant conditioning principle in which reinforcement is delivered after a specific number of responses have been made. (p. 232)

**flashbulb memories** Detailed recollections of when and where we heard about shocking events. (p. 201)

**fluid intelligence** The ability to process information (see *crystallized intelligence*). (p. 348)

**foot-in-the-door technique** A strategy that uses a person's desire for consistency to influence that person's behavior. (p. 650)

**formal operations stage** The stage of development that begins around the age of 11 and lasts through adulthood, in which children gain a deeper understanding of their own and others' minds and learn to reason abstractly. (p. 416)

**fovea** An area of the retina where vision is the clearest and there are no rods at all. (p. 133)

**framing effects** When people give different answers to the same problem depending on how the problem is phrased (or framed). (p. 277)

**fraternal twins** (also called **dizygotic twins**) Twins who develop from two different eggs that were fertilized by two different sperm (see *identical twins*). (p. 352)

**frequency distribution** A graphical representation of the measurements of a sample that are arranged by the number of times each measurement was observed. (p. 46)

**frequency format hypothesis** The proposal that our minds evolved to notice how frequently things occur, not how likely they are to occur. (p. 280)

**frontal lobe** A region of the cerebral cortex that has specialized areas for movement, abstract thinking, planning, memory, and judgment. (p. 99)

**frustration-aggression principle** A principle stating that people aggress when their goals are thwarted. (p. 623)

**full consciousness** Consciousness in which you know and are able to report your mental state. (p. 300)

**functional fixedness** The tendency to perceive the functions of objects as fixed. (p. 284)

**functionalism** The study of the purpose mental processes serve in enabling people to adapt to their environment. (p. 10)

**fundamental attribution error** See *correspondence bias.*

**GABA (gamma-aminobutyric acid)** The primary inhibitory neurotransmitter in the brain. (p. 84)

**gate-control theory** A theory of pain perception based on the idea that signals arriving from pain receptors in the body can be stopped, or *gated*, by interneurons in the spinal cord via feedback from two directions. (p. 157)

**gene** The unit of hereditary transmission. (p. 104)

**general adaptation syndrome (GAS)** A three-stage physiological response that appears regardless of the stressor that is encountered. (p. 587)

**generalization** A process in which the CR is observed even though the CS is slightly different from the original one used during acquisition. (p. 217)

**generalized anxiety disorder (GAD)** A disorder characterized by chronic excessive worry accompanied by three or more of the following symptoms: restlessness, fatigue, concentration problems, irritability, muscle tension, and sleep disturbance. (p. 502)

**genetic dysphasia** A syndrome characterized by an inability to learn the grammatical structure of language despite having otherwise normal intelligence. (p. 260)

**genital stage** The final psychosexual stage, a time for the coming together of the mature adult personality with a capacity to love, work, and relate to others in a mutually satisfying and reciprocal manner. (p. 470)

**germinal stage** The 2-week period of prenatal development that begins at conception. (p. 407)

**Gestalt psychology** A psychological approach that emphasizes that we often perceive the whole rather than the sum of the parts. (p. 13)

**Gestalt therapy** An existentialist approach to treatment with the goal of helping the client become aware of his or her thoughts, behaviors, experiences, and feelings and to "own" or take responsibility for them. (p. 555)

**glial cells** Support cells found in the nervous system. (p. 76)

**glutamate** A major excitatory neurotransmitter involved in information transmission throughout the brain. (p. 84)

**grammar** A set of rules that specify how the units of language can be combined to produce meaningful messages. (p. 255)

**grossly disorganized behavior** Behavior that is inappropriate for the situation or ineffective in attaining goals, often with specific motor disturbances. (p. 521)

**group** A collection of two or more people who believe they have something in common. (p. 628)

**group polarization** The tendency for a group's initial leaning to get stronger over time. (p. 629)

**group therapy** Therapy in which multiple participants (who often do not know one another at the outset) work on their individual problems in a group atmosphere. (p. 557)

**habituation** A general process in which repeated or prolonged exposure to a stimulus results in a gradual reduction in responding. (p. 211)

**hair cells** Specialized auditory receptor neurons embedded in the basilar membrane. (p. 152)

**hallucination** A false perceptual experience that has a compelling sense of being real despite the absence of external stimulation. (p. 520)

**hallucinogens** Drugs that alter sensation and perception and often cause visual and auditory hallucinations. (p. 326)

**haptic perception** The active exploration of the environment by touching and grasping objects with our hands. (p. 155)

**harm reduction approach** A response to high-risk behaviors that focuses on reducing the harm such behaviors have on people's lives. (p. 325)

**health psychology** The subfield of psychology concerned with ways psychological factors influence the causes and treatment of physical illness and the maintenance of health. (p. 582)

**hedonic principle** The notion that all people are motivated to experience pleasure and avoid pain. (p. 388)

**helplessness theory** The idea that individuals prone to depression automatically attribute negative experiences to causes that are internal (i.e., their own fault), stable (i.e., unlikely to change), and global (i.e., widespread). (p. 514)

**heritability** A measure of the variability of behavioral traits among individuals that can be accounted for by genetic factors. (p. 106)

**heritability coefficient** A statistic (commonly denoted as $h2$) that describes the proportion of the difference between people's scores that can be explained by differences in their genetic makeup. (p. 353)

**heuristic** A fast and efficient strategy that may facilitate decision making but does not guarantee that a solution will be reached. (p. 275)

**heuristic persuasion** A change in attitudes or beliefs that is brought about by appeals to habit or emotion. (p. 647)

**hindbrain** An area of the brain that coordinates information coming into and out of the spinal cord. (p. 93)

**hippocampus** A structure critical for creating new memories and integrating them into a network of knowledge so that they can be stored indefinitely in other parts of the cerebral cortex. (p. 96)

**homeostasis** The tendency for a system to take action to keep itself in a particular state. (p. 390)

**human sexual response cycle** The stages of physiological arousal during sexual activity. (p. 396)

**humanistic psychology** An approach to understanding human nature that emphasizes the positive potential of human beings. (p. 16)

**hypnosis** An altered state of consciousness characterized by suggestibility and the feeling that one's actions are occurring involuntarily. (p. 327)

**hypnotic analgesia** The reduction of pain through hypnosis in people who are susceptible to hypnosis. (p. 330)

**hypochondriasis** A psychological disorder in which a person is preoccupied with minor symptoms and develops an exaggerated belief that the symptoms signify a life-threatening illness. (p. 607)

**hypothalamus** A subcortical structure that regulates body temperature, hunger, thirst, and sexual behavior. (p. 95)

**hypothesis** A specific and testable prediction that is usually derived from a *theory*. (p. 65)

**hysteria** A temporary loss of cognitive or motor functions, usually as a result of emotionally upsetting experiences. (p. 14)

**iatrogenic illness** A disorder or symptom that occurs as a result of a medical or psychotherapeutic treatment. (p. 576)

**iconic memory** A fast-decaying store of visual information. (p. 174)

**id** The part of the mind containing the drives present at birth; it is the source of our bodily needs, wants, desires, and impulses, particularly our sexual and aggressive drives. (p. 464)

**identical twins** (also called **monozygotic twins**) Twins who develop from the splitting of a single egg that was fertilized by a single sperm (see *fraternal twins*). (p. 352)

**identification** A defense mechanism that helps deal with feelings of threat and anxiety by enabling us unconsciously to take on the characteristics of another person who seems more powerful or better able to cope. (p. 467)

**illusions** Errors of perception, memory, or judgment in which subjective experience differs from objective reality. (p. 12)

**immune system** A complex response system that protects the body from bacteria, viruses, and other foreign substances. (p. 588)

**implicit learning** Learning that takes place largely independent of awareness of both the process and the products of information acquisition. (p. 246)

**implicit memory** The influence of past experiences on later behavior and performance, even though people are not trying to recollect them and are not aware that they are remembering them. (p. 183)

**in-group** A human category of which a person is a member. (p. 628)

**independent variable** The variable that is manipulated in an experiment. (p. 60)

**infancy** The stage of development that begins at birth and lasts between 18 and 24 months. (p. 410)

**informational influence** A phenomenon whereby a person's behavior is influenced by another person's behavior because the latter provides information about what is good or true. (p. 646)

**informed consent** A written agreement to participate in a study made by a person who has been informed of all the risks that participation may entail. (p. 68)

**insomnia** Difficulty in falling asleep or staying asleep. (p. 313)

**intelligence** A hypothetical mental ability that enables people to direct their thinking, adapt to their circumstances, and learn from their experiences. (p. 351)

**intermittent reinforcement** An operant conditioning principle in which only some of the responses made are followed by reinforcement. (p. 233)

**intermittent-reinforcement effect** The fact that operant behaviors that are maintained under intermittent reinforcement schedules resist extinction better than those maintained under continuous reinforcement. (p. 233)

**internal validity** The characteristic of an experiment that allows one to draw accurate inferences about the causal relationship between an independent and dependent variable. (p. 64)

**internal working model of attachment** A set of expectations about how the primary caregiver will respond when the child feels insecure. (p. 424)

**interneurons** Neurons that connect sensory neurons, motor neurons, or other interneurons. (p. 77)

**interpersonal psychotherapy (IPT)** A form of psychotherapy that focuses on helping clients improve their social relationships. (p. 547)

**intrinsic motivation** A motivation to take actions that are themselves rewarding. (p. 397)

**introspection** The subjective observation of one's own experience. (p. 8)

**ironic processes of mental control** Mental processes that can produce ironic errors because monitoring for errors can itself produce them. (p. 304)

**James-Lange theory** A theory about the relationship between emotional experience and physiological activity suggesting that stimuli trigger activity in the autonomic nervous sys-

tem, which in turn produces an emotional experience in the brain. (p. 370)

**just noticeable difference (JND)** The minimal change in a stimulus that can just barely be detected. (p. 126)

**kin selection** The process by which evolution selects for genes that cause individuals to provide benefits to their relatives. (p. 627)

**language** A system for communicating with others using signals that convey meaning and are combined according to rules of grammar. (p. 254)

**language acquisition device (LAD)** A collection of processes that facilitate language learning. (p. 260)

**latency stage** The fourth psychosexual stage, in which the primary focus is on the further development of intellectual, creative, interpersonal, and athletic skills. (p. 469)

**latent content** A dream's true underlying meaning. (p. 317)

**latent learning** A condition in which something is learned but it is not manifested as a behavioral change until sometime in the future. (p. 238)

**law of effect** The principle that behaviors that are followed by a "satisfying state of affairs" tend to be repeated and those that produce an "unpleasant state of affairs" are less likely to be repeated. (p. 225)

**law of large numbers** A statistical law stating that as sample size increases, the attributes of a sample will more closely reflect the attributes of the population from which it was drawn. (p. 45)

**learning** Some experience that results in a relatively permanent change in the state of the learner. (p. 210)

**limbic system** A group of forebrain structures including the hypothalamus, the amygdala, and the hippocampus, which are involved in motivation, emotion, learning, and memory. (p. 96)

**linguistic relativity hypothesis** The proposal that language shapes the nature of thought. (p. 266)

**locus of control** A person's tendency to perceive the control of rewards as internal to the self or external in the environment. (p. 476)

**long-term memory store** A place where information can be kept for hours, days, weeks, or years. (p. 177)

**long-term potentiation (LTP)** Enhanced neural processing that results from the strengthening of synaptic connections. (p. 178)

**loudness** A sound's intensity. (p. 150)

**lymphocytes** White blood cells that produce antibodies that fight infection. (p. 588)

**major depressive disorder** A disorder characterized by a severely depressed mood that lasts 2 weeks or more and is accompanied by

feelings of worthlessness and lack of pleasure, lethargy, and sleep and appetite disturbances. (p. 512)

**manifest content** A dream's apparent topic or superficial meaning. (p. 317)

**manipulation** A characteristic of experimentation in which the researcher artificially creates a pattern of variation in an independent variable in order to determine its causal powers. Manipulation usually results in the creation of an *experimental group* and a *control group*. (p. 59)

**marijuana** The leaves and buds of the hemp plant. (p. 326)

**matched pairs** An observational technique that involves matching each participant in the experimental group with a specific participant in the control group in order to eliminate the possibility that a third variable (and not the independent variable) caused changes in the dependent variable. (p. 57)

**matched samples** An observational technique that involves matching the average of the participants in the experimental and control groups in order to eliminate the possibility that a third variable (and not the independent variable) caused changes in the dependent variable. (p. 57)

**mean** The average of the measurements in a frequency distribution. (p. 47)

**means-ends analysis** A process of searching for the means or steps to reduce differences between the current situation and the desired goal. (p. 281)

**measure** A device that can detect the measurable events to which an operational definition refers. (p. 42)

**median** The "middle" measurement in a frequency distribution. Half the measurements in a frequency distribution are greater than or equal to the median and half are less than or equal to the median. (p. 47)

**medical model** The conceptualization of psychological abnormalities as diseases that, like biological diseases, have symptoms and causes and possible cures. (p. 491)

**meditation** The practice of intentional contemplation. (p. 332)

**medulla** An extension of the spinal cord into the skull that coordinates heart rate, circulation, and respiration. (p. 93)

**memory** The ability to store and retrieve information over time. (p. 168)

**memory misattribution** Assigning a recollection or an idea to the wrong source. (p. 193)

**memory storage** The process of maintaining information in memory over time. (p. 173)

**mental control** The attempt to change conscious states of mind. (p. 303)

**mere exposure effect** The tendency for liking to increase with the frequency of exposure. (p. 632)

**metabolism** The rate at which energy is used by the body. (p. 394)

**method** A set of rules and techniques for observation that allow researchers to avoid the illusions, mistakes, and erroneous conclusions that simple observation can produce. (p. 40)

**mind** Our private inner experience of perceptions, thoughts, memories, and feelings. (p. 2)

**mind/body problem** The issue of how the mind is related to the brain and body. (p. 297)

**mindfulness meditation** A form of cognitive therapy that teaches an individual to be fully present in each moment; to be aware of his or her thoughts, feelings and sensations; and to detect symptoms before they become a problem. (p. 551)

**minimal consciousness** A low-level kind of sensory awareness and responsiveness that occurs when the mind inputs sensations and may output behavior. (p. 300)

**Minnesota Multiphasic Personality Inventory (MMPI)** A well-researched, clinical questionnaire used to assess personality and psychological problems. (p. 452)

**mode** The "most frequent" measurement in a frequency distribution. (p. 47)

**monocular depth cues** Aspects of a scene that yield information about depth when viewed with only one eye. (p. 145)

**mood disorders** Mental disorders that have a disturbance in mood as their predominant feature. (p. 511)

**morphemes** The smallest meaningful units of language. (p. 255)

**morphological rules** A set of rules that indicate how morphemes can be combined to form words. (p. 255)

**motion parallax** A depth cue based on the movement of the head over time. (p. 147)

**motivation** The purpose for or cause of an action. (p. 386)

**motor development** The emergence of the ability to execute physical action. (p. 411)

**motor neurons** Neurons that carry signals from the spinal cord to the muscles to produce movement. (p. 77)

**myelin sheath** An insulating layer of fatty material. (p. 76)

**myelination** The formation of a fatty sheath around the axons of a brain cell. (p. 408)

**narcissism** A trait that reflects a grandiose view of the self combined with a tendency to seek admiration from and exploit others. (p. 484)

**narcolepsy** A disorder in which sudden sleep attacks occur in the middle of waking activities. (p. 314)

**narcotics** or **opiates** Highly addictive drugs derived from opium that relieve pain. (p. 324)

**nativism** The philosophical view that certain kinds of knowledge are innate or inborn. (p. 5)

**nativist theory** The view that language development is best explained as an innate, biological capacity. (p. 260)

**natural correlation** A correlation observed between naturally occurring variables. (p. 56)

**natural selection** Charles Darwin's theory that the features of an organism that help it survive and reproduce are more likely than other features to be passed on to subsequent generations. (p. 10)

**naturalistic observation** A method of gathering scientific knowledge by unobtrusively observing people in their natural environments. (p. 49)

**need for achievement** The motivation to solve worthwhile problems. (p. 399)

**negative symptoms** Emotional and social withdrawal, apathy, poverty of speech, and other indications of the absence or insufficiency of normal behavior, motivation, and emotion. (p. 521)

**nervous system** An interacting network of neurons that conveys electrochemical information throughout the body. (p. 87)

**neurons** Cells in the nervous system that communicate with one another to perform information-processing tasks. (p. 74)

**neurotransmitters** Chemicals that transmit information across the synapse to a receiving neuron's dendrites. (p. 81)

**night terrors** (or sleep terrors) Abrupt awakenings with panic and intense emotional arousal. (p. 314)

**NMDA receptor** A hippocampal receptor site that influences the flow of information from one neuron to another across the synapse by controlling the initiation of long-term potentiation. (p. 178)

**nonshared environment** Those environmental factors that are not experienced by all relevant members of a household (see *shared environment*). (p. 355)

**norepinephrine** A neurotransmitter that influences mood and arousal. (p. 84)

**norm** A customary standard for behavior that is widely shared by members of a culture. (p. 642)

**norm of reciprocity** The norm that people should benefit those who have benefited them. (p. 642)

**normal distribution** A frequency distribution in which most measurements are concentrated around the mean and fall off toward the tails, and the two sides of the distribution are symmetrical. (p. 47)

**normative influence** A phenomenon whereby one person's behavior is influenced by another person's behavior because the latter provides information about what is appropriate. (p. 642)

**obedience** The tendency to do what authorities tell us to do simply because they tell us to do it. (p. 644)

**object permanence** The idea that objects continue to exist even when they are not visible. (p. 413)

**observational learning** A condition in which learning takes place by watching the actions of others. (p. 243)

**observational learning** Learning that occurs when one person observes another person being rewarded or punished. (p. 641)

**obsessive-compulsive disorder (OCD)** A disorder in which repetitive, intrusive thoughts (obsessions) and ritualistic behaviors (compulsions) designed to fend off those thoughts interfere significantly with an individual's functioning. (p. 507)

**occipital lobe** A region of the cerebral cortex that processes visual information. (p. 98)

**Oedipus conflict** A developmental experience in which a child's conflicting feelings toward the opposite-sex parent is (usually) resolved by identifying with the same-sex parent. (p. 469)

**olfactory bulb** A brain structure located above the nasal cavity beneath the frontal lobes. (p. 159)

**olfactory receptor neurons (ORNs)** Receptor cells that initiate the sense of smell. (p. 158)

**operant behavior** Behavior that an organism produces that has some impact on the environment. (p. 225)

**operant conditioning** A type of learning in which the consequences of an organism's behavior determine whether it will be repeated in the future. (p. 224)

**operational definition** A description of an abstract property in terms of a concrete condition that can be measured. (p. 41)

**oral stage** The first psychosexual stage, in which experience centers on the pleasures and frustrations associated with the mouth, sucking, and being fed. (p. 468)

**organizational encoding** The act of categorizing information by noticing the relationships among a series of items. (p. 172)

**out-group** A human category of which a person is not a member. (p. 628)

**outcome expectancies** A person's assumptions about the likely consequences of a future behavior. (p. 476)

**overjustification effect** Circumstances when external rewards can undermine the intrinsic satisfaction of performing a behavior. (p. 229)

**panic disorder** A disorder characterized by the sudden occurrence of multiple psychological and physiological symptoms that contribute to a feeling of stark terror. (p. 505)

**parasympathetic nervous system** A set of nerves that helps the body return to a normal resting state. (p. 88)

**parietal lobe** A region of the cerebral cortex whose functions include processing information about touch. (p. 98)

**passionate love** An experience involving feelings of euphoria, intimacy, and intense sexual attraction. (p. 638)

**perception** The organization, identification, and interpretation of a sensation in order to form a mental representation. (p. 123)

**perceptual confirmation** A phenomenon that occurs when observers perceive what they expect to perceive. (p. 655)

**perceptual constancy** A perceptual principle stating that even as aspects of sensory signals change, perception remains consistent. (p. 142)

**peripheral nervous system (PNS)** The part of the nervous system that connects the central nervous system to the body's organs and muscles. (p. 87)

**persistence** The intrusive recollection of events that we wish we could forget. (p. 201)

**person-centered therapy** An approach to therapy that assumes all individuals have a tendency toward growth and that this growth can be facilitated by acceptance and genuine reactions from the therapist. (p. 553)

**person-situation controversy** The question of whether behavior is caused more by personality or by situational factors. (p. 474)

**personal constructs** Dimensions people use in making sense of their experiences. (p. 475)

**personality** An individual's characteristic style of behaving, thinking, and feeling. (p. 450)

**personality disorder** A disorder characterized by deeply ingrained, inflexible patterns of thinking, feeling, relating to others, or controlling impulses that causes distress or impaired functioning. (p. 526)

**persuasion** A phenomenon that occurs when a person's attitudes or beliefs are influenced by a communication from another person. (p. 647)

**phallic stage** The third psychosexual stage, during which experience is dominated by the pleasure, conflict, and frustration associated with the phallic-genital region as well as powerful incestuous feelings of love, hate, jealousy, and conflict. (p. 469)

**phenomenology** How things seem to the conscious person. (p. 295)

**pheromones** Biochemical odorants emitted by other members of their species that can affect an animal's behavior or physiology. (p. 160)

**philosophical empiricism** The philosophical view that all knowledge is acquired through experience. (p. 5)

**phobic disorders** Disorders characterized by marked, persistent, and excessive fear and avoidance of specific objects, activities, or situations. (p. 503)

**phoneme** The smallest unit of sound that is recognizable as speech rather than as random noise. (p. 254)

**phonological rules** A set of rules that indicate how phonemes can be combined to produce speech sounds. (p. 255)

**phototherapy** A treatment for seasonal depression that involves repeated exposure to bright light. (p. 568)

**phrenology** A now defunct theory that specific mental abilities and characteristics, ranging from memory to the capacity for happiness, are localized in specific regions of the brain. (p. 7)

**physiology** The study of biological processes, especially in the human body. (p. 7)

**pitch** How high or low a sound is. (p. 150)

**pituitary gland** The "master gland" of the body's hormone-producing system, which releases hormones that direct the functions of many other glands in the body. (p. 96)

**place code** The cochlea encodes different frequencies at different locations along the basilar membrane. (p. 153)

**placebo** An inert substance or procedure that has been applied with the expectation that a healing response will be produced. (p. 571)

**placebo effect** A clinically significant psychological or physiological response to a therapeutically inert substance or procedure. (p. 606)

**pleasure principle** The psychic force that motivates the tendency to seek immediate gratification of any impulse. (p. 464)

**pons** A brain structure that relays information from the cerebellum to the rest of the brain. (p. 94)

**population** The complete collection of participants who might possibly be measured. (p. 45)

**postconventional stage** A stage of moral development at which the morality of an action is determined by a set of general principles that reflect core values. (p. 427)

**posthypnotic amnesia** The failure to retrieve memories following hypnotic suggestions to forget. (p. 330)

**posttraumatic stress disorder (PTSD)** A psychological disorder characterized by chronic physiological arousal, recurrent unwanted thoughts or images of the trauma, and avoidance of things that call the trauma to mind. (p. 592)

**power** The tendency for a measure to produce different results when it is used to measure different things. (p. 44)

**practical reasoning** Figuring out what to do, or reasoning directed toward action. (p. 286)

**preconventional stage** A stage of moral development in which the morality of an action is primarily determined by its consequences for the actor. (p. 427)

**predictive validity** The tendency for an operational definition to be related to other operational definitions. (p. 43)

**prejudice** A positive or negative evaluation of another person based on their group membership. (p. 628)

**preoperational stage** The stage of development that begins at about 2 years and ends at about 6 years, in which children have a preliminary understanding of the physical world. (p. 415)

**preparedness theory** The idea that people are instinctively predisposed toward certain fears. (p. 504)

**primary sex characteristics** Bodily structures that are directly involved in reproduction. (p. 431)

**priming** An enhanced ability to think of a stimulus, such as a word or object, as a result of a recent exposure to the stimulus. (p. 184)

**proactive interference** Situations in which earlier learning impairs memory for information acquired later. (p. 189)

**problem of other minds** The fundamental difficulty we have in perceiving the consciousness of others. (p. 295)

**procedural memory** The gradual acquisition of skills as a result of practice, or "knowing how," to do things. (p. 183)

**prodigy** A person of normal intelligence who has an extraordinary ability. (p. 350)

**projection** A defense mechanism that involves attributing one's own threatening feelings, motives, or impulses to another person or group. (p. 466)

**projective techniques** A standard series of ambiguous stimuli designed to elicit unique responses that reveal inner aspects of an individual's personality. (p. 452)

**prospect theory** Proposes that people choose to take on risk when evaluating potential losses and avoid risks when evaluating potential gains. (p. 279)

**prospective memory** Remembering to do things in the future. (p. 191)

**prototype** The "best" or "most typical member" of a category. (p. 270)

**proximodistal rule** The "inside-to-outside" rule that describes the tendency for motor skills to emerge in sequence from the center to the periphery. (p. 411)

**psychoactive drug** A chemical that influences consciousness or behavior by altering the brain's chemical message system. (p. 318)

**psychoanalysis** A therapeutic approach that focuses on bringing unconscious material into conscious awareness to better understand psychological disorders. (p. 15)

**psychoanalytic theory** Sigmund Freud's approach to understanding human behavior that emphasizes the importance of unconscious mental processes in shaping feelings, thoughts, and behaviors. (p. 15)

**psychodynamic approach** An approach that regards personality as formed by needs, strivings, and desires, largely operating outside of awareness—motives that can also produce emotional disorders. (p. 463)

**psychodynamic psychotherapies** A general approach to treatment that explores childhood events and encourages individuals to develop insight into their psychological problems. (p. 543)

**psychology** The scientific study of mind and behavior. (p. 2)

**psychopharmacology** The study of drug effects on psychological states and symptoms. (p. 560)

**psychophysics** Methods that measure the strength of a stimulus and the observer's sensitivity to that stimulus. (p. 124)

**psychosexual stages** Distinct early life stages through which personality is formed as children experience sexual pleasures from specific body areas and caregivers redirect or interfere with those pleasures. (p. 468)

**psychosomatic illness** An interaction between mind and body that can produce illness. (p. 607)

**psychosurgery** Surgical destruction of specific brain areas. (p. 569)

**psychotherapy** An interaction between a therapist and someone suffering from a psychological problem with the goal of providing support or relief from the problem. (p. 541)

**puberty** The bodily changes associated with sexual maturity. (p. 431)

**punisher** Any stimulus or event that functions to decrease the likelihood of the behavior that led to it. (p. 226)

**random sampling** A technique for choosing participants that ensures that every member of a population has an equal chance of being included in the sample. (p. 66)

**randomization** A procedure to ensure that a participant's inclusion in the experimental or control group is not determined by a third variable. (p. 61)

**range** The numerical difference between the smallest and largest measurements in a frequency distribution. (p. 47)

**ratio IQ** A statistic obtained by dividing a person's mental age by the person's physical age and then multiplying the quotient by 100 (see *deviation IQ*). (p. 339)

**rational choice theory** The classical view that we make decisions by determining how likely something is to happen, judging the value of the outcome, and then multiplying the two. (p. 274)

**rational coping** Facing a stressor and working to overcome it. (p. 596)

**rationalization** A defense mechanism that involves supplying a reasonable-sounding explanation for unacceptable feelings and behavior to conceal (mostly from oneself) one's underlying motives or feelings. (p. 466)

**reaction formation** A defense mechanism that involves unconsciously replacing threatening inner wishes and fantasies with an exaggerated version of their opposite. (p. 466)

**reaction time** The amount of time taken to respond to a specific stimulus. (p. 7)

**reality principle** The regulating mechanism that enables the individual to delay gratifying immediate needs and function effectively in the real world. (p. 464)

**reappraisal** A strategy that involves changing one's emotional experience by changing the meaning of the emotion- eliciting stimulus. (p. 376)

**reasoning** A mental activity that consists of organizing information or beliefs into a series of steps to reach conclusions. (p. 285)

**rebound effect of thought suppression** The tendency of a thought to return to consciousness with greater frequency following suppression. (p. 303)

**receptive field** The region of the sensory surface that, when stimulated, causes a change in the firing rate of that neuron. (p. 134)

**receptors** Parts of the cell membrane that receive the neurotransmitter and initiate a new electric signal. (p. 81)

**reciprocal altruism** Behavior that benefits another with the expectation that those benefits will be returned in the future. (p. 627)

**referred pain** Feeling of pain when sensory information from internal and external areas converge on the same nerve cells in the spinal cord. (p. 156)

**reflexes** Specific patterns of motor response that are triggered by specific patterns of sensory stimulation. (p. 411)

**refractory period** The time following an action potential during which a new action potential cannot be initiated. (p. 81)

**reframing** Finding a new or creative way to think about a stressor that reduces its threat. (p. 597)

**regression** A defense mechanism in which the ego deals with internal conflict and perceived threat by reverting to an immature behavior or earlier stage of development. (p. 467)

**rehearsal** The process of keeping information in short-term memory by mentally repeating it. (p. 174)

**reinforcement** The consequences of a behavior that determine whether it will be more likely that the behavior will occur again. (p. 19)

**reinforcer** Any stimulus or event that functions to increase the likelihood of the behavior that led to it. (p. 226)

**relaxation response** A condition of reduced muscle tension, cortical activity, heart rate, breathing rate, and blood pressure. (p. 598)

**relaxation therapy** A technique for reducing tension by consciously relaxing muscles of the body. (p. 598)

**reliability** The tendency for a measure to produce the same result whenever it is used to measure the same thing. (p. 44)

**REM sleep** A stage of sleep characterized by rapid eye movements and a high level of brain activity. (p. 310)

**representativeness heuristic** A mental shortcut that involves making a probability judgment by comparing an object or event to a prototype of the object or event. (p. 277)

**repression** A mental process that removes unacceptable thoughts and memories from consciousness. (p. 305)

**repressive coping** Avoiding situations or thoughts that are reminders of a stressor and maintaining an artificially positive viewpoint. (p. 595)

**resistance** A reluctance to cooperate with treatment for fear of confronting unpleasant unconscious material. (p. 544)

**response** An action or physiological change elicited by a stimulus. (p. 19)

**resting potential** The difference in electric charge between the inside and outside of a neuron's cell membrane. (p. 79)

**reticular formation** A brain structure that regulates sleep, wakefulness, and levels of arousal. (p. 93)

**retina** Light-sensitive tissue lining the back of the eyeball. (p. 132)

**retrieval** The process of bringing to mind information that has been previously encoded and stored. (p. 169)

**retrieval cue** External information that is associated with stored information and helps bring it to mind. (p. 180)

**retroactive interference** Situations in which later learning impairs memory for information acquired earlier. (p. 189)

**retrograde amnesia** The inability to retrieve information that was acquired before a particular date, usually the date of an injury or operation. (p. 177)

**rods** Photoreceptors that become active only under low-light conditions for night vision. (p. 132)

**Rorschach Inkblot Test** A projective personality test in which individual interpretations of the meaning of a set of unstructured inkblots are analyzed to identify a respondent's inner feelings and interpret his or her personality structure. (p. 453)

**sample** The partial collection of people who actually were measured in a study. (p. 45)

**savant** A person of low intelligence who has an extraordinary ability. (p. 350)

**schemas** Theories or models of the way the world works. (p. 413)

**schizophrenia** A disorder characterized by the profound disruption of basic psychological processes, a distorted perception of reality, altered or blunted emotion, and disturbances in thought, motivation, and behavior. (p. 519)

**seasonal affective disorder (SAD)** Depression that involves recurrent depressive episodes in a seasonal pattern. (p. 512)

**second-order conditioning** Conditioning where the US is a stimulus that acquired its ability to produce learning from an earlier procedure in which it was used as a CS. (p. 215)

**secondary sex characteristics** Bodily structures that change dramatically with sexual maturity but that are not directly involved in reproduction. (p. 431)

**self-actualizing tendency** The human motive toward realizing our inner potential. (p. 471)

**self-concept** A person's explicit knowledge of his or her own behaviors, traits, and other personal characteristics. (p. 478)

**self-consciousness** A distinct level of consciousness in which the person's attention is drawn to the self as an object. (p. 301)

**self-esteem** The extent to which an individual likes, values, and accepts the self. (p. 480)

**self-fulfilling prophecy** A phenomenon whereby observers bring about what they expect to perceive. (p. 655)

**self-regulation** The exercise of voluntary control over the self to bring the self into line with preferred standards. (p. 613)

**self-report** A series of answers to a questionnaire that asks people to indicate the extent to which sets of statements or adjectives accurately describe their own behavior or mental state. (p. 452)

**self-selection** The case in which a participant's inclusion in the experimental or control group is determined by the participant. (p. 61)

**self-serving bias** People's tendency to take credit for their successes but downplay responsibility for their failures. (p. 484)

**self-verification** The tendency to seek evidence to confirm the self-concept. (p. 480)

**semantic memory** A network of associated facts and concepts that make up our general knowledge of the world. (p. 185)

**sensation** Simple awareness due to the stimulation of a sense organ. (p. 123)

**sensorimotor stage** A stage of development that begins at birth and lasts through infancy in which infants acquire information about the world by sensing it and moving around within it. (p. 413)

**sensory adaptation** Sensitivity to prolonged stimulation tends to decline over time as an organism adapts to current conditions. (p. 128)

**sensory memory store** The place in which sensory information is kept for a few seconds or less. (p. 173)

**sensory neurons** Neurons that receive information from the external world and convey this information to the brain via the spinal cord. (p. 77)

**serotonin** A neurotransmitter that is involved in the regulation of sleep and wakefulness, eating, and aggressive behavior. (p. 84)

**shaping** Learning that results from the reinforcement of successive approximations to a final desired behavior. (p. 233)

**shared environment** Those environmental factors that are experienced by all relevant members of a household (see *nonshared environment*). (p. 355)

**short-term memory store** A place where nonsensory information is kept for more than a few seconds but less than a minute. (p. 174)

**sick role** A socially recognized set of rights and obligations linked with illness. (p. 608)

**signal detection theory** An observation that the response to a stimulus depends both on a person's sensitivity to the stimulus in the presence of noise and on a person's response criterion. (p. 127)

**sleep apnea** A disorder in which the person stops breathing for brief periods while asleep. (p. 313)

**sleep paralysis** The experience of waking up unable to move. (p. 314)

**social cognition** The processes by which people come to understand others. (p. 650)

**social cognitive approach** An approach that views personality in terms of how the person thinks about the situations encountered in daily life and behaves in response to them. (p. 473)

**social exchange** The hypothesis that people remain in relationships only as long as they perceive a favorable ratio of costs to benefits. (p. 639)

**social influence** The control of one person's behavior by another. (p. 640)

**social loafing** The tendency for people to expend less effort when in a group than alone. (p. 629)

**social phobia** A disorder that involves an irrational fear of being publicly humiliated or embarrassed. (p. 504)

**social psychology** A subfield of psychology that studies the causes and consequences of interpersonal behavior. (p. 28)

**social support** The aid gained through interacting with others. (p. 601)

**somatic nervous system** A set of nerves that conveys information into and out of the central nervous system. (p. 87)

**somatization disorder** A psychological disorder involving combinations of multiple physical complaints with no medical explanation. (p. 607)

**somatoform disorders** The set of psychological disorders in which the person displays physical symptoms not fully explained by a general medical condition. (p. 607)

**somnambulism** (sleepwalking) Occurs when the person arises and walks around while asleep. (p. 313)

**source memory** Recall of when, where, and how information was acquired. (p. 194)

**specific phobia** A disorder that involves an irrational fear of a particular object or situation that markedly interferes with an individual's ability to function. (p. 503)

**spinal reflexes** Simple pathways in the nervous system that rapidly generate muscle contractions. (p. 90)

**spontaneous recovery** The tendency of a learned behavior to recover from extinction after a rest period. (p. 216)

**state-dependent retrieval** The tendency for information to be better recalled when the person is in the same state during encoding and retrieval. (p. 181)

**stereotyping** The process by which people draw inferences about others based on their knowledge of the categories to which others belong. (p. 650)

**stimulants** Substances that excite the central nervous system, heightening arousal and activity levels. (p. 323)

**stimulus** Sensory input from the environment. (p. 7)

**storage** The process of maintaining information in memory over time. (p. 169)

**strange situation** A behavioral test developed by Mary Ainsworth that is used to determine a child's attachment style. (p. 423)

**stress inoculation training (SIT)** A therapy that helps people to cope with stressful situations by developing positive ways to think about the situation. (p. 597)

**stress** The physical and psychological response to internal or external stressors. (p. 582)

**stressors** Specific events or chronic pressures that place demands on a person or threaten the person's well-being. (p. 582)

**structuralism** The analysis of the basic elements that constitute the mind. (p. 8)

**subcortical structures** Areas of the forebrain housed under the cerebral cortex near the very center of the brain. (p. 95)

**sublimation** A defense mechanism that involves channeling unacceptable sexual or aggressive drives into socially acceptable and culturally enhancing activities. (p. 467)

**subliminal perception** A thought or behavior that is influenced by stimuli that a person cannot consciously report perceiving. (p. 306)

**suggestibility** The tendency to incorporate misleading information from external sources into personal recollections. (p. 197)

**sunk-cost fallacy** A framing effect in which people make decisions about a current situation based on what they have previously invested in the situation. (p. 277)

**superego** The mental system that reflects the internalization of cultural rules, mainly learned as parents exercise their authority. (p. 464)

**surface structure** How a sentence is worded. (p. 256)

**syllogistic reasoning** Determining whether a conclusion follows from two statements that are assumed to be true. (p. 287)

**sympathetic nervous system** A set of nerves that prepares the body for action in threatening situations. (p. 88)

**synapse** The junction or region between the axon of one neuron and the dendrites or cell body of another. (p. 76)

**synesthesia** The perceptual experience of one sense that is evoked by another sense. (p. 122)

**syntactical rules** A set of rules that indicate how words can be combined to form phrases and sentences. (p. 255)

**systematic desensitization** A procedure in which a client relaxes all the muscles of his or her body while imagining being in increasingly frightening situations. (p. 549)

**systematic persuasion** A change in attitudes or beliefs that is brought about by appeals to reason. (p. 647)

**taste buds** The organ of taste transduction. (p. 161)

**tectum** A part of the midbrain that orients an organism in the environment. (p. 94)

**tegmentum** A part of the midbrain that is involved in movement and arousal. (p. 94)

**telegraphic speech** Speech that is devoid of function morphemes and consists mostly of content words. (p. 258)

**temperaments** Characteristic patterns of emotional reactivity. (p. 424)

**template** A mental representation that can be directly compared to a viewed shape in the retinal image. (p. 143)

**temporal code** The cochlea registers low frequencies via the firing rate of action potentials entering the auditory nerve. (p. 153)

**temporal lobe** A region of the cerebral cortex responsible for hearing and language. (p. 99)

**teratogens** Agents that damage the process of development, such as drugs and viruses. (p. 408)

**terminal buttons** Knoblike structures that branch out from an axon. (p. 81)

**thalamus** A subcortical structure that relays and filters information from the senses and transmits the information to the cerebral cortex. (p. 95)

**Thematic Apperception Test (TAT)** A projective personality test in which respondents reveal underlying motives, concerns, and the way they see the social world through the stories they make up about ambiguous pictures of people. (p. 453)

**theoretical reasoning** Reasoning directed toward arriving at a belief. (p. 286)

**theory** A hypothetical account of how and why a phenomenon occurs, usually in the form of a statement about the causal relationship between two or more properties. Theories lead to *hypotheses*. (p. 65)

**theory of mind** The idea that human behavior is guided by mental representation, which gives rise to the realization that the world is not always the way it looks and that different people see it differently. (p. 416)

**third-variable correlation** The fact that two variables may be correlated only because they are both caused by a third variable. (p. 57)

**third-variable problem** The fact that the causal relationship between two variables cannot be inferred from the correlation between them because of the ever-present possibility of third-variable correlation. (p. 58)

**thought suppression** The conscious avoidance of a thought. (p. 303)

**timbre** A listener's experience of sound quality or resonance. (p. 151)

**tip-of-the-tongue experience** The temporary inability to retrieve information that is stored in memory, accompanied by the feeling that you are on the verge of recovering the information. (p. 192)

**token economy** A form of behavior therapy in which clients are given "tokens" for desirable behavior, which they can later trade for rewards. (p. 549)

**trait** A relatively stable disposition to behave in a particular and consistent way. (p. 454)

**transcranial magnetic stimulation (TMS)** A treatment that involves placing a powerful pulsed magnet over a person's scalp, which alters neuronal activity in the brain. (p. 568)

**transduction** What takes place when many sensors in the body convert physical signals from the environment into neural signals sent to the central nervous system. (p. 123)

**transfer-appropriate processing** The idea that memory is likely to transfer from one situation to another when we process information in a way that is appropriate to the retrieval cues that will be available later. (p. 181)

**transference** An event that occurs in psychoanalysis when the therapist begins to assume a major significance in the client's life and the client reacts to the therapist based on unconscious childhood fantasies. (p. 546)

**transience** Forgetting what occurs with the passage of time. (p. 187)

**trichromatic color representation** The pattern of responding across the three types of cones that provides a unique code for each color. (p. 137)

**two-factor theory** A theory about the relationship between emotional experience and physiological activity suggesting that emotions are inferences about the causes of undifferentiated physiological arousal. (p. 371)

**two-factor theory of intelligence** Spearman's theory suggesting that every task requires a combination of a general ability (which he called $g$) and skills that are specific to the task (which he called $s$). (p. 346)

**Type A behavior pattern** The tendency toward easily aroused hostility, impatience, a sense of time urgency, and competitive achievement strivings. (p. 590)

**unconditional positive regard** An attitude of nonjudgmental acceptance toward another person. (p. 471)

**unconditioned response (UR)** A reflexive reaction that is reliably elicited by an unconditioned stimulus. (p. 212)

**unconditioned stimulus (US)** Something that reliably produces a naturally occurring reaction in an organism. (p. 212)

**unconscious** The part of the mind that operates outside of conscious awareness but influences conscious thoughts, feelings, and actions. (p. 15)

**unconscious motivation** A motivation of which one is not aware. (p. 399)

**universality hypothesis** The hypothesis that emotional expressions have the same meaning for everyone. (p. 379)

**validity** The characteristic of an observation that allows one to draw accurate inferences from it. (p. 43)

**variable** A property whose value can vary or change. (p. 53)

**variable interval schedule (VI)** An operant conditioning principle in which behavior is reinforced based on an average time that has expired since the last reinforcement. (p. 231)

**variable ratio schedule (VR)** An operant conditioning principle in which the delivery of reinforcement is based on a particular average number of responses. (p. 232)

**vestibular system** The three fluid-filled semicircular canals and adjacent organs located next to the cochlea in each inner ear. (p. 158)

**visual acuity** The ability to see fine detail. (p. 130)

**visual-form agnosia** The inability to recognize objects by sight. (p. 140)

**visual imagery encoding** The process of storing new information by converting it into mental pictures. (p. 171)

**Weber's law** The just noticeable difference of a stimulus is a constant proportion despite variations in intensity. (p. 126)

**working memory** Active maintenance of information in short-term storage. (p. 175)

**zygote** A single cell that contains chromosomes from both a sperm and an egg. (p. 407)

# References

Abel, T., Alberini, C., Ghirardi, M., Huang, Y.-Y., Nguyen, P., & Kandel, E. R. (1995). Steps toward a molecular definition of memory consolidation. In D. L. Schacter (Ed.), *Memory distortion: How minds, brains and societies reconstruct the past* (pp. 298–328). Cambridge, MA: Harvard University Press.

Abrams, M., & Reber, A. S. (1988). Implicit learning: Robustness in the face of psychiatric disorders. *Journal of Psycholinguistic Research, 17,* 425–439.

Abramson, L. Y., Alloy, L. B., Hankin, B. L., Haeffel, G. J., MacCoon, D. G., & Gibb, B. E. (2002). Cognitive vulnerability-stress models of depression in a self-regulatory and psychobiological context. In I. H. Gotlib & C. L. Hammen (Eds.), *Handbook of depression* (pp. 268–294). New York: Guilford Press.

Abramson, L. Y., Seligman, M. E. P., & Teasdale, J. D. (1978). Learned helplessness in humans: Critique and reformulation. *Journal of Abnormal Psychology, 87,* 49–74.

Abromov, I., & Gordon, J. (1994). Color appearance: On seeing red—or yellow, or green, or blue. *Annual Review of Psychology, 45,* 451–485.

Acevedo-Garcia, D., McArdle, N., Osypuk, T. L., Lefkowitz, B., & Krimgold, B. K. (2007). *Children left behind: How metropolitan areas are failing America's children.* Boston: Harvard School of Public Health.

Achter, J. A., Lubinski, D., & Benbow, C. P. (1996). Multipotentiality among the intellectually gifted: "It was never there and already it's vanishing." *Journal of Counseling Psychology, 43,* 65–76.

Ackroff, K., Luxas, F., & Sclafani, A. (2005). Flavor preference conditioning as a function of fat source. *Physiology and Behavior, 85,* 448–460.

Acocella, J. (1999). *Creating hysteria: Women and multiple personality disorder.* San Francisco: Jossey-Bass.

Acton, G. S., & Schroeder, D. H. (2001). Sensory discrimination as related to general intelligence. *Intelligence, 29,* 263–271.

Adams, H. E., Wright, L. W., Jr., & Lohr, B. A. (1996). Is homophobia associated with homosexual arousal? *Journal of Abnormal Psychology, 105,* 440–445.

Addis, D. R., Wong, A. T., & Schacter, D. L. (2007). Remembering the past and imagining the future: Common and distinct neural substrates during event construction and elaboration. *Neuropsychologia, 45,* 1363–1377.

Adelmann, P. K., & Zajonc, R. B. (1989). Facial efference and the experience of emotion. *Annual Review of Psychology, 40,* 249–280.

Adler, A. (1927). *Understanding human nature.* Greenwich, CT: Fawcett.

Adolph, K. E., & Avoilio, A. M. (2000). Walking infants adapt locomotion to changing body dimensions. *Journal of Experimental Psychology: Human Perception and Performance, 26,* 1148–1166.

Adolphs, R., Cahil, L., Schul, R., & Babinsky, R. (1997). Impaired declarative memory for emotional material following bilateral amygdala damage in humans. *Learning and Memory, 4,* 291–300.

Adolphs, R., Russell, J. A., & Tranel, D. (1999). A role for the human amygdala in recognizing emotional arousal from unpleasant stimuli. *Psychological Science, 10,* 167–171.

Adolphs, R., Tranel, D., Damasio, H., & Damasio, A. R. (1995). Fear and the human amygdala. *Journal of Neuroscience 15,* 5879–5891.

Adorno, T. W., Frenkel-Brunswik, E., Levinson, D. J., & Sanford, R. N. (1950). *The authoritarian personality.* New York: Harper & Row.

Aggleton, J. (Ed.). (1992). *The amygdala: Neurobiological aspects of emotion, memory and mental dysfunction.* New York: Wiley-Liss.

Aharon, I., Etcoff, N., Ariely, D., Chabris, C. F., O'Conner, E., & Breiter, H. C. (2001). Beautiful faces have variable reward value: fMRI and behavioral evidence. *Neuron, 32,* 537–551.

Ahern, J., Galea, S., Resnick, H., Kilpatrick D., Bucuvalas, M., Gold, J., et al. (2003). Television images and psychological symptoms after the September 11 terrorist attacks. *Psychiatry, 65*(4), 289–300.

Ahlers, M. (2003, September 23). Bitter divorce blamed for sniper shootings. *CNN.com.* Retrieved September 15, 2007, from http://www.cnn.com/2003/LAW/09/23/sprj.dcsp.sniper.hearing/index.html

Ainslie, G. (2001). *Breakdown of will.* New York: Cambridge University Press.

Ainsworth, M. D. S., Blehar, M. C., Waters, E., & Wall, S. (1978). *Patterns of attachment: A psychological study of the strange situation.* Hillsdale, NJ: Erlbaum.

Albarracin, D., & Kumkale, G. T. (2003). Affect as information in persuasion: A model of affect identification and discounting. *Journal of Personality & Social Psychology, 84,* 453–469.

Albee, E. (1962). *Who's afraid of Virginia Woolf?* New York: Atheneum.

Alicke, M. D., Klotz, M. L., Breitenbecher, D. L., Yurak, T. J., & Vredenburg, D. S. (1995). Personal contact, individuation, and the better-than-average effect. *Journal of Personality and Social Psychology, 68,* 804–824.

Allison, D. B., Fontaine, K. R., Manson, J. E., Stevens, J., & VanItallie, T. B. (1999). Annual deaths attributable to obesity in the United States. *Journal of the American Medical Association, 282,* 1530–1538.

Alloy, L. B., Jacobson, N. H., & Acocella, J. (1999). *Casebook in abnormal psychology* (4th ed.). New York: McGraw-Hill.

Allport, G. W. (1937). *Personality: A psychological interpretation.* New York: Holt.

Allport, G. W. (1954). *The nature of prejudice.* Cambridge, MA: Addison-Wesley.

Allport, G. W., & Odbert, H. S. (1936). Trait-names: A psycholexical study. *Psychological Monographs, 47,* 592.

Alt, K. W., Jeunesse, C., Buitrago-Téllez, C. H., Wächter, R., Boës, E., & Pichler, S. L. (1997). Evidence for stone age cranial surgery. *Nature, 387,* 360.

Alvarez, L. W. (1965). A pseudo experience in parapsychology. *Science, 148,* 1541.

Amabile, T. M. (1996). *Creativity in context.* Boulder, CO: Westview Press.

American Psychiatric Association. (2000). *Diagnostic and statistical manual of mental disorders DSM-IV-TR* (4th ed.). Washington, DC: American Psychiatric Press.

American Psychological Association. (2002). *Ethical principles of psychologists and code of conduct.* Washington, DC: Author.

American Psychological Association. (2005). Resolution in favor of empirically supported sex education and HIV prevention programs for adolescents. Washington, DC.

Andersen, S. M., & Berk, J. S. (1998). Transference in everyday experience: Implications of experimental research for relevant clinical phenomena. *Review of General Psychology, 2,* 81–120.

Anderson, C. A. (1989). Temperature and aggression: Ubiquitous effects of heat on occurrence of human violence. *Psychological Bulletin, 106,* 74–96.

Anderson, C. A., Berkowitz, L., Donnerstein, E., Huesmann, L. R., Johnson, J. D., Linz, D., et al. (2003). The influence of media violence on youth. *Psychological Science in the Public Interest, 4,* 81–110.

Anderson, C. A., & Bushman, B. J. (2001). Effects of violent video games on aggressive behavior, aggressive cognition, aggressive affect, physiological arousal, and prosocial behavior: A meta-analytic review of the scientific literature. *Psychological Science, 12,* 353–359.

Anderson, C. A., & Bushman, B. J. (2002). Human aggression. *Annual Review of Psychology, 53,* 27–51.

Anderson, C. A., Bushman, B. J., & Groom, R. W. (1997). Hot years and serious and deadly assault: Empirical tests of the heat hypothesis. *Journal of Personality and Social Psychology, 73,* 1213–1223.

Anderson, C. A., Lepper, M. R., & Ross, L. (1980). Perseverance of social theories: The role of explanation in the persistence of discredited information. *Journal of Personality and Social Psychology, 39,* 1037–1049.

Anderson, J. R., & Fincham, J. M. (1994). Acquisition of procedural skills from examples. *Journal of Experimental Psychology: Learning, Memory, and Cognition, 20,* 1322–1340.

Anderson, J. R., & Schooler, L. J. (1991). Reflections of the environment in memory. *Psychological Science, 2,* 396–408.

Anderson, J. R., & Schooler, L. J. (2000). The adaptive nature of memory. In E. Tulving & F. I. M. Craik (Eds.), *The Oxford handbook of memory* (pp. 557–570). Oxford, England: Oxford University Press.

Anderson, M. C., Ochsner, K. N., Kuhl, B., Cooper, J., Robertson, E., Gabrieli, S. W., et al. (2004). Neural systems underlying the suppression of unwanted memories. *Science, 303,* 232–235.

Anderson, R. C., Pichert, J. W., Goetz, E. T., Schallert, D. L., Stevens, K. V., & Trollip, S. R. (1976). Instantiation of general terms. *Journal of Verbal Learning and Verbal Behavior, 15,* 667–679.

Andrewes, D. (2001). *Neuropsychology: From theory to practice.* Hove, England: Psychology Press.

Andrews, I. (1982). Bilinguals out of focus: A critical discussion. *IRAL: International Review of Applied Linguistics in Language Teaching, 20,* 297–305.

Angermeyer, M. C., & Matschinger, H. (1996a). Lay beliefs about the causes of mental disorders: A new methodological approach. *Social Psychiatry & Psychiatric Epidemiology, 21,* 309–315.

Angermeyer, M. C., & Matschinger, H. (1996b). The effect of violent attacks by schizophrenic persons on the attitude of the public towards the mentally ill. *Social Science and Medicine, 43,* 1721–1728.

Angier, N. (1997, December 23). Joined for life, and living life to the full. *New York Times,* p. F1.

Ansfield, M., Wegner, D. M., & Bowser, R. (1996). Ironic effects of sleep urgency. *Behavior Research and Therapy, 34,* 523–531.

Ansuini, C. G., Fiddler-Woite, J., & Woite, R. S. (1996). The source, accuracy, and impact of initial sexuality information on lifetime wellness. *Adolescence, 31,* 283–289.

Antoni, M. H., Lehman, J. M., Klibourn, K. M., Boyers, A. E., Culver, J. L., Alferi, S. M., et al. (2001). Cognitive-behavioral stress management intervention decreases the prevalence of depression and enhances benefit finding among women under treatment for early-stage breast cancer. *Health Psychology, 20,* 20–32.

Antony, M. M., Downie, F., & Swinson, R. (1998). Diagnostic issues and epidemiology in obsessive-compulsive disorder. In R. Swinson, M. Antony, S. Rachman, & M. Richter (Eds.), *Obsessive-compulsive disorder: Theory, research, and treatment* (pp. 3–32). New York: Guilford Press.

Antony, M. M., Roth, D., Swinson, R. P., Huta, V., & Devins, G. M. (1998). Illness intrusiveness in individuals with panic disorder, obsessive compulsive disorder, or social phobia. *Journal of Nervous and Mental Disease, 186,* 311–315.

Antony, M. M., & Swinson, R. P. (2000). *Phobic disorders and panic in adults: A guide to assessment and treatment.* Washington, DC: American Psychological Association.

Archer, J. E. (Ed.). (1994). *Male violence.* London: Routledge.

Archibold, R. C. (2006, July 17). Arizona ballot could become lottery ticket. *New York Times,* pp. A1/A15.

Aristotle. (1998). *The Nichomachean ethics* (D. W. Ross, Trans.). Oxford, England: Oxford University Press.

Ariyasu, H., Takaya, K., Tagami, T., Ogawa, Y., Hosoda, K., Akamizu, T., et al. (2001). Stomach is a major source of circulating ghrelin, and feeding state determines plasma ghrelin-like immunoreactivity levels in humans. *Journal of Clinical Endocrinology and Metabolism, 86,* 4753–4758.

Arkes, H. R., Boehm, L. E., & Xu, G. (1991). Determinants of judged validity. *Journal of Experimental Social Psychology, 27,* 576–605.

Arlitt, A. H. (1921). On the need for caution in establishing race norms. *Journal of Applied Psychology, 5,* 179–183.

Arlow, J. A. (2000). Psychoanalysis. In R. J. Corsini & D. Wedding (Eds.), *Current psychotherapies* (6th ed., pp. 16–53). Itasca, IL: F. E. Peacock, Publishers.

Armstrong, D. M. (1980). *The nature of mind.* Ithaca, NY: Cornell University Press.

Arnold, M. B. (Ed.). (1960). *Emotion and personality: Psychological aspects* (Vol. 1). New York: Columbia University Press.

Arnold, S. E., Trojanowski, J. Q., Gur, R. E., Blackwell, P., Han, L., & Choi, C. (1998). Absence of neurodegeneration and neural injury in the cerebral cortex in a sample of elderly patients with schizophrenia. *Archives of General Psychiatry, 55,* 225–232.

Aronson, E. (1963). Effect of the severity of threat on the devaluation of forbidden behavior. *Journal of Abnormal and Social Psychology, 66,* 584–588.

Aronson, E. (1969). The theory of cognitive dissonance: A current perspective. In L. Berkowitz (Ed.), *Advances in experimental social psychology* (Vol. 4, pp. 1–34): Academic Press.

Aronson, E., & Mills, J. (1958). The effect of severity of initiation on liking for a group. *Journal of Abnormal and Social Psychology, 59,* 177–181.

Aronson, E., Willerman, B., & Floyd, J. (1966). The effect of a pratfall on increasing interpersonal attractiveness. *Psychonomic Science, 4,* 227–228.

Aronson, E., & Worchel, P. (1966). Similarity versus liking as determinants of interpersonal attractiveness. *Psychonomic Science, 5,* 157–158.

Asch, S. E. (1946). Forming impressions of personality. *Journal of Abnormal and Social Psychology, 41,* 258–290.

Asch, S. E. (1951). Effects of group pressure on the modification and distortion of judgments. In H. Guetzkow (Ed.), *Groups, leadership, and men* (pp. 177–190). Pittsburgh: Carnegie Press.

Asch, S. E. (1955). Opinions and social pressure. *Scientific American, 193,* 31–35.

Asch, S. E. (1956). Studies of independence and conformity: 1 A minority of one against a unanimous majority. *Psychological Monographs: General and Applied, 70,* 1–70.

Aschoff, J. (1965). Circadian rhythms in man. *Science, 148,* 1427–1432.

Aserinsky, E., & Kleitman, N. (1953). Regularly occurring periods of eye motility, and concomitant phenomena, during sleep. *Science, 118,* 273–274.

Ashby, F. G., & Ell, S. W. (2001). The neurobiology of human category learning. *Trends in Cognitive Sciences, 5,* 204–210.

Ashcraft, M. H. (1998). *Fundamentals of cognition.* New York: Longman.

Associated Press. (2007). Former stripper guilty of posing as psychologist. Boston: BostonHerald.com.

Astington, J. W., & Baird, J. (2005). *Why language matters for theory of mind.* Oxford, England: Oxford University Press.

Atkinson, J. W., & Litwin, G. H. (1960). Achievement motive and test anxiety conceived as motive to approach success and motive to avoid failure. *Journal of Abnormal and Social Psychology, 60,* 52–63.

Avolio, B. J., & Waldman, D. A. (1994). Variations in cognitive, perceptual, and psychomotor abilities across the working life span: Examining the effects of race, sex, experience, education, and occupational type. *Psychology and Aging, 9,* 430–442.

Axelrod, R. (1984). *The evolution of cooperation.* New York: Basic Books.

Axelrod, R., & Hamilton, W. D. (1981). The evolution of cooperation. *Science, 211,* 1390–1396.

Ayres, C. E. (1921). Instinct and capacity. 1. The instinct of belief-in-instincts. *Journal of Philosophy, 18,* 561–565.

Azam, E. (1876). Dé doublement de la personnalité: Suite de l'histoié de Felida X. *Revue Scientifique, 6,* 265–269.

Azuma, H., & Kashiwagi, K. (1987). Descriptors for an intelligent person: A Japanese study. *Japanese Psychological Research, 29,* 17–26.

Baars, B. J. (1986). *The cognitive revolution in psychology.* New York: Guilford Press.

Backman, C. W., & Secord, P. F. (1959). The effect of perceived liking on interpersonal attraction. *Human Relations, 12,* 379–384.

Bäckman, L., & Dixon, R. A. (1992). Psychological compensation: A theoretical framework. *Psychological Bulletin, 112,* 259–283.

Baddeley, A. D., & Hitch, G. J. (1974). Working memory. In S. Dornic (Ed.), *Attention and performance.* Hillsdale, NJ: Erlbaum.

Baer, L., Rauch, S. L., Ballantine, H. T., Jr., Martuza, R., Cosgrove, R., Cassem, E., et al. (1995). Cingulotomy for intractable obsessive-compulsive disorder: Prospective long-term follow-up of 18 patients. *Archives of General Psychiatry, 52,* 384–392.

Bagby, R. M., Levitan, R. D., Kennedy, S. H., Levitt, A. J., & Joffe, R. T. (1999). Selective alteration of personality in response to noradrenergic and serotonergic antidepressant medication in depressed sample: Evidence of non-specificity. *Psychiatry Research, 86,* 211–216.

Bahrick, H. P. (1984). Semantic memory content in permastore: 50 years of memory for Spanish learned in school. *Journal of Experimental Psychology: General, 113,* 1–29.

Bahrick, H. P. (2000). Long-term maintenance of knowledge. In E. Tulving & F. I. M. Craik (Eds.), *The Oxford handbook of memory* (pp. 347–362). New York: Oxford University Press.

Bahrick, H. P., Hall, L. K., & Berger, S. A. (1996). Accuracy and distortion in memory for high school grades. *Psychological Science, 7,* 265–271.

Bailey, J. M., & Pillard, R. C. (1991). A genetic study of male sexual orientation. *Archives of General Psychiatry, 48,* 1089–1096.

Bailey, J. M., Pillard, R. C., Dawood, K., Miller, M. B., Farrer, L. A., Trivedi, S., et al. (1999). A family history study of make sexual orientation using three independent samples. *Behavior Genetics, 29,* 79–86.

Bailey, J. M., Pillard, R. C., Neale, M. C., & Agyes, Y. (1993). Heritable factors influence sexual orientation in women. *Archives of General Psychiatry, 50,* 217–223.

Bailey, R. (2002, March 6). Hooray for designer babies! *Reason.com.* Retrieved September 30, 2007, from http://www.reason.com/news/show/34776.html

Baillargeon, R., Spelke, E. S., & Wasserman, S. (1985). Object permanence in 5-month-old infants. *Cognition, 20,* 191–208.

Baldwin, M. W., Carrell, S. E., & Lopez, D. F. (1989). Priming relationship schemas: My advisor and the Pope are watching me from the back of my mind. *Journal of Experimental Social Psychology, 26,* 435–454.

Baler, R. D., & Volkow, N. D. (2006). Drug addiction: the neurobiology of disrupted self-control. *Trends in Molecular Medicine 12,* 559–566.

Baltes, P. B., & Reinert, G. (1969). Cohort effects in cognitive development of children as revealed by cross-sectional sequences. *Developmental Psychology, 1,* 169–177.

Bandura, A. (1965). Influence of models' reinforcement contingencies on the acquisition of imitative responses. *Journal of Social and Personality Psychology, 1,* 589–595.

Bandura, A. (1977). *Social learning theory.* Englewood Cliffs, NJ: Prentice Hall.

Bandura, A. (1986). *Social foundations of thought and action: A social cognitive theory.* Englewood Cliffs, NJ: Prentice Hall.

Bandura, A. (1994). Social cognitive theory of mass communication. In J. Bryant & D. Zillmann (Eds.), *Media effects: Advances in theory and research* (pp. 61–90). Hillsdale, NJ: Erlbaum.

Bandura, A., Ross, D., & Ross, S. (1961). Transmission of aggression through imitation of adult models. *Journal of Abnormal and Social Psychology, 63,* 575–582.

Bandura, A., Ross, D., & Ross, S. (1963). Vicarious reinforcement and imitative learning. *Journal of Abnormal and Social Psychology, 67,* 601–607.

Banks, M. S., & Salapatek, P. (1983). Infant visual perception. In M. Haith & J. Campos (Eds.), *Handbook of child psychology: Biology and infancy.* New York: Wiley.

Banse, R., & Scherer, K. R. (1996). Acoustic profiles in vocal emotion expression. *Journal of Personality and Social Psychology, 70,* 614–636.

Barchas, J. D., Berger, P. A., Ciranello, R. D., & Elliot, G. R. (1980). *Psychopharmacology: From theory to practice.* New York: Oxford University Press.

Bard, P. (1934). On emotional experience after decortication with some remarks on theoretical views. *Psychological Review, 41,* 309–329.

Bargh, J. A., & Chartrand, T. L. (1999). The unbearable automaticity of being. *American Psychologist, 54,* 462–479.

Bargh, J. A., Chen, M., & Burrows, L. (1996). The automaticity of social behavior: Direct effects of trait concept and stereotype activation on action. *Journal of Personality and Social Psychology, 71,* 230–244.

Bargh, J. A., Gollwitzer, P. M., Lee-Chai, A., Barndollar, K., & Trötschel, R. (2001). Bypassing the will: Automatic and controlled self-regulation. *Journal of Personality and Social Psychology, 81,* 1014–1027.

Barker, A. T., Jalinous, R., & Freeston, I. L. (1985). Noninvasive magnetic stimulation of the human motor cortex. *Lancet, 2,* 1106–1107.

Barkow, J. (1980). Prestige and self-esteem: A biosocial interpretation. In D. R. Omark, F. F. Stayer, & D. G. Freedman (Eds.), *Dominance relations* (pp. 319–322). New York: Garland.

Barlow, D. H., Gorman, J. M., Shear, M. K., & Woods, S. W. (2000). Cognitive-behavioral therapy, imipramine, or their combination for panic disorder: A randomized controlled trial. *Journal of the American Medical Association, 283*(19), 2529–2536.

Barlow, D. H., O'Brien, G. T., & Last, C. G. (1984). Couples treatment of agoraphobia. *Behavior Therapy, 15,* 41–58.

Barnier, A. J., Levin, K., & Maher, A. (2004). Suppressing thoughts of past events: Are repressive copers good suppressors? *Cognition and Emotion, 18,* 457–477.

Baron-Cohen, S. (1991). Do people with autism understand what causes emotion? *Child Development, 62,* 385–395.

Baron-Cohen, S., Leslie, A., & Frith, U. (1985). Does the autistic child have a "theory of mind"? *Cognition, 21,* 37–46.

Barondes, S. (2003). *Better than Prozac.* New York: Oxford University Press.

Barrett, T. R., & Etheridge, J. B. (1992). Verbal hallucinations in normals: I: People who hear voices. *Applied Cognitive Psychology, 6,* 379–387.

Barsalou, L. W., & Ross, B. H. (1986). The roles of automatic and strategic processing in sensitivity to superordinate and property frequency. *Journal of Experimental Psychology: Learning, Memory, & Cognition, 12,* 116–134.

Bartlett, F. C. (1932). *Remembering.* Cambridge, England: Cambridge University Press.

Bartol, C. R., & Costello, N. (1976). Extraversion as a function of temporal duration of electric shock: An exploratory study. *Perceptual and Motor Skills, 42,* 1174.

Bartoshuk, L. M. (2000). Comparing sensory experiences across individuals: Recent psychophysical advances illuminate genetic variation in taste perception. *Chemical Senses, 25,* 447–460.

Bartoshuk, L. M., & Beauchamp, G. K. (1994). Chemical senses. *Annual Review of Psychology, 45,* 419–445.

Bartoshuk, L. M., Duffy, V. B., & Miller, I. J. (1994). PTC/PROP tasting: Anatomy, psychophysics, and sex effects. *Physiology and Behavior, 56,* 1165–1171.

Batson, C. D. (2002). Addressing the altruism question experimentally. In S. G. Post & L. G. Underwood (Eds.), *Altruism & altruistic love: Science, philosophy, & religion in dialogue* (pp. 89–105). London: Oxford University Press.

Baumeister, R. F. (1999). *Evil: Inside human violence and cruelty.* New York: Freeman.

Baumeister, R. F. (2004). Gender and erotic plasticity: Sociocultural influences on the sex drive. *Sexual & Relationship Therapy, 19,* 133–139.

Baumeister, R. F., Bratslavsky, E., Muraven, M., & Tice, D. M. (1998). Ego depletion: Is the active self a limited resource? *Journal of Personality and Social Psychology, 74,* 1252–1265.

Baumeister, R. F., Campbell, J. D., Krueger, J. I., & Vohs, K. D. (2003). Does high self-esteem cause better performance, interpersonal success, happiness, or healthier lifestyles? *Psychological Science in the Public Interest, 4,* 1–44.

Baumeister, R. F., Cantanese, K. R., & Vohs, K. D. (2001). Is there a gender difference in strength of sex drive? Theoretical views, conceptual distinctions, and a review of relevant evidence. *Personality and Social Psychology Review, 5,* 242–273.

Baumeister, R. F., & Leary, M. R. (1995). The need to belong: Desire for interpersonal attachments as a fundamental human motivation. *Psychological Bulletin, 117,* 497–529.

Baumeister, R. F., Smart, L., & Boden, J. M. (1996). Relation of threatened egotism to violence and aggression: The dark side of high self-esteem. *Psychological Review, 103,* 5–33.

Baumeister, R. F., & Tice, D. M. (1990). Anxiety and social exclusion. *Journal of Social and Clinical Psychology, 9,* 165–195.

Baxter, L. R., Schwartz, J. M., Bergman, K. S., Szuba, M. P., Guze, B. H., Mazziotta, J. C., Alazraki, A., et al. (1992). Caudate glucose metabolic rate changes with both drug behavior therapy for obsessive-compulsive disorder. *Archives of General Psychiatry, 49,* 681–689.

Bayley, P. J., Gold, J. J., Hopkins, R. O., & Squire, L. R. (2005). The neuroanatomy of remote memory. *Neuron, 46,* 799–810.

Bechara, A., Damasio, A. R., Damasio, H., & Anderson, S. W. (1994). Insensitivity to future consequences following damage to human prefrontal cortex. *Cognition, 50,* 7–15.

Bechara, A., Damasio, H., Tranel, D., & Damasio, A. R. (1997). Deciding advantageously before knowing the advantageous strategy. *Science, 275,* 1293–1295.

Bechara, A., Dolan, S., Denburg, N., Hindes, A., & Anderson, S. W. (2001). Decision-making deficits, linked to a dysfunctional ventromedial prefrontal cortex, revealed in alcohol and stimulant abusers. *Neuropsychologia, 39,* 376–389.

Bechara, A., Tranel, D., & Damasio, H. (2000). Characterization of the decision-making deficit of patients with ventromedial prefrontal cortex lesions. *Brain, 123,* 2189–2202.

Beck, A. T. (1967). *Depression: Causes and treatment.* Philadelphia: University of Pennsylvania Press.

Beck, A. T., & Weishaar, M. (2000). Cognitive therapy. In R. J. Corsini & D. Wedding (Eds.), *Current psychotherapies* (6th ed., pp. 241–272). Itasca, IL: F. E. Peacock, Publishers.

Beckers, G., & Zeki, S. (1995). The consequences of inactivating areas V1 and V5 on visual motion perception. *Brain, 118,* 49–60.

Békésy, G. von. (1960). *Experiments in hearing.* New York: McGraw-Hill.

Bell, A. P., Weinberg, M. S., & Hammersmith, S. K. (1981). *Sexual preference: Its development in men and women.* Bloomington: Indiana University Press.

Belsky, G., & Gilovich, T. (2000). *Why smart people make big money mistakes—and how to correct them: Lessons from the new science of behavioral economics.* New York: Fireside.

Belsky, J., Spritz, B., & Crnic, K. (1996). Infant attachment security and affective-cognitive information processing at age 3. *Psychological Science, 7,* 111–114.

Bem, S. L. (1974). The measure of psychological androgyny. *Journal of Consulting & Clinical Psychology, 42,* 155–162.

Benedetti, F., Maggi, G., & Lopiano, L. (2003). Open versus hidden medical treatment: The patient's knowledge about a therapy affects the therapy outcome. *Prevention & Treatment, 6,* Article 1. Retrieved June 23, 2003, from http://content.apa.org/psycarticles/2003-07872-001

Benes, F. M. (1998). Model generation and testing to probe neural circuitry in the cingulated cortex of postmortem schizophrenia brain. *Schizophrenia Bulletin, 24,* 219–230.

Benjamin, L. T., Jr. (Ed.). (1988). *A history of psychology: Original sources and contemporary research.* New York: McGraw-Hill.

Bennett, D. J. (1998). *Randomness.* Cambridge, MA: Harvard University Press.

Benson, H. (Ed.). (1990). *The relaxation response.* New York: Harper Torch.

Bereczkei, T., Vorgos, S., Gal, A., & Bernath, L. (1997). Resources, attractiveness, family commitment; reproductive decisions in human mate choice. *Journal of Ethology, 103,* 681–699.

Berger, H. (1929). Über das Elektroenkephalogram des Menschen. *Archiv fuer Psychiatrie, 87,* 527–570.

Berglund, H., Lindstrom, P., & Savic, I. (2006). Brain response to putative pheromones in lesbian women. *Proceedings of the National Academy of Sciences, 103,* 8269–8274.

Berkerian, D. A., & Bowers, J. M. (1983). Eyewitness testimony: Were we misled? *Journal of Experimental Psychology: Learning, Memory, and Cognition, 9,* 139–145.

Berkowitz, L. (1989). Frustration-aggression hypothesis: Examination and reformulation. *Psychological Bulletin, 106,* 59–73.

Berkowitz, L. (1990). On the formation and regulation of anger and aggression: A cognitive-neoassociationistic analysis. *American Psychologist, 45,* 494–503.

Berkowitz, L. (1993). Pain and aggression: Some findings and implications. *Motivation and Emotion, 17,* 277–293.

Berman, D. (2005, January 10). *Berman's bits.* Retrieved March 3, 2007, from http://www.bermansbits.com/archive/2005/v10n_02.html

Bernard, L. L. (1924). *Instinct: A study in social psychology.* New York: Holt.

Berry, D. S., & McArthur, L. Z. (1985). Some components and consequences of a babyface. *Journal of Personality and Social Psychology, 48,* 312–323.

Berry, J. W., Poortinga, Y. H., Segall, M. H., & Dasen, P. R. (1992). *Cross-cultural psychology: Research and applications.* New York: Cambridge University Press.

Berscheid, E., & Reiss, H. T. (1998). Interpersonal attraction and close relationships. In D. T. Gilbert, S. T. Fiske, & G. Lindzey (Eds.), *The handbook of social psychology* (4th ed., Vol. 2, pp. 193–281). New York: McGraw-Hill.

Bertelsen, A. (1999). Reflections on the clinical utility of the ICD-10 and DSM-IV classifications and their diagnostic criteria. *Australian and New Zealand Journal of Psychiatry, 33,* 166–173.

Bertelsen, B., Harvald, B., & Hauge, M. (1977). A Danish twin study of manic-depressive disorders. *British Journal of Psychiatry, 130,* 330–351.

Bertenthal, B. I., Rose, J. L., & Bai, D. L. (1997). Perception-action coupling in the development of visual control of posture. *Journal of Experimental Psychology: Human Perception & Performance, 23,* 1631–1643.

Best, J. B. (1992). *Cognitive psychology* (3rd ed.). New York: West Publishing.

Bettencourt, B. A., & Miller, N. (1996). Gender differences in aggression as a function of provocation: A meta-analysis. *Psychological Bulletin, 119,* 422–447.

Beutler, L. E. (2002). The dodo bird is extinct. *Clinical Psychology: Science and Practice, 9,* 30–34.

Bialystok, E. (1999). Cognitive complexity and attentional control in the bilingual mind. *Child Development, 70,* 636–644.

Bialystok, E., & Hakuta, K. (1994). *In other words: The science and psychology of second-language acquisition.* New York: Basic Books.

Bickerton, D. (1990). *Language and species.* Chicago: Chicago University Press.

Biederman, I. (1987). Recognition-by-components: A theory of human image understanding. *Psychological Review, 94,* 115–147.

Bierce, A. (1911). *The devil's dictionary.* New York: A. & C. Boni.

Billet, E., Richter, J., & Kennedy, J. (1998). Genetics of obsessive-compulsive disorder. In R. Swinson, M. Anthony, S. Rachman & M. Richter (Eds.), *Obsessive-compulsive disorder: Theory, research, and treatment* (pp. 181–206). New York: Guilford Press.

Binet, A. (1905). New methods for the diagnosis of the intellectual level of subnormals. *L'Année Psychologique, 12,* 191–244.

Binet, A. (1909). *Les idées modernes sur les enfants.* Paris: Flammarion.

Binswanger, L. (1958). The existential analysis school of thought. In R. May (Ed.), *Existence: A new dimension in psychiatry and psychology.* New York: Basic Books.

Bjork, D. W. (1983). *The compromised scientist: William James in the development of American psychology.* New York: Columbia University Press.

Bjork, D. W. (1993). *B. F. Skinner: A life.* New York: Basic Books.

Bjork, R. A., & Bjork, E. L. (1988). On the adaptive aspects of retrieval failure in autobiographical memory. In M. M. Gruneberg, P. E. Morris, R. N. Sykes (Eds.), *Practical aspects of memory: Current research and issues* (pp. 283–288). Chichester, England: Wiley.

Blackmore, S. (2004). *Consciousness: An introduction.* New York: Oxford University Press.

Blair, I. V. (2002). The malleability of automatic stereotypes and prejudice. *Personality and Social Psychology Review, 6,* 242–261.

Blair, J., Peschardt, K., & Mitchell, D. R. (2005). *Psychopath: Emotion and the brain.* Oxford, England: Blackwell.

Blascovich, J., Mendes, W. B., Hunter, S. B., Lickel, B., & Kowai-Bell, N. (2001). Perceiver threat in social interactions with stigmatized others. *Journal of Personality and Social Psychology, 80,* 253–267.

Blascovich, J., & Tomaka, J. (1996). The biopsychosocial model of arousal regulation. In M. P. Zanna (Ed.), *Advances in experimental social psychology* (Vol. 28, pp. 1–51). San Diego, CA: Academic Press.

Blasi, A. (1980). Bridging moral cognition and moral action: A critical review of the literature. *Psychological Bulletin, 88,* 1–45.

Blatt, S. J., & Homann, E. (1992). Parent-child interaction in the etiology of dependent and self-critical depression. *Clinical Psychology Review, 12,* 47–91.

Blatt, S. J., & Zuroff, D. C. (1992). Interpersonal relatedness and self-definition: Two prototypes for depression. *Clinical Psychology Review, 12,* 527–562.

Blazer, D. G., Hughes, D., & George, L. D. (1987). Stressful life events and the onset of a generalized anxiety syndrome. *American Journal of Psychiatry, 144,* 1178–1183.

Blazer, D. G., Hughes, D. J., George, L. K., Swartz, M., & Boyer, R. (1991). Generalized anxiety disorder. In L. N. Robins & D. A. Regier (Eds.), *Psychiatric disorders in America* (Vol. 180–203). New York: Free Press.

Bliss, T. V. P. (1999). Young receptors make smart mice. *Nature, 401,* 25–27.

Bliss, T. V. P., & Lømo, W. T. (1973). Long-lasting potentiation of synaptic transmission in the dentate area of the anesthetized rabbit following stimulation of the perforant path. *Journal of Physiology, 232,* 331–356.

Bloom, P. (2004). *Descartes' baby: How the science of child development explains what makes us human.* New York: Basic Books.

Bohan, J. S. (1996). *Psychology and sexual orientation: Coming to terms.* New York: Routledge.

Boisvert, C. M., & Faust, D. (2002). Iatrogenic symptoms in psychotherapy: A theoretical exploration of the potential impact of labels, language, and belief systems. *American Journal of Psychotherapy, 56,* 244–259.

Boomsma, D., Busjahn, A., & Peltonen, L. (2002). Classical twin studies and beyond. *Nature Reviews Genetics, 3,* 872–882.

Bootzin, R. R., Manber, R., Perlis, M. L., Salvio, M. A., & Wyatt, J. K. (1993). Sleep disorders. In P. B. Sutker & H. E. Adams (Eds.), *Comprehensive handbook of psychopathology* (2nd ed.). New York: Plenum Press.

Borkenau, P., & Liebler, A. (1995). Observable attributes as manifestations and cues of personality and intelligence. *Journal of Personality, 63,* 1–25.

Borkevec, T. D. (1982). Insomnia. *Journal of Consulting and Clinical Psychology, 50,* 880–895.

Born, R. T., & Bradley, D. C. (2005). Structure and function of visual area MT. *Annual Review of Neuroscience, 28,* 157–189.

Bornstein, R. F. (1989). Exposure and affect: Overview and meta-analysis of research, 1968–1987. *Psychological Bulletin, 106,* 265–289.

Boroditsky, L. (2001). Does language shape thought? Mandarin and English speakers' conceptions of time. *Cognitive Psychology, 43*, 1–22.

Bostwick, J. M., & Pankratz, S. (2000). Affective disorders and suicide risk: A reexamination. *American Journal of Psychiatry, 157*, 1925–1932.

Botwin, M. D., Buss, D. M., & Shackelford, T. K. (1997). Personality and mate preferences: Five factors in mate selection and marital satisfaction. *Journal of Personality, 65*, 107–136.

Bouchard, T. J., & Loehlin, J. C. (2001). Genes, evolution, and personality. *Behavioral Genetics, 31*, 243–273.

Bouchard, T. J., & McGue, M. (1981). Familial studies of intelligence: A review. *Science, 212*, 1055–1059.

Boucher, J. D., & Carlson, G. E. (1980). Recognition of facial expressions in three cultures. *Journal of Cross-Cultural Psychology, 11*, 263–280.

Bourguignon, E. (1968). World distribution and patterns of possession states. In R. Prince (Ed.), *Trance and possession states* (pp. 3–34). Montreal, Canada: R. M. Burke Memorial Society.

Bower, B. (1999, Oct. 30). The mental butler did it—research suggests that subconscious affects behavior more than thought. *Science News.*

Bower, G. H. (1981). Mood and memory. *American Psychologist, 36*, 129–148.

Bower, G. H., Clark, M. C., Lesgold, A. M., & Winzenz, D. (1969). Hierarchical retrieval schemes in recall of categorical word lists. *Journal of Verbal Learning and Verbal Behavior, 8*, 323–343.

Bowers, K. S., Regehr, G., Balthazard, C., & Parker, D. (1990). Intuition in the context of discovery. *Cognitive Psychology, 22*, 72–110.

Bowlby, J. (1969). *Attachment and loss: Vol. 1. Attachment.* New York: Basic Books.

Bowlby, J. (1973). *Attachment and loss: Vol. 2. Separation.* New York: Basic Books.

Bowlby, J. (1980). *Attachment and loss: Vol. 3. Loss: Sadness and depression.* New York: Basic Books.

Bozarth, M. A. (Ed.). (1987). *Methods of assessing the reinforcing properties of abused drugs.* New York: Springer-Verlag.

Bozarth, M. A., & Wise, R. A. (1985). Toxicity associated with long-term intravenous heroin and cocaine self-administration in the rat. *Journal of the American Medical Association, 254*, 81–83.

Bradford, D., Stroup, S., & Lieberman, J. (2002). Pharmacological treatments for schizophrenia. In P. E. Nathan & J. M. Gorman (Eds.), *A guide to treatments that work* (2nd ed., pp. 169–199). New York: Oxford University Press.

Bradmetz, J., & Schneider, R. (2004). The role of the counterfactually satisfied desire in the lag between false-belief and false-emotion attributions in children aged 4–7. *British Journal of Developmental Psychology, 22*, 185–196.

Brainerd, C. J., & Reyna, V. E. (2005). *The science of false memory.* New York: Oxford University Press.

Bramlett, M. D., & Mosher, W. D. (2001). *First marriage dissolution, divorce, and remarriage: United States.* (Advance data from vital and health statistics, 323.) Hyattsville, MD: National Center for Health Statistics.

Bramlett, M. D., & Mosher, W. D. (2002). *Cohabitation, marriage, divorce, and remarriage in the United States* (Vital and Health Statistics Series 23, No. 22). Hyattsville, MD: National Center for Health Statistics.

Braun, A. R., Balkin, T. J., Wesensten, N. J., Gwadry, F., Carson, R. E., Varga, M., et al. (1998). Dissociated pattern of activity in visual cortices and their projections during rapid eye movement sleep. *Science, 279*, 91–95.

Breckler, S. J. (1994). Memory for the experiment of donating blood: Just how bad was it? *Basic and Applied Social Psychology, 15*, 467–488.

Brédart, S., & Valentine, T. (1998). Descriptiveness and proper name retrieval. *Memory, 6*, 199–206.

Breggin, P. R. (1990). Brain damage, dementia, and persistent cognitive dysfunction associated with neuroleptic drugs: Evidence, etiology, implications. *Journal of Mind and Behavior, 11*, 425–463.

Breggin, P. R. (2000). *Reclaiming our children.* Cambridge, MA: Perseus Books.

Brehm, J. W. (1956). Post-decision changes in the desirability of alternatives. *Journal of Abnormal and Social Psychology, 52*, 384–389.

Brehm, S. S. (1992). *Intimate relationships* (2nd ed.). New York: McGraw-Hill.

Breland, K., & Breland, M. (1961). The misbehavior of organisms. *American Psychologist, 16*, 681–684.

Brennan, P. A., & Zufall, F. (2006). Pheromonal communication in vertebrates. *Nature, 444*, 308–315.

Brenneis, C. B. (2000). Evaluating the evidence: Can we find authenticated recovered memory? *Journal of the American Psychoanalytic Association, 17*, 61–77.

Brenninkmeijer, V., Vanyperen, N. W., & Buunk, B. P. (2001). I am not a better teacher, but others are doing worse: Burnout and perceptions of superiority among teachers. *Social Psychology of Education, 4*(3–4), 259–274.

Brewer, M. B. (1979). In-group bias in the minimal intergroup situation: A cognitive-motivational analysis. *Psychological Bulletin, 86*, 307–324.

Brewer, W. F. (1996). What is recollective memory? In D. C. Rubin (Ed.), *Remembering our past: Studies in autobiographical memory* (pp. 19–66). New York: Cambridge University Press.

Brickman, P., Coates, D., & Janoff-Bulman, R. J. (1978). Lottery winners and accident victims: Is happiness relative? *Journal of Personality and Social Psychology, 36*, 917–927.

Bridges, P. K., Bartlett, J. R., Hale, A. S., Poynton, A. M., Malizia, A. L., & Hodgkiss, A. D. (1994). Psychosurgery: stereotactic subcaudate tractomy: An indispensable treatment. *British Journal of Psychiatry, 165*, 599–611.

Broadbent, D. E. (1958). *Perception and communication.* London: Pergamon Press.

Broberg, D. J., & Bernstein, I. L. (1987). Candy as a scapegoat in the prevention of food aversions in children receiving chemotherapy. *Cancer, 60*, 2344–2347.

Broca, P. (1861). Remarques sur le siège de la faculté du langage articulé; suivies d'une observation d'aphemie (perte de la parole). *Bulletin de la société anatomique de Paris, 36*, 330–357.

Broca, P. (1863). Localisation des fonction cerebrales: Siège du langage articulé. *Bulletin de la société d'anthropologie de Paris, 4*, 200–202.

Brock, A. (1993). Something old, something new: The "reappraisal" of Wilhelm Wundt in textbooks. *Theory & Psychology, 3*(2), 235–242.

Brockner, J., & Swap, W. C. (1976). Effects of repeated exposure and attitudinal similarity on self-disclosure and interpersonal attraction. *Journal of Personality and Social Psychology, 33*, 531–540.

Broderick, C. B., & Schrader, S. S. (1991). The history of professional marriage and family therapy. In A. S. Gurman & D. P. Kniskern (Eds.), *Handbook of family therapy* (pp. 3–40). New York: Brunner/Mazel.

Brody, N. (2003). Construct validation of the Sternberg Triarchic Abilities Test: Comment and reanalysis. *Intelligence, 31*(4), 319–329.

Brooks-Gunn, J., Graber, J. A., & Paikoff, R. L. (1994). Studying links between hormones and negative affect: Models and measures. *Journal of Research on Adolescence, 4*, 469–486.

Brosnan, S. F., & DeWaal, F. B. M. (2003). Monkeys reject unequal pay. *Nature, 425*, 297–299.

Brown, B. B., Mory, M., & Kinney, D. (1994). Casting crowds in a relational perspective: Caricature, channel, and context. In G. A. R.

Montemayor & T. Gullotta (Eds.), *Advances in adolescent development: Personal relationships during adolescence* (Vol. 5, pp. 123–167). Newbury Park, CA: Sage.

Brown, J. D. (1993). Self-esteem and self-evaluation: Feeling is believing. In J. M. Suls (Ed.), *The self in social perspective: Psychological perspectives on the self* (Vol. 4, pp. 27–58). Hillsdale, NJ: Erlbaum.

Brown, J. D., & McGill, K. L. (1989). The cost of good fortune: When positive life events produce negative health consequences. *Journal of Personality & Social Psychology, 57,* 1103–1110.

Brown, R. (1958). *Words and things.* New York: Free Press.

Brown, R., & Hanlon, C. (1970). Derivational complexity and order of acquisition in child speech. In J. R. Hayes (Ed.), *Cognition and the development of language* (pp. 11–53). New York: Wiley.

Brown, R., & Kulik, J. (1977). Flashbulb memories. *Cognition, 5,* 73–99.

Brown, R., & McNeill, D. (1966). The "tip-of-the-tongue" phenomenon. *Journal of Verbal Learning and Verbal Behavior, 5,* 325–337.

Brown, S. C., & Craik, F. I. M. (2000). Encoding and retrieval of information. In E. Tulving & F. I. M. Craik (Eds.), *The Oxford handbook of memory* (pp. 93–107). New York: Oxford University Press.

Brown, T. A., & Barlow, D. H. (2002). Classification of anxiety and mood disorders. In D. H. Barlow (Ed.), *Anxiety and its disorders: The nature and treatment of anxiety and panic* (2nd ed.). New York: Guilford Press.

Brown, T. A., Campbell, L. A., Lehman, C. L., Grisham, J. R., & Mancill, R. B. (2001). Current and lifetime comorbidity of the *DSM-IV* anxiety and mood disorders in a large clinical sample. *Journal of Abnormal Psychology, 110,* 585–599.

Brownell, K. D., Greenwood, M. R. C., Stellar, E., & Shrager, E. E. (1986). The effects of repeated cycles of weight loss and regain in rats. *Physiology and Behavior, 38,* 459–464.

Brownlee, S. (2002, March). Designer babies. *The Washington Monthly.*

Bruner, J. S. (1983). Education as social invention. *Journal of Social Issues, 39,* 129–141.

Brunner, D. P., Dijk, D. J., Tobler, I., & Borbely, A. A. (1990). Effect of partial sleep deprivation on sleep stages and EEG power spectra. *Electroencephalography and Clinical Neurophysiology, 75,* 492–499.

Buchanan, C. M., Eccles, J. S., & Becker, J. B. (1992). Are adolescents the victims of raging hormones? Evidence for activational effects of hormones on moods and behavior at adolescence. *Psychological Bulletin, 111,* 62–107.

Buchanan, P. J. (2002, October 30). The Beltway sniper and the media. Retrieved September 15, 2006, from http://www.townhall.com/columnists/PatrickJBuchanan/2002/10/30/the_beltway_sniper_and_the_media

Buck, L., & Axel, R. (1991). A novel multigene family may encode odorant receptors: A molecular basis for odor recognition. *Cell, 65,* 175–187.

Buckley, K. W. (1989). *Mechanical man: John Broadus Watson and the beginnings of behaviorism.* New York: Guilford Press.

Buckner, R. L., Petersen, S. E., Ojemann, J. G., Miezin, F. M., Squire, L. R., & Raichle, M. E. (1995). Functional anatomical studies of explicit and implicit memory retrieval tasks. *Journal of Neuroscience, 15,* 12–29.

Buckner, R. L., Snyder, A. Z., Shannon, B. J., LaRossa, G., Sachs, R., Fotenos, A. F., et al. (2005). Molecular, structural, and functional characterization of Alzheimer's disease: Evidence for a relationship between default activity, amyloid, and memory. *Journal of Neuroscience, 25,* 7709–7717.

Bureau of Justice Statistics. (2001). *Prisoners in 2000* (No. NCJ 188207). Washington, DC: U.S. Department of Justice.

Burger, J. M. (1999). The foot-in-the-door compliance procedure: A multiple-process analysis and review. *Personality and Social Psychology Review, 3,* 303–325.

Burger, J. M., & Burns, L. (1988). The illusion of unique invulnerability and the use of effective contraception. *Personality and Social Psychology Bulletin, 14,* 264–270.

Burke, D., MacKay, D. G., Worthley, J. S., & Wade, E. (1991). On the tip of the tongue: What causes word failure in young and older adults? *Journal of Memory and Language, 30,* 237–246.

Burnstein, E., Crandall, C., & Kitayama, S. (1994). Some neo-Darwinian decision rules for altruism: Weighing cues for inclusive fitness as a function of the biological importance of the decision. *Journal of Personality & Social Psychology, 67,* 773–789.

Burris, C. T., & Branscombe, N. R. (2005). Distorted distance estimation induced by a self-relevant national boundary. *Journal of Experimental Social Psychology, 41,* 305–312.

Bushman, B. J., & Baumeister, R. F. (1998). Threatened egotism, narcissism, self-esteem, and direct and displaced aggression: Does self-love or self-hate lead to violence? *Journal of Personality and Social Psychology, 75,* 219–229.

Buss, D. M. (1985). Human mate selection. *American Scientist, 73,* 47–51.

Buss, D. M. (1989). Sex differences in human mate preferences: Evolutionary hypotheses tested in 37 cultures. *Behavioral and Brain Sciences, 12,* 1–49.

Buss, D. M. (1994). *The evolution of desire: Strategies of human mating.* New York: Basic Books.

Buss, D. M. (1996). Social adaptation and five major factors of personality. In J. S. Wiggins (Ed.), *The five-factor model of personality: Theoretical perspectives* (pp. 180–208). New York: Guilford Press.

Buss, D. M. (1999). *Evolutionary psychology: The new science of the mind.* Boston: Allyn and Bacon.

Buss, D. M. (2000). *The dangerous passion: Why jealousy is as necessary as love and sex.* New York: Free Press.

Buss, D. M., Abbott, M., Angleitner, A., Asherian, A., Biaggio, A., Blanco-Villasenor, A., et al. (1990). International preferences in selecting mates: A study of 37 cultures. *Journal of Cross-Cultural Psychology, 21,* 5–47.

Buss, D. M., Haselton, M. G., Shackelford, T. K., Bleske, A. L., & Wakefield, J. C. (1998). Adaptations, exaptations, and spandrels. *American Psychologist, 53,* 533–548.

Buss, D. M., & Kenrick, D. T. (1998). Evolutionary social psychology. In D. T. Gilbert, S. T. Fiske, & G. Lindzey (Eds.), *The handbook of social psychology* (4th ed., pp. 982–1026). New York: McGraw-Hill.

Buss, D. M., & Schmitt, D. P. (1993). Sexual strategies theory: An evolutionary perspective on human mating. *Psychological Review, 100,* 204–232.

Butzlaff, R. L., & Hooley, J. M. (1998). Expressed emotion and psychiatric relapse: A meta-analysis. *Archives of General Psychiatry, 55,* 547–552.

Buys, C. J. (1978). Humans would do better without groups. *Personality and Social Psychology Bulletin, 4,* 123–125.

Byrne, D., Allgeier, A. R., Winslow, L., & Buckman, J. (1975). The situational facilitation of interpersonal attraction: A three-factor hypothesis. *Journal of Applied Social Psychology, 5,* 1–15.

Byrne, D., & Clore, G. L. (1970). A reinforcement model of evaluative responses. *Personality: An International Journal, 1,* 103–128.

Byrne, D., Ervin, C. R., & Lamberth, J. (1970). Continuity between the experimental study of attraction and real-life computer dating. *Journal of Personality and Social Psychology, 16,* 157–165.

Byrne, D., & Nelson, D. (1965). Attraction as a linear function of proportion of positive reinforcements. *Journal of Personality and Social Psychology, 1,* 659–663.

Cabeza, R. (2002). Hemispheric asymmetry reduction in older adults: The HAROLD model. *Psychology and Aging, 17,* 85–100.

Cabeza, R., Rao, S., Wagner, A. D., Mayer, A., & Schacter, D. L. (2001). Can medial temporal lobe regions distinguish true from false? An event-related fMRI study of veridical and illusory recognition memory. *Proceedings of the National Academy of Sciences (USA), 98,* 4805–4810.

Cacioppo, J. T., Hawkley, L. C., & Berntson, G. G. (2003). The anatomy of loneliness. *Current Directions in Psychological Science, 12,* 71–74.

Cahill, L., Haier, R. J., Fallon, J., Alkire, M. T., Tang, C., Keator, D., et al. (1996). Amygdala activity at encoding correlated with long-term, free recall of emotional information. *Proceedings of the National Academy of Sciences (USA), 93,* 8016–8021.

Cahill, L., & McGaugh, J. L. (1998). Mechanisms of emotional arousal and lasting declarative memory. *Trends in Neurosciences, 21,* 294–299.

Calder, A. J., Young, A. W., Rowland, D., Perrett, D. I., Hodges, J. R., & Etcoff, N. L. (1996). Facial emotion recognition after bilateral amygdala damage: Differentially severe impairment of fear. *Cognitive Neuropsychology, 13,* 699–745.

Calkins, M. W. (Ed.). (1930). *Mary Whiton Calkins* (Vol. 1). Worcester, MA: Clark University Press.

Callaghan, T., Rochat, P., Lillard, A., Claux, M. L., Odden, H., Itakura, S., et al. (2005). Synchrony in the onset of mental-state reasoning: Evidence from five cultures. *Psychological Science, 16,* 378–384.

Campbell, A. (1999). Staying alive: Evolution, culture, and women's intra-sexual aggression. *Behavioral & Brain Sciences, 22,* 203–252.

Campbell, C. M., Edward, R. R., & Fillingim, R. B. (2005). Ethnic differences in responses to multiple experimental pain stimuli. *Pain, 113,* 20–26.

Campbell, D. T. (1965). Ethnocentric and other altruistic motives. In D. Levine (Ed.), *Nebraska symposium on motivation* (pp. 283–311). Lincoln: University of Nebraska Press.

Campbell, R., & Sais, E. (1995). Accelerated metalinguistic (phonological) awareness in bilingual children. *British Journal of Developmental Psychology, 13,* 61–68.

Canetto, S., & Lester, D. (1995). Gender and the primary prevention of suicide mortality. *Suicide and Life Threatening Behavior, 25,* 85–89.

Cannon, W. B. (1927). The James-Lange theory of emotion: A critical examination and alternate theory. *American Journal of Psychology, 39,* 106–124.

Cannon, W. B. (1929). *Bodily changes in pain, hunger, fear, and rage: An account of recent research into the function of emotional excitement* (2nd ed.). New York: Appleton-Century-Crofts.

Cannon, W. B. (1942). "Voodoo" death. *American Anthropologist, 44,* 182–190.

Cantor, N. (1990). From thought to behavior: "Having" and "doing" in the study of personality and cognition. *American Psychologist, 45,* 735–750.

Caplan, A. L. (Ed.). (1992). *When medicine went mad: Bioethics and the Holocaust.* Totowa, NJ: Humana Press.

Carlson, C., & Hoyle, R. (1993). Efficacy of abbreviated progressive muscle relaxation training: A quantitative review of behavioral medicine research. *Journal of Consulting & Clinical Psychology, 61,* 1059–1067.

Carmena, J. M., Lebedev, M. A., Crist, R. E., O'Doherty, J. E., Santucci, D. M., Dimitrov, D. F., et al. (2003). Learning to control a brain-machine interface for reaching and grasping by primates. *Public Library of Science Biology, 1,* 193–208.

Carmichael Olson, H., Streissguth, A. P., Sampson, P. D., Barr, H. M., Bookstein, F. L., & Thiede, K. (1997). Association of prenatal alcohol exposure with behavioral and learning problems in early adolescence. *Journal of the American Academy of Child and Adolescent Psychiatry, 36,* 1187–1194.

Carolson, E. A. (1998). A prospective longitudinal study of attachment disorganization/disorientation. *Child Development, 69,* 1107–1128.

Carr, L., Iacoboni, M., Dubeau, M., Mazziotta, J. C., & Lenzi, G. L. (2003). Neural mechanisms of empathy in humans: A relay from neural systems for imitation to limbic areas. *Proceedings of the National Academy of Sciences, 100,* 5497–5502.

Carroll, J. B. (1993). *Human cognitive abilities.* Cambridge, England: Cambridge University Press.

Carson, R. C., Butcher, J. N., & Mineka, S. (2000). *Abnormal psychology and modern life* (11th ed.). Boston: Allyn and Bacon.

Carstensen, L. L. (1992). Social and emotional patterns in adulthood: Support for socioemotional selectivity theory. *Psychology and Aging, 7,* 331–338.

Carstensen, L. L., & Fredrickson, B. L. (1998). Influence of HIV status and age on cognitive representations of others. *Health Psychology, 17,* 1–10.

Carstensen, L. L., Isaacowitz, D. M., & Charles, S. T. (1999). Taking time seriously: A theory of socioemotional selectivity. *American Psychologist, 54,* 165–181.

Carstensen, L. L., Pasupathi, M., Mayr, U., & Nesselroade, J. R. (2000). Emotional experience in everyday life across the adult life span. *Journal of Personality & Social Psychology, 79,* 644–655.

Carstensen, L. L., & Turk-Charles, S. (1994). The salience of emotion across the adult life span. *Psychology and Aging, 9,* 259–264.

Carver, C. S., Lehman, J. M., & Antoni, M. H. (2003). Dispositional pessimism predicts illness-related disruption of social and recreational activities among breast cancer patients. *Journal of Personality & Social Psychology, 84,* 813–821.

Carver, C. S., & Scheier, M. F. (2001). Optimism, pessimism, and self-regulation. In E. C. Chang (Ed.), *Optimism and pessimism: Implications for theory, research, and practice.* Washington, DC: American Psychological Association.

Caspi, A., Henry, B., McGee, R. O., Moffitt, T. E., & Silva, P. A. (1995). Temperamental origins of child and adolescent behavior problems: From age three to age fifteen. *Child Development, 66,* 55–68.

Caspi, A., & Herbener, E. S. (1990). Continuity and change: Assortative marriage and the consistency of personality in adulthood. *Journal of Personality and Social Psychology, 58,* 250–258.

Caspi, A., Lynam, D., Moffitt, T. E., & Silva, P. A. (1993). Unraveling girls' delinquency: Biological, dispositional, and contextual contributions to adolescent misbehavior. *Developmental Psychology, 29,* 19–30.

Caspi, A., & Moffitt, T. E. (1991). Individual differences are accentuated during periods of social change: The sample case of girls at puberty. *Journal of Personality and Social Psychology, 61,* 157–168.

Caspi, A., Roberts, B. W., & Shiner, R. L. (2005). Personality development: Stability and change. *Annual Review of Psychology, 56,* 453–484.

Cassidy, K. W., Fineberg, D. S., Brown, K., & Perkins, A. (2005). Theory of mind may be contagious, but you don't catch it from your twin. *Child Development, 76,* 97–106.

Castro-Martin, T., & Bumpass, L. (1989). Recent trends in marital disruption. *Demography, 26,* 37–51.

Cates, W. (1999). Estimates of the incidence and prevalence of sexually transmitted diseases in the United States. *Sexually Transmitted Disease, 26*(Suppl.), S2–S7.

Catrambone, R. (2002). The effects of surface and structural feature matches on the access of story analogs. *Journal of Experimental Psychology: Learning, Memory, & Cognition, 28,* 318–334.

**Cattell, R. B.** (1950). *Personality: A systematic, theoretical, and factual study.* New York: McGraw-Hill.

**CBS.** (2000). *Survivor.* Retrieved July 2, 2003, from http://www.cbs.com/primetime/survivor

**Ceci, S. J.** (1991). How much does schooling influence general intelligence and its cognitive components? A reassessment of the evidence. *Developmental Psychology, 27,* 703–722.

**Ceci, S. J., DeSimone, M., & Johnson, S.** (1992). Memory in context: A case study of "Bubbles P.," a gifted but uneven memorizer. In D. J. Herrmann, H. Weingartner, A. Searleman, & C. McEvoy (Eds.), *Memory improvement: Implications for memory theory* (pp. 169–186). New York: Springer-Verlag.

**Ceci, S. J., & Williams, W. M.** (1997). Schooling, intelligence, and income. *American Psychologist, 52,* 1051–1058.

**Centers for Disease Control (CDC).** (1988). Health status of Vietnam veterans: I. Psychosocial characteristics. *Journal of the American Medical Association, 259,* 2701–2708.

**Centers for Disease Control (CDC).** (2000). *Tracking the hidden epidemics.* Washington, DC: author.

**Centers for Disease Control (CDC).** (August 18, 2000). Surveillance summary. *49* (No. SS-8). Washington, DC: author.

**Centers for Disease Control (CDC).** (June 28, 2002). Surveillance summary. *51* (No. SS-54). Washington, DC: author.

**Centers for Disease Control (CDC).** (2006). Epidemiology of HIV/AIDS—United States, 1981–2005. *Morbidity and Mortality Weekly Report, 55,* 589–592.

**Chaiken, S.** (1980). Heuristic versus systematic information processing and the use of source versus message cues in persuasion. *Journal of Personality and Social Psychology, 39,* 752–766.

**Chalmers, D.** (1996). *The conscious mind: In search of a fundamental theory.* New York: Oxford University Press.

**Chambless, D. L., Baker, M. J., Baucom, D. H., Beutler, L. E., Calhoun, K. S., Crits-Christoph, P., et al.** (1998). Update on empirically validated therapies, II. *Clinical Psychologist, 51*(1), 3–14.

**Chandrashekar, J., Hoon, M. A., Ryba, N. J., & Zuker, C. S.** (2006). The receptors and cells for human tastes. *Nature, 444,* 288–294.

**Chang, P. P., Ford, D. E., Meoni, L. A., Wang, N., & Klag, M. J.** (2002). Anger in young men and subsequent premature cardiovascular disease. *Archives of Internal Medicine, 162,* 901–906.

**Charles, S. T., Reynolds, C. A., & Gatz, M.** (2001). Age-related differences and change in positive and negative affect over 23 years. *Journal of Personality and Social Psychology, 80,* 136–151.

**Charness, N.** (1981). Aging and skilled problem solving. *Journal of Experimental Psychology: General, 110,* 21–38.

**Chartrand, T. L., & Bargh, J. A.** (1999). The chameleon effect: The perception-behavior link and social interaction. *Journal of Personality and Social Psychology, 76,* 893–910.

**Chartrand, T. L., & Kay, A.** (in press). Mystery moods and perplexing performance: Consequences of succeeding and failing at a nonconscious goal.

**Chebium, R.** (2000). Kirk Bloodsworth, twice convicted of rape and murder, exonerated by DNA evidence. *CNN.com.* Retrieved June 20, 2000, from http://www.cnn.com/2000/LAW/06/20/bloodsworth.profile

**Cheney, D. L., & Seyfarth, R. M.** (1990). *How monkeys see the world.* Chicago: University of Chicago Press.

**Cheng, P. W., & Holyoak, K. J.** (1989). On the natural selection of reasoning theories. *Cognition, 33,* 285–313.

**Cherlin, A. J.** (Ed.). (1992). *Marriage, divorce, remarriage* (2nd ed.). Cambridge, MA: Harvard University Press.

**Cherry, A., Dillon, M. E., & Rugh, D.** (Eds.). (2002). *Substance abuse: A global view.* Westport, CT: Greenwood.

**Cherry, C.** (1953). Some experiments on the recognition of speech with one and two ears. *Journal of the Acoustical Society of America, 25,* 275–279.

**Choi, I., Nisbett, R. E., & Norenzayan, A.** (1999). Causal attribution across cultures: Variation and universality. *Psychological Bulletin, 125,* 47–63.

**Chomsky, N.** (1957). *Syntactic structures.* The Hague: Mouton.

**Chomsky, N.** (1959). A review of *Verbal Behavior* by B. F. Skinner. *Language, 35,* 26–58.

**Chomsky, N.** (1986). *Knowledge of language: Its nature, origin, and use.* New York: Praeger.

**Chorover, S. L.** (1980). *From Genesis to genocide : The meaning of human nature and the power of behavior control.* Cambridge, MA: MIT Press.

**Christianson, S.-Å., & Loftus, E. F.** (1987). Memory for traumatic events. *Applied Cognitive Psychology, 1,* 225–239.

**Cialdini, R. B.** (2000). *Influence: Science and practice* (4th ed.). New York: Morrow.

**Cialdini, R. B.** (2005). Don't throw in the towel: Use social influence research. *American Psychological Society, 18,* 33–34.

**Cialdini, R. B., & Trost, M. R.** (1998). Social influence: Social norms, conformity, and compliance. In D. T. Gilbert, S. T. Fiske, & G. Lindzey (Eds.), *The handbook of social psychology* (4th ed., Vol. 2, pp. 151–192). New York: McGraw-Hill.

**Cialdini, R. B., Trost, M. R., & Newsom, J. T.** (1995). Preference for consistency: The development of a valid measure and the discovery of surprising behavioral implications. *Journal of Personality and Social Psychology, 69,* 318–328.

**Cialdini, R. B., Vincent, J. E., Lewis, S. K., Catalan, J., Wheeler, D., & Darby, B. L.** (1975). Reciprocal concessions procedure for inducing compliance: The door-in-the-face technique. *Journal of Personality and Social Psychology, 31,* 206–215.

**Cicchetti, D., & Toth, S. L.** (1998). Perspectives on research and practice in developmental psychopathology. In I. E. Sigel & K. A. Renninger (Eds.), *Handbook of child psychology: Vol. 4. Child psychology in practice* (5th ed., pp. 479–583). New York: Wiley.

**Clancy, S. A.** (2005). *Abducted: How people come to believe they were kidnapped by aliens.* Cambridge. MA: Harvard University Press.

**Clark, L. A.** (2007). Assessment and diagnosis of personality disorder: Perennial issues and emerging conceptualization. *Annual Review of Psychology, 58,* 227–257.

**Clark, R. D., & Hatfield, E.** (1989). Gender differences in receptivity to sexual offers. *Journal of Psychology and Human Sexuality, 2,* 39–55.

**Clayton, N. S., & Dickinson, A.** (1998). Episodic-like memory during cache recovery by scrub jays. *Nature, 395,* 272–274.

**Cleckley, H. M.** (1976). *The mask of sanity* (5th ed.). St. Louis: Mosby.

**Coe, C.** (1993). Psychosocial factors and immunity in nonhuman primates: A review. *Psychosomatic Medicine, 55,* 298–308.

**Cogan, R., Cogan, D., Waltz, W., & McCue, M.** (1987). Effects of laughter and relaxation on discomfort thresholds. *Journal of Behavioral Medicine, 10,* 139–144.

**Coghill, R. C., McHaffie, J. G., & Yen, Y.** (2003). Neural correlates of individual differences in the subjective experience of pain. *Proceedings of the National Academy of Sciences, (USA), 100,* 8538–8542.

**Cohen, D.** (1997). A critique of the use of neuroleptic drugs in psychiatry. In S. Fisher & R. P. Greenberg (Eds.), *From placebo to panacea: Putting psychiatric drugs to test* (pp. 173–228). New York: Wiley.

**Cohen, D., Nisbett, R. E., Bowdle, B. F., & Schwarz, N.** (1996). Insult, aggression, and the southern culture of honor: An "experimental ethnography." *Journal of Personality and Social Psychology, 70,* 945–960.

**Cohen, G.** (1990). Why is it difficult to put names to faces? *British Journal of Psychology, 81,* 287–297.

**Cohen, N. J., & Squire, L. R.** (1980). Preserved learning and retention of pattern analyzing skill in amnesics: Dissociation of knowing how and knowing that. *Science, 210,* 207–210.

**Cohen, S.** (1988). Psychosocial models of the role of social support in the etiology of physical disease. *Health Psychology, 7,* 269–297.

**Cohen, S.** (1999). Social status and susceptibility to respiratory infections. *New York Academy of Sciences, 896,* 246–253.

**Cohen, S., Evans, G. W., Krantz, D. S., & Stokols, D.** (1980). Physiological, motivational, and cognitive effects of aircraft noise on children. *American Psychologist, 35,* 231–243.

**Cohen, S., Frank, E., Doyle, W. J., Skoner, D. P., Rabin, B. S., & Gwaltney, J. M., Jr.** (1998). Types of stressors that increase susceptibility to the common cold in healthy adults. *Health Psychology, 17,* 214–223.

**Cohen, S., Kaplan, J. R., Cunnick, J. E., Manuck, S. B., & Rabin, B. S.** (1992). Chronic social stress, affiliation, and cellular immune response in nonhuman primates. *Psychological Science, 3,* 301–304.

**Cohen, S. J. (Ed.).** (1979). *New directions in patient compliance.* Lexington, MA: Heath.

**Cole, M.** (1996). *Cultural psychology: A once and future discipline.* Cambridge, MA: Belknap Press of Harvard University Press.

**Coley, R. L., & Chase-Landale, P. L.** (1998). Adolescent pregnancy and parenthood: Recent evidence and future directions. *American Psychologist, 53,* 152–166.

**Condon, J. W., & Crano, W. D.** (1988). Inferred evaluation and the relation between attitude similarity and interpersonal attraction. *Journal of Personality and Social Psychology, 54,* 789–797.

**Connors, E., Lundregan, T., Miller, N., & McEwen, T.** (1997). *Convicted by juries, exonerated by science: Case studies in the use of DNA evidence to establish innocence after trial.* Collingdale, PA: Diane Publishing.

**Conway, M., & Ross, M.** (1984). Getting what you want by revising what you had. *Journal of Personality and Social Psychology, 47,* 738–748.

**Conwell, Y., Duberstein, P. R., Cox, C., Hermmann, J. H., Forbes, N. T., & Caine, E. D.** (1996). Relationships of age and axis I diagnoses in victims of completed suicide: A psychological autopsy study. *American Journal of Psychiatry, 153,* 1001–1008.

**Cook, E. P.** (1985). *Psychological androgyny.* New York: Pergamon Press.

**Cook, M., & Mineka, S.** (1989). Observational conditioning of fear to fear-relevant versus fear-irrelevant stimuli in rhesus monkeys. *Journal of Abnormal Psychology, 98,* 448–459.

**Cook, M., & Mineka, S.** (1990). Selective associations in the observational conditioning of fear in rhesus monkeys. *Journal of Experimental Psychology: Animal Behavior Process, 16,* 372–389.

**Coombs, R. H.** (1991). Marital status and personal well-being: A literature review. *Family Relations, 40,* 97–102.

**Coons, P. M.** (1994). Confirmation of childhood abuse in child and adolescent cases of multiple personality disorder and dissociative disorder not otherwise specified. *Journal of Nervous and Mental Disease, 182,* 461–464.

**Cooper, J., & Fazio, R. H.** (1984). A new look at dissonance theory. In L. Berkowitz (Ed.), *Advances in experimental social psychology* (Vol. 17, pp. 229–266). New York: Academic Press.

**Cooper, J. R., Bloom, F. E., & Roth, R. H.** (2003). *Biochemical basis of neuropharmacology.* New York: Oxford University Press.

**Cooper, M. L., Shapiro, C. M., & Powers, A. M.** (1998). Motivations for sex and risky sexual behavior among adolescents and young adults: A functional perspective. *Journal of Personality and Social Psychology, 75,* 1528–1558.

**Coren, S.** (1997). *Sleep thieves.* New York: Free Press.

**Corkin, S.** (1984). Lasting consequences of bilateral medial temporal lobectomy: Clinical course and experimental findings in H. M. *Seminars in Neurology, 4,* 249–259.

**Corkin, S.** (2002). What's new with the amnesic patient HM? *Nature Reviews Neuroscience, 3,* 153–160.

**Correll, J., Park, B., Judd, C. M., & Wittenbrink, B.** (2002). The police officer's dilemma: Using ethnicity to disambiguate potentially threatening individuals. *Journal of Personality and Social Psychology, 83,* 1314–1329.

**Corsi, P.** (1991). *The enchanted loom: Chapters in the history of neuroscience.* New York: Oxford University Press.

**Corsini, R. J.** (2000). Introduction. In R. J. Corsini & D. Wedding (Eds.), *Current psychotherapies* (6th ed., pp. 1–15). Itasca, IL: F. E. Peacock, Publishers.

**Corti, E.** (1931). *A history of smoking* (P. England, Trans.). London: Harrap.

**Coryell, W., Endicott, J., Maser, J. D., Mueller, T., Lavori, P., & Keller, M.** (1995). The likelihood of recurrence in bipolar affective disorder: The importance of episode recency. *Journal of Affective Disorders, 33,* 201–206.

**Cosmides, L.** (1989). The logic of social exchange: Has natural selection shaped how humans reason? Studies with the Wason selection task. *Cognition, 31,* 187–276.

**Cox, D., & Cowling, P.** (1989). *Are you normal?* London: Tower Press.

**Coyne, J. A.** (2000, April 3). Of vice and men: Review of R. Tornhill and C. Palmer, *A natural history of rape. The New Republic,* 27–34.

**Coyne, J. C., & Whiffen, V. E.** (1995). Issues in personality as diathesis for depression: The case of sociotropy-dependency and autonomy self-criticism. *Psychological Bulletin, 118,* 358–378.

**Craik, F. I. M., Govoni, R., Naveh-Benjamin, M., & Anderson, N. D.** (1996). The effects of divided attention on encoding and retrieval processes in human memory. *Journal of Experimental Psychology: General, 125,* 159–180.

**Craik, F. I. M., & Tulving, E.** (1975). Depth of processing and the retention of words in episodic memory. *Journal of Experimental Psychology: General, 104,* 268–294.

**Cramer, R. E., Schaefer, J. T., & Reid, S.** (1996). Identifying the ideal mate: More evidence for male-female convergence. *Current Psychology: Developmental, Learning, Personality, Social, 15,* 157–166.

**Craske, M. G.** (1999). *Anxiety disorders: Psychological approaches to theory and treatment.* Boulder, CO: Westview.

**Crespi, L. P.** (1942). Quantitative variation in incentive and performance in the white rat. *American Journal of Psychology, 55,* 467–517.

**Crick, N. R., & Grotpeter, J. K.** (1995). Relational aggression, gender, and social-psychological adjustment. *Child Development, 66,* 710–722.

**Critelli, J. W., & Ee, J. S.** (1996). Stress and physical illness: Development of an integrative model. In T. W. Miller (Ed.), *Theory and assessment of stressful life events* (pp. 139–159). Madison, CT: International Universities Press.

**Crocker, J., & Luhtanen, R.** (1990). Collective self-esteem and in-group bias. *Journal of Personality and Social Psychology, 58,* 60–67.

**Crocker, J., & Wolfe, C. T.** (2001). Contingencies of self-worth. *Psychological Review, 108*(3), 593–623.

**Crombag, H. F. M., Wagenaar, W. A., & Van Koppen, P. J.** (1996). Crashing memories and the problem of "source monitoring." *Applied Cognitive Psychology, 10,* 95–104.

**Cross, P.** (1977). Not can but will college teachers be improved? *New Directions for Higher Education, 17,* 1–15.

**Cross-National Collaborative Research Group.** (1992). The changing rate of major depression: Cross-national comparison. *Journal of the American Medical Association, 268,* 3098–3105.

Crowe, R. (1990). Panic disorder: Genetic considerations. *Journal of Psychiatric Researchers, 24,* 129–134.

Csermansky, J. G., & Grace, A. A. (1998). New models of the pathophysiology of schizophrenia: Editor's introduction. *Schizophrenia Bulletin, 24,* 185–187.

Csikszentmihalyi, M. (1990). *Flow: The psychology of optimal experience.* New York: Harper & Row.

Csikszentmihalyi, M., & Larson, R. (1987). Validity and reliability of the experience-sampling method. *Journal of Nervous & Mental Disease, 175,* 526–536.

Cumming, S., Hay, P., Lee, T., & Sachdev, P. (1995). Neuropsychological outcome from psychosurgery for obsessive-compulsive disorder. *Australian and New Zealand Journal of Psychiatry, 29,* 293–298.

Cummings, D. E., Purnell, J. Q., Frayo, R. S., Schmidova, K., Wisse, B. E., & Weigle, D. S. (2001). A preprandial rise in plasma ghrelin levels suggests a role in meal initiation in humans. *Diabetes, 50,* 1714–1719.

Cummins, D. D., & Allen, C. A. (2000). *The evolution of mind.* New York: Oxford University Press.

Cunningham, M. R., Barbee, A. P., & Pike, C. L. (1990). What do women want? Facialmetric assessment of multiple motives in the perception of male facial physical attractiveness. *Journal of Personality & Social Psychology, 59,* 61–72.

Cunningham, M. R., Roberts, A. R., Barbee, A. P., Druen, P. B., & Wu, C.-H. (1995). "Their ideas of beauty are, on the whole, the same as ours": Consistency and variability in the cross-cultural perception of female physical attractiveness. *Journal of Personality and Social Psychology, 68,* 261–279.

Curran, J. P., & Lippold, S. (1975). The effects of physical attraction and attitude similarity on attraction in dating dyads. *Journal of Personality, 43,* 528–539.

Curtiss, S. (1977). Genie: A psycholinguistic study of a modern-day "wild-child." New York: Academic Press.

Cutler, D. L., Bevilacqua, J., & McFarland, B. H. (2003). Four decades of community mental health: A symphony in four movements. *Community Mental Health Journal, 39,* 381–398.

Cutler, S., & Nolen-Hoeksema, S. (1991). Accounting for sex differences in depression through female victimization: Childhood sexual abuse. *Sex Roles, 24,* 425–438.

Cytowic, R. (2003). *The man who tasted shapes.* Cambridge, MA: MIT Press.

Dabbs, J. M., Bernieri, F. J., Strong, R. K., Campo, R., & Milun, R. (2001). Going on stage: Testosterone in greetings and meetings. *Journal of Research in Personality, 35,* 27–40.

Dabbs, J. M., Carr, T. S., Frady, R. L., & Riad, J. K. (1995). Testosterone, crime, and misbehavior among 692 male prison inmates. *Personality and Individual Differences, 18,* 627–633.

Dabbs, J. M., Strong, R., & Milun, R. (1997). Exploring the mind of testosterone: A beeper study. *Journal of Research in Personality, 31,* 577–587.

D'Agostino, P. R., & Fincher-Kiefer, R. (1992). Need for cognition and correspondence bias. *Social Cognition, 10,* 151–163.

Dally, P. (1999). *The marriage of heaven and hell: Manic depression and the life of Virginia Woolf.* New York: St. Martin's Griffin.

Dalton, P. (2003). Olfaction. In H. Pashler & S. Yantis (Eds.), *Stevens' handbook of experimental psychology: Vol. 1. Sensation and perception* (3rd ed., pp. 691–746). New York: Wiley.

Daly, M., & Wilson, M. (1988). Evolutionary social psychology and family homicide. *Science, 242,* 519–524.

Damasio, A. R. (1989). Time-locked multiregional retroactivation: A systems-level proposal for the neural substrates of recall and recognition. *Cognition, 33,* 25–62.

Damasio, A. R. (1994). *Descartes' error: Emotion, reason, and the human brain.* New York: Putnam.

Damasio, A. R. (2005). *Descartes' error: Emotion, reason, and the human brain.* (ppbk. ed.). New York: Penguin.

Damasio, A. R., Grabowski, T. J., Bechara, A., Damasio, H., Ponto, L. L. B., Parvisi, J., et al. (2000). Subcortical and cortical brain activity during the feeling of self-generated emotions. *Nature Neuroscience, 3,* 1049–1056.

Damasio, H., Grabowski, T. J., Tranel, D., Hichwa, R. D., & Damasio, A. R. (1996). A neural basis for lexical retrieval. *Nature, 380,* 499–505.

Damsma, G., Pfaus, J. G., Wenkstern, D., Phillips, A. G., & Fibiger, H. C. (1992). Sexual behavior increases dopamine transmission in the nucleus accumbens and striatum of male rats: Comparison with novelty and locomotion. *Behavioral Neurosciences, 106,* 181–191.

Daniel, H. J., O'Brien, K. F., McCabe, R. B., & Quinter, V. E. (1985). Values in mate selection: A 1984 campus survey. *College Student Journal, 19,* 44–50.

Darley, J. M., & Berscheid, E. (1967). Increased liking caused by the anticipation of interpersonal contact. *Human Relations, 10,* 29–40.

Darley, J. M., & Latané, B. (1968). Bystander intervention in emergencies: Diffusion of responsibility. *Journal of Personality and Social Psychology, 8,* 377–383.

Dar-Nimrod, I., & Heine, S. J. (2006). Exposure to scientific theories affects women's math performance. *Science, 314,* 435.

Darroch, J. E., Singh, S., Frost, J. J., & Study Team. (2001). Differences in teenage pregnancy rates among five developed countries: The roles of sexuality and contraceptive use. *Family Planning Perspectives, 33,* 244–250.

Darwin, C. (1859). *On the origin of species by means of natural selection.* London: J. Murray.

Darwin, C. (1998). *The expression of the emotions in man and animals.* (P. Ekman, Ed.) New York: Oxford University Press. (Originally published 1872)

Darwin, C. J., Turvey, M. T., & Crowder, R. G. (1972). An auditory analogue of the Sperling partial report procedure: Evidence for brief auditory storage. *Cognitive Psychology, 3,* 255–267.

Dauer, W., & Przedborski, S. (2003). Parkinson's disease: Mechanisms and models. *Neuron, 39,* 889–909.

Davidson, P. R., & Parker, K. C. H. (2001). Eye movement desensitization and reprocessing (EMDR): A meta-analysis. *Journal of Consulting and Clinical Psychology, 69,* 305–316.

Davidson, R. J. (2004). What does the prefrontal cortex "do" in affect: Perspectives on frontal EEG asymmetry research. *Biological Psychology, 67,* 219–233.

Davidson, R. J., Ekman, P., Saron, C., Senulis, J., & Friesen, W. V. (1990). Emotional expression and brain physiology I: Approach/withdrawal and cerebral asymmetry. *Journal of Personality and Social Psychology, 58,* 330–341.

Davidson, R. J., Pizzagalli, D., Nitschke, J. B., & Putnam, K. (2002). Depression: Perspectives from affective neuroscience. *Annual Review of Psychology, 53,* 545–574.

Davidson, R. J., Putnam, K. M., & Larson, C. L. (2000). Dysfunction in the neural circuitry of emotion regulation—a possible prelude to violence. *Science, 289,* 591–594.

Davies, G. (1988). Faces and places: Laboratory research on context and face recognition. In G. M. Davies & D. M. Thomson (Eds.), *Memory in context: Context in memory* (pp. 35–53). New York: Wiley.

Davis, K. (1947). Final note on a case of extreme social isolation. *American Journal of Sociology, 52,* 432–437.

Dawes, R. M. (1986). Representative thinking in clinical judgment. *Clinical Psychology Review, 6,* 425–441.

Dawes, R. M. (1994). *House of cards: Psychology and psychotherapy built on myth.* New York: Free Press.

Dawes, R. M. (2001). *Everyday irrationality: How pseudo scientists, lunatics, and the rest of us systematically fail to think rationally.* Boulder, CO: Westview Press.

Dawkins, R. J. (1976). *The selfish gene.* Oxford, England: Oxford University Press.

Dawood, K., Kirk, K. M., Bailey, J. M., Andrews, P. W., & Martin, N. G. (2005). Genetic and environmental influences on the frequency of orgasm in women. *Twin Research, 8,* 27–33.

de Craen, A. J. M., Moerman, D. E., Heisterkamp, S. H., Tytgat, G. N. J., Tijssen, J. G. P., & Kleijnen, J. (1999). Placebo effect in the treatment of duodenal ulcer. *British Journal of Clinical Pharmacology, 48,* 853–860.

De Valois, R. L., Abramov, I., & Jacobs, G. (1966). Analysis of response patterns of LGN cells. *Journal of the Optical Society of America [A], 56,* 966–977.

De Witte, P. (1996). The role of neurotransmitters in alcohol dependency. *Alcohol & Alcoholism, 31*(Suppl. 1), 13–16.

De Wolff, M., & van IJzendoorn, M. H. (1997). Sensitivity and attachment: A meta-analysis on parental antecedents of infant attachment. *Child Development, 68,* 571–591.

Deary, I. J. (2000). *Looking down on human intelligence: From psychometrics to the brain.* New York: Oxford University Press.

Deary, I. J. (2001). *Intelligence: A very short introduction.* Oxford, England: Oxford University Press.

Deary, I. J., Der, G., & Ford, G. (2001). Reaction time and intelligence differences: A population based cohort study. *Intelligence, 29,* 389–399.

Deary, I. J., & Stough, C. (1996). Intelligence and inspection time: Achievements, prospects, and problems. *American Psychologist, 51,* 599–608.

Deary, I. J., Whalley, L. J., Lemmon, H., Crawford, J. R., & Starr, J. M. (2000). The stability of individual differences in mental ability from childhood to old age: Follow-up of the 1932 Scottish Mental Survey. *Intelligence, 28,* 49–55.

Deary, I. J., Whiteman, M. C., Starr, J. M., Whalley, L. J., & Fox, H. C. (2004). The impact of childhood intelligence on later life: Following up the Scottish mental surveys of 1932 and 1947. *Journal of Personality and Social Psychology, 86,* 130–147.

DeCasper, A. J., & Spence, M. J. (1986). Prenatal maternal speech influences newborns' perception of speech sounds. *Infant Behavior and Development, 9,* 133–150.

Deci, E. L. (1971). Effects of externally mediated rewards on intrinsic motivation. *Journal of Personality and Social Psychology, 18,* 105–115.

Deci, E. L., Koestner, R., & Ryan, R. M. (1999). A meta-analytic review of experiments examining the effects of extrinsic rewards on intrinsic motivation. *Psychological Bulletin, 125,* 627–668.

Deese, J. (1959). On the prediction of occurrence of particular verbal intrusions in immediate recall. *Journal of Experimental Psychology, 58,* 17–22.

DeFelipe, J., & Jones, E. G. (1988). *Cajal on the cerebral cortex: An annotated translation of the complete writings.* New York: Oxford University Press.

DeLisi, L. E., Crow, T. J., & Hirsch, S. R. (1986). The third biannual workshops on schizophrenia. *Archives of General Psychiatry, 43,* 706–711.

DeLoache, J. S., & Gottlieb, A. (2000). *A world of babies: Imagined childcare guides for seven societies.* Cambridge, England: Cambridge University Press.

Delongis, A., Coyne, J. C., Dakof, G., Folkman, S., & Lazarus, R. S. (1982). Relationship of daily hassles, uplifts, and major life events to health status. *Health Psychology, 1,* 119–136.

Demb, J. B., Desmond, J. E., Wagner, A. D., Vaidya, C. J., Glover, G. H., & Gabrieli, J. D. E. (1995). Semantic encoding and retrieval in the left inferior prefrontal cortex: A functional MRI study of task difficulty and process specificity. *Journal of Neuroscience, 15,* 5870–5878.

Dement, W. C. (1959, Nov. 30). Dreams. *Time.*

Dement, W. C. (1978). *Some must watch while some must sleep.* New York: Norton.

Dement, W. C. (1999). *The promise of sleep.* New York: Delacorte Press.

Dement, W. C., & Kleitman, N. (1957). The relation of eye movements during sleep to dream activity: An objective method for the study of dreaming. *Journal of Experimental Psychology, 53,* 339–346.

Dement, W. C., & Wolpert, E. (1958). Relation of eye movements, body motility, and external stimuli to dream content. *Journal of Experimental Psychology, 55,* 543–553.

Dennett, D. (1991). *Consciousness explained.* New York: Basic Books.

DePaulo, B. M., Charlton, K., Cooper, H., Lindsay, J. J., & Muhlenbruck, L. (1997). The accuracy-confidence correlation in the detection of deception. *Personality and Social Psychology Review, 1,* 346–357.

DePaulo, B. M., Lindsay, J. J., Malone, B. E., Muhlenbruck, L., Charlton, K., & Cooper, H. (2003). Cues to deception. *Psychological Bulletin, 129,* 74–118.

DePaulo, B. M., Stone, J. I., & Lassiter, G. D. (1985). Deceiving and detecting deceit. In B. R. Schlenker (Ed.), *The self and social life* (pp. 323–370). New York: McGraw-Hill.

DeRosnay, M., Pons, F., Harris, P. L., & Morrell, J. M. B. (2004). A lag between understanding false belief and emotion attribution in young children: Relationships with linguistic ability and mothers' mental-state language. *British Journal of Developmental Psychology,* 197–218.

DesJardin, J. L., Eisenberg, L. S., & Hodapp, R. M. (2006). Sound beginnings: Supporting families of young deaf children with cochlear implants. *Infants and Young Children, 19,* 179–189.

Deuenwald, M. (2003, June 12). Students find another staple of campus life: Stress. *New York Times.*

Deutsch, M. (1949). A theory of cooperation and competition. *Human Relations, 2,* 129–152.

DeVilliers, P. (2005). The role of language in theory-of-mind development: What deaf children tell us. In J. W. Astington & J. A. Baird (Eds.), *Why language matters for theory of mind* (pp. 266–297). Oxford, England: Oxford University Press.

Diaconis, P., & Mosteller, F. (1989). Methods for studying coincidences. *Journal of the American Statistical Association, 84,* 853–861.

Diamond, M., & Schiebel, A. B. (1986). *The human brain coloring book.* New York: Collins.

Dickens, W. T., & Flynn, J. R. (2001). Heritability estimates versus large environmental effects: The IQ paradox resolved. *Psychological Review, 108,* 346–369.

Didi-Huberman, G. (2003). *Invention of hysteria: Charcot and the photographic iconography of the Sâlpetrière* (A. Hartz, Trans.). Cambridge, MA: MIT Press.

Diener, E., & Biswas-Diener, R. (2002). Will money increase subjective well-being? *Social Indicators Research, 57,* 119–169.

Diener, E., Horwitz, J., & Emmons, R. A. (1985). Happiness of the very wealthy. *Social Indicators Research, 16,* 263–274.

Diener, E., & Wallbom, M. (1976). Effects of self-awareness on anti-normative behavior. *Journal of Research in Personality, 10,* 107–111.

Dienstbier, R. A. (1979). Attraction increases and decreases as a function of emotion-attribution and appropriate social cues. *Motivation and Emotion, 3,* 201–218.

Dietary Guidelines Advisory Committee. (2005). Dietary guidelines for Americans 2005. Retrieved October 15, 2007, from http://www.health.gov/dietaryguidelines

Dijksterhuis, A. (2004). Think different: The merits of unconscious thought in preference development and decision making. *Journal of Personality and Social Psychology, 87,* 586–598.

Dijksterhuis, A., Aarts, H., & Smith, P. K. (2005). The power of the subliminal: On subliminal persuasion and other potential applications. In J. S. U. R. Hassin & J. A. Bargh (Eds.), *The new unconscious* (pp. 77–106). New York: Oxford University Press.

Dillbeck, M. C., & Orme-Johnson, D. W. (1987). Physiological differences between Transcendental Meditation and rest. *American Psychologist, 42,* 879–881.

Dimberg, U. (1982). Facial reactions to facial expressions. *Psychophysiology, 19,* 643–647.

Dion, K., Berscheid, E., & Walster, E. (1972). What is beautiful is good. *Journal of Personality and Social Psychology, 24,* 285–290.

DiTella, R., MacCulloch, R. J., & Oswald, A. J. (2003). The macroeconomics of happiness. *Review of Economics and Statistics, 85,* 809–827.

Dittrich, W. H., Troscianko, T., Lea, S., & Morgan, D. (1996). Perception of emotion from dynamic point-light displays represented in dance. *Perception, 25,* 727–738.

Dohrenwend, B. S., Dohrenwend, B. P., Dodson, M., & Shrout, P. E. (1984). Symptoms, hassles, social supports, and life events: Problem of confounded measures. *Journal of Abnormal Psychology, 93,* 222–230.

Dollard, J., Doob, L. W., Miller, N. E., Mowrer, O. H., & Sears, R. R. (1939). *Frustration and aggression.* Oxford, England: Yale University Press.

Domjan, M. (2005). Pavlovian conditioning: A functional perspective. *Annual Review of Psychology, 56,* 179–206.

Dorahy, M. J. (2001). Dissociative identity disorder and memory dysfunction: The current state of experimental research and its future directions. *Clinical Psychology Review, 21,* 771–795.

Dornbusch, S. M., Hastorf, A. H., Richardson, S. A., Muzzy, R. E., & Vreeland, R. S. (1965). The perceiver and perceived: Their relative influence on categories of interpersonal perception. *Journal of Personality and Social Psychology, 1,* 434–440.

Dorus, S., Vallender, E. J., Evans, P. D., Anderson, J. R., Gilbert, S. L., Mahowald, M., et al. (2004). Accelerated evolution of nervous system genes in the origin of *Homo sapiens. Cell, 119,* 1027–1040.

Dostoevsky, F. (1955). *Winter notes on summer impressions* (R. L. Reinfield, Trans.). New York: Criterion Books. (Original work published 1863)

Dowling, J. E. (1992). *Neurons and networks: An introduction to neuroscience.* Cambridge, MA: Harvard University Press.

Downer, J. D. C. (1961). Changes in visual gnostic function and emotional behavior following unilateral temporal damage in the "split-brain" monkey. *Nature, 191,* 50–51.

Downing, P. E., Chan, A. W. Y., Peelen, M. V., Dodds, C. M., & Kanwisher, N. (2006). Domain specificity in visual cortex. *Cerebral Cortex, 16,* 1453–1461.

Draguns, J. G. (1980). Psychological disorders of clinical severity. In H. C. Triandis & J. G. Draguns (Eds.), *Handbook of cross-cultural psychology* (Vol. 6, pp. 99–174). Boston: Allyn and Bacon.

Dreger, A. D. (1998). The limits of individuality: Ritual and sacrifice in the lives and medical treatment of conjoined twins. *Studies in History and Philosophy of Biological and Biomedical Sciences, 29,* 1–29.

Dreifus, C. (2003, May 20). Living one disaster after another, and then sharing the experience. *New York Times,* p. D2.

Drigotas, S. M., & Rusbult, C. E. (1992). Should I stay or should I go? A dependence model of breakups. *Journal of Personality and Social Psychology, 62,* 62–87.

Driscoll, R., Davis, K. E., & Lipetz, M. E. (1972). Parental interference and romantic love: The Romeo and Juliet effect. *Journal of Personality and Social Psychology, 24,* 1–10.

Druckman, D., & Bjork, R. A. (1994). *Learning, remembering, believing: Enhancing human performance.* Washington, DC: National Academy Press.

Drummond, E. (2000). *The complete guide to psychiatric drugs: Straight talk for best results.* New York: Wiley.

Duchaine, B. C., Yovel, G., Butterworth, E. J., & Nakayama, K. (2006). Prosopagnosia as an impairment to face-specific mechanisms: Elimination of the alternative hypotheses in a developmental case. *Cognitive Neuropsychology, 23,* 714–747.

Duckworth, A. L., & Seligman, M. E. P. (2005). Self-discipline outdoes IQ in predicting academic performance of adolescents. *Psychological Science, 16,* 939–944.

Dudycha, G. J., & Dudycha, M. M. (1933). Some factors and characteristics of childhood memories. *Child Development, 4,* 265–278.

Duncker, K. (1945). On problem-solving. *Psychological Monographs, 58,* No. 5.

Dunlap, K. (1919). Are there any instincts? *Journal of Abnormal Psychology, 14,* 307–311.

Dunphy, D. C. (1963). The social structure of urban adolescent peer groups. *Sociometry, 26,* 230–246.

Durkheim, E. (1951). *Suicide: A study in sociology* (G. Simpson, Trans.). New York: Free Press.

Dutton, D. G., & Aron, A. P. (1974). Some evidence for heightened sexual attraction under conditions of high anxiety. *Journal of Personality and Social Psychology, 30,* 510–517.

Duval, S., & Wicklund, R. A. (1972). *A theory of objective self awareness.* New York: Academic Press.

Eacott, M. J., & Crawley, R. A. (1998). The offset of childhood amnesia: Memory for events that occurred before age 3. *Journal of Experimental Psychology: General, 127,* 22–33.

Eagly, A. H., Ashmore, R. D., Makhijani, M. G., & Longo, L. C. (1991). What is beautiful is good, but . . . : A meta-analytic review of research on the physical attractiveness stereotype. *Psychological Bulletin, 110,* 109–128.

Eagly, A. H., & Steffen, V. J. (1986). Gender and aggressive behavior: A meta-analytic review of the social psychological literature. *Psychological Bulletin, 100,* 309–330.

Eagly, A. H., & Wood, W. (1999). The origins of sex differences in human behavior: Evolved dispositions versus social roles. *American Psychologist, 54,* 408–423.

Eaton, W. W., Kessler, R. C., Wittchen, H. U., & McGee, W. J. (1994). Panic and panic disorder in the United States. *American Journal of Psychiatry, 151,* 413–420.

Eaton, W. W., Romanoski, A., Anthony, J. C., & Nestadt, G. (1991). Screening for psychosis in the general population with a self-report interview. *Journal of Nervous and Mental Disease, 179,* 689–693.

Ebbinghaus, H. (1964). *Memory: A contribution to experimental psychology.* New York: Dover. (Originally published 1885)

Eberhardt, J. L. (2005). Imaging race. *American Psychologist, 60,* 181–190.

Eddy, D. M. (1982). Probabilistic reasoning in clinical medicine: Problems and opportunities. In D. Kahneman, P. Slovic, & A. Tversky (Eds.), *Judgments under uncertainty: Heuristics and biases* (pp. 249–267). Cambridge, MA: Cambridge University Press.

Edgerton, V. R., Tillakaratne, J. K. T., Bigbee, A. J., deLeon, R. D., & Roy, R. R. (2004). Plasticity of the spinal neural circuitry after injury. *Annual Review of Neuroscience, 27,* 145–167.

Edwards, W. (1955). The theory of decision making. *Psychological Bulletin, 51,* 201–214.

Eich, J. E. (1980). The cue-dependent nature of state-dependent retention. *Memory & Cognition, 8,* 157–173.

Eich, J. E. (1995). Searching for mood dependent memory. *Psychological Science, 6,* 67–75.

Eichenbaum, H., & Cohen, N. J. (2001). *From conditioning to conscious recollection: Memory systems of the brain.* New York: Oxford University Press.

Eimas, P. D., Siqueland, E. R., Jusczyk, P., & Vigorito, J. (1971). Speech perception in infants. *Science, 171,* 303–306.

Einstein, G. O., & McDaniel, M. A. (1990). Normal aging and prospective memory. *Journal of Experimental Psychology: Learning, Memory, and Cognition, 16,* 717–726.

Eisenberger, N. I., Lieberman, M. D., & Williams, K. D. (2003). Does rejection hurt? An fMRI study of social exclusion. *Science, 302,* 290–292.

Ekman, P. (1965). Differential communication of affect by head and body cues. *Journal of Personality and Social Psychology, 2,* 726–735.

Ekman, P. (1972). Universals and cultural differences in facial expressions of emotion. In J. K. Cole (Ed.), *Nebraska Symposium on Motivation, 1971* (pp. 207–283). Lincoln: University of Nebraska Press.

Ekman, P. (1992). *Telling lies.* New York: Norton.

Ekman, P. (2003a). Darwin, deception, and facial expression. *Annals of the New York Academy of Science, 1000,* 205–221.

Ekman, P. (2003b). *Emotions revealed: Recognizing faces and feelings to improve communication and emotional life.* New York: Times Books.

Ekman, P., & Friesen, W. V. (1968). Nonverbal behavior in psychotherapy research. In J. M. Shlien (Ed.), *Research in psychotherapy* (Vol. 3, pp. 179–216). Washington, DC: American Psychological Association.

Ekman, P., & Friesen, W. V. (1971). Constants across cultures in the face and emotion. *Journal of Personality and Social Psychology, 17,* 124–129.

Ekman, P., & Friesen, W. V. (1978). *The Facial Action Coding System.* Palo Alto, CA: Consulting Psychologists Press.

Ekman, P., & Friesen, W. V. (1982). Felt, false, and miserable smiles. *Journal of Nonverbal Behavior, 6,* 238–252.

Ekman, P., Friesen, W. V., O'Sullivan, M., Chan, A., Diacoyanni-Tarlatzis, I., Heider, K., et al. (1987). Universals and cultural differences in the judgments of facial expressions of emotion. *Journal of Personality and Social Psychology, 53,* 712–717.

Ekman, P., Levenson, R. W., & Friesen, W. V. (1983). Autonomic nervous system activity distinguishes among emotions. *Science, 221,* 1208–1210.

Ekman, P., & O'Sullivan, M. (1991). Who can catch a liar? *American Psychologist, 46*(9), 913–920.

Ekman, P., O'Sullivan, M., & Frank, M. G. (1999). A few can catch a liar. *Psychological Science, 10,* 263–266.

Elder, G. H., & Conger, R. D. (2000). *Children of the land: Adversity and success in rural America.* Chicago: University of Chicago Press.

Eldridge, L. L., Knowlton, B. J., Furmanski, C. S., Bookheimer, S. Y., & Engel, S. A. (2000). Remembering episodes: A selective role for the hippocampus during retrieval. *Nature Neuroscience, 3,* 1149–1152.

Eldridge, M. A., Barnard, P. J., & Bekerian, D. A. (1994). Autobiographical memory and daily schemas at work. *Memory, 2,* 51–74.

Elfenbein, H. A., & Ambady, N. (2002). On the universality and cultural specificity of emotion recognition: A meta-analysis. *Psychological Bulletin, 128,* 203–235.

El-Hai, J. (2005). *The lobotomist: A maverick medical genius and his tragic quest to rid the world of mental illness.* New York: Wiley.

Ellenberger, H. F. (1954). The life and work of Hermann Rorschach (1884–1922). *Bulletin of the Menninger Clinic, 18,* 173–213.

Ellicot, A., Hammen, C., Gitlin, M., Brown, G., & Jaminson, K. (1990). Life events and course of bipolar disorder. *American Journal of Psychiatry, 147,* 1194–1198.

Elliott, R., Sahakian, B. J., Matthews, K., Bannerjea, A., Rimmer, J., & Robbins, T. W. (1997). Effects of methylphenidate on spatial working memory and planning in healthy young adults. *Psychopharmacology, 131,* 196–206.

Ellis, A. (2000). Rational emotive behavior therapy. In R. J. Corsini & D. Wedding (Eds.), *Current psychotherapies* (6th ed., pp. 168–204). Itasca, IL: F. E. Peacock, Publishers.

Ellis, B. J., & Garber, J. (2000). Psychosocial antecedents of variation in girls' pubertal timing: Maternal depression, stepfather presence, and marital and family stress. *Child Development, 71,* 485–501.

Ellis, E. M. (1983). A review of empirical rape research: Victim reactions and response to treatment. *Clinical Psychology Review, 3,* 473–490.

Ellis, L., & Ames, M. A. (1987). Neurohormonal functioning in sexual orientation: A theory of homosexuality-heterosexuality. *Psychological Bulletin, 101,* 233–258.

Ellman, S. J., Spielman, A. J., Luck, D., Steiner, S. S., & Halperin, R. (1991). REM deprivation: A review. In S. J. Ellman & J. S. Antrobus (Eds.), *The mind in sleep: Psychology and psychophysiology* (2nd ed., pp. 329–376). New York: Wiley.

Emerson, R. C., Bergen, J. R., & Adelson, E. H. (1992). Directionally selective complex cells and the computation of motion energy in cat visual cortex. *Vision Research, 32,* 203–218.

Emmelkamp, P. M. G., Krijn, M., Hulsbosch, A. M., de Vries, S., Schuemie, M. J., & van der Mast, C. A. (2002). Virtual reality treatment versus exposure in vivo: A comparative evaluation in acrophobia. *Behaviour Research and Therapy, 40*(5), 509–516.

Emmelkamp, P. M. G., & Wessels, H. (1975). Flooding in imagination vs. flooding in vivo: A comparison with agoraphobics. *Behaviour Research and Therapy, 13,* 7–15.

Empson, J. A. (1984). Sleep and its disorders. In R. Stevens (Ed.), *Aspects of consciousness.* New York: Academic Press.

Enns, J. T. (2004). *The thinking eye, the seeing brain.* New York: Norton.

Epley, N., Savitsky, K., & Kachelski, R. A. (1999). What every skeptic should know about subliminal persuasion. *Skeptical Inquirer, 23,* 40–45, 58.

Erber, R., Wegner, D. M., & Therriault, N. (1996). On being cool and collected: Mood regulation in anticipation of social interaction. *Journal of Personality and Social Psychology, 70,* 757–766.

Erffmeyer, E. S. (1984). Rule-violating behavior on the golf course. *Perceptual and Motor Skills, 59,* 591–596.

Erickson, E. (1959). *Identity and the life cycle: Selected papers.* New York: International Universities Press.

Ericsson, K. A., & Charness, N. (1999). Expert performance: Its structure and acquisition. In S. J. Ceci & W. M. Williams (Eds.), *The nature-nurture debate: The essential readings* (pp. 200–256). Oxford, England: Blackwell.

Eronen, M., Angermeyer, M. C., & Schulze, B. (1998). The psychiatric epidemiology of violent behavior. In *Social Psychiatry & Psychiatric Epidemiology* (Vol. 33). Leipzig, Germany: Springer.

Esser, J. K. (1998). Alive and well after 25 years: A review of groupthink research. *Organizational Behavior and Human Decision Processes, 73,* 116–141.

Etcoff, N. (1999). *Survival of the prettiest: The science of beauty.* New York: Doubleday.

Evans, J. St. B., Barston, J. L., & Pollard, P. (1983). On the conflict between logic and belief in syllogistic reasoning. *Memory & Cognition, 11,* 295–306.

Evans, P. D., Gilbert, S. L, Mekel-Bobrov, N., Vallender, E. J., Anderson, J. R., Vaez-Azizi, L. M., et al. (2005). Microcephalin, a gene regulating brain size, continues to evolve adaptively in humans. *Science, 309,* 1717–1720.

Everson, S. A., Lynch, J. W., Chesney, M. A., Kaplan, G. A., Goldberg, D. E., Shade, S. B., et al. (1997). Interaction of workplace demands and cardiovascular reactivity in progression of carotid atherosclerosis: Population based study. *British Medical Journal, 314,* 553–558.

Exner, J. E. (1993). *The Rorschach: A comprehensive system: Vol. 1. Basic foundations.* New York: Wiley.

Eysenck, H. J. (1957). The effects of psychotherapy: An evaluation. *Journal of Consulting Psychology, 16,* 319–324.

Eysenck, H. J. (1960). *Behavior therapy and the neuroses.* Oxford, England: Pergamon Press.

Eysenck, H. J. (1967). *The biological basis of personality.* Springfield, IL: Charles C. Thomas.

Eysenck, H. J. (1990). Biological dimensions of personality. In L. A. Pervin (Ed.), *Handbook of personality: Theory and research* (pp. 244–276). New York: Guilford Press.

Eysenck, S. B. G., & Eysenck, H. J. (1963). The validity of questionnaire and rating assessments of extraversion and neuroticism, and their factorial stability. *British Journal of Psychology, 54,* 51–62.

Eysenck, S. B. G., & Eysenck, H. J. (1985). *Personality and individual differences: A natural science approach.* New York: Plenum Press.


Falk, R., & McGregor, D. (1983). The surprisingness of coincidences. In P. Humphreys, O. Svenson, & A. Vari (Eds.), *Analysing and aiding decision processes* (pp. 489–502). New York: North Holland.

Fancher, R. E. (1979). *Pioneers of psychology.* New York: Norton.

Fantz, R. L. (1964). Visual experience in infants: Decreased attention to familiar patterns relative to novel ones. *Science, 164,* 668–670.

Farah, M. J., Illes, J. Cook-Deegan, R., Gardner, H., Kandel, E., King, P., et al. (2004). Neurocognitive enhancement: What can we do and what should we do? *Nature Reviews Neuroscience, 5,* 421–426.

Farah, M. J., & Rabinowitz, C. (2003). Genetic and environmental influences on the organization of semantic memory in the brain: Is "living things" an innate category? *Cognitive Neuropsychology, 20,* 401–408.

Farrar, M. J. (1990). Discourse and the acquisition of grammatical morphemes. *Journal of Child Language, 17,* 607–624.

Farries, M. A. (2004). The avian song system in comparative perspective. *Annals of the New York Academy of Sciences, 1016,* 61–76.

Fazel, S., & Danesh, J. (2002). Serious mental disorder in 23,000 prisoners: A review of 62 surveys. *Lancet, 359,* 545–550.

Fechner, G. T. (1966). *Elements of psychophysics.* (H. E. Alder, Trans.). New York: Holt, Reinhart and Wilson. (Original work published 1860)

Fehr, E., & Gaechter, S. (2002). Altruistic punishment in humans. *Nature, 415,* 137–140.

Fein, S., Hilton, J. L., & Miller, D. T. (1990). Suspicion of ulterior motivation and the correspondence bias. *Journal of Personality and Social Psychology, 58,* 753–764.

Fein, S., & Spencer, S. J. (1997). Prejudice as self-image maintenance: Affirming the self through derogating others. *Journal of Personality and Social Psychology, 73,* 31–44.

Feinberg, T. E. (2001). *Altered egos: How the brain creates the self.* New York: Oxford University Press.

Feingold, A. (1990). Gender differences in effects of physical attractiveness on romantic attraction: A comparison across five research paradigms. *Journal of Personality and Social Psychology, 59,* 981–993.

Feingold, A. (1992a). Gender differences in mate selection preferences: A test of the parental investment model. *Psychological Bulletin, 112,* 125–139.

Feingold, A. (1992b). Good-looking people are not what we think. *Psychological Bulletin, 111,* 304–341.

Feingold, A. (1994). Gender differences in personality: A meta-analysis. *Psychological Bulletin, 116,* 429–456.

Feldman, M. D. (2004). *Playing sick.* New York: Brunner-Routledge.

Ferster, C. B., & Skinner, B. F. (1957). *Schedules of reinforcement.* New York: Appleton-Century-Crofts.

Feske, U. (1998). Eye movement desensitization and reprocessing treatment for posttraumatic stress disorder. *Clinical Psychology: Science and Practice, 5,* 171–181.

Festinger, L. (1957). *A theory of cognitive dissonance.* Stanford, CA: Stanford University Press.

Festinger, L., & Carlsmith, J. M. (1959). Cognitive consequences of forced compliance. *Journal of Abnormal and Social Psychology, 58,* 203–210.

Festinger, L., Schachter, S., & Back, K. (1950). *Social pressures in informal groups: A study of human factors in housing.* Oxford, England: Harper & Row.

Fiedler, E. R., Oltmanns, T. F., & Turkheimer, E. (2004). Traits associated with personality disorders and adjustment to military life: Predictive validity of self and peer reports. *Military Medicine, 169,* 32–40.

Field, G. C. (1921). Faculty psychology and instinct psychology. *Mind, 30,* 257–270.

Fields, H. L., & Levine, J. D. (1984). Placebo analgesia: A role for endorphins? *Trends in Neurosciences, 7,* 271–273.

Fiering, C., & Taft, L. (1985). The gifted learning disabled: Not a paradox. *Pediatric Annals, 14,* 729–732.

Fink, M. (2001) Convulsive therapy: A review of the first 55 years. *Journal of Affective Disorders, 63,* 1–15.

Finkelstein, K. E. (1999, October 17). Yo-Yo Ma's lost Stradivarius is found after wild search. *New York Times,* p. 34.

Finn, R. (1991). Different minds. *Discover, 12,* 54–59.

Fiorentine, R. (1999). After drug treatment: Are 12-step programs effective in maintaining abstinence? *American Journal of Drug and Alcohol Abuse, 25,* 93–116.

Fisher, H. E. (1993). *Anatomy of love: The mysteries of mating, marriage, and why we stray.* New York: Fawcett.

Fisher, R. P., & Craik, F. I. M. (1977). The interaction between encoding and retrieval operations in cued recall. *Journal of Experimental Psychology: Human Learning and Perception, 3,* 153–171.

Fiske, S. T. (1998). Stereotyping, prejudice, and discrimination. In D. T. Gilbert, S. T. Fiske, & G. Lindzey (Eds.), *The handbook of social psychology* (4th ed., Vol. 2, pp. 357–411). New York: McGraw-Hill.

Fitzgerald, P. B., Brown, T. L., Marston, N. A. U., Daskalakis, Z. J., de Castella, A., Kulkarni, J., et al. (2003). Transcranial magnetic stimulation in the treatment of depression: A double-blind, placebo-controlled trial. *Archives of General Psychiatry, 60,* 1002–1008.

Fleming, R., Baum, A., Gisriel, M. M., & Gatchel, R. J. (1985). Mediating influences of social support on stress at Three Mile Island. In A. Monat & R. S. Lazarus (Eds.), *Stress and coping: An anthology* (2nd ed.) (pp. 95–106). New York: Columbia University Press.

Fletcher, P. C., Shallice, T., & Dolan, R. J. (1998). The functional roles of prefrontal cortex in episodic memory. I. Encoding. *Brain, 121,* 1239–1248.

Flor, H., Nikolajsen, L., & Jensen, T. S. (2006). Phantom limb pain: A case of maladaptive CNS plasticity? *Nature Reviews Neuroscience, 7,* 873–881.

Florian, V., Mikulciner, M., & Taubman, O. (1995). Does hardiness contribute to mental health during a stressful real-life situation? The roles of appraisal and coping. *Journal of Personality and Social Psychology, 68,* 687–695.

Flynn, J. R. (1984). The mean IQ of Americans: Massive gains 1932 to 1978. *Psychological Bulletin, 95,* 29–51.

Foa, E. B., Dancu, C. V., Hembree, E. A., Jaycox, L. H., Meadows, E. A., & Street, G. P. (1999). A comparison of exposure therapy, stress inoculation training, and their combination for reducing posttraumatic stress disorder in female assault victims. *Journal of Consulting & Clinical Psychology, 67,* 194–200.

Foa, E. B, & Meadows, E. A. (1997). Psychosocial treatments for posttraumatic stress disorder: A critical review. *Annual Review of Psychology, 48,* 449–480.

Foa, E. B., & Rothbaum, B. O. (1998). *Treating the trauma of rape: Cognitive-behavioral therapy for PTSD.* New York: Guilford Press.

Fodor, J. (2000). Why we are so good at catching cheaters. *Cognition, 75,* 2932.

Fogassi, L., Ferrari, P. F., Gesierich, B., Rozzi, S., Chersi, F., & Rizzolatti, G. (2005). Parietal lobe: From action organization to intention understanding. *Science, 308,* 662–667.

Fornazzari, L., Wilkinson, D. A., Kapur, B. M., & Carlen, P. L. (1983). Cerebellar, cortical and functional impairment in toluene abusers. *Acta Neurologica Scandinavica, 67,* 319–329.

Fouts, R. S., & Bodamer, M. (1987). Preliminary report to the National Geographic Society on "Chimpanzee intrapersonal signing." *Friends of Washoe, 7,* 4–12.

Fowler, D. (1985). Landmarks in computer-assisted psychological assessment. *Journal of Consulting and Clinical Psychology, 53,* 748–759.

Fox, P. T., Mintun, M. A., Raichle, M. E., Miezin, F. M., Allman, J. M., & Van Essen, D. C., et al. (1986). Mapping human visual cortex with positron emission tomography. *Nature, 323,* 806–809.

Frank, M. G., Ekman, P., & Friesen, W. V. (1993). Behavioral markers and recognizability of the smile of enjoyment. *Journal of Personality and Social Psychology, 64,* 83–93.

Frank, M. G., & Stennet, J. (2001). The forced-choice paradigm and the perception of facial expressions of emotion. *Journal of Personality and Social Psychology, 80,* 75–85.

Frankl, V. (2000). *Man's search for meaning.* New York: Beacon Press.

Fredrickson, B. L. (2000). Cultivating positive emotions to optimize health and well-being. *Prevention and Treatment, 3.*

Fredrickson, B. L. (2001). The role of positive emotions in positive psychology: The broaden-and-build theory of positive emotions. *American Psychologist, 56,* 218–226.

Freedman, J. (1978). *Happy people: What happiness is, who has it, and why.* New York: Harcourt Brace Jovanovich.

Freedman, J. L., & Fraser, S. C. (1966). Compliance without pressure: The foot-in-the-door technique. *Journal of Personality and Social Psychology, 4,* 195–202.

Freeman, S., Walker, M. R., Borden, R., & Latané, B. (1975). Diffusion of responsibility and restaurant tipping: Cheaper by the bunch. *Personality and Social Psychology Bulletin, 1,* 584–587.

Freud, A. (1936). *The ego and the mechanisms of defense.* New York: International Universities Press.

Freud, S. (1938). The psychopathology of everyday life. In A. A. Brill (Ed.), *The basic writings of Sigmund Freud.* New York: Basic Books. (Originally published 1901)

Freud, S. (1952). *A general introduction to psychoanalysis.* New York: Pocket Books. (Originally published 1920)

Freud, S. (1953). Three essays on the theory of sexuality. In J. Strachey (Ed.), *The standard edition of the complete psychological works of Sigmund Freud* (Vol. 7, pp. 135–243). London: Hogarth Press. (Originally published 1905)

Freud, S. (1965). *The interpretation of dreams* (J. Strachey, Trans.). New York: Avon. (Originally published 1900)

Freudenberger, H. J. (1974). Staff burnout. *Journal of Social Issues, 30,* 159–165.

Freyd, J. J. (1996). *Betrayal trauma: The logic of forgetting childhood abuse.* Cambridge, MA: Harvard University Press.

Frick, R. W. (1985). Communicating emotion: The role of prosodic features. *Psychological Bulletin, 97,* 412–429.

Fried, P. A., & Watkinson, B. (2000). Visuoperceptual functioning differs in 9- to 12-year-olds prenatally exposed to cigarettes and marijuana. *Neurotoxicology and Teratology, 22,* 11–20.

Friedberg, F. (2001). *Do-it-yourself eye movement technique for emotional healing.* Oakland, CA: New Harbinger Publications.

Friedman, M., & Rosenman, R. H. (1974). *Type A behavior and your heart.* New York: Knopf.

Friedman, W. J. (1993). Memory for the time of past events. *Psychological Bulletin, 113,* 44–66.

Friesen, W. V. (1972). Cultural differences in facial expressions in a social situation: An experimental test of the concept of display rules. Unpublished doctoral dissertation, University of California, San Francisco.

Frith, C. D., & Fletcher, P. (1995). Voices from nowhere. *Critical Quarterly, 37,* 71–83.

Frith, U. (2001). Mind blindness and the brain in autism. *Neuron, 32,* 969–979.

Frith, U. (2003). *Autism: Explaining the enigma.* Oxford, England: Blackwell.

Fryer, A. J., Mannuzza, S., Gallops, M. S., Martin, L. Y., Aaronson, C., Gorman, J. M., et al. (1990). Familial transmission of simple phobias and fears: A preliminary report. *Archives of General Psychiatry, 47,* 252–256.

Furmark, T., Tillfors, M., Marteinsdottir, I., Fischer, H., Pissiota, A., Långström, B., et al. (2002). Common changes in cerebral blood flow in patients with social phobia treated with citalopram or cognitive-behavioral therapy. *Archives of General Psychiatry, 59*(5), 425–433.

Fuster, J. M. (2003). *Cortex and mind.* New York: Oxford University Press.

Gable, S. L., & Haidt, J. (2005). What (and why) is positive psychology? *Review of General Psychology, 9,* 102–110.

Gais, S., & Born, J. (2004). Low acetylcholine during slow-wave sleep is critical for declarative memory consolidation. *Proceedings of the National Academy of Sciences (USA), 101,* 2140–2144.

Galanter, E. (1962). Contemporary psychophysics. In R. Brown, E. Galanter, E. H. Hess, & G. Mandler (Eds.), *New directions in psychology* (pp. 87–156). New York: Holt, Rinehart, & Winston.

Galati, D., Scherer, K. R., & Ricci-Bitt, P. E. (1997). Voluntary facial expression of emotion: Comparing congenitally blind with normally sighted encoders. *Journal of Personality and Social Psychology, 73,* 1363–1379.

Galea, S., Ahern, J., Resnick, H., Kilpatrick, D., Bucuvalas, M., Gold, J., et al. (2002). Psychological sequelae of the September 11 terrorist attacks in New York City. *New England Journal of Medicine, 346*(13), 982–987.

**Galef, B.** (1998). Edward Thorndike: Revolutionary psychologist, ambiguous biologist. *American Psychologist, 53,* 1128–1134.

**Gallistel, C. R.** (2000). The replacement of general-purpose learning models with adaptively specialized learning modules. In M. S. Gazzaniga (Ed.), *The new cognitive neurosciences* (pp. 1179–1191). Cambridge, MA: MIT Press.

**Gallistel, C. R., & Gelman, R.** (1992). Preverbal and verbal counting and computation. *Cognition,* Special issue: *Numerical Cognition, 44,* 43–74.

**Gallup, G. G.** (1977). Self-recognition in primates: A comparative approach to the bidirectional properties of consciousness. *American Psychologist, 32,* 329–338.

**Gallup, G. G.** (1997). On the rise and fall of self-conception in primates. *Annals of the New York Academy of Sciences, 818,* 73–84.

**Galton, F.** (1869). *Hereditary genius: An inquiry into its laws and consequences.* London: Macmillan/Fontana.

**Gangestad, S. W., & Simpson, J. A.** (2000). On the evolutionary psychology of human mating: Trade-offs and strategic pluralism. *Behavioral and Brain Sciences, 23,* 573–587.

**Garb, H. N.** (1998). *Studying the clinician: Judgment research and psychological assessment.* Washington, DC: American Psychological Association.

**Garb, H. N.** (1999). Call for a moratorium on the use of the Rorschach inkblot test in clinical and forensic settings. *Assessment, 6,* 313–315.

**Garcia, J.** (1981). Tilting at the windmills of academe. *American Psychologist, 36,* 149–158.

**Garcia, J., & Koelling, R. A.** (1966). Relation of cue to consequence in avoidance learning. *Psychonomic Science, 4,* 123–124.

**Gardner, R. A., & Gardner, B. T.** (1969). Teaching sign language to a chimpanzee. *Science, 165,* 664–672.

**Garofalo, R., Cameon, W., Wissow, L. S., Woods, E. R., & Goodman, E.** (1999). Sexual orientation and risk of suicide. *Archives of Pediatrics and Adolescent Medicine, 513,* 487.

**Garry, M., Manning, C., Loftus, E. F., & Sherman, S. J.** (1996). Imagination inflation: Imagining a childhood event inflates confidence that it occurred. *Psychonomic Bulletin and Review, 3,* 208–214.

**Gauld, A.** (1992). *The history of hypnotism.* Cambridge, England: Cambridge University Press.

**Gazzaniga, M. S. (Ed.).** (2000). *The new cognitive neurosciences.* Cambridge, MA: MIT Press.

**Gazzaniga, M. S.** (2006). Forty-five years of split brain research and still going strong. *Nature Reviews Neuroscience, 6,* 653–659.

**Ge, X. J., Conger, R. D., & Elder, G. H.** (1996). Coming of age too early: Pubertal influences on girls' vulnerability to psychological distress. *Child Development, 67,* 3386–3400.

**Geen, R. G.** (1984). Preferred stimulation levels in introverts and extraverts: Effects on arousal and performance. *Journal of Personality and Social Psychology, 46,* 1303–1312.

**Geen, R. G.** (1998). Aggression and antisocial behavior., *The handbook of social psychology,* (4th ed., Vol. 2, pp. 317–356). New York: McGraw-Hill.

**Gegenfurtner, K. R., & Kiper, D. C.** (2003). Color vision. *Annual Review of Neuroscience, 26,* 181–206.

**Geller, D. A., Hoog, S. L., Heiligenstein, J. H., Ricardi, R. K., Tamura, R., Kluszynski, S., Jacobson, J. G., et al.** (2001). Fluoxetine treatment for obsessive-compulsive disorder in children and adolescents: A placebo-controlled clinical trial. *Journal of the American Academy of Child and Adolescent Psychiatry, 40,* 773–779.

**George, D.** (1981). *Sweet man: The real Duke Ellington.* New York: Putnam.

**George, M. S., Lisanby, S. H., Sackeim, H. A.** (1999), Transcranial magnetic stimulation: Applications in neuropsychiatry. *Archives of General Psychiatry, 56,* 300–311.

**Gerard, H. B., & White, G. L.** (1983). Post-decisional reevaluation of choice alternatives. *Personality and Social Psychology Bulletin, 9,* 365–369.

**Gershoff, E. T.** (2002). Corporal punishment by parents and associated child behaviors and experiences: A meta-analytic and theoretical review. *Psychological Bulletin, 128,* 539–579.

**Gerull, F. C., & Rapee, R. M.** (2002). Mother knows best: The effects of maternal modelling on the acquisition of fear and avoidance behaviour in toddlers. *Behaviour Research and Therapy, 40,* 279–287.

**Gibb, B. E., Alloy, L. B., & Tierney, S.** (2001). History of childhood maltreatment, negative cognitive styles, and episodes of depression in adulthood. *Cognitive Therapy and Research, 25,* 425–446.

**Gibbons, F. X.** (1990). Self-attention and behavior: A review and theoretical update. In M. P. Zanna (Ed.), *Advances in experimental social psychology* (Vol. 23, pp. 249–303). San Diego, CA: Academic Press.

**Gibbs, N. A.** (1996). Nonclinical populations in research on obsessive-compulsive disorder: A critical review. *Clinical Psychology Review, 16,* 729–773.

**Gick, M. L., & Holyoak, K. J.** (1980). Analogical problem solving. *Cognitive Psychology, 12,* 306–355.

**Giedd, J. N., Blumenthal, J., Jeffries, N. O., Castellanos, F. X., Liu, H., Zijdenbos, A., et al.** (1999). Brain development during childhood and adolescence: A longitudinal MRI study. *Nature Neuroscience, 2,* 861–863.

**Giesler, R. B., Josephs, R. A., & Swann, W. B., Jr.** (1996). Self-verification in clinical depression: The desire for negative evaluation. *Journal of Abnormal Psychology, 105,* 358–368.

**Gigerenzer, G.** (1996). The psychology of good judgment: Frequency formats and simple algorithms. *Journal of Medical Decision Making, 16,* 273–280.

**Gigerenzer, G.** (2002). *Calculated risks: How to know when numbers deceive you.* New York: Simon & Schuster.

**Gigerenzer, G., & Hoffrage, U.** (1995). How to improve Bayesian reasoning without instruction: Frequency formats. *Psychological Review, 102,* 684–704.

**Gigerenzer, G., & Hug, K.** (1992). Domain-specific reasoning: Social contracts, cheating, and perspective change. *Cognition, 43,* 127–171.

**Gigone, D., & Hastie, R.** (1996). The impact of information on group judgment: A model and computer simulation. In E. H. Witte & J. H. Davis (Eds.), *Understanding group behavior: Consensual action by small groups* (Vol. 1, pp. 221–251). Mahwah, NJ: Erlbaum.

**Gigone, D., & Hastie, R.** (1997). Proper analysis of the accuracy of group judgments. *Psychological Bulletin, 121,* 149–167.

**Gilbert, D. T.** (1991). How mental systems believe. *American Psychologist, 46,* 107–119.

**Gilbert, D. T.** (1998). Ordinary personology. In D. T. Gilbert, S. T. Fiske, & G. Lindzey (Eds.), *The handbook of social psychology* (4th ed., Vol. 2, pp. 89–150). New York: McGraw-Hill.

**Gilbert, D. T.** (2006). *Stumbling on happiness.* New York: Knopf.

**Gilbert, D. T., Brown, R. P., Pinel, E. C., & Wilson, T. D.** (2000). The illusion of external agency. *Journal of Personality and Social Psychology, 79,* 690–700.

**Gilbert, D. T., Driver-Linn, E., & Wilson, T. D.** (2002). The trouble with Vronsky: Impact bias in the forecasting of future affective states. In L. F. Barrett & P. Salovey (Eds.), *The wisdom in feeling: Psychological processes in emotional intelligence* (pp. 114–143). New York: Guilford Press.

**Gilbert, D. T., Gill, M. J., & Wilson, T. D.** (2002). The future is now: Temporal correction in affective forecasting. *Organizational Behavior and Human Decision Processes, 88,* 430–444.

**Gilbert, D. T., & Jones, E. E.** (1986). Perceiver-induced constraint: Interpretations of self-generated reality. *Journal of Personality and Social Psychology, 50,* 269–280.

**Gilbert, D. T., Krull, D. S., & Malone, P. S.** (1990). Unbelieving the unbelievable: Some problems in the rejection of false information. *Journal of Personality and Social Psychology, 59*, 601–613.

**Gilbert, D. T., & Malone, P. S.** (1995). The correspondence bias. *Psychological Bulletin, 117*, 21–38.

**Gilbert, D. T., Pelham, B. W., & Krull, D. S.** (1988). On cognitive busyness: When persons perceive meet persons perceived. *Journal of Personality and Social Psychology, 54*, 733–740.

**Gilbert, D. T., Pinel, E. C., Wilson, T. D., Blumberg, S. J., & Wheatley, T. P.** (1998). Immune neglect: A source of durability bias in affective forecasting. *Journal of Personality and Social Psychology, 75*, 617–638.

**Gilbert, D. T., Tafarodi, R. W., & Malone, P. S.** (1993). You can't not believe everything you read. *Journal of Personality and Social Psychology, 65*, 221–233.

**Gilbert, G. M.** (1951). Stereotype persistence and change among college students. *Journal of Abnormal and Social Psychology, 46*, 245–254.

**Gilbertson, M. W., Shenton, M. E., Ciszewski, A., Kasai, K., Lasko, N. B., Orr, S. P., et al.** (2002). Smaller hippocampal volume predicts pathological vulnerability to psychological trauma. *Nature Neuroscience, 5*, 1242–1247.

**Gillham, J. E. (Ed.).** (2000). *The science of optimism and hope: Research essays in honor of Martin E. P. Seligman.* West Conshohoken, PA: Templeton Foundation Press.

**Gilligan, C.** (1982). *In a different voice: Psychological theory and women's development.* Cambridge, MA: Harvard University Press.

**Gilovich, T.** (1991). *How we know what isn't so: The fallibility of human reason in everyday life.* New York: Free Press.

**Gilovich, T., Kruger, J., & Savitsky, K.** (1999). Everyday egocentrism and everyday interpersonal problems. In R. M. Kowalski & M. R. Leary (Eds.), *The social psychology of emotional and behavioral problems: Interfaces of social and clinical psychology* (pp. 69–95). Washington, DC: American Psychological Association.

**Ginzburg, K., Solomon, Z., & Bleich, A.** (2002). Repressive coping style, acute stress disorder, and posttraumatic stress disorder after myocardial infarction. *Psychosomatic Medicine, 64*, 748–757.

**Gladue, B. A.** (1994). The biopsychology of sexual orientation. *Current Directions in Psychological Science, 3*, 150–154.

**Glass, D. C., & Singer, J. E.** (1972). *Urban stress.* New York: Academic Press.

**Gleaves, D. H., Smith, S. M., Butler, L. D., & Spiegel, D.** (2004). False and recovered memories in the laboratory and clinic: A review of experimental and clinical evidence. *Clinical Psychology: Science and Practice, 11*, 3–28.

**Glenwick, D. S., Jason, L. A., & Elman, D.** (1978). Physical attractiveness and social contact in the singles bar. *Journal of Social Psychology, 105*, 311–312.

**Glick, P., Gottesman, D., & Jolton, J.** (1989). The fault is not in the stars: Susceptibility of skeptics and believers in astrology to the Barnum effect. *Personality & Social Psychology Bulletin, 15*, 572–583.

**Glisky, E. L., Schacter, D. L., & Tulving, E.** (1986). Computer learning by memory-impaired patients: Acquisition and retention of complex knowledge. *Neuropsychologia, 24*, 313–328.

**Glynn, S. M.** (1990). Token economy approaches for psychiatric patients: Progress and pitfalls over 25 years. *Behavior Modification, 14*, 383–407.

**Gneezy, U., & Rustichini, A.** (2000). A fine is a price. *Journal of Legal Studies, 29*, 1–17.

**Gobert, A., Rivet, J. M., Cistarelli, L., Melon, C., & Millan, M. J.** (1999). Buspirone modulates basal and fluoxetine-stimulated dialysate levels of dopamine, noradrenaline, and serotonin in the frontal cortex of freely moving rats: Activation of serotonin 1A receptors and blockade of alpha2-adrenergic receptors underlie its actions. *Neuroscience, 93*, 1251–1262.

**Goddard, H. H.** (1913). *The Kallikak family: A study in the heredity of feeble-mindedness.* New York: Macmillan.

**Godden, D. R., & Baddeley, A. D.** (1975). Context-dependent memory in two natural environments: On land and underwater. *British Journal of Psychology, 66*, 325–331.

**Goehler, L. E., Gaykema, R. P. A., Hansen, M. K., Anderson, K., Maier, S. F., & Watkins, L. R.** (2000). Vagal immune-to-brain communication: A visceral chemosensory pathway. *Autonomic Neuroscience: Basic and Clinical, 85*, 49–59.

**Goel, V., & Dolan, R. J.** (2003). Explaining modulation of reasoning by belief. *Cognition, 87*, 11–22.

**Goetzman, E. S., Hughes, T., & Klinger, E.** (1994). *Current concerns of college students in a midwestern sample.* Unpublished report, University of Minnesota, Morris.

**Goff, L. M., & Roediger, H. L., III.** (1998). Imagination inflation for action events—Repeated imaginings lead to illusory recollections. *Memory & Cognition, 26*, 20–33.

**Gold, R. B., & Nash, E.** (2001). State-level policies on sexuality, STD education. *The Guttmacher Report on Public Policy, 4*, 4–7.

**Goldman, M. S., Brown, S. A., & Christiansen, B. A.** (1987). Expectancy theory: Thinking about drinking. In H. T. Blane & K. E. Leonard (Eds.), *Psychological theories of drinking and alcoholism* (pp. 181–266). New York: Guilford Press.

**Gollaher, D.** (1995). *Voice for the mad: The life of Dorothea Dix.* New York: Free Press.

**Gomez, C., Argandota, E. D., Solier, R. G., Angulo, J. C., & Vazquez, M.** (1995). Timing and competition in networks representing ambiguous figures. *Brain and Cognition, 29*, 103–114.

**Goodale, M. A., & Milner, A. D.** (1992). Separate visual pathways for perception and action. *Trends in Neurosciences, 15*, 20–25.

**Goodale, M. A., Milner, A. D., Jakobson, L. S., & Carey, D. P.** (1991). A neurological dissociation between perceiving objects and grasping them. *Nature, 349*, 154–156.

**Goodale, M. A., & Milner, D.** (2004). *Sight unseen.* Oxford, England: Oxford University Press.

**Goodwin, F. K., & Ghaemi, S. N.** (1998). Understanding manic-depressive illness. *Archives of General Psychiatry, 55*, 23–25.

**Goodwin, F. K., & Jamison, K. R.** (1990). *Manic depressive illness.* New York: Oxford University Press.

**Gopnik, A., & Astington, J. W.** (1988). Children's understanding of representational change and its relation to the understanding of false belief and the appearance reality distinction. *Child Development, 59*, 26–37.

**Gopnik, A., Meltzoff, A., & Kuhl, P.** (1999). *The scientist in the crib: What early learning tells us about the mind.* New York: HarperCollins.

**Gopnik, M.** (1990a). Feature-blind grammar and dysphasia. *Nature, 344*, 715.

**Gopnik, M.** (1990b). Feature blindness: A case study. *Language Acquisition: A Journal of Developmental Linguistics, 1*, 139–164.

**Gordon, P.** (2004). Numerical cognition without words: Evidence from Amazonia. *Science, 306*, 496–499.

**Gosling, S. D.** (1998). Personality dimensions in spotted hyenas (*Crocuta crocuta*). *Journal of Comparative Psychology, 112*, 107–118.

**Gosling, S. D., & John, O. P.** (1999). Personality dimensions in non-human animals: A cross-species review. *Current Directions in Psychological Science, 8*, 69–75.

**Gottesman, I. I.** (1991). *Schizophrenia genesis: The origins of madness.* New York: Freeman.

Gottesman, I. I., & Hanson, D. R. (2005). Human development: Biological and genetic processes. *Annual Review of Psychology, 56*, 263–286.

Gottfredson, L. S. (1997). Mainstream science on intelligence: An editorial with 52 signatories, history, and bibliography. *Intelligence, 24*, 13–23.

Gottfredson, L. S. (1998). The general intelligence factor. *Scientific American Presents, 9*, 24–29.

Gottfredson, L. S. (2003). Dissecting practical intelligence theory: Its claims and evidence. *Intelligence, 31*(4), 343–397.

Gottfredson, L. S., & Deary, I. J. (2004). Intelligence predicts health and longevity, but why? *Current Directions in Psychological Science, 13*, 1–4.

Gottman, J. M. (1994). *What predicts divorce? The relationship between marital processes and marital outcomes.* Hillsdale, NJ: Erlbaum.

Gould, M. S. (1990). Suicide clusters and media exposure. In S. J. Blumenthal & D. J. Kupfer (Eds.), *Suicide over the life cycle: Risk factors, assessment, and treatment of suicidal patients* (pp. 517–532). Washington, DC: American Psychiatric Press.

Gouldner, A. W. (1960). The norm of reciprocity. *American Sociological Review, 25*, 161–178.

Grace, A. A., & Moore, H. (1998). Regulation of information flow in the nucleus accumbens: A model for the pathophysiology of schizophrenia. In M. F. Lanzenweger & R. H. Dworkin (Eds.), *Origins and development of schizophrenia* (pp. 123–160). Washington, DC: American Psychological Association.

Graf, P., & Schacter, D. L. (1985). Implicit and explicit memory for new associations in normal subjects and amnesic patients. *Journal of Experimental Psychology: Learning, Memory, and Cognition, 11*, 501–518.

Graf, P., Squire, L. R., & Mandler, G. (1984). The information that amnesic patients do not forget. *Journal of Experimental Psychology: Learning, Memory, and Cognition, 10*, 164–178.

Grant, B. F., Hasin, D. S., Stinson, F. S., Dawson, D. A., Chou, S. P., & Ruan, W. J. (2004). Prevalence, correlates, and disability of personality disorders in the U.S.: Results from the National Epidemiologic Survey on Alcohol and Related Conditions. *Journal of Clinical Psychiatry, 65*, 948–958.

Gray, H. M., Gray, K., & Wegner, D. M. (2007). Dimensions of mind perception. *Science, 315*, 619.

Gray, J. A. (1970). The psychophysiological basis of introversion-extraversion. *Behavior Research and Therapy, 8*, 249–266.

Greeley, A. M. (1975). *The sociology of the paranormal: A reconnaissance.* Beverly Hills, CA: Sage.

Green, D. A., & Swets, J. A. (1966). *Signal detection theory and psychophysics.* New York: Wiley.

Green, L. W., Tryon, W. W., Marks, B., & Huryn, J. (1986). Periodontal disease as a function of life events. *Journal of Human Stress, 12*, 32–36.

Green, S. K., Buchanan, D. R., & Heuer, S. K. (1984). Winners, losers, and choosers: A field investigation of dating initiation. *Personality & Social Psychology Bulletin, 10*, 502–511.

Greenberg, J., Pyszczynski, T., Solomon, S., Rosenblatt, A., Veeder, M., Kirkland, S., et al. (1990). Evidence for terror management theory II: The effects of mortality salience on reactions to those who threaten or bolster the cultural worldview. *Journal of Personality and Social Psychology, 58*, 308–318.

Greenberg, P. E., Sisitsky, T., Kessler, R. C., Finkelstein, S. N., Berndt, E. R., Davidson, J. R. T., et al. (1999). The economic burden of anxiety disorders in the 1990s. *Journal of Clinical Psychiatry, 60*, 427–435.

Greene, J. D., Sommerville, R. B., Nystrom, L. E., Darley, J. M., & Cohen, J. D. (2001). An fMRI investigation of emotional engagement in moral judgment. *Science, 293*, 2105–2108.

Greenfield, P. M., Keller, H., Fuligni, A., & Maynard, A. (2003). Cultural pathways through universal development. *Annual Review of Psychology, 54*, 461–490.

Greenwald, A. G. (1992). New Look 3: Unconscious cognition reclaimed. *American Psychologist, 47*, 766–779.

Greenwald, A. G., Banaji, M. R., Rudman, L. A., Farnham, S. D., Nosek, B. A., & Mellott, D. S. (2002). A unified theory of implicit attitudes, stereotypes, self-esteem, and self-concept. *Psychological Review, 109*, 3–25.

Greenwald, A. G., McGhee, D. E., & Schwartz, J. L. K. (1998). Measuring individual differences in implicit cognition: The implicit association test. *Journal of Personality & Social Psychology, 74*, 1464–1480.

Greenwald, A. G., & Nosek, B. A. (2001). Health of the Implicit Association Test at age 3. *Zeitschrift für Experimentelle Psychologie, 48*, 85–93.

Gropp, E., Shanabrough, M., Borok, E., Xu, A. W., Janoschek, R., Buch, T., et al. (2005). Agouti-related peptide-expressing neurons are mandatory for feeding. *Nature Neuroscience, 8*, 1289–1291.

Gross, J. J. (1998). Antecedent- and response-focused emotion regulation: Divergent consequences for experience, expression, and physiology. *Journal of Personality and Social Psychology, 74*, 224–237.

Gross, J. J., & Munoz, R. F. (1995). Emotion regulation and mental health. *Clinical Psychology: Science and Practice, 2*, 151–164.

Groves, B. (2004, August 2). Unwelcome awareness. *The San Diego Union-Tribune*, p. 24.

Grudnick, J. L., & Kranzler, J. H. (2001). Meta-analysis of the relationship between intelligence and inspection time. *Intelligence, 29*, 523–535.

Guillery, R. W., & Sherman, S. M. (2002). Thalamic relay functions and their role in corticocortical communication: Generalizations from the visual system. *Neuron, 33*, 163–175.

Gur, R. E., Cowell, P., Turetsky, B. I., Gallacher, F., Cannon, T., Bilker, W., et al. (1998). A follow-up magnetic resonance imaging study of schizophrenia: Relationship of neuranatomical changes to clinical and neurobehavioral measures. *Archives of General Psychiatry, 55*, 145–152.

Gurman, A. S., & Messer, S. B. (Eds.). (2003). *Essential psychotherapies*, (2nd ed). New York: Guilford Press.

Gurwitz, J. H., McLaughlin, T. J., Willison, D. J., Guadagnoli, E., Hauptman, P. J., Gao, X., et al. (1997). Delayed hospital presentation in patients who have had acute myocardial infarction. *Annals of Internal Medicine, 126*, 593–599.

Gusnard, D. A., & Raichle, M. E. (2001). Searching for a baseline: Functional imaging and the resting human brain. *Nature Reviews: Neuroscience, 2*, 685–694.

Gustafsson, J.-E. (1984). A unifying model for the structure of intellectual abilities. *Intelligence, 8*, 179–203.

Guthrie, R. V. (2000). Kenneth Bancroft Clark (1914– ). In A. E. Kazdin (Ed.), *Encyclopedia of Psychology* (Vol. 2, p. 91). Washington, DC: American Psychological Association.

Hackett, T. P., & Cassem, N. H. (1975). Psychological management of the myocardial infarction patient. *Journal of Human Stress, 1*, 25–38.

Hacking, I. (1975). *The emergence of probability.* Cambridge, MA: Cambridge University Press.

Haidt, J. (2001). The emotional dog and its rational tail: A social intuitionist approach to moral judgment. *Psychological Review, 108*, 814–834.

Haidt, J. (2006). *The happiness hypothesis: Finding modern truth in ancient wisdom.* New York: Basic Books.

Haidt, J., & Keltner, D. (1999). Culture and facial expression: Open-ended methods find more expressions and a gradient of recognition. *Cognition and Emotion, 13*, 225–266.

Hajek, P., & Belcher, M. (1991). Dream of absent-minded transgression: An empirical study of a cognitive withdrawal symptom. *Journal of Abnormal Psychology, 100,* 487–491.

Hakuta, K. (1986). *Cognitive development of bilingual children.* Center for Language Education and Research, University of California, Los Angeles.

Hakuta, K. (1999). The debate on bilingual education. *Journal of Developmental and Behavioral Pediatrics, 20,* 36–37.

Hallett, M. (2000). Transcranial magnetic stimulation and the human brain. *Nature, 406,* 147–150.

Hallett, M., Cloninger, C. R., Fahn, S., & Jankovic, J. J. (Eds.). (2005). *The psychogenic movement disorders: Neurology and neuropsychiatry.* Philadelphia: Lippincott, Williams & Wilkins.

Halliday, R., Naylor, H., Brandeis, D., Callaway, E., Yano, L., & Herzig, K. (1994). The effect of D-amphetamine, clonidine, and yohimbine on human information processing. *Psychophysiology, 31,* 331–337.

Halpern, B. (2002). Taste. In H. Pashler & S. Yantis (Eds.), *Stevens' handbook of experimental psychology: Vol 1. Sensation and perception* (3rd ed., pp. 653–690). New York: Wiley.

Halpern, D. F. (1997). Sex differences in intelligence: Implications for education. *American Psychologist, 52,* 1091–1102.

Hamermesh, D. S., & Biddle, J. E. (1994). Beauty and the labor market. *American Economic Review, 84,* 1174–1195.

Hamilton, D. L., & Gifford, R. K. (1976). Illusory correlation in interpersonal perception: A cognitive basis of stereotypic judgements. *Journal of Experimental Social Psychology, 12,* 392–407.

Hamilton, W. D. (1964). The genetical evolution of social behaviour. *Journal of Theoretical Biology, 7,* 1–16.

Hammen, C. L. (1995). Stress and the course of unipolar disorders. In C. M. Mazure (Ed.), *Does stress cause psychiatric illness?* Washington, DC: American Psychiatric Press.

Hammersla, J. F., & Frease-McMahan, L. (1990). University students' priorities: Life goals vs. relationships. *Sex Roles, 23,* 1–14.

Haney, C., Banks, C., & Zimbardo, P. G. (1973). Interpersonal dynamics in a simulated prison. *International Journal of Criminology and Penology, 1,* 69–97.

Hansen, E. S., Hasselbalch, S., Law, I., & Bolwig, T. G. (2002). The caudate nucleus in obsessive-compulsive disorder. Reduced metabolism following treatment with paroxetine: A PET study. *International Journal of Neuropsychopharmacology, 5,* 1–10.

Hanson, C. J., Stevens, L. C., & Coast, J. R. (2001). Exercise duration and mood state: How much is enough to feel better? *Health Psychology, 20,* 267–275.

Happe, F. G. E. (1995). The role of age and verbal ability in the theory-of-mind performance of subjects with autism. *Child Development, 66,* 843–855.

Hare, R. D. (1998). *Without conscience: The disturbing world of the psychopaths among us.* New York: Guilford Press.

Harkness, S., Edwards, C. P., & Super, C. M. (1981). Social roles and moral reasoning: A case study in a rural African community. *Developmental Psychology, 17,* 595–603.

Harlow, H. F. (1958). The nature of love. *American Psychologist, 13,* 573–685.

Harlow, H. F., & Harlow, M. L. (1965). The affectional systems. In A. M. Schrier, H. F. Harlow, & F. Stollnitz (Eds.), *Behavior of nonhuman primates* (Vol. 2). New York: Academic Press.

Harlow, J. M. (1848). Passage of an iron rod through the head. *Boston Medical and Surgical Journal, 39,* 389–393.

Harris, B. (1979). Whatever happened to Little Albert? *American Psychologist, 34,* 151–160.

Harris, M. J., & Rosenthal, R. (1985). Mediation of interpersonal expectancy effects: 31 meta-analyses. *Psychological Bulletin, 97,* 363–386.

Harris, P. L., de Rosnay, M., & Pons, F. (2005). Language and children's understanding of mental states. *Current Directions in Psychological Science, 14,* 69–73.

Harris, P. L., Johnson, C. N., Hutton, D., Andrews, G., & Cooke, T. (1989). Young children's theory of mind and emotion. *Cognition and Emotion, 3,* 379–400.

Hart, B. L. (1988). Biological basis of the behavior of sick animals. *Neuroscience and Biobehavioral Reviews, 12,* 123–137.

Hartley, M., & Commire, A. (1990). *Breaking the silence.* New York: Putnam Group.

Hartshorne, H., & May, M. (1928). *Studies in deceit.* New York: Macmillan.

Hasher, L., & Zacks, R. T. (1984). Automatic processing of fundamental information: The case of frequency of occurrence. *American Psychologist, 39,* 1372–1388.

Hasselmo, M. E. (2006). The role of acetylcholine in learning and memory. *Current Opinion in Neurobiology, 16,* 710–715.

Hassmen, P., Koivula, N., & Uutela, A. (2000). Physical exercise and psychological well-being: A population study in Finland. *Preventive Medicine, 30,* 17–25.

Hasson, U., Hendler, T., Bashat, D. B., & Malach, R. (2001). Vase or face? A neural correlate of shape-selective grouping processes in the human brain. *Journal of Cognitive Neuroscience, 13,* 744–753.

Hatch, R. (2005). *Richard Hatch homepage.* Retrieved August 24, 2005, from http://www.richardhatch.com

Hatfield, E. (1988). Passionate and companionate love. In R. J. Sternberg & M. L. Barnes (Eds.), *The psychology of love* (pp. 191–217). New Haven, CT: Yale University Press.

Hatfield, E., & Rapson, R. L. (1992). Similarity and attraction in close relationships. *Communication Monographs, 59,* 209–212.

Hathaway, S. R., & McKinley, J. C. (1951). *Minnesota Multiphasic Personality Inventory manual.* New York: Psychological Corporation.

Hausser, M. (2000). The Hodgkin-Huxley theory of the action potential. *Nature Neuroscience, 3,* 1165.

Haxby, J. V., Gobbini, M. I., Furey, M. L. Ishai, A., Schouten, J. L., & Pietrini, P. (2001). Distributed and overlapping representations of faces and objects in ventral temporal cortex. *Science, 293,* 2425–2430.

Hay, P., Sachdev, P., Cumming, S., Smith, J. S., Lee, T., Kitchener, P., et al. (1993). Treatment of obsessive-compulsive disorder by psychosurgery. *Acta Psychiatrica Scandinavica, 87,* 197–207.

Hayes, D. P., & Grether, J. (1983). The school year and vacations: When do students learn? *Cornell Journal of Social Relations, 17,* 56–71.

Hayes, K., & Hayes, C. (1951). The intellectual development of a home-raised chimpanzee. *Proceedings of the American Philosophical Society, 95,* 105–109.

Hayes, S. C., Strosahl, K., & Wilson, K. G. (1999). *Acceptance and commitment therapy: An experiential approach to behavior change.* New York: Guilford Press.

*Health,* United States. (2001). Hyattsville, MD: National Center for Health Statistics.

Heatherton, T. F., Herman, C. P., & Polivy, J. (1991). Effects of physical threat and ego threat on eating behavior. *Journal of Personality and Social Psychology, 60,* 138–143.

Heatherton, T. F., & Weinberger, J. L. (Eds.). (1994). *Can personality change?* Washington, DC: American Psychological Association.

Heaton, R., Paulsen, J. S., McAdams, L. A., Kuck, J., Zisook, S., Bra, D., et al. (1994). Neuropsychological deficits in schizophrenia: Relationship to age, chronicity, and dementia. *Archives of General Psychiatry, 51,* 469–476.

Hebb, D. O. (1949). *The organization of behavior.* New York: Wiley.

**Hebl, M. R., & Heatherton, T. F.** (1997). The stigma of obesity in women: The difference is Black and White. *Personality and Social Psychology Bulletin, 24,* 417–426.

**Hebl, M. R., & Mannix, L. M.** (2003). The weight of obesity in evaluating others: A mere proximity effect. *Personality and Social Psychology Bulletin, 29,* 28–38.

**Hecht, S., & Mandelbaum, M.** (1938). Rod-cone dark adaptation and vitamin A. *Science, 88,* 219–221.

**Heerey, E. A., Keltner, D., & Capps, L. M.** (2003). Making sense of self-conscious emotion: Linking theory of mind and emotion in children with autism. *Emotion, 3,* 394–400.

**Heiby, E. M.** (2002). Prescription privileges for psychologists: Can differing views be reconciled? *Journal of Clinical Psychology, 58,* 589–597.

**Heider, F.** (1958). *The psychology of interpersonal relations.* New York: Wiley.

**Heider, F., & Simmel, M.** (1944). An experimental study of apparent behavior. *American Journal of Psychology, 57,* 243–259.

**Hemingway, H., & Marmot, M.** (1999). Evidence-based cardiology: Psychosocial factors in the aetiology and prognosis of coronary heart disease: Systematic review of prospective cohort studies. *British Medical Journal, 318,* 1460–1467.

**Henderlong, J., & Lepper, M. R.** (2002). The effects of praise on children's intrinsic motivation: A review and synthesis. *Psychological Bulletin, 128,* 774–795.

**Henig, R. M.** (2004, April 4). The quest to forget. *New York Times Magazine,* 32–37.

**Henriques, J. B., & Davidson, R. J.** (1990). Regional brain electrical asymmetries discriminate between previously depressed and healthy control subjects. *Journal of Abnormal Psychology, 99,* 22–31.

**Henry, W. P., Strupp, H. H., Schacht, T. E., & Gaston, L.** (1994). Psychodynamic approaches. In A. E. Bergin & S. L. Garfield (Eds.), *Handbook of psychotherapy and behavior change* (pp. 467–508). New York: Wiley.

**Herbert, J. D., Lilienfeld, S. O., Lohr, J. M., Montgomery, R. W., O'Donohue, W. T., Rosen, G. M., et al.** (2000). Science and pseudoscience in the development of eye movement desensitization and reprocessing: Implications for clinical psychology. *Clinical Psychology Review, 20,* 945–971.

**Herek, G. M.** (2002). Gender gaps in public opinion about lesbians and gay men. *Public Opinion Quarterly, 66,* 40–67.

**Herman, J. L.** (1992). *Trauma and recovery.* New York: Basic Books.

**Herman-Giddens, M. E., Slora, E. J., Wasserman, R. C., Bourdony, C. J., Bhapkar, M. V., Koch, G. G., et al.** (1997). Secondary sexual characteristics and menses in young girls seen in office practice: A study from the pediatric research in office settings network. *Pediatrics and Perinatal Epidemiology, 99,* 505–512.

**Herrmann, D. J., Raybeck, D., & Gruneberg, M.** (2002). *Improving memory and study skills: Advances in theory and practice.* Seattle: Hogrefe and Huber.

**Herrnstein, R. J.** (1972). Nature as nurture: Behaviorism and the instinct doctrine. *Behaviorism, 1,* 23–52.

**Herrnstein, R. J.** (1977). The evolution of behaviorism. *American Psychologist, 32,* 593–603.

**Herrnstein, R. J., & Murray, C.** (1994). *The bell curve.* New York: Free Press.

**Hershenson, M. (Ed.).** (1989). *The moon illusion.* Hillsdale, NJ: Erlbaum.

**Hertwig, R., & Gigerenzer, G.** (1999). The "conjunction fallacy" revisited: How intelligent inferences look like reasoning errors. *Journal of Behavioral Decision Making, 12,* 275–305.

**Hess, T. M.** (2005). Memory and aging in context. *Psychological Bulletin, 131,* 383–406.

**Hettema, J. M., Neale, M. C., & Kendler, K. S.** (2001). A review and meta-analysis of the genetic epidemiology of anxiety disorders. *American Journal of Psychiatry, 158,* 1568–1578.

**Hewstone, M., Rubin, M., & Willis, H.** (2002). Intergroup bias. *Annual Review of Psychology, 53,* 575–604.

**Heyns, B.** (1978). *Summer learning and the effects of schooling.* New York: Academic Press.

**Higgins, E. T.** (1987). Self-discrepancy theory: A theory relating self and affect. *Psychological Review, 94,* 319–340.

**Hilgard, E. R.** (1965). *Hypnotic susceptibility.* New York: Harcourt, Brace and World.

**Hilgard, E. R.** (1986). *Divided consciousness: Multiple controls in human thought and action.* New York: Wiley-Interscience.

**Hill, G. W.** (1982). Group versus individual performance: Are N + 1 heads better than one? *Psychological Bulletin, 91,* 517–539.

**Hilts, P.** (1995). *Memory's ghost: The strange tale of Mr. M and the nature of memory.* New York: Simon & Schuster.

**Hintzman, D. L., Asher, S. J., & Stern, L. D.** (1978). Incidental retrieval and memory for coincidences. In M. M. Gruneberg, P. E. Morris, & R. N. Sykes (Eds.), *Practical aspects of memory* (pp. 61–68). New York: Academic Press.

**Hirschberger, G., Florian, V., & Mikulincer, M.** (2002). The anxiety buffering function of close relationships: Mortality salience effects on the readiness to compromise mate selection standards. *European Journal of Social Psychology, 32,* 609–625.

**Hirschfeld, D. R., Rosenbaum, J. F., Biederman, J., Bolduc, E. A., Faraone, S. V., Snidman, N., et al.** (1992). Stable behavioral inhibition and its association with anxiety disorder. *Journal of the American Academy of Child and Adolescent Psychiatry, 31,* 103–111.

**Hirschfeld, R. M. A.** (1996). Panic disorder: Diagnosis, epidemiology, and clinical course. *Journal of Clinical Psychiatry, 57,* 3–8.

**Hirstein, W., & Ramachandran, V. S.** (1997). Capgras syndrome: A novel probe for understanding the neural representation of the identity and familiarity of persons. *Proceedings: Biological Sciences, 264,* 437–444.

**Hishakawa, Y.** (1976). Sleep paralysis. In C. Guilleminault, W. C. Dement, & P. Passouant (Eds.), *Narcolepsy: Advances in sleep research* (Vol. 3, pp. 97–124). New York: Spectrum.

**Hitchcock, S. T.** (2005). *Mad Mary Lamb: Lunacy and murder in literary London.* New York: Norton.

**Hobson, J. A.** (1988). *The dreaming brain.* New York: Basic Books.

**Hobson, J. A., & McCarley, R. W.** (1977). The brain as a dream-state generator: An activation-synthesis hypothesis of the dream process. *American Journal of Psychiatry, 134,* 1335–1368.

**Hodgkin, A. L., & Huxley, A. F.** (1939). Action potential recorded from inside a nerve fibre. *Nature, 144,* 710–712.

**Hodson, G., & Sorrentino, R. M.** (2001). Just who favors in in-group? Personality differences in reactions to uncertainty in the minimal group paradigm. *Group Dynamics, 5,* 92–101.

**Hoek, H. W., & van Hoeken, D.** (2003). Review of the prevalence and incidence of eating disorders. *International Journal of Eating Disorders, 34,* 383–396.

**Hoffman, R. E., Hawkins, K. A., Gueorguieva, R., Boutros, N. N., Rachid, F., Carroll, K., et al.** (2003). Transcranial magnetic stimulation of left temporoparietal cortex and medication-resistant auditory hallucinations. *Archives of General Psychiatry, 60,* 49–56.

**Hoffrage, U., & Gigerenzer, G.** (1996). The impact of information representation on Bayesian reasoning. In G. Cottrell (Ed.), *Proceedings of the Eighteenth Annual Conference of the Cognitive Science Society* (pp. 126–130). Mahwah, NJ: Erlbaum.

Hoffrage, U., & Gigerenzer, G. (1998). Using natural frequencies to improve diagnostic inferences. *Academic Medicine, 73,* 538–540.

Hogan, D. P., Sun, R., & Cornwell, G. T. (2000). Sexual and fertility behaviors of American females age 15–19 years: 1985, 1990 and 1995. *American Journal of Public Health, 90,* 1421–1425.

Hollander, E. P. (1964). *Leaders, groups, and influence.* Oxford, England: Oxford University Press.

Holloway, G. (2001). *The complete dream book: What your dreams tell about you and your life.* Naperville, IL: Sourcebooks.

Holloway, M. (1999). Flynn's effect. *Scientific American, 280*(1), 37–38.

Holmbeck, G. N., & O'Donnell, K. (1991). Discrepancies between perceptions of decision making and behavioral autonomy. In R. L. Paikoff (Ed.), *New directions for child development: No. 51. Shared views in the family during adolescence.* San Francisco: Jossey-Bass.

Holmes, T. H., & Rahe, R. H. (1967). The social readjustment rating scale. *Journal of Psychosomatic Research, 11,* 213–318.

Homans, G. C. (1961). *Social behavior.* New York: Harcourt, Brace and World.

Hooley, J. M., & Hiller, J. B. (1998). Expressed emotion and the pathogenesis of relapse in schizophrenia. In M. F. Lenzenweger & R. H. Dworkin (Eds.), *Origins and development of schizophrenia* (pp. 447–468). Washington, DC: American Psychological Association.

Horn, J. L., & Cattell, R. B. (1966). Refinement and test of the theory of fluid and crystallized general intelligences. *Journal of Educational Psychology, 5,* 253–270.

Horney, K. (1937). *The neurotic personality of our time.* New York: Norton.

Horta, B. L., Victoria, C. G., Menezes, A. M., Halpern, R., & Barros, F. C. (1997). Low birthweight, preterm births and intrauterine growth retardation in relation to maternal smoking. *Pediatrics and Perinatal Epidemiology, 11,* 140–151.

Horwitz, S., & Ruane, M. (2003). *Sniper: Inside the hunt for the killers who terrorized the nation.* New York: Ballantine Books.

House, J., Landis, K., & Umberson, D. (1988). Social relationships and health. *Science, 241,* 540–545.

Hovland, C. I., Lumsdaine, A. A., & Sheffield, F. D. (1949). *Experiments on mass communications.* Princeton, NJ: Princeton University Press.

Hovland, C. I., & Weiss, W. (1951). The influence of source credibility on communication effectiveness. *Public Opinion Quarterly, 15,* 635–650.

Howard, I. P. (2002). Depth perception. In S. Yantis & H. Pashler (Eds.), *Stevens' handbook of experimental psychology: Vol 1. Sensation and perception* (3rd ed., pp. 77–120). New York: Wiley.

Howard, J. H., Jr., & Howard, D. V. (1997). Age differences in implicit learning of higher order dependencies in serial patterns. *Psychology and Aging, 12,* 634–656.

Howes, M., Siegel, M., & Brown, F. (1993). Early childhood memories—accuracy and affect. *Cognition, 47,* 95–119.

Hróbjartsson, A., & Gøtzsche, P. C. (2001). Is the placebo powerless? An analysis of clinical trials comparing placebo with no treatment. *New England Journal of Medicine, 344,* 1594–1602.

Hsu, L. K. G. (1990). *Eating disorders.* New York: Guilford Press.

Hubbard, E. M., & Ramachandran, V. S. (2003). Refining the experimental lever. *Journal of Consciousness Studies, 10,* 77–84.

Hubbard, E. M., & Ramachandran, V. S. (2005). Neurocognitive mechanisms of synesthesia. *Neuron, 48,* 509–520.

Hubel, D. H. (1988). *Eye, brain, and vision.* New York: Freeman.

Hubel, D. H., & Wiesel, T. N. (1962). Receptive fields, binocular interaction and functional architecture in the cat's visual cortex. *Journal of Physiology, 160,* 106–154.

Hubel, D. H., & Wiesel, T. N. (1998). Early exploration of the visual cortex. *Neuron, 20,* 401–412.

Huesmann, L. R., Moise-Titus, J., Podolski, C.-L., & Eron, L. D. (2003). Longitudinal relations between children's exposure to TV violence and their aggressive and violent behavior in young adulthood: 1977–1992. *Developmental Psychology, 39,* 201–221.

Hughs, S., Power, T., & Francis, D. (1992). Defining patterns of drinking in adolescence: A cluster analytic approach. *Journal of Studies on Alcohol, 53,* 40–47.

Humphreys, N., & Dennett, D. C. (1989). Speaking for our selves. *Raritan: A Quarterly Review, 9,* 68–98.

Hunsley, J., & Di Giulio, G. (2002). Dodo bird, phoenix, or urban legend? The question of psychotherapy equivalence. *Scientific Review of Mental Health Practice, 1,* 13–24.

Hunt, M. (1959). *The natural history of love.* New York: Knopf.

Hunt, R. R., & McDaniel, M. A. (1993). The enigma of organization and distinctiveness. *Journal of Memory and Language, 32,* 421–445.

Hunter, J. E., & Hunter, R. F. (1984). Validity and utility of alternative predictors of job performance. *Psychological Bulletin, 96,* 72–98.

Hurvich, L. M., & Jameson, D. (1957). An opponent process theory of color vision. *Psychological Review, 64,* 384–404.

Huttenlocher, P. R. (1979). Synaptic density in human frontal cortex—developmental changes and effects of aging. *Brain Research, 163,* 195–205.

Huxley, A. (1954). *The doors of perception.* New York: Harper & Row.

Hyman, I. E., Jr., & Billings, F. J. (1998). Individual differences and the creation of false childhood memories. *Memory, 6,* 1–20.

Hyman, I. E., Jr., & Pentland, J. (1996). The role of mental imagery in the creation of false childhood memories. *Journal of Memory and Language, 35,* 101–117.

Hypericum Depression Trial Study Group. (2002). Effect of *Hypericum perforatum* (St. John's wort) in major depressive disorder: A randomized controlled trial. *Journal of the American Medical Association, 287,* 1807–1814.

Iacoboni, M., & Dapretto, M. (2006). The mirror neuron system and the consequences of its dysfunction. *Nature Reviews Neuroscience, 7,* 942–951.

Iacoboni, M., Molnar-Szakacs, I., Gallese, V., Buccino, G., Mazziotta, J. C., & Rizzolatti, G. (2005). Grasping the intentions of others with one's own mirror neuron system. *PLoS Biology, 3,* 529–535.

Iacono, W. G., & Beiser, M. (1992). Where are women in first-episode studies of schizophrenia? *Schizophrenia Bulletin, 18,* 471–480.

Ichheiser, G. (1949). Misunderstandings in human relations: A study in false social perceptions. *American Journal of Sociology, 55* (Part 2):1–70.

Inciardi, J. A. (2001). *The war on drugs III.* New York: Allyn and Bacon.

Ingram, R. E., Miranda, J., & Segal, Z. V. (1998). *Cognitive vulnerability to depression.* New York: Guilford Press.

Ingvar, M., Ambros-Ingerson, J., Davis, M., Granger, R., Kessler, M., Rogers, G. A., et al. (1997). Enhancement by an ampakine of memory encoding in humans. *Experimental Neurology, 146,* 553–559.

Inoff-Germain, G., Arnold, G. S., Nottelmann, E. D., & Susman, E. J. (1988). Relations between hormone levels and observational measures of aggressive behavior of young adolescents in family interactions. *Developmental Psychology, 24,* 129–139.

Inui, A. (2001). Ghrelin: An orexigenic and somatotrophic signal from the stomach. *Nature Reviews Neuroscience, 2,* 551–560.

Irvine, J. T. (1978). Wolof magical thinking: Culture and conservation revisited. *Journal of Cross Cultural Psychology, 9,* 300–310.

Isabelle, R. A. (1993). Origins of attachment: Maternal interactive behavior across the first year. *Child Development, 64,* 605–621.

Isacsson, G., & Rich, C. L. (1997). Depression and antidepressants, and suicide: Pharmacoepidemiological evidence for suicide prevention. In R. W. Maris, M. M. Silverman, & S. S. Canetton (Eds.), *Review of suicidology* (pp. 168–201). New York: Guilford Press.

Isen, A. M., & Patrick, R. (1983). The effect of positive feelings on risk-taking: When the chips are down. *Organizational Behavior and Human Performance, 31,* 194–202.

Ittelson, W. H. (1952). *The Ames demonstrations in perception.* Princeton, NJ: Princeton University Press.

Izard, C. E. (1971). *The face of emotion.* New York: Appleton-Century-Crofts.

Jablensky, A. (1997). The 100-year epidemiology of schizophrenia. *Schizophrenia Research, 28,* 111–125.

Jaccard, J., Dittus, P. J., & Gordon, V. V. (1998). Parent-adolescent congruency in reports of adolescent sexual behavior and in communications about sexual behavior. *Child Development, 69,* 247–261.

Jacobs, B. L. (1994). Serotonin, motor activity, and depression-related disorders. *American Scientist, 82,* 456–463.

Jacobson, E. (1932). The electrophysiology of mental activities. *American Journal of Psychology, 44,* 677–694.

Jacobson, T., & Hoffman, V. (1997). Children's attachment representations: Longitudinal relations to school behavior and academic competency in middle childhood and adolescence. *Developmental Psychology, 33,* 703–710.

Jaffee, S., & Hyde, J. S. (2000). Gender differences in moral orientation: A meta-analysis. *Psychological Bulletin, 126,* 703–726.

Jahoda, G. (1993). *Crossroads between culture and mind.* Cambridge, MA: Harvard University Press.

James, T. W., Culham, J., Humphrey, G. K., Milner, A. D., & Goodale, M. A. (2003). Ventral occipital lesions impair object recognition but not object-directed grasping: An fMRI study. *Brain, 126,* 2463–2475.

James, W. (1884). What is an emotion? *Mind, 9,* 188–205.

James, W. (1890). *The principles of psychology.* Cambridge, MA: Harvard University Press.

James, W. (1902). *The varieties of religious experience: A study in human nature.* New York: Longman.

James, W. (1911). *Memories and studies.* New York: Longman.

Jamison, K. R. (1999). *Night falls fast: Understanding suicide.* New York: Random House.

Janicak, P. G., Dowd, S. M., Martis, B., Alam, D., Beedle, D., Krasuski, J., et al. (2002). Repetitive transcranial magnetic stimulation versus electroconvulsive therapy for major depression: Preliminary results of a randomized trial. *Biological Psychiatry, 51,* 659–667.

Janis, I. L. (1982). *Groupthink: Scientific studies of policy decisions and fiascoes* (2nd ed.). Boston: Houghton Mifflin.

Jarvella, R. J. (1970). Effects of syntax on running memory span for connected discourse. *Psychonomic Science, 19,* 235–236.

Jarvella, R. J. (1971). Syntactic processing of connected speech. *Journal of Verbal Learning & Verbal Behavior, 10,* 409–416.

Jaynes, J. (1976). *The origin of consciousness in the breakdown of the bicameral mind.* London: Allen Lane.

Jencks, C. (1979). *Who gets ahead? The determinants of economic success in America.* New York: Wiley.

Jenike, M. A., Baer, L., & Minichiello, W. E. (1986). *Obsessive-compulsive disorders: Theory and management.* Littleton, MA: PSG Publishing.

Jenkins, H. M., Barrera, F. J., Ireland, C., & Woodside, B. (1978). Signal-centered action patterns of dogs in appetitive classical conditioning. *Learning and Motivation, 9,* 272–296.

Jobes, D. A., Berman, A. L., O'Carroll, P. W., Eastgard, S., & Knickmeyer, S. (1996). The Kurt Cobain suicide crisis: Perspectives from research, public health, and the news media. *Suicide and Life-Threatening Behavior, 26,* 269–271.

John, O. P., & Srivastava, S. (1999). The Big Five trait taxonomy: History, measurement, and theoretical perspectives. In L. A. Pervin & O. P. John (Eds.), *Handbook of personality: Theory and research* (2nd ed., pp. 102–138). New York: Guilford Press.

Johnson, D. H. (1980). The relationship between spike rate and synchrony in responses of auditory-nerve fibers to single tones. *Journal of the Acoustical Society of America, 68,* 1115–1122.

Johnson, D. R., & Wu, J. (2002). An empirical test of crisis, social selection, and role explanations of the relationship between marital disruption and psychological distress: A pooled time-series analysis of four-wave panel data. *Journal of Marriage and the Family, 64,* 211–224.

Johnson, J. D., Noel, N. E., & Sutter-Hernandez, J. (2000). Alcohol and male sexual aggression: A cognitive disruption analysis. *Journal of Applied Social Psychology, 30,* 1186–1200.

Johnson, J. S., & Newport, E. L. (1989). Critical period effects in second language learning: The influence of maturational state on the acquisition of English as a second language. *Cognitive Psychology, 21,* 60–99.

Johnson, K. (2002). Neural basis of haptic perception. In H. Pashler & S. Yantis (Eds.), *Stevens' handbook of experimental psychology: Vol. 1. Sensation and perception* (3rd ed., pp. 537–583). New York: Wiley.

Johnson, M. H., Dziurawiec, S., Ellis, H. D., & Morton, J. (1991). Newborns' preferential tracking of face-like stimuli and its subsequent decline. *Cognition, 40,* 1–19.

Johnson, M. K., Hashtroudi, S., & Lindsay, D. S. (1993). Source monitoring. *Psychological Bulletin, 114,* 3–28.

Johnson, N. J., Backlund, E., Sorlie, P. D., & Loveless, C. A. (2000). Marital status and mortality: The National Longitudinal Mortality Study. *Annual Review of Epidemiology, 10,* 224–238.

Johnson, R. (2005, February 12). A genius explains. *The Guardian.*

Johnson, S. (2004). *Mind wide open: Your brain and the neuroscience of everyday life.* New York: Scribner.

Johnson, S. L., & Miller, I. (1997). Negative life events and time to recover from episodes of bipolar disorder. *Journal of Abnormal Psychology, 106,* 449–457.

Johnston, L., Bachman, J., & O'Malley, P. (1997). *Monitoring the future.* Ann Arbor, MI: Institute for Social Research.

Johnstone, E. C., Crow, T. J., Frith, C., Husband, J., & Kreel, L. (1976). Cerebral ventricular size and cognitive impairment in chronic schizophrenia. *Lancet, 2,* 924–926.

Joiner, T. E., Jr. (2002). Depression in its interpersonal context. In I. H. Gotlib & C. Hammen (Eds.), *Handbook of depression* (pp. 295–313). New York: Guilford Press.

Joiner, T. E., Jr. (2006). *Why people die by suicide.* Cambridge, MA: Harvard University Press.

Joiner, T. E., Jr., Katz, J., & Lew, A. S. (1997). Self-verification and depression among youth psychiatric inpatients. *Journal of Abnormal Psychology, 106,* 608–618.

Joiner, T. E., Jr., & Metalsky, G. I. (1995). A prospective test of an integrative interpersonal theory of depression: A naturalistic study of college roommates. *Journal of Personality and Social Psychology, 69,* 778–788.

Joiner, T. E., Jr., Metalsky, G. I., Katz, J., & Beach, S. R. H. (1999). Be (re)assured: Excessive reassurance-seeking has (at least) some explanatory power regarding depression. *Psychological Inquiry, 10,* 305–308.

Jones, B. C., Little, A. C., Penton-Voak, I. S., Tiddeman, B. P., Burt, D. M., & Perrett, D. I. (2001). Facial symmetry and judgements of apparent health: Support for a "good genes" explanation of the attractiveness-symmetry relationship. *Evolution and Human Behavior, 22,* 417–429.

Jones, E. E., & Davis, K. E. (1965). From acts to dispositions: The attribution process in person perception. In L. Berkowitz (Ed.), *Advances in experimental social psychology* (Vol. 2, pp. 219–266). New York: Academic Press.

Jones, E. E., & Harris, V. A. (1967). The attribution of attitudes. *Journal of Experimental Social Psychology, 3,* 1–24.

Jones, E. E., & Nisbett, R. E. (1972). The actor and the observer: Divergent perceptions of the causes of behavior. In E. E. Jones, D. E. Kanouse, H. H. Kelley, R. E. Nisbett, S. Valins, & B. Weiner (Eds.), *Attribution: Perceiving the causes of behavior* (pp. 79–94). Morristown, NJ: General Learning Press.

Jones, J. T., Pelham, B. W., Carvallo, M., & Mirenberg, M. C. (2004). How do I love thee? Let me count the Js: Implicit egotism and interpersonal attraction. *Journal of Personality and Social Psychology, 87,* 665–683.

Jones, K. (1972). *A history of mental health services.* London: Routledge and Kegan Paul.

Jones, L. M., & Foshay, N. N. (1984). Diffusion of responsibility in a nonemergency situation: Response to a greeting from a stranger. *Journal of Social Psychology, 123,* 155–158.

Jost, J. T., Glaser, J., Kruglanski, A. W., & Sullaway, F. J. (2003). Political conservatism as motivated social cognition. *Psychological Bulletin, 129,* 339–375.

Jouvet, M., & Mounier, D. (1961). Identification of the neural structures responsible for rapid cortical activity during normal sleep. *Journal de Physiologie, 53,* 379–380.

Joyce, J. (1994). *Ulysses: The 1922 Text.* Introduction and notes by Jeri Johnson. New York: Oxford University Press.

Judd, L. L. (1997). The clinical course of unipolar major depressive disorders. *Archives of General Psychiatry, 54,* 989–991.

Jurewicz, I., Owen, R. J., & O'Donovan, M. C. (2001). Searching for susceptibility genes in schizophrenia. *European Neuropsychopharmacology, 11,* 395–398.

Kaas, J. H. (1991). Plasticity of sensory and motor maps in adult mammals. *Annual Review of Neuroscience, 14,* 137–167.

Kagan, J. (1997). Temperament and the reactions to unfamiliarity. *Child Development, 68,* 139–143.

Kahneman, D., Krueger, A. B., Schkade, D. A., Schwarz, N., & Stone, A. A. (2004). A survey method for characterizing daily life experience: The day reconstruction method. *Science, 306,* 1776–1780.

Kahneman, D., & Tversky, A. (1973). On the psychology of prediction. *Psychological Review, 80,* 237–251.

Kahneman, D., & Tversky, A. (1979). Prospect theory: An analysis of decision under risk. *Econometrica, 47,* 263–291.

Kalman, M., & Meyerowitz, R. (2003, September 8). What's new in pharmacology. *New Yorker,* back cover.

Kamil, A. C., & Jones, J. E. (1997). The seed-storing corvid Clark's nutcracker learns geometric relationships among landmarks. *Nature, 390,* 276–279.

Kaminski, J., Call, J., & Fischer, J. (2004). Word learning in a domestic dog: Evidence for "fast mapping." *Science, 304,* 1682–1683.

Kamiya, J. (1969). Operant control of the EEG alpha rhythm and some of its reported effects on consciousness. In C. S. Tart (Ed.), *Altered states of consciousness* (pp. 519–529). Garden City, NY: Anchor Books.

Kandel, E. R. (2000). Nerve cells and behavior. In E. R. Kandel, G. H. Schwartz, & T. M. Jessell (Eds.), *Principles of neural science* (pp. 19–35). New York. McGraw-Hill.

Kanner, A. D., Coyne, J. C., Schaefer, C., & Lazarus, R. S. (1981). Comparison of two modes of stress management: Daily hassles and uplifts versus major life events. *Journal of Behavioral Medicine, 4,* 1–39.

Kant, I. (1965). *Critique of pure reason* (N. K. Smith, Trans.). New York: St. Martin's Press. (Originally published 1781)

Kanwisher, N. (2000). Domain specificity in face perception. *Nature Neuroscience, 3,* 759–763.

Kanwisher, N., McDermott, J., & Chun, M. M. (1997). The fusiform face area: A module in human extrastriate cortex specialized for face perception. *Journal of Neuroscience, 17,* 4302–4311.

Kanwisher, N., & Yovel, G. (2006). The fusiform face area: A cortical region specialized for the perception of faces. *Philosophical Transactions of the Royal Society (B), 361,* 2109–2128.

Kapur, S., Craik, F. I. M., Tulving, E., Wilson, A. A., Houle, S., & Brown, G. M. (1994). Neuroanatomical correlates of encoding in episodic memory: Levels of processing effects. *Proceedings of the National Academy of Sciences (USA), 91,* 2008–2011.

Karlins, M., Coffman, T. L., & Walters, G. (1969). On the fading of social stereotypes: Studies in three generations of college students. *Journal of Personality and Social Psychology, 13,* 1–16.

Karney, B. R., & Bradbury, T. N. (1995). The longitudinal course of marital quality and stability: A review of theory, methods, and research. *Psychological Bulletin, 118,* 3–34.

Karno, M., & Golding, J. M. (1991). Obsessive-compulsive disorder. In L. N. Robins & D. A. Regier (Eds.), *Psychiatric disorders in America: The epidemiologic catchment area study.* New York: Free Press.

Kaslow, N. J., & Celano, M. P. (1995). The family therapies. In A. S. Gurman, & A. S. Messer (Eds.), *Essential psychotherapies* (6th ed., pp. 343–402). New York: Guilford Press.

Kasser, T., & Sharma, Y. S. (1999). Reproductive freedom, educational equality, and females' preference for resource-acquisition characteristics in mates. *Psychological Science, 10,* 374–377.

Katon, W. (1994). Primary care–psychiatry panic disorder management. In B. E. Wolfe & J. D. Maser (Eds.), *Treatment of panic disorder: A consensus development conference* (pp. 41–56). Washington, DC: American Psychiatric Press.

Katz, D., & Braly, K. (1933). Racial stereotypes of one hundred college students. *Journal of Abnormal and Social Psychology, 28,* 280–290.

Katz, R., & McGuffin, P. (1993). The genetics of affective disorders. In J. P. Chapman & D. C. Fowles (Eds.), *Progress in experimental personality and psychopathology research* (Vol. 16). New York: Springer.

Kauffmann, C. D., Cheema, M. A., & Miller, B. E. (2004). Slow right prefrontal transcranial magnetic stimulation as a treatment for medication-resistant depression: A double-blind, placebo-controlled study. *Depression and Anxiety, 19,* 59–62.

Kawakami, K., Dovidio, J. F., Moll, J., Hermsen, S., & Russin, A. (2000). Just say no (to stereotyping): Effects of training in the negation of stereotypic associations on stereotype activation. *Journal of Personality and Social Psychology, 78,* 871–888.

Keefe, F. J., Abernathy, A. P., & Campbell, L. C. (2005). Psychological approaches to understanding and treating disease-related pain. *Annual Review of Psychology, 56,* 601–630.

Keefe, F. J., Lumley, M., Anderson, T., Lynch, T., & Carson, K. L. (2001). Pain and emotion: New research directions. *Journal of Clinical Psychology, 57,* 587–607.

Keisler, D. J. (1999). *Beyond the disease model of mental disorders.* New York: Praeger.

Keller, M. B., Klein, D. N., Hirschfeld, R. M., Kocsis, J. H., McCullough, J. P., Miller, I., et al. (1995). Results of the *DSM-IV* mood disorders field trial. *American Journal of Psychiatry, 152,* 843–849.

Kelley, H. H. (1967). Attribution theory in social psychology. In D. Levine (Ed.), *Nebraska Symposium on Motivation.* (Vol. 15, pp. 192–238). Lincoln: University of Nebraska Press.

Kelley, H. H. (1983). Love and commitment. In H. H. Kelley, E. Berscheid, A. Christensen, & J. H. Harvey (Eds.), *Close relationships* (pp. 265–314). New York: Freeman.

Kelley, W. M., Macrae, C. N., Wyland, C. L., Caglar, S., Inati, S., & Heatherton, T. F. (2002). Finding the self? An event-related fMRI study. *Journal of Cognitive Neuroscience, 14,* 785–794.

Kellman, P. J., & Spelke, E. S. (1983). Perception of partly occluded objects in infancy. *Cognitive Psychology, 15,* 483–524.

Kelly, C., & McCreadie, R. (2000). Cigarette smoking and schizophrenia. *Advances in Psychiatric Treatment, 6,* 327–331.

Kelly, G. (1955). *The psychology of personal constructs.* New York: Norton.

Keltner, D. (1995). Signs of appeasement: Evidence for the distinct displays of embarrassment, amusement, and shame. *Journal of Personality and Social Psychology, 68,* 441–454.

Keltner, D., & Buswell, B. N. (1996). Evidence for the distinctness of embarrassment, shame, and guilt: A study of recalled antecedents and facial expressions of emotion. *Cognition and Emotion, 10,* 155–171.

Keltner, D., & Haidt, J. (1999). Social functions of emotions at four levels of analysis. *Cognition and Emotion, 13,* 505–521.

Keltner, D., & Harker, L. A. (1998). The forms and functions of the nonverbal signal of shame. In P. Gilbert & B. Andrews (Eds.), *Shame: Interpersonal behavior, psychopathology, and culture* (pp. 78–98). New York: Oxford University Press.

Keltner, D., & Shiota, M. N. (2003). New displays and new emotions: A commentary on Rozin and Cohen (2003). *Emotion, 3,* 86–91.

Kendler, K. S., Myers, J., & Prescott, C. A. (2002). The etiology of phobias: An evaluation of the stress-diathesis model. *Archives of General Psychiatry, 59,* 242–248.

Kendler, K. S., Neale, M., Kessler, R. C., & Heath, A. (1992). Generalized anxiety disorder in women: A population-based twin study. *Archives of General Psychiatry, 49,* 267–272.

Kendler, K. S., Walters, E. E., Neale, M. C., Kessler, R. C., Heath, A. C., & Eaves, L. J. (1995). The structure of the genetic and environmental risk factors for six major psychiatric disorders in women: Phobia, generalized anxiety disorder, panic disorder, bulimia, major depression, and alcoholism. *Archives of General Psychiatry, 52,* 374–383.

Kennedy, Q., Mather, M., & Carstensen, L. L. (2004). The role of motivation in the age-related positivity effect in autobiographical memory. *Psychological Science, 15,* 208–214.

Kenrick, D. T., Sadalla, E. K., Groth, G., & Trost, M. R. (1990). Evolution, traits, and the stages of human courtship: Qualifying the parental investment model. *Journal of Personality, 58,* 97–116.

Kensinger, E. A., & Schacter, D. L. (2005). Emotional content and reality monitoring ability: fMRI evidence for the influence of encoding processes. *Neuropsychologia, 43,* 1429–1443.

Kephart, W. M. (1967). Some correlates of romantic love. *Journal of Marriage and the Family, 29,* 470–474.

Kernis, M. H. (2003). Toward a conceptualization of optimal self-esteem. *Psychological Inquiry, 14,* 1–26.

Kessler, R. C. (1997). The effects of stressful life events on depression. *Annual Review of Psychology, 48,* 191–214.

Kessler, R. C., McGonagle, K. A., Zhao, S., Nelson, C. B., Hughes, M., Eshleman, S., et al. (1994). Lifetime and 12-month prevalence of *DSM-III-R* psychiatric disorders in the United States: Results from the National Comorbidity Study. *Archives of General Psychiatry, 51,* 8–19.

Kessler, R. C., Nelson, C. B., McGonagle, K. A., Liu, J., Swartz, M., & Blazer, D. (1996). Comorbidity of *DSM-III-R* major depressive disorder in the general population: Results from the U.S. national comorbidity survey. *British Journal of Psychiatry, 168,* 17–30.

Kessler, R. C., Sonnega, A., Bromet, E., Hughes, M., & Nelson, C. B. (1995). Posttraumatic stress disorder in the National Comorbidity Survey. *Archives of General Psychiatry, 52,* 1048–1060.

Kessler, R. C., Soukup, J., Davis, R. B., Foster, D. F., Wilkey, S. A., Van Rompay, M. I., et al. (2001). The use of complementary and alternative therapies to treat anxiety and depression in the United States. *American Journal of Psychiatry, 158,* 289–294.

Kety, S. S. (1990). Genetic factors in suicide: Family, twin, and adoption studies. In S. J. Blumenthal & D. J. Kupfer (Eds.), *Suicide over the life cycle: Risk factors, assessment, and treatment of suicidal patients* (pp. 127–133). Washington, DC: American Psychiatric Press.

Keuler, D. J., & Safer, M. A. (1998). Memory bias in the assessment and recall of pre-exam anxiety: How anxious was I? *Applied Cognitive Psychology, 12,* S127–S137.

Khalid, R. (1991). Personality and academic achievement: A thematic apperception perspective. *British Journal of Projective Psychology, 36,* 25–34.

Kiecolt-Glaser, J. K., Garner, W., Speicher, C., Penn, G., & Glaser, R. (1984). Psychosocial modifiers of immunocompetence in medical students. *Psychosomatic Medicine, 46,* 7–14.

Kiehl, K. A., Smith, A. M., Hare, R. D., Mendrek, A., Forster, B. B., Brink, J., et al. (2001). Limbic abnormalities in affective processing by criminal psychopaths as revealed by functional magnetic resonance imaging. *Biological Psychiatry, 50,* 677–684.

Kihlstrom, J. F. (1985). Hypnosis. *Annual Review of Psychology, 36,* 385–418.

Kihlstrom, J. F. (1987). The cognitive unconscious. *Science, 237,* 1445–1452.

Kihlstrom, J. F. (2005). Dissociative disorders. *Annual Review of Clinical Psychology, 1,* 227–253.

Kihlstrom, J. F., & Klein, S. B. (1994). The self as a knowledge structure. In R. S. Wyer & T. K. Srull (Eds.), *Handbook of social cognition* (2nd ed., Vol. 1, pp. 153–208). Hillsdale, NJ: Erlbaum.

Kim, K., & Smith, P. K. (1998). Childhood stress, behavioural symptoms and mother-daughter pubertal development. *Journal of Adolescence, 21,* 231–240.

King, C. A. (1997). Suicidal behavior in adolescence. In R. W. Maris, M. M. Silverman, & S. S. Canetton (Eds.), *Review of suicidology, 1997* (pp. 61–95). New York: Guilford Press.

King, F. (1990). *Lump it or leave it.* New York: St. Martin's Press.

Kinney, D. A. (1993). From nerds to normals—The recovery of identity among adolescents from middle school to high school. *Sociology of Education, 66,* 21–40.

Kirchner, W. H., & Towne, W. F. (1994). The sensory basis of the honeybee's dance language. *Scientific American, 270*(6), 74–80.

Kirsch, I., & Sapirstein, G. (1998). Listening to Prozac but hearing placebo: A meta-analysis of antidepressant medication. *Prevention and Treatment, 1,* Article 0002. Retrieved May 18, 2007, from www.journals.apa.org/pt/prevention/volume1/pre0010002a.html

Klein, S. B. (2004). The cognitive neuroscience of knowing one's self. In M. Gazzaniga (Ed.), *The cognitive neurosciences* (3rd ed.). Cambridge, MA: MIT Press.

Kleinman, A. M. (1986). *Social origins of distress and disease: Depression, neurasthenia and pain in modern China.* New Haven: Yale University Press.

Kleinman, A. M. (1988). *Rethinking psychiatry: From cultural category to personal experience.* New York: Free Press.

Kleinschmidt, A., & Cohen, L. (2006). The neural bases of prosopagnosia and pure alexia: Recent insights from functional neuroimaging. *Current Opinion in Neurology, 19,* 386–391.

Klinger, E. (1975). Consequences of commitment to and disengagement from incentives. *Psychological Review, 82,* 1–25.

Klinger, E. (1977). *Meaning and void.* Minneapolis: University of Minnesota Press.

Klopfer, B., & Kelley, D. (1942). *The Rorschach technique.* Yonkers, NY: World Book.

Kluft, R. P. (1984). Treatment of multiple personality. *Psychiatric Clinics of North America, 7,* 9–29.

Kluft, R. P. (1991). Multiple personality disorder. In A. Tasman & S. M. Goldfinger (Eds.), *American Psychiatric Press Review of Psychiatry* (Vol. 10, pp. 161–188). Washington, DC: American Psychiatric Press.

Klüver, H. (1951). Functional differences between the occipital and temporal lobes with special reference to the interrelations of behavior and extracerebral mechanisms. In L. A. Jeffress (Ed.), *Cerebral mechanisms in behavior* (pp. 147–199). New York: Wiley.

Klüver, H., & Bucy, P. C. (1937). "Psychic blindness" and other symptoms following bilateral temporary lobectomy in rhesus monkeys. *American Journal of Physiology, 119,* 352–353.

Klüver, H., & Bucy, P. C. (1939). Preliminary analysis of functions of the temporal lobes in monkeys. *Archives of Neurology and Psychiatry, 42,* 979–1000.

Knowlton, B. J., Ramus, S. J., & Squire, L. R. (1992). Intact artificial grammar learning in amnesia: Dissociation of classification learning and explicit memory for specific instances. *Psychological Science, 3,* 173–179.

Knutson, B., Adams, C. M., Fong, G. W., & Hommer, D. (2001). Anticipation of increasing monetary reward selectively recruits nucleus accumbens. *Journal of Neurosciences, 21,* 1–5.

Knutson, B., Wolkowitz, O. M., Cole, S. W., Chan, T., Moore, E. A., Johnson, R. C., et al. (1998). Selective alteration of personality and social behavior by serotonergic intervention. *American Journal of Psychiatry, 155,* 373–379.

Kobasa, S. (1979). Stressful life events, personality, and health: An inquiry into hardiness. *Journal of Personality and Social Psychology, 37,* 1–11.

Koch, C. (2004). *The quest for consciousness: A neurobiological approach.* Englewood, CO: Roberts & Co.

Koffka, K. (1935). *Principles of Gestalt psychology.* New York: Harcourt, Brace and World.

Kohlberg, L. (1963). Development of children's orientation towards a moral order (Part I). Sequencing in the development of moral thought. *Vita Humana, 6,* 11–36.

Kohlberg, L. (1986). A current statement on some theoretical issues. In S. Modgil & C. Modgil (Eds.), *Lawrence Kohlberg.* Philadelphia: Falmer.

Kolb, B., & Whishaw, I. Q. (2003). *Fundamentals of human neuropsychology* (5th ed.). New York: Worth.

Kolotkin, R. L., Meter, K., & Williams, G. R. (2001). Quality of life and obesity. *Obesity Reviews,* 219–229.

Komiya, N., Good, G. E., & Sherrod, N. B. (2000). Emotional openness as a predictor of college students' attitudes toward seeking psychological help. *Journal of Counseling Psychology, 47,* 138–143.

Koole, S. L., Dijksterhuis, A., & van Knippenberg, A. (2001). What's in a name: Implicit self-esteem and the automatic self. *Journal of Personality and Social Psychology, 80,* 669–685.

Koss, M. P. (1990). The women's mental health research agenda: Violence against women. *American Psychologist, 45,* 374–380.

Kosslyn, S. M., Alpert, N. M., Thompson, W. L., Chabris, C. F., Rauch, S. L., & Anderson, A. K. (1993). Visual mental imagery activates topographically organized visual cortex: PET investigations. *Journal of Cognitive Neuroscience, 5,* 263–287.

Kosslyn, S. M., Pascual-Leone, A., Felician, O., Camposano, S., Keenan, J. P., Thompson, W. L., et al. (1999). The role of area 17 in visual imagery: Convergent evidence from PET and rTMS. *Science, 284,* 167–170.

Kraepelin, E. (1899). *Psychiatrie.* Leipzig, Germany: Barth.

Kramer, P. D. (1997). *Listening to Prozac* (Rev. ed.). New York: Penguin.

Kramer, R. M. (1998). Revisiting the Bay of Pigs and Vietnam decisions 25 years later: How well has the groupthink hypothesis stood the test of time? *Organizational Behavior and Human Decision Processes, 73,* 236–271.

Krantz, D. S., & McCeney, M. K. (2002). Effects of psychological and social factors on organic disease: A critical assessment of research on coronary heart disease. *Annual Review of Psychology, 53,* 341–369.

Krebs, J. R., & Davies, N. B. (1991). *Behavioural ecology: An evolutionary approach* (3rd ed.). Sutherland, MA: Sinauer Associates.

Kreider, R. M., & Fields, J. M. (2002). *Number, timing, and duration of marriages and divorces: 1996.* Washington, DC: U.S. Census Bureau, Current Population Reports.

Kressmann, S., Muller, W. E., & Blume, H. H. (2002). Pharmaceutical quality of different Ginkgo biloba brands. *Journal of Pharmacy and Pharmacology, 54,* 661–669.

Krings, T., Topper, R., Foltys, H., Erberich, S., Sparing, R., Willmes, K., et al. (2000). Cortical activation patterns during complex motor tasks in piano players and control subjects. A functional magnetic resonance imaging study. *Neuroscience Letters, 278,* 189–193.

Kroeze, W. K., & Roth, B. L. (1998). The molecular biology of serotonin receptors: Therapeutic implications for the interface of mood and psychosis. *Biological Psychiatry, 44,* 1128–1142.

Kronig, M. H., Apter, J., Asnis, G., Bystritsky, A., Curtis, G., Ferguson, J., et al. (1999). Placebo-controlled multicenter study of sertraline treatment for obsessive-compulsive disorder. *Journal of Clinical Psychopharmacology, 19,* 172–176.

Kruk, M. R., Halasz, J., Meelis, W., & Haller, J. (2004). Fast positive feedback between the adrenocortical stress response and a brain mechanism involved in aggressive behavior. *Behavioral Neuroscience, 118,* 1062–1070.

Kubovy, M. (1981). Concurrent-Pitch segregation and the theory of indispensable attributes. In M. Kubovy & J. R. Pomerantz (Eds.), *Perceptual organization* (pp. 55–96). Hillsdale, NJ: Erlbaum.

Kuffler, S. W. (1953). Discharge patterns and function organization of mammalian retina. *Journal of Neurophysiology, 16,* 37–68.

Kunda, Z., & Oleson, K. C. (1997). When exceptions prove the rule: How extremity of deviance determines the impact of deviant examples on stereotypes. *Journal of Personality and Social Psychology, 72,* 965–979.

Kunugi, H., Urushibara, T., Murray, R. M., Nanko, S., & Hirose, T. (2003). Prenatal underdevelopment and schizophrenia: A case report of monozygotic twins. *Psychiatry and Clinical Neurosciences, 57,* 271–274.

Kunz, P. R., & Woolcott, M. (1976). Season's greetings: From my status to yours. *Social Science Research, 5,* 269–278.

Kutchins, H., & Kirk, S. A. (1997). *Making us crazy: DSM: The psychiatric bible and the creation of mental disorders.* New York: Free Press.

LaBar, K. S., & Phelps, E. A. (1998). Arousal-mediated memory consolidation: Role of the medial temporal lobe in humans. *Psychological Science, 9,* 490–493.

LaBerge, S., & Rheingold, H. (1990). *Exploring the world of lucid dreaming.* New York: Ballantine.

**Lachman, R., Lachman, J. L., & Butterfield, E. C.** (1979). *Cognitive psychology and information processing: An introduction.* Hillsdale, NJ: Erlbaum.

**Lackner, J. R., & DiZio, P.** (2005). Vestibular, proprioceptive, and haptic contributions to spatial orientation. *Annual Review of Psychology, 56,* 115–147.

**Lai, Y., & Siegal, J.** (1999). Muscle atonia in REM sleep. In B. Mallick & S. Inoue (Eds.), *Rapid eye movement sleep* (pp. 69–90). New Delhi, India: Narosa Publishing House.

**Lalonde, J. K., Hudson, J. I., Gigante, R. A., & Pope, H. G., Jr.** (2001). Canadian and American psychiatrists' attitudes toward dissociative disorders diagnoses. *Canadian Journal of Psychiatry, 46,* 407–412.

**Lamb, M. E., Sternberg, K. J., & Prodromidis, M.** (1992). Nonmaternal care and the security of infant/mother attachment: A reanalysis of the data. *Infant Behavior & Development, 15,* 71–83.

**Lamb, M. E., Thompson, R. A., Gardner, W., & Charnov, E. L.** (1985). *Infant-mother attachment: The origins and developmental significance of individual differences in strange situation behavior.* Hillsdale, NJ: Erlbaum.

**Lamm, H., & Myers, D. G.** (1978). Group-induced polarization of attitudes and behavior. *Advances in Experimental Social Psychology, 11,* 145–195.

**Landauer, T. K., & Bjork, R. A.** (1978). Optimum rehearsal patterns and name learning. In M. M. Gruneberg, P. E. Morris, & R. N. Sykes (Eds.), *Practical aspects of memory.* (pp. 625–632). New York: Academic Press.

**Lang, F. R., & Carstensen, L. L.** (1994). Close emotional relationships in late life: Further support for proactive aging in the social domain. *Psychology and Aging, 9,* 315–324.

**Lange, C. G., & James, W.** (1922). *The emotions.* Baltimore: Williams and Wilkins.

**Langer, E. J., & Abelson, R. P.** (1974). A patient by any other name . . . Clinician group difference in labeling bias. *Journal of Consulting & Clinical Psychology, 42,* 4–9.

**Langleben, D. D., Loughead, J. W., Bilker, W. B., Ruparel, K., Childress, A. R., Busch, S. I., et al.** (2005). Telling truth from lie in individual subjects with fast event-related fMRI. *Human Brain Mapping 26,* 262–272.

**Langlois, J. H., Kalakanis, L., Rubenstein, A. J., Larson, A., Hallam, M., & Smoot, M.** (2000). Maxims or myths of beauty? A meta-analytic and theoretical review. *Psychological Bulletin, 126,* 390–423.

**Langlois, J. H., Ritter, J. M., Casey, R. J., & Sawin, D. B.** (1995). Infant attractiveness predicts maternal behaviors and attitudes. *Developmental Psychology, 31,* 464–472.

**Langlois, J. H., & Roggman, L. A.** (1990). Attractive faces are only average. *Psychological Science, 1,* 115–121.

**Langlois, J. H., Roggman, L. A., & Musselman, L.** (1994). What is average and what is not average about attractive faces? *Psychological Science, 5,* 214–220.

**Langlois, J. H., Roggman, L. A., & Rieser-Danner, L. A.** (1990). Infants' differential social responses to attractive and unattractive faces. *Developmental Psychology, 26,* 153–159.

**Langston, J. W.** (1995). *The case of the frozen addicts.* New York: Pantheon.

**Larsen, S. F.** (1992). Potential flashbulbs: Memories of ordinary news as baseline. In E. Winograd & U. Neisser (Eds.), *Affect and accuracy in recall: Studies of "flashbulb memories"* (pp. 32–64). New York: Cambridge University Press.

**Larson, J. R., Foster-Fishman, P. G., & Keys, C. B.** (1994). Discussion of shared and unshared information in decision-making groups. *Journal of Personality & Social Psychology, 67,* 446–461.

**Larson, R., & Richards, M. H.** (1991). Daily companionship in late childhood and early adolescence—changing developmental contexts. *Child Development, 62,* 284–300.

**Lashley, K. S.** (1960). In search of the engram. In F. A. Beach, D. O. Hebb, C. T. Morgan, & H. W. Nissen (Eds.), *The neuropsychology of Lashley.* New York: McGraw-Hill.

**Latané, B., & Nida, S.** (1981). Ten years of research on group size and helping. *Psychological Bulletin, 89,* 308–324.

**Latané, B., Williams, K., & Harkins, S.** (1979). Many hands make light the work: The causes and consequences of social loafing. *Journal of Personality and Social Psychology, 37,* 822–832.

**Laupa, M., & Turiel, E.** (1986). Children's conceptions of adult and peer authority. *Child Development, 57,* 405–412.

**Laurence, J., & Perry, C.** (1983). Hypnotically created memory among high hypnotizable subjects. *Science, 222,* 523–524.

**Laureys, S., Giacino, J. T., Schiff, N. D., Schabus, M., & Owen, A. M.** (2006). How should functional imaging of patients with disorders of consciousness contribute to their clinical rehabilitation needs? *Current Opinion in Neurology, 19,* 520–527.

**Lavie, P.** (2001). Sleep-wake as a biological rhythm. *Annual Review of Psychology, 52,* 277–303.

**Lavoie, K. L., & Fleet, R. P.** (2002). Should psychologists be granted prescription privileges? A review of the prescription privilege debate for psychiatrists. *Canadian Journal of Psychiatry, 47*(5), 443–449.

**Lavori, P. W., Klerman, G. L., Keller, M. B., Reich, T., Rice, J., & Endicott, J.** (1987). Age-period-cohort analysis of secular trends in onset of major depression: Findings in siblings of patients with major affective disorder. *Journal of Psychiatric Researchers, 21,* 23–25.

**Lawton, M. P., Kleban, M. H., Rajagopal, D., & Dean, J.** (1992). The dimensions of affective experience in three age groups. *Psychology and Aging, 7,* 171–184.

**Lazarus, R. S.** (1984). On the primacy of cognition. *American Psychologist, 39,* 124–129.

**Lazarus, R. S., & Alfert, E.** (1964). Short-circuiting of threat by experimentally altering cognitive appraisal. *Journal of Abnormal and Social Psychology, 69,* 195–205.

**Lazarus, R. S., & Folkman, S.** (1984). *Stress, appraisal, and coping.* New York: Springer.

**Leary, M. R.** (1990). Responses to social exclusion: Social anxiety, jealousy, loneliness, depression, and low self-esteem. *Journal of Social and Clinical Psychology, 9,* 221–229.

**Leary, M. R., & Baumeister, R. F.** (2000). The nature and function of self-esteem: Sociometer theory. In M. P. Zanna (Ed.), *Advances in experimental social psychology* (Vol. 32, pp. 1–62). San Diego: Academic Press.

**Leary, M. R., Britt, T. W., Cutlip, W. D., & Templeton, J. L.** (1992). Social blushing. *Psychological Bulletin, 112,* 446–460.

**Leary, M. R., Tambor, E. S., Terdal, S. K., & Downs, D. L.** (1995). Self-esteem as an interpersonal monitor: The sociometer hypothesis. *Journal of Personality and Social Psychology, 68,* 518–530.

**Leaton, R. N.** (1976). Long-term retention of the habituation of lick suppression and startle response produced by a single auditory stimulus. *Journal of Experimental Psychology: Animal Behavior Processes, 2,* 248–259.

**Lecky, P.** (1945). *Self-consistency: A theory of personality.* New York: Island Press.

**Lecrubier, Y., Clerc, G., Didi, R., & Kieser, M.** (2002). Efficacy of St. John's Wort Extract WS 5570 in major depression: A double-blind, placebo-controlled trial. *American Journal of Psychiatry, 159,* 1361–1366.

**LeDoux, J. E.** (1992). Brain mechanisms of emotion and emotional learning. *Current Opinion in Neurobiology, 2,* 191–197.

**LeDoux, J. E.** (1996). *The emotional brain: The mysterious underpinnings of emotional life.* New York: Simon & Schuster.

**LeDoux, J. E.** (1998). Fear and the brain: Where have we been, and where are we going? *Biological Psychiatry, 153,* 1229–1238.

LeDoux, J. E. (2000). Emotion circuits in the brain. *Annual Review of Neuroscience, 23,* 155–184.

LeDoux, J. E. (2002). *The synaptic self: How our brains become who we are.* New York: Viking.

LeDoux, J. E., Iwata, J., Cicchetti, P., & Reis, D. J. (1988). Different projections of the central amygdaloid nucleus mediate autonomic and behavioral correlates of conditioned fear. *Journal of Neuroscience, 8,* 2517–2529.

Lee, D. N., & Aronson, E. (1974). Visual proprioceptive control of standing in human infants. *Perception & Psychophysics, 15,* 529–532.

Lefcourt, H. M. (1982). *Locus of control: Current trends in theory and research* (2nd ed.). Hillsdale, NJ: Erlbaum.

Leighton, J. P., & Sternberg, R. J. (Eds.). (2003). *The nature of reasoning.* Cambridge, England: Cambridge University Press.

Lemyre, L., & Smith, P. M. (1985). Intergroup discrimination and self-esteem in the minimal group paradigm. *Journal of Personality and Social Psychology, 49,* 660–670.

Lentz, M. J., Landis, C. A., Rothermel, J., & Shaver, J. L. (1999). Effects of selective slow wave sleep disruption on musculoskeletal pain and fatigue in middle aged women. *Journal of Rheumatology, 26,* 1586–1592.

Leonard, M. (2002, October 27). Arrest in sniper case; sniper suspect defies profile. *Boston Globe,* p. A1.

Lepage, M., Ghaffar, O., Nyberg, L., & Tulving, E. (2000). Prefrontal cortex and episodic memory retrieval mode. *Proceedings of the National Academy of Sciences (USA), 97,* 506–511.

Lepper, M. R., & Greene, D. (1976). *The hidden costs of reward.* Hillsdale, NJ: Erlbaum.

Lepper, M. R., & Greene, D. (1978). Overjustification research and beyond: Toward a means-end analysis of intrinsic and extrinsic motivation. In M. R. Lepper & D. Greene (Eds.), *The hidden costs of reward: New perspectives on the psychology of human motivation.* New York: Wiley.

Lepper, M. R., Greene, D., & Nisbett, R. E. (1973). Undermining children's intrinsic interest with extrinsic rewards: A test of the "overjustification" hypothesis. *Journal of Personality and Social Psychology, 28,* 129–137.

Levenson, R. W., Cartensen, L. L., Friesen, W. V., & Ekman, P. (1991). Emotion physiology, and expression in old age. *Psychology and Aging, 6,* 28–35.

Levenson, R. W., Ekman, P., & Friesen, W. V. (1990). Voluntary facial action generates emotion-specific autonomic nervous system activity. *Psychophysiology, 27,* 363–384.

Levenson, R. W., Ekman, P., Heider, K., & Friesen, W. V. (1992). Emotion and automatic nervous system activity in the Minangkabau of West Sumatra. *Journal of Personality and Social Psychology, 62,* 972–988.

Levine, J. M., & Moreland, R. L. (1998). Small groups. In D. T. Gilbert, S. T. Fiske, & G. Lindzey (Eds.), *The handbook of social psychology* (4th ed., Vol. 2, pp. 415–469). New York: McGraw-Hill.

Levine, M. (1981). *History and politics of community mental health.* New York: Oxford University Press.

Levy, J., Trevarthen, C., & Sperry, R. W. (1972). Perception of bilateral chimeric figures following hemispheric disconnection. *Brain, 95,* 61–78.

Lewin, K. (1936). *Principles of topological psychology.* New York: McGraw-Hill.

Lewin, K. (1951). Behavior and development as a function of the total situation. In K. Lewin, *Field theory in social science: Selected theoretical papers* (pp. 791–843). New York: Harper & Row.

Lewis, M., & Brooks-Gunn, J. (1979). *Social cognition and the acquisition of self.* New York: Plenum Press.

Lewis, R., Kapur, S., Jones, C., DaSilva, J., M. Brown, G. M., Wilson, A. A., et al. (1999). Serotonin 5-HT-sub-2 receptors in schizophrenia: A PET study using [-sup-1-sup-8F] setoperone in neuroleptic-naive patients and normal subjects. *American Journal of Psychiatry, 156,* 72–78.

Lewontin, R., Rose, S., & Kamin, L. J. (1984). *Not in our genes.* New York: Pantheon.

Li, H. Z., & Browne, A. J. (2000). Defining mental illness and accessing mental health services: Perspectives of Asian Canadians. *Canadian Journal of Community Mental Health, 19,* 143–159.

Li, W., Lexenberg, E., Parrish, T., & Gottfried, J. A. (2006). Learning to smell the roses: Experience-dependent neural plasticity in human piriform and orbitofrontal cortices. *Neuron, 52,* 1097–1108.

Libet, B. (1985). Unconscious cerebral initiative and the role of conscious will in voluntary action. *Behavioral and Brain Sciences, 8,* 529–566.

Liebenluft, E. (1996). Women with bipolar illness: Clinical and research issues. *American Journal of Psychiatry, 153,* 163–173.

Lieberman, M. D., Hariri, A., Jarcho, J. M., Eisenberger, N. I., & Bookheimer, S. Y. (2005). An fMRI investigation of race-related amygdala activity in African American and Caucasian-American individuals. *Nature Neuroscience, 8,* 720–722.

Lieberman, M. D., Ochsner, K. N., Gilbert, D. T., & Schacter, D. L. (2001). Do amnesics exhibit cognitive dissonance reduction? The role of explicit memory and attention in attitude change. *Psychological Science, 12,* 135–140.

Lieberman, M. D., & Rosenthal, R. (2001). Why introverts can't always tell who likes them: Multitasking and nonverbal decoding. *Journal of Personality and Social Psychology, 80,* 294–310.

Liebowitz, M. R., Fyer, A. J., Gorman, J. M., Dillon, D., Davies, S., Stein, J. M., et al. (1985a). Specificity of lactate infusions in social phobia versus panic disorders. *American Journal of Psychiatry, 142,* 947–950.

Liebowitz, M. R., Gorman, J. M., Fyer, A. J., Levitt, M., Dillon, D., Levy, G., et al. (1985b). Lactate provocation of panic attacks: II. Biochemical and physiological findings. *Archives of General Psychiatry, 42,* 709–719.

Lilienfeld, S. O., Lynn, S. J., & Lohr, J. M. (Eds.). (2003). *Science and pseudoscience in clinical psychology.* New York: Guilford Press.

Lilienfeld, S. O., Wood, J. M., & Garb, H. N. (2000). The scientific status of projective techniques. *Psychological Science in the Public Interest, 1,* 27–66.

Lillard, L. A., & Waite, L. J. (1995). 'Til death do us part: Marital disruption and mortality. *American Journal of Sociology, 100,* 1131–1156.

Lindenberger, U., & Baltes, P. B. (1997). Intellectual functioning in old and very old age: Cross-sectional results from the Berling aging study. *Psychology and Aging, 12,* 410–432.

Lindsay, D. S., & Read, J. D. (1994). Psychotherapy and memories of childhood sexual abuse: A cognitive perspective. *Applied Cognitive Psychology, 8,* 281–338.

Lindsley, O. R., Skinner, B. F., & Solomon, H. C. (1953). *Studies in behavior therapy (status report 1).* Waltham, MA: Metropolitan State Hospital.

Lindstrom, M. (2005). *Brand sense: How to build powerful brands through touch, taste, smell, sight and sound.* London: Kogan Page.

Link, B. G., Phelan, J. C., Bresnahan, M., Stueve, A., & Pescosolido, B. A. (1999). Public conceptions of mental illness: Labels, causes, dangerousness, and social distance. *American Journal of Public Health, 89,* 1328–1333.

Link, S. W. (1994). Rediscovering the past: Gustav Fechner and signal detection theory. *Psychological Science, 5,* 335–340.

Linszen, D. H., Dingemans, P. M., Nugter, M. A., Van der Does, A. J., Scholte, W. F., & Lenoir, M. A. (1997). Patient attributes and expressed emotion as risk factors for psychotic relapse. *Schizophrenia Bulletin, 23,* 119–130.

Lipps, T. (1907). Das Wissen von fremden Ichen. In T. Lipps (Ed.), *Psychologische Untersuchungen* (Vol. 1, pp. 694–722). Leipzig: Engelmann.

Little, B. R. (1983). Personal projects: A rationale and method for investigation. *Environment and Behavior, 15,* 273–309.

Little, B. R. (1993). Personal projects and the distributed self: Aspects of a conative psychology. In J. R. Suls (Ed.), *Psychological perspectives on the self* (Vol. 4, pp. 157–185). Hillsdale, NJ: Erlbaum.

Livingstone, M., & Hubel, D. (1988). Segregation of form, color, movement, and depth: Anatomy, physiology, and perception. *Science, 240,* 740–749.

Locksley, A., Ortiz, V., & Hepburn, C. (1980). Social categorization and discriminatory behavior: Extinguishing the minimal intergroup discrimination effect. *Journal of Personality and Social Psychology, 39,* 773–783.

Loehlin, J. C. (1992). *Genes and environment in personality development.* Newbury Park, CA: Sage.

Loftus, E. F. (1975). Leading questions and eyewitness report. *Cognitive Psychology, 7,* 560–572.

Loftus, E. F. (1993). The reality of repressed memories. *American Psychologist, 48,* 518–537.

Loftus, E. F. (2003). Make-believe memories. *American Psychologist, 58,* 867–873.

Loftus, E., & Ketcham, K. (1994). *The myth of repressed memory.* New York: St. Martin's Press.

Loftus, E. F., & Klinger, M. R. (1992). Is the unconscious smart or dumb? *American Psychologist, 47,* 761–765.

Loftus, E. F., Miller, D. G., & Burns, H. J. (1978). Semantic integration of verbal information into a visual memory. *Journal of Experimental Psychology: Human Learning and Memory, 4,* 19–31.

Loftus, E. F., & Pickrell, J. E. (1995). The formation of false memories. *Psychiatric Annals, 25,* 720–725.

Logan, G. D. (1988). Toward an instance theory of automatization. *Psychological Review, 95,* 492–527.

Lohr, J. M., Tolin, D. F., & Lilienfeld, S. O. (1998). Efficacy of eye movement desensitization and reprocessing: Implications for behavior therapy. *Behavior Therapy, 29,* 123–156.

Lorenz, K. (1952). *King Solomon's ring.* New York: Crowell.

Lorge, I. (1936). Prestige, suggestion, and attitudes. *Journal of Social Psychology, 7,* 386–402.

Lozano, B. E., & Johnson, S. L. (2001). Can personality traits predict increases in manic and depressive symptoms? *Journal of Affective Disorders, 63,* 103–111.

Lubinski, D., Webb, R. M., Morelock, M. J., & Benbow, C. P. (2001). Top 1 in 10,000: A 10-year follow-up of the profoundly gifted. *Journal of Applied Psychology, 86,* 718–729.

Luborsky, L., Rosenthal, R., Diguer, L., Andrusyna, T. P., Berman, J. S., Levitt, J. T., et al. (2002). The dodo bird verdict is alive and well—mostly. *Clinical Psychology: Science and Practice, 9,* 2–12.

Luborsky, L., & Singer, B. (1975). Comparative studies of psychotherapies: Is it true that "everywon has one and all must have prizes"? *Archives of General Psychiatry, 32*(8), 995–1008.

Lucas, R. E., Clark, A. E., Georgellis, Y., & Diener, E. (2003). Reexamining adaptation and the set point model of happiness: Reactions to changes in marital status. *Journal of Personality and Social Psychology, 84,* 527–539.

Ludwig, A. M. (1966). Altered states of consciousness. *Archives of General Psychiatry, 15,* 225–234.

Luria, A. R. (1968). *The mind of a mnemonist: A little book about a vast memory* (L. Solotaroff, Trans.). New York: Basic Books.

Lustman, P. J., Caudle, M. L., & Clouse, R. E. (2002). Case study: Nondysphoric depression in a man with type 2 diabetes. *Clinical Diabetes, 20,* 122–123.

Lykken, D. T. (1995). *The antisocial personalities.* Hillsdale, NJ: Erlbaum.

Lykken, D. T., & Tellegen, A. (1996). Happiness is a stochastic phenomenon. *Psychological Science, 7,* 186–189.

Lynn, M., & Shurgot, B. A. (1984). Responses to lonely hearts advertisements: Effects of reported physical attractiveness, physique, and coloration. *Personality and Social Psychology Bulletin, 10,* 349–357.

Lynn, R., & Vanhanen, T. (2002). *IQ and the wealth of nations.* Westport, CT: Praeger/Greenwood.

Lynn, S. J., Rhue, J. W., & Weekes, J. R. (1990). Hypnotic involuntariness: A social cognitive analysis. *Psychological Review, 97,* 169–184.

MacDonald, S., Uesiliana, K., & Hayne, H. (2000). Cross-cultural and gender differences in childhood amnesia. *Memory, 8,* 365–376.

MacDonald, T. K., Zanna, M. P., & Fong, G. T. (1996). Why common sense goes out the window: Effects of alcohol on intentions to use condoms. *Personality and Social Psychology Bulletin, 22,* 763–775.

MacGregor, J. N., Ormerod, T. C., & Chronicle, E. P. (2001). Information processing and insight: A process model of performance on the nine-dot and related problems. *Journal of Experimental Psychology: Learning, Memory, & Cognition, 27,* 176–201.

Mack, A. H., Franklin, J. E., Jr., & Frances, R. J. (2003). Substance use disorders. In R. E. Hales & S. C. Yudofsky (Eds.), *The American Psychiatric Publishing textbook of clinical psychiatry* (4th ed., pp. 309–377). Washington, DC: American Psychiatric Publishing.

Mackinnon, A., & Foley, D. (1996). The genetics of anxiety disorders. In H. G. Westenberg, J. A. Den Boer & D. L. Murphy (Eds.), *Advances in the neurobiology of anxiety disorders* (pp. 39–59). Chichester, England: Wiley.

Maclean, P. D. (1970). The triune brain, emotion, and scientific bias. In F. O. Schmitt (Ed.), *The neurosciences: A second study program* (pp. 336–349). New York: Rockefeller University Press.

Macmillan, M. (2000). *An odd kind of fame: Stories of Phineas Gage.* Cambridge, MA: MIT Press.

Macmillan, N. A., & Creelman, C. D. (2005). *Detection theory.* Mahwah, NJ: Erlbaum.

Macrae, C. N., Bodenhausen, G. V., Milne, A. B., & Jetten, J. (1994). Out of mind but back in sight: Stereotypes on the rebound. *Journal of Personality and Social Psychology, 67,* 808–817.

Macrae, C. N., Moran, J. M., Heatherton, T. F., Banfield, J. F., & Kelley, W. M. (2004). Medial prefrontal activity predicts memory for self. *Cerebral Cortex, 14,* 647–654.

Maddi, S. R., Kahn, S., & Maddi, K. L. (1998). The effectiveness of hardiness training. *Consulting Psychology Journal: Practice and Research, 50,* 78–86.

Maddi, S. R., & Kobasa, S. (1984). *The hardy executive: Health under stress.* Homewood, IL: Dow Jones–Irwin.

Maes, M. (1995). Evidence for an immune response in major depression: A review and hypothesis. *Progress in Neuro-Psychopharmacology and Biological Psychiatry, 19,* 11–38.

Magee, W. J., Eaton, W. W., Wittchen, H.-U., McGonagle, K. A., & Kessler, R. C. (1996). Agoraphobia, simple phobia, and social phobia in the National Comorbidity Survey. *Archives of General Psychiatry, 53,* 159–168.

Maguire, E. A., Woollett, K., & Spiers, H. J. (2006). London taxi drivers and bus drivers: A structural MRI and neuropsychological analysis. *Hippocampus, 16,* 1091–1101.

Mah, K., & Binik, Y. M. (2002). Do all orgasms feel alike? Evaluating a two-dimensional model of the orgasm experience across gender and sexual context. *Journal of Sex Research, 39,* 104–113.

Maier, S. F., & Watkins, L. R. (1998). Cytokines for psychologists: Implications of bidirectional immune-to-brain communication for understanding behavior, mood, and cognition. *Psychological Review, 105,* 83–107.

Maier, S. F., & Watkins, L. R. (2000). The immune system as a sensory system: Implications for psychology. *Current Directions in Psychological Science, 9,* 98–102.

Makin, J. E., Fried, P. A., & Watkinson, B. (1991). A comparison of active and passive smoking during pregnancy: Long-term effects. *Neurotoxicology and Teratology, 16,* 5–12.

Maldonado, J. R., & Butler, L. D. (1998). *Treatments for dissociative disorders.* New York: Oxford University Press.

Malina, R. M., Bouchard, C., & Beunen, G. (1988). Human growth: Selected aspects of current research on well-nourished children. *Annual Review of Anthropology, 17,* 187–219.

Malinoski, P. T., & Lynn, S. J. (1999). The plasticity of early memory reports: Social pressure, hypnotizability, compliance, and interrogative suggestibility. *The International Journal of Clinical and Experimental Hypnosis, 47,* 320–345.

Mandel, D. R., & Lehman, D. R. (1998). Integration of contingency information in judgments of cause, covariation, and probability. *Journal of Experimental Psychology: General, 127,* 269–285.

Mandle, C. L., Jacobs, S. C., Arcari, P. M., & Domar, A. D. (1996). The efficacy of relaxation response interventions with adult patients: A review of the literature. *Journal of Cardiovascular Nursing, 10,* 4–26.

Mandler, G. (1967). Organization and memory. In K. W. Spence & J. T. Spence (Eds.), *The psychology of learning and motivation* (Vol. 1, pp. 327–372). New York: Academic Press.

Mann, J. J., Waternaux, C., Haas, G. L, & Malone, K. M. (1999). Toward a clinical model of suicidal behavior in psychiatric patients. *American Journal of Psychiatry, 156,* 181–189.

Marangell, L. B., Silver, J. M., Goff, D. M., & Yudofsky, S. C. (2003). Psychopharmacology and electroconvulsive therapy. In R. E. Hales & S. C. Yudofsky (Eds.), *The American Psychiatric Publishing textbook of clinical psychiatry* (4th ed., pp. 1047–1149). Washington, DC: American Psychiatric Publishing.

Marcus, G. B. (1986). Stability and change in political attitudes: Observe, recall, and "explain." *Political Behavior, 8,* 21–44.

Marcus, J., Hans, S. L., Auerbach, J. G., & Auerbach, A. G. (1993). Children at risk for schizophrenia: The Jerusalem infant development study: II. Neurological deficits at school age. *Archives of General Psychiatry, 50,* 797–809.

Marks, I. M., & Nesse, R. M. (1994). Fear and fitness: An evolutionary analysis of anxiety disorders. *Ethology and Sociobiology, 15,* 247–261.

Markus, H. (1977). Self-schemata and processing information about the self. *Journal of Personality and Social Psychology, 35,* 63–78.

Marlatt, G. A. (Ed.). (1998). *Harm reduction: Pragmatic strategies for managing high-risk behaviors.* New York: Guilford Press.

Marlatt, G. A., Larimer, M. E., Baer, J. S., & Quigley, L. A. (1993). Harm reduction for alcohol problems: Moving beyond the controlled drinking controversy. *Behavior Therapy, 24,* 461–504.

Marlatt, G. A., & Rohsenow, D. (1980). Cognitive processes in alcohol use: Expectancy and the balanced placebo design. In N. K. Mello (Ed.), *Advances in substance abuse: Behavioral and biological research* (pp. 159–199). Greenwich, CT: JAI Press.

Marmot, M. G., Stansfeld, S., Patel, C., North, F., Head, J., White, L., et al. (1991). Health inequalities among British civil servants: The Whitehall II study. *Lancet, 337,* 1387–1393.

Marr, D., & Nishihara, H. K. (1978). Representation and recognition of the spatial organization of three-dimensional shapes. *Proceedings of the Royal Society of London B, 200,* 269–294.

Marsolek, C. J. (1995). Abstract visual-form representations in the left cerebral hemispheres. *Journal of Experimental Psychology: Human Perception and Performance, 21,* 375–386.

Martin, A. (2007). The representation of object concepts in the brain. *Annual Review of Psychology, 58,* 25–45.

Martin, A., & Caramazza, A. (2003). Neuropsychological and neuroimaging perspectives on conceptual knowledge: An introduction. *Cognitive Neuropsychology, 20,* 195–212.

Martin, A., & Chao, L. L. (2001). Semantic memory and the brain: Structure and processes. *Current Opinion in Neurobiology, 11,* 194–201.

Martin, G., & Koo, L. (1997). Celebrity suicide: Did the death of Kurt Cobain influence young suicides in Australia? *Archives of Suicide Research, 3,* 187–198.

Martin, L. R., Friedman, H. S., Tucker, J. S., Tomlinson-Keasey, C., Criqui, M. H., & Schwartz, J. E. (2002). A life course perspective on childhood cheerfulness and its relation to mortality risk. *Personality and Social Psychology Bulletin, 28,* 1155–1165.

Martin, N. G., Eaves, L. J., Geath, A. R., Jarding, R., Feingold, L. M., & Eysenck, H. J. (1986). Transmission of social attitudes. *Proceedings of the National Academy of Sciences (USA), 83,* 4364–4368.

Marucha, P. T., Kiecolt-Glaser, J. K., & Favagehi, M. (1998). Mucosal wound healing is impaired by examination stress. *Psychosomatic Medicine, 60,* 362–365.

Maslach, C. (2003). Job burnout: New directions in research and intervention. *Current Directions in Psychological Science, 12,* 189–192.

Maslow, A. H. (1937). Dominance-feeling, behavior, and status. In R. J. Lowry (Ed.), *Dominance, self-esteem, self-actualization: Germinal papers by A. H. Maslow.* Monterey, CA: Brooks-Cole.

Maslow, A. H. (1954). *Motivation and personality.* New York: Harper & Row.

Maslow, A. H. (1962). *Toward a psychology of being.* New York: Van Nostrand Reinhold.

Maslow, A. H. (1970). *Motivation and personality* (2nd ed.). New York: Harper & Row.

Masserman, J. H. (1961). *Principles of dynamic psychiatry* (2nd ed.). Philadelphia: W. B. Saunders.

Masters, W. H., & Johnson, V. E. (1966). *Human sexual response.* Boston: Little, Brown.

Mather, M., Canli, T., English, T., Whitfield, S., Wais, P., Ochsner, K., et al. (2004). Amygdala responses to emotionally valenced stimuli in older and younger adults. *Psychological Science, 15,* 259–263.

Mather, M., & Carstensen, L. L. (2003). Aging and attentional biases for emotional faces. *Psychological Science, 14,* 409–415.

Mathis, J. L. (1964). A sophisticated version of voodoo death. *Psychosomatic Medicine, 26,* 104–107.

Matthews, G., & Gilliland, K. (1999). The personality theories of H. J. Eysenck and J. A. Gray: A comparative review. *Personality and Individual Differences, 26,* 583–626.

Maudsley, H. (1886). *Natural causes and supernatural seemings.* London: Kegan Paul, Trench.

May, R. (1983). *The discovery of being: Writings in existential psychology.* New York: Norton.

Maynard-Smith, J. (1965). The evolution of alarm calls. *American Naturalist, 100,* 637–650.

Maynard-Smith, J., & Szathmary, E. (1995). *The major transitions in evolution.* Oxford, England: Oxford University Press.

McAdams, D. (1993). *The stories we live by: Personal myths and the making of the self*. New York: Morrow.

McAndrew, F. T. (1986). A cross-cultural study of recognition thresholds for facial expression of emotion. *Journal of Cross-Cultural Psychology, 17*, 211–224.

McCann, I. L., & Holmes, D. S. (1984). Influence of aerobic exercise on depression. *Journal of Personality and Social Psychology, 46*, 1142–1147.

McClelland, D. C., Atkinson, J. W., Clark, R. A., & Lowell, E. L. (1953). *The achievement motive*. New York: Appleton-Century-Crofts.

McClintock, M. K. (1971). Menstrual synchrony and suppression. *Nature, 299*, 244–245.

McClintock, M. K., & Herdt, G. (1996). Rethinking puberty: The development of sexual attraction. *Current Directions in Psychological Science, 5*, 178–183.

McCloskey, M., & Zaragoza, M. (1985). Misleading postevent information and memory for events: Arguments and evidence against memory impairment hypotheses. *Journal of Experimental Psychology: General, 114*, 1–16.

McConkey, K. M., Barnier, A. J., & Sheehan, P. W. (1998). Hypnosis and pseudomemory: Understanding the findings and their implications. In S. J. Lynn & K. M. McConkey (Eds.), *Truth in memory* (pp. 227–259). New York: Guilford Press.

McCrae, R. R., & Costa, P. T. (1990). *Personality in adulthood*. New York: Guilford Press.

McCrae, R. R., & Costa, P. T. (1999). A five-factor theory of personality. In L. A. Pervin & O. P. John (Eds.), *Handbook of personality: Theory and research*. New York: Guilford Press.

McDaniel, M. A. (2005). Big-brained people are smarter: A meta-analysis of the relationship between in vivo brain volume and intelligence. *Intelligence, 33*, 337–346.

McDougall, W. (1930). The hormic psychology. In C. Murchison (Ed.), *Psychologies of 1930* (pp. 3–36). Worcester, MA: Clark University Press.

McDougall, W. (2003). *Introduction to social psychology*. Mineola, NY: Dover Publications. (Originally published 1908)

McEvoy, S. P., Stevenson, M. R., McCartt, A. T., Woodward, M., Haworth, C., Palamara, P., et al. (2005). Role of mobile phones in motor vehicle crashes resulting in hospital attendance: A case-crossover study. *British Medical Journal, 331*, 428–430.

McFall, R. M., & Treat, T. A. (1999). Quantifying the information value of clinical assessments with signal detection theory. *Annual Review of Psychology, 50*, 215–241.

McFarland, C., & Ross, M. (1987). The relation between current impressions and memories of self and dating partners. *Personality and Social Psychology Bulletin, 13*, 228–238.

McFarlane, A. H., Norman, G. R., Streiner, D. L., Roy, R., & Scott, D. J. (1980). A longitudinal study of the influence of the psychosocial environment on health status: A preliminary report. *Journal of Health and Social Behavior, 21*, 124–133.

McGarty, C., & Turner, J. C. (1992). The effects of categorization on social judgement. *British Journal of Social Psychology, 31*, 253–268.

McGue, M., & Bouchard, T. J. (1998). Genetic and environmental influences on human behavioral differences. *Annual Review of Neuroscience, 21*, 1–24.

McGuire, P. K., Shah, G. M., & Murray, R. M. (1993). Increased blood flow in Broca's area during auditory hallucinations in schizophrenia. *Lancet, 342*, 703–706.

McHugh, P. R., Lief, H. I., Freyd, P. P., & Fetkewicz, J. M. (2004). From refusal to recollection: Family relationships after an accusation based on recovered memories. *Journal of Nervous and Mental Disease, 192*, 525–532.

McKetin, R., McLaren, J., Lubman, D. I., & Hides, L. (2006). The prevalence of psychotic symptoms among methamphetamine users. *Addiction, 101*, 1473–1478.

McKetin, R., Ward, P. B., Catts, S. V., Mattick, R. P., & Bell, J. R. (1999). Changes in auditory selective attention and event-related potentials following oral administration of D-amphetamine in humans. *Neuropsychopharmacology*, 380–390.

McKinney, C. H., Antoni, M. H., Kumar, M., Tims, F. C., & McCabe, P. M. (1997). Effects of guided imagery and music (GIM) therapy on mood and cortisol in healthy adults. *Health Psychology, 16*, 390–400.

McNally, R. J. (2003). *Remembering trauma*. Cambridge, MA: Belknap Press/Harvard University Press.

McNally, R. J., & Steketee, G. S. (1985). Etiology and maintenance of severe animal phobias. *Behavioral Research and Therapy, 23*, 431–435.

McNamara, B., Ray, J. L., Arthurs, O. J., & Boniface, S. (2001). Transcranial magnetic stimulation for depression and other psychiatric disorders. *Psychological Medicine, 31*, 1141–1146.

McNeilly, A. S., Robinson, I. C., Houston, M. J., & Howie, P. W. (1983). Release of oxytocin and prolactin in response to suckling. *British Medical Journal, 286*, 257–259.

McWilliams, N. (1994). *Psychoanalytic diagnosis: Understanding personality structure in the clinical process*. New York: Guilford Press.

McWilliams, P. (1993). *Ain't nobody's business if you do: The absurdity of consensual crimes in a free society*. Los Angeles: Prelude Press.

Mead, G. H. (1934). *Mind, self, and society*. Chicago: University of Chicago Press.

Mead, M. (1968). *Sex and temperament in three primitive societies*. New York: Dell. (Originally published 1935)

Mechelli, A., Crinion, J. T., Noppeney, U., O'Doherty, J., Ashburner, J., Frackowiak, R. S., et al. (2004). Neurolinguistics: Structural plasticity in the human brain. *Nature, 431*, 757.

Medin, D. L., & Schaffer, M. M. (1978). Context theory of classification learning. *Psychological Review, 85*, 207–238.

Medvec, V. H., Madey, S. F., & Gilovich, T. (1995). When less is more: Counterfactual thinking and satisfaction among Olympic medalists. *Journal of Personality and Social Psychology, 69*, 603–610.

Meins, E. (2003). Emotional development and attachment relationships. In A. Slater & G. Bremner (Eds.), *An introduction to developmental psychology* (pp. 141–164). Malden, MA: Blackwell.

Meins, E., Fernyhough, C., Fradley, E., & Tuckey, M. (2001). Rethinking maternal sensitivity: Mothers' comments on infants' mental processes predict security of attachment at 12 months. *Journal of Child Psychology & Psychiatry & Allied Disciplines, 42*, 637–648.

Meisel, S. R., Dayan, K. I., Pauzner, H., Chetboun, I., Arbel, Y., David, D., et al. (1991). Effect of Iraqi missile war on incidence of acute myocardial infarction and sudden death in Israeli citizens. *Lancet, 338*, 660–661.

Mekel-Bobrov, N., Gilbert, S. L., Evans, P. D., Vallender, E. J., Anderson, J. R., Hudson, R. R., et al. (2005). Ongoing adaptive evolution of ASPM, a brain size determinant in *Homo sapiens*. *Science, 309*, 1720–1722.

Meltzoff, A. N., & Moore, M. K. (1977). Imitation of facial and manual gestures by human neonates. *Science, 198*, 75–78.

Melzack, R., & Wall, P. D. (1965). Pain mechanisms: A new theory. *Science, 150*, 971–979.

Mendes, W. B., Blascovich, J., Lickel, B., & Hunter, S. (2002). Challenge and threat during social interaction with white and black men. *Personality & Social Psychology Bulletin, 28*, 939–952.

Merikangas, K. R., Wicki, W., & Angst, J. (1994). Heterogeneity of depression: Classification of depressive subtype by longitudinal course. *British Journal of Psychiatry, 164*, 342–348.

Mervis, C. B., & Bertrand, J. (1994). Acquisition of the "Novel Name" Nameless Category (N3C) principle. *Child Development, 65,* 1646–1662.

Merzenich, M. M., Recanzone, G. H., Jenkins, W. M., & Grajski, K. A. (1990). Adaptive mechanisms in cortical networks underlying cortical contributions to learning and nondeclarative memory. *Cold Spring Harbor Symposia on Quantitative Biology, 55,* 873–887.

Messick, D. M., & Cook, K. S. (1983). *Equity theory: Psychological and sociological perspectives.* New York: Praeger.

Metcalfe, J., & Wiebe, D. (1987). Intuition in insight and noninsight problem solving. *Memory & Cognition, 15,* 238–246.

Meyer-Bahlberg, H. F. L., Ehrhardt, A. A., Rosen, L. R., & Gruen, R. S. (1995). Prenatal estrogens and the development of homosexual orientation. *Developmental Psychology, 31,* 12–21.

Michael, R. T. (1994). *Sex in America: A definitive survey.* Boston: Little, Brown.

Michelson, D., Pollack, M., Lydiard, R. D., Tamura, R., Tepner, R., & Tollefson, G. (1999). Continuing treatment of panic disorder after acute responses: Randomized, placebo-controlled trail with fluoxetine. The Fluoxitine Panic Disorder Study Group. *British Journal of Psychiatry, 174,* 213–218.

Michotte, A. (1963). *The perception of causality.* New York: Basic Books.

Miklowitz, D. J., Goldstein, M. J., Nuechterlein, K. H., Snyder, K. S., & Mintz, J. (1988). Family factors and the course of bipolar affective disorder. *Archives of General Psychiatry, 45,* 225–231.

Milgram, S. (1963). Behavioral study of obedience. *Journal of Abnormal and Social Psychology, 67,* 371–378.

Milgram, S. (1974). *Obedience to authority.* New York: Harper & Row.

Milgram, S., Bickman, L., & Berkowitz, O. (1969). Note on the drawing power of crowds of different size. *Journal of Personality and Social Psychology, 13,* 79–82.

Milgram, S., & Toch, H. (1968). Collective behavior: Crowds and social movements. In G. Lindzey & E. Aronson (Eds.), *The handbook of social psychology* (2nd ed., Vol. 4, pp. 507–610). Reading, MA: Addison-Wesley.

Miller, A. J. (1986). *The obedience experiments: A case study of controversy in social science.* New York: Praeger.

Miller, D. T., & Prentice, D. A. (1996). The construction of social norms and standards. In E. T. Higgins, & A. W. Kruglanski (Ed.), *Social psychology: Handbook of basic principles* (pp. 799–829). New York: Guilford Press.

Miller, D. T., & Ratner, R. K. (1998). The disparity between the actual and assumed power of self-interest. *Journal of Personality and Social Psychology, 74,* 53–62.

Miller, G. A. (1956). The magical number seven, plus or minus two: Some limits on our capacity for processing information. *Psychological Review, 63,* 81–96.

Miller, J. (1994). On the internal structure of phonetic categories: A progress report. *Cognition, 50,* 271–285.

Miller, K. F., Smith, C. M., & Zhu, J. (1995). Preschool origins of cross-national differences in mathematical competence: The role of number-naming systems. *Psychological Science, 6,* 56–60.

Miller, N. E. (1960). Motivational effects of brain stimulation and drugs. *Federation Proceedings, 19,* 846–854.

Miller, N. E. (1978). Biofeedback and visceral learning. *Annual Review of Psychology, 29,* 373–404.

Miller, N. E., & Campbell, D. T. (1959). Recency and primacy in persuasion as a function of the timing of speeches and measurements. *Journal of Abnormal & Social Psychology, 59,* 1–9.

Miller, T. W. (Ed.). (1996). *Theory and assessment of stressful life events.* Madison, CT: International Universities Press.

Miller, W. R. (1978). Behavioral treatment of problem drinkers: A comparative outcome study of three controlled drinking therapies. *Journal of Consulting and Clinical Psychology, 46,* 74–86.

Mills, P. J., & Dimsdale, J. E. (1991). Cardiovascular reactivity to psychosocial stressors. A review of the effects of beta-blockade. *Psychosomatics, 32,* 209–220.

Milne, E., & Grafman, J. (2001). Ventromedial prefrontal cortex lesions in humans eliminate implicit gender stereotyping. *Journal of Neuroscience, 21,* 1–6.

Milner, A. D., & Goodale, M. A. (1995). *The visual brain in action.* Oxford, England: Oxford University Press.

Milner, B. (1962). Laterality effects in audition. In V. B. Mountcastle (Ed.), *Interhemispheric relations and cerebral dominance* (pp. 177–195). Baltimore: Johns Hopkins University Press.

Mineka, S., & Cook, M. (1988). Social learning and the acquisition of snake fear in monkeys. In T. Zentall & B. G. Galef, Jr. (Eds.), *Social learning* (pp. 51–73). Hillsdale, NJ: Erlbaum.

Mineka, S., & Ohman, A. (2002). Born to fear: Non-associative vs. associative factors in the etiology of phobia. *Behaviour Research and Therapy, 40,* 173–184.

Minsky, M. (1986). *The society of mind.* New York: Simon & Schuster.

Mischel, W. (1968). *Personality and assessment.* New York: Wiley.

Mischel, W., & Shoda, Y. (1999). Integrating dispositions and processing dynamics within a unified theory of personality: The Cognitive-Affective Personality System. In L. A. Pervin & O. P. John (Eds.), *Handbook of personality: Theory and research.* New York: Guilford Press.

Mischel, W., Shoda, Y., & Rodriguez, M. L. (1989). Delay of gratification in children. *Science, 244,* 933–938.

Mita, T. H., Dermer, M., & Knight, J. (1977). Reversed facial images and the mere-exposure hypothesis. *Journal of Personality and Social Psychology, 35,* 597–601.

Mitchell, J. P., Heatherton, T. F., & Macrae, C. N. (2002). Distinct neural systems subserve person and object knowledge. *Proceedings of the National Academy of Sciences (USA), 99,* 15238–15243.

Miura, I. T., Okamoto, Y., Kim, C. C., & Chang, C. M. (1994). Comparisons of children's cognitive representation of number: China, France, Japan, Korea, Sweden and the United States. *International Journal of Behavioral Development, 17,* 401–411.

Moffitt, T. E. (1993). Adolescence-limited and life-course-persistent antisocial behavior: A developmental taxonomy. *Psychological Review, 100,* 674–701.

Moghaddam, B., & Bunney, B. S. (1989). Differential effect of cocaine on extracellular dopamine levels in rat medial prefrontal cortex and nucleus accumbens: Comparison to amphetamine. *Synapse, 4,* 156–161.

Mokdad, A. H. P., Ford, E. S., Bowman, B. A., Dietz, W. H., Vinicor, F., Bales, V. S., et al. (2003). Prevalence of obesity, diabetes, and obesity-related health risk factors, 2001. *Journal of the American Medical Association, 289*(1), 76–79.

Monahan, J. L., Murphy, S. T., & Zajonc, R. B. (2000). Subliminal mere exposure: Specific, general, and diffuse effects. *Psychological Science, 11,* 462–466.

Mook, D. G. (1983). In defense of external invalidity. *American Psychologist, 38,* 379–387.

Mook, D. G. (1996). *Motivation.* New York: Norton.

Moore, K. L. (1977). *The developing human* (2nd ed.). Philadelphia: Saunders.

Moray, N. (1959). Attention in dichotic listening: Affective cues and the influence of instructions. *Quarterly Journal of Experimental Psychology, 11,* 56–60.

Morgan, H. (1990). Dostoevsky's epilepsy: A case report and comparison. *Surgical Neurology, 33,* 413–416.

Morgenstern, J., Labouvie, E., McCrady, B. S., Kahler, C. W., & Frey, R. M. (1997). Affiliation with Alcoholics Anonymous after treatment: A study of its therapeutic effects and mechanisms of action. *Journal of Consulting and Clinical Psychology, 65,* 768–777.

Morin, A. (2002). Right hemisphere self-awareness: A critical assessment. *Consciousness & Cognition, 11,* 396–401.

Morris, C. D., Bransford, J. D., & Franks, J. J. (1977). Levels of processing versus transfer-appropriate processing. *Journal of Verbal Learning and Verbal Behavior, 16,* 519–533.

Morris, R. G., Anderson, E., Lynch, G. S., & Baudry, M. ( 1986). Selective impairment of learning and blockade of long-term potentiation by an N-methyl-D-aspartate receptor antagonist, AP5. *Nature, 319,* 774–776.

Morris, T. L. (2001). Social phobia. In M. W. Vasey & M. R. Dadds (Eds.), *The developmental psychopathology of anxiety* (pp. 435–458). New York: Oxford University Press.

Morrow, D., Leirer, V., Altiteri, P., & Fitzsimmons, C. (1994). When expertise reduces age differences in performance. *Psychology and Aging, 9,* 134–148.

Moruzzi, G., & Magoun, H. W. (1949). Brain stem reticular formation and activation of the EEG. *Electroencephalography and Clinical Neurophysiology, 1,* 455–473.

Moscovitch, M. (1994). Memory and working-with-memory: Evaluation of a component process model and comparisons with other models. In D. L. Schacter & E. Tulving (Eds.), *Memory systems 1994* (pp. 269–310). Cambridge, MA: MIT Press.

Moscovitch, M., Nadel, L., Winocur, G., Gilboa, A., & Rosenbaum, R. S. (2006). The cognitive neuroscience of remote episodic, semantic and spatial memory. *Current Opinion in Neurobiology, 16,* 179–190.

Moss, D., McGrady, A., Davies, T., & Wickramasekera, I. (2002). *Handbook of mind-body medicine for primary care.* Newbury Park, CA: Sage.

Motley, M. T., & Baars, B. J. (1979). Effects of cognitive set upon laboratory induced verbal (Freudian) slips. *Journal of Speech & Hearing Research, 22,* 421–432.

Moyer, C. A., Rounds, J., & Hannum, J. W. (2004). A meta-analysis of massage therapy research. *Psychological Bulletin, 130,* 3–18.

Mroczek, D. K., & Spiro, A. (2005). Change in life satisfaction during adulthood: Findings from the Veterans Affairs Normative Aging Study. *Journal of Personality and Social Psychology, 88,* 189.

Mueller, E. T. (1990). *Daydreaming in humans and machines : A computer model of the stream of thought.* New York: Ablex.

Mueller, T. I., Leon, A. C., Keller, M. B., Solomon, D. A., Endicott, J., Coryell, W., et al. (1999). Recurrence after recovery from major depressive disorder during 15 years of observational follow-up. *American Journal of Psychiatry, 156,* 1000–1006.

Muenter, M. D., & Tyce, G. M. (1971). L-dopa therapy of Parkinson's disease: Plasma L-dopa concentration, therapeutic response, and side effects. *Mayo Clinic Proceedings, 46,* 231–239.

Mukherjee, S., Sackeim, H. A., & Schnur, D. B. (1994). Electroconvulsive therapy of acute manic episodes: a review of 50 years' experience. *American Journal of Psychiatry, 151,* 169–176.

Mullen, B. (1986). Atrocity as a function of lynch mob composition: A self-attention perspective. *Personality and Social Psychology Bulletin, 12,* 187–197.

Mullen, B., Chapman, J. G., & Peaugh, S. (1989). Focus of attention in groups: A self-attention perspective. *Journal of Social Psychology, 129,* 807–817.

Mullen, M. K. (1994). Earliest recollections of childhood: A demographic analysis. *Cognition, 52,* 55–79.

Muller, M. N., & Wrangham, R. W. (2004). Dominance, aggression and testosterone in wild chimpanzees: A test of the "challenge hypothesis." *Animal Behaviour, 67,* 113–123.

Multhaup, K. S., Johnson, M. D., & Tetirick, J. C. (2005). The wane of childhood amnesia for autobiographical and public event memories. *Memory, 13,* 161–173.

Mumford, D. B., Whitehouse, A. M., & Platts, M. (1991). Sociocultural correlates of eating disorders among Asian schoolgirls in Bradford. *British Journal of Psychiatry, 158,* 222–228.

Mumme, D. L., & Fernald, A. (2003). The infant as onlooker: Learning from emotional reactions observed in a television scenario. *Child Development, 74,* 221–237.

Murphy, N. A., Hall, J. A., & Colvin, C. R. (2003). Accurate intelligence assessments in social interactions: Mediators and gender effects. *Journal of Personality, 71,* 465–493.

Murray, C. J. L., & Lopez, A. D. (1996). *The global burden of disease: A comprehensive assessment of mortality and disability from diseases, injuries, and risk factors in 1990 and projected to 2020.* Cambridge, MA: Harvard School of Public Health.

Murray, H. A. (1938). *Explorations in personality.* New York: Oxford University Press.

Murray, H. A. (1943). *Thematic Apperception Test Manual.* Cambridge, MA: Harvard University Press.

Murray, H. A., & Kluckhohn, C. (1953). Outline of a conception of personality. In C. Kluckhohn, Murray, H. A., & Schneider, D. M. (Eds.), *Personality in nature, society, and culture* (2nd ed., pp. 3–52). New York: Knopf.

Myers, D. G., & Diener, E. (1995). Who is happy? *Psychological Science, 6,* 10–19.

Nadasdy, A. (1995). Phonetics, phonology, and applied linguistics. *Annual Review of Applied Linguistics, 15,* 68–77.

Nadel, L., & Zola-Morgan, S. (1984). Infantile amnesia: A neurobiological perspective. In M. Moscovitch (Ed.), *Infant memory* (pp. 145–172). New York: Plenum Press.

Nagasako, E. M., Oaklander, A. L., & Dworkin, R. H. (2003). Congenital insensitivity to pain: An update. *Pain, 101,* 213–219.

Nagel, T. (1974). What is it like to be a bat? *Philosophical Review, 83,* 433–450.

Nahemow, L., & Lawton, M. P. (1975). Similarity and propinquity in friendship formation. *Journal of Personality and Social Psychology, 32,* 205–213.

Nakazato, M., Murakami, N., Date, Y., Kojima, M., Matsuo, H., Kangawa, K., et al. (2001). A role for ghrelin in the central regulation of feeding. *Nature, 409,* 194–198.

Narrow, W. E., Rae, D. S., Robins, L. N., & Regier, D. A. (2002). Revised prevalence estimates of mental disorders in the United States: Using a clinical significance criterion to reconcile 2 surveys' estimates. *Archives of General Psychiatry, 59,* 115–123.

Nasar, S. (1998). *A beautiful mind.* New York: Simon & Schuster.

Nash, M. (1987). What, if anything, is regressed about hypnotic age regression? A review of the empirical literature. *Psychological Bulletin, 102,* 42–52.

Nasser, M. (1986). Comparative study of the prevalence of abnormal eating attitudes among Arab female students of both London and Cairo universities. *Psychological Medicine, 16,* 621–625.

Nathan, P. E., & Lagenbucher, J. W. (1999). Psychopathology: Description and classification. *Annual Review of Psychology, 50,* 79–107.

National Center for Health Statistics. (2001). *Health, United States.* Hyattsville, MD: National Center for Health Statistics.

National Center for Health Statistics. (2004). *Health, United States, 2004, with chartbook on trends in the health of Americans*. Hyattsville, MD: Author.

National Center for Injury Prevention and Control. (2001–2002). *Injury Fact Book*. Atlanta, GA: Centers for Disease Control and Prevention.

National Household Survey on Drug Abuse. (2001). Washington, DC: Substance Abuse and Mental Health Services Administration.

National Institute of Mental Health. (2003). In harm's way (NIH Publication No. 03-4594). Washington, DC: National Institutes of Health, U.S. Department of Health and Human Services.

National Research Council. (2003). *The polygraph and lie detection*. Washington, DC: National Academies Press.

Neilson, T. A., Deslauriers, D., & Baylor, G. W. (1991). Emotions in dream and waking event reports. *Dreaming, 1,* 287–300.

Neimeyer, R. A., & Mitchell, K. A. (1988). Similarity and attraction: A longitudinal study. *Journal of Social and Personal Relationships, 5,* 131–148.

Neisser, U. (1967). *Cognitive psychology*. New York: Appleton-Century-Crofts.

Neisser, U. (Ed.). (1998). *The rising curve: Long-term gains in IQ and related measures*. Washington, DC: American Psychological Association.

Neisser, U., & Becklen, R. (1975). Selective looking: Attending to visually significant events. *Cognitive Psychology, 7,* 480–494.

Neisser, U., Boodoo, G., Bouchard, T. J., Jr., Boykin, A. W., Brody, N., Ceci, S. J., et al. (1996). Intelligence: Knowns and unknowns. *American Psychologist, 51,* 77–101.

Neisser, U., & Harsch, N. (1992). Phantom flashbulbs: False recollections of hearing the news about Challenger. In E. Winograd & U. Neisser (Eds.), *Affect and accuracy in recall: Studies of "flashbulb memories"* (pp. 9–31). Cambridge, England: Cambridge University Press.

Neisser, U., & Hyman, I. E. (Eds.). (2000). *Memory observed: Remembering in natural contexts*. New York: Worth.

Nemeth, C., & Chiles, C. (1988). Modelling courage: The role of dissent in fostering independence. *European Journal of Social Psychology, 18,* 275–280.

Netherlands Ministry of Justice. (1999). *Fact Sheet: Dutch Drugs Policy*. Utrecht, Netherlands: Trimbos Institute, Netherlands Institute of Mental Health and Addiction.

Nettleback, T., & Lally, M. (1976). Inspection time and measured intelligence. *British Journal of Psychology, 67,* 17–22.

Neugebauer, R., Hoek, H. W., & Susser, E. (1999). Prenatal exposure to wartime famine and development of antisocial personality in early adulthood. *Journal of the American Medical Association, 282,* 455–462.

Newberg, A., Alavi, A., Baime, M., Pourdehnad, M., Santanna, J., & d'Aquili, E. (2001). The measurement of regional cerebral blood flow during the complex cognitive task of meditation: A preliminary SPECT study. *Psychiatry Research: Neuroimaging, 106,* 113–122.

Newell, A., Shaw, J. C., & Simon, H. A. (1958). Elements of a theory of human problem solving. *Psychological Review, 65,* 151–166.

Newman, A. J., Bavelier, D., Corina, D., Jezzard, P., & Neville, H. J. (2002). A critical period for right hemisphere recruitment in American Sign Language processing. *Nature Neuroscience, 5,* 76–80.

Newman, L. S., Baumeister, R. F., & Duff, K. J. (1995). A new look at defensive projection: Thought suppression, accessibility, and biased person perception, *Journal of Personality and Social Psychology, 72,* 980–1001.

Newman, M. G., & Stone, A. A. (1996). Does humor moderate the effects of experimentally induced stress? *Annals of Behavioral Medicine, 18,* 101–109.

Newsome, W. T., & Paré, E. B. (1988). A selective impairment of motion perception following lesions of the middle temporal visual area (MT). *Journal of Neuroscience, 8,* 2201–2211.

Neylan, T. C., Metzler, T. J., Best, S. R., Weiss, D. S., Fagan, J. A., Libermans, A., et al. (2002). Critical incident exposure and sleep quality in police officers. *Psychosomatic Medicine, 64,* 345–352.

Niaura, R., Todaro, J. F., Stroud, L., Spiro III, A., Ward, K. D., Weiss, S., et al. (2002). Hostility, the metabolic syndrome, and incident coronary heart disease. *Health Psychology, 21,* 588–593.

NICHD Early Child Care Research Network. (1997). The effects of infant child care on infant-mother attachment security: Results of the NICHD study of early child care. *Child Development, 68,* 860–879.

NICHD Early Child Care Research Network. (1999). Child care and mother-infant interaction in the first three years of life. *Developmental Psyclogy, 35,* 1399–1413.

NICHD Early Child Care Research Network. (2002). Child-care structure to process to outcome: Direct and indirect effects of child-care quality on young children's development. *Psychological Science, 13,* 199–206.

Nicoladis, E., & Genesee, F. (1997). Language development in preschool bilingual children. *Journal of Speech-Language Pathology & Audiology, 21,* 258–270.

Nicolelis, M. A. L. (2001). Actions from thoughts. *Nature, 409,* 403–407.

Nikles, C. D., II, Brecht, D. L., Klinger, E., & Bursell, A. L. (1998). The effects of current concern- and nonconcern-related waking suggestions on nocturnal dream content. *Journal of Personality and Social Psychology, 75,* 242–255.

Nikula, R., Klinger, E., & Larson-Gutman, M. K. (1993). Current concerns and electrodermal reactivity: Responses to words and thoughts. *Journal of Personality, 61,* 63–84.

Ninan, P. T. (1999). The functional anatomy, neurochemistry, and pharmacology of anxiety. *Journal of Clinical Psychiatry, 60,* 12–17.

Nisbett, R. E., Caputo, C., Legant, P., & Maracek, J. (1973). Behavior as seen by the actor and as seen by the observer. *Journal of Personality and Social Psychology, 27,* 154–164.

Nisbett, R. E., & Cohen, D. (1996). *Culture of honor: The psychology of violence in the south*. Boulder, CO: Westview Press.

Nisbett, R. E., & Wilson, T. D. (1977). Telling more than we can know: Verbal reports on mental processes. *Psychological Review, 84,* 231–259.

Nishino, S., Mignot, E., & Dement, W. C. (1995). Sedative-hypnotics. In A. F. Schatzberg & C. B. Nemeroff (Eds.), *American Psychiatric Press textbook of psychopharmacology*. (pp. 405–416). Washington, DC: American Psychiatric Press.

Nissen, M. J., & Bullemer, P. (1987). Attentional requirements of learning: Evidence from performance measures. *Cognitive Psychology, 19,* 1–32.

Nolen-Hoeksema, S. (1987). Sex differences in unipolar depression: Evidence and theory. *Psychological Bulletin, 101,* 259–282.

Nolen-Hoeksema, S. (1990). *Sex differences in depression*. Stanford: Stanford University Press.

Norcross, J. C., Hedges, M., & Castle, P. H. (2002). Psychologists conducting psychotherapy in 2001: A study of the Division 29 membership. *Psychotherapy: Theory/Research/Practice/Training, 39,* 97–102.

Norton, A. J. (1987). Families and children in the year 2000. *Children Today,* July–August, 6–9.

Norton, G. R., Harrison, B., Hauch, J., & Rhodes, L. (1985). Characteristics of people with infrequent panic attacks. *Journal of Abnormal Psychology, 94,* 216–221.

Nosanchuk, T. A., & Lightstone, J. (1974). Canned laughter and public and private conformity. *Journal of Personality & Social Psychology, 29,* 153–156.

Novaco, R. W. (1977). Stress inoculation: A cognitive therapy for anger. *Journal of Consulting & Clinical Psychology, 45,* 600–608.

Nunn, J. A., Gregory, L. J., & Brammer, M. (2002). Functional magnetic resonance imaging of synesthesia: Activation of V4/V8 by spoken words. *Nature Neuroscience, 5,* 371–375.

Nuttin, J. M. (1985). Narcissism beyond Gestalt and awareness: The name letter effect. *European Journal of Social Psychology, 15,* 353–361.

Nyberg, L., McIntosh, A. R., Houle, S., Nilsson, L.-G., & Tulving, E. (1996). Activation of medial temporal structures during episodic memory retrieval. *Nature, 380,* 715–717.

O'Connor, T. G., & Ruter, M. (2000). Attachment disorder following early severe deprivation: Extension and longitudinal follow-up. *Journal of the American Academy of Child and Adolescent Psychiatry, 39,* 703–712.

O'Laughlin, M. J., & Malle, B. F. (2002). How people explain actions performed by groups and individuals. *Journal of Personality and Social Psychology, 82,* 33–48.

O'Sullivan, L. F., & Allegeier, E. R. (1998). Feigning sexual desire: Consenting to unwanted sexual activity in heterosexual dating relationships. *Journal of Sex Research, 35,* 234–243.

Oakes, L. M., & Cohen, L. B. (1990). Infant perception of a causal event. *Cognitive Development, 5,* 193–207.

Oately, K., Keltner, D., & Jenkins, J. M. (2006). *Understanding emotions* (2nd ed.). Malden, MA: Blackwell.

Ochsner, K. N. (2000). Are affective events richly recollected or simply familiar? The experience and process of recognizing feelings past. *Journal of Experimental Psychology: General, 129,* 242–261.

Ochsner, K. N., Bunge, S. A., Gross, J. J., & Gabrieli, J. D. E. (2002). Rethinking feelings: An fMRI study of the cognitive regulation of emotion. *Journal of Cognitive Neuroscience, 14,* 1215–1229.

Office of the Press Secretary. (2002, July 21). Homeland Security presidential directive 3. Retrieved August 2007 from http://www.whitehouse.gov/news/releases/2002/03/20020312-5.html

Ofshe, R. J. (1992). Inadvertent hypnosis during interrogation: False confession due to dissociative state, misidentified multiple personality, and the satanic cult hypothesis. *International Journal of Clinical and Experimental Hypnosis, 40,* 125–126.

Ofshe, R., & Watters, E. (1994). *Making monsters: False memories, psychotherapy, and sexual hysteria.* New York: Scribner/Macmillan.

Öhman, A., & Dimberg, U. (1978). Facial expressions as conditioned stimuli for electrodermal responses: A case of preparedness? *Journal of Personality and Social Psychology, 36,* 1251–1258.

Öhman, A., Dimberg, U., & Öst, L. G. (1985). Animal and social phobias: Biological constraints on learned fear responses. In S. Reiss & R. Bootzin (Eds.), *Theoretical issues in behavior therapy* (pp. 123–175). New York: Academic Press.

Öhman, A., & Mineka, S. (2001). Fears, phobias, and preparedness: Toward an evolved model of fear and fear learning. *Psychological Review, 108,* 483–522.

Okagaki, L., & Sternberg, R. J. (1993). Parental beliefs and children's school performance. *Child Development, 64,* 36–56.

Olausson, P. O., Haglund, B., Weitoft, G. R., & Cnattingius, S. (2001). Teenage child-bearing and long-term socioeconomic consequences: A case study in Sweden. *Family Planning Perspectives, 33,* 70–74.

Oldham, J. M., Skodol, A. E., & Bender, D. S. (2005). *The American Psychiatric Publishing textbook of personality disorders.* Washington, DC: American Psychiatric Publishing.

Olds, J. (1956, October). Pleasure center in the brain. *Scientific American, 195,* 105–116.

Olds, J., & Fobes, J. I. (1981). The central basis of motivation: Intracranial self-stimulation studies. *Annual Review of Psychology, 32,* 523–574.

Olds, J., & Milner, P. (1954). Positive reinforcement produced by electrical stimulation of septal areas and other regions of rat brains. *Journal of Comparative and Physiological Psychology, 47,* 419–427.

Ollers, D. K., & Eilers, R. E. (1988). The role of audition in infant babbling. *Child Development, 59,* 441–449.

Oltmanns, T. F., Neale, J. M., & Davison, G. C. (1991). *Case studies in abnormal psychology* (3rd ed.). New York: Wiley.

Oltmanns, T. F., & Turkheimer, E. (2006). Perceptions of self and others regarding pathological personality traits. In R. Kreuger & J. Tackett (Eds.), *Personality and psychopathology* (pp. 71–111). New York: Guilford Press.

Olton, D. S., & Samuelson, R. J. (1976). Remembrance of places passed: Spatial memory in rats. *Journal of Experimental Psychology: Animal Behavior Processes, 2,* 97–116.

Orban, G. A., Van Essen, D., & Vanduffel, W. (2004). Comparative mapping of higher visual areas in monkeys and humans. *Trends in Cognitive Sciences, 8,* 315–324.

Orne, M. T., & Evans, F. J. (1965). Social control in the psychological experiment: Antisocial behavior and hypnosis. *Journal of Personality and Social Psychology, 1,* 189–200.

Öst, L.-G., Lindahl, I.-L., Sterner, U., & Jerremalm, A. (1984). Exposure in vivo vs. applied relaxation in the treatment of blood phobia. *Behaviour Research and Therapy, 22,* 205–216.

Oswald, L., Taylor, A. M., & Triesman, M. (1960). Discriminative responses to stimulation during human sleep. *Brain, 83,* 440–453.

Owen, A. M., Coleman, M. R., Boly, M., Davis, M. H., Laureys, S., & Pickard, J. D. (2006). Detecting awareness in the vegetative state. *Science, 313,* 1402.

Owens, W. A. (1966). Age and mental abilities: A second adult follow-up. *Journal of Educational Psychology, 57,* 311–325.

Paivio, A. (1969). Mental imagery in associative learning and memory. *Psychological Review, 76,* 241–263.

Paivio, A. (1971). *Imagery and verbal processes.* New York: Holt, Reinhart and Winston.

Paivio, A. (1986). *Mental representations: A dual coding approach.* New York: Oxford University Press.

Palmieri, R. M., Ingersoll, C. D., & Stone, M. B. (2002). Center-of-pressure parameters used in the assessment of postural control. *Journal of Sport Rehabilitation, 11,* 51–66.

Pande, A. C., Davidson, J. R. T., Jefferson, J. W., Janney, C. A., Katzelnick, D. J., Weisler, R. H., et al. (1999). Treatment of social phobia with gabapentin: A placebo-controlled study. *Journal of Clinical Psychopharmacology, 19,* 341–348.

Pande, A. C., Pollack, M. H., Crockatt, J., Greiner, M., Chouinard, G., R. Bruce Lydiard, R., et al. (2000). Placebo-controlled study of gabapentin treatment of panic disorder. *Journal of Clinical Psychopharmacology, 20,* 467–471.

Papez, J. W. (1937). A proposed mechanism of emotion. *Archives of Neurology and Pathology, 38,* 725–743.

Parkinson, B., & Totterdell, P. (1999). Classifying affect-regulation strategies. *Cognition and Emotion, 13,* 277–303.

Parrott, A. C. (2001). Human psychopharmacology of Ecstasy (MDMA): A review of 15 years of empirical research. *Human Psychopharmacology, 16,* 557–577.

Parrott, A. C., Morinan, A., Moss, M., & Scholey, A. (2004). *Understanding drugs and behavior.* Chichester, England: Wiley.

Parrott, W. G. (1993). Beyond hedonism: Motives for inhibiting good moods and for maintaining bad moods. In D. M. Wegner & J. W. Pennebaker (Eds.), *Handbook of mental control* (pp. 278–308). Englewood Cliffs, NJ: Prentice Hall.

**Parsons, T.** (1951). *The social system.* Glencoe, IL: Free Press.

**Partinen, M.** (1994). Epidemiology of sleep disorders. In M. H. Kryger, T. Roth, & W. C. Dement (Eds.), *Principles and practice of sleep medicine* (2nd ed.). Philadelphia: Saunders.

**Pasqual-Leone, A., Amedi, A., Fregni, F., & Merabet, L. B.** (2005). The plastic human brain cortex. *Annual Review of Neuroscience, 28,* 377–401.

**Pascual-Leone, A., Houser, C. M., Reese, K., Shotland, L. I., Grafman, J., Sato, S., et al.** (1993). Safety of rapid-rate transcranial magnetic stimulation in normal volunteers. *Electroencephalography and Clinical Neurophysiology, 89,* 120–130.

**Passini, F. T., & Norman, W. T.** (1966). A universal conception of personality structure? *Journal of Personality and Social Psychology, 4,* 44–49.

**Patrick, C. J., Cuthbert, B. N., & Lang, P. J.** (1994). Emotion in the criminal psychopath: Fear image processing. *Journal of Abnormal Psychology, 103,* 523–534.

**Patterson, C. J.** (1995). Lesbian mothers, gay fathers, and their children. In A. R. D'Augelli & C. J. Patterson (Eds.), *Lesbian, gay and bisexual identities across the lifespan: Psychological perspectives* (pp. 262–290). New York: Oxford University Press.

**Paul, A. M.** (2004). *The cult of personality testing.* New York: Free Press.

**Pavlidis, I., Eberhardt, N. L., & Levine, J. A.** (2002). Human behaviour: Seeing through the face of deception. *Nature, 415,* 35.

**Pavlov, I. P.** (1923a). New researches on conditioned reflexes. *Science, 58,* 359–361.

**Pavlov, I. P.** (1923b, July 23). Pavloff. *Time, 1*(21), 20–21.

**Pavlov, I. P.** (1927). *Conditioned reflexes.* Oxford, England: Oxford University Press.

**Pawlowski, B., Dunbar, R. I. M., & Lipowicz, A.** (2000). Tall men have more reproductive success. *Nature, 362,* 156.

**Pearce, J. M.** (1987). A model of stimulus generalization for Pavlovian conditioning. *Psychological Review, 84,* 61–73.

**Peissig, J. J., & Tarr, M. J.** (2007). Visual object recognition: Do we know more now than we did 20 years ago? *Annual Review of Psychology, 58,* 75–96.

**Pelham, B. W.** (1985). Self-investment and self-esteem: Evidence for a Jamesian model of self-worth. *Journal of Personality and Social Psychology, 69,* 1141–1150.

**Pelham, B. W., & Blanton, H.** (2003). *Conducting research in psychology: Measuring the weight of smoke* (2nd ed.). Pacific Grove, CA: Thomson Wadsworth.

**Pelham, B. W., Carvallo, M., & Jones, J. T.** (2005). Implicit egotism. *Current Directions in Psychological Science, 14,* 106–110.

**Pelham, B. W., Mirenberg, M. C., & Jones, J. T.** (2002). Why Susie sells seashells by the seashore: Implicit egotism and major life decisions. *Journal of Personality and Social Psychology, 82,* 469–487.

**Pendergrast, M.** (1995). *Victims of memory: Incest accusations and shattered lives.* Hinesburg, VT: Upper Access.

**Penfield, W., & Rasmussen, T.** (1950). *The cerebral cortex of man: A clinical study of localization of function.* New York: Macmillan.

**Pennebaker, J. W.** (1980). Perceptual and environmental determinants of coughing. *Basic and Applied Social Psychology, 1,* 83–91.

**Pennebaker, J. W.** (1982). *The psychology of physical symptoms.* New York: Springer.

**Pennebaker, J. W.** (1989). Confession, inhibition, and disease. *Advances in Experimental Social Psychology, 22,* 211–244.

**Pennebaker, J. W.** (1990). *Opening up: The healing power of confiding in others.* New York: Morrow.

**Pennebaker, J. W., & Beall, S. K.** (1986). Confronting a traumatic event: Toward an understanding of inhibition and disease. *Journal of Abnormal Psychology, 95,* 274–281.

**Pennebaker, J. W., Colder, M., & Sharp, L. K.** (1990). Accelerating the coping process. *Journal of Personality and Social Psychology, 58,* 528–537.

**Pennebaker, J. W., Dyer, M. A., Caulkins, R. S., Litowitz, D. L., Ackreman, P. L., Anderson, D. B., et al.** (1979). Don't the girls get prettier at closing time: A country and western application to psychology. *Personality and Social Psychology Bulletin, 5,* 122–125.

**Pennebaker, J. W., Kiecolt-Glaser, J. K., & Glaser, R.** (1988). Disclosure of traumas and immune function: Health implications for psychotherapy. *Journal of Consulting and Clinical Psychology, 56,* 239–245.

**Pennebaker, J. W., & Lightner, J. M.** (1980). Competition of internal and external information in an exercise setting. *Journal of Personality and Social Psychology, 39,* 165–174.

**Pennebaker, J. W., & Sanders, D. Y.** (1976). American graffiti: Effects of authority and reactance arousal. *Personality and Social Psychology Bulletin, 2,* 264–267.

**Perenin, M.-T., & Vighetto, A.** (1988). Optic ataxia: A specific disruption in visuomotor mechanisms. I. Different aspects of the deficit in reaching for objects. *Brain, 111,* 643–674.

**Perina, K.** (2002, May–June). Rx without the M.D. *Psychology Today, 46.*

**Perkins, D. N., & Grotzer, T. A.** (1997). Teaching intelligence. *American Psychologist, 52,* 1125–1133.

**Perloff, L. S., & Fetzer, B. K.** (1986). Self-other judgments and perceived vulnerability to victimization. *Journal of Personality and Social Psychology, 50,* 502–510.

**Perls, F. S., Hefferkine, R., & Goodman, P.** (1951). *Gestalt therapy: Excitement and growth in the human personality.* New York: Julian Press.

**Perrett, D. I., Burt, D. M., Penton-Voak, I. S., Lee, K. J., Rowland, D. A., & Edwards, R.** (1999). Symmetry and human facial attractiveness. *Evolution and Human Behavior, 20,* 295–307.

**Perrett, D. I., Rolls, E. T., & Caan, W.** (1982). Visual neurons responsive to faces in the monkey temporal cortex. *Experimental Brain Research, 47,* 329–342.

**Perris, C.** (1992). *Bipolar-unipolar distinction* (2nd ed.). New York: Guilford Press.

**Persons, J. B.** (1986). The advantages of studying psychological phenomena rather than psychiatric diagnoses. *American Psychologist, 41,* 1252–1260.

**Peskin, H.** (1973). Influence of the developmental schedule of puberty on learning and ego functioning. *Journal of Youth and Adolescence, 2,* 273–290.

**Peters, E. R., Joseph, S. A., & Garety, P. A.** (1999). Measurement of delusional ideation in the normal population: Introducing the PDI (Peters et al. Delusions Inventory). *Schizophrenia Bulletin, 25,* 553–576.

**Petersen, A. C.** (1985). Pubertal development as a cause of disturbance—Myths, realities, and unanswered questions. *Genetic Social and General Psychology Monographs, 111,* 205–232.

**Petersen, A. C., & Grockett, L.** (1985). Pubertal timing and grade effects on adjustment. *Journal of Youth and Adolescence, 14,* 191–206.

**Peterson, C., & Seligman, M. E. P.** (2004). *Character strengths and virtues: A handbook and classification.* Washington, DC: American Psychological Association.

**Peterson, C., & Siegal, M.** (1999). Representing inner worlds: Theory of mind in autistic, deaf and normal hearing children. *Psychological Science, 10,* 126–129.

**Peterson, L. R., & Peterson, M. J.** (1959). Short-term retention of individual verbal items. *Journal of Experimental Psychology, 58,* 193–198.

Peterson, S. E., Fox, P. T., Posner, M. I., Mintun, M. A., & Raichle, M. E. (1989). Positron emission tomographic studies of the processing of single words. *Journal of Cognitive Neuroscience, 1,* 154–170.

Petitto, L. A., & Marentette, P. F. (1991). Babbling in the manual mode: Evidence for the ontogeny of language. *Science, 251,* 1493–1496.

Petrie, K. P., Booth, R. J., & Pennebaker, J. W. (1998). The immunological effects of thought suppression. *Journal of Personality and Social Psychology, 75,* 1264–1272.

Petty, R. E., & Cacioppo, J. T. (1986). The elaboration likelihood model of persuasion. In L. Berkowitz (Ed.), *Advances in experimental social psychology* (Vol. 19, pp. 123–205). New York: Academic Press.

Petty, R. E., Cacioppo, J. T., & Goldman, R. (1981). Personal involvement as a determinant of argument-based persuasion. *Journal of Personality & Social Psychology, 41,* 847–855.

Petty, R. E., & Wegener, D. T. (1998). Attitude change: Multiple roles for persuasion variables. In D. T. Gilbert, S. T. Fiske, & G. Lindzey (Eds.), *The handbook of social psychology* (4th ed., Vol. 1, pp. 323–390). Boston: McGraw-Hill.

Pew Research Center for the People & the Press. (1997). *Motherhood today: A tougher job, less ably done.* Pew Research Center: Author.

Pew Research Center for the People & the Press. (2006). *Attitudes toward homosexuality in African countries.* Pew Research Center: Author.

Phelan, J., Link, B., Stueve, A., & Pescosolido, B. (1997). *Public conceptions of mental illness in 1950 in 1996: Has sophistication increased? Has stigma declined?* Paper presented at the American Sociological Association, Toronto, Ontario.

Phelan, J., Link, B., Stueve, A., & Pescosolido, B. (2000). Public conceptions of mental illness in 1950 and 1996: What is mental illness and is it to be feared? *Journal of Health and Social Behavior, 41,* 188–207.

Phelps, E. A. (2006). Emotion and cognition: Insights from studies of the human amygdala. *Annual Review of Psychology, 24,* 27–53.

Phelps, E. A., & LeDoux, J. L. (2005). Contributions of the amygdala to emotion processing: From animal models to human behavior. *Neuron, 48,* 175–187.

Phelps, E. A., O'Connor, K. J., Cunningham, W. A., Funayama, E. S., Gatenby, J. C., Gore, J. C., et al. (2000). Performance on indirect measures of race evaluation predicts amygdala activation. *Journal of Cognitive Neuroscience, 12,* 729–738.

Phillips, D. P., & Carstensen, L. L. (1986). Clustering of teenage suicides after television news stories about suicide. *New England Journal of Medicine, 315,* 685–689.

Phillips, F. (2002, January 24). Jump in cigarette sales tied to Sept. 11 attacks. *Boston Globe,* p. B1.

Piaf, E. (1990). *My life.* London: Peter Owen.

Piaget, J. (1954a). *The construction of reality in the child.* New York: Basic Books.

Piaget, J. (1954b). *The child's concept of number.* New York: Norton.

Piaget, J. (1965). *The moral judgment of the child.* New York: Free Press. (Originally published 1932)

Piaget, J. (1977). The first year of life of the child. In H. E. Gruber & J. J. Voneche (Eds.), *The essential Piaget: An interpretative reference and guide* (pp. 198–214). New York: Basic Books. (Originally published 1927)

Piaget, J., & Inhelder, B. (1969). *The psychology of the child* (H. Weaver, Trans.). New York: Basic Books.

Pinel, J. P. J., Assanand, S., & Lehman, D. R. (2000). Hunger, eating, and ill health. *American Psychologist, 55,* 1105–1116.

Pines, A. M. (1993). Burnout: An existential perspective. In W. B. Schaufeli, C. Maslach & T. Marek (Eds.), *Professional burnout: Recent developments in theory and research* (pp. 33–51). Washington, DC: Taylor & Francis.

Pines, A., M., & Aronson, E. (1988). *Career burnout: Causes and cures* (2nd ed.). New York: Free Press.

Pinker, S. (1994). *The language instinct.* New York: Morrow.

Pinker, S. (1997a). *How the mind works.* New York: Norton.

Pinker, S. (1997b). Evolutionary psychology: An exchange. *New York Review of Books, 44,* 55–58.

Pinker, S., & Bloom, P. (1990). Natural language and natural selection. *Behavioral & Brain Sciences, 13,* 707–784.

Pipes, D. (2002, October 29). The snipers: Crazy or jihadis? *New York Post.* Retrieved September 15, 2007, from http://www.danielpipes.org/article/493

Pitman, R. K., Sanders, K. M., Zusman, R. M., Healy, A. R., Cheema, F., Lasko, N. B., Cahill, L., et al. (2002). Pilot study of secondary prevention of posttraumatic stress disorder with propranolol. *Biological Psychiatry, 51,* 189–192.

Plato. (1956). *Protagoras* (O. Jowett, Trans.). New York: Prentice Hall.

Plomin, R., & Caspi, A. (1999). Behavioral genetics and personality. In L. A. Pervin & O. P. John (Eds.), *Handbook of personality: Theory and research* (Vol. 2, pp. 251–276). New York: Guilford Press.

Plomin, R., De Fries, J. C., McClearn, G. E., & Rutter, M. (1997). *Behavior genetics* (3rd ed.). New York: Freeman.

Plomin, R., DeFries, J. C., McClearn, G. E., & McGuffin, P. (2001a). *Behavioral genetics.* (4th ed.). New York: Freeman.

Plomin, R., Hill, L., Craig, I. W., McGuffin, P., Purcell, S., Sham, P., et al. (2001b). A genome-wide scan of 1842 DNA markers for allelic associations with general cognitive ability: A five-stage design using DNA pooling and extreme selected groups. *Behavior Genetics, 31,* 497–509.

Plomin, R., Scheier, M. F., Bergeman, C. S., Pedersen, N. L., Nesselroade, J. R., & McClearn, G. E. (1992). Optimism, pessimism, and mental health: A twin/adoption analysis. *Personality and Individual Differences, 13,* 921–930.

Plomin, R., & Spinath, F. M. (2004). Intelligence: Genetics, genes, and genomics. *Journal of Personality and Social Psychology, 86,* 112–129.

Plotnik, J. M., de Waal, F. B. M., & Reiss, D. (2006). Self-recognition in an Asian elephant. *Proceedings of the National Academy of Science, 103,* 17053–17057.

Polivy, J., & Herman, C. P. (1992). Undieting: A program to help people stop dieting. *International Journal of Eating Disorders, 11,* 261–268.

Poole, D. A., Lindsay, S. D., Memon, A., & Bull, R. (1995). Psychotherapy and the recovery of memories of childhood sexual abuse: U.S. and British practitioners' opinions, practices, and experiences. *Journal of Consulting and Clinical Psychology, 63,* 426–487.

Pope, A. W., & Bierman, K. L. (1999). Predicting adolescent peer problems and antisocial activities: The relative roles of aggression and dysregulation. *Developmental Psychology, 35,* 335–346.

Posey, T. B., & Losch, M. E. (1983). Auditory hallucinations of hearing voices in 375 normal subjects. *Imagination, Cognition and Personality, 3,* 99–113.

Posner, M. I., & Raichle, M. E. (1994). *Images of mind.* New York: Freeman.

Post, R. M. (2004). Differing psychotropic profiles of the anticonvulsants in bipolar and other psychiatric disorders. *Clinical Neuroscience Research, 4,* 9–30.

Posthuma, D., & de Geus, E. J. C. (2006). Progress in the molecular-genetic study of intelligence. *Current Directions in Psychological Science, 15,* 151–155.

Postman, L., & Underwood, B. J. (1973). Critical issues in interference theory. *Memory & Cognition, 1,* 19–40.

Prasada, S., & Pinker, S. (1993). Generalizations of regular and irregular morphology. *Language and Cognitive Processes, 8,* 1–56.

Pratkanis, A. R. (1992). The cargo-cult science of subliminal persuasion. *Skeptical Inquirer, 16,* 260–272.

Pratkanis, A. R., Greenwald, A. G., Leippe, M. R., & Baumgardner, M. H. (1988). In search of reliable persuasion effects: III. The sleeper effect is dead: Long live the sleeper effect. *Journal of Personality and Social Psychology, 54,* 203–218.

Premack, D. (1962). Reversibility of the reinforcement relation. *Science, 136,* 255–257.

Pressman, S. D., Cohen, S., Miller, G. E., Barkin, A., Rabin, B. S., & Treanor, J. J. (2005). Loneliness, social network size, and immune response to influenza vaccination in college freshmen. *Health Psychology, 24,* 297–306.

Prochaska, J. J., & Sallis, J. F. (2004). A randomized controlled trial of single versus multiple health behavior change: Promoting physical activity and nutrition among adolescents. *Health Psychology, 23,* 314–318.

Provine, R. R. (2000). *Laughter: A scientific investigation.* New York: Viking.

Prudic, J., Haskett, R. F., Mulsant, B., Malone, K. M., Pettinati, H. M., Stephens, S., et al. (1996). Resistance to antidepressant medications and short-term clinical response to ECT. *American Journal of Psychiatry, 153,* 985–992.

Pruitt, D. G. (1998). Social conflict. In D. T. Gilbert, S. T. Fiske, & G. Lindzey (Eds.), *The handbook of social psychology* (4th ed., Vol. 2, pp. 470–503). New York: McGraw-Hill.

Putnam, F. W., Guroff, J. J., Silberman, E. K., Barban, L., & Post, R. M. (1986). The clinical phenomenology of multiple personality disorder: Review of 100 recent cases. *Journal of Clinical Psychiatry, 47,* 285–293.

Pyszczynski, T., Holt, J., & Greenberg, J. (1987). Depression, self-focused attention, and expectancy for positive and negative future life events for self and others. *Journal of Personality and Social Psychology, 52,* 994–1001.

Pyszczynski, T., Solomon, S., & Greenberg, J. (2003). *In the wake of 9/11: The psychology of terror.* Washington, DC: American Psychological Association.

Quattrone, G. A. (1982). Behavioral consequences of attributional bias. *Social Cognition, 1,* 358–378.

Quattrone, G. A., & Jones, E. E. (1980). The perception of variability within in-groups and out-groups: Implications for the law of small numbers. *Journal of Personality and Social Psychology, 38,* 141–152.

Querleu, D., Lefebvre, C., Titran, M., Renard, X., Morillon, M., & Crepin, G. (1984). Reactivite de bouveau-ne de moins de deux heures de vie a la voix maternelle. *Journal de Gynecologie Obstetrique et de Biologie de la Reproduction, 13,* 125–134.

Quiroga, R. Q., Reddy, L., Kreiman, G., Koch, C., & Fried, I. (2005). Invariant visual representation by single neurons in the human brain. *Nature, 435,* 1102–1107.

Rabin, B. M., & Rabin, J. S. (1984) Acquisition of radiation- and lithium chloride-induced conditioned taste aversions in anesthetized rats. *Animal Learning & Behavior, 12,* 439–441.

Rachman, S. J., & DeSilva, P. (1978). Abnormal and normal obsessions. *Behavioral Research and Therapy, 16,* 223–248.

Radford, E., & Radford, M. A. (1949). *Encyclopedia of superstitions.* New York: Philosophical Library.

Rahe, R. H., Meyer, M., Smith, M., Klaer, G., & Holmes, T. H. (1964). Social stress and illness onset. *Journal of Psychosomatic Research, 8,* 35–44.

Raichle, M. E., Fiez, J. A., Videen, T. O., MacLeod, A.-M. K., Pardo, J. V., Fox, P. T., et al. (1994). Practice-related changes in human brain functional anatomy during nonmotor learning. *Cerebral Cortex, 4,* 8–26.

Raichle, M. E., & Mintun, M. A. (2006). Brain work and brain imaging. *Annual Review of Neuroscience, 29,* 449–476.

Ramachandran, V. S., & Blakeslee, S. (1998). *Phantoms in the brain: Probing the mysteries of the human mind.* New York: Morrow.

Ramachandran, V. S., & Hubbard, E. M. (2003). Hearing colors, tasting shapes. *Scientific American, 288,* 52–59.

Ramachandran, V. S., Rodgers-Ramachandran, D., & Stewart, M. (1992). Perceptual correlates of massive cortical reorganization. *Science, 258,* 1159–1160.

Rapaport, D. (1946). *Diagnostic Psychological Testing: The theory, statistical evaluation, and diagnostic application of a battery of tests.* Chicago: Year Book Publishers.

Rapoport, J. (1989). *The boy who couldn't stop washing: The experience and treatment of obsessive-compulsive disorder.* New York: Penguin.

Rapport, R. (2005). *Nerve endings: The discovery of the synapse.* New York: Norton.

Raskin, N. J., & Rogers, C. R. (2000). Person-centered therapy. In R. J. Corsini & D. Wedding (Eds.), *Current psychotherapies* (6th ed., pp. 133–167). Itasca, IL: F. E. Peacock, Publishers.

Raz, N. (2000). Aging of the brain and its impact on cognitive performance: Integration of structural and functional findings. In F. I. M. Craik & T. A. Salthouse (Eds.), *The handbook of aging and cognition* (pp. 1–90). Mahwah, NJ: Erlbaum.

Read, K. E. (1965). *The high valley.* London: Allen and Unwin.

Reason, J., & Mycielska, K. (1982). *Absent-minded?: The psychology of mental lapses and everyday errors.* Englewood Cliffs: Prentice-Hall.

Reber, A. S. (1967). Implicit learning of artificial grammars. *Journal of Verbal Learning and Verbal Behavior, 6,* 855–863.

Reber, A. S. (1996). *Implicit learning and tacit knowledge: An essay on the cognitive unconscious.* New York: Oxford University Press.

Reber, A. S., & Allen, R. (2000). Individual differences in implicit learning. In R. G. Kunzendorf & B. Wallace (Eds.), *Individual differences in conscious experience.* Philadelphia: John Benjamins.

Reber, A. S., Walkenfeld, F. F., & Hernstadt, R. (1991). Implicit learning: Individual differences and IQ. *Journal of Experimental Psychology: Learning, Memory, and Cognition, 17,* 888–896.

Reber, P. J., Gitelman, D. R., Parrish, T. B., & Mesulam, M. M. (2003). Dissociating explicit and implicit category knowledge with fMRI. *Journal of Cognitive Neuroscience, 15,* 574–583.

Rechsthaffen, A., Gilliland, M. A., Bergmann, B. M., & Winter, J. B. (1983). Physiological correlates of prolonged sleep deprivation in rats. *Science, 221,* 182–184.

Reed, G. (1988). *The psychology of anomalous experience* (Rev. ed.). Buffalo, NY: Prometheus Books.

Regan, P. C. (1998). What if you can't get what you want? Willingness to compromise ideal mate selection standards as a function of sex, mate value, and relationship context. *Personality and Social Psychology Bulletin, 24,* 1294–1303.

Regier, D. A., Narrow, W. E., Rae, D. S., Manderscheid, R. W., Locke, B. Z., & Goodwin, F. K. (1993). The de facto US mental and addictive disorders service system: Epidemiologic Catchment Area prospective 1-year prevalence rates of disorders and services. *Archives of General Psychiatry, 41,* 934–941.

Reichhardt, T. (2003). Playing with fire? *Nature, 424,* 367–368.

Reinarman, C., Cohen, P. D. A., & Kaal, H. L. (2004). The limited relevance of drug policy: Cannabis in Amsterdam and San Francisco. *American Journal of Public Health, 94,* 836–842.

Reis, S. M., Neu, T. W., & McGuire, J. M. (1995). *Talents in two places: Case studies of high ability students with learning disabilities who have achieved.* Storrs, CT: University of Connecticut, National Research Center on the Gifted and Talented.

Reiss, D., & Marino, L. (2001). Mirror self-recognition in the bottlenose dolphin: A case of cognitive convergence. *Proceedings of the National Academy of Sciences, 98,* 5937–5942.

Reissland, N. (1988). Neonatal imitation in the first hour of life: Observations in rural Nepal. *Developmental Psychology, 24,* 464–469.

Reiter, E. O., & Lee, P. A. (2001). Have the onset and tempo of puberty changed? *Archives of Pediatrics and Adolescent Medicine, 155,* 988–989.

Renner, M. J., & Mackin, R. (1998). A life stress instrument for classroom use. *Teaching of Psychology, 25,* 46–48.

Repacholi, B. M., & Gopnik, A. (1997). Early reasoning about desires: Evidence from 14- and 18-month-olds. *Developmental Psychology, 33,* 12–21.

Rescorla, R. A. (1966). Predictability and number of pairings in Pavlovian fear conditioning. *Psychonomic Science, 4,* 383–384.

Rescorla, R. A. (1988). Classical conditioning: It's not what you think it is. *American Psychologist, 43,* 151–160.

Rescorla, R. A. (2006). Stimulus generalization of excitation and inhibition. *Quarterly Journal of Experimental Psychology, 59,* 53–67.

Rescorla, R. A., & Wagner, A. R. (1972). A theory of Pavlovian conditioning: Variations in effectiveness of reinforcement and nonreinforcement. In A. Black & W. F. Prokasky, Jr. (Eds.), *Classical conditioning II.* New York: Appleton-Century-Crofts.

Ressler, K. J., & Nemeroff, C. B. (1999) Role of norepinephrine in the pathophysiology and treatment of mood disorders. *Biological Psychiatry, 46,* 1219–1233.

Rhodes, G., Yoshikawa, S., Clark, A., Lee, K., McKay, R., & Akamatsu, S. (2001). Attractiveness of facial averageness and symmetry in non-Western cultures: In search of biologically based standards of beauty. *Perception, 30,* 611–625.

Richards, M. H., Crowe, P. A., Larson, R., & Swarr, A. (1998). Developmental patterns and gender differences in the experience of peer companionship during adolescence. *Child Development, 69,* 154–163.

Richert, E. S. (1997). Excellence with equity in identification and programming. In N. Colangelo & G. A. Davis (Eds.), *Handbook of gifted education* (2nd ed., pp. 75–88). Boston: Allyn & Bacon.

Richters, J., de Visser, R., Rissel, C., & Smith, A. (2006). Sexual practices at last heterosexual encounter and occurrence of orgasm in a national survey. *Journal of Sex Research, 43,* 217–226.

Rieber, R. W. (Ed.). (1980). *Wilhelm Wundt and the making of scientific psychology.* New York: Plenum Press.

Riefer, D. M., Kevari, M. K., & Kramer, D. L. F. (1995). Name that tune: Eliciting the tip-of-the-tongue experience using auditory stimuli. *Psychological Reports, 77,* 1379–1390.

Rizzolatti, G. (2004). The mirror-neuron system and imitation. In S. Hurley & N. Chater (Eds.), *Perspectives on imitation: From mirror neurons to memes* (pp. 55–76). Cambridge, MA: MIT Press.

Rizzolatti, G., & Craighero, L. (2004.) The mirror-neuron system. *Annual Review of Neuroscience, 27,* 169–192.

Roberson, D., Davidoff, J., Davies, I. R. L., & Shapiro, L. R. (2004). The development of color categories in two languages: A longitudinal study. *Journal of Experimental Psychology: General, 133,* 554–571.

Roberts, G. A. (1991). Delusional belief and meaning in life: A preferred reality? *British Journal of Psychiatry, 159,* 20–29.

Roberts, G. A., & McGrady, A. (1996). Racial and gender effects on the relaxation response: Implications for the development of hypertension. *Biofeedback and Self-Regulation, 21,* 51–62.

Robins, E., & Guze, S. B. (1972). Classification of affective disorders: The primary-secondary, the endogenous-reactive, and the neurotic-psychotic concepts. In T. A. Williams, M. M. Katz & J. A. Shields (Eds.), *Recent advances in the psychobiology of depressive illnesses* (pp. 283–293). Washington, DC: U.S. Government Printing Office.

Robins, L. N., Helzer, J. E., Hesselbrock, M., & Wish, E. (1980). Vietnam veterans three years after Vietnam. In L. Brill & C. Winick (Eds.), *The yearbook of substance use and abuse* (Vol. 11). New York: Human Sciences Press.

Robins, L. N., Helzer, J. E., Weissman, M. M., Orvaschel, H., Gruenberg, E., Burke, J. D., et al. (1984). Lifetime prevalence of specific psychiatric disorders in three sites. *Archives of General Psychiatry, 41,* 949–958.

Robins, L. N., & Regier, D. A. (1991). *Psychiatric disorders in America.* New York: Free Press.

Robinson, A., & Clinkenbeard, P. R. (1998). Giftedness: An exceptionality examined. *Annual Review of Psychology, 49,* 117–139.

Robinson, D. N. (1995). *An intellectual history of psychology.* Madison: University of Wisconsin Press.

Robinson, R. G., & Downhill, J. E. (1995). Lateralization of psychopathology in response to focal brain injury. In R. J. Davidson & K. Hugdahl (Eds.), *Brain asymmetry* (pp. 693–711). Cambridge, MA: MIT Press.

Robinson, W. A. (2006). *The last man who knew everything: Thomas Young.* London: Pi Press.

Rodieck, R. W. (1998). *The first steps in seeing.* Sunderland, MA: Sinauer.

Roediger III, H. L. (2000). Why retrieval is the key process to understanding human memory. In E. Tulving (Ed.), *Memory, consciousness, and the brain: The Tallinn conference* (pp. 52–75). Philadelphia: Psychology Press.

Roediger III, H. L., & McDermott, K. B. (1995). Creating false memories: Remembering words not presented in lists. *Journal of Experimental Psychology: Learning, Memory, and Cognition, 21,* 803–814.

Roediger III, H. L., & McDermott, K. B. (2000). Tricks of memory. *Current Directions in Psychological Science, 9,* 123–127.

Roediger III, H. L., Weldon, M. S., & Challis, B. H. (1989). Explaining dissociations between implicit and explicit measures of retention: A processing account. In H. L. I. Roediger & F. I. M. Craik (Eds.), *Varieties of memory and consciousness: Essays in honor of Endel Tulving* (pp. 3–41). Hillsdale, NJ: Erlbaum.

Rogers, C. R. (1951). *Client-centered therapy: Its current practice, implications, and theory.* Boston: Houghton Mifflin.

Rogers, C. R. (1957). The necessary and sufficient conditions for therapeutic personality change. *Journal of Consulting Psychology, 21,* 95–103.

Rogers, C. R. (1961). *On becoming a person.* Boston: Houghton Mifflin.

Rogers, T. B., Kuiper, N. A., & Kirker, W. S. (1977). Self-reference and the encoding of personal information. *Journal of Personality and Social Psychology, 35,* 677–688.

Rosa, L., Rosa, E., Sarner, L., & Barrett, S. (1998). A close look at therapeutic touch. *Journal of the American Medical Association, 279,* 1005–1010.

Rosch, E. H. (1973). Natural categories. *Cognitive Psychology, 4,* 328–350.

Rosch, E. H. (1975). Cognitive representations of semantic categories. *Journal of Experimental Psychology: General, 104,* 192–233.

Rosch, E. H., & Mervis, C. B. (1975). Family resemblances: Studies in the internal structure of categories. *Cognitive Psychology, 7,* 573–605.

Rose, S. P. R. (2002). Smart drugs: Do they work? Are they ethical? Will they be legal? *Nature Reviews Neuroscience 3,* 975–979.

Roseman, I. J. (1984). Cognitive determinants of emotion: A structural theory. *Review of Personality and Social Psychology, 5,* 11–36.

**Roseman, I. J., & Smith, C. A.** (2001). Appraisal theory: Overview, assumptions, varieties and controversies. In K. R. Scherer, A. Schorr, & T. Johnstone (Eds.), *Appraisal processes in emotion: Theory, methods, research* (pp. 3–19). New York: Oxford University Press.

**Rosenberg, M.** (1965). *Society and the adolescent self-image.* Princeton, NJ: Princeton University Press.

**Rosenhan, D.** (1973). On being sane in insane places. *Science, 179,* 250–258.

**Rosenstein, M. J., Milazzo-Sayre, L. J., & Manderscheid, R. W.** (1990). Characteristics of persons using specifically inpatient, outpatient, and partial care programs in 1986. In M. A. Sonnenschein (Ed.), *Mental health in the United States* (pp. 139–172). Washington, DC: U.S. Government Printing Office.

**Rosenthal, R., & Fode, K. L.** (1963). The effect of experimenter bias on the performance of the albino rat. *Behavioral Science, 8,* 183–189.

**Ross, B. H.** (1984). Remindings and their effects in learning a cognitive skill. *Cognitive Psychology, 16,* 371–416.

**Ross, D. F., Ceci, S. J., Dunning, D., & Toglia, M. P.** (1994). Unconscious transference and mistaken identity: When a witness misidentifies a familiar but innocent person. *Journal of Applied Psychology, 79,* 918–930.

**Ross, L.** (1977). The intuitive psychologist and his shortcomings: Distortions in the attribution process. *Advances in Experimental Social Psychology, 10,* 173–220.

**Ross, L., Amabile, T. M., & Steinmetz, J. L.** (1977). Social roles, social control, and biases in social-perception processes. *Journal of Personality and Social Psychology, 35,* 485–494.

**Ross, L., Lepper, M. R., & Hubbard, M.** (1975). Perseverance in self-perception and social perception: Biased attribution processes in the debriefing paradigm. *Journal of Personality and Social Psychology, 32,* 880–892.

**Ross, L., & Nisbett, R. E.** (1991). *The person and the situation.* New York: McGraw-Hill.

**Roth, H. P., & Caron, H. S.** (1978). Accuracy of doctors' estimates and patients' statements on adherence to a drug regimen. *Clinical Pharmacology and Therapeutics, 23,* 361–370.

**Roth, M., & Mountjoy, C. Q.** (1997). The need for the concept of neurotic depression. In G. B. C. H. S. Akiskal (Ed.), *Dysthymia and the spectrum of chronic depressions* (pp. 96–129). New York: Guilford Press.

**Rothbart, M. K., & Bates, J. E.** (1998). Temperament. In W. Damon (Series Ed.) & N. Eisenberg (Vol. Ed.), *Handbook of child psychology: Vol. 3. Social emotional and personality development* (5th ed., pp. 105–176). New York: Wiley.

**Rothbaum, B. O., Hodges, L., Watson, B. A., Kessler, G. D., & Opdyke, D.** (1996). Virtual reality exposure therapy in the treatment of fear of flying: A case report. *Behaviour Research & Therapy, 34,* 477–481.

**Rothbaum, B. O., Meadows, E. A., Resick, P., & Foy, D. W.** (2000). Cognitive-behavioral therapy. In E. B. Foa, T. M. Keane, & M. J. Friedman (Eds.), *Effective treatments for PTSD* (pp. 60–83). New York: Guilford Press.

**Rothermundt, M., Arolt, V., & Bayer, T. A.** (2001). Review of immunological and immunopathological findings in schizophrenia. *Brain, Behavior, and Immunity, 15,* 319–339.

**Rotstein, A. H.** (2006, November 11). Despite 2–1 defeat on Election Day, backer of $1 million voter lottery still likes the idea. *Associated Press.*

**Rotter, J. B.** (1966). Generalized expectancies for internal versus external locus of control of reinforcement. *Psychological Monographs: General and Applied, 80.* 1–28.

**Rotton, L.** (1992). Trait humor and longevity: Do comics have the last laugh? *Health Psychology, 11,* 262–266.

**Rowa, K., Antony, M. M., Brar, S., Summerfeldt, L. J., & Swinson, R. P.** (2000). Treatment histories of patients with three anxiety disorders. *Depression and Anxiety, 12,* 92–98.

**Rowland, L. W.** (1939). Will hypnotized persons try to harm themselves or others? *Journal of Abnormal and Social Psychology, 34,* 114–117.

**Roy-Byrne, P. P., & Cowley, D.** (1998). *Pharmacological treatment of panic, generalized anxiety, and phobic disorders.* New York: Oxford University Press.

**Roy-Byrne, P. P., & Cowley, D. S.** (2002). Pharmacological treatments for panic disorder, generalized anxiety disorder, specific phobia, and social anxiety disorder. In P. E. Nathan & J. M. Gorman (Eds.), *A guide to treatments that work* (2nd ed., pp. 337–365). New York: Oxford University Press.

**Royzman, E. B., Cassidy, K. W., & Baron, J.** (2003). "I know, you know": Epistemic egocentrism in children and adults. *Review of General Psychology, 7,* 38–65.

**Rozanski, A., Blumenthal, J. A., & Kaplan, J.** (1999). Impact of psychological factors on the pathogenesis of cardiovascular disease and implications for therapy. *Circulation, 99,* 2192–2217.

**Rozin, P.** (1968). Are carbohydrate and protein intakes separately regulated? *Journal of Comparative and Physiological Psychology, 65,* 23–29.

**Rozin, P., Bauer, R., & Catanese, D.** (2003). Food and life, pleasure and worry, among American college students: Gender differences and regional similarities. *Journal of Personality and Social Psychology, 85,* 132–141.

**Rozin, P., Dow, S., Moscovitch, M., & Rajaram, S.** (1998). What causes humans to begin and end a meal? A role for memory for what has been eaten, as evidenced by a study of multiple meal eating in amnesic patients. *Psychological Science, 9,* 392–396.

**Rozin, P., & Fallon, A. E.** (1987). A perspective on disgust. *Psychological Review, 94,* 23–41.

**Rozin, P., Haidt, J., & McCauley, C. R.** (1999). Disgust: The body and soul emotion. In T. Dalgleish & M. J. Power (Eds.), *Handbook of cognition and emotion* (pp. 429–445). New York: Wiley.

**Rozin, P., Hammer, L., Oster, H., Horowitz, T., & Marmora, V.** (1986a). The child's concept of food: Differentiation of categories of rejected substances in the 1.4 to 5 years range. *Appetite, 7,* 141–151.

**Rozin, P., Kabnick, K., Pete, E., Fischler, C., & Schields, C.** (2003). The ecology of eating: Smaller portion sizes in France than in the United States help explain the French paradox. *Psychological Science, 14,* 450–454.

**Rozin, P., & Kalat, J. W.** (1971). Specific hungers and poison avoidance as adaptive specializations of learning. *Psychological Review, 78,* 459–486.

**Rozin, P., Millman, L., & Nemeroff, C.** (1986b). Operation of the laws of sympathetic magic in disgust and other domains. *Journal of Personality and Social Psychology, 50,* 703–712.

**Rozin, P., Trachtenberg, S., & Cohen, A. B.** (2001). Stability of body image and body image dissatisfaction in American college students over about the last 15 years. *Appetite, 37,* 245–248.

**Rubenstein, A. J., Kalakanis, L., & Langlois, J. H.** (1999). Infant preferences for attractive faces: A cognitive explanation. *Developmental Psychology, 35,* 848–855.

**Rubin, B. D., & Katz, L. C.** (1999). Optical imaging of odorant representations in the mammalian olfactory bulb. *Neuron, 23,* 499–511.

**Rubin, Z.** (1973). *Liking and loving.* New York: Holt, Reinhart and Winston.

**Rude, S. S., Wenzlaff, R. M., Gibbs, B., Vane, J., & Whitney, T.** (2002). Negative processing biases predict subsequent depressive symptoms. *Cognition and Emotion, 16,* 423–440.

Rudman, L. A., Ashmore, R. D., & Gary, M. L. (2001). "Unlearning" automatic biases: The malleability of implicit prejudice and stereotypes. *Journal of Personality and Social Psychology, 81,* 856–868.

Rusbult, C. E. (1983). A longitudinal test of the investment model: The development (and deterioration) of satisfaction and commitment in heterosexual involvements. *Journal of Personality and Social Psychology, 45,* 101–117.

Rusbult, C. E., & Van Lange, P. A. M. (2003). Interdependence, interaction and relationships. *Annual Review of Psychology, 54,* 351–375.

Rusbult, C. E., Verette, J., Whitney, G. A., & Slovik, L. F. (1991). Accommodation processes in close relationships: Theory and preliminary empirical evidence. *Journal of Personality and Social Psychology, 60,* 53–78.

Rushton, J. P. (1995). Asian achievement, brain size, and evolution: Comment on A. H. Yee. *Educational Psychology Review, 7,* 373–380.

Russell, J. A. (1980). A circumplex model of affect. *Journal of Personality and Social Psychology, 39,* 1161–1178.

Rutter, M., O'Connor, T. G., & the English and Romanian Adoptees Study Team (2004). Are there biological programming effects for psychological development? Findings from a study of Romanian adoptees. *Developmental Psychology, 40,* 81–94.

Rutter, M., & Silberg, J. (2002). Gene-environment interplay in relation to emotional and behavioral disturbance. *Annual Review of Psychology, 53,* 463–490.

Ryan, R. M., & Deci, E. L. (2000). Self-determination theory and the facilitation of intrinsic motivation, social development, and well-being. *American Psychologist, 55,* 68–78.

Sachs, J. S. (1967). Recognition of semantic, syntactic, and lexical changes in sentences. *Psychonomic Bulletin, 1,* 17–18.

Sackeim, H. A., & Devanand, D. P. (1991). Dissociative disorders. In M. Hersen & S. M. Turner (Eds.), *Adult psychopathology and diagnosis* (2nd ed., pp. 279–322). New York: Wiley.

Sacks, O. (1995). *An anthropologist on Mars.* New York: Knopf.

Saffran, J. R., Aslin, R. N., & Newport, E. I. (1996). Statistical learning by 8-month-old infants. *Science, 274,* 1926–1928.

Salge, R. A., Beck, J. G., & Logan, A. (1988). A community survey of panic. *Journal of Anxiety Disorder, 2,* 157–167.

Salthouse, T. A. (1984). Effects of age and skill in typing. *Journal of Experimental Psychology: General, 113,* 345–371.

Salthouse, T. A. (1987). Age, experience, and compensation. In C. Schooler & K. W. Schaie (Eds.), *Cognitive functioning and social structure over the life course* (pp. 142–150). New York: Ablex.

Salthouse, T. A. (1996a). General and specific mediation of adult age differences in memory. *Journal of Gerontology: Series B: Psychological Sciences and Social Sciences, 51B,* P30–P42.

Salthouse, T. A. (1996b). The processing-speed theory of adult age differences in cognition. *Psychological Review, 103,* 403–428.

Salthouse, T. A. (2000). Pressing issues in cognitive aging. In D. Park & N. Schwartz (Eds.), *Cognitive aging: A primer.* Philadelphia: Psychology Press.

Salthouse, T. A. (2001). Structural models of the relations between age and measures of cognitive functioning. *Intelligence, 29,* 93–115.

Sammons, M. T., Paige, R. U., & Levant, R. F. (Eds.). (2003). *Prescriptive authority for psychologists: A history and guide.* Washington, DC: American Psychological Association.

Sampson, R. J., & Laub, J. H. (1995). Understanding variability in lives through time: Contributions of life-course criminology. *Studies of Crime Prevention, 4,* 143–158.

Sandberg, S., Paton, J. Y., Ahola, S., McCann, D. C., McGuinness, D., Hillary, C. R., et al. (2000). The role of acute and chronic stress in asthma attacks in children. *Lancet, 356,* 982–987.

Sandin, R. H., Enlund, G., Samuelsson, P., & Lenmarken, C. (2000). Awareness during anesthesia: A prospective case study. *The Lancet, 355,* 707–711.

Sapolsky, R. M. (1992). *Stress, the aging brain, and the mechanisms of neuron death.* Cambridge, MA: MIT Press.

Sapolsky, R. M. (1998). *Why zebras don't get ulcers: An updated guide to stress, stress-related diseases, and coping.* New York: Freeman.

Sapolsky, R. M., & Share, L. J. (2004). A pacific culture among wild baboons: Its emergence and transmission. *PLoS Biology, 2,* e106.

Sarris, V. (1989). Max Wertheimer on seen motion: Theory and evidence. *Psychological Research, 51,* 58–68.

Sarter, M. (2006). Preclinical research into cognition enhancers. *Trends in Pharmacological Sciences, 27,* 602–608.

Satcher, D. (2001). *The Surgeon General's call to action to promote sexual health and responsible sexual behavior.* Washington, DC: U.S. Government Printing Office.

Savage, C. R., Deckersbach, T., Heckers, S., Wagner, A. D., Schacter, D. L., Alpert, N. M., et al. (2001). Prefrontal regions supporting spontaneous and directed application of verbal learning strategies: Evidence from PET. *Brain, 124,* 219–231.

Savage-Rumbaugh, S., & Lewin, R. (1996). *Kanzi: The ape on the brink of the human mind.* New York: Wiley.

Savage-Rumbaugh, S., Shanker, S. G., & Taylor, T. J. (1998). *Apes, language, and the human mind.* Oxford, England: Oxford University Press.

Saver, J. L., & Rabin, J. (1997). The neural substrates of religious experience. *Journal of Neuropsychiatry and Clinical Neurosciences, 9,* 498–510.

Savic, I., Berglund, H., & Lindstrom, P. (2005). Brain response to putative pheromones in homosexual men. *Proceedings of the National Academy of Sciences, 102,* 7356–7361.

Savin-Williams, R. C. (1998). Disclosure to families of same-sex attraction by lesbian, gay and bisexual youth. *Journal of Research on Adolescence, 8,* 49–68.

Sawa, A., & Snyder, S. H. (2002). Schizophrenia: Diverse approaches to a complex disease. *Science, 295,* 692–695.

Sawyer, T. F. (2000). Francis Cecil Sumner: His views and influence on African American higher education. *History of Psychology, 3(2),* 122–141.

Scarborough, E., & Furumoto, L. (1987). *Untold lives: The first generation of American women psychologists.* New York: Columbia University Press.

Scarr, S., & McCartney, K. (1983). How people make their own environments: A theory of genotype-to-environment factors. *Child Development, 54,* 424–435.

Scazufca, M., & Kuipers, E. (1998). Stability of expressed emotion in relatives of those with schizophrenia and its relationship with burden of care and perception of patients' social functioning. *Psychological Medicine, 28,* 453–461.

Schachter, S. (1982). Recidivism and self-cure of smoking and obesity. *American Psychologist, 37,* 436–444.

Schachter, S., & Singer, J. E. (1962). Cognitive, social, and psychological determinants of emotional state. *Physiological Review, 69,* 379–399.

Schacter, D. L. (1987). Implicit memory: History and current status. *Journal of Experimental Psychology: Learning, Memory, and Cognition, 13,* 501–518.

Schacter, D. L. (1996). *Searching for memory: The brain, the mind, and the past.* New York: Basic Books.

Schacter, D. L. (1999). The seven sins of memory: Insights from psychology and cognitive neuroscience. *American Psychologist, 54(3),* 182–203.

Schacter, D. L. (2001a). *Forgotten ideas, neglected pioneers: Richard Semon and the story of memory*. Philadelphia: Psychology Press.

Schacter, D. L. (2001b). *The seven sins of memory: How the mind forgets and remembers*. Boston: Houghton Mifflin.

Schacter, D. L., Alpert, N. M., Savage, C. R., Rauch, S. L., & Albert, M. S. (1996a). Conscious recollection and the human hippocampal formation: Evidence from positron emission tomography. *Proceedings of the National Academy of Sciences (USA) 93*, 321–325.

Schacter, D. L., & Buckner, R. L. (1998). Priming and the brain. *Neuron, 20*, 185–195.

Schacter, D. L., & Curran, T. (2000). Memory without remembering and remembering without memory: Implicit and false memories. In M. S. Gazzaniga (Ed.), *The new cognitive neurosciences* (2nd ed.). Cambridge, MA: MIT Press.

Schacter, D. L., Dobbins, I. G., & Schnyer, D. M. (2004). Specificity of priming: A cognitive neuroscience perspective. *Nature Reviews Neuroscience, 5*, 853–862.

Schacter, D. L., Harbluk, J. L., & McLachlan, D. R. (1984). Retrieval without recollection: An experimental analysis of source amnesia. *Journal of Verbal Learning and Verbal Behavior, 23*, 593–611.

Schacter, D. L., Israel, L., & Racine, C. A. (1999). Suppressing false recognition in younger and older adults: The distinctiveness heuristic. *Journal of Memory and Language, 40*, 1–24.

Schacter, D. L., & Moscovitch, M. (1984). Infants, amnesics, and dissociable memory systems. In M. Moscovitch (Ed.), *Infant memory* (pp. 173–216). New York: Plenum Press.

Schacter, D. L., Reiman, E., Curran, T., Yun, L. S., Bandy, D., McDermott, K. B., et al. (1996b). Neuroanatomical correlates of veridical and illusory recognition memory: Evidence from positron emission tomography. *Neuron, 17*, 267–274.

Schacter, D. L., & Tulving, E. (1994). *Memory systems 1994*. Cambridge, MA: MIT Press.

Schacter, D. L., Wagner, A. D., & Buckner, R. L. (2000). Memory systems of 1999. In E. Tulving & F. I. M. Craik (Eds.), *The Oxford handbook of memory*. New York: Oxford University Press.

Schaeffer, M. A., McKinnon, W., Baum, A., Reynolds, C. P., Rikli, P., & Davidson, L. M. (1985). Immune status as a function of chronic stress at Three-Mile Island [Abstract]. *Psychosomatic Medicine, 47*, 85.

Schafer, R. B., & Keith, P. M. (1980). Equity and depression among married couples. *Social Psychology Quarterly, 43*, 430–435.

Schaie, K. W. (1996). *Intellectual development in adulthood: The Seattle longitudinal study*. New York: Cambridge University Press.

Schaie, K. W. (2005). *Developmental influences on adult intelligence: The Seattle longitudinal study*. New York: Oxford University Press.

Schatzberg, A. F., Cole, J. O., & DeBattista, C. (2003). *Manual of clinical psychopharmacology* (4th ed.). Washington, DC: American Psychiatric Publishing.

Scheff, T. J. (1984). *Being mentally ill: A sociological theory*. Chicago: Aldine.

Scheier, M. F., Matthews, K. A., Owens, J. F., Schulz, R., Bridges, M. W., Magovern, Sr., G. J., et al. (1999). Optimism and rehospitalization after coronary artery bypass graft surgery. *Archives of Internal Medicine, 159*, 829–835.

Scherer, K. R. (1999). Appraisal theory. In T. Dalgleish & M. Power (Eds.), *Handbook of cognition and emotion* (pp. 637–663). New York: Wiley.

Scherer, K. R. (2001). The nature and study of appraisal: A review of the issues. In K. R. Scherer, A. Schorr, & T. Johnstone (Eds.), *Appraisal processes in emotion: Theory, methods, research* (pp. 369–391). New York: Oxford University Press.

Schildkraut, J. J. (1965). The catecholamine hypothesis of affective disorders: A review of supporting evidence. *American Journal of Psychiatry, 122*, 509–522.

Schlafly, P. (2001, May 2). Daycare bombshell hits the "village." Retrieved October 7, 2007, from http://www.eagleforum.org/column/2001/may01/01-05-02.shtml

Schmeichel, B. J., & Baumeister, R. F. (2004). Self-regulatory strength. In R. F. Baumeister & K. D. Vohs (Eds.), *Handbook of self-regulation* (pp. 84–98). New York: Guilford Press.

Schmidt, F. L., & Hunter, J. E. (1998). The validity and utility of selection methods in personnel psychology: Practical and theoretical implications of 85 years of research findings. *Psychological Bulletin, 124*, 262–274.

Schmidt, N. B., Lerew, D. R., & Jackson R. J. (1997). The role of anxiety sensitivity in the pathogenesis of panic: Prospective evaluation of spontaneous panic attacks during acute stress. *Journal of Abnormal Psychology, 106*, 355–365.

Schmitt, W. B., Deacon, R. M. J., Reisel, D., Sprengel, R., Seeburg, P. H., Rawlins, J. N. P., et al. (2004). Spatial reference memory in GluR-A.-deficient mice using a novel hippocampal-dependent paddling pool escape task. *Hippocampus, 14*, 216–223.

Schnapf, J. L., Kraft, T. W., & Baylor, D. A. (1987). Spectral sensitivity of human cone photoreceptors. *Nature, 325*, 439–441.

Schneider, B. H., Atkinson, L., & Tardif, C. (2001). Child-parent attachment and children's peer relations: A quantitative review. *Developmental Psychology, 37*, 86–100.

Schneider, M. (2001). Toward a reconceptualization of the coming-out process for adolescent females. In A. R. D'Augelli & C. J. Patterson (Eds.), *Lesbian, gay and bisexual identities and youth: Psychological perspectives* (pp. 71–96). New York: Oxford University Press.

Schneier, F., Johnson, J., Hornig, C. D., Liebowitz, M. R., & Weissman, M. M. (1992). Social phobia: Comorbidity and morbidity in an epidemiologic sample. *Archives of General Psychiatry, 49*, 282–288.

Schnorr, J. A., & Atkinson, R. C. (1969). Repetition versus imagery instructions in the short- and long-term retention of paired associates. *Psychonomic Science, 15*, 183–184.

Schooler, J. W., Bendiksen, M., & Ambadar, Z. (1997). Taking the middle line: Can we accommodate both fabricated and recovered memories of sexual abuse? In M. A. Conway (Ed.), *Recovered memories and false memories* (pp. 251–292). Oxford, England: Oxford University Press.

Schooler, J. W., Reichle, E. D., & Halpern, D. V. (2001). *Zoning-out during reading: Evidence for dissociations between experience and meta-consciousness*. Paper presented at the Annual Meeting of the Psychonomic Society, Orlando, FL.

Schouwenburg, H. C. (1995). Academic procrastination: Theoretical notions, measurement, and research. In J. R. Ferrari, J. L. Johnson, & W. G. McCown (Eds.), *Procrastination and task avoidance: Theory, research, and treatment*. New York: Plenum Press.

Schreiner, C. E., Read, H. L., & Sutter, M. L. (2000). Modular organization of frequency integration in primary auditory cortex. *Annual Review of Neuroscience, 23*, 501–529.

Schultz, D. P., & Schultz, S. E. (1987). *A history of modern psychology* (4th ed.). San Diego: Harcourt Brace Jovanovich.

Schwartz, C. E., Wright, C. I., Shin, L. M., Kagan, J., & Rauch, S. L. (2003). Inhibited and uninhibited infants "grown up": Adult amygdalar response to novelty. *Science, 300*, 1952–1953.

Schwartz, J. H., & Westbrook, G. L. (2000). The cytology of neurons. In E. R. Kandel, G. H. Schwartz, & T. M. Jessell (Eds.), *Principles of neural science* (pp. 67–104). New York: McGraw-Hill.

Schwartz, S., & Maquet, P. (2002). Sleep imaging and the neuropsychological assessment of dreams. *Trends in Cognitive Sciences, 6*, 23–30.

Schwartzman, A. E., Gold, D., & Andres, D. (1987). Stability of intelligence: A 40-year follow-up. *Canadian Journal of Psychology, 41*, 244–256.

Schwarz, N., & Clore, G. L. (1983). Mood, misattribution, and judgments of well-being: Informative and directive functions of affective states. *Journal of Personality and Social Psychology, 45,* 513–523.

Schwarz, N., Mannheim, Z., & Clore, G. L. (1988). How do I feel about it? The informative function of affective states. In K. Fiedler & J. Forgas (Eds.), *Affect cognition and social behavior: New evidence and integrative attempts* (pp. 44–62). Toronto: C. J. Hogrefe.

Sclafani, A. (1995). How food preferences are learned—laboratory animal models. *Proceedings of the Nutrition Society, 54,* 419–427.

Scoville, W. B., & Milner, B. (1957). Loss of recent memory after bilateral hippocampal lesions. *Journal of Neurology, Neurosurgery, and Psychiatry, 20,* 11–21.

Scribner, S. (1975). Recall of classical syllogisms: A cross-cultural investigation of errors on logical problems. In R. J. Falmagne (Ed.), *Reasoning: Representation and process in children and adults.* Hillsdale, NJ: Erlbaum.

Scribner, S. (1984). Studying working intelligence. In B. Rogoff & J. Lave (Eds.), *Everyday cognition: Its development in social context* (pp. 9–40). Cambridge, MA: Harvard University Press.

Segal, M. W. (1974). Alphabet and attraction: An unobtrusive measure of the effect of propinquity in a field setting. *Journal of Personality and Social Psychology, 30,* 654–657.

Segall, M. H., Lonner, W. J., & Berry, J. W. (1998). Cross-cultural psychology as a scholarly discipline: On the flowering of culture in behavioral research. *American Psychologist, 53*(10), 1101–1110.

Segerstrom, S. C. (2005). Optimism and immunity: Do positive thoughts always lead to positive effects? *Brain, Behavior, and Immunity, 19,* 195–200.

Seligman, M. E. P. (1971). Phobias and preparedness. *Behavior Therapy, 2,* 307–320.

Seligman, M. E. P. (1995). The effectiveness of psychotherapy: The consumer reports study. *American Psychologist, 48,* 966–971.

Selikoff, I. J., Robitzek, E. H., & Ornstein, G. G. (1952). Toxicity of hydrazine derivatives of isonicotinic acid in the chemotherapy of human tuberculosis. *Quarterly Bulletin of SeaView Hospital, 13,* 17–26.

Selye, H. (1936). A syndrome produced by diverse nocuous agents. *Nature, 138,* 32.

Selye, H. (1956). *The stress of life.* New York: McGraw-Hill.

Selye, H., & Fortier, C. (1950). Adaptive reaction to stress. *Psychosomatic Medicine, 12,* 149–157.

Semenza, C., & Zettin, M. (1989). Evidence from aphasia from proper names as pure referring expressions. *Nature, 342,* 678–679.

Senghas, A., Kita, S., & Ozyurek, A. (2004). Children create core properties of language: Evidence from an emerging sign language in Nicaragua. *Science, 305,* 1782.

Serpell, R. (1974). Aspects of intelligence in a developing country. *African Social Research, 17,* 578–596.

Shackelford, T. K., & Larsen, R. J. (1999). Facial attractiveness and physical health. *Evolution and Human Behavior, 20,* 71–76.

Shah, J., Higgins, E. T., & Friedman, R. S. (1998). Performance incentives and means: How regulatory focus influences goal attainment. *Journal of Personality and Social Psychology, 74,* 285–293.

Shallice, T., Fletcher, P., Frith, C. D., Grasby, P., Frackowiak, R. S. J., & Dolan, R. J. (1994). Brain regions associated with acquisition and retrieval of verbal episodic memory. *Nature, 368,* 633–635.

Shapiro, F., & Forrest, M. S. (2001). *EMDR: The breakthrough therapy for overcoming anxiety, stress, and trauma.* New York: Basic Books.

Shapiro, N. (2005, October 5–11). The day care scare. *Seattle Weekly.*

Shaw, P., Greenstein, D., Lerch, J., Clasen, L., Lenroot, R., N. Gogtay, N., et al. (2006). Intellectual ability and cortical development in children and adolescents. *Nature, 440,* 676–679.

Shedler, J., & Block, J. (1990). Adolescent drug use and psychological health: A longitudinal inquiry. *American Psychologist, 45,* 612–630.

Sheehan, P. (1979). Hypnosis and the process of imagination. In E. Fromm & R. S. Shor (Eds.), *Hypnosis: Developments in research and new perspectives.* Chicago: Aldine.

Sheese, B. E., & Graziano, W. G. (2005). Deciding to defect: The effects of video-game violence on cooperative behavior. *Psychological Science, 16,* 354–357.

Sheingold, K., & Tenney, Y. J. (1982). Memory for a salient childhood event. In U. Neisser (Ed.), *Memory observed* (pp. 201–212). New York: Freeman.

Shenton, M. E., Dickey, C. C., Frumin, M., & McCarley, R. W. (2001). A review of MRI findings in schizophrenia. *Schizophrenia Research, 49,* 1–52.

Shepherd, G. M. (1988). *Neurobiology.* New York: Oxford University Press.

Sherif, M., Harvey, O. J., White, B. J., Hood, W. R., & Sherif, C. (1961). *Intergroup conflict and cooperation: The Robbers Cave experiment.* Norman, OK: University of Oklahoma Book Exchange.

Sherrod, D. (1974). Crowding, perceived control, and behavioral aftereffects. *Journal of Applied Social Psychology, 4,* 171–186.

Shettleworth, S. J. (1995). Memory in food-storing birds: From the field to the Skinner box. In E. Alleva, A. Fasolo, H. P. Lipp, L. Nadel, & L. Ricceri (Eds.), *Behavioural brain research in naturalistic and seminaturalistic settings* (pp. 159–192). Boston: Kluwer Academic Publishers.

Shiffman, S., Gnys, M., Richards, T. J., Paty, J. A., & Hickcox, M. (1996). Temptations to smoke after quitting: A comparison of lapsers and maintainers. *Health Psychology, 15,* 455–461.

Shih, M., Pittinsky, T. L., & Ambady, N. (1999). Stereotype susceptibility: Identity salience and shifts in quantitative performance. *Psychological Science, 10,* 80–83.

Shimamura, A. P., & Squire, L. R. (1987). A neuropsychological study of fact memory and source amnesia. *Journal of Experimental Psychology: Learning, Memory, and Cognition, 13,* 464–473.

Shimoda, K., Argyle, M., & Ricci-Bitt, P. E. (1978). The intercultural recognition of emotional expressions by three national racial groups: English, Italian, and Japanese. *European Journal of Social Psychology, 8,* 169–179.

Shiv, B., Loewenstein, G., Bechara, A., Damasio, H., & Damasio, A. R. (2005). Investment behavior and the negative side of emotion. *Psychological Science, 16,* 435–439.

Shomstein, S., & Yantis, S. (2004). Control of attention shifts between vision and audition in human cortex. *Journal of Neuroscience, 24,* 10702–10706.

Shweder, R. A. (1991). *Thinking through cultures: Expeditions in cultural psychology.* Cambridge, MA: Harvard University Press.

Shweder, R. A., & Sullivan, M. A. (1993). Cultural psychology: Who needs it? *Annual Review of Psychology, 44,* 497–523.

Siegel, A., Roeling, T. A. P., Gregg, T. R., & Kruk, M. R. (1999). Neuropharmacology of brain-stimulation-evoked aggression. *Neuroscience and Biobehavioral Reviews, 23,* 359–389.

Siegel, B. (1988, October 30). Can evil beget good? Nazi data: A dilemma for science. *Los Angeles Times.*

Siegel, S. (1976). Morphine analgesia tolerance: Its situational specificity supports a Pavlovian conditioning model. *Science, 193,* 323–325.

Siegel, S. (1984). Pavlovian conditioning and heroin overdose: Reports by overdose victims. *Bulletin of the Psychonomic Society, 22,* 428–430.

Sigl, J. C., & Chamoun, N. (1994). An introduction to bispectral analysis for the electroencephalogram. *Journal of Clinical Monitoring, 10,* 392–404.

Silver, R. L., Boon, C., & Stones, M. H. (1983). Searching for meaning in misfortune: Making sense of incest. *Journal of Social Issues, 39,* 81–102.

Simon, L. (1998). *Genuine reality: A life of William James.* New York: Harcourt Brace.

Simpson, E. L. (1974). Moral development research: A case study of scientific cultural bias. *Human Development, 17,* 81–106.

Simpson, J. A., Campbell, B., & Berscheid, E. (1986). The association between romantic love and marriage: Kephart (1967) twice revisited. *Personality and Social Psychology Bulletin, 12,* 363–372.

Singer, T., Seymour, B., O'Doherty, J., Kaube, H., Dolan, R. J., & Frith, C. D. (2004). Empathy for pain involves the affective but not sensory components of pain. *Science, 303,* 1157–1162.

Singh, D. (1993). Adaptive significance of female physical attractiveness: Role of waist-to-hip ratio. *Journal of Personality and Social Psychology, 65,* 293–307.

Sipe, K. (2006). Muhammad trial journal. Retrieved September 15, 2007, from http://home.hamptonroads.com/guestbook/journal.cfm?startrow=11&question=1&id=53

Skinner, B. F. (1932a). Drive and reflex strength. *Journal of General Psychology, 6,* 22–37.

Skinner, B. F. (1932b). Drive and reflex strength II. *Journal of General Psychology, 6,* 38–48.

Skinner, B. F. (1938). *The behavior of organisms: An experimental analysis.* New York: Appleton-Century-Crofts.

Skinner, B. F. (1947). "Superstition" in the pigeon. *Journal of Experimental Psychology, 38,* 168–172.

Skinner, B. F. (1948/1986). *Walden II.* Englewood Cliffs, NJ: Prentice Hall.

Skinner, B. F. (1950). Are theories of learning necessary? *Psychological Review, 57,* 193–216.

Skinner, B. F. (1953). *Science and human behavior.* New York: Macmillan.

Skinner, B. F. (1957). *Verbal behavior.* New York: Appleton-Century-Crofts.

Skinner, B. F. (1958). Teaching machines. *Science, 129,* 969–977.

Skinner, B. F. (1971). *Beyond freedom and dignity.* New York: Bantam Books.

Skinner, B. F. (1979). The shaping of a behaviorist: Part two of an autobiography. New York: Knopf.

Slater, A., Morison, V., & Somers, M. (1988). Orientation discrimination and cortical function in the human newborn. *Perception, 17,* 597–602.

Sleepwalker found dozing high atop crane. (2005, July 6). Retrieved March 3, 2007, from http://www.accessmylibrary.com

Slone, M. (2000). Responses to media coverage of terrorism. *Journal of Conflict Resolution, 44,* 508–522.

Slotnick, S. D., & Schacter, D. L. (2004). A sensory signature that distinguished true from false memories. *Nature Neuroscience, 7,* 664–672.

Smetacek, V. (2002). Balance: Mind-grasping gravity. *Nature, 415,* 481.

Smetana, J. G. (1981). Preschool children's conceptions of moral and social rules. *Child Development, 52,* 1333–1336.

Smetana, J. G., & Braeges, J. L. (1990). The development of toddler's moral and conventional judgments. *Merrill-Palmer Quarterly, 36,* 329–346.

Smith, E. E., & Jonides, J. (1997). Working memory: A view from neuroimaging. *Cognitive Psychology, 33,* 5–42.

Smith, M. L., Glass, G. V., & Miller, T. I. (1980). *The benefits of psychotherapy.* Baltimore: Johns Hopkins University Press.

Smith, N., & Tsimpli, I-M. (1995). *The mind of a savant.* Oxford, England: Oxford University Press.

Snyder, M., & Swann, W. B., Jr. (1978). Hypothesis testing processes in social interaction. *Journal of Personality and Social Psychology, 36,* 1202–1212.

Sobel, D. (1995). *Longitude: The true story of a lone genius who solved the greatest scientific problem of his time.* New York: Walker.

Sobell, M. B., & Sobell, L. C. (1995). Controlled drinking after 25 years: How important was the great debate? *Addiction, 90,* 1149–1153.

Solomon, J., & George, C. (1999). The measurement of attachment security in infancy and childhood. In J. Cassidy & P. R. Shaver (Eds.), *Handbook of attachment: Theory, research and clinical applications* (pp. 287–316). New York: Guilford Press.

Solomon, S., Greenberg, J., & Pyszczynski, T. (1991). A terror management theory of social behavior: The psychological functions of self-esteem and cultural worldviews. In M. P. Zanna (Ed.), *Advances in experimental social psychology* (Vol. 24, pp. 93–159). New York: Academic Press.

Sonnby-Borgstrom, M., Jonsson, P., & Svensson, O. (2003). Emotional empathy as related to mimicry reactions at different levels of information processing. *Journal of Nonverbal Behavior, 27,* 3–23.

Spanos, N. P. (1994). Multiple identity enactments and multiple personality disorder: A sociocognitive perspective. *Psychological Bulletin, 116,* 143–165.

Spearman, C. (1904). "General intelligence," objectively determined and measured. *American Journal of Psychology, 15,* 201–293.

Spector, J., & Read, J. (1999). The current status of eye movement desensitization and reprocessing (EMDR). *Clinical Psychology and Psychotherapy, 6,* 165–174.

Speisman, J. C., Lazarus, R. S., Moddkoff, A., & Davison, L. (1964). Experimental reduction of stress based on ego-defense theory. *Journal of Abnormal and Social Psychology, 68,* 367–380.

Spellman, B. A. (1996). Acting as intuitive scientists: Contingency judgments are made while controlling for alternative potential causes. *Psychological Science, 7,* 337–342.

Spencer, L. G. (1929). *Illustrated phenomenology: The science and art of teaching how to read character—A manual of mental science.* London: Fowler.

Sperling, G. (1960). The information available in brief visual presentations. *Psychological Monographs, 74* (Whole No. 48).

Sperry, R. W. (1964). The great cerebral commissure. *Scientific American, 210,* 42–52.

Spinoza, B. (1982). *The ethics and selected letters* (S. Feldman, Ed., & S. Shirley, Trans.). Indianapolis, IN: Hackett. (Original work published 1677)

Spiro, H. M., McCrea Curnan, M. G., Peschel, E., & St. James, D. (1994). *Empathy and the practice of medicine: Beyond pills and the scalpel.* New Haven, CT: Yale University Press.

Spitz, R. A. (1949). Motherless infants. *Child Development, 20,* 145–155.

Spitzer, R. L., Gibbon, M., Skodol, A. E., Williams, J. B. W., & First, M. B. (1994). DSM-IV Casebook: *A learning companion to the diagnostic & statistical manual of mental disorders* (4th ed.). Washington, DC: American Psychiatric Press.

Sprecher, S. (1999). "I love you more today than yesterday": Romantic partners' perceptions of changes in love and related affect over time. *Journal of Personality and Social Psychology, 76,* 46–53.

Squire, L. R. (1992). Memory and the hippocampus: A synthesis from findings with rats, monkeys, and humans. *Psychological Review, 99,* 195–231.

Squire, L. R., & Kandel, E. R. (1999). *Memory: From mind to molecules.* New York: Scientific American Library.

Squire, L. R., Knowlton, B., & Musen, G. (1993). The structure and organization of memory. *Annual Review of Psychology, 44,* 453–495.

**Squire, L. R., Ojemann, J. G., Miezin, F. M., Petersen, S. E., Videen, T. O., & Raichle, M. E.** (1992). Activation of the hippocampus in normal humans: A functional anatomical study of memory. *Proceedings of the National Academy of Sciences (USA), 89,* 1837–1841.

**Sroufe, L. A., Egeland, B., & Kruetzer, T.** (1990). The fate of early experience following developmental change: Longitudinal approaches to individual adaptation in childhood. *Child Development, 61,* 1363–1373.

**Stadler, M. A., & Frensch, P. A. (Eds.).** (1998). *Handbook of implicit learning.* Thousand Oaks, CA: Sage.

**Stangor, C., & McMillan, D.** (1992). Memory for expectancy-congruent and expectancy-incongruent information: A review of the social and social developmental literature. *Psychological Bulletin, 111,* 42–61.

**Starkey, P., Spelke, E. S., & Gelman, R.** (1983). Detection of intermodal numerical correspondences by human infants. *Science, 222,* 179–181.

**Starkey, P., Spelke, E. S., & Gelman, R.** (1990). Numerical abstraction by human infants. *Cognition, 36,* 97–127.

**Stasser, G., & Titus, W.** (1985). Pooling of unshared information in group decision making: Biased information sampling during discussion. *Journal of Personality and Social Psychology, 48,* 1467–1478.

**Staw, B. M., & Hoang, H.** (1995). Sunk costs in the NBA: Why draft order affects playing time and survival in professional basketball. *Administrative Science Quarterly 40,* 474–494.

**Steadman, H. J., Mulvey, E. P., Monahan, J., Robbins, P. C., Appelbaum, P. S., Grisso, T., et al.** (1998). Violence by people discharged from acute psychiatric inpatient facilities and by others in the same neighborhoods. *Archives of General Psychiatry, 55,* 393–401.

**Steele, C. M., & Aronson, J.** (1995). Stereotype threat and the intellectual test performance of African Americans. *Journal of Personality and Social Psychology, 69,* 797–811.

**Steele, C. M., & Josephs, R. A.** (1990). Alcohol myopia: Its prized and dangerous effects. *American Psychologist, 45,* 921–933.

**Steele, H., Steele, M., Croft, C., & Fonagy, P.** (1999). Infant-mother attachment at one year predicts children's understanding of mixed emotions at six years. *Social Development, 8,* 161–178.

**Stein, M. B.** (1998). Neurobiological perspectives on social phobia: From affiliation to zoology. *Biological Psychiatry, 44,* 1277–1285.

**Stein, M. B., Chavira, D. A., & Jang, K. L.** (2001). Bringing up bashful baby: Developmental pathways to social phobia. *Psychiatric Clinics of North America, 24,* 661–675.

**Stein, M. B., Koverola, C., Hanna, C., Torchia, M. G., & McClarty, B.** (1997). Hippocampal volume in women victimized by childhood sexual abuse. *Psychological Medicine, 27,* 951–959.

**Stein, Z., Susser, M., Saenger, G., & Marolla, F.** (1975). *Famine and development: The Dutch hunger winter of 1944–1945.* Oxford, England: Oxford University Press.

**Steinbaum, E. A., & Miller, N. E.** (1965). Obesity from eating elicited by daily stimulation of hypothalamus. *American Journal of Physiology, 208,* 1–5.

**Steinberg, L.** (1999). *Adolescence* (5th ed.). Boston: McGraw-Hill.

**Steinberg, L., & Morris, A. S.** (2001). Adolescent development. *Annual Review of Psychology, 52,* 83–110.

**Steinem, G.** (1970). Testimony on May 6, 1970, *Subcommittee on Constitutional Amendments of the Committee on the Judiciary* (2nd Session on S. J. Res. 61 5–7 ed., pp. 335–337). Washington, DC: U.S. Government Printing Office.

**Steiner, F.** (1986). Differentiating smiles. In E. Branniger-Huber & F. Steiner (Eds.), *FACS in psychotherapy research* (pp. 139–148). Zurich: Department of Clinical Psychology, Universität Zürich.

**Steiner, J. E.** (1973). The gustofacial response: Observation on normal and anencephalic newborn infants. In J. F. Bosma (Ed.), *Fourth symposium on oral sensation and perception: Development in the fetus and infant* (pp. 254–278). Bethesda, MD: U.S. Department of Heath, Education, and Welfare (DHEW 73-546).

**Steiner, J. E.** (1979). Human facial expressions in response to taste and smell stimulation. *Advances in Child Development and Behavior, 13,* 257–295.

**Steinman, R. B., Pizlo, Z., & Pizlo, F. J.** (2000). Phi is not beta, and why Wertheimer's discovery launched the Gestalt revolution. *Vision Research, 40,* 2257–2264.

**Stellar, J. R., Kelley, A. E., & Corbett, D.** (1983). Effects of peripheral and central dopamine blockade on lateral hypothalamic self-stimulation: Evidence for both reward and motor deficits. *Pharmacology, Biochemistry, and Behavior, 18,* 433–442.

**Stellar, J. R., & Stellar, E.** (1985). *The neurobiology of motivation and reward.* New York: Springer-Verlag.

**Stelmack, R. M.** (1990). Biological bases of extraversion: Psychophysiological evidence. *Journal of Personality, 58,* 293–311.

**Stephens, R. S.** (1999). Cannabis and hallucinogens. In B. S. McCrady & E. E. Epstein (Eds.), *Addictions: A comprehensive guidebook.* New York: Oxford University Press.

**Sterelny, K., & Griffiths, P. E.** (1999). *Sex and death: An introduction to philosophy of biology.* University of Chicago Press.

**Stern, J. A., Brown, M., Ulett, A., & Sletten, I.** (1977). A comparison of hypnosis, acupuncture, morphine, valium, aspirin, and placebo in the management of experimentally induced pain. In W. E. Edmonston (Ed.), *Conceptual and investigative approaches to hypnosis and hypnotic phenomena* (Vol. 296, pp. 175–193). New York: Annals of the New York Academy of Sciences.

**Stern, R., & Marks, I.** (1973). Brief and prolonged flooding: A comparison in agoraphobic patients. *Archives of General Psychiatry, 28,* 270–276.

**Stern, W.** (1914). *The psychological methods of testing intelligence* (G. M. Whipple, Trans.). Baltimore: Warwick & York.

**Sternberg, R. J.** (1986). A triangular theory of love. *Psychological Review, 93,* 119–135.

**Stevens, G., & Gardner, S.** (1982). *The women of psychology* (Vol. 1). Rochester: Schenkman Books.

**Stevens, J.** (1988). An activity approach to practical memory. In M. M. Gruneberg, P. E. Morris, & R. N. Sykes (Eds.), *Practical aspects of memory: Current research and issues* (Vol. 1, pp. 335–341). New York: Wiley.

**Stevens, L. A.** (1971). *Explorers of the brain.* New York: Knopf.

**Stevenson, R. L.** (1886). *Strange Case of Dr. Jekyll and Mr. Hyde.* London: Longmans, Green & Co.

**Stewart-Williams, S.** (2004). The placebo puzzle: Putting together the pieces. *Health Psychology, 23,* 198–206.

**Stickgold, R., Hobson, J. A., Fosse, R., & Fosse, M.** (2001). Sleep, learning, and dreams: Off-line memory reprocessing. *Science, 294,* 1052–1057.

**Stickgold, R., James, L., & Hobson, J. A.** (2000). Visual discrimination learning requires post-training sleep. *Nature Neuroscience, 3,* 1237–1238.

**Stickgold, R., Malia, A., Maguire, D., Roddenberry, D., & O'Connor, M.** (2000). Replaying the game: Hypnagogic images in normals and amnesics. *Science, 290,* 350–353.

**Stigler, J. W., Shweder, R., & Herdt, G. (Eds.).** (1990). *Cultural psychology: Essays on comparative human development.* Cambridge, England: Cambridge University Press.

**Stone, J., Perry, Z. W., & Darley, J. M.** (1997). "White men can't jump": Evidence for the perceptual confirmation of racial stereotypes following a basketball game. *Basic and Applied Social Psychology, 19,* 291–306.

**Storms, M. D.** (1973). Videotape and the attribution process: Reversing actors' and observers' points of view. *Journal of Personality and Social Psychology, 27,* 165–175.

Strack, F., Martin, L. L., & Stepper, S. (1988). Inhibiting and facilitating conditions of the human smile: A nonobtrusive test of the facial feedback hypothesis. *Journal of Personality and Social Psychology, 54,* 768–777.

Strahan, E. J., Spencer, S. J., & Zanna, M. P. (2002). Subliminal priming and persuasion: Striking while the iron is hot. *Journal of Experimental Social Psychology, 38,* 556–568.

Strayer, D. L., Drews, F. A., & Johnston, W. A. (2003). Cell phone induced failures of visual attention during simulated driving. *Journal of Experimental Psychology: Applied, 9,* 23–32.

Streissguth, A. P., Barr, H. M., Bookstein, F. L., Sampson, P. D., & Carmichael Olson, H. (1999). The long-term neurocognitive consequences of prenatal alcohol exposure: A 14-year study. *Psychological Science, 10,* 186–190.

Strickland, L. H. (1991). Russian and Soviet social psychology. *Canadian Psychology, 32,* 580–595.

Strohmetz, D. B., Rind, B., Fisher, R., & Lynn, M. (2002). Sweetening the till: The use of candy to increase restaurant tipping. *Journal of Applied Social Psychology, 32,* 300–309.

Stuss, D. T., & Benson, D. F. (1986). *The frontal lobes.* New York: Raven Press.

Substance Abuse and Mental Health Services Administration. (2005). *Suicide warning signs.* Washington, DC: U.S. Department of Health and Human Services.

Suchman, A. L., Markakis, K., Beckman, H. B., & Frankel, R. (1997). A model of empathic communication in the medical interview. *Journal of the American Medical Association, 277,* 678–682.

Sue, S., Fujino, D. C., Hu, L., Takeuchi, D. T., & Zane, N. W. S. (1991). Community mental health services for ethnic minority groups: A test of the cultural responsiveness hypothesis. *Journal of Counseling and Clinical Psychology, 59,* 533–540.

Sullivan, A. (2000, April 2). The he hormone. *New York Times Magazine,* pp. SM46.

Sullivan, H. S. (1953). *The interpersonal theory of psychiatry.* New York: Norton.

Sulloway, F. J. (1992). *Freud, biologist of the mind.* Cambridge, MA: Harvard University Press.

Suls, J., & Fletcher, B. (1985). The relative efficacy of avoidant and nonavoidant coping strategies: A meta-analysis. *Health Psychology, 4,* 249–288.

Sumner, W. (1906). *Folkways.* New York: Ginn.

Susman, S., Dent, C., McAdams, L., Stacy, A., Burton, D., & Flay, B. (1994). Group self-identification and adolescent cigarette smoking: a 1-year prospective study. *Journal of Abnormal Psychology, 103,* 576–580.

Susser, E. B., Brown, A., & Matte, T. D. (1999). Prenatal factors and adult mental and physical health. *Canadian Journal of Psychiatry, 44*(4) 326–334.

Sussman, L. K., Robins, L. N., & Earls, F. (1987). Treatment-seeking for depression by black and white Americans. *Social Science and Medicine, 24,* 187–196.

Suzuki, L. A., & Valencia, R. R. (1997). Race-ethnicity and measured intelligence: Educational implications. *American Psychologist, 52,* 1103–1114.

Swann, W. B. (1983). Self-verification: Bringing social reality into harmony with the self. In J. M. Suls & Greenwald, A. G. (Eds.), *Psychological perspectives on the self* (Vol. 2, pp. 33–66). Hillsdale, NJ: Erlbaum.

Swann, W. B., Wenzlaff, R. M., & Tafarodi, R. W. (1992). Depression and the search for negative evaluations: More evidence of the role of self-verification strivings. *Journal of Abnormal Psychology, 10,* 314–317.

Swanson, J. W. (1994). Mental disorder, substance abuse, and community violence: An epidemiological approach. In J. Monahan & H. J.

Steadman (Eds.), *Violence and mental disorder: Developments in risk assessment* (pp. 101–136). Chicago: University of Chicago Press.

Swayze II, V. W. (1995). Frontal leukotomy and related psychosurgical procedures before antipsychotics (1935–1954): A historical overview. *American Journal of Psychiatry, 152,* 505–515.

Swednsen, J., Hammen, C., Heller, T., & Gitlin, M. (1995). Correlates of stress reactivity in patients with bipolar disorder. *American Journal of Psychiatry, 152,* 795–797.

Swets, J. A., Dawes, R. M., & Monahan, J. (2000). Psychological science can improve diagnostic decisions. *Psychological Science in the Public Interest, 1,* 1–26.

Swinkels, A. (2003). An effective exercise for teaching cognitive heuristics. *Teaching of Psychology, 30,* 120–122.

Szasz, T. (1960). The myth of mental illness. *American Psychologist, 15,* 113–118.

Szechtman, H., Woody, E., Bowers, K. S., & Nahmias, C. (1998). Where the imaginal appears real: A positron emission tomography study of auditory hallucinations. *Proceedings of the National Academy of Sciences, 95,* 1956–1960.

Szpunar, K. K., Watson, J. M., & McDermott, K. B. (2007). Neural substrates of envisioning the future. *Proceedings of the National Academy of Sciences (USA), 104,* 642–647.

Tajfel, H. (1970). Experiments in intergroup discrimination. *Scientific American, 223,* 96–102.

Tajfel, H., Billig, M. G., Bundy, R. P., & Flament, C. (1971). Social categorization and intergroup behaviour. *European Journal of Social Psychology, 1,* 149–178.

Tajfel, H., & Turner, J. C. (1986). The social identity theory of intergroup behavior. In S. Worchel & W. G. Austin (Eds.), *Psychology of intergroup relations* (pp. 7–24). Chicago: Nelson.

Tajfel, H., & Wilkes, A. L. (1963). Classification and quantitative judgement. *British Journal of Psychology, 54,* 101–114.

Takahashi, K. (1986). Examining the strange-situation procedure with Japanese mothers and 12-month-old infants. *Developmental Psychlogy, 22,* 265–270.

Tam, E. M., Lam, R. W., & Levitt, A. J. (1995). Treatment of seasonal affective disorder: A review. *Canadian Journal of Psychiatry, 40,* 457–466.

Tamminga, C. A. (2006). The neurobiology of cognition in schizophrenia. *Journal of Clinical Psychiatry, 67*(Suppl. 9), 9–13.

Tamminga, C. A., Nemeroff, C. B., Blakely, R. D., Brady, L., Carter, C. S., Davis, K. L, Dingledine, R., et al. (2002). Developing novel treatments for mood disorders: Accelerating discovery. *Biological Psychiatry, 52,* 589–609.

Tanaka, K. (1996). Inferotemporal cortex and object vision. *Annual Review of Neuroscience, 19,* 109–139.

Tang, Y.-P., Shimizu, E., Dube, G. R., Rampon, C., Kerchner, G. A., Zhuo, M., et al. (1999). Genetic enhancement of learning and memory in mice. *Nature, 401,* 63–69.

Tanner, L. (February 7, 2002). Woman gives birth after pre-pregnancy test is used to screen for early Alzheimer's gene. Associated Press.

Tapert, S. F., Brown, G. G., Kindermann, S., Cheung, E. Frank, L. R., & Brown, S. A. (2001). fMRI measurement of brain dysfunction in alcohol-dependent young women. *Alcoholism: Clinical and Experimental Research, 25,* 236–245.

Tarr, M. J., & Vuong, Q. C. (2002). Visual object recognition. In S. Yantis & H. Pashler (Eds.), *Stevens' handbook of experimental psychology: Vol. 1. Sensation and perception* (3rd ed., pp. 287–314). New York: Wiley.

Tart, C. T. (Ed.). (1969). *Altered states of consciousness.* New York: Wiley.

**Task Force on Promotion and Dissemination of Psychological Procedures.** (1995). Training in and dissemination of empirically-validated psychological treatments: Report and recommendations. *Clinical Psychologist, 48,* 3–23.

**Tavris, C.** (1989). *Anger: The misunderstood emotion* (Rev. ed.). New York: Simon & Schuster.

**Taylor, D., & Lambert, W.** (1990). *Language and culture in the lives of immigrants and refugees.* Austin, TX: Hogg Foundation for Mental Health.

**Taylor, E.** (2001). *William James on consciousness beyond the margin.* Princeton, NJ: Princeton University Press.

**Taylor, S. E.** (1986). *Health psychology.* New York: Random House.

**Taylor, S. E.** (1989). *Positive illusions.* New York: Basic Books.

**Taylor, S. E.** (2002). *The tending instinct: How nurturing is essential to who we are and how we live.* New York: Times Books.

**Taylor, S. E.** (2003). *The tending instinct: Women, men, and the biology of relationships.* New York: Owl Books.

**Taylor, S. E., & Brown, J. D.** (1988). Illusion and well-being: A social psychological perspective on mental health. *Psychological Bulletin, 103,* 193–210.

**Taylor, S. E., & Fiske, S. T.** (1975). Point-of-view and perceptions of causality. *Journal of Personality and Social Psychology, 32,* 439–445.

**Taylor, S. E., & Fiske, S. T.** (1978). Salience, attention, and attribution: Top of the head phenomena. In L. Berkowitz (Ed.), *Advances in experimental social psychology* (Vol. 11, pp. 249–288). New York: Academic Press.

**Teasdale, J. D., Segal, Z. V., & Williams, J. M. G.** (2000). Prevention of relapse/recurrence in major depression by Mindfulness-Based Cognitive Therapy. *Journal of Consulting and Clinical Psychology, 68,* 615–623.

**Telch, M. J., Lucas, J. A., & Nelson, P.** (1989). Non-clinical panic in college students: An investigation of prevalence and symptomology. *Journal of Abnormal Psychology, 98,* 300–306.

**Tellegen, A., & Atkinson, G.** (1974). Openness to absorbing and self-altering experiences ("absorption"), a trait related to hypnotic susceptibility. *Journal of Abnormal Psychology, 83,* 268–277.

**Tellegen, A., Lykken, D. T., Bouchard, T. J., Wilcox, K., Segal, N., & Rich, A.** (1988). Personality similarity in twins reared together and apart. *Journal of Personality and Social Psychology, 54,* 1031–1039.

**Temerlin, M. K., & Trousdale, W. W.** (1969). The social psychology of clinical diagnosis. *Psychotherapy: Theory, Research & Practice, 6,* 24–29.

**Tempini, M. L., Price, C. J., Josephs, O., Vandenberghe, R., Cappa, S. F., Kapur, N., et al.** (1998). The neural systems sustaining face and proper-name processing. *Brain, 121,* 2103–2118.

**Terman, L. M.** (1916). *The measurement of intelligence.* Boston: Houghton Mifflin.

**Terman, L. M., & Oden, M. H.** (1959). *Genetic studies of genius: Vol. 5. The gifted group at mid-life.* Stanford, CA: Stanford University Press.

**Terman, M., Terman, J. S., Quitkin, F. M., McGrath, P. J., Stewart, J. W., & Rafferty, B.** (1989). Light therapy for seasonal affective disorder. A review of efficacy. *Neuropsychopharmacology, 2,* 1–22.

**Tesser, A.** (1991). Emotion in social comparison and reflection processes. In J. Suls, & T. A. Wills (Ed.), *Social comparison: Contemporary theory and research* (pp. 117–148). Hillsdale, NJ: Erlbaum.

**Tesser, A.** (1993). The importance of heritability in psychological research: The case of attitudes. *Psychological Review, 100,* 129–142.

**Teyler, T. J., & DiScenna, P.** (1986). The hippocampal memory indexing theory. *Behavioral Neuroscience, 100,* 147–154.

**Thaker, G. K.** (2002). Current progress in schizophrenia research. Search for genes of schizophrenia: Back to defining valid phenes. *Journal of Nervous and Mental Disease, 190,* 411–412.

**Thaler, R. H.** (1988). The ultimatum game. *Journal of Economic Perspectives, 2,* 195–206.

**Tharp, R. G.** (1991). Cultural diversity and treatment of children. *Journal of Counseling and Clinical Psychology, 59,* 799–812.

**Thase, M. E., & Howland, R. H.** (1995). Biological processes in depression: An updated review and integration. In E. E. Beckham & W. R. Leber (Eds.), *Handbook of depression* (2nd ed., pp. 213–279). New York: Guilford Press.

**The UP Series: *Seven up, Seven plus seven, 21 up, 28 up, 35 up, 42 up, 49 up.*** (1964–2005). Paul Almond, dir./Michael Apted, dir. Granada Television of England Productions.

**Thelen, E., Corbetta, D., Kamm, K., Spencer, J. P., Schneider, K., & Zernicke, R. F.** (1993). The transition to reaching: Mapping intention and intrinsic dynamics. *Child Development, 64,* 1058–1098.

**Thibaut, J. W., & Kelley, H. H.** (1959). *The social psychology of groups.* New Brunswick, NJ: Transaction Publishers.

**Thoma, S. J., Narvaez, D., Rest, J., & Derryberry, P.** (1999). Does moral judgment development reduce to political attitudes or verbal ability? Evidence using the defining issues test. *Educational Psychology Review,* 325–341.

**Thomas, A., & Chess, S.** (1977). *Temperament and development.* New York: Brunner/Mazel.

**Thomas, G. V.** (1981). Contiguity, reinforcement rate and the law of effect. *Quarterly Journal of Experimental Psychology, 33B,* 33–43.

**Thompson, C. P., Skowronski, J., Larsen, S. F., & Betz, A.** (1996). *Autobiographical memory: Remembering what and remembering when.* Mahwah, NJ: Erlbaum.

**Thompson, P. M., Giedd, J. N., Woods, R. P., MacDonald, D., Evans, A. C., & Toga, A. W.** (2000). Growth patterns in the developing brain detected by using continuum mechanical tensor maps. *Nature, 404,* 190–193.

**Thompson, P. M., Vidal, C., Giedd, J. N., Gochman, P., Blumenthal, J., Nicolson, R., et al.** (2001). Accelerated gray matter loss in very early-onset schizophrenia. *Proceedings of the National Academy of Science (USA), 98,* 11650–11655.

**Thomson, D. M.** (1988). Context and false recognition. In G. M. Davies & D. M. Thomson (Eds.), *Memory in context: Context in memory* (pp. 285–304). Chichester, England: Wiley.

**Thorndike, E. L.** (1898). Animal intelligence: An experimental study of associative processes in animals. *Psychological Review Monograph Supplements, 2,* 4–160.

**Thornhill, R., & Gangestad, S. W.** (1993). Human facial beauty: Averageness, symmetry, and parasite resistance. *Human Nature, 4,* 237–269.

**Thornhill, R., & Gangestad, S. W.** (1999). The scent of symmetry: A human sex pheromone that signals fitness? *Evolution and Human Behavior, 20,* 175–201.

**Thurber, J.** (1956). *Further fables of our time.* New York: Simon & Schuster.

**Thurstone, L. L.** (1938). *Primary mental abilities.* Chicago: University of Chicago Press.

**Tice, D. M., & Baumeister, R. F.** (1997). Longitudinal study of procrastination, performance, stress, and health: The costs and benefits of dawdling. *Psychological Science, 8*(6), 454–458.

**Tienari, P., Wynne, L. C., Sorri, A., Lahti, I., Läksy, K., Moring, J., et al.** (2004). Genotype-environment interaction in schizophrenia-spectrum disorder: Long-term follow-up study of Finnish adoptees. *British Journal of Psychiatry, 184,* 216–222.

***Time* poll.** (2005, January 17). Just how happy are we? *Time,* A4.

**Titchener, E. B.** (1896). *An outline of psychology.* New York: Macmillan.

**Tittle, P. (Ed.).** (2004). *Should parents be licensed?: Debating the issues.* New York: Prometheus Books.

**Todd, J. T., & Morris, E. K.** (1992). Case histories in the great power of steady misrepresentation. *American Psychologist, 47*(11), 1441–1453.

Todes, D. P. (2000). Pavlov: *Exploring the animal machine*. New York: Oxford University Press.

Tolman, E. C., & Honzik, C. H. (1930a). Introduction and removal of reward and maze performance in rats. *University of California Publications in Psychology, 4*, 257–275.

Tolman, E. C., & Honzik, C. H. (1930b). "Insight" in rats. *University of California Publications in Psychology, 4*, 215–232.

Tolman, E. C., Ritchie, B. F., & Kalish, D. (1946). Studies in spatial learning: I: Orientation and short cut. *Journal of Experimental Psychology, 36*, 13–24.

Tomarken, A. J., Simien, C., & Garber, J. (1994). Retesting frontal brain asymmetry discriminates adolescent children of depressed mothers from low-risk controls. *Psychophysiology, 31*, 97–98.

Tomkins, S. S. (1981). The role of facial response in the experience of emotion. *Journal of Personality and Social Psychology, 40*, 351–357.

Tooby, J., & Cosmides, L. (2000). Mapping the evolved functional organization of mind and brain. In M. S. Gazzaniga (Ed.), *The cognitive neurosciences* (pp. 1185–1198). Cambridge, MA: MIT Press.

Tootell, R. B. H., Reppas, J. B., Dale, A. M., Look, R. B., Sereno, M. I., Malach, R., et al. (1995). Visual-motion aftereffect in human cortical area MT revealed by functional magnetic resonance imaging. *Nature, 375*, 139–141.

Torgensen, S. (1983). Genetic factors in anxiety disorders. *Archives of General Psychiatry, 40*, 1085–1089.

Torgensen, S. (1986). Childhood and family characteristics in panic and generalized anxiety disorder. *American Journal of Psychiatry, 143*, 630–639.

Torrey, E. F. (1994). Violent behavior by individuals with serious mental illness. *Hospital & Community Psychiatry, 45*, 653–662.

Torrey, E. F., Bower, A. E., Taylor, E. H., & Gottesman, I. I. (1994). *Schizophrenia and manic-depressive disorder: The biological roots of mental illness as revealed by the landmark study of identical twins.* New York: Basic Books.

Trebach, A. S., & Zeese, K. B. (Eds.). (1992). *Friedman and Szasz on liberty and drugs: Essays on the free market and prohibition.* Washington, DC: Drug Policy Foundation Press.

Treede, R. D., Kenshalo, D. R., Gracely, R. H., & Jones, A. K. (1999). The cortical representation of pain. *Pain, 79*, 105–111.

Trevelyan, A. J., Sussillo, D., Watson, B. O., & Yuste, R. (2006). Modular propagation of epileptiform activity: Evidence for an inhibitory veto in neocortex. *Journal of Neuroscience, 26*, 12447–12455.

Trivers, R. L. (1972a). Parental investment and sexual selection. In B. Campbell (Ed.), *Sexual selection and the descent of man, 1871–1971* (pp. 139–179). Chicago: Aldine.

Trivers, R. L. (1972b). The evolution of reciprocal altruism. *The Quarterly Review of Biology, 46*, 35–57.

Trull, T. J., & Durrett, C. A. (2005). Categorical and dimensional models of personality disorder. *Annual Review of Clinical Psychology, 1*, 355–380.

Tucker, E. (2003, June 25). Move over, Fido! Chickens are becoming hip suburban pets. *USA Today.*

Tuerlinckx, F., De Boeck, P., & Lens, W. (2002). Measuring needs with the Thematic Apperception Test: A psychometric study. *Journal of Personality and Social Psychology, 82*, 448–461.

Tulving, E. (1972). Episodic and semantic memory. In E. Tulving & W. Donaldson (Eds.), *Organization of memory* (pp. 381–403). New York: Academic Press.

Tulving, E. (1983). *Elements of episodic memory.* Oxford, England: Clarendon Press.

Tulving, E. (1998). Neurocognitive processes of human memory. In C. von Euler & I. Lundberg & R. Llins (Eds.), *Basic mechanisms in cognition and language* (pp. 261–281). Amsterdam: Elsevier.

Tulving, E., Kapur, S., Craik, F. I. M., Moscovitch, M., & Houle, S. (1994). Hemispheric encoding/retrieval asymmetry in episodic memory: Positron emission tomography findings. *Proceedings of the National Academy of Sciences (USA), 91*, 2016–2020.

Tulving, E., & Pearlstone, Z. (1966). Availability versus accessibility of information in memory for words. *Journal of Verbal Learning & Verbal Behavior, 5*, 381–391.

Tulving, E., & Schacter, D. L. (1990). Priming and human memory systems. *Science, 247*, 301–306.

Tulving, E., Schacter, D. L., & Stark, H. (1982). Priming effects in word-fragment completion are independent of recognition memory. *Journal of Experimental Psychology: Learning, Memory, and Cognition, 8*, 336–342.

Tulving, E., & Thompson, D. M. (1973). Encoding specificity and retrieval processes in episodic memory. *Psychological Review, 80*, 352–373.

Turiel, E. (1998). The development of morality. In N. Eisenberg (Ed.), *Handbook of child psychology: Vol. 3. Social, emotional and personality development* (pp. 863–932). New York: Wiley.

Turkheimer, E. (2000). Three laws of behavior genetics and what they mean. *Current Directions in Psychological Science, 9*, 160–164.

Turkheimer, E., Haley, A., Waldron, M., D'Onofrio, B., & Gottesman, I. I. (2003). Socioeconomic status modifies heritability of IQ in young children. *Psychological Science, 14*, 623–628.

Turkheimer, E., & Waldron, M. (2000). Nonshared environment: A theoretical, methodological, and quantitative review. *Psychological Bulletin, 126*, 78–108.

Turner, D. C., Robbins, T. W., Clark, L., Aron, A. R., Dowson, J., & Sahakian, B. J. (2003). Cognitive enhancing effects of modafinil in healthy volunteers. *Psychopharmacology, 165*, 260–269.

Turner, D. C., & Sahakian, B. J. (2006). Neuroethics of cognitive enhancement. *BioSocieties, 1*, 113–123.

Tversky, A., & Kahneman, D. (1973). Availability: A heuristic for judging frequency and probability. *Cognitive Psychology, 5*, 207–232.

Tversky, A., & Kahneman, D. (1974). Judgment under uncertainty: Heuristics and biases. *Science, 185*, 1124–1131.

Tversky, A., & Kahneman, D. (1981). The framing of decisions and the psychology of choice. *Science, 211*, 453–458.

Tversky, A., & Kahneman, D. (1983). Extensional versus intuitive reasoning: The conjunction fallacy in probability judgment. *Psychological Review, 90*, 293–315.

Tversky, A., & Kahneman, D. (1992). Advances in prospect theory: Cumulative representation of uncertainty. *Journal of Risk and Uncertainty, 5*, 297–323.

Twenge, J. M., Campbell, W. K., & Foster, C. A. (2003). Parenthood and marital satisfaction: A meta-analytic review. *Journal of Marriage and Family, 65*, 574–583.

Tyler, T. R. (1990). *Why people obey the law.* New Haven, CT: Yale University Press.

Ungerleider, L. G., & Mishkin, M. (1982). Two cortical visual systems. In D. J. Ingle, M. A. Goodale, & R. J. W. Mansfield (Eds.), *Analysis of visual behavior* (pp. 549–586). Cambridge, MA: MIT Press.

Ursano, R. J., & Silberman, E. K. (2003). Psychoanalysis, psychoanalytic psychotherapy, and supportive psychotherapy. In R. E. Hales & S. C. Yudofsky (Eds.), *The American Psychiatric Publishing textbook of clinical psychiatry* (4th ed., pp. 1177–1203). Washington, DC: American Psychiatric Publishing.

Usher, J. A., & Neisser, U. (1993). Childhood amnesia and the beginnings of memory for four early life events. *Journal of Experimental Psychology: General, 122*, 155–165.

Valenstein, E. S. (1973). *Brain control: A critical examination of brain stimulation and psychosurgery.* New York: Wiley.

Valenstein, E. S. (1986). *Great and desperate cures: The rise and decline of psychosurgery and other radical treatments for mental illness.* New York: Basic Books.

Valentine, T., Brennen, T., & Brédart, S. (1996). *The cognitive psychology of proper names: On the importance of being Ernest.* London: Routledge.

Valins, S. (1966). Cognitive effects of false heart-rate feedback. *Journal of Personality and Social Psychology, 4,* 400–408.

Vallacher, R. R., & Solodky, M. (1979). Objective self-awareness, standards of evaluation, and moral behavior. *Journal of Experimental Social Psychology, 15,* 254–262.

Vallacher, R. R., & Wegner, D. M. (1985). *A theory of action identification.* Hillsdale, NJ: Erlbaum.

Vallacher, R. R., & Wegner, D. M. (1987). What do people think they're doing? Action identification and human behavior. *Psychological Review, 94,* 3–15.

van den Boon, D. C. (1994). The influence of temperament and mothering on attachment and exploration: An experimental manipulation of sensitive responsiveness among lower-class mothers with irritable infants. *Child Development, 65,* 1457–1477.

van den Boon, D. C. (1995). Do first year intervention effects endure? Follow-up during toddlerhood of a sample of Dutch irritable infants. *Child Development, 66,* 1798–1816.

Van Essen, D. C., Anderson, C. H., & Felleman, D. J. (1992). Information processing in the primate visual system: An integrated systems perspective. *Science, 255,* 419–423.

van IJzendoorn, M. H. (1995). Adult attachment representations, parental responsiveness, and infant attachment: A meta-analysis on the predictive validity of the Adult Attachment Interview. *Psychological Bulletin, 117,* 387–403.

van IJzendoorn, M. H., & Kroonenberg, P. M. (1988). Cross-cultural patterns of attachment: A meta-analysis of the strange situation. *Child Development, 59,* 147–156.

van IJzendoorn, M. H., & Sagi, A. (1999). Cross-cultural patterns of attachment: Universal and contextual dimensions. In J. Cassidy & P. R. Shaver (Eds.), *Handbook of attachment: Theory, research and clinical applications* (pp. 713–734). New York: Guilford Press.

van Stegeren, A. H., Everaerd, W., Cahill, L., McGaugh, J. L., & Gooren, L. J. G. (1998). Memory for emotional events: Differential effects of centrally versus peripherally acting blocking agents. *Psychopharmacology, 138,* 305–310.

Van Velzen, C. J. M., & Emmelkamp, P. M. G. (1996). The assessment of personality disorders: Implications for cognitive and behavior therapy. *Behaviour Research and Therapy, 34,* 655–668.

Vance, E. B., & Wagner, N. N. (1976). Written descriptions of orgasm: A study of sex differences. *Archives of Sexual Behavior, 5,* 87–98.

Vanderplate, C., Aral, S. O., & Magder, L. (1988). The relationship among genital herpes simplex virus, stress, and social support. *Health Psychology, 7,* 159–168.

Vargha-Khadem, F., Gadian, D. G., Watkins, K. E., Connelly, A., Van Paesschen, W., & Mishkin, M. (1997). Differential effects of early hippocampal pathology on episodic and semantic memory. *Science, 277,* 376–380.

Vitkus, J. (1996). *Casebook in abnormal psychology* (3rd ed.). New York: McGraw-Hill.

Vitkus, J. (1999). *Casebook in abnormal psychology* (4th ed.). New York: McGraw-Hill.

Von Frisch, K. (1974). Decoding the language of the bee. *Science, 185,* 663–668.

von Restorff, H. (1933). Analyse von Vörgangen in Spurenfeld. I. Über die Wirkung von Bereichsbildung im Spurenfeld. *Psychologische Forschung, 18,* 299–342.

Vondra, J. I., Shaw, D. S., Swearingen, L., Cohen, M., & Owens, E. B. (2001). Attachment stability and emotional and behavioral regulation from infancy to preschool age. *Development and Psychopathology, 13,* 13–33.

Vonnegut, M. (1976). *The Eden express.* New York: Bantam.

Vortac, O. U., Edwards, M. B., & Manning, C. A. (1995). Functions of external cues in prospective memory. *Memory, 3,* 201–219.

Wade, N. J. (2005). *Perception and illusion: Historical perspectives.* New York: Springer.

Wager, T. D., Rilling, J., K., Smith, E. E., Sokolik, A., Casey, K. L., Davidson, R. J., et al. (2004). Placebo-induced changes in fMRI in the anticipation and experience of pain. *Science, 303,* 1162–1167.

Wagner, A. D., Schacter, D. L., Rotte, M., Koutstaal, W., Maril, A., Dale, A. M., et al. (1998). Remembering and forgetting of verbal experiences as predicted by brain activity. *Science, 281,* 1188–1190.

Wagner, U., Gais, S., Haider, H., Verleiger, R., & Born, J. (2004). Sleep inspires insight. *Nature, 427,* 352–355.

Wahba, M. A., & Bridwell, L. G. (1976). Maslow reconsidered: A review of research on the need hierarchy theory. *Organizational Behavior & Human Performance, 15,* 212–240.

Wahl, O. F. (1976). Monozygotic twins discordant for schizophrenia: A review. *Psychological Bulletin, 83,* 91–106.

Waite, L. J. (1995). Does marriage matter? *Demography, 32,* 483–507.

Waldfogel, S. (1948). The frequency and affective character of childhood memories. *Psychological Monographs, 62* (Whole No. 291).

Waldmann, M. R. (2000). Competition among causes but not effects in predictive and diagnostic learning. *Journal of Experimental Psychology: Learning, Memory, and Cognition, 26,* 53–76.

Walker, C. (1977). Some variations in marital satisfaction. In R. C. J. Peel (Ed.), *Equalities and inequalities in family life* (pp. 127–139). London: Academic Press.

Walker, L. J. (1988). The development of moral reasoning. *Annals of Child Development, 55,* 677–691.

Wall, P. (2000). *Pain: The science of suffering.* New York: Columbia University Press.

Wallace, J., Schnieder, T., & McGuffin, P. (2002). Genetics of depression. In I. H. Gottlieb & C. L. Hammen (Eds.), *Handbook of depression* (pp. 169–191). New York: Guilford Press.

Wallbott, H. G. (1998). Bodily expression of emotion. *European Journal of Social Psychology, 28,* 879–896.

Walster, E., Aronson, V., Abrahams, D., & Rottmann, L. (1966). Importance of physical attractiveness in dating behavior. *Journal of Personality and Social Psychology, 4,* 508–516.

Walster, E., Walster, G. W., & Berscheid, E. (1978). *Equity: Theory and research.* Boston: Allyn and Bacon.

Walster, E., Walster, G. W., Piliavin, J., & Schmidt, L. (1973). "Playing hard to get": Understanding an elusive phenomenon. *Journal of Personality and Social Psychology, 26,* 113–121.

Walton, D. N. (1990). What is reasoning? What is an argument? *Journal of Philosophy, 87,* 399–419.

Waltzman, S. B. (2006). Cochlear implants: Current status. *Expert Review of Medical Devices, 3,* 647–655.

Wang, L. H., McCarthy, G., Song, A. W., & LaBar, K. S. (2005). Amygdala activation to sad pictures during high-field (4 tesla) functional magnetic resonance imaging. *Emotion, 5,* 12–22.

Ward, J., Parkin, A. J., Powell, G., Squires, E. J., Townshend, J., & Bradley, V. (1999). False recognition of unfamiliar people: "Seeing film stars everywhere." *Cognitive Neuropsychology, 16,* 293–315.

Warnock, M. (2003). *Making babies: Is there a right to have children?* Oxford, England: Oxford University Press.

Warrington, E. K., & McCarthy, R. A. (1983). Category specific access dysphasia. *Brain, 106,* 859–878.

Warrington, E. K., & Shallice, T. (1984). Category specific semantic impairments. *Brain, 107,* 829–854.

Watanabe, S., Sakamoto, J., & Wakita, M. (1995). Pigeons' discrimination of painting by Monet and Picasso. *Journal of the Experimental Analysis of Behavior, 63,* 165–174.

Waters, E., & Cummings, E. M. (2000). A secure base from which to explore close relationships. *Child Development, 71,* 164–173.

Watkins, L. R., & Maier, S. F. (2005). Immune regulation of central nervous system functions: From sickness responses to pathological pain. *Journal of Internal Medicine, 257,* 139–155.

Watson, D., & Pennebaker, J. W. (1989). Health complaints, stress, and distress: Exploring the central role of negative affectivity. *Psychological Review, 96,* 234–254.

Watson, D., & Tellegen, A. (1985). Toward a consensual structure of mood. *Psychological Bulletin, 98,* 219–235.

Watson, J. B. (1913). Psychology as the behaviorist views it. *Psychological Review, 20,* 158–177.

Watson, J. B. (1924a). *Behaviorism.* New York: People's Institute.

Watson, J. B. (1924b). The unverbalized in human behavior. *Psychological Review, 31,* 339–347.

Watson, J. B. (1928). *Psychological care of infant and child.* New York: Norton.

Watson, J. B. (1930). *Behaviorism* (Rev. ed.). Chicago: University of Chicago Press.

Watson, J. B., & Rayner, R. (1920). Conditioned emotional reactions. *Journal of Experimental Psychology, 3,* 1–14.

Watson, R. I. (1978). *The great psychologists.* New York: Lippincott.

Watt, H. J. (1905). Experimentelle Beitraege zu einer Theorie des Denkens (Experimental contributions to a theory of thinking). *Archiv fuer die gesamte Psychologie, 4,* 289–436.

Watzlawick, P., Beavin, J., & Jackson, D. D. (1967). *Pragmatics of human communication: A study of interactional patterns, pathologies, and paradoxes.* New York: Norton.

Wearing, D. (2006). *Forever today.* London: Corgi Books.

Weber, R., & Crocker, J. (1983). Cognitive processes in the revision of stereotypic beliefs. *Journal of Personality and Social Psychology, 45,* 961–977.

Wechsler, H., Davenport, A., Dowdall, G., Moeykens, B., & Castillo, S. (1994). Health and behavioral consequences of binge drinking in college: A national survey of students at 140 campuses. *Journal of the American Medical Association, 272,* 1672–1677.

Wechsler, H., Rigotti, N. A., Gledhill-Hoyt, J., & Lee, H. (1998). Increased levels of cigarette use among college students: A cause for national concern. *Journal of the American Medical Association, 280,* 1673–1678.

Wegner, D. M. (1994a). Ironic processes of mental control. *Psychological Review, 101,* 34–52.

Wegner, D. M. (1994b). *White bears and other unwanted thoughts: Suppression, obsession, and the psychology of mental control.* New York: Guilford Press.

Wegner, D. M. (1997). Why the mind wanders. In J. D. Cohen & J. W. Schooler (Eds.), *Scientific approaches to consciousness* (pp. 295–315). Mahwah, NJ: Erlbaum.

Wegner, D. M. (2002). *The illusion of conscious will.* Cambridge, MA: MIT Press.

Wegner, D. M., Ansfield, M., & Pilloff, D. (1998). The putt and the pendulum: Ironic effects of the mental control of action. *Psychological Science, 9,* 196–199.

Wegner, D. M., Broome, A., & Blumberg, S. J. (1997). Ironic effects of trying to relax under stress. *Behavior Research and Therapy, 35,* 11–21.

Wegner, D. M., Erber, R. E., & Zanakos, S. (1993). Ironic processes in the mental control of mood and mood-related thought. *Journal of Personality and Social Psychology, 65,* 1093–1104.

Wegner, D. M., & Gilbert, D. T. (2000). Social psychology: The science of human experience. In H. Bless & J. Forgas (Eds.), *The message within: Subjective experience in social cognition and behavior* (pp. 1–9). Philadelphia: Psychology Press.

Wegner, D. M., & Gold, D. B. (1995). Fanning old flames: Emotional and cognitive effects of suppressing thoughts of a past relationship. *Journal of Personality and Social Psychology, 68,* 782–792.

Wegner, D. M., Lane, J. D., & Dimitri, S. (1994). The allure of secret relationships. *Journal of Personality and Social Psychology, 66,* 287–300.

Wegner, D. M., & Pennebaker, J. W. (Eds.). (1993). *Handbook of mental control.* Englewood Cliffs, NJ: Prentice Hall.

Wegner, D. M., & Schaefer, D. (1978). The concentration of responsibility: An objective self-awareness analysis of group size effects in helping situations. *Journal of Personality and Social Psychology, 36,* 147–155.

Wegner, D. M., Schneider, D. J., Carter, S. R., & White, T. L. (1987). Paradoxical effects of thought suppression. *Journal of Personality and Social Psychology, 53,* 5–13.

Wegner, D. M., Vallacher, R. R., Macomber, G., Wood, R., & Arps, K. (1984). The emergence of action. *Journal of Personality and Social Psychology, 46,* 269–279.

Wegner, D. M., & Wenzlaff, R. M. (1996). Mental control. In E. T. Higgins & A. Kruglanski (Eds.), *Social psychology: Handbook of basic mechanisms and processes* (pp. 466–492). New York: Guilford Press.

Wegner, D. M., Wenzlaff, R. M., & Kozak, M. (2004). Dream rebound: The return of suppressed thoughts in dreams. *Psychological Science, 15,* 232–236.

Wegner, D. M., & Wheatley, T. (1999). Apparent mental causation: Sources of the experience of will. *American Psychologist, 54,* 480–492.

Weinberg, R. A. (1989). Intelligence and IQ: Landmark issues and great debates. *American Psychologist, 44,* 98–104.

Weinberger, D. A., Schwartz, G. E., & Davidson, R. J. (1979). Low-anxious, high-anxious, and repressive coping styles: Psychometric patterns and behavioral and physiological responses to stress. *Journal of Abnormal Psychology, 88,* 369–380.

Weir, C., Toland, C., King, R. A., & Martin, L. M. (2005). Infant contingency/extinction performance after observing partial reinforcement. *Infancy, 8,* 63–80.

Weisfeld, G. (1999). *Evolutionary principles of human adolescence.* New York: Basic Books.

Weiskrantz, L. (1956). Behavioral changes associated with ablation of the amygdaloid complex in monkeys. *Journal of Comparative and Physiological Psychology, 4,* 381–391.

Weissenborn, R. (2000). State-dependent effects of alcohol on explicit memory: The role of semantic associations. *Psychopharmacology, 149,* 98–106.

Weissman, M. M., Bland, R. C., Canino, G. J., Faravelli, C., Greenwald, S., Hwu, H. G., et al. (1997). The cross-national epidemiology of panic disorder. *Archives of General Psychiatry, 54,* 305–309.

Weissman, M. M., & Markowitz, J. C. (2002). Interpersonal psychotherapy for depression. In I. H. Gotlib & C. L. Hammen (Eds.), *Handbook of depression* (pp. 404–421). New York: Guilford Press.

Weissman, M. M., Markowitz, J. C., & Klerman, G. L. (2000). *Comprehensive guide to interpersonal psychotherapy.* New York: Basic Books.

Wells, G. L., Malpass, R. S., Lindsay, R. C. L., Fisher, R. P., Turtle, J. W., & Fulero, S. M. (2000). From the lab to the police station: A successful application of eyewitness research. *American Psychologist, 55,* 581–598.

Wells, G. L., Small, M., Penrod, S., Malpass, R. S., Fulero, S. M., & Brimacombe, C. A. E. (1998). Eyewitness identification procedures: Recommendations for lineups and photospreads. *Law and Human Behavior, 22,* 603–647.

Wenner, L. A. (2004). On the ethics of product placement in media entertainment. In M. L. Galacian (Ed.), *Handbook of product placement in the mass media* (pp. 101–132). Binghamton, NY: Haworth Press.

Wenzlaff, R. M. (2005). Seeking solace but finding despair: The persistence of intrusive thoughts in depression. In D. A. Clark (Ed.), *Intrusive thoughts in clinical disorders: Theory, research, and treatment* (pp. 54–85). New York: Guilford Press.

Wenzlaff, R. M., & Bates, D. E. (1998). Unmasking a cognitive vulnerability to depression: How lapses in mental control reveal depressive thinking. *Journal of Personality and Social Psychology, 75,* 1559–1571.

Wenzlaff, R. M., & Eisenberg, A. R. (2001). Mental control after dysphoria: Evidence of a suppressed, depressive bias. *Behavior Therapy, 32,* 27–45.

Wenzlaff, R. M., & Grozier, S. A. (1988). Depression and the magnification of failure. *Journal of Abnormal Psychology, 97,* 90–93.

Wenzlaff, R. M., & Wegner, D. M. (2000). Thought suppression. In S. T. Fiske (Ed.), *Annual Review of Psychology* (Vol. 51, pp. 51–91). Palo Alto, CA: Annual Reviews.

Wernicke, K. (1874). *Der Aphasische Symptomenkomplex.* Breslau: Cohn and Weigart.

Wertheimer, M. (1982). *Productive thinking.* Chicago: University of Chicago Press. (Originally published 1945)

Westen, D. (1991). Social cognition and object relations. *Psychological Bulletin, 109,* 429–455.

Whalen, P. J., Rauch, S. L., Etcoff, N. L., McInerney, S. C., Lee, M. B., & Jenike, M. A. (1998). Masked presentations of emotional facial expressions modulate amygdala activity without explicit knowledge. *Journal of Neuroscience, 18,* 411–418.

Whalley, L. J., & Deary, I. J. (2001). Longitudinal cohort study of childhood IQ and survival up to age 76. *British Medical Journal, 322,* 1–5.

Wheatley, T., & Haidt, J. (2005). Hypnotic disgust makes moral judgments more severe. *Psychological Science, 16,* 780–784.

Wheeler, M. A., Petersen, S. E., & Buckner, R. L. (2000). Memory's echo: Vivid recollection activates modality-specific cortex. *Proceedings of the National Academy of Sciences (USA), 97,* 11125–11129.

White, B. L., & Held, R. (1966). Plasticity of motor development in the human infant. In J. F. Rosenblith & W. Allinsmith (Eds.), *The cause of behavior* (pp. 60–70). Boston: Allyn and Bacon.

White, F. J. (1996). Synaptic regulation of mesocorticolimbic dopamine neurons. *Annual Review of Neuroscience, 19,* 405–436.

White, G. M., & Kirkpatrick, J. (Eds.). (1985). *Person, self, and experience: Exploring pacific ethnopsychologies.* Berkeley: University of California Press.

White, N. M., & Milner, P. M. (1992). The psychobiology of reinforcers. *Annual Review of Psychology, 41,* 443–471.

Whorf, B. (1956). *Language, thought, and reality.* Cambridge, MA: MIT Press.

Whybrow, P. C. (1997). *A mood apart.* New York: Basic Books.

Wicker, B., Keysers, C., Plailly, J., Royet, J.-P., Gallese, V., & Rizzolatti, G. (2003). Both of us disgusted in *my* insula: The common neural basis of seeing and feeling disgust. *Neuron, 40,* 655–664.

Wicklund, R. (1975). Objective self-awareness. In L. Berkowitz (Ed.), *Advances in experimental social psychology* (Vol. 8, pp. 233–275). New York: Academic Press.

Widiger, T. A. (2001). The best and the worst of us? *Clinical Psychology: Science and Practice, 8,* 374–377.

Widiger, T. A., & Sankis, L. M. (2000). Adult psychopathology: Issues and controversies. *An Annual Review of Psychology, 51,* 377–404.

Wiederman, M. W. (1997). Pretending orgasm during sexual intercourse: Correlates in a sample of young adult women. *Journal of Sex & Marital Therapy, 23,* 131–139.

Wiener, D. N. (1996). *B. F. Skinner: Benign anarchist.* Boston: Allyn and Beacon.

Wiesenthal, D. L., Austrom, D., & Silverman, I. (1983). Diffusion of responsibility in charitable donations. *Basic and Applied Social Psychology, 4,* 17–27.

Wiggs, C. L., & Martin, A. (1998). Properties and mechanisms of perceptual priming. *Current Opinion in Neurobiology, 8,* 227–233.

Wilcoxon, H. C., Dragoin, W. B., & Kral, P. A. (1971). Illness-induced aversions in rats and quail: Relative salience of visual and gustatory cues. *Science, 171,* 826–828.

Wiley, J. L. (1999). Cannabis: Discrimination of "internal bliss"? *Pharmacology, Biochemistry, & Behavior, 64,* 257–260.

Williams, A. C. (2002). Facial expression of pain: An evolutionary account. *Behavioral and Brain Sciences, 25,* 439–488.

Williams, C. M., & Kirkham, T. C. (1999). Anandamide induces overeating: Mediation by central cannabinoid (CB1) receptors. *Psychopharmacology, 143,* 315–317.

Williams, K. D., Nida, S. A., Baca, L. D., & Latané, B. (1989). Social loafing and swimming: Effects of identifiability on individual and relay performance of intercollegiate swimmers. *Basic and Applied Social Psychology, 10,* 73–81.

Wilson, T. D. (2002). *Strangers to ourselves: Discovering the adaptive unconscious.* Cambridge, MA: Harvard University Press.

Wilson, T. D., Centerbar, D. B., Kermer, D. A., & Gilbert, D. T. (2005). The pleasures of uncertainty: Prolonging positive moods in ways people do not anticipate. *Journal of Personality and Social Psychology, 88,* 5–21.

Wilson, T. D., & Gilbert, D. T. (2003). Affective forecasting. In M. P. Zanna (Ed.), *Advances in experimental social psychology* (Vol. 35, pp. 345–411). New York: Elsevier.

Wilson, T. D., & Lassiter, G. D. (1982). Increasing intrinsic interest with superfluous extrinsic constraints. *Journal of Personality and Social Psychology, 42,* 811–819.

Wilson, T. D., Lindsey, S., & Schooler, T. Y. (2000). A model of dual attitudes. *Psychological Review, 107,* 101–126.

Wilson, T. D., Meyers, J., & Gilbert, D. T. (2003). "How happy was I, anyway?" A retrospective impact bias. *Social Cognition, 21,* 421–446.

Wilson, T. D., & Schooler, J. W. (1991). Thinking too much: Introspection can reduce the quality of preferences and decisions. *Journal of Personality & Social Psychology, 60,* 181–192.

Wilson, T. D., Wheatley, T., Meyers, J., Gilbert, D. T., & Axsom, D. (2000). Focalism: A source of durability bias in affective forecasting. *Journal of Personality and Social Psychology, 78,* 821–836.

Wimmer, H., & Perner, J. (1983). Beliefs about beliefs: Representations and constraining function of wrong beliefs in young children's understanding of deception. *Cognition, 13,* 103–128.

Windeler, J., & Kobberling, J. (1986). Empirische Untersuchung zur Einschatzung diagnostischer Verfahren am Beispiel des Haemoccult-Tests. [An empirical study of the value of diagnostic procedures using the example of the hemoccult test.] *Klinische Wochenscrhrift, 64,* 1106–1112.

Windham, G. C., Eaton, A., & Hopkins, B. (1999). Evidence for an association between environmental tobacco smoke exposure and birthweight: A meta-analysis and new data. *Pediatrics and Perinatal Epidemiology, 13,* 35–57.

Winner, E. (1997). Exceptionally high intelligence and schooling. *American Psychologist, 52,* 1070–1081.

Winter, L., & Uleman, J. S. (1984). When are social judgments made? Evidence for the spontaneousness of trait inferences. *Journal of Personality and Social Psychology, 47,* 237–252.

Winterer, G., & Weinberger, D. R. (2004). Genes, dopamine and cortical signal-to-noise ratio in schizophrenia. *Trends in Neuroscience, 27,* 683–690.

Wise, R. A. (1989). Brain dopamine and reward. *Annual Review of Psychology, 40,* 191–225.

Wise, R. A. (2005). Forebrain substrates of reward and motivation. *Journal of Comparative Neurology, 493,* 115–121.

Wittchen, H., Knauper, B., & Kessler, R. C. (1994). Lifetime risk of depression. *British Journal of Psychiatry, 165,* 16–22.

Wittgenstein, L. (1999). *Philosophical investigations.* Upper Saddle River, NJ: Prentice Hall. (Originally published 1953)

Wixted, J. T., & Ebbensen, E. (1991). On the form of forgetting. *Psychological Science, 2,* 409–415.

Wolf, J. (2003, May 18). Through the looking glass. *The New York Times Magazine,* p. 120.

Wolff, G., Pathare, S., Craig, T., & Leff, J. (1996). Community knowledge of mental illness and reaction to mentally ill people. *British Journal of Psychiatry, 168,* 191–198.

Wollen, K. A., Weber, A., & Lowry, D. (1972). Bizarreness versus interaction of mental images as determinants of learning. *Cognitive Psychology, 3,* 518–523.

Wolpe, J. (1958). *Psychotherapy by reciprocal inhibition.* Stanford, CA: Stanford University Press.

Wong, D. T., Bymaster, F. P., & Engleman, E. A. (1995). Prozac (fluoxetine, Lilly 110140), the first selective serotonin uptake inhibitor and an antidepressant drug: Twenty years since its first publication. *Life Sciences, 57,* 411–441.

Wood, J. M., & Bootzin, R. R. (1990). Prevalence of nightmares and their independence from anxiety. *Journal of Abnormal Psychology, 99,* 64–68.

Wood, J. M., Bootzin, R. R., Rosenhan, D., Nolen-Hoeksema, S., & Jourden, F. (1992). Effects of the 1989 San Francisco earthquake on frequency and content of nightmares. *Journal of Abnormal Psychology, 101,* 219–224.

Wood, J. M., Nezworski, M. T., Lilienfeld, S. O., & Garb, H. N. (2003). *What's wrong with the Rorschach? Science confronts the controversial inkblot test.* New York: Wiley.

Wood, J. M., Nezworski, M. T., & Stejskal, W. J. (1996). The comprehensive system for the Rorschach: A critical examination. *Psychological Science, 7,* 3–10.

Woods, E. R., Lin, Y. G., Middleman, A., Beckford, P., Chase, L., & DuRant, R. H. (1997). The associations of suicide attempts in adolescents. *Pediatrics, 99,* 791–796.

Woods, S. C., Seeley, R. J., Porte, D., Jr., & Schwartz, M. W. (1998). Signals that regulate food intake and energy homeostasis. *Science, 280,* 1378–1383.

Woods, S. M., Natterson, J., & Silverman, J. (1966). Medical students' disease: hypochondriasis in medical education. *Journal of Medical Education, 41,* 785–790.

Woody, S. R., & Sanderson, W. C. (1998). Manuals for empirically supported treatments: 1998 update. *Clinical Psychologist, 51,* 17–21.

Wrangham, R., & Peterson, D. (1997). *Demonic males: Apes and the origin of human violence.* New York: Mariner.

Wren, A. M., Seal, L. J., Cohen, M. A., Brynes, A. E., Frost, G. S., Murphy, K. G., et al. (2001). Ghrelin enhances appetite and increases food intake in humans. *Journal of Clinical Endocrinology and Metabolism, 86,* 5992–5995.

Wrenn, C. C., Turchi, J. N., Schlosser, S., Dreiling, J. L., Stephenson, D. A., Crawley, J. N. (2006). Performance of galanin transgenic mice in the 5-choice serial reaction time attentional task. *Pharmacology Biochemistry and Behavior, 83,* 428–440.

Wright, L. (1994). *Remembering Satan: A case of recovered memory and the shattering of an American family.* New York: Knopf.

Wright, P., Takei, N., Rifkin, L., & Murray, R. M. (1995). Maternal influenza, obstetric complications, and schizophrenia. *American Journal of Psychiatry, 152,* 1714–1720.

Wulf, S. (1994, March 14). Err Jordan. *Sports Illustrated.*

Wundt, W. (1900–20). *Völkerpsychologie. Eine untersuchung der entwicklungsgesetze von sprache, mythos und sitte* [Völkerpsychologie: An examination of the developmental laws of language, myth, and custom]. Leipzig, Germany: Engelmann & Kroner.

Wynn, K. (1992). Addition and subtraction by human infants. *Nature, 358,* 749–750.

Xiaohe, X., & Whyte, K. J. (1990). Love matches and arranged marriages: A Chinese replication. *Journal of Marriage and the Family, 52,* 709–722.

Yamaguchi, S. (1998). Basic properties of umami and its effects in humans. *Physiology and Behavior, 49,* 833–841.

Yamasue, H., Kasai, K., Iwanami, A., Ohtani, T., Yamada, H., Abe, O., et al. (2003). Voxel-based analysis of MRI reveals anterior cingulate gray-matter volume reduction in posttraumatic stress disorder due to terrorism. *Proceedings of the National Academy of Sciences (USA), 100,* 9039–9043.

Yang, S., & Sternberg, R. J. (1997). Conceptions of intelligence in ancient Chinese philosophy. *Journal of Theoretical and Philosophical Psychology, 17,* 101–119.

Yeh, M., Takeuchi, D. T., & Sue, S. (1994). Asian-American children treated in the mental health system: A comparison of parallel and mainstream outpatient service centers. *Journal of Clinical Child Psychology, 23,* 5–12.

Yelsma, P., & Athappilly, K. (1988). Marital satisfaction and communication practices: Comparisons among Indian and American couples. *Journal of Comparative Family Studies, 19,* 37–53.

Yewchuk, C. (1985). Gifted/learning disabled children: An overview. *Gifted Education International, 3,* 122–126.

Yin, R. K. (1970). Face recognition by brain-injured patients: A dissociable ability. *Neuropsychologia, 8,* 395–402.

Young, A. S., Klap, R., Sherbourne, C. D., & Wells, K. B. (2001). The quality of care for depressive and anxiety disorders in the United States. *Archives of General Psychiatry, 58,* 55–61.

Young, P. C. (1948). Antisocial uses of hypnosis. In L. M. LeCron (Ed.), *Experimental hypnosis* (pp. 376–409). New York: Macmillan.

Young, R. M. (1990). *Mind, brain, and adaptation in the nineteenth century: Cerebral localization and its biological context from Gall to Ferrier.* New York: Oxford University Press.

Yucha, C., & Gilbert, C. D. (2004). *Evidence-based practice in biofeedback and neurofeedback.* Colorado Springs, CO: Association for Applied Psychophysiology and Biofeedback.

Yuill, N., & Perner, J. (1988). Intentionality and knowledge in children's judgments of actor's responsibility and recipient's emotional reaction. *Developmental Psychology, 24,* 358–365.

*Yuma* (Arizona) *Sun.* (2006, May 31). Bribing people to vote will not benefit system. (Retrieved from YumaSun.com on May 31, 2007).

Zahn-Waxler, C., Radke-Yarrow, M., Wagner, E., & Chapman, M. (1992). Development of concern for others. *Developmental Psychology, 28,* 126–136.

Zajonc, R. B. (1968). Attitudinal effects of mere exposure. *Journal of Personality and Social Psychology, 9,* 1–27.

Zajonc, R. B. (1980). Feeling and thinking: Preferences need no inferences. *American Psychologist, 35,* 151–175.

Zajonc, R. B. (1984). On the primacy of affect. In K. R. Scherer & P. Ekman (Eds.), *Approaches to emotion* (pp. 259–270). Hillsdale, NJ: Erlbaum.

Zajonc, R. B. (1989). Feeling the facial efference: Implications of the vascular theory of emotion. *Psychological Review, 96,* 395–416.

Zebrowitz, L. A., Hall, J. A., Murphy, N. A., & Rhodes, G. (2002). Looking smart and looking good: Facial cues to intelligence and their origins. *Personality and Social Psychology Bulletin, 28,* 238–249.

Zebrowitz, L. A., & Montepare, J. M. (1992). Impressions of baby-faced individuals across the life span. *Developmental Psychology, 28,* 1143–1152.

Zeki, S. (1993). *A vision of the brain.* London: Blackwell Scientific Publications.

Zeki, S. (2001). Localization and globalization in conscious vision. *Annual Review of Neuroscience, 24,* 57–86.

Zeman, A. (2002). *Consciousness: A user's guide.* New Haven, CT: Yale University Press.

Zentall, T. R., Sutton, J. E., & Sherburne, L. M. (1996). True imitative learning in pigeons. *Psychological Science, 7,* 343–346.

Zhang, J. (2004, October 2). Prof. Zimbardo faults Rumsfeld for Abu Ghraib. *Stanford Daily.* Retrieved August 2007 from http://daily.stanford.edu/article/2004/10/29/profZimbardoFaultsRumsfeldForAbuGhraib.

Zihl, J., von Cramon, D., & Mai, N. (1983). Selective disturbance of movement vision after bilateral brain damage. *Brain 106,* 313–340.

Zillmann, D., Katcher, A. H., & Milavsky, B. (1972). Excitation transfer from physical exercise to subsequent aggressive behavior. *Journal of Experimental Psychology, 8,* 247–259.

Zimprich, D., & Martin, M. (2002). Can longitudinal changes in processing speed explain longitudinal age changes in fluid intelligence? *Psychology and Aging, 17,* 690–695.

Zola, S. M., & Squire, L. R. (2000). The medial temporal lobe and the hippocampus. In E. Tulving & F. I. M. Craik (Eds.), *The Oxford handbook of memory* (pp. 485–500). New York: Oxford University Press.

Zuckerman, M., DePaulo, B. M., & Rosenthal, R. (1981). Verbal and nonverbal communication of deception. In L. Berkowitz (Ed.), *Advances in experimental social psychology* (Vol. 14, pp. 1–59). New York: Academic Press.

Zuckerman, M., & Driver, R. E. (1985). Telling lies: Verbal and nonverbal correlates of deception. In W. Seigman & S. Feldstein (Eds.), *Multichannel integrations of nonverbal behavior* (pp. 129–147). Hillsdale, NJ: Erlbaum.

Zuckerman, M., Kolin, E. A., Price, L., & Zoob, I. (1964). Development of a sensation-seeking scale. *Journal of Consulting Psychology, 28,* 477–482.

# Name Index

# Subject Index

Note: Page numbers followed by f indicate figures; those followed by t indicate tables.

A1 auditory area, 99, 152, 153f
A1 visual area, 99, 113, 138–139, 138f, 139f
  feature detectors in, 113
Absentmindedness, 4, 189–191, 203
Absolute intelligence, 360
Absolute threshold, 124–125, 125f, 125t
Absolutism, 30
Abstract ideas, understanding of, 416
Abuse, sexual, recovered memories of, 198–199, 576
Academic careers, 33
Accommodation, 132, 132f
  in cognitive development, 413
Accuracy motive, in social influence, 645–651
Acetylcholine, 83, 83t
Achievement tests. *See also* Testing
  vs. aptitude tests, 339
Acquired immunodeficiency syndrome, prevention of, 615–616
Acquisition, in classical conditioning, 214, 214f
ACTH, 96
  in stress response, 586, 586f
Action potential, 80–81, 80f
  in signaling, 82, 82f
  spontaneous, 127
Activation-synthesis model, 317
Actor-observer effect, 659–660
Adaptation, sensory, 128–129
  dark, 134
  light, 131
Addiction, 318–320. *See also* Alcohol use/abuse; Drug abuse
Additive color mixing, 136–137, 136f
A-delta fibers, 156
Adler, Alfred, 15, 546–547, 546f
Adolescence
  brain development in, 431, 431f
  common goals in, 476
  cultural aspects of, 432, 434, 437
  definition of, 430
  emotions in, 433
  Erikson's developmental tasks of, 436t
  family conflict in, 433, 436–437
  identity formation in, 436–437
  peer relations in, 436–437
  pregnancy in, 434
  protraction of, 432–433
  sexual development in, 430–431, 431f
  storm and stress of, 433

Adrenal androgens
  in sexual desire, 395
  in sexual development, 433–434
  in sexual orientation, 435
Adrenal glands, 96
  in stress response, 586, 586f, 588
Adrenocorticotropic hormone (ACTH), 96
  in stress response, 586, 586f
Adulthood, 438–445. *See also* Age-related changes
  changing orientations in, 441–443
  cognitive performance in, 439–441
  common goals in, 476
  definition of, 438
  emotional experiences in, 442
  Erikson's developmental tasks of, 436t
  marriage in, 443–444, 443f
  memory changes in, 439–441, 441f
  parenthood in, 443–444
  physical decline in, 439–440
  social activity in, 442–443
  temporal orientation in, 441
Advertising
  heuristic persuasion in, 648
  informational influence in, 646
  product placement in, 163
  sensory branding in, 163
  subliminal, 163, 306–308, 308f
Aerobic exercise, in stress management, 600–601
Affective forecasting, 378
African Americans. *See* Blacks; Race/ethnicity
Afterimages, color, 137–138, 137f
Age-related changes
  cognitive, 439–440
  in cortical lateralization, 440, 440f
  in happiness, 441, 442–443
  in memory, 193, 439–441, 441f
  physical, 439
Aggression, 623–625. *See also* Crime; Violence
  alcohol and, 322
  ambient temperature and, 623, 623f
  antisocial personality disorder and, 527t, 529–530
  causes of, 623–624
  cultural aspects of, 625
  definition of, 623
  frustration and, 623
  gender differences in, 624–625
  group, 628–630
  impulsive, 623–624
  modeling of, 243–244, 244f
  observational learning in, 641

  oral, 468
  premeditated, 623
  status and, 625
  testosterone and, 625
  video games and, 244
Agnosia
  facial, 73, 108, 113
  visual-form, 140
Agonist drugs, 85, 85t
Agoraphobia, 505–506
Agreeableness, 457–458, 457t
AIDS, prevention of, 615–616
Alcohol myopia, 322
Alcohol use/abuse, 321–322, 321t
  abstinence in, 558–559
  in adolescence, 433
  aversion therapy for, 548
  effects of, 321–322
  expectancy theory and, 321–322
  harm reduction approach to, 325
  memory and, 180–181
  in pregnancy, 408–409
  Prohibition and, 324
  risks of, 321t
  self-help groups for, 558–559
  sexual behavior and, 615–616
  suicide and, 517
Alcoholics Anonymous, 558–559
Alertness, intraversion/extraversion and, 461–462
Algorithms, 275
Allport, Gordon, 29
Alpha waves, 310
  during meditation, 332
Alprazolam, 562
Altered states of consciousness. *See also* Consciousness
  definition of, 309
  drug-induced, 318–327. *See also* Drug abuse; Psychoactive drugs
  in meditation, 331–333, 551, 598
  in peak experiences, 331–333, 471
  religious, 332–333
  sleep as, 309. *See also* Sleep
Alternative therapies, 564–565
Altruism, 627–628
Alzheimer's disease
  brain activity in, 439f
  daydreaming and, 439f
Ambient temperature, aggression and, 623, 623f
Ambivalent attachment style, 423
*American Journal of Psychology*, 10